FASHION LAW AND BUSINESS

PLI PRESS

FASHION LAW AND BUSINESS

Brands & Retailers

Second Edition

Howard S. Hogan
Jennifer Bellah Maguire

Practising Law Institute
New York City
#240525

This work is designed to provide practical and useful information on the subject matter covered. However, it is sold with the understanding that neither the publisher nor the author is engaged in rendering legal, accounting or other professional services. If legal advice or other expert assistance is required, the services of a competent professional should be sought.

Legal Editor: Carol Benedicto

First edition 2013, by Lois F. Herzeca and Howard S. Hogan
Second edition 2019, by Howard S. Hogan and Jennifer Bellah Maguire

LCCN: 2019934930

ISBN: 978-1-4024-3123-4

About the Authors

HOWARD S. HOGAN is a partner in the Washington, D.C. office of Gibson, Dunn & Crutcher LLP and is Co-Chair of the firm's Fashion, Retail and Consumer Products Practice Group. Mr. Hogan focuses on intellectual property litigation and counseling, including trademark, copyright, patent, false advertising, right of publicity, licensing, and trade secret matters.

Mr. Hogan represents many luxury brands and other prominent companies in the retail and consumer products space in prosecution and defense of intellectual property infringement actions. Many of Mr. Hogan's matters have tested the application of traditional legal principles to the Internet and new media, and Mr. Hogan regularly assists clients with data privacy and information technology matters. *World Trademark Review* has recognized him as "a force to be reckoned with, combining top-flight skills with innovative thinking."

Mr. Hogan is a frequent lecturer and writer on intellectual property issues. He has provided commentary for CBS News, Bloomberg TV, and National Public Radio, and has been quoted in publications such as *The Wall Street Journal, The Washington Post,* and *USA Today.* He is the author of the trademark and domain name chapters of *Intellectual Property Law in Cyberspace,* published by BNA in conjunction with the American Intellectual Property Law Association.

Mr. Hogan received his J.D., *cum laude,* from NYU School of Law, and he clerked for the Honorable Naomi Reice Buchwald, U.S. District Judge for the Southern District of New York, from 1999–2000. In 1994, Mr. Hogan helped to initiate the AmeriCorps National Civilian Community Corps, and he now spends significant time assisting not-for-profit organizations *pro bono.* Mr. Hogan has served on the Boards of Directors for the Meals on Wheels Association of America Foundation, the National Foundation to End Senior Hunger, and the Washington Lawyers' Committee for Civil Rights and Urban Affairs, among others.

JENNIFER BELLAH MAGUIRE is a partner in the Los Angeles office of Gibson, Dunn & Crutcher and is Co-Chair of the firm's Investment Fund Group. Ms. Bellah Maguire's practice focuses on private equity fund formation and mergers and acquisitions, including public company transactions and divestitures. Ms. Bellah Maguire was shortlisted for the *Chambers USA* "Women in Law" Awards in the Corporate M&A Lawyer of the Year category, 2012. She has also been named as one of the "Most Influential M&A Advisors" (2013) and ranked among "The Best of the Bar" for Corporate Transactions (2007) by *The Los Angeles Business Journal.* The National Diversity Council recognized Ms. Bellah Maguire on the "2016 Top 50 Women Lawyers" list highlighting the most extraordinary female leaders in the industry.

Ms. Bellah Maguire holds a bachelor of arts from Bryn Mawr College, *magna cum laude,* and studied for one year at Sorbonne University in Paris, France. She was awarded a Watson Foundation Fellowship following college. She graduated from the University of California, Berkeley, School of Law, where she was a member of the *Order of the Coif* and served as an Associate Editor for the *California Law Review.* She speaks and writes French fluently, and practiced in the firm's Paris office. Prior to joining the firm, she served as law clerk for the Honorable Mary M. Schroeder in the United States Court of Appeals for the Ninth Circuit.

Ms. Bellah Maguire speaks frequently on corporate and securities topics. Ms. Bellah Maguire is a member of the Board of Trustees of the Otis College of Art and Design and a founding member of the board of the Los Angeles Ballet.

Table of Chapters

Chapter 1 Starting a Fashion Company

Chapter 2 Trademarks and Trade Dress

Chapter 3 Patents

Chapter 4 Copyrights

Chapter 5 International Design Protections

Chapter 6 Unfair Competition, Misappropriation, and Trade Secrets

Chapter 7 Counterfeiting

Chapter 8 The Gray Market and The First Sale Doctrine

Chapter 9 Design and Manufacturing

Chapter 10 Licensing Arrangements

Chapter 11 Retail Sales

Chapter 12 Antitrust

Chapter 13 Real Estate

Chapter 14 E-Commerce and Mobile Commerce

Chapter 15 False Advertising

Chapter 16 Labor and Employment

Chapter 17 Employment Agreements

Chapter 18 Rights of Publicity

Chapter 19 Customs and International Trade Issues

Chapter 20 Foreign Corrupt Practices Act

Chapter 21 Going Public

Chapter 22 Selling a Fashion Company or Fashion Brand

Chapter 23 Distressed Fashion Businesses, Restructuring, and Bankruptcy

Table of Contents

About the Authors ... v

Table of Chapters ... vii

Preface to the First Edition ... xxix

Acknowledgments ... xxxi

Introduction ... xxxv

Chapter 1 Starting a Fashion Company

§ 1:1 Introduction ... 1-2
§ 1:1.1 Planning and Preparation ... 1-2
§ 1:1.2 Drafting the Business Plan ... 1-6
[A] Executive Summary ... 1-7
[B] Business Description ... 1-7
[C] Industry and Market Analysis ... 1-8
[D] Competition ... 1-8
[E] Implementation ... 1-8
[F] Organization and Management ... 1-9
[G] Financial Projections ... 1-9
§ 1:2 Forming and Structuring the Business ... 1-12
§ 1:2.1 Initial Considerations ... 1-12
§ 1:2.2 Sole Proprietorship ... 1-13
§ 1:2.3 General Partnership ... 1-15
§ 1:2.4 C Corporation ... 1-19
§ 1:2.5 S Corporation ... 1-23
§ 1:2.6 Public Benefit Corporation ... 1-25
§ 1:2.7 Limited Liability Company ... 1-26
§ 1:2.8 Limited Partnership ... 1-29
§ 1:2.9 Cooperatives ... 1-31
§ 1:2.10 Piercing the Corporate Veil ... 1-31
§ 1:2.11 Organizational Structure ... 1-33
§ 1:3 Financing the Business ... 1-36
§ 1:3.1 Capital Structure ... 1-36
§ 1:3.2 Equity ... 1-37
§ 1:3.3 Debt ... 1-49

§ 1:4 Sources of Financing 1-50
§ 1:4.1 Financing in Stages 1-50
§ 1:4.2 Personal Funds 1-50
§ 1:4.3 Friends and Family 1-51
§ 1:4.4 Factoring 1-53
§ 1:4.5 Bank Financing and Commercial Credit 1-54
§ 1:4.6 Angel Investors 1-56
§ 1:4.7 Venture Capital Investors 1-59
§ 1:4.8 Private Equity 1-64
Appendix 1A Sample Creative Control Provisions .... App. 1A-1

Chapter 2 Trademarks and Trade Dress

§ 2:1 Introduction 2-3
§ 2:2 History 2-4
§ 2:3 Trademarks Defined 2-7
§ 2:4 Recurring Trademark Issues 2-9
§ 2:4.1 Letters and Numbers in Trademarks 2-9
§ 2:4.2 Personal Names 2-9
§ 2:4.3 Geographic Terms and Foreign Words 2-11
§ 2:4.4 Generic Terms and Common Phrases 2-12
§ 2:4.5 Deceptive Words 2-13
§ 2:5 Trade Dress 2-13
§ 2:6 Clearing and Registering a Trademark 2-16
§ 2:6.1 Registration Generally 2-16
§ 2:6.2 What Can Be Registered 2-18
§ 2:6.3 Overview of the Registration Process 2-19
[A] Trademark Searching 2-19
[B] The Application 2-20
[C] Use-Based and Intent-to-Use Applications 2-21
[D] Examination 2-22
[E] Opposition Proceedings 2-23
[F] Post-Registration 2-23
[G] International Aspects 2-25
§ 2:7 Trademark Infringement 2-25
§ 2:7.1 First Element: Establishing That the Trademark Is Entitled to Protection 2-27
§ 2:7.2 Second Element: Establishing Likelihood of Confusion 2-29
[A] The Confusion Factors 2-30
[B] Types of Confusion 2-32
[C] Likelihood of Confusion Analysis 2-37

§ 2:8 Trademark Dilution 2-52
§ 2:8.1 Dilution by Blurring 2-54
§ 2:8.2 Dilution by Tarnishment 2-56
§ 2:9 Remedies for Trademark Infringement 2-58
§ 2:9.1 Injunctive Relief 2-58
[A] Permanent Injunction 2-58
[B] Preliminary Injunction 2-59
§ 2:9.2 Monetary Relief 2-65
[A] Defendant's Profits 2-65
[B] Plaintiff's Damages 2-67
[C] Costs of the Action and Attorneys' Fees 2-67
§ 2:9.3 Accounting of Profits 2-68
§ 2:9.4 Remedies for Infringing Domain Names 2-69
§ 2:9.5 International Trade Commission 2-70
§ 2:10 Defenses to Infringement 2-74
§ 2:10.1 Invalidity of the Trademark 2-74
§ 2:10.2 Lack of Standing 2-75
§ 2:10.3 Fraud in Procuring the Trademark 2-76
§ 2:10.4 Unclean Hands 2-77
§ 2:10.5 Nominative Fair Use 2-78
§ 2:10.6 Laches 2-80
§ 2:10.7 Naked Licensing 2-82
§ 2:10.8 Parody 2-84
§ 2:10.9 Aesthetic Functionality 2-87
[A] The *Louboutin* Case 2-89
[B] *Eliya v. Steven Madden* 2-90
[C] *PUMA v. Forever 21* 2-91
§ 2:11 Search Engine and Internet Advertising as Infringement 2-92
§ 2:11.1 Use of Trademarks as Metatags 2-93
§ 2:11.2 Use of Trademarks in Search Engine Advertising 2-95
§ 2:11.3 Use of Trademarks in Hashtags 2-101
§ 2:12 Duty to Protect a Mark 2-102
§ 2:13 Developing an Enforcement Strategy 2-103
§ 2:13.1 Private Co-Existence Agreements 2-105
§ 2:14 Trademark Licensing 2-106
§ 2:15 International Trademark Issues 2-108
§ 2:15.1 The World Intellectual Property Organization 2-108
§ 2:15.2 The Madrid Protocol 2-109
Appendix 2A International Trademark Classification of Goods and Services .... App. 2A-1
Appendix 2B Signatory Nations to the Madrid Agreement Concerning the International Registration Marks and Related Protocol .... App. 2B-1

Chapter 3 Patents

§ 3:1 Introduction 3-2
Figure 3-1 Trends in Fashion-Related Patents 3-4
§ 3:2 Overview of Patent Protection 3-4
§ 3:2.1 What Is a Utility Patent? 3-4
Figure 3-2 Sample Utility Patents in Fashion 3-7
§ 3:2.2 What Is a Design Patent? 3-7
Figure 3-3 Sample Design Patents in Fashion 3-8
§ 3:3 Applying for Patent Protection 3-10
§ 3:3.1 Application Requirements 3-10
§ 3:3.2 Prior Art Searches 3-12
§ 3:3.3 Costs and Fees 3-12
§ 3:3.4 Examination 3-13
§ 3:3.5 Design Patent Applications 3-15
§ 3:3.6 Marking 3-15
§ 3:4 Patent Enforcement and Remedies 3-16
§ 3:4.1 Patent Infringement 3-16
§ 3:4.2 Remedies 3-18
[A] Monetary Damages 3-19
[B] Injunctive Relief 3-21
[C] Attorneys' Fees 3-22
[D] Prejudgment Interest 3-22
[E] Enhanced Damages for Willful Infringement 3-23
§ 3:5 Territoriality of Patent Protection 3-23
§ 3:5.1 Patent Enforcement in the United States 3-24
§ 3:5.2 Patent Protection Outside the United States 3-25
§ 3:6 Patent Protection in Fashion 3-26
§ 3:6.1 Design Patent Protection in Fashion: Trends in Use and Enforcement 3-26
Figure 3-4 Sample Patents Held by Columbia Sportswear North America, Inc. Covering Related Designs 3-29
Figure 3-5 Sample Patents Held by Times Three Clothier, LLC Covering Related Designs 3-30
Figure 3-6 Sample Design Patents Held by Lululemon Athletica Canada Inc. 3-32
Figure 3-7 Design Patents Held by Skechers U.S.A. 3-33
Figure 3-8 Design Patents Held by Deckers Outdoor Corporation 3-34
§ 3:6.2 Utility Patent Protection in Fashion: Trends in Use and Enforcement 3-35
[A] High Performance Fabrics and Athletic Attire 3-36
Figure 3-9 Sample Utility Patents in Fashion 3-37
[B] Other Uses of Utility Patents 3-37

Figure 3-10 U.S. Patent No. 6,109,747 (Eyeglass frames with magnets in flanges) ... 3-39
[C] Integration of Technology and Fashion ... 3-41
Figure 3-11 Sample Utility Patents in Fashion Using RFIDs ... 3-42
Figure 3-12 Biosensing Garment—U.S. Patent D832,556 (OMsignal Inc.) ... 3-43
Figure 3-13 U.S. Patent Application Publ. No. 2018/0256115 (Sony Interactive Entertainment) (Display to Mitigate "Virtual Reality Sickness") ... 3-45
Figure 3-14 U.S. Patent Application Publ. No. 2018/0078183 (Apple, Inc.) ... 3-46
§ 3:7 Conclusion ... 3-47
Appendix 3A-1 Illustrative Design Patent 1: Seamans, March 28, 2006 ... App. 3A-1-1
Appendix 3A-2 Illustrative Design Patent 2: Iamartino, June 26, 2012 ... App. 3A-2-1
Appendix 3B-1 Illustrative Utility Patent 1: Seamans, February 7, 2006 ... App. 3B-1-1
Appendix 3B-2 Illustrative Utility Patent 2: Drab et al., September 11, 2012 ... App. 3B-2-1

Chapter 4 Copyrights

§ 4:1 Introduction ... 4-2
§ 4:2 Development of Copyright Law in the Fashion Industry ... 4-3
§ 4:3 Elements of Copyright Protection ... 4-5
§ 4:3.1 Originality ... 4-5
§ 4:3.2 Separability ... 4-9
[A] Development of the Separability Doctrine ... 4-9
[B] Useful Articles in the Fashion Industry ... 4-10
[C] "Separable" Elements of Useful Articles ... 4-11
[D] Evaluating Whether Design Elements are "Separable" ... 4-12
§ 4:3.3 Idea and Expression ... 4-16
§ 4:4 Efforts to Protect Fashion More Vigorously ... 4-19
§ 4:5 Joint Ownership and Works Made for Hire ... 4-21
§ 4:6 Copyright Registration Procedures ... 4-24
§ 4:6.1 Elements of a Copyright Application ... 4-25
§ 4:6.2 Renewals and Change of Ownership ... 4-27
§ 4:6.3 Copyright Notice ... 4-27
§ 4:6.4 Length of Copyright ... 4-28
§ 4:7 Copyright Infringement ... 4-29
§ 4:7.1 Access ... 4-31

§ 4:7.2 Substantial Similarity 4-32
[A] The Ordinary Observer and Related Tests 4-32
[B] The Extrinsic/Intrinsic Tests 4-34
[C] Other Substantial Similarity Tests 4-38
[D] The Use of Characters in Apparel 4-39
§ 4:8 Defenses 4-40
§ 4:8.1 Fair Use 4-40
§ 4:8.2 The *De Minimis* Doctrine 4-43
§ 4:9 Remedies 4-44
§ 4:9.1 Injunctive Relief 4-44
§ 4:9.2 Impoundment and Disposition 4-45
§ 4:9.3 Damages and Profits 4-45
[A] Actual Damages and Profits 4-45
[B] Statutory Damages 4-46
§ 4:9.4 Costs and Attorneys' Fees 4-47

Chapter 5 International Design Protections

§ 5:1 Introduction 5-1
§ 5:2 The European Union 5-2
§ 5:3 Geneva Act of the Hague Agreement Concerning the International Registration of Industrial Designs 5-5
§ 5:4 Individual European Countries 5-6
§ 5:4.1 France 5-6
§ 5:4.2 United Kingdom 5-7
§ 5:4.3 Italy 5-9
§ 5:5 Non-European Countries 5-10
§ 5:5.1 Japan 5-10
§ 5:5.2 China 5-11
§ 5:5.3 Australia 5-12
§ 5:5.4 New Zealand 5-13
§ 5:5.5 Canada 5-14
§ 5:5.6 Singapore 5-16
§ 5:5.7 India 5-17
§ 5:5.8 United Arab Emirates 5-17
§ 5:6 Conclusion 5-17

Chapter 6 Unfair Competition, Misappropriation, and Trade Secrets

§ 6:1 Introduction 6-1
§ 6:2 California Law 6-3
§ 6:2.1 California's Statutory Unfair Competition Law 6-3
§ 6:2.2 California's Common Law of Misappropriation 6-7
§ 6:2.3 California Uniform Trade Secrets Act 6-8

§ 6:3 New York Law 6-9
§ 6:3.1 New York Common Law Unfair Competition 6-9
[A] Passing Off 6-10
[B] Misappropriation 6-10
§ 6:3.2 New York Statutory Unfair Competition Law 6-13
§ 6:4 Federal Law 6-14
§ 6:4.1 Federal Unfair Competition 6-14
§ 6:4.2 The Federal Trade Secrets Statute 6-15
§ 6:5 Illustrative Cases in the Fashion Industry 6-16
§ 6:5.1 Trade Secrets Cases 6-16
§ 6:5.2 *J. Crew Group Inc. v. Fenton* 6-18
§ 6:5.3 *Burch v. Burch* 6-20

Chapter 7 Counterfeiting

§ 7:1 Introduction 7-2
§ 7:2 Government Enforcement 7-2
§ 7:3 Civil Litigation 7-6
§ 7:3.1 Establishing Personal Jurisdiction over Counterfeiters 7-6
[A] Websites Selling Goods in the Forum 7-7
[B] Providing Services to Website Selling Counterfeit Goods in the Forum 7-8
[C] Alternative Service of Process 7-8
§ 7:3.2 Likelihood of Confusion 7-9
§ 7:3.3 Ex Parte Injunctive Relief 7-11
[A] Restraint of Third-Party Suppliers and Domain Name Registries 7-13
[B] Restraint of Counterfeiters' Assets 7-14
[C] Expedited and International Discovery 7-16
§ 7:3.4 Contributory Infringement 7-19
[A] The *Inwood* Decision and Its Progeny 7-20
[B] Secondary Liability in the Online Context 7-21
[B][1] *Perfect 10 v. Visa International Service Association* 7-24
[B][2] *Gucci America, Inc. v. Frontline Processing Corp.* 7-25
§ 7:3.5 Monetary Remedies 7-29
[A] Counterfeiters' Profits 7-30
[B] Statutory Damages 7-31
§ 7:4 Additional Remedies for Trademark Owners 7-33
§ 7:4.1 Technological Solutions 7-33
§ 7:4.2 Cooperation Among Trademark Owners, Credit Card Companies, and E-Commerce Servicers 7-34
§ 7:4.3 Public Education 7-35

Chapter 8 The Gray Market and The First Sale Doctrine

§ 8:1 Introduction 8-1
§ 8:2 Overview of the First Sale Doctrine 8-3
§ 8:2.1 Purpose of the First Sale Doctrine 8-3
§ 8:2.2 First Sale Doctrine in Copyright Law 8-5
§ 8:2.3 First Sale Doctrine in Trademark Law 8-7
§ 8:2.4 First Sale Doctrine in Patent Law 8-8
§ 8:3 Development of First Sale Doctrine and "Gray Market" Case Law 8-9
§ 8:3.1 *Parfums Givenchy, Inc. v. Drug Emporium, Inc.* 8-9
§ 8:3.2 *Quality King Distributors, Inc. v. L'anza Research International, Inc.* 8-11
§ 8:3.3 *Abercrombie & Fitch v. Fashion Shops of Kentucky, Inc.* 8-12
§ 8:3.4 *Omega S.A. v. Costco Wholesale Corp.* 8-13
§ 8:3.5 *John Wiley & Sons, Inc. v. Kirtsaeng* 8-14
§ 8:4 First Sale Doctrine in the Fashion and Apparel Context 8-16
§ 8:4.1 Unauthorized Production and the "Genuine" Goods Doctrine 8-16
§ 8:4.2 Failure to Transfer Ownership of Goods 8-19
§ 8:5 Strategies Used by Fashion Brands to Combat Gray Market Sales 8-21

Chapter 9 Design and Manufacturing

§ 9:1 Introduction 9-1
§ 9:2 Fashion Design and Luxury 9-6
§ 9:3 Design and Production 9-11
§ 9:4 Supply Contracts 9-18
§ 9:5 Governmental Regulation and Industry Initiatives 9-18
§ 9:5.1 Federal and State Regulation 9-18
§ 9:5.2 Industry Initiatives 9-28
§ 9:6 Conclusion 9-31
Appendix 9A Sample Manufacturing Agreement .... App. 9A-1

Chapter 10 Licensing Arrangements

§ 10:1 Introduction 10-1
§ 10:2 License Agreements for the Manufacture and Sale of Products 10-3
§ 10:2.1 Using a Term Sheet 10-3

§ 10:2.2 Drafting the License Agreement 10-4
[A] Nature and Scope of the License 10-4
[B] Rights of First Negotiation, First Offer or First Refusal 10-8
[C] Term 10-9
[D] Production Process and Quality Control 10-10
[E] Royalties and Sales Volume 10-12
[F] Reporting and Accounting 10-13
[G] Advertising and Marketing 10-14
[H] Intellectual Property Rights 10-14
[I] Termination and Its Consequences 10-15
[J] Buy-Out Rights 10-18
[K] Representations and Warranties 10-19
[L] Indemnification and Insurance 10-19
[M] Other Provisions 10-20
§ 10:3 License Agreements for Retail Stores 10-20
§ 10:3.1 Nature and Scope of the License 10-20
§ 10:3.2 Development of the Stores 10-21
§ 10:3.3 Other Terms 10-22
Appendix 10A Sample License Agreement .... App. 10A-1

Chapter 11 Retail Sales

§ 11:1 Introduction 11-1
§ 11:1.1 Department Stores 11-5
§ 11:1.2 Specialty Stores 11-10
§ 11:1.3 Discount Department Stores 11-11
§ 11:1.4 Off-Price Stores 11-13
[A] Factory Outlets 11-13
[B] Off-Price Retailers 11-14
[C] Retailer-Owned Off-Price Stores 11-15
§ 11:1.5 Boutiques 11-15
§ 11:1.6 Pop-Up Shops 11-16
§ 11:1.7 Internet Retailers 11-17
§ 11:1.8 Mail-Order (Catalog) Retailers and Television Retailers 11-21
§ 11:1.9 Transition to Brick-and-Mortar Stores and the Growth of Omni-Channel Retailing 11-22
§ 11:1.10 Shopping for the Experience 11-26
§ 11:2 Arrangements Between Retailers and Vendors 11-29
§ 11:2.1 Vendor Standards 11-31
§ 11:2.2 Selecting Products; Discounts and Markdown Allowances 11-33
§ 11:2.3 Purchase Orders 11-35

§ 11:2.4 Shipping, Delivery and Risk of Loss 11-36
§ 11:2.5 Acceptance and Terms of Payment 11-38
§ 11:2.6 Chargebacks 11-39
§ 11:2.7 Consignments 11-41
§ 11:3 Distribution Agreements 11-42
§ 11:4 Conclusion 11-42

Chapter 12 Antitrust

§ 12:1 Introduction 12-1
§ 12:2 Basics of Antitrust Claims 12-2
§ 12:3 Horizontal Relationships 12-6
§ 12:4 Vertical Relationships 12-7
§ 12:4.1 Vertical Price Restraints 12-8
[A] Resale Price Maintenance 12-8
[B] Suggested Retail Prices 12-10
[C] Persuasion and Refusals to Deal 12-10
[D] Consignment 12-11
[E] Promotional Programs and Direct Rebates 12-12
[F] Cooperative Advertising 12-13
§ 12:4.2 Non-Price Vertical Agreements 12-13
[A] Exclusive Dealing and Exclusive Distribution 12-14
[B] Territorial and Customer Restrictions 12-15
[C] Tying 12-16
§ 12:5 Price Discrimination—The Robinson-Patman Act 12-17
§ 12:6 Antitrust Review 12-19

Chapter 13 Real Estate

§ 13:1 Introduction 13-1
§ 13:2 A Brick-and-Mortar Presence: Initial Considerations 13-4
§ 13:2.1 Finding a Suitable Space 13-4
§ 13:2.2 Forms of Real Property Interests 13-5
§ 13:2.3 Holding Real Property Interests; Guaranties and Security Deposits 13-8
§ 13:3 Drafting Lease Provisions 13-9
§ 13:3.1 Space 13-9
§ 13:3.2 Term 13-11
§ 13:3.3 Use Provisions 13-14
§ 13:3.4 Exclusive Use and Use Restrictions 13-15
§ 13:3.5 Rent 13-16
§ 13:3.6 Rent Abatements 13-19

§ 13:3.7 Visibility and Signage 13-21
§ 13:3.8 Practical Considerations; Alterations 13-25
§ 13:3.9 Assignments and Subleases 13-29
§ 13:3.10 Other Provisions 13-31
§ 13:4 Special Considerations With Respect to Fashion Shows 13-32

Chapter 14 E-Commerce and Mobile Commerce

§ 14:1 Introduction 14-1
§ 14:2 Developing E-Commerce and Mobile Commerce Platforms 14-5
§ 14:2.1 E-Commerce Stores 14-5
§ 14:2.2 Mobile Commerce 14-8
§ 14:3 Legal Issues Affecting E-Commerce and Mobile Commerce 14-10
§ 14:3.1 Contract Issues 14-10
§ 14:3.2 Data Privacy and Security Issues 14-16
[A] Regulatory Privacy Issues 14-17
[B] Private Privacy Litigation 14-28
§ 14:3.3 State Taxation and *South Dakota v. Wayfair* 14-31
§ 14:3.4 Other E-Commerce Issues 14-34
§ 14:4 Payment Methods 14-35

Chapter 15 False Advertising

§ 15:1 Introduction 15-2
§ 15:2 What Constitutes Actionable "False or Misleading" Advertising? 15-2
§ 15:2.1 Commercial Speech Versus Non-Commercial Speech 15-3
§ 15:2.2 "Advertising" Defined 15-3
§ 15:2.3 Non-Actionable Statements of Opinion Versus Actionable Statements of Fact 15-5
§ 15:2.4 Material Versus Immaterial False and Misleading Statements 15-7
§ 15:2.5 Literally False Advertisements Versus Ambiguous But Misleading Advertisements 15-8
§ 15:2.6 Specific Claims (or Disclaimers) Must Be Considered Within the Context of the Larger Advertisement 15-10
§ 15:3 Historical Regulation of False Advertising 15-13
§ 15:4 Federal Regulation of False Advertising Today 15-14

§ 15:4.1 Private Litigation Under the Lanham Act 15-15
[A] Establishing Standing to Sue Under Section 43(a) 15-15
[B] Prima Facie Elements of a Section 43(a) Claim for False Advertising 15-16
[C] "Establishment Claims": A Special Case 15-17
[D] Remedies for False Advertising Available Under the Lanham Act 15-19
[E] Common Defenses to a Section 43(a) Claim 15-21
§ 15:4.2 Administrative Regulation: FTC Oversight of "Unfair or Deceptive Acts of Practices" 15-21
[A] The FTC's Mandate and Structure 15-21
[B] Broad Scope of the FTC's Investigative and Prosecutorial Powers 15-22
[C] FTC Administrative Proceedings 15-22
[D] FTC Prosecutions in Federal Court 15-24
[E] FTC Enforcement of Labeling Regulations 15-24
[F] "Made in the USA" Labeling 15-25
§ 15:4.3 Administrative Regulation: Concurrent FDA Oversight of Cosmetic Products 15-26
[A] FDA and "Misbranding and Mislabeling" of "Cosmetic" Products 15-26
[B] FDA Administrative Proceedings and Prosecutions in Federal Court 15-29
§ 15:5 State Regulation of False Advertising 15-30
§ 15:5.1 "Little FTC Act" Jurisdictions 15-30
§ 15:5.2 "Little UDTP Act" Jurisdictions 15-31
§ 15:5.3 California's Approach to Regulation 15-32
§ 15:5.4 Cosmetics Consumer Class Actions 15-32
§ 15:6 Private Self-Regulation of False Advertising 15-34
§ 15:7 "The New Horizon": False Advertising on Social Media Platforms 15-37
§ 15:7.1 Section 43(a) Suits Involving Digital Communications 15-38
§ 15:7.2 FTC Oversight of Social Media Advertisements 15-39
§ 15:7.3 Communications Decency Act 15-42
Appendix 15A Examples of Effective and Ineffective Disclosures in Digital Advertising .... App. 15A-1

Chapter 16 Labor and Employment

§ 16:1 Introduction 16-2
§ 16:2 Wages and Hours 16-3

§ 16:2.1 Overview 16-4
§ 16:2.2 Overtime Exemptions 16-7
[A] Executive Exemption 16-8
[B] Administrative Exemption 16-8
[C] Learned Professional Exemption 16-9
[D] Creative Professional Exemption 16-10
[E] Computer Professional Exemption 16-10
[F] Outside Sales Exemption 16-11
[G] Combination Exemption 16-11
[H] Highly Compensated Employee Exemption 16-12
§ 16:2.3 Unpaid Trainees or Interns 16-12
§ 16:2.4 Restrictions on Home Workers 16-15
§ 16:2.5 "Hot Goods" and Combating Unfair Labor Practices 16-15
§ 16:3 Child Labor Laws and Sweatshop Practices 16-16
§ 16:3.1 Federal Child Labor Law 16-16
[A] Employer-Employee Relationship 16-16
[B] Age of the Minor 16-17
[C] Wages 16-18
[D] Work Prohibitions 16-19
[E] Enforcement, Penalties and Contesting Penalties 16-19
§ 16:3.2 State Child Labor Laws 16-20
§ 16:3.3 Concerns Over Sweatshop Practices 16-20
§ 16:3.4 Addressing Labor Problems Through Self-Regulation: Corporate Codes of Conduct 16-21
§ 16:4 Anti-Discrimination Laws 16-22
§ 16:4.1 Role of the EEOC 16-24
§ 16:4.2 Defense to Sex and Age Claims: Bona Fide Occupational Qualifications 16-27
§ 16:4.3 Pregnancy Discrimination 16-28
§ 16:4.4 Family and Medical Leave Act 16-28
§ 16:5 Health Issues in the Fashion Industry and Implications for Employers 16-29
§ 16:6 Use of Sales Representatives 16-31
§ 16:7 Bargaining Units 16-33
§ 16:8 Social Media Usage 16-34

Chapter 17 Employment Agreements

§ 17:1 Introduction 17-1
§ 17:2 Basic Employment Terms 17-2
§ 17:2.1 Title and Scope 17-2
§ 17:2.2 Term 17-3

§ 17:2.3 Compensation 17-5
§ 17:2.4 Ownership of Creations 17-7
§ 17:2.5 Other Matters 17-7
§ 17:3 Confidentiality Covenants 17-8
§ 17:3.1 Confidentiality in the Fashion Industry 17-8
§ 17:3.2 Drafting Confidentiality Agreements 17-9
§ 17:4 Covenants Not to Compete and Related Restrictive Covenants 17-13
§ 17:4.1 Covenants Not to Compete 17-13
§ 17:4.2 Related Restrictive Covenants 17-19

Chapter 18 Rights of Publicity

§ 18:1 Introduction 18-1
§ 18:2 Overview of Right of Publicity Law 18-2
§ 18:3 History of the Right of Publicity 18-4
§ 18:4 Leading Examples of State Right of Publicity Law 18-8
§ 18:4.1 California 18-8
§ 18:4.2 New York 18-11
§ 18:4.3 Indiana 18-15
§ 18:5 Practical Implications for the Fashion Industry 18-17

Chapter 19 Customs and International Trade Issues

§ 19:1 Introduction 19-2
§ 19:2 Importer Responsibilities 19-3
§ 19:2.1 Reasonable Care 19-4
[A] Generally 19-4
[B] Forced Labor 19-5
[C] Intellectual Property Rights 19-6
§ 19:2.2 Recordkeeping Requirements 19-7
§ 19:3 Entry of Merchandise 19-9
§ 19:4 Classification 19-11
§ 19:5 Valuation 19-14
§ 19:5.1 Assists 19-15
§ 19:5.2 Royalties 19-16
§ 19:5.3 Buying Agents 19-16
§ 19:5.4 Related Parties 19-17
§ 19:5.5 Alternative Means of Valuation 19-18
§ 19:5.6 Reconciliation 19-19
§ 19:6 Country of Origin Rules and Marking 19-20
§ 19:6.1 Non-Preferential Rules of Origin 19-21
§ 19:6.2 Textile and Apparel Rules of Origin 19-22
§ 19:6.3 Preferential Rules of Origin 19-23

§ 19:6.4 Country of Origin Marking 19-24
§ 19:7 Administrative Process 19-25
§ 19:8 Penalties and Enforcement of the Customs Laws 19-26
§ 19:8.1 Seizure and Forfeiture 19-27
§ 19:8.2 Monetary Penalties 19-29
Table 19-1 U.S. Customs and Border Protection Mitigation Guidelines Mitigation 19-31
§ 19:9 Exporting From the United States 19-32
§ 19:9.1 Economic Sanctions 19-33
§ 19:9.2 Export Controls 19-34
Appendix 19A Department of Homeland Security U.S. Customs and Border Protection: Entry Summary .... App. 19A-1
Appendix 19B Sample Page from Harmonized Tariff Schedule of the United States (2013) .... App. 19B-1

Chapter 20 Foreign Corrupt Practices Act

§ 20:1 Introduction 20-2
§ 20:2 Foreign Corrupt Practices Act: Origins 20-2
§ 20:3 Foreign Corrupt Practices Act: Central Provisions 20-3
§ 20:3.1 Anti-Bribery Provisions 20-4
[A] Who Is Covered? 20-5
[B] What Conduct Is Covered? 20-7
[C] Affirmative Defenses and Statutory Exception 20-11
§ 20:3.2 Accounting Provisions 20-11
[A] Books and Records Provision 20-13
[B] Internal Controls Provision 20-13
§ 20:4 FCPA Enforcement 20-14
§ 20:4.1 Case Study: Ralph Lauren 20-14
§ 20:4.2 Case Study: Avon 20-17
[A] History of the Avon Investigation 20-18
[B] Ramifications of the Avon Investigation 20-20
§ 20:4.3 Case Study: Nu Skin 20-21
§ 20:4.4 Supply Chain Risks 20-22
[A] Third-Party Manufacturers 20-23
[B] Transportation Service Providers 20-23
[C] Distributors 20-24
§ 20:5 Issue-Spotting in FCPA Enforcement 20-25
§ 20:5.1 Issuers vs. Non-Issuers 20-25
§ 20:5.2 Third-Party Payments 20-27
§ 20:5.3 Successor Liability 20-29
§ 20:5.4 Foreign Officials 20-31
§ 20:5.5 Gifts and Entertainment 20-35

§ 20:5.6 Crafting an Effective Compliance Program 20-36
§ 20:5.7 Responding to a Potential Violation 20-37

Chapter 21 Going Public

§ 21:1 Introduction 21-2
§ 21:2 Preparing for an IPO 21-5
§ 21:2.1 The Underwriters 21-5
§ 21:2.2 The Trading Market 21-6
§ 21:2.3 Work Streams 21-7
§ 21:3 IPO Process and Timeline 21-9
§ 21:3.1 The Registration Statement and SEC Review 21-9
§ 21:3.2 The Road Show and Pricing 21-11
§ 21:3.3 Gun Jumping 21-11
§ 21:4 Drafting the Prospectus 21-12
§ 21:4.1 Prospectus Summary 21-13
§ 21:4.2 Risk Factors 21-13
§ 21:4.3 Use of Proceeds 21-14
§ 21:4.4 Capitalization, Dilution and Selected Financial Data 21-14
§ 21:4.5 Management's Discussion & Analysis of Financial Condition and Results of Operations 21-14
§ 21:4.6 Business 21-14
§ 21:4.7 Management and Compensation 21-15
§ 21:4.8 Principal Stockholders and Transactions with Related Parties 21-15
§ 21:4.9 Description of Securities 21-16
§ 21:4.10 Underwriting 21-16
§ 21:4.11 Financial Statements and Other Data 21-16
§ 21:5 Conducting the Road Show 21-16
§ 21:6 Additional Documentation 21-18
§ 21:6.1 The Underwriting Agreement 21-18
§ 21:6.2 Lock-Up Agreements 21-18
§ 21:6.3 Additional Filings 21-18
§ 21:7 Life after an IPO 21-19
Appendix 21A Sample Risk Factors .... App. 21A-1

Chapter 22 Selling a Fashion Company or Fashion Brand

§ 22:1 Introduction 22-2
§ 22:2 The Sale Process 22-5
§ 22:2.1 Potential Buyers 22-5
§ 22:2.2 Due Diligence 22-7
§ 22:2.3 Confidentiality and Standstill Agreements 22-8

§ 22:3 The Transaction Structure 22-8
§ 22:3.1 Form of Transaction 22-8
§ 22:3.2 Purchase Price 22-9
[A] Cash 22-9
[B] Equity Securities of the Buyer 22-10
[C] Buyer Promissory Notes 22-10
§ 22:3.3 Purchase Price Adjustment Mechanisms 22-11
§ 22:3.4 Contingent Payment Mechanisms 22-12
[A] Earn-Outs 22-12
[B] Sale of Brand or Royalty Rights 22-13
§ 22:4 Ancillary Agreements 22-15
§ 22:5 Risk Allocation 22-16
§ 22:5.1 Representations and Warranties 22-16
§ 22:5.2 Covenants 22-19
§ 22:5.3 Indemnities 22-19
§ 22:5.4 Escrow Arrangements 22-20
§ 22:6 Closing Conditions and Termination Rights 22-21
§ 22:7 Illustrative Acquisitions in the Fashion Industry 22-22
§ 22:7.1 Classic Stock Purchase Agreement 22-23
§ 22:7.2 Public Company Tender Offer 22-23

Appendix 22A Sample Earn-Out Provision .... App. 22A-1
Appendix 22B Sample Fashion Industry Representations and Warranties .... App. 22B-1

Chapter 23 Distressed Fashion Businesses, Restructuring, and Bankruptcy

§ 23:1 Introduction 23-3
§ 23:2 Preparation for a Bankruptcy Case 23-4
§ 23:2.1 Fiduciary Duties 23-4
[A] Insolvency and the Standing of Creditors 23-5
[B] Determining Solvency 23-6
[C] Special Considerations for Private Equity Portfolio Companies 23-7
§ 23:2.2 D&O Coverage 23-7
§ 23:2.3 Liquidity Needs 23-9
[A] Typical Financing Arrangements 23-9
[A][1] Asset-Backed Lending (ABL) Financing 23-9
[A][2] Term Loan Financing 23-10
[A][3] Factoring Arrangements 23-12
[B] Cash Collateral 23-13
[C] DIP Financing 23-14

§ 23:2.4 Venue Considerations 23-15
[A] Third-Party Releases 23-16
[B] Stub Rent Obligations Under Section 365(d)(3) 23-19
[C] Assumption of Intellectual Property Licenses 23-20
§ 23:3 Filing a Bankruptcy Case 23-21
§ 23:3.1 Automatic Stay 23-21
§ 23:3.2 First Day Relief 23-22
[A] Employee Wages and Benefits 23-23
[B] Insurance 23-23
[C] Shippers, Warehousemen, and Goods in Transit 23-24
[D] Reclamation and Section 503(b)(9) Claims 23-25
§ 23:4 Issues in a Bankruptcy Case 23-26
§ 23:4.1 First Day Relief 23-26
[A] Property of the Estate 23-26
[B] Post-Petition Value Creation 23-28
[B][1] Source of Revenue and Prepetition Liens 23-28
[B][2] Oversecured Creditors' Right to Postpetition Interest 23-30
§ 23:4.2 Treatment of Non-Residential Real Property Leases 23-32
[A] Deadline to Assume or Reject 23-33
[B] Assumption 23-35
[B][1] Cure & Compensation 23-35
[B][1][a] Defaults Under Ipso Facto Clauses 23-35
[B][1][b] Defaults for Non-Monetary Breaches 23-36
[B][2] Adequate Assurance 23-36
[C] Assignment 23-37
[C][1] Adequate Assurance 23-38
[C][2] Non-Assignability of Leases 23-38
[C][3] Special Rules for Shopping Center Leases 23-39
[C][4] Designation Rights 23-40
[D] Rejection and Damages Cap 23-41
[E] Rent Obligations and Stub Rent 23-42
[F] Special Rules if Debtor Is Landlord 23-43
§ 23:4.3 Treatment of Executory Contracts 23-43
§ 23:4.4 Intellectual Property 23-44
[A] Limitations on Assignment 23-44
[A][1] Whether an Intellectual Property License is an Executory Contract 23-45
[A][2] Applicable Law Exception 23-46
[B] Limitations on Assumption 23-47

[C] Special Rules if Debtor Is Licensor 23-48
[C][1] Non-Trademark Licensees 23-48
[C][2] Trademark Licensees 23-49
§ 23:4.5 Treatment of Consignments in Bankruptcy 23-50
[A] Consignments Governed by Article 9 of the U.C.C. 23-50
[A][1] Definition of Article 9 Consignment 23-50
[A][2] Consignor's Right to Obtain Senior Security Interest in Consigned Goods 23-53
[A][3] If a Consignor Does Not Obtain a PMSI in Consigned Goods 23-55
[B] Consignments Not Governed by Article 9 of the U.C.C. 23-58
§ 23:5 Bankruptcy Outcomes 23-60
§ 23:5.1 Reorganization or Liquidation Under Chapter 11 23-61
§ 23:5.2 Sales Authorized by Section 363 23-62
[A] The Basics of a Section 363 Sale 23-63
[B] Advantages of a 363 Sale to Buyers and Sellers 23-64
[B][1] Going Out of Business Sales 23-65
[B][1][a] Compliance with Federal and State Law 23-66
[B][1][b] Merchandise Augmentation 23-67
[B][1][c] Duration 23-67
[B][1][d] Lease Restrictions 23-68

Table of Authorities T-1

Index I-1

Preface to the First Edition

Fashion presents a compelling challenge as it is a mix of art and commerce. How we clothe ourselves defines us. The medium is the message. *Fashion Law and Business: Brands and Retailers* takes a unique approach to the challenges faced by the fashion industry by integrating the nuts and bolts of the fashion business with the laws and contractual arrangements that define it. It encompasses a broad range of substantive legal issues faced by brands and retailers operating in an increasingly global and technological world.

As a partner at the law firm of Stroock & Stroock & Lavan specializing in transactional work, I was truly surprised by the various legal disciplines that I needed to be cognizant of when my son, Zac Posen, his sister Alexandra, and I founded his business in 2001. From the outset it was well defined that in building a global luxury brand, Zac, with his sister as his Creative Director, would be in charge of all things "creative." The rest was in my bailiwick—finance, hiring, establishing the atelier, finding production capability, producing fashion shows, you name it. While I thought that I had worked effectively and hard on large complex transactions in my law practice, nothing quite prepared me for the challenges involved in the process of taking a design for one of Zac's dresses and acquiring the proper amount of fabric for a sample, having a pattern made, having the atelier produce a sample that was true to the design, making sure it fit, sending it down the runway, taking orders from retailers, finding production factories, and getting production orders of fabrics to arrive on time—all on a global basis. And believe me, I encountered something going awry at each step of the way over the course of the next 10 years. Flooding in Mumbai? Delivery of hand beading delayed. Exchange rate fluctuations? Italian fabric costs increase by 20%. The ultimate challenge: achieving season after season what I call the "trinity," that is, quality, fit, and on-time delivery. It is not for the faint of heart. Compared to this, a contested proxy fight or a project finance deal now looked like a walk in the shade. I must confess, I never look at a designer garment hanging at Bergdorf's or Saks in the same way. My appreciation is intense and immense, not only for the design talent exhibited, but also for the myriad steps and the vast range of legal considerations encountered along the way. *Fashion Law and Business: Brands and Retailers* will serve as an important and practical guide for the lawyer, executive, or investor working with an emerging or an established fashion brand or retailer.

SUSAN O. POSEN, ESQ.
Chairman of the Board, House of Z LLC/Zac Posen
2013

Acknowledgments

"Fashion is not something that exists in dresses only. Fashion is in the sky, in the street, fashion has to do with ideas, the way we live, what is happening."

— Coco Chanel

We would like to express our profound appreciation to our former colleague and partner, Lois Herzeca, who was the moving force behind the first edition of this book. Lois has been a pioneer in the study of the legal issues that affect fashion, apparel, and retail companies, and the designers, executives, and other creative contributors that make the industry work. She was chiefly responsible for organizing the fashion law practice at our firm, Gibson, Dunn & Crutcher LLP. As the co-author of the first edition of this book, we are indebted to Lois for her contributions to so much of the content reflected in this book. Lois continues her involvement in fashion law through the University of Pennsylvania Law School, where she is a Lecturer in Law, and at the Benjamin N. Cardozo School of Law, where she serves on the Advisory Board of the Fashion, Arts, Media & Entertainment Law Center. We are grateful for her leadership, guidance, and support.

We also must express sincere gratitude to our partners and counsel at Gibson Dunn, who have imparted so much critical wisdom in identifying and explaining the most important legal topics for the fashion and retail industry in each of their respective practice areas, including:

Daniel Angel (licensing arrangements)
Michael Collins (employment agreements)
Michael Diamant (Foreign Corrupt Practices Act)
Andrew L. Fabens (capital markets)
Baruch A. Fellner (consumer product safety)
Benjamin Hershkowitz (patents)
Matthew Kelsey (restructuring and bankruptcy)
Andrew Lance (real estate)
Joshua Lipton (antitrust)
Samuel A. Newman (restructuring and bankruptcy)
Jason Schwartz (labor and employment)
Akiva Shapiro (the gray market and the first sale doctrine)
Peter Sullivan (antitrust)

Christopher T. Timura (international trade and customs)
Romina Weiss (tax)
Greta Williams (labor and employment)
Chris Wood (international trade and customs)

And this book would not have been produced were it not for the singular contributions of the following Gibson Dunn attorneys—past and present—who took leading roles in researching, developing, and updating the chapters of this book listed below: Jennifer Wang, Deandra Mann, Brittany N. Schmeltz, and Lorna Wilson (Chapter 1—Starting a Fashion Company); Jennifer Colgan Halter, Ashley S. Boizelle, Ilissa Samplin, Kaitlin Zumwalt, Marissa Moshell, and Peter Weinberg (Chapter 2—Trademarks and Trade Dress); Brooke Myers Wallace, Raymond A. LaMagna, Meredith Simons, and Madelyn La France (Chapter 3—Patents); Jessica Lyn Lund, Connor Sullivan, Aidan Grano, and Sheri Pan (Chapter 4—Copyrights); Piers Plumptre, Matt Aleksic, Charlie W.S. Griggs, and Katie Mills (Chapter 5—International Design Protections); Sarah M. Vacchiano, Claudia Barrett, and Michael Springer (Chapter 6—Unfair Competition, Misappropriation, and Trade Secrets); Anne Coyle, Alex Grossbaum, Lauren Nagin, Kristin Mathews, and Kayla Wieche (Chapter 7—Counterfeiting); Michael Policastro (Chapter 8—The Gray Market and The First Sale Doctrine); Danielle Villoch, Brian A. Castelloe, Sam King, Breana Love, Deandra Mann, and Brittany N. Schmeltz (Chapter 9—Design and Manufacturing); H. Joseph Pinto III (Chapter 12—Antitrust); Krista L. Patterson and Ben Imdieke (Chapter 13—Real Estate); Alison Watkins (Chapter 14—E-Commerce and Mobile Commerce); Adam L. Yarian and Stephanie Silvano (Chapter 15—False Advertising); Thomas M. Johnson, Jr. and Zoe Klein (Chapter 16—Labor and Employment); Jennifer A. Nelson and Christine Demana (Chapter 18—Rights of Publicity); Christina Dahlman and Allison K. Lewis (Chapter 20—Foreign Corrupt Practices Act); Sean Sullivan (Chapter 21—Going Public); Sean Sullivan, Sam King, and Breana Love (Chapter 22—Selling a Fashion Company or Fashion Brand); and Daniel Denny and Sabina Jacobs Margot (Chapter 23—Distressed Fashion Businesses, Restructuring, and Bankruptcy); and Amanda J. Finkelstein.

Thank you also to the Gibson, Dunn & Crutcher Information Processing Department, our wonderful assistants, Angel Taylor, Penny P. Murphy, and Christina Perez, and the management of our firm, especially Ken Doran and Charles Woodhouse.

In addition, we appreciate the assistance of Carol Benedicto and William C. Cubberley of the Practising Law Institute in bringing this project to fruition.

Finally, we are grateful for the encouragement, patience, and understanding of our respective families, Karen Gurnitz, Emma, Abby and Sam Hogan; and Melissa and Stephen Maguire and Paul Romon.

Dedicated to the memories of our mothers, Evelyn Hogan and Melanie Bellah. We would not be here without you.

Howard S. Hogan and Jennifer Bellah Maguire

Introduction

There is no single, universally accepted or precise definition of the "fashion industry." Historically, the fashion industry was most closely identified with those celebrated fashion houses that mount elaborate and highly publicized runway shows, featuring luxurious collections of apparel, in the major fashion capitals of the world. In reality, the fashion industry has evolved to be considerably more diverse, complex, and global, and the advent of Instagram and influencers, coupled with the retreat of print magazines and journalism, has resulted in the democratization and decentralization of fashion imagery.

A Brief History of the Modern Fashion Industry

Historically, the production of a garment was a laborious process in which the fabrics (or textiles) and garments were produced by hand and custom-made. Yarn was spun from raw fibers of animal or plant material (such as wool and cotton), dyed, and woven into fabrics by hand.[1] These fabrics were then cut into patterns and hand-stitched into individual garments using needles and thread.[2] Inventions such as the spinning machine and the power loom in eighteenth century England,[3] followed a century later by the invention of the sewing machine in the United States,[4] mechanized the production of textiles and apparel, and facilitated mass production. The growth of the apparel industry was fueled by expanding infrastructure, transportation, and communication networks within individual countries and internationally, and by increasing efficiencies in manufacturing techniques.[5]

---

1. LESLIE DAVIS BURNS ET AL., THE BUSINESS OF FASHION: DESIGNING, MANUFACTURING, AND MARKETING 3–4 (Olga T. Kontzias ed., 4th ed. 2011) [hereinafter BURNS].
2. GRACE ROGERS COOPER, THE INVENTION OF THE SEWING MACHINE (The Smithsonian Institute Press, 1968) [hereinafter COOPER], at 3, http://www.gutenberg.org/files/32677/32677-h/32677-h.htm.
3. BURNS, *supra* note 1.
4. COOPER, *supra* note 2, at 11; Michael Zakim, *A Ready-Made Business: The Birth of the Clothing Industry in America*, 73 BUS. HIST. REV. 61, 64 (1999) [hereinafter Zakim], https://www.jstor.org/stable/3116101?seq=1#page_scan_tab_contents.
5. BURNS, *supra* note 1, at 5; Zakim, *supra* note 4, at 62.

In the United States, men's ready-to-wear (RTW) apparel, as opposed to custom-made or home-sewn clothing from pattern books, became generally available beginning in the mid-nineteenth century.[6] Notably, in 1873, Levi Strauss & Co. began selling riveted-for-strength work wear made out of blue denim (which came to be known as "blue jeans") to gold prospectors in the western United States.[7] Men's RTW became increasingly available as sewing machines allowed work to be performed by unskilled laborers in large factories.[8] Dry goods stores (which were the predecessors of modern department stores) began selling apparel directly to consumers in cities, and through mail order to consumers in rural communities.[9] The men's RTW industry was also stimulated by the Civil War (1861–1865), as the demand for soldiers' uniforms led to significant investments in machinery, garment workers, and factories to increase the rate of production, as well as the development of standard sizes for men's apparel.[10]

The origin of the modern women's fashion industry can be traced to mid-eighteenth century France, where Parisian suppliers provided special fabrics and trim to customers seeking the most "fashionable" apparel.[11] Beginning in the nineteenth century, and increasingly during the Second Empire through the grand vision of Napoleon III and the patronage of Empress Eugénie, Paris became the international center for women's fashion design.[12] It was home to the haute couture fashion houses, beginning with the legendary House of Worth established by the designer Charles Frederick Worth (1825–1895). Worth relocated from England to Paris in 1845 and opened his own firm in 1858; he was noted for such novel practices as placing his own labels in his garments and showing his designs on live models.[13] Worth, and other Parisian fashion designers, headed teams of expert tailors working with lavish fabrics on custom-made garments for wealthy

---

6. Burns, *supra* note 1, at 6; Steven Fraser, *Combined and Uneven Development in the Men's Clothing Industry*, 57 Bus. Hist. Rev. 522 (1983) [hereinafter Fraser], at 526, https://www.jstor.org/stable/3114812?seq=1#page_scan_tab_contents.
7. Fraser, *supra* note 6; Lynn Downey, Levi Strauss: A Biography (2014), http://www.levistrauss.com/wp-content/uploads/2014/01/Levi-Strauss-Full-Biography.pdf.
8. Burns, *supra* note 1, at 6; Fraser, *supra* note 6.
9. Burns, *supra* note 1, at 6–7.
10. Burns, *supra* note 1, at 526–27.
11. Impressionism, Fashion & Modernity 62 (Gloria Groom ed., Art Institute of Chicago, 2012).
12. Jessa Krick, Charles Frederick Worth (1825-1895) and the House of Worth, Metro. Museum of Art, Heilbrunn Timeline of Art History (Oct. 2004), https://www.metmuseum.org/toah/hd/wrth/hd_wrth.htm.
13. *Id.*

clients, including Americans.[14] The Chambre Syndicale de la Haute Couture, established in 1868, imposed stringent membership rules limiting the number of haute couture houses that could operate in Paris and thereby reinforced the quality, exclusivity, and high prices of haute couture.[15] Haute couture continues to be a legally protected and highly controlled label that can be used only by fashion houses that have been officially granted the designation.

Women's RTW emerged more slowly in the United States in the late nineteenth century, beginning with loose-fitting outerwear that did not require precise measurements to accommodate the variation in women's body sizes.[16] The growing women's magazine industry brought images of the latest European styles, along with printed patterns, to American women. Consumer magazines, such as *Vogue* (1892), and trade publications, such as *Women's Wear Daily* (1910), helped to significantly increase demand for new women's apparel and accessories.[17] In particular, urban working women viewed RTW apparel as a convenient and affordable alternative to home-sewn garments.

The late nineteenth century also saw the emergence of the modern department store. John Wanamaker (1838–1922), known as the father of the American department store and modern advertising, opened the Grand Depot (later known as Wanamaker's) in Philadelphia in 1875.[18] He instituted such novel retail practices as uniform pricing (no bargaining), returns and exchanges, and specialized departments within the store.[19] Marshall Field (1834–1906) founded Marshall Field & Co. in Chicago in 1865, which became one of the most influential and innovative American wholesale and retail companies.[20] It began primarily as a wholesale company that sold merchandise to small merchants in other parts of the country.[21] In 1887, Harry Selfridge (who later founded his eponymous store in London) was appointed

---

14. THE GOLDEN AGE OF COUTURE: PARIS AND LONDON 1947–1957, 12–14 (Claire Wilcox ed., 2007).
15. *Id.* at 14.
16. BURNS, *supra* note 1, at 11.
17. *Id.* at 13; Christopher Breward, *Femininity and Consumption: the Problem of the Late Nineteenth Century Fashion Journal,* 7 J. DESIGN HIST. 71 (1994).
18. THE PHILADELPHIA HISTORY MUSEUM, FEATURED PHILADELPHIAN: JOHN WANAMAKER.
19. *Id.*
20. CHICAGO POSTCARD MUSEUM, MARSHALL FIELD AND COMPANY, FOUNDED 1865, www.chicagopostcardmuseum.org/assets/Marshall_Field_and_Company_History.pdf.
21. *Id.*

head of the company's retail operations.[22] Selfridge increased the number of individual departments from 50 to 150, started annual sales to clear out excess inventory, introduced a bargain basement, offered personal shopping services and easy credit, and added a lady's tea room to the store.[23]

The demand for RTW apparel, fostered by women's magazines, urbanization, and the expanding retail industry, led to the growth of urban garment factories, particularly in New York City. These factories employed primarily female immigrant labor, and often had unsafe and unsanitary working conditions.[24] The International Ladies' Garment Workers' Union was formed in 1900 specifically to advocate for workers' rights and to improve industry working conditions for these female garment workers.[25]

By the 1920s, the fashion industry was firmly established in the United States. New York City was the center of the women's apparel industry in the United States, accounting for approximately 80% of women's RTW apparel production.[26] Major American cities had large department stores (including Wanamaker's in Philadelphia, Marshall Field's in Chicago, and Saks Fifth Avenue in New York City), and became centers for retail shopping. However, Paris still largely dictated the principal fashion trends for women, with Paris-based designers like Coco Chanel and Italian-born Elsa Schiaparelli achieving international fame.[27] The American fascination with French fashion began to diminish after the 1929 stock market crash and ensuing Great Depression, which caused American consumers and importers to cancel shipments of expensive European goods.[28] At the same time, the American apparel industry began to focus on "sportswear," consisting of casual, comfortable separates (often made of cotton) that were easier to store, care for, and wear throughout the day.[29]

The European fashion houses, which suffered through World War II, re-emerged as powerful luxury brands after the war.[30] In particular, French designer Christian Dior (1905–1957) helped to reestablish Paris as an international fashion capital. Dior's New Look collection of 1947, featuring a full skirt, cinched waist, and round shoulders,

---

22. *Id.*
23. *Id.*
24. BURNS, *supra* note 1, at 11.
25. *Id.* at 12.
26. *Id.* at 15.
27. *Id.*
28. *Id.* at 15–16.
29. RICHARD MARTIN, METRO. MUSEUM OF ART, HEILBRUNN TIMELINE OF ART HISTORY, AMERICAN INGENUITY: SPORTSWEAR, 1930S–1970S (2000), https://www.metmuseum.org/toah/hd/amsp/hd_amsp.htm.
30. BURNS, *supra* note 1, at 17.

launched his reputation as one of the most important designers of the twentieth century.[31] Dior also was instrumental in introducing licensing agreements to the fashion industry, licensing his name during his lifetime for such diverse products as furs, hosiery, and fragrances.[32]

The period after World War II saw the beginning of the American baby boom generation (children born between 1946 and 1964), and a rise in demand for consumer goods, including apparel. By the middle of the twentieth century, American RTW apparel was being produced in modern factories (largely outside of New York City due to rising costs) and was widely available for purchase in retail stores.[33] Although French designers still influenced fashion trends, French designs could be copied and mass-produced in American factories at lower costs. Moreover, new developments in textiles yielded low-cost, low weight synthetic fabrics, such as spandex fibers, which were easily integrated into popular American styles.[34]

The growing teen population in the 1960s fueled renewed demand for affordable clothing and accessories. These items could be conveniently purchased in the new shopping malls rising in American suburbs.[35] Apparel brands specifically targeted teens with fashions that often bore little similarity to the styles worn by previous generations.[36] The 1960s produced such novel fashion items as the bikini, go-go boots, and the mini-skirt. By the end of the decade, fashion was heavily inspired by the hippies, including bell bottoms, tie-dye and batik fabrics, and psychedelic and paisley prints. American designers gained new prominence. Both Calvin Klein and Ralph Lauren established their companies in the late 1960s. In Italy, in 1962, the Camera Nazionale della Moda Italiana was formally established to represent the highest values of Italian fashion, and to coordinate and strengthen Italian fashion ("Made in Italy") both in Italy and abroad. During the 1960s, London also emerged as another modern fashion capital.[37]

---

31. BETH DUNCUFF CHARLESTON, METRO. MUSEUM OF ART, HEILBRUNN TIMELINE OF ART HISTORY, CHRISTIAN DIOR (1905–1957) (2004), https://www.metmuseum.org/toah/hd/dior/hd_dior.htm.
32. *Id.*
33. Elizabeth Cline, *The History of a Cheap Dress*, THE ETSY BLOG (May 31, 2011) [hereinafter Cline], https://www.etsy.com/blog/en/2011/the-history-of-a-cheap-dress/.
34. BURNS, *supra* note 1, at 19, 23.
35. *Id.* at 21.
36. *See* FASHION INSTITUTE OF TECHNOLOGY, YOUTHQUAKE! THE 1960S FASHION REVOLUTION, GALLERY AND CLASSROOM LESSON PLAN, at 4 (2012) [hereinafter YOUTHQUAKE!], http://sites.fitnyc.edu/depts/museum/Youthquake/YouthquakeLessonPlan.pdf.
37. *Id.*

By the end of the 1960s, there were five times as many publicly held apparel companies in the United States as there had been at the end of the previous decade.[38] Large mass-market retailers such as Wal-Mart Stores, Inc. and Target Corporation, each of which first opened stores in 1962, began to add apparel to their product offerings.[39] The American fashion industry was evolving into a new era of mass merchandise and corporate conglomerates.[40]

In the mid-1970s, the punk movement emerged in New York City and London, with a focus on punk rock music, do-it-yourself designs, and nonconformist political views. As illuminated in the Spring 2013 Metropolitan Museum of Art Costume Institute show "Punk—Chaos to Couture," punk design elements (such as ripped and torn garments, safety pins, and studs) had an enduring impact on popular fashion as well as couture designs.[41]

Global events in the 1970s and the early 1980s led to rising oil prices, and increasing labor and material costs; at the same time, consumer demand for apparel slowed.[42] American companies that had facilitated mass fashion by developing cheaper fabrics began to face growing competition from overseas companies importing inexpensive textiles to the United States.[43] New business strategies were deployed, including vertical integration (such as integrating manufacturing with retail operations) and the sourcing and production of apparel in factories in developing nations, where labor rates were lower.[44] Quick Response techniques, pioneered in the 1980s and early 1990s, focused on improving accuracy, quality, and speed, and helped companies respond more quickly to consumer demands and increase efficiencies.[45] The emergence of new technologies, such as the bar code and electronic communications, also enabled the fashion industry to streamline operations between manufacturing and retail sales.[46]

Nonetheless, during this period, many large department store retailers either failed or were acquired and re-branded. The consolidation of American department store retailers is epitomized in the history of Federated Department Stores. Federated was originally formed

38. BURNS, *supra* note 1, at 21.
39. *Id.* at 23.
40. *See* YOUTHQUAKE!, *supra* note 36; BURNS, *supra* note 1, at 21–22.
41. Press Release, Metropolitan Museum of Art, Punk Fashion Will be Focus of Spring 2013 Costume Institute Exhibition at Metropolitan Museum, May 9–August 14, 2013 (May 9, 2013), https://www.metmuseum.org/about-the-museum/press-room/exhibitions/2012/punk-chaos-to-couture.
42. BURNS, *supra* note 1, at 24.
43. *Id.* at 22.
44. *See id.* at 25; Cline, *supra* note 33.
45. *Id.*
46. *Id.*

in 1929 as a holding company for Abraham & Straus and Filene's, and then acquired Bloomingdale's in 1930.[47] Federated entered bankruptcy in 1990, emerged in 1992 as the new public company Federated Department Stores, Inc., acquired Macy's in 1994, and then acquired May Department Stores in 2005.[48] Federated began operating primarily through its Bloomingdale's and Macy's stores, and was renamed Macy's, Inc. in 2007.[49]

The Fashion Industry Today

Since the mid-1990s, the fashion industry has experienced a retail revolution. Prior to 1995, most retailers had a single distribution channel—brick-and-mortar stores. Beginning in 1995, with the launch of Amazon and eBay, and the creation of search engines such as Google and Yahoo, e-commerce became another viable distribution channel. The launch of the Apple iPhone in 2007, and the rapid adoption of smartphones generally, followed by the subsequent development of the tablet device, spurred the growth of mobile commerce. Many retailers began to adopt a multi-channel approach, selling products in brick-and-mortar stores, online and through mobile devices; however, they generally were not integrating their data, inventory, processing, and delivery systems. Accordingly, the same product might have a different price in a physical store than on a website and products purchased online could not be returned in a brick-and-mortar store. Since 2010, retailers have been moving towards omni-channel retailing, which is aimed at providing a seamless customer experience, integrated across all channels. Typically, this requires a restructuring of management and operational functions, as well as the adoption of new technologies that facilitate data sharing and interaction across the company.

At the same time, fashion brands are engaging in more direct-to-consumer retail sales, in their own brick-and mortar stores and through e-commerce and mobile commerce. The launch of social networks, including MySpace in 2003, Facebook in 2004, Twitter in 2006, Tumblr in 2007, and Pinterest in 2010, created new ways for fashion brands to interact with consumers and build brand loyalty. According to one study, globally more than a third of all consumers have purchased products directly from brands or manufacturers.[50]

---

47. *See* MACY'S, INC., https://www.macysinc.com/about-us/.
48. *Id.*
49. *Id.*
50. PWC, DEMYSTIFYING THE ONLINE SHOPPER, 10 MYTHS OF MULTICHANNEL RETAILING, at 28 (Jan. 2013), https://www.pwc.com/en_US/us/retail-consumer/publications/assets/pwc-multi-channel-shopper-survey.pdf [hereinafter PwC]. Furthermore, McKinsey & Company reported a four times greater

This may be due to a combination of more favorable pricing, wider selection, and brand loyalty.[51]

Fashion brands and fashion retailers also have been affected by the emergence of the millennial generation (also known as "Generation Y"), generally considered to be those people born after 1980. Millennials are more ethnically and racially diverse, and more educated, than any generation in American history.[52] They are more fashion savvy (finding styles from a variety of offline and online sources), are drawn to brands that embrace their voice and social agenda, engage heavily on social media networks, and are more selective about what they purchase.[53] This new generation is dramatically impacting the ways in which brands design, produce, market, and advertise their products, and the very nature of the retail experience. There is a greater focus on curating collections specifically for millennials, delivering fast fashion, using sustainable materials and manufacturing processes, connecting and providing self-display opportunities through social media, and incorporating innovative technologies into the shopping experience.

The fashion industry, like most other industries, is changing to better address the growth of emerging international markets and shifting global demographics. Asia and, to a lesser extent, South America have become the growth markets for both luxury goods and more affordable products. Indeed, according to McKinsey FashionScope, Greater China is expected to overtake the United States as the largest fashion market in the world in 2019.[54] The focus on emerging markets has been accompanied by renewed concern about corporate social responsibility and transparency throughout the global supply and retail chain.

---

compound annual growth Revenue CAGR of fashion e-commerce retailers over traditional fashion retailers from 2013 to 2017. BUS. OF FASHION & MCKINSEY & CO., THE STATE OF FASHION 2019 (2019) [hereinafter BOF & MCKINSEY], https://www.mckinsey.com/~/media/McKinsey/Industries/Retail/Our%20Insights/The%20State%20of%20Fashion%202019%20A%20year%20of%20awakening/The-State-of-Fashion-2019-final.ashx.

51. PwC, *supra* note 50.

52. PEW RESEARCH CENTER, THE MILLENNIALS, A PORTRAIT OF GENERATION NEXT: CONFIDENT. CONNECTED. OPEN TO CHANGE (Feb. 2010), https://www.pewresearch.org/wp-content/uploads/sites/3/2010/10/millennials-confident-connected-open-to-change.pdf .

53. Emanuella Grinberg, *Cash-Strapped Millennials Curate Style Via Social Media*, CNN (Oct. 16, 2012), https://www.cnn.com/2012/10/12/living/millennials-shopping.

54. BOF & MCKINSEY, *supra* note 50.

Fueled by new technologies and new consumer markets, the fashion industry has evolved to encompass a range of global industry participants. These industry participants reflect the journey of fashion products from their point of origin, typically outside the United States, to the eventual consumer. The fashion industry can be said to include the designers of fashion products (which increasingly include celebrities branding and building fashion/life-style brands such as Tory Burch and Draper James (Reese Witherspoon)); the textile suppliers and manufacturers involved in the production of fashion products; the retailers that sell these products to the consumer; and the innovative technology companies that facilitate or enhance the production, marketing, and sale of fashion products. Fashion products include not only the general categories of apparel and accessories (such as footwear, handbags, hosiery, headwear, scarves, belts, gloves, and jewelry), but may also include other highly designed products, such as certain home furnishings. They are sold at a range of price points, from couture to RTW to mass-market.

The fashion industry is also inextricably linked to, and serviced by, other related industries and organizations. In particular, the fashion industry is tied to the fashion media (including magazines and, increasingly, blogs and social media) that continually report and editorialize on, as well as advertise, display, and sometime sell, fashion products. The merging of editorial content and e-commerce has blurred the traditional distinction between the fashion industry and the fashion media, as retailers now generate their own fashion blogs and fashion magazines have e-commerce sites. The fashion industry has also spawned a vast array of consultants (such as publicists, branding agents, and fashion forecasters) that specialize in advising and representing fashion companies. The industry is supported by a large number of trade associations, such as the American Apparel and Footwear Association, the National Retail Federation, the Retail Industry Leaders Association, and the invitation only Council of Fashion Designers of America.

Fashion Law and Business

Fashion law has become as diverse, complex, and global as the fashion industry itself. Fashion law can be analogized to entertainment, art, or sports law, in that it is circumscribed by the nature of a particular industry, but is comprised of many distinct substantive practice areas of law. One way to describe fashion law is to say that it is the body of law and legal principles that governs the relationships among the various participants in the fashion industry, the relationships between such participants and the consumer, and the relationship between such participants and various governmental entities.

Accordingly, this book is structured on the presumption that fashion law can be best examined in the context of an understanding of the business and operations of the fashion industry. Each chapter focuses on an aspect of the fashion business and the related legal issues under U.S. federal and state law and, to a more limited extent, foreign law:

Chapter 1, Starting a Fashion Company, discusses the many considerations involved in starting a company in the fashion industry. It focuses on developing a business plan, determining the form and structure of the legal entity for the business, and then funding the growth of the business through equity and debt financings.

Chapter 2, Trademarks and Trade Dress; Chapter 3, Patents; and **Chapter 4, Copyrights**, discuss the evolving legal principles applicable to the types of intellectual property that are most commonly invoked in, and significant for, the fashion industry as a matter of United States law. These chapters focus specifically on the ground rules for trademarks and trade dress, patents, and copyrights, and provide an overview of how these legal regimes have been applied with respect to fashion products, as well as the legal principles that make these doctrines particularly relevant to the fashion industry in some cases and limit their applicability in other cases.

Chapter 5, International Design Protections, provides a broad overview of how fashion designs are protected outside the United States. Most countries in the industrialized world, to one extent or another, recognize design rights as an independent intellectual property discipline. The rights and remedies afforded by these regimes, however, vary widely.

Chapter 6, Unfair Competition, Misappropriation, and Trade Secrets, addresses the legal principles applicable to the common law torts of unfair competition and misappropriation in the fashion industry. The federal government and every state, moreover, also provide some form of protection for information that is held in close confidence and derives commercial value from not being widely known. Given the competitive environment in the retail and apparel industries, all fashion companies need to understand the interplay between these doctrines and the instances in which these doctrines may provide an applicable remedy in instances where traditional doctrines of intellectual property do not.

Chapter 7, Counterfeiting, focuses on the pervasive fashion industry problem of counterfeiting. It discusses the applicable legal principles and cases, as well as innovative strategies employed by the public and private sectors to combat global counterfeiters.

Chapter 8, The Gray Market Issues and The First Sale Doctrine, focuses on the issue of fashion goods that are manufactured and sold through particular channels, and the legal doctrines that limit manufacturers' ability to control those channels once products are sold and released into the stream of international commerce.

Chapter 9, Design and Manufacturing, addresses apparel design and manufacturing. It reviews the dynamics of the apparel manufacturing industry, the importance of luxury in the fashion industry, and the actual design and manufacturing process. In addition, it discusses the contractual relationships and regulatory issues applicable to the design and production of fashion products.

Chapter 10, Licensing Arrangements, focuses on the importance of licensing in the fashion industry. It discusses the principal business and legal terms of license agreements in connection with manufacturing apparel and accessories and establishing retail stores.

Chapter 11, Retail Sales, discusses retailing, which is the final step in the delivery of fashion products to the consumer. It addresses the dynamics of the retail apparel industry, as well as contractual matters applicable to transactions between apparel brands and retailers.

Chapter 12, Antitrust, addresses the principal antitrust issues applicable to brands and retailers in the fashion industry. It discusses the types of horizontal and vertical conduct in the fashion industry that may raise particular concerns under federal and state antitrust laws.

Chapter 13, Real Estate, discusses the legal issues applicable to leasing and licensing brick-and-mortar retail stores. It addresses both the significant contractual terms and the regulatory issues that should be considered in connection with such real estate transactions.

Chapter 14, E-Commerce and Mobile Commerce, addresses the growth of e-commerce and mobile commerce in the fashion industry. It describes the business and legal issues relating to the launch of e-commerce and mobile commerce businesses. It also focuses on the significant legal issues associated with operating such businesses, particularly with respect to the collection, use and storage of consumer information.

Chapter 15, False Advertising, discusses the legal regimes that govern advertising and marketing fashion goods. It also focuses on the specific legal issues relating to marketing through social media.

Chapter 16, Labor and Employment, explores labor and employment law considerations as they relate to the fashion industry. It addresses fundamental issues related to working conditions, wages and hours, and child labor. It also discusses the use of independent contractors (such as sales representatives), developments in collective bargaining in the fashion industry, and social media usage in the workplace.

Chapter 17, Employment Agreements, discusses the special considerations applicable to employment agreements in the fashion industry. It addresses the principal terms of such employment agreements, as well as the enforceability of restrictive covenants such as confidentiality provisions, non-competes and non-solicitation provisions.

Chapter 18, Rights of Publicity, addresses rights conferred by law over a person's image, name, or persona, including the use of models and celebrities, as well as the issues that may arise in the case of fashion designers who are closely associated with their fashion brand.

Chapter 19, Customs and International Trade Issues, addresses the relevant legal issues to be considered in connection with international trade and the international expansion of a fashion business.

Chapter 20, Foreign Corrupt Practices Act, addresses the increasing importance of the Foreign Corrupt Practices Act and related compliance issues for fashion brands and retailers, particularly in the international context, and provides a basic overview of the law's requirements and application.

Chapter 21, Going Public, discusses initial public offerings of companies in the fashion industry. It describes the process of going public, the applicable disclosure documents, and the distinctive issues applicable to public companies in the fashion industry.

Chapter 22, Selling a Fashion Company or Fashion Brand, addresses strategic transactions in the fashion industry. It discusses the important structural, valuation, diligence, and contractual issues involved in the sale of fashion companies and brands to strategic and financial buyers.

Chapter 23, Distressed Fashion Businesses, Restructuring, and Bankruptcy, provides a useful overview of the legal regime that affects fashion companies in distress. It discusses the options and protections that may be available to help a company restructure and recover, and the rights of creditors and other stakeholders in the event of a restructuring or liquidation.

Fashion Law and Business does not purport to cover every aspect of fashion law and business. There are undoubtedly other legal and business issues that currently confront the fashion industry, and the fast pace of change in the fashion industry ensures that new legal and business issues will continue to arise with the passage of time. Moreover, *Fashion Law and Business*, of course, is not a substitute for specific legal, tax, accounting, or other professional advice with respect to specific factual circumstances. Although the views expressed in this book are those of the authors and should not be attributed to, or construed as policies of, the law firm of Gibson, Dunn & Crutcher LLP, the authors do invite readers to contact them through Gibson

Dunn to provide any commentary on this book. It is our hope that *Fashion Law and Business* will provide lawyers, fashion designers, brand owners, retailers, and investors, with a helpful framework to better understand how the law impacts the business of fashion.

Chapter 1

Starting a Fashion Company

§ 1:1 Introduction
- § 1:1.1 Planning and Preparation
- § 1:1.2 Drafting the Business Plan
  - [A] Executive Summary
  - [B] Business Description
  - [C] Industry and Market Analysis
  - [D] Competition
  - [E] Implementation
  - [F] Organization and Management
  - [G] Financial Projections

§ 1:2 Forming and Structuring the Business
- § 1:2.1 Initial Considerations
- § 1:2.2 Sole Proprietorship
- § 1:2.3 General Partnership
- § 1:2.4 C Corporation
- § 1:2.5 S Corporation
- § 1:2.6 Public Benefit Corporation
- § 1:2.7 Limited Liability Company
- § 1:2.8 Limited Partnership
- § 1:2.9 Cooperatives
- § 1:2.10 Piercing the Corporate Veil
- § 1:2.11 Organizational Structure

§ 1:3 Financing the Business
- § 1:3.1 Capital Structure
- § 1:3.2 Equity
- § 1:3.3 Debt

§ 1:4 Sources of Financing
- § 1:4.1 Financing in Stages
- § 1:4.2 Personal Funds
- § 1:4.3 Friends and Family

§ 1:4.4 **Factoring**
§ 1:4.5 **Bank Financing and Commercial Credit**
§ 1:4.6 **Angel Investors**
§ 1:4.7 **Venture Capital Investors**
§ 1:4.8 **Private Equity**
Appendix 1A **Sample Creative Control Provisions**

§ 1:1 Introduction

§ 1:1.1 Planning and Preparation

Despite dips in the economy following the Great Recession, entrepreneurship is thriving in the United States.[1] This may reflect a confluence of factors, including still stagnating wages in traditional employment, the advent of the gig economy, lifestyle preferences for self-employment, cultural phenomena such as *Shark Tank*, ongoing developments in technology and social media, and a robust financing environment that is experienced in funding new ventures. The growth of entrepreneurship is being propelled by the development of university entrepreneurship programs, nonprofit organizations and media focused on increasing diversity amongst entrepreneurs, start-up accelerators, and serial entrepreneurs returning for another round.[2]

The global fashion industry presents a broad range of opportunities for new business ventures. Historically, the quintessential fashion start-up consisted of a fashion designer seeking to create a new brand of apparel or accessories. In recent years, however, creative entrepreneurs have started companies that offer diverse and innovative products and services using new business models to address inefficiencies or explore unexploited opportunities in the fashion industry. Venture capital firms have invested heavily in innovative fashion technology

1. *American Entrepreneurship Is Flourishing, if You Know Where to Look*, ECONOMIST (Sept. 30, 2017), https://www.economist.com/business/2017/09/30/american-entrepreneurship-is-flourishing-if-you-know-where-to-look; KAUFFMAN, KAUFFMAN INDEX OF ENTREPRENEURIAL ACTIVITY (1996–2017) (Oct. 2017).
2. *See, e.g.*, Ginger O'Donnell, *Incubators and Accelerators Open Doors for Female, Immigrant, and Underrepresented Entrepreneurs*, INSIGHT INTO DIVERSITY (Sept. 17, 2018), http://www.insightintodiversity.com/incubators-and-accelerators-open-doors-for-female-immigrant-and-underrepresented-entrepreneurs/.

companies such as Nasty Gal,[3] Poshmark[4] and Thread.[5] The highly publicized success of companies started by fashion designers such as Gucci, as well as companies with innovative business models such as Everlane and Aday, are inspiring new generations of fashion industry entrepreneurs.[6]

The publicity surrounding successful new businesses in the fashion industry tends to obscure the challenges and difficulties of starting a new business. Available data suggest that new businesses started in the United States fail at a relatively high rate. Approximately half of small businesses fail within the first five years.[7] And according to the 2017 Small Business Credit Survey Report, sixty-four percent of firms surveyed said they experienced financial hardship within the past year, with the response most acute among start-ups that were five years old or younger.[8]

The high failure rate, while it is nothing new, can be attributed to certain fundamental problems, primarily insufficient capital to support growth and weather unforeseen difficulties, inadequate demand for the company's products or services at prices that will generate profits, operational inefficiencies, and management weaknesses.[9] Many new fashion technology companies face significant financial and strategic difficulties within just a few years of commencing operations.[10]

---

3. Grace Whelan, *Thread Receives $22m in Funding*, DRAPERS (Oct. 16, 2018), https://www.drapersonline.com/news/thread-receives-22m-in-funding/7032611.article.
4. Alex Konrad, *Poshmark Raises $87.5 Million to Take Its Social Clothes Marketplace Global*, FORBES (Nov. 14, 2017), https://www.forbes.com/sites/alexkonrad/2017/11/14/poshmark-raises-87-million-for-its-social-clothes-marketplace/#3962c0333246.
5. Shona Ghosh, *Thread, the Fashion Startup That Helps Lazy Guys Buy Clothes, Has Raised $22 Million*, BUS. INSIDER (Oct. 15, 2018), https://www.businessinsider.com/men-fashion-startup-thread-raises-22-million-2018-10.
6. Leonie Barrie, *12 of the World's Most Innovative Fashion Companies*, JUSTSTYLE (Feb. 26, 2018), https://www.just-style.com/analysis/12-of-the-worlds-most-innovative-fashion-companies_id132938.aspx.
7. John Gallagher, *Financial Literacy Key for Small Businesses*, PORTLAND PRESS HERALD (Aug. 3, 2018).
8. *United States Small Business Demand for Credit Drops in 2017*, THAI NEWS SERV. (July 24, 2018).
9. Nicole Walters, *9 Reasons Why Small Businesses Fail (And How to Avoid It)*, SHOPKEEP (Apr. 30, 2018), https://www.shopkeep.com/blog/why-small-businesses-fail.
10. Vikram Alexi Kansara, *Is There a Fashion-Tech Bubble?*, BUS. OF FASHION (Mar. 25, 2013), https://www.businessoffashion.com/articles/fashion-tech/is-there-a-fashion-tech-bubble.

The likelihood that a new business venture in the fashion industry will succeed can be improved by thorough planning and preparation.[11] This section outlines the planning process for a new business and describes the specific elements that should be considered by an entrepreneur. For illustrative purposes, it focuses on a business that designs, produces, and sells women's ready-to-wear apparel. Although the specific details of the planning process will vary with the nature of the business (for example, a new apparel company may focus on design and production processes, while a technology start-up may focus on the development of its software), the general principles discussed here are broadly applicable to other new business ventures in the fashion industry.

The business of designing, producing, and selling women's apparel is particularly challenging. As more fully discussed in the following chapters, the apparel design and production process is complex, garment deliveries must be timed to the appropriate selling season, and the market is highly competitive. Accordingly, an entrepreneur contemplating a new women's apparel business should become familiar with the dynamics of the women's apparel industry and then carefully prepare the foundation for the business before committing substantial resources to the venture. An entrepreneur might consider taking some or all of the following preparatory steps, depending upon the nature and extent of his or her prior experience in the fashion industry:[12]

1. Develop an understanding of the elements of the design, production, distribution, and sales process for women's apparel, as well as a familiarity with business fundamentals such as accounting, marketing, and financial management. This experience can be gained by attending fashion and business courses at local fashion institutes, visiting industry events and trade shows, and, in particular, by working with an established fashion designer or retailer.[13]
2. Define the company's product lines by determining: the design, fabric, or other elements that will make the products unique

---

11. For general guidance on building a new company and launching products, see ERIC RIES, THE LEAN STARTUP (Crown Bus., 1st ed. 2011).
12. For a more detailed description of the planning process for an apparel company, see Toby Meadows, HOW TO SET UP & RUN A FASHION LABEL (Lawrence King Publ. Ltd., 2d ed. 2012).
13. Notable fashion institutes in the United States include: Parsons School of Design; the Fashion Institute of Technology; the Pratt Institute; the Fashion School at Kent State University; the Fashion Institute of Design & Merchandising; Massachusetts College of Art and Design; Savannah College of Art and Design; and Rhode Island School of Design.

or create functionality; the range of the products (the number of styles); and the depth of the products (the number of colors and fabrics). It may be helpful to prepare preliminary two-dimensional designs of each of the primary products (even if the designs do not have all of the technical specifications necessary for production purposes).

3. Identify a specific target market for the company's products. Then conduct preliminary research on that market to determine if the market is well served (including identifying actual and potential competitors) or if there is an unmet need.

4. Develop a unique brand identity that will resonate with the company's target market by identifying the distinctive qualities that will differentiate the brand from its competitors. Select the company name and the brand name and the logo for the products. Consider whether the brand name will be included in the company name and cover all of the company's products, or whether the company will have a distinct name, but individual product lines will have separate brand names. An entrepreneur may be tempted to use elements of his or her personal name for the name of the company or the brand. This can prove to be problematic if the entrepreneur later sells the company or the brand. The entrepreneur may lose the right to use his or her name in future business endeavors because the intellectual property rights associated with the name will belong to the company (and not the entrepreneur). And of course, it is important to pick a trademark that is unlikely to create consumer confusion with existing market players, which will make the mark difficult to protect, invite litigation, or otherwise complicate the process of creating a separate brand identity. For a further discussion of these issues, see chapters 2, 18, and 22.

5. Consider which design and production methods will be used for the apparel and review possible locations for the sourcing of fabrics and trim and the production of the products, packaging, and labels. Particular attention should be given to the possibility of initially producing the products in-house or through a small local business, as opposed to a foreign manufacturing facility (which may have substantial order minimums and longer production and delivery times).

6. Determine which channels of distribution will be used to sell the products (both initially and over the longer term) and whether the company will employ an internal sales staff or use sales agents or distributors. For example, some apparel and

accessory companies begin with sales to private clients or trunk shows before embarking on wider distribution strategies. Consider whether to have a brick-and-mortar retail store and review the types of possible stores (such as a temporary pop-up store or longer term leased spaces), as well as possible locations. Consider what type of e-commerce/mobile commerce presence and platform to maintain (whether through wholesalers or a stand-alone presence) and the different elements required to create and operate such platforms. For a further discussion of these issues, see chapters 13 and 14.

7. Find one or more trustworthy and experienced colleagues who can supply the fashion, financial, operational, or management expertise necessary to supplement the entrepreneur's own expertise. Many successful fashion brands began with a partnership between a creative fashion designer and an experienced business executive.

8. Develop relationships with experienced fashion executives, editors and bloggers, Instagram influencers, and other influential industry leaders who can serve as business advisors and advocates.

9. Create a network of contacts who can perform essential services (such as publicists, stylists, models, and photographers) at a price that is affordable for a new business, and find accountants and legal advisors who are experienced in the fashion industry and can establish the business on a sound foundation.[14]

10. Identify potential sources of initial financing so that the business can commence operations with sufficient funds to produce the first product lines (see section 1:4 of this chapter for a detailed discussion of financing sources).

§ 1:1.2 *Drafting the Business Plan*

Thorough initial preliminary planning and focused preparatory activities can facilitate the development of an effective business plan. A business plan is a written blueprint for the business and may serve multiple functions for a company. It can serve as a guide for the company's internal planning, can be used to recruit new employees, and can be

---

14. For example, in New York City, the Fashion Law Institute at Fordham Law School, New York City Small Business Services, and Volunteer Lawyers for the Arts offer pro bono legal and business services to entrepreneurs in the fashion industry.

used for the purpose of attracting external investment. Some potential investors prefer to see a short digital presentation prior to reviewing a detailed written business plan; in such cases, elements of the business plan can be used to create a compelling slide presentation. A business plan is not necessarily a static instrument; it can be modified as the business grows and circumstances warrant. Although the structure, complexity and style of business plans vary, a business plan typically ranges from fifteen to thirty-five pages and includes the following important elements.[15] The U.S. Small Business Administration also offers guidance on the preparation of a business plan, available at https://www.sba.gov/business-guide/plan-your-business/write-your-business-plan. Further, venture funds and other financing constituents may be able to provide templates or sample business plans.

[A] Executive Summary

The Executive Summary is the concise summary of the company's strategy, products, and market opportunities, which are all more fully described in the remainder of the business plan. It should contain a clear statement of the company's mission, emphasizing the company's uniqueness and commitment to certain core values and principles. In total, it should not be more than one or two pages.

[B] Business Description

The Business Description contains the more detailed description of the company's product lines and business strategy. It should include a discussion of product design, fabrics and functionality, product range, and product depth. It should address the company's pricing strategy for the products, including target wholesale and retail prices. It also should explain the company's unique brand identity and target audience. For a women's apparel and accessories company, this section of the plan might describe the type of woman who would purchase the company's products—her age, geographic location, personality and style, income, retail shopping habits, and preferences. In addition, this section should describe the company's distribution strategy (wholesale and/or direct to consumer) and indicate why that strategy has been adopted.

This section should identify the important intellectual property (such as trademarks, domain names, or design patents) owned by the

---

15. For more detailed information about preparing a business plan, and sample business plans, see U.S. SMALL BUS. ADMIN., WRITE YOUR BUSINESS PLAN, https://www.sba.gov/business-guide/plan-your-business/write-your-business-plan.

company or the entrepreneur, and identify the geographic locations where such intellectual property is registered or where registration is pending.

[C] Industry and Market Analysis

The Industry and Market Analysis is the research-driven portion of the business plan. The industry analysis should focus on the characteristics of the industry in which the business will operate, including the size of the industry (the estimated sales and the number and type of industry participants), the industry demographics, the market segments within the industry, the factors and trends affecting the industry, and the historic growth rate and growth potential of the industry.

The Market Analysis should focus specifically on the characteristics of the particular market segment applicable to the business. It should discuss the results of any market research on that segment and of any focus groups in the target market conducted by independent research companies and/or by the entrepreneur.

[D] Competition

The Competition section identifies and describes the principal current and potential competitors in the company's market segment, the barriers to entry into that market segment (such as any required patents), and the basis on which market participants compete. It should identify any unique features or competitive advantages of the company's products. It should also indicate whether the products will occupy a niche where there is currently an unfulfilled demand in the market.

[E] Implementation

The Implementation section describes the specific steps the entrepreneur intends to take to develop and grow the business. It should identify each stage of development and address the financial, management, and operational resources that will be necessary to achieve each developmental goal.

For a women's apparel and accessories business, this section might describe the expected design process, the sourcing of fabrics and trim, the manufacturing and production process, the distribution channels and sales process, and the advertising and marketing strategy. It should detail the types of expertise necessary for the business to grow (including design, technology, finance, human resources, sales, and marketing) and explain when and how that expertise is expected to be obtained. It should address any significant capital expenditures or operational expenses that are contemplated.

This section should focus in particular on retail sales. If the company will be a wholesale business, it should indicate which types of retailers it intends to sell to (such as e-commerce retailers, department stores, or boutiques). If the business is expected to have brick-and-mortar retail stores, this section should discuss the time frame for opening stores, possible locations, and the expected costs associated with those locations (such as rent, sales staff, and furniture and fixtures). This section should also discuss the anticipated e-commerce/mobile commerce presence and/or platform. If the business is expected to sell direct to consumer through e-commerce and/or mobile commerce, or an e-commerce and/or mobile commerce platform is expected to be used in connection with another sales methodology, this section should indicate whether such platforms will be developed internally or through third-party design and development arrangements, and the expected time frame and costs.

[F] Organization and Management

The Organization and Management section describes the legal structure of the company and might include an organization chart, particularly if the organization includes multiple entities. It should describe the background of the entrepreneur and the other principals in the business, highlighting all relevant experience. It may be helpful to list any business advisors and any experienced industry professionals who have agreed to serve on the company's Board of Directors. It should note any professional services firms (for example, legal and accounting) that have been retained.

It also might include a description of each of the company's equity holders, including any outside investors with significant equity ownership positions.

[G] Financial Projections

The Financial Projections section should include at least three, but preferably five, years of projected financial results for the company, including balance sheets, income statements, and cash flow statements. Since cash flow is an important issue for an apparel and accessories business (which has high up-front costs of production), the projections might also include projected cash flow statements on a monthly or quarterly basis. These projections should be conservatively prepared, based on expected revenue and expenses.

The entrepreneur should begin the preparation of the financial projections by creating an initial balance sheet for the company. The balance sheet reflects the company's assets (including all items of value such as physical property, intellectual property, investments, and cash); the company's liabilities (including all obligations owed to third parties such as bank borrowings, rent, wages, and taxes); and the company's stockholders' equity or shareholders' equity (the amount that would remain if all of the company's assets were sold and all liabilities satisfied) at a specified point in time (usually a fiscal month, quarter, or year-end).[16] The balance sheet provides a starting point for the future financial results of the company.

The entrepreneur should then prepare the projected income statements and cash flow statements for the company. An income statement reflects the revenue that the company has earned, the costs and expenses associated with earning that revenue, and the company's resulting net income or loss over a specified period of time (usually a fiscal month, quarter, or year).[17] The related cash flow statements reflect the cash flowing into the company and the cash expenditures flowing out of the company over a specified period of time (usually a fiscal month, quarter, or year) and indicate whether a company is generating positive cash flow.[18]

Preparation of the income statements and cash flow statements requires an estimate of when the company's products will be first available for sale. Prior to the first product sales, the company will generally have expenses without revenues, since revenues are generated primarily or exclusively from the sale of products.

For each year of the projections in which sales are expected to occur, the entrepreneur should estimate the company's revenue by considering: the number of collections to be produced in such year; the number of individual pieces in each collection; and the wholesale price per piece. If the entrepreneur reasonably anticipates royalty income from license agreements or other sources of revenue, such revenue should be included in the revenue estimates.

The estimation of projected expenses requires an estimate of both start-up and annual operating expenses, including items such as: rent; utilities; salaries and wages; equipment; supplies; manufacturing and packaging costs; distribution and sales costs; advertising and marketing costs; website design and maintenance; business travel; taxes; insurance; and legal and accounting fees. Especially during the early years, the entrepreneur should endeavor to monitor and control the company's costs.

A new entrepreneur can take steps to avoid common financial mistakes: for example, a new entrepreneur can automate business tasks, invest in talented, reliable employees, and cut back on the physical

---

16. U.S. SEC. & EXCH. COMM'N, BEGINNERS' GUIDE TO FINANCIAL STATEMENT, https://www.sec.gov/reportspubs/investor-publications/investorpubs begfinstmtguidehtm.html.
17. *Id.*
18. *Id.*

space used.[19] Reasonable steps can also be taken to control costs in advertising and marketing. A skillful company can use influencers, social media, and editorial coverage as relatively low-cost substitutes for expensive advertising. Even with careful monitoring of expenses, however, the first few years of the projections may indicate a loss for the company.

Once a preliminary version of the financial projections has been prepared, it is helpful to compare it to the historical financial statements of similar companies, to the extent they are available either from public sources or through industry contacts.[20] In addition, the projections should be reviewed by someone with an accounting or financial background, who is knowledgeable about the fashion industry.

If the business plan is being used to solicit funding, it should also contain a separate section discussing the contemplated financing. This section typically contains a "sources and uses" table, which describes the anticipated sources of funds (such as bank borrowings and/or equity investments) and the anticipated uses of the funds (such as production costs and salaries) over a specified time period. It should also detail the specific terms of the equity and/or debt being sought, as more fully described in section 1:3 later in this chapter.

Depending on the nature of the financial projections and associated factual representations, it may be advisable to include in the business plan sufficient caveats or other disclosures of potential risks that would be reasonably expected to affect an investment decision. By their nature, financial projections are subject to change, and it may serve the interests of both principals and investors to have a mutual understanding of foreseeable material risks to those projections.

---

19. For additional suggestions, see David Finkel, *23 Tips to Reduce Your Biggest Business Expenses*, INC. (Sept. 28, 2016), https://www.inc.com/david-finkel/23-tips-to-reduce-you-biggest-business-expenses.html; *Fourteen Financial Mistakes All Entrepreneurs Should Avoid*, FORBES (May 30, 2017, 9:00 AM), https://www.forbes.com/sites/forbesfinancecouncil/2017/05/30/fourteen-financial-mistakes-all-entrepreneurs-should-avoid/#27882eee4faf.

20. Financial statements of public companies can be found in their Annual Reports on Form 10-K or Quarterly Reports on Form 10-Q at the U.S. Securities and Exchange Commission website at SEC. & EXCH. COMM'N, EDGAR/COMPANY FILINGS, https://www.sec.gov/edgar/searchedgar/companysearch.html.

§ 1:2 Forming and Structuring the Business

§ 1:2.1 Initial Considerations

An entrepreneur establishing a new business (a "founder") may consider applying for certain governmental licenses or entering into contractual arrangements with third parties on behalf of the business. As these business opportunities are pursued, the founder should consider whether the business will have a separate legal identity from the founder, which is desirable both in order to limit the liability of the founder and in order to structure third-party funding. Thus, assuming the business will have a separate legal identity, the founder should consider which form of business organization is most appropriate. The principal forms of business organization for companies in the fashion industry are: sole proprietorship; general partnership; corporation ("C" or "S"); limited partnership; and the most popular, limited liability company.[21] There are important differences in the legal requirements and legal attributes, the tax treatment, and the advantages and disadvantages of each of these forms of business organization. The legal requirements and legal principles applicable to the formation and operation of each type of business organization derive from state law, and may vary from state to state. Unless otherwise indicated, the discussion below assumes that the business is formed under the laws of the State of Delaware, where a majority of the Fortune 500 companies (and many smaller companies) are incorporated[22] and the laws of which have served as a model for the business statutes of many other states.

When choosing an ownership structure, a founder should carefully assess the objectives and intended scope, scale, and operations of the new business. A designer of women's apparel may have very different legal and financial needs in the early stages of its business than a fashion technology company. The following factors are relevant to determining which organizational structure best satisfies the requirements of the new business:

- nature of the assets held by the business;
- potential liabilities of the business (including contractual obligations and third-party claims);

---

21. Useful information for starting a business, including descriptions of basic business forms, can be found at the U.S. Small Business Administration's website at SMALL BUS. ADMIN., https://www.sba.gov.

22. *Why Businesses Choose Delaware*, DELAWARE.GOV, https://corplaw.delaware.gov/why-businesses-choose-delaware/ ("[M]ore than 60 percent of the Fortune 500 companies are incorporated in Delaware.").

- tax treatment of the business, its owners, and its employees;
- number of co-owners, type of co-owners (individuals or other business entities), and relationships among co-owners;
- short- and long-term capital needs of the business;
- corporate control matters;
- transferability of ownership interests;
- costs associated with formation and operation of the entity;
- recruitment of employees and compensation;
- recordkeeping requirements; and
- continuity of the business.

§ 1:2.2 Sole Proprietorship

A sole proprietorship is the simplest form for operating a business. If a founder has started a business without any co-owners, but has not yet formed a legal entity for the business, then the business is already being operated as a sole proprietorship. A sole proprietorship may be used only by an individual who both owns and operates the business. The sole proprietorship is not a separate legal entity and there is no legal distinction between the owner and the business—all of the assets and liabilities of the business are the assets and liabilities of the owner. While the sole proprietor receives all of the profits of the business, the founder is also responsible, and has full and unlimited personal liability, for the losses, debts, and other liabilities of the business,[23] which can be recovered from the founder's other assets by creditors. Because a sole proprietorship is not a separate legal entity, it would also be more difficult to transfer ownership of the business enterprise (as opposed to ownership of the individual assets) and to ensure continuity of the business after the sole proprietor's death. Sole proprietorships are often used by businesses that do not have employees other than the owner, are not using external financing, and prefer not to expend funds on formation and other organizational costs. An example of such a business might be a fashion blog built around an individual that is slowly adding e-commerce features. As the business grows and its requirements change, the sole proprietorship can be converted into a different ownership structure.

---

23. U.S. SMALL BUS. ADMIN., SOLE PROPRIETORSHIP, https://www.sba.gov/starting-business/choose-your-business-structure/sole-proprietorship%20.

There are no organizational documents to be prepared and no organizational filings required with state authorities for sole proprietorships. The sole proprietor may incur certain costs in order to obtain licenses and permits necessary to operate the business, however, depending on the industry and the location of the business.[24] Further, while a sole proprietor can use his or her own name as the name of the business, sole proprietors often choose a fictitious name under which to operate the business (a trade name, or a "doing business as" name), which may require certain additional filings to ensure that others cannot use the same name.[25]

From a federal income tax perspective, the sole proprietor and the business are treated as a single person. All of the profits and losses of the business are treated as those of the sole proprietor and, along with any other income earned by the sole proprietor, are taxed to the sole proprietor at the sole proprietor's applicable income tax rate. Depending on the type of business, the sole proprietor may, however, be entitled to a deduction generally of 20% of certain qualified business income earned in respect of the business, subject to the satisfaction of certain requirements.[26] Because there is no legal entity, no annual franchise tax is imposed on the business. The sole proprietor is required to report and calculate the income of the business on Schedule C of Internal Revenue Service (IRS) Form 1040, the annual income tax return that is filed with the IRS, and on any applicable state and local tax returns. In addition, a sole proprietor generally must pay quarterly estimated income taxes and self-employment taxes, which include Social Security and Medicare taxes.[27] If the sole proprietorship has employees, the sole proprietorship must obtain an employer identification number for purposes of reporting and paying

---

24. *See, e.g.*, CAL. FISH & GAME §§ 4030–43; ALASKA DEP'T OF FISH & GAME, FUR DEALER LICENSES, http://www.adfg.alaska.gov/index.cfm?adfg=prolicenses.fur; CAL. DEP'T OF INDUS. RELATIONS, GARMENT REGISTRATION, https://www.dir.ca.gov/dlse/howtoobtaingarmentregistration.htm; MD. DEP'T OF NATURAL RESOURCES, FUR DEALER PERMIT/LICENSE, http://dnr.maryland.gov/wildlife/Pages/Licenses/furdealer.aspx; N.Y. DEP'T OF LABOR, APPAREL INDUSTRY TASK FORCE, http://www.labor.ny.gov/workerprotection/laborstandards/workprot/garment.asp; OR. DEP'T OF FISH & WILDLIFE, FUR DEALER LICENSE, http://www.dfw.state.or.us/wildlife/license_permits_apps/faq/fur_faq.asp.
25. *See, e.g.*, N.Y. DEP'T OF STATE, CERTIFICATE OF ASSUMED NAME, http://www.dos.ny.gov/corps/assdnmins.html.
26. 26 U.S.C. § 199A. This deduction is, however, set to expire in 2026. 26 U.S.C. § 199A(i).
27. 26 U.S.C. §§ 1401–1403. Fifty percent of the Social Security and Medicare taxes paid under section 1401 are deductible. 26 U.S.C. § 164(f).

payroll taxes.[28] A sole proprietorship may also have state or local filing or payment obligations.[29]

A summary of the principal advantages and disadvantages of using a sole proprietorship is set forth below:

Advantages:

- ease and low cost of formation;
- least-regulated ownership structure;
- sole control of the business;
- tax simplicity; and
- ease of termination (the sole proprietor can simply cease carrying on any actions of the business).

Disadvantages:

- unlimited personal liability (unless mitigated by other means);
- potential difficulty in raising capital and attracting investors (there is no ability to issue equity, and it is more difficult to borrow funds from commercial lenders);
- potential difficulty in attracting talented employees (there is no clear path to a future ownership interest in the business);
- lack of continuity (if the owner is ill, the business can be disrupted, or if the owner dies, the sole proprietorship automatically terminates); and
- lack of transferability, except through a sale of assets used in the business.

§ 1:2.3 General Partnership

A general partnership is similar to a sole proprietorship, but permits ownership by more than one party. It is the simplest form (like a sole proprietorship for a solo owner) that can be used by individuals who desire to jointly manage a company. Partners in a general partnership can include individuals or other business entities, including corporations, limited liability companies, trusts, and estates. A general partnership is the form of ownership that is often used in the early stages of a new business venture started by more than one party. In Delaware, general partnerships are subject to the provisions of the

28. 26 C.F.R. § 301.6109-1(a)(1)(ii)(D).

29. *See, e.g.*, N.Y. DEP'T OF TAXATION & FIN., PUBL'N NO. 20, at 5–6 (Nov. 2012); CAL. SBE INFO. PUBL'N 170 (May 2016).

Delaware Revised Uniform Partnership Act (DRUPA).[30] A general partnership is also similar to a sole proprietorship in that each partner has full and unlimited personal liability for the losses, debts, and other liabilities of the business. Like a sole proprietorship, there is no legal entity providing a limitation on liability. Furthermore, each partner is jointly and severally liable for such losses, debts, and liabilities.[31] As a result, one partner can be fully liable for all of the liabilities of the general partnership, including those resulting from the decisions and actions of another partner, if the general partnership does not satisfy those obligations. Personal assets of a partner can also be used to satisfy the partnership's obligations.[32] But like any business, regardless of its structure, appropriate insurance against likely claims and risks can help to mitigate this concern.

The management and operation of a general partnership are more complex than that of a sole proprietorship because there are multiple owners. It is therefore advisable for the partners to enter into a partnership agreement that governs the relationship among the partners, and between the partners and the general partnership. The partnership agreement may also contain provisions that specifically deviate from or modify certain default requirements or standards set forth in the DRUPA.

Similar to a sole proprietorship, a general partnership does not need to be established through organizational documents or filings with state authorities, and a general partnership can be inferred from the conduct of the relevant parties under section 202 of the DRUPA. If two or more parties are engaged in a business relationship that could be construed as a general partnership, but is not intended to be one, the parties should be careful to affirm, in appropriate documents between them and with third parties, that they are not acting as partners.[33]

---

30. DEL. CODE ANN. tit. 6, § 15.
31. DEL. CODE ANN. tit. 6, § 15-306(a).
32. *See* FINDLAW, PARTNERSHIP RULES: FAQS, http://smallbusiness.findlaw.com/incorporation-and-legal-structures/partnership-rules-and-faqs.html ("Partners are personally liable for the business obligations of the partnership. This means that if the partnership can't afford to pay creditors or the business fails, the partners are individually responsible to pay for the debts and creditors can go after personal assets such as bank accounts, cars, and even homes.").
33. "Partnership by estoppel, although accepted in Delaware before the adoption of the Uniform Partnership Act, is now codified under [DEL. CODE ANN. tit. 6, § 15-308]. Under this section, a person can subject himself or herself to partnership liability, even though not in actuality a partner, by representing

Although filings with a state authority are not required to form a general partnership, section 105 of the DRUPA provides for permissive filings to establish a general partnership. A general partnership may choose to file a statement or certificate with the Delaware Secretary of State because it may facilitate establishing bank accounts for the partnership, securing commercial loans, or carrying out additional business activities.[34] Similar to a sole proprietorship, a general partnership is free from certain of the reporting and recordkeeping obligations common to other legal entities. DRUPA does not contain any specific recordkeeping requirements, though each partner or former partner is to be given access to certain information, and a general partnership should, therefore, establish certain recordkeeping guidelines.[35] In addition, the appropriate licenses and permits necessary to operate the business, which will depend on the industry and location of the business, must also be obtained.

From a federal income tax perspective, a general partnership is generally not subject to tax as an entity.[36] However, a general partnership is required to file a partnership income tax return on IRS Form 1065 and any applicable state and local tax returns.[37] Each partner's share of the profits and losses of the partnership are reported to both the partner and the IRS on a Schedule K-1. The profits and losses of the partnership are "passed through" to its partners and are reported by the partners on their respective income tax returns.[38] A partner in a partnership must pay tax on the income of the partnership allocated to that partner whether or not cash is distributed to the partner. The partner

---

himself or herself through words or conduct, or allowing another to so represent him or her as a partner to another person." O. A. Newton & Son Co. v. Horsey, 1987 WL 8879, at *1 (Del. Super. Ct. 1987).

34. Registered Agents Legal Servs., LLC, General Partnership ("In Delaware, a statement of partnership existence may be filed with the Secretary of State if the partners opt to do so; such a filing may be needed for the partnership to open bank accounts, secure business loans, and carry out other business functions."), https://www.inclegal.com/general-partnership/; David M. Steingold, *Opening a Business Bank Account*, NOLO, https://www.nolo.com/legal-encyclopedia/opening-business-bank-account.html.

35. Del. Code Ann. tit. 6, § 15-403.

36. 26 U.S.C. § 701. A general partnership (and a limited partnership, discussed below) are, however, generally permitted to elect to be classified as associations taxable as corporations for federal income tax purposes. 26 C.F.R. § 301.7701-3(a). A partnership that has made the election and that otherwise meets the applicable requirements may elect to be treated as an S corporation.

37. 26 U.S.C. § 6031(a); Instructions to Form IT-204; Instructions to Form NYC-204.

38. 26 U.S.C. §§ 701, 702.

is taxed on such income at the partner's applicable income tax rate. Similar to a sole proprietorship, discussed above, depending on the type of business and subject to the satisfaction of certain requirements, the partner may be entitled to a deduction generally of 20% of certain qualified business income of the partnership. In order to provide the partners with sufficient cash to pay their tax liabilities arising from their ownership of interests in the partnership, a partnership may make "tax distributions" to its partners, that is, distributions of cash sufficient to enable the partners to pay their tax liabilities arising from their ownership of interests in the partnership. When the income of the partnership is distributed to the partners, subject to certain exceptions, it is not generally subject to tax, because the partners have already paid tax on these amounts.[39] If a partnership distributes appreciated assets to its partners, neither the partnership nor its partners will generally recognize gain on the distribution.[40]

If an individual partner of a partnership receives a "salary" from the partnership, the income is not subject to withholding by the partnership and is not reported to the partner on a Form W-2. Rather, it is included on the partner's Schedule K-1. Like a sole proprietor, discussed above, the partner must pay self-employment taxes, including Social Security and Medicare taxes, and pay estimated income taxes.[41]

If the partnership has filed a statement of partnership existence in Delaware, then the partnership must also pay an annual franchise tax.[42]

A summary of the principal advantages and disadvantages of using a general partnership is set forth below:

Advantages:

- ease and low cost of formation (although there may be legal and accounting costs involved in creating a partnership agreement, and the partners may elect a permissive filing with state authorities);
- lightly regulated ownership structure;
- single level of taxation;
- ability to offer partnership interests to attract talent;
- ability to raise capital through admission of new partners; and

39. 26 U.S.C. § 731.
40. 26 U.S.C. § 731. *But see* 26 U.S.C. § 751 (relating to distributions of "hot assets," *i.e.*, unrealized receivables and inventory).
41. See discussion on Sole Proprietorships, *supra* section 1:2.2.
42. DEL. CODE ANN. tit. 6, § 15-1208.

- continuity (in most states, including Delaware, the partnership does not automatically dissolve upon the death, retirement, or withdrawal of a partner from the partnership; the remaining partners may purchase such partner's interest in the partnership).

Disadvantages:

- unlimited joint and individual personal liability;
- potential difficulty in raising capital (no ability to issue equity to parties without admission as a general partner);
- shared and decentralized management control; and
- possibility of disagreements arising among partners (which can disrupt the business).

Typically, the greatest disincentive to using either a sole proprietorship or a general partnership is the unlimited personal liability associated with these forms of ownership. For this reason, many businesses prefer to use a form of legal entity that creates a greater distinction between the owners of the business personally and the business itself. In such a legal entity, the owners are protected from unlimited personal liability because the law treats the business as a separate entity, and the assets and liabilities of the owners are legally distinct from the assets and liabilities of the business. That said, if a company operates without sufficient capital or the legal distinction between the owners and the legal entity is blurred, a court may choose to "pierce the corporate veil," a concept discussed further below in section 1:2.10, and treat the owners as if there were no separate legal entity. In addition to issues of limiting liability, there may be business reasons to use a more robust legal entity. For example, if several of the founders of the business own intellectual property rights (such as trademark brand names or design patents) that are integral to the new business, it may be desirable to convey those rights to the legal entity that owns the business, to shield them from an individual owner's own debts, marital dissolution proceedings amongst owners, and the like. A summary of the principal types of entities with separate legal identities follows.

§ 1:2.4 C Corporation

A C corporation (as referred to in this section, a "corporation") is an incorporated business entity of which the owners' liability is limited to their investment in its shares. It has a legal identity that is separate from that of its owners. Owners of the corporation are known as stockholders (or shareholders) and may include individuals and other business entities, including other corporations, limited liability companies, partnerships, trusts, and estates. By statute, stockholders are insulated from personal liability for the obligations of, or actions taken by, the corporation. Delaware corporations are subject to the provisions of the Delaware General Corporation Law (DGCL).[43]

Most publicly traded companies are organized as corporations, and many businesses using other entity structures convert into corporations prior to their initial public offerings.[44] Corporations can also offer equity-based incentives to employees, which can help to attract talented personnel. A corporation, however, is a regulated form of business entity, and financial and other management resources must be dedicated to complying with the applicable regulatory and legal formalities.

Section 141 of the DGCL vests the corporation's Board of Directors with authority over the management of the corporation. Section 211(b) of the DGCL provides that the corporation's stockholders indirectly exercise control over the corporation by electing the members of the corporation's Board of Directors. Although the Board of Directors generally authorizes designated officers of the corporation to control the day-to-day operations of the corporation, the Board ultimately has a fiduciary duty to protect the interests of the stockholders and, therefore, must adequately exercise oversight over the corporation.[45] Directors owe the fiduciary duties of due care and loyalty to the stockholders of the corporation. The scope of these duties has been shaped by Delaware case law and continues to evolve. The duty of due care generally requires directors to act on an informed basis and with "that amount of care which ordinarily careful and prudent men would use in similar circumstances."[46] Prior to making a business decision, the directors must be "informed"; in determining whether this standard is met, courts look to "the material or advice the board had available to it and whether it had sufficient opportunity to acquire knowledge concerning the problem before acting."[47] The Delaware courts have

---

43. DEL. CODE ANN. tit. 8, §§ 101–398.
44. Davis Wright Tremaine, *Choice of Entity*, STARTUP LAW BLOG, http://www.startuplawblog.com/choice-of-entity/.
45. *See In re* Caremark Int'l Inc. Derivative Litig., 698 A.2d 959 (Del. Ch. 1996).
46. *See* EDWARD P. WELCH ET AL., FOLK ON THE DELAWARE GENERAL CORPORATION LAW § 141.02 (6th ed. Supp. 3 2018) (discussing fiduciary duty of directors and the business judgment rule); *see also* Smith v. Van Gorkom, 488 A.2d 858, 872 (Del. 1985); Graham v. Allis-Chambers Mfg. Co., 188 A.2d 125, 130 (Del. Ch. 1963).
47. Moran v. Household Int'l Inc., 490 A.2d 1059, 1075 (Del. Ch.), *aff'd*, 500 A.2d 1346 (Del. 1985).

also held that officers and directors have a duty of loyalty, "[c]orporate officers and directors are not permitted to use their position of trust and confidence to further their private interests"[48] and "directors can neither appear on both sides of a transaction nor expect to derive any personal financial benefit from it in the sense of self-dealing, as opposed to a benefit which devolves upon the corporation or all stockholders generally."[49]

A corporation is formed in Delaware when a properly executed certificate of incorporation is filed with the Delaware Secretary of State. Upon filing the certificate of incorporation, the corporation must pay fees to the State of Delaware in an amount based on the number of authorized shares.[50] Once legally formed, a corporation should adopt bylaws, which, according to section 109(b) of the DGCL, "may contain any provision, not inconsistent with law or with the certificate of incorporation, relating to the business of the corporation, the conduct of its affairs, and its rights or powers or the rights or powers of its stockholders, directors, officers or employees." Bylaws typically address the following principal areas: (i) annual and special stockholders' meetings; (ii) Board of Director meetings and Board committees; (iii) appointment of officers and their duties; and (iv) indemnification of directors and officers in their roles as such. In addition, certain stockholders may decide to enter into a stockholders' agreement with the corporation and with each other, which may cover the issues discussed in section 1:3 of this chapter.

Corporations are required to comply with certain legal formalities during the period of their legal existence. For example, an organizational meeting must be held after the certificate of incorporation is filed,[51] meetings of stockholders generally must be held at least annually,[52] and meetings of the Board of Directors should be held at least quarterly thereafter. Significant transactions involving the corporation must be formally approved by the Board of Directors and, depending on their significance, by the stockholders as well. Actions of the Board and stockholders should be recorded, either in the form of minutes of meetings or in written consents, and maintained in the corporation's records, which must be made available to stockholders.[53] In addition, the appropriate licenses and permits necessary to operate the business, which will depend on the industry and location of the business, must also be obtained.

---

48. *See* Guth v. Loft, Inc., 5 A.2d 503, 510 (Del. 1939).
49. *See* Aronson v. Lewis, 473 A.2d 805, 812 (Del. 1984).
50. DEL. CODE ANN. tit. 8, § 391.
51. DEL. CODE ANN. tit. 8, § 108.
52. DEL. CODE ANN. tit. 8, § 211(b).
53. DEL. CODE ANN. tit. 8, § 220.

From a federal income tax perspective, a corporation is a separate taxpayer that is required to pay tax on its income.[54] A C corporation must file an IRS Form 1120 annually with the IRS and pay tax at the rates applicable to corporations.[55] In addition, when a C corporation pays dividends to its stockholders, the stockholders are required to report the dividends on their income tax returns and pay tax at the applicable rates.[56] Thus, the result is two layers of tax: one at the corporate level and a second at the shareholder level.

Stockholders of a C corporation who are also employees of the corporation are treated in the same manner as all other employees of the corporation. Therefore, their salaries are subject to withholding for federal, state, and local income taxes, and Social Security and Medicare taxes, and the corporation must pay the employer's share of Social Security and Medicare taxes on their behalf as well as unemployment taxes. Their salaries (including any bonuses) are reported on a Form W-2, and they must include this income in calculating their personal income tax liabilities.[57]

All corporations organized in Delaware must file an annual franchise tax report and pay an annual tax to the Delaware Secretary of State.[58]

A summary of the principal advantages and disadvantages of using a C corporation is set forth below:

Advantages:

- limited personal liability for stockholders (a stockholder's liability is generally limited to the amount of its investment in the corporation);
- capital can be raised through private placements or public offerings of stock;
- ability to offer equity ownership incentives to attract and retain talent;
- perpetual existence;

---

54. S corporations are generally exempt from paying U.S. federal income tax. Not all states recognize S corporations as exempt from tax. For example, in New York State, N.Y. Tax Law § 210(1) requires a New York S Corporation to pay a fixed-dollar minimum tax as set forth in § 210(1)(d). *See* 26 C.F.R. § 301.6109-1.
55. A C corporation may also be required to file state and local tax returns, and pay applicable income taxes to the applicable jurisdictions. *See, e.g.*, N.Y. Tax Law § 209; N.Y.C. ADMIN. CODE § 11-603.
56. 26 U.S.C. §§ 301(a), 302(a).
57. Instructions to IRS Form W-2, https://www.irs.gov/pub/irs-pdf/fw2.pdf.
58. *See* DEL. CODE ANN. tit. 8, §§ 502–503.

- ease of transferability of ownership interests; and
- investment firms often prefer to invest in corporations for their investors' tax reasons.

Disadvantages:

- higher formation costs;
- ongoing recordkeeping requirements and need to maintain corporate formalities;
- potential for double taxation (at the corporate and stockholder level); and
- need to comply with the fiduciary duties of directors.

§ 1:2.5 S Corporation

An S corporation is a corporation that satisfies certain requirements under the Internal Revenue Code of 1986 (the "Code") that permit it to obtain certain tax advantages.[59] Accordingly, the distinctions between an S corporation and a C corporation are relevant only for income tax purposes. To become an S corporation, the corporation itself must affirmatively elect S corporation status on Form 2553, and all stockholders of the corporation must consent to the election.[60] The election must be made no later than the fifteenth day of the third month of the taxable year for which the election is to take effect.[61] If the election is not timely made, the corporation may apply to the IRS for relief to make a late election.[62] Only "small business corporations" meeting the requirements set forth in the Code are eligible to elect to be treated as S corporations.[63] Some of the requirements include that there can be no more than 100 stockholders, there can be no more than one class of stock (although there can be differences in voting rights among shares of common stock[64]), and stockholders must be individual citizens or residents of the United States for federal income tax purposes, certain trusts, and certain tax-exempt organizations, and cannot be other business entities. If an S corporation does not meet these ownership requirements, it generally will automatically become a C corporation.[65]

---

59. 26 U.S.C. § 1361.
60. 26 U.S.C. § 1362(a).
61. 26 U.S.C. § 1362(b)(1)(B).
62. 26 U.S.C. § 1362(b)(5); Rev. Proc. 2013-30, 2013-36 I.R.B. 173.
63. 26 U.S.C. §§ 1361(b), 1362(a).
64. 26 U.S.C. § 1361(c)(4).
65. 26 U.S.C. § 1361(a)(2).

From a federal income tax perspective,[66] an S corporation, like a partnership, does not generally pay taxes.[67] The profits and losses of an S corporation are generally "passed through" to its stockholders, are reported to the IRS and the stockholders on a Schedule K-1, and are reported by the stockholders on the IRS Form 1040 (or other applicable IRS form) that they are required to file annually and are taxed at the stockholders' applicable federal income tax rates.

A stockholder of an S corporation must pay tax on the income of the S corporation, whether or not cash is distributed to the stockholder. The stockholder is taxed on such income at the stockholder's applicable income tax rate. Similar to a sole proprietorship and partnership, discussed above, depending on the type of business and subject to the satisfaction of certain requirements, the stockholder may be entitled to a deduction generally of 20% of certain qualified business income of the S corporation. In order to provide the stockholders with sufficient cash to pay their tax liabilities arising from their ownership of shares of an S corporation, the S corporation may make "tax distributions" to its stockholders, that is, distributions of cash sufficient to enable the stockholders to pay their tax liabilities arising from their ownership of shares in the S corporation. When the income of the S corporation is distributed to the stockholders, subject to certain exceptions, it is not generally subject to tax because the stockholders have already paid tax on these amounts.

If a stockholder provides services to the S corporation, unlike in the case of a partnership, the stockholder is treated like an employee of the corporation, and, subject to certain exceptions,[68] is subject to tax in the same manner as a stockholder-employee of a C corporation, as described above. Because a stockholder of an S corporation may pay a lower rate of tax on income that is earned by the S corporation and distributed to the stockholders than on any salary paid to him or her by the S corporation, stockholders of S corporations often have the incentive to treat all amounts received by them from an S corporation as distributions from the S corporation. If a stockholder does so, he or she is subject to the risk that the IRS will claim that the stockholder has not been paid "reasonable compensation" for his or her services by the

---

66. State laws may differ, and states (for example, New York) may require that the election be made separately for state income tax purposes. N.Y. Tax Law § 660(a).

67. If the S corporation was previously a C corporation, there may be circumstances under which the S corporation would be required to pay federal income taxes. 26 U.S.C. §§ 1374(a), 1375(a).

68. 26 U.S.C. § 1372(a).

S corporation, and some or all of the distribution to the stockholder may be recharacterized as compensation.[69]

If a corporation satisfies the applicable requirements for becoming an S corporation, an S corporation generally provides all of the advantages of a C corporation described above, but without the disadvantage of double taxation. Nevertheless, the requirements for being an S corporation pose the following disadvantages:

- significant ownership restrictions (business entities and non-U.S. individuals may not be owners);
- 100-stockholder limitation restricts the ability to raise capital in the public market;
- one-class-of-stock rule limits flexibility in raising capital; and
- it is subject to administratively complex tax compliance requirements.

§ 1:2.6 Public Benefit Corporation

The intersection of social impact and the corporate form has a long history in the United States. Concerns about the social effect of corporations caused states to begin granting shareholders limited liability as far back as the nineteenth century,[70] and early corporate charters were granted for enterprises seen to benefit the public good, such as building railroads or canals.[71] In the twenty-first century, the social enterprise movement has caused more and more for-profit entities to craft their business models on the foundation of positive social impact. One of the earliest and best-known examples of this movement is TOMS, which was founded in 2006 with its "One for One" mission, under which the company matches every pair of shoes purchased with a pair of shoes donated to a child in need.[72]

In August 2013, the state of Delaware solidified the movement's entry into state law by passing an amendment to the Delaware General Corporation Law that allows for-profit corporations to incorporate in Delaware as "public benefit corporations."[73] Pursuant to the statute, public benefit corporations are for-profit entities intended to "produce a public benefit or public benefits, and to operate in a responsible and

---

69. *See, e.g.*, David E. Watson, P.C. v. United States, 668 F.3d 1008 (8th Cir. 2012).
70. RALPH NADER ET AL., TAMING THE GIANT CORPORATION 34–35 (1976).
71. JOHN MICKLETHWAIT & ADRIAN WOOLRIDGE, THE COMPANY—A SHORT HISTORY OF A REVOLUTIONARY IDEA 43 (2003).
72. TOMS, THE TOMS® STORY, https://www.toms.com/about-toms.
73. DEL. CODE ANN. tit. 8, § 362(a).

sustainable manner."[74] "'Public benefit' means a positive effect (or reduction of negative effects) on one or more categories of persons, entities, communities or interests (other than stockholders in their capacities as stockholders) including, but not limited to, effects of an artistic, charitable, cultural, economic, educational, environmental, literary, medical, religious, scientific or technological nature."[75] Directors of public benefit corporation are obligated to manage the business in a manner that "balances the pecuniary interests of the stockholders, the best interests of those materially affected by the corporation's conduct, and the specific public benefit or public benefits identified in its certificate of incorporation."[76] Additionally, corporations are required to prepare statements every two (2) years for their stockholders to set forth the business's promotion of its public benefit and the interests of its stakeholders.[77]

Benefits of the public benefit corporation structure include alignment with corporation missions that focus on stakeholders rather than shareholders, and built-in protection for director liability when decisions are made to prioritize the mission over monetary value.[78] On the other hand, the reporting obligations to stockholders can potentially be burdensome. Regardless, the public benefit corporation structure will likely grow in its presence in the retail and other industries.

§ 1:2.7 Limited Liability Company

A limited liability company (LLC) provides limited personal liability similar to a corporation.[79] In Delaware, LLCs are subject to the provisions of the Limited Liability Company Act (DLLCA).[80] An LLC is considered to be a separate legal entity, distinct from its owners, who have limited personal liability for the obligations and actions of the LLC. An LLC can be formed with only one owner or with multiple owners and often provides more structural and regulatory flexibility than a corporation. Owners of the LLC are referred to as members, and members can include individuals as well as business entities such as other LLCs, corporations, partnerships, trusts, and estates. The members of the LLC control and manage the LLC, unless provided

---

74. *Id.* § 362(a).
75. *Id.* § 362(b).
76. *Id.* § 365.
77. *Id.* § 366(b).
78. Dennis O'Reilly & Luciana Aquino-Hagedorn, *Benefit Corporations: An Introduction*, BLOOMBERG LAW (Feb. 6, 2018).
79. 26 C.F.R. § 301.7701-3(b). A "check-the-box" election may be made to have an LLC subject to tax as a corporation. 26 C.F.R. § 301.7701-3(a).
80. DEL. CODE ANN. tit. 6, § 18.

otherwise in an LLC operating agreement. For example, in multi-member LLCs, managers are often appointed to oversee the business, similar to a Board of Directors of a corporation. Like a corporation, the LLC can provide for different classes of securities, known as membership interests, with varying rights (including voting rights) and powers as set forth in the LLC operating agreement.

Pursuant to section 201 of the DLLCA, to form an LLC in Delaware, one or more authorized persons must execute a certificate of formation, which is filed with the Delaware Secretary of State. The LLC is considered to be formed at the time the initial certificate of formation is filed, or at any later time as specified in the certificate.

Delaware law does not require that an LLC have an operating agreement, but certain other states, including New York, do require an operating agreement.[81] Even if an operating agreement is not required, if an LLC has more than one member, it is desirable to adopt an LLC operating agreement to govern the internal affairs of the LLC, as well as the rights, powers, and duties of its members. It is unclear under Delaware law whether the managers or controlling members of an LLC owe fiduciary duties to the other members of the LLC under the LLCA.[82] Therefore, if the members of an LLC desire to have fiduciary duties apply to the managers or controlling members of the LLC, then the operating agreement should be drafted to explicitly provide for, and describe, such fiduciary duties.

Although Delaware does not have a "publication" requirement, certain states still require public notice of the formation of an LLC.[83] In addition, the appropriate licenses and permits necessary to operate the business, which will depend on the industry and location of the business, must also be obtained.

From a federal income tax perspective, an LLC that has more than one member may be treated as either a partnership or a corporation.[84] And an LLC that has one member may be treated as a disregarded

---

81. *See* N.Y. LTD. LIAB. CO. LAW § 417.
82. *See* Auriga Capital Corp. v. Gatz Props, LLC, 40 A.3d 839 (Del. Ch. 2012) (Court of Chancery of Delaware held that the Delaware LLC Act created default fiduciary duties owed by managers of Delaware LLCs); *see also* Gatz Props., LLC v. Auriga Capital Corp., 59 A.3d 1206 (Del. 2012) (The Supreme Court of Delaware affirmed *Auriga Capital Corp. v. Gatz Props, LLC*, but stated that it was "improvident and unnecessary" for the Court of Chancery to interpret the LLC Act and explicitly stated that the issue of whether the LLC Act contains default fiduciary duties is one where "reasonable minds could differ" and that it was up to the General Assembly to resolve any statutory ambiguity.).
83. *See, e.g.*, N.Y. LTD. LIAB. CO. LAW § 206.
84. 26 C.F.R. § 301.7701-3(a).

entity or a corporation.[85] An election on IRS Form 8832 is required to be made within the required period in order for an LLC to elect to be treated as a corporation. If an LLC elects to be treated like a corporation, it may elect to be an S corporation if it satisfies all of the applicable requirements. If no election is made, the LLC will, by default, be treated as a partnership (if it has more than one member) or a disregarded entity (if it has one member). If an LLC is treated as a disregarded entity, it is generally treated like a sole proprietorship and is subject to the rules discussed above. If an LLC is treated as a partnership, a C corporation, or an S corporation, it will be subject to the rules applicable to those entities and their owners, discussed above.

LLCs organized in Delaware must pay an annual franchise tax to the Delaware Secretary of State.[86]

A summary of the principal advantages and disadvantages of using an LLC is set forth below:

Advantages:

- limited personal liability for members (similar to a corporation);
- flexibility in management structure, legal formalities, and recordkeeping (need not have a separate Board of Directors or managers);
- ability to elect a single level of taxation; and
- distributions to owners do not need to be proportionate to equity ownership.

Disadvantages:

- some uncertainty regarding applicable legal standards since this is a more recent business form;
- lack of a public market for LLC interests generally (LLCs must generally issue new membership interests through private placements);
- limited life in some states; and
- venture capital firms often prefer to invest in corporations (but they may be willing to invest in an LLC by using an intermediate corporation to hold the LLC investment).

---

85. *Id.*

86. DEL. CODE ANN. tit. 6, § 18-1107.

§ 1:2.8 Limited Partnership

A limited partnership (LP), while similar in many ways to a general partnership, is a statutory entity that offers the protections of limited personal liability to its limited partners. LPs in Delaware are subject to the provisions of the Delaware Revised Uniform Limited Partnership Act (DRULPA).[87] An LP must have at least two partners, at least one of which must be the general partner, which is subject to unlimited liability for the obligations of the business.[88] LPs differ from general partnerships in that at least one partner must be a limited partner. A limited partner generally relinquishes managerial control in exchange for the protections of limited personal liability; such personal liability is limited to the amount of the limited partner's investment. Partners may be any combination of individuals and business entities, including LLCs, other partnerships, corporations, trusts, and estates.

Management of a limited partnership is centralized in the general partner. If a limited partner does act in a managerial capacity, the limited partner may be deemed to be a general partner and lose limited liability. Section 303(b) of the DRULPA sets forth a list of circumstances in which a limited partner is not considered to be participating in control of the business, including, among other things: when consulting with or advising a general partner with respect to any matter; when requesting, calling, or participating in meetings of the partners; or when serving on a committee of the LP. In an LP, certain material decisions may also require the approval of the limited partners.

Pursuant to section 201 of the DRULPA, one or more persons (but not less than all of the general partners) file an executed certificate of limited partnership with the Delaware Secretary of State to form an LP. The limited partnership is formed when the certificate of limited partnership is filed with the Secretary of State, or at a later time if specified in the certificate of limited partnership. Furthermore, section 201(d) of the DRULPA states that a partnership agreement can be entered into before, after, or at the time of the filing of the certificate of limited partnership and may be made effective as of the time of the filing of the certificate of limited partnership or at such other time as provided by the partnership agreement. Similar to a partnership agreement for a general partnership, the partnership agreement for a limited partnership governs the internal affairs of the partnership and defines the relationship among the partners,

87. DEL. CODE ANN. tit. 6, § 17.

88. It is also possible for the general partner to be an entity that itself has limited liability.

especially between the general partner and the limited partners and between the partners and the limited partnership.

Delaware case law has long recognized that a general partner of an LP owes fiduciary duties to the LP and its limited partners, which are similar to the duties owed by a director to the stockholders of a corporation.[89] More specifically, the Delaware Court of Chancery has stated that "Delaware law requires the general partners of limited partnerships to exercise due care and to act in the best interests of the partnership and the limited partners."[90] Delaware law (under section 1101(d) of the DRULPA) recognizes, however, that any fiduciary duties created under the DRULPA may be modified by the partnership agreement. Therefore, to the extent the parties desire to modify or eliminate any of the fiduciary duties of a general partner created under the DRULPA, such changes should be specifically set forth and described in the partnership agreement. For example, partnership agreements often specifically include exculpation and indemnification provisions limiting the liability of the general partner (unless the general partner acted with gross negligence or willful misconduct).[91]

Pursuant to section 1107 of the DRULPA, a filing fee is due when the certificate of limited partnership is filed with the Delaware Secretary of State. In addition, the appropriate licenses and permits necessary to operate the business, which will depend on the industry and location of the business, must also be obtained.

The income tax treatment of a limited partnership is generally the same as that for a general partnership. Pursuant to section 1109 of the DRULPA, Delaware limited partnerships must also pay an annual franchise tax to the Delaware Secretary of State.

A summary of the principal advantages and disadvantages of using a limited partnership is set forth below:

Advantages:

- limited liability of limited partners (limited partners are generally only liable up to the amount of their respective capital contributions to the LP);
- single level of taxation;
- centralized control and management of the business in the general partner;

---

89. Boxer v. Husky Oil Co., 429 A.2d 995 (Del. Ch. 1981).
90. *In re* Boston Celtics Ltd. P'ship S'holders Litig., C.A. No. 16511, 1999 WL 641902, at *9 (Del. Ch. Aug. 6, 1999).
91. MARTIN I. LUBAROFF & PAUL M. ALTMAN, LUBAROFF AND ALTMAN ON DELAWARE LIMITED PARTNERSHIPS § 11.2.6.2 (1st ed. Supp. 2018).

- continuity of business when a limited partner withdraws; and
- distributions to partners do not need to be proportionate to equity ownership.

Disadvantages:

- unlimited personal liability for the general partner (the general partner, however, can itself be an entity with limited liability, such as a corporation or LLC);
- risk of dissolution when a general partner withdraws, unless there remains at least one other general partner; and
- difficulty in raising capital (no ability to issue equity to parties without admission of a partner).

§ 1:2.9 Cooperatives

A cooperative (coop) is another possible business structure, although it is not widely used in the fashion industry. The principal feature of a coop is that it is owned by, and operated for, the benefit of its members, and the members are both users and owners of the business.[92] Members become part of the coop by purchasing shares in the coop and have the voting power to control the direction of the coop, although an elected Board of Directors and/or officers may manage the coop on a day-to-day basis.[93] Recreational Equipment Inc., or REI, a business selling outdoor recreational gear, apparel and sporting goods, is an example of a consumer products coop in the United States.[94]

§ 1:2.10 Piercing the Corporate Veil

Founders generally elect to form corporations, limited liability companies, or limited partnerships for the primary purpose of establishing a legal distinction, often referred to as "the corporate veil" of limited liability, between their personal assets and liabilities and those of the business. In certain circumstances, however, courts will "pierce the corporate veil" and hold the owner of a business personally responsible for the business's obligations, despite the limited liability entity structure. Creditors of the business can then proceed directly against an owner's personal assets, which may include the owner's

---

92. *See* U.S. SMALL BUS. ADMIN., COOPERATIVE, https://www.sba.gov/starting-business/choose-your-business-structure/cooperative.
93. *See id.*
94. *See* REI CO-OP, REI CO-OP MEMBERSHIP BENEFITS, https://www.rei.com/membership/benefits; *see also* REI CO-OP, ABOUT REI, https://www.rei.com/about-rei/business.

home, investments, and bank accounts, in order to satisfy debts of the business.

In determining whether to pierce the corporate veil in a particular circumstance, courts have considered the following matters:

1. *Comingling of funds*. Courts have pierced the corporate veil in cases when the owner and the company do not have separate bank accounts, when the owner personally cashes the checks of the company, or when funds of the company are used for the owner's personal purposes.[95]

2. *Lack of compliance with legal formalities*. Courts have also pierced the corporate veil in instances where the company did not comply with appropriate legal formalities and record-keeping, such as a failure to hold Board meetings, keep corporate minutes, or adopt corporate resolutions for important decisions.[96]

3. *Undercapitalization*. If the company was not adequately capitalized to meet its expected obligations, then a court may find that the company was never a separate legal entity.[97] Note that maintaining adequate insurance for foreseeable risks of the business is one of the most important ways to limit claims of this type.

4. *Closely held*. Smaller companies with fewer equity holders are more likely to have their corporate veils pierced than larger, publicly traded corporations, which tend to have a deeper balance sheet and well-developed risk management.

5. *Wrongful or fraudulent behavior*. If the owner of a company acted recklessly or dishonestly, for example by knowingly incurring indebtedness that the company could not satisfy, then a

---

95. *See* Harco Nat. Ins. Co. v. Green Farms. Inc., CIV. A. No. 1131, 1989 WL 110537 (Del. Ch. Sept. 19, 1989). *See also* United States v. Golden Acres, Inc., 702 F. Supp. 1097, 1104 (D. Del. 1988) ("[A]n alter ego analysis must start with an examination of factors which reveal how the corporation operates and the particular defendant's relationship to that operation. These factors include whether the corporation was adequately capitalized for the corporate undertaking; whether the corporation was solvent; whether dividends were paid, corporate records kept, officers and directors functioned properly, and other corporate formalities were observed; whether the dominant shareholder siphoned corporate funds; and whether, in general, the corporation simply functioned as a facade for the dominant shareholder.").

96. *Harco Nat. Ins. Co.*, 1989 WL 110537.

97. *Id.*

court may find that limited liability protection should not apply to such conduct.[98]

Accordingly, owners of interests in a separate legal entity should carefully maintain the entity's separate legal status, including by:

- complying with the legal formalities applicable to the form of the entity, including adopting the proper organizational documents and, if applicable, holding regular Board of Director and stockholder meetings;
- maintaining separate bank accounts for the company;
- maintaining complete records of all company actions and copies of all contracts and other legal documents of the company;
- applying for a taxpayer identification number, which the company will use in its tax filings and correspondence with the IRS;
- obtaining necessary business permits and licenses in the company's name;
- establishing company protocols for acting on the company's behalf and using the company's name in all business correspondence and transactions; and
- adequately capitalizing and insuring the company in light of its reasonably anticipated business requirements.

§ 1:2.11 *Organizational Structure*

As a company grows, it becomes increasingly important to adapt the company's internal configuration to the operational requirements of the business. Some companies are divided into separate divisions, some use a series of subsidiaries, and some use a combination of divisions and subsidiaries. For companies with international operations, the local laws of a particular country may make it necessary or desirable to use a separate subsidiary, rather than a division, for business operations in that country.

---

98. Piercing cases "inevitably tend to evaluate the specific facts with a standard of 'fraud' or 'misuse' or some other general term of reproach in mind." Irwin & Leighton, Inc. v. W.M. Anderson Co., 532 A.2d 983, 989 (Del. Ch. 1987). The corporate veil can be pierced "in the interest of justice, when such matters as fraud, contravention of law or contract, public wrong, or where equitable consideration among members of the corporation require it, are involved." Pauley Petroleum, Inc. v. Cont'l Oil Co., 239 A.2d 629, 633 (Del. 1968).

A division of a company is not necessarily a separate legal entity, but rather a separate administrative entity within the company. A company can be divided into separate divisions in ways that make operational sense for the particular business. For example, in an apparel company, manufacturing activities might be separated into one division, while retail sales activities might be separated into another division. Alternatively, when a company produces several different product lines, each product line might be separated into a separate division.[99] For example, a fashion retailer could separate its business into an apparel division and an accessories division. Divisions of a company may operate under separate business plans, have separate management teams, or have separate financial reporting systems, even though they are all part of the same larger legal entity.

Advantages of a Division:

- *Ease of formation, operation, and termination.* Because a division is not a separate legal entity, no formation documents or registrations must be prepared, complied with, or filed in order to create, operate, or terminate a division.
- *Flexibility of staffing.* Because the personnel working within separate divisions are all employed by one legal entity, it may be easier to transfer employees in and out of divisions as needed.
- *Tax simplicity.* Because a division is not a separate legal entity, for federal income tax purposes, all of the profits and losses of the various divisions are combined in determining the profits and losses of the business.

Companies also often form separate subsidiaries to conduct different aspects of their businesses, which are also sometimes considered to be "divisions" in an operating sense. Legally, however, a subsidiary is an entity that is legally separate from its parent entity and from the other subsidiaries of its parent entity. A subsidiary will have a separate Board of Directors and separate executive officers (although the individuals assigned to those roles may also serve the parent company). Subsidiaries can be wholly owned or partially owned by the parent entity. In the case of a wholly owned subsidiary, the parent entity retains sole voting control and economic ownership of the subsidiary.

99. Erin Schreiner, *Differences Between Wholly Owned Subsidiaries & Divisions*, HOUS. CHRON., http://smallbusiness.chron.com/differences-between-wholly-owned-subsidiaries-divisions-32631.html ("Particularly when businesses produce more than one product or offer more than one service, they often divide into divisions.").

In the case of a partially owned subsidiary, the parent entity would have less than full voting or economic ownership of the subsidiary, and may be either a majority or a minority owner. Some companies are structured so that all operational activities of the business are conducted through subsidiaries and the parent entity serves only as a holding company that directly or indirectly owns stock in subsidiaries. A subsidiary can generally be any type of business entity, including an LP, an LLC, a general partnership, or a corporation. Furthermore, when a company acquires another company, it will often hold it in a subsidiary, which enables it to provide some insulation to the acquiring business from problems the new entity may have.

Advantages of a Subsidiary:

- *Isolation of risks.* The parent entity and each subsidiary are separate legal entities, so the losses and liabilities of one subsidiary do not necessarily transfer to the parent or each other subsidiary. For example, a single subsidiary can declare bankruptcy while other parts of the company are outside of the bankruptcy, although the parent entity will need to consider the ramifications of such bankruptcy on, and the resulting exposure to, the parent entity and the rest of the company. There may be claims, for instance, based on piercing the corporate veil or breaches of fiduciary duties, and certain state or federal statutes and contractual obligations may expose the parent or the rest of the company to the subsidiary's creditors.[100]
- *Transfer or spin-off of a business.* It may be easier to sell a subsidiary than a division, since all of the employees and assets of the business unit are legally contained within the subsidiary.
- *Utilization of equity interests.* Equity interests in a subsidiary can be sold to raise funds or to achieve a strategic objective involving a third party. Similarly, equity interests in the subsidiary can be used as collateral for debt financings.

---

100. Brad B. Erens et al., *Bankrupt Subsidiaries: The Challenges to the Parent of Legal Separation*, 25 EMORY BANKR. DEV. J. 61 (2008), https://www.jonesday.com/ files/Publication/ ce51ed78-4f3d-4bd3-b1c6-49a1d7d500ac/ Presentation/PublicationAttachment/ 0ed7d582-1bff-42e4-8eff-a5cdcd5e3a39/ Emory%20Article.pdf. As an example of a subsidiary filing for bankruptcy, see Press Release, Ally Financial Inc., Ally Financial Announces Key Strategic Actions to Strengthen Company and Accelerate Ability to Repay U.S. Treasury (May 14, 2012), https://media.ally.com/press-releases?item=122889.

Disadvantages of a Subsidiary:

- *Tax Complexity.* A subsidiary that is not wholly owned by its parent may be required to file a separate income tax return and, in certain cases, the profits and losses of a subsidiary may not be used to offset the profits and losses of another subsidiary or the parent entity. In many cases, such as through the use of subsidiary LLCs that are treated as disregarded entities, or 80% owned and controlled corporate subsidiaries that elect to file a consolidated federal income tax return with the parent corporation, this disadvantage can be mitigated or avoided.

- *Corporate Complexity.* A subsidiary must have its own board of directors or other governing body, and must make state filings, keep minutes and other corporate records, and take other measures to prevent a third party from seeking to "pierce the veil."

§ 1:3 Financing the Business

§ 1:3.1 Capital Structure

The cost of starting any new business, including a business in the fashion industry, can be substantial.[101] Although some companies are financed solely by the founders, most companies will seek external financing at an early stage of the business. A company can raise funds from third parties by issuing equity (in the form of common or preferred stock), by incurring debt, or by issuing debt that is convertible into equity. There are important distinctions between equity and debt, and the advantages and disadvantages of each should be carefully considered. Throughout a company's existence, its capital structure should be periodically evaluated and adjusted to reflect an

---

101. The U.S. Small Business Administration provides an outline to follow in calculating the start-up costs for a new business. *See* U.S. SMALL BUS. ADMIN., CALCULATE YOUR STARTUP COSTS, https://www.sba.gov/business-guide/plan-your-business/calculate-your-startup-costs. For a practical example illustrating the costs of starting a retail shop several years ago, see Darren Dahl, *The Cost of Starting Up a Retail Shop*, INC. (Aug. 8, 2011), https://www.inc.com/articles/201108/business-start-up-costs-retail-store.html. *See also* Ray Masaki, *Costs of Starting a Clothing Company*, HOW TO START A CLOTHING COMPANY (for estimated funds necessary to start a clothing company in approximately 2009), https://www.howtostartaclothingcompany.com/costs-starting-clothing-company/; Anne Field, 7 *Great Ways to Finance a Startup*, FSB MAG. (Oct. 18, 2007, 9:53 AM), http://money.cnn.com/2007/05/03/magazines/fsb/raising.money.fsb/.

optimal mix of equity and debt, which can strengthen the financial position of the company and facilitate its growth.[102]

§ 1:3.2 Equity

Equity financing is the sale of an ownership interest in a company. An equity investor is one of the owners of the business (though the terms of the equity holder's participation in the day-to-day operations of the company can be limited) and is entitled to a share of the profits of the business.[103] The purchase price that an equity investor pays for its equity investment reflects a proportionate share of the total value of the company. There are many factors that influence the value of a company, including its historical financial performance, the value of its tangible and intangible assets and liabilities, its management team, its competitive advantages, and the opportunity for growth. Valuing a company before it has significant earnings or revenues can be challenging. In such situations, potential investors may informally compare the company to more established businesses with which they are familiar on the basis of such factors as the caliber and experience of the management team, the strength of the idea and any new technologies, and the extent of the market opportunity. More established companies are typically valued on the basis of more traditional financial valuation metrics, and they may engage an experienced investment banker or other financial advisor to determine the company's valuation. Although an equity investor can receive an economic return during the period of its equity ownership in the form of a dividend,[104] the eventual sale of the equity interest by the investor

---

102. *See* CORP. FIN. INST., CAPITAL STRUCTURE: FINANCING ASSETS WITH DEBT AND EQUITY, https://corporatefinanceinstitute.com/resources/knowledge/finance/capital-structure-overview/; Michael Milken, *The Corporate Financing Cube: Matching Capital Structure to Business Risk*, MICHAEL MILKEN ("Building the right capital structure can be as important as managing other parts of a business."), http://www.mikemilken.com/articles.taf?page=1; *see also* Fraser Sherman, *How Does Business Risk Affect Decisions About Capital Structure?*, HOUS. CHRON., https://smallbusiness.chron.com/business-risk-affect-decisions-capital-structure-45278.html.

103. *See* NAT'L FED'N OF INDEP. BUS., DEBT VS. EQUITY FINANCING: WHICH IS BEST FOR YOUR BUSINESS?, https://www.nfib.com/content/resources/money/ital-50036/.

104. A dividend is a portion of the company's profits distributed to the owners of the company either in the form of cash, additional ownership interests, or other non-cash consideration. *See What Is a Dividend?*, INVESTING DAILY (Aug. 4, 2012), https://www.investingdaily.com/15550/what-is-a-dividend; *see also* Todd Wenning, *Dividend Masterclass No. 1: What Is a Dividend?*, THE MOTLEY FOOL (Dec. 30, 2010), https://www.fool.com/investing/dividends-income/2010/12/30/dividend-masterclass-no-1-what-is-a-dividend.aspx.

for a price higher than the original purchase price is the primary economic motivation for an equity investment.

While the equity investor shares in the potential growth of a company, the equity investor also shares in any losses, to the extent of its equity contribution. Absent a contractual agreement to the contrary, a company is not required to return to its equity investors the money invested in the business; the equity investor assumes the risk of losing its full investment.[105] Equity financing, in comparison to debt financing, can be attractive to a founder for this very reason; without the requirement of regularly scheduled interest and principal repayments, more cash flow is available for use in the operation and growth of the business.

The primary risk associated with equity financing is that the founder loses exclusive ownership of, and potentially exclusive control over, the business. Not only will the founder share the company's future profits with the other equity investors, but some equity investors may insist on certain control rights with respect to the business. From the perspective of the founder, this managerial involvement can be either a benefit or a detriment. An equity investor familiar with the industry could bring valuable expertise and industry experience to the business. For example, Andrew Rosen, the founder of the brand Theory, is an investor in many smaller fashion companies.[106] Alternatively, an equity investor who is unfamiliar with the industry

---

105. *See* U.S. SMALL BUS. ADMIN. OFFICE OF ADVOCACY, FREQUENTLY ASKED QUESTIONS ABOUT SMALL BUSINESS 2 (Aug. 2018) ("Four out of five establishments that started in 2016 survived until 2017 (79.8%), https://www.sba.gov/sites/default/files/advocacy/Frequently-Asked-Questions-Small-Business-2018.pdf. From 2005 to 2017, an average of 78.6% of new establishments survived one year. About half of all establishments survive five years or longer. In the past decade, this ranged from a low of 45.4% for establishments started in 2006, and a high of 51.0% for those started in 2011. About one-third of establishments survive 10 years or longer."); *see also* Matt Mansfield, *Startup Statistics—The Numbers You Need to Know*, SMALL BUS. TRENDS (May 15, 2018), https://smallbiztrends.com/2016/11/startup-statistics-small-business.html ("40 percent of small businesses are profitable, 30 percent break even and 30 percent are continually losing money."); Neil Patel, *90% of Startups Fail: Here's What You Need to Know About the 10%*, FORBES (Jan. 16, 2015, 10:00 AM) ("Nine out of ten startups will fail."), https://www.forbes.com/sites/neilpatel/2015/01/16/90-of-startups-will-fail-heres-what-you-need-to-know-about-the-10/#f750e4366792.

106. Divia Harilela, *Theory's Andrew Rosen Drops Contemporary Fashion Crown in Favour of Investing in People*, S. CHINA MORNING POST (Apr. 9, 2018), https://www.scmp.com/lifestyle/fashion-beauty/article/2140854/theorys-andrew-rosen-drops-contemporary-fashion-crown.

could influence the company in ways that conflict with the founder's vision or are harmful to the business.

If the founder is a fashion designer (or is otherwise providing creative direction for the business), issues of managerial control can be particularly challenging. Although the founder started the business based on a creative vision, and potential investors presumably are attracted by the market opportunities inherent in that vision, those investors may seek to impose operational and financial constraints on the founder's ability to execute on the vision. A common approach to resolving these issues is to provide the founder with "creative control rights," subject to compliance with an annual business plan and budget approved by the Board of Directors. For a fashion designer, such creative control rights might include the right to approve all product designs, fabrics, production sources, advertising and promotional material, retail store designs, and similar matters. Under this formulation, the fashion designer can exercise creative control only to the extent that the proposed expenditures fall within the approved business plan and budget. For example, if a women's luxury footwear designer prefers to have shoes produced in Italy, but the cost of production exceeds the budgeted costs, the designer may have to find a more cost-effective production location. Appendix 1A contains sample creative control provisions addressing the issues discussed above.

The specific economic terms of, and control rights associated with, an equity investment are typically reflected in a formal agreement between the company and the investor (usually called a purchase agreement) and a formal agreement among the company and all of the equity investors (usually called a stockholders agreement, in the case of a corporation, and an operating agreement in the case of an LLC). As in all negotiations, the terms of any final agreement will be influenced by the leverage of the parties, the interests and priorities of each party, the specific facts and circumstances of the company, the industry standards, if any, and the context of the negotiations generally. It is important for entrepreneurs to understand that even if an investor or an investor group proposes to provide all necessary documentation, their documentation is being prepared only with their interests in mind, and a lawyer representing the founder may raise a number of important issues and concerns that would not otherwise be addressed in a favorable way. It is important not to let the excitement of a successful pitch lead to a rushed, one-sided negotiation. A wise entrepreneur will seek advice and counsel from a lawyer and possibly from other mentors and advisors before entering into agreements that may result in them losing partial or complete control of their dream.

The following issues are typically addressed in negotiations with potential equity investors (reference is made to shares of stock and

Boards of Directors; however, these points apply equally to partnerships and LLCs):

1. *Representation on the governing body*. If an investor is acquiring a substantial percentage of the company's outstanding equity securities, the investor is likely to seek representation on the company's Board of Directors (or similar governing body) by obtaining the right to appoint one or more directors. Representation on the Board of Directors will allow the investor to participate in Board discussions and vote on the important decisions relating to the business. In some cases, the investor may condition its investment on the ability to maintain its Board representation rights, unless its investment falls below an ownership level. Venture capital and private equity firms are more likely to ask for Board positions than friends and family. In cases of a majority investment by a venture capital firm or private equity firm, the firm may demand such number of Board positions as to give the firm control of the Board and, accordingly, control over the management of the company.[107] In cases of a smaller investment, or in which a Board position for the investor is not desirable, an investor may be granted observer rights on the Board of Directors. Board observers generally have the right to attend and observe Board meetings, receive Board materials, and may, in some cases, participate in Board discussions; however, observers do not have the right to vote on any matters brought before the Board. Board observers also may be asked not to participate in certain portions of Board meetings, including during "executive sessions" of the Board, when management directors are excused from the meeting so that highly sensitive or confidential information can be discussed. Board observers do not owe fiduciary duties to the company or its stockholders,[108] which means that, generally, Board observers are not liable to the company or the stockholders for actions of the company's Board of Directors. Some investors prefer Board observer status to Board representation specifically for this reason.

2. *Consent rights*. In addition to, or in lieu of, representation on the Board of Directors, an investor may request consent rights

---

107. *See, e.g.*, Scott Edward Walker, *Demystifying the VC Term Sheet: Board Control*, VENTUREBEAT (Mar. 14, 2011), http://venturebeat.com/2011/03/14/demystifying-the-vc-term-sheet-board-control/.

108. For a definition of "board observer," see PRACTICAL L. CO., BOARD OBSERVER (Thomson Reuters 2018), http://uslf.practicallaw.com/2-501-5854?q=*&qp=&qo=&qe=.

with respect to certain fundamental decisions of the company. These consent rights can include the right to approve the following matters:

- changes in control of the company;
- significant sales, transfers, or other dispositions of assets;
- equity issuances, including additional rounds of equity financing or an initial public offering;
- repurchases of securities;
- dissolution, bankruptcy, or liquidation of the company;
- entering into or amendment of significant employment agreements or material increases in executive compensation;
- incurrence of material indebtedness;
- amendment of the company's organizational documents and stockholders' rights agreements in any way that would adversely affect the investor;
- entering into transactions with affiliates;
- changes in lines of business or major strategic changes;
- material acquisitions ;
- declarations of dividends over a certain threshold or to a certain class of securities;
- changing the company's accounting policies, other than as required by generally accepted accounting principles; and/or
- changes that would otherwise adversely affect the rights, preferences, and privileges of the shares or equity interests held by the investor.

A founder must balance the need to attract investors and allow them to protect their investments against the need to retain flexibility to operate the business. For example, the types and amounts of asset dispositions that trigger an investor's consent right should be formulated to avoid capturing ordinary course dispositions of inventory. Similarly, the threshold for what constitutes a material level of indebtedness should be formulated to exclude the use of existing credit lines.

3. *Access to information*. An investor may request the periodic delivery of important information regarding the business. For example, investors may ask to receive annual audited financial statements, quarterly unaudited financial statements, or even monthly capsule financial statements by a specific date after each completed fiscal period. It is also common for investors to request copies of the company's annual budgets or strategic forecasts. As discussed in greater detail below, stockholders in Delaware have the right to inspect and copy certain books and records of the business, but an investor may request enhanced inspection rights relative to what is statutorily provided. An investor may also require the company to notify it of certain material events or occurrences, such as materially adverse changes in the company's financial results or the commencement of litigation by or against the company.

4. *Preemptive rights*. Investors often request preemptive rights, which give the investor the right to purchase a portion of any future share issuances so as to maintain its proportionate ownership interest in the company. (For example, Company has 1,000 shares outstanding and Investor owns 20% of Company, or 200 shares. Company plans to issue 1,000 additional shares to third parties, which would leave Investor with 200 of the 2,000 outstanding shares, or 10% of Company. In order to prevent this dilution, Investor exercises its preemptive right to purchase its pro rata portion of shares in the stock issuance. Investor now has the opportunity to purchase 20% of the 1,000 new shares being issued, equaling an additional 200 shares. After the right is exercised and the purchase consummated, Investor owns 400 out of 2,000 shares, or 20% of Company. Investor's pro rata ownership stake in Company remains unchanged.)[109] When a company is subject to preemptive rights, it must undertake a notification process prior to issuing new shares of capital stock (subject to certain exceptions, such as issuances to employees). The investors with preemptive rights must be notified of a potential new stock issuance, and granted a specified amount of time to decide whether to exercise preemptive rights, before such issuance can be consummated. This can significantly delay the process

---

109. Joshua Kennon, *Understanding Shareholders Preemptive Rights*, ABOUT.COM GUIDE, http://beginnersinvest.about.com/od/stocksoptionswarrants/f/preemptive.htm.

of raising equity in the future and may impair the ability of the company to add new investors who may be advantageous to the business.[110]

5. *Restrictions on transfers and lock-up periods*. Founders may seek to impose restrictions on the ability of investors to transfer equity interests to third parties. The founder may seek approval rights over all future transfers, except in cases where the shares are transferred to an affiliate of the investor. Alternatively, the founder may designate certain persons to whom transfers cannot be made, such as competitors. A founder may also seek to limit the number of total investors in the business, and accordingly may impose minimum transfer amounts to limit stockholder diffusion.[111] Moreover, no-transfer periods (or "lock-up periods") may be imposed to prohibit individual stockholders from exiting the company without the company's permission for a specified period after the initial investment. A substantial equity investor may seek to restrict transfers of equity interests by the founder until the occurrence of specified events or the achievement of certain financial thresholds.

6. *Tag-along rights and drag-along rights*. A tag-along right, or a co-sale right, gives the owner of the right (usually a minority owner) the opportunity to participate, typically on a pro rata basis, in any future sale of shares by another equity investor (usually the majority owner) to a third party, at the same price and on the same other terms. The majority owner therefore cannot exit the business without also considering the interests of the minority owners. This right protects the minority owners from circumstances in which the majority owner exits the business and leaves the minority owners in a potentially undesirable situation with a new majority owner.[112] A drag-along right gives the owner of the right (usually a majority owner) the ability to compel the other owners (usually the minority owners) to sell their shares in the company to a third party,

---

110. *See id.* (describing the inconvenience of preemptive rights with respect to raising cash from equity interest).

111. An entrepreneur may desire to limit the number of shareholders in order to avoid the reporting requirements under the federal securities laws. *See* 15 U.S.C. § 78(g)(1) (describing the general registration requirements for securities).

112. John D. Agogliati III, *Tag-Along and Drag-Along Rights: A Valuation Analyst's View*, LAW360 (May 12, 2015), https://www.law360.com/articles/653263/tag-along-and-drag-along-rights-a-valuation-analyst-s-view.

alongside the selling owner for the same price and on the same other terms. Often, third-party purchasers desire to purchase all of the outstanding shares in a company. Drag-along rights ensure that, in the event such a third-party purchaser emerges and the majority stockholders accept the terms of the purchaser's acquisition, all minority stockholders will sell their shares.[113] Both tag-along and drag-along rights are fairly common.[114]

7. *Registration rights*. Registration rights are the contractual rights of an equity holder to require the company to register such holder's shares with the U.S. Securities and Exchange Commission (SEC), allowing the holder to sell its shares in the public market.[115]

   - *Piggyback registration rights*. Piggyback registration rights grant an equity holder the right to include its unregistered shares in a public offering of securities conducted by the company. These rights apply only in the event that the company, or another stockholder, first initiates a registration process and may be subject to certain limitations to allow the company to conduct a successful public offering.

   - *Demand registration rights*. Demand registration rights grant an equity holder one or more rights to require the company to register such holder's shares, typically at the company's expense. In most cases, these rights apply only after the company has already completed an initial public offering. In rare situations, demand rights are granted to an investor in a private company prior to an initial public offering.[116] In this situation, the investor can compel the company to undertake an initial public offering, which is an expensive and time-consuming process. Accordingly, such rights typically may not be exercised until a designated period of time has elapsed since the grant of the right or certain conditions have been satisfied (such as specified financial benchmarks).

---

113. *Id.*

114. *Id.*

115. Eric A. Koester, *Venture Capital Term Sheet: Registration Rights*, AVVO (Jan. 1, 2009), https://www.avvo.com/legal-guides/ugc/venture-capital-term-sheet-registration-rights.

116. *What Are Registration Rights?*, VC EXPERTS (Apr. 11, 2017), https://blog.vcexperts.com/2017/04/11/what-are-registration-rights-2/.

8. *Rights of first refusal and rights of first offer.* Rights of first refusal provide the company and existing investors with the opportunity to purchase additional shares of the company in connection with any sale of shares by another investor before a third party is permitted to consummate a purchase of the shares. Generally, the selling investor is obligated to notify the company and the other investors when a third party offers to purchase the investor's shares, and must provide the company and such other investors with an opportunity to purchase all or a portion of those shares for the same price and on the same other terms as set forth in the third-party offer. A right of first offer obligates an investor to negotiate the possible sale of its shares with the company, or the other investors, prior to offering such shares for sale to a third party. Typically, if the company and the other investors do not purchase the investor's offered shares, the investor is free, for a limited period of time, to sell those shares to a third party on terms no more favorable to the third party than those offered to the company and the other investors.
9. *Standstill provisions*. The founder of a company may seek to limit the amount of investment by any single investor through a standstill provision. A standstill provision limits the amount of shares or voting power that an investor can accumulate in the company, thereby limiting the extent of the investor's economic interest or control. For example, the company may restrict any single investor from accumulating more than 50% of the shares of the company, or from entering into voting agreements with other investors of the company so as to effectively control decision making.
10. *Call and put options*. A call option gives the holder of the option the ability to buy additional shares of the company in the future. The exercise price of the option is preset, but adjustable under certain circumstances, and exercise is typically contingent on the occurrence of certain future events, the passage of time, or the company's achieving certain performance targets. If an investor exercises its call option, this could dilute the other investors' ownership stake in the company at a time when the business is doing well. Conversely, a put option gives the holder of the option the ability to require the company (or other investors) to buy its shares in the future. The exercise price of the option is preset, also often adjustable, and exercise typically is also contingent on the happening of certain future events, the passage of time, or the company's achieving certain performance targets. If

an investor exercises its put option, the founder may have to increase its ownership stake in the company at a time when the investment is not as attractive and may be compelled to raise the funds necessary to repurchase the shares.

Equity investors often seek to purchase preferred stock instead of common stock. Preferred stock has a designated liquidation preference; in the event of a liquidation of the company or certain other events, such as a sale of the business, the preferred stockholders will get paid the amount of their liquidation preference (plus accrued but unpaid dividends) prior to any pay-out to the common stockholders. Preferred stock may also be participating, which means that upon the happening of certain events (such as a sale of the business), the preferred stockholders will get paid their liquidation preference (plus accrued but unpaid dividends), and a pro rata percentage of any remaining consideration calculated as if the preferred stock had been converted to common stock. The use of preferred stock results in a more complicated capital structure, and disqualifies a corporation from making an election to be an S corporation.[117] Holders of preferred stock might have different voting, consent, or other rights that are not granted to common stockholders. Often, dividend rates on preferred stock are fixed, while dividend rates on common stock are subject to the discretion of the Board of Directors. Preferred stock may be subject to mandatory redemption by the company, at a specified date, or optional redemption at the option of the company or the holder.

A company also may issue convertible preferred stock, which is preferred stock that can be converted into common stock of the company, at a specified conversion price (for example, each share of preferred stock converts into one share of common stock), either upon the occurrence of certain events (such as an initial public offering) or at the election of the company or the holders. Holders of convertible preferred stock may vote as a separate class with respect to certain issues affecting the preferred stock, but they may also vote with the common stock on an "as converted" basis. Investors purchasing convertible preferred stock typically request anti-dilution protection. Anti-dilution provisions adjust the conversion price to protect the original investment upon the happening of certain future events affecting the value of a share of the company's common stock (such as stock splits, distributions of rights to purchase common stock, and dilutive issuances of common stock). Convertible preferred stock may have "pay

117. Terry Masters, *Can an S Corporation Sell Preferred Shares?*, POCKET SENSE (Apr. 9, 2017), https://pocketsense.com/can-s-corporation-sell-preferred-shares-3299.html.

to play" provisions, which provide that holders must participate in subsequent financing rounds on a pro rata basis or they will lose their anti-dilution protection (or other rights such as the right to participate in future rounds or the right to have board representation). Angel investors and venture capital investors often expect to purchase convertible preferred stock.[118] Convertible preferred stock can offer external investors the benefits of debt (preferential treatment and seniority over common stock and fixed payments in the form of pre-set dividends), while retaining the characteristics of common stock (sharing in the upside if the business does well).[119]

In addition to contractual rights that may be negotiated by equity investors, state laws generally provide certain non-contractual protections to stockholders in a corporation.[120] Under Delaware law, the principal protections afforded to stockholders in Delaware corporations include the following:

1. *Inspection rights*. Under section 220 of the DGCL, any stockholder has the right, exercisable pursuant to specified procedures (including making a written demand "under oath" and having a "proper purpose") and during normal business hours, to inspect and make copies of the corporation's stock ledger, list of stockholders, and other books and records, as well as the books and records of the corporation's subsidiaries, in certain circumstances. A proper purpose is defined as "a purpose reasonably related to such person's interest as a stockholder." Delaware courts have interpreted this term broadly to allow stockholders to protect their investments.[121] Similar rights to inspect books and records exist for limited partnerships and limited liability companies, although they can be tailored by the governing agreement.

2. *Derivative suits*. Stockholders have the right to bring derivative suits, on behalf of the corporation, to enforce a claim that the corporation may have against its directors and officers for

---

118. Mike Sullivan & Richard Harroch, *A Guide to Venture Capital Financings for Startups*, FORBES (Mar. 29, 2018), https://www.forbes.com/sites/allbusiness/2018/03/29/a-guide-to-venture-capital-financings-for-startups/#255efc8051c9.

119. Kimberly Amadeo, *Preferred Stock and How It Differs From Common Stock*, THE BALANCE (updated Nov. 11, 2018), https://www.thebalance.com/preferred-stock-definition-vs-common-stock-types-3305954.

120. Scott Edward Walker, *What Are the Rights of Minority Stockholders?*, VENTUREBEAT (July 18, 2011), http://venturebeat.com/2011/07/18/what-are-the-rights-of-minority-stockholders/ [hereinafter Walker, *Minority Stockholders*].

121. *Id.*

breaches of their fiduciary duties to the corporation. In order to bring a derivative suit, the stockholder must show, under section 327 of the DGCL, that it "was a stockholder of the corporation at the time of the transaction of which such stockholder complains or that such stockholder's stock thereafter devolved upon such stockholder by operation of law." In order to proceed with the derivative suit, the stockholder must also first make a written demand to the corporation's Board of Directors, unless it would have been futile to do so.[122] Recovery in a derivative suit goes to the corporation and not to the stockholders directly, although it can benefit the stockholders by increasing the value of the corporation. Derivative suits are more common in large publicly held corporations than in smaller privately held corporations.

3. *Suits against controlling stockholders.* Under Delaware law, a controlling stockholder of a corporation may also owe certain fiduciary duties to its fellow stockholders. While Delaware does not have a statutory cause of action for oppression claims, Delaware courts have created a common law cause of action "when a [stockholder] presumes to exercise control over a corporation, to direct its actions, that [stockholder] assumes a fiduciary duty of the same kind as that owed by a director."[123] Stockholders can bring actions directly against such controlling stockholders claiming a breach of fiduciary duties. These claims often arise when the controlling stockholder has a conflict of interest, or will derive a special benefit, not shared by the other stockholders, from a transaction. Breaches of fiduciary duty have been found where a controlling stockholder:[124]

    - forced minority stockholders to sell their shares at a price below fair market value;
    - caused the corporation to issue additional shares of capital stock to the controlling stockholder at an inadequate price;
    - disproportionately reduced the economic value or voting rights of the minority stockholder's shares; and/or

122. Kamen v. Kemper Fin. Servs., 500 U.S. 90, 95 (1991).
123. Sterling v. Mayflower Hotel Corp., 93 A.2d 107, 109–10 (Del. 1952).
124. Samuel Goldman, *Shareholder Oppression in Delaware*, EZINE ARTICLES (Apr. 27, 2010), http://EzineArticles.com/4188732; Walker, *Minority Stockholders*, *supra* note 120.

- sold its own shares to an improper or fraudulent buyer, without first conducting proper diligence.

4. *Appraisal rights*. Subject to certain exceptions, stockholders of a Delaware corporation that is acquired in a merger, who are dissatisfied with the merger consideration, have a right to seek a court appraisal of the value of their shares pursuant to the procedures set forth in section 262 of the DGCL.

§ 1:3.3 Debt

Debt financing is the borrowing of funds from a third-party lender. Borrowings accrue interest and are required to be repaid to the lender on demand or on a predetermined schedule. Debt can come from various financing sources, including commercial banks, institutional investors, and individuals. It may be referred to as a loan, a promissory note, a bond, or a debenture. It may be transferable or non-transferable by the lender. Debt is senior to equity in the capital structure of a company in bankruptcy, and different classes of debt may be senior or subordinated to each other. Principal and interest payments on debt reduce the amount of available cash that can be used to operate and invest in a business, and interest payments reduce the profits available for distribution to the equity investors.

In order to obtain a loan, a founder may have to personally guarantee the loan or secure the loan with "collateral" (which may include assets of the business or personal assets of the founder as in the case of a home equity loan). If the borrower fails to pay installments of principal or interest on the loan when such payments become due, the entire loan may be accelerated and become immediately due and payable in full, and the lender may be allowed to take control of and sell the assets used as collateral to secure the loan.

Debt financing, as opposed to equity financing, does not transfer an ownership interest in the company and is non-dilutive. Accordingly, lenders generally will not seek to control the management of the business or ask for the voting rights typically requested by equity investors. However, lenders will often require the borrower to agree to certain covenants imposing restrictions on the ability of the company to incur additional indebtedness, pay dividends, or take other actions, and require the company to maintain certain financial ratios (for example, debt to equity). Failure to satisfy these covenants may accelerate the maturity of the loan.

Debt can be structured so that it is convertible into common or preferred stock of a company either upon the occurrence of certain events or at the election of the company or the holder. The holders of a convertible debt may be entitled to convert the debt into common stock at a specified conversion price or at a price that is tied to the market price of the common stock at the time of conversion. Holders of convertible debt also typically request anti-dilution protections.

§ 1:4 Sources of Financing

§ 1:4.1 Financing in Stages

A new company typically raises capital in stages, or "rounds," that correlate with the development and financial requirements of the business. Although the timing and amount of capital rounds vary considerably by company, the principal sources of investment capital for new and growing companies are: personal savings; friends and family; angel investors; venture capital and private equity capital, each of which are discussed in more detail below.

Eloquii, a plus-size fashion retailer, is an example of a start-up in the fashion industry that has rapidly raised capital in multiple investment rounds. The company has been through two rounds of venture capital funding, and now has a funding of close to $40 million.[125] A more typical but very successful example of the cadence of funding rounds is the athleisure company Bandier, which was founded in 2014 and received a significant ($34 million) investment from prestigious international firm Eurazeo in early 2019.[126] For most fashion industry start-ups, however, the financing process may be slower and more challenging, and the founder will need to rely more heavily on personal funds and friends and family.

§ 1:4.2 Personal Funds

Like Jennifer Bandier, the founder of the athleisure company Bandier, the founder of a new business often uses personal savings (or funds obtained from a personal home equity loan) as an immediate source of capital to commence operations. The funds can be used without dilution of the founder's ownership, and can fund the establishment of the company's "proof of concept."[127] Financing an early stage of the business from external sources might be expensive, since investors typically demand higher returns for seed round

---

125. Ellen Rose, *Bringing a Personal Touch to Plus-Size Fashion*, N.Y. TIMES (Feb. 8, 2018), https://www.nytimes.com/2018/02/08/business/smallbusiness/plus-size-fashion.html.

126. Jaweon Kang, *Activewear Retailer Bandier Collects $34.4 Million from Eurazeo, C Ventures*, WALL ST. J (Feb. 28, 2019), https://www.wsj.com/articles/activewear-retailer-bandier-collects-34-4-million-from-eurazeo-c-ventures-11551389778.

127. Gregory C. Smith, START-UP & EMERGING COMPANIES: PLANNING, FINANCING AND OPERATING THE SUCCESSFUL BUSINESS, § 7.02 (Law Journal Press 2017) [hereinafter Smith].

financing given the significantly higher risk profile.[128] Using personal funds for the initial development of the business can ultimately help attract future rounds of financing, since the founder can offer a more advanced product or service and demonstrate the founder's personal commitment to the venture.[129] A company that produces apparel, for example, typically cannot attract external capital until it has sold one or more seasonal collections and proven the marketability of its products.

§ 1:4.3 Friends and Family

Friends and family also can be a source of financing in the early stages of a business. Friends and family often are the first source of external financing for a new business because they know and trust the founder, and accordingly may offer better terms and fewer conditions than other sources.[130] It is generally preferable to raise funds from family and friends through an unsecured loan, rather than convertible securities or common stock. A loan is non-dilutive (unlike convertible securities or common stock) and typically can be prepared and executed more quickly than other forms of financing. Moreover, friends and family may agree to lower interest rates and more flexible repayment structures in a loan than may be available from an institutional or commercial lender.[131] If the loan is structured properly, it may not be deemed to be a "security" under federal and state securities laws, and so will not be subject to registration requirements, as discussed below.

Obtaining financing from informal sources, however, poses challenges. Friends and family may not have previously invested in a start-up and may not be financially sophisticated. As a result, they may not understand the risks associated with financing a start-up, and might have unrealistic expectations about the return on investment.[132] Their expectations may have been influenced by the media publicity surrounding successful start-ups (such as Instagram) and the media's relative silence on start-ups that failed (such as Yik Yak and Sprig).[133] Friends and family also might not appreciate or understand the

---

128. *Id.*

129. *Id.*

130. *How to Borrow from Family and Friends*, WALL ST. J. [hereinafter *How to Borrow from Family and Friends*], http://guides.wsj.com/small-business/funding/how-to-borrow-from-family-and-friends.

131. *Id.*

132. Smith, *supra* note 127.

133. Becky Peterson, *10 Startups That Died in 2017*, BUSINESS INSIDER (Dec 2, 2017), https://www.businessinsider.com/startups-that-raised-148-billion-have-shut-down-or-may-soon-2017-11.

amount of time required to develop a business. Moreover, they may expect to have an active role in the management of the company and the design of the products, particularly if they are acquiring an equity interest in the company. Accordingly, when a founder obtains capital from friends or family, there is a risk of both straining personal relationships and negatively affecting the business.

If the founder obtains funds from friends or family without proper documentation and, in the case of a loan, does not observe the formalities of paying interest, the IRS could potentially argue that a purported "loan" is a gift to the founder, thereby triggering gift tax consequences, or determine that the purported loan should be treated as equity, thereby potentially eliminating any interest deduction associated with the loan and causing distributions to be treated for tax purposes as dividends.[134] An alternative structure would be to characterize the forgone interest as an annual gift, assuming that is the intention of the parties, which can confer tax benefits on the donor by reducing the size of the donor's estate.[135] Because the maximum annual gift amount is limited to a relatively small amount, using this strategy may not be possible for anything but small cash infusions.[136]

Founders who sell common stock in a start-up can create potential governance, tax, and valuation difficulties.[137] If common stock is issued to friends and family or employees, the company will need to address governance issues (such as voting rights and rights to elect directors) and transfer rights (including between the equity holders and to third parties) in a stockholder's agreement or an LLC agreement. If an angel investor or venture capital investor later seeks to invest in the company, it may be difficult to unwind or revise these arrangements to facilitate the investment. On the other hand, if convertible preferred stock or convertible debt is issued to friends and family, the governing instruments can provide that appropriate arrangements among the equity holders will be entered into at the time of a subsequent investment from angel investors or venture capital investors. If common stock is sold at a lower price to employees or founders than to third-party investors during the same general time frame, the employees and founders may be treated as having received compensation in an amount equal to the discount they received.[138]

---

134. *How to Borrow from Family and Friends*, *supra* note 130.
135. *Id.*
136. The annual gift tax exclusion amount for gifts to an individual in 2018 was $15,000. Press Release IR-2018-94, IRS Inflation Adjustments Under Recently Enacted Tax Law (Apr. 13, 2018), https://www.irs.gov/newsroom/inflation-adjustments-under-recently-enacted-tax-law.
137. Smith, *supra* note 127.
138. *Id.*

Also, the higher price of the common stock sold to non-employees might establish a market value for the shares that would impair the ability of the company to issue restricted stock, options, or other equity incentives to attract talented employees.[139]

In addition, as discussed below, the sale of debt or equity securities in a company must comply with the federal securities laws, which generally prohibit the sale of securities that have not been registered with the SEC, subject to exceptions for certain private placements and certain other types of transactions.[140] Registration is a time-consuming and costly process, and sales of securities to friends and family are not necessarily exempt, though certain exemptions are available for non-public offerings of securities that comply with specific requirements as more fully discussed below.[141] Issuances of securities to friends and family that have not been properly documented, that are inappropriately priced, or that fail to comply with the federal securities laws can impair the ability of the company to obtain capital from other financing sources in the future.[142]

§ 1:4.4 Factoring

A fashion company that generates revenues from product sales, but is not yet ready to raise capital, may use factoring to finance its growth. In a typical factoring arrangement, the fashion company assigns to a factoring company, or a "factor," the right to receive the proceeds from a set of customer invoices in the future. The factor will then advance a certain portion of the invoiced amounts, generally between 60% and 90%, to the fashion company within twenty-four (24) to forty-eight (48) hours.[143] There are two principal types of factoring, recourse (or "discount") factoring and non-recourse (or "traditional") factoring. In recourse factoring, which is less expensive than non-recourse factoring, the factor pays the company the remainder of an invoiced amount only after the customer has paid the invoice. In non-recourse factoring, if a customer's credit has been approved, the factor will pay the company the remainder of an invoiced amount for that customer at maturity, whether or not the customer actually paid the invoice.

---

139. *Id.*

140. Securities Act of 1933 § 5, 15 U.S.C. § 77e.

141. Securities Act of 1933 § 4(2), 15 U.S.C. § 77d; Rule 506 of Regulation D, 17 C.F.R. § 230.506.

142. Smith, *supra* note 127.

143. Charles Klein, *Examining the Agreements of Fashion Law, in* NAVIGATING FASHION LAW, at 247 (Aspatore 2012) [hereinafter Klein]; and *How to Use Factoring for Cash Flow*, WALL ST. J. [hereinafter *How to Use Factoring for Cash Flow*], http://guides.wsj.com/small-business/funding/how-to-use-factoring-for-cash-flow.

Factoring arrangements are advantageous for fashion companies that sell a reasonable volume of apparel and accessories, because they allow the company to obtain cash from its invoices more quickly. Also, because factors analyze the creditworthiness of the company's customers rather than the creditworthiness of the company itself, companies may be able to enter into factoring arrangements even when other forms of financing may not be available on favorable terms.[144]

Factoring is typically several percentage points more expensive than conventional borrowing,[145] and the fees and other terms of each factoring arrangement are based on considerations including the creditworthiness of the company's customers, and the size and age of the invoices (with large and current receivables obtaining better terms).[146] Factors impose a fee, which can be between 2% and 10% of sales,[147] for each invoice that is assigned by the fashion company.[148] Annual minimum fees are typical in many factoring arrangements, and fashion companies should generally avoid more frequent minimum fee payments, assessed each month or quarter.[149] Because sales of apparel are seasonal, and certain periods may be busier than others, committing to a minimum fee in a slow month can raise costs unnecessarily.[150] A fashion company should also consider the following points in negotiating factoring arrangements: minimizing the number of days it takes for the factor to credit the company's account after the customer has paid an invoice; shrinking the amount of time that the invoice must remain unpaid before the factor pays the remainder of the invoice; limiting the factor's rights to inspect the company; and limiting the fees and reimbursements payable to the factor.[151]

§ 1:4.5 Bank Financing and Commercial Credit

Because early-stage fashion companies may not have an established credit history or established revenue or profit stream, it can be difficult for such companies to secure commercial loans. Nevertheless, commercial lending is an important source of capital for a business seeking to expand. In 2018, for example, 56% of small nonemployer businesses (businesses without full-time or part-time workers on the

---

144. *How to Use Factoring for Cash Flow*, *supra* note 143.
145. *Id.*
146. US LEGAL, FACTOR LAW & LEGAL DEFINITION, http://definitions.uslegal.com/f/factor/.
147. *Id.*
148. *How to Use Factoring for Cash Flow*, *supra* note 143.
149. Klein, *supra* note 143.
150. *Id.*
151. *Id.*

payroll, and with only one or more owners as full-time employees, along with contracted workers) reported they had applied for business loans.[152]

There are measures that a fashion company may be in a position to take to facilitate obtaining a favorable commercial loan. A local bank may be inclined to provide loans to neighborhood businesses, especially if the founder has a long-standing relationship with the bank. When applying for a loan, a founder should include in its application a copy of the company's recent financial statements (including a balance sheet, income statement, and cash flow statement) to provide support for the company's ability to repay the loan.[153] Prospective borrowers should solicit offers from several banks and encourage the banks to compete for their business in the negotiation of key terms such as interest rates, loan fees, limits on the amount of the borrower's personal guarantee, default terms, and prepayment penalties.

There are several types of commercial bank financing. A revolving line of credit, or a revolving loan, is a multi-use source of financing that companies can use for start-up costs, capital purchases, or operating costs.[154] A revolving line of credit, or a revolving loan, allows a business to borrow up to a certain amount and, after the outstanding debt is paid off, borrow up to that amount again. Typically, interest is paid only on the portion of the loan that has been borrowed. A revolving line of credit, or a revolving loan, is often secured, or collateralized, by the company's assets.[155] If the company defaults on the loan, the lender can take possession of the collateral securing the loan. Because the collateral in a secured loan reduces the risk of default to the lender, interest rates for secured loans are usually lower than for unsecured loans.[156]

A term loan usually has a fixed or formula-based interest rate, quarterly or monthly repayment requirements, and a fixed maturity date.[157] Because term loans typically have more stringent financial and

152. FED. RESERVE BANKS OF NEW YORK, CLEVELAND AND RICHMOND, SMALL BUSINESS CREDIT SURVEY—REPORT ON NONEMPLOYER FIRMS (2018), https://www.fedsmallbusiness.org/medialibrary/fedsmallbusiness/files/2018/sbcs-nonemployer-firms-report.pdf.

153. Richard Harroch, *10 Keys Steps To Getting A Small Business Loan*, FORBES (Mar. 22, 2017), https://www.forbes.com/sites/allbusiness/2017/03/22/10-key-steps-to-getting-a-small-business-loan/#79d9c1a940f6.

154. Kristie Lorette, *Line of Credit vs. Revolving Credit*, HOUS. CHRON., http://smallbusiness.chron.com/line-credit-vs-revolving-credit-3697.html.

155. *Id.*

156. *Id.*

157. *Bank-Term Loans*, ENTREPRENEUR, http://www.entrepreneur.com/article/52728.

collateral requirements, they tend to be better suited for established businesses.[158]

§ 1:4.6 Angel Investors

Angel investors are individuals who invest their own capital in nascent start-ups, often at a stage of development and profitability that many venture capitalists would consider too risky or small to finance.[159] As a result, many start-ups use angel financing from wealthy individuals, acting alone or in investment pools, to bridge the gap between funds contributed by friends and family, discussed above, and more formal venture capital funding, discussed below.[160] Individual angel investors typically make investments between $25,000 and $100,000, though some investments can be much higher depending on the business industry and its potential growth.[161]

It can be challenging for a company to find angel investors, in part because the federal securities laws typically applicable to issuances of securities to angel investors prohibit advertising or other forms of general solicitation.[162] Founders generally begin the investor recruitment process by contacting their network of friends and family for names of potential investors.[163] Angel investor networks such as Golden Seeds (which focuses on women entrepreneurs) can also provide assistance.[164] These organizations introduce entrepreneurs to potential investors and assist early-stage entrepreneurs in finding capital. Some angel investors invest specifically in the fashion or fashion technology industry, and those investors are typically well known in a local fashion community. Although locating angel investors and securing angel financing can be a difficult task for company founders, founders should be selective about whom they select as angel investors.

---

158. *Id.*

159. DAVID MANGUM, BRINGING ANGEL INVESTING OUT OF THE SHADOWS (Colorado Law May 2012) [hereinafter MANGUM], http://siliconflatirons.com/documents/publications/report/AngelReport2012.pdf.

160. *Id.* at 10.

161. Roman Shteyn, *Weighing the Pros and Cons of Angel Investors for Your Business*, BUS. (Jan. 22, 2018), https://www.business.com/articles/pros-and-cons-of-angel-investors/.

162. Rule 506(a), 17 C.F.R. § 230.506(a); Rule 502(c) of Regulation D, 17 C.F.R. § 230.502(c).

163. Imran Amed, *The Basics Part 3—How Do I Find the Right Investors and Partners?*, BUS. OF FASHION (June 8, 2007), https://www.businessoffashion.com/2007/06/the-business-of-fashion-basics-3-how-do-i-find-the-right-investors-and-partners.html.

164. GOLDEN SEEDS, ANGEL INVESTOR NETWORK, https://goldenseeds.com/angel-network/.

Angel investors should understand and be committed to the founder's vision for the company, offer guidance and business contacts to facilitate the company's growth, and collaborate effectively with the founder. Moreover, angel investors should be "accredited," as defined under the federal securities laws, to simplify compliance requirements in future rounds of financing. Generally, under the federal securities laws, accredited investors must have either:

- individual net worth (or joint net worth with a spouse) exceeding $1 million, not counting the value of the investor's primary residence; or
- individual income exceeding $200,000 or joint income with a spouse exceeding $300,000 in each of the two (2) most recent years, and a reasonable expectation of the same income level in the current year.[165]

When documenting an angel investment, it is customary for the founder to obtain a representation in writing from the angel investor that the investor meets "accredited" investor requirements.

As a practical consideration, an angel investor who can contribute mentoring, professional connections, and expertise is more beneficial than an investor who is solely a funding source.[166] Additionally, avoiding equity issuances to numerous unaccredited, unsophisticated investors can make future venture funding easier. Judicious selection of investors reduces the total number of investors in the start-up, which makes future financing rounds easier to negotiate and consummate.

Although angel investors may have a higher risk tolerance than traditional venture capitalists and private equity investors, angel investors nonetheless typically have their own criteria for investing in a start-up. Angel investors have become more thorough in their information requests prior to investment, as they increasingly work together in groups to review potential investment targets and syndicate deals among multiple members to spread risk.[167] As a result, a founder is more likely to be successful if he or she approaches an angel investor with a well-developed and tested product—confirmed sales of one or more seasonal collections in the context of an apparel company or a beta-tested website in the context of an e-commerce

---

165. Rule 501(a) of Regulation D, 17 C.F.R. § 230.501(a) (2012).

166. Rebecca Wessell, *Through Mentoring, Angel Investors Offer More than Just Money*, START UP NATION (Jan. 25, 2018), https://startupnation.com/grow-your-business/mentoring-angel-investors-money/.

167. Doug White & Polly White, *10 Ways to Fund Your Small Business*, ENTREPRENEUR (Feb. 9, 2016), https://www.entrepreneur.com/article/270556.

company. Angel investors may expect to see evidence of an established customer base or a pipeline of future purchase orders, a well-developed and cogent business plan, and investment by the founder in the project. Start-ups that are attractive to angel investors typically have a competent and experienced management team, a unique product with a large addressable market, and a plan for swift and scalable market penetration.[168]

Angel investor groups typically follow procedures in making investment decisions, although the order of the procedures is unique to each investor or investor group. The process generally begins with the founder submitting an initial application (which may include a summary of the business plan); several stages of internal analysis and screening (in which the angel group eliminates applications that are incomplete or do not meet the angel's investment preferences); one or more investment meetings (in which the founder formally pitches to the investor, almost always in person); a due diligence phase (to validate the quality of the business, its prospects, and its management team); and finally, a term sheet negotiation prior to investment.[169] While the founder may seek rapid access to capital, securing capital from angel investors often takes several months. It is advisable for the founder to consult with experienced legal counsel in connection with an angel investment.

Angel investment usually takes one of the following forms: preferred stock, convertible preferred stock, or convertible debt. The preferred stock or convertible preferred stock issued in angel investments typically does not confer as many protective rights as the securities issued in connection with venture capital financings.[170] In a convertible preferred stock or convertible debt financing, the angel investor can convert the preferred stock into common shares or the debt into common or preferred shares of the company upon the occurrence of certain future events. These trigger events may include the company receiving additional investor financing in excess of a certain amount or the sale of the company. Typically, the preferred stock or debt will convert at a discount compared to the value of the new financing, or the angel investor will receive warrants to purchase more shares of the company at a fixed price on a future date.[171] These favorable conversion terms are meant to reward the angel investor for the additional risk of making an early-stage investment.[172]

168. *Id.*
169. *Id.*
170. MANGUM, *supra* note 159, at 36.
171. *Id.*
172. *Id.*

§ 1:4.7 Venture Capital Investors

In contrast to angel investors, venture capital funds typically invest the capital of third parties, invest larger amounts, and invest in later financing rounds.[173] They generally have an expected rate of return that they seek in the particular categories of investments in which they participate. In addition to providing capital, venture capitalists can provide the following important benefits to companies and their founders:[174]

- *Assistance in arranging a syndicate of co-investors for current and subsequent financing rounds.* Two or more venture funds may invest together in a start-up in order to diversify their risk and divide the work of advising the company. Ideally, the initial venture capital investors will continue to participate in future financing rounds, typically with the addition of new investors.
- *Advice, business connections, and professional experience.* Venture capital investors often require representation on the Board of Directors of the company as part of their investment. Their knowledge and experience can be instrumental to the company's growth and development.
- *Validation of the business to third parties.* After a start-up has received venture capital financing, it often has greater credibility with vendors and business partners.

The founder of a fashion company who is seeking funding from a specific venture capital investor should attempt to secure an introduction from someone whom the venture capital investor knows—an executive of a company in the investor's portfolio, a fashion industry contact, or legal counsel.[175] In addition, the founder should research venture capital firms to identify each firm's sector preferences, reputation, capital resources for future financings, and size-of-investment history.[176] For example, Menlo Ventures invested in the following innovative fashion industry start-ups: Warby Parker and Poshmark.[177] Performing a targeted venture capital search allows the founder to

---

173. *Id.*
174. Smith, *supra* note 127, §§ 7.04, 8.02.
175. Alejandro Cremades, *How Venture Capital Works*, FORBES (Aug. 2, 2018), https://www.forbes.com/sites/alejandrocremades/2018/08/02/how-venture-capital-works/#2b64016c1b14 [hereinafter Cremades].
176. Smith, *supra* note 127, § 7.04.
177. Lauren Sherman, *The Top 10 Venture-Backed Fashion Startups*, CAMPFIRE-CAPITAL (May 4, 2017), http://campfire-capital.com/apparel/top-10-vc-backed-fashion-startups/.

tailor his or her pitch more closely to a particular venture capital firm, and increase the chances of securing financing from the most aligned investors.[178]

Venture capitalists typically focus on start-ups that can demonstrate measurable success in a large potential market. This concept, often referred to as "traction" in the venture community, can be demonstrated through quantifiable increases in the company's business metrics such as revenues, profits, customers, subscribers, active users, or partners.[179] Founders should be prepared to show venture capital firms data in support of the potential addressable market, and a plan for a quick and sustained quantifiable increase in key business metrics. Venture capitalists also typically consider the competence and business experience of the company's management. Many venture capitalists find management quality to be the most important factor in deciding to invest and will carefully evaluate the management team's prior experience (including previous involvement in a successful start-up), business knowledge, management ability, integrity, and ambition.[180]

The process of obtaining venture capital financing is similar to obtaining angel investor financing. If the venture capital firm is interested in the investment based on a preliminary review of the company's business plan, it may invite the founder to meet with the principals to discuss a potential financing. At the meeting, the founder of a company in the fashion industry should be prepared to discuss such matters as the business and fashion industry experience of the management team, current market trends, industry or demographic changes that could affect the company's profitability, the uniqueness of the company, competition and barriers to entry, the potential for brand-name recognition, and quality control.[181] If the meeting is successful, the venture capital firm may commence a formal legal and business diligence review to confirm that there are no significant legal issues, that all equity and contractual arrangements are properly documented, and that the company's financial projections and underlying assumptions are reasonable. The types of legal issues that are frequently discovered in the course of a due diligence review

---

178. Cremades, *supra* note 175.

179. Collin Horan, *Key Elements of a Pitch Deck*, MEDIUM (May 16, 2017), https://medium.com/laveer-growth-capital/key-elements-of-a-pitch-deck-9db953aa3c3.

180. Martin J. Smith, *Do Funders Care More About Your Team, Your Idea, or Your Passion?*, INSIGHTS STAN. BUS. (Jan. 12, 2017), https://www.gsb.stanford.edu/insights/do-funders-care-more-about-your-team-your-idea-or-your-passion.

181. MADISON PARK GRP., GUIDE TO VENTURE CAPITAL, http://upload.madisonparkgrp.com/news/gtvc.pdf.

include: claims by third parties alleging ownership of particular assets or intellectual property rights (such as patents or trademarks) that are fundamental to the value of the company and its brand; issuances of common stock to unaccredited investors, such as friends or family (which could trigger additional disclosure requirements[182] or violate legal limitations on the number of participating unaccredited investors);[183] and ongoing disputes with disaffected co-founders or employees (which could cast doubt on the value of the enterprise and foreshadow troublesome management disputes).[184]

During the diligence process or shortly thereafter, the investors and the company (and their respective legal counsel) negotiate a term sheet for the financing, which typically provides for the issuance of convertible preferred stock. A number of venture capitalists will request that a company execute a standstill agreement in conjunction with term sheet negotiations. The standstill agreement grants an option to the venture capitalist to invest in the company on agreed terms if the diligence review does not reveal any material problems with the company.[185] The standstill typically bars the company from negotiating with other venture capital firms, locks in certain investment terms, and prohibits a sale of the company to another party during the diligence period.[186] Standstill agreements create additional pressure on the founder to complete the financing with the venture capital firm that is party to the standstill agreement. A standstill agreement, followed by a diligence process typically lasting four to six weeks, may exacerbate the company's capital constraints. As a result, a company should consider negotiating a bridge financing as part of a term sheet containing a standstill.[187] A bridge financing is a short-term loan to the company in anticipation of a future infusion of capital.[188]

As noted above, issuances of securities (equity or debt) are subject to federal and state securities laws. In order to issue securities without registering them with the SEC, the securities must be exempt from registration, or the transaction by which the securities are sold must be exempt from registration. Section 3(b) of the Securities Act of 1933, as amended (the "Securities Act"), empowers the SEC to promulgate rules for specific exemptions from registration for small issuances of

182. Rule 502(b) of Regulation D, 17 C.F.R. § 230.502(b).
183. Rule 506(b)(2) of Regulation D, 17 C.F.R. § 230.506(b)(2).
184. Gary Tan, *Co-founder conflict*, TECHCRUNCH (Feb. 18, 2017), https://techcrunch.com/2017/02/18/co-founder-conflict/.
185. Smith, *supra* note 127, § 7.04.
186. *Id.*
187. *Id.*
188. *Id.* § 17.01.

securities.[189] Section 4(2) of the Securities Act exempts "transactions by an issuer not involving any public offering" from the registration requirements of section 5 of the Securities Act.[190] Regulation D promulgated under the Securities Act contains two section 3(b) exemptions (Rules 504 and 505) as well as a safe harbor under the section 4(2) non-public offering exemption (Rule 506). [191] If a transaction does not comply with the provisions of Regulation D, a legal analysis of the facts and circumstances of the offering must be made to determine whether the issuance of securities was properly a private placement that did not require registration under the securities laws.[192] Issuances of securities pursuant to the exemptions contained in Rules 504, 505, and 506 require the filing of a notice on Form D with the SEC.

Rule 506 of Regulation D provides an exemption from registration that is often used for venture capital investments.[193] Pursuant to Rule 506, a company may sell an unlimited amount of securities in a private placement to an unlimited number of "accredited investors" (defined in Rule 501, and discussed above) and up to thirty-five non-accredited investors (based on the issuer's reasonable belief as to their status). Non-accredited investors, either individually or with the aid of advisors, must have sufficient knowledge and experience in business and finance to evaluate the risks of the prospective investment. Compliance with Rule 506 requires that the company provide disclosure documents, including financial statements and a description of the business, to non-accredited investors in the offering.[194] The process of preparing appropriate disclosure documents may not be cost-effective in a financing round if the information is difficult or time-consuming to gather and verify. Moreover, if the company provides disclosure documents to non-accredited investors, it should also provide such documents to accredited investors in the offering. In addition, securities issued under Regulation D are subject to certain resale restrictions such as holding period requirements. These apply unless the securities are subsequently registered with the SEC, for example, pursuant to an initial public offering. Rule 506 previously prohibited issuers from offering or selling securities using any form of general solicitation or advertising. Typically, this includes

---

189. Securities Act § 3(b), 15 U.S.C. § 77c(b).
190. Securities Act § 5, 15 U.S.C. § 77e.
191. Regulation D, 17 C.F.R. § 230.
192. LOUIS LOSS, JOEL SELIGMAN & TROY PAREDES, SECURITIES REGULATION § 7.b (2018).
193. Regulation D, 17 C.F.R. § 230.500.
194. Rule 506(b) of Regulation D, 17 C.F.R. § 230.506(b); Rule 502(b) of Regulation D, 17 C.F.R. § 230.502(b).

advertisements or notices published in newspapers or magazines or broadcast through television or radio. It also includes seminars or meetings where participants were invited through general solicitation or advertisements. This prohibition has been modified upon the implementation of the Jumpstart Our Business Startups Act (H.R. 3606, the "JOBS Act"), which was enacted in 2012.[195] Under the JOBS Act and Rule 506(c), issuers relying on Rule 506 will be permitted to engage in general solicitations and advertising if (i) the issuer takes reasonable steps to verify that the purchasers are accredited investors and (ii) all of the purchasers fall within one of the eight categories of persons who are accredited investors under Rule 501(a) or the issuer reasonably believes that the purchasers fall within one of those categories.[196] Securities issued under Rule 506 are not subject to state securities laws, called "blue sky laws," because they are "preempted" by the federal National Securities Markets Improvement Act of 1996.[197] Accordingly, securities issued under Rule 506 are subject only to the federal securities regulatory regime.[198]

Rules 504 and 505 of Regulation D also provide exemptions for non-public companies, but contain notable limitations. Under Rule 504, the size of an offering is limited to $1 million per twelve-month period, with no restrictions on the number and nature of potential investors. Under Rule 504, a disclosure document need not be delivered to investors. Under Rule 505, the size of an offering is limited to $5 million per twelve-month period, and an unlimited number of accredited investors are permitted to invest, but the number of non-accredited investors is limited to thirty-five. Additionally, the company issuing securities is required to provide disclosure documents, including financial statements and a description of the business, to any participating non-accredited investors, and should provide such information to accredited investors in the offering as well. The restrictions on general solicitation will apply to Rules 504 and 505 offerings, even after implementation of the JOBS Act.[199] Importantly,

---

195. For a fuller discussion of the JOBS Act, see *infra* chapter 21.

196. Rule 506(c) of Regulation D, 17 C.F.R. § 230.506(c).

197. Smith, *supra* note 127, § 8.02.

198. *See also* Maria Bartiromo, *A Rough Week for Socialism*, REALCLEAR POLITICS (Apr. 1, 2019) (crediting 2012 JOBS Act for creating "a more welcoming environment" for start-ups by making "it easier for young companies to prepare for a public offering and test investor appetite before having to make wholesale public disclosures"), https://www.realclearpolitics.com/articles/2019/04/01/a_rough_week_for_socialism_139917.html.

199. Rule 504 of Regulation D, 17 C.F.R. § 230.504; Rule 505 of Regulation D, 17 C.F.R. § 230.505.

securities issued under Rule 504 or 505 remain subject to state securities regulation.[200]

Securities offerings pursuant to Rules 504, 505, and 506 under Regulation D may be "integrated," meaning that a series of related Regulation D offerings may be considered by the SEC to be a single offering.[201] Offerings that individually may comply with the requirements of a rule under Regulation D may fail to comply if they are integrated, and the company may lose the availability of an exemption from registration. The federal securities laws generally provide a safe harbor against integration for Regulation D offerings that are completed more than six (6) months apart from one another.[202]

Following the adoption of Regulation D, the SEC has adopted two additional sets of rules that permit general solicitation and advertising of unregistered securities and facilitate smaller company access to capital: Regulation A+ ("Reg A+")[203] and Regulation Crowdfunding.[204]

Reg A+ provides for two tiers of offerings: Tier 1 offerings are limited to $20 million in any twelve- (12-)month period and Tier 2 offerings are limited to $50 million in any twelve- (12-)month period.[205] Purchasers under Tier 2 offerings that are not accredited investors under Rule 501 of Regulation D may not invest in amounts that exceed 10% of their annual income or annual revenue, as applicable.

The SEC's Regulation Crowdfunding rules are set forth in section 4(a)(6) of the Securities Act, and allow an exemption for registration from crowdfunding transactions where (i) the amount raised does not exceed $1 million in a twelve- (12-)month period; (2) individual investments from all crowdfunding issuers in such period are limited to the greater of $2,000 or 5% of the annual income of investors with a net worth less than $100,000, or 10% of the annual income of investors with worth of $100,000 or more; and (3) transactions are conducting through an intermediary funding portal.[206]

§ 1:4.8 *Private Equity*

Although several brand-oriented private equity firms such as Eurazeo Brands may be active in earlier-stage companies, many private equity firms invest in larger, later-stage companies, typically Series

200. Smith, *supra* note 127, § 8.02.
201. Rule 502(a) of Regulation D, 17 C.F.R. § 230.502(a).
202. *Id.*
203. 17 C.F.R. § 230.251 *et seq.*; Amendments for Small and Additional Issues Exemptions under the Securities Act (Regulation A). 75 Fed. Reg. 218,069 (Apr. 2015).
204. Securities Act § 4(a)(6); 80 Fed. Reg. 71,399 (Nov. 2015).
205. 17 C.F.R. § 230.251.
206. Securities Act § 2(a)(6), 15 U.S.C. § 77b(a)(6).

C and beyond.[207] Therefore, start-ups may find it difficult to access private equity funding in their early stages. Traditional private equity firms individually, or as part of a consortium with other private equity firms, may take minority or majority equity positions or participate in management buy-outs of fashion companies.[208] TSG Consumer Partners, LLC, for example, focuses on consumer brands and has invested in such well-known fashion companies as Revolve and Privé Revaux.[209] Accordingly, traditional private equity financing may provide capital and exit opportunities for fashion companies that have matured beyond the start-up stage.

There is also a category of private equity firms that specializes in small business funding. These firms are called "small business investment companies," or SBICs.[210] While privately owned, SBICs are licensed by the U.S. Small Business Administration, or SBA, and use money borrowed from the SBA to supplement their own funds in order to invest.[211] SBICs typically make small business investments in the form of debt, or debt with equity features.[212] Equity financing also may be available.[213] SBICs can only invest in companies defined as "small" by the SBA;[214] depending on the industry, a small business could be defined as a business with a maximum of 250 employees or a maximum of 1,500 employees.[215] Because SBICs must repay their loans to the SBA, SBICs usually invest in companies that are developed sufficiently to make interest payments on the invested capital.[216] Online resources such as the Small Business Investor Alliance[217] are helpful in locating SBICs within a geographical area and with a specific industry focus.

---

207. *Glossary of Investor Types*, CRUNCHBASE, https://support.crunchbase.com/hc/en-us/articles/115010624128-Glossary-of-Investor-Types.
208. PRACTICAL L. CO., VENTURE CAPITAL INVESTMENT IN UNITED STATES: MARKET AND REGULATORY OVERVIEW (Mar. 1, 2015), http://us.practicallaw.com/7-501-0057.
209. TSG CONSUMER PARTNERS, PORTFOLIO, http://www.tsgconsumer.com/portfolio.
210. U.S. SMALL BUS. ADMIN., SBIC INVESTMENT CAPITAL [hereinafter SBIC PROGRAM], https://www.sba.gov/funding-programs/investment-capital.
211. *Id.*
212. *Id.*
213. U.S. SMALL BUS. ADMIN., SBIC DIRECTOR, https://www.sba.gov/content/all-sbic-licensees-state.
214. SBIC PROGRAM, *supra* note 210.
215. Georgia McIntyre, *What Is the SBA's Definition of Small Business (And Why)?*, FUNDERA (June 20 2018), https://www.fundera.com/blog/sba-definition-of-small-business.
216. SBIC PROGRAM, *supra* note 210.
217. SMALL BUS. INV. ALL., https://www.sbia.org.

Appendix 1A

Sample Creative Control Provisions

Creative Control. The Stockholders and the Company agree that, subject to the Business Plan and Annual Budget (each as defined below), so long as Founder is employed by the Company, Founder shall have ultimate authority and final approval rights with respect to all "creative" matters relating to the Company and its products. In furtherance thereof, the Stockholders agree that all material decisions of the Company with respect to each of the following matters will require the prior consent of Founder (or his designees) so long as Founder is employed by the Company:

(i) the design of each product sold by the Company, including, without limitation, the manufacturing specifications, such as all fabrics and materials to be used, colors, cut, detailing, stitching, and labeling;

(ii) the prototype or sample of each product produced for the purpose of demonstrating (internally and/or to third parties such as customers and the press) the execution of each design and the manufacturing, quality, and workmanship of the manufactured version of such product;

(iii) the products to be included in each collection in each season;

(iv) the design, layout, format, style, look, typefaces, graphic design, color and placement of each trademark of the Company, including, without limitation, any modifications or variations of any existing trademark, or the creation of any new trademark, or the elimination of any trademark;

(v) the design, layout, format, style, look, typefaces, graphic design, color, materials, and construction of all packaging and labeling used in connection with the products sold by the Company;

(vi) the concept, style, production, presentation, and location of each defile, if any, for each product collection in each season, as well as the particular products to be presented, the particular persons to be employed to model the products, and the production team to be used to mount such defile (as used herein, the term "defile" shall refer to each formal presentation or event staged for the purpose of presenting collections and/or products to customers, the press and/or the trade, whether staged "live" (*i.e.*, a traditional "runway fashion show") or made available in a recorded or other form);

(vii) the design, decoration, style of furnishing, style of signage, and overall look and image of all spaces and facilities associated with the Company's business to which the public, the trade, and/or the press are granted regular access, including, without limitation, the Company's headquarters, each showroom, each press office, and each dedicated shop (*e.g.*, a store, boutique, or similar retail outlet or in-store shop);

(viii) the advertising and media plan for all co-op advertising, trade advertising, and other advertising, and all promotional activities and events in each season relating to the Company's business, including, without limitation, the dates, publications, placement, format, and size of each proposed advertisement, activity, or event;

(ix) the design, layout, formats, style, look, typefaces, graphic design, text, themes, content, and subjects of all advertising materials, including, without limitation, all advertising copy, layouts, artwork, graphic design, photographs, texts, catalogues, in-store or point-of-purchase displays, and similar audiovisual materials that are used for advertising or promotional purposes in connection with the Company's business, in any medium;

(x) all material aspects of the press and publicity strategy for the Company's business, including, with respect to worldwide press communications and events, and the press and public relations policies, strategies and guidelines to be implemented by each press office of the Company, including all general and/or model press and public relations materials to be used in connection with the Company's business; and

(xi) the hiring, firing and compensation of all Company personnel (other than executive officers) involved in any of the foregoing activities.

The Company shall provide, and Founder shall take all actions within his control to cause the Company to provide, to Founder all matters required to be submitted to him for his review and approval under this Section on a timely basis, to allow sufficient time for meaningful consideration of each such matter. Founder shall not unreasonably withhold, delay or condition any approval required under this Section. The Company shall not make use of any item that is subject to the approval of Founder under this Section until such approval has been granted or in any manner other than in the manner for which approval was granted.

<u>*Press and Publicity*</u>. The Stockholders and the Company agree as follows:

(i) without the prior approval of Founder so long as he is employed by the Company, unless otherwise agreed to by him, no person other than Founder shall be identified as having the ultimate right of approval over the "creative" aspects of the business of the Company or as being the "creative director" or "designer" of the Company, or as having any similar title that in the international fashion industry would tend to be perceived as indicating the person having primary responsibility for creative matters;

(ii) the Company shall submit to Founder so long as he is employed by the Company, for his advance review and approval, each proposed material "press communication." As used herein, a "press communication" shall refer to any statement or item of information provided to the press with regard to the Company, the products of the Company or Founder personally, whether provided orally or in writing, live or recorded, including, without limitation, press releases related primarily to the Company, interviews granted by any person likely to be perceived to be speaking on behalf of the Company, and plans for press events relating to the Company;

(iii) the Company shall not make use of any image, likeness, photograph, or graphic depiction of Founder (a "<u>Portrait</u>"), or provide any Portrait to the press or to any third party, without Founder's prior express approval, as applicable. Approval granted with respect to the use of a particular Portrait for a particular purpose shall not be deemed to extend to the use of such Portrait for any other purpose, or to the use of a different Portrait for the same purpose, or to any subsequent use of the Portrait for the same purpose;

(iv) the Company shall make no public use of the name of Founder, without his prior express approval; and

(v) the Company shall not refer to or provide any information with respect to Founder in the course of any oral or written interview intended for publication without Founder's prior express approval. If such authorization is granted, the Company shall use its best efforts to obtain the right to review and approve the final version of such interview prior to its publication, and to provide Founder with an opportunity to do the same.

Founder shall not unreasonably condition, delay or withhold any agreement or approval required under this Section. Where possible, the Company and Founder shall formulate and agree upon guidelines and general parameters within which particular usages, information and/or materials will be deemed pre-approved. The Company shall implement at each of its press offices such procedures and policies as may be reasonably necessary to ensure that all items required to be submitted to Founder under this Section for review and approval are delivered on a timely basis, sufficient to allow meaningful consideration of each item submitted.

Business Plan. The Stockholders have agreed on an initial business plan for the Company, substantially in the form attached as an Exhibit hereto, covering, without limitation, strategy, organizational structure improvement, product extension, development of a second line, retail development, distribution development, scheduling of strategic steps and financial projections (such business plan, as it may be amended from time to time pursuant to this Agreement, the "Business Plan"). At least ninety (90) days prior to the end of the period covered by the initial and any subsequent Business Plan, an updated Business Plan shall be presented to the Board for its review and approval. The Business Plan may also be subject to periodic review and adjustment by the Board.

Annual Budget. At least thirty (30) days prior to the end of each fiscal year of the Company, an annual budget for the next fiscal year of the Company (each, an "Annual Budget"), consistent with the Business Plan then in effect and this Agreement, shall be presented to the Board for its review and approval.

Chapter 2

Trademarks and Trade Dress

§ 2:1 Introduction
§ 2:2 History
§ 2:3 Trademarks Defined
§ 2:4 Recurring Trademark Issues
§ 2:4.1 Letters and Numbers in Trademarks
§ 2:4.2 Personal Names
§ 2:4.3 Geographic Terms and Foreign Words
§ 2:4.4 Generic Terms and Common Phrases
§ 2:4.5 Deceptive Words
§ 2:5 Trade Dress
§ 2:6 Clearing and Registering a Trademark
§ 2:6.1 Registration Generally
§ 2:6.2 What Can Be Registered
§ 2:6.3 Overview of the Registration Process
[A] Trademark Searching
[B] The Application
[C] Use-Based and Intent-to-Use Applications
[D] Examination
[E] Opposition Proceedings
[F] Post-Registration
[G] International Aspects
§ 2:7 Trademark Infringement
§ 2:7.1 First Element: Establishing That the Trademark Is Entitled to Protection
§ 2:7.2 Second Element: Establishing Likelihood of Confusion
[A] The Confusion Factors
[B] Types of Confusion
[C] Likelihood of Confusion Analysis
§ 2:8 Trademark Dilution
§ 2:8.1 Dilution by Blurring
§ 2:8.2 Dilution by Tarnishment

§ 2:9 Remedies for Trademark Infringement
§ 2:9.1 Injunctive Relief
[A] Permanent Injunction
[B] Preliminary Injunction
§ 2:9.2 Monetary Relief
[A] Defendant's Profits
[B] Plaintiff's Damages
[C] Costs of the Action and Attorneys' Fees
§ 2:9.3 Accounting of Profits
§ 2:9.4 Remedies for Infringing Domain Names
§ 2:9.5 International Trade Commission
§ 2:10 Defenses to Infringement
§ 2:10.1 Invalidity of the Trademark
§ 2:10.2 Lack of Standing
§ 2:10.3 Fraud in Procuring the Trademark
§ 2:10.4 Unclean Hands
§ 2:10.5 Nominative Fair Use
§ 2:10.6 Laches
§ 2:10.7 Naked Licensing
§ 2:10.8 Parody
§ 2:10.9 Aesthetic Functionality
[A] The *Louboutin* Case
[B] *Eliya v. Steven Madden*
[C] *PUMA v. Forever 21*
§ 2:11 Search Engine and Internet Advertising as Infringement
§ 2:11.1 Use of Trademarks as Metatags
§ 2:11.2 Use of Trademarks in Search Engine Advertising
§ 2:11.3 Use of Trademarks in Hashtags
§ 2:12 Duty to Protect a Mark
§ 2:13 Developing an Enforcement Strategy
§ 2:13.1 Private Co-Existence Agreements
§ 2:14 Trademark Licensing
§ 2:15 International Trademark Issues
§ 2:15.1 The World Intellectual Property Organization
§ 2:15.2 The Madrid Protocol
Appendix 2A International Trademark Classification of Goods and Services
Appendix 2B Signatory Nations to the Madrid Agreement Concerning the International Registration Marks and Related Protocol

§ 2:1 Introduction

"What's in a name? That which we call a rose
By any other name would smell as sweet."
–William Shakespeare, *Romeo and Juliet* (II, ii, 1–2)

While Shakespeare's pithy musing on the insignificance of a name makes for memorable poetry, trademark law is based on the premise that names *are* important. Trademark law, indeed, is based on the notion that for a free market economy to function, it is necessary for the law to protect the names that consumers use to identify the source of a particular good or service—as well as logos, packaging, and other ways that consumers distinguish one product maker from another.

To qualify as a trademark, a word or symbol must satisfy three elements: (1) it must be a specified and definable word, name, symbol, or device or any combination of these; (2) it must be used in commerce to sell or promote goods or services to potential consumers; and (3) its function must be to identify and distinguish the seller's goods from those offered by others.

The functions of trademarks include: (1) identifying and distinguishing one seller's goods from another's; (2) signifying that all goods bearing the trademark come from or are controlled by a single source; (3) signifying that all goods bearing the trademark are of an equal level of quality; and (4) as a tool to advertise and market the goods.

Trademark law, moreover, is uniquely important in the fashion industry. As discussed in the chapters that follow, there are instances in which copyright and patent law will not protect fashion. And even where these alternate forms of protection are applicable, they can only protect the work of an owner for a limited time period. Trademark protection, in contrast, can go on forever, as long as consumers actually use the mark to identify a specific source.[1]

Although trademark law is certainly motivated by a desire to protect the investments that companies make in building their brands, it is the need to protect consumers from erroneous purchasing decisions that makes trademark law so powerful. As long as a designer, manufacturer, or retailer uses a mark to tell consumers, "I made this," the law affords a potent mechanism to restrict the use of marks that are similar enough to be likely to confuse potential consumers. Trademark law is, accordingly, often the legal regime of first resort for brand owners who find themselves victimized by knockoffs and copies.

---

1. Kellogg Co. v. Nat'l Biscuit Co., 305 U.S. 111, 119–20 (1938) (Brandeis, J.).

This chapter provides an overview of U.S. trademark law as it relates to fashion design, including a brief history of trademark law and a discussion of the types of trademarks that the law recognizes, the basic elements of trademark infringement, defenses against infringement claims, and other important related concepts for participants in the fashion industry.

§ 2:2 History

Though trademarks are the oldest form of intellectual property, they were the last to receive federal statutory protection in the United States.[2] The U.S. Congress enacted the first federal trademark statute in 1870,[3] but the law was struck down as a violation of the patent and copyright clause of the U.S. Constitution in 1879.[4] A few years later, Congress passed the Trademark Act of 1881, which focused on trademarks used in commerce with other nations and Indian tribes.[5] In 1905, Congress passed an act that provided trademark protection for marks used in interstate commerce, but that act limited trademark registration to fanciful and arbitrary marks in use for ten years prior to February 20, 1905.[6]

In 1946, Congress passed the Lanham Act, which created a new framework for protecting trademarks and preventing unfair competition.[7] The Lanham Act defines a "trademark" as a designation used to "identify and distinguish" the goods of a person.[8] Among other things, the Lanham Act establishes the procedure for federal registration of trademarks. Though registration is not required in order to enforce a trademark, registered federal trademarks receive greater procedural protections than their unregistered counterparts. For example, federal courts have automatic jurisdiction to hear claims brought by the owner of a mark that was registered by the U.S. Patent and Trademark Office (PTO) to enforce that trademark. In addition, the owner of a registered mark may enjoy certain factual presumptions if the

2. *See* FRANK ISAAC SCHECHTER, THE HISTORICAL FOUNDATIONS OF THE LAW RELATING TO TRADEMARKS (Columbia Legal Studies 1925).
3. "An Act to Revise, Consolidate and Amend the Statutes Relating to Patents and Copyrights Act (July 8, 1870), 16 Stat. at L 198, §§ 77–84." Ch. 2, tit. 60, §§ 4937–4974, Revised Stats.
4. The Trade Mark Cases, 100 U.S. 82 (1879).
5. Trademark Act of 1881, 21 Stat. 502 (Mar. 3, 1881).
6. Act of Feb. 20, 1905, 33 Stat. 724, 15 U.S.C. §§ 81 *et seq.* "An Act to authorize the registration of trademarks used in commerce with foreign nations or among the several States or with Indian Tribes, and to protect the same."
7. Lanham Act § 1, 15 U.S.C. §§ 1051 *et seq.* (July 6, 1946).
8. 15 U.S.C. § 1127.

registration has lasted long enough, and can recover statutory damages in certain instances. The owner of an unregistered mark, in contrast, is limited to remedies based in the Lanham Act's provision on false advertising and unfair competition, with no statutory presumptions or ability to recover statutory damages.

Unlike patent and copyright law, moreover, the Lanham Act does not establish exclusive jurisdiction in the federal courts to hear claims of trademark infringement. In fact, each state has developed its own trademark registration regime. Most states follow the federal system, and do not require state registration to receive trademark protection under state law, but state registration can provide advantages in enforcing trademark rights in certain states. Under the complementary federal and state regimes, it is possible for the owner of a state-registered trademark, or a common law unregistered trademark, to have rights superior to the owner of a registered federal trademark. The key is that the owner of the older, "senior" mark must have actually and continuously used the mark in commerce to allow consumers to identify the source of particular goods longer than the younger mark that happened to be registered first.

The Lanham Act of 1946 was amended over two dozen times between its 1947 effective date and the end of the twentieth century. One of the more substantial amendments was the Trademark Law Revision Act of 1988 (TLRA), which afforded applicants an opportunity to apply to register a mark based on an "intent-to-use" that trademark, and to complete that registration once the actual use of that mark in commerce has commenced.[9] This change eliminated the need to make a showing of a token use in order to kick start the federal application process. The TLRA also introduced the concept of "constructive use," which begins when an application to register a mark is filed.

In 1995, Congress passed the Federal Trademark Dilution Act, which, for the first time, created a federal cause of action for "dilution" of a trademark in addition to the more familiar cause of action for "infringement."[10] The remedy was designed to protect owners of trademarks from acts that slowly whittle away or detract from the value of a mark, as opposed to acts that infringe by creating immediate confusion.[11] The statute was amended in 2006, in the Trademark Dilution Revision Act, to make clear that a trademark owner need

---

9. Trademark Law Revision Act of 1988, Pub. L. No. 100-667, 102 Stat. 3935 (Nov. 16, 1988).

10. Federal Trademark Dilution Act, Pub. L. No. 104-98, 109 Stat. 985 (enacted and effective Jan. 16, 1996); *see* Moseley v. V Secret Catalogue, Inc., 537 U.S. 418 (2003).

11. *See also infra* section 2:8.

only establish a *likelihood of* dilution rather than *actual* dilution of the famous mark. The 2006 law clarified the parameters of actionable dilution under the federal statute and set forth factors to assist courts in determining when dilution has occurred.

In 1996, Congress passed the Anticounterfeiting Consumer Protection Act, which introduced changes designed to strengthen the penalties and procedures available to combat counterfeiting.[12] Congress was motivated in part by a gap in the law: Plaintiffs who were victorious on their civil counterfeiting claims were often unable to obtain an adequate recovery in actual damages because counterfeiters generally maintain sparse business records.[13] The statute introduced statutory damages as an alternative to proving actual damages in civil counterfeiting litigation.[14]

Another important amendment to the Lanham Act was the 1999 Anticybersquatting Consumer Protection Act (ACPA), which is directed at preventing the registration and use of domain names that are confusingly similar to trademarks and people's names.[15] The trademark portions of the ACPA define cybersquatting as reserving, with bad faith intent to profit, a domain name that is confusingly similar to a registered or unregistered mark or dilutive of a famous mark. The standard under ACPA is not whether there is a likelihood of confusion between two specific websites, but rather whether the allegedly offending website "creat[es] a likelihood of confusion as to the source, sponsorship, affiliation, or endorsement of the site."[16] ACPA is relevant to fashion brands seeking to prevent others from using their trademarks as domain names.[17]

Together, these statutes form the foundation of trademark law in the United States. This chapter provides as detailed an examination of these provisions as this format will allow, focusing on the concepts most salient in the fashion and retail space.

---

12. Anticounterfeiting Consumer Protection Act of 1996, § 7, Pub. L. No. 104-153, 110 Stat. 1386 (codified at 15 U.S.C. § 1117(c)).
13. Louis Vuitton Malletier S.A. v. LY USA, Inc., 676 F.3d 83, 110 (2d Cir. 2012) (citing S. Rep. 104-177, at 10 (1995)).
14. *See also infra* chapter 7.
15. Anticybersquatting Consumer Protection Act § 1000(a) (1999), 15 U.S.C. § 1125(d).
16. 15 U.S.C. § 1125(d)(1)(B)(v).
17. *See, e.g.*, Newport News Holdings Corp. v. Virtual City Vision, Inc., 650 F.3d 423 (4th Cir. 2011) (holding that domain name created a likelihood of confusion as to the source of the website and therefore infringed a clothing company's trademark).

§ 2:3 Trademarks Defined

As a technical matter, a trademark is a designation used "to identify and distinguish" goods, as opposed to a "service mark," which is used to identify and distinguish the source of services.[18] In practice, however, courts and businesses use the term "trademark" to cover both goods and services. Indeed, to the extent there was once a justification for distinguishing between the two types of marks, it is now a distinction without a difference.

The keystones of trademark law are distinctiveness of the mark and avoidance of "a likelihood of confusion" in the minds of the purchasing public. The more likely it is that a mark will be remembered and associated in the public mind with the mark's owner, the greater protection the mark is accorded by trademark laws.[19] Distinctive marks serve to identify a particular source. Louis Vuitton's interlocking "LV" logo, Nike's "Just Do It" slogan, and Ralph Lauren's polo insignia are examples of distinctive marks that cannot be copied without violating the owner's trademark.

Less distinctive marks, like personal names or geographic locations, can also be protected if they have acquired "secondary meaning" among members of the public.[20] "Secondary meaning" refers to the public's understanding that a mark is affiliated with a particular source of goods or services, in contrast to the literal, or "primary" meaning of the mark.[21] The public does not have to know the specific corporate identity of the single source as long as the public associates the product bearing the mark with a single source.[22]

In addition to identifying the goods or services of a person or company, trademarks can be used to indicate sponsorship or authorization by a recognized entity. For example, the name of a sports team or institution on clothing can signify that the referenced team or institution authorizes, endorses, and licenses the sale of such apparel

---

18. Lanham Act § 45, 15 U.S.C. § 1127.

19. Kenner Parker Toys Inc. v. Rose Art Indus., Inc., 963 F.2d 350, 353 (Fed. Cir. 1992).

20. Inwood Labs., Inc. v. Ives Labs., Inc., 456 U.S. 844, 851 n.11 (1982) (a mark has acquired "secondary meaning" when, "in the minds of the public, the primary significance of a product feature . . . is to identify the source of the product rather than the product itself.").

21. Levi Strauss & Co. v. Blue Bell, Inc., 632 F.2d 817 (9th Cir. 1980); *see also* Paul Frank Indus., Inc. v. Sunich, 502 F. Supp. 2d 1094, 1098–99 (C.D. Cal. 2007) (Paul Frank Sunich was not permitted to use his personal name to market clothing because Paul Frank Industries, Inc. owned the Paul Frank mark, and that mark had "achieved significant recognition and fame").

22. Union Carbide Corp. v. Ever-Ready, Inc., 531 F.2d 366, 380 (7th Cir.), *cert. denied*, 429 U.S. 830 (1976).

by the manufacturer. The University of Pittsburgh's suit against the manufacturer of Champion T-shirts is an example of this phenomenon. There, the U.S. Court of Appeals for the Third Circuit noted that "the crucial element [in purchasing a Champion T-shirt] is consumer desire to associate with the entity whose imprint is reproduced [on the Champion T-shirt]," not the shirt itself. Champion's use of the University of Pittsburgh's trademark therefore constituted trademark infringement.[23] A similar situation arose when a company called New World Creation Inc. began selling imitation jerseys and replica dresses that mimicked the famous uniform designs of the National Basketball Association (NBA).[24] The NBA sued, alleging trademark infringement on grounds that New World Creation was purporting to profit from the NBA's famous marks by falsely suggesting affiliation or sponsorship.

Other types of marks defined by law include the following:

A **certification mark** is any word, name, symbol, or device used or intended to be used in commerce by someone other than its owner, to certify particular characteristics of the goods or services offered in connection with the marks, such as the geographic location of origin, material used, mode of manufacture, or a certification attained as to the quality of the goods or accuracy of the services offered.[25] In the fashion industry, familiar certification marks include the "union label," indicating that a particular item of apparel was created in a unionized facility,[26] and the woolmark, which indicates that an item is made 100% out of wool.[27]

Collective marks are trademarks or service marks used, or intended to be used, in commerce, by the members of a cooperative, an association, or other collective group or organization, including a mark that indicates membership in a union, an association, or other organization.[28]

---

23. Univ. of Pittsburgh v. Champion Prods., Inc., 686 F.2d 1040 (3d Cir. 1982).
24. NBA v. New World Creation Inc. of N.Y., No. 03 Civ. 5180 (S.D.N.Y. July 16, 2003).
25. 15 U.S.C. § 1127.
26. *See* UNION LABEL & SERV. TRADES DEP'T, AFL-CIO, https://unionlabel.org/.
27. *See* THE WOOLMARK COMPANY, https://www.woolmark.com/certification/.
28. 15 U.S.C. § 1127.

§ 2:4 Recurring Trademark Issues

§ 2:4.1 Letters and Numbers in Trademarks

An individual letter or arbitrary grouping of letters, not functioning as a recognizable word, can function as a protectable mark.[29] This is especially true if the letters or numbers in combination have no inherent meaning.[30] This is why courts have repeatedly enforced rights in numbers that are used to form an arbitrary composite mark, like Chanel No. 5 or Seven Jeans.[31] And at least one court was willing to protect the use of the number "05" when placed on an athletic jersey, on the theory that because numbers on athletic jerseys had not conventionally used a zero before the main number, the "05" was recognizable to consumers as indicating a particular source.[32] If, however, numbers are used only to indicate size, capacity, model, style, or grade, they are not being used in a trademark sense and are not subject to trademark protection.

§ 2:4.2 Personal Names

The law also allows the use of personal names as trademarks. Ralph Lauren, Christian Dior, Alexander Wang, Brian Atwood, and Tory Burch—all use personal names as trademarks. A few words of caution are appropriate, though. First, personal names are not always inherently distinctive. Many people may have the same or similar names. Second, courts often prefer to permit people to use their own names in commerce, and may fashion a remedy that is designed to allow an individual as much leeway as possible in using his or her own name while still preventing the likelihood of consumer confusion. This issue has arisen repeatedly in the fashion context.

One example involves the menswear designer, Joseph Abboud. After registering his personal name as a trademark in 1987, Abboud licensed the use of his name to a company called JA Apparel, which manufactured, marketed, and sold products under the Joseph Abboud trademark. After JA Apparel was purchased by a private equity firm, Abboud signed an agreement that transferred the license to his personal name to JA's new owners. Several years later, Abboud undertook preparations to start a new line of high-end men's clothing. JA Apparel brought suit alleging trademark infringement. Evaluating

29. *See, e.g.*, K2 Advisors, LLC v. K2 Volatility Fund, LP, No. 02 CIV. 3984(AGS), 2002 WL 31235701 (S.D.N.Y. Oct. 4, 2002) ("K2").

30. J. Thomas McCarthy, McCarthy on Trademarks and Unfair Competition § 7.16 (4th ed. 1996) [hereinafter McCarthy].

31. Chanel, Inc. v. Suttner, 109 U.S.P.Q. 493 (S.D.N.Y. 1956) (mark "C No. 5" held infringement).

32. GTFM, Inc. v. Solid Clothing, Inc., 215 F. Supp. 2d 273 (S.D.N.Y. 2002).

the licensing agreement and the likelihood of confusion, the district court ruled in favor of JA Apparel and enjoined Abboud from using his personal name to sell, market, or otherwise promote goods, products, and services.[33] The Second Circuit reversed, holding that the agreement that licensed Abboud's name to JA Apparel was ambiguous.[34] On remand, after analyzing the ambiguities in the agreement, the district court permanently enjoined Abboud from using his personal name as a trademark, service mark, trade name, or brand name for any competing line of clothing to avoid confusing consumers.[35] The court noted that "injunctions in trademark cases involving use of an individual's personal name should be narrowly tailored," and the court "must seek to avoid confusion in the marketplace, protect a prior company's property interest in its name, and permit an individual to exploit his own identity and reputation in a legitimate manner."[36] In striking this balance, the court prohibited Abboud from using his name unless it was employed "in the context of a complete sentence or descriptive phrase" or was accompanied by a disclaimer of any affiliation with the products sold under the other Joseph Abboud trademarks.[37]

In another case, a member of the Gucci family, Paolo Gucci, sued Gucci Shops, Inc., seeking a declaration that he had the right to use his personal name to sell products.[38] Evaluating the likelihood of confusion with the Gucci trademark, the district court enjoined Paolo Gucci from using his name as a trademark or trade name to sell products he had designed.[39] Sensitive to Paolo's desire to use his name, however, the court tailored the injunction to *exclude* his use of his name to identify himself as the designer of products sold under separate trademarks that did not include the name "Gucci." Accordingly, Paolo's name could be used only if it appeared after the non-Gucci trademark in advertisements and on labels, and was no more prominent than the non-Gucci trademark.[40]

Generally speaking, individuals can obtain stronger trademark protection for personal names by demonstrating that the mark has acquired "secondary meaning."[41] As mentioned earlier, secondary

---

33. JA Apparel Corp. v. Abboud, 591 F. Supp. 2d 306 (S.D.N.Y. 2008).
34. JA Apparel Corp. v. Abboud, 568 F.3d 390 (2d Cir. 2009).
35. JA Apparel Corp. v. Abboud, 682 F. Supp. 2d 294 (S.D.N.Y. 2010).
36. *Id.* at 318 (internal quotation marks omitted).
37. *Id.*
38. Gucci v. Gucci Shops, Inc., 688 F. Supp. 916 (S.D.N.Y. 1988).
39. *Id.* at 927.
40. *Id.* at 928.
41. E. & J. Gallo Winery v. Gallo Cattle Co., 967 F.2d 1280 (9th Cir. 1992); *see also* Cairns v. Franklin Mint Co., 24 F. Supp. 2d 1013, 1043–45 (C.D. Cal. 1998).

meaning has been defined by courts as the consumer's association of the mark with a particular source or sponsor.[42] Secondary meaning can be established by showing long, continued use of the mark, the mark's widespread, national public recognition, and extensive and expensive advertising and promotion of products bearing the marks.[43] Accordingly, even if Calvin Klein were a common name, the fact that consumers associate the Calvin Klein mark with a particular American designer entitles it to greater trademark protection. Indeed, the name "Tiffany" has been deemed a strong trademark for the Tiffany and Co. jewelry brand, as evidence has demonstrated that Tiffany '"claims the largest share of the female mind in the U.S.' with respect to name recognition in jewelry brands."[44]

The lesson of these cases is that personal names must have secondary meaning to be protectable. But because courts often look for a way to permit the newcomer to use his or her name in commerce, the most successful fashion companies often develop symbols and other consistent and unique branding elements that distinguish their products from others with similar names.

§ 2:4.3 Geographic Terms and Foreign Words

Fashion companies should also be conscious of the risks that arise when a geographic term or a foreign word is used as a mark.

For example, geographic terms can be characterized as merely descriptive when they provide accurate information about the geographic location where a product or service originates. As a result, they receive less rigorous trademark protection. When used in an arbitrary way—unconnected with the good or service at issue—a geographic term can be protectable though,[45] especially when combined with other non-generic, non-descriptive words. Similarly, when a geographic term is used widely over a long period of time to point consumers to one particular company, such as "American Airlines," the mark also can be strong and protectable.[46]

The use of foreign words as trademarks can also be problematic at times. Pursuant to the "doctrine of equivalents," most foreign words

---

42. *Id.* at 1291.
43. *Id.*
44. Tiffany & Co. v. Costco Wholesale Corp., 127 F. Supp. 3d 241, 248 (S.D.N.Y. 2015) (finding that any "generic" uses of "Tiffany" have not undermined the uncontroverted strength of the TIFFANY mark).
45. *See, e.g.*, Atl. Monthly Co. v. Frederick Ungar Publ'g Co., 197 F. Supp. 524 (S.D.N.Y. 1964).
46. *See, e.g.*, Metro. Opera Ass'n v. Metro. Opera Ass'n of Chi., 81 F. Supp. 127 (N.D. Ill. 1948) (concluding that the term METROPOLITAN had acquired secondary meaning because consumers identify it only with the New York Metropolitan Opera).

will be translated into their English counterparts and then analyzed for descriptiveness purposes. As a result, it is generally advisable to use marks based on geographic terms and foreign words in combination with other source-identifying branding elements.

§ 2:4.4 Generic Terms and Common Phrases

Courts are also careful to avoid granting trademark protection to words or phrases that have dictionary meanings. The Supreme Court has warned against "allowing anyone to obtain a complete monopoly on use of a descriptive term simply by grabbing it first."[47] When a trademark owner consciously "decide[s] to identify [their] product with a mark that [also doubles as] a well-known descriptive phrase" it assumes the risk that others would continue to use the same phrase in that ordinary sense.[48]

In particular, courts refuse to register—or refuse to enforce—trademarks that consist of terms that merely describe the particular product. For example, in the fashion world, the Court of Appeals for the Federal Circuit affirmed a decision of the U.S. Patent and Trademark Office (PTO) refusing to allow a company called Branded LLC to renew a registration for the trademark TWEEDS because it is a generic term for shirts and sweaters made of tweed.[49] In contrast, the PTO's Trademark Trial and Appeal Board (TTAB) allowed designer Stella McCartney to register the trademark FUR FREE FUR for handbags and related products.[50] Although the Board's majority held that "there is no dispute as to the meaning of the constituent terms," the combination of "fur free" and "fur" "creates a "logical paradox" that "is likely to give consumers pause." Because this "incongruous phrase" then "requires some imagination, thought, or perception to reach a conclusion as to the nature of the goods," the majority concluded that the phrase should be merely "suggestive" and thus capable of conveying the source of the goods to consumers rather than the nature of the goods themselves.[51]

It is important to remember that not every word or symbol that appears in connection with an entity's goods or services functions as a trademark. Courts often refuse to register or enforce claimed slogans if they conclude that there is no evidence that the expression serves a source-identifying function. For example, in 2019, the TTAB rejected a prominent retailer's attempt to register the expression INVESTING

---

47. KP Permanent Make-Up, Inc. v. Lasting Impression I, Inc., 543 U.S. 111, 122 (2004).
48. *Id.*
49. *In re* Branded LLC, No. 18-1828 (Fed. Cir. Apr. 8, 2019).
50. *In re* Stella McCartney Ltd., Ser. No. 87410072 (TTAB Mar. 29, 2019).
51. *Id.*

IN AMERICAN JOBS as a trademark.[52] After examining the retailer's evidence of online and in-store use of the phrase and extensive use of similar phrases by third parties, the Board concluded that "the public would perceive INVESTING IN AMERICAN JOBS merely as an informational slogan rather than as a source indicator."[53] As a result, the application to register the slogan was denied.

§ 2:4.5 Deceptive Words

Fashion companies also should be conscious of the opposite risk, that terms that may be associated with materials or fabrics, or other qualities of a product may also be rejected if the term does *not* accurately describe the product.

For example, terms that are similar to the names of materials or fabrics may be deemed too deceptive to serve as trademarks when they are used to signify the source of clothing that is not made of those materials or fabrics. That is what happened when a Trademark Examining Attorney initially refused to register "L.A.M.B." as a mark on the ground that the mark was "deceptive" for clothing, footwear, and accessories not made of lamb.[54] The Trademark Trial and Appeal Board reversed, however, concluding that the "L.A.M.B." mark was perceived by relevant consumers and the trade as an acronym for "LOVE ANGEL MUSIC BABY," which is "arbitrary with respect to Applicant's identified clothing, headwear and footwear."[55] As a result, the Trademark Trial and Appeal Board concluded that prospective purchasers will not believe that "L.A.M.B." is only intended to identify clothing and footwear made of lamb, and permitted registration.[56]

§ 2:5 Trade Dress

A product's trade dress is defined as the signature design and appearance of the product, together with all the elements comprising the product's overall image, which serve to identify the product to consumers.[57] Tiffany's signature use of one specific shade of light medium robin egg blue to package its jewelry and other products in distinctive boxes is a quintessential example of trade dress. Tiffany's

---

52. *In re* Wal-Mart Stores, Inc., Ser. No. 86261962 (TTAB Jan. 11, 2019).
53. *Id.*
54. *In re* Lamb-Grs, LLC, No. 77756492, 2014 WL 5282244, at *1 (Sept. 30, 2014).
55. *Id.* at *6.
56. *Id.*
57. Fun-Damental Too, Ltd. v. Gemmy Indus. Corp., 111 F.3d 993, 999 (2d Cir. 1997) (citing Jeffrey Milstein, Inc. v. Greger, Lawlor, Roth, Inc., 58 F.3d 27, 31 (2d Cir. 1995)).

investment in its trade dress is such that when someone receives a gift in a Tiffany box, there should be no doubt where it came from. In effect, the packaging conjures the name of the company that sells the products.

Trade dress, moreover, has been expanded to protect nonfunctional aspects of the design or configuration of a product itself, where the design communicates a unique source to consumers.[58] The components that make up a company's trade dress may include features like size, shape, color (or color combinations), texture, graphics, or even sales techniques. In the fashion industry, trade dress has been recognized for goods like handbags,[59] tennis shoes,[60] jewelry,[61] children's clothing,[62] and watches.[63]

A plaintiff asserting trade dress rights in the design of a product under the Lanham Act must establish: (1) a precise expression of the character and scope of the claimed trade dress, either in words or images; (2) that the claimed trade dress is nonfunctional, meaning it is not essential to the product's function; (3) that the claimed trade dress has secondary meaning; and (4) that there is a likelihood of confusion between the plaintiff's goods and the defendant's.[64]

A trade dress that is either "generic, non-specific, or inconsistent among its products cannot be distinctive."[65] In *Yurman Designs v. PAJ*, for example, the U.S. Court of Appeals for the Second Circuit reversed a jury's finding of trade dress infringement and unfair competition arising out of the defendant's "manufacture and sale of

---

58. Yurman Design v. PAJ, Inc., 262 F.3d 101, 114 (2d Cir. 2001) (quoting Wal-Mart Stores, Inc. v. Samara Bros., Inc., 529 U.S. 205, 209 (2000)).

59. Hermès Int'l v. Lederer de Paris Fifth Ave., Inc., 219 F.3d 104, 109 (2d Cir. 2000) (post-sale confusion could occur); Louis Vuitton Malletier S.A. v. Dooney & Bourke, 454 F.3d 108 (2d Cir. 2006) (reversing denial of preliminary injunction against alleged infringement of Louis Vuitton's "Multicolore" style handbag).

60. L.A. Gear v. Thom McAn Shoe Co., No. 88 Civ. 6444(RJW), 1989 WL 282850 (S.D.N.Y. July 5, 1989), *rev'd*, 988 F.2d 1117 (Fed. Cir. 1993) (no likely confusion because of defendant's use of its word mark on look-alike shoe).

61. Cosmos Jewelry v. Po Sun Hon Co., 470 F. Supp. 2d 1072 (C.D. Cal. 2006), *aff'd without op.*, No. 06-56338 (9th Cir. Mar. 24, 2009) (infringement found and $2 million in profits awarded).

62. Wal-Mart v. Samara Bros., 165 F.3d 120 (2d Cir. 1998), *rev'd*, 529 U.S. 205 (2000).

63. Gucci Timepieces Am. Inc. v. Yidah Watch Co., No. CV-97-6985-KMW (MANx), 1998 WL 650078 (C.D. Cal. Aug. 8, 1998).

64. *See, e.g.*, Abercrombie & Fitch Stores, Inc. v. Am. Eagle Outfitters, Inc., 280 F.3d 619 (6th Cir. 2002).

65. Maharishi Hardy Blechman Ltd. v. Abercrombie & Fitch Co., 292 F. Supp. 2d 535, 542 (S.D.N.Y. 2003).

jewelry featuring the use of twisted, multi-strand cable together with other design elements, including gemstones" because the plaintiff failed to adequately describe the trade dress at issue.[66]

In discussing the legal standard guiding trade dress infringement claims for Yurman's jewelry, the court noted that it "exercise[d] particular caution, when extending protection to product designs."[67] The court's sensitivity to over-extending trade dress protection reflects general anxiety about limiting creativity in the marketplace by recognizing intellectual property rights in functional design elements. Accordingly, any designer seeking to develop a recognizable trade dress should be aware that courts will often deny protection to an asserted trade dress if important elements of the trade dress are purely functional.

On the other hand, where a court finds a trade dress to be distinctive and protectable, it can enjoin infringement of the trade dress via a specific injunction that lists in detail the elements that make up the protected trade dress and that a defendant cannot use in combination. A broad injunction that forbids use of a product with the "same overall appearance" as plaintiff's trade dress, however, may not be enforceable if it is too broad to be easily understood.[68]

In evaluating whether an alleged trade dress is distinctive enough to be enforceable, the Federal Circuit has noted that eleven different circuit courts of appeal had each "formulated some version of a multifactor test" to analyze whether an asserted trade dress is enforceable because it has achieved source identifying "secondary meaning" in the minds of consumers.[69] After reviewing these tests, the Federal Circuit panel adopted the following factors that courts should consider in evaluating a claim of secondary meaning:

(1) association of the trade dress with a particular source by actual purchasers (typically measured by customer surveys);

(2) length, degree, and exclusivity of use;

(3) amount and manner of advertising;

(4) amount of sales and number of customers;

---

66. Yurman Design v. PAJ, Inc., 262 F.3d 101, 107 (2d Cir. 2001).

67. *Id.* at 114 (internal quotation marks omitted).

68. Gasser Chair Co. v. Infanti Chair Mfg. Corp., 95 F.3d 1165, 40 U.S.P.Q.2d 1700 (Fed. Cir. 1996), *injunction defined on remand*, 40 U.S.P.Q.2d 1701 (E.D.N.Y. 1996), *aff'd without op.*, 155 F.3d 565, 47 U.S.P.Q.2d 1208 (Fed. Cir. 1998) (district court on remand had sufficiently defined the protected trade dress by dividing designs into three groups and providing descriptions and pictures for each group).

69. Converse Inc. v. ITC, No. 16-2497 (Fed. Cir. Oct. 30, 2018).

(5) intentional copying; and

(6) unsolicited media coverage of the product embodying the mark.[70]

Because the Federal Circuit governs the U.S. Patent and Trademark Office and its Trademark Trial and Appeal Board, this test is likely to continue to be influential.

The Federal Circuit's decision reversed an order that had concluded that footwear manufacturer Converse could not enforce its trade dress in its famous white Chuck Taylor sneakers. Of particular importance, the court of appeals held that the only relevant time period was the five years' before the first allegedly infringing use and that it was wrong to rely too heavily on older designs that may no longer be in the minds of consumers.[71] The court stated that "[u]ses older than five years should only be considered relevant if there is evidence that such uses were likely to have impacted consumers' perceptions of the mark as of the relevant date."[72]

§ 2:6 Clearing and Registering a Trademark

§ 2:6.1 Registration Generally

In the United States, the process of registering a trademark involves several steps. First, an applicant files an application to register a specific trademark with the PTO. Second, the PTO assigns one of its reviewing attorneys to review the application and ensure that it is complete and satisfies procedural and substantive requirements. If there are any deficiencies in the application, the reviewing attorney will notify the applicant and require him or her to rectify them in order for the application to proceed. Third, if the reviewing attorney accepts the registration application, it is published for opposition. During a thirty-day period, third parties who may be affected by the registration are permitted to file an opposition proceeding to stop the registration of the mark. If no third party opposes registration during the opposition period or if the opposition is decided in the applicant's favor, the mark is registered to the applicant. The PTO maintains a database of registered trademarks, which is open to the public.

Under section 2(d) of the Lanham Act, the PTO may refuse to register a trademark if it is so similar to a registered mark "as to be likely, when used on or in connection with the goods of the applicant,

---

70. *Id.*
71. *Id.*
72. *Id.*

to cause confusion, or to cause mistake, or to deceive."[73] Whether a likelihood of confusion exists between an applied-for mark and a prior mark is determined on a case-by-case basis applying thirteen non-exclusive factors set forth in *In re E.I. DuPont DeNemours & Co.*[74]

The *DuPont* factors include: (1) the similarity or dissimilarity of the marks in their entireties as to appearance, sound, connotation, and commercial impression; (2) the similarity or dissimilarity and nature of the goods or services as described in an application or registration or in connection with which a prior mark is in use; (3) the similarity or dissimilarity of established, likely-to-continue trade channels; (4) the conditions under which, and buyers to whom, sales are made, that is, "impulse" buys versus careful, sophisticated purchasing; (5) the fame of the prior mark (sales, advertising, length of use); (6) the number and nature of similar marks in use on similar goods; (7) the nature and extent of any actual confusion; (8) the length of time during and conditions under which there has been concurrent use without evidence of actual confusion; (9) the variety of goods on which a mark is or is not used; (10) the market interface between applicant and the owner of a prior mark; (11) the extent to which the applicant has a right to exclude others from use of its mark on its goods; (12) the extent of potential confusion, that is, whether *de minimis* or substantial; and (13) any other established fact probative of the effect of use.[75]

The *DuPont* factors are applied flexibly. Even where the marks are identical, registration may be permitted if the registrants are in different commercial channels. In *Coach Services, Inc. v. Triumph Learning LLC*, for example, the Court of Appeals for the Federal Circuit held that a test preparation company's use of the mark "COACH" for educational materials used to prepare students for standardized tests was not likely to cause confusion with the luxury good manufacturer's prior use of "COACH" as a mark for fashion accessories because the goods were unrelated, the channels of trade were distinct, and the prior mark brought to mind traveling by carriage, while the applied-for mark brought to mind someone who instructed students.[76]

Registration is not required to obtain trademark rights. Rather, trademark rights are generally created by using a mark in connection with selling goods or services. Nevertheless, federal registration of a

---

73. 15 U.S.C. § 1052(d).
74. *In re* E.I. DuPont DeNemours & Co., 476 F.2d 1357, 1361 (C.C.P.A. 1973).
75. *Id.*
76. Coach Servs., Inc. v. Triumph Learning LLC, 668 F.3d 1356 (Fed. Cir. 2012).

mark on the Principal Register confers a number of important benefits. Among others:

- Registration creates a presumption of validity and of the registrant's exclusive right to use the mark in commerce in connection with the specified goods and services;
- Registration also provides the world with at least constructive notice of the registrant's rights throughout the United States;
- The owner of a registered mark can seek enhanced damages for counterfeiting and to stop importation of infringing goods;
- Federal courts have subject matter jurisdiction to hear claims of infringement of a registered mark; and
- Owners of a registered mark are allowed to signal their rights by using the ® symbol when displayed next to the mark as registered.

Registration at the state level confers benefits as a matter of state law and, depending on the state involved, there may be some benefits to state registration of marks that are not eligible for federal registration. The remainder of this section, however, uses "registration" to refer to federal registration.

§ 2:6.2 *What Can Be Registered*

The federal trademark laws define "mark" expansively: a mark includes any "word, name, symbol, or device, or any combination thereof" that identifies and distinguishes a person's goods or services from those of other sellers.[77] The most commonly registered marks are brand names and logos. Brand names can be registered either simply as words (that is, without being written in any particular format) or in stylized letters with or without other design elements. For example, the COACH mark is registered simply as a word and also in a distinctive logo format:[78]

COACH

77. *See* 15 U.S.C. § 1127.
78. *See* U.S. Trademark Reg. No. 1,309,779.

Logos, such as Nike's well-known "swoosh," are also commonly registered. The mark can also be an integral element of the product, such as Levi Strauss's arcuate stitching design.[79]

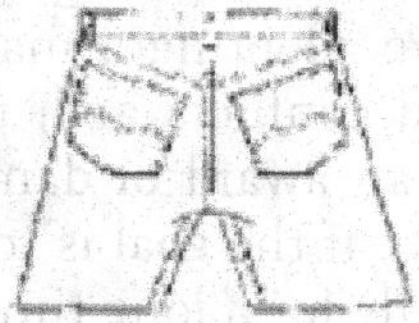

Trade dress can also be registered—for example, the familiar Tiffany blue box.[80] Indeed, it is well established that colors and color schemes can be protectable where there is evidence of secondary meaning based on long-standing use of particular color schemes, and well-known association between the colors and particular athletic teams, schools, or patterns that appear over and over on a company's products, such as Gucci's familiar green-red-green stripes.[81]

Although sounds can also be registered as trademarks, the PTO's Trademark Trial and Appeal Board has held that sounds made in their normal course of operation of a product are not inherently distinctive and may be registered only upon proof of acquired distinctiveness. This rule doomed an application to register the sound of a watch alarm where the maker did not provide evidence that the sound actually had secondary meaning for consumers.[82] Even smells may be registered when they are not related to the function of a product, as in a perfume. Although perfume scents may not be registrable, the PTO has approved registrations for the "grape scent" of motor oil products.[83]

Registration of these unconventional types of marks may often raise issues of lack of distinctiveness, being "merely ornamental," and/or failing to serve as a mark.

§ 2:6.3 *Overview of the Registration Process*

[A] Trademark Searching

It is common to search the records of the PTO and other sources of trademark information before filing a trademark application,

79. *See* U.S. Trademark Reg. No. 0,404,248.
80. *See* U.S. Trademark Reg. Nos. 2,184,128; 2,359,351; 2,416,794–95.
81. *See* U.S. Trademark Reg. No. 1,222,780; Bd. of Supervisors for La. St. Univ. v. Smack Apparel Co., 550 F.3d 465 (5th Cir. 2008).
82. *See In re* Vertex Grp. LLC, 89 U.S.P.Q.2d 1694 (TTAB 2009).
83. *See* U.S. Trademark Reg. No. 2,568,512.

although there is no strict legal requirement to do so. The question of whether to search for potentially conflicting third-party rights before filing an application cannot be completely separated from the question of whether to do such a search in connection with the decision to adopt a mark in the first instance. It is generally advisable to search for trademark rights before adopting a mark, and the failure to do so can lead to unexpected conflicts and, perhaps, a finding of bad faith, which can support an award of damages if trademark litigation ensues.[84] Nevertheless, if the goal is to register a mark that has already been used, especially for a long time, there may be little reason to do more than a cursory search before filing an application.

The most comprehensive trademark searches are generally performed by specialist service providers such as Thomson Compumark, Corporation Service Company, and their competitors. Before ordering a comprehensive search, it is common to do some preliminary screening such as Internet searching and reviewing available online records of the PTO at www.uspto.gov. The key is not only to investigate registered trademarks, but also to find unregistered marks that are in use in the relevant marketplace. If international transactions are contemplated, foreign trademark registries should also be consulted.

The goal is to identify any potentially confusing marks—to allow an appropriate legal analysis of the question of whether the proposed new mark is likely to cause consumer confusion with, or otherwise dilute, an existing trademark. If a screening search reveals obvious problems, it may be desirable to reconsider using or registering the proposed mark. The PTO generally only considers marks that have been registered with it (or pending applications) when reviewing a trademark application, but as discussed below, the owner of an unregistered trademark can assert a trademark infringement claim.

[B] The Application

A trademark application is most commonly filed online with the PTO. The application identifies the owner of the mark, the mark, the goods and services that the mark is used to promote, and information regarding the first use of the mark (if the application is based on use, discussed below). The PTO encourages applicants to use its online application system. As of January 14, 2017, the filing fees are $225 per class of goods or services for applicants who choose the streamlined "TEAS Plus" process, $275 for applicants who choose the "TEAS Reduced Fee" process, or $400 per class for applicants who choose the "TEAS Regular" option. It is also still possible to file by

84. *See* Int'l Star Class Yacht Racing v. Tommy Hilfiger U.S.A., 146 F.3d 66 (2d Cir. 1998).

paper and the fees per class of goods or services are $600. The more expensive options are generally preferable for creative or customized applications, and the less expensive options are available for applications that adopt pre-approved elements, such as descriptions for goods and services.[85] The classification of goods and services used by the PTO, now forty-five separate classes, is based on an internationally agreed taxonomy of goods and services. Filing fees and other aspects of trademark applications are handled on a class-by-class basis. An applicant does not need to specify all of the goods and services it provides in connection with a mark; it is the applicant's discretion to decide what goods and services it wants a registration to cover. In general, a "broad" application covering all of the goods and services provided in connection with a mark is desirable so that the registration covers as many goods or services as possible in any subsequent litigation. Still, it is important not to misstate to the PTO what goods and services are being offered in connection with a mark—willful false statements can be a basis to invalidate a trademark registration.

A full line of fashion-related goods and services may involve multiple classes: for example, clothing, sunglasses, handbags, jewelry, and retail store services are all in separate classes. Appendix 2-A contains description of the international classification of goods and services utilized by the PTO, with additional detail provided for classes related to the fashion industry.

[C] Use-Based and Intent-to-Use Applications

A trademark application can be filed before or after a mark is used in commerce. An advantage of filing an application before the mark is used is that, if the PTO eventually accepts the application for registration, the registration confers a presumption that the right to use the mark extends back to the filing date rather than the date the applicant later starts selling goods or services using the mark. If an applicant fears there may be a substantial delay between selection of a mark and launch of the goods or services that will use the mark, an Intent-to-Use (ITU) application can be helpful to mitigate the possibility that a third party will start to develop intervening rights in the interim. But in any event, and subject to exceptions for marks based on foreign registrations, the mark must be used in commerce in the United States before the PTO will issue the certificate of registration.

85. *See* U.S. PATENT & TRADEMARK OFFICE, INDEX OF ALL TEAS FORMS, https://www.uspto.gov/trademarks-application-process/filing-online/index-all-teas-forms.

[D] Examination

An application is examined by a trademark examiner sometime after the application is filed. The current delay from filing until the initial examination averages three to four months, although this may fluctuate depending on the workload and resources of the PTO.

The examiner will reject the application if he or she concludes that there is some flaw in the application. Some types of rejections are generally easy to overcome. For example, an examiner may object to the identification of goods or services set forth in an application as being "vague and indefinite" if an applicant uses an identification that is not included in the PTO's Trademark ID Manual. An applicant can usually overcome this objection by amending the description of goods to something the examiner deems acceptable.

Other rejections may be more difficult or impossible to overcome. For example, if an examining attorney concludes that a proposed mark is likely to cause confusion with a previously registered mark, or concludes that the proposed mark is merely descriptive of the identified goods or services, it will be necessary to make a factual showing that the examining attorney's initial conclusion was incorrect. Many registrations, however, result from applications that were initially rejected. If an applicant believes an examiner is improperly rejecting an application even after the examiner has considered the applicant's counter arguments, the applicant may appeal to the PTO's Trademark Trial and Appeal Board (TTAB) and ultimately to the federal courts, although appeals beyond the TTAB-level are not common.[86]

If the examiner is satisfied that an application meets statutory requirements for registrability, the application is published in the PTO's *Trademark Official Gazette* for opposition by any interested third party.

If no opposition is filed or is successfully resolved, the application will mature into a registration. If the application is based on an intent-to-use, the PTO will issue a Notice of Allowance, setting a six-month deadline to file a Statement of Use that proves the registrant has actually started to use the mark in commerce or, alternately, to request a six-month extension of time.

86. It is important to keep in mind that the rejection of the trademark application is not a rejection of the applicant's rights per se but only a denial of the benefits of a registration. The PTO cannot prevent anyone from using a mark, and only courts ultimately decide rival parties' rights to use a mark when a dispute arises. The PTO actions can, however, influence a court's evaluation of a given mark.

[E] Opposition Proceedings

An interested third party has thirty days from the date of an application's publication to file either a Notice of Opposition or a request for extension of time to oppose. A third party with standing may oppose a registration application on any basis that the examiner could rely on in rejecting the application, but the most common opposition basis is that the third party believes that the mark in the application conflicts with the third party's prior trademark rights. Trademark owners, especially sophisticated ones, often use automated watch services that monitor the *Official Gazette* for the publication of similar marks.

An opposition proceeding is an adversarial administrative proceeding held before the TTAB and is analogous to a court case, except that jurisdiction is strictly limited to a question of whether the application will be approved; the TTAB cannot enjoin a party from using a mark, award damages (including any costs or fees), or order the respondent take any particular action. Accordingly, a party that believes it is damaged by an applicant's use of a mark in a pending trademark application may also file a lawsuit in a state or federal court, in addition to the opposition proceeding. The conduct of an opposition proceeding mirrors a court case, in that the parties are entitled to take discovery, and ultimately develop and present evidence to the TTAB. There is no live trial, though, as witness testimony is taken by deposition and then presented to the TTAB along with arguments in a "trial brief." Approximately 4% of applications are opposed. As with civil litigation, the large majority of opposition proceedings are settled.

[F] Post-Registration

Trademark registrations remain in effect for periods of ten years, and a renewal application must be filed during a window that extends from the ninth anniversary of registration to six months after the tenth anniversary (with a surcharge due if the filing is made after the ten-year anniversary). Additionally, a maintenance filing is due between the fifth-year anniversary and six months after the sixth-year anniversaries (with a surcharge due if the filing is made after the sixth-year anniversary).

The PTO will cancel the registration if these filings are not submitted, so it is essential to maintain a reliable long-term calendar and/or to outsource the calendaring function to a reputable entity. Each maintenance filing includes the payment of fees, plus a declaration that the mark is still in use for the goods and services identified in the registration, and evidence of current use. In some instances, a filing can be made on the basis of excusable non-use. For example, it would be excusable non-use if a factory that produced goods were destroyed and being rebuilt. A general economic downturn coupled with a hope for better times, however, generally does not qualify as excusable non-use.

After a registration has been in force for five years and the owner has used the mark for five consecutive years with no unresolved adverse trademark litigation, the owner may file an optional Declaration of Incontestability. While "incontestability" is a term of art under the federal trademark laws and not as absolute as the word suggests, it provides additional benefits and limits the grounds upon which the registration may be attacked.

As with other aspects of the trademark registration process, the existence of the trademark registration does not strictly equate to the existence of common-law trademark rights, and there can be important distinctions. In particular, trademark rights can be abandoned if the mark is no longer used, notwithstanding a registration's ten-year term. The Lanham Act creates a rebuttable presumption that if a federally registered mark is not used for a period of three years, then it has been abandoned.[87] A registrant, however, may be able to overcome this presumption, depending on the strength of the evidence that the trademark owner intended to resume use.[88]

Trademark registrations can also be canceled if someone files a proceeding before the PTO to cancel the mark. A cancellation proceeding is similar to an opposition proceeding, but is filed after a registration issues. If a registration has been in existence for less than five years, it may be canceled for any reason that would have properly barred its registration. Registrations in existence for more than five years may only be challenged for limited reasons; notably, a likelihood of confusion with a prior trademark is not a basis for the PTO to cancel a registration deemed "incontestable" because it has been

---

87. *See* 15 U.S.C. § 1127. *See also* E. Remy Martin & Co., S.A. v. Shaw-Ross Int'l Imports, Inc., 756 F.2d 1525, 1532 (11th Cir. 1985) (explaining that once a party establishes a case of prima facie abandonment, "[t]he burden of proof then shift[s] to [the mark holder] to demonstrate that circumstances d[o] not justify the inference of intent not to resume use").

88. *See, e.g.*, Emmpresa Cubana Del Tabaco v. Culbro Corp., 213 F. Supp. 2d 247, 268 (S.D.N.Y. 2002) ("Defendants must come forward with objective, hard evidence of actual 'concrete plans to resume use' in the 'reasonably foreseeable future when the conditions requiring suspension abate.'"; "'A bare assertion of possible future use is not enough' to prove an intent to resume use.") (quoting Silverman v. CBS, Inc., 870 F.2d 40, 45 (2d Cir. 1989)); Société de Developments et D'Innovations des Marches Agricoles et Alimentaires-Sodima-Union de Cooperatives Agricoles v. Int'l Yogurt Co., 662 F. Supp. 839 (D. Or. 1987) ("[w]hen the registrant has come forward with evidence [of an intent to resume use], the burden of proof remains with the challenger," but an intent not to use a mark "may be inferred from circumstances" such as merely token use or "prolonged indecision").

registered for more than five years. Federal courts, however, also have the power to cancel registrations.

[G] International Aspects

A trademark registration generally only has force in the nation that awarded it. A trademark owner that seeks to obtain the benefits of registration in more than one country must therefore register the mark in each jurisdiction where it seeks to register its rights. It is important to note that, in contrast to the U.S. approach, many foreign jurisdictions have limited or no recognition of common-law rights and require registration in order to obtain trademark protection.

A U.S. applicant may be able to benefit from an "International Application." U.S. trademark applicants can file an application to have their mark registered in other countries under a process administered by the World Intellectual Property Organization under an international agreement referred to as the "Madrid Protocol" (and applicants from other Madrid Protocol nations have the same benefit).[89] In general, it is much simpler (and can be less costly) to file one International Application than it is to file numerous applications with separate national authorities. In the United States, the International Application is filed with the PTO and, provided the application satisfies formal requirements, the PTO forwards the application to the national trademark authorities in the Madrid Protocol countries that the applicant designates. If the trademark office of a designated nation rejects the application, local counsel will likely need to be engaged. If the application is accepted, however, the applicant can avoid fees required to engage local counsel, which quickly escalate when multiple jurisdictions are involved. A current list of Madrid Protocol members in set forth in Appendix 2-B.[90]

Another simplification of international registration is that the European Union maintains a common trademark registration, which stands alongside the national trademark offices of the member countries. International trademark issues are discussed further below in section 2:15.

§ 2:7 Trademark Infringement

The U.S. Lanham Act provides two parallel causes of action for a trademark's owner to seek relief for the infringement of a mark. First,

---

89. *See also infra* section 2:15.2.

90. *See also* Madrid Agreement Concerning the International Registration of Marks (Mar. 17, 2019), https://www.wipo.int/export/sites/www/treaties/en/documents/pdf/madrid_marks.pdf.

section 32(1) of the Lanham Act provides a right of action against anyone who, without the consent of the owner of a registered mark, shall:

> (a) use in commerce any reproduction, counterfeit, copy, or colorable imitation of a registered mark in connection with the sale, offering for sale, distribution, or advertising of any goods or services on or in connection with which such use is likely to cause confusion, or to cause mistake, or to deceive; or
>
> (b) reproduce, counterfeit, copy, or colorably imitate a registered mark and apply such reproduction, counterfeit, copy, or colorable imitation to labels, signs, prints, packages, wrappers, receptacles or advertisements intended to be used in commerce upon or in connection with the sale, offering for sale, distribution, or advertising of goods or services on or in connection with which such use is likely to cause confusion, or to cause mistake, or to deceive . . . .[91]

Second, section 43(a) of the Lanham Act provides a right of action against:

> Any person who, on or in connection with any goods or services, or any container for goods, uses in commerce any work, term, name, symbol, or device, or any combination thereof, or any false designation of origin, false or misleading description of fact, or false or misleading representation of fact, which—
>
> (A) is likely to cause confusion, or to cause mistake, or to deceive as to the affiliation, connection, or association of such person with another person, or as to the origin, sponsorship, or approval of his or her goods, services, or commercial activities by another person . . . .[92]

In practice, the standards for both causes of action are the same, although section 32(1) is only applicable to registered marks.[93] To prevail on a claim for trademark infringement, the plaintiff must

---

91. 15 U.S.C. § 1114(1).
92. 15 U.S.C. § 1125(a)(1)(A).
93. *See, e.g.*, Lois Sportswear U.S.A., Inc. v. Levi Strauss & Co., 799 F.2d 867, 871 (2d Cir. 1986) ("[I]n either a claim for trademark infringement under § 32 or a claim of unfair competition under § 43, a prima facie case is made out by showing the use of one's trademark by another in a way that is likely to confuse as to the source of the product."); Gen. Motors Corp. v. Keystone Auto. Corp., 453 F.3d 351, 354 (6th Cir. 2006) ("In many factual situations, the same result is reached whether the legal wrong is called trademark infringement or unfair competition. In such cases the courts often lump them together and speak of them as identical concepts.") (quoting MCCARTHY, *supra* note 30, §§ 2:7–2:8).

establish: (1) that its mark is valid and entitled to protection; and (2) that the defendant's unauthorized use of the mark in commerce is likely to cause confusion as to the source of defendant's goods, or deception as to affiliation, connection, or sponsorship of the defendant's goods.[94]

§ 2:7.1 First Element: Establishing That the Trademark Is Entitled to Protection

A plaintiff can assert a claim for trademark infringement for registered and unregistered trademarks, so long as the unregistered mark could qualify for registration under the Lanham Act.[95] The validity of the trademark, therefore, is a threshold issue in proving infringement and one on which the plaintiff bears the burden of proof.[96]

The plaintiff can establish the validity of its trademark by demonstrating priority of use (that is, that the plaintiff was the first to use the mark in commerce).[97] A federally registered trademark provides the plaintiff with a presumption that the mark is valid.[98] For purposes

---

94. Gruner + Jahr USA Publ'g v. Meredith Corp., 991 F.2d 1072 (2d Cir. 1993); Louis Vuitton Malletier S.A. v. Haute Diggity Dog, LLC, 507 F.3d 252 (4th Cir. 2007); The Gap, Inc. v. G.A.P. Adventures Inc., No. 07 Civ. 9614(AKH), 2011 WL 2946384, at *12 (S.D.N.Y. June 24, 2011).

95. *See* Rescuecom Corp. v. Google Inc., No. 562 F.3d 123, 128 n.3 (2d Cir. 2009) (citing Two Pesos, Inc. v. Taco Cabana, Inc., 505 U.S. 763, 768 (1992)).

96. Bauer Bros. LLC v. Nike, Inc., No. 09cv500–WQH–BGS, 2012 WL 1900047, at *5, *7 (S.D. Cal. May 24, 2012) ("'A necessary concomitant to proving infringement is, of course, having a valid trademark.'") (quoting Tie Tech, Inc. v. Kinedyne Corp., 296 F.3d 778, 783 (9th Cir. 2002)); *see* also GTFM, Inc. v. Solid Clothing Inc., 215 F. Supp. 2d 273, 293 (S.D.N.Y. 2002) ("The owner of an unregistered mark bears the burden of proving that the mark is valid and entitled to protection.").

97. *Bauer*, 2012 WL 1900047, at *6–7 ("To acquire ownership of a trademark, it is not enough to have invented the mark first or even to have registered it first; the party claiming ownership must have been the first to actually use the mark in the sale of goods or services.").

98. *Id.*; *see also* Solid 21, Inc. v. Breitling USA, Inc., No. 11-56439, 2013 WL 1116539, at *1 (9th Cir. Mar. 19, 2013) (dismissal of claims was improper because federally registered "Red Gold" trademark was entitled to "presumption of validity [that] is difficult to overcome, even at the summary judgment stage"); Pretty Girl, Inc. v. Pretty Girl Fashions, Inc., 778 F. Supp. 2d 261, 266–67 (E.D.N.Y. 2011) ("'A certificate of registration with the PTO is prima facie evidence that the mark is registered and valid (*i.e.*, protectable), that the registrant owns the mark, and that the registrant has the exclusive right to use the mark in commerce.'") (quoting Lane Capital Mgmt., Inc. v. Lane Capital Mgmt., Inc., 192 F.3d 337, 345 (2d Cir. 1999)); Urban Outfitters, Inc. v. BCBG Max Azria Grp., Inc., 511 F. Supp. 2d 482, 491 (E.D. Pa. 2007) ("Validity and legal

of determining priority of use, the federal registration of the mark also entitles the plaintiff to a presumption that the mark was first used in commerce as of the date the trademark application was filed.[99] If the plaintiff establishes that the mark is properly registered, the burden then shifts to the defendant to show by a preponderance of evidence that the trademark actually was not used as set forth in the registration, or is otherwise not protectable as a matter of law.[100]

In contrast, the owner of an unregistered mark is not entitled to any presumption as to the mark's validity.[101] To be valid and protectable, a mark must be capable of distinguishing the products it marks from those of others.[102] A mark is entitled to protection if it is either inherently distinctive or it has acquired distinctiveness through secondary meaning.[103]

A mark is inherently distinctive if it is so arbitrary, fanciful, or suggestive that it can serve to identify a particular source without a need for consumers to be educated that the name functions as a trademark.[104] Marks that are not inherently distinctive, such as descriptive marks, merit protection only if they have developed a secondary meaning in the mind of the public (that is, the mark has come to identify the source of the product rather than the product itself).[105]

In assessing the acquired distinctiveness or secondary meaning of a mark, courts consider the following factors: (1) advertising expenditures; (2) consumer studies linking the mark to a source; (3) unsolicited media coverage of the product; (4) sales success; (5) attempts to plagiarize the mark; and (6) the length and exclusivity of the mark's use.[106] The plaintiff does not need to satisfy every factor and no one factor is determinative.[107]

For example, in *GTFM, Inc. v. Solid Clothing, Inc.*, the court concluded that the plaintiff's "05" trademark had acquired secondary meaning even though the plaintiff had relatively low advertising expenditures as compared to other apparel brands, and the plaintiff

---

protectability are established when a mark is federally registered and has become incontestable under the Lanham Act").

99. *Bauer*, 2012 WL 1900047, at *7.
100. *Id.*
101. *See GTFM, Inc.*, 215 F. Supp. 2d at 293.
102. *Id.*
103. *Id.*
104. *Id.*
105. *Id.* at 294. ("Because the '05' mark is descriptive, [plaintiff] must show that it had acquired secondary meaning during the period when it was infringed.").
106. *Id.* at 294 (plaintiff established that its "05" mark, applied to jerseys, had acquired distinctiveness).
107. *Id.*

did not provide consumer survey evidence.[108] Weighing in favor of a finding of secondary meaning was the "widespread public exposure" of the "05" mark through its affiliation with prominent celebrities, the plaintiff's sales of more than three million garments bearing the mark, and the plaintiff's consistent use of the mark.[109] The court further observed that the efforts of defendants and others to copy the mark suggested recognition that the mark had achieved secondary meaning.[110]

Registration of a mark, however, does not mean that a defendant cannot argue that a mark should not be protected, even where the allegedly infringing mark has attained "incontestable" status.[111]

§ 2:7.2 Second Element: Establishing Likelihood of Confusion

If a mark is entitled to protection, courts seek to determine "whether [the] defendant's use of a similar mark is likely to cause consumer confusion."[112] Confusion exists if it is likely that "ordinary prudent purchasers" will be misled or confused as to the source of the goods or services in question, or where consumers are likely to believe that the plaintiff sponsored, endorsed, or otherwise approved of the defendant's use of the mark.[113] A claim of trademark infringement cannot be sustained unless there is a likelihood of confusion.[114]

---

108. *Id.*
109. *Id.*
110. *Id.*
111. *See* Urban Outfitters, Inc. v. BCBG Max Azria Grp., Inc., 511 F. Supp. 2d 482, 487 n.1 (E.D. Pa. 2007) ("[T]he Defendant's True People mark is not incontestable to the extent that it infringes on Plaintiff's Free People mark, notwithstanding the Defendant's federal registration of the True People Mark in 2001.").
112. Louis Vuitton Malletier v. Dooney & Bourke, Inc., 454 F.3d 108, 115 (2d Cir. 2006); *see also* RESTATEMENT (THIRD) OF UNFAIR COMPETITION § 21 cmt. a (1995) ("The test for infringement is whether the actor's use of a designation as a trademark . . . creates a likelihood of confusion . . . .").
113. Estée Lauder, Inc. v. The Gap, Inc., 108 F.3d 1503, 1510 (2d Cir. 1997); *see also* A&H Sportswear, Inc. v. Victoria's Secret Stores, Inc., 237 F.3d 198, 211 (3d Cir. 2000) (plaintiff must show that "consumers viewing the mark would probably assume that the product or service it represents is associated with the source of a different product or service identified by a similar mark") (internal quotation omitted).
114. Swarovski Aktiengesellschaft v. Bldg. No. 19, 704 F.3d 44 (1st Cir. 2013) (per curiam) ("The Supreme Court has made clear that a trademark infringement action 'requires a showing that the defendant's actual practice is likely to produce confusion in the minds of consumers'. . . . Without such a showing, no trademark infringement has occurred and so the trademark holder has no cause of action.") (quoting KP Permanent

[A] The Confusion Factors

To determine whether there is a likelihood of confusion, courts conduct an analysis based on factors originally derived from the *Restatement of Torts*.[115]

The specific factors applied by the courts can vary from circuit to circuit.[116] Two of the most well-known multi-factor tests were developed by the Second Circuit in *Polaroid Corporation v. Polarad Electronics Corporation*,[117] and the Ninth Circuit in *AMF, Incorporated v. Sleekcraft Boats*.[118] While the specific factors considered by the

---

Make-Up, Inc. v. Lasting Impression I, Inc., 543 U.S. 111, 117–18 (2004)).

115. *See, e.g.*, Polaroid Corp. v. Polarad Elecs. Corp., 287 F.2d 492, 495 (2d Cir. 1961) (Friendly, J.) (citing RESTATEMENT OF THE LAW OF TORTS §§ 729, 730, 731).

116. MCCARTHY, *supra* note 30, § 23.19, n.2 ("Each circuit has created its own list of factors and the litigator is well-advised not to rely upon a list from a 'foreign' circuit."). *First Circuit:* I.P. Lund Trading ApS v. Kohler Co., 13 F.3d 27, 43 (1st Cir. 1998). *Second Circuit:* Polaroid Corp. v. Polarad Elecs. Corp., 287 F.2d 492 (2d Cir. 1961). *Third Circuit:* Interpace Corp. v. Lapp, Inc., 721 F.2d 460, 462–63 (3d Cir. 1983). *Fourth Circuit:* Pizzeria Uno Corp. v. Temple, 747 F.2d 1522, 1527 (4th Cir. 1984). *Fifth Circuit:* Roto-Rooter Corp. v. O'Neal, 513 F.2d 44, 45 (5th Cir. 1975). *Sixth Circuit:* Frisch's Rests., Inc. v. Elby's Big Boy, 670 F.2d 642, 648 (6th Cir. 1982). *Seventh Circuit:* Helene Curtis Indus., Inc. v. Church & Dwight Co., 560 F.2d 1325, 1330 (7th Cir. 1977). *Eighth Circuit:* SquirtCo v. Seven-Up Co., 628 F.2d 1086, 1091 (8th Cir. 1980). *Ninth Circuit:* AMF, Inc. v. Sleekcraft Boats, 599 F.2d 341, 348–49 (9th Cir. 1979). *Tenth Circuit:* Sally Beauty Co. v. Beautyco, Inc., 304 F.3d 964, 972 (10th Cir. 2002). *Eleventh Circuit:* Alliance Metals, Inc. v. Hinely Indus., Inc., 222 F.3d 895, 907 (11th Cir. 2000). *D.C. Circuit:* Basile, S.p.A. v. Basile, 899 F.2d 35, 37 (D.C. Cir. 1990). *Federal Circuit: In re* E. I. Du Pont de Nemours & Co., 476 F.2d 1357, 1361 (C.C.P.A. 1973).

117. *Polaroid*, 287 F.2d 492; *see also* U.S. Polo Ass'n, Inc. v. PRL USA Holdings, Inc., 800 F. Supp. 2d 515, 526 (S.D.N.Y. 2011) ("It is well-established that the eight factors set forth in *Polaroid* . . . control the analysis of whether there is a likelihood of confusion in trademark infringement cases in this Circuit.") (citing *Polaroid*, 287 F.2d 492). The "*Polaroid* factors" include: (1) the strength of the senior mark; (2) the degree of similarity between the marks; (3) the proximity of the goods; (4) the likelihood that the senior user will enter the same market as the junior user (*i.e.*, "bridge the gap"); (5) actual confusion generated by the junior mark; (6) whether the junior mark was adopted in good faith; (7) the quality of the defendant's product; and (8) consumer sophistication. *Polaroid*, 287 F.2d 492.

118. *Sleekcraft*, 599 F.2d 341. The "*Sleekcraft* factors" include: (1) the strength of the contested mark, (2) the proximity of the goods, (3) the similarity of the marks, (4) evidence of actual confusion, (5) the marketing channels used, (6) the type of goods and the degree of care used to purchase

various circuit courts range in number from six to thirteen, factors that are typically common across the circuits include:

- the strength of the contested mark;
- the degree of similarity between the marks;
- the proximity of the goods;
- the likelihood that the plaintiff will enter the same market as the defendant (that is, "bridge the gap");
- the marketing channels used;
- evidence of actual confusion;
- the defendant's intent in adopting the contested mark;
- the quality of the defendant's product; and
- consumer sophistication in purchasing the particular goods or services.

Although the courts in different areas of the country have adopted their own unique names for the likelihood of confusion criteria—for example, the "*Polaroid* factors" in the Second Circuit and "*Sleekcraft* factors" in the Ninth Circuit—the factors listed above will be collectively referred to in the text below as the "Confusion Factors." The most commonly discussed factors are examined in further detail below.

It is important to note, however, that this likelihood of confusion criteria is not the sole criteria by which courts will analyze trademark infringement claims, although it is the most common. In *Multi Time Machine, Inc. v. Amazon.com, Inc.*, for example, the Ninth Circuit held that the *Sleekcraft* factors were inapplicable to the infringement claim at issue. Multi Time Machine alleged that Amazon infringed its trademark by displaying competitors' trademarks in search results when Multi Time Machine's mark was searched (because Amazon did not carry Multi Time Machine watches). The Ninth Circuit held that the *Sleekcraft* factors were inapplicable to the particular dispute because the *Sleekcraft* test was "developed for a different problem—that is, for analyzing whether two competing brands' marks are sufficiently similar to cause consumer confusion."[119] Multi Time Machine was not alleging that its competitors' marks were confusingly similar to its mark, but rather that the design of Amazon's webpage

---

them, (7) the alleged infringer's intent, and (8) the likelihood of expansion of the product lines. *Id.* at 348–49.

119. Multi Time Mach., Inc. v. Amazon.com, Inc., 804 F.3d 930, 936 (9th Cir. 2015).

confused consumers. The Ninth Circuit held that the "ultimate test" for determining the likelihood of confusion in that scenario was whether a "reasonably prudent consumer" would likely be confused as to the origin of the goods.[120] Because Amazon displayed the competing marks with clear brand labels and images that displayed the competitors' watches, the court concluded that a reasonably prudent consumer would not be confused into believing Amazon was selling Multi Time Machine watches.[121]

[B] Types of Confusion

In assessing whether the defendant's use of a mark is likely to cause confusion among actual and prospective customers, the courts recognize that there are different types of consumer confusion, some of which overlap, and some of which do not. Before applying the relevant Confusion Factors, courts will often seek to determine exactly what *type* of source confusion is at issue, as this can influence the weight of certain factors.[122] Commonly recognized types of confusion include:

- source confusion
- endorsement confusion
- initial interest confusion
- point-of-sale confusion
- post-sale confusion
- forward confusion
- reverse confusion

1. ***Source Confusion and Endorsement Confusion.*** The Lanham Act not only prohibits confusion as to the origin or source of a good or service ("source confusion") but also confusion as to whether a particular good, service, or commercial activity is affiliated with, connected to, associated with, sponsored by, or approved by another person or entity ("endorsement confusion"). As the Second Circuit has described these principles,

---

120. *Id.* at 937.
121. *Id.* at 938.
122. *See* Lois Sportswear U.S.A., Inc. v. Levi Strauss & Co., 799 F.2d 867, 872 (2d Cir. 1986) (observing that it "is critical first to determine just what type of actionable confusion as to source is presented"); Gibson Guitar Corp. v. Paul Reed Smith Guitars, LP, 423 F.3d 539, 551 n.15 (6th Cir. 2005) ("[E]vidence of initial-interest confusion comes into the [likelihood of confusion] test as a substitute for evidence of actual confusion.").

"[a] consumer 'need not believe that the owner of the mark actually produced the item and placed it on the market' in order to satisfy [the Lanham Act's] confusion requirement" (that is, source confusion), because the Lanham Act also prohibits activity likely to cause "[t]he public's belief that the mark's owner sponsored or otherwise approved the use of the trademark" (that is, endorsement confusion).[123]

2. ***Initial Interest Confusion.*** "Initial interest confusion," also known as "foot in the door" confusion, refers to the use of another's trademark in a manner calculated to capture initial consumer attention.[124] If the prospective buyer believes that the product is from a well-known brand, he or she may be more willing to stop and consider making the purchase. By the time of the purchase, it is most likely that the buyer will know exactly from whom he is buying the product and has no misconceptions. But the seller would have arguably never made that sale but for the brief time when the buyer thought the product was related to a well-known brand.

   Where the two marks are similar in sound for example, courts have recognized that the famous, similar-sounding name "would attract potential customers based on the reputation built up by [the trademark owner] in this country for many years."[125] Such use may constitute infringement even though no actual sale is completed as a result of the confusion.[126] Courts have recognized that initial interest confusion can harm a trademark owner in a number of ways, including: the defendant may receive unearned consumer interest as a result of goodwill associated with plaintiff's brand and marks; consumers may impute to the defendant many of the positive traits associated with the plaintiff's brand due to the time and expense the plaintiff has spent advertising its marks; the defendant may divert sales from buyers seeking to acquire

---

123. Famous Horse Inc. v. 5th Ave. Photo Inc., 624 F.3d 106, 109 (2d Cir. 2010) (quoting Dallas Cowboys Cheerleaders, Inc. v. Pussycat Cinema, Ltd., 604 F.2d 200, 204 (2d Cir. 1979)).

124. *See Lois Sportswear*, 799 F.2d at 872 ("[T]he Lanham Act was designed to prevent a competitor from such a bootstrapping of a trademark owner's goodwill by the use of a substantially similar mark."); adidas-Am., Inc. v. Payless Shoesource, Inc., 546 F. Supp. 2d 1029, 1058 (D. Or. 2008) (observing the Ninth Circuit's explicit recognition that initial interest confusion could be actionable).

125. *Lois Sportswear*, 799 F.2d at 872 (quotation marks omitted; alteration in original).

126. *adidas-Am., Inc.*, 546 F. Supp. 2d at 1058.

the prestige associated with plaintiff's brand at a cheaper price, and consumers searching for the plaintiff's goods or services may become distracted or discouraged and abandon their search for the plaintiff's products.[127]

3. ***Point-of-Sale Confusion.*** "Point-of-sale confusion" is confusion that occurs at the time of purchase as to a product's origin or sponsorship.[128] Confusion at the point of sale may be avoided by attaching conspicuous labels to the merchandise or placing signage in the retail store clearly and unambiguously informing the consumer that the famous mark owner is not affiliated with the junior user's product.[129] The fact that a junior user took steps to prevent confusion at the point of sale, however, is not sufficient to avoid a claim that confusion is likely either prior to or after the point of sale.[130]

In some instances, the nature of the product at issue will determine how the court analyzes when and where confusion is most likely to occur.

In *Munsingwear, Inc. v. Jockey International, Inc.*, the plaintiff alleged that Jockey had infringed its common law trademark in a "horizontal-fly" style of men's underwear.[131] In determining how to examine the similarity of the marks, the court and the parties drew a distinction between how consumers interact with the "pre-sale product" (the underwear as packaged and sold in retail stores) and the "post-sale product" (the individual briefs alone).[132] The court concluded that the

---

127. *See, e.g., id.*; People for the Ethical Treatment of Animals v. Doughney, 263 F.3d 359, 366 (4th Cir. 2001).

128. Gen. Motors Corp. v. Keystone Auto. Corp., 453 F.3d 351, 355 (6th Cir. 2006).

129. *See id.* (finding no point-of-sale confusion where, among other things, the defendant's invoice included a "conspicuous" disclaimer).

130. *Id.* at 356 ("'Since Congress intended to protect the reputation of the manufacturer as well as to protect purchasers, the [Lanham] Act's protection is not limited to confusion at the point of sale.'") (quoting Ferrari S.P.A. Esercizio v. Roberts, 944 F.2d 1235, 1245 (6th Cir. 1991)); *Lois Sportswear*, 799 F.2d at 872 (noting that labeling of the Lois Sportswear jeans may prevent "confusing consumers at the point of sale into believing that [Lois Sportswear] manufactured and marketed [Levi]'s jeans, the labeling does nothing to alleviate other forms of likely confusion that are equally actionable"); Keds Corp. v. Renee Int'l Trading Corp., 888 F.2d 215, 222 ("[P]oint of sale confusion [is] not the only issue.").

131. Munsingwear, Inc. v. Jockey Int'l, Inc., No. 4-93-538, 1994 WL 422280, at *1 (D. Minn. Apr. 21, 1994), *aff'd*, 39 F.3d 1184 (8th Cir. 1994) (per curiam).

132. *Id.* at *3.

pre-sale products were most appropriate for comparison in a likelihood of confusion analysis because "[t]he general public does not ordinarily see underwear in the same manner and to the extent that it views outerwear." Because of the "lack of post-sale exposure" to the product, the possibility of confusion "is not as great as it could be for other articles of clothing."[133]

4. ***Post-Sale Confusion.*** "Post-sale confusion" occurs when consumers view a product outside the context in which it is originally sold and confuse it with another, similar product.[134] Even if the immediate consumer is not confused as to the source of the defendant's product, a plaintiff may be able to demonstrate that the "person on the street" is likely to be confused as to the origin of defendant's product.[135] Specifically, the passer-by who views the defendant's product on the street may believe the product is associated with the plaintiff.[136] The post-sale confusion doctrine prototypically applies to counterfeits and copies where the intention is to "pass[] it off to the public as the genuine article."[137]

For example, in *Polo Fashions, Inc. v. Craftex, Inc.*, the plaintiff demonstrated likelihood of confusion, including post-sale confusion, between its products and the counterfeit shirts manufactured by the defendant, because anyone seeing the

---

133. *Id.* at *4.

134. *Lois Sportswear*, 799 F.2d at 872 ("[P]ost-sale confusion as to source is actionable under the Lanham Act."); *see also* Levi Strauss & Co. v. Blue Bell, Inc., 632 F.2d 817 (9th Cir. 1980) (enjoining Wrangler's use of a small tab protruding from the back pocket of its blue jeans as infringing Levi's red pocket tab trademark because, mitigation of point-of-sale confusion did not obviate confusion by prospective purchasers); Gen. Motors Corp. v. Keystone Auto. Corp., 453 F.3d 351, 356 (6th Cir. 2006) ("[A] likelihood of downstream confusion, also called 'post-sale confusion' is actionable."); Payless Shoesource, Inc. v. Reebok Int'l Ltd., 998 F.2d 985, 989 (Fed. Cir. 1993) ("[S]everal of our sister circuits have recognized that an action for trademark infringement may be based on confusion of consumers other than direct purchasers, including observers of those wearing an accused article.") (collecting cases).

135. *See, e.g.*, Fortune Dynamic, Inc. v. Victoria's Secret Store Brand Mgmt., 618 F.3d 1025, 1032 (9th Cir. 2010) (holding that, while knowledgeable consumers would be unlikely to confuse a footwear designer's trademark on a tank top in a Victoria's Secret store, observers of a tank top worn outside the store could be confused about its source).

136. *Lois Sportswear*, 799 F.2d at 872–73.

137. Hermès Int'l v. Lederer de Paris Fifth Ave., Inc., 219 F.3d 104, 109 (2d Cir. 2000).

counterfeit shirt bearing plaintiff's trademark logo being worn by its owner would not see the defendant's label on the inside back of the neck.[138] Thus, it was likely that observers would identify the shirt with the plaintiff, and the plaintiff's reputation would suffer damage if the shirt appeared to be of poor quality.[139]

In the post-sale context, any steps that the defendant took to avoid confusion at the point-of-sale, such as attaching labels that the consumer discards before wearing, will be of little use in avoiding confusion.[140] Courts have also recognized that the goodwill of a brand can be adversely impacted by post-sale confusion if consumers believe that a once "exclusive" brand has become over-exposed and is therefore no longer desirable.[141]

5. ***Forward Confusion.*** "Forward confusion" is the "typical" type of confusion alleged in an infringement action. Forward confusion occurs when customers mistakenly think that a junior user's product originates with or is affiliated with the senior user.[142]

6. ***Reverse Confusion.*** "Reverse confusion," by contrast, is a unique type of confusion that occurs where, "rather than trying to profit from the senior user's mark, the junior user saturates the market and overwhelms the senior user."[143] In a reverse confusion case, the junior user will usually have the stronger mark and is not seeking to profit from the goodwill associated with the senior user's mark.[144] Courts recognize "reverse confusion" as actionable under the Lanham Act due to the potential harm faced by the senior user—loss of the

138. Polo Fashions, Inc. v. Craftex, Inc., 816 F.2d 145, 148 (4th Cir. 1987).

139. *Id.*; *see also* Beacon Mut. Ins. Co. v. OneBeacon Ins. Grp., 376 F.3d 8, 17 (1st Cir. 2004); adidas-Am., Inc. v. Payless Shoesource, Inc., 546 F. Supp. 2d 1029, 1059 (D. Or. 2008) ("[C]onsumers who view Payless' shoes in the post-sale context may attribute any perceived inferior quality of Payless shoes to adidas.") (quotation marks omitted).

140. *Lois Sportswear*, 799 F.2d at 873.

141. *Id.* at 875–76; *see also* RESTATEMENT OF THE LAW (THIRD): UNFAIR COMPETITION § 20 cmt. b (1995); *infra* section 7:3.2.

142. Sands, Taylor & Wood Co. v. Quaker Oats Co., 978 F.2d 947, 957 (7th Cir. 1992).

143. MCCARTHY, *supra* note 30, § 23:10; *see also* Big O Tire Dealers, Inc. v. Goodyear Tire & Rubber Co., 408 F. Supp. 1219 (D. Colo. 1976) (recognizing the doctrine of "reverse confusion"), *aff'd and award modified*, 561 F.2d 1365 (10th Cir. 1977), *cert. dismissed*, 454 U.S. 1052 (1978).

144. *See Quaker Oats Co.*, 978 F.2d at 957.

value of its trademark and identity, loss of the ability to move into new markets, and loss of the ability to control its reputation.[145] Reverse confusion most typically presents a risk for a junior user who expends significant resources on advertising only to learn that the marks at issue are already in use.[146]

[C] Likelihood of Confusion Analysis

The Confusion Factors are not evaluated in a rigid, formulaic fashion and no one factor is controlling.[147] Rather, "each factor must be evaluated in the context of how it bears on the ultimate question of likelihood of confusion as to the source of the product."[148]

1. ***Strength of the Plaintiff's Trademarks.*** In most contexts, courts consider the strength of a mark to be "crucial" in a likelihood of confusion analysis because the stronger the mark, the more likely it is that consumers will believe there is a connection between the mark's owner and the infringing product.[149]

   The strength of the mark depends on its capacity to function as an identifier for the source of a good or service.[150] The stronger the mark, the broader the protection that the law will afford the mark. To measure the strength of a mark, courts generally look to two factors: (1) the extent to which the mark

---

145. *See, e.g., id.* (finding that defendant's advertising slogan "Gatorade is Thirst Aid" infringed plaintiff's "Thirst-Aid" based on reverse confusion); Banff, Ltd. v. Federated Dep't Stores, Inc., 841 F.2d 486 (2d Cir. 1988) ("[T]he objectives of the Lanham Act—to protect an owner's interest in its trademark by keeping the public free from confusion as to the source of goods and ensuring fair competition—are as important in a case of reverse confusion as in typical trademark infringement.").

146. M2 Software, Inc. v. Madacy Entm't, 421 F.3d 1073, 1089 (9th Cir. 2005), *cert. denied*, 126 S. Ct. 1772, *reh'g denied*, 126 S. Ct. 2885 (2006) (upholding a jury instruction that reverse confusion occurs when "consumers doing business with the senior user mistakenly believe that they are dealing with the larger user").

147. Estée Lauder, Inc. v. The Gap, Inc., 108 F.3d 1503, 1510 (2d Cir. 1997) ("[T]he analysis of the [*Polaroid*] factors is not a mechanical process.") (quotation marks omitted); *see also* Brookfield Commc'ns v. W. Coast Entm't, 174 F.3d 1036, 1054 (9th Cir. 1999); A&H Sportswear, Inc. v. Victoria's Secret Stores, Inc., 237 F.3d 198, 215–16 (3d Cir. 2000).

148. Lois Sportswear U.S.A., Inc. v. Levi Strauss & Co., 799 F.2d 867, 872 (2d Cir. 1986).

149. *Id.* at 873 (evidence indicated "as a matter of law that [Levi]'s stitching pattern is a very strong mark").

150. *Estée Lauder*, 108 F.3d at 1510; Gucci Am., Inc. v. Action Activewear, 759 F. Supp. 1060, 1063 (S.D.N.Y. 1991).

is inherently distinctive; and (2) the recognition value of the mark in the marketplace in identifying the source of the goods or services.[151]

There are four levels of trademark protection, ranging from classes of marks that are least distinctive to those that are most distinctive. The more distinctive a mark is, the more the law considers it to be "strong" and protectable, ranging from (1) generic, to (2) descriptive, (3) suggestive, and (4) fanciful or arbitrary.[152] In other words, the more that a mark is unique and unrelated to the goods or the services offered, the more protection it receives.

Federally registered trademarks are presumed to be distinctive and are provided the utmost protection by courts.[153] The fact that the mark has been federally registered and has "incontestable" status, however, does not alone establish how strong the mark is.[154] The relevant inquiry is whether the mark has come to "identify not only the goods but the source of the goods," that is, whether the mark has acquired secondary meaning in the minds of the public.[155] One way to examine this question is to review evidence of marketplace recognition and commercial strength of the mark.[156] For example,

---

151. *Id.*

152. Abercrombie & Fitch Co. v. Hunting World, Inc., 537 F.2d 4, 9 (2d Cir. 1976) (setting forth classification of trademarks according to degree of protection accorded under the law); *see also Gucci Am., Inc. v. Action Activewear*, 759 F. Supp. at 1063–64 (concluding that the trademarks "POLO" and "RALPH LAUREN" in combination with a representation of a "polo player on a horse" are "clearly fanciful rather than descriptive or suggestive of the goods so marked" and "are accorded the broadest protection against infringement").

153. *Lois Sportswear*, 799 F.2d at 871 ("[R]egistered marks are presumed to be distinctive and should be afforded the utmost protection.").

154. Sports Auth. v. Prime Hosp. Corp., 89 F.3d 955, 964 (2d Cir. 1996) ("We agree that independent indicia of strength is relevant to deciding whether the strength of the mark weighs in favor or against a finding of likelihood of confusion under *Polaroid*.").

155. *Id.* at 1064.

156. *See* The Gap, Inc. v. G.A.P. Adventures Inc., No. 07 Civ. 9614 (AKH), 2011 WL 2946384, at *13 (S.D.N.Y. June 24, 2011) ("Because Gap's marks have been long, prominently, and notoriously used in commerce, there is an increased likelihood that a consumer who encounters G.A.P. Adventures' website or concept store will assume incorrectly that it is affiliated with or sponsored by Gap.") (quotations and citation omitted); Urban Outfitters, Inc. v. BCBG Max Azria Grp., Inc., 511 F. Supp. 2d 482, 493 (E.D. Pa. 2007) ("Notwithstanding the frequency with which the words 'Free' and 'People' appear in marks in the apparel industry, the

evidence that a trademark owner committed significant resources to advertising its mark or attained significant sales levels can help establish the strength of a mark.[157]

A claim for trademark infringement can turn upon the strength of the mark allegedly being infringed. In *Estée Lauder, Inc. v. The Gap, Inc.*, for example, the Second Circuit reversed a district court's order granting a permanent injunction where there was no evidence to support the district court's finding that Estée Lauder's "100%" mark was inherently distinctive or that the mark had acquired secondary meaning.[158] The Second Circuit also took issue with the district court's weighing of several other factors, but noted that its disagreement was with the lower court's conclusion as to the strength of the mark.[159]

On the other hand, in *Tiffany and Co. v. Costco Wholesale Corp.*, a district court focused first and foremost on the strength, fame, and value of the "Tiffany" mark when analyzing a claim of trademark infringement, relying on reports from consultancy firms finding that Tiffany is "one of the strongest luxury brands," and "claims the largest share of the female mind in the U.S." for jewelry brand recognition.[160] The court rejected the notion that the strength of the "Tiffany" mark had been undermined by potential generic uses of the term.[161]

2. ***Similarity of the Two Marks.*** In evaluating the similarity of the marks at issue, the question is not only whether the marks are similar, but also whether the similarity is likely to cause

---

[plaintiff]'s substantial investment in the Free People brand and its position in the national marketplace, along with its status as an arbitrary and fanciful mark, both support a finding that Free People is a strong mark entitled to a high level of protection.").

157. Gucci Shops, Inc. v. Dreyfoos & Assocs., Inc., No. 83 Civ. 709 (ALH), 1983 WL 425, at *1–2 (S.D. Fla. Nov. 7, 1983) (because Gucci's "extensive media advertising reaches millions of retail customers throughout the United States," the "Gucci Marks have acquired and now enjoy distinctiveness, goodwill, and a secondary meaning").

158. Estée Lauder, Inc. v. The Gap, Inc., 108 F.3d 1503, 1511 (2d Cir. 1997) (finding that Estée Lauder's "100%" mark was suggestive and protectable, but reversing the district court's finding as to likelihood of confusion and entry of permanent injunction).

159. *Id.*

160. Tiffany & Co. v. Costco Wholesale Corp., 127 F. Supp. 3d 241, 248 (S.D.N.Y. 2015).

161. *Id.*

customer confusion.[162] To make this determination, courts consider whether the marks give the same "overall impression."[163] A mark's overall impression is created by the sight, sound, and meaning of the mark.[164]

There are three axioms in evaluating the similarity of trademarks. First, the marks must be evaluated in their entirety and as they appear in the marketplace.[165] For this reason, district courts have been cautioned not to over-emphasize a side-by-side comparison of the marks because this is not how they appear to consumers in the marketplace.[166] Second, the marks

---

162. Sports Auth. v. Prime Hosp. Corp., 89 F.3d 955, 962 (2d Cir. 1996) ("In considering this factor, we look to two key questions: 1) whether the similarity between the two marks is likely to cause confusion and 2) what effect the similarity has upon prospective purchasers.").

163. The Gap, Inc. v. G.A.P. Adventures Inc., No. 07 Civ. 9614(AKH), 2011 WL 2946384, at *14 (S.D.N.Y. June 24, 2011) (courts "look to the overall impression created by the logos and the context in which they are found and consider the totality of the factors that could cause confusion among prospective purchasers") (quoting Gruner + Jahr USA Publ'g v. Meredith Corp., 991 F.2d 1072, 1078 (2d Cir. 1993); Paddington Corp. v. Attiki Importers & Distribs., Inc., 996 F.2d 577, 586 (2d Cir. 1993) (differences in the details of parties' products did not matter because "[e]ach label's lettering style, layout, and coloration, taken together, convey the same impression").

164. U.S. Polo Ass'n, Inc. v. PRL USA Holdings, Inc., 800 F. Supp. 2d 515, 528 (S.D.N.Y. 2011) ("An assessment of the similarity of marks examines the similarity between them in appearance, sound, and meaning.") (citing Grotrian, Helfferih, Schulz, Th. Steinweg Nachf. v. Steinway & Sons, 523 F.2d 1331 (2d Cir. 1975)); Urban Outfitters, Inc. v. BCBG Max Azria Grp., Inc., 511 F. Supp. 2d 482, 491 (E.D. Pa. 2007).

165. *See, e.g.*, Jordache Enters., Inc. v. Hogg Wyld, Ltd., 828 F.2d 1482, 1485 (10th Cir. 1987) (holding that similarity of "Lardashe" to "Jordache" on jeans label would support inference of likelihood of confusion but for striking dissimilarities in the designs used in the marks); Abercrombie & Fitch Co. v. Moose Creek, Inc., 486 F.3d 629, 636 (9th Cir. 2007) (holding that district court erred by using defendant's mark printed on masthead of catalog rather than the mark as it appeared on a substantial portion of the company's apparel as object of comparison in evaluating similarity of marks).

166. *See* Louis Vuitton Malletier v. Dooney & Bourke, Inc., 454 F.3d 108, 117 (2d Cir. 2006) ("[T]he trial court made the same mistake that we criticized in *Burlington Coat Factory*: inappropriately focusing on the similarity of the marks in a side-by-side comparison instead of when viewed sequentially in the context of the marketplace.") (citing Louis Vuitton Malletier v. Burlington Coat Factory Warehouse Corp., 426 F.3d 532, 537–38 (2d Cir. 2005)).

must be evaluated by sight, sound, and meaning.[167] Third, similarities are weighed more heavily than differences.[168] Taken together, similarity is determined by the "overall impression created by the mark as a whole rather than simply comparing individual features."[169]

The marks at issue do not have to be identical to be found confusingly similar.[170] And even where the marks are similar or even identical, the court may nevertheless conclude that the remaining factors do not support a finding that confusion is likely.[171] In *Estée Lauder, Inc. v. The Gap, Inc.*, for example, the parties used the same "100%" mark in connection with moisturizers and bath products, but the Second Circuit still reversed the district court's grant of a permanent injunction to Estée Lauder.[172] Among other facts weighing in favor of reversal, the Second Circuit observed that while the mark was the same, there were noticeable differences in the appearance

---

167. adidas-Am., Inc. v. Payless Shoesource, Inc., 546 F. Supp. 2d 1029, 1052 (D. Or. 2008) (quoting Entrepreneur Media, Inc. v. Smith, 279 F.3d 1135, 1144 (9th Cir. 2002)); Tommy Hilfiger Licensing, Inc. v. Nature Labs, LLC, 221 F. Supp. 2d 410, 417–18 (S.D.N.Y. 2002) (observing "visual and phonetic similarities between the words 'Tommy Hilfiger' and 'Tommy Holedigger'").

168. GoTo.com, Inc. v. Walt Disney Co., 202 F.3d 1199, 1206 (9th Cir. 2000).

169. Exxon Corp. v. Texas Motor Exch., Inc., 628 F.2d 500, 505 (5th Cir. 1980); *see also adidas-America, Inc.*, 546 F. Supp. 2d at 1053 ("Payless cannot avoid liability for infringement merely by adding (or subtracting) an identical, parallel stripe to adidas' Three-Stripe Mark."); Saks & Co. v. Hill, 843 F. Supp. 620, 622 (S.D. Cal. 1993) (finding that "Saks Thrift Avenue" was likely to be confused with "Saks Fifth Avenue").

170. Londontown Mfg. Co. v. Cable Raincoat Co., 371 F. Supp. 1114 (S.D.N.Y. 1974) (enjoining defendant's use of "SMOG" on raincoats as confusingly similar to plaintiff raincoat manufacturer's "LONDON FOG" mark); *see also Sleekcraft Boats*, 599 F.2d at 352 ("Closeness in meaning can itself substantiate a claim for similarity of trademarks.").

171. *See, e.g.*, Estée Lauder, Inc. v. The Gap, Inc., 108 F.3d 1503, 1503 (2d Cir. 1997); Rolex Watch U.S.A., Inc. v. Rolex Deli Corp., No. 11 Civ. 9321 (BSJ), 2012 WL 5177517, at *2 (S.D.N.Y. Oct. 18, 2012) (despite identical use of the "ROLEX" mark, there was "simply no confusing correlation" between plaintiff's use of the mark on watches and defendant's use in the name of a delicatessen); Louis Vuitton Malletier S.A. v. Haute Diggity Dog, LLC, 507 F.3d 252, 263 (4th Cir. 2007) (no likelihood of confusion despite similarity of marks where defendant's "Chewy Vuiton" dog toy was "an obvious parody" of Louis Vuitton's famous marks).

172. *Estée Lauder*, 108 F.3d at 1507.

of both marks (that is, how the marks were rendered) and the packaging for the products.[173]

By the same token, even where the marks are not inherently confusingly similar, the remaining Confusion Factors can nevertheless support a finding of infringement where an examination of the competing marks in context leads to a conclusion that confusion is likely.[174]

3. ***Competitive Proximity of the Products.*** This factor addresses the extent to which the parties' products compete with each other.[175] The closer the defendant's goods are to those the consumer has seen marketed under the plaintiff's brand, the more likely it is that the court will conclude that consumers will mistakenly assume that the defendant's goods are associated with the plaintiff's brand or made by the plaintiff.[176] Where both parties manufacture apparel for the same target consumer group, there may be a likelihood of consumer confusion if the purchaser could reasonably conclude that the related products are being sold by one company.[177] Even where the products are not in direct competition, courts may consider whether there

---

173. *Id.* at 1512 (concluding that the district court erred in finding a likelihood of confusion given "that the rendering of '100%' in the two sets of marks is different in appearance; that the appearance of the of packaging overall is quite different in graphic design; that on each package the purveyor of the product is expressly identified; that the use of '100%' is not original; that the companies' products are sold in disparate types of stores; that the per-ounce price of Gap's body care products would likely be less than five percent of the per-ounce price of Lauder's product; that Lauder does not plan to enter Gap's market; that Gap did not act in bad faith; and that . . . no knowledgeable consumer would be likely to buy one product thinking it was the other").

174. *See* Urban Outfitters, Inc. v. BCBG Max Azria Grp., Inc., 511 F. Supp. 2d 482, 492 (E.D. Pa. 2007) (even though "the similarity of the marks [did] not, standing alone, lead to a likelihood of confusion," the other factors weighed in favor of granting plaintiff's request for a preliminary injunction).

175. Lois Sportswear U.S.A., Inc. v. Levi Strauss & Co., 799 F.2d 867, 874 (2d Cir. 1986).

176. Gucci Am., Inc. v. Action Activewear, 759 F. Supp. 1060, 1060 (S.D.N.Y. 1991) (because both plaintiffs and defendant sold sportswear with the Gucci and Polo logos, even though defendant's products were of inferior quality, "a likelihood of confusion exists because customers could have mistakenly assumed that plaintiffs had begun producing such items, or licensing their marks to the producers of those items.").

177. *Urban Outfitters, Inc.*, 511 F.2d at 505–06; adidas-Am., Inc. v. Payless Shoesource, Inc., 546 F. Supp. 2d 1029, 1055 (D. Or. 2008) ("Aside from arguable differences in quality, the parties' products are

is any overlap between the parties' customers, and whether consumers would reasonably expect the goods and services at issue to emanate from the same source.[178]

Courts will also take note where the products are sold through "markedly different channels of distribution," as this can be relevant for determining "whether confusion is probable among numerous consumers who are ordinarily prudent."[179] In *Estée Lauder, Inc. v. The Gap, Inc.*, for example, the Second Circuit reversed the district court's grant of a permanent injunction banning The Gap from using the term "100%" as a trademark in connection with the sale of personal products, including body lotion. The Second Circuit found no support for the district court's conclusion that consumers were likely to confuse Estée Lauder as the source of products sold by The Gap.[180] Among other things, there were noticeable differences in price between the products, and they were sold in "mutually exclusive types of stores."[181] Estée Lauder's product sold for $32.50 for less than two ounces through upscale retailers, whereas The Gap sold its product through its Old Navy retail store at a fraction of the price.[182] The Second Circuit concluded that even though the products were "closely-related" (that is, moisturizers and bath products) and that some consumers shop in both types of stores, the remaining factors did not support a finding of likelihood of confusion.[183]

'reasonably interchangeable by buyers for the same purposes,' and thus competitive.") (quoting MCCARTHY, *supra* note 30, § 24.23).

178. The Gap, Inc. v. G.A.P. Adventures Inc., No. 07 Civ. 9614(AKH), 2011 WL 2946384, at *14 (S.D.N.Y. June 24, 2011) ("In assessing 'the structure of the market,' I consider 'the class of customers to whom the goods [and services] are sold, the manner in which the products are advertised and the channels through which the goods [and services] are sold.'") (quoting Cadbury Beverages v. Cott Corp., 73 F.2d 474, 480 (2d Cir. 1996) (alteration in original)); *but see* Sports Auth. v. Prime Hosp. Corp., 89 F.3d 955, 963 (2d Cir. 1996) ("TSA and Prime are attempting to reach the same market of sports aficionados and are using at least one advertising medium simultaneously. Nonetheless, the parties' services—restaurants and sporting goods stores—are sufficiently different . . . to find that this factor weighs against TSA.").

179. Estée Lauder, Inc. v. The Gap, Inc., 108 F.3d 1503, 1507, 1511 (2d Cir. 1997).

180. *Id.*

181. *Id.*

182. *Id.*

183. *Id.*

4. ***Likelihood that Plaintiff Will "Bridge the Gap."*** "Bridging the gap" refers to the plaintiff's interest in preserving avenues of expansion and entering into related fields.[184] This factor looks to whether the plaintiff is likely to enter the market in which the defendant is operating in order to determine whether there is a "future likelihood of confusion as to source."[185] Courts may also look at "the average customer's perception of the likelihood that the plaintiff would enter the defendant's market."[186]

   A strong possibility that either party may expand its business to directly compete with the other would weigh in favor of finding that the defendant's present use is infringing.[187] Where the competing products are similar and the parties are engaged in the same segment of commerce, for example, both plaintiff and defendant sell handbags, there is no gap to bridge.[188]

5. ***Marketing Channels.*** The "marketing channels" factor involves two considerations: (1) whether the parties' products are sold through the same marketing channels; and (2) whether the "predominant customers" are the same.[189] Courts look at whether the products use the same, parallel, or

---

184. Lois Sportswear U.S.A., Inc. v. Levi Strauss & Co., 799 F.2d 867, 874 (2d Cir. 1986) (quoting Scarves By Vera, Inc. v. Todo Imports, Ltd., 544 F.2d 1167, 1172 (2d Cir. 1976)).

185. *Id.*

186. Sports Auth. v. Prime Hosp. Corp., 89 F.3d 955, 963 (2d Cir. 1996) (finding that this factor weighed against the plaintiff where "TSA admits that it presently has no plans to enter the restaurant business, nor has [plaintiff] provided any evidence that the public believes that it will do so").

187. Sands, Taylor & Wood Co. v. Quaker Oats Co., 978 F.2d 947, 958 (7th Cir. 1992) ("'When it appears extremely likely . . . that the trademark owner will soon enter the defendant's field, this . . . factor weighs heavily in favor of injunctive relief.'") (quoting Interpace Corp. v. Lapp, Inc., 721 F.2d 460, 464 (3d Cir. 1983).

188. Gucci Am., Inc. v. Action Activewear, 759 F. Supp. 1060, 1065 (S.D.N.Y. 1991) ("Where, as here, the parties are selling very closely related, if not identical products, there is no gap to bridge."); GTFM, Inc. v. Solid Clothing, Inc., 215 F. Supp. 2d 273, 296 (S.D.N.Y. 2002) (where both plaintiff and defendant sell jerseys, "[b]oth of these factors weigh heavily in favor of" finding a likelihood of confusion); *Lois Sportswear*, 799 F.2d at 874; Scarves By Vera, Inc. v. Todo Imports, Ltd., 544 F.2d 1167, 1174 (2d Cir. 1976).

189. Gen. Motors Corp. v. Keystone Auto. Corp., 453 F.3d 351, 357 (6th Cir. 2006).

distinct channels based on the understanding that convergent marketing channels increase the likelihood of confusion.[190] In examining the products' marketing channels, the court conducts a fact-intensive inquiry to examine how the parties market their products, whether through trade shows, print advertisements, the Internet, catalogues, or other forms of media.[191] The channels of trade inquiry, however, is relevant only to pre-sale confusion and is "immaterial to . . . whether actionable confusion is likely to occur *after* the marked product has entered the public arena."[192] This is because "post-sale observers may be unaware that [the products] are sold in different stores or at different prices, yet their confusion may be detrimental to [plaintiff]."[193]

With clothing designers and manufacturers, the marketing channels are similar where the parties sell their products through the same department stores, the same Internet websites, or the same magazines.[194] In identifying "parallel" marketing channels, courts will look to see whether the same sales methods are employed, the price ranges are proximate, the scope of advertising is similar, and the target audiences are the same.

Courts will also examine the images used by the parties in connection with their marketing efforts to determine if there is any similarity in the style of the parties' catalogues or advertisements. In *Urban Outfitters, Inc. v. BCBG Max Azria Group, Inc.*, for example, the parties had marketed their products at the same trade show, and the court credited testimony regarding the defendant's use of "iconic elements" in its catalogues that were long-associated with the marketing images

---

190. *Sleekcraft Boats*, 599 F.2d at 353 ("Convergent marketing channels increase the likelihood of confusion.").

191. Urban Outfitters, Inc. v. BCBG Max Azria Grp., Inc., 511 F. Supp. 2d 482, 502–03 (E.D. Pa. 2007).

192. adidas-Am., Inc. v. Payless Shoesource, Inc., 546 F. Supp. 2d 1029, 1055 (D. Or. 2008) (quoting Payless v. Reebok, 988 F.2d 985, 989–90 (Fed. Cir. 1993)); *General Motors*, 453 F.3d at 357 ("Since this factor focuses on the point of sale, it has little bearing on the question of downstream confusion.").

193. *adidas-America, Inc.*, 546 F. Supp. 2d at 1055 (quoting *Reebok*, 988 F.2d at 990).

194. *See adidas-America, Inc.*, 546 F. Supp. 2d at 1055 (parties' marketing channels partially overlapped where "adidas and Payless place advertisements for their respective products in the same magazines and on the same Internet websites").

used in plaintiff's catalogues, including the layered use of Polaroid photos over other art, the hair style of the models, and the use of handwritten text, including a handwritten version of the brand name.[195]

6. ***Evidence of Actual Confusion.*** It is well-established that a showing of actual confusion is not required to prove a claim for trademark infringement.[196] Evidence of actual confusion can be persuasive, however, in the likelihood of confusion analysis.[197] To show "actual confusion," the plaintiff must demonstrate that the defendant's use of the mark could cause plaintiff commercial injury in the form of sales diversion, damage to goodwill, or a loss of control over reputation. The confusion requirement is satisfied if the public might believe that the trademark owner "sponsored or otherwise approved of the use of the trademark."[198]

In some instances, there may be little or no evidence of actual confusion. For example, in *Urban Outfitters, Inc. v. BCBG Max Azria Group, Inc.*, the "new incarnation" of the defendant's True People brand—that plaintiff allegedly infringed with its own Free People brand—had not yet appeared in the marketplace.[199] The court nevertheless granted plaintiff's request for a preliminary injunction, in light of queries received at a fashion trade show, evidence of the defendant's intent, and consumer survey evidence.[200]

A trademark owner may wish to use surveys to provide evidence of actual confusion, although courts have concluded

---

195. *Urban Outfitters*, 511 F. Supp. 2d at 503–04 ("This evidence, together with the intent factor which the Court finds weighs in favor of Plaintiffs, suggests that Defendants may attempt to market their products in a similar manner to those employed by Free People in the future.").

196. Lois Sportswear U.S.A., Inc. v. Levi Strauss & Co., 799 F.2d 867, 875 (2d Cir. 1986) ("[I]t is black letter law that actual confusion need not be shown to prevail under the Lanham Act since actual confusion is difficult to prove and the Act requires only a likelihood of confusion as to source.").

197. Louis Vuitton Malletier S.A. v. Haute Diggity Dog, LLC, 507 F.3d 252, 263 (4th Cir. 2007); Jordache Enters., Inc. v. Hogg Wyld, Ltd., 828 F.2d 1482, 1487 (10th Cir. 1987) ("Obviously, the best evidence of likelihood of confusion in the marketplace is actual confusion.").

198. Dallas Cowboys Cheerleaders, Inc. v. Pussycat Cinemas, Ltd., 604 F.2d 200, 205 (2d Cir. 1979).

199. *Urban Outfitters*, 511 F. Supp. 2d at 496; *see also* MCCARTHY, *supra* note 30, § 23.18 ("If the junior user's mark has not yet appeared on the market, the lack of actual confusion evidence is irrelevant.").

200. *Id.*

that survey evidence is not required so long as there is other evidence of likely confusion.[201] Survey evidence that is methodologically sound can be particularly persuasive evidence of confusion, though.[202] Where survey evidence is offered, the plaintiff should be prepared for either the defendant or the court to question both the survey's methodology and the resulting data. Any perceived defects in the survey's methodology will necessarily affect the evidentiary weight of the survey data,[203] or whether it is admissible at all.[204] One of the most influential discussions of the appropriate standards for litigation surveys is found in the *Reference Guide on Survey Research* prepared by Shari Siedman Diamond for the Federal Judicial Center's Reference Manual on Scientific Evidence.[205]

A useful illustration is the Tenth Circuit's treatment of a confusion survey in *Jordache Enterprises, Inc. v. Hogg Wyld, Ltd.*, where the court concluded that the plaintiff's survey was entitled to little weight because the survey's use of a "side-by-side" comparison of two jeans "bears little resemblance to

---

201. Jordache Enters., Inc. v. Levi Strauss & Co., 841 F. Supp. 506, 518 (S.D.N.Y. 1993) ("Evidence of actual confusion consists of (1) anecdotal evidence of confused consumers in the marketplace; and (2) consumer survey evidence."); *see also* Sports Auth. v. Prime Hosp. Corp., 89 F.3d 955, 964 (2d Cir. 1996) ("TSA's evidence of misdirected phone calls between TSA's stores and Prime's restaurants, and especially the evidence that customers have believed there to be a connection between the restaurants and the stores, is sufficient to create a genuine issue of fact on this factor.").

202. *See adidas-America, Inc.*, 546 F. Supp. 2d at 1059 ("[C]onsumer surveys have generally been accepted as proxies for actual confusion.").

203. *See, e.g.*, *Jordache Enters.*, 828 F.3d at 1487 ("[T]he evidentiary value of such surveys depends on the relevance of the questions asked and the technical adequacy of the survey procedures."); Lois Sportswear U.S.A., Inc. v. Levi Strauss & Co., 799 F.2d 867, 875 (2d Cir. 1986) (consumer survey was discounted by the district court "due to methodological defects in simulating the post-sale environment"); Louis Vuitton Malletier, S.A. v. Dooney & Bourke, Inc., 340 F. Supp. 2d 415, 444–45 & 445 n.161 (S.D.N.Y. 2004), *vacated in part on other grounds*, 454 F.3d 108 (2d Cir. 2007) (concluding that a consumer confusion survey premised on a question that required participants to draw a legal conclusion carried little weight).

204. FED. R. EVID. 702; CytoSport, Inc. v. Vital Pharm., Inc., No. 2:08-CV-02632-JAM-GGH, 2012 WL 3881599 (E.D. Cal. Sept. 6, 2012) ("A district court must exclude [survey] evidence that is either not 'relevant,' or not conducted according to accepted principles.") (citing cases).

205. Shari Siedman Diamond, *Reference Guide on Survey Research*, *in* REFERENCE MANUAL ON SCIENTIFIC EVIDENCE 359–424 (3d ed. 2011).

the actual workings of the marketplace."[206] Because a consumer does not ordinarily carry a sample of the well-known product with them into the marketplace, surveys based on side-by-side comparison were of little use in determining whether the infringing mark was likely to cause confusion when seen "singly presented" to consumers.[207] Instead, the court endorsed the type of survey used in *Union Carbide Corp. v. Ever-Ready, Inc.*,[208] where the plaintiff showed consumers the product bearing the confusing mark, asked the consumers to identify the manufacturer of the product, and asked consumers to identify any other products sold by that manufacturer.[209]

Other courts, however, have criticized the use of an "*Ever-Ready*" survey format where "consumers have a reasonable likelihood of encountering the marks at issue one after the other in a store or mall."[210] In such circumstances, a survey based on a sequential presentation or "line-up" of competing products in the marketplace may better test a consumer's perceptions of associations between the products at issue.[211]

7. ***The Defendant's Intent.*** This factor looks at whether the defendant adopted the mark with the intention of capitalizing on the reputation and goodwill associated with plaintiff to take advantage of any confusion between the defendant's product and that of the plaintiff.[212] When the defendant knowingly adopts a mark similar to an existing mark, courts may

---

206. *Jordache Enters.*, 828 F.3d at 1487.

207. *Id.* at 1488 (quotations and citation omitted); *see also* U.S. Polo Ass'n, Inc. v. PRL USA Holdings, Inc., 800 F. Supp. 2d 515, 534–35 (S.D.N.Y. 2011) ("Studies using that methodology [side-by-side comparisons] generally produce higher levels of confusion.") (citing Phyllis J. Welter, TRADE MARK SURVEYS § 6.01[4]).

208. Union Carbide Corp. v. Ever-Ready, Inc., 531 F.2d 366 (7th Cir.), *cert. denied*, 429 U.S. 830 (1976).

209. *Jordache Enters.*, 828 F.3d at 1487 n.5 (citing *Union Carbide*, 531 F.2d at 385–86).

210. Louis Vuitton Malletier v. Dooney & Bourke, Inc., 525 F. Supp. 2d 558, 633 (S.D.N.Y. 2007).

211. *Id.*

212. Sports Auth. v. Prime Hosp. Corp., 89 F.3d 955, 964 (2d Cir. 1996); Jordache Enters., Inc. v. Hogg Wyld, Ltd., 828 F.2d 1482, 1485 (10th Cir. 1987) ("The deliberate adoption of a similar mark may lead to an inference of intent to pass off goods as those of another which in turn supports a finding of likelihood of confusion.") (quotation marks omitted).

infer that the defendant intended to confuse the public.[213] At the same time, "adoption of a trademark with actual knowledge of another's prior registration of a very similar mark may be consistent with good faith" where there was no "evidence that [defendant] intended to promote confusion between the products or appropriate [plaintiff's] good will."[214]

In determining whether the defendant acted in bad faith, courts will consider whether the defendant knew of the plaintiff's mark before the alleged infringement took place, the care that the defendant took in evaluating and investigating its own proposed mark, and how the defendant reacted when it learned of the existence of the plaintiff's mark.[215] The court is under no obligation to accept the defendant's explanation of how it came to adopt a mark, particularly where the defendant offers "an elaborately fantastic and strained scenario of how it 'coincidentally' hit upon its symbol."[216] Where the defendant's explanation is not credible, the court may conclude that the defendant intended to trade off of the plaintiff's well-known name and mark.[217]

A finding of bad faith is not required to prove a claim for trademark infringement because the Lanham Act does not

---

213. *Jordache Enters.*, 828 F.3d at 1486 ("Given the unlimited number of possible names and symbols that could serve as a trademark, it is understandable that a court generally presumes one who chooses a mark similar to an existing mark intends to confuse the public."). There are, however, exceptions to this general rule, such as parody, which are discussed further in *infra* section 2:10.8. As the Tenth Circuit explained in *Jordache*, "where a party chooses a mark as a parody of an existing mark, the intent is not necessarily to confuse the public but rather to amuse." *Id.*

214. W.W.W. Pharm. Co. v. Gillette Co., 984 F.2d 567, 575 (2d Cir. 1993).

215. Urban Outfitters, Inc. v. BCBG Max Azria Grp., Inc., 511 F. Supp. 2d 482, 501 (E.D. Pa. 2007) ("[E]vidence of a defendant's carelessness in evaluating the potential confusion caused by its mark with that of a senior user is 'highly relevant' and will tend to favor a finding of likelihood of confusion.") (citing *A & H Sportswear*, 237 F.3d at 226).

216. *Jordache Enters.*, 828 F.3d at 1486 n.3 (quoting MCCARTHY, *supra* note 30, § 23:35 at 156) ("[J]udges are not amused when asked to swallow fantastic fabrications about coincidental, unknowing usage.").

217. Sears, Roebuck & Co. v. Sears Fin. Network, 576 F. Supp. 857, 863 (D.D.C. 1983) (court did not accept defendant's claim that he chose the name "Sears" for his financial services company as a tribute to a woman named "Patricia Sears," with whom the defendant "had long ago been smitten").

require that copying be "intentional" to be actionable.[218] Nevertheless, evidence of a defendant's bad faith can weigh heavily in a likelihood of confusion analysis.[219] Good faith is less probative of the likelihood of confusion, but it may be given considerable weight in fashioning a remedy. A finding of good faith may be made where "a defendant has selected a mark which reflects the product's characteristics, has requested a trademark search or has relied on the advice of counsel."[220]

8. ***Quality of Defendant's Product.*** This factor looks at whether the plaintiff's reputation may be harmed because the defendant's product is of an inferior quality.[221] The inferior nature of the infringing products or services will strengthen the plaintiff's interest in protecting its reputation from harm.[222] At the same time, courts have concluded that confusion is more likely when the goods are *not* of an inferior quality.[223] The actual quality of the goods, however, is less important than the fact that the trademark holder is entitled to maintain control over the quality of goods associated with its mark.[224]

9. ***Consumer Sophistication.*** This factor relates to the level of care that a reasonably prudent consumer is likely to employ when selecting the relevant product or service. Courts expect the typical consumer to be more discerning and less easily

---

218. Lois Sportswear U.S.A., Inc. v. Levi Strauss & Co., 799 F.2d 867, 875 (2d Cir. 1986) ("[I]ntent is largely irrelevant in determining if consumers will likely be confused as to source.").

219. *Urban Outfitters, Inc.*, 511 F. Supp. 2d at 501 ("Although evidence that a defendant intentionally used a mark to cause confusion is not a prerequisite to determining that the defendant committed a Lanham Act violation, such evidence weighs heavily in favor of finding a likelihood of confusion.").

220. Sports Auth. v. Prime Hosp. Corp., 89 F.3d 955, 964 (2d Cir. 1996).

221. Gucci Am., Inc. v. Action Activewear, 759 F. Supp. 1060, 1066 (S.D.N.Y. 1991) ("the existence of inferior infringing goods strengthens a plaintiff's 'interest in protecting its reputation from debasement'") (citation omitted).

222. *Id.* ("the existence of inferior infringing goods strengthens a plaintiff's 'interest in protecting its reputation from debasement'") (citation omitted).

223. Lois Sportswear U.S.A., Inc. v. Levi Strauss & Co., 799 F.2d 867, 875 (2d Cir. 1986) ("[T]he good quality of appellants' product actually may increase the likelihood of confusion as to source.").

224. El Greco Leather Prods. Co. v. ShoeWorld, Inc., 806 F.2d 392, 395 (2d Cir. 1986).

confused when he or she is purchasing expensive items.[225] Conversely, consumers are expected to exercise less care when dealing with inexpensive products.[226]

Courts also consider what type of consumer is purchasing the goods or services at issue—ordinary consumers or trained professionals making a purchase relating to their chosen field.[227] Courts expect that trained professionals, such as professional clothing buyers, are generally more sophisticated and exercise a higher degree of discernment than the average retail consumer.[228] Where the purchasers are made up of a "mixed class" of consumers and professionals, the court evaluates this factor based on the sophistication of the consumer rather than the professional.[229]

In the fashion context, where there are both retail consumers and professional buyers, the court will consider the degree of care given by the retail consumer rather than the professional. In *Urban Outfitters, Inc. v. BCBG Max Azria Group, Inc.*, for example, the court concluded that the relatively high retail price at which plaintiff's "Free People" goods were sold (between $68 and $188) made consumers of those goods

---

225. *See, e.g.*, Urban Outfitters, Inc. v. BCBG Max Azria Grp., Inc., 511 F. Supp. 2d 482, 493 (E.D. Pa. 2007) ("[D]epending on the price and durability of a product, consumers will spend more or less time evaluating different options before settling on one to purchase."); Louis Vuitton Malletier, S.A. v. Hyundai Motor Am., No. 10 Civ. 1611 (PKC), 2012 WL 1022247, at *25 (S.D.N.Y. Mar. 22, 2012) ("Given the expense of purchasing a new automobile and the market niche for Louis Vuitton's luxury products, the consumers of both . . . products . . . are likely to be sophisticated and attentive to their respective purchases.").

226. *See* Munsingwear, Inc. v. Jockey Int'l, Inc., No. Civ. No. 4-93-538, 1994 WL 422280, at *6 (D. Minn. Apr. 21, 1994), *aff'd*, 39 F.3d 1184 (8th Cir. 1994) (per curiam) ("[D]ue to the inexpensive nature of the products, the court finds that the relevant consumer is not generally sophisticated and gives little thought to the purchasing decision."); adidas-Am., Inc. v. Payless Shoesource, Inc., 546 F. Supp. 2d 1029, 1060 (D. Or. 2008) ("Relatively unsophisticated value-conscious consumers are more likely to be attracted to, and confused by imitations of [plaintiff's marks]."); MCCARTHY, *supra* note 30, § 23:96 ("The reasonably prudent purchaser is assumed to take more care in purchasing 'expensive' items which he buys infrequently, than in buying everyday, relatively inexpensive items.").

227. *Urban Outfitters, Inc.*, 511 F. Supp. 2d at 493–94.

228. *Id.*

229. *Id.* at 494 ("[C]onfusion within the lowest stratum of 'reasonably prudent buyers' may give rise to liability even if professional buyers in the market are not confused.").

"particularly likely to be discriminating in selecting clothing."[230] Contrary to the general rule that the cost of goods correlates with the sophistication of the consumer, however, the *Urban Outfitters* court found that the purchasers of defendant's inexpensive apparel (average retail price $18) were "likely to be discerning in distinguishing between brands" based on hearing testimony that supported the conclusion that "teenaged girl[s] . . . place a significant amount of importance on clothing brands and styles."[231]

Similarly, another court opined that "fashion-conscious" young women "are likely to exercise a significant degree of care in purchasing their clothing, since the name of the particular designer is important in the fashion world."[232] Yet another court, however, has rejected such assumptions about the relative sophistication of consumers based on gender and noted that, in many cases, such determinations should be made by a jury.[233] And still another court concluded that the sophistication of consumers would actually weigh in favor of a finding that confusion is likely because the sophisticated consumer is the one most likely to notice the similarity between two marks and presume that it is indicative of an association between the plaintiff and defendant.[234]

§ 2:8 Trademark Dilution

In addition to asserting a claim for infringement, owners of famous trademarks can seek relief for trademark dilution under the Lanham Act.[235] In 1995, Congress enacted the Federal Trademark Dilution Act (FTDA),[236] subsequently amended by the Trademark Dilution Revision Act of 2006 (TDRA).[237] Congress sought to "protect famous

---

230. *Id.* at 494.
231. *Id.*
232. Kookai S.A. v. Shabo, 950 F. Supp. 605, 609 (S.D.N.Y. 1997).
233. Fortune Dynamic, Inc. v. Victoria's Secret Stores Brand Mgmt., Inc., 618 F.3d 1025, 1038 (9th Cir. 2010).
234. *See* Coach Leatherware Co. v. AnnTaylor, Inc., 933 F.2d 162, 170 (2d Cir. 1991) (quoting Lois Sportswear U.S.A., Inc. v. Levi Strauss & Co., 799 F.2d 867, 875 (2d Cir. 1986)).
235. 15 U.S.C. § 1125(c).
236. Federal Trademark Dilution Act, Pub. L. No. 104-98, 109 Stat. 985 (effective Jan. 16, 1996).
237. Trademark Dilution Revision Act of 2006, Pub. L. No. 109-312, 120 Stat. 1730 (2006), codified at 15 U.S.C. § 1125(c)(1). Congress enacted the TDRA in response to the U.S. Supreme Court's ruling in Moseley v. V. Secret Catalogue, Inc., 537 U.S. 418, 433 (2003), in which the Court held

marks from subsequent uses that blur the distinctiveness of the mark or tarnish or disparage it, even in the absence of a likelihood of confusion."[238] In explaining the need for legislation to protect trademark owners from dilution, Congress reasoned that "[c]onfusion leads to immediate injury, while dilution is an infection, which if allowed to spread, will inevitably destroy the advertising value of the mark."[239]

Dilution is defined as "the lessening of the capacity of a famous mark to identify and distinguish goods or services."[240] The TDRA explicitly provides relief for two different types of dilution—dilution by "blurring" and dilution by "tarnishment"—which are discussed in further detail below.[241] In addition to providing injunctive relief as a remedy for dilution, the statute also permits monetary damages in cases where the violation was willful.[242]

The main purpose of the TDRA is to protect the interests of owners of famous marks in maintaining the value of their marks, rather than to protect the consuming public from confusion.[243] Indeed, unlike a claim for trademark infringement, the statute permits a plaintiff to maintain a claim for dilution "regardless of the presence or absence of (1) competition between the owner of the famous mark and other parties; or (2) likelihood of confusion, mistake, or deception."[244]

---

that the text of the FTDA required a showing of actual dilution, rather than a likelihood of dilution. With the TDRA, Congress made plain that a claim for dilution required only a showing of likely dilution, not actual dilution.); Louis Vuitton Malletier S.A. v. Haute Diggity Dog, LLC, 507 F.3d 252, 264 (4th Cir. 2007) ("Congress amended the [TDRA] principally to overrule *Moseley* and to require that only a *likelihood* of dilution need be proved.").

238. H.R. Rep. No. 104-374, at 3 (1995).

239. *Id.* at 2.

240. 15 U.S.C. § 1127.

241. 15 U.S.C. § 1125(c)(1)–(2).

242. *See* Louis Vuitton Malletier v. Dooney & Bourke, Inc., 454 F.3d 108, 118 (2d Cir. 2006) ("[T]he only relief a plaintiff may obtain is an injunction upon a finding of defendant's liability for diluting the distinctive quality of a famous mark, except in cases of willful dilution where damages may also be awarded.") (citing 15 U.S.C. § 1127(c)(2)).

243. Louis Vuitton Malletier, S.A. v. Hyundai Motor Am., No. 10 Civ. 1611 (PKC), 2012 WL 1022247, at *5 (S.D.N.Y. Mar. 22, 2012) ("[The TDRA's] purpose is to protect the owners of famous marks from the kind of dilution that is permitted by the trademark laws when a junior user uses the same mark in a non-confusing way in an unrelated area of commerce.") (quoting TCPIP Holding Co. v. Hoar Comm'ns, Inc., 244 F.3d 88, 91 (2d Cir. 2001)).

244. 15 U.S.C. § 1127; *see also* Louis Vuitton Malletier S.A. v. Haute Diggity Dog, LLC, 507 F.3d 252, 265 (4th Cir. 2007); *Hyundai Motor Am.*, 2012 WL 1022247, at *5 ("[The TDRA] applies 'regardless of the absence of competition or confusion'") (quoting *TCPIP Holding Co.*, 244 F.3d at 95)).

Courts have described dilution as a cause of action reserved for a "select class of marks—those marks with such powerful consumer association that even non-competing uses can impinge on their value."[245] The same defenses that are available against a claim for trademark infringement are also available against claims for dilution under the TRDA.[246]

§ 2:8.1 Dilution by Blurring

Dilution by blurring occurs when a mark previously associated with one product also becomes associated with a second mark, thus creating "an association arising from the similarity between a mark or trade name and a famous mark that impairs the distinctiveness of the famous mark."[247] In this context, "distinctiveness" refers to the ability of the famous mark to identify a single source and thus maintain its selling power.[248] Where blurring occurs, "the 'commercial magnetism' of these marks and . . . their ability to evoke their original association" is weakened.[249]

To prevail on a claim for dilution by blurring, the plaintiff must show that:

- the mark is famous;
- the mark is distinctive;
- the defendant's use of the mark is "commercial";

---

245. adidas-Am., Inc. v. Payless Shoesource, Inc., 546 F. Supp. 2d 1029, 1060 (D. Or. 2008) (quoting Avery Dennison Corp. v. Sumpton, 189 F.3d 868, 875 (9th Cir. 1999)).

246. *See* 14 U.S.C. § 1125(c)(3)(A) ("Any fair use, including a nominative or descriptive fair use, or facilitation of such fair use, of a famous mark by another person other than as a designation of source for the person's own goods or services" is not "actionable as dilution by blurring or dilution by tarnishment").

247. 15 U.S.C. § 1125(c)(2)(B); *see also* Starbucks Corp. v. Wolfe's Borough Coffee, Inc., 588 F.3d 97, 105 (2d Cir. 2009) (quoting 15 U.S.C. § 1127(c)(2)(B)); Tiffany (NJ) Inc. v. eBay Inc., 600 F.3d 93, 111 (2d Cir. 2010) (describing blurring as "the whittling away of [the] established trademark's selling power through its unauthorized use by others") (alteration in original; quotation mark omitted).

248. *Haute Diggity Dog*, 507 F.3d at 265.

249. Levi Strauss & Co. v. Abercrombie & Fitch Trading Co., 633 F.3d 1158, 1169 (9th Cir. 2011) (citation omitted) (judgment reversed where the district court incorrectly applied the "identical or nearly identical" standard to plaintiff's TDRA claim for blurring); *Hyundai Motor Am.*, 2012 WL 1022247, at *5 (using "Buick aspirin tablets" and "Kodak pianos" as "classic examples of blurring") (quotation marks omitted).

- the defendant's use began after plaintiff's mark was famous; and
- the defendant is likely to cause dilution of the distinctive quality of plaintiff's mark.[250]

The TDRA sets forth a list of non-exclusive factors for courts to consider when evaluating the fifth element of the test (likelihood of dilution):

- the degree of similarity between the mark or trade name and the famous mark;
- the degree of inherent or acquired distinctiveness of the famous mark;
- the extent to which the owner of the famous mark is engaging in substantially exclusive use of the mark;
- the degree of recognition of the famous mark;
- whether the user of the mark or trade name intended to create an association with the famous mark; and
- any actual association between the mark or trade name and the famous mark.[251]

Under the TDRA, the marks need only be "similar" to establish a claim for blurring, rather than "identical or nearly identical," as was the requirement under the FTDA.[252] No single factor is outcome-determinative.[253] While "[a] sufficiently strong showing of similarity

---

250. *Haute Diggity Dog*, 507 F.3d at 264; *see also* Rolex Watch U.S.A., Inc. v. Rolex Deli Corp., No. 11 Civ. 9321 (BSJ), 2012 WL 5177517, at *3 (S.D.N.Y. Oct. 18, 2012); The Gap, Inc. v. G.A.P. Adventures Inc., No. 07 Civ. 9614(AKH), 2011 WL 2946384, at *16 (S.D.N.Y. June 24, 2011).

251. 15 U.S.C. § 1125(c)(2)(B).

252. *Levi Strauss & Co.*, 633 F.3d at 1171 ("The word chosen by Congress [in the TDRA], 'similarity,' sets forth a less demanding standard than that employed by many courts under the FTDA."); *see also* Tiffany (NJ) Inc. v. eBay, Inc., 600 F.3d 93, 111 n.18 (2d Cir. 2010) ("We have recently explained that under the [TDRA] the similarity between the famous mark and the allegedly blurring mark need not be 'substantial' in order for the dilution by blurring claim to succeed.").

253. Starbucks Corp. v. Wolfe's Borough Coffee, Inc., 588 F.3d 97, 108–09 (2d Cir. 2009); *Levi Strauss & Co.*, 633 F.3d at 1173; *see also Haute Diggity Dog*, 507 F.3d at 266 ("Not every factor will be relevant in every case . . . . [b]ut a trial court must offer a sufficient indication of which factors it has found persuasive so that the court's decision can be reviewed.").

can overcome all other relevant factors,"[254] districts courts have been cautioned not to place undue weight on the lack of similarity between two marks to the exclusion of the other factors.[255]

Determining whether a mark has been blurred is a fact-intensive inquiry. As a result, courts do not often resolve such claims on motions for summary judgment.[256] Where critical facts are not in dispute, however, a motion for summary judgment may be appropriately granted. In *Louis Vuitton Malletier, S.A. v. Hyundai Motor America*,[257] for example, the court granted summary judgment to Louis Vuitton on its claim for dilution by blurring after finding that Louis Vuitton had proffered evidence satisfying each of the six blurring factors set forth in the TDRA. Among other things, the marks were "virtually indistinguishable," the defendant admitted that it "specifically intended to create an association with Louis Vuitton," and there was evidence of "actual association."[258]

§ 2:8.2 Dilution by Tarnishment

Dilution by tarnishment occurs when a famous mark is disparaged as a result of being linked to products of poor quality or portrayed in an unwholesome manner.[259] That association can cause

---

254. *Levi Strauss & Co.*, 633 F.3d at 1173; *see also Haute Diggity Dog*, 507 F.3d at 266 ("If [defendant] used the actual marks of LVM (as a parody or otherwise), it could dilute LVM's marks by blurring, regardless of whether [defendant]'s use was confusingly similar, whether it was in competition with LVM, or whether LVM sustained actual injury.").

255. *Starbucks Corp.*, 588 F.3d at 108–09.

256. *See Levi Strauss & Co.*, 633 F.3d at 1173 ("[L]ikelihood of dilution is a factual inquiry generally not appropriate for decision on summary judgment.") (quotations omitted).

257. Louis Vuitton Malletier, S.A. v. Hyundai Motor Am., No. 10 Civ. 1611 (PKC), 2012 WL 1022247, at *14 (S.D.N.Y. Mar. 22, 2012) (granting summary judgment to Louis Vuitton on federal and state law claim for dilution by blurring where Hyundai's automobile commercial featured a basketball bearing marks similar to Louis Vuitton's famous monogram mark).

258. *Id.* at *7, *9, *10. The court also rejected Hyundai's reliance on *Tiffany (NJ) Inc.*, 600 F.3d at 93, in which the Second Circuit held that an online auction site could not be held liable for dilution when it displayed Tiffany's mark to advertise the availability of authentic Tiffany merchandise. "Unlike *Tiffany*, Hyundai, as the ad's creators testified, was 'definitely laddering and borrowing equity from Louis Vuitton.'" *Id.* at *13.

259. *See Haute Diggity Dog*, 507 F.3d at 268 (a claim for dilution by tarnishment requires a showing that the defendant's use "harms the reputation" of plaintiff); *Tiffany (NJ) Inc.*, 600 F.3d at 93 ("[D]ilution by tarnishment is an association arising from the similarity between a mark or trade name and a famous mark that harms the reputation of the famous mark.") (quotation marks omitted); GTFM, Inc. v. Solid Clothing Inc.,

immense harm to the trademark owner's brand and reputation if the public comes to associate the "lack of quality or lack of prestige in the defendant's goods with the plaintiffs' unrelated goods."[260] For example, Burberry reportedly faced a concern of dilution by tarnishment when its trademark plaid color scheme was adopted by Britain's mainstream football fans, and sales in the United Kingdom dropped, reportedly because luxury consumers did not want to be associated with members of "lower" social strata.[261]

Unlike a claim for dilution by blurring, the TDRA does not set forth a list of factors for courts to consider in connection with claims for dilution by tarnishment. In general, however, courts look to whether the defendant is using the mark: (1) in connection with products or services of an inferior quality;[262] or (2) in an unsavory manner, such that the defendant's use impairs the ability of the famous mark to serve as a "wholesome identifier" of the plaintiff's product.[263] Where the mark is being used in either of these ways, and in the absence of any defense such as fair use, courts may find that a defendant's use is likely to tarnish the famous mark.

The more "unwholesome" the defendant's use, moreover, the more likely the court is to conclude that the famous mark is likely to be tarnished. This is particularly true where the famous mark is being used in connection with adult-themed products, and there is a "semantic association" with the famous mark and the defendant's mark.[264]

---

215 F. Supp. 2d 273, 301 (S.D.N.Y. 2002) ("Tarnishment occurs where a trademark is 'linked to products of shoddy quality, or is portrayed in an unwholesome or unsavory context, with the result that the public will associate the lack of quality and lack of prestige with the plaintiff's unrelated goods.'") (quoting N.Y. Stock Exch., Inc. v. N.Y., N.Y. Hotel, LLC, 293 F.3d 550, 558 (2d Cir. 2002)).

260. *GTFM, Inc.*, 215 F. Supp. 2d at 301 (quoting *N.Y. Stock Exch.*, 293 F.3d at 558); *see also* Rosetta Stone Ltd. v. Google, Inc., 676 F.3d 144, 167 (4th Cir. 2012) ("Tarnishment . . . creates consumer aversion to the famous brand.").

261. Erika Myers, *Justice in Fashion: Cheap Chic and the IP Equilibrium in the United Kingdom and the United States*, 37 AIPLA Q.J. 47, 56 (2009).

262. *GTFM, Inc.*, 215 F. Supp. 2d at 301 (finding tarnishment likely where plaintiff's "apparel is generally of higher quality" than that of the defendant).

263. Starbucks Corp. v. Wolfe's Borough Coffee, Inc., 588 F.3d 97, 110 (2d Cir. 2009) (collecting cases).

264. *See, e.g.*, Moseley v. V Secret Catalogue, Inc., 605 F.3d 382, 388 (6th Cir. 2010), *rehr'g and rehr'g en banc denied* (Aug. 5, 2010), *cert. denied*, 131 S. Ct. 1003 (Jan. 18, 2011), *rehr'g denied*, 131 S. Ct. 1627 (Mar. 7, 2011) ("There have been at least eight federal cases in six jurisdictions that conclude that a famous mark is tarnished when the mark is semantically associated with a new mark that is used to sell sex-related products.")

In such a case, the defendant must present evidence to rebut the presumption that its "new mark" will cause harm to the reputation of the famous mark.[265]

§ 2:9 Remedies for Trademark Infringement

§ 2:9.1 *Injunctive Relief*

The Lanham Act grants federal courts broad powers to fashion injunctive relief to prevent harm to plaintiffs and the consuming public, in the form of a preliminary injunction, a permanent injunction, or both.[266] In particular, courts have the discretion to fashion relief appropriate for the circumstances of each case, including prohibiting the defendant from continuing its infringing use of the marks, restraining the defendant's assets, and requiring the defendant to undertake corrective advertising. Whether a specific type of relief is appropriate will depend on the particular facts of the case.

[A] Permanent Injunction

A permanent injunction issues to a party after winning on the merits and has traditionally been granted upon a finding of trademark infringement.[267] In *eBay Inc. v. MercExchange, LLC*, the Supreme Court emphasized that before issuing an injunction, courts should weigh the four factors traditionally used to determine if an injunction should issue.[268] This four-part test requires a plaintiff to demonstrate: "(1) that it has suffered an irreparable injury; (2) that remedies available at law, such as monetary damages, are inadequate to compensate for that injury; (3) that, considering the balance of hardships between the plaintiff and defendant, a remedy in equity is warranted; and (4) that the public interest would not be disserved by a permanent injunction."[269] Although *eBay* arose in the patent context, courts

---

(collecting cases and upholding injunction barring defendant from using "Victor's Little Secret" and "Victor's Secret" in connection with adult-themed store).

265. *Id.*

266. *See* U.S. Polo Ass'n, Inc. v. PRL USA Holdings, Inc., 800 F. Supp. 2d 515, 540 (S.D.N.Y. 2011) ("The Lanham Act expressly provides that federal courts 'have power to grant injunctions, according to the principles of equity' in trademark infringement and [trademark] dilution cases.") (quoting 15 U.S.C. § 1116(a)).

267. *See* MCCARTHY, *supra* note 30, § 30.01, at 30–35; Estée Lauder, Inc. v. The Gap, Inc., 108 F.3d 1503, 1511 (2d Cir. 1997) (reversing grant of permanent injunction where plaintiff failed to establish likelihood of confusion necessary for a claim of infringement).

268. eBay Inc. v. MercExchange, LLC, 547 U.S. 388, 391 (2006).

269. *Id.*

have been evaluating the same factors in connection with trademark injunctions.[270] The test substantially overlaps with the showing required for a preliminary injunction, except that a plaintiff who has succeeded on the merits no longer needs to establish that he or she is "likely to succeed."[271] Each of the remaining injunction factors are discussed in greater detail below.

[B] Preliminary Injunction

To obtain a preliminary injunction, a plaintiff must establish: (1) irreparable harm and (2) either (a) a likelihood of success on the merits or (b) a sufficiently serious question going to the merits and a balance of hardships tipping decidedly in the moving party's favor.[272]

Before *eBay v. MercExchange, LLC,*[273] courts widely accepted that proof of likelihood of confusion sufficed to establish both a likelihood of success on the merits and irreparable harm.[274] In *Salinger v. Colting,*[275] however, the Second Circuit evaluated these assumptions in light of *eBay,* and concluded that there is "no reason that *eBay* would not apply with equal force to an injunction in any type of case."[276] The test, articulated in *Salinger* for copyright cases, is that a preliminary injunction could not be granted unless the plaintiff established: (1) a likelihood of success on the merits; (2) a likelihood of irreparable injury in the absence of an injunction; (3) that "remedies at law," such as monetary damages, are inadequate to compensate for

---

270. *See, e.g.,* The Gap, Inc. v. G.A.P. Adventures, Inc., No. 07 Civ. 9614(AKH), 2011 WL 2946384, at *18 (S.D.N.Y. June 24, 2011).

271. *See, e.g.,* Urban Outfitters, Inc. v. BCBG Max Azria Grp., Inc., 511 F. Supp. 2d 482, 489 (E.D. Pa. 2007) ("There is a four part test for evaluating whether a court should issue a preliminary injunction in a trademark case: (1) the likelihood that the applicant will prevail on the merits at a final hearing; (2) the extent to which the plaintiffs are being irreparably harmed by the conduct complained of; (3) the extent to which the defendants will suffer irreparable harm if the preliminary injunction is issued; and (4) the public interest.") (citing Opticians Ass'n of Am. v. Indep. Opticians of Am., 920 F.2d 187, 191–92 (3d Cir. 1990)).

272. Christian Louboutin S.A. v. Yves Saint Laurent Am. Holding, Inc., 696 F.3d 206, 215 (2d Cir. 2012); *see also* Swarovski Aktiengesellschaft v. Bldg. No. 19, 704 F.3d 44, 48 (1st Cir. 2013) (per curiam) (phrasing the factors to be demonstrated by the plaintiff as: "(1) the plaintiff's likelihood of success on the merits; (2) the potential for irreparable harm in the absence of an injunction; (3) whether issuing an injunction will burden the defendants less than denying an injunction would burden the plaintiffs; and (4) the effect, if any, on the public interest").

273. eBay v. MercExchange, LLC, 547 U.S. 388, 391 (2006).

274. *See* Hasbro, Inc. v. Lanard Toys, Ltd., 858 F.2d 70, 73 (2d Cir. 1988).

275. Salinger v. Colting, 607 F.3d 68 (2d Cir. 2010).

276. *Id.* at 78 n.7.

that injury; (4) that the balance of the hardships tips in the plaintiff's favor; and (5) that the public interest would not be disserved by the issuance of the injunction.[277] District courts have already followed *Salinger* in applying the test to requests for trademark injunctions.[278]

Even after *eBay*, though, a number of courts have concluded that the same factual concerns that support a finding of likelihood of consumer confusion also support a finding that the balance of the hardships weighs in the plaintiff's favor.[279]

1. ***Likelihood of Success on the Merits.*** For the court to conclude that a plaintiff is likely to succeed on the merits of its claims, it must be "probable" that the plaintiff will be able to establish a likelihood of confusion.[280] To make this determination, courts examine the Confusion Factors set forth in section 2:7.2[A] above.[281] Because resolution of questions concerning irreparable harm and the balance of the hardships depend in large part on the plaintiff's likelihood of success, it can be reversible error for a court to issue an injunction without first determining whether the defendant's use of the marks is likely to cause confusion.[282]

---

277. *Id.* at 80.

278. *See* Pretty Girl, Inc. v. Pretty Girl Fashions, Inc., 778 F. Supp. 2d 261, 265 (E.D.N.Y. 2011) ("The Second Circuit has not yet spoken on this issue in the context of a trademark case; but the court agrees that there is no principled reason not to adopt the newly announced standard in the trademark context."); U.S. Polo Ass'n, Inc. v. PRL USA Holdings, Inc., 800 F. Supp. 2d 515, 539 (S.D.N.Y. 2011); Rolex Watch U.S.A., Inc. v. Rolex Deli Corp., No. 11 Civ. 9321 (BSJ), 2012 WL 5177517, at *4 (S.D.N.Y. Oct. 18, 2012) (although district courts were initially "split as to whether the new standard should be applied in trademark cases. . . . [f]ollowing the application of the *eBay* standard to copyright actions, . . . its relevance in trademark cases appears to stand on firmer ground") (citations omitted).

279. *See, e.g., id.*; New York City Triathlon v. NYC Triathlon Club, 704 F. Supp. 2d 305 (S.D.N.Y. 2010).

280. *See* Louis Vuitton Malletier v. Dooney & Bourke, Inc., 454 F.3d 108, 114 (2d Cir. 2006) (finding that "the district court placed too high a burden on plaintiff" by requiring a "strong" likelihood of success rather than "just a likelihood of success"); Gucci Shops, Inc. v. R.H. Macy & Co., 446 F. Supp. 838, 839 (S.D.N.Y. 1977) (granting preliminary injunction to Gucci prohibiting manufacture and sale of diaper bag labeled "Gucchi Goo" that had a version of Gucci's trademarked "green-red-green" stripe).

281. *See* Swarovski Aktiengesellschaft v. Bldg. No. 19, 704 F.3d 44, 48 (1st Cir. 2013); *Louis Vuitton Malletier*, 454 F.3d at 116 (citing to *Polaroid* factors in reviewing district court's order denying preliminary injunction).

282. *Swarovski*, 704 F.3d at 48 (per curiam) (reversing grant of preliminary injunction where the district court did not find that defendant's use of

In *Urban Outfitters, Inc. v. BCBG Max Azria Group, Inc.*, the court partially granted the plaintiff's request for a preliminary injunction.[283] There, the defendant sold low-priced clothing for years under the brand "True People" despite plaintiff's rights in its "Free People" mark, but the plaintiff provided no evidence that consumers had actually confused the two brands.[284] Although the court declined to enjoin the defendant from selling clothing in its already established retail outlets, it granted the plaintiff's request to enjoin the defendant from establishing new or different retail outlets as part of the defendant's effort to "upgrade" the True People brand, both in price and marketing method.[285] Despite the price gap between the clothing sold by the parties, the court concluded that there was a "very strong" possibility that the defendant's strategy and plans would confuse consumers given the significant overlap in the parties' customers and products.[286]

2. ***Likelihood of Irreparable Harm and Inadequacy of Monetary Damages.*** The requirement of "irreparable harm" overlaps with the requirement that the party seeking injunctive relief demonstrate the "lack of an adequate remedy at law" because of the particular types of harm that can occur as a result of trademark infringement.[287] Irreparable harm is harm that cannot be compensated by monetary damages.[288] In the context of a trademark infringement claim, courts consider

---

the mark was likely to confuse consumers or that plaintiff would suffer irreparable harm).

283. Urban Outfitters, Inc. v. BCBG Max Azria Grp., Inc., 511 F. Supp. 2d 482, 491 (E.D. Pa. 2007).

284. *Id.* at 506.

285. *Id.* at 507.

286. *Id.*

287. U.S. Polo Ass'n, Inc. v. PRL USA Holdings, Inc., 800 F. Supp. 2d 515, 541 (S.D.N.Y. 2011) (quoting Nw. Nat'l Ins. Co. of Milwaukee, Wis. v. Alberts, 923 F.2d 77, 80 (2d Cir. 1991)).

288. *Id.* at 540 ("Irreparable harm . . . is neither calculable nor precisely compensable.") (quotation marks omitted); *see also* The Gap, Inc. v. G.A.P. Adventures, Inc., No. 07 Civ. 9614(AKH), 2011 WL 2946384, at *18 (S.D.N.Y. June 24, 2011) (granting permanent injunction where Gap, Inc. would suffer "irreparable injury because consumers are likely to be confused initially or deceived as to a connection or affiliation" with defendant and "[r]emedies at law will not compensate Gap for the boost in credibility that [defendant] receives as a result of this initial confusion as to its affiliation").

the following types of injury to be "irreparable": loss of control of reputation, loss of sales, and loss of goodwill.[289]

A plaintiff does not need to show actual injury to its reputation; merely the threat of such harm is sufficient for purposes of obtaining a preliminary injunction.[290] Courts have recognized that "[o]ne of the most valuable and important protections afforded by the Lanham Act is the right to control the quality of the goods manufactured and sold under the holder's trademark."[291]

Many courts had traditionally based a finding of irreparable injury upon a showing of likelihood of confusion.[292] In light of the Supreme Court's decision in *eBay v. MercExchange*, however, courts cannot rely on a simple presumption that liability for trademark infringement supports injunctive relief.[293]

In the Second Circuit, to establish irreparable injury in a trademark case, a plaintiff must separately conclude "that it

---

289. *Urban Outfitters, Inc.*, 511 F. Supp. 2d at 507; Gucci Shops, Inc. v. R.H. Macy & Co., 446 F. Supp. 838, 841 (S.D.N.Y. 1977) (possibility of irreparable harm existed where defendant's product "either misleads the public into mistakenly associating plaintiff's quality products with defendant's or ridicules plaintiff's marks, damages plaintiff's reputation and the value of plaintiff's marks"); *U.S. Polo Players Ass'n*, 800 F. Supp. 2d at 541 (because harm to "reputation and goodwill cannot be quantified," irreparable harm would result in the absence of injunctive relief).

290. *Urban Outfitters, Inc.*, at 507; Gayle Martz, Inc. v. Sherpa Pet Grp., LLC, 651 F. Supp. 2d 72, 85 (S.D.N.Y. 2009) (granting permanent injunction because "[t]he unauthorized use of a mark . . . invariably threatens injury to the economic value of the goodwill and reputation associated with a . . . mark").

291. Zino Davidoff SA v. CVS Corp., 571 F.3d 238, 243 (2d Cir. 2009) (quotation marks and citation omitted) (affirming district court's grant of preliminary injunction).

292. *See, e.g.*, *Urban Outfitters, Inc.*, 511 F. Supp. 2d at 507 ("When a plaintiff demonstrates a strong likelihood of confusion, irreparable injury results as a matter of course.") (citing Opticians Ass'n of Am. v. Indep. Opticians of Am., 92 F.2d 187, 196 (3d Cir. 1990)); GoTo.com, Inc. v. Walt Disney Co., 202 F.3d 1199, 1205 n.4 (9th Cir. 2000) ("This presumption effectively conflates the dual inquiries of this prong into the single question of whether the plaintiff has shown a likelihood of success on the merits.").

293. Salinger v. Colting, 607 F.3d 68 (2d Cir. 2010); *see also U.S. Polo Ass'n*, 800 F. Supp. 2d at 540 ("In light of *Salinger*'s clarification that '*eBay*'s central lesson is that, unless Congress intended a major departure from the long tradition of equity practice, a court must not adopt categorical or general rules or presume that a party has met an element of the injunction standard,' the presumption of irreparable injury in trademark cases is no longer appropriate.") (quoting *Salinger*, 607 F.3d at 77–78 & n.7).

will lose control over the reputation of its trademark pending trial, because loss of control over one's reputation is neither calculable nor precisely compensable."[294] Of course, courts may continue to take the likelihood of consumer confusion into account when considering the question of irreparable injury.[295] If consumers may be confused as to the source of a product, the plaintiff's reputation and goodwill may suffer because he is not in control of the impression being given to consumers.[296] Harm to a company's reputation and goodwill often cannot be quantified, and can be considered irreparable.[297]

Following *eBay*, the Ninth Circuit held that there is no longer a presumption of irreparable harm in trademark infringement cases, and that trademark plaintiffs must demonstrate a likelihood of irreparable harm with detailed, substantiated supporting evidence to obtain injunctive relief.[298] In *adidas America, Inc. v. Skechers USA, Inc.*, for example, adidas sought a preliminary injunction to prevent Skechers from selling shoes that adidas claimed were confusingly similar to it's registered "Stan Smith" and "three-stripe" trade dress. Adidas supported its motion with testimony from a Director who described the "significant efforts" his team undertook in promoting its Stan Smith shoe through social media campaigns and product placement. Adidas also presented evidence demonstrating how it controls the supply of the Stan Smith shoe, to ensure that it does not flood the marketplace with similar styles, and produced customer surveys illustrating that approximately 20% of consumers believed Skechers's shoe was affiliated with adidas's Stan Smith shoe. The Ninth Circuit upheld the district court's finding of a likelihood of irreparable harm to the Stan Smith trade dress, based on sufficient evidence.

---

294. Pretty Girl, Inc. v. Pretty Girl Fashions, Inc., 778 F. Supp. 2d 261, 269 (E.D.N.Y. 2011); *see also U.S. Polo Ass'n*, 800 F. Supp. 2d at 540.

295. *U.S. Polo Ass'n*, 800 F. Supp. 2d at 541 ("[G]iven the likelihood of confusion between the Polo Player Logo and USPA's Double Horseman Trademark, the reputation and goodwill cultivated by PRL's would be out its hands.").

296. *Id.* ("The [defendants]' product may or may not be of high quality, sold with sufficient customer service, or convey the same branding image that has been highly cultivated by Ralph Lauren.").

297. *Id.*

298. *See* Herb Reed Enters., LLC v. Fla. Entm't Mgmt., Inc., 736 F.3d 1239, 1249 (9th Cir. 2013); *see also, e.g.*, adidas Am., Inc. v. Skechers USA, Inc., 890 F.3d 747, 756 (9th Cir. 2018); Puma SE v. Forever 21, Inc., No. 17-cv-2523 PSG E, 2017 WL 4771003, at *2 (C.D. Cal. June 2, 2017).

However, the Ninth Circuit reversed the district court's holding that adidas would be irreparably harmed by Skechers's sale of a shoe that allegedly infringed on its "three-stripe" trade dress. The Ninth Circuit rejected adidas's argument that consumers who saw others wearing the allegedly counterfeit and lesser-quality shoe would associate it with the adidas "three-stripe" shoe. First, it held that adidas had failed to present evidence from general consumers demonstrating that they find Skechers to be an inferior brand, aside from a "generalized statement" from an adidas employee about Skechers's lower price point. Second, the Ninth Circuit rejected adidas's argument that consumers would, from afar, associate a lesser-quality shoe with adidas's three-stripe mark. The Ninth Circuit reasoned that if the Skechers shoe truly is similar enough to be confused with the adidas three-stripe from afar, then consumers would not be able to assess the inferior quality from afar, and the adidas brand would not be harmed.

3. ***Balance of the Hardships.*** The "balance of the hardships" prong requires the court to consider whether the issuance of the injunction would harm the alleged infringer more than the mark's owner.[299] Where there is a likelihood of consumer confusion and potential loss to the trademark owner in the form of sales, loss of control of reputation and loss of goodwill, the equities will likely weigh in favor of granting a request for injunctive relief.[300] On the other hand, courts need not enter an injunction that will inflict harm on an accused infringer that "outweighs any conceivable injury" allegedly caused by the infringement.[301]

4. ***Public Interest.*** It is well-established that the purpose of trademark law is to protect the public from confusion.[302] Courts recognize that the consuming public has a "protectable interest in being free from confusion, deception, and mistake."[303]

---

299. Urban Outfitters, Inc. v. BCBG Max Azria Grp., Inc., 511 F. Supp. 2d 482, 507–08 (E.D. Pa. 2007).
300. *See U.S. Polo Players Ass'n*, 800 F. Supp. 2d at 541.
301. Mushroom Makers, Inc. v. R.G. Barry Corp., 580 F.2d 44, 48–49 (2d Cir. 1978).
302. *See, e.g.*, Hermès Int'l v. Lederer de Paris Fifth Ave., Inc., 219 F.3d 104, 107–08 (2d Cir. 2000); United States v. Torkington, 812 F.2d 1347, 1353 n.6 (11th Cir. 1987) ("[T]he enforcement of trademark laws benefits consumers even in cases where there is no possibility that consumers will be defrauded.").
303. *See, e.g.*, *U.S. Polo Players Ass'n*, 800 F. Supp. 2d at 541 (citation omitted).

Where the plaintiff establishes that there is a likelihood of success on the merits—and, by extension, a likelihood of confusion—the public interest will almost always favor issuance of an injunction.[304] If, on the other hand, the requested injunction will harm the public and therefore will be contrary to the public interest, the injunction should be denied.[305]

§ 2:9.2 Monetary Relief

Section 35(a) of the Lanham Act permits a plaintiff who successfully establishes a claim for trademark infringement to recover: (1) the defendant's profits; (2) any damages sustained by the plaintiff as a result of the infringement; and (3) the costs of the action.[306]

[A] Defendant's Profits

An award of profits is subject to principles of equity and is not automatic.[307] In determining the defendant's profits, the plaintiff is required to prove the defendant's sales, but not the defendant's net profit after costs.[308] Once liability and defendant's gross profits are established, the defendant must set forth evidence demonstrating any deductions to its profits.[309]

---

304. *See id.*; *see also* Gayle Martz, Inc. v. Sherpa Pet Grp., LLC, 651 F. Supp. 2d 72, 85 (S.D.N.Y. 2009) ("[T]he public interest lies in the enforcement of the Acts of Congress, especially the prevention of consumer confusion as espoused by the Lanham Act."); Bausch & Lomb, Inc. v. Allergan, Inc., No. 87 Civ. 1284 (RO), 1987 WL 12080, at *1 (S.D.N.Y. June 4, 1987) (awarding injunctive relief to plaintiff on showing of health risk to consumers who may confuse defendants' product with that of plaintiff's).

305. Winter v. NRDC, 555 U.S. 7 (2008) (vacating injunction where public interest favored continuation of challenger's activity notwithstanding finding that challenger had violated statute).

306. 15 U.S.C. § 1117(a); *see also* MCCARTHY, *supra* note 30, § 30:57.

307. Quick Techs., Inc. v. Sage Grp. PLC, 313 F.3d 338, 349 (5th Cir. 2002) ("Section 1117(a) remedies are awarded 'subject to the principles of equity.' Thus, an award of the defendant's profits is not automatic.").

308. 15 U.S.C. § 1117(a).

309. *Id.*; *see also* Venture Tape Corp. v. McGills Glass Warehouse, 540 F.3d 56, 64 (1st Cir. 2008) (defendant bore "the burden of producing evidentiary documentation that [the] sales were unrelated to and unaided by [defendant]'s illicit use of [plaintiff]'s marks"); *accord* Banjo Buddies, Inc. v. Renosky, 399 F.3d 168, 177 (3d Cir. 2005); *see also* Troublé v. Wet Seal, Inc., 179 F. Supp. 2d 291, 304–05 (S.D.N.Y. 2001) ("There is a general presumption that an infringer's sales of goods bearing the infringing mark were due to the selling power of the mark and not any other cause. . . . If [defendant] can prove that certain 'non-infringing elements' somehow contributed to the profits of the alleged infringing goods, it is entitled to deduct this from the profits it must disgorge to [plaintiff].").

The Lanham Act provides courts with broad discretion in awarding damages. The statute permits the court to enter an award representing up to three times the amount of provable actual damages.[310] If the amount of recovery a plaintiff would obtain based on the defendant's profits is either inadequate or excessive, the court has discretion under the Lanham Act to adjust the award upward or downward to "such sum as the court shall find to be just."[311] The statute makes clear, however, that the sum to be awarded is considered "compensation and not a penalty."[312]

In providing the courts with flexibility to adjust the plaintiff's damages awards, the Lanham Act accounts for the fact that it may be difficult in some circumstances to accurately assess the defendant's profits. Courts have upheld such awards on appeal, finding that "[w]here the mark owner cannot prove actual damages attributable to the infringer's misconduct (for example, specific instances of lost sales), its recovery of an equitable share of the infringer's profits serves, *inter alia*, as a 'rough measure' of the likely harm that the mark owner incurred because of the infringement, while also preventing the infringer's unjust enrichment and deterring future infringement."[313]

In some circuits, courts will only allow a trademark plaintiff to obtain an award of the defendant's profits if the plaintiff can show that the defendant acted willfully.[314] In other circuits, courts will

---

310. 15 U.S.C. § 1117(a).
311. *Id.*
312. *Id.*
313. *Venture Tape Corp.*, 540 F.3d at 63 (affirming district court's award of an equitable share of defendant's profits, costs and attorneys' fees).
314. *See, e.g.*, Stone Creek, Inc. v. Omnia Italian Design, Inc., 875 F.3d 426, 441 (9th Cir. 2017) ("willfulness remains a prerequisite for awarding a defendant's profits"), *cert. denied*, 138 S. Ct. 1984 (2018); Merck Eprova AG v. Gnosis S.p.A., 760 F.3d 247, 261 (2d Cir. 2014) ("a finding of defendant's willful deceptiveness is a prerequisite for awarding profits"); W. Diversified Servs., Inc. v. Hyundai Motor Am., Inc., 427 F.3d 1269, 1273 (10th Cir. 2005) (courts "require a showing that Defendant's actions were willful to support an award of profits under 15 U.S.C. § 1117(a)"); Minn. Pet Breeders, Inc. v. Schell & Kampeter, Inc., 41 F.3d 1242, 1247 (8th Cir. 1994) (an accounting of profits is available only "[i]f a registered owner proves willful, deliberate infringement or deception"); ALPO Petfoods, Inc. v. Ralston Purina Co., 913 F.2d 958, 968 (D.C. Cir. 1990) ("an award based on a defendant's profits requires proof that the defendant acted willfully or in bad faith"). The First Circuit requires a showing of willfulness where the plaintiff and defendant are not direct competitors. Tamko Roofing Prods., Inc. v. Ideal Roofing Co., 282 F.3d 23 (1st Cir. 2002).

weigh the question of willfulness as part of a broader analysis.[315] In 2019, Romag Fasteners, Inc. filed a petition for a writ of certiorari, asking the U.S. Supreme Court to resolve this split in a dispute with Fossil, Inc. and Macy's, Inc.[316] As of the date of publication, the Court had not acted on the petition.

[B] Plaintiff's Damages

The plaintiff may seek compensation for any damages resulting from the defendant's infringing use of plaintiff's mark, such as "(1) lost sales or revenue; (2) sales at lower prices; (3) harm to market reputation; or (4) expenditures to prevent, correct, or mitigate consumer confusion."[317] Courts may require the plaintiff to submit proof of actual confusion in order to recover for monetary loss.[318]

[C] Costs of the Action and Attorneys' Fees

An award of "costs" under the Lanham Act generally involves the same kind of expenses itemized in 28 U.S.C. § 1920: court fees,

---

315. *See, e.g.*, Laukus v. Rio Brands, Inc., 391 F. App'x 416, 424 (6th Cir. 2010) (willfulness is "not required" but is rather "one element that courts may consider in weighing the equities"); Optimum Techs., Inc. v. Home Depot U.S.A., Inc., 217 F. App'x 899, 902 (11th Cir. 2007) (per curiam) ("an accounting of a defendant's profits is appropriate" in any one of three circumstances: where "(1) the defendant's conduct was willful and deliberate, (2) the defendant was unjustly enriched, or (3) it is necessary to deter future conduct."); Synergistic Int'l, LLC v. Korman, 470 F.3d 162, 175 (4th Cir. 2006) ("although willfulness is a proper and important factor in an assessment of whether to make a damages award, it is not an essential predicate thereto"); Banjo Buddies, Inc. v. Renosky, 399 F.3d 168, 171 (3d Cir. 2005) ("willfulness is an important equitable factor but not a prerequisite" to recovery of profits); Roulo v. Russ Berrie & Co., 886 F.2d 931, 941 (7th Cir. 1989) ("[o]ther than general equitable considerations, there is no express requirement that . . . the infringer wilfully [sic] infringe the trade dress to justify an award of profits").

316. Romag Fasteners, Inc. v. Fossil, Inc., No. 18-1233 (U.S. cert. petition filed Mar. 20, 2019).

317. Int'l Star Class Yacht Racing Ass'n v. Tommy Hilfiger, U.S.A., Inc., 80 F.3d 749, 753 (2d Cir. 1996).

318. *Id.* at 753 (citing RESTATEMENT (THIRD) OF UNFAIR COMPETITION § 36 cmt. i (1995)); Zelinski v. Columbia 300, Inc., 335 F.3d 633, 639 (7th Cir. 2003) ("To recover damages, [the plaintiff] must show that the violation caused actual confusion among his customers and, as a result, he suffered actual injury."); Teaching Co. P'ship v. Unapix Entm't, Inc., 87 F. Supp. 2d 567, 588–89 (E.D. Va. 2000) ("[T]o recover monetary damages, a plaintiff must prove actual confusion; however, to recover a monetary award of the defendant's profits, a plaintiff need not prove actual confusion.").

disbursements for printing and witnesses, and compensation of court appointed experts and interpreters.

In "exceptional cases," the court may also award reasonable attorney's fees to the prevailing party.[319] Factors that courts consider in determining whether a case is "exceptional" include "frivolousness, motivation, objective unreasonableness (both in the factual and legal components of the case) and the need in particular circumstances to advance considerations of compensation and deterrence." These factors, however, are not exhaustive.[320] Courts consider a case to be "exceptional" if, based on the totality of the circumstances, the court concludes that the infringement was malicious, fraudulent, deliberate, or willful.[321] Courts may also award attorneys' fees to defendants in Lanham Act cases where "the plaintiff has no reasonable or legal basis to believe in success on the merits."[322]

§ 2:9.3 Accounting of Profits

The plaintiff may also seek an accounting of the defendant's profits even if actual damages are not available.[323] Although some courts have treated an award of defendants' profits as a damages award at law, the correct interpretation is to treat an accounting of profits as an equitable remedy, available to courts to cure any unjust enrichment

---

319. 15 U.S.C. § 1117(a).

320. Octane Fitness, LLC v. ICON Health & Fitness, Inc., 134 S. Ct. 1749, 1756 n.6 (2014) (internal citations omitted) (discussing the "exceptional case" standard under the Patent Act, 35 U.S.C. § 285). Most courts have held that the *Octane Fitness* factors apply equally to the "exceptional case" standard under the Lanham Act. *See, e.g.*, Sleepy's LLC v. Select Comfort Wholesale Corp., 909 F.3d 519 (2d Cir. 2018); SunEarth, Inc. v. Sun Earth Solar Power Co., 839 F.3d 1179, 1181 (9th Cir. 2016); Baker v. DeShong, 821 F.3d 620, 624 (5th Cir. 2016); Georgia-Pac. Consumer Prods. LP v. Von Drehle Corp., 781 F.3d 710, 721 (4th Cir. 2015); Slep-Tone Entm't Corp. v. Karaoke Kandy Store, Inc., 782 F.3d 313, 317–18 (3d Cir. 2014).

321. *Venture Tape Corp.*, 540 F.3d at 64; Guess?, Inc. v. Gold Ctr. Jewelry, 997 F. Supp. 409, 412 (S.D.N.Y. 1998) ("Usually, the type of conduct that has sufficed to make out an 'exceptional case' is intentional, deliberate, or willful infringement."); Nike, Inc. v. Just Did It Enters., 799 F. Supp. 894 (N.D. Ill. 1992) (granting attorney's fees to plaintiff where defendant's infringement was willful).

322. Secalt S.A. v. Wuxi Shenxi Constr. Mach. Co., 668 F.3d 677, 687 (9th Cir. 2012).

323. *Int'l Star Class Yacht Racing Ass'n*, 80 F.3d. at 753 ("The unavailability of actual damages as a remedy . . . does not preclude [plaintiff] from recovering an accounting of [defendant]'s profits or attorney fees.").

gained by the defendant as a result of its unauthorized use of plaintiff's mark and as a deterrent to future infringement.[324]

The prevailing party in an infringement action does not have an automatic right to obtain an accounting of a defendant's profits, and it is within the court's discretion to deny a request for an accounting.[325] An accounting is appropriate if it is likely that the defendant's use of the plaintiff's mark resulted in a diversion of sales or if an assessment of profits is necessary to avoid a speculative determination of damages.[326]

§ 2:9.4 Remedies for Infringing Domain Names

Where the defendant's infringement includes using the plaintiff's marks in the domain name of a website, there is a risk that the domain name may confuse consumers as to the source of defendant's products. In such circumstances, the plaintiff may seek relief under the Anticybersquatting Consumer Protection Act or "ACPA," 15 U.S.C. § 1125(d), which imposes liability for registering or using a domain name that is identical or confusingly similar to, or dilutive of, someone else's mark with a bad faith intent to profit off that person's mark.[327] When Congress enacted the ACPA, it noted the many

---

324. Gucci Am., Inc. v. Weixing Li, 768 F.3d 122, 131–32 (2d Cir. 2014) ("as plaintiffs correctly contend, the common law action of 'account' is one of the earliest examples of a restitutionary action in equity, imposing on a defendant the obligation to disclose and return profits from the use of the plaintiff's property"). *See also* Animale Grp. Inc. v. Sunny's Perfume Inc., 256 F. App'x 707, 709 (5th Cir. 2007) (per curiam) (ruling that the district court was "authorized to preserve the status quo by entering a limited asset freeze" in a Lanham Act infringement case); Levi Strauss & Co. v. Sunrise Int'l Trading Inc., 51 F.3d 982, 987 (11th Cir. 1995) (concluding that the "district court had the authority to freeze those assets which could have been used to satisfy an equitable award of profits" in a Lanham Act case); Reebok Int'l, Ltd. v. Marnatech Enters., Inc., 970 F.2d 552, 562 (9th Cir. 1992) ("The district court's inherent equitable power to freeze defendants' assets in cases in which an accounting is the ultimate relief sought is therefore not limited by the Lanham Act.").

325. Gucci Am., Inc. v. Daffy's, Inc., 354 F.3d 228, 241–43 (3d Cir. 2003) (district court did not abuse its discretion in refusing to order an accounting); L & L Wings, Inc. v. Marco-Destin Inc., 756 F. Supp. 2d 359 (S.D.N.Y. 2010) (concluding that "the equities weigh against an accounting" where, among other things, there was no head-to-head competition between the parties and it was "not at all certain" that the defendant's continued use of the mark "led to any substantial additional profits").

326. Banjo Buddies, Inc. v. Renosky, 399 F.3d 168, 175–76 (3d Cir. 2005) ("[W]e conclude that the District Court did not abuse its discretion in deciding to order an accounting of [defendant]'s profits.").

327. *See* 15 U.S.C. § 1125(d).

problems associated with cybersquatting, including attempts to sell domain names to trademark holders at exorbitant prices, lost business opportunities for the mark holder, and dilution of the mark.[328]

To prevail on a claim under the ACPA, a plaintiff must show that "(1) its marks were distinctive at the time the domain name was registered; (2) the infringing domain names complained of are identical to or confusingly similar to plaintiff's mark; and (3) the defendant has a bad faith intent to profit from the mark."[329]

Various forms of relief are available for claims arising under the ACPA, including injunctive and monetary relief. The plaintiff can request an order from the court requiring that the infringing domain name be turned over to the trademark owner. This order can be requested as part of preliminary injunctive relief or ultimate relief once the plaintiff has established its claim for trademark infringement.[330]

Further, the Lanham Act provides for monetary damages in connection with claims arising under the ACPA that are separate from the other types of monetary relief discussed above. At any time prior to entry of final judgment, the plaintiff can elect to recover either the defendant's actual damages and profits, or an award of statutory damages.[331] The available statutory damages range from a minimum of $1,000 per infringing domain name up to a maximum of $100,000 per domain name, to be awarded as the court deems just.[332]

§ 2:9.5 *International Trade Commission*

The United States International Trade Commission (ITC) offers yet another avenue for trademark owners to enforce their rights against infringers.[333] The ITC is a quasi-judicial federal agency charged with administering U.S. trade remedy laws, serving as a resource for the President, Congress, and the U.S. Trade Representative, and

328. H.R. REP. No. 106-412, at 5–6 (1999).

329. *See* N.Y.C. Triathlon, LLC v. N.Y.C. Triathlon Club, Inc., 704 F. Supp. 2d 305, 324 (S.D.N.Y. 2010) (citations omitted).

330. *See, e.g.*, Webadviso v. Bank of Am. Corp., No. 09 Civ. 5769 (DC), 2009 WL 5177997, at *4 (S.D.N.Y. Dec. 31, 2009) (finding defendants' loss of control over domain name using its trademark could cause irreparable loss of goodwill).

331. 15 U.S.C. § 1117(d).

332. *Id. See also* Elecs. Boutique Holdings Corp. v. Zuccarini, 56 U.S.P.Q.2d 1705 (E.D. Pa. 2000) (awarding $500,000 damages under Lanham Act section 43(d) against registrant of domain names confusingly similar to distinctive marks), *motion to set aside verdict denied*, 2001 U.S. Dist. LEXIS 765 (E.D. Pa. Jan. 25, 2001).

333. A discussion of additional international trademark enforcement options, including the World Intellectual Property Organization (WIPO) and the Madrid Protocol, appears in *infra* section 2:15.2.

maintaining the U.S. Harmonized Tariff Schedule. Pursuant to section 337 of the Tariff Act of 1930, as amended, the ITC is vested with authority to adjudicate claims of infringement and unfair competition in connection with imports into the United States.[334] Among other things, section 337 prohibits the import of infringing goods into the United States, the sale of infringing goods for import into the United States, and the sale of infringing goods within the United States.[335]

Actions arising under section 337 are referred to as "Section 337 Investigations." To request a Section 337 Investigation, the trademark owner must meet the "domestic industry requirement," by demonstrating that it has made a significant investment in the United States with respect to the goods and marks at issue.[336] The remedies available to a trademark owner in a Section 337 Investigation include preliminary injunctive relief,[337] cease and desist orders,[338] and exclusion orders directing U.S. Customs and Border Protection to prevent the infringing goods from entering the United States.[339] Prior to the issuance of such orders, the ITC must conclude that the order is in the public interest.[340]

While the majority of the ITC's intellectual property investigations concern patent-based claims relating to telecommunications and computer equipment,[341] Louis Vuitton has utilized section 337 remedies to enforce its trademark rights. In 2010, Louis Vuitton filed a complaint with the ITC against various entities based in China

---

334. *See* 19 U.S.C. § 1337.

335. 19 U.S.C. § 1337(a)(1)(C).

336. *See, e.g.*, 19 U.S.C. § 1337(a)(3) ("[A]n industry in the United States shall be considered to exist if there is in the United States, with respect to the articles protected by the patent, copyright, trademark, mask work, or design concerned—(A) significant investment in plant and equipment; (B) significant employment of labor or capital; or (C) substantial investment in its exploitation, including engineering, research and development, or licensing.").

337. 19 U.S.C. § 1337(e)(2) ("The Commission may grant preliminary relief under this subsection or subsection (f) of this section to the same extent as preliminary injunctions and temporary restraining orders may be granted under the Federal Rules of Civil Procedure.").

338. 19 U.S.C. § 1337(f).

339. 19 U.S.C. § 1337(d), (g).

340. 19 U.S.C. § 1337(e)–(g) (requiring the ITC to "consider[] the effect of such exclusion or order upon the public health and welfare, competitive conditions in the United States economy, the production of like or directly competitive articles in the United States, and United States consumers").

341. *See, e.g.*, U.S. INT'L TRADE COMM'N, FY 2011 AT A GLANCE, OPERATION 2: INTELLECTUAL PROPERTY IMPORT INVESTIGATIONS, https://www.usitc.gov/press_room/documents/op2_transition.pdf.

and the United States.[342] Louis Vuitton alleged that the respondents manufactured counterfeit Louis Vuitton products in China, which were then imported into the United States for sale by various retailers, who were also named in the complaint.[343] This was not Louis Vuitton's first encounter with these counterfeiters, some of whom Louis Vuitton had previously sued in China.[344] During the course of the Chinese litigation, Louis Vuitton learned that the counterfeiters had applied to the Chinese customs authorities to export nearly 10,000 counterfeit Louis Vuitton handbags out of the country.[345] The Chinese litigants continued to infringe Louis Vuitton's mark, which led the brand to seek relief from the ITC.

Following the Section 337 Investigation, the ITC issued a general exclusion order in Louis Vuitton's favor, finding that the order was "necessary because there is a pattern of violation of section 337 and it is difficult to identify the source of infringing products."[346] Recognizing that "there may be numerous ways to manipulate the trademarks so as to create infringements," the ITC attached photographs of certain infringing products to the exclusion order in an effort to assist Customs and Border Protection personnel in enforcing the order.[347] Importantly, the ITC's general exclusion order operates to exclude *all* infringing products, regardless of whether the importer was named as a respondent in the ITC proceedings.[348]

While there are benefits to seeking relief through the ITC, there are also certain limitations that trademark owners should be aware of. First, while Section 337 Investigations provide an alternative route for trademark owners to secure injunctive relief against infringers, the ITC does not have the authority to award monetary damages to claimants.

Second, the trademark owner will be required to post a bond "in an amount determined by the Commission to be sufficient to protect the complainant from any injury" in order to obtain a cease and desist order or preliminary relief during the pendency of the Section 337

342. Verified Am. Compl., *In re* Certain Handbags, Luggage, Accessories and Packaging Thereof, Inv. No. 337-TA-754 (Dec. 10, 2010).

343. *Id.* ¶¶ 10–26.

344. *Id.* ¶ 56.

345. *Id.*

346. General Exclusion Order, *In re* Certain Handbags, Inv. No. 337-TA-754, at 1 (Int'l Trade Comm'n May 30, 2012).

347. *Id.* ¶ 3.

348. *See* Kyocera Wireless Corp. v. Int'l Trade Comm'n, 545 F.3d 1340, 1356 (Fed. Cir. 2008) ("If a complainant wishes to obtain an exclusion order operative against articles of non-respondents, it must seek a GEO by satisfying the heightened burden of §§ 1337(d)(2)(A) and (B).").

Investigation.[349] While the amount of the bond can vary, the ITC required Louis Vuitton to post a bond equal to 100% of the value of the imported goods.[350]

Third, the injunctive relief afforded by the ITC is limited to activity in the United States. While an exclusion order can prohibit infringing goods from entering the United States, it does not reach the infringer's conduct outside of the United States. An order from the ITC, for example, would not prevent the infringer from importing their goods to countries other than the U.S. In contrast, federal courts have authority to enjoin infringing conduct taking place in foreign countries where the infringer's conduct could cause harm in the United States.[351]

Fourth, certain infringers—particularly, counterfeiters—ship their products directly to consumers in small packages precisely to avoid detection by Customs and Border Protection, and to minimize loss if the counterfeiters' packages are confiscated.[352] Because the contents of these packages are often falsely labeled by the counterfeiters as "gifts" and shipped in innocuous packaging, they can be hard to detect (and seize). In such circumstances, an exclusion order may be of limited use in stemming the flow of the infringer's goods into the United States. The exclusion order can be of great value, however, where the facts suggest that the infringer is shipping large quantities of goods into the United States, as was the case in a Section 337 Investigation involving the Louis Vuitton trademarks.

Finally, the ITC can rule against the trademark owner. For example, in 2016, the ITC concluded that Converse, Inc. could not enforce rights in the midsole design of its Chuck Taylor All Star shoes because the design lacked secondary meaning and could not function as a trademark. In a procedurally complex decision, a split panel of the U.S. Court of Appeals for the Federal Circuit eventually reversed the

---

349. *See* 19 U.S.C. § 1337(e)(1), (f).

350. Notice of Commission Final Determination of Violation of Section 337; Termination of Investigation; Issuance of General Exclusion Order, *In re* Certain Handbags, Inv. No. 337-TA-754, at 3 (Int'l Trade Comm'n May 30, 2012).

351. A.V. by Versace, Inc. v. Gianni Versace, S.p.A., 126 F. Supp. 2d 328, 336 (S.D.N.Y. 2001) ("It is well-established that United States courts have jurisdiction to apply the Lanham Act to infringing conduct occurring outside the United States when necessary to prevent harm to United States commerce.") (citing Steele v. Bulova Watch Co., 344 U.S. 280 (1952)).

352. *See, e.g.*, NAT'L INTELLECTUAL PROP. RIGHTS COORDINATION CTR., INTELLECTUAL PROPERTY RIGHTS VIOLATIONS: A REPORT ON THREATS TO UNITED STATES INTERESTS AT HOME AND ABROAD 53–54 (Nov. 2011).

ITC's decision, remanding the case back to the ITC to be reconsidered again, two years later.[353]

§ 2:10 Defenses to Infringement

There are a number of defenses that can be asserted in response to a claim of trademark infringement. Most obviously, a defendant can contest the elements of the plaintiff's claim, by making a showing that its activities are not likely to cause consumer confusion. Procedural defenses, such as lack of personal jurisdiction, are beyond the scope of this chapter but are important defenses that should also be considered alongside the trademark-specific defenses discussed herein. Additional potential defenses are discussed below.

§ 2:10.1 *Invalidity of the Trademark*

Although a plaintiff is entitled to a presumption as to the validity of a federally registered trademark, a defendant who demonstrates by a preponderance of evidence that the mark is invalid can defeat a claim for infringement.[354]

One of the grounds on which a defendant can challenge the validity of plaintiff's trademark is by asserting a defense of "prior use," that is, that because the plaintiff was not the first to use the mark in commerce, the trademark is invalid and cannot form the basis of a claim for trademark infringement.[355]

Indeed, under 15 U.S.C. § 1065, a defendant can even challenge the validity of a federally registered trademark that is considered "incontestable" because it has existed on the federal register for more than five years, as long as it can support the particular grounds to challenge the mark listed in section 1065.[356]

For example, in *Bauer Bros. LLC v. Nike, Inc.*, defendant Nike rebutted the presumption of validity and demonstrated its own priority of use through the submission of detailed evidence regarding

---

353. Converse Inc. v. ITC, No. 16-2497 (Fed. Cir. Oct. 30, 2018).

354. Bauer Bros. LLC v. Nike, Inc., No. 09cv500–WQH–BGS, 2012 WL 1900047, at *7 (S.D. Cal. May 24, 2012) (the defendant "must demonstrate through undisputed facts, or a combination thereof that the registrant had not established valid ownership rights in the mark at the time of registration") (quotation marks and citation omitted).

355. *Id.* at *6 ("Failure to meet the prior use requirement renders the mark *void ab initio*").

356. *See* Urban Outfitters, Inc. v. BCBG Max Azria Grp., Inc., 511 F. Supp. 2d 482, 487 n.1 (E.D. Pa. 2007) ("[T]he incontestability of the Defendant's mark does not shield it from an infringement action when the Plaintiff has established common law rights to the mark preceding the registration of the Defendant's mark.").

its use of the marks in commerce, including sales records, internal emails, marketing and development materials, and samples of the goods sold.[357] In contrast, Bauer Bros. failed to "produce[] any evidence of bona fide use of the marks or sale of the marks in commerce either at the time [it] filed the respective applications or at any time before Nike's first use."[358] As a result, the court concluded that Bauer Bros.'s trademark registrations were invalid and granted Nike's motion for summary judgment.[359]

The U.S. Supreme Court's 2013 decision in *Already LLC v. Nike, Inc.*,[360] suggests, however, that a plaintiff may be able to avoid a judicial determination as to the validity of its marks by voluntarily removing any threat of an infringement suit against a particular infringer through the issuance of a broad covenant not to sue.[361]

§ 2:10.2 *Lack of Standing*

In most trademark cases, standing is not an issue because the claims are asserted by the same entity that owns the trademark registration and markets the goods or services sold in connection with that trademark. But when the plaintiff is not the trademark owner, defendants should carefully consider a lack of standing defense.

---

357. *Bauer*, 2012 WL 1900047, at *7–8.
358. *Id.* at *8.
359. *Id.*
360. Already LLC v. Nike, Inc., 133 S. Ct. 721 (2013).
361. *Id.* In *Already LLC*, in response to Nike's claim of trademark infringement, the defendant asserted a counterclaim challenging the validity of Nike's "Air Force 1" trademark. Months later, Nike determined that Already's shoe lines were unlikely to threaten its Air Force 1 mark "at a level sufficient to warrant the substantial time and expense of continued litigation," and issued a covenant not to sue Already or any of its affiliates based on any of Already's existing footwear designs, or any future Already designs that constitute a "colorable imitation" of Already's current products. Nike then asked the district court to dismiss its own claims with prejudice, and to dismiss Already's invalidity counterclaim without prejudice on the ground that the covenant rendered the case moot. Already objected to the dismissal of its counterclaim, but both the district court and the Second Circuit held that Nike's covenant eliminated any justiciable case or controversy. The Supreme Court unanimously affirmed, holding that Already's counterclaims were moot because the covenant assured that Nike could not later claim that Already's footwear infringed Nike's trademark. Although the concurring opinion counseled caution and suggested limits on the availability of this tactic, the Court's main opinion reaffirms the longstanding principle that courts lack jurisdiction to hear a challenge to intellectual property that is not asserted in a real "case or controversy."

Trademark standing can be distinguished from Constitutional standing, which requires the plaintiff to establish that there has been an injury in fact, causation, and redressability to overcome Article III's "case or controversy" requirement.[362] The Lanham Act creates a cause of action for "any person who believes that he or she is likely to be damaged,"[363] but courts have created a judicial doctrine of "statutory standing," that restricts trademark claims to those who have sufficient "rights in the name" to sue under the Lanham Act.[364]

An example of statutory standing arose in a case brought by Kroma Makeup EU LLC against companies associated with reality television celebrities the Kardashians.[365] Kroma alleged that the Kardashians' makeup line infringed its rights in the KROMA trademark. Kroma, however, did not own the KROMA mark. It merely sought to enforce the mark as the former European distributor of cosmetics products that used the mark. The Kardashians moved to dismiss on the ground that the license did not explicitly give Kroma the authority to enforce the mark. Both the district court and the court of appeals for the Eleventh Circuit agreed.[366] Reading the plain language of the license "only vested Kroma EU with the obligation to 'inform [the mark's owner] of any illegal use of the trademark,' prompting [the mark owner] to file suit against the infringer—at which point [the mark owner] would be required to compensate Kroma for its losses resulting from the infringement." Because these provisions indicate that only the mark owner had the exclusive right to sue for infringement, the case was dismissed.[367]

§ 2:10.3 *Fraud in Procuring the Trademark*

An alleged infringer may also assert that the trademark registration was procured by fraud and should be cancelled. Defenses based on a charge of fraud, however, require the defendant to meet a heavy burden of proof.[368] Courts will require a charge of fraud to "be proven to the hilt with clear and convincing evidence," with "any doubt . . . resolved against the charging party."[369]

---

362. *See, e.g.*, Lujan v. Defenders of Wildlife, 504 U.S. 555 (1992).
363. 15 U.S.C. § 1125(a)(1).
364. Kroma Makeup EU LLC v. Boldface Licensing + Branding Inc., No. 17-14211 (11th Cir. Apr. 1, 2019).
365. *Id.*
366. *Id.*
367. *Id.*
368. Bauer Bros. LLC v. Nike, Inc., No. 09cv500–WQH–BGS, 2012 WL 1900047, at *10 (S.D. Cal. May 24, 2012).
369. *Id.* at *10 (denying plaintiff's motion for summary judgment on counterclaim for fraud where "Nike has shown sufficient evidence to support an

A defendant seeking to cancel a trademark registration based on fraud must establish the following: (1) a false representation to the PTO regarding a material fact; (2) the registrant's knowledge or belief that the representation is false; (3) the intent to induce reliance upon the misrepresentation and reasonable reliance thereon; and (4) damages proximately caused from resulting on the reliance.[370] It is important to note that a false representation alone is not sufficient—there also must be a willful intent to deceive the PTO.[371]

§ 2:10.4 Unclean Hands

Another defense to trademark infringement is "unclean hands," which has been characterized by the Supreme Court as "rooted in the historical concept of equity as a vehicle for affirmatively enforcing the requirements of conscience and good faith."[372] In the trademark context, there are limits to the kind of conduct that can be labeled "unclean hands." First, the plaintiff's misconduct must relate to the subject matter of the litigation.[373] Second, at least one court has said that the conduct must be serious enough to rise to the level of "egregious" misconduct.[374] Third, because "unclean hands" is an equitable defense, courts will balance the parties' conduct against one another. Accordingly, the plaintiff's alleged "unclean hands" cannot be considered in a vacuum without also evaluating the nature of defendant's conduct that gave rise to the litigation.[375]

In *Levi Strauss & Company v. Shilon*, the Ninth Circuit held that a counterfeiter had no unclean hands entrapment defense where the only proof of infringement was that the defendant offered to sell counterfeit goods to a private investigator. The Ninth Circuit reasoned that even if entrapment were a valid defense to a trademark claim, there was sufficient evidence that the defendant "was predisposed to sell or produce counterfeit clothing."[376]

---

inference that [plaintiff] committed fraud on the PTO in obtaining federal registrations for the trademarks").

370. *Id.* at *9 (quoting Robi v. Five Platters, Inc., 918 F.2d 1439, 1444 (9th Cir. 1990)).

371. *Bauer*, 2012 WL 1900047, at *9 ("There is no fraud if a false misrepresentation is occasioned by an honest misunderstanding or inadvertence") (quotation marks omitted).

372. Precision Instrument Mfg. Co. v. Auto. Maint. Mach. Co., 324 U.S. 806, 814 (1945).

373. Keystone Driller Co. v. General Excavator Co., 290 U.S. 240, 245 (1933).

374. Citizens Fin. Grp., Inc. v. Citizens Nat'l. Bank of Evans City, 383 F.3d 110 (3d Cir. 2004).

375. Republic Molding Corp. v. B.W. Photo Utils., 319 F.2d 347 (9th Cir. 1963).

376. Levi Strauss & Co. v. Shilon, 121 F.3d 1309, 313 (1997).

§ 2:10.5 Nominative Fair Use

The nominative fair use doctrine is another affirmative defense to trademark infringement. The concept of nominative fair use for trademarks was first articulated by the Ninth Circuit in *New Kids on the Block v. News America Publishing, Inc.*, in which the court crafted a special "nominative fair use" analysis for a certain class of cases of alleged infringement, usually involving a competitive need to use another's trademark to identify the plaintiff in a way that was not likely to confuse consumers.[377] This kind of use includes, for example, use in comparative advertising, use in expressive works like film and music, and use in parodies. In *New Kids on the Block*, the defendant conducted a "New Kids on the Block" survey, in which it solicited people's opinions about the band. Recognizing that the suit was "not the classic fair use case where the defendant has used the plaintiff's mark to describe the defendant's *own* product," the court articulated a three-part test for "nominative fair use."[378] First, the product or service in question must be one not readily identifiable without use of the trademark; second, only so much of the mark or marks may be used as is reasonably necessary to identify the product or service; and third, the user must not use the mark in a way that suggests sponsorship or endorsement by the trademark holder.[379] Finding that there was no way to ask people their opinion of the band without using the band's name, the court held that the defendant had not infringed New Kids on the Block's trademark.

In *Playboy Enterprises, Inc. v. Welles*, the Ninth Circuit addressed the concept of nominative fair use once more.[380] Playboy Enterprises, Inc. brought suit against former Playboy Playmate Terri Welles for using the trademarked term "Playmate of the Year" in the metatags on her personal website. Evaluating the likelihood of confusion, the court held that certain uses of the term were non-infringing and "nominative" because Welles could not accurately describe her previous designation as "Playmate of the Year" without using the term. The court further held, however, that repeated uses of the term were excessive and "not necessary" to describe Welles's goods and services.[381]

The Fifth Circuit, in contrast, has held that courts "ordinarily should consider a nominative fair use claim in conjunction with its likelihood-of-confusion analysis in order to avoid lowering the standard for confusion" and that to avail itself of the doctrine, a defendant

---

377. New Kids on the Block v. News Am. Publ'g, Inc., 971 F.2d 302, 305 (9th Cir. 1992).
378. *Id.* at 308.
379. *Id.* (footnote omitted).
380. Playboy Enters., Inc. v. Welles, 279 F.3d 796 (9th Cir. 2002).
381. *Id.* at 801, 805.

must establish that: (1) it only used so much of the plaintiff's marks as was necessary to identify its products or services, and (2) it did not do anything that suggests affiliation, sponsorship, or endorsement by the plaintiff.[382]

In *Century 21 v. Lending Tree*, a divided Third Circuit panel took yet another approach, holding that the "nominative fair use" analysis should not replace the likelihood of confusion analysis, but instead should be analyzed as an affirmative defense to infringement, if the plaintiff can separately establish a likelihood of consumer confusion.[383] Specifically, the Third Circuit held that even if confusion is likely, a defendant can still show that its use of the mark is nevertheless "fair" if it can establish that (1) the use of the plaintiff's mark was necessary to describe plaintiff's product or service, or defendant's product or service; (2) the defendant only used as much of the plaintiff's mark as necessary to describe plaintiff's products or services; and (3) the defendant's conduct or language reflected the true and accurate relationship between the plaintiff and defendant's products or services.[384]

The Court of Appeals Second Circuit, in contrast, has held that courts must consider nominative fair use in the first instance, when deciding the fundamental element of likelihood of confusion, using not only the traditional likelihood of confusion factors, but also (1) whether the use of the plaintiff's mark is necessary to describe both the plaintiff's and the defendant's goods or services; (2) whether the defendant only uses so much of the mark as is necessary; and (3) whether the defendant did anything would suggest sponsorship or endorsement by the plaintiff.[385] The First and Fourth Circuits have declined to endorse any particular test for nominative fair use.[386]

The defense of nominative fair use, however, was explicitly adopted by Congress in devising the Trademark Dilution Revision Act in 2006.[387] As a result, mark owners in all circuits should be aware that use of a trademark to describe a product can result in a finding of nominative fair use that will bar an infringement or dilution action.

---

382. Bd. of Supers. for La. St. Univ. Ag. & Mech. Coll. v. Smack Apparel Co., 550 F.3d 465, 489 (5th Cir. 2008).

383. Century 21 Real Estate Corp. v. Lendingtree, Inc., 425 F.3d 211 (3d Cir. 2005).

384. *Id.*

385. Int'l Info. Sys. Sec. Certification Consortium v. Sec. Univ., LLC, 823 F.3d 153, 168 (2d Cir. 2016).

386. *See, e.g.*, Swarovski Aktiengesellschaft v. Bldg. No. 19, 704 F.3d 44 (1st Cir. 2013); Rosetta Stone Ltd. v. Google, Inc., 676 F.3d 144 (4th Cir. 2012).

387. *See* 15 U.S.C. § 1125(c)(3)(A).

The defense involves a fact-intensive inquiry that often is not suitable for resolution on the pleadings. For example, in 2015, a Brooklyn-based artist Joseph Tierney (a.k.a. "Rime") sued Moschino SpA alleging that the dress Katy Perry wore to the Metropolitan Museum of Art's annual Costume Institute Gala copied his 2012 mural "Vandal Eyes" without his knowledge or consent.[388] Tierney accused Moschino and its designer, Jeremy Scott, of literal misappropriation of his work, including his distinctive signature "Rime," in connection with Moschino's fall/winter 2015 collection. The defendants moved to dismiss Tierney's trademark infringement claim on the basis that, *inter alia,* its use of "Rime" alongside the highlight piece of the collection, which featured "Vandal Eyes," was simply nominative. The court concluded that it could not resolve that fact-intensive inquiry on the pleadings, and stated that any such inquiry "would be better suited in a motion for summary judgment."[389] The parties ultimately settled the lawsuit before the court decided summary judgment.

§ 2:10.6 Laches

Laches is an equitable defense that is available when a trademark owner delays in asserting its rights without excuse, thereby causing prejudice to the defendant. In order to establish a laches defense, a defendant must show that the plaintiff had knowledge of the defendant's use of its marks, that the plaintiff inexcusably delayed in taking action with respect to those marks, and that the defendant will be prejudiced by permitting the plaintiff to assert its rights at this time.[390]

In one case, Chattanooga Manufacturing, Inc. sued Nike, Inc. and basketball star Michael Jordan, alleging infringement of its JORDAN trademark and unfair competition in violation of the Lanham Act.[391] The district court dismissed the claims, finding that the plaintiff had constructive notice of Nike's sale and promotion of Michael Jordan-endorsed products.[392] The Seventh Circuit affirmed, noting that the plaintiff had notice of Nike's sale of "Jordan" products and that it had unreasonably delayed in bringing suit. The court emphasized the fact that Nike had invested substantial sums of money in promoting its

388. Tierney v. Moschino S.p.A., No. 15-cv-05900-SVW-PJW (C.D. Cal. filed Aug. 5, 2015).
389. *Id.*, Dkt. 49, at 7–8.
390. Cuban Cigar Brands N.V. v. Upmann Int'l, Inc., 457 F. Supp. 1090, 1096 (S.D.N.Y. 1978), *aff'd*, 607 F.2d 995 (2d Cir. 1979).
391. Chattanoga Mfg., Inc. v. Nike, Inc., 301 F.3d 789 (7th Cir. 2002).
392. *Id.* at 793.

Jordan products and therefore would suffer extreme prejudice if forced to defend against Chattanooga Manufacturing, Inc.'s claims.[393]

Under the doctrine of "progressive encroachment," however, courts may, under appropriate circumstances, excuse a party's delay in bringing claims against a particular potential infringer.[394] As a general rule, progressive encroachment requires proof that (1) during the period of the delay the plaintiff could reasonably conclude that it should not bring suit to challenge the allegedly infringing activity; (2) the defendant materially altered its infringing activities; and (3) suit was not unreasonably delayed after the alteration in infringing activity.[395] The first and third requirements are self-explanatory. The second requirement "turns . . . on the likelihood of confusion resulting from the defendant's moving into the same or similar market area and placing itself more squarely in competition with the plaintiff."[396] Put succinctly, courts ask "whether [the] defendant, after beginning its use of the mark, redirected its business so that it more squarely competed with plaintiff and thereby increased the likelihood of public confusion of the marks."[397] The second requirement can also be satisfied on a showing that the defendant's use of the mark has changed. For example, where a defendant used a non-infringing mark for years and then changes the mark to an infringing use, the years of non-infringing use are not counted toward laches.[398]

---

393. *Id.* at 795.

394. Oriental Fin. Grp., Inc. v. Cooperativa de Ahorro y Credito Oriental, 698 F.3d 9, 21–22 (1st Cir. 2012); Roederer v. J. Garcia Carrion, S.A., 569 F.3d 855, 859–60 (8th Cir. 2009); Tillamook Country Smoker, Inc. v. Tillamook Cty. Creamery Ass'n, 465 F.3d 1102, 1110 (9th Cir. 2006); ProFitness Physical Therapy Ctr. v. Pro–Fit Orthopedic & Sports Physical Therapy P.C., 314 F.3d 62, 69–70 (2d Cir. 2002); Chattanoga Mfg., Inc. v. Nike, Inc., 301 F.3d 789, 794 (7th Cir. 2002); Kellogg Co. v. Exxon Corp., 209 F.3d 562, 571 (6th Cir. 2000); Kason Indus., Inc. v. Component Hardware Grp., Inc., 120 F.3d 1199, 1205–06 (11th Cir. 1997).

395. *Oriental Fin. Grp.*, Inc., 698 F.3d at 21–22.

396. *Kellogg*, 209 F.3d at 573.

397. ProFitness Physical Therapy, 314 F.3d at 70.

398. Mead Johnson & Co. v. Baby's Formula Svc., Inc., 402 F.2d 19 (5th Cir. 1968) (holding that, where the defendant used a non-infringing mark for years and then changed the mark to an infringing use, the years of non-infringing use are not counted towards laches); Indep. Nail & Packing Co. v. Stronghold Screw Prods., Inc., 205 F.2d 921 (7th Cir. 1953) (rejecting laches defense under the doctrine of progressive encroachment where plaintiff knew that the defendant was making a minimal use of an infringing mark but did not sue until the defendant changed its corporate name to include the infringing mark); O. & W. Thum Co. v. Dickinson, 245 F. 609, 623 (6th Cir. 1917) (rejecting laches defense under progressive encroachment theory where plaintiff "took definite action" after the

In *Newport News Holdings Corp. v. Virtual City Vision, Inc.*, the Fourth Circuit held that the doctrine of laches did not bar a clothing company's infringement claim against the owner of the "newportnews.com" domain name because the clothing company did not unreasonably delay in bringing its claim alleging violation of the ACPA with respect to the company's "Newport News" trademarks.[399] Rather, the company brought its claim one year after the owner of the domain name changed its website from one offering city information to one that competed with the clothing company by advertising women's apparel.[400] Accordingly, there was no laches defense because it was not until the Internet domain owner advertised women's apparel that it became clear that the clothing company had a viable ACPA claim based on the domain owner's bad-faith intent to profit from its infringing domain name.[401]

A related defense is acquiescence, which occurs when a trademark owner consents to infringing conduct. While many cases refer to laches and acquiescence interchangeably, at least one commentator has said that the word "acquiescence" should be used as a defense only in those cases where the trademark owner, by affirmative word or deed, conveys its implied consent to another.[402]

The law associated with laches, acquiescence, and progressive encroachment teaches that any trademark owner wishing to retain the ability to bring an infringement claim must actively police its trademarks and should not sit on its rights when it has notice of infringing activities.

§ 2:10.7 Naked Licensing

Another defense to infringement is called "naked licensing." Naked licensing occurs when a mark owner licenses its mark without acting to protect the quality of the goods or services provided under the licensed mark.[403] The defense is based on the notion that when a trademark owner allows licensees to depart from specific quality

---

defendant had made "radical and apparently permanent changes in [its] trademark and trade dress").

399. Newport News Holdings Corp. v. Virtual City Vision, Inc., 650 F.3d 423, 438 (4th Cir. 2011).

400. *Id.*

401. *Id.*

402. MCCARTHY, *supra* note 30, § 31.41 (2012); *see also* Sara Lee Corp. v. Kayser-Roth Corp., 81 F.3d 455 (4th Cir. 1996).

403. Exxon Corp. v. Oxxford Clothes, Inc., 109 F.3d 1070, 1075 (5th Cir. 1997).

standards, the public will be misled, and the trademark will cease to have utility as an informational device.[404]

Indeed, where a trademark owner has failed to exercise appropriate control and supervision over its licensees, courts can find that the mark holder has effectively abandoned the licensed mark. A finding of abandonment can result in cancellation of all trademark rights against the world,[405] a particular geographic area,[406] or against specific licensees.[407] Indeed, courts have found that abandonment of a mark through naked licensing may have different effects on the validity of the mark in different markets. For example, a finding of naked licensing in the retail market might not result in the loss of trademark rights in the wholesale market.[408]

Because naked licensing is generally relevant only to establish an unintentional abandonment of a trademark, courts place the burden of proof on third parties to show abandonment.[409]

A licensee in a purported naked license may also invoke the defense of naked licensing as a form of estoppel or acquiescence to estop the trademark owner from challenging the use of the mark and business that the licensee has developed during the period of unsupervised use.[410]

There are several examples of naked licensing in the fashion context. In *Eva's Bridal Ltd. v. Halanick Enterprises, Inc.*, for example,

404. Kentucky Fried Chicken Corp. v. Diversified Packaging Corp., 549 F.2d 368, 387 (5th Cir. 1977).

405. *Id.*; *see also* Carl Zeiss Stiftung v. V.E.B. Carl Zeiss, Jena, 293 F. Supp. 892, 918 (S.D.N.Y. 1968) ("a 'naked' license may be the basis for an inference of abandonment where the licensor maintains no control over the quality of goods made by the licensee") (emphasis added; citation omitted), *aff'd as modified*, 433 F.2d 686 (2d Cir. 1970), *cert. denied*, 403 U.S. 905 (1971); 15 U.S.C. § 1115(b)(2).

406. Patsy's Italian Rest., Inc. v. Banas, 658 F.3d 254, 265 (2d Cir. 2011) (mark owner can abandon a mark through naked licensing in a particular geographic area without abandoning its rights throughout the United States).

407. Sweetheart Plastics, Inc. v. Detroit Forming, Inc., 743 F.2d 1039, 1046 (4th Cir. 1984) ("[w]hile abandonment results in a loss of rights as against the whole world, . . . acquiescence is a personal defense which merely results in a loss of rights as against one defendant") (citation omitted).

408. *See* Dawn Donut Co. v. Hart's Food Stores, Inc., 267 F.2d 358, 369 (2d Cir. 1959) (a finding of naked licensing in the retail market would not result in the loss of trademark rights in the wholesale market).

409. *Exxon Corp.*, 109 F.3d at 1075–76.

410. Sheila's Shine Prods., Inc. v. Sheila Shine, Inc., 486 F.2d 114, 123–124 (5th Cir. 1973); Health Indus. v. European Health Spas, 489 F. Supp. 860, 868 (D.S.D. 1980) (discussing claim that reciprocity agreement with trademark owner's employee is sufficient to estop trademark owner from contesting defendant's use of that mark).

the Seventh Circuit addressed a claim of naked licensing in the context of an infringement action brought by the owner of a bridal boutique.[411] The plaintiff owned the mark, "Eva's Bridal," and licensed it to other purveyors of bridal dresses in exchange for royalties. Several years after the license agreement expired, the defendant continued to use the mark, and the owners of the Eva's Bridal mark filed a claim for trademark infringement. The Seventh Circuit held that the mark owner had engaged in naked licensing because it "never tried to control any aspect of how defendants' shop operated or how the mark was used."[412] In defining the level of control necessary to avoid a naked licensing claim, the Seventh Circuit opined that the control must be such that it is "sufficient under the circumstances to insure that the licensee's goods or services would meet the expectations created by the presence of the trademark."[413] Because the mark holder had failed to exercise any control at all, the mark had been abandoned.

To avoid naked licensing concerns, mark holders who license their marks should be careful to ensure that there are comprehensive quality control provisions in any license agreement, but also that such licensee quality controls are applied and enforced. Additional details on this subject may be found below in section 2:14 and in chapter 10.

§ 2:10.8 Parody

Parody is a form of speech protected by the First Amendment and is a defense to trademark infringement on grounds that a parody does not create any likelihood of confusion because consumers are in on the joke. Ultimately, the question is whether the use of plaintiff's trademark—even if the use is a parody—creates a likelihood of confusion. Accordingly, if a defendant charged with infringement claims that it was engaged in a parody of the plaintiff or its trademark, courts must engage in an analysis that reviews the elements of traditional trademark analysis in light of free speech concerns.

There are numerous examples of the parody defense in the fashion context. For example, a federal district court in New Mexico held that use of a LARDASHE mark for pants for plus-size women was not an infringement of the JORDACHE mark for jeans because, while the defendant intentionally parodied the JORDACHE mark, it did not intend any source confusion, and there was no evidence of likely confusion.[414] Likewise, a New York district court dismissed on

411. Eva's Bridal Ltd. v. Halanick Enters., Inc., 639 F.3d 788 (7th Cir. 2011).
412. *Id.* at 790.
413. *Id.* (quoting RESTATEMENT (THIRD) OF UNFAIR COMPETITION § 33 cmt. a (1995)).
414. Jordache Enters. Inc. v. Hogg Wyld, Ltd., 625 F. Supp. 48 (D.N.M. 1985), *aff'd*, 828 F.2d 1482 (10th Cir. 1987).

summary judgment an infringement action brought by the owner of the TOMMY HILFIGER mark against a manufacturer of pet perfume called, TIMMY HOLEDIGGER.[415] The court held that the "defendant's use of the mark is an obvious parody or pun, readily so perceived and unlikely to cause confusion among consumers."[416]

And in *Louis Vuitton Malletier S.A. v. Haute Diggity Dog, LLC*, Louis Vuitton sued a manufacturer of pet products with names like CHEWY VUITON, CHEWNEL #5, DOG PERIGNON, and SNIFFANY & CO.[417] The Fourth Circuit affirmed dismissal on summary judgment on grounds that the defendant's product names were parodies and because there was no likelihood of confusion, there was no actionable trademark infringement. The court noted that "the [defendant's] 'Chewy Vuiton' dog toy undoubtedly and deliberately conjures up the famous LVM marks and trade dress, but at the same time, it communicates that it is not the LVM product."[418] The court went on to observe that

> the juxtaposition of the similar and dissimilar—the irreverent representation and the idealized image of an LVM handbag—immediately conveys a joking and amusing parody. The furry little "Chewy Vuiton" imitation, as something to be chewed by a dog, pokes fun at the elegance and expensiveness of a LOUIS VUITTON handbag, which must not be chewed by a dog.[419]

The lesson of these cases is that parodies of famous marks do not constitute trademark infringement if there is no likelihood of confusion among consumers. Owners of fashion-related trademarks should keep in mind that the more famous the mark, the greater the likelihood of parodies, and under appropriate circumstances, the best reaction to a parody of a mark may be a sense of humor.

There are times, however, when a parody product may run afoul of a trademark owner's rights. In *Anheuser-Busch, Inc. v. VIP Products, LLC*, for example, the owner of the "Budweiser" trademark overcame a claim of parody to obtain a preliminary injunction on its claim for infringement.[420] There, Anheuser-Busch sued the manufacturer of a dog toy called "Buttwiper," a squeeze toy that was similar in shape,

---

415. Tommy Hilfiger Licensing, Inc. v. Nature Labs, LLC, 221 F. Supp. 2d 410, 420 (S.D.N.Y. 2002).
416. *Id.*
417. Louis Vuitton Malletier S.A. v. Haute Diggity Dog, LLC, 507 F.3d 252, 267 (4th Cir. 2007).
418. *Id.* at 260.
419. *Id.* at 260–61.
420. Anheuser-Busch, Inc. v. VIP Prods., LLC, 666 F. Supp. 2d 974 (E.D. Mo. 2008).

color, and labeling to a Budweiser bottle and featured a label showing a dog scooting across the floor on its bottom.[421] In concluding that Anheuser-Busch had established a likelihood of confusion, the court drew important distinctions between the evidence presented by Anheuser-Busch and the evidence put forth by Louis Vuitton and Tommy Hilfiger in the cases discussed above.[422]

First, in both *Haute Diggity Dog* and *Tommy Hilfiger*, neither plaintiff presented any survey evidence of confusion.[423] Anheuser Busch, by contrast, conducted a methodically sound survey that revealed a 30% confusion rate among potential purchasers of dog toys.[424]

Second, there was no competition between the products in *Haute Diggity Dog* or *Tommy Hilfiger*.[425] In *Haute Diggity Dog*, there was no evidence that Louis Vuitton sold dog toys, and there was a significant price difference between the products sold by Louis Vuitton and the dog toy at issue.[426] In *Tommy Hilfiger*, there was no evidence that the plaintiff made a pet perfume or that it intended to do so in the future.[427] Anheuser-Busch, however, demonstrated that it sold a number of pet-related items bearing the Budweiser trademark that were in the same price range as defendant's "Buttwiper" squeaker toy.[428] Several months after the court issued the preliminary injunction, the parties agreed to dismiss with prejudice all claims and defenses.[429]

This line of cases suggests that, as in other areas of trademark law, the success or failure of a parody defense is likely to turn on the strength of a trademark owner's evidence that consumers are likely to be confused as to source, sponsorship, or approval of the defendant's parody. And even in cases where the parody defense succeeds, the courts have recognized that "the doctrinal tests for trademark infringement and trademark dilution by blurring both 'required the application of a fact-intensive, multifactor analysis, making it difficult for [brand owners like] Louis Vuitton to predict the likelihood of success on the merits,'" and "the use of a mark as parody does not necessarily resolve either a dilution or an infringement claim."[430]

---

421. *Id.* at 980–81.
422. *Id.* at 985–86.
423. *Id.*
424. *Id.* at 983.
425. *Id.* at 985–86.
426. *Id.* at 985.
427. *See id.* at 985–86.
428. *Id.* at 985.
429. Order of Dismissal, Anheuser-Busch, Inc. v. VIP Prods., LLC, No. 04 Civ. 0358 (E.D. Mo. Jan. 28, 2009).
430. Louis Vuitton Malletier, S.A. v. My Other Bag, Inc., No. 18-293-cv (2d Cir. Mar. 15, 2019) (quoting opinion of district court below).

§ 2:10.9 Aesthetic Functionality

The doctrine of "aesthetic functionality" is one of the most important concepts in evaluating trademark protection for fashion designs. The doctrine comes into play where the aesthetic design of a product is *itself* the mark for which protection is sought, but giving the mark holder the right to use that mark exclusively would adversely affect competition in the relevant market. In other words, "aesthetic functionality" is a doctrine created by courts to balance the need to protect inventive designs with the need to preserve competition between designers. The Supreme Court has confirmed this objective, observing that the doctrine "prevents trademark law, which seeks to promote competition by protecting a firm's reputation, from instead inhibiting legitimate competition by allowing a producer to control a useful product feature."[431]

The term "aesthetic functionality" was proposed as early as 1938,[432] but the first court to adopt the doctrine as a basis for denying protection of a design was the U.S. Court of Appeals for the Ninth Circuit in 1952.[433] There, the court determined that the Wallace China Company was not entitled to the exclusive use of a floral design on hotel china, despite its creation of "a substantial market" for its designs "by virtue of extensive advertising"[434] because the design satisfied "a demand for the aesthetic as well as for the utilitarian."[435] The court reasoned that because the "particular feature is an important ingredient in the commercial success of the product, the interest in free competition permits its imitation in the absence of a patent or copyright."[436]

In 1995, the Supreme Court expressly endorsed the aesthetic functionality doctrine, holding that "[t]he ultimate test of aesthetic functionality . . . is whether the recognition of trademark rights [in an

---

431. Qualitex Co. v. Jacobson Prods. Co., 514 U.S. 159, 164 (1995).

432. In 1938, the *Restatement of Torts* stated that "[a] feature of goods is functional . . . if it affects their purpose, action or performance, or the facility or economy of processing, handling or using them; it is non-functional if it does not have any of such effects." RESTATEMENT OF TORTS § 742 (1938). In the official comment to that section, the Restatement identified several characteristics of "functional" goods. With regard to "goods [that] are bought largely for their aesthetic value," the Restatement suggested that "their features may be functional because they definitely contribute to that value and thus aid the performance of an object for which the goods are intended." *Id.* § 742, cmt. a.

433. Pagliero v. Wallace China Co., 198 F.2d 339 (9th Cir. 1952).

434. *Id.* at 340.

435. *Id.* at 343–44.

436. *Id.* at 343.

aesthetic design feature] would significantly hinder competition."[437] In *Qualitex Company v. Jacobson Products Co., Inc.*, a manufacturer of green and gold press pads used in dry cleaning establishments brought an action against a competitor alleging trademark infringement and unfair competition.[438] The Court held that the green and gold color of the pads could be registered as a trademark because the color was not a functional component of the underlying product. The Court explained that, "'[i]n general terms, a product feature is functional,' and cannot serve as a trademark, 'if it is essential to the use or purpose of the article or if it affects the cost or quality of the article,' that is, if exclusive use of the feature would put competitors at a significant non-reputation-related disadvantage."[439]

Six years later, the Supreme Court reiterated its *Qualitex* analysis, declaring that where "[a]esthetic functionality [is] the central question," courts must "inquire" as to whether recognizing the trademark "would put competitors at a significant non-reputation-related disadvantage."[440]

Based on these cases, the test for aesthetic functionality is highly fact-specific and has three components. First, courts ask whether the design feature is "essential to the use or purpose" or whether it "affects the cost or quality" of the product at issue. If a design feature falls into either category, it is "functional" and not subject to trademark protection.[441] If, on the contrary, the design feature is not "functional" under this rubric, it must be shown *not* to have a significant effect on competition in order to receive trademark protection. In conducting this inquiry, courts must consider both the markholder's right to enjoy the benefits of its effort to distinguish and brand its product, as well as the public's right to a "vigorously competitive market" protected by the Lanham Act, which an overly broad trademark might hinder.[442]

The manner in which the doctrine is applied depends on the circuit in which the case is litigated. The Second Circuit applies the doctrine

---

437. Qualitex Co. v. Jacobson Prods. Co., 514 U.S. 159, 170 (1995) (quoting RESTATEMENT (THIRD) OF UNFAIR COMPETITION § 17 cmt. c, at 176 (1993)) (internal quotation marks omitted).

438. *Id.*

439. *Qualitex*, 514 U.S. at 165 (quoting Inwood Labs., Inc. v. Ives Labs., Inc., 456 U.S. 844, 850 n.10 (1982)).

440. TrafFix Devices, Inc. v. Mktg. Displays, Inc., 532 U.S. 23, 32–33 (2001).

441. *See, e.g.*, Industria Arredamenti Fratelli Saporiti v. Charles Craig, Ltd., 725 F.2d 18, 19 (2d Cir. 1984) (interlocking design of couch cushions was a visual "label" but served a utilitarian purpose by keeping cushions in place and was therefore functional).

442. Christian Louboutin, S.A. v. Yves Saint Laurent Am. Holdings, Inc., 696 F.3d 206, 222 (2d Cir. 2012).

consistent with the Supreme Court's analysis. The Fifth Circuit, on the other hand, has expressly rejected the doctrine, though it applies a variant, which it calls, "the competitive necessity test."[443] The Sixth Circuit has acknowledged the doctrine but never formally adopted it.[444] The Seventh Circuit has held that "[f]ashion is a form of function" and applies the doctrine liberally, sometimes relying on utility patents as "cheat sheets" on the theory that any design claimed in a patent is supposed to be useful.[445] And the Ninth Circuit has applied the doctrine inconsistently.[446]

[A] The *Louboutin* Case

In *Christian Louboutin S.A. v. Yves Saint Laurent America Holding, Inc.*, two fashion icons went head to head over the question whether a single color may serve as a legally protected trademark in the fashion industry.[447]

Christian Louboutin stormed onto the shoe scene in the 1990s with red-soled shoes reminiscent of Louis XIV. After two decades of commercial success, Yves Saint Laurent (YSL) began selling a collection of monochromatic footwear featuring colored insoles, heels, uppers, and outsoles in various colors, including red. Perceiving a threat to its red-soled signature, Louboutin sued YSL seeking disgorgement of profits, actual damages, statutory damages, reasonable attorney's fees and costs, and an injunction prohibiting YSL from selling red-soled shoes.

The district court ruled for YSL.[448] Citing famous trademark cases involving Louis Vuitton's multi-colored monogram and Burberry's signature plaid, the trial court determined that the Lanham Act permitted registration of color as a trademark only in distinct patterns or

---

443. Bd. of Supervisors for La. State Univ. Agric. & Mech. Coll. v. Smack Apparel Co., 550 F.3d 465, 487–88 (5th Cir. 2008) (arguing that the Supreme Court has recognized the aesthetic functionality doctrine only in dicta, and that therefore the Fifth Circuit's long-standing rejection of the doctrine was not abrogated). The "competitive necessity" test is simply the final prong of the "aesthetic functionality" inquiry and asks whether the feature is one "the exclusive use of which would put competitors at a significant non-reputation-related disadvantage." *Id.* at 486 (internal quotation marks omitted).

444. Maker's Mark Distillery, Inc. v. Diageo N. Am., Inc., 679 F.3d 410, 417–19 (6th Cir. 2012).

445. Jay Franco & Sons, Inc. v. Franek, 615 F.3d 855, 860 (7th Cir. 2010) (collecting cases for the proposition that "fashionable designs can be freely copied unless protected by patent law").

446. MCCARTHY, *supra* note 30, § 7.80 (collecting cases).

447. Christian Louboutin, S.A. v. Yves Saint Laurent Am. Holdings, Inc., 778 F. Supp. 2d 445 (S.D.N.Y. 2011).

448. *Id.*

combinations.[449] The district court reasoned that "color serves ornamental and aesthetic functions vital to robust competition [in the fashion industry]," and therefore "Louboutin is unlikely to be able to prove that its red outsole brand is entitled to trademark protection, even if it has gained enough public recognition in the market to have acquired secondary meaning."

The Second Circuit reversed this determination as inconsistent with *Qualitex*, holding that Louboutin's registered red-sole trademark, which consisted of "a red, lacquered outsole on a high fashion woman's shoe," had acquired secondary meaning as a distinctive symbol. Citing Louboutin's considerable advertising and marketing expenditures and the successful fame and association of the red soles with Louboutin, the Second Circuit concluded that the red outsole, when used with a contrasting upper shoe, had come to identify and distinguish the Louboutin brand and thus was a distinctive symbol that qualified for trademark protection under the Lanham Act.[450]

Nevertheless, the Second Circuit *affirmed* the district court's decision to deny Louboutin's request for an injunction of YSL's sale of monochromatic red shoes. Importantly, the Second Circuit concluded that Louboutin was not likely to succeed in its ultimate infringement claim, as YSL's buyers were unlikely to conclude that red-only shoes emanate from the same source as Louboutin's shoes, because Louboutin's shoes are known for contrasting red soles from the color scheme of the rest of the shoe.[451]

[B] *Eliya v. Steven Madden*

In *Eliya, Inc. v. Steven Madden, Ltd.*, Eliya sued Madden for copying three shoe designs: the Lulia shoe, the Comfi shoe, and the Catwalk shoe. Each of these shoes had one-fourth inch multi-color or multi-shaded wide straps that "form[ed] a distinctive alternating pattern on the upper portion of the shoe, and an appendage on the heel that extends higher than the weave portion and includes cutouts through which the weave can be seen."[452] Eliya alleged that, through the aforementioned features, Eliya gave its shoes an "innovative and unique look" and that "consumers have come to identify Eliya as their

---

449. *Id.* at 451 (citing Louis Vuitton Malletier S.A. v. Dooney & Bourke, 454 F.3d 108, 116 (2d Cir. 2006); Burberry Ltd. v. Euro Moda, Inc., No. 08 Civ. 5781(CM), 2009 WL 1675080, at *5 (S.D.N.Y. June 10, 2009)).

450. Christian Louboutin S.A. v. Yves Saint Laurent Am. Holding, Inc., 696 F.3d 206, 225–27 (2d Cir. 2012).

451. *Id.* at 228.

452. Eliya, Inc. v. Steven Madden, Ltd., No. 15-1272 (DRH)(SIL), 2018 WL 1027157, at *1 (E.D.N.Y. Feb 22, 2018).

source . . . ."[453] Eliya accused Madden of copying the design on its Bernie Mev shoes. The magistrate judge issued a report and recommendation that Eliya's complaint be dismissed for failure to state a claim of trade dress infringement.

In considering Eliya's objections to the magistrate judge's recommendation, the district court first explained that a party alleging trade dress infringement of a product design must allege "a precise expression of the character and scope of the claimed trade dress," and facts that plausibly demonstrate that "the claimed trade dress i[s] non-functional," "the claimed trade dress has acquired secondary meaning" and "there is a likelihood of confusion between the plaintiff's goods and the defendant's."[454] With respect to functionality, the court noted that there "is a statutory presumption that features are deemed functional until proved otherwise by the party seeking trade dress protection."[455] Analyzing the shoes at issue, the court concluded that there was no evidence to support non-functionality because the components at issue were functional—that is, straps and a raised heel appendage. And as for the ornamental features of the straps, such as their multi-colors, the court concluded that those features did not serve to identify the shoes' source. As such, the court adopted the magistrate judge's report and recommendation, and granted Madden's motion to dismiss. The Second Circuit affirmed the dismissal.[456]

[C] *PUMA v. Forever 21*

The aesthetic functionality doctrine has important implications for fashion designers at the pleadings stage. While functionality is a question of fact not generally suitable for resolution on a motion to dismiss, courts are careful to scrutinize whether a trade dress plaintiff has adequately pled non-functionality in the first place. That is, courts agree that even though the doctrine implicates questions of fact, non-functionality must be sufficiently pled in order to permit a trade dress infringement action to proceed beyond the pleadings.

In *Puma SE v. Forever 21, Inc.*, the Puma fashion brand alleged that retailer Forever 21 copied three of the most prominent footwear designs from singer Rihanna's Fenty collection for Puma in an attempt to trade on the substantial goodwill of Rihanna, Puma, and the Fenty shoes.[457] Puma alleged that Forever 21 copied the Fur Slide and Bow Slide styles of its shoes, among others, and, accordingly,

453. *Id.*
454. *Id.* at *2 (citations omitted).
455. *Id.* at *3 (internal citations omitted).
456. Eliya, Inc. v. Steven Madden, Ltd., No. 18-831 (2d Cir. Oct. 23, 2018).
457. Puma SE v. Forever 21, Inc., No. 17-cv-02523-PSG-E (C.D. Cal. filed Mar. 31, 2017, terminated Nov. 13, 2018).

brought claims of trademark, copyright, and patent infringement. With respect to the trade dress infringement claim, Puma argued that Forever 21's designs were confusingly similar to those of Rihanna's Fenty line. Specifically, for the "Fur Slide," Puma claimed that the "trade dress consists of, at least, a thick sandal base with a wide plush fur strap extending to the base of the sandal, and a satin foam backing, and shares the deep bowl for the foot (albeit in a sandal)." And for the "Bow Slide," Puma claimed that the trade dress consists of "a thick sandal base decorated by a wide, casually knotted satin bow with pointed endings atop the side strap in addition to satin foam backing, and the same deep bowl for the foot."

Forever 21 moved to dismiss the trade dress claim on the basis that Puma failed to plead facts supporting that the Fenty shoes' trade dress is non-functional because Puma fails to even address non-functionality in its complaint. In opposition, Puma argued that non-functionality had been asserted in allegations such as the Bow Slide having a "casually knotted bow with pointed endings," or the Fenty Shoes being associated with their brand ambassador Rihanna. The court rejected Puma's argument. The court noted that it has long held that non-functionality is not implicitly pleaded when the complaint provides a description of an overall aesthetic look of a product, and that plaintiffs are required to allege *how* their trade dress is non-functional.[458] Accordingly, the court granted Forever 21's motion to dismiss the trade dress claim, with leave to amend. The parties subsequently announced a settlement, dismissing all claims with prejudice.[459]

§ 2:11 Search Engine and Internet Advertising as Infringement

In recent decades, the Internet and the rise of e-commerce has allowed brand owners to reach a wider audience and sell directly to consumers. At the same time, the Internet has presented unique challenges for brand owners seeking to enforce their trademark rights. One of the biggest challenges facing trademark owners is, of course, the use of the Internet to sell counterfeit goods bearing unauthorized copies of protected marks, a topic that is discussed in detail in chapter 7. In addition to grappling with the ongoing problem of counterfeits, trademark owners also face the possibility of consumer

458. *Id.*, Dkt. 61, at 9–10.

459. Hilary George-Parkin, *Puma and Forever 21 Settle Contentious Fenty Footwear Lawsuit*, FOOTWEAR NEWS (Nov. 9, 2018), https://footwearnews.com/2018/business/news/puma-forever-21-fenty-lawsuit-settlement-1202704966/.

confusion in connection with the use of trademarks in search engine and Internet advertising.

§ 2:11.1 Use of Trademarks as Metatags

One of the earliest unique forms of trademark disputes in the online context arose when websites started to use the trademarks of others in metatags. A metatag is Hyper Text Markup Language (HTML) code that describes the content of a website. The use of a trademark term in a metatag is typically challenged as an act of trademark infringement, unfair competition, or trademark dilution because the express purpose of using a trademark in a metatag is to cause the website to appear among search engine results when Internet users search for that trademark online and thus divert the users from the website of the trademark owner.[460] Challenges of this kind have declined, as modern search engines have moved away from the use of metatags.

The majority of courts that have analyzed use of trademark terms in metatags generally have concluded that such a practice results in actionable "initial interest confusion." Even though consumers eventually become aware that they have not reached the website they initially sought, they still have been momentarily led astray and may not attempt to reach their previously intended target.[461] In the leading case discussing the use of metatags, *Brookfield Communications, Inc. v. West Coast Entertainment Corp.*, the court applied this idea of initial interest confusion.[462] Internet users who are taken to a defendant's website by a search engine relying on metatags may find a substantially similar website or service to the plaintiff's and may choose to remain at the defendant's site due to convenience. Therefore,

---

460. *See, e.g.*, Bayer Corp. v. Custom Sch. Frames, LLC, 259 F. Supp. 2d 503 (E.D. La. 2003).

461. *See, e.g.*, Eli Lilly & Co. v. Natural Answers, Inc., 233 F.3d 456, 464 (7th Cir. 2000) ("Such confusion, which is actionable under the Lanham Act, occurs when a consumer is lured to a product by its similarity to a known mark, even though the consumer realizes the true identity and origin of the product before consummating a purchase."); Nespresso USA, Inc. v. Africa Am. Coffee Trading Co., No. 15 Civ. 5553 (LTS), 2016 WL 3162118, at *6 n.6 (S.D.N.Y. June 2, 2016) (inferring defendant's intent to cause initial interest confusion by using plaintiff's mark in metatags, which "might lead consumers from the trademark holder's website to the website of a competitor" and, in turn, "might cause the consumer to remain on the competitor's website and utilize the competitor's goods or services instead of returning to the initially-sought mark holder's website").

462. Brookfield Commc's, Inc. v. West Coast Entm't Corp., 174 F.3d 1036 (9th Cir. 1999).

"[a]lthough there is no source confusion in the sense that consumers know they are patronizing [the defendant] West Coast rather than [the plaintiff] Brookfield, there is nevertheless initial interest confusion in the sense that, by using 'moviebuff.com' or 'MovieBuff' to divert people looking for 'MovieBuff' to its web site, West Coast improperly benefits from the goodwill that Brookfield developed in its mark."[463] In embedding trademark terms in its website metatags, the defendant utilized another's trademark "in a manner calculated 'to capture initial consumer attention.'"[464] As a result of this behavior, even if "no actual sale is finally completed as a result of the confusion, [there] may be still an infringement."[465] The court analogized the metatagging behavior to "posting a sign with another's trademark in front of one's store."[466] This view of metatagging has been adopted by numerous courts.[467]

The use of trademarks in metatags has also been interpreted by courts as evidence of bad faith and intent to confuse consumers, thus invalidating various affirmative defenses offered by defendants. For example, in *Australian Gold, Inc. v. Hatfield*, the court rejected the first sale defense offered by the defendants because the use of trademarks in the site's metatags "[gave] the impression that they are favored or authorized dealers for a product when in fact they are not."[468]

---

463. *Id.* at 1062.
464. *Id.* (citation omitted).
465. *Id.*
466. *Id.* at 1064.
467. *See, e.g.*, North Am. Med. Corp. v. Axiom Worldwide, Inc., 522 F.3d 1211, 1222 (11th Cir. 2008) ("a company's use in meta tags of its competitor's trademarks may result in a likelihood of confusion"); Australian Gold, Inc. v. Hatfield, 436 F.3d 1228, 1239 (10th Cir. 2006) (in using trademarks in metatags, "Defendants used the goodwill associated with Plaintiffs' trademarks in such a way that consumers might be lured to the lotions from Plaintiffs' competitors"); Promatek Indus., Ltd. v. Equitrac Corp., 300 F.3d 808, 814 (7th Cir. 2002) (affirming district court's grant of a preliminary injunction where plaintiff alleged Lanham Act violation based on defendant's use of the trademark in metatags); L&A Designs v. Xtreme ATVs, Inc., No. 03:10-CV-627, 2012 U.S. Dist. LEXIS 60760, at *24 (D. Or. Apr. 30, 2012) ("Because the metatags are not visible to the consumer, initial interest confusion is more likely here."); Soilworks, LLC v. Midwest Indus. Supply, Inc., 575 F. Supp. 2d 1118, 1132 (D. Ariz. 2008) (finding for defendant in its counterclaim, court held that use of trademarks in metatags "divert[ed] the initial attention of potential Internet customers to [plaintiff's] websites"); Fin. Express LLC v. Nowcom Corp., 564 F. Supp. 2d 1160 (C.D. Cal. 2008) (concluding that the use of trademarks in metatags was not descriptive and instead intended to confuse consumers and capitalize from plaintiff's goodwill).
468. *Australian Gold*, 436 F.3d at 1241.

§ 2:11.2 Use of Trademarks in Search Engine Advertising

Search engine advertising is a form of Internet marketing in which advertisers pay to have advertisements for their goods or services appear when Internet users enter specific terms—or related terms—into a search engine. The most prominent example of this is Google AdWords. In addition to generating search results based on a "natural" keyword search, Google also displays paid advertisements known as "sponsored links." Google allows multiple advertisers to bid on the same keyword, and then ranks their placement on the page, in part, based on how much each advertiser is willing to pay Google if an Internet user clicks on its sponsored link to be taken to a website of the advertiser's choosing. This is commonly referred to as the "pay-per-click" model, meaning that the advertiser pays whenever a user of Google's search engine clicks on the sponsored link. When consumers type the keywords into the search engine's browser, the results will include a sponsored link to the advertiser's website.

Search engine advertising, moreover, is particularly important for fashion, luxury, and other brand owners because of the number of online retailers. For example, a user searching the term "Prada handbag" will be shown results for advertisers that have bid on the "Prada handbag" keyword (or another term that Google's "broad match" algorithm has determined is related to the term "Prada handbag"). And although Google is willing to allow a brand owner like Prada to bid on their own marks, Google simultaneously allows or encourages other advertisers to bid on the same terms, whether to resell genuine trademark goods or to compete directly against the trademark owner. Brand owners have expressed concern about this practice, asserting that many Internet users do not understand that the "search results" that Google and others prominently display are, in fact, paid advertising that may make it more difficult for consumers to reach the legitimate websites of the brands they search. When sponsored links also use the mark in the text of the links, the likelihood of confusion may be even more acute.

Claims of trademark infringement began to arise soon after search engines began selling trademarked keywords to third-party advertisers without the consent of the marks' owners. Although some courts initially struggled with the question of whether selling a trademark term as a keyword could even give rise to potential trademark liability, the universal consensus is now that the sale of a mark as a search keyword constitutes a "use in commerce" that triggers liability under the Lanham Act if the trademark owner can establish the likelihood of consumer confusion.[469]

Courts have varied, however, in analyzing the likelihood of confusion question in the keyword context. Separate courts, for example, have emphasized different specific Confusion Factors in analyzing allegations of online trademark infringement.[470] For a time, the Ninth Circuit in particular had emphasized the so-called Internet "troika" factors: (1) the similarity of the marks, (2) the relatedness of the goods and services, and (3) the simultaneous use of the Internet as a marketing channel.[471] In 2010 and 2011, however, the Ninth Circuit and other circuit courts made clear that courts' analyses of these issues must remain flexible and depend on the specific facts of the case alleged.[472] As a result, a plaintiff seeking relief for the unauthorized use of its marks as keywords should be prepared to

---

469. *See, e.g.*, Rescuecom Corp. v. Google Inc., 562 F.3d 127 (2d Cir. 2009) (holding that the sale of trademarks as keywords constitutes a use in commerce); Network Automation, Inc. v. Advanced Sys. Concepts, Inc., 638 F.3d 1137, 1144 (9th Cir. 2011) (holding that "the use of a trademark as a search engine keyword that triggers the display of a competitor's advertisement is a 'use in commerce' under the Lanham Act").

470. *Network Automation, Inc.*, 638 F.3d at 1148 (emphasizing certain likelihood of confusion factors to consider in keyword advertising cases; "Given the multifaceted nature of the Internet and the ever-expanding ways in which we all use the technology . . . it makes no sense to prioritize the same three factors for every type of potential online community activity"); Playboy Enters., Inc. v. Netscape Commc'ns, Inc., 354 F.3d 1020, 1026 (9th Cir. 2004) ("In the Internet context, courts must be flexible in the factors, as some may not apply. Moreover, some factors are more important than others."); Checkpoint Sys. Inc. v. Check Point Software Techs., Inc., 269 F.3d 270 280 (3d Cir. 2001) (no single factor is "determinative" and "each factor must be weighed and balanced one against the other[,]" although the weight given to each factor will depend on the individual circumstances of the specific case); Hearts on Fire Co. v. Blue Nile, Inc., 603 F. Supp. 2d 264, 289 (D. Mass. 2009) (offering multi-factored test in the context of sponsored links as a supplement to the traditional likelihood of confusion factors); Trans Union LLC v. Credit Research, Inc., 142 F. Supp. 2d 1029, 1044 (N.D. Ill. 2001) (emphasizing certain factors as "the most important considerations" when considering online confusion.).

471. GoTo.com, Inc. v. Walt Disney Co., 202 F.3d 1199, 1205 (9th Cir. 2000).

472. *Network Automation, Inc.*, 638 F.3d at 1144, 1154 (focusing on a subset of the traditional likelihood-of-confusion factors as "the most relevant factors" for courts to consider in keyword cases: (i) the strength of the plaintiff's mark; (ii) the evidence of actual confusion; (iii) the type of goods and degree of care likely to be exercised by the purchaser; and (iv) the labeling and appearance of the advertisements and the surrounding context on the screen displaying the results); Coll. Network, Inc. v. Moore Educ. Publishers, Inc., 38 F. App'x 403 (5th Cir. 2010).

demonstrate likelihood of confusion using the traditional Confusion Factors.

In *Rosetta Stone Ltd. v. Google Inc.*, Rosetta Stone sued Google claiming that it had directly and secondarily infringed Rosetta Stone's trademark by selling it as a keyword for Internet searches.[473] Rosetta Stone alleged that Google's policy concerning the use of trademarks in keywords and ad text created a likelihood of confusion and also led to some consumers unknowingly purchasing counterfeit Rosetta Stone software. The trial court, however, concluded that there was no likelihood of confusion and granted summary judgment to Google.[474]

On appeal, the Fourth Circuit reversed, concluding that "there [was] sufficient evidence in the record to create a question of fact . . . to preclude summary judgment," and that the trial court had incorrectly applied trademark law.[475] Specifically, the Fourth Circuit held that "[m]ore than just source confusion is at issue in an infringement claim" and confusion as to "'*sponsorship* of the goods'" can give rise to a claim under the Lanham Act.[476] In determining whether confusion is likely, the Fourth Circuit emphasized that courts should continue to use the traditional likelihood-of-confusion multi-factor test and, in particular, to provide "at least a brief explanation of its reasons"[477] for concluding that certain factors are not relevant, even if "there is no hard and fast rule that obligates the district court to discuss each non-mandatory factor."[478] Importantly, the Court of Appeals noted Rosetta's Stone's evidence—including internal Google studies—indicating that when consumers search for a trademark term, many are likely to be confused into believing that the links most prominently displayed by Google would take them to Rosetta Stone's company websites or a website endorsed by Rosetta Stone.[479] Viewing the contested facts in the light most favorable to Rosetta Stone, as required on a motion for summary judgment, the Fourth Circuit

473. Rosetta Stone Ltd. v. Google, Inc., 730 F. Supp. 2d 531, 541, 97 U.S.P.Q.2d 1855 (E.D. Va. 2010), *aff'd in part, rev'd in part*, 676 F.3d 144 (4th Cir. 2012) (remanding for further proceedings on plaintiff's claims for direct infringement, contributory infringement and dilution).

474. *Id.*

475. Rosetta Stone Ltd. v. Google, Inc., 676 F.3d 144, 160 (4th Cir. 2012).

476. *Id.* at 157 (quoting PETA v. Doughney, 263 F.3d 359, 366 (4th Cir. 2001)) (emphasis added by the court).

477. *Id.* at 155.

478. *Id.* at 154.

479. *Id.* at 156–58 (describing "both survey and anecdotal evidence of actual confusion in connection with Google's use of trademarks in its AdWords program"); *see also* Expert Reports in Am. Airlines, Inc. v. Google Inc., No. 4:07-CV-487-A (N.D. Tex. May 22, 2008); Am. Airlines, Inc. v. Yahoo! Inc., No. 4:08-CV-626-A (N.D. Tex. Aug. 17, 2009).

concluded that Rosetta Stone had proffered enough evidence that a reasonable jury could reach a finding of infringement.[480]

After the case was remanded to the trial court, the parties reached a settlement that Rosetta Stone's general counsel described as "a significant victory for consumer protection" that "goes a long way toward advancing our goal to strengthen the Rosetta Stone brand and trademarks around the world," by "enlist[ing] Google in our ongoing fight against online piracy and counterfeiting . . . ."[481] The specifics of the settlement, however, remain undisclosed.[482]

Not all trademark holders have sued search engines, however. Indeed, many have sued their competitors based on allegations that the *advertisers'* purchases of trademarks were likely to cause consumer confusion. In some of these lawsuits, courts accepted the theory that consumers are likely to be confused.[483] And courts

---

480. *Rosetta Stone*, 676 F.3d at 160.

481. Megan Leonhardt, *Rosetta Stone, Google Settle AdWords Trademark Row*, LAW360 (Oct. 31, 2012), https://www.law360.com/articles/390911/rosetta-stone-google-settle-adwords-trademark-row.

482. Google had also settled claims brought by American Airlines over Google's use of American's trademarks in its AdWords program on the eve of a hearing into American's allegations of discovery misconduct. Order, Am. Airlines, Inc. v. Google Inc., No. 4:07-CV-487-A (N.D. Tex. July 3, 2008) ("The court's preliminary review causes the court to believe that defendant, Google, Inc., has declined to comply with [the court's discovery orders]."); Brendan Pierson, *American Airlines, Google Settle Trademark Dispute*, LAW360 (July 18, 2008); Craig Anderson, *In a War of AdWords, Google Scores Many Victories*, L.A. DAILY J., Oct. 11, 2010 ("a quick look at Google's search results suggests one possible term of the deal: While the search results for other airlines include a long list of 'sponsored links,' American Airlines' search result has no advertisements at all").

483. *See, e.g.*, Coachella Music Festival, LLC v. Simms, No. 2:17-cv-06059 RGK (GJSx), 2018 WL 1409739, at *2 (C.D. Cal. Jan. 4, 2018) (preliminarily enjoining defendant from using "Coachella" as a metatag); Nat'l Grange of the Order of Patrons of Husbandry v. California Guild, 334 F. Supp. 3d 1057, 1071 (E.D. Cal. 2018) (preliminarily enjoining defendant from using plaintiff's trademark and other similar marks as advertising keywords); Feldenkrais Guild of N. Am. v. Wildman, No. 18-CV-2340-YGR, 2018 WL 2331905, at *6 (N.D. Cal. May 23, 2018) (preliminarily enjoining defendant from using plaintiff's trademarks as a keyword or metatag); FenF, LLC v. Smarthingz, Inc., No. 12-cv-14770, 2014 WL 1304779, at *2 (E.D. Mich. Mar. 28, 2014) (granting summary judgment for trademark holder where defendant sold a "product that compete[d]" with the plaintiff's product in "the same on-line channels" and the defendant's purchase of the plaintiff's mark as a keyword meant that the defendant's "website would be listed and advertised before FenF's website when internet users searched for [the mark] through Google's search engine"); Binder v. Disability Grp., Inc., 772 F. Supp. 2d 1172, 1176–77

continue to hold that trademark complaints based on the use of keywords to trigger sponsored link advertising state a claim for which relief may be granted if they allege that consumers are not able to distinguish between links to the website of the advertiser and links to the website of the trademark owner.[484]

(C.D. Cal. 2011) (holding that trademark holder established infringement where parties provided "identical" services and the defendants "intentionally chose Plaintiff's mark based on its strength and appeal in the market," and the parties "market[ed] their products through the Internet and rel[ied] upon it to obtain clients"); Storus Corp. v. Aroa Mktg., Inc., No. 4:2006cv07376, 2008 WL 449835 (N.D. Cal. Feb. 15, 2008); World Entm't, Inc. v. Brown, No. 09-5365, 2011 WL 2036686 (E.D. Pa. May 20, 2011) (enjoining defendant from using keywords "containing plaintiffs' CTO trademark, or any mark incorporating plaintiffs' CTO trademark, colorable imitations thereof or any confusingly similar mark"); Quidgeon v. Olsen, No. 10-cv-1168, 2011 WL 1480537 (C.D. Ill. Apr. 19, 2011) (enjoining defendant from using plaintiff's mark, "or any similar or confusing variations thereof," as keywords for Internet search engines); Partners for Health & Home, L.P. v. Yang, No. CV 09-07849 (CBM) (RZx) (C.D. Cal. Sept. 13, 2010) (granting preliminary injunction enjoining the purchase of hyphenated and non-hyphenated versions of mark as keywords); Skydive Ariz., Inc. v. Quattrocchi, No. CV–05–2656–PHX–MHM, 2010 WL 1743189 (D. Ariz. Apr. 29, 2010) (enjoining defendant from using "Skydive Arizona" mark, as well as "Skydiving Arizona" and "Arizona Skydiving" as search keywords); *see also, e.g.*, Australian Gold, Inc. v. Hatfield, 436 F.3d 1228, 1239 (10th Cir. 2006) (holding that when an advertiser paid a search engine to list the advertiser "in a preferred position whenever a computer use searched for Plaintiffs' trademarks," it was an "attempt[] to divert traffic to Defendants' web sites" that "used the goodwill associated with Plaintiffs' trademarks in such a way that consumers might be lured to the" products of the trademark owner's "competitors" in a way that constituted a "violation of the Lanham Act").

484. *See, e.g.*, Xymogen, Inc. v. Digitalev, LLC, No: 6:17-cv-869-Orl-31KRS, 2018 WL 659723, at *4 (M.D. Fla. Feb. 1, 2018) ("Plaintiff's allegations" that products were similar and that Google AdWords "do not always clearly identify themselves as advertisements," among others, were "more than enough to raise [Plaintiff's] right to relief above the speculative level" and survive a motion to dismiss); St. George Exec. Shuttle, LLC v. W. Trails Charters & Tours LLC, No. 2:17-CV-900-DN, 2018 WL 3350348, at *3 (D. Utah July 9, 2018) (denying defendant's motion to dismiss, finding the purchase of plaintiff's trademark as an AdWord keyword constitutes a use in commerce); Julian Bakery, Inc. v. Healthsource Int'l, Inc., No. 16-cv-2594-JAH (KSC), 2018 WL 1524499, at *5 (S.D. Cal. Mar. 28, 2018) (denying defendant's motion to dismiss plaintiff's trademark infringement claim, finding the facts alleged support an inference that defendant's online advertising that utilizes plaintiff's trademark as a keyword is likely to confuse consumers).

In other suits, however, courts have rejected the claim.[485] One court even "agree[d] with" a party's "assessment" that "there is a growing consensus in the case authorities that purchasing trademarked keywords for the purpose of competitive keyword advertising does not violate the Lanham Act."[486] While that *dictum* appears to be an outlier among courts, it is true that some courts have been particularly skeptical of trademark infringement claims in certain circumstances, especially (1) where defendants incorporate prominent disclaimers or courts believe that Internet consumers are particularly savvy or skeptical of associating search terms with search results, and (2) where consumers are sophisticated or products are particularly expensive, such that consumers would exercise a higher degree of care than in the average situation.[487] In 2015, for example, one court was "unpersuaded" that a party infringed by purchasing another's trademark as a keyword because the "advertisements" triggered "d[id] not use [the plaintiff's marks] in the advertisement itself," and "each [advertisement was] either separated from the search results or plainly labeled as a sponsored advertisement."[488] And in 2013, the Court of Appeals for the Tenth Circuit found that trademark owner 1-800 Contacts, Inc. did not meet its evidentiary burden of proving a likelihood of confusion where only twenty-five Internet users (1.5%) clicked on the competitor's sponsored link.[489]

Although most of the attention in these cases has focused on basic trademark infringement claims, courts have considered other related theories as well. For example, courts have allowed trademark dilution claims based on blurring—on the theory that an advertiser's use of a famous trademark as a keyword lessens the mark's ability to identify and distinguish goods and services—to proceed beyond the pleading

485. *See, e.g.*, Coll. Network, Inc. v. Moore Educ. Publishers, Inc., 38 F. App'x 403 (5th Cir. 2010); AK Metals L.L.C. v. Norman Indus. Materials Inc., No. 3:12-cv-02595-IEGWVG,IEG (WVG), 2013 WL 417323 (S.D. Cal. Jan. 31, 2013).

486. Guardian Pool Fence Sys. Inc. v. Sunwest Indus., Inc., No.: SACV 16-0824-DOC, 2017 WL 2931413, at *7 (C.D. Cal. June 1, 2017).

487. *See, e.g.*, CollegeSource, Inc. v. AcademyOne, Inc., 597 F. App'x 116, 130 (3d Cir. 2015) (affirming grant of summary judgment for defendant in part due to "the expected savviness of internet users seeking out college-transfer information"); General Steel Domestic Sales, LLC v. Chumley, No. 10–cv–01398–PAB–KLM, 2013 WL 1900562, at *9 (D. Colo. May 7, 2013) (rejecting claim in part because parties sold "expensive" and "complicated" "steel buildings," "not the type of purchase that would be made without a thorough consideration of the available options").

488. Infogroup, Inc. v. DatabaseLLC, 95 F. Supp. 3d 1170, 1191 (2015).

489. 1-800 Contacts, Inc. v. Lens.com, Inc., No. 11-4114, slip op. (10th Cir. July 16, 2013).

stage and even past a defendant's motion for summary judgment.[490] Plaintiffs have also survived pleadings challenges with unfair competition claims in this context.[491]

In short, the outcomes of trademark infringement cases in this context are highly context-sensitive. But at a high level, many courts have appeared sympathetic to these claims, particularly where a putative infringer competes directly with a mark holder and does not take affirmative steps to prevent or dispel confusion. Loss of Internet traffic to competitors due to the use of trademark keywords is only one kind of loss associated with search engine advertising. Fashion companies in particular have to worry about dilution of their brand and the loss of aspirational customers where those customers are diverted to sites selling similar or counterfeit products. An aspirational customer is someone who, had they not purchased a similar or replica bag online, may have instead purchased an authentic luxury product on sale, or alternatively, may have simply delayed the purchase of an authentic luxury product until saving up additional money. When those customers are diverted to sites selling competing or even counterfeit products, that sale is lost.

§ 2:11.3 Use of Trademarks in Hashtags

As hashtags have become a prominent feature of social media marketing and advertising, they have also entered into the conversation about trademark infringement in Internet advertising.

In 2018, luxury fashion brand Chanel brought a lawsuit against What Goes Around Comes Around (WGACA), a luxury reseller, alleging that the defendant's advertising and marketing improperly trades upon Chanel's famous brand and trademark to create the false

---

490. *See, e.g.*, Rosetta Stone Ltd. v. Google, Inc., 676 F.3d 144, 169–71 (4th Cir. 2012) (reversing district court's grant of summary judgment to defendant on dilution-by-blurring claim); Edible Arrangements, LLC v. Provide Commerce, Inc., No. 3:14-CV-00250, 2016 WL 4074121, at *16 (D. Conn. July 29, 2016) (denying defendant's motion for summary judgment on blurring and tarnishment claims based on defendant's purchase of plaintiff's mark as keyword); Google Inc. v. Am. Blind & Wallpaper Factory, Inc., No. C 03–05340, 2005 WL 832398 (N.D. Cal. Mar. 30, 2005) (denying motion to dismiss trademark claims, including dilution claim, based on keyword purchases).

491. *See, e.g.*, Morningware, Inc. v. Hearthware Home Prods., Inc., 673 F. Supp. 2d 630, 638 (N.D. Ill. 2009) (holding that plaintiff sufficiently alleged unfair competition because defendant's advertisements triggered by plaintiff's mark allegedly "could mislead consumer[s] to believe that the link is associated with [plaintiff]"); Edina Realty, Inc. v. TheMLSonline.com, No. Civ. 04–4371, 2006 WL 737064, at *6 (D. Minn. Mar. 20, 2006) (denying defendant's motion for summary judgment on unfair-competition claim).

impression that WGACA is affiliated with Chanel or that Chanel endorses WGACA's products.[492] WGACA moved to dismiss the complaint and the court largely sided with Chanel, upholding Chanel's claims for federal counterfeiting and trademark infringement, false advertising, and unfair competition and false endorsement, all of which, the court stated, center on whether defendant's use of Chanel's trademarks have caused confusion, deception, or mistake about the source of its goods.

With respect to hashtags in particular, the court held that Chanel adequately stated infringement claims by alleging that defendant's use of the #WGACACHANEL hashtag inaccurately "create[s] the impression that WGACA is affiliated with Chanel or is an authorized Chanel retailer."[493] The court also found that Chanel "adequately allege[d] that WGACA's extensive unauthorized use of the Chanel brand and trademarks constitutes false advertising or endorsement."[494] The court explained that "such extensive use of Chanel's trademarks" by WGACA—such as its "use of pictures from Chanel advertising campaigns, the #WGACACHANEL hashtag on social media, and the prominence and large volume of Chanel trademarks that WGACA displays in stores and online . . . may form the basis for a Lanham Act violation."[495]

§ 2:12 Duty to Protect a Mark

While a trademark can be a valuable commodity, its value is only realized and preserved if it is used in commerce. In other words, if you don't use it, you lose it.[496] Indeed, "[w]hen a senior user delays in

---

492. Chanel, Inc. v. WGACA, LLC, No. 18 Civ. 2253 (LLS), 2018 WL 4440507 (S.D.N.Y. Sept. 14, 2018).

493. *Id.* at *2.

494. *Id.* at *3.

495. *Id.*

496. *See, e.g.*, MCCARTHY, *supra* note 30, § 31:38; Du Pont de Nemours & Co. v. Yoshida Int'l, Inc., 393 F. Supp. 502, 512 (E.D.N.Y. 1975) (noting the importance of policing efforts "to ensure that whatever distinctiveness or exclusivity has been achieved is not lost through neglect, inattention or consent to infringing use"); Bachellerie v. Z. Cavaricci, Inc., 762 F. Supp. 1070 (S.D.N.Y. 1991) (concluding that failure of plaintiff to enforce its mark against third-party users "diminishes the strength of the mark"); Morningside Grp. Ltd. v. Morningside Capital Grp., L.L.C., 182 F.3d 133 (2d Cir. 1999) (observing that successful policing of a mark adds to its strength by preventing weakening of the mark's distinctiveness in the relevant market); Dictaphone Corp. v. Dictamatic Corp., 199 U.S.P.Q. 437 (D. Or. 1978) (same).

enforcing its rights, a junior user may acquire a valid trademark in a related field, enforceable against even the senior user."[497]

Though a trademark owner must be vigilant in protecting its trademarks, an owner is only required to fight one infringer at a time.[498] For example, in one case, the court held that a cigar manufacturer's multi-decade delay in bringing an infringement action against a competitor was excused where the trademark owner had been embroiled in litigation with the Cuban government and other entities over a period of ten years in the interim.[499] The court observed that the plaintiff's involvement in other trademark actions "establishe[d] that plaintiff was a vigilant defender of its rights."[500] As a result, it is important that a trademark owner take steps and prioritize its enforcement efforts in ways that are reasonable in light of the company's resources and the threat posed by alleged infringers.

Trademark owners in the fashion industry, therefore, are well-advised to make substantial efforts to police their trademarks even if it means engaging in a proverbial game of whack-a-mole. This is particularly true for the fashion industry because brand image is a significant driver of value, and customers will refuse to pay premium prices if they do not believe that they are purchasing something special.

While the sale of counterfeit luxury products may not result in a one-for-one loss of genuine product sales by the luxury retailer, the unauthorized sale might result in the loss of aspirational customers, as described above. Indeed, this problem is particularly acute in the luxury goods industry because the incentive to pay premium prices for a genuine product is reduced if knockoffs are widely available. For this reason, luxury brands must be vigilant in using and policing their marks.

§ 2:13 Developing an Enforcement Strategy

The goals of a trademark enforcement strategy are: (1) to protect the mark; (2) to challenge any marks that could cause confusion among consumers; and (3) to strengthen the mark.

---

497. Patsy's Brand, Inc. v. I.O.B. Realty, Inc., 317 F.3d 209, 216–217 (2d Cir. 2003).

498. Cuban Cigar Brands N.V. v. Upmann Int'l, Inc., 457 F. Supp. 1090, 1097 n.28 (S.D.N.Y. 1978), *aff'd*, 607 F.2d 995 (2d Cir. 1979).

499. *Id.* at 1098–99.

500. *Id.* at 1098; *see also* Elec. Comm'ns, Inc. v. Elec. Components for Indus. Co., 443 F.2d 487, 490 (8th Cir.), *cert. denied*, 404 U.S. 833 (1971); Alfred Dunhill of London, Inc. v. Kasser Distillers Prods. Corp., 350 F. Supp. 1341, 1365 (E.D. Pa. 1972), *aff'd mem.*, 480 F.2d 917 (3d Cir. 1973).

Trademark owners have a number of options available to them when it comes to enforcing their trademarks, but enforcement can be a costly and time-consuming process. For this reason, trademark owners should carefully evaluate the costs and benefits of each option to determine the most effective enforcement method.

The first step in the enforcement process is to assess potential infringements to determine whether and how to take action. The trademark owner should engage in reasonable oversight of the marketplace to determine how its marks may be being used by third parties in ways that overlap with the trademark owner's mark. If troublesome third-party uses are discovered, the trademark owner should assess the nature of goods or services being offered by the third party in connection with the use of the mark, determine whether the third party has registered the mark at issue, and determine how long the third party has been using the mark.

If, after conducting this assessment, the trademark owner believes that its mark is being infringed by the third party, the second step in the enforcement process is to decide upon a strategy for addressing the infringement. One commonly used and often effective strategy is for the trademark owner to send a "cease-and-desist" letter to the unauthorized user of the mark. The goal of the cease-and-desist letter is to put the unauthorized user on notice of the trademark owner's exclusive right to use the mark. The letter provides the unauthorized user with an opportunity to cease using the mark and may enable the trademark owner to avoid litigation. Ignoring a cease and desist letter, in contrast, can serve as evidence that an infringers??? conduct is willful.

A trademark owner can also take legal action by filing a complaint against an infringer in court.[501] There is no requirement that the trademark owner send a cease-and-desist letter to the unauthorized user prior to commencing litigation. In addition to asserting a claim for trademark infringement, the complaint can also assert claims for dilution, false designation of origin, and unfair competition.[502] The

501. Federal courts have jurisdiction over claims arising under the Lanham Act, such as infringement of a federally registered trademark or for false advertising in violation of section 43(a). MCCARTHY, *supra* note 30, § 34.1. Even if the mark is not federally registered, however, a plaintiff may still have its action heard in federal court. *Id.* § 34.3.

502. 15 U.S.C. § 1114(1); *see also* Lois Sportswear U.S.A., Inc. v. Levi Strauss & Co., 799 F.2d 867, 871 (2d Cir. 1986) ("[I]n either a claim for trademark infringement under § 32 or a claim of unfair competition under § 43, a prima facie case is made out by showing the use of one's trademark by another in a way that is likely to confuse as to the source of the product."); Gen. Motors Corp. v. Keystone Auto. Corp., 453 F.3d 351, 354 (6th Cir. 2006) ("In many factual situations, the same result is reached

trademark owner can also seek injunctive relief from the court in the form of a court order requiring the defendant to cease its unauthorized use of the plaintiff's marks.[503]

§ 2:13.1 Private Co-Existence Agreements

Private co-existence agreements can be used either to pre-empt a claim for infringement or to settle a claim for infringement. Often, a co-existence agreement will allow both parties to continue using the trademark at issue but will place certain restrictions on that use, such as a geographic limitation or a constraint on the types of goods or services that can be associated with the trademarks, in order to minimize the possibility of consumer confusion.

A co-existence agreement can represent a reasonable (and less expensive) alternative to litigation, and typical considerations regarding entering into any contract will apply. Co-existence agreements, like any other contract, are subject to claim of breach by either side.[504] Therefore, when drafting the co-existence agreement, the parties should consider what state's laws should govern the interpretation and enforcement of the agreement and the venue for any litigation that may arise from the agreement. Brand owners should also take care to ensure that the terms of the co-existence agreement do not run afoul of any laws governing anti-competitive behavior.[505]

Importantly, courts have not viewed co-existence agreements as inherently inconsistent with a brand owner's duty to police its mark.[506] Rather, courts have, under appropriate circumstances, viewed such

---

whether the legal wrong is called trademark infringement or unfair competition. In such cases the courts often lump them together and speak of them as identical concepts.") (quoting MCCARTHY, *supra* note 30, §§ 2:7–2:8).

503. 15 U.S.C. § 1125(c)(1) ("The owner of a famous mark shall be entitled . . . to an injunction against another person's commercial use in commerce of a mark or trade name, if such use begins after the mark has become famous and causes dilution of the distinctive quality of the mark . . . .").

504. *See, e.g.*, Original Petition, filed on February 8, 2013, Mary Kay, Inc. v. Michael Kors LLC, No. DC-13-01663 (68th Judicial Dist., Dallas Cty., Tex.) (alleging breach of contract for violation of co-existence agreement and requesting injunctive relief); Kerana Todorov, *Duckhorn Asks N.Y. Winery to Modify Labels and Sales*, NAPA V. REG. (Jan. 24, 2013), http://napavalleyregister.com/lifestyles/food-and-cooking/wine/duckhorn-asks-n-y-winery-to-modify-label-and-sales/article_d4ccdbca-669a-11e2-b6a1-001a4bcf887a.html.

505. *See infra* chapter 12.

506. Anthony's Pizza Hldg. Co. v. Anthony's Pizza & Pasta Int'l, Inc., 415 F. App'x 222, 225 (Fed. Cir. Nov. 18, 2010) ("This court has specifically endorsed co-existence agreements that accept the parties' reasonable appraisal of marketplace conditions.").

agreements as an important tool in avoiding consumer confusion. In *Anthony's Pizza Holding Co., Inc. v. Anthony's Pizza & Pasta Int'l, Inc.*, for example, the Federal Circuit noted that the trademark owner's prior co-existence agreement "reflected the parties' agreement to avoid confusion by limiting their operations to distinct channels of trade."[507] As a result, appropriately designed co-existence agreements should not prevent a brand owner from taking action against unauthorized users of the same mark (that is, users who are not parties to a co-existence agreement).[508]

§ 2:14 Trademark Licensing

Trademarks can be bought, sold, and licensed, but because trademarks are symbols of commercial and reputational goodwill, special rules apply to trademark assignment and licensing. For example, a trademark cannot be assigned to another party without the goodwill to which it is attached. And a trademark cannot be licensed to another without the original owner exercising a degree of control over the nature and quality of the licensee's sales of goods and services under the mark.

A trademark license is an agreement between a trademark owner (the "licensor") and another person (the "licensee"), in which the licensor grants permission to the licensee to use its trademark for specified commercial purposes. Generally, a license agreement is a written contract that specifies the scope and duration of the license.

A trademark license must identify:

- The trademark being licensed;
- The licensor and licensee;
- The territory in which the marks are being licensed and the duration of the license; and
- The specific categories, and qualities, of goods and services the licensee can offer under the licensed trademark.

Trademark licenses also generally include terms addressing:

- Royalty and other payments made by the licensee to the licensor for use of the license;
- The renewal terms and grounds for termination of the license; and

---

507. *Id.*
508. *See id.*

- Whether the license is exclusive (meaning the trademark may be licensed exclusively to a single licensee for certain purposes) or non-exclusive (meaning the licensor retains the right to use the trademark itself and/or to license it to others for such purposes).

In the fashion realm, it is crucial that any trademark license agreement contain provisions detailing the licensor's right to regulate and oversee the quality of the goods and services provided under the licensed trademark. This kind of control is essential, particularly for luxury goods, because trademarks retain and preserve reputational capital, and consumers will pay premium prices, only where they can expect to receive high-quality goods. It is also important because where a licensor fails to exercise sufficient control over the quality of goods and services offered by the licensee, the trademark may become vulnerable to attack by the licensee or a third party under the doctrine of "naked licensing," which can result in a determination that the licensor's trademark has been abandoned.[509]

Quality control provisions in a trademark license agreement should cover the licensee's use of the trademark, as well as ongoing quality control monitoring by the licensor. To ensure control of trademark usage, the licensor should specify the manner in which the trademark will be used on the goods and services, as well as advertising and promotional materials, to which the mark may be attached. Another way to ensure the quality of the licensee's goods is to include warranties from the licensee promising to adhere to particular quality standards. The licensor might also require the licensee to obtain the licensor's permission before using the mark in any manner not specified by the license agreement. To ensure ongoing quality control monitoring, the licensor may require access to the licensee's facilities, materials, finished products, personnel, and records to monitor the licensee's compliance with the licensor's quality standards.

License agreements can be useful and lucrative in terms of expanding a business, delegating production or sales, and generating revenue. The RoyaltySource Intellectual Property Database indicates that for trademark license agreements of luxury and apparel brands, royalty rates range from 4.5% to 10% of sales.[510] While licenses can generate valuable royalties, would-be licensors should also consider the cost of policing and overseeing licensees. Oversight and monitoring is essential to ensure that the licensed trademark retains its value and to safeguard the price of the underlying goods and services.

---

509. Eva's Bridal Ltd. v. Halanick Enters., Inc., 639 F.3d 788 (7th Cir. 2011). *See also supra* section 2:10.7.

510. *See* ROYALTY SOURCE, https://www.royaltysource.com/.

For a fuller discussion of the licensing process, see chapter 10.

§ 2:15 International Trademark Issues

§ 2:15.1 The World Intellectual Property Organization

On July 14, 1967 the United Nations passed the Convention Establishing the World Intellectual Property Organization (the "Convention"), which was designed, among other things, to "promote the protection of intellectual property throughout the world."[511] The Convention thus transformed the United International Bureaux for the Protection of Intellectual Property,[512] or BIRPI, into the World Intellectual Property Organization (WIPO). Today, WIPO is the United Nations agency dedicated to "the development of a balanced and effective international intellectual property (IP) system that enables innovation and creativity for the benefit of all."[513] WIPO is focused on resolving intellectual property disputes, developing an international legal framework to address intellectual property rights protection, utilizing intellectual property to support economic growth, and creating systems which will make it easier for individuals to obtain international protection for their designs, trademarks, patents etc. Additionally, WIPO works to develop a cohesive and common network of intellectual property laws and practices among member countries.

WIPO offers alternative dispute resolution services through its Arbitration and Mediation Center. This center is experienced in resolving international commercial disputes, including contractual disputes, and is internationally known for its resolution of Internet

---

511. Convention Establishing the World Intellectual Property Organization (July 14, 1967), https://www.wipo.int/treaties/en/convention/trtdocs_wo029.html.

512. The BIRPI was established in 1893 and was a combination of two international bureaus previously established to handle administrative tasks related to the protection of patent, copyright and trademark rights. The first bureau had been established as part of the Paris Convention for the Protection of Industrial Property ("Paris Convention") in 1883. *See* Paris Convention for the Protection of Industrial Property (Mar. 20, 1883), https://www.wipo.int/treaties/en/ip/paris/trtdocs_wo020.html. The Paris Convention was focused on patents, trademarks and industrial designs. *Id.* at Article 1. In 1886, the Berne Convention for the Protection of Literary and Artistic Works (the "Berne Convention") was enacted; bringing copyright into the realm of international protection. *See* Berne Convention for the Protection of Literary and Artistic Works (Sept. 9, 1886), https://www.wipo.int/treaties/en/ip/berne/trtdocs_wo001.html.

513. WORLD INTELLECTUAL PROP. ORG., ABOUT WIPO, https://www.wipo.int/about-wipo/en/.

domain name challenges, which is an issue of particular importance for brand owners in the fashion and luxury goods industries.[514]

As an example of the WIPO process, in *Balenciaga v. liu zhixian, zhixian liu*, Balenciaga filed a complaint with the Arbitration and Meditation Center disputing the use of the domain name balenciaga-bags.com by the Defendant, liu zhixian. The domain name had been registered with Name.com LLC.[515] Balenciaga contended that the Defendant had no right to use the BALENCIAGA trademark and that the items being offered for sale through balenciaga-bags.com were likely counterfeit.[516]

In response to the complaint, the Arbitration and Mediation Center contacted Name.com LLC in order to obtain a verification of the registration of the disputed domain name.[517] Although the panel had some question as to whether the defendant had, in fact, sold counterfeit goods, the panel found that the defendant had "no rights or legitimate interests" in balenciaga-bags.com.[518] Further, the panel held that the defendant had registered the domain name in bad faith as the defendant had "no rights or legitimate interests" in the name.[519] The panel ultimately ordered the transfer of balenciaga-bags.com to Balenciaga under the Uniform Domain-Name Dispute-Resolution Policy (often referred to as the "UDRP"), which governs the terms of domain name registrations for popular top-level domains, such as .com.

§ 2:15.2 The Madrid Protocol

In 1891, a system for the international registration of trademarks was established.[520] As discussed above in section 2:6.3[G], the Madrid System allows a trademark holder to expedite the process of registering his or her mark in multiple countries.[521] Today, the Madrid System is made up of two treaties. The most recent treaty, the Madrid

---

514. Specifically, the WIPO Arbitration and Mediation Center is known for resolving challenges to the registration and use of domain names referred to as "cybersquatting."

515. *See* Balenciaga v. liu zhixian, zhixian liu, WIPO No. D2010-1831 (2010), https://www.wipo.int/amc/en/domains/search/text.jsp?case=d2010-1831.

516. *Id.*

517. *Id.*

518. *Id.*

519. *Id.*

520. The Madrid system operates under two separate agreements: the Madrid Agreement of 1891 and the Madrid Protocol of 1989.

521. For additional information and an online tool for using the Madrid system, please review WIPO's Internet website for the Madrid System, see WORLD INTELLECTUAL PROP. ORG., MADRID–THE INTERNATIONAL TRADEMARK SYSTEM, https://www.wipo.int/madrid/en/ [hereinafter WIPO, MADRID–THE INTERNATIONAL TRADEMARK SYSTEM].

Protocol, was enacted in 1989 and is principally a filing treaty. The Madrid Protocol became effective in the United States on November 2, 2003. Today, approximately ninety countries have joined the Madrid Protocol.[522] A full list of these countries is set forth at Appendix 2-B.

The Madrid Protocol provides an efficient system by which a trademark holder fills out a single application in his or her home trademark office for international protection.[523] The applicant is able to designate on the application the countries in which he or she is seeking protection for the marks. In the United States, the applicant must have already applied for a trademark through a basic application. This system is particularly useful for the fashion industry as a designer or brand is able to easily seek protection of their marks in multiple countries in an efficient and simple process. In the United States, a trademark holder may submit an international application to the U.S. Patent and Trademark Office who will then forward the application to the International Bureau.[524] In order to apply through the Madrid System, and individual must be "a national of, be domiciled in, or have a real and effective business or commercial establishment" in a country that is a member to the Madrid Protocol.[525] The application must be for the same mark that the applicant has protection over in his or her home country.[526] Also, the application must include the same list of goods and/or services that was listed on the original application in the home country. Each country that has been designated for potential protection has the right to determine whether or not protection over the mark will be granted. If a trademark office in a designated country grants protection, then the trademark is afforded the same level of protection as if the applicant had applied directly in that country.

---

522. A list of the 90 countries, known as "Contracting Parties" may be found at WORLD INTELLECTUAL PROP. ORG., WIPO–ADMINISTERED TREATIES, https://www.wipo.int/treaties/en/ShowResults.jsp?lang=en&treaty_id=8.

523. Applicants in the United States may utilize electronic forms available through the PTO, *see* U.S. PATENT & TRADEMARK OFFICE, MADRID–ELECTRONIC FORMS FOR MADRID-PROTOCOL RELATED SUBMISSIONS, https://www.uspto.gov/trademarks/law/madrid/forms/index.jsp.

524. Additional information on submitting an international application through the PTO is available on their website, *see* U.S. PATENT & TRADEMARK OFFICE, MADRID FAQS, https://www.uspto.gov/trademarks/law/madrid/madridfaqs.jsp.

525. *See* Rules for Practice for Trademark-Related Filings Under the Madrid Protocol Implementation Act, 68 Fed. Reg. 55,748 (Sept. 26, 2003).

526. *Id.*

The Madrid Protocol also simplified the management of trademarks. Under the protocol, a trademark holder may make subsequent changes or renew a trademark registration through the same procedure.[527]

527. *See* WIPO, MADRID–THE INTERNATIONAL TRADEMARK SYSTEM, *supra* note 521. Additional tips for holders of international marks regarding seeking extensions of protection in the United States can be found through WIPO. *See* WORLD INTELLECTUAL PROP. ORG., Information Notice No. 4/2009: Madrid Protocol Concerning the International Registration of Marks, Tips for Holders of International Registrations Seeking Extension of Protection to the United States of America: Avoiding Provisional Refusals, https://www.wipo.int/edocs/madrdocs/en/2009/madrid_2009_4.pdf.

Appendix 2A

International Trademark Classification of Goods and Services

The United States Patent and Trademark Office associates the following word titles with the respective international trademark class numbers (additional details/explanatory notes added for certain classes):

<u>GOODS</u>

1. Chemicals
2. Paints
3. Cosmetics and cleaning preparations

Includes: Non-medicated cosmetics and toiletry preparations; non-medicated dentifrices; perfumery, essential oils; bleaching preparations and other substances for laundry use; cleaning, polishing, scouring, and abrasive preparations.

Explanatory Note

Class 3 includes mainly non-medicated toiletry preparations as well as cleaning preparations for use in the home and other environments.

This Class includes, in particular:

- sanitary preparations being toiletries;
- tissues impregnated with cosmetic lotions;
- deodorants for human beings or for animals;
- room fragrancing preparations;
- nail art stickers;
- polishing wax;
- sandpaper.

This Class does not include, in particular:

- ingredients for use in the manufacture of cosmetics, for example, vitamins, preservatives, and antioxidants (Cl. 1);
- degreasing preparations for use in manufacturing processes (Cl. 1);

- chemical chimney cleaners (Cl. 1);
- deodorants, other than for human beings or for animals (Cl. 5);
- medicated shampoos, soaps, lotions, and dentifrices (Cl. 5);
- emery boards, energy files, sharpening stones, and grindstones (hand tools (Cl. 8);
- cosmetic and cleaning instruments, for example, make-up brushes (Cl. 21), cloths, pads, and rags for cleaning (Cl. 21).

4. Lubricants and fuels
5. Pharmaceuticals
6. Metal goods
7. Machinery
8. Hand tools
9. Electrical and scientific apparatus
10. Medical apparatus
11. Environmental control apparatus
12. Vehicles
13. Firearms
14. Jewelry

Includes: Precious metals and their alloys; jewellery, precious and semi-precious stones; horological and chronometric instruments.

Explanatory Note

Class 14 includes mainly precious metals and certain goods made of precious metals or coated therewith, as well as jewellery, clocks, and watches, and component parts therefor.

This Class includes, in particular:

- jewellery, including imitation jewellery, for example, paste jewellery;
- cuff links, tie pins, tie clips;
- key rings , key chains and charms therefor;
- jewellery charms;
- jewellery boxes;

- component parts for jewellery, clocks and watches, for example, clasps and beads for jewellery, movements for clocks and watches, clock hands, watch springs, watch crystals.

This Class does not include, in particular:

- smart watches (Cl. 9);
- charms, other than for jewellery, key rings, or key chains (Cl. 26);
- objects of art not made of precious metals or coated therewith that are classified according to the material of which they are made, for example, works of art of metal (Cl. 6); of stone, concrete, or marble (Cl. 19); of wood, wax, plaster, or plastic (Cl. 20); of porcelain, ceramic, earthenware, terracotta, or glass (Cl. 21).
- certain good made of precious metals or coated therewith that are classified according to their function or purpose, for example, metals in foil and powder form for use in painting, decorating, printing, and art (Cl. 2); dental amalgams of gold (Cl. 5); cutlery (Cl. 8); electric contacts (Cl. 9); pen nibs of gold (Cl. 16), teapots (Cl. 21); gold and silver embroidery (Cl. 26); cigar boxes (Cl. 34).

15. Musical instruments
16. Paper goods and printed matter
17. Rubber goods
18. Leather goods

Includes: Leather and imitations of leather; animal skins and hides; luggage and carrying bags, umbrellas and parasols; walking sticks; whips, harness and saddlery; collars, leashes, and clothing for animals.

Explanatory Note

Class 18 includes mainly leather, imitations of leather and certain goods made of those materials.

This Class includes, in particular:

- luggage and carrying bags, for example, suitcases, trunks, traveling bags, sling bags for carrying infants, school bags;
- luggage tags;

- business card cases and pocket wallets;
- boxes and cases of leather or leatherboard.

This Class does not include, in particular:

- walking sticks or canes for medical purposes (Cl. 10);
- clothing, footwear and headgear for humans (Cl. 25);
- bags and cases adapted to the product they are intended to contain, for example, bags adapted for laptops (Cl. 9), bags and cases for cameras and photographic equipment (Cl. 9), cases for musical instruments (Cl. 15), golf bags with or without wheels, bags especially designed for skis and surfboards (Cl. 28);
- certain good made of leather, imitations of leather, animal skins and hides that are classified according to their function or purpose, for example, leather strops (Cl. 8), polishing leather (Cl. 21), chamois leather for cleaning (Cl. 21), leather belts for clothing (Cl. 25).

19. Non-metallic building materials
20. Furniture and articles not otherwise classified
21. Housewares and glass
22. Cordage and fibers

Includes: Ropes and string; nets; tents and tarpaulins; awnings of textile or synthetic materials; sails; sacks for the transport and storage of materials in bulk; padding, cushioning and stuffing materials, except of paper, cardboard, rubber or plastics; raw fibrous textile materials and substitute therefor.

Explanatory Note

Class 22 includes mainly canvas and other materials for making sails, rope, padding, cushioning and stuffing materials and raw fibrous textile materials.

This Class includes, in particular:

- cords and twines made of natural or artificial textile fibers, paper or plastics;
- fishing nets, hammocks, rope ladders;
- vehicle covers, not fitted;
- certain sacks and bags not otherwise classified by function or purpose, for example, bags for washing hosiery, body bags, mail bags;

- packaging bags of textile;
- animal fibres and raw textile fibres, for example, animal hair, cocoons, jute, raw or treated wool, raw silk.

This Class does not include, in particular:

- metal ropes (Cl. 6);
- strings for musical instruments (Cl. 15) and for sports rackets (Cl. 28);
- padding and stuffing materials of paper or cardboard (Cl. 16), rubber or plastic (Cl. 17);
- certain nets and bags that are classified according to their function or purpose, for example, safety nets (Cl. 9), luggage nets for vehicles (Cl. 12), garment bags for travel (Cl. 18), hair nets (Cl. 26), golf bags (Cl. 28), net for sports (Cl. 28);
- packaging bags, not of textile, which are classified according to the material of which they are made, for example, packaging bags of paper or plastic (Cl. 16), of rubber (Cl. 17), of leather (Cl. 18).

23. Yarns and threads

Includes: Yarns and threads, for textile use.

24. Fabrics

Includes: Textiles and substitutes for textiles; household linen; curtains of textile or plastic.

Explanatory Note

Class 24 includes mainly fabric covers for household use.

This Class includes, in particular:

- household linen, for example, bedspreads, pillow shams, towels of textile;
- bed linen of paper;
- sleeping bags, sleeping bag liners;
- mosquito nets

This Class does not include, in particular:

- electrically heated blankets, for medical purposes (Cl. 10) and not for medical purposes (Cl. 11);
- table linen of paper (Cl. 16);

- asbestos safety curtains (Cl. 17), bamboo curtains and bead curtains for decoration (Cl. 20);
- horse blankets (Cl. 18);
- certain textiles and fabrics for specific uses, for example, fabrics for bookbinding (Cl. 16), insulating fabrics (Cl. 17) geotextiles (Cl. 19).

25. Clothing

Includes: Clothing, footwear, headgear.

Explanatory Note

This Class does not include, in particular:

- certain clothing and footwear for special use (consult the Alphabetical List).

26. Fancy goods

Includes: Lace and embroidery, ribbons and braid; buttons, hooks and eyes, pins and needles; artificial flowers; hair decorations; false hair.

Explanatory Note

Class 26 includes mainly dressmakers' articles, natural or synthetic hair for wear, and hair adornments, as well as small decorative items intended to adorn a variety of objects, not included in other classes.

This Class includes, in particular:

- wigs, toupees, and false beards;
- barrettes and hair bands;
- hair nets;
- buckles and zippers;
- charms, other than for jewelry, key rings or key chains.

This Class does not include, in particular:

- certain special types of hooks (consult the Alphabetical List of Goods);
- certain special types of needles (consult the Alphabetical List of Goods);
- false eyelashes (Cl. 3);
- hair prostheses (Cl. 10);

- jewellery charms, charms for key rings or key chains (Cl. 14);
- yarns and threads for textile use (Cl. 23).

27. Floor coverings
28. Toys and sporting goods
29. Meats and processed foods
30. Staple foods
31. Natural agricultural products
32. Light beverages
33. Wines and spirits
34. Smokers' articles

SERVICES

35. Advertising and business
36. Insurance and financial
37. Building construction and repair
38. Telecommunications
39. Transportation and storage
40. Treatment of materials
41. Education and entertainment
42. Computer and scientific
43. Hotels and restaurants
44. Medical, beauty and agricultural

Includes: Medical services; veterinary services; hygienic and beauty care for human beings or animals; agriculture, horticulture and forestry services.

Explanatory Note

Class 44 includes mainly medical care, hygienic and beauty care given by persons or establishments to human beings and animals; it also includes services relating to the fields of agriculture, horticulture and forestry.

This Class includes, in particular:

- medical analysis services relating to the treatment of persons (such as x-ray examinations and taking of blood samples);

- artificial insemination services;
- pharmacy advice;
- animal breeding;
- services relating to the growing of plants such as gardening;
- services relating to floral art such as floral compositions as well as garden design.

This Class does not include, in particular:

- vermin exterminating (other than for agriculture, aquaculture, horticulture and forestry) (Cl. 37);
- installation and repair services for irrigation systems (Cl. 37);
- ambulance transport (Cl. 39);
- animal slaughtering services and taxidermy (Cl. 40);
- timber felling and processing (Cl. 40);
- animal training services (Cl. 41);
- health clubs for physical exercise (Cl. 41);
- scientific research services for medical purposes (Cl. 42);
- boarding for animals (Cl. 43);
- retirement homes (Cl. 43).

45. Personal and legal

Appendix 2B

Signatory Nations to the Madrid Agreement Concerning the International Registration Marks and Related Protocol

5. Madrid Agreement Concerning the International Registration of Marks

Madrid Agreement (Marks) (1891), revised at Brussels (1900), at Washington (1911), at The Hague (1925), at London (1934), Nice (1957) and at Stockholm (1967), and amended in 1979

and

6. Protocol Relating to the Madrid Agreement Concerning the International Registration of Marks

Madrid Protocol (1989), amended in 2006 and in 2007

(Madrid Union)[1]

Status on March 17, 2019

State/IGO	Date on which State became party to the Madrid Agreement[2]	Date on which State/IGO became party to the Madrid Protocol (1989)
Afghanistan	–	June 26, 2018
African Intellectual Property Organization (OAPI)	–	March 5, 2015[5,6]
Albania	October 4, 1995	July 30, 2003
Algeria	July 5, 1972	October 31, 2015
Antigua and Barbuda	–	March 17, 2000[5,6]
Armenia	December 25, 1991	October 19, 2000[6,10]
Australia	–	July 11, 2001[5,6]
Austria	January 1, 1909	April 13, 1999
Azerbaijan	December 25, 1995	April 15, 2007
Bahrain	–	December 15, 2005[10]
Belarus	December 25, 1991	January 18, 2002[6,10]
Belgium	July 15, 1892[3]	April 1, 1998[3,6]
Bhutan	August 4, 2000	August 4, 2000
Bosnia and Herzegovina	March 1, 1992	January 27, 2009
Botswana	–	December 5, 2006
Brunei Darussalam	–	January 6, 2017[5,6]
Bulgaria	August 1, 1985	October 2, 2001[6,]
Cambodia	–	June 5, 2015[5,6]
Canada	–	June 17, 2019[5,6]
China	October 4, 1989[4]	December 1, 1995[4,5]
Colombia	–	August 29, 2012[5,6]
Croatia	October 8, 1991	January 23, 2004
Cuba	December 6, 1989	December 26, 1995
Cyprus	November 4, 2003	November 4, 2003[5]
Czech Republic	January 1, 1993	September 25, 1996
Democratic People's Republic of Korea	June 10, 1980	October 3, 1996
Denmark	–	February 13, 1996[5,6,7]
Egypt	July 1, 1952	September 3, 2009
Estonia	–	November 18, 1998[5,6,8]
Eswatini	December 14, 1998	December 14, 1998
European Union	–	October 1, 2004[6,10]
Finland	–	April 1, 1996[5,6]
France	July 15, 1892[9]	November 7, 1997[9]
Gambia	–	December 18, 2015[5,6]
Georgia	–	August 20, 1998[6,10]
Germany	December 1, 1922	March 20, 1996
Ghana	–	September 16, 2008[5,6]
Greece	–	August 10, 2000[5,6]
Hungary	January 1, 1909	October 3, 1997
Iceland	–	April 15, 1997[6,10]
India	–	July 8, 2013[5,6,8]
Indonesia	–	January 2, 2018[6,10]
Iran (Islamic Republic of)	December 25, 2003	December 25, 2003[5]
Ireland	–	October 19, 2001[5,6]
Israel	–	September 1, 2010[5,6]
Italy	October 15, 1894	April 17, 2000[5,6]
Japan	–	March 14, 2000[6,10]
Kazakhstan	December 25, 1991	December 8, 2010
Kenya	June 26, 1998	June 26, 1998[5,6]
Kyrgyzstan	December 25, 1991	June 17, 2004[6]
Lao People's Democratic Republic	–	March 7, 2016[6,10]

5. Madrid Agreement Concerning the International Registration of Marks

Madrid Agreement (Marks) (1891), revised at Brussels (1900), at Washington (1911), at The Hague (1925), at London (1934), Nice (1957) and at Stockholm (1967), and amended in 1979

and

6. Protocol Relating to the Madrid Agreement Concerning the International Registration of Marks

Madrid Protocol (1989), amended in 2006 and in 2007

(Madrid Union)

(continuation)

State/IGO	Date on which State became party to the Madrid Agreement[2]	Date on which State/IGO became party to the Madrid Protocol (1989)
Latvia	January 1, 1995	January 5, 2000
Lesotho	February 12, 1999	February 12, 1999
Liberia	December 25, 1995	December 11, 2009
Liechtenstein	July 14, 1933	March 17, 1998
Lithuania	–	November 15, 1997[5]
Luxembourg	September 1, 1924[3]	April 1, 1998[3,6]
Madagascar	–	April 28, 2008[10]
Malawi	–	December 25, 2018[5]
Mexico	–	February 19, 2013[6,10]
Monaco	April 29, 1956	September 27, 1996
Mongolia	April 21, 1985	June 16, 2001
Montenegro	June 3, 2006	June 3, 2006
Morocco	July 30, 1917	October 8, 1999[6]
Mozambique	October 7, 1998	October 7, 1998
Namibia	June 30, 2004	June 30, 2004[8]
Netherlands	March 1, 1893[3,11]	April 1, 1998[3,6,11]
New Zealand	–	December 10, 2012[5,6,12]
North Macedonia	September 8, 1991	August 30, 2002
Norway	–	March 29, 1996[5,6]
Oman	–	October 16, 2007[10]
Philippines	–	July 25, 2012[5,6,8]
Poland	March 18, 1991	March 4, 1997[10]
Portugal	October 31, 1893	March 20, 1997
Republic of Korea	–	April 10, 2003[5,6]
Republic of Moldova	December 25, 1991	December 1, 1997[6]
Romania	October 6, 1920	July 28, 1998
Russian Federation	July 1, 1976[13]	June 10, 1997
Rwanda	–	August 17, 2013
Samoa	–	March 4, 2019[5,6]
San Marino	September 25, 1960	September 12, 2007[6,10]
Sao Tome and Principe	–	December 8, 2008
Serbia[14]	April 27, 1992	February 17, 1998
Sierra Leone	June 17, 1997	December 28, 1999
Singapore	–	October 31, 2000[5,6]
Slovakia	January 1, 1993	September 13, 1997[10]
Slovenia	June 25, 1991	March 12, 1998
Spain	July 15, 1892	December 1, 1995
Sudan	May 16, 1984	February 16, 2010
Sweden	–	December 1, 1995[5,6]
Switzerland	July 15, 1892	May 1, 1997[6,10]
Syrian Arab Republic	–	August 5, 2004[5]
Tajikistan	December 25, 1991	June 30, 2011[6,10]
Thailand	–	November 7, 2017[5,6]
Tunisia	–	October 16, 2013[5,6]
Turkey	–	January 1, 1999 [5,6,8]
Turkmenistan	–	September 28, 1999[6,10]
Ukraine	December 25, 1991	December 29, 2000[5,6]
United Kingdom	–	December 1, 1995[5,6,15]
United States of America	–	November 2, 2003[5,6]
Uzbekistan	–	December 27, 2006[6,10]
Viet Nam	March 8, 1949	July 11, 2006[6]

- 18 -

5. Madrid Agreement Concerning the International Registration of Marks

Madrid Agreement (Marks) (1891), revised at Brussels (1900), at Washington (1911), at The Hague (1925), at London (1934), Nice (1957) and at Stockholm (1967), and amended in 1979

and

6. Protocol Relating to the Madrid Agreement Concerning the International Registration of Marks

Madrid Protocol (1989), amended in 2006 and in 2007

(Madrid Union)

(continuation)

State/IGO	Date on which State became party to the Madrid Agreement[2]	Date on which State/IGO became party to the Madrid Protocol (1989)
Zambia	–	November 15, 2001[6]
Zimbabwe	–	March 11, 2015[5,6]
Total: (104)	(55)	(104)

[1] The Madrid Union is composed of the States party to the Madrid Agreement and the Contracting Parties to the Madrid Protocol.

[2] All the States party to the Madrid Agreement have declared, under Article 3*bis* of the Nice or Stockholm Act, that the protection arising from international registration shall not extend to them unless the proprietor of the mark so requests.

[3] The territories of Belgium, Luxembourg and the Kingdom of the Netherlands in Europe are to be deemed a single country, for the application of the Madrid Agreement as from January 1, 1971, and for the application of the Protocol as from April 1, 1998.

[4] Not applicable to either Hong Kong, China or Macao, China.

[5] In accordance with Article 5(2)(b) and (c) of the Protocol, this Contracting Party has declared that the time limit to notify a refusal of protection shall be 18 months and that, where a refusal of protection results from an opposition to the granting of protection, such refusal may be notified after the expiry of the 18–month time limit.

[6] In accordance with Article 8(7)(a) of the Protocol, this Contracting Party has declared that, in connection with each request for territorial extension to it of the protection of an international registration and the renewal of any such international registration, it wants to receive an individual fee, instead of a share in the revenue produced by the supplementary and complementary fees.

[7] Applicable to Greenland as of January 11, 2011 and the Faroe Islands as of April 13, 2016.

[8] In accordance with Article 14(5) of the Protocol, this Contracting Party has declared that the protection resulting from any international registration effected under this Protocol before the date of entry into force of this Protocol with respect to it cannot be extended to it.

[9] Including all Overseas Departments and Territories.

[10] In accordance with Article 5(2)(b) of the Protocol, this Contracting Party has declared that the time limit to notify a refusal of protection shall be 18 months.

[11] The instrument of ratification of the Stockholm Act and the instrument of acceptance of the Protocol were deposited for the Kingdom in Europe. The Netherlands extended the application of the Madrid Protocol to the Netherlands Antilles with effect from April 28, 2003. The Netherlands Antilles ceased to exist on October 10, 2010. As from that date, the Protocol continues to apply to Curaçao and Sint Maarten. The Protocol also continues to apply to the islands of Bonaire, Sint Eustatius and Saba which, with effect from October 10, 2010, have become part of the territory of the Kingdom of the Netherlands in Europe.

[12] With a declaration that this accession shall not extend to Tokelau unless and until a declaration to this effect is lodged by the Government of New Zealand with the depositary on the basis of appropriate consultation with that territory.

[13] Date of accession by the Soviet Union, continued by the Russian Federation as from December 25, 1991.

[14] Serbia is the continuing State from Serbia and Montenegro as from June 3, 2006.

[15] Ratification in respect of the United Kingdom and the Isle of Man.

Chapter 3

Patents

§ 3:1 Introduction
Figure 3-1 Trends in Fashion-Related Patents
§ 3:2 Overview of Patent Protection
§ 3:2.1 What Is a Utility Patent?
Figure 3-2 Sample Utility Patents in Fashion
§ 3:2.2 What Is a Design Patent?
Figure 3-3 Sample Design Patents in Fashion
§ 3:3 Applying for Patent Protection
§ 3:3.1 Application Requirements
§ 3:3.2 Prior Art Searches
§ 3:3.3 Costs and Fees
§ 3:3.4 Examination
§ 3:3.5 Design Patent Applications
§ 3:3.6 Marking
§ 3:4 Patent Enforcement and Remedies
§ 3:4.1 Patent Infringement
§ 3:4.2 Remedies
[A] Monetary Damages
[B] Injunctive Relief
[C] Attorneys' Fees
[D] Prejudgment Interest
[E] Enhanced Damages for Willful Infringement
§ 3:5 Territoriality of Patent Protection
§ 3:5.1 Patent Enforcement in the United States
§ 3:5.2 Patent Protection Outside the United States
§ 3:6 Patent Protection in Fashion
§ 3:6.1 Design Patent Protection in Fashion: Trends in Use and Enforcement
Figure 3-4 Sample Patents Held by Columbia Sportswear North America, Inc. Covering Related Designs
Figure 3-5 Sample Patents Held by Times Three Clothier, LLC Covering Related Designs

Figure 3-6 Sample Design Patents Held by Lululemon Athletica Canada Inc.
Figure 3-7 Design Patents Held by Skechers U.S.A.
Figure 3-8 Design Patents Held by Deckers Outdoor Corporation
§ 3:6.2 Utility Patent Protection in Fashion: Trends in Use and Enforcement
[A] High Performance Fabrics and Athletic Attire
Figure 3-9 Sample Utility Patents in Fashion
[B] Other Uses of Utility Patents
Figure 3-10 U.S. Patent No. 6,109,747 (Eyeglass frames with magnets in flanges)
[C] Integration of Technology and Fashion
Figure 3-11 Sample Utility Patents in Fashion Using RFIDs
Figure 3-12 Biosensing Garment—U.S. Patent D832,556 (OMsignal Inc.)
Figure 3-13 U.S. Patent Application Publ. No. 2018/0256115 (Sony Interactive Entertainment) (Display to Mitigate "Virtual Reality Sickness")
Figure 3-14 U.S. Patent Application Publ. No. 2018/0078183 (Apple, Inc.)
§ 3:7 Conclusion
Appendix 3A-1 Illustrative Design Patent 1: Seamans, March 28, 2006
Appendix 3A-2 Illustrative Design Patent 2: Iamartino, June 26, 2012
Appendix 3B-1 Illustrative Utility Patent 1: Seamans, February 7, 2006
Appendix 3B-2 Illustrative Utility Patent 2: Drab et al., September 11, 2012

§ 3:1 Introduction

This chapter provides a brief overview of U.S. patent law, with an eye toward trends in the exploitation and enforcement of patents in the fashion industry. Although patent disputes are less common in the fashion industry than more familiar trademark or copyright disputes, patents play an important—and increasingly utilized—role in the overall basket of remedies available to designers and retailers in protecting new and unique designs and inventions in the fashion world. Indeed, depending on the design or invention at issue, patent law may provide the ideal legal paradigm to protect innovative designs and new products from copying by others. Although no single chapter can provide comprehensive coverage of patent law, the goal of this chapter is to provide fashion industry participants with the basic information necessary to start the process of evaluating whether patent issues may exist in a given fashion business and, if necessary, to seek the advice and assistance of competent legal counsel.

There are two types of patents relevant to fashion—utility patents and design patents. "Utility patents" protect new, nonobvious, useful inventions, while "design patents" protect new, nonobvious, non-functional, and ornamental designs. Both types of patents confer the right to exclude others from making, using or selling the claimed invention in the United States (or from importing the claimed invention item into the United States) for a specified period of time after the patent's application (utility patents) or issuance (design patents). To obtain a patent, the patent owner (or "patentee") must timely file an application with the U.S. Patent and Trademark Office (PTO). An application for a utility patent must include a "specification" that describes the invention and one or more "claims" that precisely define the invention's scope.[1] An application for a design patent always has one claim, the scope of which is typically determined by the drawings of the patented design; it contains no additional specification. If the PTO official assigned to the application (the "examiner") determines that the patent should issue, the claims are "allowed." From the date of issuance until the patent expires, the patentee may file a civil suit for infringement in federal court or an administrative action in the International Trade Commission (ITC) (with appeals to the U.S. Court of Appeals for the Federal Circuit, and eventually to the U.S. Supreme Court) to stop anyone who, without authority, makes, uses, sells, offers to sell, or imports the patented invention (the "accused product"). Remedies generally include monetary damages, as well as preliminary and permanent injunctions, although courts have issued such injunctions less frequently since the Supreme Court's 2006 decision in *eBay Inc. v. MercExchange*.[2]

For reasons discussed in this chapter, the fashion industry historically has not relied on either type of patent protection to any great degree. Nonetheless, a review of recently issued patents, patent applications, and relevant enforcement actions seems to indicate that patents are playing an increasingly important role in the fashion business.

---

1. Each claim is comprised of one or more phrases or clauses describing the claimed invention. Each of these phrases or clauses is often referred to as a "limitation." For example, for the following claim, "A chair comprising three legs, a seat with the legs connected on a bottom side and a back connected to a top side," there are three limitations: the chair must have (a) three legs, (b) a seat and (c) a back.
2. eBay Inc. v. MercExchange, 547 U.S. 388 (2006).

Figure 3-1
Trends in Fashion-Related Patents

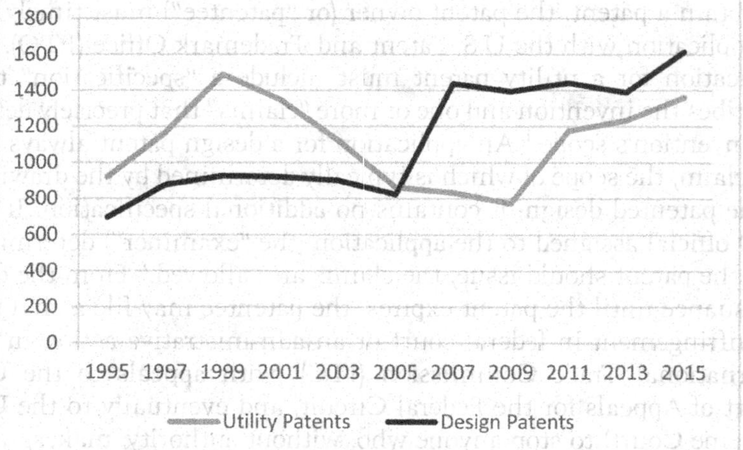

Source: USPTO, *Patent Counts by Class by Year*, https://www.uspto.gov/web/offices/ac/ido/oeip/taf/cbcby.htm. Fashion-related utility patents include classification nos. 2 (Apparel), 24 (Buckles, Buttons, and Clasps), 36 (Boots, Shoes, and Leggings), 63 (Jewelry), 87 (Textiles: Braiding, Netting, and Lace making), 150 (Purses, Wallets and Protective covers), 442 (Fabric: Woven, Knitted, or Nonwoven Textile or Cloth, Etc.), and 450 (Foundation Garments). Fashion-related design patents include classification nos. D02 (Apparel and Haberdashery) and D11 (Jewelry, Symbolic Insignia and Ornaments).

§ 3:2 Overview of Patent Protection

§ 3:2.1 *What Is a Utility Patent?*

A "utility patent" may be granted for inventions of new and useful processes, machines, manufactures, or compositions of matter, as well as for improvements thereon.[3] There are three requirements for patentability:

3. *See* 35 U.S.C. § 101 ("Whoever invents or discovers any new and useful process, machine, manufacture, or composition of matter, or any new and useful improvement thereof, may obtain a patent therefore, subject to the conditions and requirements of this title.").

First, the invention must be just that—an invention. It must be new, having never been disclosed in the "prior art."[4] "Prior art" generally includes devices or methods described in a printed publication, or in public use, on sale, or otherwise available to the public before the effective filing date of the invention, as well as any patents filed and/or issued before the patent application.[5] Further, the invention must not be an obvious development to a person skilled in the relevant field.[6]

Second, the invention must be useful,[7] that is, it must have a "specific and substantial utility that is credible."[8]

Third, the invention must be directed to patent-eligible subject matter.[9] This includes machines, "article[s] of manufacture" (something human-made), compositions of matter (like a drug), or an improvements thereon.[10] Patent law also protects innovative methods or processes, subject to important limitations.[11] "Laws of nature, natural phenomena, and abstract ideas are not patentable."[12] Whether a method, system, or process constitutes patentable subject matter is determined by a two-part analysis set forth by the U.S. Supreme

---

4. *See* 35 U.S.C. § 102(a).
5. *See generally* 35 U.S.C. § 102(a), (d). Limited exceptions are made to allow an inventor to disclose his or her own invention for up to a year prior to filing, and to account for disclosures from the inventor in other patents or applications. *Id.* § 102(b), (c). *See also infra* section 3:4.1. A different definition of prior art applies to patents filed or claiming priority before March 16, 2013. *See generally id.* § 102 (pre-America Invents Act).
6. *See generally* 35 U.S.C. § 103.
7. 35 U.S.C. § 101.
8. U.S. Patent & Trademark Office, Manual of Patent Examining Procedure (9th ed. Mar. 2014, rev. Jan. 2018) [hereinafter MPEP], § 2107, pt. II(B), https://www.uspto.gov/web/offices/pac/mpep/index.html. The Manual of Patent Examining Procedure is the manual written by the PTO to guide its patent examiners in patent application procedure.
9. 35 U.S.C. § 101.
10. *See id.*
11. *See, e.g., id.*; Mayo Collaborative Servs. v. Prometheus Labs., Inc., 566 U.S. 66 (2012); Bilski v. Kappos, 561 U.S. 593 (2010).
12. Alice Corp. v. CLS Bank, Int'l, 573 U.S. 208, 216 (2014) (internal quote omitted).

Court in *Alice Corp. v. CLS Bank, International*.[13] At step one, a court determines if a patent claim is "directed to a patent-ineligible concept," such as an abstract idea.[14] If so, at step two, the court determines if the claim "contains an 'inventive concept' sufficient to 'transform' the claimed abstract idea into a patent-eligible application."[15] A claim can be shown to be patent eligible if it includes "additional features" establishing that it "in practice amounts to significantly more than a patent upon the [ineligible concept] itself."[16]

By way of example concerning wearable technology, in 2015, Fitbit, Inc. sued Aliphcom, makers of Jawbone, contending that its wearable fitness trackers infringed three Fitbit patents related to methods of wirelessly pairing biometric devices.[17] In reviewing patent eligibility, the court found it to be a "close call" at step one as to whether the patents focused on a "specific asserted improvement in computer capabilities" instead of "a process that qualifies as an 'abstract idea' for which computers are invoked merely as a tool."[18] On step two, the court noted that limiting Fitbit's patents to "wearable" technology did not itself make its claims patent eligible.[19] But the court also found that the "ordered combination of claim elements" contained inventive concepts, namely incorporating means of "tapping" the device to pair it, and use of a computer server to minimize user interaction in pairing.[20]

---

13. *Id.* at 217–21. The authors' law firm, Gibson, Dunn & Crutcher LLP, successfully represented CLS Bank in the Supreme Court in this matter, resulting in the rule and test stated here.
14. *Id.* at 218.
15. *Id.* at 221.
16. *Id.* at 218, 221
17. Complaint, Fitbit, Inc. v. Aliphcom, No. 15-cv-04073 (N.D. Cal. Sept. 8, 2015) (asserting U.S. Pat. Nos. 9,026,053, 9,106,307, 9,048,923).
18. Fitbit, Inc. v. Aliphcom, 233 F. Supp. 3d 799, 806, 810 (N.D. Cal. 2017) (quoting Enfish LLC v. Microsoft Corp., 822 F.3d 1327, 1335–36, 1339 (Fed. Cir. 2016)).
19. *Fitbit, Inc.*, 233 F. Supp. 3d at 812.
20. *Id.* at 812–13.

Figure 3-2
Sample Utility Patents in Fashion

U.S. Patent No. 6,016,613 U.S. Patent No. 7,367,669 U.S. Patent No. 7,946,322 U.S. Patent No. 6,427,242

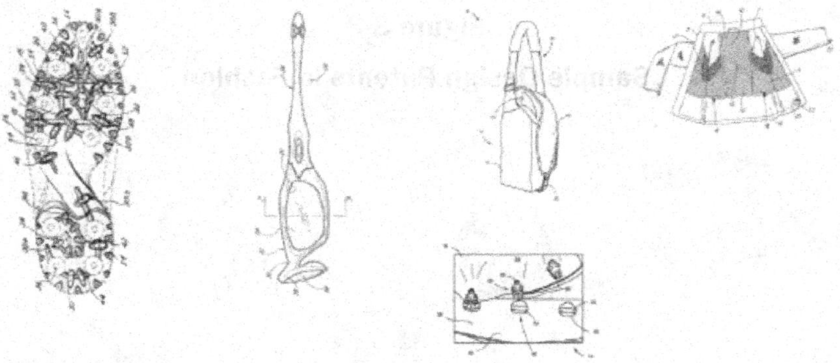

In sum, the subject matter of utility patents has covered a wide range of technologies both within and without the fashion industry, including, for example, the cotton gin,[21] battery-operated smoke detectors,[22] automatic bread slicers,[23] and electronic voting machines,[24] as well as chemical compounds used as antidepressants.[25] In the area of fashion, utility patents have been issued for golf shoes,[26] sunglasses,[27] purses,[28] and high-performance outerwear,[29] among others, as discussed further in this chapter.

§ 3:2.2 *What Is a Design Patent?*

Design patents are issued for new, original, and ornamental designs,[30] and as such, are often colloquially referred to as "picture

---

21. U.S. Patent No. 72X (filed Oct. 28, 1793).
22. *E.g.*, U.S. Patent No. 3,460,124 (filed June 6, 1966).
23. *E.g.*, U.S. Patent No. 1,867,377 (filed Nov. 26, 1928).
24. *E.g.*, U.S. Patent No. 4,015,106 (filed May 20, 1975).
25. *E.g.*, U.S. Patent No. 4,314,081 (filed Jan. 10, 1974).
26. *E.g.*, U.S. Patent No. 6,016,613 (filed Nov. 5, 1997).
27. *E.g.*, U.S. Patent No. 7,367,669 (filed Jan. 1, 2007).
28. *E.g.*, U.S. Patent No. 7,946,322 (filed Apr. 20, 2009).
29. *E.g.*, U.S. Patent No. 6,427,242 (filed Jan. 5, 2000).
30. *See* 35 U.S.C. § 171. According to the PTO, "[i]n a design patent application, the subject matter which is claimed is the design embodied in or applied to an article of manufacture (or portion thereof) and not the article itself." MPEP, *supra* note 8, § 1502. "[35 U.S.C. §] 171 refers, not

patents." Iconic design patents include those for the Statue of Liberty[31] and the classic Coca-Cola bottle.[32] In the area of fashion, design patents have been issued for eyeglass frames,[33] watches,[34] shoes,[35] and jeans,[36] among others.

Figure 3-3

Sample Design Patents in Fashion

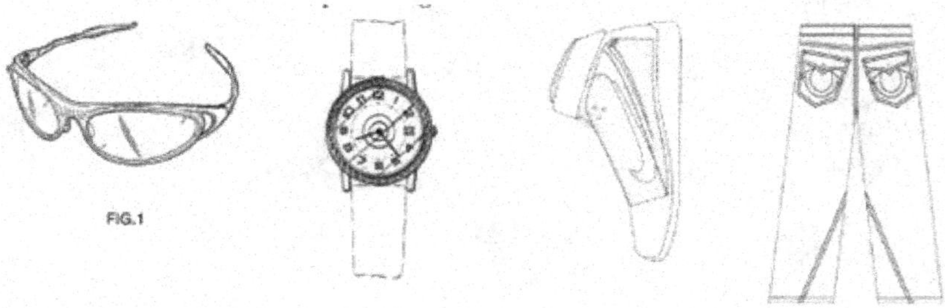

To be patentable, the design must be both (1) "aesthetically pleasing," and (2) "not . . . dictated by function alone."[37] It should be noted that decisions by the U.S. Court of Appeals for the Federal Circuit (the federal appeals court with exclusive appellate jurisdiction over patent cases) reflect a shift away from emphasizing the aesthetic beauty of an article of manufacture as a "requirement" for patentability.[38] But

---

to the design *of* an article, but *to* the design for an article, and is inclusive of ornamental designs of all kinds including surface ornamentation as well as configuration of goods." *In re* Zahn, 617 F.2d 261 (C.C.P.A. 1980). "Design is inseparable from the article to which it is applied and cannot exist alone merely as a scheme of surface ornamentation. It must be a definite, preconceived thing, capable of reproduction and not merely the chance result of a method . . . ." MPEP, *supra* note 8, § 1504.01 (citing Blisscraft of Hollywood v. United Plastics Co., 189 F. Supp. 333 (S.D.N.Y. 1960), 294 F.2d 694 (2d Cir. 1961)).

31. *E.g.*, U.S. Patent No. D11,023 (filed Jan. 2, 1879) (Statute of Liberty).
32. *E.g.*, U.S. Patent No. D48,160 (filed Aug. 18, 1915) (Coca-Cola bottle).
33. *E.g.*, U.S. Patent No. D436,119 (filed Nov. 12, 1999) (Bolle eyeglasses).
34. *E.g.*, U.S. Patent No. D265,632 (filed Apr. 2, 1979), D314,154 (filed Feb. 18, 1988).
35. *E.g.*, U.S. Patent No. D546,540 (filed Jan. 15, 2007).
36. *E.g.*, U.S. Patent No. D547,530 (filed Dec. 9, 2005).
37. Bonito Boats Inc. v. Thunder Craft Boats Inc., 489 U.S. 141, 148 (1989).
38. *See* Seiko Epson Corp. v. Nu-Kote Int'l, Inc., 190 F.3d 1360, 1368 (Fed. Cir. 1999) ("Nor need the design be aesthetically pleasing. The 'ornamental'

because the second requirement provides that the patented design be dictated by something other than function, designs rendered valuable simply as a result of functional considerations are not patentable.[39] For example, in *Best Lock Corp. v. Ilco Unican Corp.*,[40] the design patent claimed the portion of the key that was designed to fit into the matching front face of a key plug (the "key blade"). The Federal Circuit held the patent invalid because the key blade's design was dictated by its function—the key blade had to fit into the matching key plug in order for the lock to function properly—and not solely by any decorative influence.

It is important to note that a single invention may be eligible for patent protection from *both* a utility patent *and* a design patent. For example, if an invention has a unique structure or function and also has a unique ornamental design, it may be appropriate to seek both a utility patent (to protect the functional aspect of the product), as well as a design patent (to protect the appearance of the product), as long as the design is not dictated by the function. Indeed, a single product may be covered by more than one utility patent and/or more than

---

requirement of the design statute means that the design must not be governed solely by function, *i.e.*, that this is not the only possible form of the article that could perform its function.") (citing L.A. Gear v. Thom McAn Shoe Co., 988 F.2d 1117, 1123 (Fed. Cir. 1993)). "A design patent is for a useful article, but patentability is based on the design of the article, not the use. The design may contribute distinctiveness or consumer recognition to the design, but an absence of artistic merit does not mean that the design is purely functional." *Id.* An article in the *Journal of Intellectual Property* concluded that this doctrinal shift matched a larger shift in court outcomes. The study purported to measure the average attractiveness of patented designs (as rated in a controlled experiment) and concluded that although the "average attractiveness" of design patents has remained stable over the last three decades, the average attractiveness of the designs found to be invalid has grown. Andrew W. Torrance, *Beauty Fades: An Experimental Study of Federal Court Design Patent Aesthetics*, 19 J. INTELL. PROP. L. 2, 389 (2012). Thus, according to the author, "both legal doctrine and empirical data reflect a decline in the importance of aesthetic considerations in design patent decisions by federal courts over the last three decades." *Id.*, Abstract. The author concluded that "[d]esign beauty appears to have ceased to be a useful predictor of judicial outcome in design patent litigation." *Id.* at 392.

39. *E.g.*, Door-Master Corp. v. Yorktown, Inc., 256 F.3d 1308, 1312 (Fed. Cir. 2001); Best Lock Corp. v. Ilco Unican Corp., 94 F.3d 1563, 1566 (Fed. Cir. 1996) ("If the design claimed in a design patent is dictated solely by the function of the article of manufacture, the patent is invalid because the design is not ornamental . . . . A design is not dictated solely by its function when alternative designs for the article of manufacture are available.").

40. *Best Lock Corp.*, 94 F.3d at 1566.

one design patent. As another example, in the case of design patents, the claimed design may be a portion of the ultimate product sold (for example, the waistband of the yoga pant), the entire product sold (for example, the entire design of the yoga pant), or the ornamentation applied to the design (for example, a particular pattern of fabric used to make the yoga pant).

§ 3:3 Applying for Patent Protection

§ 3:3.1 *Application Requirements*

Both utility and design patents have stringent application requirements that must be met in order for a valid patent to issue.

Although, traditionally the PTO awarded a patent to the person or people who could prove that they were the first to invent patentable subject matter, the United States transitioned to primarily a first-to-file system, pursuant to the America Invents Act (AIA), passed by Congress in 2011 and signed into law by President Obama. Under the pre-AIA law, the date of invention was just as significant as the application filing date, indeed, in most cases, more so. But since passage of the AIA, the date of invention has limited importance for any application filed and claiming priority on or after March 16, 2013.

Early filing of an application for an invention, therefore, is extremely useful, as a patent applicant cannot know when a third party may file its own patent application or publicly disclose the same or a similar invention, which could prevent the issuance of a valid patent.[41] Moreover, the patent applicant's own sale or public disclosure of an invention can bar a patent unless the applicant files a patent within one year (the "grace period") of the first sale or public disclosure.[42]

A utility patent application must have a "specification" that includes a written description of the invention that enables those skilled in the art to make and use the claimed invention.[43] This can be seen as one aspect of the "bargain" under which a patentee gets a limited monopoly on an invention in exchange for public disclosure.[44] The specification is required to state the "best mode" contemplated by the inventor for practicing the invention, but changes in the AIA expressly state that failure to disclose the best mode is no longer a basis to invalidate a patent or otherwise render it unenforceable.[45]

---

41. *See* 35 U.S.C. § 102(a).
42. *Id.*; 35 U.S.C. § 102(b).
43. 35 U.S.C. § 112.
44. *See* Pfaff v. Wells Elecs., Inc., 525 U.S. 55, 64 (1998).
45. 35 U.S.C. § 282(b)(3)(A).

In addition to a written description, an application must include one or more drawings "where necessary for the understanding of the subject matter sought to be patented."[46] The vast majority of patent applications, including those relevant to the fashion industry, will have drawings, as shown in the illustrative examples set forth in the appendices to this chapter.

The purpose of the written specification and the drawings is to set the stage for the most legally significant part of a utility patent, which are the "claims." Every patent concludes with a list of specific numbered paragraphs that define the scope of the patent, that is, the subject matter over which the patentee has exclusive rights.[47] While a patent need only include a single claim, most patents include a number of claims that define the invention in somewhat different terms and in different levels of detail. Including multiple claims helps a patent owner protect its own products and also bring as many potentially infringing products within the scope of the patent and also to provide multiple layers of protection if the validity of the patent is challenged (which nearly always occurs in litigation). A broad claim is more difficult to defend than a narrower claim.

A patent application must also include an oath (or declaration) from the inventor(s) stating that he or she authorizes the patent application and believes himself or herself to be the original inventor.[48] An assignee of an inventor's rights may file a patent application without the oath if the inventor cannot be found or refuses to execute the oath. This situation typically arises in the employment context. For this and other reasons, it is important—and quite commonplace—for employers to have employees execute written agreements vesting patent ownership in the employer for all inventions created within the scope of their employment. Unlike other forms of intellectual

---

46. 15 U.S.C. § 113.

47. *See* 35 U.S.C. § 112(b); Corning Glass Works v. Sumitomo Elec. USA, Inc., 868 F.2d 1251, 1257 (Fed. Cir. 1989) ("A claim in a patent provides the metes and bounds of the right which the patent confers on the patentee to exclude others from making, using, or selling the protected invention.").

48. 35 U.S.C. § 115. Where there are multiple inventors for a patent application, each must provide a declaration. *See* U.S. PATENT & TRADEMARK OFFICE, AIA INVENTOR'S OATH OR DECLARATION QUICK REFERENCE GUIDE, § II ("an inventor's oath or declaration . . . executed by or with respect to each inventor must be submitted on the same day as the nonprovisional application is filed"), http://www.uspto.gov/aia_implementation/inventors-oath-or-declaration-quick-reference-guide.pdf.

property, and subject to exceptions, an employer does *not* in general own inventions created by employees absent such an agreement.[49]

§ 3:3.2 *Prior Art Searches*

The PTO does not require that a patent applicant perform any searching to see what other public information may already exist that is relevant to the applicant's claim of originality (the "prior art") before filing a patent application. Nevertheless, a prior art search can help determine if a patent application is likely to be approved and also determine the appropriate "scope" of the claimed invention. It may also help in crafting a more effective application. For example, it is generally not useful to explain in detail features that are already known in the art; rather, it is more productive to focus on the new features. This can only be done when the drafter of the application has a sense of the most relevant prior art.

The PTO does, however, require that the applicant and those involved in the application process disclose prior art material to the application that is known to each of them, and an intentional failure to do so can be classified as "inequitable conduct" and serve as a basis to hold a patent unenforceable.[50]

§ 3:3.3 *Costs and Fees*

A complete patent application must also include the required fee. Fees vary depending on the status of the applicant:

(1) An applicant not entitled to any special reduction (a "large entity") pays the full fee;

(2) An applicant that is a "small entity" (essentially, independent inventors with income above a certain level, small business concerns, and nonprofits) pays 50% of most fees; and

(3) An applicant that is classified as a "micro entity" (an independent inventor who has gross income below a specified level and has filed fewer than a certain number of patent applications, and employees of institutions of higher education where the institution owns the invention) is entitled to pay 25% of most fees.[51]

---

49. *See, e.g.*, Ethicon, Inc. v. U.S. Surgical Corp., 135 F.3d 1456, 1460 (Fed. Cir. 1998).

50. *See* Therasense, Inc. v. Becton, Dickinson & Co., 649 F.3d 1276 (Fed. Cir. 2011) (en banc); 37 C.F.R. § 1.56.

51. 35 U.S.C. §§ 41, 123; 37 C.F.R. § 1.27; MPEP, *supra* note 8, § 509.02.

An applicant is not entitled to small entity or micro entity status if someone who does not fit one of these categories also has rights to the same patent. There can be significant consequences (including loss of patent rights in some circumstances) for improperly claiming reduced fee status, so it is important to ensure that an applicant does in fact meet the relevant criteria.[52]

As of January 1, 2019, the full fee for filing a utility patent application (including the "filing" fee, "search" fee, and "examination" fee) was over $1,700. If the patent application is allowed (and the applicant still desires to obtain a patent), a $1,000 issue fee must be paid.[53] The full fee for filing a design patent application (including the "filing" fee, "search" fee, and "examination" fee) is $960, and the issue fee is $700.[54] Additional fees are often due for any number of reasons (for example, to file disclosure statements identifying prior art, to file excess claims, to file delayed responses to official actions, etc.).

In addition to fees due to the PTO, the more significant costs may be those charged by patent attorneys and other professionals to prepare and file patent applications. Fees vary by the professional and the complexity of the invention, with design patent applications being typically significantly less expensive than utility applications. Typical professional fees have historically varied, between the order of $1,000 for a design patent application to up to $10,000 or more for complex utility patent applications, although most applications in the fashion industry will probably not command the premium fees charged for highly complex technology.

§ 3:3.4 Examination

After a complete patent application is filed, it awaits review by a patent examiner, which primarily consists of searching for related art and evaluating the patentability of the claims over that art. The delay before the first substantive review (the first "Office Action") depends on the backlog of applications in the PTO. In 2018, the delay was estimated to last, on average, about sixteen (16) months, although less technical patent applications may be examined somewhat more quickly.[55]

---

52. *See* 37 C.F.R. § 1.27; MPEP, *supra* note 8, § 509.02.

53. *See* U.S. PATENT & TRADEMARK OFFICE, USPTO FEE SCHEDULE (2019), https://www.uspto.gov/learning-and-resources/fees-and-payment/uspto-fee-schedule.

54. *Id.*

55. *See* U.S. PATENT & TRADEMARK OFFICE, NOVEMBER 2018 PATENTS DATA, AT A GLANCE [hereinafter PTO, NOVEMBER 2018 PATENTS DATA], https://www.uspto.gov/dashboards/patents/main.dashxml. Applications for design patents are processed somewhat quicker, with the initial response time averaging just under fourteen (14) months. *Id.* at "Design Data."

If the examiner rejects the application, the applicant's options are:

- amend the claims in an effort to overcome the rejection;
- attempt to persuade the examiner that the rejection is incorrect and should be withdrawn;
- some combination of the foregoing; or
- take no action and allow the application to go abandoned.

The choice as to the best course of action will usually depend on the merits of the examiner's rejection, which is usually determined by the seriousness of the concerns raised by the examiner.

An applicant may go through repeated rounds of PTO rejections and responsive arguments before a patent issues, and the procedure of arguments and amendments may require filing additional applications that claim priority to the initial application or taking other procedural steps, with additional fees.[56] Patent "prosecution" (that is, the actions taken in filing one or more patent applications and interacting with the PTO to secure the allowance of one or more patents) may involve complicated strategies and is often handled by attorneys (or sometimes patent agents) who specialize in that work.

A patent applicant who is dissatisfied with an examiner's continued rejection of a patent application may file an appeal within the PTO and ultimately to the federal courts.[57] Appeals within the PTO are common and have a reasonable success rate; appeals to the courts are less common and generally reserved to inventions seen as having significant commercial potential.

Once (and if) the patent examiner allows the application, the PTO issues a Notice of Allowance, and the patent applicant may pay the issue fee and receive the patent. As of November 2018, the average utility patent application pendency was twenty-four (24) months.[58]

The term of a utility patent is twenty (20) years from its effective U.S. filing date (although the term of older patents may be different due to a change in the law operative in 1995).[59] The term is subject to the payment of maintenance fees due three-and-a-half (3½), seven-and-a-half (7½), and eleven-and-a-half (11½) years after the date of patent grant. Failure to pay a maintenance fee results in the abandonment of the patent, although the PTO has provided a grace period and a

---

56. *See* 35 U.S.C. § 120 (continuation applications); § 132 (continued examination).

57. *See* 35 U.S.C. §§ 134, 141, 145.

58. *See* PTO, NOVEMBER 2018 PATENTS DATA, *supra* note 55. The average pendency of prosecution extends past thirty (30) months when "Requests for Continued Examination" (RCE) are considered.

59. *See* 35 U.S.C. § 154.

procedural mechanism to cure an inadvertent or unavoidable failure to make a payment.[60]

§ 3:3.5 Design Patent Applications

Design patent applications are simpler than utility patent applications, as the application essentially consists of drawings of the design to be patented, without significant additional verbiage. Design patents are valid for fifteen (15) years from grant, unless filed before May 13, 2015, in which case a fourteen- (14-)year term applies.[61] A design patent does not have maintenance fees. Design patents are not published before issuance.

The average design patent application pendency is about fourteen months, and the patent grant rate is over 80%.[62]

§ 3:3.6 Marking

It is permissible, but not required, to mark a physical object covered by a pending patent application with the words "patent pending," or the like. Once a patent has been granted, it is advantageous to "mark" the article with the words "patent" or the abbreviation "pat.", together with the patent number(s) (or a Web address containing that information).[63] If the physical article cannot be marked (for example, due to its size), the marking can be done on packaging or labels.[64] For patent claims covering physical products or objects (such as articles of apparel), failure to mark may limit the patentee to damages accrued only after the infringer has been notified of the infringement.[65] The marking requirement does not apply, however, to patent claims covering processes or methods of manufacturing products, or to instances where a patentee has not yet made or licensed the manufacturer of patented products.[66] On the other hand, it should

---

60. 37 C.F.R. § 1.378.
61. 35 U.S.C. § 173; MPEP, *supra* note 8, § 1505.
62. *See* PTO, NOVEMBER 2018 PATENTS DATA, *supra* note 55.
63. 35 U.S.C. § 287.
64. *Id.*
65. *Id. See also infra* section 3:4.2.
66. 35 U.S.C. § 287; ActiveVideo Networks v. Verizon Commc'ns, 694 F.3d 1312, 1335 (Fed. Cir. 2012) ("[P]atents which contain only method claims are not subject to the section 287 marking requirements[.]"); Crown Packaging Tech., Inc. v. Rexam Beverage Can Co., 559 F.3d 1308, 1316 (Fed. Cir. 2009) (35 U.S.C. § 287(a) does not apply if "the patentee only asserted the method claims of a patent which included both method and apparatus claims.").

be noted that marking products with expired or plainly inapplicable patents ("false marking") carries its own penalties.[67]

§ 3:4 Patent Enforcement and Remedies

§ 3:4.1 *Patent Infringement*

A patent gives its owner the right to exclude others from making, using, selling, or offering for sale the invention within the United States or importing the invention into the United States.[68] A utility patent bestows this right for twenty (20) years after the application is filed;[69] a design patent for fifteen (15) years after the application is issued.[70] Thus, a patent is infringed when one makes, uses, sells,

---

67. 35 U.S.C. § 292(a) ("Whoever, without the consent of the patentee, marks upon, or affixes to, or uses in advertising . . . the name or any imitation of the name of the patentee, the patent number, or the words 'patent,' 'patentee,' or the like, with the intent of counterfeiting or imitating the mark of the patentee, or of deceiving the public . . . ; or Whoever marks upon, or affixes to, or uses in advertising in connection with any unpatented article, the word 'patent' or any word or number importing that the same is patented, for the purpose of deceiving the public; or Whoever marks upon, or affixes to, or uses in advertising in connection with any article, the words 'patent applied for,' 'patent pending,' or any word importing that an application for patent has been made, when no application for patent has been made . . . [s]hall be fined not more than $500 for every such offense. Only the United States may sue for the penalty authorized by this subsection."); *id.* § 292(b) ("A person who has suffered a competitive injury as a result of a violation of this section may file a civil action in a district court of the United States for recovery of damages adequate to compensate for the injury.").

68. 35 U.S.C. § 271(a) ("[W]hoever without authority makes, uses, offers to sell or sells any patented invention, within the United States or imports into the United States any patented invention during the term of the patent therefor, infringes the patent."). A claim for infringement is limited to reaching back six (6) years from the filing of the complaint. 35 U.S.C. § 286. But that six- (6-)year period cannot be reduced under equitable doctrines asserting unfair delay in enforcement (that is, laches). Hygiene Prods. Aktiebolag v. First Quality Baby Prods., LLC, 580 U.S. __ (2017).

69. If a utility patent could claim "priority" to the filing date of an earlier patent application, the twenty- (20-)year period would be calculated based on that earlier date. Priority may be claimed where the earlier-filed application adequately describes the invention claimed in the later-filed patent. Historically, for a utility patent whose application had been filed before June 8, 1995, such patent was entitled to a term of the longer of seventeen (17) years from its issue date or twenty (20) years from the filing date of the earliest U.S. or international application to which it could claim priority.

70. 35 U.S.C. § 173.

or imports the patented invention without the patentee's permission during the life of the patent (often referred to as the "patent term").

In the case of a utility patent, the patent is infringed simply if the accused product does ("practices") what the claim's limitations describe as the invention. In the case of design patents, however, there is only one claim, the scope of which is determined by the patent's drawings.[71] A design patent is infringed if, from the perspective of an "ordinary observer," the accused design appears to be "substantially similar" to the non-functional aspects of the patented design:[72]

"[I]f, in the eye of an ordinary observer, giving such attention as a purchaser usually gives, two designs are substantially the same, if the resemblance is such as to deceive such an observer, inducing him to purchase one supposing it to be the other, the first one patented is infringed by the other."[73]

Accordingly, the object or product does not need to be an exact match for the patent to be infringed.[74]

---

71. *See* Crocs, Inc. v. Int'l Trade Comm'n, 598 F.3d 1294, 1302 (Fed. Cir. 2010); *see also* L.A. Gear, Inc. v. McAn Shoe Co., 988 F.2d 1117, 1122 (Fed. Cir. 1993) ("A patented design is ordinarily claimed as shown, that is, by its drawing.").

72. Gorham Mfg. Co. v. White, 81 U.S. 511 (1872). This assessment should be made as if the ordinary observer is seeing the patented design for the first time, rather than long after the patented design has become familiar to the viewer (because, for example, it has sold well). *See, e.g.*, Sanson Hosiery Mills v. Warren Knitting Mills, 202 F.2d 383, 395 (3d Cir. 1953); Contessa Food Prods. v. Conagra, Inc., 282 F.3d 1370, 1375, 1381 (Fed. Cir. 2002). On the other hand, an accused product may infringe even if it differs from the plaintiff's own commercialized design, just as long as it is substantially similar to the design that was patented. *E.g.*, OddzOn Prods., Inc. v. Just Toys, Inc., 122 F.3d 1396, 1404 (Fed. Cir. 1997). The similarity must also arise from the non-functional aspects of the patented design. *E.g.*, *id.*; Richardson v. Stanley Works, Inc., 597 F.3d 1288, 1293 (Fed. Cir. 2010) ("In *OddzOn*, we affirmed a district court's claim construction wherein the court had carefully distinguished the ornamental features of the patented design from the overall 'rocket-like' appearance of the design of a football-shaped foam ball with a tail and fin structure. . . . We held that '[w]here a design contains both functional and non-functional elements, the scope of the claim must be construed in order to identify the non-functional aspects of the design as shown in the patent.' . . . The district court here properly factored out the functional aspects of Richardon's design as part of its claim construction.").

73. *Gorham Mfg. Co.*, 81 U.S. at 528.

74. *See Crocs*, 598 F.3d at 1303. In *Crocs*, the Federal Circuit overruled an ITC finding of non-infringement on the basis that the ITC put "undue emphasis on particular details of its written description of the patented design," *id.* at 1303, rather than taking a "view to the design as a whole," *id.* at 1304. "In other words, the concentration on small differences in isolation distracted from the overall impression of the claimed

Traditionally, a finding of design patent infringement also required the patentee to satisfy a test referred to as the "point of novelty test."[75] While the newer "ordinary observer" test still assumes that the observer is familiar with the prior art,[76] the patentee no longer needs to show that the accused design "appropriate[d] the novelty in the patented device which distinguishes it from the prior art."[77] Because the "point of novelty test" was perceived as a difficult hurdle for patentees to clear, the abolishment of the test was widely seen as a boon to design patent holders.[78] In addition to simplifying the infringement test, at least one author has predicted that removing the "point of novelty" test from the equation will make "competitors less likely to design 'close to the line' because the ordinary observer test's standard of 'substantial similarity' is very difficult to assess before the fact. . . . Thus, competitors will shy away from close design-arounds,[79] leaving design patents with a *de facto* increase in scope of protection."[80]

§ 3:4.2 Remedies

Upon a finding of infringement, several remedies are available to compensate the patentee including monetary damages,[81] an injunction

ornamental features. The proper comparison requires a side-by-side view of the drawings of the [patent-in-suit] and the accused products." *Id.*

75. Egyptian Goddess, Inc. v. Swisa, Inc., 543 F.3d 665, 681 (Fed. Cir. 2008) (en banc), *cert. denied*, 129 S. Ct. 1917 (2009) (rejecting the "point of novelty" test articulated in Litton Sys., Inc. v. Whirlpool Corp., 728 F.2d 1423 (Fed. Cir. 1984)).

76. *See Crocs*, 598 F.3d at 1303; *Egyptian Goddess*, 543 F.3d at 681; Smith v. Whitman Saddle Co., 148 U.S. 674, 674–75 (1893). If the claimed design is similar to the prior art, then the ordinary observer may pay more attention to those aspects of the claimed design that distinguish it from the prior art. *Crocs*, 598 F.3d at 1303.

77. *Litton Sys.*, 728 F.2d at 1444.

78. *E.g.*, Perry J. Saidman, *Egyptian Goddess Exposed!: But Not in the Buff(er)*, 90 J. PAT. & TRADEMARK OFFICE SOC'Y 859, 884–85 (2008); Christopher V. Carani, *Design Law & Footwear: Landmark Case Fundamentally Alters Design Patent Enforcement*, SHOE RETAILING TODAY, 26–27 (July–Aug. 2009) [hereinafter Carani] ("With the troublesome point of novelty test eliminated, design patentees undoubtedly received a significant boost.").

79. A "design around" is a phrase typically used to describe a would-be infringer's attempt to design his or her product around the patent's claims.

80. Carani, *supra* note 78, at 26.

81. 35 U.S.C. § 284 ("Upon finding for the claimant the court shall award the claimant damages adequate to compensate for the infringement, but in no event less than a reasonable royalty for the use made of the invention by the infringer, together with interest and costs as fixed by the court."); 35 U.S.C. § 289 ("Whoever during the term of a patent for a design

(preliminary or permanent),[82] attorneys' fees in exceptional cases,[83] and/or prejudgment interest,[84] although some of these remedies are awarded more frequently than others. In addition, if the infringement is "willful," as discussed further below, enhanced damages may also be available.[85]

[A] Monetary Damages

An award of monetary damages as a remedy for patent infringement serves two alternative purposes: first, to compensate the patentee for any injury suffered by way of the infringement, and second, to punish the infringer. Regarding the first category of monetary damages, the award will attempt to approximate the amount necessary to restore the owner to the financial position he or she would have enjoyed absent any infringement (the "lost profits" approach).[86] Regarding the second category of monetary damages, the award is in the form of a royalty: either an "established royalty," if the established royalty can be known by a history of prior actual licenses for acts comparable to those engaged in by the infringer, or a "reasonable royalty," the amount that would have been set in a hypothetical negotiation between a willing patent owner and a willing potential licensee (now infringer) if the

---

[infringes the design] . . . shall be liable to the owner to the extent of his total profit, but not less than $250, recoverable in any United States district court having jurisdiction of the parties.").

82. 35 U.S.C. § 283 ("[The court] . . . may grant injunctions in accordance with the principles of equity to prevent the violation of any right secured by patent, on such terms as the court deems reasonable.").

83. 35 U.S.C. § 285 ("The court in exceptional cases may award reasonable attorney fees to the prevailing party.").

84. 35 U.S.C. § 284 ("Upon finding for the claimant the court shall award the claimant damages adequate to compensate for the infringement, but in no event less than a reasonable royalty for the use made of the invention by the infringer, *together with interest* and costs as fixed by the court.") (emphasis added).

85. *Id.* ("the court may increase the damages up to three times the amount found or assessed."); *see also, e.g.*, Halo Elecs., Inc. v. Pulse Elecs., Inc., 136 S. Ct. 1923, 1933 (2016) ("[T]he subjective willfulness of a patent infringer, intentional or knowing, may warrant enhanced damages, without regard to whether his infringement was objectively reckless.").

86. *See, e.g.*, Depuy Spine, Inc. v. Medtronic Sofamor Danek, Inc., 567 F.3d 1314, 1329 (Fed. Cir. 2009) (applying a four-factor test from Panduit Corp. v. Stahlin Bros. Fibre Works, Inc., 575 F.2d 1152, 1156 (6th Cir. 1978) to affirm a jury award of lost profits). In certain cases, lost *foreign* profits may be recoverable for infringing activities caused by exportation of specially designed components for assembly abroad. *See* WesternGeco LLC v. ION Geophysical Corp., 579 U.S. ___ (2018) (allowing the recovery of lost foreign profits due to infringement under 35 U.S.C. § 271(f)(2)).

license had been negotiated before the infringement began.[87] The most common remedy sought by patentees is the reasonable royalty.

In the case of design patents, however, a fourth option is available—an accounting of the infringer's total illicit profits.[88] A design patent owner can therefore choose either to recover the infringer's profits, or to seek one of the traditional patent remedies (but not both). Seeking total profits can be an especially attractive option when the damages would otherwise be difficult to prove.

For the accrual of monetary damages to begin, however, the would-be infringer must be on actual or constructive notice of the patentee's rights if the patent owner has already made or sold goods covered by the patent.[89] The patent owner can satisfy this requirement by showing that the infringer knew about the patent at issue, but a patentee may also be able to provide constructive notice of the patent at an earlier date if it marked its own commercial products with

---

87. *See, e.g.*, Mars, Inc. v. Coin Acceptors, Inc., 527 F.3d 1359 (Fed. Cir. 2008). Where a patent covers just one or a limited number of features in a multi-feature device, the "reasonable royalty" must be apportioned to account for the contribution of the patented aspects versus other features. *See* VirnetX, Inc. v. Cisco Sys., Inc., 767 F.3d 1308, 1327–28 (Fed. Cir. 2014); LaserDynamics, Inc. v. Quanta Comput., Inc., 694 F.3d 51, 68–69 (Fed. Cir. 2012). This prevents the patentee from obtaining a royalty on the infringing product's unpatented features. CSIRO v. Cisco Sys., Inc., 809 F.3d 1295, 1302 (Fed. Cir. 2015).

88. 35 U.S.C. § 289 ("Whoever during the term of a patent for a design [infringes the design] . . . shall be liable to the owner to the extent of his total profit, but not less than $250, recoverable in any United States district court having jurisdiction of the parties."). The "article of manufacture" used as the base for profit disgorgement need not be the end product sold to consumers; it can be just a component of that product. Samsung Elecs. Co. v. Apple Inc., 137 S. Ct. 429, 434 (2016). To measure disgorgement under section 289, a court must "[f]irst, identify the 'article of manufacture' to which the infringed design has been applied [and second,] calculate the infringer's total profit made on that article of manufacture." *Id.* at 434. To identify the article of manufacture (that is, the product as a whole or a component), courts have considered four factors: "[1] The scope of the design claimed in the plaintiff's patent, including the drawing and written description; [2] The relative prominence of the design within the product as a whole; [3] Whether the design is conceptually distinct from the product as a whole; and [4] The physical relationship between the patented design and the rest of the product, including whether the design pertains to a component that a user or seller can physically separate from the product as a whole, and whether the design is embodied in a component that is manufactured separately from the rest of the product, or if the component can be sold separately." Apple Inc. v. Samsung Elecs. Co., No. 11-CV-01846-LHK, 2017 U.S. Dist. LEXIS 177199, at *111 (N.D. Cal. Oct. 22, 2017).

89. *See supra* section 3:3.6.

the applicable patent numbers.[90] As noted earlier, this is why products offered for sale in the marketplace embodying a patent are often marked with the word "patent" or the abbreviation "pat." followed by the patent number affixed to the product. Marking a product this way gives constructive notice of the patent to the world. In the absence of such marking, pre-suit monetary damages may be limited.[91]

[B] Injunctive Relief

In some cases, a patent owner may also be able to obtain an injunction prohibiting infringing activity by the accused infringer.[92] The injunction may be preliminary (prohibiting the infringing behavior while the lawsuit is pending) or permanent (prohibiting the behavior after the patentee prevails on the merits). In order to obtain a preliminary injunction, the patentee must establish a strong probability of success on the merits and that the patentee will be irreparably injured if the infringer were permitted to continue the infringement.[93] The trial court has considerable discretion whether to issue a preliminary injunction, and will consider other factors, such as the relative hardships that the parties will suffer from granting or withholding the injunction, and possible effects on third parties or the public interest.[94] Once a patent owner has prevailed on the merits of a patent infringement claim, it may request either a permanent injunction against future infringement or monetary damages for

---

90. 35 U.S.C. § 287(a) ("Patentees, and persons making, offering for sale, or selling within the United States any patented article for or under them, or importing any patented article into the United States, may give notice to the public that the same is patented, either by fixing thereon the word 'patent' or the abbreviation 'pat.', together with the number of the patent, or by fixing thereon the word 'patent' or the abbreviation 'pat.' together with an address of a posting on the Internet, accessible to the public without charge for accessing the address, that associates the patented article with the number of the patent, or when, from the character of the article, this cannot be done, by fixing to it, or to the package wherein one or more of them is contained, a label containing a like notice. In the event of failure so to mark, no damages shall be recovered by the patentee in any action for infringement, except on proof that the infringer was notified of the infringement and continued to infringe thereafter, in which event damages may be recovered only for infringement occurring after such notice. Filing of an action for infringement shall constitute such notice.").
91. *Id. See also supra* section 3:3.6.
92. 35 U.S.C. § 283 ("[The court] . . . may grant injunctions in accordance with the principles of equity to prevent the violation of any right secured by patent, on such terms as the court deems reasonable.").
93. *See* Apple, Inc. v. Samsung Elecs. Co., 695 F.3d 1370, 1374 (Fed. Cir. 2012).
94. *Id.*

future infringement, but not both.[95] As permanent injunctions are relatively rare, most often monetary damages are sought.

[C] Attorneys' Fees

Typically, each party bears its own costs in patent infringement litigations. However, in exceptional cases, the court may award reasonable attorneys' fees to the prevailing party.[96] This applies to both plaintiffs and defendants. A case is "exceptional" if it is "simply one that stands out from others with respect to the substantive strength of a party's litigating position (considering both the governing law and the facts of the case) or the unreasonable manner in which the case was litigated."[97]

[D] Prejudgment Interest

In addition to monetary damages, a patent owner whose patent has been infringed may also be entitled to prejudgment interest. Because damage awards for patent infringement are meant to place the patent owner in as good a position as he would have been had the infringer entered into a reasonable royalty agreement, an award of prejudgment interest is necessary in a typical case.[98] On the other hand, if the patent owner is responsible for undue delay in prosecuting the lawsuit, prejudgment interest may be limited or denied completely.[99]

---

95. *See, e.g.*, Trans-World Mfg. Corp. v. Al Nyman & Sons, Inc., 750 F.2d 1552, 1565 (Fed. Cir. 1984) ("Where the damage award is based upon an assumed license for the life of the patent, there is no need to enjoin use, because the license fee authorizes use. The propriety of an injunction against use, however, arises only if the damages are based upon a flat amount giving the licensee the right to use the patent for its life."). Injunctions are, however, not granted as a matter of right. eBay Inc. v. MercExchange, L.L.C., 547 U.S. 388, 391 (2006). The harm of future infringement must be irreparable and not remediable by royalty damages. *Id.* Courts also must consider the respective hardships on the parties, as well as whether the public's interest would be served by an injunction. *Id.* This contrasts with the laws in other countries (for example, Germany), where patent injunctions are routine.
96. 35 U.S.C. § 285.
97. *See, e.g.*, Octane Fitness, LLC v. ICON Health & Fitness, Inc., 572 U.S. 545, 554 (2014). An award of attorney's fees is reviewed for abuse of discretion. Highmark Inc. v. Allcare Health Mgmt. Sys., Inc., 572 U.S. 559, 564 (2014).
98. Gen. Motors Corp. v. Devex Corp., 461 U.S. 648, 655–56 (1983).
99. *Id.* at 656–57.

[E] Enhanced Damages for Willful Infringement

Courts also have the discretion to "increase the damages up to three times the amount found or assessed"[100] if the court determines that the infringer should be penalized for his or her increased culpability from acting "willfully" or in "bad faith."[101] In order to obtain these "treble damages," the plaintiff/patentee must show by a preponderance of evidence that, given the particular circumstances of the case, the infringement went beyond that done in ignorance or good faith, but instead constituted egregious conduct based on the accused infringer's "subjective willfulness."[102] One way a company may try to reduce the likelihood that a court would find that its sale of the accused products constitutes "willful" infringement is for the company to obtain an opinion by legal counsel concluding that the products do not infringe a particular patent or patents.[103]

§ 3:5 Territoriality of Patent Protection

Under U.S. patent law, the right to exclude granted by a patent is limited to "exclud[ing] others from making, using, offering for sale, or selling the invention *throughout the United States* or importing the invention *into the United States* . . . ."[104] Accordingly, patent infringement can generally be found only where the activity at issue—the "making, using, offering for sale, or selling"—occurs "within the

---

100. 35 U.S.C. § 284.

101. *See* Halo Elecs., Inc. v. Pulse Elecs., Inc., 136 S. Ct. 1923, 1932–33 (2016).

102. *See id.* at 1933.

103. *See In re* Seagate Tech., L.L.C., 497 F.3d 1360, 1369 (Fed. Cir. 2007) ("[A]ccused willful infringers commonly assert an advice of counsel defense. Under this defense, an accused willful infringer aims to establish that due to reasonable reliance on advice from counsel, its continued accused activities were done in good faith. Typically, counsel's opinion concludes that the patent is invalid, unenforceable, and/or not infringed. Although an infringer's reliance on favorable advice of counsel, or conversely his failure to proffer any favorable advice, is not dispositive of the willfulness inquiry, it is crucial to the analysis."), *abrogated on other grounds by Halo Elecs.*, 136 S. Ct. at 1928.

104. 35 U.S.C. § 154(a)(1) (emphases added) ("Every patent shall contain a short title of the invention and a grant to the patentee, his heirs or assigns, of the right to exclude others from making, using, offering for sale, or selling the invention throughout the United States or importing the invention into the United States, and, if the invention is a process, of the right to exclude others from using, offering for sale or selling throughout the United States, or importing into the United States, products made by that process, referring to the specification for the particulars thereof.").

United States" or where the patented invention is "import[ed] into the United States."[105] By contrast, where the "making" or "using" of the patentee's invention is occurring in another country, say Italy or China, U.S. patent law is unlikely to reach such activity for products that are not imported into the United States.[106] Instead, the patentee would have to first obtain a patent in that other country, and then enforce it in that country's courts.[107]

§ 3:5.1 Patent Enforcement in the United States

The U.S. court system provides several places ("jurisdictions," "venues," or "forum/fora") in which patentees may attempt to enforce their patent rights. First, as discussed above, a patentee can sue for patent infringement in a federal district court.[108] Second, the patentee can pursue a "Section 337 investigation" in the ITC.[109] The ITC is a federal agency with broad statutory authority over trade-related matters, including the authority to issue orders excluding the importation of infringing products into the United States. While the ITC cannot issue an award of monetary damages, an ITC exclusion order effectively makes it impossible to lawfully import and then sell infringing products in the United States.[110] That is, if the ITC determines that the accused products infringed the asserted patents, an ITC exclusion

---

105. 35 U.S.C. § 271(a) ("[W]hoever without authority makes, uses, offers to sell or sells any patented invention, within the United States or imports into the United States any patented invention during the term of the patent therefore, infringes the patent."). Limited exceptions are made to address specially designed components made in the United States, but exported for assembly to avoid infringement, and for imported products that were made abroad by a patented process. *Id.* § 271(f), (g). Where those limited exceptions apply, remedies (including potentially lost profits) may be available based on foreign conduct. *See, e.g.*, WesternGeco LLC v. ION Geophysical Corp., 579 U.S. ___ (2018).

106. *See* Microsoft Corp. v. AT&T Corp., 550 U.S. 437, 441 (2007) ("It is the general rule under United States patent law that no infringement occurs when a patented product is made and sold in another country."). But see exceptions stated in 35 U.S.C. § 271(f), (g).

107. *See, e.g.*, Voda v. Cordis Corp., 476 F.3d 887 (Fed. Cir. 2007) (holding that a district court abused its discretion in exercising supplemental jurisdiction to consider foreign patent claims asserted by the patent owner).

108. *See supra* section 3:4.2; *see also* 28 U.S.C. § 1338(a) ("The district courts shall have original jurisdiction of any civil action arising under any Act of Congress relating to patents, plant variety protection, copyrights and trademarks."); 28 U.S.C. § § 1331, 1391.

109. 19 U.S.C. § 1337.

110. *See supra* section 2:9.5 (discussing ITC orders in the context of trademark infringement).

order will direct the U.S. Customs and Border Protection to stop the importation of infringing products at the U.S. border, and a cease and desist order targeting activities already occurring in the United States.[111] Given the relatively rare issuance of preliminary or permanent injunctions by federal district courts, the ITC has become a hotspot for patent infringement litigation. However, in order to receive the ITC's assistance and relief, the patentee must engage in a substantial "domestic industry" in the United States with respect to the asserted patents. For an example of a recent enforcement of design patents in the ITC, see section 3:6.2 below.

The following hypothetical situation illustrates a patentee's enforcement rights. American company M has a patent on a particular process for making women's stiletto pumps; foreign company F does not have a license to M's patent, but is using that patented process to make pumps in Japan for import into the United States. M could enforce its patent rights in the following ways. First, M could sue F in federal district court for patent infringement. In that suit, M could sue for the monetary damages resulting from F's sales of its pumps in the United States, as well as seek an injunction to prevent F from continuing to sell its pumps in the United States. Second, M could bring a Section 337 Investigation in the ITC, seeking to stop the importation of F's pumps at the U.S. border. These two enforcement avenues are not mutually exclusive, and patentees often seek relief in both jurisdictions.

§ 3:5.2 Patent Protection Outside the United States

Because patent law is a creature of national law rather than international registration and enforcement, a U.S. patent does not provide a patentee with the ability to stop the manufacture, sale or distribution of goods that never enter the United States. In the hypothetical discussed above, company M would not be able to sue F for patent infringement if F made and sold its pumps exclusively in Japan. To entirely prevent F from continuing to make its stiletto pumps in Japan, M would have to obtain a Japanese patent covering its shoe-making process and enforce that Japanese patent against F in Japanese courts.

There are, however, various international agreements that provide patentees with certain advantages when applying for patents in other countries. For example, the Paris Convention for the Protection of Industrial Property requires its member countries to recognize "a right of priority" to patent applications filed domestically, as well as patent applications filed in the other member countries.[112] As a result,

---

111. 19 U.S.C. § 1337; 19 C.F.R. § § 210.1 *et seq.*

112. Paris Convention for the Protection of Industrial Property (Mar. 20, 1883, as revised at Stockholm, July 14, 1967), 21 U.S.T. 1583, 828 U.N.T.S.

when a patent owner in one country that is a signatory to the Paris Convention seeks a patent for the same invention in another signatory country, the second country should treat the patent owner as if he or she had applied for the patent on the same date as in the first country. This recognition of an earlier date can be important if someone else in the second country later makes a claim to the same invention.[113]

The Patent Cooperation Treaty (PCT) provides a more concrete recognition of these international benefits: it enables the filing of a single "international application"—the PCT application—that would have the effect of a domestic patent application for each of the PCT contracting countries, subject to certain national or regional limitations.[114] Filing a PCT application, then, can be a practical and beneficial first step towards obtaining certain foreign patent protection.

§ 3:6 Patent Protection in Fashion

§ 3:6.1 Design Patent Protection in Fashion: Trends in Use and Enforcement

This section examines the formal requirements for issuance and infringement of a design patent in the specific context of the fashion industry. As noted earlier in this chapter, design patents protect only the "ornamental" attributes of a product. This has limited their value to the fashion industry for at least two reasons. First, because even a novel design may be rejected if its novelty is also functional, function-based designs can be difficult to protect. Second, because the protectable subject matter of a design patent is limited to its aesthetic attributes, its value to the patent holder depends upon the constancy of visual design elements over time, whereas the fashion industry thrives

---

305. Article 4 of the Paris Convention, for example, provides: "Any person who has duly filed an application for a patent, or for the registration of a utility model, or of an industrial design, or of a trademark, in one of the countries of the Union, or his successor in title, shall enjoy, for the purpose of filing in the other countries, a right of priority during the periods hereinafter fixed."

113. The earlier priority date is significant because in most countries, the law gives superior rights to the inventor who files her patent application first, even if someone else came up with the idea first. As discussed above, U.S. law had traditionally given priority to the "first to invent" rather than the "first to file." In 2011, Congress passed the America Invents Act (AIA), which, among other things, brought the United States in line with the majority approach by adopting a "first-to-file" system. *See* Changes to Implement the First Inventor to File Provisions of the Leahy-Smith AIA, 78 Fed. Reg. 11,024 (Feb. 14, 2013) (codified at 37 C.F.R. pt. 1).

114. Patent Cooperation Treaty (June 19, 1970), 28 U.S.T. 7645, 1160 U.N.T.S. 231, https://www.wipo.int./pct/en/texts/articles/atoc/htm.

on change. And, although the PTO issues design patents on a comparatively expedited schedule, pendencies still average around nineteen months. By this time, an ornamental feature that was once on-trend may no longer be desirable to its targeted consumer. When one adds in the time and expense of prosecuting an obstinate infringer, it is perhaps understandable that design patents and the protection they afford have traditionally been sought only for enduring or "signature" aesthetic features and pieces with multi-year staying power.

Design patents, therefore, have been used to protect products with demonstrated longevity, such as handbags, footwear, timepieces, eyewear, and other accessories, as well as designs for cosmetic and fragrance packaging. To name just a few, Christian Dior Couture, S.A., Yves Saint Laurent, Louis Vuitton Malletier, Stuart Weitzman IP, LLC, Bulgari Time (Switzerland) S.A., Bottega Veneta International S.A.R.L., and Oakley, Inc. hold such patents, and several major brands regularly invoke the PTO's protection.[115] For example, J. Choo, more commonly known as Jimmy Choo, holds hundreds of design patents related to its luxury footwear, while Nike, Inc.'s patents number in the thousands.[116] Similarly, in recent years, Christian Louboutin has increasingly turned to design patents to protect his shoe styling,[117] as well as his shoe sole,[118] handbag,[119] and beauty product packaging designs.[120]

---

115. *See, e.g.*, U.S. Patent No. D498,589 (filed Dec. 3, 2003); U.S. Patent No. D518,627 (filed Dec. 3, 2004); U.S. Patent No. D324,771 (filed Aug. 12, 1988); U.S. Patent No. D583,404 (filed Jan. 22, 2008); U.S. Patent No. D376,545 (filed Sept. 29, 1995); U.S. Patent No. D657,952 (filed Apr. 12, 2010); U.S. Patent No. D820586 (filed June 12, 2017).

116. *See, e.g.*, U.S. Patent No. D664,756 (filed Mar. 21, 2011); U.S. Patent No. D618,449 (filed Dec. 17, 2008); U.S. Patent No. D582,653 (filed July 12, 2007); U.S. Patent No. D661,886 (filed Feb. 29, 2012); U.S. Patent No. D545,044 (filed Jan. 29, 2007); U.S. Patent No. D466,277 (filed Feb. 28, 2002); U.S. Patent No. D407,200 (filed Oct. 15, 1998).

117. *See, e.g.*, U.S. Patent No. D712,641 (filed May 10, 2013); U.S. Patent No. D713,132 (May 10, 2013); U.S. Patent No. D715,034 (filed June 28, 2012); U.S. Patent No. D729,506 (filed May 10, 2013); U.S. Patent No. D734,597 (filed Sept. 6, 2013); U.S. Patent No. D734,599 (filed Sept. 6, 2013); U.S. Patent No. D735,981 (filed Sept. 6, 2013); U.S. Patent No. D735,986 (filed Sept. 6, 2013).

118. *See, e.g.*, U.S. Patent No. D831,318 (filed Apr. 12, 2017). Christian Louboutin's iconic red sole design (specifically, Pantone 1801663TP) is also trademarked in the United States and abroad.

119. *See, e.g.*, U.S. Patent No. D751,814 (filed Aug. 7, 2014); U.S. Patent No. D784,012 (filed Jan. 15, 2016); U.S. Patent No. D785,931 (filed Feb. 16, 2016); U.S. Patent No. D785,933 (filed Feb. 16, 2016); U.S. Patent No. D825,918 (filed Mar. 17, 2017).

120. *See, e.g.*, U.S. Patent No. D805,915 (filed Dec. 3, 2014); U.S. Patent No. D804,812 (filed Jan. 15, 2016).

Although the many design patents issued in the fashion industry fall into the aforementioned categories, there are outliers. Levi Strauss & Co. has patented a number of its denim designs, and Guess? Inc., True Religion Apparel, Inc., and Alexander Wang Inc. all hold patents covering clothing design *elements*, such as signature stitching, pocket style, and stud work.[121] Christian Louboutin has separately patented one of his signature ornamental handbag clasps,[122] and Missoni S.p.A. has patented eponymous designer Rosita Missoni's fabric designs used in its iconic apparel.[123]

Perhaps most interestingly, the use of design patents by major clothing manufacturers appears to be on the rise, particularly in the realms of shapewear and sports and active apparel. Lululemon Athletica Canada Inc., a leading manufacturer of high-end yoga and active apparel, has been relatively aggressive in patenting its staple pieces. From 2010 to 2012 alone, the Canadian company obtained at least sixteen design patents covering its pants, shorts, tank tops, and jackets, as well as its signature waistband design, with a similar pace of grants coming in subsequent years.[124] Similarly, sports and outerwear company Columbia Sportswear North America, Inc. was issued more than forty design patents over an eighteen-month period, including at least ten relating to pants, shorts, pocket designs, and jackets, with dozens more issuing in the years that followed.[125]

---

121. *See, e.g.*, U.S. Patent No. D660,199 (filed Sept. 30, 2011); U.S. Patent No. D547,530 (filed Dec. 9, 2005); U.S. Patent No. D440,028 (filed Sept. 15, 1999); U.S. Patent No. D437,102 (filed Sept. 15, 1999); U.S. Patent No. D436,714 (filed Sept. 15, 1999); U.S. Patent No. D337,193 (filed Aug. 12, 1991).

122. *See* U.S. Patent No. D804,812 (filed Jan. 15, 2016).

123. *See, e.g.*, U.S. Patent No. D647,704 (filed Sept. 13, 2010); U.S. Patent No. D647,705 (filed Sept. 13, 2010); U.S. Patent No. D647,706 (filed Sept. 13, 2010)

124. *See, e.g.*, U.S. Patent No. D612,129 (filed Apr. 29, 2009); U.S. Patent No. D613,037 (filed Apr. 29, 2009); U.S. Patent No. D613,928 (filed Apr. 29, 2009); U.S. Patent No. D615,279 (filed Sept. 2, 2009); U.S. Patent No. D618,434 (filed Jan. 12, 2010); U.S. Patent No. D618,435 (filed Jan. 12, 2010); U.S. Patent No. D639,023 (filed Mar. 26, 2010); U.S. Patent No. D645,644 (filed Apr. 16, 2010); U.S. Patent No. D654,661 (filed June 30, 2011); U.S. Patent No. D654,665 (filed Aug. 17, 2010); U.S. Patent No. D661,871 (filed July 27, 2011); U.S. Patent No. D661,872 (filed Sept. 23, 2011); U.S. Patent No. D662,281 (filed Feb. 6, 2012); U.S. Patent No. D662,284 (filed Mar. 16, 2011); U.S. Patent No. D668,434 (filed Apr. 23, 2012); U.S. Patent No. D669,660 (filed June 29, 2011). For a full list of patents assigned to Lululemon or any company, search function is available at the U.S.P.T.O. website, https://assignment.uspto.gov/patent/index.hml#/patent/search.

125. *See, e.g.*, U.S. Patent No. D637,794 (filed Oct. 21, 2010); U.S. Patent No. D638,200 (filed Oct. 20, 2010); U.S. Patent No. D638,201 (filed Oct. 21,

And while the vast majority of Nike, Inc.'s design patents relate to footwear, it, too, has obtained a number of design patents covering articles of clothing, including jerseys, jackets, compression shorts and shirts, and sports bras.[126]

Figure 3-4
Sample Patents Held by Columbia Sportswear North America, Inc. Covering Related Designs

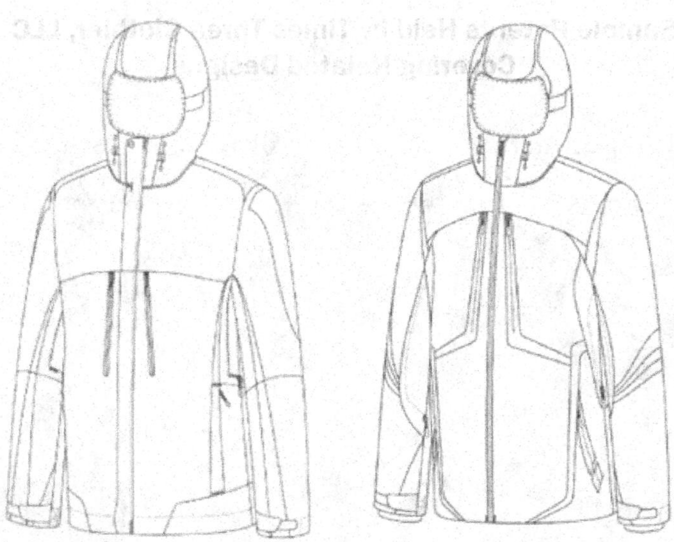

FIG. 1 FIG. 1

2010); U.S. Patent No. D638,202 (filed Oct. 21, 2010); U.S. Patent No. D638,608 (filed Apr. 23, 2010); U.S. Patent No. D639,529 (filed July 22, 2009); U.S. Patent No. D643,597 (filed May 7, 2010); U.S. Patent No. D648,924 (filed Oct. 20, 2010); U.S. Patent No. D655,070 (filed Sept. 23, 2011); U.S. Patent No. D657,532 (filed July 15, 2011). For a full list of patents assigned to Columbia Sportswear, the search function is available at the U.S.P.T.O. website, https://assignment.uspto.gov/patent/index.html#/patent/search.

126. *See, e.g.*, U.S. Patent No. D654,659 (filed Nov. 25, 2009); U.S. Patent No. D633,692 (filed Apr. 19, 2010); U.S. Patent No. D633,688 (filed Dec. 18, 2009); U.S. Patent No. D629,999 (filed Dec. 18, 2009); U.S. Patent No. D629,588 (filed Nov. 25, 2009); U.S. Patent No. D628,769 (filed Dec. 18, 2009); U.S. Patent No. D627,135 (filed Dec. 18, 2009); U.S. Patent No. D594,631 (filed Jan. 28, 2009).

Other major companies that currently have design patents on articles of clothing include Christian Dior Couture, S.A., Under Armour, Inc., and M. J. Soffe LLC.[127] In the shapewear arena, Times Three Clothier, LLC, which does business as Yummie Tummie, has been issued at least eleven patents covering its stomach-slimming designs, several of which were issued after the company reached a settlement with Maidenform Brands, Inc. to end competing infringement and invalidity lawsuits related to a few of Times Three's design patents.[128]

Figure 3-5

Sample Patents Held by Times Three Clothier, LLC Covering Related Designs

U.S. PATENT NO. D632,052

U.S. Patent Feb. 8, 2011 Sheet 2 of 12 US D632,052 S

FIG. 2

U.S. PATENT NO. D632,053

U.S. Patent Feb. 8, 2011 Sheet 2 of 12 US D632,053 S

FIG. 2

---

127. *See, e.g.*, U.S. Patent No. D660,553 (filed Nov. 21, 2011); U.S. Patent No. D659,951 (filed Sept. 23, 2011); U.S. Patent No. D571,080 (filed Aug. 17, 2006).

128. *See* U.S. Patent No. D606,285 (filed Jan. 17, 2008); U.S. Patent No. D616,627 (filed Nov. 12, 2009); U.S. Patent No. D622,477 (filed May 26, 2010); U.S. Patent No. D623,377 (filed May 25, 2010); U.S. Patent No. D632,051 (filed Dec. 21, 2009); U.S. Patent No. D632,052 (filed Dec. 21, 2009); U.S. Patent No. D632,053 (filed Dec. 21, 2009); U.S. Patent No. D656,298 (filed Dec. 21, 2009); U.S. Patent No. D665,558 (filed Nov. 13, 2009); U.S. Patent No. D666,384 (filed May 26, 2011); U.S. Patent No. D667,607 (filed Nov. 13, 2009); *see also* Amended Answer and Counterclaim, Maidenform Brands Inc. v. Times Three Clothier LLC, No. 1:10-cv-01661-GBD-HBP (S.D.N.Y. Mar. 9, 2011), ECF No. 67; Agreed Order of Dismissal With Prejudice, Maidenform Brands Inc. v. Times Three Clothier LLC, No. 1:10-cv-01661-GBD-HBP (S.D.N.Y. Aug. 10, 2011), ECF No. 88.

A number of companies in the fashion industry, in fact, have applied for separate patents that cover different variations on similar products. This trend, combined with the comparatively limited scope of a design patent's protection, suggests that it may prove beneficial for a holder to pursue more than one patent in order to adequately protect minor variations on a signature style and guard against close copies.

In sum, although far from ubiquitous, fashion has an established history of employing design patents to protect signature pieces and design elements, particularly as applied to handbags, shoes, cosmetics, and other accessories. Design patents, moreover, appear poised to take on a more diverse role. The fashion industry's renewed interest in design patents mirrors a general trend, perhaps spurred on by the PTO's efforts to expedite the application process and the decision in *Egyptian Goddess, Inc. v. Swisa, Inc.*,[129] which, as noted in section 3:4.1, above, abolished the point of novelty test and simplified the standard for proving infringement. An estimated 40,406 design patent applications were filed in FY 2016, up from 19,706 in FY 2002 and 12,907 in FY 1992.[130] In fact, with the exception of FY 2009 (when the recessionary economy reduced profits for many companies in the fashion industry), the total number of design patent applications filed steadily increased from 1997 to 2016.[131]

Along with the growth in design patent applications and issuances in the fashion industry, there seems to be a corresponding growth in the effort expended to enforce design patents. One well-known such dispute occurred between Lululemon Athletica and Calvin Klein. In August 2012, Lululemon sued Calvin Klein for patent infringement claiming that the waistband of Calvin Klein's "performance knee length running tights" infringes U.S. Patent Nos. D645,644, D661,872, and D662,281, embodied in Lululemon's signature "Astro" pant. The case drew attention because of Lululemon's strategy of seeking to enforce a design patent rather than its trademarks, and the parties settled under undisclosed terms in November 2012.[132]

---

129. Egyptian Goddess, Inc. v. Swisa, Inc., 543 F.3d 665, 681 (Fed. Cir. 2008) (en banc), *cert. denied*, 129 S. Ct. 1917 (2009).

130. U.S. Patent & Trademark Office, Performance and Accountability Report: Fiscal Year 2016 (2016) [hereinafter PTO, Performance and Accountability Report: Fiscal Year 2016], at 178–79.

131. *Id.*

132. Ben Fox Rubin, Lululemon, *Calvin Klein Agree to Settle Yoga-Pants Suit*, Wall St. J., Nov. 20, 2012.

Figure 3-6
Sample Design Patents Held by Lululemon Athletica Canada Inc.

U.S. PATENT NO. D662,281 U.S. PATENT NO. D645,644 U.S. PATENT NO. D661,872

Companies in the footwear industry have also vigorously pursued alleged infringers. From 2010 to 2012 alone, footwear manufacturers Crocs, Skechers, Nike/Converse, and Brooke Hollow, Inc. all instituted design patent enforcement actions against a variety of, and sometimes multiple, alleged infringers,[133] with later similar litigation following. For example, Crocs has enforced its design patents, along with its utility patents, in long-running disputes against a variety of alleged infringers, including competitor U.S.A. Dawgs, Inc. and retail chains CVS and Walgreens.[134] This enforcement came at a price, however, with Crocs's design patents for its iconic foam shoe being then subjected to reexamination and

133. *See, e.g.*, Complaint, Crocs, Inc. v. Skechers U.S.A., Inc., No. 11-cv-01330 (D. Colo. May 19, 2011) (suing to enforce U.S. Pat. No. D610,784); Complaint, NIKE, Inc. v. Superstar Int'l Inc., No. 12-cv-05240 (C.D. Cal. June 15, 2012) (suing to enforce NIKE, Inc. U.S. Pat. Nos. D398,762, D498,912, D504,562, D511,884, D512,214, D529,273, D530,904, D531,396, and Converse, Inc. U.S. Pat. Nos. D555,332, D618,897, D619,797); Complaint, Brooke Hollow Inc. v. Antebi Footwear Grp. LLC, No. 2:09-cv-01824 (W.D. Wash. Dec. 23, 2009) (to enforce U.S. Pat. No. D579,642); complaints listed *infra* notes 136–139.

134. *See, e.g.*, Order, Crocs, Inc. v. Effervescent, Inc., No. 06-cv-00605, 2017 WL 4286148, at pt. I (D. Colo. Sept. 25, 2017) (summarizing in part Crocs assertion of its design patents against competitors and retailers); Complaint, Crocs, Inc. v. CVS Caremark, Corp., No. 12-cv-02096 (D. Colo. Aug. 8, 2012) (suing to enforce U.S. Pat. No. D517,789); Complaint, Crocs, Inc. v. Walgreen Co., No. 11-cv-02954 (D. Colo. Nov. 14, 2011) (suing to enforce U.S. Pat. No. D610784).

later rejections at the U.S. Patent and Trademark Office.[135] Skechers U.S.A., Inc., maker of the popular Shape-Ups and Twinkle Toes shoes, similarly instituted actions against shoewear giant Steve Madden, Sears, and The Children's Place all within just an eight-month span between 2011 and 2012,[136] with numerous later actions against others in following years.[137]

Figure 3-7

Design Patents Held by Skechers U.S.A.

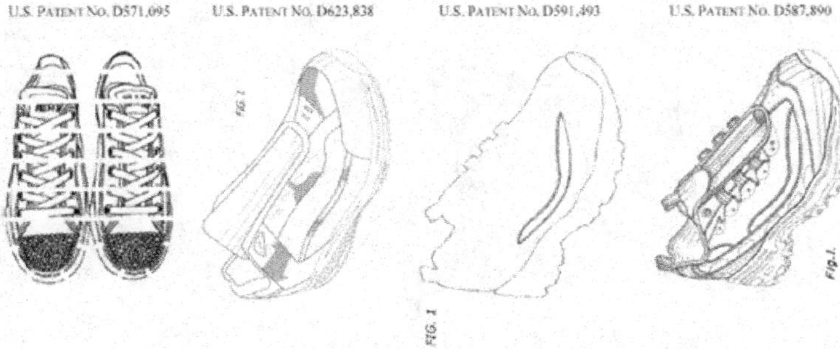

135. *See, e.g.*, Effervescent, Inc., No. 06-cv-00605, at pt. I (summarizing reexamination proceedings for U.S. Patents D 517,789 and D 6,993,858).

136. Complaint, Skechers U.S.A., Inc. v. The Children's Place Retail Stores, Inc., No. 12CV00928 (C.D. Cal. Feb. 2, 2012) (suing to enforce U.S. Patent No. D571,095 covering the Twinkle Toes designs); Complaint, Skechers U.S.A., Inc. v. Steve Madden, Ltd., No. 11-cv-07295 (C.D. Cal. Sept. 2, 2011) (suing to enforce U.S. Patent No. D571,095 covering the Twinkle Toes designs); Complaint, Skechers U.S.A., Inc. v. Sears Holding Corp., No. 11-cv-01893 (C.D. Cal. July 20, 2011) (suing to enforce U.S. Patent Nos. D623,838, D591,493 and D587,890).

137. *See, e.g.*, Complaint, Skechers U.S.A., Inc. v. Eliya Inc., No. 16-cv-02820 (C.D. Cal. Apr. 25, 2016) (suing to enforce U.S. Pat. Nos. D655,901, D682,522, D708,430); Complaint, Skechers U.S.A., Inc. v. DB Shoe Co., No. 14-cv-07009 (C.D. Cal. Sept. 8, 2014) (suing to enforce U.S. Pat. Nos. D651,788, D652,613, D652,614, D661,880, D661,884, D680,309, D680,312); Complaint, Skechers U.S.A., Inc. v. FILA U.S.A. Inc., No. 14-cv-05123 (C.D. Cal. July 1, 2014) (suing to enforce U.S. Pat. Nos. D661,884, D688,446); Complaint, Skechers U.S.A., Inc. v. Reebok Int'l Ltd., No. 14-cv-04722 (C.D. Cal. June 18, 2014) (suing to enforce U.S. Pat. No. D661,884); Complaint, Skechers U.S.A., Inc. v. Shoe Confession, LLC, No. 13-cv-07573 (C.D. Cal. Oct. 11, 2013) (suing to enforce U.S. Pat. Nos. D650,980, D651,788, D652,613, D652,614); Complaint, Skechers U.S.A. Inc. v. Anthony L & S LLC, No. 13-cv-03768 (C.D. Cal. May 28, 2013) (suing to enforce U.S. Pat. Nos. D661,880, D680,309).

Likewise, in 2012 alone, Deckers Outdoor Corporation, the owner of the popular UGG brand, instituted design patent infringement actions against shoe retailers Sears, Kmart and Ash Footwear USA, as well as against multiple other competitors and retailers.[138] Since then, from 2013 through mid-2018, Deckers has filed over fifty more lawsuits asserting its design patents.

Figure 3-8

Design Patents Held by Deckers Outdoor Corporation

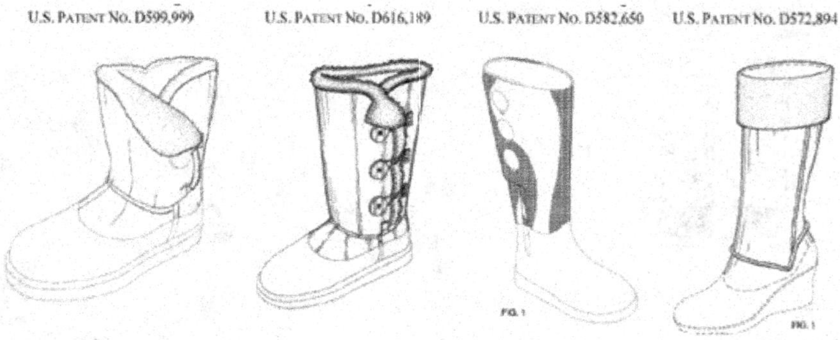

Similarly, eyewear designer Oakley Inc. instituted ten design patent litigations between 2010 and 2012.[139] Since then, Oakley

---

138. *E.g.*, Complaint, Deckers Outdoor Corp. v. Sears Holding Corp., No. 12-cv-8723 (C.D. Cal. Oct. 11, 2012) (suing to enforce U.S. Patent Nos. D599,999, D616,189, D582,650, D572,894); Complaint, Deckers Outdoor Corp. v. Minnetonka Moccasin, No. 12-cv-11022 (C.D. Cal. Dec. 28, 2012) (suing to enforce U.S. Patent No. D599,999); Complaint, Deckers Outdoor Corp. v. Lamo Sheepskin Inc., No. 12-cv-02282 (C.D. Cal. Dec. 28, 2012) (suing to enforce U.S. Patent No. D634,109); Complaint, Deckers Outdoor Corp. v. Ollie's Bargain Outlet, Inc., No. 12-cv-09114 (S.D.N.Y. Dec. 14, 2012) (suing to enforce U.S. Patent Nos. D599,999, D616,189); Complaint, Deckers Outdoor Corp. v. Ash Int'l Grp., No. 12-cv-09848 (C.D. Cal. Nov. 16, 2012) (suing to enforce U.S. Patent No. D594,639); Complaint, Deckers Outdoor Corp. v. Walgreens Co., No. 12-cv-08579 (C.D. Cal. Oct. 5, 2012) (suing to enforce U.S. Patent Nos. D599,999, D616,189); Complaint, Deckers Outdoor Corp. v. Conscious Corp., No. 12-cv-07687 (C.D. Cal. Sept. 7, 2012) (same); Complaint, Deckers Outdoor Corp. v. ShoesScandal.com LLC, No. 12-cv-07382 (C.D. Cal. Aug. 28, 2012) (same).
139. *See, e.g.*, Complaint, Oakley, Inc. v. NY Eyewear Trading Co., No. 10-cv-00338 (S.D. Cal. Feb. 11, 2010) (suing to enforce U.S. Patent Nos. 5,387,949; D415,188; 5,137,342; D473,892; D470,166; D561,813;

has increased its assertion of design patents, filing nearly seventy additional suits from 2013 through mid-2018.

The existence of these design patent lawsuits seems to indicate that at least some companies have determined that enforcing design patents for their most important signature looks against alleged large-scale infringers makes good business sense, however uncommon these lawsuits had been in the fashion industry previously. The power of design patent protection and enforcement is perhaps best illustrated in the fashion-adjacent world of smartphones, where Apple's well-publicized and long-running battle against Samsung ultimately resulted in a jury verdict in Apple's favor of $533 million on its asserted design patents, *one hundred times* the award the jury gave Apple for its utility patents.[140] Industry participants would be well advised to consider whether judicious use of design patents and enforcement makes business sense, and to consider their potential liability for products that may be seen as substantially similar to an existing design patent.

§ 3:6.2 Utility Patent Protection in Fashion: Trends in Use and Enforcement

Utility patents make up the vast majority of patents issued by the PTO. In FY 2016, for example, the PTO issued 304,568 utility patents, compared with only 27,830 design patents.[141] And while utility patents are perhaps used less obviously than design patents in the fashion industry, they nonetheless play a significant role. Instead of protecting aspects of a product that are ornamental, like the design patents discussed above, utility patents protect the functional (or utilitarian) aspects of products like clothing, shoes, and eyewear. In addition, as discussed in greater detail below, as technology becomes miniaturized and increasingly ubiquitous, novel uses of technology in fashion may presage a growing importance of utility patents in the fashion industry.

D581,443; D581,444); Complaint, Oakley, Inc. v. Mountain View Mktg., Inc., No. 11-cv-01607 (S.D. Cal. Aug. 1, 2012) (suing to enforce U.S. Patent Nos. 5,387,949; D543,572; D616,919; D581,450; D469,458; D581,451; D554,689; D404,754; D572,747).

140. *See, e.g.*, *Jury Awards Apple $539 Million in Samsung Patent Case*, N.Y. TIMES (May 24, 2018), https://www.nytimes.com/2018/05/24/business/apple-samsung-patent-trial.html.

141. PTO, PERFORMANCE AND ACCOUNTABILITY REPORT: FISCAL YEAR 2016, *supra* note 130, at 178.

[A] High Performance Fabrics and Athletic Attire

Sports and athletic wear manufacturers often obtain utility patents for their clothing and accessories. Under Armour, Inc. is an excellent example—the company has patented or is patenting its golf gloves,[142] detachable cleats,[143] and zipper arrangements.[144] Moreover, one of its patents describes a deodorizing device that is inserted into clothing for use while wearing.[145] In addition, certain elements of the high-performance fabrics are quite often patented, including flame resistant fabric,[146] fabric intended for use by military personnel,[147] and other niche inventions like hunting garments that are designed to capture human odors.[148] Another of Under Armour's patents covers a "[r]eversible garment with warming side and cooling side."[149] The texture of the fabric—substantially smooth on one side and textured on the other—allows the cooling side (the smooth side) to "eliminate airgaps" between the user's body and the fabric, while the other side "traps air and heat" between the user's body and the fabric.[150]

Waterproof breathable materials also fall under the category of patentable high-performance fabrics. Although Gore-Tex's original patents on the popular material have expired,[151] other clothing retailers have attempted to build upon Gore-Tex's patents, and have patented or are in the process of patenting their own materials.[152] This innovative functionality as applied to clothing can be a fertile source of enhanced intellectual property protection in the fashion arena.

---

142. U.S. Patent No. 8,261,372 (filed Nov 10, 2008).
143. U.S. Patent No. 8,234,799 (filed Sept. 10, 2008).
144. U.S. Patent No. 8,484,811 (filed Nov. 16, 2010).
145. U.S. Patent No. 8,337,773 (filed Oct. 15, 2010).
146. U.S. Patent No. 8,209,785 (filed Feb. 9, 2010).
147. *Id.*
148. U.S. Patent No. 7,805,769 (filed Mar. 8, 2007).
149. U.S. Patent No. 8,813,525 (filed May 10, 2010).
150. *Id.*
151. *See* U.S. Patent No. 3,953,566 (continuation from Application No. 39,753, filed May 21, 1970) ("Process for producing porous products") and U.S. Patent No. 4,187,390 (continuation from Application No. 39,753, filed May 21, 1970) ("Porous products and process therefor").
152. *See* U.S. Patent No. 8,518,207 (filed May 11, 2011) ("Waterproof breathable fabric and method of making the same").

Figure 3-9
Sample Utility Patents in Fashion

U.S. PATENT APP. NO. 20120093685 U.S. PATENT NO. 8,209,785

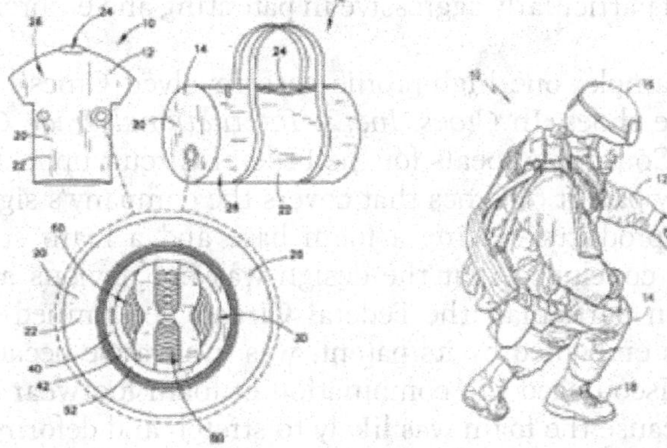

[B] Other Uses of Utility Patents

Other entities have been able to obtain utility patents for a wide variety of inventions. Some more popular areas of invention are in the arena of maternity garments[153] and bras whose "utility" is to shape and lift breasts.[154] In the children's clothing industry, one utility patent application described "improved sleeves" that facilitate the dressing of a baby or child.[155]

One rather unique patent owned by Levi Strauss & Co. is for a "[s]haped fit sizing system"—a "revolutionary, new sizing and fitting system for jeans . . . . based on the concept of shape, not size."[156] The inventor describes the basic body shapes around which the system is organized: "slight curve (straighter figure, flatter fanny), demi curve (evenly proportioned hip and seat) and bold curve (smaller waist, larger seat)."[157] This demonstrates the various creative ways that utility

153. *See, e.g.*, U.S. Patent No. 8,276,216 (filed June 22, 2011) (describing a garment that "accommodates the changing shape of a woman's body during pregnancy, minimizing the need for maternity clothes").
154. *See, e.g.*, U.S. Patent No. 8,241,088 (filed Feb. 10, 2009) (a brassiere with an interchangeable modesty panel, allowing for more or less cleavage to show).
155. U.S. Patent App. No. 13/370,418 (filed Feb. 10, 2012) (now abandoned).
156. U.S. Patent No. 8,307,560 (filed Nov. 2, 2010).
157. *Id.*

patents can be used in the clothing industry. What the above-mentioned utility patents and patent applications have in common is a functional element that draws them under the umbrella of utility patents.

Utility patents related to the fashion industry are also routinely enforced, particularly when they cover the owner's signature or blockbuster products. In particular, the footwear and eyewear industries have been particularly aggressive in patenting and enforcing their patent rights.

For example, one high-profile case involved Crocs's famous and distinctive shoes. In *Crocs, Inc. v. International Trade Commission*, the U.S. Court of Appeals for the Federal Circuit upheld the validity of a utility patent of Crocs that covers the company's signature foam footwear products, having a foam base and a foam strap, because the court concluded that the design was not obvious and therefore valid.[158] In particular, the Federal Circuit determined that Crocs's design, as embodied by its patent, was innovative because the prior art had discouraged the combination of foam footwear with a foam strap "because the foam was likely to stretch and deform, in addition to causing discomfort for the wearer."[159] And, of particular interest to innovative designers, the Federal Circuit used the copying by infringers as evidence that the design was innovative, and therefore not obvious. "Copying may indeed be another form of flattering praise for inventive features."[160] On remand, the ITC determined that Crocs's utility patent was infringed and issued a Final Commission Determination of Violation, issuing a General Exclusion Order to bar the importation of infringing articles.[161] Crocs since instituted other patent lawsuits, asserting the same patent.[162]

In another instance of utility patent enforcement in the footwear industry, the owner of two patents covering orthopedic shoe inserts for running and jogging shoes sued Reebok for infringement in the District of Massachusetts after Reebok introduced its DMX Series 2000 Cushioning Technology.[163]

---

158. Crocs, Inc. v. Int'l Trade Comm'n, 598 F.3d 1294 (Fed. Cir. 2010).

159. *Id.* at 1308.

160. *Id.* at 1311.

161. *See* Crocs, Inc. v. Cheng's Enters., No. 06-cv-00605, 2012 U.S. Dist. LEXIS 161954, at *2–3 (Oct. 16, 2012).

162. *E.g.*, Complaint for Patent Infringement, Crocs, Inc. v. Walgreen, Co., No. 11CV02954 (D. Colo. Nov. 14, 2011); Complaint for Patent Infringement, Crocs, Inc. v. CVS Caremark Corp., No. 12CV02096 (D. Colo. Aug. 8, 2012).

163. *See* Weiss v. Reebok Int'l, Ltd., No. 02-1471, 2004 WL 434158 (Fed. Cir. Mar. 9, 2004).

Eyewear has been another industry impacted by litigation involving the alleged infringement of utility patents. For example, in *Aspex Eyewear Inc. v. Clariti Eyewear, Inc.*, plaintiff Aspex asserted its patent covering magnetically attachable auxiliary lenses, like sunshades, against defendant Clariti's magnetic eyewear designs.[164] Aspex had previously sued Clariti in 1999 for infringement of a different patent that ultimately reissued as the patent-in-suit. That litigation resulted in a consent judgment by which Clariti agreed to a permanent injunction against the accused designs and any other magnetic eyewear. In 2003, however, Clariti launched a new line of magnetic eyewear, AirMag.

Figure 3-10

U.S. Patent No. 6,109,747 (Eyeglass frames with magnets in flanges)

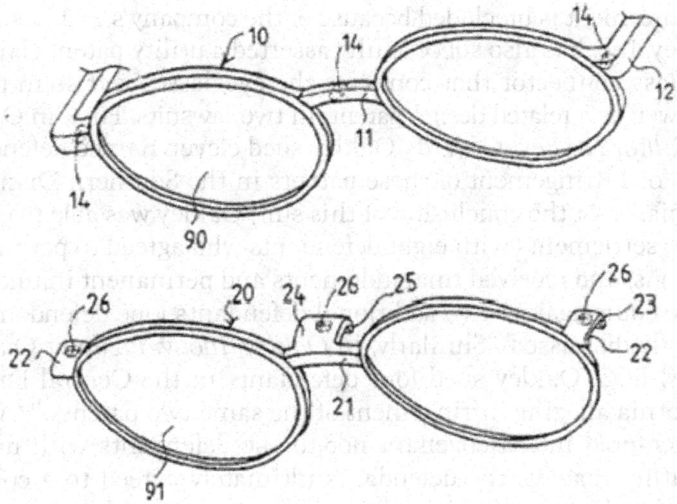

After Clariti launched its new product line, the parties engaged in a letter exchange, with Aspex requesting that Clariti cease selling the AirMag line as infringing several of Aspex's patents. Clariti, in turn, maintained that it did not infringe Aspex's patents and continued to market the AirMag line.

164. Aspex Eyewear Inc. v. Clariti Eyewear, Inc., 605 F.3d 1305, 1312 (Fed. Cir. 2010).

Aspex did not contact Clariti again until 2006, and ultimately brought suit against Clariti in the Southern District of New York in 2007. The district court granted Clariti's motion to dismiss on the basis of equitable estoppel, finding that Aspex engaged in misleading conduct by following what could reasonably be understood as a threat of an infringement suit with three years of silence. When Aspex appealed, the Federal Circuit agreed that Clariti reasonably relied on Aspex's silence to expand the AirMag product line, and further that:

> Clariti's development of its AirMag® business, in reliance on Aspex's silence after its aggressive letters, represents a significant change in economic position and constitutes material prejudice sufficient to support equitable estoppel.[165]

In brief, Aspex's delay in bringing suit caused it to be equitably estopped from pursuing its infringement claim against Clariti. The clear lesson from this case is that a company must be prepared to follow through on threats of infringement, or risk a later court finding that enforcement is precluded because of the company's earlier silence.

Oakley, Inc. has also successfully asserted a utility patent claiming an eyeglass connector that connects the eyeglasses' ear stem to the lens, as well as a related design patent, in two lawsuits. First, in *Oakley, Inc. v. Talitor Far East Co. Ltd.*, Oakley sued eleven named defendants in 2011 for infringement of these patents in the Southern District of California.[166] At the conclusion of this suit, Oakley was able to obtain favorable settlements with eight defendants who agreed to permanent injunctions, and received final judgments and permanent injunctions from the court against two additional defendants (one defendant was voluntarily dismissed). Similarly, in *Oakley, Inc. v. Predator Outdoor Products, LLC*, Oakley sued four defendants in the Central District of California alleging infringement of the same two patents.[167] While Oakley entered into a covenant not to sue defendants with respect to the utility patent, the defendants ultimately agreed to a consent judgment and permanent injunction against continued infringement of the design patent. Oakley has asserted its design and utility patents against numerous other companies as well.

---

165. *Id.* The less strict equitable doctrine of laches, which does not require the accused infringer's reliance on misleading statements by the patent owner, is not available in patent actions. SCA Hygiene Prods. Aktiebolag v. First Quality Baby Prods., LLC, 137 U.S. 954 (2017).

166. Oakley, Inc. v. Talitor Far East Co., No. 3:11-cv-01305 (S.D. Cal. filed June 14, 2011).

167. Oakley, Inc. v. Predator Outdoor Prods., LLC, No. 8:11-cv-00456 (C.D. Cal. filed Mar. 22, 2011).

[C] Integration of Technology and Fashion

Another trend in the fashion industry comes from the integration of technology and articles of apparel, footwear, and accessories. Shoes are one such popular example. Nike, Inc., the company that famously paired with Apple in 2006 to market the Nike + iPod Sports Kit,[168] has patented shoe inserts and other devices to track the GPS coordinates, heart rates and other bodily indicators of runners while the wearer exercises.[169] U.S. Patent No. 8,112,251 claimed a "Multi-sensor monitoring of athletic performance," one embodiment including a portable/wearable display.[170]

Radio Frequency Identification (RFID) tags are also technological items that have been embedded into apparel and patented, for varying purposes. These tags are most commonly used to keep track of merchandise in the supply chain, which is accomplished by embedding RFID tags into clothing palettes.[171] RFID tags can also be used to track data about a person wearing a tag. For example, racers often wear bibs with RFID tags (which can also be attached to a racer's shoes) while racing to keep track of and store the participants' locations, speeds and times.[172] Another patented use of RFIDs in apparel is to automatically immobilize a machine, like a bulldozer, when the RFID senses the RFID tag's proximity to a portion of the equipment.[173]

---

168. Press Release, Apple, Inc., Nike and Apple Team Up to Launch Nike+iPod (May 23, 2006), https://www.apple.com/newsroom/2006/05/23Nike-and-Apple-Team-Up-to-Launch-Nike-iPod/.

169. *See, e.g.*, U.S. Patent No. 8,112,251 (continuation from Application No. 11/014,241, filed Dec. 17, 2004); *see also* U.S. Patent No. 7,983,876 (filed Aug. 7, 2009) ("Shoes and garments employing one or more of accelerometers, wireless transmitters, processors altimeters, to determine information such as speed to persons wearing the shoes or garments.").

170. U.S. Patent No. 8,112,251 (continuation from Application No. 11/014,241, filed Dec. 17, 2004).

171. *See, e.g.*, U.S. Patent No. 5,500,650 (filed Dec. 15, 1992); U.S. Patent No. 5,627,544 (continuation from Application No. 990,915, filed Dec. 15, 1992); U.S. Patent No. 5,974,078 (continuation from Application No. 08/032,384, filed Mar. 17, 1993); U.S. Patent No. 6,459,726 (filed Apr. 24, 1998); U.S. Patent No. RE41,531 (continuation from Application No. 09/026,043, filed Feb. 19, 1998).

172. U.S. Patent No. 8,174,393 (continuation from Application No. 12/136, 805, filed on June 11, 2008).

173. U.S. Patent No. 8,115,650 (filed Feb. 14, 2012) (RFID-based personal safety system).

Figure 3-11

Sample Utility Patents in Fashion Using RFIDs

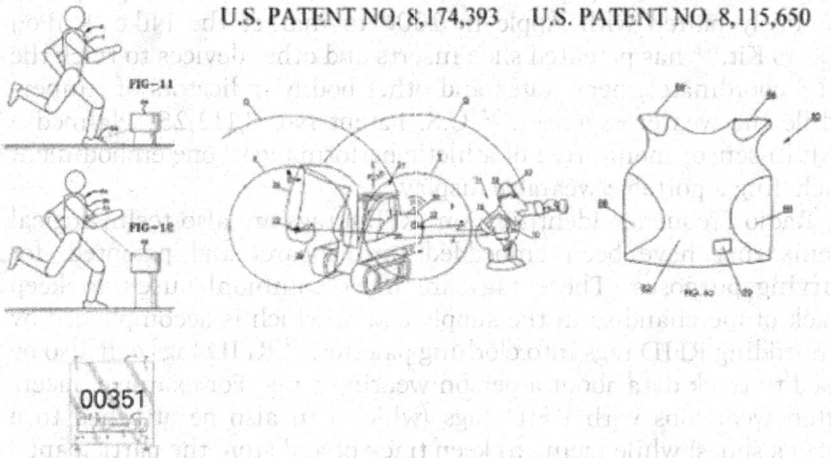

Now, "smart fabrics" are emerging at the intersection of utility and design protection. For example, OMsignal, Inc. has a utility patent for a textile-based electrode system using sensors in fabric contacting the wearer's skin to communicate with conductive pathways that interface computer analytics.[174] Coupled with its design patents for a "biosensing" sports bra and "smart textile controller,"[175] OMsignal's OMbra offers to communicate running distance, cadence, pace, heart rate, calories, and breathing metrics to the wearer's smartphone.[176]

---

174. *See* U.S. Patent No. 9,993,199 (filed Apr. 9, 2014).
175. *See* U.S. Patent No. D832,556 (filed Dec. 12, 2017); U.S. Patent No. D781,811 (filed Jan. 6, 2015).
176. Robert Nazarian, *This Sports Bra Is Not Only Comfortable, It Can Track Your Fitness Data*, DIG.TRENDS (Jan. 4, 2016), https://www.digitaltrends.com/health-fitness/ombra-omrun-news/.

Figure 3-12

Biosensing Garment—U.S. Patent D832,556 (OMsignal Inc.)

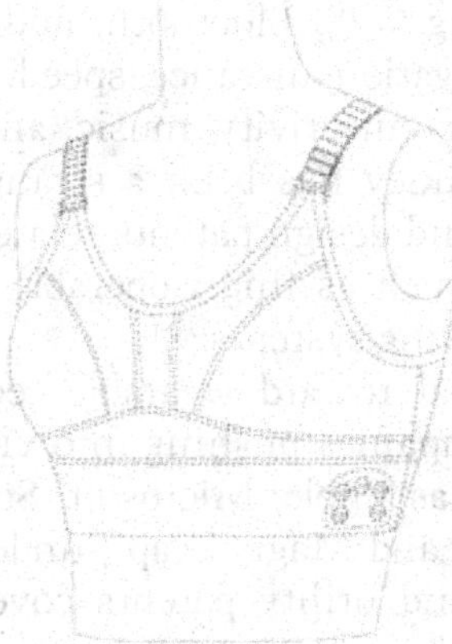

FIG. 1

As a complement to smart fabric, Google, Inc. has patented a smart "interactive cord"—a controller cable that can be covered with fabric woven of conductive thread, capable of registering multiple touchpoints or gestures.[177] And Apple Inc. now has a patent covering "Force Sensing" fabric-based devices.[178] Apple's patent discloses that its invention can use intertwined strands of conductive material and force-sensing electrodes in apparel like gloves to transmit pressure data to related computer devices or other wearables.[179]

CASE STUDY: MODERN INTERSECTIONS OF FASHION AND TECHNOLOGY

A number of products presently in development by several large technology companies illustrate the convergence between fashion and technology, and the emerging combined role of utility and design patents in protecting these hybrid products.

An early volley in the marriage of fashion and technology started with a race between two unlikely competitors—technology leader Google, Inc. and sports and eyewear brand Oakley, Inc.—to develop the first set of "smart glasses" for meaningful consumer use. The "Google Glass," a wearable computer with a head-mounted display,

---

177. *See* U.S. Patent No. 10,047,459 (filed Jan. 27, 2017).
178. *See* U.S. Patent No. 10,180,721 (filed Mar. 28, 2018).
179. *See id.*; Mark Jansen, *Apple Patents 'Force Sensing' Fabric for Clever Clothing*, DIG.TRENDS.COM (Dec. 20, 2018), https://www.digitaltrends.com/mobile/apple-smart-fabric-patent-2018/.

was developed by Google[180] and publicly demonstrated in 2013 by none other than cofounder Sergey Brin.[181] In turn, Oakley, Inc. had been working on smart glasses for a decade.[182] Its "Airwave" smart ski and snowboard goggles first hit the market in October 2012[183] and were touted as featuring GPS, Bluetooth, and onboard sensor technologies to provide navigation, distance, speed, and motion analytics, as well as smartphone connectivity, music, and tracking features.[184] Neither Google nor Oakley has been a stranger to the PTO, with both obtaining utility and design patents related to their products,[185] including for features such as finger-operable inputs,[186] nose-bridge sensors,[187] and eye-tracking systems.[188]

Since then, the trend toward wearable technology has accelerated, with multiple companies pushing into virtual reality headsets, including entities such as Apple, Microsoft, Sony, Occulus VR (now a division of Facebook), and Magic Leap (funded by Google and others) obtaining design and utility patents covering both immersive and mixed "augmented" reality experiences.[189] Thalmic Labs, Inc., funded by Amazon and Intel, has also been granted multiple utility

---

180. *See* GOOGLE, INC., GOOGLE GLASS, https://plus.google.com/+GoogleGlass.
181. Ryan Mac, *No One Is More Excited for Google Glass than Facebook CEO Mark Zuckerberg*, FORBES (Feb. 21, 2013), http://www.forbes.com/sites/ryanmac/2013/02/21/no-one-is-more-excited-for-google-glass-than-facebook-ceo-mark-zuckerberg/.
182. *See* U.S. Patent No. 6,966,647 (filed Dec. 4, 2001).
183. Ian Hamilton, *Smart Goggles Hit the Slopes*, O.C. REG. (Nov. 1, 2012), http://www.ocregister.com/articles/goggles-376342-oakley-company.html.
184. Trevor Mogg, *High-Tech Airwave Ski Goggles from Oakley Bring Augmented Reality to the Slopes*, DIG. TRENDS (Nov. 11, 2012), https://www.digitaltrends.com/cool-tech/high-tech-airwave-ski-goggles-from-oakley-bring-augmented-reality-to-the-slopes/.
185. *See, e.g.*, U.S. Patent No. 9,285,592 (filed Feb. 21, 2013); U.S. Patent No. 8,313,192 (filed Sept. 26, 2011); U.S. Patent No. 8,020,989 (filed Oct. 9, 2007); U.S. Patent No. 7,461,936 (filed Feb. 13, 2006); U.S. Patent No. 6,966,647 (filed Dec. 4, 2001); U.S. Patent No. D671,589 (filed May 16, 2012); U.S. Patent No. D669,066 (filed Apr. 20, 2012); U.S. Patent No. 8,217,856 (filed July 27, 2011).
186. U.S. Patent No. 8,203,502 (filed May 25, 2011).
187. U.S. Patent No. 8,184,067 (filed July 20, 2011).
188. U.S. Patent No. 8,235,529 (filed Nov. 30, 2011).
189. *See, e.g.*, U.S. Patent Application Publ. No. 2018-0039052 (filed Aug. 18, 2011) (Apple utility application); U.S. Patent No. 10,032,314 (filed Oct. 11, 2016) (Microsoft utility patent); U.S. Patent Application No. 2018-0256115 (filed Mar. 7, 2017) (Sony Interactive Entertainment utility application); U.S. Patent No. D701,206 (filed June 4, 2013) (Occulus design patent); U.S. Patent No 10,140,695 (filed Oct. 4, 2016) (Facebook utility patent); U.S. Patent Application No. 2018-0053284 (filed Aug. 22, 2016) (Magic Leap utility application); U.S. Patent No. D795,952 (filed Sept. 2, 2015) (Magic Leap design patent).

patents for its "Integrated Eye Tracker" technology that powers its holographic projection glasses that adjust for the wearer's field of view and eye movement.[190]

Figure 3-13
U.S. Patent Application Publ. No. 2018/0256115 (Sony Interactive Entertainment) (Display to Mitigate "Virtual Reality Sickness")

FIG. 2B

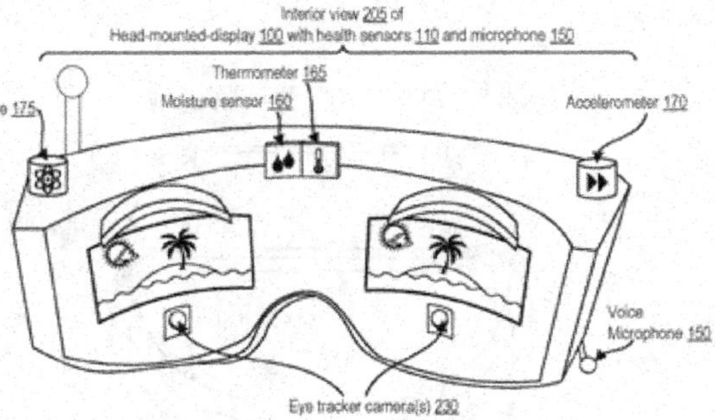

Moreover, glasses and headsets appear to be just the start of the burgeoning market for wearable computers and other "smart" accessories. Competition among purveyors of "smart watches" is heating up, with models like the Apple Watch and Samsung Galaxy Watch battling head-to-head.[191] Companies hold patents related to smart watches dating back over a decade,[192] with recent development

190. *See* U.S. Patent No. 10,078,219 (filed May 27, 2016); U.S. Patent No. 10,031,338 (filed Feb. 17, 2016); U.S. Patent No. 10,054,788 (continuation from Application No. 14/749,351, filed June 24, 2015); U.S. Patent No. 10,078,220 (filed May 27, 2016); Douglas Soltys, *Thalmic Has Been Issued US Patents for Its Hologram Lenses as Company Preps for Launch*, BETAKIT (Sept. 19, 2018), https://betakit.com/thalmic-has-been-issued-us-patents-for-its-hologram-lenses/.

191. *See, e.g.*, Lexy Savvides & Vanessa Hand Orellana, *Apple Watch vs. Samsung Galaxy Watch: Which Should You Buy?*, CNET (Dec. 20, 2018), https://www.cnet.com/news/apple-watch-vs-samsung-galaxy-watch-which-should-you-buy/.

192. *See, e.g.*, U.S. Patent No. 6,549,791 (filed Nov. 8, 1999) (assigned to Samsung Electronics Co.); U.S. Patent No. 8,374,852 (filed Apr. 22, 2009) (assigned to Apple Inc.); U.S. Patent No. 8,279,716 (filed Oct. 26, 2011) (assigned to Google, LLC).

directed to the crossover between health and fashion.[193] Apple in particular has taken a lead in this area, embedding sensors in the Apple Watch to measure the electrical activity of a wearer's heart and offering companion electrocardiogram (EKG) apps that are both approved by the Food and Drug Administration (FDA) and supported by the American Heart Association.[194] Among potential benefits touted for the Apple Watch is the ability to detect atrial fibrillation in previously undiagnosed individuals.[195]

Figure 3-14

U.S. Patent Application Publ. No. 2018/0078183 (Apple, Inc.)

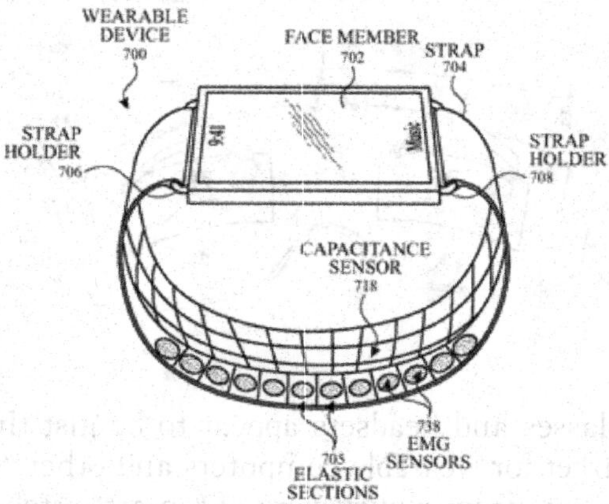

FIG. 7B

Empatica has similarly received approval from the FDA for its Embrace smart watch that doubles as an epilepsy monitor, capable

193. *See, e.g.*, U.S. Patent Application No. 2018/0078183 (filed Sept. 15, 2017) (assigned to Apple, Inc. and disclosing a watch band embedded with electromyography (EMG) sensors to measure electrical activity of a wearer's heart).

194. *See, e.g.*, Maggie Fox, *The New Apple Watch Has a Heart Monitor and the FDA Approves*, NBC NEWS (Sept. 12, 2018), https://www.nbcnews.com/health/health-news/new-apple-watch-has-heart-monitor-fda-approves-n908976; *ECG App and Irregular Heart Rhythm Notification Available Today on Apple Watch*, APPLE NEWSROOM (Dec. 6, 2018), https://www.apple.com/newsroom/2018/12/ecg-app-and-irregular-heart-rhythm-notification-available-today-on-apple-watch/.

195. *See, e.g.*, Christopher Worsham & Anupam B. Hena, *Why Doctors Shouldn't Dismiss the Apple Watch's New ECG App*, HARV. BUS. REV. (Oct. 5, 2018), https://hbr.org/2018/10/why-doctors-shouldnt-dismiss-the-apple-watchs-new-ecg-app.

of alerting caregivers and recording seizure activity.[196] Empatica has obtained a design patent for its Embrace line, with a utility patent pending for its devices and methods of measuring electrodermal activity (EDA).[197] Healthcare applications are not, of course, the only growth area for technology-enhanced fashion. An unexpected entrant into the smart wearables field is Carnival Cruise Lines, whose parent has a utility patent to wearable devices and accessories "for use in wireless guest engagement systems."[198] Carnival's "Ocean Medallion" uses near field communication and Bluetooth, can be worn as a necklace or bracelet, and can open staterooms, purchase goods, or place wagers at the ship's casino.[199] Similar wearable fashion technology may have crossover application for security uses in schools, hospitals, and corporate campuses.

§ 3:7 Conclusion

Once viewed as too expensive and cumbersome to protect the lightning-fast developments in the fashion industry, both design and utility patents are proving increasingly important in the industry. As discussed in this chapter, using patents appropriately means that the creator of a novel fashion design or invention can reap the benefits of its innovative work long after the creator (now patentee) is off designing the "next big thing" by either licensing the design to others or enforcing legitimate patent rights against others to obtain, for example, a reasonable royalty on the illicit sales of infringing products. Thus, patent enforcement can become an alternative, additional way to monetize a designer's signature work above and beyond the original sales of the products embodying the patents themselves. On the flip side, companies in the fashion industry need to be increasingly wary of launching products that may infringe another company's design or utility patents.

---

196. *See, e.g.*, Emily Matchar, *This Smartwatch Can Help Detect Seizures in Kids*, SMITHONIAN MAG. (Jan. 30, 2019), https://www.smithsonianmag.com/innovation/smartwatch-can-help-detect-seizures-kids-180971352/.

197. *See* U.S. Patent D760,395 (filed Nov. 19, 2014); U.S. Patent Application No. 14/215,613 (filed Mar. 17, 2014).

198. *See, e.g.*, U.S. Patent No. 10,037,642 (filed July 20, 2017) (assigned to Carnival Corp.).

199. *See, e.g.*, *id.*; *Carnival Corporation Awarded Three U.S. Patents for Guest Experience Innovations*, PRNEWSWIRE (Oct. 31, 2018), https://www.prnewswire.com/news-releases/carnival-corporation-awarded-three-us-patents-for-guest-experience-innovations-300741385.html.

Appendix 3A-1

Illustrative Design Patent 1: Seamans, March 28, 2006

US00D517789S

(12) **United States Design Patent** (10) **Patent No.:** **US D517,789 S**
Seamans (45) **Date of Patent:** ** **Mar. 28, 2006**

(54) **FOOTWEAR**

(75) Inventor: **Scott Seamans**, Boulder, CO (US)

(73) Assignee: **Crocs, Inc.**, Niwot, CO (US)

(**) Term: **14 Years**

(21) Appl. No.: **29/206,427**

(22) Filed: **May 28, 2004**

Related U.S. Application Data

(63) Continuation-in-part of application No. 10/803,569, filed on Mar. 17, 2004, which is a continuation-in-part of application No. 10/602,416, filed on Jun. 23, 2003, and a continuation-in-part of application No. 10/603,126, filed on Jun. 23, 2003.

(51) **LOC (8) Cl.** **02-99**
(52) **U.S. Cl.** **D2/969**
(58) **Field of Classification Search** D2/903, D2/916–918, 919, 969, 926, 932; 36/4, 8.1, 36/10, 11.5
See application file for complete search history.

(56) **References Cited**

U.S. PATENT DOCUMENTS

1,392,350 A		10/1921	O'Brien	
2,180,924 A		11/1939	Dunbar	
2,470,089 A		5/1949	Booth	
3,407,517 A	*	10/1968	Gessner	36/11.5
3,698,107 A		10/1972	Fukuoka	
4,032,611 A		6/1977	Fukuoka	
4,100,685 A		7/1978	Dassler	
4,408,401 A		10/1983	Seidel et al.	
4,476,600 A		10/1984	Seidel et al.	
4,888,887 A		12/1989	Solow	
4,967,750 A		11/1990	Cherniak	
D350,021 S	*	8/1994	Stein	D2/969
5,369,895 A		12/1994	Hammerschmidt	
5,438,767 A		8/1995	Stein	
5,528,841 A		6/1996	Pozzobon	
5,561,919 A		10/1996	Gill	
D381,794 S		8/1997	Gelli	

(Continued)

FOREIGN PATENT DOCUMENTS

CA	2375957	9/2002
EP	0 802 039 A2	10/1997
EP	0 802 040 A2	10/1997
EP	0 802 041 A2	10/1997
EP	0 884 005 A1	12/1998
GB	2322286	8/1998

OTHER PUBLICATIONS

http://web.archive.org/web/19980420230857/www.birkenstock.com/featprof.htm (3 pages).
Birkenstock®, Spring & Summer 2003 Catalog, Birkenstock Orthopudie GMbh, Germany (82 pages).
Cindy MacDonald, *The Entrepreneurs: they're bilingual, multicultural and talented. Distance and language present no barriers to Quebec plastics processors and mold makers as the province's plastics industry continues to increase its level of exports and welcome new companies*, Canadian Plastics, O'99, v. 57(10), pp. 35–50 (9 pages).
Comfortable Walking, Italian Technology, Oct. 1999, n. 3, p. 168 (abstract, 1 page).

(Continued)

Primary Examiner—Dominc Simone
(74) *Attorney, Agent, or Firm*—Faegre & Benson, LLP

(57) **CLAIM**

The ornamental design for footwear, as shown and described.

DESCRIPTION

FIG. **1** is a front perspective view.
FIG. **2** is a right side view.
FIG. **3** is a left side view.
FIG. **4** is a front view.
FIG. **5** is a rear view.
FIG. **6** is a top view; and,
FIG. **7** is a bottom view.
The broken line showing of the sole and surface treatment of the upper is for illustrative purpose only and forms no part of the claim design.

1 Claim, 4 Drawing Sheets

U.S. PATENT DOCUMENTS

5,814,254 A		9/1998	Bisconti	
D416,667 S		11/1999	Lamstein	
6,052,920 A		4/2000	Bathum	
D431,346 S		10/2000	Birkenstock	
6,237,249 B1		5/2001	Aguerre	
6,237,250 B1		5/2001	Aguerre	
6,256,906 B1		7/2001	Matis et al.	
6,416,610 B1		7/2002	Matis et al.	
6,439,536 B1		8/2002	Piccolo	
D473,040 S	*	4/2003	Hawker et al.	D2/932
D476,797 S		7/2003	Schenone	
D479,034 S	*	9/2003	Tzenos	D2/926
D479,906 S	*	9/2003	Hawker et al.	D2/969
6,640,464 B1		11/2003	Hsin et al.	
D499,234 S	*	12/2004	Dal Magro et al.	D2/916
6,860,035 B1		3/2005	Girard	
2002/0124434 A1		9/2002	Hsin et al.	
2003/0074806 A1		4/2003	Urie et al.	

OTHER PUBLICATIONS

Defendant's Response to Request for Particulars, Foam Creations Inc. vs. *Holey Soles Holdings Ltd.*, Ontario, Canada Federal Court, Court File No. T–161–05, Apr. 22, 2005, Oyen Wiggs Green & Mutala LLP (including Appendices A–C, 236 pages).

Defendant's Statement of Defence, Foam Creations Inc. vs. *Holey Soles Holdings Ltd.*, Ontario, Canada Federal Court, Court File No. T–161–05, Mar. 10, 2005, Oyen Wiggs Green & Mutala LLP (9 pages).

Engage® polyolefin elastomers, the critical ingredient for Success, DuPont Dow Elastomers, Copyright© 2000, DuPont Dow Elastomers, www.dupont–dow.com/engage (12 pages).

FinProject Brews an Extralight (*Evasol Plastics and Finproject signed a joint venture agreement to introduce a range of new–block and net–fit soles for shoes*), Footwear News, World Week, Aug. 4, 1997, v. 53, n. 31, p. 8 (3 pages).

Injected Eva, Macplas International, Aug. 1999, n. 10, p. 90. (abstract, 1 page).

Luisa Zargani, *One Fine Year; Anton Magnani's Quirky Dry–Shod Designs have Gained the Italian Designer Respect, Recognition and a Deal with Comme Des Garcons*, Footwear News, Aug. 2, 1999, p. 102 (2 pages).

Plaintiff's Further Request for Particulars, Foam Creations Inc. vs. *Holey Soles Holdings Ltd.*, Ontario, Canada Federal Court, Court File No. T–161–05, May 12, 2005, Ridout & Maybee (including Schedule A, 6 pages).

Plantiff's Reply, Foam Creations Inc. vs. *Holey Soles Holdings Ltd.*, Ontario, Canada Federal Court, Court File No. T–161–05, Ridout & Maybee (7 pages).

Plantiff's Request for Particulars of Defence, Foam Creations Inc. vs. *Holey Soles Holdings Ltd.*, Ontario, Canada Federal Court, Court File No. T–161–05, May 1, 2005, Ridout & Maybee (5 pages).

Plantiff's Statement of Claim, Foam Creations Inc. vs. *Holey Soles Holdings Ltd.*, Ontario, Canada Federal Court, Jan. 28, 2005, Ridout & Maybee LLP (8 pages).

Rhoda Miel, *Snowshoe Walks Away with Best Design*, Plastic News, Apr. 22, 2002, v. 14, n. 8, p. 4 (2 pages).

The Elastomers Times: Engage Adds Comfort to Sporting Components, Chemical Business New Base: The Elastomers Times; Dec. 1, 2000 (2 pages).

Trade Name Record, Official Gazette of the U.S. Patents and Trademarks Office, Mar. 24, 1998, 1208, n. 4, p. 73, (abstract, 1 page).

waldenstore.com, *Footwear Waldies*, Aug. 4, 2003, http://www.waldenstore.com/waldies.html, (1 page).

Walking on Modified Eva, Italian Technology, May 1999, n. 2, p. 121, (abstract, 1 page).

* cited by examiner

U.S. Patent **Mar. 28, 2006** **Sheet 1 of 4** **US D517,789 S**

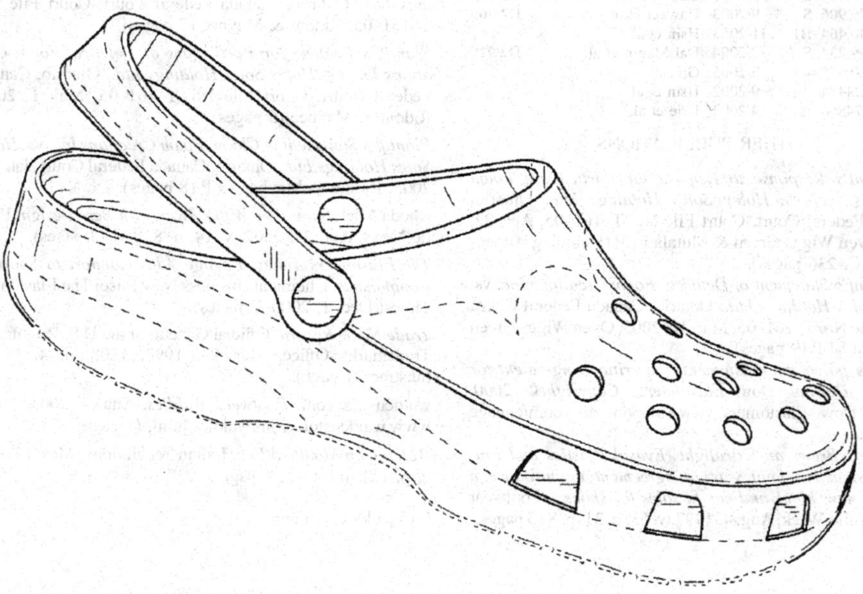

FIG.1

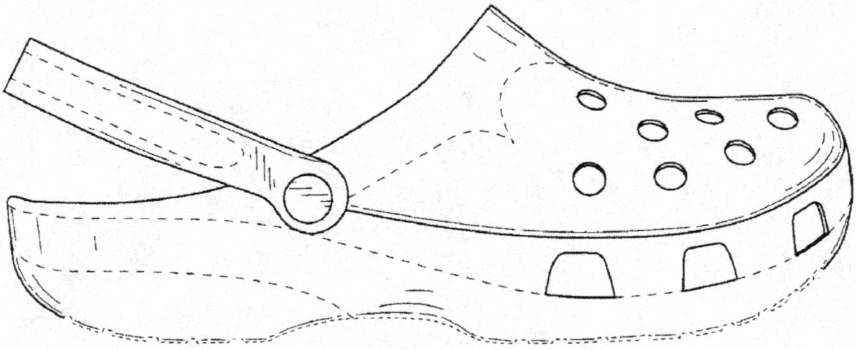

FIG.2

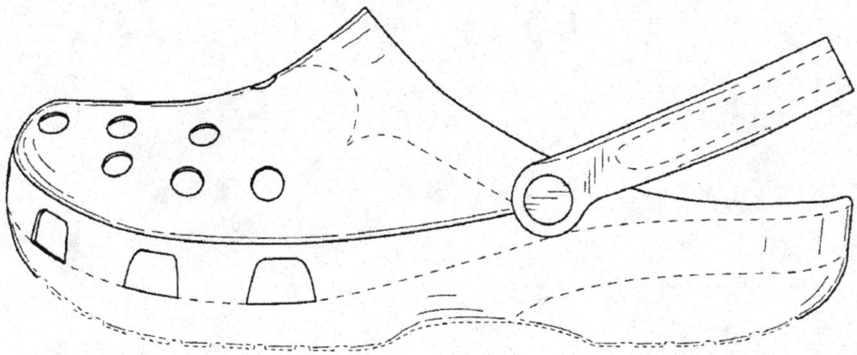

FIG.3

Appendix 3A-2

Illustrative Design Patent 2: Iamartino, June 26, 2012

US00D662281S

(12) **United States Design Patent**
Iamartino

(10) **Patent No.:** **US D662,281 S**
(45) **Date of Patent:** ** **Jun. 26, 2012**

(54) **PANTS**

(75) Inventor: **Antonia Iamartino**, Vancouver (CA)

(73) Assignee: **Lululemon Athletica Canada Inc.**, Vancouver (CA)

(**) Term: **14 Years**

(21) Appl. No.: **29/412,581**

(22) Filed: **Feb. 6, 2012**

Related U.S. Application Data

(63) Continuation-in-part of application No. 29/402,465, filed on Sep. 23, 2011, which is a continuation of application No. 29/359,858, filed on Apr. 16, 2010, now Pat. No. Des. 645,644.

(51) **LOC (9) Cl.** **02-02**
(52) **U.S. Cl.** **D2/742**
(58) **Field of Classification Search** D2/712, D2/731, 738, 742; 2/406, 227, 228, 234–238, 2/242
See application file for complete search history.

(56) **References Cited**

U.S. PATENT DOCUMENTS

1,825,271 A		9/1931	Karberg	
D132,058 S	*	4/1942	Barge	D2/712
2,417,529 A		3/1947	Terry	
RE23,334 E		1/1951	Montmarquet	
3,073,312 A		1/1963	Lobbenberg	
3,396,730 A		8/1968	Fox	
D252,656 S		8/1979	Bergh	
4,466,137 A		8/1984	Carnaghi	
5,143,092 A		9/1992	Flowers	
D461,943 S		8/2002	Lyden	
6,430,752 B1	*	8/2002	Bay	2/228
D473,694 S	*	4/2003	Lyden	D2/742
D486,954 S		2/2004	Mori	
D552,328 S		10/2007	Smith et al.	
D571,530 S	*	6/2008	De Palma	D2/712
D580,126 S		11/2008	Rieder	
D600,883 S		9/2009	Blumenfeld	
D606,284 S		12/2009	Caten et al.	
D609,881 S		2/2010	Chen et al.	
D612,129 S		3/2010	Iamartino et al.	
D612,581 S		3/2010	Ramirez	
D641,127 S	*	7/2011	Zarabi	D2/701
D641,135 S	*	7/2011	Zarabi	D2/712
D641,539 S	*	7/2011	Zarabi	D2/701
D642,768 S		8/2011	Sawle et al.	
D645,644 S	*	9/2011	Iamartino	D2/742
D654,661 S	*	2/2012	Savage	D2/742
2009/0293167 A1	*	12/2009	Kottler	2/23
2012/0036615 A1	*	2/2012	Bradstreet et al.	2/236

OTHER PUBLICATIONS

U.S. Appl. No. 29/402,465, Iamartino.
Kosher Casual. http://www koshercasual.com/baggy-cropped-pants-yoga-exercise31319-p-152.html?osCsid= 67i5o5igmqu2vehgdhu4gs1ar7. Date Unknown: Viewed Sep. 2010.
An American Girl (blog). http://anamericangirlmovestovienna.blogspotcom/2010/08/i-just-ironed-my-yoga-pants.html. Aug. 2010, Yoga Pants.

(Continued)

Primary Examiner — Rashida Johnson
(74) *Attorney, Agent, or Firm* — Joseph Conneely; McCarthy Tetrault LLP

(57) **CLAIM**

The ornamental design for pants, as shown and described.

DESCRIPTION

FIG. **1** is a front view of pants according to a first embodiment of the design;
FIG. **2** is a rear view thereof;
FIG. **3** is a right side view thereof;
FIG. **4** is a left side view thereof;
FIG. **5** is a front perspective view thereof;
FIG. **6** is a front view of pants according to a second embodiment of the design;
FIG. **7** is a rear view thereof;
FIG. **8** is a right side view thereof;
FIG. **9** is a left side view thereof; and,
FIG. **10** is a front perspective view thereof.
The symbol depicted in FIGS. **2** and **3** forming part of the claimed design is a registered trademark of Lululemon Athletica Canada Inc.

1 Claim, 10 Drawing Sheets

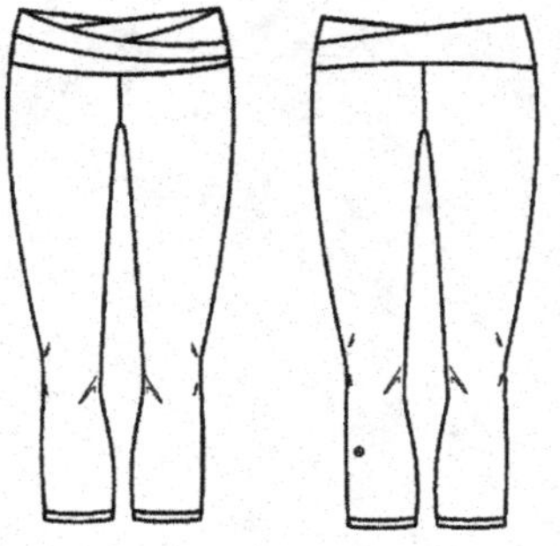

OTHER PUBLICATIONS

Yoga Pants, Etc. http://www.yogapantsetc.com/yocrlomipa.html. Copyright 2008. "Low-Rise Microfiber Capri Youth Yoga Pants".

Old Navy. http://oldnavy.gap.com/browse/ . Date Unknown: Viewed Sep. 2010. "Women's Plus Stretch-Jersey Yoga Pants".

* cited by examiner

Fig. 1

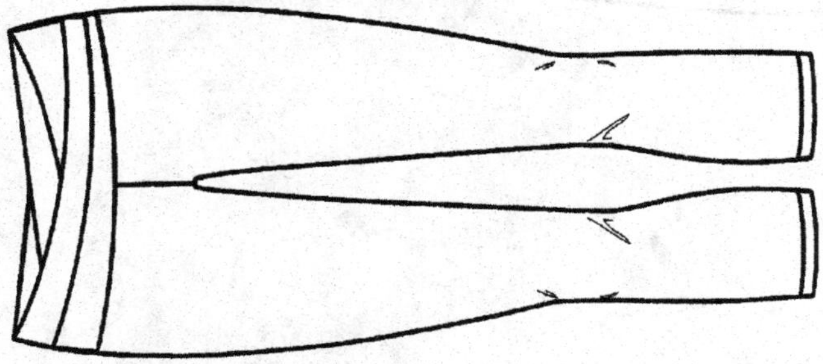

U.S. Patent Jun. 26, 2012 Sheet 2 of 10 US D662,281 S

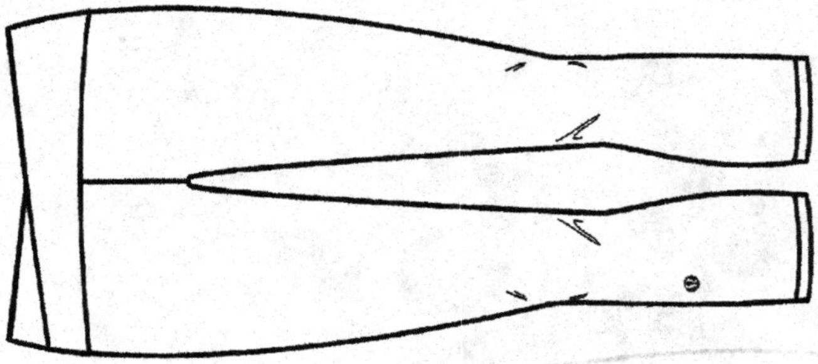

Fig. 2

Fig. 3

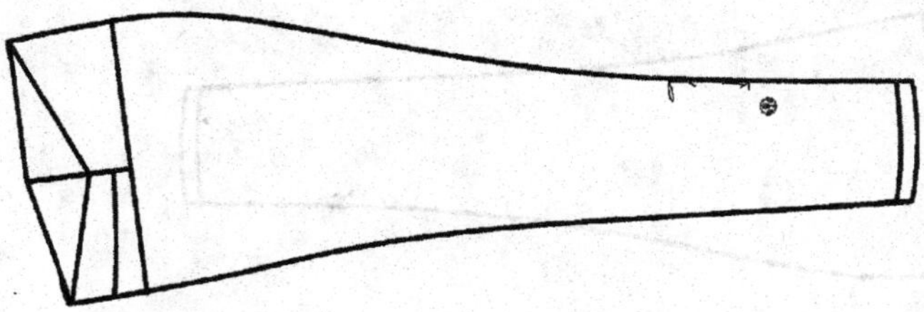

U.S. Patent **Jun. 26, 2012** **Sheet 4 of 10** **US D662,281 S**

Fig. 4

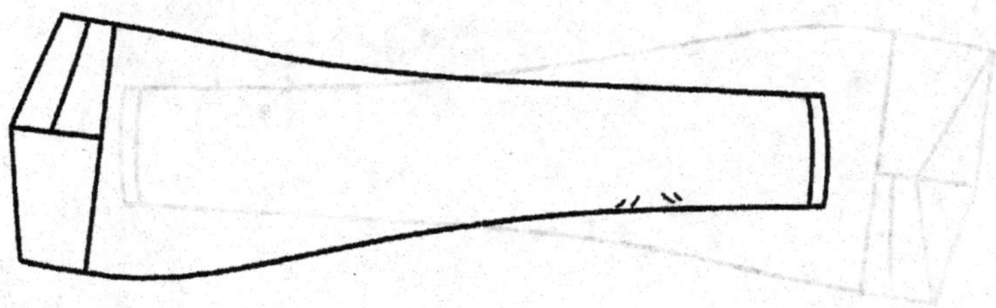

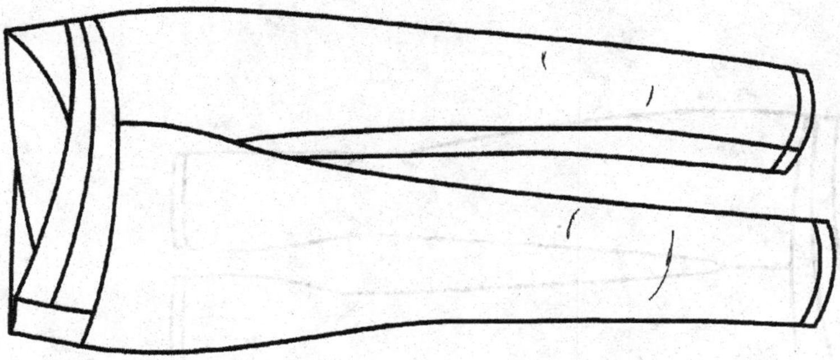

Fig. 5

U.S. Patent Jun. 26, 2012 Sheet 6 of 10 US D662,281 S

Fig. 6

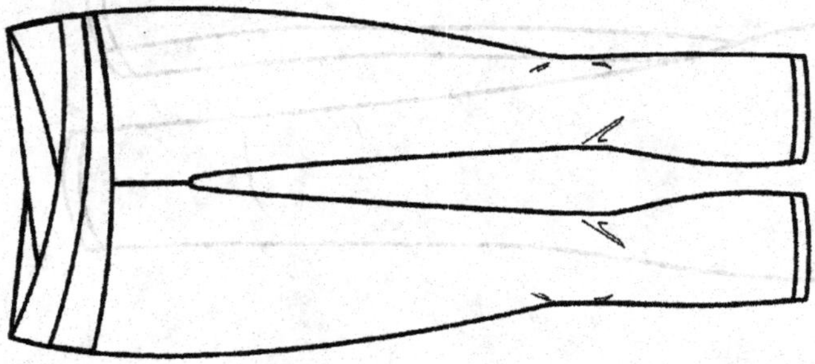

Fig. 7

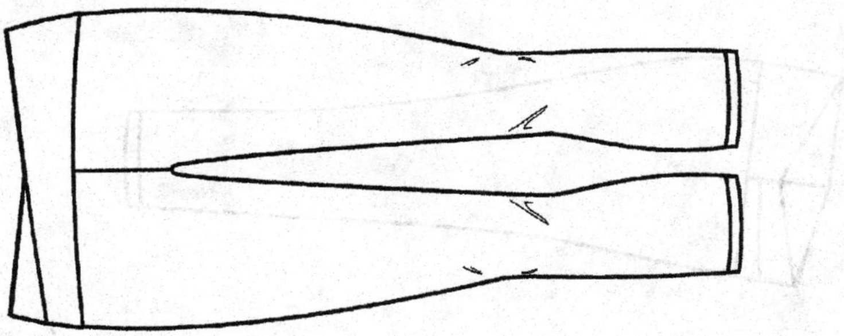

U.S. Patent **Jun. 26, 2012** **Sheet 8 of 10** **US D662,281 S**

Fig. 8

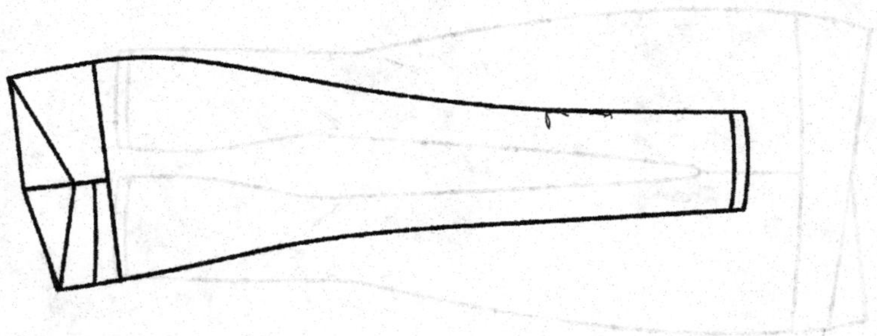

Fig. 9

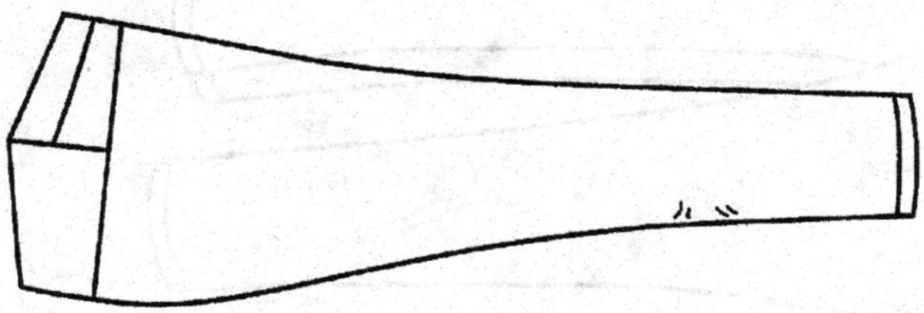

U.S. Patent **Jun. 26, 2012** **Sheet 10 of 10** **US D662,281 S**

Fig. 10

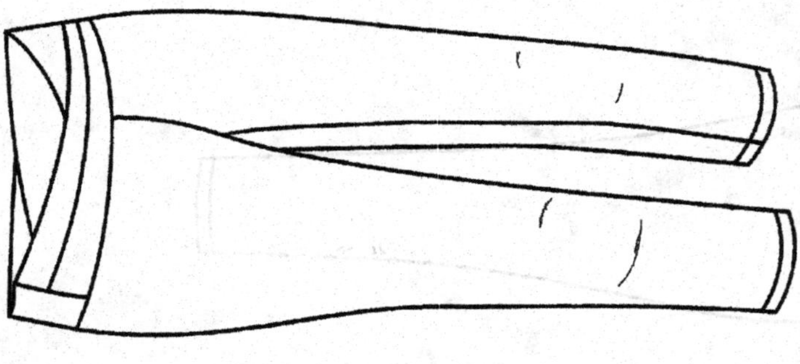

Appendix 3B-1

Illustrative Utility Patent 1: Seamans, February 7, 2006

US006993858B2

(12) United States Patent
Seamans

(10) **Patent No.: US 6,993,858 B2**
(45) **Date of Patent: Feb. 7, 2006**

(54) **BREATHABLE FOOTWEAR PIECES**

(75) Inventor: **Scott Seamans**, Longmont, CO (US)

(73) Assignee: **Crocs, Inc.**, Niwot, CO (US)

(*) Notice: Subject to any disclaimer, the term of this patent is extended or adjusted under 35 U.S.C. 154(b) by 133 days.

(21) Appl. No.: **10/603,126**

(22) Filed: **Jun. 23, 2003**

(65) **Prior Publication Data**

US 2004/0231189 A1 Nov. 25, 2004

Related U.S. Application Data

(60) Provisional application No. 60/473,360, filed on May 23, 2003, provisional application No. 60/473,371, filed on May 23, 2003.

(51) **Int. Cl.**
A43B 7/06 (2006.01)
A43B 3/12 (2006.01)

(52) **U.S. Cl.** .... **36/3 A**; 36/11.5; 36/50.1

(58) **Field of Classification Search** .... 36/3 R, 36/3 A, 3 B, 7.5, 11.5, 98, 29
See application file for complete search history.

(56) **References Cited**

U.S. PATENT DOCUMENTS

2,180,924 A * 11/1939 Dunbar .... 36/3 B
4,476,600 A * 10/1984 Seidel et al. .... 12/142 V
4,888,887 A * 12/1989 Solow .... 36/3 R
4,967,750 A * 11/1990 Cherniak 36/140
5,369,895 A * 12/1994 Hammerschmidt .... 36/3 A
D381,794 S * 8/1997 Gelli D2/916
5,814,254 A 9/1998 Bisconti
D416,667 S * 11/1999 Lamstein D2/916
D431,346 S * 10/2000 Birkenstock D2/916
6,237,249 B1 * 5/2001 Aguerre 36/11.5
6,256,906 B1 * 7/2001 Matis et al. 36/11.5
6,640,464 B2 * 11/2003 Hsin et al. 36/11.5

FOREIGN PATENT DOCUMENTS

EP 0802039 A2 10/1997
EP 0802040 A2 10/1997
EP 0802041 A2 10/1997
EP 0884005 A1 12/1998

OTHER FUBLICATIONS

Rhoda Miel, *Snowshoe walks away with best design, Plastics News*, Apr. 22, 2002, v14, n8, p4 (2 pages).
Luisa Zargani, *One Fine Year; Anton Magnani's Quirky Dry-Shod Designs Have Gained the Italian Designer Respect, Recognition and a Deal With Comme Des Garcons, Footwear News*, Aug. 2, 1999, p. 102 (2 pages).
Finproject Brews an Extralight (Evasol Plastics and Finproject signed a joint venture agreement to introduce a range of new block and net-fit soles for shoes), FN World, Aug. 4, 1997, v. 53, n.31, p. 8 (1 page).

(Continued)

Primary Examiner—Jila M. Mohandesi
(74) *Attorney, Agent, or Firm*—Townsend and Townsend and Crew LLP

(57) **ABSTRACT**

Among other things, the present invention provides various footwear pieces, and methods for manufacturing such pieces. In various cases, the footwear pieces are molded from a lofting material. Further, in various cases, the footwear pieces include one or more ventilators formed in the footwear piece that are surrounded by liquid conductors capable of channeling liquid spilled on the surface of the footwear pieces away from a foot within the footwear pieces.

2 Claims, 12 Drawing Sheets

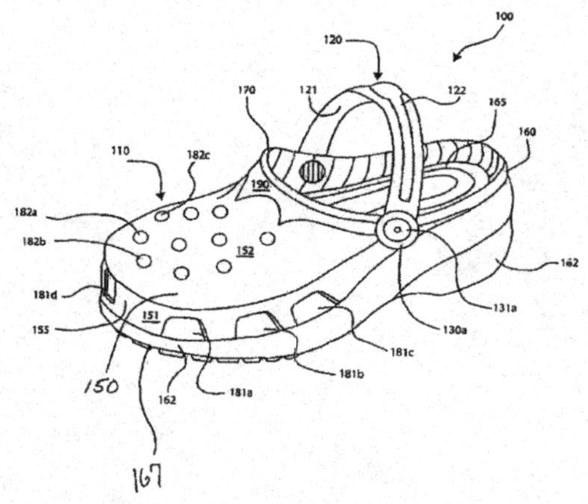

OTHER PUBLICATIONS

Cindy Macdonald, *The entrepreneurs: they're bilingual, multicultural and talented. Distance and language present no barries to Quebec plastics processors and moldmakers as the province's plastics industry continues to increase its level of exports and welcome new companies, Canadian Plastics*, O'99, v. 57(10), p. 35-50 (9 pages).
The Elastomers Times: Engage Adds Comfort to Sporting Components, Chemical Business NewsBase: The Elastomers Times, Friday, Dec. 1, 2000, (1 page).
Comfortable Walking, Italian Technology, Oct., 1999, No. 3, p. 168, (abstract, 1 page).
Injected Eva, Macplas International, Aug., 1999, No. 10, p. 90, (abstract, 1 page).
Walking on Modified Eva, Italian Technology, May 1999, No. 2, p. 121, (abstract, 1 page).
Trade Name Record, Official Gazette of the US Patent and Trademarks Office, Mar. 24, 1998, 1208, No. 4, p. 73, (abstract, 1 page).
Engage® polyolefin elastomers, the critical ingredient for success, DuPont Dow elastomers, Copyright @ 2000 DuPont Dow Elastomers, www.dupont-dow.com/engage (12 pages).
waldenstore.com, *Footwear, Watdies*, Aug. 4, 2003, http://www.waldenstore.com/waldies.html, (1 page).
Birkenstock®, Spring & Summer 2003 Catalog,Birkenstock Orthopudie GMbh, Germany.

* cited by examiner

U.S. Patent **Feb. 7, 2006** **Sheet 1 of 12** **US 6,993,858 B2**

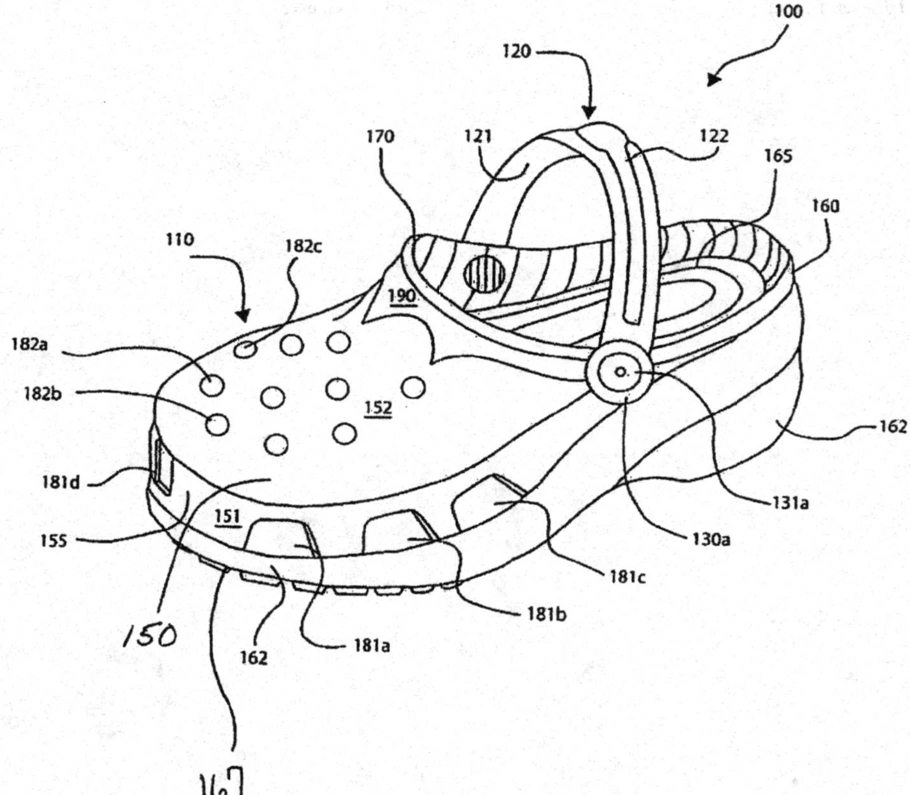

Fig. 1

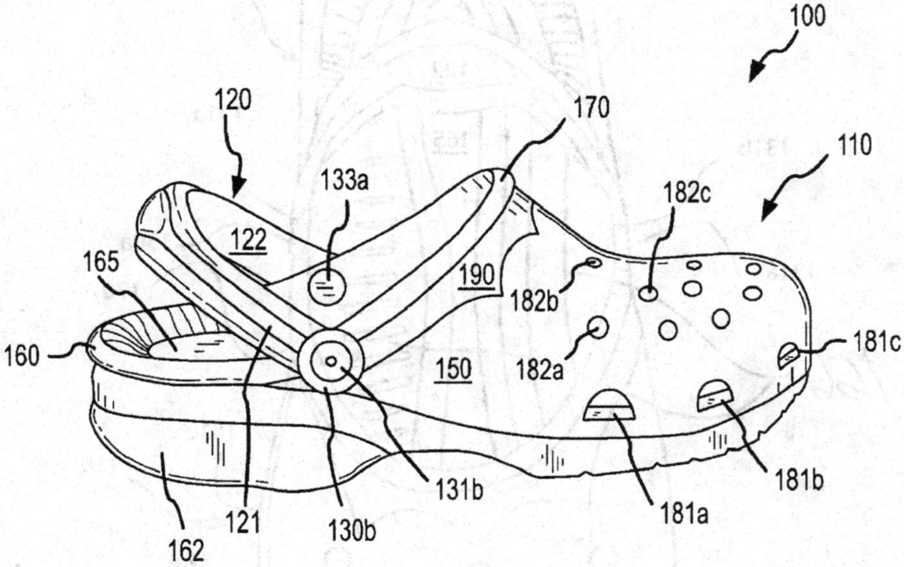
100
120
170
110
133a
182c
122
190
165
182b
160
150
182a
181c
121
131b
181b
130b
181a
162

FIG.2

U.S. Patent Feb. 7, 2006 Sheet 3 of 12 US 6,993,858 B2

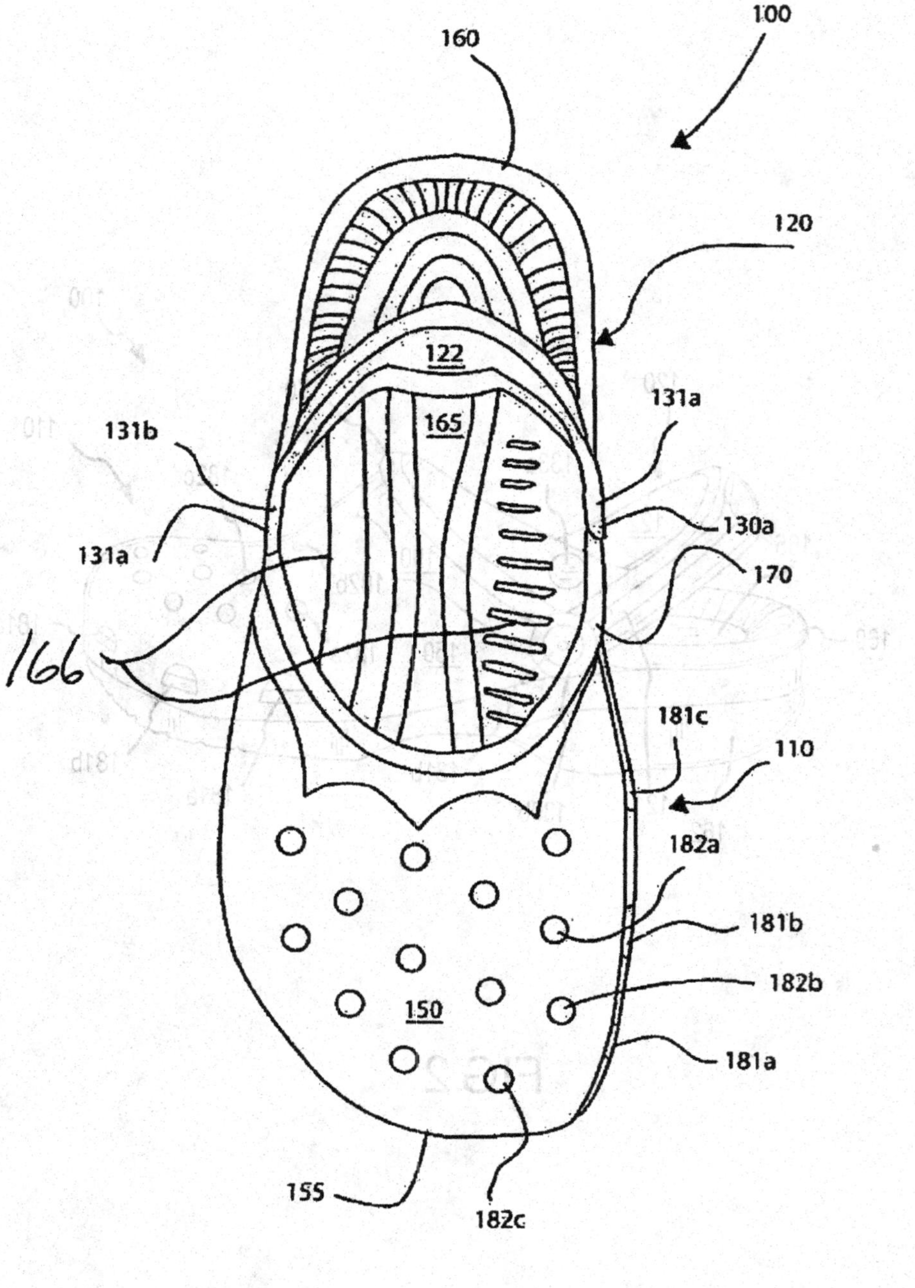

Fig. 3

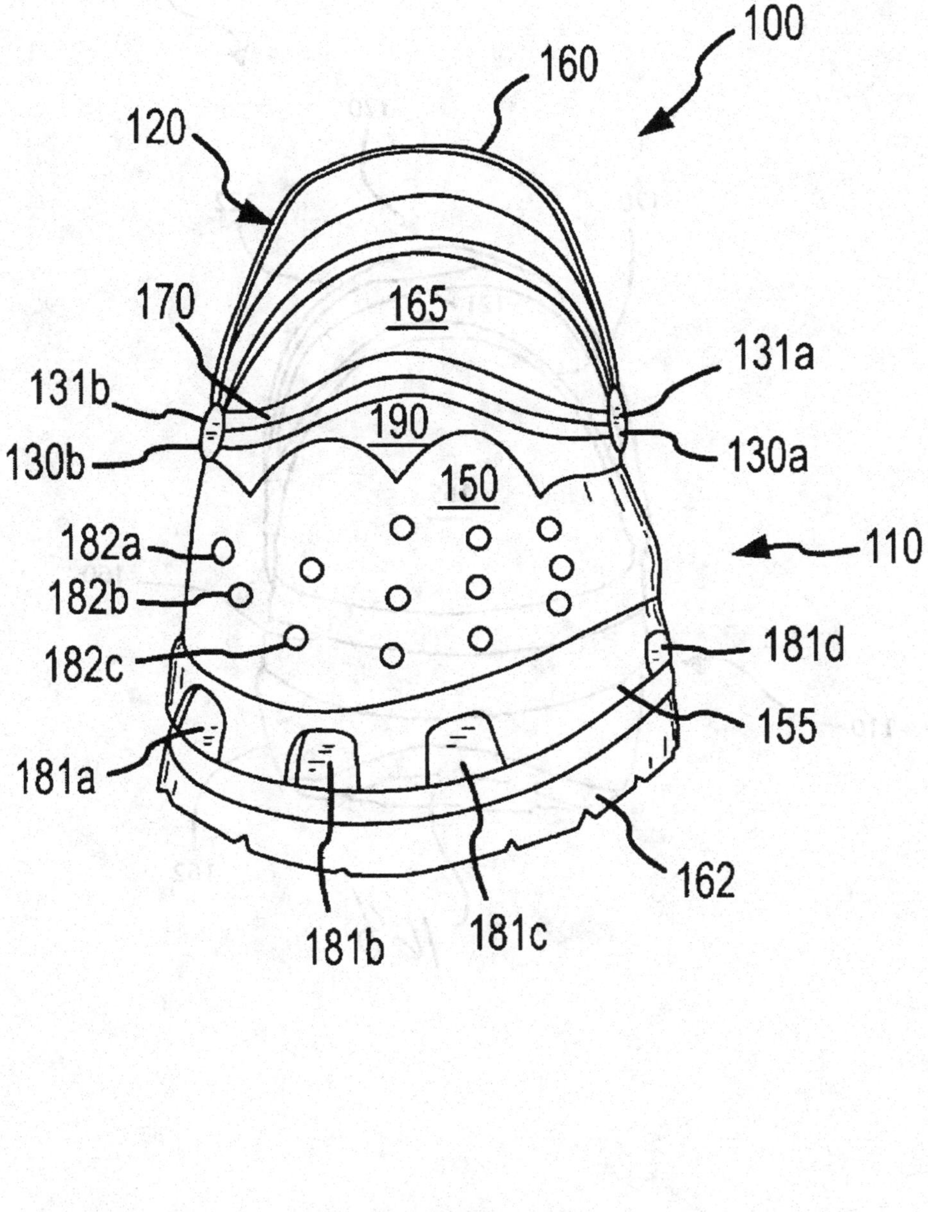
100
160
120
170
165
131a
131b
190
130b
130a
150
182a
110
182b
182c
181d
155
181a
162
181b
181c

FIG.4

U.S. Patent Feb. 7, 2006 Sheet 5 of 12 US 6,993,858 B2

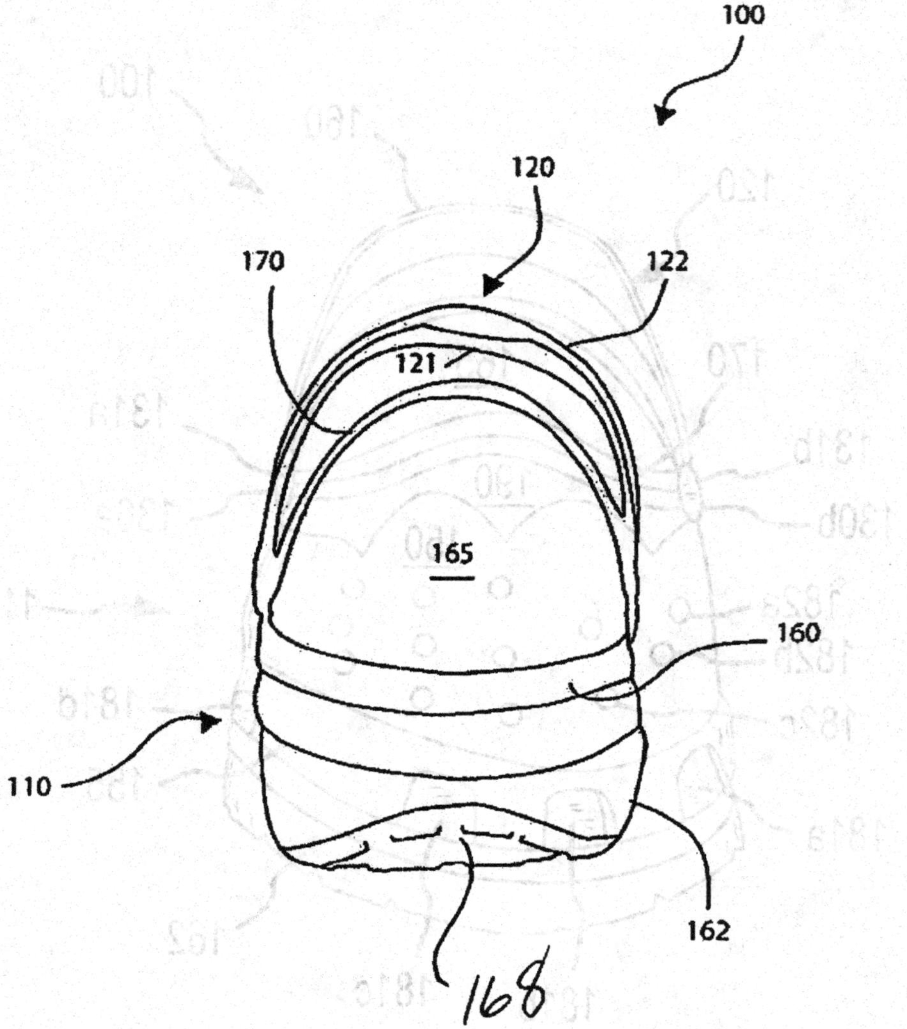

Fig. 5

U.S. Patent **Feb. 7, 2006** **Sheet 6 of 12** **US 6,993,858 B2**

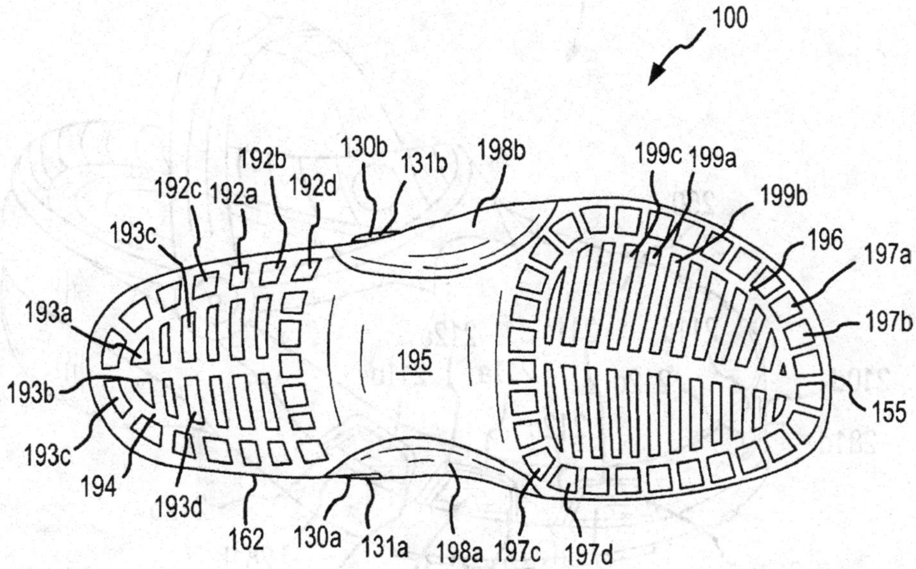

FIG.6

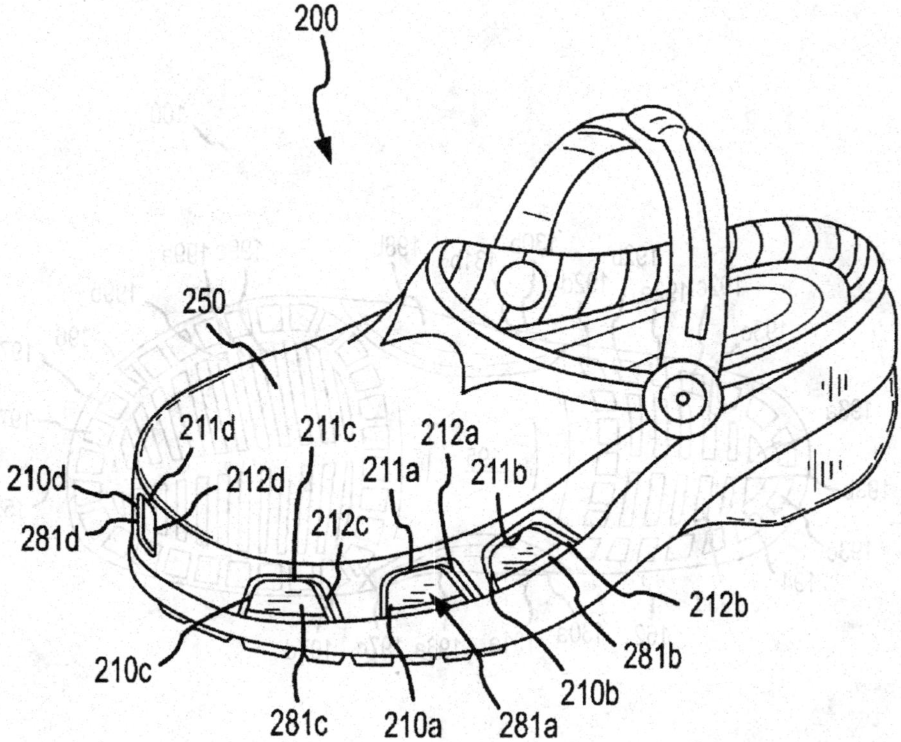

200
250
211d
211c
212a
211a
211b
210d
212d
281d
212c
212b
281b
210c
210b
281c
210a
281a

FIG.7

U.S. Patent Feb. 7, 2006 Sheet 8 of 12 US 6,993,858 B2

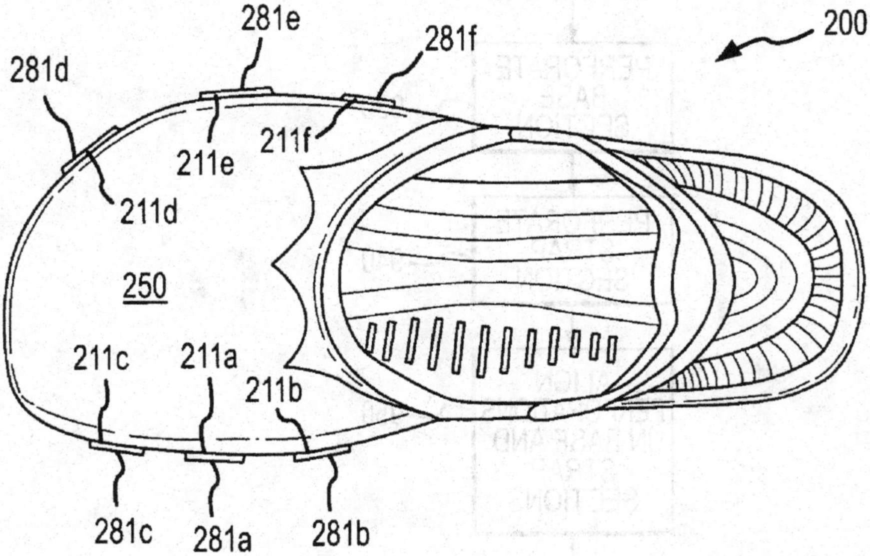

FIG.8

U.S. Patent Feb. 7, 2006 Sheet 9 of 12 US 6,993,858 B2

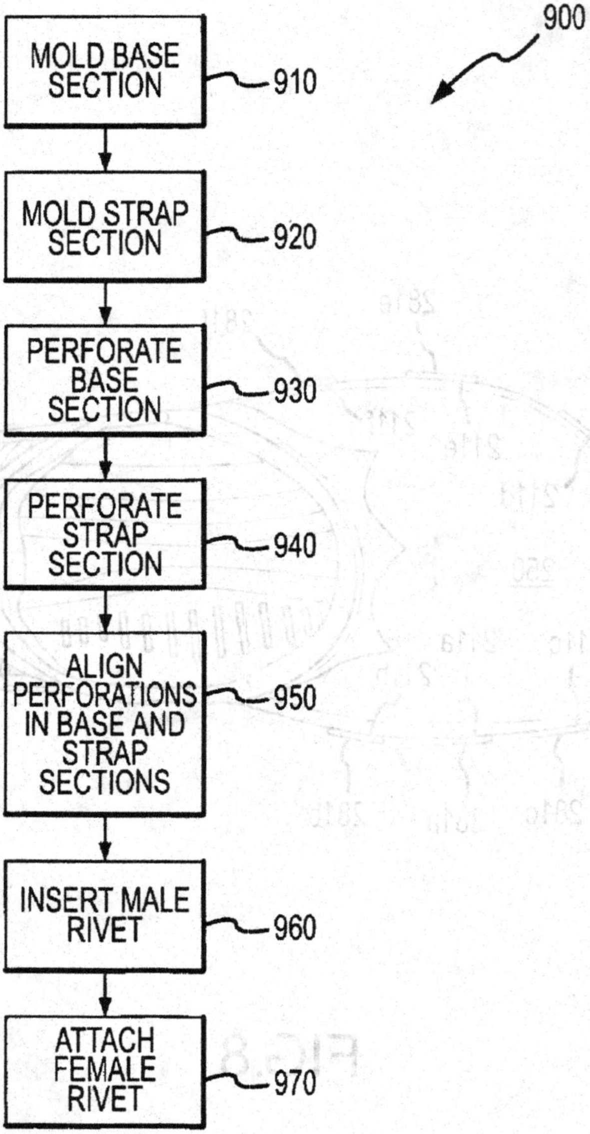

FIG.9

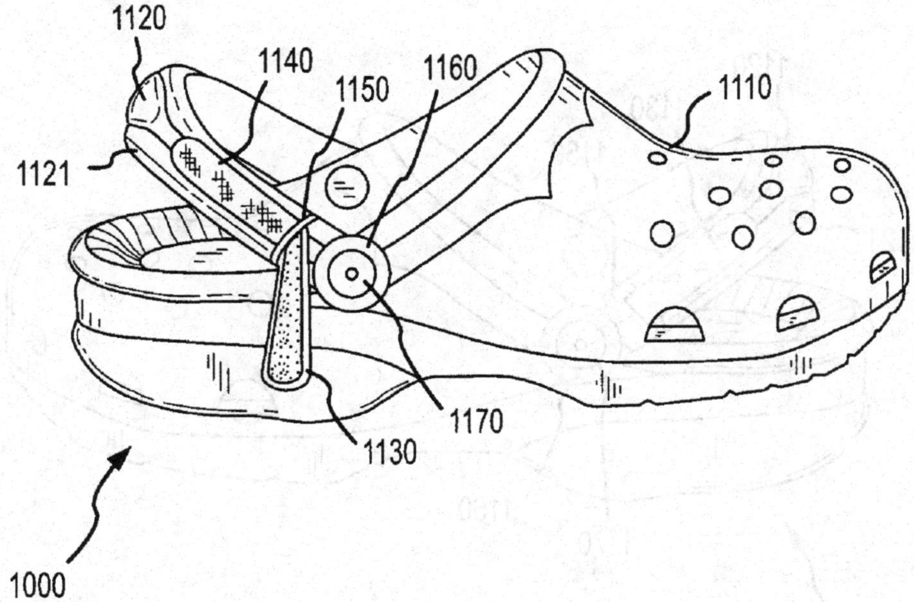

FIG.10a

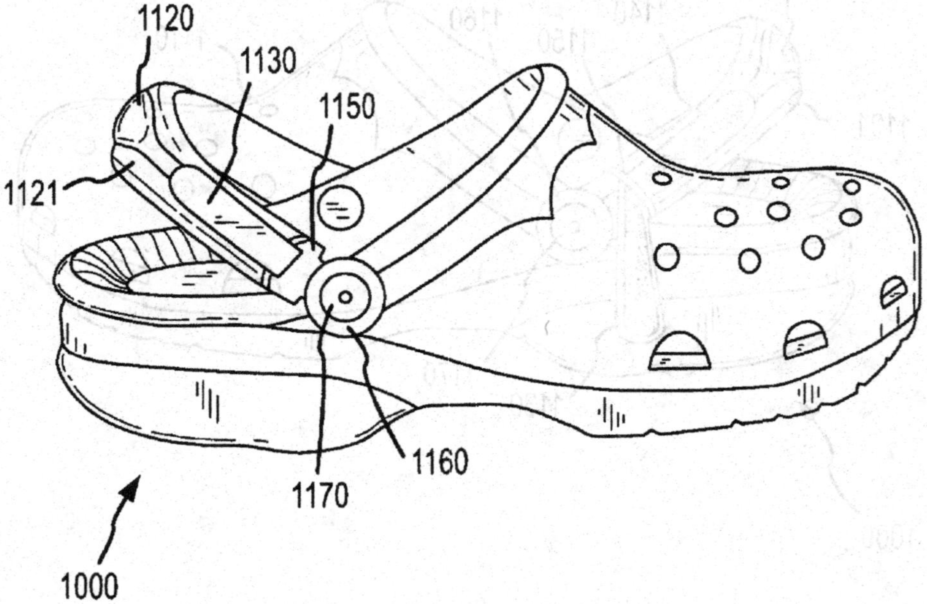

FIG. 10b

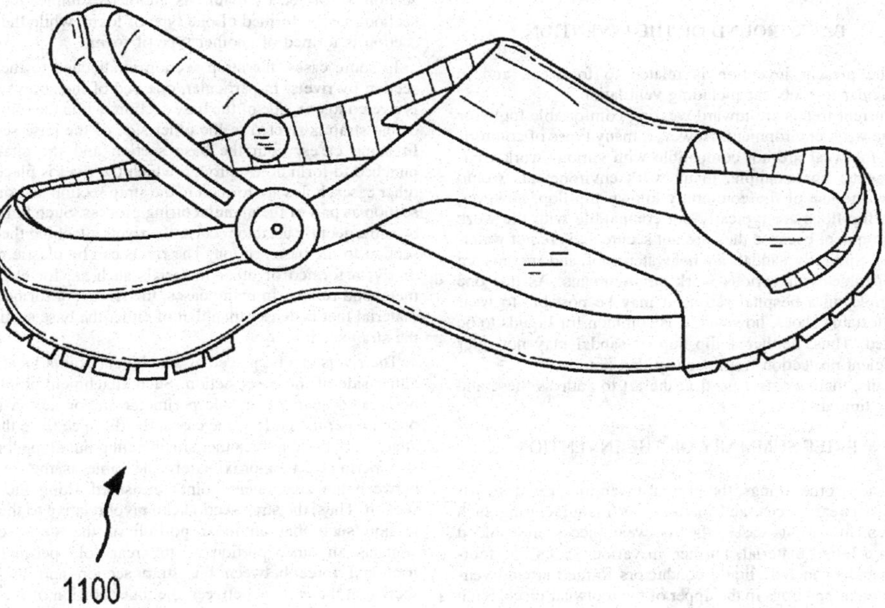

FIG. 11

BREATHABLE FOOTWEAR PIECES

The present application claims priority to U.S. Provisional Pat. Appl. No. 60/473,360, entitled "FOOTWEAR PIECES AND METHODS FOR MANUFACTURING SUCH," filed May 23, 2003 and assigned to an entity common herewith; and U.S. Provisional Pat. Appl. No. 60/473,371, entitled "METHODS AND COMPOSITES FOR MANUFACTURING FOOTWEAR PIECES," also filed May 23, 2003 and assigned to an entity common herewith. Further, the present application is related to U.S. Pat. Appl. No. 10/602,416, entitled "FOOTWEAR PIECES AND METHODS FOR MANUFACTURING SUCH", filed on a date even herewith and assigned to an entity common herewith. The entirety of each of the aforementioned patent applications are incorporated herein by reference for all purposes.

BACKGROUND OF THE INVENTION

The present invention is related to footwear, and in particular to footwear including ventilation.

Current trends are toward wearing comfortable footwear in the work environment. However, many types of comfortable footwear are not compatible with various work environments. For example, many work environments would allow the use of the commonly known flip-flop, however, such flip-flops are typically not compatible with the work environment because they are not secure and are not waterproof. Similarly, sandals are not waterproof, and are thus not compatible with various work environments. As just one example, in a hospital setting it may be possible to wear comfortable shoes, however, it is common for liquids to be spilled. Thus, neither a flip-flop or sandal may not offer sufficient protection from such spilled liquids.

Thus, there exists a need in the art to address these and other limitations.

BRIEF SUMMARY OF THE INVENTION

Among other things, the present invention provides various footwear pieces, and methods for manufacturing such pieces. In various cases, the footwear pieces are molded from a lofted material. Further, in various cases, the footwear pieces include liquid conductors formed around ventilators, or openings in the upper of the footwear piece. Such liquid conductors operate to disperse liquids away from a foot inserted in the footwear piece.

Some embodiments of the present invention provide breathable footwear pieces that include a base section comprising an upper and a sole. The upper includes a substantially horizontal portion and a substantially vertical portion. The substantially horizontal portion is a solid portion, while the substantially vertical portion includes one or more ventilators formed in the substantially vertical portion. In particular instances, liquid conductors are formed around each of the ventilators. In some cases, the liquid conductors are molded as part of the upper, while in other cases, the liquid conductors are attached to the upper after the upper is otherwise formed. In one particular case, the material used to form the base section exhibits a final growth value of approximately 1.51. Such a growth value provides a lightweight, comfortable footwear piece that floats in water, and is slip resistant when used on, for example, wet floors.

Other embodiments of the present invention provide sectional shoe pieces that include a base section and a strap section. The base section includes an upper and a sole formed as a part. The strap section is formed as a second part

that is attached to the base section such that the strap pivots relative to the base section. In some instances, the base section is molded of a continuous piece of foam material. Such foam material can be lofted material manufactured using a resin. Where a resin material is used, it can be mixed to exhibit an expansion coefficient, and a contraction coefficient. In particular cases, multiplying the expansion coefficient and the contraction coefficient results in a product of between 1.46 and 1.58, inclusively.

In various instances, the base section and the strap section are formed of the same material. Such material can be the aforementioned foam material formed into different shapes. In other cases, the strap section and the base section are formed of different materials. For example, the base section may be formed of leather and/or rubber, while the strap section is formed of foam. As another example, the base section may be formed of one type of foam, while the strap section is formed of another type of foam.

In some cases, the strap section is attached to the base section by rivets. In particular, one end of the strap section is riveted to one side of the base section, while the other end of the strap is riveted to the other side of the base section. In some cases, both the base section and the strap are punched to form holes through which the rivet is placed. In other cases, holes are formed in the strap section and/or base section as part of the manufacturing process. Such holes can be subsequently used to receive the rivets attaching the strap section to the base section. The rivets can be plastic rivets, or rivets formed of other materials such as, for example, metal and rubber. In many cases, the rivets are formed of a material that is denser than that of either the base section or the strap section.

The rivets can be placed at attachment points located on either side of the base section. Such attachment points can be located near a rear sole perimeter and/or near a upper opening perimeter. In some cases, the distance from the one attachment point to the other attachment point along the rear sole perimeter is approximately the same as the distance between the attachment points measured along the strap section. Thus, the strap section can pivot relative to the base section such that an inner portion of the strap section contacts an outer portion of the rear sole perimeter. A frictional force between the strap section and the base section at the contact between the inner portion of the strap section and the outer portion of the rear sole perimeter maintains the strap section fixed relative to the base section. In such a position, the strap section forms what appears to be a decorative portion of the base section, and does not interfere with inserting and removing a foot from the base section.

Similarly, the distance from one attachment point to the other attachment point along the upper opening perimeter is approximately the same as the distance between the attachment points measured along the strap section. Thus, the strap section can pivot relative to the base section such that an inner portion of the strap section contacts an outer portion of the upper opening perimeter. A frictional force between the strap section and the base section at the contact between the inner portion of the strap section and the outer portion of the upper opening perimeter maintains the strap section fixed relative to the base section. Again, in such a position, the strap section forms what appears to be a decorative portion of the base section, and does not interfere with inserting and removing a foot from the base section. Further, in some cases, the strap can be fixed in contact with either the upper opening perimeter or the rear sole perimeter.

In various cases, a number of ventilators are formed in the upper. Such ventilators can be holes of varying sizes that allow liquid and or air to pass through at prescribed locations in the upper. In some cases, such ventilators are formed in both a substantially horizontal portion of the upper and a substantially vertical portion of the upper. This provides for a significant amount of ventilation for applications where it is not necessary to protect the foot from exposure to liquids entering through the ventilators. Such applications can include, but are not limited to, boating, beach use, fishing, and the like.

Alternatively, some instances include a solid covering over the substantially horizontal portion of the upper, while including ventilators formed in the vertical portions of the uppers. This provides for sufficient ventilation, while at the same time protecting a foot from spilled liquids. Such an approach may be desirable for applications including use by medical personnel, chefs, and the like. Further, in some cases, a liquid conductor is formed around at least a portion of a perimeter of each of the plurality of ventilators. Such a liquid conductor transfers a liquid spilled on the upper around and away from the various ventilators formed in the substantially vertical portion. Such conductors can thus further protect the foot from exposure to spilled liquids.

In particular cases, the toe region of the upper is extended at a location corresponding to the larger toes of the human foot. Thus, the toe region of the upper generally follows the contour of a human foot from larger toes on the inside of the shoe to smaller toes on the outside of the shoe. Such an approach can provide increased comfort and/or functionality. Further, the rear perimeter of the sole can be raised above a support base further increasing the functionality of the shoe. This support base can include a raised pattern where the foot contacts the shoe.

Other embodiments of the present invention provide sectional shoe pieces that include a base section and a strap section. The strap section is attached to the base section using a rivet such that the strap is pivotable relative to the base section. The rivet can be made of metal, plastic, or some other material. In some cases, the base section is formed of a continuous piece of foam, while in other cases, the base section includes an assemblage of multiple constituent parts. The parts can be formed of various materials including, but not limited to, foam, plastic, rubber, leather, and/or the like.

Yet other embodiments of the present invention provide methods for manufacturing a sectional shoe. The methods include molding a base section and a strap section. The methods further include attaching the strap section to the base section such that the strap pivots relative to the base section. In some cases, the strap section is attached to the base section by riveting opposite ends of the strap to opposing sides of the base section. In various cases, holes are punched through the base section and the strap section prior to riveting the strap section in place. In other cases, the holes through which the rivet are placed are formed during the molding of the base section and/or strap section.

The base section can include a sole and an upper. The sole includes a rear sole perimeter, and the upper includes an upper opening perimeter. In particular cases, rivet holes are placed approximately equidistant from a midway point of the rear sole perimeter and from a midway point of the upper opening perimeter. Thus, the strap can be folded over the upper and the sole and worn as a decorative feature, or in contrast worn away from either the sole or the upper as a functional strap.

This summary provides only a general outline of some embodiments according to the present invention. Many other objects, features, advantages and other embodiments of the present invention will become more fully apparent from the following detailed description, the appended claims and the accompanying drawings.

BRIEF DESCRIPTION OF THE DRAWINGS

A further understanding of the various embodiments of the present invention may be realized by reference to the figures which are described in remaining portions of the specification. In the figures, like reference numerals are used throughout several to refer to similar components. In some instances, a sub-label consisting of a lower case letter is associated with a reference numeral to denote one of multiple similar components. When reference is made to a reference numeral without specification to an existing sub-label, it is intended to refer to all such multiple similar components.

FIGS. **1–6** are views of a footwear piece in accordance with embodiments of the present invention;

FIGS. **7–8** are views of another footwear piece in accordance with other embodiments of the present invention;

FIG. **9** is a flow diagram illustrating methods for manufacturing in accordance with embodiments of the present invention;

FIG. **10** illustrates another footwear piece in accordance with other embodiments of the present invention; and

FIG. **11** illustrates yet another footwear piece in accordance with various embodiments of the present invention.

DETAILED DESCRIPTION OF THE INVENTION

Among other things, the present invention provides various footwear pieces, and methods for manufacturing such pieces. In various cases, the footwear pieces are molded from a lofted, or foam material material. Further, in various cases, the footwear pieces include liquid conductors formed around ventilators, or holes, in the footwear piece. Such liquid conductors operate to disperse liquids away from a foot inserted in the footwear piece.

Turning to FIG. **1**, a footwear piece **100** in accordance with some embodiments of the present invention is illustrated. Footwear piece **100** includes a base section **110** and a strap section **120**. Base section **110** includes an upper **150** and a sole **162**. In some embodiments, base section **110** is molded as a single piece of foam material. In other embodiments, sole **162** is molded from a foam or other foam like material, while upper **150** is manufactured of a different material that is later assembled with sole **162** to form base section **110**.

Upper **150** includes a substantially horizontal portion **152** that can include one or more ventilators **182**. Ventilators **182** can be, but are not limited to, openings that are formed in upper **150** as base section **110** is being molded. Alternatively, ventilators **182** can be openings formed in upper **150** after formation and/or assembly of upper **150**. As yet another alternative, ventilators **182** can be formed as part of an assembly process associated with upper **150**. Thus, for example, ventilators **182** can be openings between assembled parts of upper **150**. Based on the disclosure provided herein, one of ordinary skill in the art will appreciate a number of different ventilator types and methods for forming such.

Upper **150** further includes a substantially vertical region **151** that includes one or more ventilators **181**. FIG. **1** illustrates a preferred embodiment wherein each of the ventilators **181** extend up a majority of the height of vertical region **151**. As with ventilators **182**, ventilators **181** can be, but are not limited to, openings that are formed in upper **150** as base section **110** is being molded. Alternatively, ventilators **181** can be openings formed in upper **150** after formation and/or assembly of upper **150**. As yet another alternative, ventilators **181** can be formed as part of an assembly process associated with upper **150**. Thus, for example, ventilators **181** can be openings between assembled parts of upper **150**. Based on the disclosure provided herein, one of ordinary skill in the art will appreciate a number of different ventilator types and methods for forming such.

Upper **150** further includes a toe region **155** that surrounds the toes of a human foot inserted into base section **110**. In some embodiments, toe region **155** tapers from the inner area of base section **110** to the outer area of base section **110** such that it generally follows the contour of a human foot where larger toes exist at the inside of the foot, and the foot tapers to smaller toes on the outside. This can be functionally advantageous as the footwear piece **100** conforms to the shape of the human foot. In other embodiments, toe region **155** is a square cross section that does not exhibit tapering, while yet other embodiments provide a rounded square where the toe section has its greatest extension near the a central point of base section **110**, and tapers in both directions from the central point. Based on the disclosure provided herein, one of ordinary skill in the art will appreciate a number of shapes for toe region **155**.

As depicted, upper **150** includes a substantially horizontal region **152** that rises toward an upper opening perimeter **170**. When worn, the upper opening perimeter can contact an area of the human foot in front of, and below the ankle. Upper **150** can be designed such that upper opening perimeter **170** is disposed only a short distance from toe region **155**, in which case it will be formed in substantially horizontal region **152**. Alternatively, upper **150** can be designed to extend farther up the foot toward the ankle, in which cases it will be in a more vertical region of upper **150**. A decorative pattern **190** may or may not be molded or otherwise created near upper opening perimeter **170**. As depicted, upper opening perimeter **170** and decorative pattern **190** can extend from the location of rivet **131***a* to that of rivet **131***b* (shown in other figures).

Sole **162** includes a rear sole perimeter **160** that defines the rear portion of sole **160**. In some cases, this region is raised above a support base **165** that is the area that is in contact with the bottom part of the human foot. Such a raised rear sole perimeter provides some support to the heel of the human foot and helps maintain footwear piece **100** in position. In other embodiments, rear sole perimeter **160** is not raised. In addition, support base **165** includes a raised pattern **166** throughout the surface where the foot contacts support base **165**. As shown in FIG. **1**, the bottom surface of sole **162** includes a toe portion **167** that is raised slightly from the generally flat plane of sole **162**. As best shown in FIG. **5**, the bottom surface of sole **162** also preferably includes a heel portion **168** that is raised slightly from the generally flat plane of sole **162**.

Strap section **120** includes an outer region **122**, an inner region **121**, and rounded ends **130**. In some cases, strap section **120** is attached to base section **110** by rivets **131** that are placed through holes in both strap ends **130**, and in upper **150** at an attachment point. Strap section **120** can be pivoted in relation to base section **110** such that strap section **120** can contact upper opening perimeter **170** when pivoted in one direction, and rear sole perimeter **160** when pivoted in the other direction. In some embodiments strap section **120** includes dimensions such that when strap section **120** is pivoted forward, inner region **121** contacts an outer surface of upper opening perimeter **170**. A frictional force at the contact of inner region **121** and upper opening perimeter **170** maintains strap section **120** in a fixed position relative to base section **110**.

Alternatively, strap section **120** can include dimensions such that when strap section **120** is pivoted backward, inner region **121** contacts an outer surface of rear sole perimeter **160**. A frictional force at the contact of inner region **121** and rear sole perimeter **160** maintains strap section **120** in a fixed position relative to base section **110**. In such positions, strap **120** can be a decorative portion of footwear piece **100**.

As yet another alternative, strap section **120** can be placed in an intermediary position between rear sole perimeter **160** upper opening perimeter **170**. In this position, the strap serves the utilitarian purpose of lending support to the Achilles portion of the human foot, thus helping to maintain footwear piece **100** in position on the human foot. In some embodiments, a frictional force developed between strap **120** and upper **150** at the location of the rivets is sufficient to maintain strap **120** in place. This helps to assure that strap **120** remains in place even when the Achilles part of the foot is not pressing against strap **120**. Without such friction, strap **120** would succumb to gravity and fall to a position where the foot would not be supported. At the same time, it can be desirable to reduce the friction at the contact point sufficient to allow strap **120** to be readily moved.

In particular embodiments, strap **120** is formed of a foam material capable of significant deformation making footwear piece **100** comfortable for a large number of foot types. In other embodiments, strap **120** is form of a less deformable material that provides a stronger security for the foot. Yet other embodiments include an adjustable strap that includes significant deformability, yet is capable of capable of being securely strapped to the foot. Such embodiments are discussed further in relation to FIG. **10** below.

FIG. **2** depicts a side view of footwear piece **100**, while FIG. **3** provides a top view of footwear piece **100**. FIGS. **4** and **5** provide front and rear views, respectively, of footwear piece **100**. Further, FIG. **6** illustrates the bottom of sole **162**. As illustrated, sole **162** includes raised side portions **198**, front tread pattern **196**, and rear tread pattern **194**. Front tread pattern **196** includes inner longitudinal tread portions **199**, and outer rectangular tread portions **197**. Similarly, rear tread pattern **194** includes inner longitudinal tread portions **193**, and outer rectangular tread portions **192**. Based on this, one of ordinary skill in the art will appreciate a number of other trade patterns and/or formations that can be used in relation to footwear piece **100**.

Turning to FIG. **7**, another footwear piece **200** in accordance with other embodiments of the present invention is illustrated. Footwear piece **200** includes a number of features similar to that of the previously described footwear piece **100**. In contrast, however, substantially horizontal portion **250** of the upper is of solid construction. As such, liquid materials that are spilled or otherwise contact substantially horizontal portion **250** do not permeate footwear piece **200**. This can be advantageous in medical or other commercial applications where the foot needs at least some protection from spilled materials. Further, a number of ventilators **281** are formed in the substantially vertical portion of the upper. Liquid conductive portions **210, 211, 212** are formed around each of ventilators **281**. Liquid conductive portions **210**, **211**, **212** can be any formation or structure that can divert a liquid falling from above footwear piece **200** from entering through ventilators **281**. In one embodiment, liquid conductive portions **210**, **211**, **212** are molded as part of the upper. FIG. **8** is a top view of footwear piece depicting the various liquid conductive portions.

FIG. **9** is a flow diagram **900** illustrating a method in accordance with the present invention for manufacturing footwear pieces. Following flow diagram **900**, a base section and strap section are molded (blocks **910**, **920**). The base section and strap section are perforated at the location where the two pieces are to be connected (blocks **930**, **940**). The perforations in the strap and base section are aligned (block **950**), a male portion of a rivet is inserted through the aligned perforations (block **960**), and a female portion of the rivet is mated to the male portion, thus securing the strap to the base section.

Turning to FIG. **10**, another footwear piece **1000** in accordance with other embodiments of the present invention is illustrated. Footwear piece **1000** is similar to previously described footwear piece **100**, except that strap **1120** has been modified to allow for adjustment. As illustrated, strap **1120** includes a main portion **1121** and a connection portion **1160**. Connection portion **1160** is attached to a base section **1110** of footwear piece **1000** by a rivet **1170**, or some other pivotable connection as is known in the art. Main portion **1121** is attached to the opposite side via a rivet (not shown), and includes a male Velcro portion **1140** attached thereon, and a female Velcro portion **1130** extending like a tongue therefrom.

Female Velcro portion **1130** is fed through a buckle **1150** that is attached to connection portion **1160** and pulled until the desired tightness is achieved. Female Velcro portion **1130** is then laid over male Velcro portion **1140** as depicted in FIG. **10***b*. One of ordinary skill in the art will appreciate that other connection materials can be used in place of Velcro and that the male **1140** and female **1130** Velcro portions can be interchanged. Further, based on the disclosure provided herein, one of ordinary skill in the art will appreciate that an adjustment can be used on either or both sides of strap **1120**, or can be placed in the center of strap **1120**.

FIG. **11** illustrates yet another footwear piece **1100** in accordance with some embodiments of the present invention. Footwear piece **1100** is an open toe model with a pivotable strap. Based on the disclosure provided herein, one of ordinary skill in the art will appreciate that adjustable strap **1120** depicted in FIG. **10** can also be used in relation to footwear piece **1100**.

As previously suggested, the footwear pieces disclosed herein can be made of a lofted foam material. Manufacturing footwear pieces using such a lofted foam material can include providing a resin that includes a pre-mixture of resin, pigment, and a growth additive. The resin, originally in pellet form, is heated to a liquid state. This liquid resin is screwed into a mold that has been heated prior to receiving the resin. The volume of resin injected into the mold is controlled by the pitch of the screw that drives the liquid resin into the mold. The liquid resin is allowed to set, at which time the mold is opened and the formed footwear piece is removed from the mold. The formed footwear piece is then placed on a cooling last, where it is allowed to air dry.

During this process, a relatively small footwear piece confirming to the size of the mold is created, but when the mold opens, the footwear piece springs out as it expands in size. Then, as the footwear piece is air cooled, it contracts to a final size. Thus, the process involves both an expansion characteristic and a contraction characteristic. Multiplying the size of the shoe in the mold by the expansion characteristic yields the size of the footwear piece after the mold is opened. Multiplying the expansion characteristic by the contraction characteristic provides a final growth value representative of the final size of the shoe relative to the mold.

In such a manufacturing process, a number of elements can be controlled to achieve the desired end result. These elements include, the volume of material introduced into the mold, the size of the mold, the composition of the material being used, and the size of the cooling last. Previous manufacturers of molded footwear products have used, for example, four sizes of molds to create six different sizes of footwear pieces. Thus, for example, to create two different sized shoes from the same mold, one volume of a material is screwed into a mold to create one shoe size, and another volume of the same material is screwed into the same mold to create a different shoe size. Once removed from the mold, the shoes are cooled on cooling lasts of different sizes. Thus, the process uses a modified volume and cooling last size to control the end product, while keeping the mold size and the composition fixed. While this creates shoes of different sizes, it has been found that control of the final sizes is somewhat limited and/or unpredictable.

In part to address this, embodiments of the present invention use a fixed volume and composition of material, and cooling last size, while varying mold sizes to control the size of the end product. It has been found that such an approach results in a heightened degree of control, when compared to the previously described approach. This approach is particularly valuable for shoes manufactured of the same color resin. Where different colors are involved, the composition of the resin may be varied across the colors to achieve size control between colors. This composition adjustment is more fully described below.

In one particular embodiment, the resin is Ethylene Vinyl Acetate copolymer (EVA) based material. In this particular case, additives are included with the EVA base to create an expansible and cross-linking material. More particularly, an expanding powder is added which decomposes at a specific temperature to produce gases which cause the material to rise as it sets within a mold. Accordingly, when the mold is opened, an instantaneous expansion of the molded part results. During this expansion, the dimensions of the part increase rapidly, while the proportions and shape remain reasonably constant providing a consistent shape of the end part relative to the original mold. Additional disclosure of such cross-linking and expansion is provided in European Patent 0 802 039 A2, filed on Mar. 25, 1997, and assigned to FINPROJECT™ of Italy.

Some embodiments of the present invention utilize an EVA as previously described that is known commercially as LEVIREX™, and is marketed by FINPROJECT™ of Italy. It has been found desirable to create a mixture of LEVIREX™ that exhibits a final growth value of between 1.47 and 1.58. In one particularly desirable embodiment, a final growth value of approximately 1.51 is used. This includes an expansion characteristic of approximately 2.5, and a contraction characteristic of approximately 0.6. This provides a relatively soft footwear piece that has very good anti-slip capabilities, and at the same time, size reproducibility and durability.

In some cases, the resin mixture (LEVIREX™, growth additive such as ENGAGE™ by DUPONT™, and pigment) is modified depending upon the desired color of the footwear piece. This is at least in part due to the density of the pigment associated with certain colors. Were the resin mixture not adjusted, a green shoe would be produced appreciably smaller than a khaki shoe where all other factors remain constant. This can be unacceptable where, for example, the footwear pieces are to be sold over the Internet and the consumer is not capable of trying the footwear piece on before purchasing. To alleviate this, the final growth value for a green resin is adjusted to approximately 1.515, where the final growth value for the khaki resin is adjusted to approximately 1.505. Thus, by modifying the mixture, shoes of accurate sizes across multiple colors can be produced.

While footwear pieces can be molded as previously described, based on the disclosure provided herein, one of ordinary skill in the art will appreciate that various embodiments of the present invention can be utilized in relation to other molding processes, and or assembly methods. For example, a hard plastic footwear piece could be injection molded using techniques known in the art, or a footwear piece could be at least partially made of leather or other natural materials. As another example, the footwear piece could be Freon cooled, rather than air cooled. This could be used to speed the manufacturing process.

The invention has now been described in detail for purposes of clarity and understanding. However, it will be appreciated that certain changes and modifications may be practiced within the scope of the appended claims. Accordingly, it should be recognized that many other systems, functions, methods, and combinations thereof are possible in accordance with the present invention. Thus, although the invention is described with reference to specific embodiments and figures thereof, the embodiments and figures are merely illustrative, and not limiting of the invention. Rather, the scope of the invention is to be determined solely by the appended claims.

What is claimed is:

1. A footwear piece comprising:

a base section including an upper and a sole formed as a single part manufactured from a moldable foam material; and

a strap section formed of a moldable material that is attached at opposite ends thereof to the upper of the base section with plastic connectors such that the moldable foam material of the strap section is in direct contact with the moldable material of the base section and pivots relative to the base section at the connectors;

wherein the upper includes an open rear region defined by an upper opening perimeter, and wherein frictional forces developed by the contact between the strap section and the base section at the plastic connectors are sufficient to maintain the strap section in place in an intermediary position after pivoting, whereby the strap section lends support to the Achilles portion of the human foot inserted in the open rear region; and

wherein the upper includes a substantially horizontal portion and a substantially vertical portion forming a toe region that generally follows the contour of a human foot, wherein the toe region tapers from an inner area of the base section where the larger toes exist to an outer area of the base section where the smaller toes exist; and

wherein the sole includes a bottom surface having front and rear tread patterns longitudinally connected by a flat section.

2. A footwear piece comprising:

a base section including an upper and a sole formed as a single part manufactured from a moldable foam material; and

a strap section formed of a molded foam material attached at opposite ends thereof to the base section such that the strap section is in direct contact with the base section and pivots relative to the base section; and

wherein the upper includes an open rear region defined by an upper opening perimeter; and wherein the sole includes a rear perimeter; and wherein the strap section pivots between a first contact point on the upper opening perimeter and a second contact point on the rear perimeter, and wherein frictional forces developed by the contact between the strap section and the base section at the points of attachment are sufficient to maintain the strap section in place in an intermediary position after pivoting whereby the strap section lends support to the Achilles portion of a human foot inserted in the open rear region; and

wherein the upper includes a substantially horizontal portion and a substantially vertical portion forming a toe region that generally follows the contour of a human foot, wherein the toe region tapers from the inner area of the base section where the larger toes exist to the outer area of the base section where the smaller toes exist; and

wherein a decorative pattern of raised bumps is molded or otherwise created in the upper near to and extending the length of the upper opening perimeter; and

wherein a plurality of ventilators are formed in both the substantially vertical portion and the substantially horizontal portion, and wherein the ventilators extend up a majority of the height of the vertical portion;

wherein the vertical portion of the upper includes an upper strip, wherein the ventilators are formed in the upper strip, and wherein the upper strip extends from the toe region to the points of attachment for the strap section, and wherein the sole includes a lower strip that parallels the upper strip and is separated by a line that extends from the toe region to a heel of the footwear piece, and wherein the lower strip vertically rises in a direction toward the heel; and

wherein the sole includes a bottom surface having front and rear tread patterns longitudinally connected by a flat section without tread patterns bounded by raised side portions; and

wherein the sole further includes a top surface having a support base including a raised pattern where a foot contacts the support base.

* * * * *

Appendix 3B-2

Illustrative Utility Patent 2: Drab et al., September 11, 2012

US008261372B2

(12) **United States Patent**
Drab et al.

(10) **Patent No.: US 8,261,372 B2**
(45) **Date of Patent: Sep. 11, 2012**

(54) **GOLF GLOVE**

(75) Inventors: **John Drab**, Pasadena, MD (US); **Tim Dennis**, Bowie, MD (US); **Raphael Peck**, Baltimore, MD (US)

(73) Assignee: **Under Armour, Inc.**, Baltimore, MD (US)

(*) Notice: Subject to any disclaimer, the term of this patent is extended or adjusted under 35 U.S.C. 154(b) by 493 days.

(21) Appl. No.: **12/268,087**

(22) Filed: **Nov. 10, 2008**

(65) **Prior Publication Data**

US 2009/0139008 A1 Jun. 4, 2009

Related U.S. Application Data

(60) Provisional application No. 61/002,665, filed on Nov. 9, 2007.

(51) **Int. Cl.**
A63B 71/14 (2006.01)

(52) **U.S. Cl.** **2/161.3**; 2/161.2; 2/161.1

(58) **Field of Classification Search** 2/20, 159, 2/160, 161.1, 161.2, 161.3, 161.6, 161.8, 2/167, 168

See application file for complete search history.

(56) **References Cited**

U.S. PATENT DOCUMENTS

5,423,089 A		6/1995	Chun et al.	
5,644,795 A		7/1997	Landis et al.	
5,926,847 A		7/1999	Eibert	
5,983,395 A	*	11/1999	Lei	2/159
6,044,494 A	*	4/2000	Kang	2/167
6,209,138 B1	*	4/2001	Kang	2/167
6,408,442 B1	*	6/2002	Kang	2/167
6,675,392 B2	*	1/2004	Albert	2/161.1
D549,397 S	*	8/2007	VanErmen	D29/113
D560,037 S	*	1/2008	VanErmen	D29/117.2
D560,040 S	*	1/2008	VanErmen	D29/117.2
D594,159 S	*	6/2009	Drab et al.	D29/117.2
7,625,625 B2	*	12/2009	Rios et al.	428/141
2007/0148409 A1	*	6/2007	Rios et al.	428/167
2009/0162651 A1	*	6/2009	Rios et al.	428/354
2010/0077526 A1	*	4/2010	Smeltzer	2/16
2010/0183814 A1	*	7/2010	Rios et al.	427/387

* cited by examiner

Primary Examiner — Khoa Huynh
Assistant Examiner — Sally Haden
(74) *Attorney, Agent, or Firm* — Maginot, Moore & Beck

(57) **ABSTRACT**

A golf glove comprises a palm portion and a plurality of digits comprised of a first material. A plurality of grip pads of a second material such as silicone is provided on the digits and/or the palm portion. The grip pads comprise a plurality of bumps having geometric shapes. In at least one embodiment, the bumps are hexagonal in shape. The bumps may be provided directly on the first material of the glove or may be provided on a thin base layer. The bumps are arranged on the glove such that they contact the grip of a golf club when the golf club is gripped by a golfer. Accordingly, the bumps may be positioned on tip portions of the fingers and thumb and also along a line extending between a hypothenar region of the palm and a portion of the palm located between the finger and thumb.

16 Claims, 3 Drawing Sheets

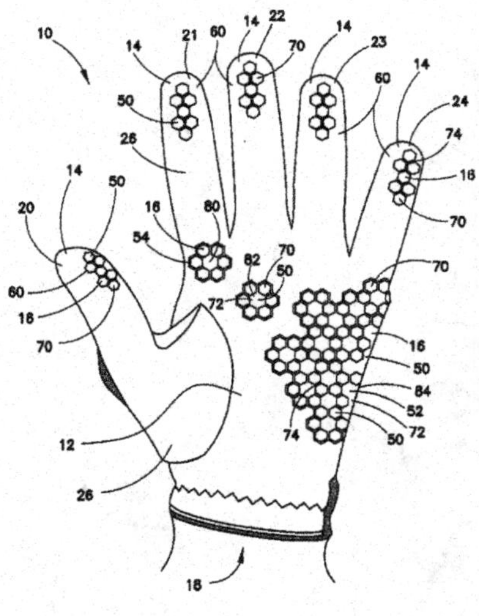

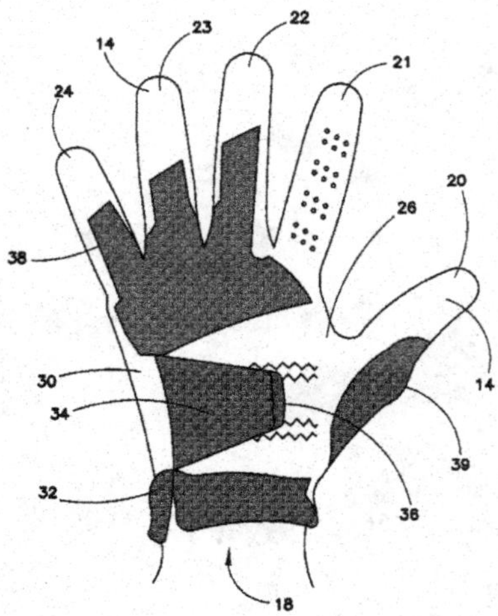

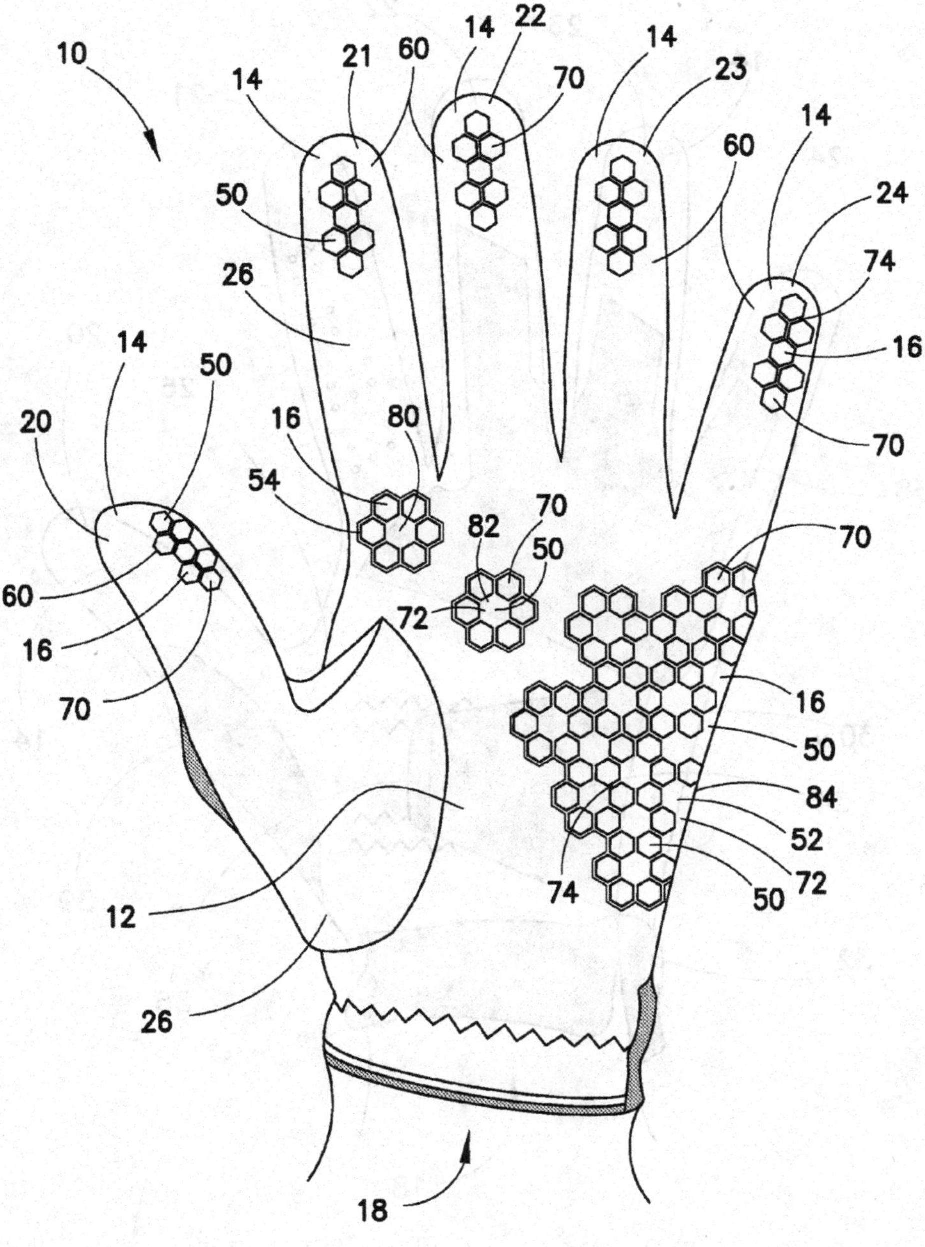
10
14
21
60
14
22
70
14
23
14
60
24
74
16
70
50
26
14
50
20
16
80
54
82
70
50
72
60
16
70
70
16
50
84
52
72
50
74
12
26
18

FIG. 1

U.S. Patent **Sep. 11, 2012** **Sheet 2 of 3** **US 8,261,372 B2**

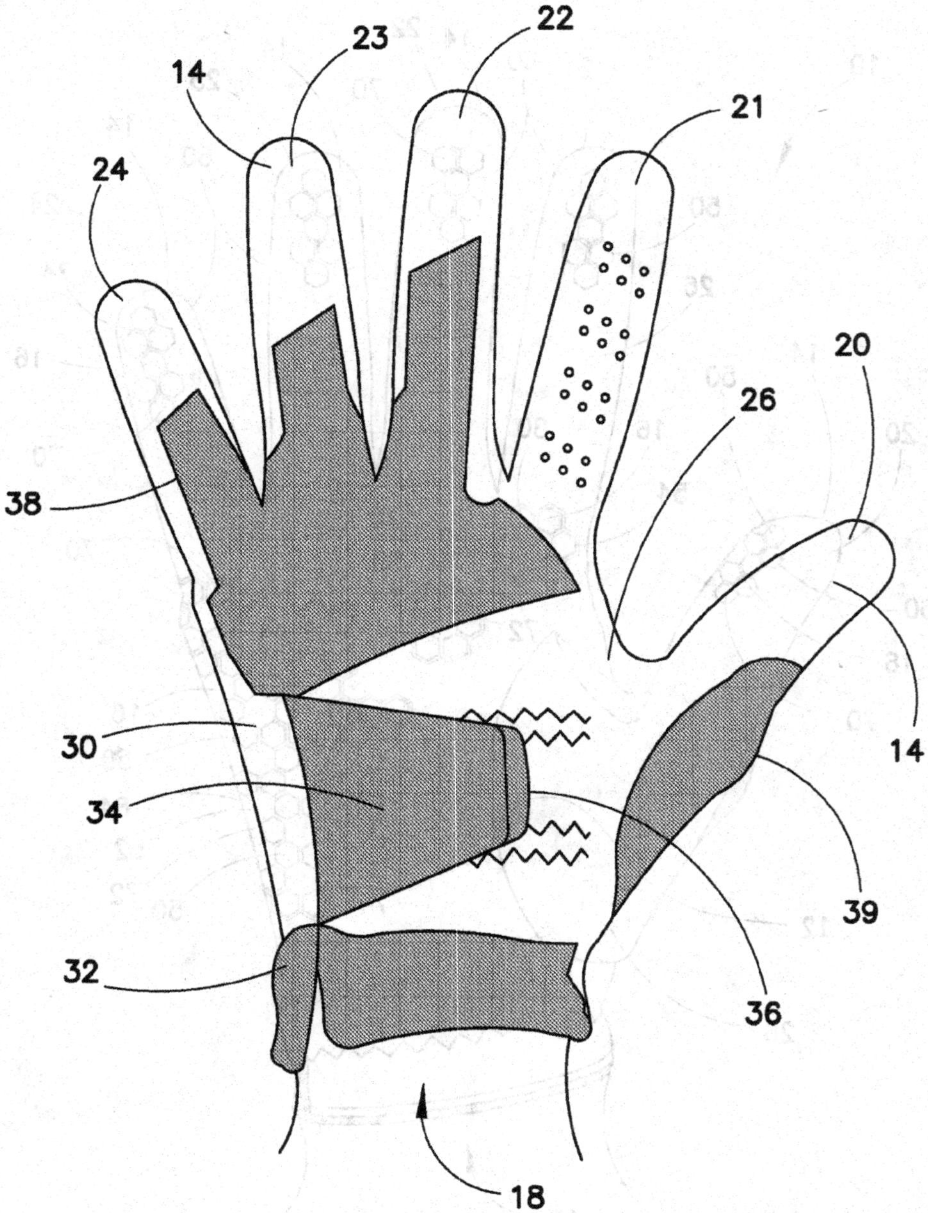

FIG. 2

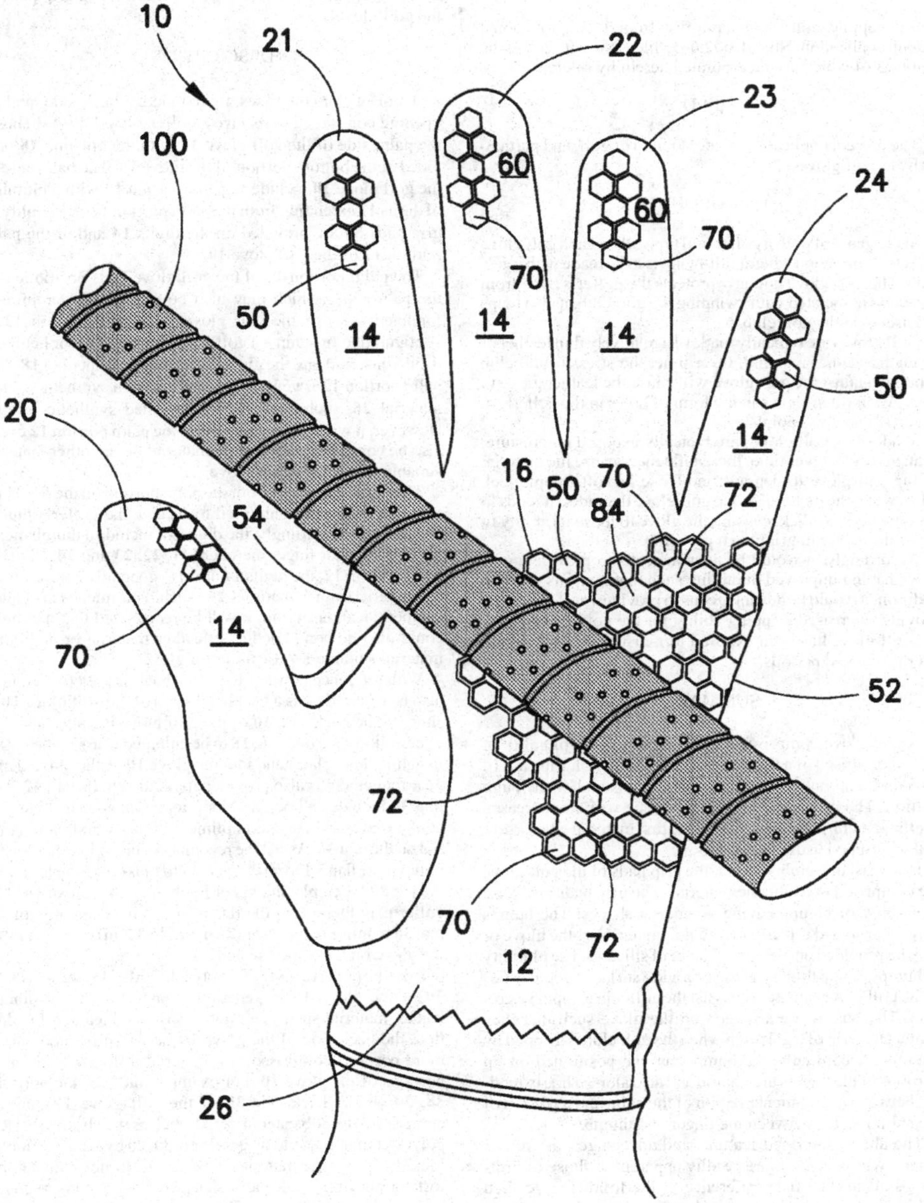
10
21
22
23
24
100
60
60
70
70
50
14
14
14
50
14
20
16
50
70
84
72
54
14
70
52
72
70
72
12
26

FIG. 3

GOLF GLOVE

CROSS-REFERENCE TO RELATED APPLICATIONS

This application claims priority from U.S. provisional patent application No. 61/002,665, filed Nov. 9, 2007, the contents of which are incorporated herein by reference.

FIELD

The present application relates to field of golf, and particularly, to golf gloves.

BACKGROUND

In the game of golf, a golfer will typically wear a golf glove on at least one hand when a full swing is to be made with a golf club. The golf glove not only protects the golfer's hand from the stress associated with swinging the golf club, it also helps the user grip the golf club.

Golf gloves are typically made of a relatively thin leather or synthetic leather material. Over time, the stress of the club rubbing against the golf glove will cause the leather glove to wear. Wear often shows in the form of holes in the golf glove at particular stress points.

In addition, golf gloves are typically exposed to moisture, heat, and cold. Over time, these influences cause the material of the golf glove to degrade and loose its soft, supple feel. Also, when the material of the golf glove degrades, it tends to become dry and slick, causing the glove to loose its ability to assist the golfer in gripping a golf club.

Accordingly, it would be advantageous to provide a golf glove having improved durability such that it resists wear. In addition, it would be advantageous to provide a golf glove that provides increased gripping ability for the golfer, even after the golf glove has been exposed to moisture, heat and cold over prolonged periods.

SUMMARY

A golf glove comprises a palm portion and a plurality of digits comprised of a first material. A plurality of grip pads of a second material is provided on the digits and/or the palm portion. The grip pads provide a surface with an increased coefficient of friction over that of the first material when a golf club is gripped using the golf glove.

In at least one embodiment, the grip pads of the golf glove are comprised of a silicone material. The grip pads comprise a plurality of bumps having geometric shapes. The bumps may be provided directly on the first material of the glove or may be provided on a thin base layer of silicone. The plurality of bumps on the thin base layer provide surface irregularities in the golf glove intended to assist the golfer in gripping a golf club. The bumps are arranged on the glove such that they contact the grip of a golf club when the golf club is gripped by a golfer. Accordingly, the bumps may be positioned on tip portions of the fingers and thumb and also along a line extending between a hypothenar region of the palm and a portion of the palm located between the finger and thumb.

The above described features and advantages, as well as others, will become more readily apparent to those of ordinary skill in the art by reference to the following detailed description and accompanying drawings.

BRIEF DESCRIPTION OF THE DRAWINGS

FIG. **1** shows a perspective view of a palm side of a golf glove;

FIG. **2** shows a perspective view of a back side of the golf glove of FIG. **1**; and

FIG. **3** shows a perspective view of the golf glove of FIG. **1** with the grip of a golf glove positioned along grip pads of the golf glove.

DESCRIPTION

A golf glove comprises a palm side, a back side, and an opening configured to receive a golfer's hand. FIG. **1** shows the palm side of the golf glove **10** with the opening **18** provided at the bottom portion of the glove **10**. The palm side of the golf glove **10** includes a palm portion **12** with a plurality of digits **14** extending from the palm portion **12**. A plurality of grip pads **50** are provided on the digits **14** and/or the palm portion **12** of the golf glove **10**.

The palm portion **12** of the golf glove **10** is positioned on the palm side (which may also be referred to herein as a forehand side) of the golf glove. The palm portion **12** is configured to fit against a golfer's palm when his or her hand is fully inserted into the glove **10** through the opening **18**. The palm portion **12** is generally comprised of a synthetic leather material **26**, such as a micro-capsulated synthetic leather. However, it will be recognized that the palm portion **12** could also be comprised of a leather material or any other material suitable for use as a golf glove.

The digits **14** extend from the palm portion on the forehand side, the digits **14** configured to receive the golfer's thumb and fingers. Accordingly, the digits **14** include a thumb member **20**, and four finger members **21**, **22**, **23** and **24**. Like the palm portion **12**, the digits **14** are also generally comprised of a synthetic leather material **26**, such as a micro-capsulated synthetic leather. Again, it will be recognized that the digits could also be comprised of a leather material or any other material suitable for use as a golf glove.

With reference now to FIG. **2**, the back side **30** (which may also be referred to as a backhand side) of the golf glove **10** is shown. The back side **30** of the golf glove includes a slit **32** which allows the opening **18** to be enlarged to assist the golfer in getting his or her hand into the glove **10**. A flap **34** and mat **36** arrangement is also provided in relation to the slit **32**. The flap **34** includes a hook and loop material, such as Velcro®, configured to engage a complimentary hook and loop material on the mat **36**. As will be recognized, the golfer may easily remove the flap **34** from the mat **36** to maximize the length of the slit **32** when placing his or her hand in the glove **10**. The golfer may then bring the flap **34** into engagement with the mat **36** to minimize the length of the slit **32**, in order to tighten the glove on the golfer's hand.

Like the palm **12** and digits **14** of the glove **10**, the back side **30** of the glove **10** is generally comprised of a synthetic leather material such as a micro-capsulated leather. In addition, the back side of the glove **10** may also include one or more portions comprised of a material different from other portions of the glove **10**. For example, the knuckle portions **38**, **39** on the back side **30** of the golf glove **10** may be comprised of a polyester material, such as the HEATGEAR® polyester material sold on goods produced by Under Armour, Inc. This polyester material provides the golfer with a comfortable and breathable fabric that provides moisture management and temperature regulation in the golf glove **10**. The material may also be stretchable to provide increased range of motion for the golfer when the golfer grips a golf club. It will be recognized that other materials may be provided on the front or back side **30** of the golf glove **10**, depending on the design of the glove and desired characteristics.

Returning again to FIG. **1**, the palm portion **12** and digits **14** of the golf glove further include a plurality of grip pads **50**. The grip pads **50** provide areas of increased grip quality over other areas of the golf glove when a golfer wearing the glove grips a golf club grip. In particular, when a golfer takes hold of a golf club grip, such as club grips comprised of leather, synthetic leather, rubber or plastic material, the grip pads **50** provide areas having an increased coefficient of friction over other areas of the golf glove **10** that may be used to grip the golf club. In the disclosed embodiment of FIG. **1**, the grip pads **50** provide an increased coefficient of friction over the synthetic leather material provided on the palm portion **12** and digits **14**. With these grip pads **50** provided on the golf glove **10**, the golfer tends to experience e increased gripping ability and club control than would be experienced without such grip pads.

In at least one embodiment, the grip pads **50** are preferably comprised of silicone. However, it will be recognized that other materials may be utilized for the grip pads, and various methods may be used to provide the grip pads. For example, in one alternative embodiment, the grip pads **50** may be comprised of a PVC material or some other material instead of a silicone material. Exemplary methods for providing the grip pads include heat press, embroidery, or laser etching.

In addition to providing for increased grip qualities, the grip pads **50** may also provide other advantages. For example, the grip pads **50** may also provide areas of increased durability and wear characteristics for the golf glove. In particular, the grip pads will tend to wear longer and will generally be more durable than the other material provided on the golf glove, such as a leather or synthetic leather material. Thus, the golf glove will not develop holes at the grip pads **50** as fast as if the areas covered by the grip pads were comprised of leather or synthetic leather.

Another advantage provided by the grip pads **50** is that of increased club feel. Furthermore, the arrangement of the grip pads **50** on the glove may be used to provide the golfer with an indication of the proper grip position and help the golfer grip the club properly.

In addition to the above, in one alternative embodiment, another advantage may be realized if the material used for the grip pads provides the golfer with a better grip in wet conditions. PVC is one example of a material that may be used to provide such increased grip in wet conditions. Of course, it will be recognized that numerous other materials may be used to provide the golfer with a better grip in wet conditions.

With reference now to the embodiment of FIGS. **1** and **3**, it can be seen that the grip pads **50** are located on the golf glove **10** in locations such that the grip pads will contact the grip **100** of a golf club when a golfer takes hold of the golf club grip **100** using a conventional grip. Accordingly, the plurality of grip pads **50** are positioned on the palm portion **12** along an area that extends between a hypothenar region **52** of the palm **12** to a region **54** of the palm **12** located between the thumb **20** and the index finger **21**. The region **54** of the palm may be for example, a portion opposite the knuckle of the index finger **21**. In addition to locations on the palm **12** of the glove **10**, the grip pads **50** include locations at the distal ends **60** of the digits **14**.

In the embodiment of FIGS. **1** and **3**, the grip pads **50** comprise a plurality of geometrically shaped bumps **70**. In the disclosed embodiment, the grip pads comprise hexagonal shaped bumps **70**. Channels **74** extend in-between each of the geometrically shaped bumps **70**. At least one side of each hexagonal bump **70** faces a side of another hexagonal bump across a channel **74** with a channel **74** positioned in between the two opposing sides. The hexagonal shape of each bump **70** is defined along a perimeter of each bump **70** and a substantially flat and smooth upper surface is provided within the perimeter of each bump **70**.

The grip pads **50** are configured such that the geometrically shaped bumps **70** are either provided on a thin base layer **72** or are provided directly on the material that forms the other portions of the golf glove **10**, such as on the leather or synthetic leather forming the palm portion **12** or digits **14** of the golf glove **10**. In the embodiment of FIG. **1**, the grip pads **50** on the palm portion **12** of the glove **10** include a thin base layer **72**, while the grip pads **50** on the digits **14** do not. Thus, the bumps **70** on the palm portion **12** are situated on top of the thin base layer **72**, and the bumps **70** on the digits **14** are situated directly on the leather material forming the digits.

When the grip pads **50** comprise hexagonal bumps **70** provided on a thin silicone base layer **72**, the bumps **70** extend outward from the thin base layer **72** such that the plurality of bumps **70** provide additional surface irregularities for the grip pads **50** and thus provide additional gripping qualities for a golfer using the glove. In this case, the channels **74** extend outward from the base layer **72** and are positioned in-between the bumps **70**.

The thin base layer **72** is provided on top of the synthetic leather material, and in one embodiment the thin base layer **72** is generally between about 0.10 mm and 2.0 mm in thickness. In at least one embodiment, the thin base layer **72** is about 0.25 mm in thickness. The bumps **70** generally extend outward from the thin base layer **70** between about 0.5 mm and 2.5 mm. The In at least one embodiment, the bumps **70** extend about 1.0 mm outward from the thin base layer **70**. On the distal ends **60** of the digits **14**, the bumps **70** are provided directly on the synthetic leather without the thin base layer **72**. The diameter of the bumps, from side-to-side, is generally between 3.0 and 9.0 mm. In at least one embodiment, the bumps are about 4.0 mm to 6.0 mm in diameter. The channels **74** between the bumps are about 0.25 mm to 1.0 mm in width and have the same height as the bumps themselves. It will be appreciated that the foregoing arrangement and associated ranges for the bumps **70**, channels **74**, and base layer **72** are merely exemplary of one embodiment, and it will be recognized that numerous other arrangements and ranges for the bumps and base layer are possible.

In the embodiment of FIGS. **1** and **3**, the hexagonal shape of the bumps **70** allow for unique configuration of the bumps **70**. For example, on the palm portion **12** of the glove **10**, the hexagonal bumps **70** are arranged in a circular arrangement, as shown by pads **80** and **82**, with six bumps **70** in each circle. In the large grip pad **84** in the hypothenar region **52**, the hexagonal bumps **70** may be provided in an overlapping circular arrangement such that one or two bumps **70** are shared between adjacent circles. On the digits **14**, the bumps are provided in rows of even numbered and odd numbered bumps. In particular, the bumps are provided in a 1-2-1-2-1 arrangement along the distal end **60** of each digit **14**. As set forth above, various methods may be used to provide the grip pads **50** on the golf glove **10**. For example, the grip pads **50** may be screen printed on the glove, heat-sealed, embroidered, heat pressed, or laser etched. It will be recognized that other methods of manufacture are also possible.

Although the golf glove has been described with respect to certain preferred embodiments, it will be appreciated by those of skill in the art that other implementations and adaptations are possible. Moreover, there are advantages to individual advancements described herein that may be obtained without incorporating other aspects described above. Therefore, the

US 8,261,372 B2

5

spirit and scope of any eventual claims should not be limited to the description of the preferred embodiments contained herein.

What is claimed is:

1. A golf glove comprising:

a palm side and a back side, the palm side including a palm portion and a plurality of digits extending from the palm portion, the palm portion and the back side comprised of a first material; and

at least one silicone pad provided on the palm side, the silicone pad comprising a plurality of geometrically shaped bumps and channels formed between the geometrically shaped bumps, wherein the at least one silicone pad provides an increased coefficient of friction over that of the first material;

wherein a first plurality of the plurality of geometrically shaped bumps are positioned on tip portions of the digits in alternating rows of even numbered complete geometrically shaped bumps and odd numbered complete geometrically shaped bumps with no partial geometrically shaped bumps positioned in the alternating rows; and

wherein the geometrically shaped bumps comprise hexagonal bumps defined along a perimeter of the bumps and a substantially flat surface is provided within the perimeter of the bumps.

2. The golf glove of claim 1 wherein at least one silicone pad covers an exterior portion of the first material on the palm side.

3. The golf glove of claim 1 wherein the at least one silicone pad further includes at least one silicone pad provided on the palm portion.

4. The golf glove of claim 1 wherein the at least one silicone pad comprises a substantially smooth base layer of a silicone material and the plurality of geometrically shaped bumps are provided on the base layer and extend outward from the base layer.

5. The golf glove of claim 1 wherein the bumps are positioned on at least one of the plurality of digits and wherein the bumps are provided directly on the first material.

6. The golf glove of claim 1 wherein geometrically shaped bumps are about 4.0 mm to about 6.0 in diameter.

7. A golf glove comprising:

a palm portion comprised of a first material;

a plurality of digits extending from the palm portion, the plurality of digits also comprised of a first material; and

a plurality of grip pads comprised of a second material provided on the palm portion and on the plurality of digits, wherein the each of the plurality of grip pads include a base layer and a plurality of geometrically shaped bumps extending outward from the base layer, wherein empty channels are formed between the geometrically shaped bumps such that the plurality of geometrically shaped bumps are separated on the at least one grip pad by the empty channels;

6

wherein each of the grip pads on the plurality of digits comprise a first plurality of the plurality of geometrically shaped bumps positioned on tip portions of the digits in alternating rows of even numbered complete geometrically shaped bumps and odd numbered complete geometrically shaped bumps with no partial geometrically shaped bumps positioned in the alternating rows

wherein the geometrically shaped bumps comprise hexagonal bumps defined along a perimeter of the bumps and a substantially flat surface is provided within the perimeter of the bumps.

8. The golf glove of claim 7 wherein the plurality of geometrically shaped bumps on the palm portion are positioned a circular arrangement of bumps with no bump positioned in a center of the circular arrangement.

9. The golf glove of claim 7 wherein the base layer is provided directly on the first material.

10. The golf glove of claim 7 wherein the base layer is between about 0.10 mm and 2.0 mm in thickness.

11. The golf glove of claim 10 wherein the base layer is about 0.25 mm in thickness.

12. The golf glove of claim 7 wherein the bumps extend outward from the base layer between about 0.5 mm and 2.5 mm.

13. The golf glove of claim 12 wherein the bumps extend about 1.0 mm outward from the thin base layer.

14. The golf glove of claim 7 wherein the second material is comprised of silicone.

15. A golf glove comprising:

a backhand portion;

a forehand portion comprising a palm portion, a plurality of fingers, and a thumb; and

a plurality of hexagonal bumps comprised of a silicone material, the plurality of hexagonal bumps separated by empty channels formed between the hexagonal bumps, wherein the plurality of hexagonal bumps are positioned on the forehand portion and are arranged on the glove such that the plurality of bumps contact a grip of a golf club when the golf club is gripped by a golfer;

wherein a first plurality of the plurality of hexagonal bumps are positioned on tip portions of the fingers and thumb in alternating rows of even numbered complete hexagonal bumps and odd numbered complete hexagonal bumps with no partial hexagonal bumps positioned in the alternating rows; and

wherein a hexagonal shape of the bumps is defined along a perimeter of the bumps and a substantially flat surface is provided within the perimeter of the bumps.

16. The golf glove of claim 15 wherein a second plurality of the plurality of hexagonal bumps are positioned on the palm portion in a circular arrangement of six bumps with no hexagonal bump positioned in a center of the circular arrangement, wherein two sides of each bump in the circular arrangement are respectively opposed to a side of an adjacent bump in the circular arrangement.

* * * * *

Chapter 4

Copyrights

§ 4:1 Introduction
§ 4:2 Development of Copyright Law in the Fashion Industry
§ 4:3 Elements of Copyright Protection
§ 4:3.1 Originality
§ 4:3.2 Separability
[A] Development of the Separability Doctrine
[B] Useful Articles in the Fashion Industry
[C] "Separable" Elements of Useful Articles
[D] Evaluating Whether Design Elements are "Separable"
§ 4:3.3 Idea and Expression
§ 4:4 Efforts to Protect Fashion More Vigorously
§ 4:5 Joint Ownership and Works Made for Hire
§ 4:6 Copyright Registration Procedures
§ 4:6.1 Elements of a Copyright Application
§ 4:6.2 Renewals and Change of Ownership
§ 4:6.3 Copyright Notice
§ 4:6.4 Length of Copyright
§ 4:7 Copyright Infringement
§ 4:7.1 Access
§ 4:7.2 Substantial Similarity
[A] The Ordinary Observer and Related Tests
[B] The Extrinsic/Intrinsic Tests
[C] Other Substantial Similarity Tests
[D] The Use of Characters in Apparel
§ 4:8 Defenses
§ 4:8.1 Fair Use
§ 4:8.2 The *De Minimis* Doctrine
§ 4:9 Remedies
§ 4:9.1 Injunctive Relief
§ 4:9.2 Impoundment and Disposition

§ 4:9.3 **Damages and Profits**
[A] Actual Damages and Profits
[B] Statutory Damages
§ 4:9.4 **Costs and Attorneys' Fees**

§ 4:1 Introduction

In the fashion industry, it is common for designers to make use of the work of other designers. In the most benign instances, designers are merely inspired by the works of others and use that inspiration to create new original works. In other instances, the copying is more direct. In fact, copying is the basic business model of several large industry participants and made easier by advances in technology and social media.

Whether this phenomenon benefits or harms the industry is subject to vigorous debate. This chapter, however, focuses on the specific question of when copying is permitted—and when it is prohibited—by U.S. copyright law. For some courts, the answer had been a simple one: copyright law does not protect "useful items" such as clothing. For other courts, however, it was clear that the Copyright Act protects all original works of authorship in fixed form, even if that form happens to be an item of apparel. Courts in different jurisdictions had developed numerous, often contradictory tests to govern when a work of creative authorship is separable from its utilitarian function, and thus protectable under copyright law. In 2017, the Supreme Court waded into this debate in the unlikely context of cheerleader uniforms. The Court's decision, in *Star Athletica LLC v. Varsity Brands, Inc.*,[1] casts a large shadow over this debate.

The chapter presents a general overview of copyright law in the context of the fashion industry, continuing with a brief review of some well-documented incidents at the intersection of fashion and copyright law. Next, the chapter provides a review of the basic elements of copyright law (focusing on the largest obstacles to protecting fashion through copyright), followed by a discussion of the procedures for registration of a copyright, and the key elements of and defenses to a claim of copyright infringement.

1. Star Athletica, L.L.C. v. Varsity Brands, Inc., 137 S. Ct. 1002 (2017).

§ 4:2 Development of Copyright Law in the Fashion Industry

Article I, section 8 of the U.S. Constitution is the basis for copyright protection in the United States. It grants the U.S. Congress the power:

> [t]o promote the Progress of Science and useful Arts, by securing for limited Times to Authors and Inventors the exclusive Right to their respective Writings and Discoveries.

Two forms of copyright protection evolved from this Constitutional grant: first, common law, developed by courts in published judicial decisions, and, second, statutory protection, as recorded in laws passed by Congress.[2] At present, the 1976 Copyright Act, as subsequently amended, governs most protected works in the United States.[3] The 1976 Copyright Act identifies eight categories of protected works: (1) literary works; (2) musical works, including any accompanying words; (3) dramatic works, including any accompanying music; (4) pantomimes and choreographic works; (5) pictorial, graphic, and sculptural works; (6) motion pictures and other audiovisual works; (7) sound recordings; and (8) architectural works.[4]

While works of fashion are not specifically listed, they could, in theory, fall under the "pictorial, graphic, and sculptural works" category. In practice, however, fashion designs are included in that category "only if, and only to the extent that, such design incorporates pictorial, graphic, or sculptural features that can be identified separately from, and are capable of existing independently of, the utilitarian aspects of the article."[5]

---

2. International treaties that affect copyright protection are addressed in *infra* chapter 5.
3. Works that predate the 1976 version of the Copyright Act and that are not yet in the public domain are governed by the prior 1909 version of the Copyright Act. The 1909 Act's provisions, which differ in several respects from those of the 1976 Act, are not examined in detail in this chapter for two reasons: first, as explained in greater detail in this chapter, because of the ways that some courts have evaluated claims of copyright in fashion design, there are significant types of works in the fashion industry that receive relatively scant copyright protection; and second, as a practical matter, the fashion industry is constantly changing—trends emerge, spread, and dissipate in periods of months, not years, and in most instances, not decades. For an overview of the 1909 Act, see BRUCE P. KELLER & JEFFREY CUNARD, COPYRIGHT LAW: A PRACTITIONER'S GUIDE § 1.3 (Practising L. Inst. 2012).
4. 17 U.S.C. § 102(a).
5. 17 U.S.C. § 101 (defining "Pictorial, graphic, and sculptural works").

As discussed in greater detail in section 4:3.2 below, this "separability" requirement has caused numerous courts to conclude that certain types of works created in the fashion industry are not protected by copyright law. As a result, the industry established various less formal methods to protect fashion originators from copying by others.

In the early to mid-twentieth century, French fashion houses barred wholesalers and retailers who were not explicitly invited to their runway shows. They attempted to impose rules regulating the publication of photos and sketches, and the timing of deliveries to customers and stores as well.[6] But these informal efforts could not protect against the spread of goods bearing similar designs, as national and regional department stores, like Macy's and Marshall Fields, stocked with mass-market versions of previously unattainable fashions, began to dominate the U.S. market.[7]

The U.S. fashion industry attempted to protect designs through other private methods, but these efforts eventually foundered when they ran up against legal regimes designed to protect consumers and free competition.

For example, in the 1930s, fifteen manufacturers of expensive women's dresses organized the "Fashion Originator's Guild of America," which operated a registration system for designs.[8] Members agreed not to copy other members' designs and they extracted formal pledges from retailers who sold their dresses to boycott copies.[9] The guild extensively policed compliance, maintained a sophisticated system of trial and appellate tribunals to adjudicate whether a garment was copied, and fined (sometimes heavily) members who dealt with noncompliant retailers or manufacturers.[10] The Fashion Originator's Guild's power and reach grew. Many textile producers ultimately agreed not to sell their products to non-members as well.[11] The Fashion Originator's Guild was so successful in this initial phase that women's hat designers copied it, establishing the Millinery Creators' Guild to protect their designs.[12] The Fashion Originator's Guild's private

6. TERI AGINS, THE END OF FASHION: HOW MARKETING CHANGED THE CLOTHING BUSINESS FOREVER 24 (William Morrow 2000).
7. *Id.*
8. Robert P. Merges, *Contracting into Liability Rules: Intellectual Property Rights and Collective Rights Organizations*, 84 CAL. L. REV. 1293, 1363 (1996) [hereinafter Merges].
9. *Id.*
10. *Id.*; Safia A. Nurbhai, *Style Piracy Revisited*, 10 J.L. & POL'Y 489, 495–96 (2002).
11. Merges, *supra* note 8, at 1363.
12. *Id.*

rules effectively replaced intellectual property laws by suppressing competition from would-be copyists who would otherwise have sold knockoff dresses at lower prices.

Ultimately, however, the Fashion Originator's Guild ran afoul of U.S. antitrust laws (the Sherman and Clayton Acts), and both the Federal Trade Commission and the U.S. Supreme Court deemed the Guild's private rules to constitute unlawful anti-competitive behavior.[13] Other associations that were designed to prevent copying in the fashion industry met similar fates. The Second Circuit addressed the Millinery Creators' Guild whose purpose was "to combat the practice known as 'style piracy.'"[14] The court found that the "creator who maintains a large staff of highly paid designers . . . suffers a real loss when the design is copied as soon as it appears; the imitator in turn reaps a substantial gain by appropriating for himself the style innovations produced by the creator's investment." But despite these findings, the court reasoned that "[a]n 'original' creation is too slight a modification of a known idea to justify the grant by the government of a monopoly to the creator," and it upheld the guild's termination.[15] This line of cases took a heavy toll on the fashion industry's efforts to protect itself by private agreement.

§ 4:3 Elements of Copyright Protection

As a general matter, copyright only protects original works that exist in a *fixed* form, in a tangible medium of expression.[16] This means that only works of authorship that are rendered in sufficiently permanent and stable forms (for example, patterns on a piece of fabric, or designs sketched on a piece of paper) qualify for copyright protection. Garments are, of course, fixed in a tangible medium of expression (generally fabric), but not every work of authorship that is fixed in a tangible medium of expression qualifies for copyright protection. This section addresses common issues in determining whether a work qualifies for copyright protection.

§ 4:3.1 Originality

The 1976 Copyright Act only protects ***"original*** works of authorship."[17] The word "original" has a unique meaning in copyright law. A work may be "original" even if it would not be described as "novel" or

13. Fashion Originator's Guild of Am. v. FTC, 312 U.S. 457, 462 (1941). *See also infra* chapter 12.
14. Millinery Creators' Guild v. FTC, 109 F.2d 175, 177 (2d Cir. 1940).
15. *Id.*
16. 17 U.S.C. § 102.
17. *Id.* (emphasis added).

"innovative" in common parlance. To be "original," a work need only originate with the author and possess some modicum of creativity.[18] Works that were copied from another work are not original. But any "creative spark, no matter how crude, humble or obvious it might be," is sufficient for a work to be considered sufficiently original to merit copyright protection for the aspect of the work that is deemed original and not copied from some preexisting source.[19]

The level of creativity required for copyright protection is so low in fact that even compilations of otherwise non-protectable elements meet the standard.[20] Indeed, courts have concluded that an author's independent "selection, coordination, and arrangement" of traditionally non-protectable elements are copyrightable as long as they possess a minimal amount of creativity.[21] The limit of this doctrine is that copyright will not protect a compilation where mere ease of manufacture or functionality dictates the selection, coordination, or arrangement (as opposed to creativity).[22] For example, arranging data in alphabetical order would not qualify as original.[23] And even where the selection, coordination, and arrangement of elements are protectable, the copyright is limited to that arrangement, coordination, or selection, and not the constituent elements that have been selected, coordinated, or arranged.

Works that are derived from prior works may also be sufficiently original to receive copyright protection, so long as the modification to the original work is itself sufficiently original. To be protectable, modifications must originate from the author and possess a modicum of creativity, like any other work of authorship. But again, the protection only extends to the original modification and not to the underlying work modified.

In theory, many fashion designs, regardless of whether they are derivative of prior works or compilations of otherwise non-protectable

---

18. Alfred Bell & Co. v. Catalda Fine Arts, 191 F.2d 99, 102–03 (2d Cir. 1951) ("No matter how poor artistically the author's addition, it is enough if it be his own.") (internal citation omitted).
19. *See* Feist Publ'ns, Inc. v. Rural Tel. Serv. Co., 499 U.S. 340, 345 (1991) (internal citation and quotation marks omitted).
20. *See id.* at 348 (explaining that even telephone directories may be copyrightable if the selection, coordination and arrangement of the listings is original).
21. *Id.* at 358.
22. *See* Folio Impressions, Inc. v. Byer Cal., 937 F.2d 759 (2d Cir. 1991) (reasoning that "[t]he arrangement of the roses over the background . . . does not appear to be designed to ease manufacture . . . [r]ather [it] was an artistic decision" such that arrangement was sufficiently original).
23. *Feist Publ'ns, Inc.*, 499 U.S. at 345.

elements, should easily meet the originality part of the overall copyright test. In *Mon Cheri Bridals Inc. v. Wen Wu*,[24] for example, Mon Cheri Bridals, a wedding and special occasion dress designer, alleged that Wen Wu had copied an entire line of Mon Cheri's wedding dresses. The jury found for Mon Cheri, and Wen Wu appealed, claiming that Mon Cheri's wedding dress designs were not sufficiently original to receive copyright protection. The Third Circuit affirmed the jury's conclusion that the designs were, in fact, sufficiently original. Among other things, the court relied on the designer's testimony that she had been inspired by many different things, and although she had used some common elements, including a particular flower and vine drawing, she changed the size, color, and frequency of those elements to create an embroidery and bead pattern that she considered original.[25]

Various courts have also found original compilations of non-protectable elements to satisfy the originality requirement. In *Wolstenholme v. Hirst*, a federal court in New York found that the creative selection, coordination, and arrangement of pills to form a pharmaceuticals-inspired charm bracelet met the low bar of originality.[26] The court noted that the plaintiff had "selected a unique combination of pharmaceutical charms . . . [,] interspersed charms for weight and symmetry and grouped together replications of pills that are often prescribed together."[27] In *Star Fabrics, Inc. v. DKJY, Inc.*, a federal court in California noted that the plaintiff did not own a copyright in all peacock-eye patterns, but did own a copyright in its particular arrangements of peacock-feather eyes and other design elements.[28]

Although the U.S. Supreme Court has held that originality is the "*sine qua non*" of copyright,[29] some courts have appeared to require fashion to be more than merely original, as defined by copyright law, to be protected. For example, in *Todd v. Montana Silversmiths, Inc.*,[30] plaintiff, a jewelry designer with a "western-themed" focus, created a

---

24. Mon Cheri Bridals Inc. v. Wen Wu, 383 F. App'x 228, 2010 WL 2222497, at *1 (3d Cir. June 4, 2010).
25. *Id.* at *4.
26. Wolstenholme v. Hirst, 271 F. Supp. 3d 625, 636 (S.D.N.Y. 2017).
27. *Id.* (internal quotations omitted).
28. Star Fabrics, Inc. v. DKJY, Inc., No. 2:13-CV-07293-ODW, 2014 WL 102809, at *4 (C.D. Cal. Jan. 9, 2014).
29. *Feist Publ'ns, Inc.*, 499 U.S. at 362 ("Rural expended sufficient effort to make the white pages directory useful, but insufficient creativity to make it original" because the "end product is a garden-variety white pages directory.").
30. Todd v. Montana Silversmiths, Inc., 379 F. Supp. 2d 1110, 1114 (D. Colo. 2005).

barbed-wire style bracelet and set of matching earrings. A federal court in Colorado concluded that Todd's barbed-wire jewelry was not copyrightable, in part, because "[p]laintiff has not 'recast and arranged' the public domain elements of her jewelry in an original way. Instead, she has taken the constituent elements of barbed-wire and arranged them in a way that by all objective measures still matches the elemental arrangement of barbed-wire."[31] The court recognized the "artistic appeal" and "certain *'je ne sais quoi'*" of the plaintiff's jewelry and noted that "[n]o one could seriously contend that [p]laintiffs' jewelry is indistinguishable from actual barbed-wire."[32] Nevertheless, the plaintiff could not persuade the court that her jewelry had "substantial" variation from the barbed wire so as to be "truly original."[33]

Commentators have differed in attempting to explain these disparate results. There are, however, circumstances under which courts have generally been more likely to find a design to be sufficiently original to receive protection.[34] Registering a work with the U.S. Copyright Office, for example, creates a presumption that the copyright in that work is valid and the work is copyrightable.[35] Although an alleged infringer may challenge those presumptions, the burden shifts to the alleged infringer to overcome the presumption by proving that the copyright is invalid or the subject matter is not copyrightable. If the alleged infringer fails, the court will generally uphold the copyright.[36] Similarly, an original work of graphic art will not lose its protection merely because it is printed on a shirt or bag.[37]

---

31. *Id.* at 1113.
32. *Id.* at 1114.
33. *Id.* (internal quotation marks omitted).
34. *See infra* section 4:4.
35. 17 U.S.C. § 410(c).
36. *See, e.g.*, Samara Bros. v. Wal-Mart Stores, 165 F.3d 120, 132 (2d Cir. 1998) (holding that defendant had failed to overcome the presumption that appliques of strawberries, daisies, hearts and tulips were sufficiently original to receive copyright protection that arose from federal copyright registration), *rev'd on other grounds*, 529 U.S. 205 (2000); Mon Cheri Bridals, Inc. v. Wen Wu, 383 F. App'x 228, 2010 WL 2222497, at *2 (3d Cir. June 4, 2010) (registration "creates a rebuttable presumption that the work in question is copyrightable") (citing Whimsicality, Inc. v. Rubie's Costume Co., 891 F.2d 452, 455 (2d Cir. 1989)).
37. *See, e.g.*, Scarves by Vera, Inc. v. United Merchants & Mfrs. Inc., 173 F. Supp. 625, 627 (S.D.N.Y. 1959) ("Clearly the design [printed upon blouse fabric] is a proper subject of copyright."); Knitwaves, Inc. v. Lollytogs Ltd. 71 F.3d 996 (2d Cir. 1995); Folio Impressions, Inc. v. Byer Cal., 937 F.2d 759 (2d Cir. 1991); Novelty Textile Mills, Inc. v. Joan Fabrics Corp., 558 F.2d 1090 (2d Cir. 1977); Thomas Wilson & Co. v. Irving J. Dorfman Co., 433 F.2d 409 (2d Cir. 1970); H. M. Kolbe Co. v. Armgus Textile Co., 315 F.2d 70 (2d Cir. 1963); Eve of Milady v. Impression Bridal, Inc., 957 F. Supp. 484, (S.D.N.Y. 1997).

§ 4:3.2 Separability

Even fashion designs that pass the originality test, however, may still run afoul of a different requirement under copyright law. In particular, the Copyright Act provides that "useful articles"—those "having an intrinsic utilitarian function that is not merely to portray the appearance of the article or to convey information[38]—receive protection "only if, and only to the extent that, [they] incorporate[] pictorial, graphic, or sculptural features that can be identified separately from, and are capable of existing independently of, the utilitarian aspects of the article."[39] The reason for this is simple: to prevent copyright law from impeding free competition in the manufacture and sale of useful articles.[40] Whatever the motivations for this "separability" rule, it has traditionally been the single largest obstacle to protecting certain works of fashion through current copyright law.

[A] Development of the Separability Doctrine

The limitation on protecting useful articles under copyright law has a long history. Congress extended copyright protection to three-dimensional works in the Copyright Act of 1870, but it initially only covered those three-dimensional works that qualified as "fine art."[41] The 1909 version of the Copyright Act abandoned that "fine art" requirement,[42] but the Copyright Office's regulations continued to caution that "[p]roductions of the industrial arts utilitarian in purpose and character are not subject to copyright registration, even if artistically made or ornamented."[43] In 1948, the Copyright Office broadened the scope of protection for three-dimensional works of art to cover "works of artistic craftsmanship insofar as their form but not their utilitarian aspects are concerned, such as artistic jewelry . . . ."[44]

The Supreme Court addressed the copyrightability of useful articles next in the landmark case of *Mazer v. Stein*.[45] In that case, a lamp manufacturer sued one of its competitors for infringing its copyright in statuettes of dancing couples embodied in lamp bases.

---

38. 17 U.S.C. § 101.
39. *Id.*
40. *See* Esquire v. Ringer, 591 F.2d 796 (D.C. Cir. 1978).
41. Carol Barnhart Inc. v. Economy Cover Corp., 773 F.2d 411, 415 (2d Cir. 1985) (quoting Act of July 8, 1870, ch. 230, § 86, 16 Stat. 198, 212 (repealed 1916)).
42. *Id.* (citing 17 U.S.C. §§ 1–216 (1976)).
43. Copyright Office, Rules and Regulations for the Registration of Claims to Copyright, Bulletin No. 15 (1910), *reprinted in* Mazer v. Stein, 347 U.S. 201, 212 n.23 (1945).
44. 37 C.F.R. § 207(a) (1949), *reprinted in Mazer*, 347 U.S. at 212–13.
45. Mazer v. Stein, 347 U.S. 201 (1945).

The Supreme Court held that the statuettes were copyrightable even though they were embodied in useful articles.

Five years later, in 1959, the Copyright Office addressed useful articles yet again. It issued a regulation that arguably altered the scope of protection for useful articles. The 1959 regulation explained that if "the sole intrinsic function of an article is its utility, the fact that the work is unique and attractively shaped will not qualify it as a work of art."[46] It only permitted designers to copyright elements of a useful article that "can be identified separately and are capable of existing independently as a work of art."[47]

The version of the Copyright Act passed in 1976 now defines "Useful Article" to mean "an article having an intrinsic utilitarian function that is not merely to portray the appearance of the article or to convey information."[48] In fact, an "article that is ***normally a part of*** a useful article is considered a 'useful article.'"[49]

[B] Useful Articles in the Fashion Industry

Garments, of course, ***do*** serve a useful function—to cover the body for warmth or to comply with social norms. This is why so many courts have concluded that garments are, by definition, "useful articles."[50]

Not all works of authorship in the fashion industry are "useful articles," however. Fashion sketches, as distinct from the garments made from them, are not "useful articles" under copyright law. As a result, copyright law does protect sketches from the moment that they are fixed in a tangible medium. The extent of that protection, however, is necessarily limited because although the sketches are themselves protected from copying, copyright law may not protect against the development of useful articles based on those sketches, subject to the limitations discussed below.

Similarly, if a copyrighted image is imprinted on a t-shirt or on other similar apparel items, the copyright in the image is separately protectable.[51]

---

46. Pivot Point Int'l, Inc. v. Charlene Prods., Inc., 372 F.3d 913, 921 (7th Cir. 2004) (quoting 37 C.F.R. § 207.8(a) (1949) and 37 C.F.R. § 201.10(c) (1959); footnotes omitted).
47. *Id.*
48. 17 U.S.C. § 101 (definition of "useful article").
49. *Id.* (emphasis added).
50. Whimsicality, Inc. v. Rubie's Costume Co., 891 F.2d 452, 455 (2d Cir. 1989) (citing Fashion Originators' Guild v. FTC, 114 F.2d 80, 84 (2d Cir. 1940), *aff'd*, 312 U.S. 457 (1941)).
51. *See* Scarves by Vera, Inc. v. United Merchants & Mfrs. Inc., 173 F. Supp. 625, 627 (S.D.N.Y. 1959).

Additionally, accessories—including, for example, bags, jewelry, and certain items used in costumes—may not be considered "useful articles."[52]

Whether an item qualifies as a useful article is a question of fact. If there is a dispute between the parties, a jury will decide the question after hearing evidence. The parties may present evidence and expert testimony as to the question of whether or not design features are "useful" or decorative. Evidence of the creator's intent in designing the item may also be relevant.[53]

[C] "Separable" Elements of Useful Articles

Even if a garment is itself deemed a "useful article," specific features of that garment may still be protectable if they can be "identified separately" from, and exist independently of, the garment's utilitarian aspects. It is often a difficult factual question, though, to determine which features may be identified separately and exist independently.

The legislative history of the 1976 version of the Copyright Act indicates if an element is either *physically* or *conceptually* separable from its utilitarian function, then it may be protected.[54] Courts have generally considered an element to be physically separable where it "can actually be removed from the original item and separately sold,

---

52. *See, e.g.*, Miche Bag, LLC v. Ayers, No. 4-09-3261-TLW-SVH, 2010 WL 5141662, at *5 (D.S.C. Sept. 22, 2010) (recommending that the district court permanently enjoin a defendant boutique from directly or indirectly infringing on plaintiff manufacturers' rights in certain copyrighted purses, handbags, and related products); Donald Bruce & Co. v. B.H. Multi Com Corp., 964 F. Supp. 265, 267 (N.D. Ill. 1997) ("The ring is purely ornamental, its sole purpose is to portray its appearance. Accordingly, the court concludes that it is not a useful article under Section 101, and the court need not determine whether the utilitarian aspects of the mount are separable from the sculptural elements."); Masquerade Novelty, Inc. v. Unique Indus., Inc., 912 F.2d 663, 670–71 (3d Cir. 1990) (finding that nose masks are not "useful articles" and thus are entitled to copyright protection because "[u]nlike a design incorporated in a belt, which holds up the wearer's pants, or even a costume, which may serve, aside from its appearance, to clothe the wearer, nose masks have no utility that does not derive from their appearance") (internal citation omitted).

53. Poe v. Missing Persons, 745 F.2d 1238 (9th Cir. 1984) (reversing summary judgment because there was evidence in the record that item was a work of art and not a useful article, a swimsuit).

54. Kieselstein-Cord v. Accessories by Pearl, Inc., 632 F.2d 989, 993 (2d Cir. 1980) (quoting H.R. Rep. No. 94-1476, at 55 (1976)); *see also* Pivot Point Int'l Inc. v. Charlene Prods., Inc., 372 F.3d 913, 922 n.8 (7th Cir. 2004) ("circuits have been almost unanimous in interpreting the language of § 101 to include both types of separability") (collecting circuit court cases).

without adversely impacting the article's functionality,"[55] In *Chosun International, Inc. v. Chrisha Creations, Ltd.*, the Court of Appeals for the Second Circuit considered the copyrightability of animal-themed children's costumes, including a line of "plush sculpture" costumes consisting of a bodysuit and a sculpted hood.[56] The court permitted Chosun's copyright infringement case to proceed in part because "[i]t might, for example, be the case that the sculpted heads of these designs are physically separable from the overall costume in that they could be removed from the costume without adversely impacting the wearer's ability to cover his or her body."[57] Thus, when a garment's creative features are physically separable from it, like sculpted animal heads attached to a children's costume, those features may be copyrightable.

Courts have also frequently found that fabric designs may be considered separate "writings" from the garments those fabrics are used to create, which would make them protectable.[58] For example, in *Peter Pan Fabrics, Inc. v. Martin Weiner Corp.*,[59] the Court of Appeals for the Second Circuit held that certain fabric patterns from which garments were made displayed the requisite originality to be considered copyrightable. Similarly, courts have repeatedly held that lace designs used to make garments are copyrightable.[60] And in *Knitwaves, Inc. v. Lollytogs Ltd.*,[61] the Second Circuit held that felt appliqués of leaves and squirrels stitched to the surfaces of children's sweaters were also copyrightable.

[D] Evaluating Whether Design Elements are "Separable"

The separability doctrine has its limits, however, where a garment's creative features are not physically separable from its utilitarian function. For example, the cut of a garment (its neckline, sleeve,

55. Chosun Int'l, Inc. v. Chrisha Creations, Ltd., 413 F.3d 324, 329 (2d Cir. 2005).
56. *Id.* at 325.
57. *Id.* at 329–30.
58. *See, e.g.*, Folio Impressions, Inc. v. Byer Cal., 937 F.2d 759, 763 (2d Cir. 1991); Soptra Fabrics Corp. v. Stafford Knitting Mills, Inc., 490 F.2d 1092 (2d Cir. 1974); Peter Pan Fabrics, Inc. v. Martin Weiner Corp., 274 F.2d 487 (2d Cir.1960) (L. Hand, J.).
59. *Peter Pan Fabrics*, 274 F.2d at 488.
60. Eve of Milady v. Impression Bridal, 957 F. Supp. 484, 489 (S.D.N.Y. 1997); Express, LLC v. Fetish Grp. Inc., 424 F. Supp. 2d 1211, 1224–25 (C.D. Cal. 2006) (citing *Eve of Milady*, 957 F. Supp. at 489); Imperial Laces v. Westchester Lace, No. 95 Civ. 5353, 1998 WL 830630 (S.D.N.Y. Nov. 30, 1998).
61. Knitwaves, Inc. v. Lollytogs Ltd., 71 F.3d 996 (2d Cir. 1995).

or the way the fabric is draped) is often what makes it creative and valuable. And while it may be somewhat straightforward to determine whether a feature that has been superimposed on a garment (appliqués or attached sculptures, for example) or an item from which a garment was made (the fabric or lace) is physically separable from the garment's utilitarian function, evaluating *conceptual* separability has proven more challenging.[62]

In the landmark case *Kieselstein-Cord v. Accessories by Pearl, Inc.*[63]—which claimed to be "on a razor's edge of copyright law"[64]—Kieselstein-Cord, manufacturer of western-themed accessories, sued a competitor for infringing the copyright in his belt buckles. The alleged infringer argued that only physically separable elements of items of apparel are copyrightable. The Second Circuit disagreed. It held that the Kieselstein-Cord belt buckles were copyrightable, reasoning that "[t]he **primary** ornamental aspect of the Vaquero and Winchester buckles is conceptually separable from their **subsidiary** utilitarian function."[65]

Conceptual separability thus could exist under the test established by *Kieselstein-Cord* when the artistic feature to be protected is primary and the utilitarian function secondary. The *Kieselstein-Cord* court deduced that even the buckles' wearers recognized that the ornamental features of the buckles were conceptually separate from the belts' function, based on the fact that the buckles in question were not always even worn as belts around the waist. The fact that they were not always used to keep the wearer's pants up effectively undermined the argument that the copyrightable design could not be separated from the useful aspect of the belt buckles.

On the other hand, just a few years later, in a case involving parties peripherally involved in the fashion industry, the same federal court *refused* to extend copyright protection to mannequins that were used as decorating props and signs in addition to being used to model clothes.[66] The court in that case, *Carol Barnhart v. Economy Cover Corp.*, reasoned that "to the extent the forms possess aesthetically pleasing features, even when these features are considered in the aggregate, they cannot be conceptualized as existing independently

---

62. *See* Masquerade Novelty v. Unique Indus., 912 F.2d 663, 670 (3d Cir. 1990) ("Courts have twisted themselves into knots trying to create a test to effectively ascertain whether the artistic aspects of a useful article can be identified separately from and exist independently of the article's utilitarian function.").
63. Kieselstein-Cord v. Accessories by Pearl, Inc., 632 F.2d 989 (2d Cir. 1980).
64. *Id.* at 990.
65. *Id.* at 993 (emphasis added).
66. Carol Barnhart Inc. v. Economy Cover Corp., 773 F.2d 411 (2d Cir. 1985).

of their utilitarian function."[67] Judge Newman, writing in dissent in the *Carol Barnhart* case, suggested an alternate test of conceptual separability—whether the useful article (through its artistic features) stimulates in the mind of the beholder a concept that is separate from the concept evoked by its utilitarian function.[68]

Courts and commentators articulated several other tests for evaluating conceptual separability. The Court of Appeals for the Seventh Circuit, in fact, identified no fewer than six alternate tests of conceptual separability when it reviewed the law in this area in detail.[69] As a result, the outcome of a fashion-related copyright case turned in large part on the law governing in a particular circuit or jurisdiction. A test predominantly used in the Second and Seventh Circuits extended protection to features "that can be identified as reflecting the designer's artistic judgment exercised independently of functional influences."[70]

In *Jovani Fashion v. Cinderella Divine Inc.*,[71] for example, a federal court in New York reasoned that elements of a prom dress designed by Jovani Fashion were "plainly fashioned to fit the specific needs of a prom dress," and concluded that they were not conceptually separable under this test.[72] The *Jovani* court was not persuaded by the fact that Jovani could have made "different choices . . . in each area" because the "the artistic judgment was exercised with an eye toward the basic requirements of a dress . . . ."[73] On appeal, the Court of Appeals for the Second Circuit agreed, concluding that Jovani had not demonstrated and could not demonstrate conceptual separability.[74]

Another leading test as to separability was the one adopted by the Fifth Circuit, which required "a substantial likelihood that even if the article had no utilitarian use it would still be marketable to some significant segment of the community simply because of its aesthetic qualities."[75]

---

67. *Id.* at 418.
68. *Id.* at 422 (Newman, J., dissenting).
69. Pivot Point Int'l Inc. v. Charlene Prods., Inc., 372 F.3d 913, 923 (7th Cir. 2004).
70. Brandir Int'l, Inc. v. Cascade Pac. Lumber Co., 834 F.2d 1142, 1145 (2d Cir. 1987); *see also Pivot Point Int'l*, 372 F.3d at 931.
71. Jovani Fashion v. Cinderella Divine Inc., 808 F. Supp. 2d 542 (S.D.N.Y. 2011).
72. *Id.* at 550.
73. *Id.*
74. Jovani Fashion, Ltd. v. Fiesta Fashions, No. 12-598- cv, 2012 WL 4856412 (2d Cir. Oct. 15, 2012).
75. MELVILLE B. NIMMER & DAVID NIMMER, NIMMER ON COPYRIGHT (2013) [hereinafter NIMMER ON COPYRIGHT], § 2.08[B][3], at 2-101; Galiano v. Harrah's Operating Co., 416 F.3d 411, 419–21 (5th Cir. 2005).

In *Star Athletica LLC v. Varsity Brands, Inc.*, the Supreme Court clarified the test for separability.[76] Varsity Brands had filed suit accusing Star Athletica of infringing five designs for cheerleading uniforms.[77] The designs were two-dimensional renderings depicting "combinations, positionings, and arrangements of elements" that included "chevrons . . . , lines, curves, stripes, angles, diagonals, inverted [chevrons], coloring, and shapes."[78]

The district court ruled in favor of Star Athletica on the ground that the designs did not qualify as protectable pictorial, graphic or sculptural works because they served the utilitarian function of identifying the garments as cheerleading uniforms.[79] The Sixth Circuit reversed, reasoning that the graphic designs were "separately identifiable" and "capable of existing independently."[80]

The Supreme Court affirmed, and enunciated a two-part test for separability. "A feature incorporated into the design of a useful article is eligible for copyright protection only if the feature (1) can be perceived as a two- or three-dimensional work of art separate from the useful article and (2) would qualify as a protectable pictorial, graphic, or sculptural work—either on its own or fixed in some other tangible medium of expression—if it were imagined separately from the useful article into which it is incorporated."[81] The test did not reference a distinction between physical and conceptual separability, and thus seemed to reject those conceptual categories.

Applying the test to Varsity Brand's designs for cheerleading uniforms, the Court found, firstly, that the decorations clearly had pictorial, graphic, or sculptural qualities.[82] Secondly, "if the arrangement of colors, shapes, stripes, and chevrons on the surface of the cheerleading uniforms were separated from the uniform and applied in another medium—for example, on a painter's canvas—they would qualify as 'two-dimensional . . . works of . . . art.'"[83] Furthermore, applying the decorations on another medium "would not replicate the uniform itself," which underscores the conclusion that the decorations are separable.[84]

---

76. Star Athletica, L.L.C. v. Varsity Brands, Inc., 137 S. Ct. 1002 (2017).
77. *Id.* at 1007.
78. *Id.*
79. *Id.* at 1007–08.
80. *Id.* at 1008.
81. *Id.* at 1007.
82. *Id.* at 1012.
83. *Id.*
84. *Id.*

In the aftermath of the *Star Athletica* decision, a federal court in New York found that the "decorative black trim and T-shape" of bikinis were "physically separable and demonstrable as works of art."[85] The Copyright Office, relying on *Star Athletica*, approved the registration of a design for sneakers, and a judge ruled that animal designs that appeared on the surface of t-shirts were eligible for copyright protection.[86] The cutout of clothing, by contrast, did not fare as well in a case before a federal court in New Jersey.[87] That court held that the cutout holes of a banana costume served a solely utilitarian function of making the costumer wearable, and thus were not eligible for copyright protection.[88] The length, shape, color, and lines of the costume, however, were found to be unique and the result of artistic and stylistic choices.[89]

§ 4:3.3 *Idea and Expression*

Another fundamental precept of copyright law is that it does not protect abstract ideas, only their expression in a fixed form.[90] As 17 U.S.C. § 102(b) states, "[i]n no case does copyright protection for an original work of authorship ***extend to any idea***, procedure, process, system, method of operation, concept, principle, or discovery, regardless of the form in which it is described, explained, illustrated, or embodied in such work."[91]

The distinction between ideas and their expression can be particularly difficult to draw in the fashion industry. The Second Circuit addressed this issue in a case involving a fabric pattern that consisted of roses turned in various directions arranged in straight lines

---

85. Triangl Grp. Ltd. v. Jiangmen City Xinhui Dist. Lingzhi Garment Co., No. 16 CIV. 1498 PGG, 2017 WL 2829752, at *8 (S.D.N.Y. June 22, 2017).
86. U.S. Copyright Office, Letter on the Second Request for Reconsideration for Refusal to Register Yeezy Boost 350 Version 1, Yeezy Boost 350 Version 2 (May 8, 2019) (relying on *Star Athletica* to find that adidas and Kanye West's "Yeezy" sneakers contained separable designs); L.A. T-Shirt & Print, Inc. v. Rue 21, Inc., No. 16-CV-5400 (RA), 2017 WL 3575699, at *6 (S.D.N.Y. Aug. 17, 2017).
87. *See* Silvertop Assocs., Inc. v. Kangaroo Mfg., Inc., No. 117CV7919NLH-KMW, 2018 WL 2427120 (D.N.J. May 30, 2018).
88. *Id.* at *5.
89. *Id.*
90. *See, e.g.*, N.Y. Times Co. v. United States, 403 U.S. 713, 726, n.* (1971) (Brennan, J., concurring) (Copyright laws are not restrictions on freedom of speech as copyright protects only form of expression and not the ideas expressed.); Metcalf v. Bochco, 294 F.3d 1069, 1074 (9th Cir. 2002) (citing Kouf v. Walt Disney Pictures & Television, 16 F.3d 1042, 1045 (9th Cir. 1994)); NIMMER ON COPYRIGHT, *supra* note 75, § 13.03[B][2][a].
91. 17 U.S.C. § 102(b) (emphasis added).

on a generic background.[92] In that case, *Folio Impressions, Inc. v. Byer California*, an importer and purveyor of fabrics purchased the "Folio Rose" fabric design. After Byer California, a clothing manufacturer, obtained a swatch of the Folio-Rose-patterned fabric, it requested a similar fabric from one of Folio's competitors. The competitor, which did not have a similar pattern at the time, created a new one using its own reference materials and sold it to Byer. Folio sued both Byer and the competitor that offered the fabric.

The Second Circuit concluded that both the "the Folio Rose itself and the way in which that rose is arranged" were copyrightable (although the background, which was copied from a pattern in the public domain, was not). Although the court upheld Folio's copyright, the fact that there were so few ways of expressing the idea of a rose-patterned fabric ultimately doomed the plaintiff's claim of infringement.

The Second Circuit explained that "the copyright umbrella does not cover the idea of arranging roses generally in a straight line pattern."[93] Even though defendants placed roses that closely resembled the Folio Rose in a similar straight line pattern on their fabric, the court reasoned that "by the rose's very nature, one artist's rendering of it will closely resemble another artist's work." Thus, the court concluded, "an average lay observer would not recognize the alleged copy as having been appropriated from the copyrighted work" despite the similarities.[94]

Put differently, even though the plaintiff's particular expression of roses depicted in straight lines on a piece of fabric was itself original enough to merit copyright protection in the abstract, because there were only a few ways to express the idea of roses depicted in straight lines, the court found that a copy must be virtually identical to infringe the plaintiff's copyright.

In 2012, the Court of Appeals for the Ninth Circuit reached a very different decision under facially comparable facts. In *L.A. Printex Industries Inc. v. Aeropostale, Inc.*,[95] the court reasoned that there are many ways to combine "petals, buds, stems, leaves, and colors in floral fabric design." As a result, the court found that the plaintiff's particular expression of that idea "is broad and a work will infringe if it's substantially similar to the copyrighted work."[96] Unlike the Second Circuit, the Ninth Circuit concluded that the plaintiff had stated a sufficient claim that the defendant's fabric infringed the copyright

92. *See, e.g.*, Folio Impressions, Inc. v. Byer Cal., 937 F.2d 759, 765 (2d Cir. 1991).
93. *Id.* at 765.
94. *Id.* at 766.
95. L.A. Printex Indus. Inc. v. Aeropostale, Inc., 676 F.3d 841 (9th Cir. 2012) (internal quotation marks omitted).
96. *Id.* at 850.

holder's rights. The "subjective evaluation of the expressive similarities in two fabric designs, here intended for public consumption as clothing apparel, is best suited for the trier of fact," the Ninth Circuit found. The court of appeals therefore remanded the case to the trial court because "on the facts here involving stylized floral fabric designs, the issue of substantial similarity must go to the jury."[97]

When there is no distinction between an idea and its expression, copyright law will not protect the work at all. This principle—known as idea/expression "merger"—can have drastic effects on works of visual art, including fashion. In particular, courts will not enforce a plaintiff's copyright if "it is not clear that there is any real distinction between the idea in a work of art and its expression," such as where the "artist's idea, among other things, is to depict a particular subject in a particular way."[98]

A case discussed earlier, involving jewelry, demonstrates how an idea can merge with its expression. In *Todd v. Montana Silversmiths, Inc.*,[99] a federal court in Colorado concluded that copyright law did not protect the plaintiffs' barbed-wire style jewelry. In addition to finding the jewelry insufficiently original, the court reasoned that "any expression contained in Plaintiff's work is a necessary concomitant of the idea of barbed-wire jewelry."[100] Even though the court implicitly recognized that there may be "visually distinguishable" ways of making barbed-wire jewelry, it nevertheless rejected the argument that the idea and its expression could be sufficiently distinguished to justify copyright protection.[101] The court was apparently concerned that if it were to grant protection to an expression that could not be distinguished from the overall idea of barbed-wire jewelry, it would effectively be granting a monopoly to the first person to come up with the idea, a result that copyright law does not allow.

By contrast, the Fifth Circuit declined to apply the merger doctrine to jewelry containing bead dog trinkets, plastic beads twisted into the shape of a dog.[102] The court reviewed the examples of bead dogs that

---

97. *Id.* at 852.
98. Mannion v. Coors Brewing Co., 337 F. Supp. 2d 444, 458 (S.D.N.Y. 2005).
99. *Todd*, 379 F. Supp. 2d at 1110, cited at *supra* section 4:3.1.
100. *Id.* at 1114.
101. *See id.* ("[I]f a court were to grant copyright in an arrangement that is visually but not conceptually distinguishable from barbed-wire . . . [a]rguably it would be impossible for other artists to create barbed-wire style jewelry (no matter how visually distinguishable) without infringing on Plaintiff's copyrighted arrangement.") (internal citation omitted).
102. Nola Spice Designs, L.L.C. v. Haydel Enters., Inc., 783 F.3d 527 (5th Cir. 2015).

were in the record and concluded that "the idea of a bead dog may be expressed in various ways."[103]

Because this analysis is highly fact-intensive and situation-specific, it can be difficult to predict how a court will apply the idea/expression dichotomy in a particular case. Two cases involving fashion photography and marketing illustrate just how fact-specific this analysis can be.

In *Bill Diodato Photography, LLC v. Kate Spade, LLC,*[104] a federal court refused to extend copyright protection to an image of "a woman's feet, astride a toilet, in stylish, colorful shoes . . . [with] a handbag on the floor."[105] The photographer had submitted the image to Kate Spade, which then used, without authorization, a virtually identical image in its advertisements for certain fashion accessories. The court reasoned that the image was "an idea that has been used often in popular culture," and so copyright did not protect the idea.[106]

By contrast, in *LaChapelle v. Fenty,*[107] another case in the same district, also involving fashion photography, the court reached the opposite result. In *LaChapelle,* the plaintiff was a fashion photographer, who sued popular recording artist Rihanna and others for infringing his successful S&M-themed photo series in her music video for the song "S&M." The court refused to dismiss LaChapelle's copyright infringement claim at the pleading stage because he had alleged copying of more than his ideas. The court recognized that "subjects [that] flow naturally from the chosen idea . . . are not protectable," but it identified several elements of the photos that reflected the photographer's particular expression, including numerous physical elements within the photos, the level of color saturation, the lighting, focus, and mood of the photos. The court held that a jury could rely on similar elements in Rihanna's music video to conclude that defendants had infringed LaChapelle's copyright.

§ 4:4 Efforts to Protect Fashion More Vigorously

In theory, Congress could extend greater copyright protection to apparel. Indeed, Congress has already protected other useful articles that are analogous to garments. In 1990, Congress amended the Copyright Act to extend protection to a category of "architectural works," defined to include "the design of a building as embodied in any tangible medium of expression, including a building, architectural

103. *Id.* at 549–50.
104. Bill Diodato Photography, LLC v. Kate Spade, LLC, 388 F. Supp. 2d 382 (S.D.N.Y. 2005).
105. *Id.* at 384.
106. *Id.*
107. LaChapelle v. Fenty, 812 F. Supp. 2d 434 (S.D.N.Y. 2011).

plans, or drawings."[108] Until enactment of the Architectural Works Copyright Protection Act, blueprints (like fashion sketches) enjoyed copyright protection. But buildings erected based on those blueprints (like the garments manufactured from design sketches) did not. Congress also enacted separate legislation, the Vessel Hull Act, to protect boat hulls from copying above and beyond the protections that general copyright law had previously provided.[109]

Commentators have long debated how extending copyright protection to garments might affect different parts of the fashion industry.[110] Faced with the obstacles to copyright protection in the fashion industry described above, however, courts have even noted that "[w]hat [fashion designers] need is . . . a statute which will protect them against plagiarism of their designs."[111]

Consistent with that advice, there have been numerous attempts to persuade Congress to protect fashion from copying.[112] For example, on August 5, 2010, Senator Charles Schumer (D-NY) introduced the Innovative Design Protection and Piracy Prevention Act (IDPPPA) to the Senate.[113] On July 13, 2011, Representative Bob Goodlatte (R-VA) introduced the identical bill to the House.[114] These bills, however, were not passed into law.

In 2012, a slightly modified bill, the proposed Innovative Design Protection Act (IDPA), was introduced in the Senate again by Senator Schumer.[115] The bill would have amended section 1301 of the Copyright Act to extend protection to fashion designs.[116] Section 1301 currently

---

108. 17 U.S.C. § 101.

109. 17 U.S.C. §§ 1301 *et seq.* (granting *sui generis*, copyright-like protection to boat hulls, which like fashion design, would otherwise be categorized as useful articles not entitled to protection).

110. *See, e.g.*, Kal Raustiala & Christopher Sprigman, *The Piracy Paradox: Innovation and Intellectual Property in Fashion Design*, 92 VA. L. REV. 1687 (2006) ("Original ideas are few, and the existence of fashion trends typically means that many actors copy or rework the ideas of some originator (or copy a copy of the originator's design). Some may originate more than others, but all engage in some copying at some point . . . .").

111. White v. Leanore Frocks, 120 F.2d 113 (2d Cir. 1941).

112. Nat Lewis Purses v. Carole Bags, 83 F.2d 475, 476 (2d Cir. 1936) ("[e]fforts have been made to induce Congress to change the law so as to give some [limited copyright] protection, without success so far; and until it does, new designs are open to all").

113. Innovative Design Protection and Piracy Prevention Act, S. 3728, 111th Cong. (2009–2011), https://www.govtrack.us/congress/bills/111/s3728/text.

114. Innovative Design Protection and Piracy Prevention Act, H.R. 2511, 112th Cong. (2011–2013), https://www.govtrack.us/congress/bills/112/hr2511/text.

115. Innovative Design Protection Act of 2012, S. 3523, 112th Cong. (2011–2013) (IDPA), https://www.govtrack.us/congress/bills/112/s3523/text.

116. *Id.*

protects the design of boat vessel hulls and decks, despite their intrinsic utilitarian function.[117]

To qualify for protection under the IDPA, an article of apparel[118] would have had to include: (a) original elements or (b) the original arrangement or placement of original or non-original elements, either of which must be the result of an artist's own creative endeavor.[119] Only designs that provided a "unique, distinguishable, non-trivial and non-utilitarian variation over prior designs for similar types of articles" would have been entitled to protection.[120] Although it was unclear how this standard would have been applied in practice if the bill had been enacted, it would have presumably required some level of proof that a design presented a qualitative advancement over prior designs. If an article of apparel were to pass this test, the IDPA would have protected it for three (3) years from publication of the registration or the design.[121]

Under the IDPA, a design would have infringed a protected article of apparel if it was: (1) substantially identical in overall visual appearance to the overall design and the original elements of the protected design; and (2) not the result of independent creation.[122] An allegedly infringing work would have been "substantially identical" if it was "so similar in appearance as likely to be mistaken for the protected design" and contains only trivial differences in construction or design.[123]

The IDPA stalled in committee between the 112th and 113th Congresses.[124] Since then, there have not been comparable legislative efforts directed towards strengthening copyright protection for fashion.

§ 4:5 Joint Ownership and Works Made for Hire

Another issue that frequently arises in the fashion industry is who owns a copyright. Determining who owns a copyright is simple where a single artist working independently (and not as an employee of another entity) creates an original work in a tangible medium of expression. But in the fashion industry, collaborative works and works

117. 17 U.S.C. § 1301(a)(2).
118. The IDPA defines "apparel" to include clothing, undergarments, outerwear, gloves, footwear, headwear, handbags, purses, wallets, tote bags, belts, and eyeglass frames.
119. IDPA § 2(a).
120. *Id.*
121. *Id.*
122. *Id.*
123. *Id.*
124. Congress.gov, Actions Overview S.3523—112th Congress (2011–2012), https://www.congress.gov/bill/112th-congress/senate-bill/3523/actions.

made in the context of an employment relationship are common. Copyright law establishes two separate concepts—"joint ownership" and "works for hire"—that govern the analysis of ownership when there are multiple potential claimants to a copyright.

First, under the Copyright Act, "[a] 'joint work' is a work prepared by two or more authors with the intention that their contributions be merged into inseparable or interdependent parts of a unitary whole."[125] Joint ownership may be a particularly relevant aspect of copyright law in the fashion industry where fashion designers may collaborate on copyrightable components of garments, sketches, fabric designs, or in photographing and marketing fashion products. Importantly, a "joint owner of a copyright [cannot] sue his co-owner for infringement."[126] Each joint owner is entitled to "equal undivided interests in the whole work—in other words, each joint author has the right to use or to license the work as he or she wishes, subject only to account to the other joint owner for any profits that are made."[127]

Second, the employer of the creator of a copyright-eligible work is deemed to be the legal author of the work if it is "prepared by an employee within the scope of his or her employment."[128] Generally, courts require an employer to establish that it had the "right to control the manner and means by which the product is accomplished."[129] Among other factors, courts look to see that the employer retained the right to edit or amend the work, that the employee worked on the submission according to hours established by the employer, that the employee used the employer's facilities and personnel to create the work, or that the employee described himself as an "employee."[130] Conversely, if the creator of a given work, "worked on his own time, at a place other than [the employer's] offices, and . . . was paid on

---

125. 17 U.S.C. § 101.
126. Cortner v. Israel, 732 F.2d 267, 271 (2d Cir. 1984); *see generally* NIMMER ON COPYRIGHT, *supra* note 75, § 6.10[A][1][a].
127. Thomson v. Larson, 147 F.3d 195, 199 (2d Cir. 1998).
128. 17 U.S.C. § 101.
129. Cmty. for Creative Non-Violence v. Reid, 490 U.S. 730, 751 (1989).
130. *See, e.g.*, Saenger Org., Inc. v. Nationwide Ins. Licensing Assoc., Inc., 119 F.3d 55, 60–62 (1st Cir. 1997) (finding an employer to be "author" of an insurance manual drafted by an officer of the company); Langman Fabrics v. Graff Californiawear, Inc., 160 F.3d 106, 111 (2d Cir. 1998) (holding that a jury may conclude that an artist was an employee where the employer withheld taxes and paid benefits for the employee who worked at the employer's place of business so that the employer could collaborate in the creative process); Montgomery v. Alcoa, Inc., No. 99-CV-73350-DT, 2000 WL 1769526, at *7–8 (E.D. Mich. Sept. 29, 2000) (relying on fact that salaried employee developed computer system on company time and with company computers to find that an employer was "author" of the system under work-made-for-hire doctrine).

a piecemeal basis without receiving benefits or having federal taxes withheld" then courts are not likely to find the employer to be the author.[131] The analysis is not mechanical: for example, even where an employer asks an employee to perform a task, the result of that work may be deemed not "made for hire" if the employee worked on it in his off-hours and understood the project to be for the benefit of a separate company.[132]

In addition, a work may be deemed a work made for hire if it is a "work specially ordered or commissioned for," if the work falls within one of nine specifically listed categories of uses, and "if the parties expressly agree in a written instrument signed by them that the work shall be considered a work made for hire."[133] Specifically, the statute limits contractual works made for hire to the following nine itemized categories of works: "a collective work," a "part of a motion picture or other audiovisual work," a "translation," a "supplementary work," a "compilation," an "instructional text," a "test," "answer material for a test," or an "atlas."[134] Courts reject "work for hire" contract assignments if they do not fall into one of these nine categories.[135]

For these purposes:

- A "supplementary work" is defined as "a work prepared for publication as a secondary adjunct to a work by another author for the purpose of introducing, concluding, illustrating, explaining, revising, commenting upon, or assisting in the use of the other work, such as forewords, afterwords, pictorial illustrations, maps, charts, tables, editorial notes, musical arrangements, answer material for tests, bibliographies, appendixes, and indexes."
- A "compilation" is defined as a work that "collect[s] and assembl[es] preexisting materials or . . . data that are selected, coordinated, or arranged in such a way that the resulting work, as a whole constitutes an original work of authorship."

---

131. *See, e.g.*, Ludden v. Metro Weekly, 8 F. Supp. 2d 7, 18 (D.D.C. 1998); *see also* Smith v. Mikki More, LLC, 59 F. Supp. 3d 595 (S.D.N.Y. 2014).

132. *See, e.g.*, Kuryakyn Holdings, LLC v. Ciro, LLC, 242 F. Supp. 3d 789 (W.D. Wis. 2017).

133. *See* Lulirama Ltd. v. Axcess Broad. Servs., Inc., 128 F.3d 872, 877 (5th Cir. 1997).

134. 17 U.S.C. § 101.

135. *See, e.g.*, *Lulirama Ltd.*, 128 F.3d at 877 ("A work created by an independent contractor can constitute a work for hire only if it fits one of nine narrowly drawn categories of works delineated in [Section 101]"); Staggers v. Real Authentic Sound, 77 F. Supp. 2d 57, 63–64 (D.D.C. 1999) (because a sound recording does not fall into one of the nine categories, question of authorship depends on existence of employment relationship).

- An "instructional text" is defined as "a literary, pictorial, or graphic work prepared for publication with the purpose of use in systematic instructional activities."[136]

One can see how works that fall into each of these categories may arise in the fashion industry, such as in the case of books commenting on fashion designs or fashion technique, but they do not lend themselves to the designs or apparel items themselves.

Furthermore, courts have also refused to find an agreement legally sufficient even where there is a written contract between the parties if "there is no express reference in the contract that the work is 'made for hire' or is a transfer of 'copyrights.'"[137]

§ 4:6 Copyright Registration Procedures

Copyright registration is not required to obtain copyright protection. Rather, copyrights are obtained by operation of law when an author first creates a copyrightable work in tangible form.[138] Nevertheless, registration of works with the U.S. Copyright Office is important for at least a few principal reasons:

(1) Subject to possible exceptions for non-U.S. works, a work must be successfully registered before a copyright owner files an infringement lawsuit.[139]

(2) Registration that is timely (that is, within three (3) months of publication or before infringing activity commences) allows the copyright owner the possibility of recovering attorneys' fees and statutory damages in an infringement lawsuit. Otherwise, the copyright owner is limited to recovering actual economic damages.[140]

(3) Copyright registration can assist in proving that the author created the work at least as of the application filing date.

---

136. 17 U.S.C. § 101.

137. *See, e.g.*, Netnumina Sols., Inc. v. Dietrehab.com, Inc., No. Civ.A. 01-10195-PBS, 2001 WL 455842, at *5 (D. Mass. Apr. 6, 2001) (citing Baltimore Orioles, Inc. v. Major League Baseball Players Assoc., 805 F.2d 663, 671–72 (7th Cir. 1986)).

138. *See, e.g.*, U.S. COPYRIGHT OFFICE, CIRCULAR 1: COPYRIGHT BASICS [hereinafter U.S. COPYRIGHT OFFICE, CIRCULAR 1: COPYRIGHT BASICS], at 3 ("Copyright is secured automatically when the work is created, and a work is 'created' when it is fixed in a copy or phonorecord for the first time."), https://www.copyright.gov/circs/circ01.pdf.

139. *See infra* section 4:6. The Copyright Office must grant registration, and not simply have received the application, before a copyright owner files an infringement lawsuit. Fourth Est. Pub. Benefit Corp. v. Wall-Street.com, LLC, 139 S. Ct. 881 (2019).

140. *See infra* section 4:8.3.

(4) Ownership of a valid registration makes it easier for a copyright owner to monetize his or her ownership interest, and to treat the work as an asset for purposes of fundraising.

(5) Copyright registration may also be useful in that the U.S. Customs and Border Protection service is authorized to bar the importation of works that infringe registered copyrights.[141]

As a result, it is often advantageous for a copyright owner to register the work, especially in light of the relatively low costs involved in doing so.

The sole venue to register copyrights in the United States is the U.S. Copyright Office.[142] There is no equivalent at the state level, and notions such as a "poor man's copyright" (mailing the copyrighted work to establish a date) may have some evidentiary effect in certain situations, but are in no way equivalent to registration.

Unlike the process to register a trademark or patent with the U.S. Patent & Trademark Office, the U.S. Copyright Office generally does not engage in searching or other clearance before registering a work. This is because, unlike patents and trademarks, the works of others generally have no relevance to whether the copyright in a particular work of authorship can be registered. If a work is original, that is, not copied from another source, it is generally registrable, even if it may be similar to another work.

It is important to bear in mind that a product that is original and therefore protectable under copyright law could nevertheless raise infringement issues as a matter of patent or trademark law. For example, an article of jewelry may be completely original to its creator, but could so resemble some other piece of jewelry that is protected by a design patent as to constitute patent infringement. Therefore, product clearance should consider all potential infringement, not just copyright law.

§ 4:6.1 Elements of a Copyright Application

The registration process is similar for all types of works. As discussed above, however, the primary types of copyrights relevant to the fashion industry are works of visual arts (for example, artwork applied to clothing, fabric designs, and jewelry designs). And companies may register catalogs, which are classified as textual works. For example, the clothing manufacturer Patagonia, Inc. regularly publishes catalogs that not only advertise its products, but also contain articles and

---

141. *See supra* section 2:9.5.

142. *See* 19 C.F.R. §§ 133.31 *et seq*. *See* U.S. COPYRIGHT OFFICE, https://www.copyright.gov/.

other content that is of interest to its customers. Patagonia has regularly registered its copyrights in its catalogs.[143]

A copyright application has three essential elements: (1) a completed application form, (2) a "deposit," that is, a copy of the work to be registered, and (3) the filing fee. Copyright applications may be filed online, and online filing is encouraged by lower filing fees and quicker examination.[144]

The effective date of registration is the date a valid application is submitted, regardless of how long it takes the Copyright Office to issue the registration. However, in certain situations, it is necessary or useful to obtain the registration on an expedited basis. The Copyright Office will issue expedited registrations (called "Special Handling") to assist when necessary for litigation purposes, customs matters, or to meet contractual or publishing deadlines.[145]

The Copyright Office publishes forms to register various types of copyrightable works, and it is useful to review those forms before preparing to submit an electronic application in order to ensure that all the necessary information has been compiled. Forms and instructions are available online at *https://www.copyright.gov/forms/*. As of September 1, 2018, the basic online registration fee is $35. Fees are subject to change, and current fees may be found at *https://www.copyright.gov/docs/fees.html*.

Registering a work requires determining whether it has been "published," which is a term of art in copyright law. Publication requires distributing copies of the work to the public by sale or other transfer of ownership; by rental, lease, or lending; or by offering to distribute copies.[146] In general, a work that exists only its original form (such as a painting) is not regarded as being published, even when it is sold or if it is publicly displayed, although a complicated body of law developed under prior versions of the Copyright Act, when publication without notice led to forfeiture of copyrights.[147] Under the present law, publication has somewhat less significance, although it still is relevant because the timing of registration relative to publication can affect damages as noted above.

---

143. *See, e.g.*, U.S. Copyright Reg. Nos. TX0006559644, TX0006516730, TX0006440412, TX0006440411.

144. *See, e.g.*, U.S. COPYRIGHT OFFICE, ECO ONLINE SYSTEM, https://eco.copyright.gov/eService_enu/start.swe.

145. *See* U.S. COPYRIGHT OFFICE, SPECIAL HANDLING, https://www.copyright.gov/help/faq/faq-special.html.

146. *See* U.S. COPYRIGHT OFFICE, CIRCULAR 1: COPYRIGHT BASICS, *supra* note 138, at 3.

147. *Id.* at 3–4.

Under certain circumstances, a copyright owner can register multiple works in a single application and single filing fee.[148] It is relatively common to register unpublished collections of jewelry, for example. Separately published works cannot generally be registered together, with exceptions for group registrations of published photographs and contributions to periodicals.

§ 4:6.2 Renewals and Change of Ownership

Unlike patents and trademark registrations, copyright registrations no longer require any renewals or similar filings. Renewals are relevant only in connection with certain copyrights that came into being before the current 1976 Copyright Act (that is, that were first published before January 1, 1978).[149]

It is not strictly necessary to record the transfer of copyright ownership, but doing so provides constructive notice and may affect the rights between competing claimants. For example, as between two conflicting transfers, the later transferee will prevail if the first transferee does not record its rights within one (1) month after execution, and the later transferee first records and takes its interest in good faith and for consideration.[150] Moreover, perfection of a security interest in a registered copyright may require recordation with the Copyright Office.[151]

§ 4:6.3 Copyright Notice

Traditionally, U.S. law required copyright owners to affix notice of registration to copies of the protected work. Because other leading countries did not require copyright notice, however, when the United States entered into the Berne Convention for the Protection of Literary and Artistic Works, it did away with the copyright notice requirement for works published after March 1, 1989 (the effective

---

148. *See id.* at 8 (Multiple unpublished works may be registered together "if the elements are assembled in an orderly form; the combined elements bear a single title identifying the collection as a whole; the copyright claimant in all the elements and in the collection as a whole is the same; and all the elements are by the same author or, if they are by different authors, at least one of the authors has contributed copyrightable authorship to each element." Multiple published works may be registered together "if they are all first published together in the same publication on the same date and owned by the same claimant.").

149. *Id.* at 6 (describing renewal system prior to the effective date of the 1976 version of the Copyright Act).

150. 17 U.S.C. § 205.

151. *See In re* Peregrine Entm't, Ltd., 116 B.R. 194 (C.D. Cal. 1990).

date of the Berne Convention Implementation Act).[152] Even for works created after 1989, proper notice may have value in helping to dissuade potential infringers, and if an infringer possesses a copy of the work with notice, it is more difficult for that defendant to assert an "innocent infringement" defense.[153]

In general, proper copyright notice has three parts: (1) the symbol © or the word "Copyright" or its abbreviation "Copr."; (2) the year of first publication; and (3) the name of the copyright owner, which may be an abbreviation or a generally known alternative designation of the owner. Element (2) may frequently be omitted if desired, as it is not required "when a pictorial, graphic, or sculptural work, with accompanying textual matter, if any, is reproduced in or on greeting cards, postcards, stationery, jewelry, dolls, toys, or useful articles."[154]

The notice should be placed so as to give reasonable notice to the claim of copyright. The Copyright Office has guidelines relating to placement on various types of works, but in general, placement on the front or back of the relevant articles will suffice.[155] Applying copyright notice does not require filing a copyright application or other action or approval from the Copyright Office.[156]

§ 4:6.4 *Length of Copyright*

The length of a copyright is a surprisingly complicated question, and the answer depends on factors such as when the work was first created, when it was published, whether it was renewed during the time frame that renewal was required, and the life span of the work's author.[157] For a work that was created on or after January 1, 1978, though, copyright generally lasts for the length of the author's life plus an additional seventy (70) years after the author's death. In the case of "a joint work" prepared by two or more authors, the term lasts for seventy (70) years after the last surviving author's death. For works made for hire, the copyright will last ninety-five (95) years from publication or 120 years from creation, whichever is shorter. An analysis of the length of copyrights for works created before January 1, 1978, however, may require resort to Copyright Office records, to see if the registration was appropriately renewed.[158]

---

152. *See* U.S. COPYRIGHT OFFICE, CIRCULAR 1: COPYRIGHT BASICS, *supra* note 138, at 4.
153. *Id.*
154. *See* U.S. COPYRIGHT OFFICE, CIRCULAR 3: COPYRIGHT NOTICE, at 2, https://www.copyright.gov/circs/circ03.pdf.
155. *See id.*; 37 C.F.R. § 201.20.
156. *Id.*
157. *See* U.S. COPYRIGHT OFFICE, CIRCULAR 1: COPYRIGHT BASICS, *supra* note 138, at 3, 5–6 (setting forth general categories for "How Long Copyright Protection Endures").
158. *Id.*

§ 4:7 Copyright Infringement

Copyright law grants to the creator of an original work of authorship that qualifies for protection a bundle of exclusive rights. In particular, the Copyright Act lists the exclusive rights to: (1) reproduce the work; (2) prepare derivative works based on the copyrighted work; (3) distribute copies of the work; (4) perform the work publicly; (5) display the work publicly; and (6) perform the work by means of a digital audio transmission.[159] The fourth category (the public performance right) is limited to "literary, musical, dramatic, and choreographic works, pantomimes, and motion pictures and other audiovisual works."[160] Category 5 (the display right) is limited to similar categories, but also includes sculptural works.[161] Category 6 (digital audio transmission) is limited to sound recordings.[162]

Violation of any one or more of the exclusive rights of the copyright holder constitutes copyright infringement, which may provide a basis for a lawsuit. In connection with the fashion industry, however, typically, copyright infringement cases involve the exclusive right to reproduce, distribute, or, in the case of fashion photography, display a work. In those contexts, a successful infringement case requires: (1) ownership of a valid copyright; and (2) that the alleged infringer copied the copyrighted work without authorization.[163] Unlike patent law, copyright does not grant the holder of a copyright the right to prevent others from distributing a similar work, no matter how similar, if that work was developed independently and not copied. Two persons may develop the same work independently, and each may exploit it, without violating the other's copyrights.[164]

With respect to the first element of a successful copyright infringement case—ownership of a valid copyright—federal registration creates a rebuttable presumption that the registrant owns the copyright,

---

159. 17 U.S.C. § 106.
160. *Id.*
161. *Id.*
162. *Id.*
163. *See* Gibson Tex, Inc. v. Sears Roebuck & Co., 11. F. Supp. 2d 439, 443 (S.D.N.Y. 1998) (denying copyright owner's motion for summary judgment because "the repeat pattern [of the fabric] is the main protectable element of [the] design, and the variations in design available when putting a public domain fabric in repeat are limited"); *see also* Feist Publ'ns, Inc. v. Rural Tel. Serv. Co., 499 U.S. 340, 361 (1991).
164. NIMMER ON COPYRIGHT, *supra* note 75, § 10.1, at 34. *See also* Sheldon v. Metro-Goldwyn Pictures Corp., 81 F.2d 49, 54 (2d Cir. 1936), *aff'd*, 309 U.S. 390 (1940).

it is valid, and the subject matter is copyrightable.[165] The burden properly shifts to the alleged infringer to challenge those presumptions. Moreover, copyright owners may not institute a lawsuit until they have federally registered the work with the Copyright Office.[166] Under the Berne Convention, the United States does not require foreign copyright owners to register their works in the United States to commence a lawsuit,[167] but registration is permissible and in most cases advisable because of the presumptions it creates, as well as the fact that statutory damages and attorneys' fees (discussed below) are not available for infringement of unregistered works regardless of whether those works are non-U.S. Berne works.[168]

With respect to the second element of a copyright infringement action—unauthorized copying of the protected work—copyright holders may always prove that an alleged infringer copied the copyrighted work through direct eyewitness testimony or admission of the infringer, if any such evidence exists. But because such evidence is understandably difficult to come by, courts also allow copyright holders to prove copying through circumstantial evidence. A copyright holder may do so by showing that (a) the alleged infringer had *access* to the original work and (b) the allegedly infringing work is *substantially similar* to the original work rather than requiring direct evidence of the copying.[169]

---

165. 17 U.S.C. § 410; United Merchants & Mfrs., Inc. v. Sarne Co., 278 F. Supp. 162, 164 (S.D.N.Y. 1967) (preliminarily enjoining luggage distributor from infringing copyrighted fabric design).

166. 17 U.S.C. § 411(a); Fourth Est. Pub. Benefit Corp. v. Wall-Street.com, LLC, 139 S. Ct. 881 (2019). Before the Supreme Court's decision in *Fourth Estate*, the Ninth, Fifth, and Seventh Circuits had held that application to Copyright Office was sufficient to satisfy registration requirement, while the Tenth and Eleventh Circuits had found that the Copyright Office needed to approve or reject an application to satisfy the registration requirement. *See, e.g.*, Cosmetic Ideas, Inc. v. IAC/Interactivecorp, 606 F.3d 612, 614–15 (9th Cir. 2010) (listing cases on either side of the divide). District courts in the Second and Third Circuits have long followed the registration approach. *See, e.g.*, Patrick Collins Inc. v. Doe, 843 F. Supp. 2d 565, 568 (E.D. Pa. 2011); Lewinson v. Henry Holt & Co., 659 F. Supp. 2d 547 (S.D.N.Y. 2009).

167. NIMMER ON COPYRIGHT, *supra* note 75, § 7.16[B][6][c].

168. *Id.* § 7.16[B][6][d].

169. L.A. Printex Indus. Inc. v. Aeropostale, Inc., 676 F.3d 841, 846 (9th Cir. 2012); *see also* Laureyssens v. Idea Grp., Inc., 964 F.2d 131, 140 (2d Cir. 1992) (noting that copying may be established "by direct evidence of copying or by indirect evidence, including access to the copyrighted work, similarities that are probative of copying between the works, and expert testimony").

There have been some cases in which courts have concluded that an alleged copy is so *"strikingly similar"* that it is possible to infer copying even without any evidence of access.[170] These cases, however, tend to be rare and limited to extreme cases of otherwise inexplicable similarity. Many courts remain skeptical of allowing this leap.[171]

§ 4:7.1 Access

"Access" simply means that the alleged infringer had "the opportunity to view or copy plaintiff's work."[172] Although a bare possibility that an accused infringer had access to the copyrighted material is not sufficient, it is sufficient to show that there is a reasonable possibility that an alleged infringer had the chance to view the protected work.[173] Some courts permit a copyright holder to prove an alleged infringer had access to the copyrighted work through circumstantial evidence that either (1) a "chain of events" existed between the protected work and the alleged infringer's access to it, or (2) the original work was disseminated widely.[174]

Although analysis of whether a work is disseminated widely enough to constitute evidence of access is fact specific,[175] a work must be fairly ubiquitous in the relevant market to support an inference that an alleged infringer had access based simply on the work's widespread dissemination. In *Art Attacks Ink, LLC v. MGA Entertainment Inc.*,[176] Art Attacks, an airbrush art business that sold custom-made T-shirts depicting images of "Spoiled Brats," sued MGA, the maker of the "Bratz" dolls, for, among other things, infringing Art Attacks's copyright in the "Spoiled Brats" images. The Ninth Circuit held that a reasonable jury could not have concluded that the "Spoiled Brats" images were disseminated widely enough to support an inference that MGA had access to them, even though the images were displayed (1) at county fair booths and kiosks that millions of people attended,

---

170. *See* Unicolors, Inc. v. Unicolors, Inc., Urban Outfitters, Inc., 853 F.3d 980 (9th Cir. 2017) (citing Baxter v. MCA, Inc., 812 F.2d 421 (9th Cir. 1987), and Selle v. Gibb, 741 F.2d 896 (7th Cir. 1984)).

171. *See* Bouchat v. Balt. Ravens, Inc., 241 F.3d 350 (4th Cir. 2001), in which the majority and a dissenting judge dispute the operation of the doctrine.

172. *L.A. Printex Indus.*, 676 F.3d at 846 (internal quotation marks omitted).

173. *Id.* at 846–47; *see also* Art Attacks Ink, LLC v. MGA Entm't Inc., 581 F.3d 1138, 1143 (9th Cir. 2009) (affirming summary judgment for alleged infringer).

174. *L.A. Printex Indus.*, 676 F.3d at 846–47.

175. *Id.* at 847.

176. *Art Attacks Ink*, 581 F.3d at 1144.

(2) on people wearing the custom-made T-shirts, and (3) on Art Attacks's website.[177] The court reasoned that there was no evidence that a sufficient number of patrons saw the images at Art Attacks's fair booths, it only sold 2,000 T-shirts annually, and its website was not sufficiently accessible to the public for the work to be considered "widely disseminated."[178]

If, however, there is evidence that the work at issue was widely distributed in the relevant market and time period to support a conclusion of access, the plaintiff can meet its burden. In *L.A. Printex Industries Inc. v. Aeropostale, Inc.*, for example, the court held that a jury could reasonably believe that a fabric design was "widely disseminated" enough to support a presumption of access where plaintiff sold more than 50,000 feet of it in the same industry, in the same city, during the four years immediately preceding the alleged infringement.[179]

§ 4:7.2 Substantial Similarity

In addition to proving access, in order to establish an infringement claim by circumstantial evidence, the copyright holder must also prove that the two works are substantially similar.[180] There are several tests for determining whether an allegedly infringing work is substantially similar to a copyrighted work. Different courts may apply different tests depending on the case law of the governing circuit and the type of copyrighted works at issue (for example, courts have articulated different tests for computer software versus programming code).

[A] The Ordinary Observer and Related Tests

The Second Circuit, which includes courts in New York, applies an "ordinary observer test" in cases involving fabric designs.[181] Under the ordinary observer test, two works are substantially similar if "an average lay observer would recognize the alleged copy as having been

---

177. *Id.*

178. *Id.* at 1144–45.

179. *L.A. Printex Indus.*, 676 F.3d at 848 ("A reasonable jury could find that [the fabric design] was widely disseminated in the Los Angeles-area fabric industry, and hence that there was a 'reasonable possibility' that Defendants had an opportunity to view and copy L.A. Printex's design.") (internal citation omitted).

180. *See* Gibson Tex, Inc. v. Sears Roebuck & Co., 11. F. Supp. 2d 439, 443 (S.D.N.Y. 1998); *see also* Feist Publ'ns, Inc. v. Rural Tel. Serv. Co., 499 U.S. 340, 361 (1991).

181. Novelty Textile Mills v. Joan Fabrics Corp., 558 F.2d 1090, 1093 (2d Cir. 1977) (reversing denial of preliminary injunction against competing upholstery manufacturer because infringing fabric was substantially similar to protected design).

appropriated from the copyrighted work."[182] The copying "need not be of every detail so long as the copy is substantially similar to the copyrighted work."[183] Under the ordinary observer test, courts focus on the similarities, not the differences, between the works.[184]

Because courts have found that many copyrights in the fashion industry are thin because of the limited number of protectable ways to express an idea, as discussed above, those courts have applied a "modified" version of the ordinary observer test. In *Gibson Tex, Inc. v. Sears Roebuck & Co.*, for example, a federal court in New York applied a modified ordinary observer test to compare two fabric designs.[185] In that case, a fabric designer sued a department store and lingerie manufacturer for infringing its copyright in a particular fabric pattern.[186] The court altered the ordinary observer test because the fashion designer had based its design on a work in the public domain. The court explained that "where a plaintiff closely models its work after a design in the public domain, the showing of imitation must be stronger than usual and even small variations may protect a subsequent designer from infringement."[187] The court concluded that the "repeat width of the [defendant's] fabric [was] substantially different from the repeat width of [plaintiff's] fabric."[188] Based on that difference, the court refused to find that the department store and lingerie manufacturer had infringed the designer's copyright as a matter of law, because a reasonable jury could conclude that the department store and lingerie manufacturer had not copied the designer's fabric design.[189]

Similarly, in *Folio Impressions, Inc. v. Byer California*, the Second Circuit applied the ordinary observer test to find that one rose-print fabric design did not infringe a competing rose-print fabric design.[190] The court reasoned that even though the roses in both designs were similarly arranged on the fabric, the roses themselves differed in certain respects[191] and "by the rose's very nature, one artist's rendering of it will closely resemble another artist's work."[192] As a result, the court concluded that "an average lay observer would not recognize the

182. *Gibson Tex, Inc.*, 11 F. Supp. 2d at 443.
183. *Novelty Textile Mills*, 558 F.2d at 1093 (internal citation omitted).
184. *Id.*
185. *Gibson Tex, Inc.*, 11 F. Supp. 2d at 443.
186. *Id.* at 440–41.
187. *Id.* at 444.
188. *Id.*
189. *Id.*
190. *Folio Impressions*, 937 F.2d at 761.
191. *Id.* at 766.
192. *Id.*

alleged copy as having been appropriated from the copyrighted work" despite the similarities.[193]

In some cases, the Second Circuit has also articulated a "more discerning" test, in which a work with "both protectible and unprotectible" elements must be considered with an eye toward "whether the protectible elements, standing alone, are substantially similar."[194] The court, however, noted that the test remains focused on "the contested design's total concept and feel" such that the "excerpting, modifying, and arranging" of unprotectible elements may contribute to the overall similarity.[195] In a case concerning jewelry, for example, a district court concluded that a "large center stone" and "small crystal stones on thin chains" may not be protectible elements themselves but that the arrangement of these elements into an "uneven, asymmetric pattern . . . produces a specific 'look.'"[196] Because these choices were not dictated by "functionality or the choice of subject," the court concluded plaintiffs had plausibly alleged substantial similarity.[197]

[B] The Extrinsic/Intrinsic Tests

In the Ninth Circuit, which includes California, courts apply a different test—the two-part extrinsic/intrinsic test—to determine whether works are substantially similar. The extrinsic test "is an objective comparison of specific expressive elements; it focuses on the articulable similarities between the two works."[198] Where a high degree of access is shown, a lesser degree of substantial similarity is required.[199] If a copyright holder satisfies the extrinsic test—that there are articulable similarities between the two works—the jury (and, on rare occasion, the court) applies the intrinsic test.[200] At that stage, a "subjective comparison that focuses on whether the ordinary, reasonable audience

---

193. *Id.* The court also found that there was sufficient evidence to conclude that the second "design was an original work arrived at independently." *Id.* The Second Circuit reached a similar conclusion in Klauber Bros. v. Bon-Ton Stores, Inc., 557 F. App'x 77 (2d Cir. 2014), in which the court held that two lace designs both featuring flower and leaf patterns had a substantially different "aesthetic appeal" based on their arrangement.

194. Peter F. Gaito Architecture, LLC v. Simone Dev. Corp., 602 F.3d 57, 66 (2d Cir. 2010).

195. *Id.*

196. Int'l Diamond Imps., Inc. v. Oriental Gemco (N.Y.), Inc., 64 F. Supp. 3d 494, 512 (S.D.N.Y. 2014).

197. *Id.* at 522.

198. L.A. Printex Indus. Inc. v. Aeropostale, Inc., 676 F.3d 841, 848 (9th Cir. 2012) (internal quotations and citations omitted).

199. Smith v. Jackson, 84 F.3d 1213, 1218 (9th Cir. 1996).

200. *Id.* at 1218.

would find the works substantially similar in the total concept and feel of the works" is made.[201]

1. ***The Extrinsic Test.*** The Ninth Circuit compared a floral fabric design to an allegedly infringing T-shirt using the extrinsic test in *L.A. Printex Industries, Inc. v. Aeropostale, Inc.*[202] In that case, a fabric printing company sued an apparel wholesaler and a mall-based retailer for infringing the fabric designer's floral design on T-shirts.[203] To apply the extrinsic test for substantial similarity, the court distinguished between protectable and unprotectable elements of the design and examined "the similarities in [the design's] objective details in appearance, including, but not limited to, the subject matter, shapes, colors, materials, and arrangements of the representations."[204] The court noted that both designs contained: (1) two types of small bouquets of flowers, with one featuring the largest flower in profile view, and the other featuring the largest flower in an open-face view and both emerging from three buds; (2) small three-leave branches interspersed between two types of bouquets with similar shapes and numbers of flower petals; (3) flower bouquets arranged at similar angles; and (4) similar spatial combinations of the bouquets and branches on a grid of similar scale and layout.[205] In addition to these design similarities, the court also highlighted markedly similar color arrangements between the works, which is probative of copying under both Ninth and Second Circuit case law.[206]

   Although the flowers, stems, and leaves in the defendants' design were less detailed than the comparable elements in plaintiff's design, the court concluded that a rational jury could find: (1) the differences were inconsequential and the product of the fabric design process, and (2) the lack of detail was the common result of replicating a design with lower quality techniques and machinery.[207] Taking these comparisons into

201. *L.A. Printex Indus.*, 676 F.3d at 848 (internal quotation marks and citations omitted).
202. *Id.* at 849.
203. *Id.* at 845.
204. *Id.* at 849 (internal quotation marks omitted).
205. *Id.* at 851.
206. *Id.* at 851; *see also* Spotra Fabrics Corp. v. Stafford Knitting Mills, Inc., 490 F.2d 1092, 1094 (2d Cir. 1974) ("The appearance in one of defendant's fabrics of colors identical to plaintiff's is additional evidence of actual copying, as well as another factor leading to the conclusion that the aesthetic appeal of the fabrics is the same.") (internal quotation marks, citation, and alteration omitted).
207. *L.A. Printex Indus.*, 676 F.3d at 851.

consideration, the Ninth Circuit concluded that "the objective similarities in the expressive elements of Defendants' design and [the protected design] present a genuine dispute of material fact under the extrinsic test" such that a jury could conclude that defendant infringed the protected design.[208] The court of appeals thus reversed the lower court's finding for defendants as a matter of law and permitted the case to proceed to the jury for analysis of the works under the intrinsic test.

2. ***The Intrinsic Test.*** The Ninth Circuit's intrinsic test evaluates "whether the ordinary, reasonable person would find the total concept and feel of the [compared] works to be substantially similar."[209] In contrast to the extrinsic test, which requires a methodical and "analytic dissection of a work's elements," to which expert testimony is often appropriate, the intrinsic test excludes such expert analysis and dissection and instead "requires that the work's elements be viewed as a whole."[210] Although juries are often best suited to apply the intrinsic test, "where the works are so overwhelmingly identical that the possibility of independent creation is precluded," a court may apply the intrinsic test to find infringement as a matter of law without submitting the question to the jury.[211]

In *Spectravest, Inc. v. Mervyn's Inc.*, a federal court in California applied the intrinsic test in the context of an allegedly infringed "puzzle-teddy" fabric print.[212] In that case, a clothing manufacturer designed and copyrighted a puzzle-teddy fabric design (consisting of rows of flattened teddy bear shapes interlocking like a puzzle) for a line of girls' sweatshirts and dresses.[213] A buyer for the defendant retailer purchased one of the sweatshirts and gave it to the retailer, which used it as a model for

---

208. *Id.* at 852.

209. Express, LLC v. Fetish Grp., Inc., 424 F. Supp. 2d 1211, 1228 (C.D. Cal. 2006) (granting summary judgment to plaintiff copyright holder for defendant's infringement of a camisole fabric design).

210. *Id.*

211. *Id.* (granting copyright holder's motion for summary judgment on infringement claim because "there can be no question that the embroidery designs on the . . . Tunic and the Express Long Camisole are virtually identical"). *See also Unicolors*, 853 F.3d at 987 (concluding that "[w]here the extrinsic similarity is so strong that the works are near duplicates save for superficial differences," a court may properly find "so overwhelmingly similar" that summary judgment is warranted).

212. Spectravest, Inc. v. Mervyn's Inc., 673 F. Supp. 1486 (C.D. Cal. 1987).

213. *Id.* at 1488.

its own design.[214] Plaintiff clothing manufacturer sued for copyright infringement of its puzzle-teddy fabric print. The retailer contended that the designs were *not* substantially similar under the intrinsic test and submitted expert testimony as to their differences.[215] But because analytic dissection and expert analysis is inappropriate under the intrinsic test, the court refused to consider the proffered testimony.[216] Instead, the court compared the overall look and feel of the designs and found that the two puzzle-teddy designs were substantially similar. In particular, the court noted that: (1) the outstretched teddy bears and lines connecting them were "virtually indistinguishable to the viewer," (2) the designs had the same primary colors, and (3) simply stated, the two designs both "look[ed] like [the copyrighted] puzzle-teddies."[217]

In some cases, a higher standard of similarity can be required. In particular, when copyright protection is "broad" (that is, there is a "wide range of expression" for an idea), the "substantially similar" test applies; but when protection is thin (that is, there is "only a narrow range of expression"), the alleged copy must be "virtually identical" to infringe.[218] For example, in *Sophia & Chloe, Inc. v. Brighton Collectibles, LLC*, the majority of the court concluded that an original earring deserved only "thin" protection for its arrangement of "three common, unprotectable elements: (1) the henna symbol for the word kiss; (2) the image of the Buddha; and (3) the teardrop shape."[219] The judges reasoned that because "there are only a few ways to design an earring that incorporates those three elements," the "virtually identical" standard should apply.[220] By contrast, the dissenting judge concluded that broad protection should apply, citing testimony by the designer that she could have varied the earring in size, number of pendants, bracket shape, and dimension. The line between "thin" and "broad" protection is not, therefore, always easily discernible, particularly in fashion designs that may consist of independently unprotectible elements.

---

214. *Id.* at 1489.
215. *Id.* at 1489, 1491.
216. *Id.* at 1492.
217. *Id.*
218. Mattel, Inc. v. MGA Entm't, Inc., 616 F.3d 904 (9th Cir. 2010).
219. Sophia & Chloe, Inc. v. Brighton Collectibles, LLC, 708 F. App'x 460, 461 (9th Cir. 2018).
220. *Id.* at 462.

[C] Other Substantial Similarity Tests

Courts have used a number of other tests to determine whether two works are substantially similar outside the context of fashion. While these tests have not yet been applied to works in the fashion industry, a few are briefly addressed below.

1. ***The Abstractions Test.*** The abstractions test has existed in American jurisprudence since 1930. Judge Learned Hand originally formulated the test in a case involving a play. He explained:

    > Upon any work and especially upon a play a great number of patterns of increasing generality will fit equally well, as more and more of the incident is left out. The last may perhaps be no more than the most general statement of what the play is about and at times consist of only its title, but there is a point in this series of abstractions where they are no longer protected since otherwise the playwright could prevent the use of his ideas to which apart from their expression his property is never extended.[221]

    The abstractions test—while perhaps philosophically compelling—is practically difficult to administer in the context of works of fashion and may result in inconsistent decisions because it does not specify the point in the series of abstractions at which copyright no longer offers protection. However, at least one court recently concluded that "striking similarity" had been demonstrated because the copied design was a "highly original" "random collection of shapes and patterns without any attempt to imitate real life images such as flowers or animals."[222] Because of its "arbitrary, abstract design, the level of similarity is both surprising and telling," and based on that alone, the court concluded "it could not possibly have been the product of independent creation."[223]

2. ***The Successive Filtering Approach.*** Another substantial similarity test—the successive filtering approach, which has been used in computer software cases—bears some resemblance to the discerning observer test employed in the Second Circuit and the extrinsic prong of the Ninth Circuit's test. Under this approach, before determining whether works are substantially similar, the court first "eliminate[s] all non-protectable elements

221. Nichols v. Universal Pictures Co., 45 F.2d 119, 121 (2d Cir. 1930).
222. Standard Fabrics Int'l, Inc. v. Dress Barn, Inc., No 2:15-cv-08437-ODW (PJW), 2017 WL 240072 (C.D. Cal. Jan. 19, 2017).
223. *Id.* at *3.

from consideration."[224] The court then analyzes only the substantial similarity of the remaining protectable expressions (not the whole work).[225] This test may prove difficult to meet in the context of fashion considering how few elements of garments may be protectable. As discussed in section 4:3.2 above, after *Star Athletica*, the only original elements that garner protection are those that can be perceived as separable from the functional article and that could exist as protectible art in another medium.

[D] The Use of Characters in Apparel

One question that comes up in the apparel industry surprisingly frequently is whether copyright law prevents a seller of T-shirts or other apparel from marketing products that include images that are subject to copyright, such as popular film or cartoon characters. The answer, however, is fairly straightforward. For popular works like cartoons or movies that are subject to a valid copyright, a component of that copyright protection extends to the characters themselves, to the extent that such characters are sufficiently distinctive.[226] Thus, when a company affixes images of those characters on T-shirts or other similar products, it can be held liable for copyright infringement.[227] This is true even when some renderings of the same characters have fallen into the public domain for one reason or another.[228]

The Eighth Circuit has noted, however, that the law recognizes a spectrum from original, fanciful characters (who are the most protected), to characters that do not display consistent, distinctive visual characteristics (where the protection that copyright law affords may be more thin).[229] Where a character's appearance varies widely from image to image, courts may limit their protection to copies of a precise copyright-protected image.[230] And where an image does not display

224. Autoskill, Inc. v. Nat'l Educ. Support Sys., Inc., 793 F. Supp. 1557, 1565 (S.D.N.Y. 2001).

225. *Id.* at 1565.

226. *See, e.g.*, Gaiman v. McFarlane, 360 F.3d 644, 661 (7th Cir. 2004) ("[A] stock character, once he was drawn and named and given speech [in a comic book series] became sufficiently distinctive to be copyrightable."); Olson v. Nat'l Broad. Co., 855 F.2d 1446, 1452 (9th Cir.1988) ("copyright protection may be afforded to characters visually depicted in a television series or in a movie" for "characters who are especially distinctive").

227. *See, e.g.*, Warner Bros. Entm't v. X One X Prods., 644 F.3d 584 (8th Cir. 2011).

228. *Id.* at 602–04.

229. *Id.* at 599–600.

230. *Id.* at 601.

distinctive character or visual traits, but only visual characteristics typical to general archetypes such as cats and mice, copyright law will not prohibit the sale of products that display similar images.[231] The use of an image of a famous character may, however, raise separate trademark issues if the product is likely to cause confusion as to source or approval.[232]

One effective way to avoid copyright liability for use of a character on an item of apparel is to secure a license from the property's owner. The owner may, however, be unwilling to grant a license or may demand a high royalty in exchange for the license if the character is popular. Resources like Licensing.org provide information on comparable deals in the licensing industry and specifics about particular licensors and licensing agents.[233]

§ 4:8 Defenses

As discussed in section 4:7 above, in order to succeed on a copyright infringement action, a plaintiff must prove that it owns a valid copyright and that the alleged infringer copied the work. The alleged infringer, on the other hand, may defend against a copyright infringement lawsuit by producing evidence that contradicts either or both of these required elements. In addition to contesting these elements, though, an alleged infringer may assert other applicable affirmative defenses. Two of the most important of those defenses—fair use and *de minimis non curat lex*—are addressed below.

§ 4:8.1 *Fair Use*

One of the most important limitations on the law of copyright is the doctrine of "fair use," a "privilege in others than the owner of copyright to use the copyrighted material in a reasonable manner without his consent."[234] Much has been written about the fair use doctrine, and a full examination of it is beyond the scope of this chapter. A brief overview of the salient points of the fair use defense, however, merits discussion.

As a general matter, the fair use defense protects certain uses of copyrighted material. The fair use doctrine balances copyright protection with other protectable interests such as First Amendment rights, specifically "the exclusive rights of a copyright holder with the

---

231. *Id.* at 600.
232. *See generally supra* chapter 2.
233. *See* International Licensing Industry Merchandisers' Association, Licensing.org & The LIMA Directory, https://www.licensing.org.
234. HORACE G. BALL, THE LAW OF COPYRIGHT AND LITERARY PROPERTY 260 (M. Bender & Co. 1944).

public's interest in dissemination of information affecting areas of universal concern, such as art, science, and industry."[235]

Title 17 of the U.S. Code, section 107—which was intended to codify, not enlarge or alter, the common law on fair use[236]—lists several illustrative types of fair uses, including criticism, comment, news reporting, teaching (even if it requires multiple classroom copies of a protected work), scholarship, and research. It sets forth four factors to be considered in determining whether a particular use of copyrighted material will escape liability as a fair use. They are:

1. the purpose and character of the use, including whether such use is of a commercial nature or is for nonprofit educational purposes;
2. the nature of the copyrighted work;
3. the amount and substantiality of the portion used in relation to the copyrighted work as a whole; and
4. the effect of the use upon the potential market for, or on value of, the copyrighted work.[237]

Because section 107 does not contain bright-line rules and because it was intended to codify existing common law, judicial opinions remain particularly important in evaluating fair use defense arguments. The Supreme Court has addressed the fair use doctrine several times. In the seminal case in this area, *Campbell v. Acuff-Rose Music, Inc.*,[238] the Court explained that the four factors listed in section 107 must be considered together and that the first factor—"the purpose and character of the use, including whether such use is of a commercial nature or is for nonprofit educational purposes"—is the most important consideration.[239] The *Campbell* court explained that the reason courts must evaluate the purpose and character of the use "is to see . . . whether the new work merely 'supersede[s] the objects' of the original creation, or instead adds something new, with a further purpose or different character, altering the first with new expression, meaning, or message . . . ." Although a use does not have to be "transformative" to be protected by the doctrine of fair use, the goal of copyright—to promote science and the arts—is generally furthered

235. Wainwright Sec., Inc. v. Wall St. Transcript Corp., 558 F.2d 91, 94–95 (2d Cir. 1977).
236. NIMMER ON COPYRIGHT, *supra* note 75, § 13.05.
237. 17 U.S.C. § 107.
238. Campbell v. Acuff-Rose Music, Inc., 510 U.S. 569 (1994).
239. *Id.* at 578–79.

by the creation of transformative works. As a result, uses that can be characterized as transformative are more likely to be protected.[240]

In *On Davis v. The Gap, Inc.*, the Second Circuit addressed the fair use defense in the context of the fashion industry. In that case, Davis, the designer of copyrighted nonfunctional eyewear, sued The Gap for infringement because one of the models in a Gap advertisement was depicted wearing Davis's eyewear.[241] The Gap argued that the fair use defense protected its advertisement.[242]

The court rejected The Gap's argument, reasoning that there was "nothing transformative about The Gap's presentation of Davis's copyrighted work."[243] On the contrary, The Gap's advertisement showed models wearing Davis's "Onoculii" eyewear in the manner Davis intended it to be worn (as decorative eyeglasses) and it looked like an advertisement Davis himself may have sponsored to promote his Onoculii.[244] Moreover, because the use was not transformative, the commercial nature of the use gained increased importance under the first factor as well.[245] Accordingly, the most determinative factor for evaluating fair use defenses—the purpose and character of the use—weighed against a finding that the use was fair.[246]

The *Davis* court concluded that the second factor—the nature of the copyrighted work[247]—also weighed against a finding of fair use because Davis's copyrighted work was an artistic creation embodying "the core of the copyright's protective purposes."[248] The court concluded that the third factor—"the amount and substantiality of the portion used in relation to the copyrighted work as a whole"[249]—also weighed against a finding of fair use because Gap's advertisement presented "a head-on full view of Davis's piece, centered and prominently featured."[250] Finally, the court evaluated the fourth factor—"the effect of the use upon the potential market for or value of the copyrighted work."[251] The court evaluated this factor in light of its determination

---

240. *Id.* at 579 (internal citations omitted).
241. On Davis v. The Gap, Inc., 246 F.3d 152 (2d Cir. 2001).
242. *Id.* at 173.
243. *Id.* at 174.
244. *Id.*
245. *Id.* at 175 (citing Sony Corp. of Am. v. Universal City Studios, Inc., 464 U.S. 417, 449 (1984)).
246. *On Davis*, 246 F.3d at 175.
247. 17 U.S.C. § 107(2).
248. *On Davis*, 246 F.3d at 175 (citing Campbell v. Acuff-Rose Music, Inc., 510 U.S. 569, 586 (1994)).
249. 17 U.S.C. § 107(3).
250. *On Davis*, 246 F.3d at 175.
251. 17 U.S.C. § 107(4).

on the first factor that The Gap's use was not transformative,[252] and it concluded that the final factor also weighed against The Gap because The Gap could have licensed (for a fee) Davis's eyewear rather than including it in its advertisements without compensating Davis. Additionally, as the court noted, The Gap's failure to compensate Davis for its use may have further harmed Davis by diminishing his opportunity to license his design to others.[253] As the *Davis* case illustrates, the fair use analysis tends to be fact-intensive and unique to the particulars of the asserted work and the context of the alleged infringement.

§ 4:8.2 The De Minimis *Doctrine*

The doctrine *de minimis non curat lex* is another important defense to copyright infringement actions. The *de minimis* doctrine provides that "the law will not impose legal consequences" where unauthorized copying of protected matter was trivial.[254] Although the *de minimis* doctrine is not frequently applied in published judicial decisions (because suits are rarely brought over trivial instances of copying), it is an important doctrine under copyright law and it has been addressed in the fashion context.

In *On Davis v. The Gap, Inc.*, for example, The Gap argued that its use of Davis's eyeglasses was also *de minimis* because in the context of the overall advertisement, the fact that one model was wearing Davis's eyewear was trivial.[255] The court rejected The Gap's argument because the infringing item was highly noticeable.[256] Specifically, the court found that the infringement was not trivial because "Davis's design and concept are strikingly bizarre; it is startling to see the wearer peering at us over his Onoculii."[257] The court also noted that "eyes are naturally a focal point of attention, and because the wearer is at the center of the group . . . the viewer's gaze is powerfully drawn to Davis's creation."[258] Furthermore, the advertisement created the impression that the models in the advertisement "have been outfitted from top to bottom, including eyewear, with Gap merchandise."[259] Based on all of this, the court concluded that The Gap's use of Davis's eyewear was not *de minimis*.[260]

---

252. *On Davis*, 246 F.3d at 176.
253. *Id.*
254. Ringgold v. Black Entm't TV, 126 F.3d 70, 74 (2d Cir. 1977).
255. *On Davis*, 246 F.3d at 172–73.
256. *Id.*
257. *Id.*
258. *Id.*
259. *Id.*
260. *Id.*

§ 4:9 Remedies

Under the Copyright Act, the following remedies are available to a party that has proved that its copyright has been infringed: (1) injunctive relief, (2) impoundment and disposition (order of destruction), (3) actual or statutory damages and profits, and (4) costs and attorney's fees.[261] This section will review each of these remedies in turn.

§ 4:9.1 *Injunctive Relief*

The Copyright Act permits courts of competent jurisdiction to "grant temporary and final injunctions on such terms as it may deem reasonable to prevent or restrain infringement of a copyright."[262] Despite the Copyright Act's grant of authority, however, in light of the Supreme Court's holding that an injunction against patent infringement must be supported by an evaluation of the factors generally applicable to injunctions under the Federal Rules of Civil Procedure, before granting a permanent injunction, courts generally require a copyright holder to demonstrate that:

1. it has suffered an irreparable injury;
2. remedies available at law, such as monetary damages, are inadequate to compensate for that injury;
3. considering the balance of hardships between the plaintiff and defendant, a remedy in equity is warranted; and
4. the public interest would not be disserved by a permanent injunction.[263]

Federal Courts of Appeals have offered slight variations on this test.[264]

---

261. *See* 17 U.S.C. §§ 502, 503, 504, 505.

262. 17 U.S.C. § 502.

263. *See* Miche Bag, LLC v. Ayers, No. 4-09-3261-TLW-SVH, 2010 WL 5141662, at *9 (D.S.C. Sept. 22, 2010) (citing eBay Inc. v. MercExchange, L.L.C., 547 U.S. 388 (2006)) (recommending that the district court permanently enjoin a defendant boutique from directly or indirectly infringing on plaintiff manufacturers' rights in certain copyrighted purses, handbags, and related products).

264. *See, e.g.*, Cmty. of Christ Copyright Corp. v. Devon Park Restoration Branch of Jesus Christ's Church, 634 F.3d 1005 (8th Cir. 2011) ("To obtain a permanent injunction, [the moving party] is required to show: (1) its actual success on the merits; (2) that it faces irreparable harm; (3) that the harm to it outweighs any possible harm to others; and (4) that an injunction serves the public interest.") (internal citation omitted); *see also* adidas Am., Inc. v. Skechers USA, Inc., 890 F.3d 747, 761 (9th Cir. 2018) (in a trademark infringement case, requiring "concrete evidence" of irreparable harm to grant a preliminary injunction).

§ 4:9.2 Impoundment and Disposition

A party whose copyright has been infringed may seek the impoundment and destruction of the infringing articles. Under the Copyright Act, "the court may order the impounding [of certain infringing articles], on such terms as it may deem reasonable . . . [and] [a]s part of a final judgment or decree, the court may order the destruction or other reasonable disposition of all [articles] . . . found to have been made or used in violation of the copyright owner's exclusive rights[.]"[265] In *Miche Bag, LLC v. Ayers*, for example, the magistrate judge recommended awarding this relief. In that case, also discussed above, a defendant had infringed a number of plaintiff's copyrights in purses, handbags, and related products. The magistrate judge recommended that the defendant "be ordered to destroy all products, packaging, merchandise, advertisements, or other materials that violate the plaintiff's [copyrights]."[266]

§ 4:9.3 Damages and Profits

A copyright infringer is liable for either: (a) the copyright owner's actual damages and any additional profits of the infringer, or (b) statutory damages.[267] The infringed party may select between the two types of damages to best make it whole. Substantive differences between them and how they may be recovered (both of which are addressed below) make the selection of the damages remedy an important decision for an aggrieved copyright owner.

[A] Actual Damages and Profits

The Copyright Act provides that a "copyright owner is entitled to recover the actual damages suffered by him or her as a result of the infringement, and any profits of the infringer."[268] But the copyright owner should not be awarded a double recovery of both its own damages and the infringer's profits, to the extent they overlap.[269] Calculating the profits earned by the infringer is a relatively simple task. The copyright owner need only "present proof [] of the infringer's gross revenue."[270] It is the infringer who is "required to prove his or her deductible expenses and the elements of profit attributable to factors other than the copyrighted work."[271]

---

265. 17 U.S.C. § 503.
266. *Miche Bag, LLC*, 2010 WL 5141662, at *11.
267. 17 U.S.C. § 504.
268. 17 U.S.C. § 504(b).
269. *Id.*
270. *Id.*
271. *Id.*

If a copyright holder prefers to recover the actual damages it suffered, on the other hand, it must prove "with reasonable probability the existence of a causal connection between defendant's infringement and loss of anticipated revenue."[272] Once it has done so, "the burden properly shifts to the infringer to show that this damage would have occurred had there been no taking of the copyrighted expression."[273]

Courts in the Second Circuit have permitted a copyright holder to calculate the actual damages it suffered based on either: (1) lost profits that plaintiff would have realized from sales to customers who purchased from both plaintiff and defendant; or (2) lost profits based on the difference between the sales of the infringed item and the average sales of other models sold by the plaintiff, whichever sum is larger.[274] For example, in *Stevens Linen Associates, Inc. v. Mastercraft Corp.*, the Second Circuit held that a trial court should have used one of the above methods to calculate the copyright holder's actual damages from infringement of a copyright in a furniture fabric design.[275]

Nevertheless, a copyright holder may prove its actual damages through other evidence, including its own direct testimony as long as it is not too speculative. In *Stevens*, plaintiff fabric designer's Vice President and Director of Design offered oral sales projections for the infringed product as evidence that it would have sold as much fabric as the infringer. Noting that under other circumstances such testimony "might support an award for damages," the court ruled that in the circumstances of that case, the testimony was too speculative to support an award because it was "devoid of documentary support, and the witness furnished the court with no basis for the projections and hence no basis on which the court could evaluate the validity of the projections."[276]

[B] Statutory Damages

The owner of an infringed work "may elect, at any time before final judgment is rendered, to recover, instead of actual damages and profits, an award of statutory damages for all infringements involved in the action[.]"[277] It may be wise for a party to elect statutory damages

---

272. Key W. Hand Print Fabrics, Inc. v. Serbin, Inc., 269 F. Supp. 605, 613 (N.D. Tex. 1998).
273. Harper & Row, Publishers, Inc. v. Nation Enters., 471 U.S. 539, 567 (1985).
274. *See* Stevens Linen Assocs., Inc. v. Mastercraft Corp., 656 F.2d 11, 15 (2d Cir. 1981).
275. *Id.*
276. *Id.*
277. 17 U.S.C. § 504(c)(1).

where (1) it does not have (or cannot prove) actual damages, or (2) if the statutory damage award is simply more robust. The court may generally award statutory damages "in a sum of not less than $750 or more than $30,000" per infringed work.[278] If the infringement is committed willfully, then the court has discretion to increase the statutory damages award to "a sum not more than $150,000" per infringed copyright.[279] In *Miche Bag*, discussed above, the defendant boutique failed to respond to the civil action and continued to sell infringing articles after receiving plaintiff's cease and desist letters.[280] The magistrate judge therefore found the infringement to be willful and recommended statutory damages in the amount of $50,000 per infringed copyright.[281]

In setting the appropriate level of statutory damages, courts are asked to consider whether the infringement was willful or innocent, whether the infringer reasonably believed its use was a fair use, and the role of the specific defendant in the infringement.[282]

§ 4:9.4 Costs and Attorneys' Fees

The Copyright Act gives courts discretionary authority to award a prevailing party full costs and reasonable attorneys' fees stemming from an action to enforce a copyright.[283] In deciding whether to grant such fees, courts consider factors such as: (1) the motivation of the parties; (2) the objective reasonableness of the legal and factual positions advanced; (3) the need in particular circumstances to advance considerations of compensation and deterrence; and (4) any other relevant factor presented.[284]

The Supreme Court explained in *Kirtsaeng v. John Wiley & Sons, Inc.*, that courts awarding fees under the Copyright Act should first also consider whether the party seeking fees "well advance[d] the Copyright Act's goals" of "enriching the general public through access to creative works" and "encouraging and rewarding authors' creations

---

278. *Id.*
279. 17 U.S.C. § 504(c)(2).
280. Miche Bag, LLC v. Ayers, No. 4-09-3261-TLW-SVH, 2010 WL 5141662, at *4 (D.S.C. Sept. 22, 2010).
281. *Id.* at *5. *See also* Nintendo of Am. v. Ketchum, 830 F. Supp. 1443, 1445 (M.D. Fla. 1993) (awarding "statutory damages in the amount of $2,000 for each of the twelve infringements, under 17 U.S.C. § 504(c)(2), for a total of $24,000").
282. 17 U.S.C. § 504(c).
283. 17 U.S.C. § 505.
284. *Miche Bag, LLC*, 2010 WL 5141662, at *5 (citing Superior Form Builders, Inc. v. Dan Chase Taxidermy Supply Co., 74 F.3d 488, 489 (4th Cir. 1996)).

while also enabling others to build on that work."[285] To ensure that parties only receive attorneys' fees when they have advanced those roles, the Court also explained that courts should give "substantial weight to the reasonableness of a losing party's position" when deciding whether the losing party should also pay the prevailing party's fees.[286] However, "objective reasonableness" should be "only an important factor in assessing fee applications—not the controlling one," and a court may award fees even though the losing party offered reasonable arguments (or, conversely, deny fees even though the losing party made unreasonable ones)."[287]

Courts have awarded fees and costs in the fashion context. The magistrate judge in *Miche Bag*, for example, recommended an award of $384.50 in costs and $17,516 in attorneys' fees to the plaintiff as the prevailing party under the Copyright Act.[288] § 4: In contrast, the Court of Appeals for the Second Circuit applied the Supreme Court's *Kirtsaeng* standard in affirming a district court's decision to *deny* a fee award to a copyright defendant, even though the defendant contended that it had only sold an obvious parody of the plaintiff's well known handbags.[289] The court noted that an award of fees was not appropriate given that the "copyright claim [at issue] turned on the application of a fact-intensive, multifactor test" in which "one prong of the inquiry, commerciality, favored" the plaintiff.[290]

285. Kirtsaeng v. John Wiley & Sons, Inc., 136 S. Ct. 1979, 986 (2016).
286. *Id.* at 1985.
287. *Id.* at 1988.
288. *Miche Bag, LLC*, 2010 WL 5141662, at *11.
289. Louis Vuitton Malletier, S.A. v. My Other Bag, Inc., No. 18-293-cv, 2019 WL 1223089 (2d Cir. Mar. 15, 2019), *aff'g* No. 14 Civ. 3419 (JMF), 2018 WL 317850 (S.D.N.Y. Jan. 8, 2018).
290. *Id.* The authors' firm represented Louis Vuitton in this matter.

Chapter 5

International Design Protections

§ 5:1 Introduction
§ 5:2 The European Union
§ 5:3 Geneva Act of the Hague Agreement Concerning the International Registration of Industrial Designs
§ 5:4 Individual European Countries
  § 5:4.1 France
  § 5:4.2 United Kingdom
  § 5:4.3 Italy
§ 5:5 Non-European Countries
  § 5:5.1 Japan
  § 5:5.2 China
  § 5:5.3 Australia
  § 5:5.4 New Zealand
  § 5:5.5 Canada
  § 5:5.6 Singapore
  § 5:5.7 India
  § 5:5.8 United Arab Emirates
§ 5:6 Conclusion

§ 5:1 Introduction

The fashion industry is global and many of its participants act in various countries around the world. In spite of efforts to harmonize copyright protection such as the Berne Convention, differences persist in the protections various countries afford to fashion.

Perhaps the most important of these distinctions is that most of the industrialized world—unlike the United States—recognizes a distinct intellectual property discipline that protects fashion or other types of industrial designs. The scope, criteria, duration, and remedies for these protections tend to vary by country. But one thing that these design protections have in common is that they do tend to differ from the types of protections afforded by trademarks, patents, and copyrights discussed in the preceding chapters.

This chapter provides a brief introduction to design protections in a selection of key jurisdictions.

§ 5:2 The European Union[1]

The European Union offers fashion designs much stronger protection than the United States. In 2002, the European Union implemented the "Community design" system, which applied uniform design protections across all member countries.[2] The purpose of the system is to help fight piracy and counterfeiting, and "foster creativity and innovation by making it easier to protect designs throughout the [European Union] with a single application."[3]

Under the Community design system, a "design" is "the appearance of the whole or part of a product resulting from the features of, in particular, the lines, contours, colors, shape, texture and/or materials of the product itself and/or its ornamentation."[4] The Community system affords protection to both designs and to products that utilize such designs. A "product" can comprise packaging, typeface, symbols, and component parts of a larger product. To qualify for protection, designs must be "new" and have an "individual character." A design is "new" if no identical design has been produced prior to filing (for registered Community designs) and before it became available (for unregistered Community designs).[5] A design has individual character if it is apparent to an informed user that they are different from designs that existed previously.[6] There is no geographic restriction when

1. The European Union includes Germany, France, Italy, Belgium, the Netherlands, Luxembourg, Denmark, Ireland, Greece, Spain, Portugal, Austria, Finland, Sweden, the Czech Republic, Estonia, Cyprus, Latvia, Lithuania, Hungary, Malta, Poland, Slovenia, Slovakia, Bulgaria, Romania, and Croatia, with the United Kingdom debating and negotiating the terms of exit as of the date of this writing.
2. Council Regulation 6/2002, http://eur-lex.europa.eu/LexUriServ/LexUriServ.do?uri=CELEX:32002R0006:EN:NOT.
3. Press Release, Office for Harmonization in the Internal Mkt., Industrial Property: Commission Sets Registration Fees for "Community Designs" (Ref. No. IP/02/1926, Dec. 19, 2002), http://europa.eu/rapid/press-release_IP-02-1926_en.htm.
4. Council Regulation 6/2002, art. 3(a), 2002, art. 3, 2001 O.J. (L. 3) 1, 4 (EC).
5. Art 5 CDR.
6. Press Release, Office for Harmonization in the Internal Mkt., Commission Welcomes Adoption of Regulation on Community Designs (Ref. No. IP/01/1803, Dec. 12, 2001), http://europa.eu/rapid/press-release_IP-01-1803_en.htm?locale=en.

deciding if a design is "new," and a worldwide assessment is made. However, a comparison is not drawn with designs that "could not reasonably have become known in the normal course of business."[7] A design has the requisite individual character if "the overall impression produced on an informed user viewing the design clearly differs from that produced on him by the existing design corpus," while taking into consideration the nature of the product, the industry to which it belongs, and the designer's freedom in developing the design.[8] When evaluating whether a design has an individual character, courts look at the design as a whole, not its constituent elements.[9] Aspects of the design that are purely functional cannot be protected under this regime.

A holder of a Community design has the exclusive right "to use the design concerned and to prevent any third party from using it anywhere within the European Union."[10] The legislation does not, however, protect designs that are contrary to public policy or "accepted principles of morality."[11]

Although registration is not required for protection under the Community design system, registered designs receive additional protections.[12] Unregistered designs are protected for three years from the date the design was first made available to the public within the EU (by being published, exhibited, used in trade, or otherwise disclosed to the industry in which it belongs).[13] Registered designs,

---

7. Art 7.1 CDR.
8. Council Regulation 6/2002, [preface], art. 14.
9. Karen Millen Ltd. v. Dunnes Stores, [2008] 2 I.L.R.M. 368 (H. Ct.) (Ir.) (Rejecting defendants' method of comparing individual parts of plaintiff's design to prior designs, rather than comparing the overall impression of the whole design, to assess whether it was a protectable Community design), http://curia.europa.eu/juris/document/document.jsf;jsessionid=9ea7d2dc30d503def715a1f242f387a7a2fc3a1317eb.e34KaxiLc3qMb40Rch0SaxuSb3r0?text=&docid=153817&pageIndex=0&doclang=EN&mode=lst&dir=&occ=first&part=1&cid=156339.
10. Press Release, Office for Harmonization in the Internal Mkt., Industrial Property: EU-Wide Registration of Designs Moves Closer (Ref. No. IP/02/1535, Oct. 22, 2002), http://europa.eu/rapid/press-release_IP-02-1535_en.htm?locale=EN.
11. Council Regulation 6/2002, art. 9, 2001 O.J. (L 3) 5 (EC); *cf.* JAPAN EXTERNAL TRADE ORG., INVESTING IN JAPAN [hereinafter INVESTING IN JAPAN], § 5.7.1 (Japan's design law refusing to protect "designs that may breach public order and morals"), https://www.jetro.go.jp/en/invest/setting_up/section5/page7.html.
12. Those who wish to register their designs under the Community design system must file an application with the Office for Harmonization in the Internal Market (OHIM) in Alicante, Spain.
13. Council Regulation 6/2002, art. 11, 1.

by contrast, are protected for an initial period of five years from the date of registration, with four potential successive five-year renewal terms, for a maximum of twenty-five years of protection.[14] If a renewal is missed, it is possible to restore the design to the register in exceptional circumstances where renewal was missed due to unforeseeable circumstances.[15] If the registered design is reinstated, it will be treated as if renewal was not missed (that is, there is no registration gap). While unregistered designs are protected only against deliberate copying, registered designs are protected against both deliberate copying and the independent development of similar designs.[16] In addition, courts presume the validity of a registered Community design, whereas the owner of an unregistered design must produce evidence that the design qualifies for protection under the Community design system.[17]

To determine whether an alleged copy infringes a Community design holder's exclusive rights, courts compare the overall commercial impression of the two designs from the perspective of an informed user.[18] An informed user has general knowledge of the product or the industry to which the product belongs; (s)he is neither a person on the street nor a designer.[19] For registered Community designs, unless an informed user's overall impression of two designs is different, the later design infringes the Community design. Although an unregistered Community design holder must also prove that his design was actually copied, courts will infer the requisite copying if the two designs are sufficiently similar.[20] Nonetheless, an alleged infringer may rebut the inference by proving that it independently created the later work. Additionally, the Community design regime provides for fair use exceptions for personal, educational, and experimental uses

---

14. *Id.* art. 12.
15. Art 67 CDR.
16. *Id.* art. 19 [1, 2].
17. *Id.* art. 85(2).
18. Council Regulation 6/2002, art. 10; *see also* J. Choo (Jersey) Ltd. v. Towerstone Ltd., [2008] EWHC (Ch) 346 (Eng.) (applying the overall impression test to conclude that handbag infringed Jimmy Choo's unregistered community design).
19. J. Choo (Jersey) Ltd. v. Towerstone Ltd., [2008] EWHC (Ch) 346 (Eng.) (explaining that an informed user is "someone with a knowledge of handbag design; not the woman in the street, not a handbag designer"), http://www.obi.gr/obi/Portals/0/ImagesAndFiles/VIVIMAKRI_FOLDER/Design_CD/nomologia/agglia/2_UK-Handbags.pdf.
20. *Id.* ("Looking at the bags side by side, restricting my consideration to the features which appear in the design document, it appears to me that the inference of copying is overwhelming. The likelihood that these two designs could have been arrived at independently. . .seems to me to be truly fanciful.").

of Community designs.[21] The regime also provides a prior use defence for infringement of registered designs where a third party began using a design in good faith prior to filing.[22]

The jurisdiction of a court in an EU Member state to apply this regime is based on the defendant's domicile (or place of establishment in a Member State if the defendant is not domiciled in a Member State).[23] Remedies for infringement include EU-wide injunctions against the sale of infringing goods, orders seizing infringing products, damages[24] or products used to make infringing products, and sanctions according to the laws of the member country in which the infringement occurred.[25] Licensees of Community designs can claim damages for infringement if they have the right holder's consent or if the right holder refuses to take action.[26] Some EU countries, in their interpretation of the Regulation, have taken differing stances to the remedies available. For example, the United Kingdom's implementing regulations provide that unintentional infringements of registered and unregistered designs cannot give rise to damages.[27] This amendment was introduced to put the damages position in the United Kingdom for Community designs and UK designs on the same footing.

§ 5:3 Geneva Act of the Hague Agreement Concerning the International Registration of Industrial Designs

The Geneva Act of the Hague Agreement Concerning the International Registration of Industrial Designs was adopted on July 2, 1999, and became effective on December 23, 2003.[28] The Hague Agreement establishes a mechanism for registering designs in countries that have acceded to its terms.[29] In such countries, designers

---

21. Council Regulation 6/2002, art. 20, 2001 O.J. (L 3) 12 (EC).
22. Art 22 CDR.
23. Art 82(1) / 82(2) CDR.
24. Additionally, Article 13 of the EC Directive of 2004 on The Enforcement of Intellectual Property Rights provides for the recovery of damages.
25. Council Regulation 6/2002, art. 89.
26. Art 32(3) CDR.
27. The United Kingdom's Community Design (Amendment) Regulations 2014 (SI 2014/400).
28. *See* Geneva Act of the Hague Agreement Concerning the International Registration of Industrial Designs (adopted by the Diplomatic Conference on July 2, 1999), https://www.wipo.int/edocs/pubdocs/en/designs/453/wipo_pub_453.pdf; Hague Agreement Concerning the International Registration of Industrial Designs (status on Apr. 15, 2013), http://www.wipo.int/export/sites/www/treaties/en/documents/pdf/hague.pdf.
29. *See* Hague System for the International Registration of Industrial Designs, http://www.wipo.int/hague/en/.

need only file one application with the International Bureau of World Intellectual Property Organization (WIPO) in Geneva, Switzerland. Upon registration, the design obtains protection in each member country, as though the owner of the design had registered the design in each individual country.[30]

In late 2006, the European Union adopted the necessary regulations to allow EU companies to file a single application to obtain protection under both the Community design system and the Geneva Act of the Hague Agreement Concerning the International Registration of Industrial Designs.[31] The United States has not ratified the Geneva Act.

§ 5:4 Individual European Countries

The Community design system does not replace or preempt individual member countries' laws related to designs.[32] Designers may claim protection under the Community design system and/or under an individual country's laws, and often designers will rely on when bringing proceedings.

§ 5:4.1 *France*

France, long known as a center of the fashion world, first provided copyright protection to fashion designs as applied under the Copyright Act of 1793.[33] Currently, Article L. 112-2 of the French Intellectual Property Code protects articles of fashion.[34] The *Institut National de la Propriété Industrielle* is responsible for design registration.[35] To be

30. *Id.*
31. Press Release, Office for Harmonization in the Internal Mkt., Industrial Property: Commission Adopts Necessary Measures for Linking EU Design Registration System with WIPO International System (Ref. No. IP/07/1160, July 24, 2007), http://europa.eu/rapid/press-release_IP-07-1160_en.htm?locale=en.
32. Council Regulation 6/2002, art. 88.
33. *See* Leslie J. Hagin, *A Comparative Analysis of Copyright Laws Applied to Fashion Works: Renewing the Proposal for Folding Fashion Works into the United States Copyright Regime*, 26 TEX. INT'L L.J. 341, 374 (1991).
34. Article L. 112-2 of the French Intellectual Property Code [hereinafter French IPC] (protecting "creations of the seasonal industries of dress and articles of fashion" in the list of protected "works of the mind," noting that these are industries "which by reason of the demands of fashion, frequently renew the form of their products"). An English language version of the Code is http://www.wipo.int/wipolex/en/details.jsp?id=5563.
35. Articles L. 512-1 and R. 511-1 of the French IPC set out the application procedure. Information relating to this application procedure can be found on the INPI website, http://www.inpi.fr/fr.

registered, a design must be novel and have an individual character.[36] Protection starts from the date of the filing of the design application and lasts for a period of five (5) years, which may be extended for further periods of five (5) years up to a maximum of twenty-five (25) years.[37]

Remedies available for infringement actions include injunctive relief, damages, and "infringement seizure," which can involve the destruction of the infringing goods.[38] Infringers may, in some cases, also be subject to criminal penalties, including fines of €300,000 and up to three (3) years imprisonment.[39]

In *Societe Yves Saint Laurent Couture S.A. v. Societe Louis Dreyfus Retail Management S.A.*,[40] the Commercial Court held that Ralph Lauren's adaptation of Yves St. Laurent's haute couture dress, which had only slight modifications in length, fabric, and buttons on Yves St. Laurent's creation, infringed Yves St. Laurent's exclusive right to use the "creative" features of its design. Yves St. Laurent was awarded an injunction and nearly $400,000 in damages. However, Yves St. Laurent was unable to recover damages from the sale of Ralph Lauren's dresses in the United States.[41]

§ 5:4.2 United Kingdom

In the United Kingdom, fashion designs can be protected as registered or unregistered designs.[42]

The Registered Design Act of 1949 (RDA) affords protection to new designs with individual character that have been registered with

---

36. Article L. 511-2 of the French IPC. According to Article L.511-4, a design has 'individual character' if the overall impression that it produces on an informed observer differs from that produced by any prior design, taking into account the freedom of the designer in developing it.
37. Article L. 513-1 of the French IPC.
38. *See* French IPC, Art. Intellectual Property Code, art. L. 521-4123-1.
39. *See* French IPC, Art. L. 521-10. *See also* Biana Borukhovich, *Fashion Design: The Work of Art That Is Still Unrecognized in the United States*, 9 WAKE FOREST INTELL. PROP. L.J. 155, 168 (2009).
40. Societe Yves Saint Laurent Couture S.A. v. Societe Louis Dreyfus Retail Mgmt. S.A., Tribunal de Commerce Paris, [Trib. Comm.] [Commercial Court] May 8, 1994, E.C.C. 512, 514 (Fr.)
41. *See* Julie P. Tsai, *Fashioning Protection: A Note on the Protection of Fashion Designs in the United States*, 9 LEWIS & CLARK L. REV. 447, 465 (2005).
42. UK COPYRIGHT SERV., FACT SHEET P-15: DESIGNS AND DESIGN RIGHTS (July 29, 2004) [hereinafter UK FACT SHEET P-15], https://www.copyrightservice.co.uk/protect/p15_design_rights. As in the United States, designers in the United Kingdom may also claim copyright protection in drawings or pictures of the design.

the Intellectual Property Office.[43] To qualify as "new," the design cannot be identical to any design that has been made available to the public prior to the registration date.[44] A design has "individual character" if the overall impression it produces on an informed user differs from the overall impression produced on such a user by any design previously made available to the public.[45] Protection begins on the date of registration and lasts for five (5) years, with five- (5-)year term renewals up to a maximum of twenty-five (25) years.[46]

The Copyright, Designs and Patents Act, 1988 (CDPA) amended the RDA to extend design protection to include original designs that are "commonplace in the design field in question at the time of its creation." [47] Protection under the CDPA begins once the design has been recorded in a design document or an article has been made based on the design.[48] Registration is not required, although such designs may be registered with the UK Copyright Service in order to establish proof of the date and content of the work.[49] Designs are protected for fifteen (15) years beginning at the end of the calendar year in which the design was first recorded in a design document or first fixed in a tangible form; if the design is made into a marketable product anywhere in the world within five (5) years from the end of that calendar year, then the design right expires ten (10) years from the end of the calendar year in which that first occurred.[50] In the last five (5) years of the design right term, any person is entitled to apply for a license to infringe a protected design, which may include the payment of royalties to the original designer.[51]

Under the CDPA, infringement of a design includes producing an article that is "exactly or substantially to that design."[52] In addition

---

43. Registered Designs Act, 1949, 12, 13, & 14 Geo. 6, c. 88, § 1B(1), http://www.legislation.gov.uk/ukpga/Geo6/12-13-14/88.
44. Registered Designs Act, 1949, c. 88, § 1B(2).
45. *Id.*
46. Registered Designs Act, 1949, c. 88, § 8, as amended by the Copyright, Designs and Patents Act, 1988, c. 48, §§ 269, 273.
47. Copyright, Designs and Patents Act, 1988, c. 48, § 213(4), http://www.legislation.gov.uk/ukpga/1988/48, http://www.legislation.gov.uk/ukpga/1988/48/contents.
48. Copyright, Designs and Patents Act, 1988, c. 48, § 213(6), http://www.legislation.gov.uk/ukpga/1988/48, http://www.legislation.gov.uk/ukpga/1988/48/contents.
49. UK FACT SHEET P-15, *supra* note 42.
50. Copyright, Designs and Patents Act, 1988, c. 48, § 216.
51. Copyright, Designs and Patents Act, 1988, c. 48, § 237.
52. Copyright, Designs and Patents Act, 1988, c. 48, § 226(2); *see also* Intellectual Property Office, Copyright, Designs and Patents Act 1988 (Design Right), https://assets.publishing.service.gov.uk/government/uploads/system/uploads/attachment_data/file/406766/Copyright_Designs_and_Patents_Act_1988.pdf.

to remedies of damages, injunctions, and an accounting of profits, courts may, at their discretion, award additional damages based on all the circumstances of the case, in particular the flagrancy of the infringement and any benefit the defendant received by infringing on the design.[53]

Following the results of the United Kingdom EU membership referendum in June 2016,[54] the United Kingdom indicated its intention to leave the European Union by invoking Article 50 of the Lisbon Treaty with a "Brexit" that was originally scheduled for March 29, 2019.[55] At the time of writing, the European Commission withdrawal agreement has not been finalized. The draft withdrawal agreement that was published in March 2018[56] included provisions regarding the continuing protection of intellectual property rights. For example, those with internationally registered designs were given protection under the draft agreement.[57] The situation will, however, remain unclear until a final withdrawal agreement has been agreed and implemented.

§ 5:4.3 Italy

Like France, Italy has long been regarded as a key fashion center, with its first design law enacted in 1868. The current main law regulating copyright is Law No. 633 of 22 April 1941 on the protection of copyright and of other rights related to its exercise, as supplemented and amended by subsequent laws (as last amended up to Law No. 2 of January 9, 2008). This provides protection for, amongst other things "industrial design works that have creative character or inherent artistic character,"[58] which applies to fashion. A protected design must be novel and a have a degree of individual creativity.

The remedies available against an infringer include injunctive relief with the provision of a penalty for any further infringement. Any person injured by infringement of design rights belonging to him or her may seek destruction or removal of the material constituting the infringement, or damages.[59] In 2012, Italian design company Blufin S.p.A, which owns the *haute couture* trademarks Blumarine

---

53. Copyright, Designs and Patents Act, 1988, c. 48, § 229.
54. *See* EU Referendum, https://www.gov.uk/government/topical-events/eu-referendum/about.
55. *See* the UK Government website for information about EU Exit including the article 50 process, negotiations, and announcements about policy changes as a result of EU Exit, https://www.gov.uk/government/brexit.
56. *See* Draft Withdrawal Agreement (Mar. 19, 2018), https://www.gov.uk/government/publications/draft-withdrawal-agreement-19-march-2018.
57. *Id.* at Art. 52.
58. Law No. 633 of 22 Apr. 1941, Article 2(10).
59. Law No. 633 of 22 Apr. 1941, Article 158.

and Blugirl, received an order from the Court of Turin that forced the defendant in that case to immediately and permanently halt the sale of all infringing products and to buy back any infringing goods that had been sold to stores. Infringement proceedings will generally be conducted according to the Italian Code of Civil Procedure.

§ 5:5 Non-European Countries

§ 5:5.1 Japan

Japan's Design Law protects the "form, pattern, or color of an object or a combination of these, which appeals visually to the viewer's sense of aesthetics."[60] The design must visually appeal to the aesthetic sense,[61] and be able to be recreated and mass-produced (that is, it must have "industrial usability"). Registration is required with the Japan Patent Office. Under the registration criteria, the design must be novel ("completely new"), industrially applicable, creative (based on ease of creation), and unique (no other similar or identical designs registered).[62] Like the European Union's Community design system, Japanese law does not protect designs that "may break public order and morals."[63] Protection for registered designs begins on the date of registration and lasts twenty (20) years, contingent on the owner's payment of an annual fee within thirty (30) days of the rights being granted. Because of the novelty requirement and relatively long registration process of eight months, some commentators have concluded that Japan's Design Law (sometimes compared to U.S. patent law) may not provide fashion designers with effective protection against copying.[64] Design rights can be assigned in whole or in part, including the right to register.

The owner of a registered design may sue any party who uses the design or similar designs without the design owner's consent.[65] An

---

60. *See* INVESTING IN JAPAN, *supra* note 11, § 5.7.1.
61. In contrast, Italy's copyright law extends protection to "[w]orks of industrial design displaying creative character and per se artistic value." Alberto Musso & Mario Fabiam, *Italy*, *in* INTERNATIONAL COPYRIGHT LAW AND PRACTICE § 2(4)(c)(i) (Paul Edward Gellar ed., 2006) (quoting Italian Copyright Act art. 2).
62. INVESTING IN JAPAN, *supra* note 11, § 5.7.1.
63. *Id.*
64. *See* Lisa J. Hedrick, *Tearing Fashion Design Protection Apart at the Seams*, 65 WASH. & LEE L. REV. 215, 247–248 (Winter 2008). Hedrick notes that the database of registered designs appears to have few, if any, fashion designs.
65. MINAKO MIZUNO, FROM FILING TO REGISTRATION OF DESIGN, at 5 (Japan Patent Office Asia-Pac. Indus. Prop. Ctr. 2006).

infringement action can be brought on the grounds of either direct infringement (commercially producing a registered design) or indirect infringement (producing a product that will be used to infringe a registered design). Infringement is presumed to be the result of negligence.[66] Nevertheless, because it is not readily apparent to others whether a design is registered, it may be advisable for designers to indicate registration status on the product itself.[67] Infringers are liable for damages under Japanese law; other remedies that are available to registered design infringement include injunctions and measures to restore credibility.[68] The defenses of experimentation and research as well as prior use are available. If the form of the registered object becomes famous or generally known after use, design owners can sue copiers under Japan's Unfair Competition Prevention Law.[69] Unregistered designs also receive limited protection. New goods are protected for up to three (3) years from the date on which they were first sold in Japan, regardless of whether registration was obtained.[70]

§ 5:5.2 China

China has also grown into an important fashion center, although China's significant contributions to the market have historically been marred by counterfeiting issues.[71]

China currently does not have its own piece of legislation that deals exclusively with designs. Instead, designs must be protected by other means, such as patent or copyright law. As to the latter, the Copyright Law of the People's Republic of China provides protection to works, including "drawings of engineering designs, and product designs; maps, sketches and other graphic works and model works."[72] The Copyright Law includes provisions detailing infringement offences as well as remediés available to the injured party.[73] The Copyright Law

---

66. *Id.* at 6.
67. *Id.*
68. *Id.* at 5.
69. *See* INVESTING IN JAPAN, *supra* note 11, § 5.7.2.
70. *Id.*
71. *See, e.g.*, W. Shepard, *How Chinese Counterfeiters Continue Beating Amazon*, FORBES (Jan. 12, 2017), https://www.forbes.com/sites/wadeshepard/2017/01/12/why-amazon-is-losing-its-battle-against-chinese-counterfeiters/#7af7c32f585c.
72. Copyright Law of the People's Republic of China (as amended up to the Decision of February 26, 2010, by the Standing Committee of the National People's Congress on Amending the Copyright Law of the People's Republic of China), art. 3(7), http://www.wipo.int/wipolex/en/text.jsp?file_id=186569.
73. *Id.* at Chapter V.

also extends protection to foreigners under certain circumstances.[74] Major cities in China, such as Beijing, Shanghai, and Guangdong province, have their own intellectual property courts to handle such matters.

In September 2018, China enacted an e-commerce law, which will come into force in early 2019,[75] and includes protections of intellectual property rights. It remains to be seen how much these protections will be utilized by consumers and designers going forward.

§ 5:5.3 Australia

In Australia, new and distinctive fashion designs are afforded protection under the Designs Act of 2003.[76] A design is defined as "the overall appearance of the product resulting from one or more visual features of the product."[77] A right that is registered by IP Australia, the federal government agency that administers intellectual property law,[78] gives the owner exclusive rights to commercially use, license, and sell the design, and protection for the visual appearance of the product. This protection begins when the design application is filed and lasts for an initial term of five (5) years, with a renewal term of five (5) years.[79] The design right, however, will not be legally enforceable until it has also been examined and certified by IP Australia.[80] Post-registration, the owner would be required to submit another request to IP Australia to have their designed examined and certified.

To qualify for registration a design must be "new and distinctive when compared with the prior art base for the design."[81] As such, a design must not be used publicly or published in a document anywhere in the world before an application for registration is made.[82]

---

74. *Id.* at art. 2.
75. Laney Zhang, *China: E-Commerce Law Passed*, LIBRARY OF CONGRESS GLOBAL LEGAL MONITOR (Nov. 21, 2018), http://www.loc.gov/law/foreign-news/article/china-e-commerce-law-passed/.
76. *See* Designs Act of 2003, https://www.legislation.gov.au/Details/C2018C00367. Incorporating amendments by the Intellectual Property Laws Amendment (Productivity Commission Response Part 1 and Other Measures) Act 2018, https://www.legislation.gov.au/Details/C2018A0007.
77. *Id.* section 2, pt. 5.
78. *See* AUSTRALIAN GOVERNMENT, IP AUSTRALIA, https://www.ipaustralia.gov.au/.
79. Designs Act of 2003, sec. 46.
80. Designs Act of 2003, sec. 73(3).
81. Designs Act of 2003, sec. 15. The priority date is usually the date the design application is filed. *See* Designs Act of 2003, sec. 27.
82. Designs Act of 2003, sec. 15(2). *See also* AUSTRALIAN GOVERNMENT, IP AUSTRALIA, DON'T PUBLICISE YOUR DESIGN, https://www.ipaustralia.gov.au/designs/applying-design/dont-publicise-your-design.

Like Japan and the European Union, certain designs, including those featuring "scandalous graphics," may not be registered in Australia on moral grounds.[83]

Designs that are "identical to, or substantially similar in overall impression to, [a] registered design" are infringing.[84] Remedies for infringement include injunctive relief and damages.[85] Fashion designers may also protect their "works for artistic craftsmanship," such as one-of-a-kind garments and jewelry, under the Copyright Act of 1968, which does not require registration.[86]

§ 5:5.4 New Zealand

In New Zealand, the administration of rights to a design is governed by the Designs Act 1953 and the Designs Amendment Act 2010.[87] A design is defined as "features of shape, configuration, pattern, or ornament applied to an article by any industrial process or means."[88] To qualify for registration, a design must be "new or original,"[89] that is, not published before the date that the registration application is filed. Unlike the Australian process, design applications filed at the Intellectual Property Office of New Zealand are automatically examined before they are registered.[90] Once registered, the applicant

---

83. *Id.*
84. Designs Act of 2003, sec. 71.
85. Designs Act of 2003, sec. 75. *See also* Review Aus. Pty Ltd v. Innovative Lifestyle Invs. [2008] FCA 74 (requiring defendants to pay $7,500 for reputational damages, and $10,000 in punitive damages where infringer continued to sell infringing design after being put on notice original design was registered), http://www.austlii.edu.au/au/cases/cth/FCA/2008/74.html. The judge in the *Innovative Lifestyle Investments* case also ordered defendants to pay plaintiff's legal costs. *See* Anthony B. Watson, *First Victory for Australian Designer Under the Designs Registration Regime*, MONDAQ (Mar. 20, 2008), http://www.mondaq.com/australia/x/58374/Copyright/First+Victory+For+Australian+Designer+Under+The+Designs+Registration+Regime.
86. COMMONWEALTH OF AUSTRALIA, FASHION RULES: A GUIDE TO INTELLECTUAL PROPERTY FOR AUSTRALIA'S CLOTHING AND FASHION DESIGN INDUSTRY (2009), https://www.wipo.int/edocs/lexdocs/laws/en/au/au332en.pdf.
87. These Acts are accompanied by the Design Regulations 1954 and the Designs Amendment Regulations 2011. *See* NEW ZEALAND INTELLECTUAL PROPERTY OFFICE, LEGISLATION, https://www.iponz.govt.nz/about-ip/designs/legislation-hearings/.
88. Designs Act 1954, sec. 2(1), http://www.legislation.govt.nz/act/public/1953/0065/latest/whole.html#DLM281076.
89. Designs Act 1954, sec. 5(2).
90. *See* NEW ZEALAND INTELLECTUAL PROPERTY OFFICE, EXAMINATION PROCESS, https://www.iponz.govt.nz/about-ip/designs/process/.

is given the "copyright in the design"[91] (that is, the exclusive right to sell, hire, manufacture, and import any article that embodies the design), for a period of five (5) years from the date of registration.[92] This period can be extended by a further ten (10) years.[93]

For a product to infringe a registered design, it must embody a design that is the same or not substantially different to that registered.[94] Available remedies include injunctive relief and damages.

§ 5:5.5 Canada

In Canada, different intellectual property rights attach to different aspects of a fashion design. Copyrights and industrial designs may protect aesthetic aspects; a patent may protect any innovative functional features; and trademarks may protect branding.

According to the Copyright Act, "copyright shall subsist in Canada . . . in every original literary, dramatic, musical and artistic work,"[95] and fashion design is arguably an artistic work. The Copyright Act affords the owner of a copyright "the sole right to produce or reproduce the work or any substantial part of the work"[96] for a period ending fifty (50) years after the death of its creator.[97] In addition to economic rights, the author of a work has parallel moral rights, namely the right of attribution, the right to the integrity of the work, and the right to be associated with the work.[98] Moral rights may not be assigned, but may be waived.[99] The Copyright Act specifically contemplates that a copyright can overlap with an industrial design, which is defined as "features of shape, configuration, pattern or ornament and any combination of those features that, in a finished article, appeal to and are judged solely by the eye."[100] In such a case, a fashion design owner would be advised to rely on more than one form of intellectual property protection. Although the Copyright Act excludes protection for "useful articles,"[101] there are exceptions for graphic or photographic representations, trademarks, labels, and

---

91. Designs Act 1954, sec. 11(1).
92. Designs Act 1954, sec. 12(1).
93. Designs Act 1954, sec. 12(2).
94. Designs Act 1954, sec. 11(1).
95. Copyright Act, R.S.C. 1985, c. C-42, s. 5.
96. Copyright Act, R.S.C. 1985, c. C-42, s. 3.
97. Copyright Act, R.S.C. 1985, c. C-42, s. 6.
98. Copyright Act, R.S.C. 1985, c. C-42, s. 14.1(1).
99. Copyright Act, R.S.C. 1985, c. C-42, s. 14.1(2).
100. Copyright Act, R.S.C. 1985, c. C-42, s. 64(1).
101. Copyright Act, R.S.C. 1985, c. C-42, s. 64(2).

"material that has a woven or knitted pattern or that is suitable for piece goods or surface coverings or for making wearing apparel."[102]

Registered industrial designs are protected under the Industrial Design Act for a term of ten (10) years from the date of registration.[103] Industrial designs carry the same definition in this act as they do in the Copyright Act.[104] Excluded from protection are features applied to a useful article that are not "dictated solely by a utilitarian function of the article."[105] In order to qualify for registration, designs must be "substantially different from prior art."[106] They must contain "some spark of inspiration" that leads to a new design or a new use for an old design—"a higher degree of originality" than that required by copyright.[107] Similar to the European Union and Japan, designs that are "contrary to public morality or order" may be denied registration.[108] Infringement occurs when the registered design or "a design not differing substantially therefrom" is applied to an article without the designer's permission.[109] Courts, "in considering whether the differences are substantial," take into account "the extent to which the registered design differs from any previously published design."[110]

The functional aspects of a fashion design may be protected by registration under the Patent Act. The holder of a patent is afforded "the exclusive right, privilege and liberty of making, constructing and using the invention and selling it to others to be used"[111] for a term of twenty (20) years from the filing date.[112]

Lastly, trademarks can provide protection to certain features that distinguish the goods from those of others. Traditional trademark protection applies to a designer's name or logo, but protection can also be extended to distinctive design elements such as color,

---

102. Copyright Act, R.S.C. 1985, c. C-42, s. 64(3).
103. Copyright Act, R.S.C. 1985, c. C-42, ss. 9, 10(1).
104. Copyright Act, R.S.C. 1985, c. C-42, s. 2.
105. Industrial Design Act, R.S.C., 1985, c. I-9, s. 5.1(a), http://laws-lois.justice.gc.ca/eng/acts/I-9/.
106. Bodum USA, Inc. v. Trudeau Corp. (1889) Inc., 2012 FC 1128 at para. 96 [hereinafter Bodum], *citing* Clatworthy & Son Ltd v. Dale Display Fixtures Ltd, [1929] SCR 429 at page 433.
107. *Id.* at para. 97, *citing* Bata Indus. Ltd. v. Warrington Inc., [1985] FCJ No 239 at 347.
108. Industrial Design Act, R.S.C. 1985, c. 1-9, s. 6(2).
109. Industrial Design Act, R.S.C. 1985, c. 1-9, s. 11(1).
110. Industrial Design Act, R.S.C. 1985, c. 1-9, s. 11(2); *see also* Bodum, *supra* note 106 (holding that the registered product and allegedly infringing product must be viewed side-by-side from the point of view of an informed consumer).
111. Patent Act, R.S.C. 1985, c. P-4, s. 42.
112. Patent Act, R.S.C. 1985, c. P-4, s. 44.

shaping, or stitching. The owner of a trademark is protected from passing off, which is codified by the Trademarks Act: "No person shall . . . direct public attention to his goods, services or business in such a way as to cause or be likely to cause confusion in Canada, at the time he commenced so to direct attention to them, between his goods, services or business and the goods, services or business of another."[113] Trademarks may or may not be registered to benefit from protection, but registration provides national protection[114] while unregistered marks are limited to geographic use.

Remedies for infringement of the above rights include injunctive relief, damages, lost profits, punitive damages, and the destruction of the infringing products.[115]

§ 5:5.6 Singapore

Designs are protected under the Registered Designs Act.[116] Designs are defined by "features of shape, configuration, pattern or ornament applied to an article by any industrial process."[117] To qualify for registration, such designs must be "new" and therefore not published anywhere before the date of application of the first filing.[118] Once the design is registered by the Intellectual Property Office of Singapore,[119] it will be protected for an initial five (5) years from the date of filing, and this period can be extended up to ten (10) years.[120] An infringement action can be brought if a registered design is used without the consent of the registered owner.[121] Such claims are heard by the High Court of Singapore.[122] Available remedies include injunctive relief, damages, and an accounting of profits.[123]

---

113. Trademarks Act, R.S.C. 1985, c. T-13, s. 7(b).
114. Trademarks Act, R.S.C. 1985, c. T-13, s. 19.
115. Industrial Design Act, R.S.C. 1985, c. 1-9, s. 15.1; Copyright Act ss. 35-41; Trademarks Act s. 22(2).
116. Registered Designs Act (Chapter 266) Revised Edition 2005, as amended up to Intellectual Property (Miscellaneous Amendments) Act 2012 [hereinafter Registered Designs Act 2005], http://www.wipo.int/wipolex/en/text.jsp?file_id=362395.
117. Registered Designs Act 2005, sec. 2(1).
118. Registered Designs Act 2005, sec. 5(1) and 5(2).
119. *See* INTELLECTUAL PROPERTY OFFICE OF SINGAPORE, UNDERSTANDING INNOVATION & IP: DESIGN, https://www.ipos.gov.sg/understanding-innovation-ip/design.
120. Registered Designs Act 2005, sec. 21(1) and (2).
121. Registered Designs Act 2005, sec. 30(2).
122. Registered Designs Act 2005, sec. 2(1).
123. Registered Designs Act 2005, sec. 36(2).

§ 5:5.7 India

India has a registered design rights protection regime. In order to be registrable with the Design Office, designs must be new or original; relate in some way to features of shape, pattern, or ornamentation; be applicable to an article by industrial process; and use a design that can be judged unique solely by eye.[124] Registered designs can be cancelled at any time under limited grounds.[125] The registration of a design provides protection for ten (10) years, which can be extended by a further five (5) years.[126] Available remedies for infringement include an injunction, damages, an account of profits, and destruction of the infringing product. The defenses to infringement actions are the same as the grounds for cancelling a design that has been registered: previous registration; publication before registration; no originality; or, it is a non-registrable design. Unregistered designs are not covered by the Designs Act 2000, but may benefit from the protection of the common law tort of passing off.

§ 5:5.8 United Arab Emirates

The United Arab Emirates has established an Intellectual Property Protection Department, which accepts the registration of design rights for a period of ten (10) years but does not provide recognition of unregistered design rights.[127] Temporary protection is also afforded to designs exhibited at local fairs.[128] Because there is no online registry, any search of existing registrations must be conducted through intellectual property journals. The United Arab Emirates has a federal law that deals with the industrial regulation and protection of patents, industrial drawings, and designs.[129] Designs must satisfy novelty, innovation, and usability tests. Violation of design rights can be remedied by court order preventing use and damages. If the underlying rationale for using the design is criminal, then imprisonment and a fine can be imposed.

§ 5:6 Conclusion

Because of the differences between the substantive protections offered under these diverse regimes, and the varying time periods for which designs are protected, multinational fashion companies face

---

124. Section 2(d), Designs Act 2000.
125. Section 19, Designs Act 2000.
126. Section 11, Designs Act 2000.
127. Article 49, Federal Law No. 49 of 2006.
128. Article 3, Federal Law No. 31 of 2006.
129. Federal Law No. 31 of 2006.

administrative and practical burdens in managing and enforcing their intellectual property that are unfamiliar in other industries. As a result, it is advisable to consult with counsel in important international markets to make sure that appropriate steps are taken to maximize the protections and remedies that these countries' legal systems afford.

Chapter 6

Unfair Competition, Misappropriation, and Trade Secrets

§ 6:1 Introduction
§ 6:2 California Law
  § 6:2.1 California's Statutory Unfair Competition Law
  § 6:2.2 California's Common Law of Misappropriation
  § 6:2.3 California Uniform Trade Secrets Act
§ 6:3 New York Law
  § 6:3.1 New York Common Law Unfair Competition
    [A] Passing Off
    [B] Misappropriation
  § 6:3.2 New York Statutory Unfair Competition Law
§ 6:4 Federal Law
  § 6:4.1 Federal Unfair Competition
  § 6:4.2 The Federal Trade Secrets Statute
§ 6:5 Illustrative Cases in the Fashion Industry
  § 6:5.1 Trade Secrets Cases
  § 6:5.2 *J. Crew Group Inc. v. Fenton*
  § 6:5.3 *Burch v. Burch*

§ 6:1 Introduction

Apart from the doctrines of trademark, patent, and copyright law discussed above, courts have long recognized that businesses and innovators may also be protected under appropriate circumstances by the common law doctrines of unfair competition and misappropriation. In addition, the law offers "trade secret" protections for information that is gathered or developed in confidence and draws value from the fact that it is not publicly available, whether or not it is separately protectable under a different intellectual property discipline. These doctrines may be particularly important in the fashion industry where designers often encounter difficulties in protecting certain types of designs as a matter of trademark, patent, or copyright law (as discussed in chapters 2 through 4). A claim of unfair competition or misappropriation may be more applicable where a company exploits a disparity in economic position or otherwise wrongfully misappropriates the work of a creator or designer, whether or not that work qualifies for protection under more conventional intellectual property theories. And trade secrets remedies may be available to help protect confidential methods or processes that provide brands or retailers competitive advantages, or at least to give a fashion company a leg up on imitators up until the moment that a product or service is publicly launched.

Courts and commentators use the term "unfair competition" to describe a cluster of federal and state doctrines and causes of action. Broadly speaking, the law of unfair competition seeks to protect economic and creative investments that result in valuable commercial property. Historically perceived as a "catch all" cause of action, the unfair competition cause of action has "flourished in a variety of factual settings," and the general "trend of the law . . . has been to extend the scope of the doctrine of unfair competition, whose basic principle is that commercial unfairness should be restrained whenever it appears that there has been a misappropriation, for the advantage of one person, of a property right belonging to another."[1] Therefore, a claim based on unfair competition may be used offensively—at least in theory—even when other forms of federal intellectual property protection do not provide a relevant cause of action. And while these claims apply across many industries, they are often invoked in the fashion industry, where the existing legal landscape invites a think-outside-the-box approach to protecting intellectual property and commercial goodwill.

At its heart, "unfair competition" is commercial or competitive behavior that is so "unfair" that courts are willing to step in and penalize the party responsible. A variety of words and concepts describe a claim of unfair competition in plain language: disadvantageous, anti-competitive, unjust, unequal terms, or fraudulently or illegitimately gained advantages—to name just a few. But courts have stressed that a claim of unfair competition must be based on conduct that is "wrongful" in some legally cognizable sense. Within this confine, an unfair competition cause of action may potentially be crafted as creatively as some of the fashion designs it may seek to protect.

---

1. ITC Ltd. v. Punchgini Inc., 880 N.E.2d 852 (N.Y. 2007).

In the context of the fashion industry, one of the most important forms of "unfair" conduct is the misappropriation of an idea that in all right and equity belongs to someone else. Ideas, after all, are the lifeblood of the fashion industry. As a result, misappropriation claims have been litigated, either under the rubric of an "unfair competition" cause of action, or under a separately identified common law tort of misappropriation. Frequently, plaintiffs allege that an idea for a creative concept was pitched to a party that initially declined to accept the idea, then later appeared to have implemented the concept without proper compensation, credit, or attribution to the original party. In an industry that thrives on creativity and entrepreneurship, the misappropriation of ideas is one of the most common and salient risks.

This chapter summarizes the most important of these doctrines and their application to the fashion industry. It is important to keep in mind, however, that the common law of unfair competition, misappropriation, and trade secrets varies by state, so any analysis of potential liability must reflect the particular approach adopted in the relevant jurisdiction.[2] This chapter provides a closer look at the approach taken in California and New York to illustrate how each state has applied and codified the common law of unfair competition, misappropriation, and trade secrets.

§ 6:2 California Law

§ 6:2.1 *California's Statutory Unfair Competition Law*

California Business and Professions Code section 17200 is California's unfair competition statute. Section 17200 states that "unfair competition shall mean and include any unlawful, unfair or fraudulent business act or practice."[3] The breadth of this statute, and the vagueness of the term "unfair," has invited litigants to test various theories under which plaintiffs may bring an unfair competition claim in California. Because the language is disjunctive, moreover, the statute only requires a violation that is *either* unlawful, unfair, *or* fraudulent. And in contrast to other similar unfair competition statutes, the California statute does not provide an explicit intent requirement. In theory, this means that a plaintiff is not required to

---

2. *See* Carolyn L. Carter, Nat'l Consumer L. Ctr., A 50-State Report on Unfair and Deceptive Acts and Practices Statutes (Feb. 2009).
3. Cal. Bus. & Prof. Code § 17200.

show that the defendant intended to act unlawfully, unfairly, or fraudulently in a business act or practice.[4]

The California Supreme Court has defined the term "unfair" under the statute as follows:

> When a plaintiff who claims to have suffered injury from a direct competitor's "unfair" act or practice invokes section 17200, the word "unfair" in that section means conduct that threatens an incipient violation of an antitrust law, or violates the policy or spirit of one of those laws because its effects are comparable to or the same as a violation of the law, or otherwise significantly threatens or harms competition.[5]

The court was explicit that this interpretation of "unfair" business acts applies only in the context of competitors. Designers and innovators in the fashion industry may thus invoke this interpretation of section 17200 for a broad variety of injurious business practices by a competitor. In addition, one California court has held that a cause of action based on section 17200 may also, under appropriate circumstances, extend to actions challenging a breach of contractual obligations.[6]

Consider the following scenario: An innovative jewelry designer in California has launched a line of monogrammed jewelry. In lieu of a business model where the designer designs and then mass produces specific types of jewelry with various combinations of personal initials, the designer markets its line of jewelry as uniquely personal: each time a customer orders a piece of monogrammed jewelry, the designer uses an original process to create a new, monogrammed design for that customer, rather than a mass-produced design. The particular presentation of initials is therefore unique to each customer, denoting an additional level of personalization for each piece of monogrammed jewelry. The designer emphasizes this distinctive feature in its marketing strategy: each customer is purchasing a custom designed and unique piece of monogrammed jewelry. Should a competing jewelry designer choose to replicate this method of designing and selling monogrammed jewelry in such a way that the first designer's ability to compete is "significantly threaten[ed] or harm[ed]," the designer may have a viable unfair competition cause of action under section 17200, so long as the "unfair" nature of the competitor's acts

4. *See* State Farm Fire & Cas. Co. v. Super. Ct., 45 Cal. App. 4th 1093, 1102 (Ct. App. 1996).
5. Cel-Tech Commc'ns, Inc. v. L.A. Cellular Tel. Co., 20 Cal. 4th 163, 187 (Ct. App. 1999).
6. *See* Gibson v. World Sav. & Loan Ass'n, 103 Cal. App. 4th 1291 (Ct. App. 2002).

is "tethered to some legislatively declared policy or proof of some actual or threatened impact on competition."[7]

As another example, in 2013, California's Attorney Generally filed two unfair competition lawsuits against Chinese and Indian apparel manufacturers, alleging they had gained an unfair competitive advantage through the use of unlicensed, pirated software to manufacture, ship, and sell apparel imported and sold in California.[8] The lawsuits, filed under section 17200, sought injunctions that would bar the manufacturers from distributing the apparel in California until they complied with all software licensing requirements.[9] These lawsuits are notable in that the claim was not that the apparel was itself counterfeit, but that the merchants benefited from the use of counterfeit software in the production or merchandising process. The defendants' alleged piracy enabled them to reduce costs and reallocate those savings to gain unfair competitive advantages over competitors. In bringing the suit, the Attorney General took the position that California's unfair competition law is designed to ensure a level playing field and protect against practices that incentivize anti-competitive behavior.[10]

Individuals have also asserted unfair competition claims under California law. For example, street artist Joseph Tierney (a/k/a "RIME") brought suit against high-end fashion-brand Moschino, alleging, among other claims, unfair competition under California state law.[11] One of Tierney's better known murals, "Vandal Eyes," was painted on the side of a building in Detroit. Tierney alleged that Moschino used that design as part of its Fall/Winter 2015 collection and featured it on a dress worn by Katy Perry at the 2015 Met Gala.

---

7. *Cel-Tech*, 20 Cal. 4th at 186–87.
8. Press Release, State of Cal. Dep't of Justice, Office of the Att'y Gen., Attorney General Kamala D. Harris Files Unfair Competition Lawsuits Over Use of Pirated Software in Apparel Industry (Jan. 24, 2013), http://oag.ca.gov/news/press-releases/attorney-general-kamala-d-harris-files-unfair-competition-lawsuits-over-use.
9. Complaint, People v. Ningbo Beyond Home Textile Co., et al., No. BC499771, at 9 (Cal. Super. Los Angeles Cty. Jan. 24, 2013); Complaint, People v. Pratibha Syntex Ltd., et al., No. BC 499751, at 9 (Cal. Super. Los Angeles Cty. Jan. 24, 2013).
10. In contrast, Washington and Louisiana passed laws in 2012 that create a civil cause of action against manufacturers, whether local or foreign, that use unauthorized software in the course of their business operations, and which sell (or offer to sell) their products, or which have their products sold (or offered for sale) within Washington and Louisiana respectively. *See, e.g.*, WASH. REV. CODE §§ 19.330 *et seq.*; LA. REV. STAT. ANN. § 51:1427.
11. Tierney v. Moschino, No. 15-cv-5900, 2016 WL 4942033 (C.D. Cal. Jan. 13, 2016).

Tierney claimed that Moschino unfairly benefited from his work to his detriment in that he had allegedly lost his "street cred" due to the perceived association with Defendants' clothing. The case ended with a settlement in July 2016.

In an interesting application of the law, Modern Appealing Clothing, an upscale clothing boutique, brought a class action lawsuit claiming unfair competition under California law against Ivanka Trump's fashion company, alleging that Ms. Trump's company gained an unfair advantage due to her father's position as the President of the United States and her husband's position as an advisor to the President.[12] After Donald Trump's election, sales of Ivanka's brand reportedly increased by 346% in January 2017 and 557% in February 2017, compared against the same months in 2016.[13] Shortly after filing suit, Modern Appealing Clothing voluntarily dismissed the case without prejudice after it was confirmed that Ivanka Trump voluntarily agreed to abide by federal ethics rules.[14]

California unfair competition law, in particular, is affected by the tendency of California courts to infuse judicial decisions with public policy considerations. As one law review article phrased it, "[t]he judiciary in [California] has tacitly condoned the idea of basing a[n Unfair Competition Law] cause of action solely upon a violation of public policy."[15] As a result, plaintiffs have used the breadth of the statute for a tactical litigation advantage, to increase their leverage for settlement, or to expand the permissible scope of information they can get as part of the civil discovery process.[16]

There are limits to the use of California's unfair competition statute, however, and courts are not afraid to grant motions to dismiss or summary judgment when the circumstances merit it.[17] For example, plaintiffs in California must satisfy traditional

12. Modern Appealing Clothing v. Ivanka Trump Marks, LLC, No. CGC-17-557575 (filed on Mar. 16, Sup. Ct. Cal. 2017).
13. Ana Colon, *Searches for Ivanka Trump's Brand Skyrocketed in February*, REFINERY29 (Mar. 7, 2017), https://www.refinery29.com/2017/03/144206/ivanka-trump-brand-search-increase-february-2017.
14. *Modern Appealing Clothing*, No. CGC-17-557575.
15. Joshua Taylor, *Why the Increasing Role of Public Policy in California's Unfair Competition Law Is a Slippery Step in the Wrong Direction*, 52 HASTINGS L.J. 1131 (2000–2001).
16. *Id.*
17. *See, e.g.*, Levitt v. Yelp, Inc., No. C-10-1321 EMC, 2011 WL 5079526 (N.D. Cal. Mar. 22, 2011) (dismissing as "entirely speculative," claims that Yelp "deliberately manipulates" reviews to coerce businesses to advertise because "the disappearance and reappearance of various user reviews" regarding plaintiffs' businesses could not be reasonably attributed to any wrongdoing on Yelp's part).

constitutional standing requirements, namely, injury in fact, based on a loss of money or property.[18]

§ 6:2.2 *California's Common Law of Misappropriation*

California also recognizes a common law tort of misappropriation of ideas. To prevail on such a claim, a plaintiff must establish:

(1) a substantial investment of time and money in the development of property;

(2) that the defendant has appropriated the property at little or no cost; and

(3) that the defendant's conduct has caused injury to the plaintiff.[19]

As a threshold matter, California law does not recognize abstract ideas as property.[20] However, under an "implied-in-fact" contract theory, if a plaintiff can establish that he or she "prepared the work, disclosed the work to the offeree for sale, and did so under circumstances from which it could be concluded that the offeree voluntarily accepted the disclosure knowing the conditions on which it was tendered and the reasonable value of the work,"[21] contract law may protect the creative ideas pitched and then implemented unfairly. There is an important limitation on these claims, however, in that plaintiff must have had a reasonable expectation of receiving compensation for implementation of the idea *prior* to pitching the idea. In other words, the "idea man" who "blurts out his idea without having first made his bargain . . . has no one but himself to blame for the loss of his bargaining power."[22]

Accordingly, a fashion designer, entrepreneur, or vendor who pitches an idea under circumstances where it can be shown that there was a reasonable expectation of payment may similarly be able to state a claim if the idea is then used without compensation.

---

18. *See, e.g.*, Californians for Disability Rights v. Mervyn's, LLC, 39 Cal. 4th 223 (2006) (bringing California into line with requirements for unfair competition claims in all other states).
19. *See* Self Directed Placement Corp. v. Control Data Corp., 908 F.2d 462, 467 (9th Cir. 1990).
20. *See* Desny v. Wilder, 46 Cal. 2d 715 (1956).
21. Grosso v. Miramax Film, 383 F.3d 965, 967 (9th Cir. 2004) (citing Desny v. Wilder, 46 Cal. 2d 715 (1956)).
22. Gunther-Wal Prods. v. Mattel, Inc., 104 Cal. App. 4th 27, 39 (Ct. App. 2002).

§ 6:2.3 California Uniform Trade Secrets Act

California is one of forty-nine states that has adopted some version of the Uniform Trade Secrets Act (UTSA).[23] The California Trade Secrets Act (CUTSA) defines a "trade secret" as:

> information, including a formula, pattern, compilation, program, device, method, technique, or process, that: (1) Derives independent economic value, actual or potential, from not being generally known to the public or to other persons who can obtain economic value from its disclosure or use; and (2) Is the subject of efforts that are reasonable under the circumstances to maintain its secrecy.[24]

A trade secret is "misappropriated" if it was acquired by improper means, if it was acquired under circumstances giving rise to a duty to maintain its secrecy, or if it was derived from someone who owed a duty to protect its secrecy.[25] The claims will be denied if the owner of the trade secret cannot identify the nature of the trade secret with sufficient particularity, or if it cannot establish that it made reasonable efforts to protect the secrecy of the alleged trade secret.[26]

A trade secret need not be technical in nature, however, and new products—or elements of products—can be considered trade secrets if they are protected appropriately. For instance, in *Mattel, Inc. v. MGA Entertainment, Inc.*, a federal court applying CUTSA held that that the design and concept for the not-yet-released Bratz fashion dolls might qualify as a trade secret. The court reasoned that even if the individual elements of the dolls and their clothing could not be considered trade secrets alone (for example, dictionary names such as "Jade"), they might still collectively constitute a trade secret if brought together in a manner designed to be kept secret for the company's competitive advantage.[27]

---

23. CAL. CIV. CODE §§ 3426.1-3426.11. UTSA is a model law created by the National Conference of Commissioners on Uniform State Laws in the 1960s to codify and standardize the common law of trade secrets. *See* Christopher B. Seaman, *The Case Against Federalizing Trade Secrets*, 101 VA. L. REV. 317, 326 (2015).
24. CAL. CIV. CODE § 3426.1.
25. *Id.*
26. *See, e.g.*, FormFactor Inc. v. Micro-Probe Inc., No. C-10-3095-PJH, 2012 BL 159474 (N.D. Cal. June 7, 2012).
27. *See* Mattel, Inc. v. MGA Entm't, Inc., 782 F. Supp. 2d 911, 962–63 (C.D. Cal. 2011).

§ 6:3 New York Law

§ 6:3.1 New York Common Law Unfair Competition

In New York, the essence of a common law unfair competition claim is that the defendant has misappropriated the labors and expenditures of another, with some element of bad faith present.[28] This showing of bad faith or intent, coupled with a claim of misappropriation, establishes a claim for common law unfair competition.[29] In the fashion industry, this often occurs when a competitor makes an effort to deceive consumers by using recognizable characteristics of another designer or brand and passing them off as his or her own product or design.

The concept of "bad faith" has been described as showing that a defendant acted "out of a dishonest purpose."[30] Under New York law, the use of a counterfeit mark creates a presumption of bad faith.[31] For example, in 2007, Burberry Limited and Burberry USA sued a company called Designers Imports, Inc. for selling counterfeit Burberry goods. The court found that "Burberry's evidence of Defendant's sale of counterfeit Burberry-branded merchandise creates a presumption of bad faith, satisfying the elements of Burberry's common law unfair competition claim."[32] Similarly, in 2018, Burberry sued Target for unfair competition under New York common law, among other claims.[33] In the suit, Burberry alleged that Target was selling "blatant reproductions" of Burberry's famous check trademark, including eyewear, luggage, water bottles, and scarves.

While there is no concrete list of activities that constitute unfair competition under New York law, an unfair competition claim contemplates that one may not unfairly misappropriate the skill, expenditures, and labor of another person.[34] For instance, in 2012, the French luxury brand Hermès International won a $100 million judgment against thirty-four websites that sold counterfeit copies of

---

28. *See* Saratoga Vichy Spring Co. v. Lehman, 625 F.2d 1037, 1044 (2d Cir. 1980).
29. Girl Scouts of U.S.A. v. Bantam Doubleday Dell Publ'g Grp., Inc., 808 F. Supp. 1112, 1131 (S.D.N.Y. 1992).
30. Kalisch-Jarcho Inc. v. City of N.Y., 448 N.E.2d 413, 417 n.5 (N.Y. 1983).
31. Philip Morris U.S.A., Inc. v. Filizardo, No. 03 Civ. 5891(HB), 2004 WL 1375277, at *6 (S.D.N.Y. June 18, 2004).
32. Burberry v. Designers Imports, Inc., No. 07 Civ. 3997 (PAC), 2010 WL 199906, at *8 (S.D.N.Y. 2010).
33. Burberry Ltd. v. Target Corp., No. 18 Civ. 3946 (S.D.N.Y. May 2, 2018).
34. *See* Electrolux Corp. v. Val-Worth, Inc., 6 N.Y.2d 556, 567 (1959); Jeffrey Milstein, Inc. v. Greger, Lawlor, Roth, Inc., 58 F.3d 27, 34 (2d Cir. 1995).

the brand's luxury goods.[35] Among other causes of action, Hermès alleged violations of both common law and statutory New York unfair competition law.[36]

At a minimum, however, New York recognizes two theories of common law unfair competition: passing off and misappropriation.[37]

[A] Passing Off

Passing off[38] occurs when a defendant makes a form of false representation that causes consumers to believe that the defendant's goods or services come from the plaintiff. "[Passing] off"—that is, the sale of the goods of one manufacturer as those of another—was the first theory of unfair competition endorsed by New York courts, and "has been extended . . . to situations where the parties are not even in competition."[39] For example, passing off could occur where an up and coming handbag designer falsely represents that another designer's handbags are in fact his product. To prove passing off, a plaintiff must first demonstrate that a defendant deliberately copied or simulated the plaintiff's distinctive mark.[40] To support a passing off claim, the mark must be inherently distinctive or have acquired secondary meaning (that is, that consumers associate the mark with a particular source and not the dictionary, or "primary" meaning of the mark). In addition, the plaintiff must demonstrate that the copying alleged caused a likelihood of consumer confusion about the source of the goods or services of the plaintiff.[41] For a further discussion of secondary meaning and likelihood of confusion, refer to chapter 2.

[B] Misappropriation

Under New York law, a claim of misappropriation is broader than passing off. "The general principle . . . evolved from all of the cases is that commercial unfairness will be restrained when it appears that there has been a misappropriation, for the commercial advantage of one person, of a benefit or property right belonging to another."[42] "Commercial advantage" is a term of art used interchangeably with

---

35. Hermès Int'l v. John Doe, No. 12 Civ. 1623 (DLC) (S.D.N.Y. Apr. 30, 2012).
36. *Id.*
37. *Electrolux*, 6 N.Y.2d at 567–68 (discussing the acceptance of these theories of unfair competition in New York courts).
38. "Passing off" is often referred to interchangeably as "palming off."
39. *Electrolux*, 6 N.Y.2d at 567.
40. ITC Ltd. v. Punchgini Inc., 9 N.Y.3d 467, 480 (2007).
41. *Id.* at 479.
42. Telecom Int'l Am., Ltd. v. AT & T Corp., 280 F.3d 175, 197 (2d Cir. 2001).

property or know-how.[43] A misappropriation claim contemplates the taking and use of another's commercial advantage to compete against that person.[44] Indeed, "[t]he tort of unfair competition under New York law is premised on the principle that one may not misappropriate the product of the labor, skill, and expenditures of another."[45]

New York is the only state that has not adopted some version of the Uniform Trade Secrets Act.[46] As a result, claims based on an alleged misappropriation of trade secrets are frequently asserted in New York as "unfair competition" claims. As in other states, New York recognizes claims based not only on an alleged theft of technical trade secrets or ideas, but also based on the misappropriation of information that confers a commercial advantage, even if it does not necessarily rise to the level of an invention or innovative business method.[47] For example, "a claim may be based on misappropriation of information . . . such as client lists, internal company documents, and business strategies."[48] It is important to note, however, that a customer list is not subject to a trade secret or misappropriation claim if it was readily ascertainable through Internet websites such as LinkedIn, for example.[49] The New York Court of Appeals has held that compensatory damages for trade secrets claims are limited to the actual amount lost by the plaintiff and cannot include the amount

---

43. *See* Flexitized, Inc. v. Nat'l Flexitized Corp., 335 F.2d 774, 781–82 (2d Cir. 1964).
44. Roy Export Co. v. CBS, 672 F.2d 1095, 1105 (2d Cir. 1982) (unfair competition claim established where a compilation consisting of six Charlie Chaplin film clips was used to unfairly compete with a Charlie Chaplin film biography).
45. Sokol Holdings, Inc. v. BMB Munai, Inc., 726 F. Supp. 2d 291, 302–03 (S.D.N.Y. 2010).
46. In 2018, two bills that would have adopted the UTSA in New York, SB 4688 and AO 6419, died in committee in the New York State Assembly.
47. Unlike other states, New York has not yet adopted a version of the Uniform Trade Secrets Act and trade secrets are therefore governed under New York case law. New York courts consider six factors in determining whether information constitutes a trade secret: (1) the extent to which the information is known outside of the business; (2) the extent to which it is known by employees and others involved in the business; (3) the extent of measures taken by the business to guard the secrecy of the information; (4) the value of the information to the business and its competitors; (5) the amount of effort or money expended by the business in developing the information; and (6) the ease or difficulty with which the information could be properly acquired or duplicated by others. Hudson Hotels Corp. v. Choice Hotels Int'l, 995 F.2d 1173, 1177 (2d Cir. 1993).
48. Berman v. Sugo LLC, 580 F. Supp. 2d 191, 209 (S.D.N.Y. 2008).
49. *See* Sasqua Grp., Inc. v. Courtney, 2010 U.S. Dist. LEXIS 93442 (E.D.N.Y. Aug. 2, 2010).

of money saved by the defendant by using the misappropriated information, such as by saving on research and development.[50]

New York law also recognizes a claim for misappropriation of ideas, which is a broader unfair competition claim that is potentially useful given the right set of factual evidence. In order to recover under a misappropriation of ideas theory, "the plaintiff must establish the existence of a genuine issue as to the novelty and originality of the allegedly misappropriated ideas."[51] Novelty and originality *must* be established to support a claim for misappropriation because unoriginal ideas exist in the public domain and are free to be used by anyone with impunity.

For example, in *Daou v. Huffington*, the New York Supreme Court addressed claims that Arianna Huffington misappropriated ideas related to the creation of her political blog, *The Huffington Post*. As the court explained, "New York law recognizes the tort of misappropriation of ideas when a plaintiff's factual assertions establish that the misappropriated ideas were both novel and concrete."[52] In that particular case, the court declined to dismiss the plaintiff's claims for misappropriation of idea, based on the plaintiff's allegation that, at the time of the purported misappropriation, no website had yet combined the elements of a "collective of blogs by notable personalities, non-partisan news aggregation, issue-specific web pages, scoops and exclusives derived from the founders' personal relationships with Democratic Party and media insiders, and online community-building."[53] On February 14, 2013, the court ruled on *The Huffington Post*'s second motion to dismiss the plaintiff's amended complaint, in which the plaintiff reasserted the initial misappropriation of ideas claim (that had survived the first motion to dismiss). The court again denied *The Huffington Post*'s motion to dismiss, finding that it was merely repetitive of the earlier, failed motion.[54] On February 18, 2014, the court also denied *Huffington Post*'s motion for summary judgment. Shortly thereafter, the parties reached a settlement and the case was dismissed.

Under New York law, a viable claim for unfair competition under a misappropriation theory requires a showing of bad faith.[55] Therefore,

---

50. *See* E.J. Brooks Co. v. Cambridge Sec. Seals, 31 N.Y.3d 441, 454 (2018).
51. Paul v. Haley, 183 A.D.2d 44, 53 (N.Y. App. Div. 2d Dep't 1992).
52. Daou v. Huffington, No. 651997/2010 (N.Y. Cty. Sup. Ct. Oct. 25, 2011) (denying defendant's motion to dismiss cause of action for misappropriation of ideas).
53. *Id.*
54. Daou v. Huffington, No. 651997/10 2013 NY Slip Op. 30372(U) (N.Y. Sup. Ct. Feb. 14, 2013).
55. Berman v. Sugo LLC, 580 F. Supp. 2d 191, 209 (S.D.N.Y. 2008).

a claim of unfair competition must allege both that the plaintiff expended significant labor and resources *and* the bad faith acts by which the defendant misappropriated such labor and resources for its own commercial advantage.[56] "The essence of an unfair competition claim under New York law is that the defendant misappropriated the fruit of plaintiff's labors and expenditures by obtaining access to plaintiff's business idea either through fraud or deception, or an abuse of a fiduciary or confidential relationship."[57]

Under a misappropriation cause of action, the plaintiff must show that the defendant "actually misused [plaintiff's] property in a competitive setting."[58]

§ 6:3.2 New York Statutory Unfair Competition Law

New York also has a state statutory provision that provides a related form of relief to the state's common law unfair completion cause of action. General Business Law section 349 (Article 22A) protects against unfair trade acts by prohibiting "deceptive acts or practices in the conduct of any business, trade or commerce or in the furnishing of any service."[59] This statute is applied broadly to accommodate numerous types of deceptive acts that may constitute unfair competition.

New York courts have applied a three-factor test for establishing a section 349 violation: (1) that the defendant engaged in a consumer-oriented act (such as the sale of a designer's branded merchandise); (2) that the act was misleading in a material way (for example, the products were counterfeit); and (3) the plaintiff suffered injury.[60]

As one commentator has explained, "[t]he omission of unfair acts from section 349 . . . implies that such acts were not intended to be covered by the statute unless they were also deceptive" to the public at large.[61] The statute does not apply strictly to consumers, however. A competitor may allege a cause of action for unfair competition under the statute so long as the wrongful conduct alleged

56. *Id.*
57. Telecom Int'l Am., Ltd. v. AT & T Corp., 280 F.3d 175, 197 (2d Cir. 2001) (citations omitted).
58. Delville v. Firmenich Inc., No. 08 Civ. 10891, 2013 U.S. Dist. LEXIS 17461, at *60–62 (S.D.N.Y. Jan. 31, 2013).
59. N.Y. GEN. BUS. LAW § 349.
60. *See* Vitabiotics, Ltd. v. Krupka, 606 F. Supp. 779, 785 (E.D.N.Y. 1984) (sale of infringing products creates presumption of injury under section 349).
61. Peter J. Wied, *Patently Unfair: State Unfair Competition Laws and Patent Enforcement*, 12 HARV. J. L. & TECH. 2 (1999).

was "consumer-oriented."[62] But because of section 349's focus on consumer-oriented acts, private contract disputes may not be litigated under the statute.[63]

§ 6:4 Federal Law

§ 6:4.1 *Federal Unfair Competition*

Though unfair competition law is principally governed by state common law, federal law may also apply where trademarks or false advertising are at issue. In particular, the U.S. Lanham Act, best known as the federal trademark statute, may provide an additional relevant cause of action that does not fit neatly under the rubric of trademark infringement. More specifically, section 43(a) of the Lanham Act[64] "is one of the few provisions that goes beyond trademark protection."[65] It does not, however, "have boundless application as a remedy for unfair trade practices,"[66] and therefore "can never be a federal 'codification' of the overall law of 'unfair competition.'"[67]

On its face, section 43(a) covers not only infringement of unregistered trademarks,[68] but also trade dress and product design,[69] and more generally prohibits a person from using "any word, term, name, symbol, or device, or any combination thereof" that:

(A) is likely to cause confusion, or to cause mistake, or to deceive as to the affiliation, connection, or association of such person with another person, or as to the origin, sponsorship, or

---

62. N.Y. GEN. BUS. LAW § 349.
63. *See* Korn v. First Unim Life Ins. Co., 277 A.D.2d 355, 356 (N.Y. App. Div. 2000) ("Since the complaint essentially alleges a private contract dispute . . . the complaint fails to state a cause of action pursuant to General Business Law § 349."); Graham v. Eagle Distrib. Co., 224 A.D.2d 921, 921 (N.Y. App. Div. 1996) (plaintiff is not allowed to "add a cause of action alleging a violation of General Business Law § 349" that merely restates an existing contract claim); *see also* Fekete v. GA Ins. Co. of N.Y., 279 A.D.2d 300, 300 (N.Y. App. Div. 2001) (affirming denial of "motion to amend complaint to assert a claim under General Business Law § 349" based on "[p]rivate contract disputes").
64. 15 U.S.C. § 1125(a).
65. Dastar Corp. v. Twentieth Century Fox Film Corp., 539 U.S. 23, 29 (2003).
66. Alfred Dunhill, Ltd. v. Interstate Cigar Co., 499 F.2d 232, 237 (2d Cir. 1974).
67. J. MCCARTHY, TRADEMARKS AND UNFAIR COMPETITION § 27:7 (4th ed. 2012) [hereinafter J. MCCARTHY].
68. EMI Catalogue P'ship v. Hill, Holliday, Connors, Cosmopulos Inc., 228 F.3d 56, 61 (2d Cir. 2000).
69. *See* Wal-Mart Stores, Inc. v. Samara Bros., Inc., 529 U.S. 205, 209 (2000).

approval of his or her goods, services, or commercial activities by another person, or

(B) in commercial advertising or promotion, misrepresents the nature, characteristics, qualities, or geographic origin of his or her or another person's goods, services, or commercial activities. . . .[70]

Courts have applied the statute to a wide range of deceptive conduct that is likely to cause consumer confusion. For example, it is well settled that section 43(a) is "broad enough to encompass reverse passing off."[71] Reverse passing off occurs when someone markets another's product as his own product.

In addition, commentators have noted that the statute may cover instances of product disparagement, that is, false negative statements made about a seller's product. For example, the leading treatise on unfair competition states that "some courts hold that the intent required [for a statement to qualify as product disparagement] is intent that the matter published be 'reasonably understood to cast doubt'" upon the "quality" of the relevant products.[72] Under the Second Restatement of Torts, liability arises only if it is proven that the defendant made the statement with: (1) either knowledge of falsity or with a reckless disregard for truth or falsity, and (2) intent to harm plaintiff's interest or it was foreseeable that harm would result.[73] A victim of a campaign of false statements about its products may have a cause of action and an opportunity for relief if it can meet this test.

The statute does not, however, protect the "origin" of abstract ideas. The U.S. Supreme Court has interpreted "origin" under section 43(a) to refer only to the producer of tangible goods offered for sale, and not to the original "author of any idea, concept or communication embodied in those goods."[74] As a result, section 43(a) is limited to false statements made "in connection with goods or services."[75]

§ 6:4.2 *The Federal Trade Secrets Statute*

In 2016, Congress passed the Defend Trade Secrets Act (DTSA), which created a private cause of action with federal subject matter jurisdiction, allowing plaintiffs to sue in federal court for the

---

70. 15 U.S.C. § 1125(a).
71. Dastar Corp. v. Twentieth Century Fox Film Corp., 539 U.S. 23, 30 (2003).
72. J. MCCARTHY, *supra* note 67, § 27:104 (quoting Brignoli v. Balch Hardy & Scheinman, Inc., 645 F. Supp. 1201, 1208 (S.D.N.Y. 1986)).
73. RESTATEMENT (SECOND) OF TORTS § 623A (1977).
74. *Dastar*, 539 U.S. at 37.
75. *Id.* at 29.

misappropriation of trade secrets even in instances where both the plaintiff and defendant hale from the same state.[76] To qualify for federal jurisdiction, the trade secrets at issue must be "related to a product or service used in, or intended for use in, interstate or foreign commerce."[77] The Act defines "trade secrets" broadly to include patterns, formulas and designs.[78] The owner must have taken "reasonable measures" to keep the information secret, and the information must derive some sort of "independent economic value, actual or potential, from not being generally known . . . ."[79] The DTSA also defines "misappropriation" broadly to encompass either the acquisition of trade secrets by a person who "knows or has reason to know" the trade secret was improperly acquired or disclosure of a trade secret "without express or implied consent," by a party who acquired the trade secret through "improper means" or had a "duty to maintain the secret."[80] Thus, the statute permits plaintiffs to sue not only the direct thief of the alleged secret, but also anyone who improperly obtained the trade secret.

One striking feature of the DTSA is that it contains an *ex parte* civil seizure provision that allows a court to order the "seizure of property necessary to prevent the propagation or dissemination of trade secrets," provided the plaintiff is able to show "extraordinary circumstances."[81] This allows a successful plaintiff to seize computers or other forms of communications equipment that may contain the trade secret information.

§ 6:5 Illustrative Cases in the Fashion Industry

The following cases are illustrative of the ways trade secrets, misappropriation, and unfair competition claims have arisen in the context of the fashion industry.

§ 6:5.1 *Trade Secrets Cases*

Although fashion designs that are offered to the public cannot constitute a "trade secret," fashion companies can protect—or at least prolong—certain competitive advantages that are not shared with the public. For example, in *Nike v. Enter Play Sports, Inc.*, Nike alleged that

76. 18 U.S.C. § 1836. The DTSA does not preempt state causes of action. *See* 18 U.S.C. § 1838. Plaintiffs can bring suit for misappropriation of trade secrets under both state and federal law. *See id.*
77. 18 U.S.C. § 1836(b)(1).
78. 18 U.S.C. § 1839(3).
79. *Id.*
80. 18 U.S.C. § 1839(5).
81. 18 U.S.C. § 1836(b)(2).

it had "conceived of proprietary and confidential concepts" regarding a special sort of shoe design, and that it had revealed these concepts to the defendant subject to a non-disclosure agreement (NDA), with the understanding that the defendant would assist Nike in designing samples.[82] Instead, Nike alleged, the defendant sought to obtain its own patents based on Nike's shoe design, in violation of its NDA. Nike sued under the Oregon state trade secret statute; and the court rejected the defendant's motion to dismiss.[83]

Similarly, in *Marimar Textiles, Inc. v. Jude Clothing & Accessories Corp.*, the court allowed a DTSA claim to proceed based on the allegation that the defendant had misappropriated certain confidential fabric designs.[84] In particular, the plaintiff alleged that it had "supplied the U.S. and European apparel industry with original printed and novelty textile patter[n]s" and when one of its employees quit the company, she left with a laptop containing digital copies of the company's "11,000 patterns," as well as written materials containing other trade secrets about how the patterns were made.[85] Although the laptop was taken prior to the DTSA's passage, the court allowed the claims to proceed because violations relating to the claim were allegedly ongoing.[86]

The theft of secret designs and know how by former employees is a common feature of trade secrets litigation in the fashion world.[87] For instance, in May 2015, Louis Vuitton sued its former executive, Joon Ma, who left the company to work at Coach, Inc.[88] Louis Vuitton sought a preliminary injunction against Ma, alleging, that Ma violated her six-month non-compete and, on her last day at Louis Vuitton, copied files from her work laptop onto external hard drives and thumb drives before deleting emails and files to cover her tracks. The court granted the preliminary injunction, holding Ma to the terms of her non-compete and forcing her to return the proprietary information to Louis Vuitton, including material relevant to the

---

82. Nike, Inc. v. Enter Play Sports, Inc., 305 F.R.D. 642, 642–46 (D. Or. 2015).
83. *Id.*
84. Marimar Textiles, Inc. v. Jude Clothing & Accessories Corp., Civ. No. 17-2900 (JLL), 2017 WL 4391748, at *6–7 (D.N.J. 2017),
85. *Id.* at *1–2.
86. *Id.*
87. *See, e.g., Puma Hit with $57M Trade Secret Misappropriation Law Suit*, FASHION L. (Jan. 16, 2015), http://www.thefashionlaw.com/home/puma-slapped-with-57-million-trade-secret-misappropriation-lawsuit.
88. Louis Vuitton N. Am. Inc. v. Joon Ma, No. 651421/2014 (N.Y. Sup. Ct. 2014).

company's internal operations, processes, and strategic plans.[89] Other fashion brands have obtained similar results.[90]

The ecommerce side of the fashion world also offers fertile ground for trade secrets litigation. In October 2014, Lindsey Lohan and her brother were sued by Fima Potik, a technology entrepreneur.[91] Potik developed an app called Spotted Friend, that allowed users to shop the virtual wardrobes of celebrities. Potik claimed that he and the Lohans entered into an agreement to collaborate on Spotted Friend. Instead, the Lohans launched their own, competing app called Vigme, based on Potik's business model and trade secrets. The complaint asserted claims for misappropriation of trade secrets and unfair competition. Shortly after the suit was filed, the court entered a temporary restraining order against the Lohans, restraining them from promoting their app or seeking investments or partnerships in connection therewith. A year later, the parties stipulated to vacate the restraining order and, in 2017, Potik moved to voluntarily discontinue the action. Of course, these claims are less successful when the plaintiff cannot establish that the allegedly stolen information is, in fact, a trade secret.[92]

§ 6:5.2 J. Crew Group Inc. v. Fenton

Because a designer's unique perspective and creative input can drive a brand's success, highly regarded designers are frequently recruited by competitors in the fashion and retail industries. In these

---

89. *See* Kate Greene, *Louis Vuitton Claims Ex-VP Took Secrets to Coach*, LAW360 (May 8, 2014), https://www.law360.com/articles/536209; Stewart Bishop, *Ex-Louis Vuitton VP Must Return Files in Trade Secrets Fight*, LAW360 (May 21, 2014), https://www.law360.com/articles/540266/ex-louis-vuitton-vp-must-return-files-in-trade-secrets-fight.

90. *See also* Nike, Inc. v. Dekovic, No. 14 Cv. 18876 (Or. Cir. Ct. Multnomah Co., filed Dec. 8, 2014), in which Nike obtained a preliminary injunction preventing three former Nike designers from disclosing misappropriated trade secrets.

91. Spotted Friend, LLC v. Vigme, Inc., No. 653322/2014 (N.Y. Sup. Ct. 2014).

92. In *Archie MD, Inc. v. Elsevier, Inc.*, No. 16 Civ. 6614, 2017 WL 3421167 (S.D.N.Y. Mar. 13, 2017), the plaintiff corporation created three-dimensional animations of human anatomy for education purposes and licensed the right to use these animations to a company involved in medical education and the sale of textbooks. After the contract was terminated, the educational corporation hired a new company to create original animations—and these animations were based in part on those previously provided by the plaintiff. The plaintiff brought a DTSA claim and lost. The court reasoned that because the licensed designs were "distributed to consumers," they could not qualify as trade secrets and, moreover, the plaintiff failed to take "reasonable measures to keep such information secret."

instances, it is particularly important to be conscious of the risks if a designer takes proprietary information from one employer to the next.

In 2012, one of J. Crew Group Inc.'s top men's fashion designers, Dwight Fenton, resigned from J. Crew to join Bonobos, Inc., a direct J. Crew competitor. J. Crew alleged that Fenton, as the company's Senior Design Director, was integrally involved in "determining style trends and directions, selecting materials, colors, and patterns used in designs and helping create brand and sales strategies."[93] Before Fenton left J. Crew, however, he allegedly forwarded numerous internal J. Crew documents to his personal email address, in what J. Crew claims was a violation of company policy. J. Crew promptly filed a complaint, alleging claims of unfair competition, misappropriation of trade secrets, and a breach of Fenton's contractual confidentiality obligations. J. Crew alleged that Fenton improperly forwarded J. Crew's proprietary designs, product specifications, and measurements; J. Crew's production development calendar; contact information for J. Crew's key manufacturing resources; lists of J. Crew's third-party brand collaborators; presentation samples; design inspirations; and financial data relevant to J. Crew's men's design budgets.[94]

According to J. Crew, Fenton engaged in unfair competition by "unlawfully misappropriating and using this confidential information for the benefit of J. Crew's competitor, Bonobos."[95] J. Crew's success in asserting these claims, as one legal commentator noted, was tied to the question of "whether and to what extent Fenton was bound by a non-disclosure agreement" and whether "Fenton's act of sending J. Crew's confidential information to his personal computer evidences intent to use that information against J. Crew, and for Bonobos."[96]

In addition, J. Crew faced the added task of establishing that the pre-commercial ideas and designs that Fenton allegedly misappropriated had value, and that J. Crew would be harmed by its inability to keep these materials private. J. Crew's motion for a preliminary injunction, however, was withdrawn when the parties filed a stipulation of discontinuance.[97] The terms of the settlement were not disclosed. This case, however, is illustrative of the ways that unfair competition

---

93. Complaint, J. Crew Grp., Inc. v. Fenton, Index No. 650271/2013, at 2 (N.Y. Cty. Sup. Ct. Jan. 24, 2013).
94. *Id.*
95. *Id.* at 5.
96. Robert Levine, *J. Crew Complaint Illustrates Issues With Litigating Misappropriation Cases Under New York Law*, BROOKLYN L. SCH. TRADE SECRETS INST., http://tsi.brooklaw.edu/commentary/j-crew-complaint-illustrates-issues-litigating-misappropriation-cases-under-new-york-law.
97. Order, J. Crew Grp., Inc. v. Fenton, Index No. 650271/2013 (N.Y. Sup. Ct. Feb. 14, 2013).

claims arise in the context of what might otherwise be considered employment disputes.[98]

§ 6:5.3 Burch v. Burch

In other instances, unfair competition claims focus on an alleged misappropriation of a brand image or experience. For example, Chris Burch, the ex-husband of celebrated designer Tory Burch, was a founding partner of Tory Burch LLC, and served as co-chairperson of the board and as a consultant to the company. In these roles, he was privy to confidential information such as design concepts, business strategies, and customer base and performance data.[99] Tory Burch later alleged, however, that Chris Burch had always been interested in establishing his own retail brand.[100] According to Ms. Burch, Chris Burch had led the company to believe he was developing a line of stores to sell an assortment of home goods, electronics, surfboards, motor scooters, refrigerators, washers and dryers, nondescript basic apparel, coffee makers, and vacuum cleaners. After the couple separated, Ms. Burch alleged that Mr. Burch's new store was not what she had expected, but rather "copied the Tory Burch brand image—from the lacquered front doors, to the store fixtures, to the furnishings, area rugs and wall treatments, to the packing design, to the merchandising."[101]

In 2012, Chris Burch sued Tory Burch for breach of contract and interference with attempts to sell his shares in Tory Burch LLC.[102] In response, Ms. Burch filed counterclaims, describing Chris Burch's store as "a cheapened, lower-quality version of the Tory Burch brand" and ultimately a "knockoff brand."[103] Importantly, Ms. Burch not only alleged that Mr. Burch misappropriated Tory Burch LLC's confidential information to use for a rival retail establishment, but also that he misappropriated key elements of the Tory Burch brand identity itself, in such a way that consumers would perceive an undeniable association between his new brand and that of Tory Burch.[104]

For example, Ms. Burch alleged that the interior design of the C. Wonder (the name of Mr. Burch's new retail brand) retail storefronts

98. *See also infra* chapter 16.

99. Counterclaim, Burch v. Burch, C.A. No. 7921-CS, at 3, 14 (Del. Ch. Nov. 5, 2012).

100. *Id.* at 2.

101. *Id.*

102. *See Tory Burch v. Chris Burch v. Judge Strine*, BLOOMBERG BUSINESSWEEK (Nov. 14, 2012), https://www.businessweek.com/articles/2012-11-14/tory-burch-v-dot-chris-burch-v-dot-judge-strine.

103. Counterclaim, Burch v. Burch, C.A. No. 7921-CS, at 2 (Del. Ch. Nov. 5, 2012).

104. *Id.* at 27–28.

was too similar to Tory Burch boutiques. Both stores allegedly incorporated lacquered and brass furniture, with "Grecian key pattern" trim on the store awnings, and velvet curtains throughout the interior.[105] "In addition to borrowing key elements of Tory Burch's distinctive store décor," Ms. Burch alleged that "Chris [Burch] stocked his C. Wonder stores with signature products that closely resemble Tory Burch's best-selling products, displayed in a manner that accentuated their similarity to Tory Burch's iconic collection, down to the gold logo buttons. . . ."[106]

Further, Ms. Burch claimed that Mr. Burch had selected her best-selling items and copied them on a large scale: "The overall effect of the C. Wonder product line, which emphasized gold hardware, was to create the impression that C. Wonder was selling lower-quality, lower-priced Tory Burch goods" that were uniquely representative of the Tory Burch brand and therefore likely to confuse and deceive consumers as to the affiliation or connection between the Tory Burch company and C. Wonder.[107]

The lawsuits were settled in 2013 under undisclosed terms, but *Burch v. Burch* remains illustrative of the many forms that unfair competition claims can take in the fashion and retail context.[108]

---

105. *Id.* at 22–23.

106. *Id.* at 23.

107. *Id.* at 24.

108. Some unfair competition claims in the fashion industry end in failure. For example, in 2016, the Southern District of New York dismissed claims alleging that Louis Vuitton Malletier had copied the decorative aspect of a luxury sneaker line sold by LVL XIII Brands. LVL XIII Brands, Inc. v. Louis Vuitton Malletier S.A., 209 F. Supp. 3d 612, 626 (S.D.N.Y. 2016), *aff'd*, 720 F. App'x 24 (2d Cir. 2017). The court specifically noted that no federal or New York state claim of unfair competition claim could be made out without establishing bad faith. Because the plaintiff had "zero evidence that LV copied the [plaintiff's shoe]—much less that it did so with the goal of capitalizing on LVL XIII's reputation," the case was dismissed. 209 F. Supp. 3d at 674, 678 (citing Sly Magazine, LLC v. Weider Publ'ns L.L.C., 346 F. App'x 721, 723 (2d Cir. 2009)).

Chapter 7

Counterfeiting

§ 7:1 Introduction
§ 7:2 Government Enforcement
§ 7:3 Civil Litigation
§ 7:3.1 Establishing Personal Jurisdiction over Counterfeiters
[A] Websites Selling Goods in the Forum
[B] Providing Services to Website Selling Counterfeit Goods in the Forum
[C] Alternative Service of Process
§ 7:3.2 Likelihood of Confusion
§ 7:3.3 Ex Parte Injunctive Relief
[A] Restraint of Third-Party Suppliers and Domain Name Registries
[B] Restraint of Counterfeiters' Assets
[C] Expedited and International Discovery
§ 7:3.4 Contributory Infringement
[A] The *Inwood* Decision and Its Progeny
[B] Secondary Liability in the Online Context
[B][1] *Perfect 10 v. Visa International Service Association*
[B][2] *Gucci America, Inc. v. Frontline Processing Corp.*
§ 7:3.5 Monetary Remedies
[A] Counterfeiters' Profits
[B] Statutory Damages
§ 7:4 Additional Remedies for Trademark Owners
§ 7:4.1 Technological Solutions
§ 7:4.2 Cooperation Among Trademark Owners, Credit Card Companies, and E-Commerce Servicers
§ 7:4.3 Public Education

§ 7:1 Introduction

Large-scale international counterfeiting of accessories and apparel poses a significant threat to the fashion industry and intellectual property rights owners, as globalization has enhanced the ability of counterfeiters to cheaply manufacture and sell illegal merchandise to customers around the world. Counterfeiting, moreover, is no longer a problem that affects only luxury goods. Although luxury goods certainly remain an inviting target for unscrupulous counterfeiters, more and more piracy is aimed at lower-cost, higher-volume retail products.[1] Indeed, counterfeiters often succeed because many consumers do not expect counterfeiters to make counterfeit versions of lower-priced consumer products. The result is that all makers of retail goods need to be concerned about the prospect that counterfeiters are out there developing ersatz versions of their products for sale through every conceivable chain of distribution from flea markets and sidewalks, all the way to goods that find their way onto the shelves of innocent retailers who are not aware that their stores are being used to merchandise counterfeits.

The ability of counterfeiters to offer illegal goods over the Internet poses a unique challenge, as counterfeiters easily remain anonymous by using false identities in connection with websites, and can transfer their operation from one domain name to the next, as soon as one website selling counterfeits is shut down. Moreover, even when a trademark owner is able to identify and obtain a judgment against an actual person, counterfeiters often hide their assets, either in banks outside the United States or in international banks with a presence in the United States that resist complying with U.S. court process, making collection efforts difficult. Effectively tackling counterfeiting therefore requires a multi-pronged approach drawing on the tools of law enforcement, civil litigation, cooperation among private businesses, and public education. This chapter outlines some of the innovative strategies employed by both public and private actors, as well as the key legal issues that arise, in the fight against global counterfeiting.

§ 7:2 Government Enforcement

Both federal and local law enforcement have long taken steps to fight counterfeiting through seizures of counterfeit goods and the property used in connection with the sale of such goods, and criminal

---

1. *See, e.g.*, Kelli B. Grant, *Cheap Fakes: 10 Ordinary Items now Counterfeited*, MARKETWATCH (Dec. 18, 2011), https://www.marketwatch.com/story/cheap-fakes-10-ordinary-items-now-counterfeited-1322607984784.

prosecution of the offenders. One of the most important resources for intellectual property rights owners faced with rampant counterfeiting is the federal government, which has become increasingly aggressive in its pursuit of counterfeiters. For example, in August 2018, after months of investigation and undercover work by both the New York City Police Department and the Department of Homeland Security, Homeland Security Investigations Border Enforcement and Security Task Force, the Southern District of New York arrested and filed a lawsuit against five individuals responsible for hawking more than 380,000 pairs of fake Nike sneakers worth over $70 million.[2]

Federal agencies working cooperatively through the National Intellectual Property Rights Coordination Center ("IPR Center")[3] have developed at least two notable tactics to fight counterfeiting: seizure of means and forfeiture of proceeds. For example, in 2017, U.S. Customs and Border Protection (CBP) and U.S. Department of Homeland Security Immigration and Customs Enforcement (ICE) seized 34,143 shipments of counterfeit goods.[4] The Department of Justice and ICE have coordinated a law enforcement initiative coined Operation "In Our Sites."[5] In 2016, Operation in Our Sites VII included law enforcement authorities from twenty-seven countries.[6] Together, the authorities seized 15,000 illegal websites and 48,000 erroneous e-commerce links.[7] The seizure provisions of 18 U.S.C. § 981(b) allow law enforcement to obtain warrants and seize the goods offered for sale in counterfeiting schemes. The government can seek forfeiture of proceeds after a conviction. The government may also seek civil and criminal forfeiture under 18 U.S.C. § 2323 and 18 U.S.C. § 981(k) for property used to facilitate, or derived from the commission

---

2. *See* Nadia Dreid, *Counterfeit Ring Sold $73M in Fake Jordans, Feds Say*, LAW360 (Aug. 7, 2018), https://www.law360.com/retail/articles/1070974/counterfeit-ring-sold-73m-in-fake-jordans-feds-say; Complaint, *U.S. v. Suen et al.*, No. 18-mj-06658 (S.D.N.Y. Aug 3, 2018).
3. *See* NAT'L INTELLECTUAL PROP. RIGHTS COORDINATION CTR., https://www.iprcenter.gov/.
4. News Release, U.S. Customs and Border Protection, Record Number of IPR Seizures in FY17 for CBP, ICE (Mar. 5, 2018), https://www.cbp.gov/newsroom/national-media-release/record-number-ipr-seizures-fy17-cbp-ice.
5. *Website Seizure: A New Weapon Against IP Crime*, LAW360 (Apr. 5, 2011), http://www.law360.com/articles/236201/website-seizure-a-new-weapon-against-ip-crime; U.S. IMMIGRATION & CUSTOMS ENF'T, OPERATION IN OUR SITES (May 22, 2014), https://www.ice.gov/factsheets/ipr-in-our-sites.
6. *See* News Release, U.S. Immigration & Customs Enf't, 'Operation In Our Sites' Keeps Internet Clear of Fakes (Nov. 28, 2016), https://www.ice.gov/news/releases/operation-our-sites-keeps-internet-clear-fakes.
7. *Id.*

of, copyright and trademark counterfeiting offenses. Pursuant to the statute, law enforcement may seize not only the counterfeit goods themselves, but also domain names of infringing websites and any proceeds of the illegal activity. In *United States v. Zhao*, for example, a guilty verdict for importing and selling counterfeit computer equipment led to a forfeiture penalty of over $1.6 million in accounts and another $1 million in assets.[8]

The government has used a provision of the USA Patriot Act[9] to seize proceeds of counterfeit sales deposited in accounts overseas. After criminal investigation of a counterfeiting operation revealed that counterfeiters used PayPal to process payments for counterfeit goods and then wired the proceeds to bank accounts in China, the government obtained warrants to seize $826,883 from correspondent accounts held by Chinese banks that have branches in the United States.[10]

In an impressive exercise of federal enforcement power, Operation In Our Sites was able to seize funds from counterfeiters' bank accounts, even though the illegal proceeds were held in bank accounts designated as being located in bank branches in China. After an investigation revealed that counterfeiters based in China processed payments for the sale of counterfeit sports apparel using PayPal accounts and then wired their proceeds to bank accounts held at Chinese banks such as the Bank of China (BOC), law enforcement officers seized $826,883 in proceeds that had been transferred from PayPal accounts to various bank accounts at BOC and another Chinese bank by serving a warrant for seizure on the branches of these banks that are

---

8. United States v. Zhao, No. 10-cr-00317 (E.D. Va. May 26, 2011).
9. Uniting and Strengthening America by Providing Appropriate Tools Required to Intercept and Obstruct Terrorism Act (USA Patriot Act) of 2001, Pub. L. No. 107-56, 115 Stat. 272 (Oct. 26, 2001).
10. News Release, U.S. Immigration & Customs Enf't, More Than $896,000 in Proceeds Seized from the Online Sale of Counterfeit Sports Apparel Manufactured in China (Apr. 10, 2012) [hereinafter ICE News Release], https://www.ice.gov/news/releases/more-896000-proceeds-seized-online-sale-counterfeit-sports-apparel-manufactured-china; Verified Complaint for Forfeiture In Rem, U.S. v. All Funds in Indus. & Commercial Bank of China Ltd. Interbank Accounts in the United States, No. 1:12 cv 00489 (D.D.C. Mar. 22, 2012). Bank of China subsequently provided documentation that the account named in the complaint contained fewer than five U.S. dollars, and the government voluntarily dismissed the claim. Consent Motion for Release of Funds and for Voluntary Dismissal, No. 1:12-cv-00489 (D.D.C. Sept. 20, 2013).

physically located in the United States.[11] Law enforcement officers also seized $69,504 in funds remaining in three PayPal accounts used by the counterfeiters.[12] Section 2323 provides for restitution to victims of copyright and counterfeiting offenses, furnishing the intellectual property rights holder with the means to recoup some of the proceeds of the infringing activity.

The IPR Center, led by ICE and Homeland Security Investigations (HSI), is at the center of enforcement efforts.[13] The IPR Center connects twenty-three federal agencies, the governments of Canada and Mexico, and the private sector, to combat illegal trade by coordinating cross-agency task forces that identify, investigate, and prosecute counterfeiters and dismantle their illegal enterprises of manufacturers, importers, distributers, and sellers. In May 2018 in Laredo, Texas, special agents with ICE and HSI seized 79,000 counterfeit items bearing trademarks of Hermés, Louis Vuitton, adidas, Nike, Apple, Samsung and Sony—valued at $16 million.[14] In 2017, the IPR Center teamed up with a Europol coalition of twenty-seven European Union Member States to effectuate the largest e-commerce takedown in history—seizing 20,520 websites offering counterfeit goods for sale.[15]

The government relies extensively on leads from brand owners to track counterfeiters, so it is advisable for brand owners to keep in close communication with federal agencies, participate in programs that train customs agents how to spot counterfeits, and regularly report instances of suspected infringement in both brick-and-mortar and online outlets. The federal government has unique enforcement abilities, and has developed tactics both to cut off the counterfeiters' means of purveying counterfeit goods and to seize the proceeds of the illegal activity.

Of course, there are limits to the government's power. For example, law enforcement must have sufficient factual and legal bases to

---

11. ICE News Release, *supra* note 10.
12. *Id.*
13. Nat'l Intellectual Prop. Rights Coordination Ctr., About Us, https://www.iprcenter.gov/about.
14. News Release, U.S. Immigration & Customs Enf't, ICE, CBP Seize Nearly 79,000 Counterfeit Items in South Texas Valued at $16 Million (May 21, 2018), https://www.ice.gov/news/releases/ice-cbp-seize-nearly-79000-counterfeit-items-south-texas-valued-16-million.
15. News Release, EUROPOL, Biggest Hit Against Online Piracy: Over 20,520 Internet Domain Names Seized for Selling Counterfeits (Nov. 27, 2017), https://www.europol.europa.eu/newsroom/news/biggest-hit-against-online-piracy-over-20-520-internet-domain-names-seized-for-selling-counterfeits.

search and seize counterfeiters' property.[16] And, while seizures are a critical tool in enforcing intellectual property rights, law enforcement agencies do not have sufficient resources to stop all persistent counterfeiters.[17]

§ 7:3 Civil Litigation

Although not quite as far-ranging as the powers at the disposal of federal law enforcement agencies, private civil litigation also provides intellectual property rights owners with the means to shut down infringing websites, obtain discovery into the counterfeiters' business operations, and restrain the assets of counterfeiters prior to final judgment.

§ 7:3.1 *Establishing Personal Jurisdiction over Counterfeiters*

A threshold issue in many counterfeiting cases is whether the court has personal jurisdiction over a defendant operating a counterfeiting website outside the forum state. Personal jurisdiction over a foreign defendant alleged to have infringed a trademark or copyright will typically be based on specific jurisdiction under a state's long-arm statute. For instance, New York's long-arm statute extends jurisdiction for a tortious act (including trademark infringement) if: "(1) [t]he defendant committed a tortious act outside the state; (2) the cause of action arose from that act; (3) the act caused injury to a person or property within the state; (4) the defendant expected or should reasonably have expected the act to have consequences in the state; [and] (5) the defendant derives substantial revenue from interstate or international commerce."[18]

---

16. *See, e.g.*, Memorandum Order Denying the Government's Application for a Warrant to Seize and Search Electronic Devices at 1, *In re* Cunnius, No. 11-mj-00055 (W.D. Wash. Feb. 11, 2011) (denying government's application for a warrant to seize a suspected counterfeiter's digital devices and search all electronically stored information as overbroad under the Fourth Amendment).
17. *See* Press Release, U.S. Dep't of Justice, Five Individuals and Five Corporations Charged in New York for Importing and Selling Hazardous and Counterfeit Toys (Feb. 6, 2013) (announcing indictment against five individuals who continued selling hazardous counterfeiting toys for eight years although thirty-three of their shipments had been seized by the U.S. government), http://www.justice.gov/opa/pr/2013/February/13-crm-162.html.
18. Sole Resort, S.A. de C.V. v. Allure Resorts Mgmt., LLC, 450 F.3d 100, 106 (2d Cir. 2006); N.Y. C.P.L.R. 302(3).

[A] Websites Selling Goods in the Forum

In counterfeiting cases, courts have made clear that long-arm statutes may be applied to out-of-state defendants who operate an interactive website that sells counterfeit goods into the forum state. For example, in *Chloé v. Queen Bee of Beverly Hills, LLC*, the Second Circuit held that "the single act of an out-of-state defendant employee shipping an item into New York, combined with his employer's extensive business activity involving New York, gives rise to personal jurisdiction."[19] The defendant website offered Chloé handbags for sale to New York consumers, facilitated the shipment of those bags into New York, and also sold other items to New York consumers. Thus, the court held that the shipment of one item bearing the counterfeit Chloé mark was "part of a larger business plan purposefully directed at New York consumers" and imputed the company's New York activities to an individual defendant as well as the defendant website itself, finding the exercise of personal jurisdiction appropriate.[20]

Going a step further, a court in the Northern District of Illinois asserted personal jurisdiction over an out-of-state defendant that offered counterfeit products for sale in the forum state even though no sale was ever actually completed. The court, applying Illinois's long-arm statute, exercised personal jurisdiction over the Chinese defendant for operating an interactive website that offered to sell counterfeit products to customers in all fifty states—including Illinois—despite not having actually sold a single product to an Illinois resident.[21] There, the court found that asserting personal jurisdiction was fair because the defendant expressly aimed its operations at Illinois by

---

19. Chloé v. Queen Bee of Beverly Hills, LLC, 616 F.3d 158, 165 (2d Cir. 2010).

20. *Id.* at 167–68. The Second Circuit left open the "question of whether a sale of a counterfeit item to a plaintiff's investigator or agent by itself constitutes an act of trademark infringement." *Id.* at 165 n.3 (citations omitted). The Southern District of New York adopted the same jurisdictional analysis in another case in which the defendants operated an interactive website, displayed testimonials purporting to be from satisfied New York customers, and processed and delivered an investigator's purchase of a counterfeit product to a New York address. Balenciaga Am., Inc. v. Dollinger, No. 10 Civ. 2912 (LTS), 2010 WL 3952850 (S.D.N.Y. Oct. 8, 2010).

21. Monster Energy Co. v. Wensheng, 136 F. Supp. 3d 897, 906 (N.D. Ill. 2015); *but see* Am. Bridal & Prom Indus. Assoc., Inc. v. The P'ships & Unincorp. Assocs. Identified on Sched. A, 192 F. Supp. 3d 924, 932 (N.D. Ill. 2016) (declining personal jurisdiction based solely on the existence of an interactive website without evidence that defendants offered to sell counterfeit products to Illinois residents).

inviting potential buyers from Illinois to purchase its counterfeit products and therefore knew that the effects of its counterfeiting practice likely would be felt in the forum state.[22]

[B] Providing Services to Website Selling Counterfeit Goods in the Forum

In *Gucci America, Inc. v. Frontline Processing Corp.*, a district court in the Southern District of New York applied these same principles to accused *contributory* infringers who allegedly assisted merchants in obtaining credit card processing services, and processed credit card transactions, for the sale of counterfeit goods on the Internet.[23] The New York court held that it could exercise personal jurisdiction over a Wyoming corporation with a five-employee business in Colorado, a Nevada corporation with its principal place of business in Montana, and a Texas bank.[24] Plaintiff Gucci America, a New York–based corporation, alleged that it was harmed in New York by the infringing website's sale of counterfeit goods in New York.[25] The court found that the defendants expected or should have expected their businesses to have consequences in New York because defendants knew that the Internet businesses they serviced "were unrestricted by geography and available through the [I]nternet to consumers in all of the states, including New York."[26] Additionally, each of the defendants held itself out as a nationwide operation and had some clients in New York.[27]

Under the reasoning in *Frontline*, there may be a basis to assert personal jurisdiction over any knowing provider of important services to an interactive website selling counterfeit goods into the brand owner's home forum, especially where the third party is a national company that also transacted some additional business in the forum state.

[C] Alternative Service of Process

It is often difficult or impossible to serve defendants in counterfeiting cases with traditional forms of process because counterfeiters tend to supply false names and contact information in connection with their counterfeiting activities. As a result, courts have frequently allowed alternative service via the Internet to email addresses associated with specific accused infringing websites, especially where the

22. *Wensheng*, 136 F. Supp. 3d at 907–08.
23. Gucci Am., Inc. v. Frontline Processing Corp., 721 F. Supp. 2d 228 (S.D.N.Y. 2010).
24. *Id.* at 237–38.
25. *Id.* at 241.
26. *Id.* at 244.
27. *Id.* at 245.

plaintiff's agents have successfully communicated with the defendant through email in connection with the purchase of counterfeit goods.[28]

§ 7:3.2 Likelihood of Confusion

As described in greater detail above in chapter 2, to prevail on a traditional trademark infringement claim, a plaintiff must establish that the trademark is protected under the Lanham Act and that the defendant's use of a similar mark is likely to cause confusion "among the relevant consuming public."[29] The members of the consuming public in question have traditionally been assumed to be "numerous ordinary prudent purchasers."[30]

In the counterfeiting context, the concept of post-sale confusion is particularly important because, even if the immediate consumer knows he or she is buying a counterfeit item, there is still substantial danger that a gift recipient or other casual observer may be confused about the origin of the goods and that such confusion may dampen

---

28. *See, e.g.*, Rio Props., Inc. v. Rio Int'l Interlink, 284 F.3d 1007, 1017–18 (9th Cir. 2002) ("[W]hen faced with an international e-business scofflaw, playing hide-and-seek with the federal court, email may be the only means of effecting service of process."); Elsevier, Inc. v. Siew Yee Chew, 287 F. Supp. 3d 374, 378–89 (S.D.N.Y. 2018) (finding email an acceptable method to serve Chinese defendants who have "stymie[d] any effort to determine their true addresses"); Out Fit 7 Ltd. v. Nanjing 3D Info. Tech., Co., No. C 13-00050 CRB (N.D. Cal. July 29, 2013) ("Plaintiffs here have diligently, patiently, and unsuccessfully attempted service through formal international process, but failed because Defendant has made it unusually difficult to locate its physical address. . . . [Because] correspondence between the parties makes clear that Plaintiffs have identified email addresses used by Defendant that are regularly monitored by its leadership . . . the Court finds that service upon Defendant by email would be reasonable . . . ."); Order, Nike, Inc. v. Wu, No. 13-cv-8012 (SAS), 2015 WL 9450795 (S.D.N.Y. Aug. 20, 2015); Temporary Restraining Order, Asset Restraining Order, Order Authorizing Expedited Discovery and Alternative Service of Process, and Order to Show Cause, Tiffany (NJ) LLC v. Dong, No. 11 Civ. 2183 (GBD)(FM) (S.D.N.Y. Mar. 30, 2011); Temporary Restraining Order, Asset Restraining Order, Order Authorizing Expedited Discovery and Alternative Service of Process and Order to Show Cause, Gucci Am. Inc. v. Bagsmerchant, LLC, No. 10 Civ. 2911 (DAB) (S.D.N.Y. Apr. 12, 2010); Temporary Restraining Order, Asset Restraining Order, Order Authorizing Expedited Discovery and Alternative Service of Process and Order to Show Cause, Gucci Am. Inc. v. Weixing Li, No. 10 Civ. 4974 (RJS) (S.D.N.Y. July 2, 2010).
29. *E.g.*, Burberry Ltd. v. Euro Moda, Inc., No. 08 Civ. 5781, 2009 WL 1675080, at *5 (S.D.N.Y. June 10, 2009).
30. Arrow Fastener Co. v. Stanley Works, 59 F.3d 384, 390 (2d Cir. 1995).

demand for genuine trademark goods.[31] As a result, for the purposes of the likelihood of confusion analysis, the relevant audience may not be the targeted purchasers of authentic trademark goods, but rather any "person on the street." In fact, in the context of online counterfeiting, many websites specifically disclaim that the goods are "replicas" and not authentic designer merchandise, and therefore the purchasers of the goods are arguably not confused as to the origins of the products.

As the Second Circuit held, trademark law protects the public from incurring harms caused by post-sale confusion:

> Trademark laws exist to protect the public from confusion. The creation of confusion in the post-sale context can be harmful in that if there are too many knockoffs in the market, sales of the originals may decline because the public is fearful that what they are purchasing may not be an original. Furthermore, the public may be deceived in the resale market if it requires expertise to distinguish between an original and a knockoff.[32]

Under the doctrine of post-sale confusion, counterfeiters are likely to face liability even if they disclose that the counterfeit goods are not authentic.[33]

Criminal prosecution of counterfeiters includes the unauthorized use of both exact and substantially indistinguishable marks. The Fourth Circuit upheld the jury conviction of individuals who sold products using a logo found "substantially indistinguishable" from Burberry Group plc's trademark tartan plaid, even though the infringing plaid pattern differed slightly in color and shape, and bore an overlay of the trademark Burberry equestrian knight, which is not always used in connection with the plaid in authentic Burberry goods.

---

31. *See, e.g.*, Adidas Am., Inc. v. Skechers USA, Inc., No. 3:15-cv-01741, 2017 U.S. Dist. LEXIS 122459 (D. Or. Aug. 3, 2017); Louis Vuitton Malletier S.A. v. Sunny Merch. Corp., 97 F. Supp. 3d 485 (S.D.N.Y. 2015); Oralabs, Inc. v. Kind Grp., LLC, No. 13-cv-00170, 2015 U.S. Dist. LEXIS 98246 (D. Colo. July 28, 2015) (post-sale confusion).
32. Hermès Int'l v. Lederer de Paris Fifth Ave., Inc., 219 F.3d 104, 107–08 (2d Cir. 2000) (post-sale confusion standard). The Second Circuit reaffirmed the post-sale confusion standard in Louis Vuitton Malletier S.A. v. LY USA, Inc., 472 F. App'x 19, 21 (2d Cir. 2012) ("The likelihood that the use of plaintiff's marks would lead individuals other than purchasers of the knockoff products to believe that they were manufactured by the trademark-holder (so-called 'post-sale confusion') provides further support for the judgment of the district court." (citing *Hermès Int'l*, 219 F.3d at 109)).
33. *See* Rolex Watch U.S.A., Inc. v. Jones, No. 99 Civ. 2359, 2000 WL 1528263, at *3 n.1 (S.D.N.Y. Oct. 13, 2000) ("Likelihood of confusion does not focus solely on the party purchasing a product from the defendant."); *see also supra* section 2:7.2[C].

Copying a famous mark alone, however, may not trigger counterfeiting liability where the famous mark is used as part of a parody. In *Louis Vuitton Malletier S.A. v. Haute Diggity Dog, LLC*, Louis Vuitton brought trademark counterfeiting and infringement claims against the seller of "Chewy Vuiton" dog chew toys that bore colorable imitations of the Louis Vuitton marks.[34] The Fourth Circuit concluded that "the dog toys are successful parodies of LVM handbags and the LVM marks and trade dress used in connection with the marketing and sale of those handbags" because the "irreverent representation and the idealized image of an LVM handbag—immediately conveys a joking and amusing parody."[35] Although the court found that the defendant had "mimicked a part of the LVM marks," it also found "the parody sufficiently blatant" that a consumer would not be confused as to the source of the product.[36] Because the toys were a successful parody and no other factors supported a likelihood of confusion, the Fourth Circuit affirmed the district court's grant of summary judgment in favor of the defendant on the issue of trademark infringement.[37] A "subtle satire" of the original mark, however, does not constitute a fair use defense to trademark dilution.[38] And would-be parodists should be careful, because for some products, the risk that consumers will conclude that the product is approved or sponsored by the trademark owner may overcome the allegedly humorous message.[39]

§ 7:3.3 Ex Parte Injunctive Relief

An important remedy for brand owners is an ex parte temporary restraining order (TRO). Courts are authorized to issue a TRO under Rule 65 of the Federal Rules of Civil Procedure where "specific facts in an affidavit or a verified complaint clearly show that immediate and irreparable injury, loss, or damage will result to the movant before the adverse party can be heard in opposition." A TRO is a particularly potent weapon against counterfeiters. These orders typically enjoin further advertising, marketing or sale of counterfeit goods by the defendants' websites and require third-party hosts and e-commerce providers

---

34. Louis Vuitton Malletier S.A. v. Haute Diggity Dog, LLC, 507 F.3d 252 (4th Cir. 2007).
35. *Id.* at 260–61.
36. *Id.* at 262.
37. *Id.* at 263. *See also supra* section 2:10.8.
38. *See, e.g.*, Louis Vuitton Malletier S.A. v. Hyundai Motor Am., No. 10 Civ. 1611 (PKC), 2012 WL 102247 (S.D.N.Y. Mar. 22, 2012).
39. *See, e.g.*, Anheuser-Busch, Inc. v. VIP Prods., LLC, 666 F. Supp. 2d 974 (E.D. Mo. 2008) (enjoining "Buttwiper" product that mimicked Budweiser beer trade dress).

to cease providing support to the infringing websites.[40] A TRO may also enjoin further use of a domain name that makes unauthorized use of a trademark.[41] A trademark holder can therefore effectively shut down infringing websites before the defendant has even received notice of the lawsuit, as long as the trademark holder has created an evidentiary record sufficient to show that it has a likelihood of success on the merits and that it will suffer irreparable harm absent such relief.[42]

The limits of this form of relief were explored in *Juicy Couture, Inc. v. Bella International Limited*, where the court declined to apply the Lanham Act to a Hong Kong–based website, even though there were demonstrated sales of at least $3,000 of counterfeits into the United States.[43] The facts of that case were unique and appear to have contributed to the district court's decision. Specifically, the website was directed to consumers in Hong Kong, most of its customers were Chinese, and some of the marks at issue were the subject of litigation in Hong Kong, where there was already an ongoing dispute as to the rightful ownership of the trademarks at issue as a matter of Hong Kong law. The court invited reconsideration of the issue, though, if warranted by further discovery.

---

40. *See, e.g.*, Balenciaga Am. Inc. v. Dollinger, No. 10 Civ. 2912 (LTS), 2010 WL 3952850 (S.D.N.Y. Apr. 6, 2010); Temporary Restraining Order, Asset Restraining Order, Order Authorizing Expedited Discovery and Alternative Service of Process and Order to Show Cause, Gucci Am. Inc. v. Bagsmerchant, LLC, No. 10 Civ. 2911 (DAB) (S.D.N.Y. Apr. 12, 2010); Temporary Restraining Order and Order to Show Cause, Gucci Am., Inc. v. Curveal Fashion, No. 09 Civ. 8458(RJS) (S.D.N.Y. Oct. 9, 2009); Temporary Restraining Order and Order to Show Cause, Gucci Am., Inc. v. Laurette Co., No. 08 Civ. 5065 (LAK) (S.D.N.Y. June 3, 2008).

41. *See, e.g.*, Preliminary Injunction, Nike, Inc. v. Wu, No. 13-cv-8012 (SAS), 2015 WL 9450795 (S.D.N.Y. Dec. 3, 2013); Temporary Restraining Order, Asset Restraining Order, Order Authorizing Expedited Discovery and Alternative Service of Process, and Order to Show Cause, Tiffany (NJ) LLC v. Dong, No. 11 Civ. 2183 (GBD) (S.D.N.Y. Mar. 30, 2011); Temporary Restraining Order, Asset Restraining Order, Order Authorizing Expedited Discovery and Alternative Service of Process, and Order to Show Cause, Tiffany (NJ) LLC v. Andrew, No. 10 Civ. 9471 (WHP) (S.D.N.Y. Dec. 21, 2010).

42. In one case, the court granted plaintiff's request to seal its application for a temporary restraining order until the hearing on the preliminary injunction. *See* Order to Seal File, Tory Burch LLC v. Yong Sheng Int'l Trade Co., No. 10 Civ. 9336 (S.D.N.Y. Dec. 14, 2010); *see also* Application to Seal File of Plaintiffs' *Ex Parte* Application for a Temporary Restraining Order, Order to Disable Certain Websites, Asset Restraining Order, Expedited Discovery Order and Order to Show Cause for Preliminary Injunction (S.D.N.Y. Dec. 14, 2010).

43. Juicy Couture, Inc. v. Bella Int'l Ltd., 930 F. Supp. 2d 489 (S.D.N.Y. 2013).

[A] Restraint of Third-Party Suppliers and Domain Name Registries

An *ex parte* restraining order may also be directed to third parties who supply services to counterfeiters, such as financial institutions, e-commerce service providers, and domain registries, although the court must have some basis to exercise jurisdiction to bind a third party by the terms of the order. For example, in *The North Face Apparel Corp. v. Fujian Sharing Import & Export Ltd. Co.*, the district court issued an order that authorized plaintiffs to shut down new counterfeiting websites tied to the defendants and to seize newly discovered funds from the defendants' accounts without further court approval (unless the defendants challenged the seizure) "[i]n accordance with this Court's inherent equitable powers and its power to coerce compliance with its lawful orders, and due to Defendants' ongoing proliferation of domain names for operation of its counterfeiting activities."[44] The court then granted plaintiffs' motion to hold the Public Interest Registry (the registry of the ".org" Internet domains) in contempt for failing to obey the court's prior orders to disable the domain names controlled by defendants and transfer ownership of the domains to the plaintiffs.[45] The court subsequently reversed its order, however, concluding that it had lacked jurisdiction over the registry to order it to take any affirmative acts.[46] Still, the court found that once the registry was on notice—through the court's injunction—of the defendants' counterfeiting activities, "it would commit an unlawful act, by aiding and abetting in defendants' unlawful counterfeiting activities" and could subsequently be held in contempt as a result.[47]

---

44. Order for Contempt, at 8–11, The North Face Apparel Corp. v. Fujian Sharing Imp. & Exp. Ltd., No. 10 Civ. 1630 (S.D.N.Y. Dec. 21, 2010).
45. Order Denying on Reconsideration Plaintiffs' Motion to Hold Public Interest Registry in Contempt at 1, The North Face Apparel Corp. v. Fujian Sharing Import & Export Ltd., No. 10 Civ. 1630 (AKH) (S.D.N.Y. June 24, 2011).
46. *Id.* at 4.
47. *Id.* at 6. Consistent with Rule 65(d) of the Federal Rules of Civil Procedure, a non-party may be found in contempt "for violating the terms of an injunction when [the] non-party is legally identified with the defendant or when the non-party aids or abets a violation of an injunction." Blockowicz v. Williams, 630 F.3d 563, 566–67 (7th Cir. 2010). This may be so even where the aider and abettor is not within the judicial district where the order was made. Waffenschmidt v. Mackay, 763 F.2d 711, 716 (5th Cir. 1985).

[B] Restraint of Counterfeiters' Assets

Perhaps most significantly, courts throughout the United States have entered *ex parte* orders freezing the assets of defendant counterfeiters to preserve plaintiffs' equitable right to an accounting and to recover the defendants' illicit profits under the Lanham Act. Although "a court may not freeze assets solely to secure a future money judgment, where plaintiffs seek both equitable and legal relief in relation to specific funds, a court retains it[s] equitable power to freeze assets."[48] These assets may later be used to satisfy a money judgment against defendants. Notably, courts have exercised their equitable power to freeze defendants' assets anywhere in the world.[49] Given the prevalence of foreign counterfeiters exporting goods into the United States, the ability to restrain funds held abroad is crucial to a plaintiff's ability to reach the proceeds of the counterfeiter's illegal business. As noted above in section 7:2, law enforcement officials have the power to seize the proceeds of counterfeiting operations pursuant to federal statutes, but private litigants do not have a right of action under those forfeiture statutes.

In 2011, a court in the Southern District of New York held that section 35(a) of the Lanham Act (15 U.S.C. § 1117(a)), which authorizes a trademark owner to recover defendants' profits, provides district courts with the "'authority to freeze [a defendant's] assets insofar as they could be used to satisfy an award of . . . profits pursuant to Plaintiffs' Lanham Act Claims.'"[50] The court rejected the notion that it lacked authority to issue a pre-judgment asset restraint directed at assets held overseas at a Chinese bank, finding that "'[o]nce personal

---

48. *See* Balenciaga Am., Inc. v. Dollinger, No. 10 Civ. 2912 (LTS), 2010 WL 3952850, at *7 (S.D.N.Y. Oct. 8, 2010) (citation and internal quotation marks omitted) (collecting cases); *see also* Preliminary Injunction, Nike, Inc. v. Wu, No. 13 Civ. 8012 (SAS), 2015 WL 9450795 (S.D.N.Y. Dec. 3, 2013) (enjoining defendants from "transferring, disposing of, or secreting" defendants' assets based on a finding that plaintiffs were likely to succeed on the merits).

49. Gucci Am., Inc. v. Weixing Li, 768 F.3d 122, 129 (2d Cir. 2014) (citing United States v. First Nat'l City Bank, 379 U.S. 378, 384 (1965)); *see also Balenciaga*, 2010 WL 3952850, at *8 (concluding that obtaining personal jurisdiction over defendants granted the court authority to freeze their assets outside the United States); Preliminary Injunction at 7, Tiffany (NJ) LLC v. Dong, No. 2011 Civ. 2183 (GBD) (Apr. 26, 2011) (enjoining transfer of funds "into or out of any accounts associated with or utilized by any of the Defendants, regardless of whether such accounts are located in the United States or abroad").

50. *See Balenciaga*, 2010 WL 3952850, at *7; Gucci Am., Inc v. Weixing Li, No. 10 Civ. 4974 (RJS), 2011 WL 6156936, at *3 (S.D.N.Y. Aug, 23, 2011) (alteration in opinion) (quoting *Balenciaga*, 2010 WL 3952850, at *7).

jurisdiction of a party is obtained, the District Court has authority to order it to freeze property under [the party's] control, whether the property be within or without the United States.'"[51]

In *Gucci America, Inc. v. Weixing Li*, the Second Circuit affirmed, over the objections of the non-party foreign bank, that the district court had authority to restrain the defendants' assets held at a foreign bank pending trial based on the court's personal jurisdiction over the defendants and equitable principles.[52] The case suggests that the Second Circuit will continue to affirm the court's equitable power to freeze a defendant's assets, including assets maintained outside the United States, to preserve the plaintiff's equitable right to an accounting and return of the counterfeiters' profits under the Lanham Act.

Courts have also routinely upheld post-judgment asset restraints pursuant to the court's equitable powers under the Lanham Act, Federal Rule of Civil Procedure 69, and state law. Judges in the Southern District of New York have found that the court possesses the equitable powers to issue an asset restraint.[53] Although one judge in that district found that, because the plaintiff had failed to choose between an accounting of profits and statutory damages, the court could not enter a post-judgment asset restraint under its equitable powers, the court nevertheless entered a restraint pursuant to New York state law.[54]

An asset freeze order may also effectively require credit card companies and other payment processors to cease processing transactions for the defendants, which can be fatal to an Internet counterfeiting operation.[55] Because counterfeiters selling goods over the Internet rely primarily on credit card or other electronic payment transactions, disrupting a defendant's relationship with its payment processors can frustrate the defendant's ability to transfer its website to a different

---

51. *Balenciaga*, 2010 WL 3952850, at *8 (quoting *First Nat'l. City Bank*, 379 U.S. at 384).
52. *Weixing Li*, 768 F.3d at 129.
53. *See* Tiffany (NJ) LLC v. Forbse, No. 11 Civ. 4976 (NRB), 2012 WL 1918866, at *12 (S.D.N.Y. May 23, 2012); Default Judgment, Tiffany (NJ) LLC v. Dong, No. 11 CV 02183 (GBD)(FM) (Oct. 27, 2014) (ordering asset restraint pursuant to New York procedural rules as well as the court's "inherent equitable power to issue remedies" against Defendant with assets held in a Chinese bank).
54. Tiffany (NJ) LLC v. Qi Andrew, No. 10 CIV. 9471 KPF HBP, 2015 WL 3701602, at *7–12 (S.D.N.Y. June 15, 2015); Default Judgment, Tiffany (NJ) LLC v. Qi Andrew, No. 10 CIV. 9471 KPF HBP (June 23, 2015).
55. *See, e.g.*, Temporary Restraining Order at 6, Balenciaga Am., Inc. v. Dollinger, No. 2010 Civ. 2912 (LTS) (S.D.N.Y. Apr. 6, 2010); Temporary Restraining Order at 8, Tiffany (NJ) LLC v. Dong, No. 2011 Civ. 2183 (GBD) (S.D.N.Y. Mar. 30, 2011).

domain name to evade the provisions of a court order directing the defendant to stop selling counterfeits.

[C] Expedited and International Discovery

Courts also have been willing to order expedited discovery from both defendants and third parties as a form of *ex parte* relief in counterfeiting cases, allowing the plaintiff to discern the true identity of the defendants and obtain key information from defendants' financial institutions and other third parties who provide services to defendants' websites.[56] Such information can be used to trace defendants' assets, as well as to identify other participants in the counterfeiting operation and potential contributory infringers, as described below. It can also be used to identify potential victims of the counterfeit products for notice purposes.[57]

A plaintiff may also invoke the *ex parte* seizure provision of the Lanham Act to obtain business records relating to the sale of counterfeits, as the NFL did in 2013, pursuant to 15 U.S.C. § 1116(d).[58] A seizure order requires advance notice to "the United States attorney for the judicial district in which such order is sought" and sealing of the application, among other requirements.[59]

Although many counterfeiters maintain accounts at offshore banks, as long as a foreign bank is subject to the court's jurisdiction, the bank may be required to comply with a court order to produce documents. In *Gucci America, Inc. v. Curveal Fashion*, the court issued a contempt opinion against United Overseas Bank for its failure to produce documents relating to the defendant counterfeiter's accounts at its Malaysian subsidiary on the grounds that doing so would violate Malaysian bank secrecy law and that the parent company lacked the power to cause its subsidiary to turn over the documents.[60] The magistrate judge rejected the bank's secrecy argument and also concluded that "a parent company doing business in New York is required to

---

56. *See, e.g.*, Temporary Restraining Order at 10–12, *Balenciaga*, No. 2010 Civ. 2912 (LTS) (S.D.N.Y. Apr. 6, 2010).
57. *See, e.g.*, Dentsply Sirona Inc. v. L I K Supply, Corp., No. 3:16-cv-00806 (MAD/DEP), 2016 WL 3920241, at *9 (N.D.N.Y. July 15, 2016) (ordering expedited discovery because, among other factors, "[t]here is a potential that other suppliers that are not ordinarily direct purchasers of Plaintiffs' products have not been brought to Plaintiffs' attention and, thus, are unaware of the potential danger posed by Defendants' products").
58. *See* Preliminary Injunction Order, National Football League v. Sunmei, No. 13 Civ. 2572 (LGS) (S.D.N.Y. Apr. 24, 2013).
59. *See* 15 U.S.C. § 1116(d).
60. Gucci Am., Inc. v. Curveal Fashion. No. 09 Civ. 8458 (RJS) (THK), 2010 WL 808639 (S.D.N.Y. Mar. 8, 2010).

produce documents held by its subsidiary, even if located overseas."[61] After the bank continued to refuse to produce the documents, the district court held the bank in contempt and imposed a $10,000 per day coercive fine until the bank complied.[62]

In *Gucci America, Inc. v. Weixing Li*, the Second Circuit confirmed the authority of a district court to order an international bank to produce a counterfeiter's records despite the bank's claim that such a production would violate Chinese banking privacy law.[63] The court held that the district judge had properly analyzed the relevant principles of comity between international courts in finding, among other things, that the United States' "powerful interest" in protecting intellectual property outweighed China's interest in bank secrecy and that the Bank's purported exposure to liability for producing the requested information was "unduly speculative."[64] The Second Circuit, however, remanded the decision in light of *Daimler AG v. Bauman*, because the district court's decision presumed it had general jurisdiction over nonparty Bank of China.[65] On remand, the district court found specific jurisdiction over the Bank of China based on its numerous "substantial, deliberate, and recurring" contacts in New York, and the fact that "BOC frequently and deliberately used its New York correspondent account with Chase [Manhattan Bank] to effectuate wire transfers for its U.S. clients, including, critically, Defendants in this action."[66]

---

61. *Id.* at *7.
62. Order, Gucci Am., Inc. v. Curveal Fashion, No. 09 Civ. 8459 (RJS) (S.D.N.Y. May 27, 2010); *see also* Tiffany (NJ) LLC v. Dong, No. 11 Civ. 2183 (GBD), 2013 WL 4046380, at *12 (S.D.N.Y. Aug. 9, 2013) (noting that there have been "several instances" where judges in the Southern District of New York have "required Chinese banks to provide information concerning their account holders, or to turn over their assets to satisfy a judgment against one or more Chinese debtors, or both").
63. Gucci Am., Inc. v. Weixing Li, 768 F.3d 122 (2d Cir. 2014).
64. *Id.* at 141; *see* Gucci Am., Inc. v. Weixing Li, No. 10 Civ. 4974 (RJS), 2011 WL 6156936 (S.D.N.Y. Aug. 23, 2011), *aff'd in relevant part*, 768 F.3d 122 (2d Cir. 2014). On remand, the district court again weighed China's interest in bank secrecy laws against the plaintiffs' need to enforce their trademark rights and concluded that proceedings in China in the interim had "shift[ed] the balance of national interests more firmly toward the United States because they acknowledge[d] that [Bank of China] had broad contractual rights over its customers' account information" and "d[id] not provide any support for BOC's assertion that China's bank secrecy laws are rigidly enforced or a matter of strong state policy that trump the United States' interest in enforcing the Lanham Act." Gucci Am., Inc. v. Weixing Li, 135 F. Supp. 3d 87, 103 (S.D.N.Y. 2015).
65. Daimler AG v. Bauman, 134 S. Ct. 746 (2014).
66. Gucci Am., Inc. v. Weixing Li, 135 F. Supp. 3d 87, 94, 95 (S.D.N.Y. 2015) (emphasis omitted).

Nevertheless, Bank of China refused to comply with a court order compelling production of certain subpoenaed account documents. In response, the district court held the Bank in contempt and imposed a coercive fine of $50,000 per day of non-compliance.[67] The Second Circuit then effectively condoned the district court's actions by refusing to stay the contempt sanctions after full merits briefing.[68] The parties subsequently settled all claims out of court.[69]

The Hague Convention is an international agreement that provides an additional method of seeking discovery of evidence located in a foreign country.[70] While the Hague Convention is an option, the U.S. Supreme Court has specifically stated that a "rule of first resort in all cases would [] be inconsistent with the overriding interest in the just, speedy, and inexpensive determination of litigation in our courts."[71]

Some Courts have ordered parties to first attempt to obtain discovery through the Hague Convention,[72] but a consensus seems to

---

67. Gucci Am., Inc. v. Weixing Li, No. 10 Civ. 4974 (RJS), 2015 U.S. Dist. LEXIS 160842 (S.D.N.Y. Nov. 30, 2015).
68. Gucci Am., Inc. v. Weixing Li, No. 15-3850 (2d Cir. Jan. 12, 2016).
69. Letter from Robert L. Weigel, Counsel to Plaintiffs, to Judge Richard J. Sullivan, Gucci Am., Inc. v. Weixing Li, No. 10 Civ. 4974 (RJS) (S.D.N.Y. Apr. 8, 2016).
70. Société Nationale Industrielle Aérospatiale v. U.S. Dist. Court for S. Dist. of Iowa, 482 U.S. 522, 524 (1987).
71. *Id.* at 542–46.
72. In Tiffany (NJ) LLC v. Qi Andrew, 276 F.R.D. 143 (S.D.N.Y. 2011), the court ruled that the plaintiffs should first attempt to obtain discovery of the defendants' bank records maintained by three non-party banks in China through the Hague Convention in deference to Chinese bank secrecy law, although the court stated that it would reconsider compelling the banks to produce the documents if the Hague Convention process proved futile. *Id.* at 160–61. On that subsequent review, the court found that the Chinese banks had "produced relevant, responsive documents" and that the Hague Convention process had not been "futile." Tiffany (NJ) LLC v. Qi Andrew, No. 10 Civ. 947 (RA)(HBP), 2012 WL 5451259, at *2 (S.D.N.Y. Nov. 7, 2012). A different court in the Southern District of New York, however, reviewed the *Qi Andrew* production a year later, and concluded that "the Chinese Ministry of Justice's response . . . denied some of the valid discovery requested by the court's Letter of Request." Wultz v. Bank of China Ltd., 910 F. Supp. 2d 548, 557–58 (S.D.N.Y. 2012) (footnote omitted). In another case out of the Southern District of New York, the court took the middle ground, ordering the plaintiffs to seek discovery from two of three Chinese banks via the Hague Convention but requiring Bank of China to produce documents pursuant to the expedited discovery provisions of the preliminary injunction entered by the court. Tiffany (NJ) LLC v. Forbse, No. 11 Civ. 4976 (NRB), 2012 WL 1918866, at *10–11 (S.D.N.Y. May 23, 2012).

have developed that brand owners should be allowed to obtain discovery about counterfeiters in China directly through the Federal Rules of Civil Procedure if the counterfeiters use Chinese banks that take advantage of access to the New York banking market to hold the profits of sales to U.S.-based consumers and convert those profits into Chinese currency.

On September 12, 2018, Magistrate Judge Debra Freeman of the U.S. District Court for the Southern District of New York issued a 51-page opinion compelling six separate Chinese banks to produce all of their documents relating to several individual counterfeiting rings that had operated hundreds of websites that sold counterfeit products.[73]

In granting the order, Judge Freeman found that the court has specific personal jurisdiction over the Chinese banks that hold these records because they purposefully avail themselves of the privilege of transacting business in New York. Judge Freeman further found that international comity weighed in favor of compelling the banks to produce documents in response to the subpoenas and against forcing Plaintiff to seek discovery from the banks via the Hague Convention.[74]

Counsel for the Chinese banks filed an appeal of Judge Freeman's order to Chief Judge Colleen McMahon of the U.S. District Court for the Southern District of New York. After an additional round of briefing, Judge McMahon affirmed the order compelling the Chinese banks to produce the records.[75] Importantly, the court concluded that New York courts can exercise specific personal jurisdiction over Chinese banks that do business in the United States "as long as the [banks'] establishment and maintenance of [a correspondent] account [in New York to convert U.S. dollars into Chinese currency] evinces a purposeful availment of New York as a place for conducting business."[76] Judge McMahon also concured with the previous courts that had found that a formal request for evidence from Chinese authorities under the Hague Convention did not provide a reasonable "alternative to U.S. discovery" in obtaining information about the counterfeiting rings at issue.[77] The Banks' production of documents is continuing.

§ 7:3.4 Contributory Infringement

Trademark owners may assert claims for infringement not only against those who directly infringe their trademarks, but also against secondary actors who knowingly contribute to the infringement.

---

73. Nike, Inc. v. Wu, 349 F. Supp. 3d 310 (S.D.N.Y. 2018).
74. *Id.*
75. *Id.*
76. *Id.* at 356.
77. *Id.* at 365.

Asserting claims against secondary actors is often a more effective method to reduce the level of counterfeiting than bringing claims against the direct infringers themselves, because counterfeiters will often default when claims are brought against them, seek refuge in foreign countries, or otherwise prove to be judgment proof. By contrast, secondary infringers are often legitimate businesses that provide their goods or services to numerous direct infringers, and a successful claim of contributory infringement may result in both recovery of damages and cessation of the infringing activity.

[A] The *Inwood* Decision and Its Progeny

A cause of action for contributory trademark infringement arises from the doctrine articulated by the Supreme Court in *Inwood Laboratories, Inc. v. Ives Laboratories, Inc.*, in which the Court held that liability for trademark infringement could extend beyond direct infringers.[78] The defendant in *Inwood* manufactured generic pharmaceuticals that it distributed to non-party pharmacists, who then applied the plaintiff's name brand to the drugs. The plaintiff sued, alleging that the defendant knew about the infringing use of its generic drugs.[79]

The Supreme Court found that the plaintiff had stated a cause of action for contributory infringement and articulated the following standard for secondary liability:

> If a manufacturer or distributor intentionally induces another to infringe a trademark, or if it continues to supply its product to one whom it knows or has reason to know is engaging in trademark infringement, the manufacturer or distributor is contributorily liable for any harm as a result of the deceit.[80]

The *Inwood* standard was subsequently extended to providers of services as well as products—first, by the Seventh Circuit in *Hard Rock Café Licensing Corp. v. Concession Services, Inc.*, and then by the Ninth Circuit in *Fonovisa, Inc. v. Cherry Auction, Inc.*, in which secondary liability was imposed on the flea market owner or landlord who knowingly provided the necessary marketplace for the sale of infringing goods.[81]

---

78. Inwood Labs., Inc. v. Ives Labs., Inc., 456 U.S. 844 (1982).
79. *Id.* at 850.
80. *Id.* at 854.
81. Hard Rock Café Licensing Corp. v. Concession Servs., Inc., 955 F.2d 1143 (7th Cir. 1992); Fonovisa, Inc. v. Cherry Auction, Inc., 76 F.3d 259, 264 (9th Cir. 1996); *see also, e.g.*, Coach, Inc. v. Goodfellow, 717 F.3d 498 (6th Cir. 2013) (holding flea market operator contributorily liable for sales of counterfeits at vendor booths).

[B] Secondary Liability in the Online Context

Trademark holders have sought to impose secondary liability on service providers in the online context as one strategy in the fight against counterfeit sales over the Internet. Court decisions indicate that plaintiffs must be able to allege (at the motion to dismiss stage) and prove (at the summary judgment and trial stages) *specific facts* showing that defendants either knew or were willfully blind to infringement, or actively encouraged or participated in the infringement.[82]

1. ***Online Marketplaces.*** In *Tiffany (NJ) Inc. v. eBay, Inc.*, Tiffany & Co. asserted claims for contributory infringement against eBay for the sale of counterfeit Tiffany products by individuals using eBay's online auction website.[83] The court found that, for the purposes of the contributory liability analysis, "eBay is analogous to a flea market like those in *Hard Rock Café* and *Fonovisa*."[84] After a bench trial, however, the district court entered judgment for eBay, finding that it could not be held liable for contributory trademark infringement.

   The court concluded that Tiffany had established that eBay "retains significant control over the transactions conducted" and "supplies the necessary marketplace for the sale of counterfeit goods" but failed to establish that eBay had "specific knowledge of infringement" as opposed to "general knowledge" that certain unidentified sellers may be offering counterfeits, which the court found was insufficient to impose liability.[85]

   In its analysis, the court focused on eBay's efforts to remove counterfeit goods from its site, which included monitoring and removing listings "that expressly offered 'knock-off,' 'counterfeit,' 'replica,' or 'pirated' merchandise, and listings in which the seller stated he 'cannot guarantee the authenticity' of the items being offered," as well as eBay's Verified Rights Owner (VeRO) Program, through which trademark holders could

---

82. *See, e.g.*, Tiffany (NJ), Inc. v. eBay, Inc., 600 F.3d 93, 107 (2d Cir.), *cert. denied*, 131 S. Ct. 647 (2010) ("For contributory trademark infringement liability to lie, a service provider must have more than general knowledge or reason to know that its service is being used to sell counterfeit goods."); 1-800 Contacts, Inc. v. Lens.com, Inc., 755 F. Supp. 2d 1151, 1184 (D. Utah 2010) (same) (citing *Tiffany*, 600 F.3d at 107).
83. Tiffany (NJ) Inc. v. eBay, Inc., 576 F. Supp. 2d 463 (S.D.N.Y. 2008), *aff'd in part, rev'd in part*, 600 F.3d 93 (2d Cir. 2010).
84. *Id.* at 507.
85. *Id.* at 506.

submit complaints about suspected infringing listings.[86] On appeal, the Second Circuit found Tiffany's reliance on *Hard Rock Café* and *Fonovisa* "unavailing," in part because "eBay's efforts to combat counterfeiting far exceeded the efforts made by the defendants in those cases."[87]

In *Gucci America, Inc. v. Alibaba Group Holding Ltd.*, a group of luxury goods brand owners sued another Internet marketplace, Alibaba, along with the merchants that Alibaba hosted who were selling counterfeit goods.[88] The brand owners alleged that the defendants had violated the Lanham Act and the Racketeer Influenced and Corrupt Organizations Act (RICO).[89] With respect to their RICO claim, the plaintiffs alleged that Alibaba knowingly provided services to the merchant-defendants, which enabled the merchants to illegally sell counterfeit goods and that Alibaba had profited substantially from these operations. Ultimately, finding that the plaintiffs had failed adequately to allege the existence of an "enterprise" within the meaning of RICO, the court granted Alibaba's motion to dismiss the plaintiffs' RICO claim, but allowed the contributory and direct trademark infringement claims to proceed.[90] The case later settled out of court.[91]

2. ***Credit Card Processors.*** The ability to accept payment by credit card is essential for the sale of counterfeit products over the Internet because other payment options, such as bank wire transfer or check, are not convenient for consumers, who often rely on the fraud protection programs provided by credit card companies. On several occasions, and with varying results, trademark holders have attempted to impose liability on the companies involved in the processing of credit card transactions in an attempt to cut off the infringer's ability to accept payment for the infringing goods.

An understanding of the role of each player in a credit card transaction and its relationship to the infringer is helpful to evaluate the likelihood that a claim for secondary liability will be upheld. Each credit card transaction involves five key players: (1) the customer/cardholder; (2) the bank that issued

---

86. *Id.* at 477–78.
87. Tiffany (NJ), Inc. v. eBay, Inc., 600 F.3d 93, 110, n.16 (2d Cir. 2010).
88. Gucci Am., Inc. v. Alibaba Grp. Holding Ltd., No. 15-cv-3784 (PKC), 2016 WL 6110565 (S.D.N.Y. Aug. 4, 2016).
89. *Id.* at *1.
90. *Id.* at *7–9.
91. Gucci Am., Inc. v. Alibaba Grp. Holding Ltd., No. 15-CV-03784, 2017 WL 7118036 (S.D.N.Y. Aug. 3, 2017).

the customer's card ("issuing bank"); (3) the merchant; (4) the merchant's acquiring bank; and (5) the authorization network (for example, VisaNet for Visa cards).[92] The credit card transaction begins with the cardholder inserting the card's chip or swiping the card into the merchant's terminal. The merchant's terminal transmits the authorization request to the acquiring bank, which then sends the request electronically to the network. The network routes the cardholder's request to the cardholder's issuing bank. The issuing bank approves or declines the transaction, and this response is forwarded by the network to the acquiring bank, which in turn forwards it to the merchant. If approved, the merchant completes the transaction. All transactions are kept at the terminal until the merchant sends all transactions, usually at the end of each day, to the acquiring bank. The acquiring bank credits the merchant's account and submits the transactions to the network for settlement. The network pays the acquiring bank and debits the appropriate issuer accounts. The issuing bank then posts the transaction to its cardholder's account.[93] In this manner, the acquiring bank is effectively advancing funds to the merchant, and also takes on the risk that the customer will later dispute the charge, as the acquiring bank remains responsible for chargebacks that are not reimbursed by the merchant.

Whether a claim for secondary liability will be upheld appears to depend, in part, on the particular defendant's role in the

---

92. To process credit card sales, a merchant must have access to the credit card's authorization network (such as Visa or MasterCard), which it can only do through an acquiring bank that has a relationship with Visa or MasterCard. Therefore, the merchant must find an acquiring bank willing to accept the risks associated with its particular business model. If a merchant is engaged in a line of business that acquiring banks view as being particularly high risk, the merchant may enlist the help of a "merchant broker," who can assist the merchant in locating an appropriate acquiring bank. In those instances, the merchant broker becomes the sixth player in the credit card transaction, as it will receive commissions from the acquiring bank in the form of residuals from each of its merchant's credit card transactions. The acquiring bank itself may also contract with an independent sales organization (ISO) that acts as an agent for the bank in reviewing and ruling upon merchant service applications submitted either directly by the merchant or through a merchant broker. The ISO adds yet another player to the transaction that will receive a percentage of the merchant's credit card sales.

93. *See, e.g.*, CHASE, PAYMENT PROCESSING (THE BASICS), https://www.chasepaymentech.com/the_basics.html.

credit card transaction process and on whether the payment transaction is deemed necessary to the infringement.

[B][1] Perfect 10 v. Visa International Service Association

In *Perfect 10 v. Visa International Service Association*, the Ninth Circuit held that providing credit card services to a website that sold access to infringing images did not "materially contribute" to the infringement.[94] Perfect 10, the operator of an adult website, filed suit against the companies that provided payment services to a competitor adult website that allowed customers to view images for a fee. Perfect 10 alleged that the competitor was selling access to certain images in violation of Perfect 10's copyrights and trademarks, and that the defendants were aware of this infringement but nonetheless continued to provide their services to the infringing website and profited from each infringing sale. The defendants included Visa, MasterCard, and the infringer's acquiring banks that were part of the Visa and MasterCard networks.

The Ninth Circuit affirmed the district court's dismissal of the complaint, finding that the plaintiff failed to plead facts constituting contributory trademark infringement. The court rejected Perfect 10's argument that the "instrumentality" of infringement was the credit card processing network through which the defendants processed payments for the infringing images.[95] Instead, the Ninth Circuit found that "the infringement occurs without any involvement of Defendants and their payment systems."[96] According to the court, because the infringement occurred through the unauthorized display of photos, which could occur without payment, the credit card processors were not a necessary part of the infringement. The court also rejected Perfect 10's argument that the defendants had "direct control" over the infringement because they could choose to stop processing payments for the website, which would reduce the infringing activity.[97]

---

94. Perfect 10 v. Visa Int'l Serv. Ass'n, 494 F.3d 788 (9th Cir. 2007).
95. *Id.* at 807.
96. *Id.*
97. *Id.* Although Perfect 10 compared the defendants' role to that of a flea market operator, the Ninth Circuit found the analogy inapplicable. *Id.* at 807 (quoting Lockheed Martin Corp. v. Network Sols., Inc., 194 F.3d 980, 985 (9th Cir. 1999)) ("While the landlord of a flea market might reasonably be expected to monitor the merchandise sold on his premises, [defendant] NSI cannot reasonably be expected to monitor the Internet.") (citation omitted) (alteration in original).

[B][2] Gucci America, Inc. v. Frontline Processing Corp.

In *Gucci America, Inc. v. Frontline Processing Corp.* (discussed previously in section 7:3.1), the Southern District of New York reached a different conclusion than the court in *Perfect 10*.[98] Gucci alleged that two credit card processors and the merchant broker that linked Internet merchants with these processors had knowingly provided services to operators of a website selling counterfeits, against whom Gucci and Chloé had obtained a multimillion-dollar judgment a year earlier. Gucci asserted claims for contributory trademark infringement against all the credit card processors and affiliated companies listed as defendants in the subsequent action. The defendants moved to dismiss the complaint, relying heavily upon the Ninth Circuit's decision in *Perfect 10* and the district court decision in *Tiffany v. eBay*. In *Gucci*, however, the district court denied the motion to dismiss.

In upholding Gucci's claim for contributory trademark infringement, the court distinguished *Perfect 10* on the facts, noting that "the infringing conduct [in *Perfect 10*] was the publication on the website of trademarked images of nude models, and the distribution occurred via individuals viewing and taking the image directly from the website."[99] In contrast, Gucci's claim for infringement resulted from the sale of infringing *products* over the Internet, the sale of which could not be completed (nor the counterfeit products shipped) without the payment-processing services provided by the defendants.

The court concluded that Gucci had sufficiently alleged a claim against the merchant broker for contributory infringement under the "intentional inducement" theory based on its allegations that "[the broker] crafted advertisements or solicitations that broadcast a message designed to stimulate others to commit violations."[100] The court found that Gucci sufficiently alleged a claim against the credit card processors for contributory infringement because the "allegations at the very least provide a strong inference that each knew that [the infringing website] traded in counterfeit products, or [was] willfully blind to that fact."[101] The court also found that the "credit card processing services are a necessary element for the transaction of counterfeit goods online, and were essential to sales" from the website.[102]

---

98. Gucci Am., Inc. v. Frontline Processing Corp., No. 09 Civ. 6925 (HB), 2010 WL 2541367 (S.D.N.Y. June 23, 2010).
99. *Id.* at *16.
100. *Id.* at *12.
101. *Id.* at *13.
102. *Id.* at *15.

The court also noted that "the ability to literally shut down the website is not needed given the facts of this case."[103]

3. ***Internet Service Providers (ISPs).*** Although the courts initially resisted applying the holdings of *Inwood* and its progeny to find contributory liability against ISPs, trademark holders have had some success asserting claims for secondary liability against ISPs that ignore requests to cease servicing infringing websites or that knowingly and actively assist such websites. Courts have suggested, however, that there is a heightened knowledge requirement for ISPs that carry out only ministerial functions, such as domain registrars.[104]

   In *Lockheed Martin Corp. v. Network Solutions, Inc.*, Lockheed filed suit against the domain name registrar Network Solutions (NSI), alleging that it allowed third parties to register domain names that infringed Lockheed's trademarks.[105] Lockheed notified NSI once it learned of the infringing domain names and requested that NSI cancel the existing infringing registrations and cease allowing registration of domains that included Lockheed's "Skunk Works" trademark.[106] NSI did not cancel the existing infringing registrations and it permitted a new registrant to register "skunkworks.com."[107] Lockheed subsequently filed suit for, *inter alia*, contributory trademark infringement. The district court granted NSI's motion for summary judgment.[108]

---

103. *Id.* at *16.

104. *See* Petroliam Nasional Berhad v. GoDaddy.com, Inc., No. C 09-5939, 2010 WL 3619780, at *4 (N.D. Cal. Sept. 9, 2010) (citing Lockheed Martin Corp. v. Network Sols., Inc., 985 F. Supp. 949, 962–63) (C.D. Cal. 1997)) (noting that where "the facts alleged do not show any direct involvement with potentially infringing uses of domain names, it is generally inappropriate to extend contributory liability to the registrar" unless "the registrar had unequivocal knowledge that a domain name was being used to infringe a trademark"); Baidu, Inc. v. Register.com, Inc., 760 F. Supp. 2d 312 (S.D.N.Y. 2010) (noting that the immunity provided to domain name registrars under the Lanham Act (15 U.S.C. § 1114(2)(D)(iii)) for "registering and maintaining a domain name" does not necessarily defeat a claim for secondary liability).

105. Lockheed Martin Corp. v. Network Sols., Inc., 194 F.3d 980 (9th Cir. 1999).

106. *Id.* at 983.

107. *Id.*

108. Lockheed also appealed the district court's ruling denying Lockheed's request to amend its complaint to add a claim for contributory trademark dilution. *Id.* at 985–86. The Ninth Circuit upheld the district court's decision, noting in dicta that, "[a]lthough courts have discussed

On appeal, the Ninth Circuit concluded that NSI did not supply a "product" within the meaning of *Inwood*, finding instead that Lockheed's claim for contributory infringement had to be analyzed as one against a "service provider."[109] The Ninth Circuit agreed with the district court's observation that "the infringement does not result from NSI's publication of the domain name list. . . . NSI's involvement with the use of domain names does not extend beyond registration."[110] The Ninth Circuit concluded that "NSI's rote translation service does not entail the kind of direct control and monitoring required to justify an extension of the 'supplies a product' requirement."[111]

Luxury goods retailer Louis Vuitton had more success in a subsequent lawsuit against Akanoc Solutions, Inc., Managed Solutions Group, Inc. (MSG) and Steven Chen, the principal behind Akanoc. Akanoc had actually hosted websites that sold infringing Louis Vuitton products.[112] Louis Vuitton alleged that the defendants were contributorily liable for the websites' infringement because they failed to take appropriate action after being provided with notice of the specific websites on their servers selling counterfeit products. The district court denied defendants' motion for summary judgment on contributory trademark infringement, finding that there were genuine issues of material fact regarding their knowledge of the underlying infringement and their extent of control over the infringing websites.

In denying defendants' motion, the district court noted that "Defendants physically host websites on their servers and

---

contributory dilution, no appellate court or statute has yet enabled the cause of action." *Id.* at 986 (citation omitted). However, at least one decision suggests that the courts may be willing to extend theories of contributory liability beyond traditional "trademark infringement," and allow claims of secondary liability for cybersquatting and trademark dilution. *See* Microsoft Corp. v. Shah, No. C10-0653 (RSM), 2011 WL 108954, at *2–4 (W.D. Wash. Jan. 12, 2011) (denying defendants' motion to dismiss claims for contributory cybersquatting and contributory trademark dilution where defendants registered or used domains containing Microsoft trademarks for the sole purpose of infringement).

109. *Lockheed Martin*, 194 F.3d at 984.

110. *Id.* at 985 (citation omitted).

111. *Id.* at 984–85 (citation omitted).

112. Louis Vuitton Malletier, S.A. v. Akanoc Sols., Inc., 591 F. Supp. 2d 1098 (N.D. Cal. 2008), *aff'd in part, rev'd in part*, 658 F.3d 936 (9th Cir. 2012).

route internet traffic to and from those websites. This service is the internet equivalent of leasing real estate. . . . As with the flea market operators in *Fonovisa*, Defendants cannot remain 'willfully blind' to trademark infringement taking place on their servers."[113]

At trial, a jury found Akanoc, MSG, and Chen liable for willful contributory trademark infringement and awarded Louis Vuitton $10.5 million in statutory damages against each defendant, for a total of $31,500,000 in statutory damages.[114] The district court subsequently rejected defendants' attempt to set aside the award as unconstitutionally punitive.[115] The district court also denied defendants' post-trial motions for judgment as a matter of law except with respect to defendant MSG. As to MSG, the court concluded that there was no evidence that MSG did anything more than own and lease the hardware operated by Akanoc and Chen. On appeal, the Ninth Circuit largely affirmed the district court's handling of the case, but found that the defendants could be held liable for only one single joint and several statutory damages award, not three duplicative statutory damages awards.

Participation in the creation of an infringing website is also likely to result in a finding of contributory liability. In *Roger Cleveland Golf Company v. Prince*, the well-known golf equipment company alleged that a company that hosted and designed an infringing website was contributorily liable for infringement.[116] The U.S. District Court for the District of South Carolina denied the defendant's motion for summary judgment, rejecting the argument that it functioned only as a website host.[117] Plaintiff had offered evidence that the defendant was not just a host, but meaningfully participated in the creation of and development of the website and business model, including recommending that the infringer use "wholesalers" and

---

113. *Id.* at 1112.

114. *See* Jury Verdict, Louis Vuitton Malletier, S.A. v. Akanoc Sols., Inc., No. C 07-03952 JW, 2009 WL 3062893 (N.D. Cal. Aug. 28, 2009).

115. *See* Louis Vuitton Malletier, S.A. v. Akanoc Sols., Inc., No. C 07-03952 JW, 2010 WL 5598337 (N.D. Cal. Mar. 19, 2010).

116. Roger Cleveland Golf Co. v. Prince, No. 2:09-CV-2119-MBS, 2010 WL 5019260 (D.S.C. Dec. 3, 2010); *see also* Roger Cleveland Golf Co. v. Prince, No. 2:09-CV-2119-MBS, 2012 WL 1106775 (D.S.C. Mar. 30, 2012).

117. *Roger Cleveland Golf*, 2012 WL 1106775, at *1.

"drop shippers" to fulfill customer orders.[118] Roger Cleveland also adduced evidence that the company knew or should have known that its customer was selling counterfeit golf clubs, and that the name of the website, CopyCatClubs.com, should have put defendant on notice of its client's intent to infringe.[119]

After a two-day jury trial, the defendant web host was found liable for willful contributory trademark infringement, and the jury awarded the plaintiff $770,000 in statutory damages under the Lanham Act, representing $70,000 per mark infringed.[120] In contrast, the direct infringer was found liable for only $2,500 in statutory damages.

In *Schreiber v. Dunabin*, the District Court for the Eastern District of Virginia dismissed a claim of contributory infringement against various domain name registries and registrars, both because the underlying direct infringement claims failed and because the court perceived flaws in the contributory infringement theory.[121] As in *Lockheed Martin*,[122] the court found that the contributory infringement claim failed because "'the relevant tortious act is the *use* of the domain name, and not the act of registration.'"[123] As a result, "because registrars do not 'use' marks in commerce, they are not subject to liability" for registering and maintaining domain names.[124] The court methodically analyzed the *pro se* complaint, and dismissed without leave to re-plead based on numerous fundamental flaws in the plaintiff's theory of liability.[125]

§ 7:3.5 Monetary Remedies

In all Lanham Act claims, a successful plaintiff can recover the infringer's profits, any damages sustained, and the costs of the action.[126] Where there are two or more infringers, courts conclude that they jointly and severally share responsibility for the final

---

118. *Id.*
119. *Id.*
120. *Id.* at *5–6.
121. Schreiber v. Dunabin, 938 F. Supp. 2d 587 (E.D. Va. 2013).
122. Lockheed Martin v. Network Sols., 194 F.3d 980 (9th Cir. 1999).
123. *Schreiber*, 938 F. Supp. 2d at 600 (emphasis in original) (quoting Am. Online, Inc. v. Huang, 106 F. Supp. 2d 848, 854 (E.D. Va. 2000)).
124. *Schreiber*, 938 F. Supp. 2d at 600 (citing Bird v. Parsons, 289 F.3d 865, 879 (6th Cir. 2002)).
125. *Schreiber*, 938 F. Supp. 2d at 601–02.
126. 15 U.S.C. § 1117(a). *See also supra* section 2:9.2.

damages award.[127] In assessing profits, the plaintiff must prove only the gross amount of defendant's sales, and the defendant must come forward with evidence of any amounts that should be deducted.[128] And the court has the discretion to increase the amount of the award up to three times the amount of actual damages, "according to the circumstances of the case."[129]

In counterfeiting cases, however, the Lanham Act explicitly provides that "the court shall, unless the court finds extenuating circumstances, enter judgment for three times such profits or damages, whichever amount is greater, together with a reasonable attorney's fee."[130] Because a counterfeiter's profits or the harm from counterfeiting may be difficult to determine with specificity, Congress also afforded victims of counterfeiting an alternative remedy: the ability to elect statutory damages "at any time before final judgment is rendered by the trial court."[131]

[A] Counterfeiters' Profits

Courts have held that where there is evidence that a defendant has engaged in willful counterfeiting, an award of the profits *must* be trebled.[132] For example, in *Fendi Adele S.R.L. v. Ashley Reed Trading, Inc.*, because there was evidence of the counterfeiter's sales, the Second Circuit instructed the district court to *increase* its damages award after concluding that the district court's award of $10.5 million was inconsistent with the fact that Fendi had proven infringement over a five-year span.[133] On remand, the district court awarded Fendi $29,855,043 in damages, representing three times Ashley Reed's sales from 2001 to 2006.[134] There are still instances, however, where courts

---

127. *See, e.g.*, Louis Vuitton Malletier, S.A. v. Akanoc Sols., Inc., 658 F.3d 936, 947 (9th Cir. 2011); Coach, Inc. v. Celco Customs Servs. Co., No. CV-11-10787 (MMM) (FMOX), 2014 WL 12573411, at *25 (C.D. Cal. June 5, 2014); Sara Lee Corp. v. Bags of N.Y., Inc., 36 F. Supp. 2d 161, 171 (S.D.N.Y. 1999).
128. 15 U.S.C. § 1117(a)(3); Bambu Sales, Inc. v. Ozak Trading Inc., 58 F.3d 849, 854 (2d Cir. 1995).
129. 15 U.S.C. § 1117(a)(3).
130. 15 U.S.C. § 1117(b).
131. 15 U.S.C. § 1117(c).
132. *See, e.g.*, Chloe v. Zarafshan, No. 06 Civ. 03140 (RJH) (MHD), 2009 WL 2956827, at *7 (S.D.N.Y. Sept. 15, 2009) ("The trebling of [a] defendant's profits is mandatory if the court find[s] that [a] defendant['s] actions were willful, absent extenuating circumstances.").
133. Summary Order, Fendi Adele S.R.L. v. Ashley Reed Trading, Inc., No. 11-3025-cv (L) (2d Cir. Jan. 4, 2013).
134. Corrected Order, Fendi Adele S.R.L. v. Ashley Reed Trading, Inc., No. 06 Civ. 00243 (RMB) (MHD) (S.D.N.Y. Apr. 22, 2013).

find that trebled damages are not warranted because the plaintiff is fully compensated by an award of the defendant's profits alone.[135]

[B] Statutory Damages

Seeking statutory damages can be preferable where the counterfeiter's sales records are non-existent or not available. Under the Lanham Act, in a case involving the use of a counterfeit mark, plaintiffs are entitled to statutory damages of no less than $1,000, if the use of the counterfeit mark was willful, and up to $2,000,000 "per counterfeit mark per type of goods or services sold, offered for sale, or distributed, as the court considers just" pursuant to 15 U.S.C. § 1117(c). In awarding statutory damages, the amount of actual harm suffered is generally treated as irrelevant.[136] In both direct and contributory trademark infringement cases, the statutory damages are assessed by the number of works infringed upon rather than the number of times that the work is infringed.[137]

Courts have taken different approaches to awarding statutory damages in counterfeiting cases. For example, a number of courts have awarded $100,000 per mark per category of goods infringed, and then $200,000 per mark per category of good infringed after Congress doubled the mandatory minimums and maximums in 2008.[138]

---

135. *See, e.g.*, 4 Pillar Dynasty LLC v. New York & Co., 257 F. Supp. 3d 611, 624 (S.D.N.Y.) (denying a jury's treble damages award to plaintiff where the defendant did not gain an improved market position and where plaintiff did not evidence that its full compensation required treble damages and concluding instead that an award of defendant's profits was sufficient), *amended by* 16 Civ. 2823 (JSR), 2017 WL 3738442 (S.D.N.Y. Aug. 8, 2017) (addressing attorneys' fees as well as pre- and post-judgment interest).

136. *See* Luxottica Grp. S.p.A. v. Hao Li, Nos. 16 CV 487 & 16 CV 1227, 2017 WL 621966, at *5 (N.D. Ill. Feb. 15, 2017) ("Because plaintiffs elected to recover statutory damages rather than actual damages, they need not prove their actual losses. . . . Given that the proliferation of lower-quality counterfeit products can harm a trademark owner's brand and goodwill, that global exposure makes plaintiffs' actual losses difficult to calculate and reinforces the need to award damages sufficient to deter similar conduct by defendant and others.").

137. *See, e.g.*, Dentsply Sirona Inc. v. L I K Supply, Corp., No. 316 CV 806 (MAD/DEP), 2017 WL 4357462, at *9–11 (N.D.N.Y. Sept. 29, 2017) (explaining that Lanham Act's statutory damages provision applies "per counterfeit mark per type of goods or services sold, offered for sale, or distributed" and awarding statutory damages accordingly).

138. *Compare* Gucci Am., Inc. v. MyReplicaHandbag.com, No. 07 Civ. 2438 (JGK), 2008 WL 512789 (S.D.N.Y. Feb. 26, 2008) (adopting recommendation that plaintiffs be awarded $100,000 per mark per category of good infringed); Louis Vuitton Malletier v. WhenU.com, No. 05 Civ. 1325 (LAK), 2007 WL 257717, at *6 (S.D.N.Y. Jan. 26, 2007) (same), *with*

Ultimately, courts have wide discretion in awarding statutory damages up to the maximum amount and are more likely to award high damages where plaintiffs "substantiate or delineate the basis for the relief sought."[139]

Courts have been awarding increasingly high statutory damages in counterfeiting cases involving the Internet.[140] One court awarded the $2 million statutory maximum for willful trademark counterfeiting for each mark infringed (without regard to categories of goods) against each of forty-one defendants selling counterfeits online.[141] Another court awarded damages of $863.9 million against counterfeiters of True Religion jeans for willful trademark counterfeiting and copyright infringement.[142] In *4 Pillar Dynasty LLC v. New York & Company, Inc.*, an advisory jury awarded a trebled statutory damages award of $5.6 million to the plaintiff, although the judgment was later reduced after the court concluded, in the context of the defendant's motion for a judgment as a matter of law, that the plaintiff was fully compensated based on the defendant's profits alone.[143]

Statutory damages may be available not only against the primary infringer, but also against contributory infringers who assisted in the sale of counterfeit goods, such as ISPs.[144] For example, in *Roger Cleveland*

Balenciaga Am., Inc. v. Dollinger, No. 10 Civ. 2912 (PAE) (S.D.N.Y. Jan. 3, 2012) (judgment awarding $12.4 million in damages based on calculation of $200,000 per mark per category of good infringed); *see also* Prioritizing Resources and Organization for Intellectual Property Act of 2008, Pub. L. No. 110-403, § 104, 122 Stat. 4256, 4259 (codified as amended at 15 U.S.C. § 1117(c)).

139. Sennheiser Elec. Corp. v. Eichler, No. CV 12-10809 (MMM) (PLA), 2013 WL 3811775, at *7 (C.D. Cal. July 19, 2013).

140. *See* Rolex Watch U.S.A., Inc. v. Jones, No. 99 Civ. 2359, 2002 WL 596354, at *5 (S.D.N.Y. Apr. 17, 2002) (Maas, M.J.), adopted without modification by Judge Cote on June 18, 2002 (explaining that the amount of damages per mark should be higher in the case of online infringement given "the virtually limitless number of customers available to [defendant] through his Web sites").

141. Tory Burch LLC v. Yong Sheng, No. 10 Civ. 9336, 2011 WL 13042618, at *3 (S.D.N.Y. May 13, 2011).

142. *See True Religion Wins $863.9 M Cybersquatting Suit*, WOMEN'S WEAR DAILY, Mar. 30, 2012.

143. *See, e.g.*, 4 Pillar Dynasty LLC v. New York & Co., 257 F. Supp. 3d 611, 624 (S.D.N.Y.), *amended by* No. 16 Civ. 2823 (JSR), 2017 WL 3738442 (S.D.N.Y. Aug. 8, 2017).

144. *See* Louis Vuitton Malletier, S.A. v. Akanoc Sols., Inc., 658 F.3d 936, 947 (9th Cir. 2011) (clarifying that Internet website hosting service provider and manager are jointly and severally liable for $10.5 million statutory damages award against them); *see also* Cartier Int'l B.V. v. Ben-Menachem, No. 06 Civ. 3917, 2008 WL 64005, at *12 (S.D.N.Y. Jan. 3, 2008) (entering summary judgment against contributory infringers

Golf Co., discussed above, the court rejected the defendant web host's motion for relief from the judgment and a new trial, concluding that the jury award was not excessive even though the jury awarded greater damages based on the contributory infringement than it did for the direct infringement.[145]

§ 7:4 Additional Remedies for Trademark Owners

§ 7:4.1 Technological Solutions

Many brand owners are increasingly turning to technological solutions to try to reclaim market share from counterfeiters.[146] One of the most widespread methods is to affix holograms to products and hang tags that are more difficult to replicate than more traditional labels. This "overt" use of technology signals to consumers that an item is genuine and thereby reduces at least certain unwitting purchases of counterfeit items.[147] Another method is the use of "covert" tracking technologies that "show that a product is where it should be and is what it should be."[148] An example is radio frequency identification, or "RFID" tags, which are intelligent bar codes with the capacity to read and convey data. Once primarily deployed to assist in the tracking of cattle, RFID tags are increasingly used to allow manufacturers to track garments from the manufacturing process all the way to store shelves.[149] Promoters of the RFID technology claim that it can also be used to help detect counterfeits and assist in appropriate inventory maintenance. Critics say the technology continues to have flaws that limit its applicability.

Recently, online platforms have used the tagging approach to provide innovative and unique solutions to brand owners by empowering consumers to validate purchases from their smartphones. A company called Certilogo uses information supplied by brands (including manufacturing and distribution data) to generate a unique identifier (called "Certilogo Code") for authentic products registered by the brand owner that is used to authenticate goods at the point of sale.[150] Using the Certilogo application, information provided by consumers,

---

who allowed their sons to operate an online counterfeiting business from their home and office) and Order of Judgment (S.D.N.Y. Jan. 23, 2008).

145. Roger Cleveland Golf Co. v. Prince, No. 2:09-CV-2119-MBS, 2012 WL 1106775, at *10–11 (D.S.C. Mar. 30, 2012).

146. Gilly Wright, *Fake Fashion*, 5 BRAND PROTECTION & PROMOTION WORLD 10 (June 15, 2012) [hereinafter Wright, *Fake Fashion*], at 6.

147. *Id.* at 8.

148. *Id.* (quoting Ben Muis, a consultant to the fashion industry).

149. *Id.*

150. CERTILOGO, HOW IT WORKS, http://brands.certilogo.com/en/how-it-works.

retailers, and even customs agents to authenticate goods is shared with the brand, which reduces policing costs. Using a simple interface, consumers are provided the necessary tools to protect themselves and the brands they support with a few clicks from their smartphones.

In a further effort to protect brands and combat counterfeiting, platforms such as uFaker, Inc. provide consumers with the necessary tools to self-report counterfeiters using their smartphones. The uFaker application enables users to take photographs of possible counterfeits and supply information regarding the retailer's location, which uFaker then imports into a privately owned database of suspected counterfeiters that brand owners can utilize.[151]

Another technological innovation has been the use of Quick Response, or "QR" codes that are increasingly popular with users of mobile devices. QR codes are two-dimensional matrix bar codes that can be read and interpreted by an imaging device, such as a cell phone camera. Proponents of the technology tout the ability to encrypt data that will allow consumers to instantly verify a product's authenticity, while at the same time allowing the manufacturer to share information with the consumer and incorporate the consumer into an overall social networking strategy.[152] As with any use of anti-piracy technology (such as the use of digital rights management technology in the entertainment industry), it will require constant innovation to keep ahead of the counterfeiters who will undoubtedly look for opportunities to crack these codes and possibly even turn them to their own ends.

§ 7:4.2 Cooperation Among Trademark Owners, Credit Card Companies, and E-Commerce Servicers

In January 2012, the International Anti-Counterfeiting Coalition (IACC), in collaboration with the world's largest multinational brands and leading financial companies, launched "RogueBlock"—a payment processing program. RogueBlock created streamlined procedures for members to report online sellers of counterfeit or pirated goods directly to credit card and financial services companies, as well as government agencies, in connection with processing online payments. The program collects, aggregates, and shares information provided by consumers, brand owners, regulators, financial service companies, payment processors, and online e-commerce platforms and databases, to identify and track potential infringement in order

151. Laura Lorenzetti, *uFaker App Turns Consumers into Detectives*, CRAIN'S N.Y. BUS. (July 10, 2013), http://www.crainsnewyork.com/article/20130710/TECHNOLOGY/130719993.

152. Wright, *Fake Fashion*, *supra* note 147, at 9–10.

to shut down criminal counterfeiters and seize profits from their illicit businesses in real time. To date, the program has terminated over 5,000 individual counterfeiters' merchant accounts, which has impacted over 200,000 websites.[153]

Trademark owners may also report infringing websites directly to credit card companies, including Visa and MasterCard. The credit card company will investigate the website and work with the merchant's acquiring bank to terminate credit card processing accounts used in connection with illegal sales of counterfeits.[154] PayPal offers a "PayPal Purchase Protection" program that allows individual consumers to report and contest questionable transactions, including if the consumer "received a counterfeit version of [an] item" ordered.[155]

Brand owners are no longer the only parties seeking to privately enforce their intellectual property rights; indeed, litigation funders are responsible for a rise in civil litigation enforcement actions.[156] In addition, e-commerce platforms are taking a lead in bringing claims for enforcement. In 2016, marketplace Amazon.com filed lawsuits against vendors allegedly selling counterfeit goods through its website in an effort to keep fake goods off its site.[157] Amazon had originally removed the counterfeit goods from its website, but, when the vendor reappeared on the website selling counterfeit goods, Amazon targeted the vendor with a lawsuit.[158]

§ 7:4.3 Public Education

Finally, because counterfeiters rely on the demand for cheap "brand name" products and the ignorance of many consumers about the

---

153. INT'L ANTICOUNTERFEITING COAL., ONLINE INITIATIVES: ROGUEBLOCK, https://www.iacc.org/online-initiatives/rogueblock.

154. *See, e.g.*, VISA, ABOUT VISA, http://corporate.visa.com/about-visa/security-and-trust/intellectual-property-rights.shtml?ep=v_sym_ReportBrand-Abuse.

155. *See, e.g.*, PAYPAL, PAYPAL PURCHASE PROTECTION, http://www.paypal.com/us/webapps/mpp/security/safe-online-shopping.

156. *See, e.g.*, AroChen Int'l, Inc v. Buirkle, 968 F.2d 266, 272 (2d Cir. 1992); Nathan Hale, *Litigation Funding Isn't Just for the Little Guy Anymore*, LAW360 (Apr. 20, 2018), https://www.law360.com/articles/1033681/litigation-funding-isn-t-just-for-the-little-guy-anymore; AM. BAR ASS'N COMM'N ON ETHICS 20/20, INFORMATIONAL REPORT TO THE HOUSE OF DELEGATES, at 11 (2011), https://www.americanbar.org/content/dam/aba/administrative/ethics_2020/20111212_ethics_20_20_alf_white_paper_final_hod_informational_report.authcheckdam.pdf.

157. Spencer Soper, *Amazon Files Lawsuits Seeking to Keep Counterfeit Goods Off Site*, BLOOMBERG BNA (Nov. 14, 2016).

158. *Id.; see also* Amazon.com, Inc. v. Wong, No. 16-2-27556-7 (Wash. St. Super. Ct. 2016); Amazon.com, Inc. v. ToysNet, No. 16-2-27563-0 (Wash. St. Super. Ct. 2016).

nature of counterfeit goods and/or the rights of trademark owners, brand owners need to actively educate the public about the dangers associated with purchasing counterfeit goods. Indeed, many people perceive counterfeiting to be nothing more than a "victimless crime." However, the economic harm caused by counterfeiting is growing exponentially. For example, in recognition of World Anti-Counterfeiting Day, on June 6, 2018, the European Union Intellectual Property Office (EUIPO) released a synthesis research report highlighting that the EU is currently losing EUR 60 billion each year as a result of counterfeiting. For each EU citizen, this amounts to a cost of EUR 116 per year, and a loss of 434,000 jobs.[159] The economic harm value of counterfeit and pirated products is projected to increase to over $3 trillion by 2022.[160]

Consumers are encouraged to learn more about their rights so they can make smart purchasing decisions in a marketplace where the sale of counterfeit goods is on the rise and growing exponentially. Educating consumers on the impact of counterfeiting—the manufacture, distribution, import, export, and sale of goods, with a false trademark that is identical to, or substantially indistinguishable from, a registered trademark that is likely to confuse or deceive consumers—is the best place to start. As International Trademark Association (INTA) CEO Etienne Sanz de Acedo explained, "it is important for consumers to know the value of purchasing authentic goods and to understand that making informed purchasing decisions is essential to protect public safety," given that "almost every product you can think of can be counterfeited" and that counterfeit products are not just "poorly made," but also "can be dangerous, posing negative economic, health, and safety effects on individuals and society."[161]

One leading example of brand owners and their advocates banding together to counter this perception is the INTA's "Unreal Campaign."[162] The Unreal Campaign is designed to educate teenagers (ages fourteen to eighteen) about the importance of trademarks and intellectual property, and the dangers associated with counterfeit

---

159. Charles Kim, *EU Losing 60 Billion Euro Annually Due to Counterfeiting, EUIPO Reports*, International Trademark Association, INTABLOG (June 8, 2018), https://www.inta.org/INTABlog/Lists/Posts/Post.aspx?ID=490.

160. Press Release, Int'l Trademark Ass'n, Understanding Real Versus Fake Goods During National Consumer Protection Week (Mar. 1, 2018), https://www.inta.org/Press/Pages/National_Consumer_Protection_Week_2018.aspx.

161. *Id.*

162. *See* INT'L TRADEMARK ASS'N, THE UNREAL CAMPAIGN, EDUCATING TEENS ON THE DANGERS OF COUNTERFEITS, http://www.inta.org/Advocacy/Pages/UnrealCampaign.aspx.

products. The Unreal Campaign has successfully reached over 9,000 students in thirty countries since its launch in 2012.[163]

In recognition of National Consumer Protection Week, which took place in March 2018, INTA sponsored "The Power of Trademarks" exhibit at the National Investors Hall of Fame Museum in Alexandria, Virginia. Admission was free and open to the public. The exhibit provided visitors with a close-up view of counterfeit goods and an opportunity to put their shopping skills to the test in order to protect themselves with the tools they need to make quick, safe, and smart purchasing decisions.[164] From interesting facts to interactive games that encourage museumgoers to identify real versus fake products, the exhibit shined a light on why trademarks are important to companies, consumers, and communities worldwide.

Fashion magazines have also joined the cause of raising awareness about counterfeiting. For instance, *Harper's Bazaar* has an ongoing campaign called "Fakes Are Never In Fashion" devoted to raising public awareness about the dangers of counterfeit products and the association between counterfeiting and such unsavory practices as child labor and drug trafficking.[165]

---

163. *Id.*

164. *Id.*

165. *See Counterfeits Infiltrate the Military, Government Takes Charge*, FAKES ARE NEVER IN FASHION BLOG (July 28, 2011), http://fakesareneverinfashion.wordpress.com/.

Chapter 8

The Gray Market and The First Sale Doctrine

§ 8:1 Introduction
§ 8:2 Overview of the First Sale Doctrine
  § 8:2.1 Purpose of the First Sale Doctrine
  § 8:2.2 First Sale Doctrine in Copyright Law
  § 8:2.3 First Sale Doctrine in Trademark Law
  § 8:2.4 First Sale Doctrine in Patent Law
§ 8:3 Development of First Sale Doctrine and "Gray Market" Case Law
  § 8:3.1 *Parfums Givenchy, Inc. v. Drug Emporium, Inc.*
  § 8:3.2 *Quality King Distributors, Inc. v. L'anza Research International, Inc.*
  § 8:3.3 *Abercrombie & Fitch v. Fashion Shops of Kentucky, Inc.*
  § 8:3.4 *Omega S.A. v. Costco Wholesale Corp.*
  § 8:3.5 *John Wiley & Sons, Inc. v. Kirtsaeng*
§ 8:4 First Sale Doctrine in the Fashion and Apparel Context
  § 8:4.1 Unauthorized Production and the "Genuine" Goods Doctrine
  § 8:4.2 Failure to Transfer Ownership of Goods
§ 8:5 Strategies Used by Fashion Brands to Combat Gray Market Sales

§ 8:1 Introduction

In the fashion and retail industry, brand owners—particularly luxury brand owners—often employ business strategies that rely in significant part on their ability to maintain control of the chain of distribution through which their products reach consumers. Indeed, it is doubtful that consumers would be willing to pay premium prices for products if they are available, or are perceived to be available, on a mass consumer basis and/or at discount prices. Often, however, brands find it advisable or necessary to mitigate losses on unsold products through lower-price closeout sales, or to offer their goods at reduced prices in developing countries, either to maximize profits or because they are required to sell products in such countries in order to maintain their ability to enforce intellectual property rights in those products. If these reduced price goods are ultimately imported and/or resold through unapproved channels in the United States or Europe, the basic business strategy for such brands is undermined. The marketplace for these resales is often referred to as the "gray market."

The choice of the word "gray" is intentional. Resales of legitimately made and sold goods are not unlawful in the same sense as a "black" market in stolen goods. At the same time, these sales are not exactly "white" either, as they often defy a web of practical and contractual impediments that brands impose to prevent reduced price sales of their products in ways that can impair the cachet associated with such products.

"Gray market goods," thus, are broadly defined as goods that are resold or imported into the United States without the brand owner's consent, whether manufactured abroad or manufactured in the United States and then exported to foreign countries where they are acquired for re-importation. According to a report by analysts at Deloitte & Touche LLP, there are over $63 billion in annual gray market sales across industries, making this market—and the legal issues that arise in connection with it—critically important to brands in consumer products industries.[1]

Opinions about the gray market in the fashion and apparel context differ markedly. Detractors argue that the gray market illegitimately deprives brands of the opportunity to control downstream distribution of their branded goods, thereby undercutting price-point controls and product quality.[2] In contrast, supporters trumpet the gray market because, they argue, it results in a multiplicity of distribution channels, greater competition, and lower prices, to the ultimate benefit of the consumer.[3]

---

1. *See* Carol Wolf, *Losing $63 Billion to Gray Market Is Sleuth Obsession*, BLOOMBERG (Apr. 9, 2009).
2. *See generally* Kersi D. Antia, Mark Bergen & Shantanu Dutta, *Competing With Gray Markets*, MIT SLOAN MGMT. REV. (Oct. 15, 2004), https://sloanreview.mit.edu/article/competing-with-gray-markets/ [hereinafter Antia, Bergen & Dutta].
3. *See* William Richelieu, *Gray Days Ahead?: The Impact of* Quality King Distributors, Inc. v. L'anza Research International, Inc., 27 PEPP. L. REV. 827, 833 (2000).

The first sale doctrine[4] provides the legal framework within which the legality of the gray market is frequently litigated. The doctrine circumscribes certain rights in the three major areas of intellectual property law. First, under copyright law, the rule limits a copyright owner's distribution right, thereby allowing the purchaser of a copyrighted work to resell that work without violating the copyright.[5] Second—and similarly—in the trademark context, the first sale rule prevents a producer's exclusive right to distribute its trademark products from extending beyond the first sale of those products.[6] Third, "[u]nder the doctrine of patent exhaustion, the authorized sale of a patented article gives the purchaser, or any subsequent owner, a right to use or resell that article."[7]

This chapter provides an overview of the purposes and operation of the first sale doctrine and discusses the implications of the doctrine within the fashion law framework. In particular, this chapter considers the relationship among the first sale doctrine, the gray market, and the fashion industry.

§ 8:2 Overview of the First Sale Doctrine

§ 8:2.1 *Purpose of the First Sale Doctrine*

The primary rationale for the first sale rule throughout intellectual property law is to "ensure[] that the intellectual property rights holder

---

4. The "first sale doctrine" is also referred to as the "right of first sale," the "first sale rule," or the "exhaustion rule." These terms are used interchangeably throughout this chapter.
5. *See* 17 U.S.C. § 109(a) ("Notwithstanding the provisions of Section 106(3), the owner of a particular copy or phonorecord lawfully made under this title, or any person authorized by such owner, is entitled, without the authority of the copyright owner, to sell or otherwise dispose of the possession of that copy or phonorecord."). For simplicity, this chapter is phrased in terms of "copies," as opposed to "copies or phonorecords," but, for purposes of the first sale doctrine, the same considerations apply to phonorecords. *See* 2 MELVILLE B. NIMMER & DAVID NIMMER, NIMMER ON COPYRIGHT (2018) [hereinafter NIMMER ON COPYRIGHT], § 8.12[B][1], at 8-251 n.12.
6. *See* RESTATEMENT (THIRD) OF UNFAIR COMPETITION § 24 cmt. b (1995).
7. Bowman v. Monsanto Co., 569 U.S. 278, 280 (2013). *See also* David W. Barnes, *Free-Riders and Trademark Law's First Sale Rule*, 27 SANTA CLARA COMPUT. & HIGH TECH. L.J. 457, 461 (2011) [hereinafter Barnes] ("unconditioned sale of a patented item exhausts the rights of the patent holder to put any condition on the resale of that item") (citing Motion Picture Patents Co. v. Universal Film Mfg. Co., 243 U.S. 502, 516 (1917)).

earns only one fee for the sale of each object."[8] The doctrine strikes a "logical balance between transacting parties: the work's creator receives the benefit of controlling how her work reaches the public, but the public gets to enjoy the work, sell it, give it away, recycle it, or dispose of it at whim."[9]

The rule, which has common law roots dating back to at least the seventeenth century,[10] tracks the general legal policy disfavoring restraints on alienation.[11] At the moment when the intellectual property owner first consents to the distribution of his work, "the policy favoring a copyright monopoly for authors" is outweighed by "the policy opposing unduly limiting trade and restraints on alienation."[12] This is because the importance of a copyright or trademark holder's distribution right—namely, to provide the holder with adequate recourse if and when his work is "stolen or otherwise wrongfully obtained and thereafter publicly distributed"—recedes once a copyright owner "first consents to the sale or other distribution of copies . . . of his work."[13] In these situations, the copyright owner still may wish to "prevent unauthorized reproduction," but not "for the purpose of preventing distribution of the copies . . . that he has released into the public channels because . . . he has already consented to that disposition of his work."[14]

Accordingly, following a first authorized sale, the right to prohibit unauthorized distribution "is no longer a necessary supplement" to the exclusive right to reproduce goods protected by copyright.[15] The first sale doctrine thus seeks to "properly balance economic incentives of creators

---

8. Barnes, *supra* note 7, at 462 (citing Richard A. Epstein, *The Disintegration of Intellectual Property? A Classical Liberal Response to a Premature Obituary*, 62 STAN. L. REV. 455, 505 (2010)).
9. Michael Stockalper, *Is There a Foreign "Right" of Price Discrimination Under United States Copyright Law? An Examination of the First Sale Doctrine as Applied to Gray-Market Goods*, 20 DEPAUL J. ART TECH. & INTELL. PROP. L. 513, 514 (2010); *see also* Kirtsaeng v. John Wiley & Sons, Inc., 568 U.S. 519, 539 (2013) ("American law too has generally thought that competition, including freedom to resell, can work to the advantage of the consumer.").
10. *Kirtsaeng*, 568 U.S. at 538.
11. Barnes, *supra* note 7, at 462.
12. NIMMER ON COPYRIGHT, *supra* note 5, § 8.12[A], at 8-250. *See also* Brilliance Audio, Inc. v. Haights Cross Commc'ns, Inc., 474 F.3d 365, 374 (6th Cir. 2007) ("The first sale doctrine ensures that the copyright monopoly does not intrude on the personal property rights of the individual owner, given that the law generally disfavors restraints of trade and restraints on alienation.").
13. NIMMER ON COPYRIGHT, *supra* note 5, § 8.12[A], at 8-249–8-250.
14. *Id.* at 8-250.
15. *Id.*

against the rights of the public to enjoy and use the works as they please,"[16] and "follows the specific intellectual property policy limiting rights to the extent necessary to produce [meaningful] incentives . . . to encourage creative activity."[17] On a more pragmatic level, the first sale doctrine "frees courts from the administrative burden of trying to enforce restrictions upon difficult-to-trace, readily movable goods" and "avoids the selective enforcement inherent in any such effort."[18]

§ 8:2.2 First Sale Doctrine in Copyright Law

17 U.S.C. § 106(3)—subject to sections 107 through 122—grants the owner of a U.S. copyright the exclusive right "to distribute copies or phonorecords of the copyrighted work to the public by sale or other transfer of ownership, or by rental, lease, or lending . . . ."[19] As such, this distribution right "primarily protects a copyright owner's ability to control the terms on which her work enters the market by providing a remedy against persons who distribute copies of her work without permission."[20]

The first sale doctrine, currently codified at 17 U.S.C. § 109(a), limits the scope of a copyright owner's distribution right. At its core, section 109(a) "provides that the distribution right may be exercised solely with respect to the initial disposition of copies of a work, not to prevent or restrict the resale or other further transfer of possession of those copies."[21] In other words, "Section 109(a) precludes further

---

16. Thomas J. Bacon, *Caveat Bibliotheca: The First Sale Doctrine and the Future of Libraries After* Omega v. Costco, 11 J. MARSHALL REV. INTELL. PROP. L. 414, 422 (2011).

17. Barnes, *supra* note 7, at 462 (citing Twentieth Century Music Corp. v. Aiken, 422 U.S. 151, 156 (1975) ("Creative work is to be encouraged and rewarded, but private motivation must ultimately serve the cause of promoting broad public availability of literature, music, and the other arts.")).

18. Kirtsaeng v. John Wiley & Sons, Inc., 568 U.S. 519, 539 (2013).

19. 17 U.S.C. § 106(3). *See also supra* chapter 4.

20. Pearson Edu., Inc. v. Liu, 656 F. Supp. 2d 407, 409 (S.D.N.Y. 2009) (citing 2 MELVILLE B. NIMMER & DAVID NIMMER, NIMMER ON COPYRIGHT (2008), § 8.12[A], at 8-154).

21. NIMMER ON COPYRIGHT, *supra* note 5, § 8.12[B][1][a], at 8-252. The first sale doctrine was initially articulated in Bobbs-Merrill Co. v. Straus, 210 U.S. 339 (1908), where the Supreme Court interpreted the exclusive right to vend (the 1909 Copyright Act's precursor to the 1976 Act's distribution right) as applying only to the first sale such that "absent an appropriate contractual provision, there could be no restriction on resales." NIMMER ON COPYRIGHT, *supra* note 5, § 8.12[B][1], at 8-251–8-252; *see also Bobbs-Merrill Co.*, 210 U.S. at 351 ("To add to the right of exclusive sale the authority to control all future retail sales . . . would give a right not included in the terms of the [copyright] statute.").

application of the distribution right to the affected copy."[22] Thus, once a copyright owner "consents to the sale of particular copies of his work, he may not thereafter exercise the distribution right with respect to those copies."[23]

In raising a first sale defense against a copyright infringement claim, a defendant must satisfy the following four prongs:

(a) the subject physical product (the "copy") must have been lawfully manufactured with the authorization of the copyright owner;

(b) the particular copy must have been transferred under the copyright owner's authority;

(c) the defendant must qualify as the lawful owner of that particular copy; and

(d) the defendant must have thereupon disposed of that particular copy (as opposed to, for example, reproducing it).[24]

Failure to satisfy any one prong "dooms" a defense under the doctrine.[25] Although the first sale doctrine is seemingly straightforward, it has been "[t]he most frequently litigated aspect of the distribution right."[26]

In addition (and as discussed in greater detail below), the doctrine does ***not*** apply if the initial transfer fails to pass legal title in the copyrighted work from the copyright owner to the subsequent possessor of the work. In other words, "mere authorized possession of a copy, if title in the tangible copy does not pass to the possessor, does not trigger the limitation of Section 109(a) and, hence, does not affect the copyright owner's [distribution] rights under Section 106(3)."[27]

---

22. NIMMER ON COPYRIGHT, *supra* note 5, § 8.12[B][1][a], at 8-252–8-253.
23. *Id.* at 8-251. Although a copyright owner and the purchaser of the former's copyrighted work can attempt to contract around section 109(a), *id.* § 8.12[B][1][b], at 8-254, for privity of contract and notice reasons, contractual obligations preventing or restricting further disposition of the work generally do not create copyright liability for subsequent buyers of resold products. As the Fifth Circuit has explained, "[e]ven if the copyright holder places restrictions on the purchaser in a first sale . . ., the buyer's disregard of the restrictions on resale does not make the buyer or the person who buys in the secondary market liable for infringement." Am. Int'l Pictures, Inc. v. Foreman, 576 F.2d 661, 664 (5th Cir. 1978).
24. NIMMER ON COPYRIGHT, *supra* note 5, § 8.12[B][1][a], at 8-253.
25. *Id.*
26. *Id.* § 8.11[C], at 8-206.
27. *Id.* § 8.12[B][1][a], at 8-253.

§ 8:2.3 First Sale Doctrine in Trademark Law

The operation of the first sale doctrine in trademark law is similar to its counterpart in copyright law. In general, under the rule, a trademark holder "may no longer control branded goods after releasing them into the stream of commerce."[28]

Accordingly, "[a]fter the first sale, the brandholder's control is deemed exhausted. Down-the-line retailers are free to display and advertise the branded goods. Secondhand dealers may advertise the branded merchandise for resale in competition with the sales of the markholder," so long as they "do not misrepresent themselves as authorized agents."[29]

Resellers of trademark goods, therefore, have an obligation not to sell the merchandise "in a manner that which would have been likely to suggest to prospective customers that it was a part of the [trademark holder's] organization of franchisees."[30]

The doctrine's application is limited in trademark law in a unique way, as discussed in more detail below: the first sale rule applies only where the goods are "genuine," that is, manufactured and first sold with the authorization of the mark holder and without modification.[31]

Accordingly, both "the unauthorized repackaging or reconstruction or other modification of the goods by a distributor" and the unauthorized

---

28. Osawa & Co. v. B&H Photo, 589 F. Supp. 1163, 1173 (S.D.N.Y. 1984).

29. *Id.* at 1173–74. *See also* Davidoff & CIE, S.A. v. PLD Int'l Corp., 263 F.3d 1297, 1301–02 (11th Cir. 2001) (internal citations omitted) ("Under . . . the 'first sale' or 'exhaustion' doctrine, the trademark protections of the Lanham Act are exhausted after the trademark owner's first authorized sale of that product. Therefore, even though a subsequent sale is without a trademark owner's consent, the resale of a genuine good does not violate the Act."). As the leading trademark treatise explains:

> It would be absurd to hold that a manufacturer could sell a branded product to a distributor without restriction and then tell the distributor that it could not resell the branded goods without either paying for a trademark "license" or removing the trademark. . . . Some courts have stated the general rule in terms that a trademark owner who sells products, knowing that they will be resold before reaching the consumer, is held to give an implied consent to use of the mark by each dealer in the chain of distribution.

J. THOMAS MCCARTHY, 4 MCCARTHY ON TRADEMARKS AND UNFAIR COMPETITION (2012) [hereinafter MCCARTHY], § 25:41, at 25-126. *See also supra* chapter 2.

30. H.L. Hayden Co. of N.Y. v. Siemens Med. Sys., Inc., 879 F.2d 1005, 1023–24 (2d Cir. 1989). *See also* Bandag, Inc. v. Al Bolster's Tire Stores, Inc., 750 F.2d 903, 911 (Fed. Cir. 1984) (holding defendant accountable for use of plaintiff's trademark in yellow pages ad to create false suggestion of affiliation with plaintiff).

31. *See* MCCARTHY, *supra* note 29, § 25:41, at 25-124.

manufacture or first sale of goods, such as articles of apparel, render those goods non-genuine for first-sale-doctrine purposes, and thus can defeat a first sale doctrine defense.[32] Whether a good is genuine, or whether it is materially different from that sold by the trademark owner such that the first sale rule does not apply, "is a question of fact requiring an examination of the products and the desires of the target market."[33] As such, trademark cases in which first sale is raised as a defense often focus on this materiality issue.

§ 8:2.4 *First Sale Doctrine in Patent Law*

The common law "exhaustion doctrine," as the first sale doctrine is known in the patent context, circumscribes the patentee's ability to control post-sale use of a patented article. Like the first sale doctrine, the patent exhaustion doctrine is an affirmative defense against infringement claims that applies only when the initial sale was authorized by the patentee. As the U.S. Supreme Court has articulated, "[t]he authorized sale of an article that substantially embodies a patent exhausts the patent holder's rights and prevents the patent holder from invoking patent law to control postsale use of the article."[34] In 2017, the Supreme Court held that the patent holder's rights are exhausted after the first sale of a patented item regardless of its location, and that a patentee cannot retain rights to control reuse or resale of such an item once sold.[35]

The exhaustion doctrine presents an issue unique to patents with respect to the sale of incomplete or unfinished articles that do not directly embody the patent.[36] In such a case, the exhaustion doctrine applies to the authorized sale of the product if (and only if): (1) the incomplete or unfinished product's "only reasonable and intended use [is] to practice the patent," and (2) it "embodies essential features" of the patented invention.

---

32. *Id.* at 25-127 (internal citations and punctuation omitted).
33. *Id.* at 25-124.
34. Quanta Comput., Inc. v. LG Elecs., Inc., 553 U.S. 617, 638 (2008). Subsequently, however, the Federal Circuit interpreted this decision to reaffirm that the doctrine of patent exhaustion remains territorial, meaning that if an entire product is sold outside of the United States, the product did not exhaust the U.S. patent owner's rights. Fujifilm Corp. v. Benun, 605 F.3d 1366 (Fed. Cir. 2010). *See also* Bowman v. Monsanto Co., 569 U.S. 278, 284 (2013) ("the doctrine restricts a patentee's rights only as to the 'particular article' sold . . . it leaves untouched the patentee's ability to prevent a buyer from making new copies of the patented item").
35. Impression Prods., Inc. v. Lexmark Int'l, Inc., 137 S. Ct. 1523 (2017).
36. *See, e.g.*, United States v. Univis Lens Co., 316 U.S. 241 (1942).

§ 8:3 Development of First Sale Doctrine and "Gray Market" Case Law

As noted earlier, gray market goods are products that are released into channels of commerce or else imported into the United States without the approval of the owner of the intellectual property embodied in those products.[37] Often, such goods are available for purchase from authorized distributors abroad for a lower price than those same goods can be purchased from an authorized distributor in the United States. Retailers, seeking to compete on price, will purchase gray market goods—often luxury goods, such as designer apparel and watches—either from an importer or after importation, and will then resell them to consumers for prices lower than authorized U.S. distributors can offer. The legality of this practice is often fact-intensive and frequently litigated.

At times, the resale of goods in the gray market has even been prosecuted by law enforcement in connection with so-called organized retail crime. In such cases, it is alleged that sophisticated criminal rings steal, and then resell, large volumes of branded products in ways that make it difficult to tell whether or not the product was legitimately sold in the first instance.[38] Frequently stolen products range from high-end designer handbags to Tide laundry detergent.[39] This section, however, focuses on goods that were not stolen, but were instead released into channels of commerce by one or more parties to the production process. In these cases, brand owners have attempted to use a combination of trademark law, copyright law, and other legal theories to prevent the unauthorized resale of their products.

§ 8:3.1 Parfums Givenchy, Inc. v. Drug Emporium, Inc.

A prominent brand owner turned to copyright law to try to prevent resales of its products in *Parfums Givenchy, Inc. v. Drug Emporium, Inc.*[40] There, Givenchy owned the copyright to the box design of its Amarige perfume, produced in France. Third parties lawfully obtained quantities of Amarige abroad and imported the perfume into the United States without Givenchy's authorization. Once imported, the

---

37. *See* Quality King Distributors, Inc. v. L'anza Research Int'l, Inc., 523 U.S. 135, 153 (1998) ("In K Mart Corp. v. Cartier, Inc., 486 U.S. 281 (1988), we used those terms to refer to the importation of foreign-manufactured goods bearing a valid United States trademark without the consent of the trademark holder.").
38. HITHA PRABHAKAR, BLACK MARKET BILLIONS 94 (2012).
39. *See* Ben Paynter, *Suds for Drugs*, N.Y. MAG. (Jan. 6, 2013), http://nymag.com/news/features/tide-detergent-drugs-2013-1/.
40. Parfums Givenchy, Inc. v. Drug Emporium, Inc., 38 F.3d 477 (9th Cir. 1994).

retail chain Drug Emporium purchased the perfume from the third parties in the United States and marketed the perfume in its original copyright-protected packaging. Givenchy sued Drug Emporium for copyright infringement, and the district court granted summary judgment to Givenchy, finding that the first sale doctrine did not shield Drug Emporium from liability.[41]

On appeal, the U.S. Court of Appeals for the Ninth Circuit discussed the need to "harmonize" the first sale doctrine and the importation right created under 17 U.S.C. § 602, which "provides that unauthorized *importation* of *foreign* purchased copies of U.S. copyrighted materials is an infringement of the distribution rights provided in" 17 U.S.C. § 106.[42] Drug Emporium argued that the first sale doctrine supersedes the importation right and that a lawful sale abroad of a foreign good protected by U.S. copyright would terminate the exclusive right of the U.S. copyright holder to import and distribute those goods in the United States.[43] As a result, Drug Emporium claimed, Givenchy could not interfere with the U.S. distribution of Amarige products that Drug Emporium lawfully obtained abroad, even though Givenchy owned the U.S. copyright in the box design.[44] The Ninth Circuit disagreed, finding that "the importation right survives as to a particular copy unless and until there has been a 'first sale' *in the United States*."[45] The purpose of such an interpretation ensures that the exclusive distribution right afforded to copyright owners has "an extraterritorial scope" and "that a U.S. copyright owner will gain the full value of each copy sold in the United States, by preventing the unauthorized importation of copies sold abroad from being used as a means of circumventing the copyright owner's distribution rights in the United States."[46] The court, relying on its earlier decision in *BMG Music v. Perez*,[47] noted that "the words 'lawfully made under this title' in [17 U.S.C.] § 109(a) grant first sale protection only to copies legally made and sold in the United States."[48] Otherwise, the importation right created by section 602 would be rendered "virtually meaningless" because "copyright owners would no longer have an exclusive right to distribute copies or phonorecords of works manufactured abroad."[49]

41. *Id.* at 479.
42. *Id.* at 480 (emphasis in original).
43. *Id.* at 481.
44. *Id.*
45. *Id.* (emphasis in original).
46. *Id.*
47. BMG Music v. Perez, 952 F.2d 318 (9th Cir. 1991).
48. *Parfums Givenchy*, 38 F.3d at 481 (internal citations and quotation marks omitted).
49. *Id.* (internal citations and quotation marks omitted).

§ *8:3.2* Quality King Distributors, Inc. v. L'anza Research International, Inc.

The Supreme Court addressed this issue in *Quality King Distributors, Inc. v. L'anza Research International, Inc.*[50] L'anza was a California corporation that manufactured its hair care products in the United States and then sold its products to foreign distributors at much lower prices than it sold the same products to U.S. distributors. Quality King obtained L'anza products from those foreign distributors, and then sold them in the United States. L'anza brought suit on the grounds that the importation and later distribution of its products—marked with copyright-protected labels—violated its exclusive rights to reproduce and distribute those products in the United States. The Supreme Court described the case as "unusual" because, rather than claiming that a third party had copied its copyrighted material without authorization, "L'anza [was] primarily interested in protecting the integrity of its method of marketing the products to which the labels are affixed."[51] The district court and court of appeals rejected Quality King's first sale defense, holding that L'anza could control both its initial sale to foreign distributors and downstream sales.

The Supreme Court reversed, finding that because 17 U.S.C. § 602(a) "merely provides that unauthorized importation is an infringement of an exclusive right 'under section 106,' and since that limited right does not encompass resales by lawful owners, the literal text of § 602(a) is simply inapplicable to both domestic and foreign owners of L'anza's products who decide to import them and resell them in the United States."[52] In other words, the copyright holder's "exclusive" importation right does not extend so far as to limit the importation of products by lawful owners.[53] Consequently, L'anza was powerless under the Copyright Act to prevent the sale of its exported-then-imported products by Quality King. The Supreme Court did not, however, reach the question of the applicability of the first sale doctrine where goods are manufactured and first sold abroad.

---

50. Quality King Distributors, Inc. v. L'anza Research Int'l, Inc., 523 U.S. 135 (1998). L'anza promoted the domestic sales of its products "with extensive advertising in various trade magazines and at point of sale, and by providing special training to authorized retailers," while it did not engage in the same marketing campaigns abroad. *Id.* at 139.
51. *Id.* at 140.
52. *Id.* at 145.
53. *Id.* at 144. *See also* Kirtsaeng v. John Wiley & Sons, Inc., 568 U.S. 519 (2013) (holding that the first sale doctrine applies regardless of the location where the protected items are manufactured), discussed *infra*.

§ 8:3.3 Abercrombie & Fitch v. Fashion Shops of Kentucky, Inc.

In 2005, the application of the first sale doctrine in the context of foreign-manufactured apparel was at the heart of a trademark case involving the fashion retailer Abercrombie & Fitch.[54] In *Abercrombie & Fitch v. Fashion Shops of Kentucky, Inc.*, Fashion Shops operated a small off-price retail clothing chain that sold brand-name clothing, typically excess inventory and end-of-season goods at discounted prices, and was selling Abercrombie merchandise in one of its Kentucky stores.[55] Abercrombie sought to enjoin Fashion Shops from selling any articles of clothing that bore any of its trademarks.[56]

Abercrombie explained that the company's merchandise is produced by various manufacturers overseas and that all merchandise is inspected by Abercrombie; merchandise that does not meet Abercrombie's quality standards could be sold by the manufacturers, but only subject to certain restrictions.[57] Under Abercrombie's "Sell-Off Compliance Agreement," (1) no Abercrombie merchandise could be sold in the United States; (2) Abercrombie must approve of the final destination for the merchandise; and (3) all brand names on the labels and in marketing materials must be removed.[58]

The most problematic category was the merchandise that was rejected but nevertheless authorized to be resold abroad under the "Sell-Off Compliance Agreement."[59] These goods were authorized to be produced with the plaintiff's mark for sale abroad, and then were brought into the United States in violation of the sell-off agreement.[60] The district court explained that the maxim that "trademark law generally does not reach the sale of genuine goods bearing a true mark even though such sale is without the mark owner's consent" does not apply "when genuine, but unauthorized, imports differ materially from authentic goods authorized for sale in the domestic market" because "a difference in products bearing the same name confuses

54. Abercrombie & Fitch v. Fashion Shops of Kentucky, Inc., 363 F. Supp. 2d 952 (S.D. Ohio 2005).
55. *Id.* at 953.
56. *Id.* at 953, 955.
57. *Id.* at 955.
58. *Id.* Abercrombie did permit two exceptions to the prohibition against merchandise being sold within the United States: (1) manufacturers could sell denim garments within the United States, and (2) one chain of discount stores, Gabriel Brothers, could sell any end-of-season merchandise which it did not sell at their outlet stores and any damaged merchandise which came from Abercrombie retail stores. *Id.* at 955–56.
59. *Id.* at 963.
60. *Id.*

consumers and impinges on the local trademark holder's goodwill."[61] Thus, the court found it "only logical" that the first sale doctrine would not apply where unauthorized imports differ materially from goods authorized for sale in the domestic market.[62]

The district court concluded that it would extend the first sale doctrine too far to apply it as a defense to gray market goods sales in this context. The court noted that the threshold of materiality is quite low in order to "take account of potentially confusing differences—differences that are not blatant enough to make it obvious to the average consumer that the origin of the product differs from his or her expectations."[63]

Applying this low threshold for materiality, the court concluded that because the goods authorized for sale under the sell-off agreement did not meet Abercrombie's strict standards of quality and appearance, the merchandise was, in fact, materially different from authorized Abercrombie merchandise sold within the United States.[64] The court then granted the requested injunction against Fashion Shops, finding that Abercrombie was likely to succeed on the merits, and had established both irreparable injury to itself and the strong potential for harm to the public interest from the sale of unauthorized, potentially confusing goods.[65]

§ 8:3.4 Omega S.A. v. Costco Wholesale Corp.

Ten years after *Quality King*, the issue of gray market goods returned to the U.S. Supreme Court. In *Omega S.A. v. Costco Wholesale Corp.*, the Ninth Circuit considered a case in which authentic watches bearing the copyrighted Omega insignia were first manufactured and sold abroad to authorized foreign distributors and later, without Omega's permission, imported into the United States and sold to Costco.[66] Costco, in turn, sold the watches to California consumers.[67] Costco, like the defendant in *Quality King*, argued that under the first sale doctrine, Omega's first sale of its watches—albeit outside of the United States—"preclude[d] claims of infringing distribution and importation in connection with the subsequent, unauthorized sales."[68] The Ninth Circuit sided with Omega, finding that under Ninth Circuit precedent, including the *Drug Emporium* case discussed above, the

61. *Id.* at 964 (internal citations and quotation marks omitted).
62. *Id.* at 964 n.13 (citing MCCARTHY, *supra* note 29, § 29:51.2).
63. 363 F. Supp. 2d at 964 (internal citation and quotation marks omitted).
64. *Id.* at 966.
65. *Id.* at 966–68.
66. Omega S.A. v. Costco Wholesale Corp., 541 F.3d 982 (9th Cir. 2008).
67. *Id.* at 984.
68. *Id.*

first sale doctrine applies only to works made "within the United States, where the Copyright Act applies."[69] Because the watches at issue were manufactured abroad, and imported into the United States without the authorization of the copyright holder, the first sale doctrine provided no defense for Costco.[70]

The Supreme Court granted *certiorari*, but issued a 4–4 split decision without opinion, leaving the Ninth Circuit's decision in place without rendering a precedential Supreme Court decision.[71] On remand, the district court granted summary judgment to Costco, finding that "Omega misused its copyright of the Omega Globe to expand its limited monopoly impermissibly."[72] The Ninth Circuit reviewed the district court's grant of summary judgment de novo and again sided with Omega. The court found that Omega's right to control importation and distribution of its copyrighted watches expired after their first sale.[73] The Ninth Circuit thus reaffirmed that Costco's subsequent sale of watches did not constitute copyright infringement under the first sale doctrine and that "copyright holders cannot use their rights to fix resale prices in the downstream market."[74]

§ 8:3.5 John Wiley & Sons, Inc. v. Kirtsaeng

In *John Wiley & Sons, Inc. v. Kirtsaeng*, the Second Circuit (and, later, the Supreme Court) considered the same issue considered by the Ninth Circuit in *Omega*, but arising in the context of an unauthorized importation and sale of foreign edition textbooks that had

---

69. *Id.* at 988. The court noted that under some prior Ninth Circuit cases, the first sale doctrine would apply even to foreign-produced goods if the foreign-manufactured copies were sold in the United States with the authorization of the copyright holder. However, because there was "no genuine dispute" that the Omega watches were sold in the United States without Omega's authority, the court did not need to decide whether this was still good law. *Id.* at 990.

70. The court held that *Quality King* was consistent with and did not disturb the prior Ninth Circuit case law on which the court relied. In particular, the "general rule" in the Ninth Circuit that section 109(a) "refers 'only to copies legally made . . . in the United States' . . . is not clearly irreconcilable with *Quality King* [where the goods were in fact manufactured in the United States before exportation and re-importation], and, therefore, remains binding precedent." *Id.* (quoting BMG Music v. Perez, 952 F.2d 318, 319 (9th Cir. 1991)).

71. Costco Wholesale Corp. v. Omega, S.A., 562 U.S. 40 (2010). Justice Kagan recused herself because she had filed a brief supporting Omega's position during her service as Solicitor General.

72. Omega S.A. v. Costco Wholesale Corp., 776 F.3d 692, 694 (9th Cir. 2015).

73. *Id.* at 695.

74. *Id.*

been manufactured and sold to authorized distributors abroad.[75] In *Kirtsaeng*, the defendant had directed his family and friends abroad to purchase foreign editions of Wiley & Sons textbooks and ship them to him in the United States. He then sold the textbooks on eBay for profit.[76] Interpreting the "utterly ambiguous" phrase "lawfully made under this title" in section 109(a), the Second Circuit followed the Ninth Circuit in *Omega* in concluding that Kirtsaeng could not successfully rely on the first sale defense because the books were manufactured abroad.[77] Thus, in both cases, the circuit courts held that the statutory copyright first sale defense does not protect downstream retailers of imported foreign-manufactured goods, even where there was a first authorized sale abroad.

On March 19, 2013, however, the U.S. Supreme Court reversed the Second Circuit's decision, holding that the first sale doctrine *does* apply to copyrighted works lawfully made abroad and later imported into the United States.[78] Like the lower courts, the Supreme Court also focused on the phrase "lawfully made under this title" in section 109(a). Unlike the lower courts, however, the Supreme Court did not read the phrase as "imposing a form of *geographical* limitation," but rather interpreted the phrase as meaning "made 'in accordance with' or 'in compliance with'" the Copyright Act.[79] Thus, the first sale doctrine "would apply to copyrighted works as long as their manufacture met the requirements of American copyright law," that is, that they were manufactured abroad "with the permission of the copyright owner."[80] A plurality of the Court found that a non-geographical interpretation of the phrase "lawfully made under this title" made "word-by-word linguistic sense."[81] Although the Court uniformly conceded that its non-geographical interpretation would substantially limit the separate exclusive importation right conferred on copyright holders by the Copyright Act, the majority concluded that, reading the Copyright Act as a whole, copyright holders do not have "a right to divide markets or a concomitant right to charge different purchasers different prices . . . to increase or to maximize gain."[82]

---

75. John Wiley & Sons, Inc. v. Kirtsaeng, 654 F.3d 210, 213 (2d Cir. 2011).
76. *Id.*
77. *Id.* at 220, 222.
78. Kirtsaeng v. John Wiley & Sons, Inc., 568 U.S. 519, 525 (2013).
79. *Id.* at 529 (emphasis in original).
80. *Id.* at 530.
81. *Id.*
82. *Id.* at 552. The case returned to the Supreme Court in 2016 to address Kirtsaeng's claim to his attorneys' fees as the prevailing party in the underlying action. Kirtsaeng v. John Wiley & Sons, Inc., 136 S. Ct. 1979 (2016). In brief, the Court held that the attorneys' fees provision of the

§ 8:4 First Sale Doctrine in the Fashion and Apparel Context

Many disputes at the intersection of the first sale doctrine and fashion law have turned on one or both of two factual issues: (A) whether the production of the goods at issue was authorized and thus that the goods are "genuine"; and (B) whether the brand owner transferred "material ownership" of the goods. Both issues are discussed below.

§ 8:4.1 Unauthorized Production and the "Genuine" Goods Doctrine

Many trademark holders assert that if an initial sale was not "authorized," the goods then resold by an alleged infringer are rendered not "genuine," and thus not protected by the first sale doctrine. This issue usually arises in disputes between brand owners and discount retailers selling the trademark holder's branded goods, where the discount retailer obtained the goods from a source that was not authorized to sell them.

The genuine goods doctrine was explored in detail in *Liz Claiborne, Inc. v. Mademoiselle Knitwear, Inc.*[83] In that case, Claiborne, a company that designs, produces, and distributes trademark apparel, established a business relationship with Mademoiselle whereby Mademoiselle would produce knitwear for Claiborne, and Claiborne would order a specific quantity, style, and trademark to be used. Under the terms of this agreement, Mademoiselle was permitted to sell to third parties goods that did not pass a quality control test ("irregulars") and goods that exceeded the specified quantity by more than five percent ("overruns").[84] When a dispute arose as to the scope of Mademoiselle's authority to sell irregulars and overruns bearing Claiborne trademarks, Claiborne sued Mademoiselle for infringement.[85]

In response, Mademoiselle asserted that it could not infringe Claiborne's marks, because the garments in question were "genuine."[86] The court rejected this argument, finding that even though a trademark owner may authorize a distributor to use its trademark, that does not wholly deprive the trademark owner of the right to control the product sold under the trademark.[87]

Copyright Act "confers broad discretion on district courts" and requires them to "take into account a range of considerations beyond the reasonableness of litigating positions." *Id.* at 1988.

83. Liz Claiborne, Inc. v. Mademoiselle Knitwear, Inc., 979 F. Supp. 224, 226 (S.D.N.Y. 1997).

84. *Id.*

85. *Id.* at 227–28.

86. *Id.* at 230.

87. *Id.*

Delving into the first sale doctrine, the court discussed the "well settled" rule that the "sale of genuine goods without authorization by the trademark holder generally will not constitute trademark infringement."[88] The court found that the doctrine applies only when the initial sale of the trademarked goods was authorized, but the second sale is contested.[89] Trademark goods are not genuine, the court noted, unless their initial sale under the mark was authorized by the trademark owner. Thus, if the trademark owner rejects the goods, "the manufacturer may not use the mark in reselling the goods to others."[90] The case turned on the question of whether Mademoiselle's alleged sales of Claiborne garments were authorized; if those sales were not authorized, the garments could not be genuine and could not avoid potential trademark infringement liability under the guise of the first sale doctrine.[91]

The court ultimately found that there were genuine issues of material fact regarding the scope of the agreement between Claiborne and Mademoiselle and, therefore, summary judgment was improper.[92] Although the court did not reach the merits, this case illustrates the importance of an initial authorized sale in determining whether the first sale doctrine shields an alleged trademark infringer from liability.

Another district court elaborated on the issue of authorized sales and genuine goods in *Too, Inc. v. The TJX Cos., Inc.*[93] In that case, Limco, Inc. and Too, Inc. ("Limited Too")—holders of the Limited Too trademark—sought to enjoin TJX from selling or offering to sell allegedly unauthorized and/or counterfeit Limited Too merchandise. TJX acquired the merchandise from Limited Too under Limited Too's traditional practice of selling prior season merchandise to off-price retailers. Limited Too, however, claimed that TJX's possession and sale of the garments at issue violated the Lanham Act because they were either unauthorized for production or counterfeit.[94] TJX asserted that Limited Too could not obtain relief under the Lanham Act for unauthorized sales of products made by an otherwise authorized manufacturer (that is, garments made by Limited Too itself).[95]

---

88. *Id.*
89. *Id.*
90. *Id.* (citing RESTATEMENT (THIRD) OF UNFAIR COMPETITION § 24 cmt. c (1995)).
91. *Id.* at 231.
92. *Id.* at 231–32.
93. Too, Inc. v. The TJX Cos., 229 F. Supp. 2d 825, 827 (S.D. Ohio 2002).
94. *Id.* at 828.
95. *Id.*

The district court looked to the *Liz Claiborne* decision discussed above, and ultimately concluded that there was a substantial likelihood that Limited Too ***did not*** authorize the items in question to be produced.[96] The court noted that, similar to Mademoiselle in *Liz Claiborne*, TJX was a downstream retailer selling garments that bore purportedly genuine marks but, because Limited Too produced evidence showing a substantial likelihood that the garments were not authorized for production in the first instance, the garments should not be considered genuine for purposes of the Lanham Act.[97] The court, therefore, held that Limited Too was likely to prevail on its infringement claims.

The same district court again addressed the meaning of "authorized" and "genuine" goods in the case *Abercrombie & Fitch v. Fashion Shops of Kentucky, Inc.*, discussed above.[98] Abercrombie & Fitch argued that, under its "Sell Off Compliance Agreement," any merchandise not approved for sale was "non-genuine," and thus the first sale doctrine offered no protection to Fashion Shops for its sale of unauthorized merchandise.

Instead of focusing on the traditional likelihood of confusion factors that usually define a trademark infringement analysis,[99] the court discussed the more narrow question of whether the goods were "genuine" because, "as a general rule, trademark law does not reach the sale of genuine goods bearing a true mark even though the sale is not authorized by the mark owner."[100] Once the trademark owner validly authorizes a sale of the merchandise, the court held, that merchandise is "genuine," and any further downstream sales do not constitute trademark infringement. The court further clarified that "the first sale doctrine applies when a purchaser does no more than stock, display, and resell a producer's product under the producer's trademark," but "offers no defense when the reseller used the trademark in a manner likely to cause the public to believe the reseller was part of the producer's authorized sales force or one of its franchisees."[101] Because the first sale doctrine presupposes that the goods were authorized to be made in the first instance, if the plaintiff shows a substantial likelihood that the garments were not in fact authorized for production in the first place, there is a strong likelihood

96. *Id.* at 832.
97. *Id.* at 834.
98. Abercrombie & Fitch v. Fashion Shops of Ky., Inc., 363 F. Supp. 2d 952 (S.D. Ohio 2005).
99. *See supra* section 2:7.2.
100. *Fashion Shops*, 363 F. Supp. 2d at 959 & n.7 (internal citations and quotation marks omitted).
101. *Id.* at 961–62 (internal citations and quotation marks omitted).

that the garments cannot be considered "genuine" for purposes of the Lanham Act and trademark infringement.[102]

The court easily disposed of the issue of genuineness as to certain categories of merchandise. In particular, the court concluded without difficulty that counterfeit merchandise created by third parties was not genuine, and thus Fashion Shops agreed not to sell that merchandise any longer. The court also found that the first sale doctrine did not insulate from liability any merchandise manufactured without Abercrombie's approval, or rejected by Abercrombie, or sold in violation of the "Sell-Off Compliance Agreement" because such merchandise was either not authorized to be made or was not authorized to be sold.[103] The first sale doctrine did, however, apply to denim products that Abercrombie had approved for sale in the United States, and to merchandise that Abercrombie approved for sale by a different discount retailer—Gabriel Brothers—because all of this merchandise was authorized for manufacture and sale.[104]

The three cases described above illustrate the importance of an authorized first sale to the application of the first sale doctrine. If the trademarked goods were authorized by the trademark holder for sale in the United States, they are "genuine" and the first sale doctrine serves as a defense to infringement liability. If, however, the trademark owner did not authorize the initial sale of the merchandise, or authorized the initial sale subject to express limitations that were justified by defects or other material differences in the product, any downstream sales of the apparel may be considered non-genuine and not protected under the first sale rule.

§ 8:4.2 Failure to Transfer Ownership of Goods

A related issue is whether the copyright holder lawfully transferred ownership of the goods to another, such that the holder is divested of the right to control future transfers of copies of the item. This issue primarily arises in disputes between copyright holders and manufacturers that have not been authorized to distribute or sell the copyrighted goods without the express permission of the copyright holder.

This issue is illustrated in *Too, Inc. v. Kohl's Department Stores, Inc.*[105] In that case, Too, Inc. owned four copyrights on design patterns used for Limited Too girls' sleepwear. Wormser, a maker of infants' and children's sleepwear, manufactured Limited Too's designs, and

102. *Id.* at 962 (citing *TJX Cos.*, 229 F. Supp. 2d at 834).
103. *Id.*
104. *Id.*
105. Too, Inc. v. Kohl's Dep't Stores, Inc., No. 2:01-CV-1256, 2002 WL 31409852 (S.D. Ohio Sept. 4, 2002).

Wormser sold certain quantities of the sleepwear bearing those designs to Kohl's without Limited Too's authorization. Limited Too alleged that Kohl's infringed its rights in the four designs by selling sleepwear that made use of the copyright-protected designs, and Kohl's asserted the first sale doctrine as a defense.[106] Limited Too, however, responded that Wormser was never vested with an ownership interest in the sleepwear at issue and, therefore, the first sale doctrine did not apply to protect downstream sales to Kohl's from infringement liability.[107]

The Copyright Act, the court noted, provides that "once a copyright holder has transferred its 'material ownership' to another, the holder is divested of the right to control future transfers of particular copies of the copyrighted work" and the "voluntary disposition of interest in the copyrighted work negates the copyright owner's control over further 'downstream' transfers."[108] A purchaser of a copy in a secondary market may, however, be held liable for infringement if the seller in that secondary market never properly acquired title to the copyrighted merchandise. The first sale by the copyright holder must properly transfer title, or else subsequent sales do not confer good title, and the first sale doctrine does not apply. The district court, moreover, concluded that the alleged infringer bears the burden to prove proper chain of title and thus applicability of the first sale doctrine.[109]

The central question in the case was whether Limited Too's conveyance of its copyrighted designs to Wormser for the purpose of manufacturing sleepwear from Limited Too also conveyed an *ownership interest* in the finished products that Wormser eventually sold to Kohl's.[110] The court agreed with Limited Too that the right to manufacture sleepwear for Limited Too did not translate into an ownership interest in the sleepwear's designs and, therefore, Limited Too sufficiently alleged that Wormser's sales to Kohl's "were performed without the permission, license or authority of plaintiff, and/or were performed in deliberate, intentional, or reckless disregard of plaintiff's rights" in its copyrighted designs.[111] As a result, at the motion to dismiss stage, the court was not willing to apply the first sale doctrine to dismiss an infringement claim.[112]

106. *Id.* at *1–2
107. *Id.* at *3.
108. *Id.* (internal citations omitted).
109. *Id.*
110. *Id.* at *4.
111. *Id.*
112. *Id.*

§ 8:5 Strategies Used by Fashion Brands to Combat Gray Market Sales

Fashion brands have employed a wide array of strategies in an attempt to prevent or limit gray market sales of genuine products, with varying degrees of success.

The most obvious technique is to control distribution to the extent possible through vertical integration of the channels of distribution. This may not be a realistic option for most companies, so many brand owners will instead try to screen distributors carefully to ensure that authorized goods are provided only to entities that can be trusted to offer products only through authorized channels, in agreed geographic markets.[113] This technique requires that brand owners thoroughly investigate a distributor's business dealings, to gauge the likelihood that a distributor might sell products to undesirable customers or in markets that are inconsistent with the brand's strategy if demand slows. In some cases, trust and loyalty are developed over the course of a long-term relationship. In other cases, brand owners offer incentives to "prevent diversion of products" by distributors.[114]

Many brands contractually require distributors of licensed products to limit their resale activities. For example, agreements between brands and foreign distributors may contain provisions stating that the distributors are not authorized to export or sell those products in the United States.[115] If a distributor violates the terms of the agreement, the brand then has remedies to terminate its agreement with the distributor, or even to bring a breach of contract action against the noncompliant distributor under appropriate circumstances. In some instances, brands require that their distributors agree to liquidated damages provisions requiring payment of an agreed monetary sum (representing a good faith estimate of the harm caused by a breach) if the goods sold to that distributor are found in a market or geographic region that the contract prohibits.[116] Some brands have also pursued remedies against downstream resellers, on the theory that these resellers have tortiously interfered with the contractual obligation placed on the distributor to limit resales. But courts will dismiss these claims if the brand cannot identify specific business relationships with which the defendant allegedly interfered or if the brand owner

---

113. Antia, Bergen & Dutta, *supra* note 2.

114. *Id.*

115. *See* Ronald G. Dove Jr. & Hope Hamilton, *Combat Grey Market Goods in the US*, MANAGING IP (Nov. 2008) [hereinafter Dove & Hamilton], at 60.

116. Lawrence M. Friedman, *Business and Legal Strategies for Combating Grey-Market Imports*, 32 INT'L LAW. 27, 50 (1998) [hereinafter Friedman].

cannot detail the defendant's knowledge of the specific contracts allegedly breached.[117]

Many brands consciously sell different versions of their products in the United States and abroad, with an eye toward limiting gray market sales.[118] Because courts take into account whether goods are "materially" different in a Lanham Act suit, brands that sell "materially different" goods abroad can argue that the product "reaching consumers through unauthorized channels is not what the U.S. trademark is intended to represent."[119] In some cases, the differences are limited to labels, and in other cases, brand owners alter the actual products sold to specific markets. The less important that alleged differences are to consumer demand for a particular product, the harder it is for brand owners to allege that goods are "materially different." But tampering with the labeling of health and beauty products, such as removing the serial codes that allow brand owners to track the origins and age of particular products, is routinely held likely to cause consumer confusion and give rise to claims under the Lanham Act and for unfair competition.[120]

Some luxury brands, in fact, are so concerned about gray market resales that they charge the same price for their goods in all markets, regardless of the local cost of living.[121]

Not all strategies to limit resales are successful. Most notoriously, Omega S.A. affixed its copyrighted hologram "Omega Globe Design" logo to the back of its watches, in order to take advantage of the exclusive importation rights created by the Copyright Act. A U.S. district court, however, deemed this use of a copyright logo to fall under the doctrine of "copyright misuse."[122] Specifically, when Omega brought a lawsuit against Costco Wholesale Corporation asserting that Costco violated its copyright in the logo by purchasing imported Omega watches for resale, the district court held that Omega was wrongly attempting to leverage its copyright in the logo to "control

117. *See, e.g.*, Wolff v. Rare Medium, Inc., 171 F. Supp. 2d 354 (S.D.N.Y. 2001); Plasticware, LLC v. Flint Hills Res., LP, 852 F. Supp. 2d 398 (S.D.N.Y. 2012); TechnoMarine SA v. Jacob Time, Inc., No. 12 Civ. 0790 (KBF), slip op. (S.D.N.Y. July 16, 2013).

118. Dove & Hamilton, *supra* note 115, at 60.

119. Friedman, *supra* note 116, at 32–33.

120. *See, e.g.*, John Paul Mitchell Sys. v. Pete-n-Larry's Inc., 862 F. Supp. 1020 (W.D.N.Y. 1994). *See also* Martin's Herend Imports, Inc. v. Diamond & Gem Trading USA, Co., 112 F.3d 1296 (5th Cir. 1997) (affirming nearly $700,000 judgment against unauthorized distributor who sold trademarked goods that were materially different from plaintiff's product).

121. Antia, Bergen & Dutta, *supra* note 2.

122. Omega S.A. v. Costco Wholesale Corp., No. CV 04-05443 TJH, 2011 WL 8492716, at *1–2 (C.D. Cal. Nov. 9, 2011).

the importation and sale of [the] watches," because "the watches [themselves] could not be copyrighted."[123] Noting that Omega had not publicized the presence of the logo as a desirable attribute of its watches, the district court found that Omega had wrongly "leverage[d]" its "limited monopoly" and "used the defensive shield of copyright law as an offensive sword."[124] The Ninth Circuit later affirmed the district court's decision without passing judgment on the copyright misuse issue, relying on the Supreme Court's decision in *Kirtsaeng v. John Wiley & Sons*, which was decided in the interim.[125] The lesson is that brands should carefully consider where and when—and under what theory—to assert their intellectual property rights in order to limit gray market resales of their products.

---

123. *Id.*
124. *Id.*
125. Omega S.A. v. Costco Wholesale Corp., 776 F.3d 692 (9th Cir. 2015).

Chapter 9

Design and Manufacturing

§ 9:1 Introduction
§ 9:2 Fashion Design and Luxury
§ 9:3 Design and Production
§ 9:4 Supply Contracts
§ 9:5 Governmental Regulation and Industry Initiatives
  § 9:5.1 Federal and State Regulation
  § 9:5.2 Industry Initiatives
§ 9:6 Conclusion
Appendix 9A Sample Manufacturing Agreement

§ 9:1 Introduction

The business of designing and manufacturing apparel and accessories is global, segmented, and highly competitive. Apparel and accessory brands face significant challenges, including rising raw material costs, labor intensive production processes, seasonal fashion trends, and shifting consumer preferences. In light of these challenges, companies adopt a variety of strategies to produce their products. Many U.S. companies design and market their own branded products, but outsource the manufacturing to contract manufacturers. Other companies license their brands to third parties that manufacture the branded products in their own factories and/or through contract manufacturers and then market the branded products, paying the brand owner a royalty on sales to retailers. Integrated manufacturers design, manufacture, and market their branded products, using their own factories and/or contract manufacturers. The overwhelming majority of apparel and accessory companies, however, use manufacturing facilities based outside of the United States.[1]

---

1. *See* DUN & BRADSTREET, FIRST RES., INDUSTRY PROFILE: APPAREL MANUFACTURING (May 21, 2018) [hereinafter FIRST RES.]. For additional Dun

The global apparel manufacturing industry generates annual revenue of about \$515 billion.[2] China has the world's largest apparel manufacturing industry with an annual revenue of about \$200 billion, and it accounts for about 40% of the global export market.[3] Due to rising labor costs in China, however, manufacturing has migrated to countries such as Cambodia, Indonesia, and Vietnam, which have lower garment worker wages.[4] Additionally, the United States is importing more apparel products from Vietnam than China because of the current tension between the United States and China due to increased trade tariffs.[5] Despite continuing cost pressures, some U.S. and European luxury brands that emphasize craftsmanship continue to manufacture their apparel products in Europe, particularly in Italy and France.[6]

The U.S. apparel industry includes (i) national brands, produced by approximately ten companies, accounting for about 18% of U.S. wholesale apparel sales and (ii) other apparel, which includes private label retail store brands and smaller brands, accounting for approximately 82% of U.S. wholesale apparel sales.[7] The U.S. apparel manufacturing industry, which is significantly smaller than the Chinese and European industries, is comprised of approximately 7,000 companies with combined annual revenue of approximately \$11 billion.[8] It is highly fragmented, with the fifty largest companies generating less than 40% of total revenue.[9] Domestic manufacturing in the United States is concentrated in California, New York, North Carolina, Pennsylvania, Florida, and Texas.[10] The U.S. apparel manufacturing industry has lost manufacturing jobs to countries with lower labor costs, and textile mills have automated many aspects of production in order to effectively compete with foreign suppliers. U.S. apparel

---

& Bradstreet First Research Industry Profiles, including current Apparel Manufacturing Industry Profile, see DUN & BRADSTREET, FIRST RESEARCH INDUSTRY PROFILES, http://www.firstresearch.com/industry-profiles.aspx.

2. *Id.*
3. *Id.*
4. *Id.*
5. *Id.*
6. Krystina Gustafson, *'Made in the USA' Is a Tough Promise for Luxury Brands to Make*, CNBC (Feb. 14, 2017, 9:38 AM), https://www.cnbc.com/2017/02/14/made-in-the-usa-is-a-tough-promise-for-luxury-brands-to-make.html [hereinafter Gustafson].
7. Tuna Amobi, *Industry Surveys Apparel & Footwear: Retailers & Brands*, S&P CAPITAL IQ, at 10 (Sept. 2014), https://gskkr.files.wordpress.com/2015/01/apparel-footwear-retailers-brands.pdf.
8. FIRST RES., *supra* note 1.
9. *Id.*
10. *Id.*

manufacturing employment peaked in the early 1970s with more than 1.4 million employees, and U.S. textile manufacturing employment peaked in the 1950s with more than 1.2 million employees.[11] Between 2007 and 2016, the number of U.S. jobs in the apparel manufacturing industry decreased by about 40%.[12] The U.S. apparel manufacturing industry is now one of the smallest segments of the U.S. manufacturing industry.[13]

Some reports, however, indicate that the U.S. apparel manufacturing industry is showing signs of renewed growth, and the "Made in the U.S.A." movement has gained some momentum.[14] The output of U.S. apparel manufacturing, including knit and sewn apparel and accessories, is predicted to grow at an annual compounded rate of 2% through 2022.[15] The growth in U.S. manufacturing can be attributed to a combination of factors, two of which are the demand for shorter lead times on production and the demand for increased flexibility to implement changes.[16] It can take as long as ten months to receive a shipment of apparel from a manufacturer in China, thus increasing the time for the product to reach the consumer and preventing the company from making quick modifications to serve the market.[17] The "local for local" manufacturing model allows companies to serve today's on-demand e-consumer by allowing quicker delivery to customers and providing the ability to adjust orders based on fast moving fashion trends.[18] For example, the U.S. designer Rebecca

---

11. U.S. DEP'T OF COMMERCE, BUREAU OF INDUS. & SEC., THE U.S. TEXTILE AND APPAREL INDUSTRIES (Oct. 2003), https://www.bis.doc.gov/index.php/forms-documents/technology-evaluation/75-u-s-textile-and-apparel-industries-2003.
12. FIRST RES., *supra* note 1.
13. *See* Kristi Ellis & Liza Casabona, *U.S. Apparel Manufacturing Showing Signs of Life*, WOMEN'S WEAR DAILY (Jan. 10, 2011), https://wwd.com/business-news/government-trade/a-comeback-for-u-s-apparel-manufacturing-3413691/.
14. Harry Moser & Sandy Montalbano, *Why Made-in-USA Fashion Is Turning Heads*, INDUSTRY WEEK (Jan. 18, 2018), https://www.industryweek.com/economy/why-made-usa-fashion-turning-heads [hereinafter Moser & Montalbano]; *see also* Paul Davidson, *Some Apparel Manufacturing 'Reshoring' to USA*, USA TODAY (July 4, 2013), https://www.usatoday.com/story/money/business/2013/07/04/some-apparel-manufacturing-returns-to-us/2454075/ [hereinafter Davidson].
15. FIRST RES., *supra* note 1.
16. Moser & Montalbano, *supra* note 14.
17. Elizabeth Segran, *Why Clothing Startups Are Returning to American Factories*, FAST COMPANY (Mar. 16, 2016), https://www.fastcompany.com/3057738/why-clothing-startups-are-returning-to-american-factories [hereinafter Segran].
18. Moser & Montalbano, *supra* note 14.

Minkoff shifted her manufacturing to New York City and Los Angeles in order to speed up the overall process.[19] The e-commerce company Amazon went a step further by planning to manufacture in the United States and at the same facility as designers work. In 2017, Amazon obtained a U.S. patent for an automated system for on-demand apparel manufacturing that can design, produce, and ship in a matter of hours.[20] In addition, there has been an increased demand by consumers for a "Made in the U.S.A." label. A study by Consumer Reports found that almost eight in ten American consumers stated that they would rather buy American-made products than imported ones, and more than 60% of those consumers were willing to pay 10% more for it.[21] The U.S. manufacturing industry is also benefitting from the emergence of companies focused on assisting designers who want to manufacture in America. For example, Maker's Row is an e-commerce company launched in 2012 to provide an easy-to-navigate platform for connecting American designers with local American manufacturers.[22] Manufacture New York is a factory based in Brooklyn that helps emerging designers understand the manufacturing process and connect with local supply chains.[23] By bringing production back to the United States, companies may gain greater control over the production process, reduce shipping costs, and shorten lead times (and in the process, decrease vulnerability to phenomena such as trade tariffs). In addition, by working with smaller domestic manufacturers, new and independent designers may be able to produce apparel without the high minimum volume requirements often imposed by larger foreign manufacturers.[24] Yet, few experts predict that the U.S. apparel manufacturing industry will return to its historic levels, as foreign manufacturers continue to offer cost advantages and the United States no longer has the requisite apparel manufacturing infrastructure of factories and skilled labor.[25]

The apparel manufacturing process is labor intensive. The manufacturing process begins with textile mills: fiber (such as cotton and wool), yarn, and thread mills; fabric mills; and finishing and coating mills. The fabrics produced by textile mills are purchased and delivered to apparel factories, in which the fabrics are cut in sizes and

---

19. Gustafson, *supra* note 6.
20. Moser & Montalbano, *supra* note 14.
21. *Id.*
22. *See* Joseph Flaherty, *'Maker's Row' Bridges Daunting Gap Between Design and Manufacturing*, WIRED (Nov. 26, 2012), https://www.wired.com/2012/11/makers-row/; *see also* MAKER'S ROW, http://makersrow.com/.
23. Segran, *supra* note 17.
24. *Id.*
25. Gustafson, *supra* note 6.

then sewn into garments. Garment workers typically sit at individual stations and produce the garments in a sequence of steps that correspond to the garment's technical specifications.

Technological advances in the manufacturing process can reduce the labor intensity of garment production. 3D printing ("additive manufacturing" as opposed to traditional subtractive manufacturing) is a collection of technologies through which a machine creates a three dimensional and complex object by producing a succession of thin layers, one layer at a time, that are then fused with chemicals, light, or heat. 3D printing uses computer-aided design files and a computer guided laser, extruder, or printer head. Fashion designers such as threeASFOUR are working with additive manufacturing companies such as Materialise and Stratasys Ltd. to master the 3D printing of apparel.[26] Some of these designers, such as Dutch designer Iris Van Herpen, are even creating 3D printed high-end fashion apparel that has been included in runway collections.[27] 3D printed technology is quickly evolving and is frequently used to produce hard materials such as jewelry and watches, but using it to make soft materials is more challenging.[28] For instance, to create a 3D-printed dress, three-ASFOUR had to print the dress in thirty pieces and then carefully assemble all of the separate pieces.[29] Additionally, the clothing items are known to be stiff, clingy, and uncomfortable.[30] However, some companies have developed strategies to overcome these obstacles. For instance, the performance professional brand Ministry of Supply uses 3D printing to create superior knits and sells them at its Boston store.[31] Brands also use 3D printing to develop prototypes more efficiently. For example, Nike and Adidas use 3D printing in their

---

26. Roni Jacobson, *The Shattering Truth of 3D-Printed Clothing*, WIRED (May 12, 2017, 12:00 AM), https://www.wired.com/2017/05/the-shattering-truth-of-3d-printed-clothing/ [hereinafter Jaconson].
27. Mark Holgate, *Meet Iris van Herpen, the Dutch Designer Boldly Going Into the Future*, VOGUE (Apr. 28, 2016, 11:55 AM), https://www.vogue.com/article/iris-van-herpen-dutch-designer-interview-3d-printing.
28. Herbert Sim, *3D Printing in Luxury Fashion: Revolution or Evolution*, FORBES (Dec. 3, 2017, 10:56 PM), https://www.forbes.com/sites/herbertrsim/2017/12/03/3d-printing-in-luxury-fashion-revolution-or-evolution/#797093bc3f20 [hereinafter Sim].
29. Jacobson, *supra* note 26.
30. Sim, *supra* note 28.
31. Mara Leighton, *A Clothing Startup Founded by MIT Grads Is Using 3D Printing to Make Better, More Sustainable Clothes*, BUS. INSIDER (Sept. 6, 2017), https://www.businessinsider.com/ministry-of-supply-3d-printed-knits.

prototype process to accelerate the development of new, high-performance padding and soles for their athletic footwear.[32] In addition to 3D printing, apparel manufacturers may make more effective use of industrial robotic systems. These systems, which can be programmed to use their sensory and mechanical abilities to carry out routine tasks, have been used to automate the sewing process. For example, the Chinese clothing manufacturer Tianyuan Garments Company plans to produce 800,000 Adidas T-shirts per day using fully automated Sewbots supplied by SoftWear Automation.[33] Over 1.2 million industrial robots are already in use globally.[34] For example, robots produced by Kiva Systems that sort and deliver items are already in use in many U.S. warehouse fulfillment centers that serve companies such as Staples and Amazon.[35]

The following sections discuss the design and manufacturing process, the relationships among the parties to the process, and the U.S. laws and regulations applicable to the process.

§ 9:2 Fashion Design and Luxury

Fashion design has historically been associated with luxury. The origin of the modern women's fashion industry can be traced to mid-eighteenth century Paris, where women sought luxurious fabrics and trims to create "fashionable" apparel.[36] A century later, haute couture became the enduring symbol of fashion elegance, artistry, and exclusivity.

Luxury can be defined both by quantitative and qualitative measures. Industry analysts often define luxury goods as those products that represent the top sector (or highest price point) of any product

---

32. Jacobson, *supra* note 26.
33. May Zhou & Zhang Yuan, *Textile Companies Go High Tech in Arkansas*, CHINA DAILY (July 25, 2017), http://usa.chinadaily.com.cn/world/2017-07/25/content_30244657.htm?utm_campaign=T-shirt%20line&utm_source=hs_email&utm_medium=email&utm_content=54911122&_hsenc=p2ANqtz-9WyxMiFliVTrpO35Quk5KN0XpHHHj2bYn9-7WKp3Tt_iF8LUsO9Q6m6OEH892iW9QcXJ4kvAk8C1Ooiy5TffzH6URrPVnKTrvZ3TEFQ_zyt6rIjp0&_hsmi=54911122.
34. Press Release, Int'l Fed'n of Robotics, Survey: 1.3 Million Indus. Robots to Enter Serv. by 2018 (Feb. 5, 2016), https://ifr.org/ifr-press-releases/news/-survey-13-million-industrial-robots-to-enter-service-by-2018-.
35. Pablo Valerio, *Amazon Robotics: IoT in the Warehouse*, INFO. WEEK (Sept. 28, 2015, 9:06 AM), https://www.informationweek.com/strategic-cio/amazon-robotics-iot-in-the-warehouse/d/d-id/1322366.
36. ART INST. OF CHICAGO, IMPRESSIONISM, FASHION & MODERNITY 63 (Gloria Groom ed., 2012).

category.[37] The luxury industry would therefore include the most expensive fashion items, as well as the highest price points of every other sector of consumer products and experiences, including wine, cars, and travel.[38]

Luxury also can be defined by reference to aesthetic values. It has been suggested that luxury refers "to the special element of a luxury product that makes it desired for its own sake rather than any function that it may have."[39] Some commentators have noted that luxury goods share certain unifying characteristics, including quality, heritage, integrity, price, scarcity, and superfluousness or non-utility,[40] or are "items which provide extra pleasure by flattering all senses at once."[41] Many luxury fashion brands emphasize the uniqueness of their products and the craftsmanship and service associated with their brand. For example, in 2011, Louis Vuitton, one of the oldest French fashion houses, introduced La Haute Maroquinerie salons in selected Louis Vuitton boutiques where customers can purchase made-to-order bags (choosing from a selection of leathers or skins, colors, and shapes) to be produced at the Louis Vuitton workshops in Paris.[42]

Luxury brands have been slower to embrace e-commerce and some luxury brands remain reluctant to sell their apparel or accessories online. For instance, Goyard, a two-centuries-old Parisian brand, forgoes selling through e-commerce in order to maintain its sense of exclusivity.[43] Additionally, Chanel, one of the most famous luxury

---

37. *See* Bernard Dubois & Patrick Duquesne, *The Market for Luxury Goods: Income Versus Culture*, 27 EUR. J. OF MKTG. 36 (1993).

38. Press Release, Bain & Co, Global Personal Luxury Goods Market Expected to Grow by 2–4 Percent to €254–259bn in 2017, Driven By Healthier Local Consumption in China and Increased Tourism and Consumer Confidence in Europe (May 29, 2017), https://www.bain.com/about/media-center/press-releases/2017/global-personal-luxury-goods-market-expected-to-grow-by-2-4-percent/.

39. MINTEL STORE, LUXURY GOODS RETAILING—INTERNATIONAL—AUGUST 2013, https://store.mintel.com/luxury-goods-retailing-international-august-2013.

40. *See* MICHAEL CHEVALIER & GERALD MAZZALOVO, LUXURY BRAND MANAGEMENT: A WORLD OF PRIVILEGE 9-15 (Wiley, 2d ed. 2012).

41. Paurav Shukla, *Defining Luxury: The Conundrum of Perspectives*, LUXURY SOC'Y (May 13, 2010), http://luxurysociety.com/articles/2010/05/defining-luxury-the-conundrum-of-perspectives.

42. *See* Melainne Chiew, *Louis Vuitton Re-Opens Ion Store With Haute Maroquinerie Service*, LUXURY INSIDER (Feb. 4, 2016), https://www.luxury-insider.com/luxury-news/2016/02/louis-vuitton-ion-haute-maroquinerie.

43. Hillary Hoffower, *Forget Louis Vuitton and Hermes—This Luxury Brand Is the Status Symbol for the World's Richest People*, BUS. INSIDER (May 24, 2018, 8:30 AM), https://www.businessinsider.com/louis-vuitton-hermes-goyard-secret-luxury-brand-rich-people-love-2018-5.

brands in the world, formerly chose not to sell its apparel and handbags online out of concern that online sales might impair the brand's ability to convey the full experience and high quality of service available in its Chanel boutiques.[44] Despite these concerns, more brands, including Chanel, are embracing the e-commerce model so as to serve their current customers, who are increasingly shopping online, and new customers in the global market.[45] However, to preserve exclusivity, some companies, like Hermes, offers a limited number of products online and sells their more expensive and popular products in the store.[46]

Consumption of luxury goods also includes an "aspirational" element,[47] and consumers selectively trade up to higher levels of quality, taste, and aspiration. For some consumers, the purchase of a luxury fashion product serves not only a functional purpose but also represents the attainment of a certain status, lifestyle, and experience associated with the celebrated and the wealthy. Some market research firms note that as consumers become more sophisticated and discerning, they shift from displaying logos and other external signs of wealth ("bling") to more personal experiences of connoisseurship.[48]

Some luxury fashion brands (such as the French brands Louis Vuitton and Hermes) offer mainly high-end collections and do not have large wholesale businesses, diffusion lines, or outlet stores.[49] Other luxury fashion brands (such as the American brands Ralph Lauren and Michael Kors) are based on a pyramid model, with a small luxury collection and multiple diffusion brands that benefit from the brand image yet are more accessible and generate a greater share of the profits.[50]

---

44. Imran Amed, *CEO Talk: Bruno Pavlovsky, President of Fashion, Chanel*, BUS. OF FASHION (Oct. 22, 2012), https://www.businessoffashion.com/2012/10/ceo-talk-bruno-pavlovsky-president-of-fashion-chanel.html [hereinafter Amed].
45. Catalin Zorzini, *Why Are so Few Luxury Brands Sold Online?*, ECOMMERCE PLATFORMS (Aug. 14, 2017), https://ecommerce-platforms.com/ecommerce-selling-advice/why-are-so-few-luxury-brands-sold-online.
46. *Id.*
47. BAKER RETAILING CENTER, ONLINE LUXURY RETAILING: LEVERAGING DIGITAL OPPORTUNITIES, at 11 (2016), https://bakerretail.wharton.upenn.edu/wp-content/uploads/2016/06/Online_Luxury_Retail.pdf.
48. Sonia Kolesnikov-Jessop, *Toning Down the Bling Factor*, N.Y. TIMES (Sept. 10, 2012), https://www.nytimes.com/2012/09/11/business/global/toning-down-the-bling-factor.html?pagewanted=all.
49. Vanessa Friedman et al., *Fashion: Luxury's New Look*, FIN. TIMES (Dec. 23, 2012), http://www.ft.com/intl/cms/s/2/2f99fcc6-4aef-11e2-929d-00144feab49a.html#axzz2QpajL5qL.
50. *Id.*

The core categories of luxury fashion products are: apparel, accessories, and leather ("soft luxury"); watches and jewelry ("hard luxury"); and cosmetics and fragrances.[51] The soft luxury segment has traditionally represented the largest share of luxury goods revenue, but over the years, the hard luxury segment has grown at a greater pace.[52] As hard luxury goods target "high net worth individuals,"[53] revenue in this segment tends to be more robust, and has historically been more resilient during economic downturns. Hard luxury accounted for the highest sales within the luxury goods market in 2018.[54] The fragrance and cosmetics segment is generally the most affordable of the three luxury fashion segments and has generally fared better during times of economic downturn.[55]

The Internet and e-commerce have contributed to globalization, which has significantly impacted the luxury sector, allowing fashion brands and retailers to access previously untapped markets. Rising consumption in emerging markets, in particular, has impacted marketing and growth strategies as fashion companies adapt to consumer preferences in different countries.[56] In India, certain brands are tailoring their own merchandise to the Indian market and are using India's heritage and local designs for inspiration.[57] For example, at one point, the luxury brands Hermes and Canali incorporated Indian designs in their products in order to generate demand.[58] Hermes launched a sari collection and Canali offered Nawab jackets.[59] Chinese luxury consumers represent almost one

---

51. KERING, 2017 REFERENCE DOCUMENT, at 16 (2017), http://www.kering.com/sites/default/files/document/kering-ddr_va_vdef-290317-miseenligne.pdf.
52. *Id.*
53. Capgemini defines high net worth individuals as one with more than $1 million at their disposal for investing. CAPGEMINI, WORLD WEALTH REP. (2017), https://www.capgemini.com/news/capgemini-world-wealth-report-2017-high-net-worth-individual-population-and-wealth-hits-new-all-time-high/.
54. *See* DELOITTE, GLOBAL POWERS OF LUXURY GOODS, at 29 (2018), https://www2.deloitte.com/content/dam/Deloitte/mx/Documents/consumer-business/2018/Global-Power-of-Luxury-Goods-2018.pdf.
55. *What Is "the Lipstick Index" and Why Is It Important Right Now*, FASHION L. (Aug. 1, 2017), http://www.thefashionlaw.com/home/premium-beauty-what-is-it-and-why-is-it-so-important-right-now.
56. Amed, *supra* note 44.
57. Abhay Gupta, *Emerging Luxury Markets: India's Ripe Retail Market*, LUXURY SOC'Y (Apr. 12, 2016), https://www.luxurysociety.com/en/articles/2016/04/emerging-luxury-markets-indias-ripe-retail-market/.
58. *Id.*
59. *Id.*

third of the global luxury market.[60] The majority of such buyers are millennials who choose to live in provinces outside major cities like Beijing due to urbanization.[61] Thus, to capture this market, brands such as Prada and LVMH are offering more stores in these areas.[62] In addition, companies are increasing their digital offerings to serve China's online shoppers.[63] For example, Louis Vuitton and Gucci both rolled out Chinese e-commerce websites.[64]

As more fully discussed in chapter 21, in 2011, some European and American luxury fashion companies went public, or listed, on the Hong Kong Stock Exchange in recognition of the importance of the Asian consumer market to the future success of their brands.[65] For example, the traditionally family-controlled company Prada SpA, owner of the Italian luxury brands Prada and Miu, listed its initial public offering on the Hong Kong Stock Exchange.[66] However, the increase of tariffs in the ongoing trade war between China and the United States has caused some concern among public luxury brands.[67] As of October 2018, global luxury stocks were down by 11%, causing many brands to be more cautious in making future business decisions involving China.[68]

---

60. Lambert Bu et al., *Chinese Luxury Consumers: More Global, More Demanding, Still Spending*, MCKINSEY & CO. (Aug. 2017), https://www.mckinsey.com/business-functions/marketing-and-sales/our-insights/chinese-luxury-consumers-more-global-more-demanding-still-spending.
61. Farah Master & Donny Kwok, *Global Luxury Brands Again Chase China's Young, Rich and Spendthrift*, REUTERS (Aug. 19, 2018, 4:05 PM), https://www.reuters.com/article/us-china-luxury-focus/global-luxury-brands-again-chase-chinas-young-rich-and-spendthrift-idUSKCN1L40Q6.
62. *Id.*
63. *Id.*
64. *Id.*
65. James Chambers, *Sector Focus: Fashion & Luxury Goods*, INSIDE INVESTOR REL. (June 24, 2011), https://www.irmagazine.com/case-studies/sector-focus-fashion-luxury-goods.
66. Frederik Balfour, *Prada's Hong Kong Initial Offering May Raise up to $2.6 Billion*, BLOOMBERG (June 12, 2011), https://www.bloomberg.com/news/2011-06-12/prada-initial-share-sale-may-raise-up-to-2-6-billion-clsa-says.html; Prudence Ho et al., *Prada IPO Hits Bargain Bin*, WALL ST. J. (June 18, 2011), https://www.wsj.com/articles/SB10001424052702304186404576390350685422420.
67. Carol Matlack, Rachel Chang & Allen Wan, *Europe's Biggest Luxury Brands Are Nervous About China*, BLOOMBERG BUSINESSWEEK (Oct. 17, 2018, 9:01 PM), https://www.bloomberg.com/news/articles/2018-10-18/europe-s-biggest-luxury-brands-are-nervous-about-china.
68. *Id.*

§ 9:3 Design and Production

Most apparel sold in the United States is considered "ready-to-wear" (RTW). RTW apparel is made in specific sizes and is ready to be worn by the consumer when purchased through a retail store. Luxury fashion brands may produce RTW items in limited quantities, while more affordable brands may use mass manufacturing. Brands may produce groupings of RTW merchandise in seasonal collections (higher-priced) or lines (mid- or lower-priced). The number of seasonal collections or lines produced each year varies with the type of merchandise and the target customer. Although most companies produce four to six seasonal collections or lines each year, traditional fast fashion retailers, such as Zara, can produce new lines every few weeks and fast fashion on-line retailers, like Fashion Nova, can produce new lines within one to two weeks.[69] The number of individual pieces in a particular collection or line may depend upon the type of garments, the price range of the garments, the distribution strategy for the garments, and the number of collections or lines to be produced by the company.

Large apparel companies typically have design teams that are responsible for the creation, development, and coordination of products under a particular brand, or for a category of products for each collection or line. Internal design teams may be supplemented with independent contractor designers, who may be more familiar with specific geographic markets or have other specialized skills. Design teams may travel to major domestic and foreign markets to conduct market research on customer and retailer preferences and fashion research on the latest style and color trends. They may also subscribe to an online fashion and trend forecasting agency such as Trendstop.[70] Designers look for inspiration to many sources, including historical designs, different cultures, nature, and new technologies.

For a seasonal collection, design teams may begin the design process by assembling a mood board to reflect the concept of the collection. For example, mood boards for fall collections may be inspired by tweed and equestrian elements with richer colors, while mood boards for spring collections may focus on florals. Mood boards can consist of images, object samples, fabric swatches, and color schemes. Mood boards are meant to capture a certain aesthetic or

---

69. *See* LESLIE DAVIS BURNS ET AL., THE BUSINESS OF FASHION: DESIGNING, MANUFACTURING, AND MARKETING 103 (5th ed. 2016) [hereinafter BURNS]; *A Slew of New Retailers Are Killing the Fast Fashion Status Quo*, FASHION L. (Mar. 27, 2018), http://www.thefashionlaw.com/home/is-fast-fashion-dying-or-is-it-just-hm?rq=slew.

70. *See* TRENDSTOP, https://www.trendstop.com/.

story, which then serves as the thematic inspiration for a collection and starting point for designers in the design process.[71] Designers may then use hand-drawn sketches and computer-aided design and graphic software to capture their individual designs. Some designers may also drape and pin fabrics on a dress form or live model to further refine their designs.

The design and production of apparel involves a balancing of aesthetics with practicality. The garment must be produced at an acceptable cost and be available for timely retail distribution. The processes occurring after design approval and before actual production of a garment are considered preproduction. Preproduction processes include sample development, sample testing to determine care instructions, fit development, sourcing and manufacturing decisions, and production planning.[72]

As part of the preproduction process, any technical drawings produced during the design phase must be provided to the manufacturer, along with the "spec sheet."[73] Technical drawings are based on a designer's initial design sketches, but the drawings appear flat since they do not include the body silhouette.[74] Such drawings can be made by hand, but most designers use either computer-aided design software or graphics software.[75] The spec sheet lists all fabrics, trims, findings, and important construction instructions or specifications.[76] Construction specifications relate to the desired production sequence for each garment in order to be both cost- and time-efficient with production.[77] Changes or alterations that occur throughout the preproduction process must be transferred to the spec sheet, as this document is the main form of communication between the designers and the manufacturer.[78]

Generally, sourcing refers to the process of determining how and where apparel products and their components will be procured and produced.[79] Companies consider a variety of factors in addition to

---

71. Kathryn Branch, *Board Game*, N.Y. TIMES (Sept. 14, 2012), https://www.nytimes.com/interactive/2012/09/10/t-magazine/womens-fashion/20120913-mood-boards.html.
72. Prasanta Sarkar, *Pre-Production Processes in Garment Manufacturing*, ONLINE CLOTHING STUDY (June 30, 2011), https://www.onlineclothingstudy.com/2011/06/pre-production-processes-in-garment.html.
73. *See* BURNS, *supra* note 69, at 240.
74. *Id.* at 158.
75. *Id.*
76. *Id.* at 240.
77. *Id.* at 292.
78. *Id.* at 241.
79. *Id.* at 256.

aesthetics and design when making sourcing decisions. These factors include cost, labor requirements, skill and equipment requirements, fabric quality and availability, shipping distance, turn-around time and quality control, as well as external factors such as existing trade agreements with the United States, government regulations, and political and economic conditions in the countries in which the goods may be manufactured.[80] The two main sourcing decisions involve selecting (i) the fabric, findings (snaps, hooks, zippers, thread, and other embellishments used to construct or attached to a garment), and the finishing process for the garment; and (ii) the manufacturing facilities for producing the garment.

Fabric and material costs represent a large component of production costs. Accordingly, companies work with potential vendors to source components that match design specifications at an appropriate cost. Thereafter, the production or design development team works with the vendors to ensure that the color of each component of a garment matches design specifications.[81] Special considerations apply in sourcing fabric for printed pieces. Although some textile mills produce a printed fabric, in other cases the design is printed on a fabric by a textile converter according to design specifications.[82] The fabric is purchased from a textile mill and then sent to a textile converter to print before the fabric is sent to a manufacturer for cutting. Custom print fabrics require substantial lead time for orders, which requires greater planning in the design and preproduction process.[83] If stock printed fabric is used, however, a company may find that a competing brand is using the same or similar prints in its collection. In contrast to the longer lead time required for prints, staple fabrics, such as denim or tricot, require less lead time and can be purchased closer in time to production.[84] However, some brands, including Levi's and Ermenegildo Zegna, have launched services through which customers can order bespoke jeans made of customized denim, which can entail myriad customization options and require the sourcing of specific varieties of premium denim.[85]

In addition to sourcing fabric, the design and production teams must source the trims and findings for each garment. If trims are specifically tailored for a garment, they must be sourced earlier in the

---

80. *Id.* at 257.
81. *Id.* at 236.
82. *Id.* at 238.
83. *Id.*
84. *Id.* at 89.
85. Kareem Rashed, *Do Office Casual the Right Way With Expertly Custom-Crafted Jeans*, ROBB REPORT (July 25, 2017), https://robbreport.com/style/fashion/zegna-levis-j-mueser-custom-crafted-jeans-2724648/.

pre-production process than if they are in standard styles and colors.[86] While most standard findings, such as zippers, thread and hooks, tend to be kept in stock at manufacturing and production facilities, garments in new fashion colors may require special orders to match thread color and closures to the selected fabric.[87] Additionally, the selection process for findings may include testing and other research in order to ensure that the end product meets both aesthetic and quality expectations. Finally, to the extent possible, companies may choose to source components from vendors located near manufacturing sites to reduce shipping costs and lead times.[88] Preproduction decisions involving fabric, trim, and finding sourcing are reflected in the final tech pack provided to the manufacturer, which may also include fabric swatches and samples of each trim and finding to be used to produce each garment.

The production team selects a manufacturing process and a particular facility to produce the garment. The selection of a manufacturing process for a garment depends upon a balancing of various factors, including the type of garment being produced, the time required for production, the number of units being produced, and the cost. Companies also must determine whether to manufacture garments domestically or internationally. Start-up companies are especially likely to elect domestic manufacturing given their limited capital, concerns over quality control, and desire to establish a distinctive brand identity.[89] Additionally, certain American brands are committed to domestic production because they need to meet certain production requirements in order to use a "Made in the U.S.A." label on their garments.[90] There is also a modest trend of brands "reshoring" apparel production back to the United States,[91] with Los Angeles, New York, North Carolina, and South Carolina serving as hubs for domestic manufacturing.[92] According to one study of publicized cases of reshoring from 2011 to 2015, the apparel industry ranked third among industries that had moved overseas manufacturing back to

---

86. BURNS, *supra* note 69, at 240.
87. *Id.*
88. *See id.* at 259.
89. Segran, *supra* note 17.
90. BURNS, *supra* note 69, at 258; *see also infra* chapter 15 (discussing the need to ensure that representations such as "Made in the U.S.A." are accurate).
91. Davidson, *supra* note 14; *see also* Moser & Montalbano, *supra* note 14.
92. Whitney Bauck, *Where in America U.S. Designers Get Their Clothing Made*, FASHIONISTA (July 6, 2017), https://fashionista.com/2017/07/american-usa-clothing-garments-manufactured-made-where.

the United States, accounting for 12% of all publicized cases.[93] For example, Brooks Brothers, following the opening of its manufacturing plant in Haverhill, Massachusetts in 2008,[94] has placed a greater emphasis on domestic production.[95] In 2015, Brooks Brothers manufactured 70% of its suits in Massachusetts, 100% of its ties in New York City, and approximately 10% of its shirts in North Carolina.[96] Other companies view the benefits of lower labor costs outside the United States as outweighing the possible quality control issues, and higher transportation and import costs, associated with foreign manufacturing.

Generally, there are four principal options for manufacturing apparel: (i) in-house manufacturing; (ii) cottage industry manufacturing; (iii) CMT (cut, make, trim) manufacturing; and (iv) full package manufacturing.[97] Fashion designers starting their own business often begin by manufacturing their garments in-house so that they can produce small quantities and maintain control over quality, design, and production.[98] They also may use cottage industry manufacturing, in which the sampling and production processes are outsourced to technically proficient, skilled seamstresses and patternmakers often working from home.[99] In CMT manufacturing, which is used by many larger brands, the company provides the patterns, fabric, and trim, but outsources the sampling and production to a contract manufacturer that cuts the fabrics, makes (or sews) the garment, and adds trims.[100] Companies may send fabric to a CMT manufacturer pre-cut to reduce the cost of production. Full package manufacturers produce patterns; source the fabric, trims, and finishes; and sample and produce the garment.[101] Full package manufacturing is often used

---

93. A.T. KEARNEY, U.S. RESHORING: OVER BEFORE IT BEGAN?, https://www.atkearney.com/documents/20152/1497648/2015+US+Reshoring.pdf/e1432e79-c2f7-663e-7b77-26143080bda6.

94. Davidson, *supra* note 14; *see also* Teri Agins, *With a Glance Backward, Brooks Brothers Looks to the Future Image*, N.Y. TIMES (Apr. 21, 2018), https://www.nytimes.com/2018/04/21/business/brooks-brothers-looks-to-the-future.html.

95. Jessica Dineen, *Why Brooks Brothers and Other Apparel Companies Are Moving Manufacturing Back Home*, FORBES (Feb. 13, 2015), https://www.forbes.com/sites/cit/2015/02/13/why-brooks-brothers-and-other-apparel-companies-are-moving-manufacturing-back-home/#3f3f068a15bf.

96. *Id.*

97. *See* TOBY MEADOWS, HOW TO SET UP & RUN A FASHION LABEL 113–14 (Laurence King Publishing, 2d ed. 2012) [hereinafter MEADOWS].

98. *Id.*

99. *Id.*

100. *Id.*

101. *Id.*

for larger production runs for garments that require less production oversight, are brand staples, or are less fashion-sensitive.

Some companies use diversified sourcing and production strategies. The selection of a specific factory may be dependent on the type of garment and the fabric being used, as many factories have specific skills and equipment designed for particular fabrics or types of garments. Companies may prefer to use the same factory for similar products each season, since such factories would be familiar with the company's procedures and standards. Large companies with many labels may select a factory for production of a garment if such factory is already manufacturing garments for the company and has additional capacity. Once a factory is selected, it is typically reviewed by the company's compliance team to ensure that the factory complies with the company's manufacturing standards and codes, and is then subject to periodic on-site visits and inspections. After a factory has been approved, the company and the factory negotiate the cost of manufacturing the garment. Ordering less than the factory's minimum quantity requirement may result in an increase in the cost of production, which can affect profitability.

Other companies are vertically integrated manufacturers that own their manufacturing facilities. Vertically integrated manufacturers tend to produce similar products each year, using standard equipment, which allows them to maintain continuous production schedules. Examples of vertically integrated apparel companies include the Spanish company the Inditex Group, which owns Zara,[102] and the Canadian company Gildan Activewear Inc.,[103] which purchased the U.S. company American Apparel, Inc. (formerly one of the largest apparel manufacturers in North America) in 2017 following American Apparel's bankruptcy.[104]

Prior to full production, samples of each garment are produced based on patterns either prepared in-house and provided to manufacturers, or prepared by the manufacturers for designer approval. Samples are used in determining or re-evaluating production sequence, care instructions, and whether any adjustments should be made to the design or components. Production samples are sometimes used by independent fashion designers to market their collections to buyers.[105]

---

102. INDITEX: WHO WE ARE, https://www.inditex.com/about-us/who-we-are.
103. GILDAN: OUR BUSINESS, http://www.gildancorp.com/en/Our-Business.
104. Jessica DiNapoli, *Exclusive: Gildan Wins American Apparel Auction With $88 Million Bid—Source*, REUTERS (Jan. 9, 2017), https://www.reuters.com/article/us-americanapparel-bidders-bankruptcy-idUSKBN14T26J.
105. MEADOWS, *supra* note 97, at 118.

The production stage is the construction process in which the cut fabric pieces, findings, and trims are incorporated into a finished garment.[106] As described above, a company may send the factory a "tech pack" with all of the specifications for the production of the garment, and other materials such as testing results and sample items. Tech packs are intended to provide manufacturers with all the information necessary for production so they do not have to request additional information after the manufacturing process has begun.[107] Throughout production and prior to shipment, a company may conduct a sampling of the production units to ensure that each size variation of each garment meets the required technical and measurement specifications.[108]

At the end of the production stage, factories undertake several finishing steps prior to preparing the garments for shipping. Finishing includes applying topstitching or finishing edges, pressing, trimming threads, and attaching buttons or similar closures.[109] It may also include attaching any tagging devices or labels related to care or wash instructions, if such tags or labels were not already attached during the manufacturing process, and applying any special treatments, such as treatments that age and distress denim, to garments. To finish garments, some brands, including Levi's, are abandoning manual and labor-intensive processes in favor of digital laser technology, which reduces the use of chemicals and shortens lead times.[110] For example, Levi's digital process reduces the finishing time for a pair of jeans from around twenty to thirty minutes, to ninety seconds.[111] Designer jeans are often finished in Los Angeles, with the talent in Los Angeles wash houses implementing the designer rips, ironing and/or sanding the jeans, distressing and/or softening the jeans, and otherwise applying the finishing touches.[112]

---

106. *See* BURNS, *supra* note 69, at 291.

107. A more detailed explanation of what information and specifications are included in a tech pack can be found at TECH PACK DESIGN, https://www.techpackdesign.com/what-is-tech-pack-1.

108. *See* BURNS, *supra* note 69, at 243.

109. *Id.* at 297–98.

110. MCKINSEY APPAREL, FASHION & LUXURY GRP., IS APPAREL MANUFACTURING COMING HOME? 16 (Oct. 2018), https://www.mckinsey.com/~/media/mckinsey/industries/retail/our%20insights/is%20apparel%20manufacturing%20coming%20home/is-apparel-manufacturing-coming-home_vf.ashx.

111. *Id.* at 17.

112. David Greene & Kelly Mcevers, *From Pocket Lining to Jeans, A Niche Means Survival in LA Fashion*, NPR (Dec. 1, 2015), https://www.npr.org/2015/12/01/456027751/from-pocket-lining-to-jeans-a-niche-means-survival-in-la-fashion.

Factories also prepare garments for shipping in accordance with instructions from the company by folding them (either by hand or by machine) or by placing them on hangers.[113] Once items are packed and ready for shipment, employees prepare and review packing lists in order to confirm that such lists mirror the actual shipments. The factory then sends the company an advance ship notice (ASN), which is a notification of pending deliveries that describes the contents of a shipment. An ASN alerts the company that the goods have been shipped, in addition to indicating what percentage of the order has been fulfilled. Most factories expect buyers to be responsible for shipping from their factories, especially if shipping involves import or export duties.[114] Companies may request that garments be shipped to a distribution center, shipped directly to retail customers, or shipped to their own retail stores.

§ 9:4 Supply Contracts

Generally, supply contracts and individual purchase orders are the primary documents that govern the legal relationships among the parties to the production process. Supply contracts establish the general terms of the working relationship between the vendor and the company, subject to the terms of individual purchase orders. A vendor can be a provider of fabric or findings, a manufacturer, or a cutting plant. The terms of a supply contract may cover some or all of the following matters: product description; pricing; payment terms; delivery and shipping terms; quality controls and inspection rights; workplace standards; ownership of intellectual property; and non-disclosure provisions. A supply contract may also contain provisions restricting a factory or supplier from providing certain products or services to competitors of the company. The supply contract should specify the applicable governing law and might include an arbitration provision. If the vendor will not sign a full agreement, the company should include its terms and conditions of purchase in its individual purchase orders. Appendix 9A contains a sample manufacturing supply agreement.

§ 9:5 Governmental Regulation and Industry Initiatives

§ 9:5.1 *Federal and State Regulation*

The U.S. textile and apparel manufacturing industry is subject to regulation both at the federal and state levels. One of the broadest

113. BURNS, *supra* note 69, at 298–99.
114. MEADOWS, *supra* note 97, at 125.

U.S. federal statutes affecting textile and apparel manufacturers is the Consumer Products Safety Act, enacted in 1972, which established the Consumer Product Safety Commission (CPSC) in order to regulate consumer products and develop uniform safety standards.[115]

The Consumer Product Safety Improvement Act (CPSIA), enacted in 2008 and further amended in 2011, provided the CPSC with increased authority to regulate consumer products and enforce safety laws, in addition to establishing more stringent regulations for children's products.[116] While the CPSIA is primarily aimed at manufacturers of children's products, certain provisions of the statute apply to any manufacturer, importer, or private labeler of specified consumer products, which include fabrics.[117] The CPSIA imposed new testing and documentation requirements for U.S. manufacturers and imposed new levels of acceptable substances found in manufactured consumer goods.[118] The CPSIA also increased penalties and fines in connection with violations of certain requirements and regulations, and increased the budget of the CPSC. Manufacturers and importers of specified general use products (that is, non-children's products) must issue to retailers or distributors a General Certificate of Conformity (GCC) which, among other matters, identifies the product, the applicable law, the manufacturer or importer certifying compliance, the location of manufacture, and where the product was tested for compliance.[119] However, under an enforcement policy that became effective March 25, 2016, the CPSC has stated that it will not pursue any enforcement actions based on noncompliance with the GCC requirement against "makers, importers or private labelers of certain adult apparel" that is exempted from testing under the CPSC's flammability standard, which is discussed below.[120]

The CPSC promulgates regulations, mandatory safety standards, and bans of certain substances. For example, children's products, including children's apparel, must bear tracking labels and be tested

---

115. Consumer Products Safety Act, 15 U.S.C. §§ 2051–2089 (Oct. 27, 1972).

116. Consumer Product Safety Improvement Act of 2008 (CPSIA), Pub. L. No. 110-314; 122 Stat. 3016 (Aug. 14, 2008) (*amended* 2011).

117. *Id.*; U.S. CONSUMER PROD. SAFETY COMM'N (CPSC), https://www.cpsc.gov/About-CPSC.

118. CPSIA §§ 102, 108.

119. *Id.* § 108; *see also* CPSC, GENERAL CERTIFICATE OF CONFORMITY, https://www.cpsc.gov/Business--Manufacturing/Testing-Certification/General-Certificate-of-Conformity.

120. Press Release, CPSC, CPSC Approves Adult Apparel Enforcement Discretion to Reduce Paperwork Requirement on Businesses (Mar. 4, 2016), https://www.cpsc.gov/content/cpsc-approves-adult-apparel-enforcement-discretion-to-reduce-paperwork-requirement-on.

by an approved CPSC laboratory.[121] Children's products are also subject to the CPSIA's lead content regulations (though the CPSC has exempted some products made out of specified fibers, including cotton, wool, and polyester).[122] Moreover, the CPSC, tasked with enforcing the Flammable Fabrics Act,[123] has enacted a flammability standard that applies to fabrics and textiles that are used in both children's and adult "wearing apparel," which is defined to include any "garments and costumes finished for consumer use."[124] However, the standard does not apply to hats, gloves, footwear, and interlining fabrics.[125] The flammability standard mandates specified testing methods for the flammability of textiles and classifies these textiles into three classes based on their burn rate.[126] Class 1 fabrics are of "normal flammability" and may be used in clothing.[127] Class 2 fabrics exhibit "intermediate flammability" and are also permitted to be used in clothing.[128] In contrast, highly flammable Class 3 textiles "exhibit rapid and intense burning" and "shall not be used for clothing."[129] CPSC guidance clarifies that certain textiles are likely to be classified as Class 2 or Class 3 textiles, including "sheer rayon or silk, rayon chenille, reverse fleece or sherpa of cotton or cotton blend, and certain cotton terry cloth."[130] Meanwhile, the CPSC has exempted certain textiles from the flammability testing requirements because they consistently pass as Class 1 textiles, including plain-surface fabrics weighing 2.6 ounces per square yard or more and all fabrics (regardless of their weight) made entirely out of the following fibers or a combination of them: acrylic, modacrylic, nylon, olefin, polyester, and wool.[131] The CPSC also imposes special flammability testing requirements and labeling requirements on children's sleepwear when the sleepwear contains flammable materials or materials that reduce

---

121. 15 U.S.C. § 2063(a)(5); *see also* CPSC, TRACKING LABEL REQUIREMENT FOR CHILDREN'S PRODUCTS, https://www.cpsc.gov/Business--Manufacturing/Business-Education/tracking-label.
122. 16 C.F.R. § 1500.91; *see also* CPSC, TOTAL LEAD CONTENT, https://www.cpsc.gov/Business--Manufacturing/Business-Education/Lead/Total-Lead-Content.
123. CPSC, FLAMMABLE FABRICS ACT, https://www.cpsc.gov/Regulations-Laws--Standards/Statutes/Flammable-Fabrics-Act.
124. 16 C.F.R. § 1610.1.
125. *Id.*
126. *Id.*
127. *Id.* § 1610.4.
128. *Id.*
129. *Id.*
130. CPSC, CLOTHING BUSINESS GUIDE, https://www.cpsc.gov/Business--Manufacturing/Business-Education/Business-Guidance/Clothing/.
131. *Id.*

the flame resistance of the sleepwear.[132] Furthermore, the CPSC regulates the construction of bicycle helmets[133] and bans drawstrings positioned at the hood and neck (and depending on their length and other characteristics, some drawstrings positioned at the waist and below) of certain children's outerwear.[134]

In addition to promulgating mandatory standards, the CPSC actively participates in the development of "voluntary standards," or product safety standards developed by "private sector domestic or multinational organizations or groups, or combinations thereof."[135] For example, the CPSC has helped develop the ASTM International Standard ASTM F 2923-11, Standard Specification for Consumer Product Safety for Children's Jewelry.[136] Where a voluntary standard "would eliminate or adequately reduce the risk of injury addressed and it is likely that there will be substantial compliance with" the standard, the CPSC must rely on voluntary standards rather than mandatory standards.[137]

The Consumer Product Safety Act also sets forth certain requirements with respect to defective or noncomplying products. A manufacturer, distributor or retailer of a consumer product is required to make a "Section 15(b) report," pursuant to section 15(b) of the Consumer Product Safety Act, immediately after it "obtains information which reasonably supports the conclusion that such product":[138]

- "fails to comply with an applicable consumer product safety rule or with a voluntary consumer product safety standard upon which the Commission has relied under" 15 U.S.C. § 2058;

---

132. 16 C.F.R. §§ 1615.4–1615.5, 1615.31; *see also* CPSC, CPSC REINFORCES CHILDREN'S SLEEPWEAR AND LOUNGEWEAR ENFORCEMENT POLICY TO APPAREL INDUSTRY (Dec. 23, 2011), https://www.cpsc.gov/content/cpsc-reinforces-childrens-sleepwear-and-loungewear-enforcement-policy-to-apparel-industry.
133. 16 C.F.R. § 1203.5.
134. *Id.* § 1120.3(b); *see also* CPSC, DRAWSTRINGS IN CHILDREN'S UPPER OUTERWEAR, https://www.cpsc.gov/Business--Manufacturing/Business-Education/Business-Guidance/Drawstrings-in-Childrens-Upper-Outerwear.
135. 16 C.F.R. § 1031.1.
136. CPSC, CHILDREN'S JEWELRY (Feb. 23, 2012), https://www.cpsc.gov/ja/Regulations-Laws--Standards/Voluntary-Standards/Topics/Childrens-Jewelry.
137. 16 C.F.R. § 1031.2.
138. The CPSC interprets "immediately" to mean "within 24 hours." *See* CPSC, DUTY TO REPORT TO CPSC: RIGHTS AND RESPONSIBILITIES OF BUSINESSES, https://www.cpsc.gov/Business—Manufacturing/Recall-Guidance/Duty-to-Report-to-the-CPSC-Your-Rights-and-Responsibilities.

- "fails to comply with any other rule, regulation, standard, or ban under this chapter or any other Act enforced by the Commission";
- "contains a defect which could create a substantial product hazard described in" 15 U.S.C. § 2064(a); or
- "creates an unreasonable risk of serious injury or death."[139]

It is unlawful to fail to make a report required by the Consumer Product Safety Act,[140] and a knowing failure to report may result in civil penalties.[141] But if a company "has actual knowledge" that the CPSC is already fully informed of the issue, the company need not make the report.[142]

Under section 37 of the Consumer Product Safety Act, manufacturers of consumer products must also notify the CPSC if they are involved in at least three civil actions in federal or state court during a statutorily prescribed "twenty-four-month period" in which a particular model of a product they manufacture was allegedly involved "in death or grievous bodily injury," so long as each action results in a final settlement or a judgment in favor of the plaintiff during that twenty-four-month period.[143]

The CPSC oversees consumer product recalls, which are often initiated when a company submits a report mandated by the Consumer Product Safety Act that identifies a substantial product hazard. Manufacturers can engage in voluntary recalls or remedial action, with significant oversight by the CPSC, or the CPSC may initiate litigation to enforce a mandatory recall.[144] The CPSC has a "fast track" recall program for companies that speedily and voluntarily develop a plan to remediate a product hazard.[145] Companies that meet the requirements of this program can avoid the step of the standard recall procedure in which the CPSC staff makes a "preliminary determination" that the product poses "a substantial product hazard."[146] Avoiding such a finding can have substantial benefits in mitigating the economic consequences of a recall, as well as the impact of third-party litigation.

---

139. 15 U.S.C. § 2064.
140. *Id.* § 2068(a)(4).
141. *Id.* § 2069(a)(1).
142. *Id.* § 2064.
143. *Id.* § 2084(a); 16 C.F.R. § 1116.3.
144. 16 C.F.R. §§ 1115.20, 1115.21.
145. *See* CPSC, CPSC FAST TRACK RECALL PROGRAM, https://www.cpsc.gov/Business--Manufacturing/Recall-Guidance/CPSC-Fast-Track-Recall-Program.
146. 62 Fed. Reg. 39,827 (July 24, 1997).

Federal law bars any person from selling, distributing, or importing products or substances that are not in compliance with the applicable consumer safety laws and regulations.[147] Federal law also prohibits the sale, distribution, or importation of any product or substance subject to a publicly announced voluntary recall by a manufacturer or a mandatory recall ordered by the CPSC, as well as any banned hazardous substances.[148] Those who knowingly violate these laws are subject to civil penalties.[149]

Since its inception, the CPSC has occasionally disclosed information it receives about consumer products. Traditionally, the CPSC has had to comply with the rigorous disclosure requirements of section 6 of the Consumer Product Safety Act before disclosing any information that specifically identifies or will reasonably be linked to a specific manufacturer or private labeler.[150] Under the traditional procedures, the CPSC must provide a manufacturer or private labeler with fifteen (15) days' notice before disclosing such information.[151] If the manufacturer or private labeler believes the information is inaccurate or that it contains confidential information, it may object to the release of the information.[152] If the CPSC decides to publish the information over these objections, the CPSC must first notify the manufacturer or private labeler and then must wait a prescribed number of days before releasing the information.[153] After the manufacturer or private labeler receives notice that the CPSC plans to release the disputed information, it may bring suit to enjoin the disclosure in a District Court of the United States. If, after information is already disclosed, the CPSC determines that the information is inaccurate or misleading, the CPSC must take reasonable steps to issue a retraction.[154]

In the CPSIA, Congress called for the creation of a publicly available, searchable Internet database for consumer reports that would allow for a speedier release of certain types of information about consumer products. By a 3–2 vote, the CPSC promulgated a final rule governing the database on December 9, 2010, despite heated objections from companies and organizations that were concerned that inaccurate information posted on the database could cause irreparable harm to

---

147. 15 U.S.C. § 2068(a)(1).
148. *Id.* § 2068(a)(2).
149. *Id.* § 2069(a)(1).
150. *See id.* § 2055.
151. *Id.*
152. *Id.*
153. *Id.*
154. *Id.*

manufacturers' reputations.[155] The database, saferproducts.gov, went live on March 11, 2011.

Before appearing on the database, incident reports are reviewed by the CPSC. Under the terms of the CPSIA and the CPSC's regulations, consumers, government agencies, health care professionals, child service providers, and public safety entities may submit incident reports describing harms or "risk[s] of harm" related to the use of consumer products.[156] The CPSC first reviews the report to ensure that it meets minimum content requirements[157] and then transmits the report to the manufacturer or private labeler named in the report.[158] In response, the company may submit a claim to the CPSC identifying the information in the report as confidential or materially inaccurate,[159] and the CPSC determines whether such a claim is viable.[160] Unless the CPSC determines that the report contains materially inaccurate or confidential information (which cannot be resolved through editing), the CPSC will publish the report on the database.[161]

The CPSC's decision to publish a report on saferproducts.gov has been legally challenged. In *Company Doe v. Tenenbaum*, the company Ergo Baby Carrier, Inc., suing under a pseudonym, sought to enjoin the publication of a report that named the company.[162] The company persuaded the District Court that the report was "materially inaccurate" under the CPSC's regulations, given insufficient evidence establishing a causal connection between the use of the product and the harm reported.[163] Indeed, the court found that "the odds that [the

---

155. *See* 16 C.F.R. § 1102; Letter from R. Bruce Josten, U.S. Chamber of Commerce, to the Members of the United States Senate, Opposing S. 2663, the "CPSC Reform Act" (Mar. 4, 2008) ("[T]he bill's requirement for the CPSC to create a public database without any safeguards or assurances that the information posted is true and accurate will lead to consumer confusion and give rise to lawsuits based on a rumor repeated through the echo chamber of the Internet . . . . Should [the Commission] make a mistake and post something in the database that is in error, it would cause tremendous harm to a company who may have done nothing wrong."), https://www.uschamber.com/issues/letters/2008/letter-opposing-s-2663-cpsc-reform-act.

156. 16 C.F.R. § 1102.10.

157. *See id.* §§ 1102.10, 1102.20.

158. *Id.*

159. *Id.* §§ 1102.24, 1102.26.

160. *Id.* §§ 1102.24, 1102.26.

161. *Id.* § 1102.24.

162. Company Doe v. Tenenbaum, 900 F. Supp. 2d 572 (D. Md. 2012); *see also* Ergo Baby Carrier, Inc. v. Tenenbaum, No. DKC 11-2958 (D. Md. June 12, 2014).

163. *Company Doe*, 900 F. Supp. 2d at 596–98.

product] was 'involv[ed]' in [the reported harm] are significantly lower than a coin flip."[164] The court also redacted its opinion, sealed the record, and allowed the plaintiff to litigate under a pseudonym—all in order to protect plaintiff's judicial remedy.[165] However, in an appeal brought by various consumer advocacy groups, the Fourth Circuit of Appeals held that the sealing and pseudonymity orders violated the public's right of access under the First Amendment and directed the District Court to unseal the court record and to reveal the identity of the plaintiff company.[166]

The CPSC has become more aggressive in enforcing its statutes and regulations. The CPSC has increasingly pursued enforcement actions (especially for reporting violations) in a wide variety of industries, including children's toys and home appliances,[167] and has frequently brought administrative complaints[168] and litigation via the Department of Justice.[169]

This trend of robust enforcement also includes the imposition of higher civil penalties,[170] exemplified by a record-setting $27.25 million civil penalty imposed on Polaris in April 2018 for allegedly failing to report defective models of recreational off-road vehicles.[171] Examples of civil penalties assessed against apparel retailers include a 2012 penalty of $1.5 million in a settlement with Burlington Coat Factory and a 2008 penalty of $60,000 in a settlement with

---

164. *Id.* at 595.

165. *Id.* at 608–11.

166. Company Doe v. Public Citizen, 749 F.3d 246, 275 (4th Cir. 2014).

167. Erin M. Bosman, *CPSC Could Be Coming Around on a Litigation Strategy*, LAW360 (July 8, 2015), https://www.law360.com/articles/673064/cpsc-could-be-coming-around-on-a-litigation-strategy.

168. *See, e.g.*, Sheila A. Millar & Nathan A. Cardon, *Why CPSC Sued to Recall Stroller That Met Standards*, LAW360 (Apr. 11, 2018), https://www.law360.com/articles/1032031/why-cpsc-sued-to-recall-stroller-that-met-standards.

169. *Id.*; *see also* John C. Celeste & Alicia N. Ritchie, *Looking Back at Another Very Active Year for the CPSC*, LAW360 (Jan. 4, 2016), https://www.law360.com/articles/742154/looking-back-at-another-very-active-year-for-the-cpsc.

170. *See* Jonathan Judge, *CPSC Civil Penalties: A Statistical Analysis*, LAW360 (Feb. 16, 2017), https://www.law360.com/articles/892507/cpsc-civil-penalties-a-statistical-analysis; Eric A. Rubel et. al., *How CPSC Late Reporting Penalty Trends Are Evolving*, LAW360 (Apr. 17, 2018), https://www.law360.com/articles/1033550/how-cpsc-late-reporting-penalty-trends-are-evolving.

171. CPSC, POLARIS AGREES TO PAY $27.25 MILLION CIVIL PENALTY FOR FAILURE TO REPORT DEFECTIVE RECREATIONAL OFF-ROAD VEHICLES (Apr. 2, 2018), https://www.cpsc.gov/Newsroom/News-Releases/2018/Polaris-Agrees-to-Pay-27-25-Million-Civil-Penalty-for-Failure-to-Report-Defective.

Nordstrom.[172] Both of these settlements involved the retailers' alleged failure to report to the CPSC that they had sold children's outerwear that contained drawstrings at the neck.[173] Furthermore, the CPSC has demanded operational changes from noncompliant companies as conditions of their settlements. For example, in settlements in 2013 involving two companies' alleged failure to comply with reporting requirements, the CPSC mandated that the companies create specific compliance procedures in addition to paying civil fines.[174] The CPSC had not historically imposed specific compliance policies in these types of settlements.[175] However, many settlements with the CPSC, including an October 2018 settlement with Costco and a November 2017 settlement with Home Depot, have similarly mandated the implementation of compliance programs.[176]

---

172. Press Release, CPSC, Burlington Coat Factory Agrees to $1.5 Million Civil Penalty for Failure to Report Drawstrings in Children's Outerwear and for Selling Recalled Outerwear (July 26, 2012), https://www.cpsc.gov/content/burlington-coat-factory-agrees-to-15-million-civil-penalty-for-failure-to-report-drawstrings [hereinafter Burlington Coat Factory]; Press Release, CPSC, Major Apparel Retailer to Pay a $60,000 Civil Penalty for Failure to Report Drawstrings in Children's Outerwear (Dec. 3, 2008), https://www.cpsc.gov/content/major-apparel-retailer-to-pay-a-60000-civil-penalty-for-failure-to-report-drawstrings-in [hereinafter Major Apparel Retailer].

173. Burlington Coat Factory, *supra* note 172; Major Apparel Retailer, *supra* note 172.

174. Press Release, CPSC, Williams-Sonoma Agrees to $987,500 Civil Penalty, Significant Internal Compliance Improvements for Failure to Report Defective Pottery Barn Wooden Hammock Stands (May 6, 2013), https://www.cpsc.gov/en/Newsroom/News-Releases/2013/Williams-Sonoma-Agrees-to-987500-Civil-Penalty-Significant-Internal-Compliance-Improvements-for-Failure-to-Report-Defective-Pottery-Barn-Wooden-Hammock-Stands/; Press Release, CPSC, Kolcraft Agrees to $400,000 Civil Penalty, Significant Internal Compliance Improvements for Failure to Report Defective Play Yards (Mar. 11, 2013), http://cpsc.gov/en/Newsroom/News-Releases/2013/Kolcraft-Agrees-to-400000-Civil-Penalty-for-Failure-to-Report-Defective-Play-Yards/.

175. *See* Greg Ryan, *CPSC Finds Roundabout Way to Impose Pricey Policies*, LAW360 (May 6, 2013), https://www.law360.com/internationaltrade/articles/438893/cpsc-finds-roundabout-way-to-impose-pricey-policies.

176. Press Release, CPSC, Costco Agrees to $3.85 Million Civil Penalty, Compliance Program for Failure to Report Defective Trash Cans (Oct. 5, 2018), https://www.cpsc.gov/Newsroom/News-Releases/2019/costco-agrees-to-385-million-civil-penalty-compliance-program-for-failure-to-report; Press Release, CPSC, Home Depot Agrees to Pay $5.7 Million Civil Penalty, Maintain Compliance Program for Selling and Distributing Recalled Products (Aug. 30, 2017), https://www.cpsc.gov/content/home-depot-agrees-to-pay-57-million-civil-penalty-maintain-compliance-program-for-selling.

Other regulations that are particularly applicable to apparel manufacturing and labeling include regulations against deceptive trade practices. The Federal Trade Commission Act (the "FTC Act") generally regulates deceptive practices affecting commerce and specifically prohibits the use (or exclusion) of information to mislead consumers.[177] Under authority granted by the FTC Act, the Federal Trade Commission (FTC) has established regulations affecting the apparel industry, including the Textile Fiber Products Identification Act,[178] the Wool Products Labeling Act,[179] the Leather and Imitation Leather Guide,[180] and the Fur Products Labeling Act,[181] which establish labeling requirements for apparel, including requirements with respect to fiber content, country of origin, and manufacturer identification. The Rule on Care Labeling of Textile Wearing Apparel and Certain Piece Goods[182] contains requirements for apparel care instructions (washing or dry-cleaning), which must be permanently attached to the garment. Apparel products that contain fur, leather, wool, or "faux fur" are required to comply with additional guidelines. FTC regulation of labeling and advertising is discussed in greater detail in chapter 15.

The U.S. Department of Labor's Occupational Safety and Health Administration (OSHA) sets and enforces workplace health and safety standards in a wide variety of areas, including chemical exposure, employee access to information, toxic or hazardous substances, and the use of personal protective equipment.[183] Individual states are permitted to adopt their own occupational safety and health plans in lieu of OSHA's regulations, provided that they are at least as effective as OSHA.[184] Twenty-two states and territories, including California, have adopted OSHA-approved state plans that cover both private sector and public sector workers.[185] Six states and territories, including New York, have adopted OSHA-approved plans that cover only public sector employees.[186]

---

177. Federal Trade Commission Act, 15 U.S.C. §§ 41–58.
178. Textile Fiber Products Identification Act, 15 U.S.C. § 70 (2011).
179. Wool Products Labeling Act of 1939, 15 U.S.C. § 68 (2011).
180. Leather and Imitation Leather Guide, 16 C.F.R. § 24.
181. Fur Products Labeling Act, 15 U.S.C. § 69 (2011).
182. Trade Regulation Rule On Care Labeling of Textile Wearing Apparel and Certain Piece Goods, 16 C.F.R. § 423.6 (2000).
183. U.S. DEP'T OF LABOR, ABOUT OSHA, https://www.osha.gov/about.html.
184. *Id.*
185. U.S. DEP'T OF LABOR, STATE OCCUPATIONAL SAFETY AND HEALTH PLANS, https://www.osha.gov/dcsp/osp/.
186. *Id.*

Most states have laws of general applicability that regulate such matters as workplace safety, wages and hours, and the use of certain chemicals within the state; some of these state laws are more stringent than federal law. Certain states also have laws that apply specifically to apparel manufacturing. New York and California, for example, both require garment manufacturers to register with the applicable labor department and comply with specific labor and other requirements.[187]

§ 9:5.2 *Industry Initiatives*

Many U.S. companies have undertaken voluntary initiatives to bring increased transparency to their supply and manufacturing processes and improve the working conditions at their third-party foreign suppliers. The impetus for additional disclosures came in 2016 when Human Rights Watch, along with several international labor rights groups and unions, urged seventy-two of the world's leading brands to comply with a Transparency Pledge.[188] As of October 2018, seventeen of those brands have committed to the pledge by taking steps such as publishing worker numbers, factory addresses, and types of products made at each site in an easily accessible and searchable location on their websites.[189] Some companies have gone beyond these minimum standards and offered detailed information about their production lines. For example, Patagonia, a U.S. outdoor and sportswear company, dedicates a special section of its website to describing in depth the efforts it takes to reduce social and environmental harm in its supply chain.[190] These efforts are driven as much by consumer preferences as they are by concerns over governmental or regulatory concerns, as consumers continue to seek reassurance that the products they wear and use have been manufactured and sourced ethically.[191]

---

187. N.Y. LAB. LAW art. 12-A, § 341 (2011); CAL. LAB. CODE § 2670 (1981).

188. Aruna Kashyap, *Soon There Won't Be Much to Hide*, HUMAN RIGHTS WATCH (2018), https://www.hrw.org/world-report/2018/essay/transparency-in-apparel-industry.

189. *Id.*; HUMAN RIGHTS WATCH, THE TRANSPARENCY PLEDGE (2016), https://www.hrw.org/content/301844.

190. PATAGONIA, THE FOOTPRINT CHRONICLES, https://www.patagonia.com/footprint; *Patagonia Clothing: Made Where? How? Why?*, THE CLEANEST LINE, http://www.thecleanestline.com/2012/04/patagonia-clothing-made-where-how-why.html.

191. *See, e.g.*, THIRTY ONE BITS, https://31bits.com/ (jewelry company working with Ugandan craftswomen); THE CAUSE BAR, https://www.thecausebar.com/ (social good lifestyle, products, and events).

Improvements in working conditions have largely been championed by the Fair Labor Association (FLA). The FLA is an independent nonprofit organization dedicated to ensuring fair pay and safe working conditions in garment factories. In 1997, it issued a model Workplace Code of Conduct prohibiting child labor, discrimination, and subminimum wage pay and standardizing healthy and safe working conditions.[192] Over the years, the FLA has periodically revised its code as new stakeholders have become involved and advocated for higher standards.[193] Many large companies implement codes of conduct in their factories that resemble the FLA model and some require that their suppliers follow the codes as well.[194] See chapter 16 for a more detailed discussion of these codes of conduct.

Brands have searched for ways to address their environmental impact as well. In 2012, the Sustainable Apparel Coalition (the "Coalition"), an industry-wide group of over eighty apparel and footwear brands, retailers, suppliers, nonprofits, and NGO's, launched the Higg Index.[195] The Higg Index is a self-assessment tool created to measure the environmental performance of existing and proposed apparel products, through an evaluation of material types, product types, facilities, and processes based on a range of environmental and design choices.[196] The Coalition has applied the Higg Index to footwear products and expanded its repertoire to include six assessment tools that help brands reduce their environmental impact and deliver key sustainability information to consumers.[197]

At the center of many of these initiatives is Bangladesh, one of the world's largest clothing and apparel exporters. In 2012 and 2013, the country suffered a series of catastrophic disasters, including the

---

192. *Fair Labor Association Enhances Its Workplace Code of Conduct*, FAIR LABOR ASS'N BLOG (June 21, 2011), http://www.fairlabor.org/blog/entry/fair-labor-association-enhances-its-workplace-code-conduct.

193. FAIR LABOR ASS'N, WORKPLACE CODE OF CONDUCT, http://www.fairlabor.org/our-work/labor-standards.

194. FAIR LABOR ASS'N, PARTICIPATING COMPANIES, http://www.fairlabor.org/affiliates/participating-companies.

195. Amy Westervelt, *Target, Nike, Levi's Join Forces on Sustainable Clothing*, FORBES (July 26, 2012), https://www.forbes.com/sites/amywestervelt/2012/07/26/target-nike-levis-join-forces-on-sustainable-clothing/.

196. SUSTAINABLE APPAREL COAL., THE HIGG INDEX (2018), https://apparelcoalition.org/the-higg-index/.

197. Press Release, Sustainable Apparel Coal., Designers Can Use Sustainable Apparel Coalition's Materials Tool to Assess Environmental Impact (Aug. 8, 2018), https://www.prnewswire.com/news-releases/designers-can-use-sustainable-apparel-coalitions-materials-tool-to-assess-environmental-impact-300693010.html?tc=eml_cleartime.

tragic collapse of an eight story building housing five garment factories that resulted in over 1,000 deaths.[198] As was the case in U.S. fashion manufacturing's most notorious disaster, the 1911 Triangle Shirtwaist Factory fire in New York a century earlier, the victims were overwhelmingly female. In response to the Bangladesh disasters, the International Labour Organization, a specialized agency of the United Nations consisting of government representatives, employers, and workers, issued proposals for new labor laws protecting fundamental rights of Bangladeshi workers.[199] In early 2013, more than seventy primarily European brands and retailers, as well as several North American companies, including PVH Corp., one of the world's largest apparel companies, agreed to an Accord on Fire and Building Safety (the Accord) with a group of non-governmental organizations and trade unions.[200] The Accord updated and extended the 2012 Joint Memorandum of Understanding on Fire and Building Safety, which directed a multi-stakeholder task force to create training programs, review building regulations and enforcement, and develop worker complaint mechanisms in Bangladesh garment factories.[201] Between 2013 and 2018, the task force is said to have identified and fixed nearly 100,000 building safety violations, deploying the $11 million contributed annually by signatories to hire engineers, perform inspections, and devise solutions.[202] Despite this progress, however, many global brands still have not joined the Accord and proponents argue the task force should do more to address outstanding problems with wages and working conditions.[203]

In North America, an alliance of major retailers, including Gap Inc., responded with their own program, The Bangladesh Worker Safety Initiative. This five-year plan, with over $42 million of funding,

---

198. *Bangladesh Factory Collapse Toll Passes 1,000*, BBC (May 10, 2013), https://www.bbc.com/news/world-asia-22476774. For statistical information on clothing/apparel exporters, see WORLD TRADE ORG., WORLD TRADE STATISTICAL REVIEW 2018 144 (2018), https://www.wto.org/english/res_e/statis_e/wts2018_e/wts2018_e.pdf.
199. Press Release, Int'l Labour Org., ILO Report Presents a Path to Sustainable Growth in Bangladesh (Nov. 18, 2013), https://www.ilo.org/global/about-the-ilo/newsroom/news/WCMS_229135/lang--en/index.htm.
200. *See* Press Release, PVH Corp., PVH Corp. Announces it Will Join the Accord on Fire and Building Safety in Bangladesh (May 13, 2013), https://www.businesswire.com/news/home/20130513006018/en/PVH-Corp.-Announces-Join-Accord-Fire-Building.
201. *Id.*
202. Cam Wolf, *The Deadliest Garment Industry Disaster in History, Five Years Later*, GQ (Apr. 24, 2018), https://www.gq.com/story/rana-plaza-disaster-five-years-later.
203. *Id.*

established a program of factory inspections, training and safety standards, and access to $100 million in low-cost capital, for factories in Bangladesh.[204] As of September 2018, 400 affiliated factories had materially complied with the initiative's corrective action plans, while 173 remained suspended for non-compliance.[205]

§ 9:6 Conclusion

Today's fashion and garment manufacturing industry reflects extraordinary geographic and technological diversity and continues to employ large numbers of people worldwide. Its role in the fashion industry is central. In addition to addressing the complexities of cross-border, multi-jurisdictional contracting, manufacturing continues to generate the widest and often most challenging scope of legal and social issues the fashion industry faces.

---

204. Roy Maurer, *Public, Private Sectors Take Action to Improve Worker Safety in Bangladesh*, SOC'Y FOR HUMAN RESOURCE MGMT. (Aug. 29, 2013), https://www.shrm.org/resourcesandtools/hr-topics/risk-management/pages/worker-safety-bangladesh.aspx.

205. Press Release, Alliance for Bangladesh Worker Safety, Alliance Achieves Factory Safety Milestone: 400 Factories Complete Remediation (Sept. 9, 2018), https://www.bangladeshworkersafety.org/486-alliance-achieves-factory-safety-milestone-400-factories-complete-remediation.

Appendix 9A

Sample Manufacturing Agreement

This Manufacturing Agreement ("Agreement") is entered into this [ ] day of [ ] (the "Effective Date"), by and between [insert name of Buyer] ("Buyer"), and [insert name of Manufacturer] ("Manufacturer") with respect to the manufacturing of Products (as defined below).

In consideration of the mutual covenants and agreements herein contained, the parties hereto agree as follows:

1. **Nature of Manufacturing Relationship.** Manufacturer (and its approved subcontractors and sublicensees) agree to manufacture products for Buyer, and Buyer agrees to purchase those manufactured products from Manufacturer, all in accordance with the terms and subject to the conditions of this Agreement. The products manufactured by Manufacturer for Buyer will be referred to in this Agreement as "Products." The Products will be manufactured by Manufacturer using certain of Buyer's "Marks." Buyer's "Marks" are all trademarks, service marks, trade names, distinctive words, copyrights, logos, pictures, or designs which Buyer may have or acquire, including such copyrights originating from Manufacturer as described in paragraph 6.3 of this Agreement. Buyer hereby grants Manufacturer a nonexclusive, limited, and revocable license to use certain of its Marks, as instructed by Buyer, solely to manufacture the Products exclusively for Buyer in accordance with this Agreement. Manufacturer agrees not to sell, offer to sell, transfer or distribute the Products to anyone other than Buyer.

2. **Orders, Shipping Terms, and Cancellation of Orders.**

   2.1 **Orders.** Buyer will agree to purchase Products from Manufacturer by advising Manufacturer in writing of its desire to purchase Products in a written purchase order ("Order"), and Manufacturer will fill such Orders received from Buyer. Each Order will be sent to Manufacturer by facsimile, e-mail, or other agreed means of transmission and will specify the quantity, specific type, style and size of Products, price (as provided for in this Agreement), and requested delivery date. Manufacturer shall acknowledge in writing, within fifteen (15) days, that it has received the Order and will confirm the delivery date in that writing.

2.2 **Shipping Terms.** The Products will be sold and delivered to Buyer on the shipping terms specified in the Order. The Products will be labeled and packaged as Buyer instructs Manufacturer. Manufacturer will provide all customs and export documentation for shipping and customs clearance in a manner acceptable to Buyer.

2.3 **Cancellation of Orders.** Buyer may cancel any Order by giving notice to Manufacturer not later than thirty (30) days from the Order placement date. It is anticipated that, with respect to any cancelled Order, the work-in-process for the Products can be used by Manufacturer for subsequent Orders by Buyer. If there are no subsequent Orders from Buyer in the next six months, Buyer will pay Manufacturer its cost of materials and labor for the cancelled Order up to the date of cancellation, in exchange for Manufacturer's delivery of the work-in-process to Buyer in accordance with the shipping terms set forth in the Order.

3. **Pricing and Payment Terms.**

3.1 **Product Prices.** As full compensation for the Products and the performance of Manufacturer's obligations under this Agreement, Buyer shall pay Manufacturer an agreed price in United States Dollars per Product, as set forth on Schedule 1 hereto. The agreed price shall be effective for all Orders submitted by Buyer, unless otherwise agreed in writing.

3.2 **Payment Terms.** Manufacturer shall send Buyer an invoice for Products at the agreed price, including an agreed upon advance-shipment deposit and time frame in which Buyer must complete payment. Payments shall be made via wire transfer to the account provided by Manufacturer, or via other payment methods as agreed upon in advance in writing by the parties.

4. **Manufacturer's Obligations.**

4.1 **Pre-Production Sample.** Each Product shall be of the same design as, made of the same or equivalent materials as, and meet or exceed the quality standard set by, a pre-production sample of such Product ("Pre-Production Sample") to be agreed on by the parties by a mutually agreed upon date ("Pre-Production Sample Date").

4.2 **Delivery.** Manufacturer shall have the Products ready for delivery to the freight company or have such Products ready for pick up by the freight company as instructed by Buyer in writing, by the date requested by Buyer in its Order and as confirmed by Manufacturer (the "Ready Date"). In the event Products are not shipped by the Ready Date, Buyer shall have the sole discretion to require Manufacturer to air ship the Products, at Manufacturer's expense. The latest date Products may be delivered to Buyer without Manufacturer incurring any penalties shall be the "Receive by Date," as stated on each Order. Products not delivered to Buyer by the Receive by Date may be subject to one or more of the following penalties at Buyer's sole discretion:

(a) [ ] percent discount off Order price if Product is not received on the Receive by Date;

(b) [ ] percent discount penalty off Order price accrued each week after the Receive by Date; and

(c) Freight cost for late deliveries of Product.

In addition to the penalties above, if Products are not received within two (2) weeks after the Receive by Date, Buyer shall have the sole discretion to cancel the Order without any penalty or further cost to Buyer and Buyer shall be refunded all monies paid under such Order. Should Buyer elect such penalty, Buyer may request Products be destroyed, with Manufacturer certifying such destruction or Buyer may have such Product shipped to Buyer at Manufacturer's cost and at a discount negotiated between Buyer and Manufacturer.

4.3 **Production.** Manufacturer understands that, for its relationship with Buyer to be successful, Manufacturer must be able to timely fill the Orders. Buyer and Manufacturer will mutually agree upon delivery dates and the dates will be confirmed in writing. Manufacturer's failure to meet the production requirements as described in this Paragraph 4 shall entitle Buyer to terminate this Agreement as provided in Paragraph 10.

4.4 **Materials and Equipment.** All materials, equipment, and other items used in the manufacture of the Products shall be obtained by Manufacturer at its expense.

4.5 **Extras, Rejects, and Scraps.** Manufacturer shall provide Buyer with all extra Products from each Order ("Extras"), defective Products ("Rejects"), and scrap materials containing any of the Marks ("Scraps") after production of such Products has been completed. If Buyer elects not to receive any Extras, Rejects, or Scraps, Manufacturer must destroy such Products and provide certification to Buyer of such destruction. Manufacturer shall not sell or distribute any Extras, Rejects, or Scraps without the express written consent of Buyer.

4.6 **Additional Obligations.** In addition to the obligations set forth under this Agreement, Manufacturer shall comply with the obligations set forth under any Order, as accepted by Manufacturer, which shall each be incorporated by reference to this Agreement, and [insert Buyer production or quality assurance manuals, as applicable], incorporated herein by reference.

5. **Warranties, Defective Products, Indemnifications, and Limitations on Liability.**

5.1 **Manufacturer's Warranties.** Manufacturer warrants to Buyer and Buyer's customers that the Products will be manufactured, labeled, and packaged for shipment in accordance with all applicable laws and regulations, as well as the [insert Buyer production or quality assurance manual, as applicable] and Buyer's instructions. For the period ending six (6) months after Buyer has delivered a Product to a Buyer customer, Manufacturer warrants to Buyer and Buyer's customers that all Products shall (i) meet the Pre-Production sample requirements as set forth in Paragraph 4.1, and (ii) be free from defects in workmanship or materials, including, without limitation, such defects that could create a hazard to life or property. Manufacturer will provide, and will cause its approved subcontractors and approved sublicensees to provide, a safe working environment for all its employees and other persons performing services in connection with the Products. Manufacturer will comply, and will cause its approved subcontractors and approved sublicensees to comply, with Buyer's Workplace Code of Conduct. Manufacturer shall make its facilities, and the facilities of its approved subcontractors and sublicensees available to Buyer and its representatives for inspection, during normal business hours and upon 24 hours prior notice, and will allow Buyer and its representatives to meet with and interview employees and any others performing services in connection with the Products for the purposes of determining compliance with this Agreement.

5.2 **Quantity Discrepancy.** Buyer will inspect Products for accuracy of quantity within fifteen (15) days of such Products' delivery to the specified shipping destination and will advise Manufacturer of any quantity discrepancy.

5.3 **Products Nonconforming at Delivery.** Buyer will inspect Products within thirty (30) days of such Products' delivery to the specified shipping destination and will advise Manufacturer within that time period whether the Products appear to be conforming and, accordingly, accepted by Buyer. Any Products that are damaged, do not conform to the Pre-Production sample, do not conform to Manufacturer's representations and warranties as set forth in this Agreement, or do not conform to warranties implied by law, may at Buyer's option be retained by Buyer and destroyed. Buyer will have no obligation to pay Manufacturer for such Products (or, if payment has been made, Buyer shall be entitled to a full refund), provided, however, that (i) if, in Buyer's discretion, it may remanufacture or repair any nonconforming Products so as to make them conforming, it may do so and reduce the purchase price to Manufacturer for such Products by Buyer's reasonable costs in so doing (which will be negotiated and approved in advance) or (ii) if, in Buyer's discretion, it may make some use of any nonconforming Products or the materials comprising them, it shall pay Manufacturer a reasonable value (which will be negotiated and approved in advance) for any use so made. Manufacturer shall refund to Buyer any payment made for packing, shipping, and transporting all nonconforming Products and shall itself bear that expense (which will be negotiated and approved in advance). Buyer's acceptance of the Products within thirty (30) days of such Products' delivery to the specified shipping destination, as described above, does not constitute a waiver of Buyer's rights to later claim breach of Manufacturer's warranty with respect to the Products, should such a breach occur.

5.4 **Limitation of Liability.** Buyer's sole liability to Manufacturer shall be payment of amounts due hereunder for purchases of Products or cancellation of Orders, and under no circumstances shall Buyer be liable to Manufacturer for loss of prospective profits, expenditures or investments, or any other incidental, special, consequential, indirect, or punitive damages in connection with this Agreement.

5.5 **Maintenance of Data.** Manufacturer will, at all times during this Agreement and for a period of five (5) years thereafter, keep at its usual place of business, appropriate and accurate records of the manufacture and inventory of the Products and sales to Buyer. Buyer shall have reasonable access to review, audit and make extracts from (at Buyer's expense) Manufacturer's books of account and other records relating to the manufacture and sale of the Products.

6. **Intellectual Property.**

6.1 **Buyer Intellectual Property.** As between the Parties, and except as otherwise licensed under this Agreement, Buyer shall retain all right, title and interest in and to all of the intellectual property and proprietary materials developed, and Buyer's intellectual property and proprietary materials used, in connection with this Agreement, including, but not limited to, registered trademarks, registered service marks, patents, trade dress, logos, trade names, domain names and including goodwill associated therewith, trademark and patent applications, registrations and renewals, copyrightable works, copyrights, and applications, registrations and renewals, and trade secrets (collectively, including the Buyer's Marks, "Buyer Intellectual Property"). Manufacturer recognizes and respects the value in, and goodwill associated with, Buyer Intellectual Property, and except as otherwise specifically licensed under this Agreement, Manufacturer agrees that it will obtain advance written permission from Buyer for any use of Buyer Intellectual Property.

6.2 **Restrictions on Use of Buyer's Marks.** Manufacturer shall use Buyer's Marks only on the Products for which Buyer has authorized and approved the use of such Marks, and only in the manner so approved, on products that meet and are otherwise consistent with all quality specifications agreed to hereunder, and shall assert no interest in the Marks nor attempt to register the Marks.

6.3 **Ownership of Intellectual Property.** All rights in the Products, registered or unregistered, including, but not limited to, patent rights, trademark rights, trade secret rights, design rights, and copyrights created within the scope of this agreement shall be the property of Buyer ("Work"). Manufacturer represents and warrants to Buyer that it has obtained from employees, approved subcontractors, approved sublicensees, and all others involved in production of the Products the right to transfer all Work which may be developed by Manufacturer to Buyer. Manufacturer hereby assigns all rights in such Work to Buyer and agrees to execute such further instruments of assignment in recordable form as Buyer may request. Without limiting the generality of the foregoing, the parties expressly acknowledge that Work eligible for copyright protection was specially ordered or commissioned by Buyer, and that such Work is work made for hire within the meaning of the copyright laws of the United States, and that Buyer is entitled to the copyright and all the rights therein throughout the world, including, but not limited to, the right to make such changes in and such uses of the Work and all derivative works as Buyer may determine. If, however, for any reason whatsoever the Work is not considered a work made for hire under the copyright laws, then Manufacturer hereby grants and assigns to Buyer, its successors and assigns, all of Manufacturer's right, title, and interest in and to the Work and all derivative works, including, but not limited to, the copyright therein throughout the world (any renewal, extension, or reversion of copyright now or hereafter provided), and all other rights in the Work and all derivative works of any nature whatsoever whether now known or hereafter devised, including, but not limited to, the right to make such changes in and uses of the Work as it may determine.

Manufacturer acknowledges that Manufacturer is not entitled to any further payment regardless of the uses Buyer may make of the Work in the future.

7. **Knock-Offs and Infringement by Third Parties.** Manufacturer will not, with the intent to derive benefit from the designs of Buyer, directly or indirectly: (i) produce or assist others in producing products which are similar to the Products in overall commercial impression; or (ii) "knock-off" the Products or attempt to manufacture or sell (or assist others in manufacturing or selling) any products similar to the Products or that involve Confidential Material (as defined below). Manufacturer shall promptly notify Buyer upon learning of any infringing use of the Marks, or any copying or counterfeiting of the Products, by third parties. Manufacturer shall cooperate in any infringement proceeding or other action relating to the Marks or any copying or counterfeiting of the Products, and may be joined as a party if Buyer deems it necessary or desirable for purposes of enforcing Buyer's rights against any third party.

8. **Confidentiality.** Manufacturer hereby acknowledges that Buyer has made, or may make, available to Manufacturer certain customer lists, client information, pricing and cost data, supply sources, techniques, computerized data, maps, methods, product design information, drawings, market information, marketing and advertising strategy, technical information, benchmarks, performance standards and other confidential and/or proprietary information of, or licensed to, the Buyer or its clients/customers ("Customers"), including, without limitation, trade secrets, inventions, patents, and copyrighted materials (collectively, the "Confidential Material"). Manufacturer acknowledges that this information has independent economic value, actual or potential, that is not generally known to the public or to others who could obtain economic value from their disclosure or use, and that this information is subject to a commercially reasonable effort by the Buyer to maintain its secrecy and confidentiality. Except as essential to Manufacturer's obligation under this Agreement, Manufacturer shall not make any disclosure of this Agreement, the terms of this Agreement, or any of the Confidential Material. Except as essential to Manufacturer's obligations pursuant to its relationship with the Buyer, Manufacturer shall not make any duplication or other copy of the Confidential Material. Manufacturer shall

not remove Confidential Material or proprietary property or documents from its premises without written authorization.

Immediately upon request from Buyer, Manufacturer shall return to Buyer all Confidential Material or summaries thereof. Manufacturer shall notify each person to whom any disclosure is made that such disclosure is made in confidence, that the Confidential Material shall be kept in confidence by such persons, and that such persons shall be bound by the provisions of this Agreement. Manufacturer further promises and agrees not solicit Customers or potential Customers of the Buyer, for a period of one year after the termination of this Agreement, while in possession of Buyer's Confidential Material.

9. **Insurance.** To the extent commonly available in the jurisdiction of residence of Manufacturer, Manufacturer agrees to maintain in effect insurance coverage with reputable insurance companies covering workers' compensation and employers' liability, automobile liability, commercial general liability, including product liability and excess liability, and with such limits as are sufficient in Buyer's reasonable judgment, all to protect Manufacturer and Buyer from the liabilities insured against by such coverages. Manufacturer shall furnish a certificate evidencing the obligation of its insurance carriers not to cancel or materially amend such policies without thirty (30) days' prior written notice to Buyer. In addition, Buyer shall be named as an additional insured with respect to the commercial general liability policy including products liability.

10. **Term and Termination.**

10.1 **Term.** Subject to termination for default as described below, this Agreement shall commence on the Effective Date and remain in effect for an initial term of one year, unless sooner terminated ("Term"). This Agreement may be terminated by Buyer or Manufacturer on ninety (90) days' notice.

10.2 **Renewal.** This Agreement shall auto-renew for successive one-year terms unless previously terminated.

10.3 **Default and Insolvency.** This Agreement may be terminated at any time by either party on thirty (30) days' notice if the other party fails to comply with its obligations under this Agreement (including, but not limited to, Manufacturer's failure to produce Products which, in Buyer's sole discretion, conform to the requirements of this Agreement). Buyer may immediately terminate this Agreement by written notice to Manufacturer, if Manufacturer files a petition in bankruptcy or in an equivalent proceeding is adjudicated bankrupt, or a petition in bankruptcy is filed against it or if it becomes insolvent or makes an assignment for the benefit of creditors or any arrangement pursuant to any bankruptcy law, or if it discontinues its business or if a receiver is appointed for it or its assets.

10.4 **Rights on Termination.** By the effective date of any termination of this Agreement, Manufacturer shall promptly deliver to Buyer (i) all property of Buyer of any type and in any medium, including any materials used in connection with the Marks, (ii) all Pre-Production samples in Manufacturer's possession, and (iii) all Confidential Information of Buyer in Manufacturer's possession. In the event of termination by Buyer pursuant to Paragraph 10 of this Agreement, Buyer shall purchase from Manufacturer, at Manufacturer's cost, any work-in-progress, finished Products, or materials purchased by Manufacturer specifically for manufacture of the Products, provided, however, that Buyer shall not be obligated to purchase any such items which are Rejects or are in excess of what Manufacturer could reasonably have expected were necessary to fulfill Buyer's Orders and shall not be obligated to purchase any equipment specially purchased by Manufacturer for manufacture of the Products. On termination, Manufacturer shall immediately cease to use Buyer's name and Marks, and shall refrain thereafter from representing itself as a manufacturer of the Products. If Manufacturer has work-in-process or inventory of the Products at the time this Agreement terminates, Manufacturer shall not sell or in any way distribute such work-in-process or Products to any party other than Buyer. Such work-in-process shall either be purchased by Buyer or destroyed by Manufacturer (who shall provide certification of such destruction).

10.5 **Survival of Terms and Remedies.** Termination of this Agreement shall not affect any rights or obligations of either party that have accrued at the date of termination, including in particular Manufacturer's rights to payment for Products sold to Buyer pursuant to this Agreement. Provisions of this Agreement that by their context are meant to survive termination shall remain effective in accordance with their terms following termination. Termination of this Agreement for default does not limit the availability of any other remedy then available.

11. **General.**

11.1 **Conflict of Terms.** Should there be any conflict of terms between this Agreement, any accepted Order or [insert production or quality assurance manual, as applicable], such conflict shall be resolved in the following order of precedence from highest to lowest:

(a) Order;

(b) [insert production or quality assurance manual, as applicable]; and

(c) this Agreement.

11.2 **Legal Requirements.** Manufacturer shall comply with all requirements imposed by laws or regulations with respect to the Products, including not only the laws of the United States but any applicable laws in jurisdictions into which the Products (or any parts thereof), and the packaging and labels are manufactured or sold.

11.3 **Anti-Corruption Policies.** Manufacturer agrees that it will at all times comply, and cause its approved subcontractors and sublicensees to comply, with the United States Foreign Corrupt Practices Act, as amended from time to time and all successor statutes ("FCPA"), and all other applicable anti-corruption laws. Manufacturer understands that Buyer is committed to complying with the FCPA and all applicable anti-corruption laws, and Manufacturer declares its commitment to those laws as well. Manufacturer will cooperate with Buyer to provide such information as may be requested in connection with those laws.

11.4 **Language.** Manufacturer acknowledges that, although English may not be its native language, it has read and understood this Agreement in the English language and has had full opportunity to have this Agreement translated before executing it, should Manufacturer so desire.

11.5 **Dispute Resolution.** The parties shall make a reasonable effort to resolve any claims which they may have against each other by good faith negotiation; this provision, however, shall not affect a party's right to arbitrate as set forth in this paragraph. All claims arising under or relating to this Agreement, to the relationship of the parties evidenced by this Agreement, or between the parties during the term of this Agreement whether or not related to this Agreement, including any claims created by statutory law ("Claims"), shall be decided by final and binding arbitration. The arbitration will be submitted to [insert selected arbitration panel] for arbitration held in [insert selected jurisdiction] in the English language, pursuant to [insert selected jurisdiction] law. This provision shall provide the exclusive means for dispute resolution, provided, however, that Buyer shall not be prohibited from proceeding in a court to seek injunctive relief with respect to this Agreement or security pending arbitration. The parties shall share equally in the costs of any arbitration, but the prevailing party shall be entitled to receive, as a part of the award, its reasonable arbitrator and attorney fees incurred in connection with the arbitration. Final judgment on any arbitration award may be obtained in any forum having jurisdiction.

11.6 **Subcontracting, Sublicensing, and Assignment.** Manufacturer shall not directly or indirectly subcontract, sublicense, assign or transfer its rights or delegate its duties under this Agreement without prior written approval of Buyer in its sole discretion. All subcontractors and sublicensees must agree to be bound by the terms of this Agreement.

11.7 **Indemnification and Attorney Fees.** Manufacturer will indemnify, defend and hold harmless Buyer from any claim, expenses, cost, losses, damages or liability arising out of any breach of this Agreement or violation of applicable law by Manufacturer or its subcontractors or sublicensees. In any legal action or arbitration concerning this Agreement, the prevailing party shall be entitled to recover all reasonable attorney fees and expenses of litigation or arbitration incurred at trial, on appeal, and in any bankruptcy proceeding, together with other costs allowed by law.

11.8 **Injunctive Relief.** Manufacturer hereby acknowledges (1) the unique nature of the protections and provisions set forth in this Agreement, (2) that Buyer will suffer irreparable harm if Manufacturer breaches any of said protections or provisions, and (3) that monetary damages will be inadequate to compensate Buyer for such breach. Therefore, if Manufacturer breaches any of such provisions, then Buyer shall be entitled to injunctive relief, in addition to any other remedies at law or equity, to enforce such provisions.

11.9 **Governing Law and Jurisdiction.** All questions with respect to the construction of this Agreement and the rights and liabilities of the parties hereto shall be determined in accordance with the applicable provisions of the internal laws (and not the law of conflicts of laws) of the [insert applicable jurisdiction]. Any action for injunctive relief under this Agreement, shall be maintained exclusively in the state and federal courts located in the [insert applicable jurisdiction]. Manufacturer and Buyer each agree that jurisdiction in [insert applicable jurisdiction] is reasonable, appropriate and will not impose any undue hardship upon any party. Manufacturer further agrees that any judgment by such courts shall be fully enforceable in the country where Manufacturer has its principal place of business.

11.10 **Counterparts.** This Agreement may be executed in counterparts. Delivery of a signed copy by facsimile or electronic transmission shall be deemed equivalent to delivery of a signed original.

11.11 **Independent Contractor.** Buyer and Manufacturer are independent contractors, and not employees, agents, joint venturers, or partners. Neither Party has any authority to bind or act on behalf of the other, and neither shall take any action that would lead a third party to believe otherwise.

11.12 **Severability.** If any provision of this Agreement is held to be invalid, unenforceable, or void, the provision shall be enforced to the greatest extent permitted by law, and the remainder of this Agreement shall remain in full force and effect.

11.13 **Modifications.** This Agreement may be modified only by a contract in writing executed by the Party to this Agreement against whom enforcement of such modification is sought.

11.14 **Title.** Title to the Products shall pass to Buyer when the risk of loss passes to Buyer.

11.15 **Waiver.** Any waiver of a default under this Agreement must be made in writing and shall not be a waiver of any other default concerning the same or any other provision of this Agreement. No delay or omission in the exercise of any right or remedy shall impair such right or remedy or be constructed as a waiver. A consent to or approval of any act shall not be deemed to waive or render unnecessary consent to or approval of any other or subsequent act.

11.16 **Continuing Effects.** Manufacturer's obligations regarding Confidential Material shall continue in effect beyond the termination of this Agreement, and said obligation shall be binding upon Manufacturer's approved subcontractors, approved sublicensees, affiliates, assigns, spouses, heirs, executors, administrators, or other legal representatives.

11.17 **Notices.** Notices shall be given in writing or by electronic means to the address, e-mail address, or facsimile transmission number below. A party may change its address, e-mail address, or facsimile transmission number for notices by giving the other party notice of the change in accordance with this Paragraph. A copy of any notice given by e-mail or facsimile transmission must be promptly sent by first-class mail to the recipient. Notice will be deemed given at the earliest of: (i) the date received; (ii) if sent by overnight courier, the next business day; or (iii) if sent by U.S. certified mail, return receipt requested, the fourth following business day.

[BUYER NAME

Attn: ____________________

Address: ____________________

____

e-mail: ____________________]

[MANUFACTURER NAME

Attn: ____________________

Address: ____________________

____

e-mail: ____________________]

11.18. **Complete Agreement.** This Agreement, together with the Orders and [insert production or quality assurance manual, as applicable], contain the entire agreement between the Parties with respect to the subject matter of the Agreement, are intended as a final expression of the Parties' agreement with respect to such terms as are included herein and therein and are intended as a complete and exclusive statement of the terms of such agreement, and supersede all prior negotiations, stipulations, understanding, agreements, representations and warranties, if any, with respect to such subject matter, which precede or accompany the execution of this Agreement.

IN WITNESS WHEREOF, the Parties understand this Agreement and have caused this Agreement to be executed by their duly authorized representatives as of the date first set forth above.

BUYER:	**MANUFACTURER:**
By: ____________	By: ____________
Print Name: ____________	Print Name: ____________
Title: ____________	Title: ____________

Chapter 10

Licensing Arrangements

§ 10:1 Introduction
§ 10:2 License Agreements for the Manufacture and Sale of Products
§ 10:2.1 Using a Term Sheet
§ 10:2.2 Drafting the License Agreement
[A] Nature and Scope of the License
[B] Rights of First Negotiation, First Offer or First Refusal
[C] Term
[D] Production Process and Quality Control
[E] Royalties and Sales Volume
[F] Reporting and Accounting
[G] Advertising and Marketing
[H] Intellectual Property Rights
[I] Termination and Its Consequences
[J] Buy-Out Rights
[K] Representations and Warranties
[L] Indemnification and Insurance
[M] Other Provisions
§ 10:3 License Agreements for Retail Stores
§ 10:3.1 Nature and Scope of the License
§ 10:3.2 Development of the Stores
§ 10:3.3 Other Terms
Appendix 10A Sample License Agreement

§ 10:1 Introduction

Licensing arrangements are an important source of revenue for the fashion industry, generating over $19 billion of annual retail sales in North America alone.[1] Licensing is often associated with luxury

1. Kirsty Birkett-Stubbs, *An In-Depth Look at Licensing and Retail in North America*, LICENSE GLOBAL (Apr. 26, 2018), https://www.licenseglobal.com/magazine-article/depth-look-licensing-and-retail-north-america.

fashion brands, which have been licensing their trademarks since the 1950s. In recent years, however, licensing arrangements have become increasingly common in the mid-tier and mass merchandising segments of the fashion industry.[2]

Many companies with recognized fashion brands strategically utilize licensing arrangements to extend the range of their branded products into new categories or new countries. Some brands, such as Chanel, use licensing arrangements very selectively for certain products such as eyewear.[3] Other brands, like the Calvin Klein brand owned by PVH Corp., use a licensing model for both their products and their retail stores.[4] Licensing arrangements can be advantageous to a fashion brand by creating revenue streams without new investment in employees or facilities. They are intended to be invisible to the consumer, who may not be aware that a particular product is designed or made by a third party other than the company whose brand it bears. For that reason, however, licenses can be disadvantageous to a fashion brand if they dilute or damage the value of the brand. Customers may become confused about the identity of the brand if products under a single brand are sold at many different price and quality points. To minimize such customer confusion, fashion brands often use different but related names for products sold at different price points, whether or not the products are licensed (for example, Ralph Lauren offers women's apparel under the names Polo Ralph Lauren, Ralph Lauren Collection, Double RL, Lauren, and Golf).[5]

Licensing arrangements can be beneficial to the licensee, particularly if the licensed brand is well established. It generally takes many years, and a significant capital investment, to develop a trademark into a nationally or internationally recognized brand. The licensee obtains the marketing power of the brand, without having made the initial capital investment. On the other hand, the licensee takes the financial risk with respect to future sales of the licensed product, particularly if the license agreement provides for substantial advances or guaranteed payments.

---

2. *Licensing Industry Sales Jump 5% Marking First Gain in Five Years*, LIMA (June 19, 2012), https://www.licensing.org/news/licensing-industry-sales-jump-5-marking-first-gain-in-five-years/.
3. *See Luxottica and Chanel Announce New License Agreement*, LUXOTTICA (July 24, 2014), http://www.luxottica.com/en/luxottica-and-chanel-announce-new-license-agreement-0.
4. *See* Imran Amed, *Tom Murry Breaks Down Calvin Klein's Business Model*, BUS. OF FASHION (Nov. 30, 2011), https://www.businessoffashion.com/articles/ceo-talk/ceo-talk-tom-murry-president-and-chief-executive-officer-calvin-klein.
5. *See* RALPH LAUREN, https://www.ralphlauren.com/?ab=int_fd_background.

A company considering a new licensing arrangement should carefully assess the timing of entering into the arrangement and how such arrangement can advance the company's strategic objectives. Moreover, a company should research the reputation, creditworthiness, and experience of potential licensees in the specific categories and territories covered by a proposed license. Since investigating potential licensees and reviewing licensing offers can be a time-consuming process, some companies engage an experienced licensing agent to find appropriate licensees and then negotiate the business terms of the licensing arrangements on their behalf. These agents are typically compensated, if they are successful in consummating a licensing transaction, by a percentage of the royalties received by the licensor under the license.

§ 10:2 License Agreements for the Manufacture and Sale of Products

§ 10:2.1 *Using a Term Sheet*

Licensing arrangements for the manufacture and sale of products are typically formalized in a license agreement between the party owning the brand and granting the license (the "licensor") and the party paying to receive the license (the "licensee"). The scope of the license is defined and limited, and the respective rights and obligations of the licensor and licensee are set forth, in the detailed provisions of the license agreement.

In some circumstances, however, the parties negotiate a term sheet prior to negotiating a full license agreement. By focusing first on the material business terms of the proposed license, the parties can more quickly determine if they are in agreement on the fundamental business arrangement. If, during the negotiation of the term sheet, it appears that there are serious areas of disagreement, the parties can conclude their discussions without undue time and expense. If, on the other hand, the parties can agree on a term sheet, the term sheet will set the parameters for the full license agreement.

The term sheet should specifically address the issue of whether, and to what extent, the term sheet creates any binding obligations on the parties. In the absence of specific language, the term sheet might be construed under applicable state common law (which varies considerably from state to state) to create a binding obligation on the parties to either negotiate in good faith or to enter into the transaction covered by the term sheet. Accordingly, the term sheet should expressly provide that it is nonbinding on the parties, except for certain enumerated provisions that the parties intend to be binding, discussed further below. If a full license agreement is subsequently executed by the parties, the terms of the license agreement should supersede all of the terms contained in the term sheet.

A term sheet can facilitate the process of negotiating a full license agreement, but may not be sufficiently detailed to create the standards for performance under the license. A term sheet should address the essential business issues in the proposed licensing arrangement, particularly the following matters: the scope of the license; the royalty rates and, if applicable, the amount of advances; any guaranteed royalties and/or guaranteed minimum sales; and the term and renewal rights for the license. The term sheet might also address other business issues that are likely to be heavily negotiated, such as definitions of key terms (such as "Net Sales" and "Cost"), and rights of the licensee to add new products or territories. The parties should not try to address in the term sheet all of the business and legal issues that would be covered in a full license agreement, as that would undermine the benefits of negotiating a term sheet.

As noted above, the parties may seek to have certain provisions of the license agreement create a binding obligation on the parties. In particular, a licensee may seek to provide for a period of exclusivity (such as sixty days), during which the parties cannot negotiate with third parties with respect to the subject matter of the license agreement. An exclusivity provision prevents the licensor from negotiating with multiple potential licensees at the same time. For that reason, many licensors reject exclusivity provisions. Term sheets typically include confidentiality provisions (covering the confidential and proprietary information of both parties and the fact that the parties are discussing a potential licensing transaction), which should be binding on the parties for a specified time period.

An effective term sheet generally covers the key business issues between the parties, states that it is nonbinding (aside from certain enumerated provisions), and is usually only two to three pages in length.

§ 10:2.2 *Drafting the License Agreement*

This section describes the principal provisions contained in a full license agreement for the manufacture and sale of apparel or accessories. Appendix 10A contains a sample license agreement.

[A] Nature and Scope of the License

The most critical aspects of a license agreement are the provisions that address the nature and scope of the license being granted by the licensor to the licensee. The principal elements that define the nature and scope of a license include: the intellectual property being licensed; the purpose of the license; the extent of the licensee's rights and the rights retained by the licensor; the categories and nature of the products covered by the license; the standards and procedures to ensure the quality of the licensed products; the territories where the licensed products may be sold; and the distribution channels for the licensed products.

These scope provisions should be drafted to be as specific as possible. For example, the license agreement should include a detailed list (and, if applicable, graphic representations) of the licensor's intellectual property to be licensed under the agreement. This may include one or more trademarks and logos, which can be preexisting or newly created solely for the purpose of the license (such as a new trademark created to brand a high-end designer's more moderately priced diffusion line). In order to avoid any ambiguities with respect to the licensor's continuing rights in the licensed intellectual property, the license agreement should specifically state that the licensor remains the owner of the licensed intellectual property, and reserves all rights to use and grant to others the right to use such intellectual property, except to the extent such rights are specifically granted to the licensee in the license agreement.

In a license agreement for products that will be co-branded, using intellectual property of both the licensor and the licensee, the license agreement should also specifically identify the intellectual property of the licensee that will be used on the licensed products and the parties' respective rights to use each other's marks (or new blended marks) in connection with their respective marketing efforts. The agreement may include precise standards for the relative sizing and placement of each of the respective brand identifiers. For example, in an athletic footwear license, the license agreement may provide that one party's logo may appear only on the sole of the shoe and the other party's logo may appear only on the back of the shoe, and that each logo must be of the same size.

The license agreement should state the specific purpose of the license and describe in detail the range of products covered by the license. For example, it may state that the license is granted for the design, development, manufacture (directly or through third-party factories), marketing, and sale of branded women's footwear, other than women's athletic footwear. The product categories should be defined as specifically as possible, so that the parties clearly understand which product lines are included in the license. This may be a point of contention between the parties, as licensees often desire to use the licensed intellectual property on a broad range of products, whereas licensors may prefer to reserve certain related product lines for inclusion in license agreements with future licensees.

Although some license agreements are worldwide, most contain territorial limitations that identify the specific countries or regions in which the licensed products may be sold. The licensee should be prohibited from exporting the licensed products outside of the territories specified in the agreement and may also be prohibited from selling the licensed products to third parties that the licensee knows will sell the products outside of the specified territory.

A license agreement should specify the intended channels of distribution for the licensed products. The license agreement may identify a specific list of retailers where the products may be sold, or may provide specific categories of approved retailers (such as, better department stores and specialty stores), or may require that each retailer must be preapproved by the licensor prior to selling to such retailer. If specific categories of retailers are referred to, it is useful to provide illustrative examples within each category to minimize potential future disputes as to the meaning of the category. Licensors may prefer to limit distribution channels to ensure that the licensed products are sold only by retailers that have a reputation that is consistent with the quality and reputation of the licensed brand or in channels where the price points will achieve the desired revenue streams.[6] Licensees typically require some ability to manage excess or defective inventory through sales to off-price retailers, while licensors may be concerned that such sales may dilute the value of their brand and reduce royalties. Accordingly, sales of second quality products or excess inventory to off-price retailers are typically specifically addressed in the agreement. Such sales may require preapproval by the licensor, may be permitted but capped at a specified percentage of total sales in each year of the license, may be subject to different royalty terms, or may simply be prohibited.

Although some license agreements are exclusive, others may provide for nonexclusive licenses. In situations where a product line requires more than one manufacturer, a nonexclusive license may be necessary.[7] In addition, the licensor may desire to retain the right to sell all or certain licensed products in specified direct-to-consumer distribution channels, such as the licensor's own e-commerce website or retail stores. If the licensor is retaining certain rights, those rights should be carefully defined.

A good example of the importance of clearly defining the scope of the licensor's retained rights arose in a well-publicized

---

6. For an example of a dispute between a licensor and licensee over distribution channels, see Compl., Diane Von Furstenberg Studio, LP v. ID Beauty Int'l Distribution LTD, No. 8097, 2012 WL 6629994 (Del. Ch. Dec. 12, 2012).

7. For an example of the potential pitfalls to a licensor of granting an exclusive license to manufacture, see Macy's, Inc. v. J.C. Penney Corp., 45 Misc. 3d 274 (N.Y. Sup. Ct. 2014), *aff'd sub nom.*, Macy's Inc. v. Martha Stewart Living Omnimedia, Inc., 127 A.D.3d 48 (N.Y. App. Div. 2015).

dispute among J.C. Penney Company, Inc., Martha Stewart Living Omnimedia, Inc. (MSLO) and Macy's, Inc. with regard to MSLO's 2006 license and promotion agreement with Macy's. Under the agreement, MSLO licensed to Macy's specified MSLO trademarks to be used in connection with certain "exclusive" product categories, including housewares. MSLO retained the right, however, to sell such trademarked "exclusive" product categories through "any retail store branded with Martha Stewart Marks or Stewart Property that is owned or operated by MSLO or an Affiliate of MSLO or that otherwise prominently features Martha Stewart Marks or Stewart Property."[8] In 2012, Macy's filed suit in New York State court seeking to enjoin J.C. Penney from selling Martha Stewart branded products in the "exclusive" categories pursuant to a 2011 licensing agreement that was entered into between MSLO and J.C. Penney.[9] One of the disputed issues in the case was whether sales of Martha Stewart branded products in the "exclusive" categories in J.C. Penney stores fell within the retail store exception in the Macy's license agreement because they were sold in a distinctive Martha Stewart "store" within J.C. Penney. Macy's contended that they did not fall within the exception because the products were manufactured, owned, and priced by J.C. Penney, and sold in J.C. Penney stores by J.C. Penney sales associates.[10] In July 2012, the New York State Supreme Court granted a preliminary injunction preventing MSLO from selling Martha Stewart branded products in the "exclusive" categories in J.C. Penney stores.[11] In April 2013, the court declined to extend the preliminary injunction to products in the "exclusive" categories that were designed by Martha Stewart, but did not carry her brand identification.[12]

If the licensor retains the right to sell the licensed products in direct-to-consumer channels, the business arrangement typically will require the licensor to purchase the licensed products from the licensee for resale. Accordingly, the parties will need to negotiate the terms on which the licensor will purchase the licensed products from the licensee. The agreement may specify a unit price for each product, typically expressed either as a percentage discount from the regular wholesale price of the licensed product, or as the licensee's

---

8. *Macy's*, 45 Misc. 3d at 300.
9. *See* Summons, Macy's, Inc. v. J.C. Penney Corp., Inc., No. 0652861-2012, 2012 WL 3518040 (N.Y. Sup. Ct. Aug. 16, 2012).
10. *See id.*
11. *See Macy's*, 45 Misc. 3d at 288–94; *see also* Aaron Katersky & Susanna Kim, *Judge Denies Extending Preliminary Injunction Against JCP, Martha Stewart*, ABC NEWS (Apr. 12, 2013) [hereinafter Katersky & Kim], https://abcnews.go.com/Business/partial-ruling-favors-jc-penney-macys-suit-martha/story?id=18942572#.UYcK7Yfn_rc.
12. *See* Katersky & Kim, *supra* note 11.

cost of production plus an additional percentage. If the licensee's cost of production is used as the base, the parties should include a specific definition of "cost of production." Some license agreements also include a most favored nations clause, requiring that the price paid by the licensor to the licensee for the licensed products be the most favorable price offered by the licensee to any other third party. The license agreement may also address volume requirements. The licensor may be required to purchase a minimum number of licensed products quarterly or annually, the licensee may be required to satisfy all of the licensor's product orders, or the licensor may be granted priority over third-party orders. The license agreement should specifically indicate whether purchases by the licensor generate royalties (typically they do not) and whether they are applied to minimum sales volume guarantees of the licensee.

The license agreement should specifically indicate whether or not the licensee has any sublicensing rights. Sublicensing allows the licensee to re-grant its licensed rights to third parties in connection with the performance of its obligations under the license agreement. For example, a licensee may use a specialized sublicensee for the manufacture of certain of the licensed products. Some license agreements contain an express prohibition on sublicensing, with an exception only for sublicensees that are preapproved by the licensor. Other license agreements will condition the right to sublicense upon the submission to the licensor of specified financial and other information about the sublicensee, or, in the case of full sublicenses (where the licensee sublicenses the manufacture, marketing, and sale of a particular category of products), a business plan setting forth, among other matters, projected sales and royalties.

[B] Rights of First Negotiation, First Offer or First Refusal

A licensee that is making a substantial investment of time and resources in the launch or development of a brand may seek certain advantageous rights in connection with future product categories or territories for the brand. These rights may take the form of rights of first negotiation, rights of first offer, or rights of first refusal:

(1) ***Rights of first negotiation*** permit the licensee to propose to the licensor the addition of specified products or territories to the license. These rights generally provide that, during a specified period of time or throughout the term of the agreement, a licensee may submit to the licensor a business plan with respect to one or more additional product categories or territories, including a marketing plan and projected sales and royalties. Under these arrangements, the licensor

typically has a specified period of time to review the plan and respond to the licensee, either by acceptance or rejection of the business plan or by an offer to enter into further negotiations. If, after a specified negotiation period, the parties are unable to reach an agreement with respect to the proposed categories or territories, the licensor may decline to add them to the license. Thereafter, the licensee may be required to wait a specified period of time before making another proposal to the licensor, or may be permanently foreclosed from making another proposal for the same product category or territory.

(2) ***Rights of first offer*** require the licensor to offer new product categories or territories to the licensee, before offering them to third parties. If the licensee desires to pursue such an opportunity, it would be required to submit a business plan to the licensor, and the parties would enter into negotiations with respect to licensing the additional products or territories. If the parties are unable to reach agreement within a specified time period, the licensor is generally free to enter into a license agreement covering those products or territories with a third party, but usually on terms no more favorable to the third party than the terms proposed by the licensee.

(3) ***Rights of first refusal*** generally require the licensor to offer to the licensee the same license terms proposed by a third party for a new product category or territory, and the licensee has the right to accept or reject such terms. If the licensee rejects such terms, the licensor is free (usually for a specified period of time) to enter into a license agreement for the new categories or territories with the third party, but usually on terms no more favorable to the third party than those offered to the licensee.

Of these three types of rights, rights of first negotiation and first offer are the least burdensome, and rights of first refusal can be the most burdensome, to the licensor. Rights of first refusal may impair the ability of the licensor to negotiate with a third party, since a third party may be unwilling to undertake the time, effort, and expense to negotiate a licensing opportunity if the original licensee has the right to take the opportunity simply by matching the third party's terms.

[C] Term

Most license agreements contain duration provisions. These provisions may specify when the license agreement commences, when the initial term expires (unless earlier terminated by one or both of the parties), and how the term may be renewed. The initial term of an apparel or accessory license agreement is generally at least three full calendar years, in light of the long lead time required to manufacture and market the licensed products. License agreements typically also provide for one or more possible renewal periods after the expiration of the initial term. In "automatic renewals," the licensee has the right to renew the license for one or more specified periods, generally if certain factors have been met; such factors may include if the licensee has provided prior written notice to the licensor of its intent to renew, achieved the requisite minimums, and is otherwise in material compliance with all of the provisions of the license agreement.[13] In "non-automatic renewals," the parties agree that, prior to the expiration of the initial term, they will meet in good faith to negotiate the terms of a possible renewal. In a new licensing relationship, the licensor may desire to limit the initial term of the license, and provide that renewals are not automatic, in order to minimize the risk of committing to a long-term agreement with a licensee that may be meeting its minimum requirements but not actively growing the customer base and revenue stream for the licensed products. On the other hand, a licensee that is making a substantial investment in the launch or extension of a brand may prefer a longer initial term, and automatic renewal rights, in order to fully reap the economic benefits of its investment.

[D] Production Process and Quality Control

License agreements should specifically address the process, and the roles and responsibilities for developing the licensed products, from initial concept through retail sales. In some arrangements, the licensor will be responsible for the creative and design elements of the licensed products, while in other cases these functions will be provided jointly or by the licensee. In the latter case, the license agreement may require the licensee to appoint dedicated design teams for the licensed products. The most important design positions are usually filled only after consultation with, or upon the approval of, the licensor. If the licensor is providing the design services for the licensed products, the licensor may request payment of a separate initial or annual "creative" or "design" fee.

Product development generally is a collaborative process, depending upon the relative expertise of the licensor and licensee. Typically, the licensor and the licensee agree to meet at specified times each season in accordance with a design calendar to review concepts, designs, and

---

13. *See, e.g.*, Nicholas Labs. Ltd. v. Almay, Inc., 900 F.2d 19 (2d Cir. 1990), in which the court found that a trademark licensing agreement that was to continue for successive five-year periods was not terminable at will by the licensor at the conclusion of each five-year period.

marketing strategies for the licensed products. The design calendar can be attached as an exhibit to the license agreement or can be agreed upon at a later point in time.

Prior to commencement of production, the licensee may be required to supply the licensor with preproduction samples of the licensed products and packaging materials. Once the samples are submitted, the licensor will have a specified period of time in which to review the samples and to either approve them, propose modifications, or reject them (generally accompanied by a detailed explanation of the reason for rejection). To avoid delays in the production process, some license agreements state that the licensor's failure to respond by the expiration of the specified time period will be deemed tacit approval of the samples. A license agreement may provide for a more formal approval process, such as a seasonal "line review" attended by a representative of the licensor to review and approve all preproduction samples of licensed products to be manufactured, distributed, and sold during the relevant season. License agreements usually include a provision to the effect that once samples are approved by the licensor, the licensee will be prohibited from departing in any material way from the samples without the licensor's approval.

License agreements generally require the licensee to adhere to a specified standard of quality in manufacturing the licensed products. As discussed in greater detail in chapter 2, section 2:14, the failure of a trademark owner to exercise sufficient quality control over a licensee's products can impair the trademark.[14] Some licensors require the quality of the licensed products to be consistent with the reputation, image, and prestige of the other products sold under the same brand. Other licensors require the quality of the licensed products to conform to the quality of comparable products offered for sale at similar price points and in the same distribution channels.

Generally, it is the responsibility of the licensee to engage, supervise, and coordinate with the multiple third-party suppliers and contractors involved in manufacturing the licensed products. The licensor may have either approval or consultation rights with respect to the selection of such third parties. Licensors also typically require that the licensee take appropriate steps to monitor the compliance of its owned facilities, third-party suppliers, and contractors with applicable laws and industry standards for manufacturing. For example, a licensor might insist on provisions that specifically: require the use of best industry practices; prohibit the use of child labor (the employment of children who are under the applicable local

---

14. *See* ROGER M. MILGRAM & ERIC E. BENSEN, 1 MILGRIM ON LICENSING § 4.53 (33d ed. 2011).

legal minimum age for employment), prison labor, or slave labor; or require compliance with all applicable local laws (including wage-and-hour, worker safety, and environmental laws). Most large licensees have company-wide polices in effect that address these workplace conduct matters (such as health, safety, child or forced labor, and banned substances), and such policies are often referenced in (and sometimes appended to) the license agreement. The licensor may have the right, on prior notice to the licensee, to periodically visit and inspect the relevant manufacturing facilities during business hours to confirm compliance with these policies, as well as to monitor the quality of the licensed products being manufactured.

If a licensor is particularly concerned about maintaining high-quality craftsmanship (for example, for a luxury brand) or performance features (for example, for an athletic shoe) of a licensed product, it may seek product recall rights. Product recall provisions allow the licensor to request, by written notice, that the licensee withdraw, and cause its distributors and retailers to withdraw, licensed products from sale within a specified time period if such products fail to meet the requisite product specifications. Licensees are generally reluctant to agree to product recall provisions (particularly those that are in the sole discretion of the licensor) because product recalls can be time-consuming and costly.

[E] Royalties and Sales Volume

In a typical license agreement, the licensee will agree to pay specified royalties to the licensor as consideration for the grant of the license. Royalties are usually calculated as a percentage of the licensee's "net sales" of the licensed products during the term of the agreement. The definition of the term "net sales" is fundamental to the calculation of the amounts that actually will be received by the licensor. Typically, "net sales" is defined as the gross revenues from the licensee's sale of the licensed products, minus specified deductions. The categories of deductions are heavily negotiated, but might include taxes (other than income taxes); returns as credited to third-party customers; uncollected accounts; and retailer discounts, allowances, and chargebacks. Licensors seek to limit the categories and amounts of allowable deductions in various ways, including by limiting deductions to those allowed under U.S. Generally Accepted Accounting Principles, or by limiting the amount of total deductions each year to a specified percentage of that year's total gross sales of the licensed products. Licensees typically resist these efforts.

Royalty rates can be fixed throughout the term of the agreement, or can vary depending on the volume of sales or the particular distribution channels. Royalties are usually paid to the licensor in quarterly or annual installments, and interest may accrue in the event of late payments by the licensee. Prior to entering into a license agreement, the parties generally agree on a business plan that includes a set of projected revenues for each category of licensed products each year during the initial term of the agreement. The parties may use those projections as a basis to establish guaranteed minimum royalty and/or guaranteed minimum sales volume requirements for particular product categories, territories, or the license agreement as a whole. Guaranteed minimum royalties are the minimum royalty amounts that the licensee must pay to the licensor, regardless of the amount of licensed products sold. Guaranteed minimum sales volumes are more onerous requirements for the licensee because the licensee is committing to achieve actual minimum quarterly or annual "net sales" of the licensed products, although a licensee may be able to negotiate an exception for factors beyond its control. In either case, if the licensee fails to achieve the specified minimums, the licensor may have the right to terminate the agreement and/or the licensee may lose certain rights, such as the right to have the agreement renewed after the expiration of the current term. Accordingly, the minimums for a given year are usually set at a level below, sometimes significantly below, the projected revenues for such year.

If the licensor has a particularly desirable brand, it may negotiate to receive an initial advance payment upon execution of the license agreement, or upon the first shipment of the licensed products. This advance payment may be fully or partially applied against future royalty payments. If a license agreement contemplates that the licensed products will be sold in territories outside the United States, the agreement should include a provision specifying how transactions in other currencies will be handled for purposes of royalty payments. Typically, sales in other currencies are converted into the currency of the licensor by reference to either the licensee's currency conversion policies or to an independent currency conversion reference source (such as *The Wall Street Journal*).

[F] Reporting and Accounting

For those license agreements that require the licensee to pay royalties to the licensor based on the licensee's net sales, the license agreement should also contain reporting and accounting provisions so that the licensor can monitor sales and royalty levels. The licensee should be required to submit periodic reports to the licensor, detailing such items as gross revenues for all licensed products sold by category and country, calculations of "net sales," and itemization of all deductions. Sometimes, the licensee may be required to provide monthly reports on sales volumes, so that the licensor can better manage the license.

The licensor should have the right (typically at its own expense) to periodically audit the licensee's books and records relating to the licensed products during the term of the agreement in order to verify the royalty reports. To support the licensor's tax and reporting requirements, the licensee should be required to keep such books and records for a specified period of time after the license agreement is terminated. The license agreement also should provide that if, upon audit, the licensor discovers any payment deficiencies (sometimes only in excess of agreed percentages), the licensor should be reimbursed for its audit expenses and, in egregious cases, should have the right to terminate the agreement.

[G] Advertising and Marketing

License agreements typically address advertising and marketing issues because they impact future revenues. The agreement may provide that the parties will jointly develop annual marketing plans, including product launch dates, media placements, and advertising expenditures. Typically, the licensor has approval rights over the contents and appearance of marketing material and of related uses of the licensed trademarks.

License agreements may require the licensee to spend an agreed amount each year on the advertising and marketing of the licensed products. This requirement can be formulated either as a specified dollar amount (that is, $5 million in the first year and $2 million in each subsequent year) or as a specified percentage (such as one or two percent) of projected "net sales" of the licensed products in each year. The licensee may also be required to construct, or designate, a specific showroom to display the licensed products to buyers for retail stores.

In some cases, the licensor may be obligated to contribute to the cost of marketing and advertising the licensed products, or may be required to support the marketing efforts in other ways. For example, if the licensed products are being marketed under a brand associated with a particular designer or celebrity employed by the licensor, the licensor may be asked to make such individual available for various press and promotional activities. In such event, the parties may negotiate the specific number and type of activities for which the individual must be present and which party will be responsible for the individual's travel expenses.

[H] Intellectual Property Rights

License agreements should contain provisions protecting the licensor's rights to the licensed intellectual property. For example, the licensee may be prohibited from modifying or altering the licensed trademarks, using them as a corporate or trade name, combining them with any of the licensee's other trademarks, or using any new trademarks in connection with the licensed products. The license agreement might specify that any new intellectual property rights created for the licensed products during the term of the agreement become the property of the licensor. The licensee may be required to acknowledge or ratify the licensor's rights to existing intellectual property (to minimize the potential for future disputes), and might be prohibited from using or registering any other trademarks that are confusingly similar to the licensed trademarks. Typically, it will be the licensor's responsibility under the license agreement to maintain registrations, and file and prosecute any necessary applications for the licensed intellectual property in the licensed territories.

Further, it is important to remember that courts will not allow a licensee to sue to enforce an intellectual property right unless the license specifically conveys that right. For example, in 2019, the Kardashian sisters were sued as celebrity endorsers of a cosmetic line called "Kroma Beauty." The court granted summary judgment dismissing the claims because the plaintiff, as the licensee to use the KROMA trademark, lacked standing to assert trademark infringement claims. Specifically, the license provided that the licensor would "protect [the trademark] properly from any attempts of illegal use, to the best of his knowledge."[15]

In most instances, the licensor should retain the sole right to enforce its licensed intellectual property rights, but should not be obligated to do so. This is because it may not be cost-effective to use litigation to enforce the rights in certain instances, or because certain types of enforcement efforts might be disadvantageous to the overall image or reputation of the brand. Sometimes, however, the licensor specifically agrees to give a licensee exclusive rights to enforce the licensed trademarks. Moreover, a licensor may task the licensee with the specific responsibility of enforcing the licensed trademark.[16]

[I] Termination and Its Consequences

License agreements should include a list of actions or omissions that constitute a "material breach" of the license agreement. Certain material breaches of the agreement may be grounds for immediate

---

15. *See*, Kroma Makeup EU LLC v. Boldface Licensing + Branding Inc., __ F3d. __, No. 17-14211 (11th Cir. Apr. 1, 2019).

16. *See, e.g.*, Hudson Ins. Co. v. Colony Ins. Co., 624 F.3d 1264, 1266 (9th Cir. 2010) (NFL Properties LLC "has been licensed to use the trademarks of the Member Clubs [of the National Football League] for commercial purposes and is the exclusive trademark enforcement arm for the Member Clubs.").

termination by the non-breaching party. Other material breaches may be grounds for termination only if they remain uncured after notice and the expiration of a designated cure period. Generally, curable breaches might include a failure to timely pay royalties, a failure to provide royalty reports, or a failure to maintain insurance.[17] Non-curable breaches might include failure to meet guaranteed minimum sales requirements, sales by the licensee of unauthorized products, sales made outside the agreed upon territory, and sales made to unapproved distribution channels.[18]

Some license agreements provide that the licensor may terminate the license agreement if the licensee does not use its "reasonable efforts," "commercially reasonable efforts," "best efforts," or another variant of those terms, in connection with performing its obligations under the agreement. The interpretation of "efforts" clauses is governed by applicable state common law, which varies considerably from state to state; in some states, these clauses are essentially interchangeable, while in other states they may require different levels of conduct.[19] For example, under New York law, a contract "need not explicitly define 'best efforts' for its 'best efforts' provision to be enforceable."[20] In contrast, courts in states such as Illinois and Texas have held that "best efforts" is too indefinite and uncertain a term to provide an enforceable standard and thus must reference or be accompanied by objective guidelines by which to measure the "best efforts" clause.[21] Similarly, although New York courts have found that a "best efforts" obligation requires "more than 'good faith,'" other states have found no difference between the two formulations.[22]

---

17. *See* Charles Klein, *Examining the Agreements of Fashion Law, in* NAVIGATING FASHION LAW, 10, 242 (Aspatore 2012).

18. *Id.*

19. *See, e.g.*, Bloor v. Falstaff Brewing Co., 601 F.2d 609, 613–14 (2d Cir. 1979) (applying New York law and finding that a contracting party does not use "best efforts" where it fails to meet agreed sales targets or promote the product).

20. US Airways Grp., Inc. v. British Airways PLC, 989 F. Supp. 482, 491 (S.D.N.Y. 1997).

21. *See, e.g.*, Kevin M. Ehringer Enters., Inc. v. McData Servs. Corp., 646 F.3d 321, 327 (5th Cir. 2011) ("[T]hese cases make clear that 'best efforts' provisions may be enforceable under Texas law if they provide some kind of objective goal or guideline against which performance is to be measured. . . ."); Kraftco Corp. v. Kolbus, 274 N.E.2d 153, 156 (Ill. App. Ct. 1971) (applying Illinois law and finding that "[t]he mere allegation of best efforts is too indefinite and uncertain to be an enforceable standard").

22. *Compare* Kroboth v. Brent, 625 N.Y.S.2d 748, 749–50 (App. Div. 1995) ("'[B]est efforts' requires more than 'good faith'. . . ."), *with* Triple-A Baseball Club Assocs. v. Ne. Baseball, Inc., 832 F.2d 214, 225 (1st Cir. 1987) ("[T]he 'best efforts' standard has been held to be equivalent to that

New York courts had historically construed "best efforts" in the licensing context to mean "active exploitation in good faith . . . ."[23] But in interpreting "best efforts" clauses more generally, New York courts have emphasized that a "best efforts" obligation must be "reasonable," so in evaluating an alleged breach of a best efforts obligation, New York courts will typically engage in a thorough analysis of the factual context in which the best efforts obligation allegedly arises, taking into account "reasonable consideration" of the interests of the party subject to the best efforts obligation.[24] In the licensing context, this analysis may involve an evaluation of promises made during the course of negotiating the license, the nature and extent of the parties' respective expected benefits from the license, the relative costs associated with exercising alleged best efforts, and relevant industry practice. Accordingly, a licensor and licensee should understand the legal ramifications of using particular "efforts" clauses. Moreover, in determining whether to exercise one of these termination rights, it is important for the licensor to consider its own obligations to the licensee as a matter of the state common law of the relevant jurisdiction, such as an implied covenant of good faith or fair dealing.[25]

The bankruptcy or insolvency of a party is generally considered grounds for automatic termination of a license agreement.[26] In some circuits, this includes trademarks, as well as other forms of intellectual property.[27] Other courts and scholars, however, had criticized that holding.[28] In 2019, the Supreme Court held that the debtor-licensor's

---

of good faith. . . . We have been unable to find any case in which a court found, as here, that a party acted in good faith but did not use its best efforts.").

23. W. Geophysical Co. of Am., Inc. v. Bolt Assocs., Inc., 584 F.2d 1164, 1170 (2d Cir. 1978).

24. *See, e.g.*, Scott-Macon Sec., Inc. v. Zoltek Cos., No. 04 Civ. 2124, 2005 WL 1138476 (S.D.N.Y. May 12, 2005), *aff'd in relevant part*, No. 06-2711-cv, 2007 WL 2914873 (2d Cir. Oct. 4, 2007).

25. *Compare* Desco Vitro Glaze of Schenectady v. Mech. Constr. Corp., 552 N.Y.S.2d 185, 186–87 (App. Div. 1990) (finding that where contract provided clear right to terminate, claim that termination violated the implied covenant of good faith and fair dealing was subject to summary judgment), *with* Sons of Thunder, Inc. v. Borden, Inc., 690 A.2d 575, 586 (N.J. 1997) (finding that even where there is an express termination right, the court still "must determine whether" the party in question "performed its obligations in good faith").

26. 11 U.S.C. § 365.

27. *See* Lubrizol Enters., Inc. v. Richmond Metal Finishers, Inc., 756 F.2d 1043 (4th Cir. 1985).

28. *See* Sunbeam Prods., Inc. v. Chi. Am. Mfg., LLC, 686 F.3d 372, 377 (7th Cir. 2012) (Easterbrook, J.).

rejection of that contract by filing for bankruptcy does not deprive the licensee of its rights to use the trademark.[29] For a longer discussion of the implications of bankruptcy, see chapter 23.

Licensors also may seek to terminate the license agreement upon a change of control of the licensee, but licensees (particularly licensees that are public companies) often object to such provisions because they may act as a deterrent to a future strategic sale.

After termination or expiration of a license agreement, the licensee should be required to pay to the licensor any accrued but unpaid royalties. The licensee may also be required to deliver to the licensor a written report detailing the amount and nature of the remaining inventory of the licensed products (and works in progress) in the possession of the licensee or any sublicensees and distributors, and the status of any unfilled orders. The licensor may negotiate for the right to purchase from the licensee any licensed products remaining in inventory, may require the licensee to continue working on any unfinished products so that they become licensed products that can be sold, or may request that the licensee destroy any remaining inventory of licensed products.

In many cases, the licensee will have a sell-off period, which is an agreed period of time during which it may sell off its inventory of finished (or in some cases, unfinished) licensed products existing as of the date of termination or expiration. The license agreement should provide the terms for any sell-off period clearly and unambiguously, and the parties should adhere to such provisions after termination or expiration of the license agreement. Failure to do so could be found to be a modification of the license agreement.[30]

[J] Buy-Out Rights

In cases where a license agreement covers all or most of the products of a particular brand, the parties may include a buy-out right in the license agreement. A buy-out right allows the licensee to purchase the licensed intellectual property and related goodwill of the brand on specified terms. A buy-out right can create an additional incentive for the licensee to promote the brand and can provide an exit for the licensor. The buy-out right can be a "put," where the licensor has the right to force a sale, a "call," where the licensee has the right to force

29. Mission Prod. Holdings v. Tempnology, LLC, No. 17-1657 (U.S.) (argued May 20, 2019).

30. *See, e.g.*, Christian Dior-N.Y., Inc. v. Koret, Inc., 792 F.2d 34 (2d Cir. 1986) (finding genuine issues of material fact as to whether the license agreement's sell-off period and post-termination procedures were waived or modified by subsequent actions by the licensor and the licensee).

a sale, or both a put and call. The put and call rights are typically triggered either by the passage of a specified period of time or by the achievement of certain financial milestones. The put and call rights may be exercisable only once during the term of the agreement or at predetermined intervals. After a put or call is exercised, the license agreement terminates and the licensee becomes the owner of the licensed intellectual property for the brand and related goodwill associated with the licensed products. Put and call right provisions typically provide either a formula or a mechanism to establish the put or call price. For example, a formula might be based on a multiple of the prior year's royalties or revenues. Alternatively, the parties may agree that an independent third-party arbiter should determine the purchase price based on the fair market value of the brand. This approach can prove problematic, however, because the licensor and licensee are agreeing to be bound by a future third-party pricing determination that may vary materially from their expectations at the time of the determination.

[K] Representations and Warranties

License agreements typically include various representations and warranties made by the licensor and the licensee, respectively, to the other party. The most common representations and warranties of a party include the following: such party has the full right, power, and authority to enter into the license agreement, and the license agreement has been validly authorized, executed, and delivered by it; such party is duly organized as a matter of state or foreign law; such party has not entered into any other agreements that would conflict with the license agreement; and such party is not bankrupt or insolvent. The licensor may also make representations as to its ownership of the licensed intellectual property.

[L] Indemnification and Insurance

License agreements may include reciprocal indemnification provisions. Typically, each party will indemnify the other party for any losses arising out of such party's breach of the license agreement. The licensor also may indemnify the licensee for any claims that the licensee's use of the licensed intellectual property solely as permitted under the license agreement constitutes an infringement of a third party's rights. The licensee may indemnify the licensor for third-party claims relating to the manufacture and sale of the products, including product liability claims.

A license agreement may require that the licensee obtain and maintain product liability insurance in certain designated amounts, and name the licensor as an additional insured. The license agreement may further require the licensee to notify the licensor of any termination, nonrenewal, or material reduction in coverage of the insurance policies.

[M] Other Provisions

License agreements may contain additional provisions that address particular concerns of the parties. For example, a licensor that is concerned about the financial condition of the licensee may require the licensee to maintain a letter of credit or certain working capital balances for the duration of the license term. A license agreement may also include non-compete or non-solicit provisions that prevent the parties from competing with each other, or hiring key employees of the other party, during the term and for a designated period after termination of the agreement.[31] License agreements typically also contain confidentiality provisions, protecting for a specified time period the confidential information of each party that is shared with the other party during the term of the license agreement. And license agreements may have provisions setting forth dispute resolution processes, such as an agreement to submit to private arbitration, or an agreement to litigate disputes in particular states or courts.

§ 10:3 License Agreements for Retail Stores

License agreements are often used by retailers (that may also be vertically integrated manufacturers) to expand their network of stores domestically or internationally. License agreements for retail stores include many of the same provisions as manufacturing and sales license agreements. There are, however, some distinctive provisions in a retail store license agreement, which are discussed below.

§ 10:3.1 Nature and Scope of the License

A license agreement for retail stores grants the licensee the right to use the licensor's intellectual property for the development of one or more retail stores in a specific territory. The license may also extend to catalog sales of products that are also offered for sale in the licensed retail stores, which products will be shipped to addresses in the territory. The licensor may retain the right to advertise, through the Internet or otherwise, in the territory, but such advertisements

31. The enforceability of agreements limiting rights to compete varies significantly by state. *See generally infra* chapter 17. *See also* BRIAN M. MALSBERGER, COVENANT NOT TO COMPETE: A STATE-BY-STATE SURVEY (BNA Books, 2003).

are typically subject to the review of the licensee. The licensor is typically prohibited from shipping products to addresses within the licensed territory.

If the licensor is also a product brand, the licensee may be required to carry only the licensor's products in the stores and in an assortment that is consistent with the range of products available in the licensor's other retail stores. If a licensor is primarily a retailer, such as a department store, the licensor and licensee typically agree on the merchandise assortment, including the quantities and styles, to be carried in the licensed stores. In such circumstances, the licensee is generally required to use either the licensor's suppliers or other suppliers that have been approved by the licensor. The licensee may or may not be required to sell the retailer's private label products, but if it does so, typically it must use the licensor's suppliers for those products.

§ 10:3.2 Development of the Stores

The licensee is typically required to develop retail stores that are consistent with the licensor's other retail stores. To ensure consistency, the licensor has certain approval rights over the planning and operation of the stores. The license agreement may address, or the licensor may have approval rights over, the most significant features of each store, including square footage, configuration, and location. Depending on the territory covered by the agreement, the parties may prefer that the store be a stand-alone retail store or part of a larger collection of stores in a mall. The licensee typically agrees to open and operate retail stores in the territory pursuant to an agreed upon schedule. The licensee may be expected to enter into a retail lease with a third party for each of the retail stores in the territory. The licensor generally has approval rights over either the retail leases or the material terms of each retail lease. If the licensee does not enter into an acceptable retail lease in the territory within a specified time period, the licensor may have the right to terminate the license agreement. The licensor may also have approval rights over the architect and general contractor for each retail store. The licensee may be required to adhere to some or all of the licensor's proprietary systems of store décor, fixtures, and design, inventory control, standards and procedures for the quality and consistency of the store's products and services, marketing and advertising, and training. In the event that the licensor updates its systems, the licensee is typically given a specified time period to conform to the updated system.

§ 10:3.3 Other Terms

The licensee may be required to pay an initial license fee as well as royalties during the term of the license agreement. Royalties are typically calculated based on a percentage of the revenues from sales of products and services at the licensed retail stores, net of returns and specified discounts. Because retail license agreements involve the operation of a retail store, the term of a retail license agreement typically is longer than that of a manufacturing and sales license agreement, and can extend to twenty years or longer, with options for renewal.

If a license is granted for retail stores in the United States, care should be taken in drafting the license agreement to avoid inadvertently falling within the purview of federal and state franchise laws. Typically, a franchise agreement is distinguished from a license agreement by the greater degree of control that the franchisor has over the business and operations of the franchisee. Franchise laws can impose significant disclosure, registration, contractual requirements, and other costly obligations on the franchisor.[32] If a license is granted for retail stores in a foreign jurisdiction, applicable local franchise law should be reviewed.

32. For the federal franchise law, see 16 C.F.R. pts. 436–437; for the New York State franchise law, see N.Y. GEN. BUS. LAW, art. 33, §§ 680–695.

Appendix 10A

Sample License Agreement

This License Agreement ("Agreement") is entered into this [•] day of [•] (the "Effective Date"), by and between [insert name of Licensor] ("Licensor"), and [insert name of Licensee] ("Licensee"), with respect to the [design, manufacture, importation, marketing, sale and distribution] of Products (as defined below) under the Licensed Mark (as defined below). Licensor and Licensee are referred to herein as a "Party" and collectively as the "Parties."

In consideration of the mutual covenants and agreements herein contained, the Parties agree as follows:

1. **Defined Terms.** The following capitalized terms have the following meanings in this Agreement:

"Affiliate" means, with respect to a Party, any entity that directly or indirectly controls, is controlled by, or is under common control with such Party.

"Contract Year" means each period of twelve (12) consecutive months commencing, with respect to the first Contract Year, on the Effective Date, and thereafter upon the anniversary of the Effective Date.

"Confidential Information" means all of a Party's non-public information, including technical, financial and business information relating to a Party's products, research and development, design, manufacturing processes, costs, revenues, profits, employees, customers, marketing and strategy, and future business plans.

"Licensed Channels" means Retailers and Off-Price Retailers.

"Licensed Mark" means the trademark "[•]," including any derivative of the Licensed Mark.

"Licensed Territory" means the following jurisdictions: [•].

"Licensor Design-Related IP" means the design concepts and other information and materials relating to the design and marketing of Products that Licensor provides to Licensee pursuant to Section 6(a).

"Net Sales" means one hundred percent (100%) of the gross revenues, as defined in accordance with U.S. GAAP, recognized by Licensee or any of its Affiliates [or sublicensees] ("Gross Revenues") from the sale or other distribution of Products, less (a) credits or allowances actually repaid or credited to customers with respect to rejected, damaged or returned Products, (b) bona fide customary trade discounts and allowances actually given and taken that are specifically attributed to a Product (including, but not limited to, any traditional retailer deductions such as margin support and mark down allowances), (c) bona fide chargebacks with respect to a Product, (d) freight discounts earned or granted to the extent allowed and taken that are specifically attributable to a Product, and (e) sales and excise taxes collected on behalf of a governmental authority (collectively, "Deductions"). No other deductions or costs incurred by Licensee shall be deductible from Gross Revenues or included in the calculation of Net Sales. The total amount of Deductions in any Contract Year shall not exceed [•] percent of Gross Revenues for such Contract Year.

"Off-Price Retailers" means (i) retail chains or organizations known for selling nationally recognized brands at discount prices, including, but not limited to, [•]; and (ii) internet retailers known for selling nationally recognized brands at discount prices, including, but not limited to, [•].

"Products" means [insert licensed product(s)], in each case, bearing the Licensed Mark.

"Retailer" means the following retailers: [•].

2. **License.** Licensor hereby grants to Licensee during the Term [[an exclusive] | [a nonexclusive]], non-assignable, non-transferable right and license to use and display the Licensed Mark[, together with the name, likeness and signature of [•]] (in each case solely in connection with the Licensed Mark and subject to Licensor's prior written approval), and the Licensor Design-Related IP, solely in connection with the [design, manufacture, importation, marketing, sale and distribution] of the Products through the Licensed Channels in the Licensed Territory, subject to the terms and conditions of this Agreement. Licensee will not sell any Products through Licensed Channels who, to Licensee's knowledge, intend or are likely to resell such Products in any country outside of the Licensed Territory. Licensee shall not make or authorize any use of the Products outside of the Licensed Territory other than for the purpose of having Products manufactured for sale within the Licensed Territory. Licensor shall not be permitted to make any direct-to-consumer sales of the Products and shall

not knowingly place any Products into a retail channel other than through Licensee. Licensee shall provide reasonable quantities of Products to Licensor, upon Licensor's request, solely for promotional purposes or for use as charitable gifts.

3. **Standards.** Licensee may sublicense its license rights set forth in Section 2, without Licensor's prior consent, solely to third-party suppliers, factories, contractors and subcontractors for the manufacture of Products on behalf of Licensee for resale by Licensee in accordance with the terms herein. In performing its obligations under this Agreement, Licensee shall, and shall only utilize suppliers, factories, contractors and subcontractors that, to Licensee's knowledge, conduct business in compliance with all applicable laws and regulations and ethical industry standards and Licensor's Workplace Code of Conduct, a copy of which is attached hereto and incorporated by reference herein. Licensee shall be responsible for all suppliers, factories, contractors and subcontractors of Licensee hereunder and any sublicensing of Licensee's rights shall not relieve Licensee of its obligations hereunder.

4. **Right of First Offer for Additional Licensed Territories.** During the Term, should Licensor consider entering into an agreement with a non-Affiliated third party to license the Licensed Mark in connection with the [design, manufacture, importation, marketing, sale and/or distribution] of Products through Licensed Channels in a territory outside of the Licensed Territory (each, an "Additional Licensed Territory"), then Licensor shall notify Licensee in writing of such intention and provide Licensee with the opportunity to make a written offer, within twenty (20) calendar days after receipt of such notice, to Licensor with respect to the terms on which Licensee would enter into a license for such Additional Licensed Territory. If no written offer is received by Licensor from Licensee within such twenty (20) calendar day period, or if a definitive agreement between the Parties is not executed within thirty (30) calendar days after receipt of such notice, Licensor may enter into an agreement with any other party with respect to such Additional Licensed Territory. Nothing in this Section 4 shall obligate Licensor to enter into an agreement for any Additional Licensed Territory with Licensee.

5. **Right of First Offer for Additional Categories.** During the Term, should Licensor consider entering into an agreement with a non-Affiliated third party to license the Licensed Mark in connection with the manufacture and sale of product

categories other than the Products in the Licensed Territory ("Additional Products"), then Licensor shall notify Licensee in writing of such intention and provide Licensee with the opportunity to make a written offer, within twenty (20) calendar days after receipt of such notice, to Licensor with respect to the terms on which Licensee would enter into a license for such Additional Products. If no written offer is received by Licensor from Licensee within such twenty (20) calendar day period, or if a definitive agreement between the Parties is not executed within thirty (30) calendar days after receipt of such notice, Licensor may enter into an agreement with any other party with respect to such Additional Products. Nothing in this Section 5 shall obligate Licensor to enter into an agreement for any Additional Products with Licensee.

6. **Design and Line Review.**

a. Design. It is the objective of this Agreement that the Parties shall establish a broad spectrum of Products. The Parties agree that Licensor shall establish the concepts and designs for the Products, in collaboration with Licensee. Promptly after executing this Agreement, Licensee shall appoint a brand manager (the "Manager"), subject to the approval of Licensor, not to be unreasonably withheld or delayed, to work with Licensor in designing and developing the Products, including their packaging, and in marketing the Products. In the event that such Manager is no longer employed in such capacity by Licensee, then Licensee shall appoint a replacement, subject to the approval of Licensor, not to be unreasonably withheld or delayed. Licensee shall be responsible for, at Licensee's expense, the following: (i) developing strategic positioning and market strategy for the Products; (ii) the production of prototypes and samples of Products; and (iii) sourcing, manufacturing, advertising, and sale and distribution of Products in accordance with the license granted in Section 2; provided that each of the foregoing shall be subject to Licensor's final approval as outlined in Section 7. The Parties shall have an initial creative meeting on the earliest mutually convenient date following the Effective Date, during which the Parties will discuss and agree upon a fashion point of view for the collection of Products, and a timetable for the design and production of the Products. The Parties shall cooperate as reasonably necessary thereafter to create, at least once in every Contract Year, a book setting forth the guidelines for the Products, including packaging guidelines (the "Style Guide"), which Style Guide shall set forth all anticipated uses of the Licensed Mark, as well as the name, signature and likeness of [•] together with any photos or any biographical information related to [•], and any designs, sketches, prints, artwork and logos related to the foregoing (collectively, "Style Guide Items") for use in connection with advertising and promotional materials, packaging materials, hang tags, labels, and such other usages as Licensor may propose. During the Term, Licensee shall have the right to use the Style Guide Items for these purposes in the manner set forth in the then-applicable Style Guide, without requiring any further approval by Licensor, except as set forth in Section 7. Licensee shall be required to obtain such approval if Licensee proposes to deviate in any material way from the provisions of the then-applicable Style Guide.

b. Line Reviews. Prior to each selling season, Licensee shall invite a representative of Licensor to attend a line review at Licensee's showroom, so as to obtain Licensor's approval of the Product preproduction samples to be manufactured, distributed and sold during such season (a "Line Review"). Licensee shall ensure that the nature, quality, construction, styling, materials, workmanship and contents and all other characteristics of all Products shall at all times be of high quality, and consistent with the prestige and reputation of the Licensed Mark, which for purposes of this Agreement shall be at least equal to the general quality of other comparable products sold by the Retailers where the Products are sold, and at least equal in quality, construction, workmanship, styling and materials to the samples approved by Licensor at the applicable Line Review.

7. **Approvals.**

a. Licensor shall have final approval as to (i) the design and quality of final preproduction samples for the Products, with the understanding that the Products shall not differ in any material respect from such approved preproduction sample, (ii) the Style Guide and all uses of the Licensed Marks, Licensor's name or [•]'s name, likeness and signature that are not set forth in the Style Guide, and (iii) the content, style and venues of all advertising (whether or not the elements thereof are included in the

Style Guide), which approvals shall not be unreasonably withheld or delayed.

b. In the event that, at any time during the Term, Licensor is dissatisfied with the quality of Products manufactured by a particular supplier, Licensor shall provide Licensee with written notice thereof, indicating in reasonable detail the basis for its determination. Licensee shall use commercially reasonable efforts to work with the supplier in question to correct the problem, if possible, and if the problem cannot be corrected or is not corrected within thirty (30) days after receipt of Licensor's notice, then Licensee shall cease placing orders in respect of Products with the supplier in question.

c. Licensor shall provide Licensee with the reasons for rejecting any request for its approval, and approval shall in all events be deemed to have been granted if Licensor does not communicate its denial thereof to Licensee in writing within ten (10) business days after receipt of the relevant written request for approval from Licensee.

8. **Intellectual Property Rights.**

a. Licensee hereby acknowledges and agrees not to contest that Licensor owns the Licensed Mark and the Licensor Design-Related IP ("Licensor Properties") and all derivative works, rights, registrations, applications and filings with respect to such Licensor Properties, and all renewals and extensions of any such registrations, applications and filings. Licensee acknowledges that it is acquiring rights hereunder only in connection with the design, marketing, manufacture and sale of the Products in the Licensed Territory in accordance with the terms of this Agreement, and that all rights to the Licensor Properties, other than those specifically granted to Licensee herein, are reserved to Licensor for its use and benefit. Licensee acknowledges and agrees that all usages of the Licensor Properties, and goodwill arising therefrom, shall inure to the benefit of Licensor.

b. The Products and all related promotional, packaging and advertising material shall include all appropriate legal notices and markings as required herein or in writing by Licensor. Licensee shall cause the Licensed Mark to be reproduced exactly and accurately in full conformity to the sketches, drawings, samples and designs provided to

Licensee by Licensor and on the written request of Licensor, Licensee shall mark all advertising, products, packages or other materials with the letters "TM," or the encircled letters "R" and "C" or both, or as otherwise may be required in order to provide notice of Licensor's rights in and to the Licensed Mark and copyrightable materials.

c. Licensee shall not use all or any part of the Licensed Mark together or in combination with any other marks, names, logos, symbols or devices other than with the prior written consent of Licensor.

d. Licensee shall not use any device, mark, logo or symbol that may reasonably be considered to be similar to or resemble any part of the Licensed Mark as to be likely to cause deception or confusion.

e. Licensee shall not use the Licensed Mark in a manner that reasonably could be expected to be prejudicial to Licensor or in a manner that reasonably could be expected to cause material harm to the goodwill attaching to all or any part of the Licensed Mark.

f. Licensee shall not, anywhere in the world, apply to register or register any intellectual property rights that are identical with or substantially similar (using the recognized legal standard for such terms established pursuant to copyright and trademark law) to or include any part of, or could adversely affect Licensor's ownership of, the Licensed Mark.

g. Licensee agrees to cooperate with Licensor in protecting and defending the Licensed Mark in the Licensed Territory, including protection against infringement and counterfeiting[, at Licensor's cost and expense]. Licensor shall retain the exclusive right to enforce the Licensed Mark against third-party infringers (and shall retain all damages recovered in connection therewith).

h. Licensee shall (i) take commercially reasonable steps to monitor manufacturing so as to avoid overruns and shall require the manufacturer to dispose of any rejected products only after the removal of any Licensed Mark, labels, brand names or other markings identifying them as Licensor's brand, and (ii) ensure that any Retailer returns are, upon agreement of the Parties, either sold to Off-Price Retailers with labels intact (in which case Royalties shall be paid pursuant to <u>Section 10</u>) or liquidated to third parties after the removal of any Licensed Marks, labels, brand names or other markings identifying them as Licensor's brand (in which case no Royalties shall be paid).

i. Licensee shall meet delivery deadlines for the Products in a manner that is satisfactory to the Retailers and Off-Price Retailers and to Licensor so that the image of the Licensed Mark and the brand is not diminished or impaired.

9. **Personal Appearances and Promotional and Other Support by Licensor.**

a. [•] shall use his commercially reasonable efforts to participate in personal appearances or interviews ("Appearances"), photo shoots ("Photo Sessions"), promotional events, sales clinics, and other activities ("Events") as necessary to promote the sale of Products and to foster the goodwill associated with the Licensed Mark (collectively, the Appearances, Photo Sessions and Events are referred to as "Promotional Events"), subject to the terms hereof. The Promotional Events may take place at a Retailer facility or at other locations designated by either Licensee or a Retailer and approved by Licensor, such approval not to be unreasonably withheld or delayed. The Parties shall, reasonably promptly after this Agreement is executed, jointly devise a promotional plan that establishes a strategy and defines the level of individual involvement by [•] in Promotional Events (the "Promotional Plan"); provided, that [•] shall participate in a minimum of two (2) Photo Sessions per season during each Contract Year for purposes of creating an advertising campaign if requested by Licensee. The Promotional Plan shall be updated at the beginning of each Contract Year during the Term. In addition to the Photo Sessions, [•] shall be reasonably available for participation in Promotional Events, including a minimum of four (4) Appearances and two (2) Events in each Contract Year during the Term, if requested by Licensee.

b. Licensee shall promptly reimburse [•] for (i) all out-of-pocket first class hotel, first class air travel and other costs reasonably incurred by [•]; and (ii) all out-of-pocket business class hotel, coach class air travel and other costs reasonably incurred by one assistant, in connection with any activities that he may engage in pursuant to the Promotional Plan or otherwise pursuant to this

Agreement. The Parties shall include a budget in the Promotional Plan that will define the anticipated level of expenses associated with such activities.

c. [•] shall, at all times and in all material respects, engage in and maintain such personal behavior as shall enhance and promote the goodwill of the Licensed Mark and the image thereof. [•] warrants that he has not committed, and during the Term will not commit, any act which constitutes an offense involving moral turpitude under federal, state or local laws, or which is reasonably likely to materially damage the reputation of the Products or Licensee. Licensor acknowledges that any breach by [•] of his obligation under this Section 9(c) will be a basis for termination of this Agreement.

10. **Royalties and Reports.** In consideration for the [[exclusive] | [nonexclusive]] license granted under Section 2, Licensee shall pay Licensor royalties equal to [•] percent of Net Sales of Products (the "Royalties"); provided that Royalties payable for approved sales to Off-Price Retailers shall be [•] percent of Net Sales to such Off-Price Retailers. The Royalties shall be payable on a quarterly basis within sixty (60) days following the close of each calendar quarter during the Term or, with respect to the period from the end of the last calendar quarter ending prior to the expiration of the Term until the date on which the Term expires, within thirty (30) days after the expiration of the Term. Any Royalties paid more than five (5) business days after the applicable due date shall bear interest at the rate of [•] percent per annum. The obligation to pay Royalties shall accrue upon the sale of the Products. For purposes of this Agreement, a Product shall be considered sold on the date the Product is delivered to a Retailer or Off-Price Retailer. Each Royalty payment shall be accompanied by detailed reports in a form acceptable to Licensor, listing the SKU, item, units sold, description, quantity shipped, gross revenues, deductions and Royalties owing.

11. **Business Plan.** Attached hereto for informational purposes only as Exhibit A to this Agreement is Licensee's business plan with respect to the sale and distribution of Products, including Licensee's reasonable forecasts of Net Sales by season, projected advertising and promotional expenditures by season, and product range and price points by season (a "Business Plan") for the first [•] Contract Years of the Term. Licensee shall deliver an updated good faith Business Plan for each

subsequent Contract Year not later than sixty (60) days prior to the end of the preceding Contract Year.

12. **Records and Audit.** Licensee shall keep and maintain accurate books and records covering all transactions relating to this Agreement during the Term and for at least five (5) years thereafter. Licensor shall have the right to periodically, but not more than twice during any Contract Year, inspect and audit Licensee's books and records and other documents and materials in the possession or control of Licensee with respect to the subject matter of this Agreement; provided, however, that no audit shall occur later than five (5) years after the end of any applicable Contract Year. Licensor shall be provided free and full access to such items and shall be permitted to make copies thereof. In the event that such inspection and audit reveals an underpayment of Royalties owed to Licensor, Licensee shall pay such discrepancy, plus interest at a rate of [•] percent per annum measured from the end of the Contract Year to which such discrepancy relates to the date of payment. In the event such underpayment is in excess of [•] percent of the amount actually due Licensor for the period being audited, Licensee shall reimburse Licensor for the cost of such inspection and audit. In the event such underpayment is in excess of [•] percent of the amount actually due Licensor, Licensor shall have the right to immediately terminate this Agreement.

13. **Advance and Minimum Net Sales.**

    a. Licensee shall pay to Licensor a nonrefundable advance against Royalties in the amount of $[•] (the "Advance"). The Advance shall be paid within three (3) business days after execution of this Agreement. The Advance shall be credited against any Royalties that Licensee may owe to Licensor at any time during the Term.

    b. Schedule A to this Agreement sets forth certain minimum amounts of Net Sales for the Products for each Contract Year (collectively, the "Minimum Net Sales"). Licensee shall use its commercially reasonable efforts to achieve the Minimum Net Sales for each Contract Year. If the Minimum Net Sales in any Contract Year are not achieved, Licensee shall have the option, within thirty (30) days after the end of such Contract Year, to pay Licensor an amount (the "Catch-Up Amount") equal to one hundred percent (100%) of the Royalties that would have been due in such Contract Year (calculated at a rate of [•] percent of Net Sales) had the Minimum Net Sales for such Contract Year been achieved (less any Royalties in respect of such Contract Year that were previously paid to Licensor). If Licensee does not pay the Catch-Up Amount to Licensor within such thirty (30) day period, Licensor shall have the right to terminate this Agreement and retain the Advance.

14. **Term.** The term of this Agreement shall commence on the Effective Date and shall continue through [•] (the "Initial Term"). Licensee shall have the option to renew the Agreement for [•] successive renewal periods of [•] years each ("Renewal Periods") by providing written notice to Licensor at least sixty (60) days prior to the start of the applicable Renewal Period. Licensee shall only be eligible to exercise the renewal options if it has actually achieved the Minimum Net Sales in the last Contract Year of the Initial Term or applicable Renewal Period, has paid Licensor the associated Royalties and the Advance provided for hereunder and is not otherwise in material breach of this Agreement. The "Term" shall include the Initial Term, Renewal Periods and, to the extent applicable, any Disposal Period (as defined below).

15. **Termination.** This Agreement may be terminated as follows:

    a. by either Party if the other Party breaches the Agreement and fails to cure the breach within thirty (30) days after receiving written notice of the breach;

    b. by either Party upon the other Party's bankruptcy, insolvency or assignment for the benefit of creditors;

    c. by Licensee as set forth in Section 9(c);

    d. by Licensor as set forth in Section 12;

    e. by Licensor as set forth in Section 13(a) and Section 13(b);

    f. by Licensee in the event of [•]'s death or in the event of his disability such that he is incapable of performing his obligations under Section 9(a); or

    g. by Licensor if Net Sales for the [•] Contract Year are less than [•].

16. **Consequences of Termination.** Upon termination or expiration of this Agreement, Licensee shall promptly pay to Licensor all Royalties that have accrued prior to the date of termination or expiration and shall deliver to Licensor a full accounting of

the status of all Products (i.e., all orders, all items in production and all inventory). Licensee shall have [•] days (hereinafter referred to as the "Disposal Period") following the termination or expiration of this Agreement in which to use the Licensed Mark on a nonexclusive basis to make an orderly disposition of the Products in stock or in the manufacturing process (in the latter case, in respect of orders received by Licensee) prior to the termination or expiration of this Agreement. Licensee may manufacture Products during the Disposal Period solely to fill orders existing as of the effective date of termination. Upon termination or expiration of this Agreement, and except as provided above, Licensee shall cease using the Licensed Mark and other Licensor Properties, and all Confidential Information of Licensor and all materials intended for use with or bearing the Licensed Mark shall be destroyed by Licensee or, at Licensor's option, shall be returned to Licensor at Licensor's cost. Upon termination or expiration of this Agreement, the Parties shall agree as to whether Products in stock at such time will be sold by Licensee to Retailers, liquidated to third parties (only after the removal of any Licensed Mark, labels, brand names or other markings identifying them as Licensor's brand products) or sold by Licensee to Off-Price Retailers. All payments required hereunder shall continue with respect to Net Sales of Products during the Disposal Period. In the event that Licensee terminates this Agreement pursuant to a material violation by [•] of Section 9(c) with respect to [•] committing any act which constitutes an offense involving moral turpitude under Federal, state or local laws, then Licensor shall reimburse to Licensee any portion of the Advance that has been paid but not otherwise been credited against actual Royalties as of the date of termination.

17. **Advertising Allowance.** Licensee shall spend a minimum amount for each Contract Year equal to [•] percent of projected Net Sales of Products (as set forth in the applicable Business Plan) for such Contract Year on marketing and advertising the Products, including, but not limited to, print ads, Internet ads, television ads, photo-shoot costs, showroom costs, social media efforts, co-op advertising with retailers, circulars, catalogs, point of sale materials, the cost and use of marketing coordinators, and sales and trade show expenses (the "Advertising Allowance"). In addition, the Parties will agree upon an additional marketing and advertising budget with respect to the initial launch of the Products. Licensor shall have final approval on the content and venues of all advertising, which approval shall not be unreasonably withheld or delayed.

18. **Collections and Launch Date.** Each Contract Year, Licensee shall produce and sell four (4) collections of Products: pre-fall; fall; pre-spring, and spring. Licensee shall use commercially reasonable efforts to first introduce the Products to the public by [date].

19. **Confidentiality.** The Parties agree to take all steps reasonably necessary to hold in trust and confidence, and not to disclose or confirm to any third party (except to the extent required by law or regulatory process), the other Party's Confidential Information; provided that each Party may disclose such information to its representatives as necessary in connection with the transactions contemplated by this Agreement so long as such persons are informed by such Party of the confidential nature of such information and are directed by such Party to treat such information confidentially. The foregoing obligations do not apply to information that can be shown to have been (i) previously known on a nonconfidential basis by the other Party, (ii) in the public domain through no fault of such other Party, or (iii) later lawfully acquired by such other Party from a third-party source that does not have any obligation to keep such information confidential.

20. **Public Announcements and Press Releases.** The timing and content of all public announcements and press releases relating to this Agreement and the transactions contemplated herein shall be subject to the approval of both Parties.

21. **Non-Circumvention.** The Parties shall not, directly or indirectly, enter into an agreement or take any action the purpose of which would reduce, avoid or prevent the payment of Royalties, commissions, or any other compensation to the other Party.

22. **Indemnification.**

    a. Licensee agrees to indemnify, defend and hold harmless [•] and Licensor and its officers, directors, employees, agents and representatives (collectively, the "Licensor Indemnified Parties," and each, a "Licensor Indemnified Party"), against all damages, costs, expenses and losses (including reasonable attorneys' fees and costs) (collectively, "Losses") incurred in connection with third-party claims (a "Third-Party Claim") against a Licensor Indemnified Party: (i) related to the manufacture, marketing, sale or distribution of the Products, including, without limitation, actions based on product liability; or

(ii) resulting from any breach by Licensee or its representatives of any of its or their representations and obligations hereunder.

b. Licensor agrees to indemnify, defend and hold harmless Licensee and its officers, directors, employees, agents and representatives (collectively, the "Licensee Indemnified Parties," and each, a "Licensee Indemnified Party"), against all Losses incurred in connection with Third-Party Claims against a Licensee Indemnified Party: (i) resulting from the infringement or violation of the intellectual property rights of any third party as a result of Licensee's use of the Licensed Mark in accordance with the terms of this Agreement; or (ii) resulting from any breach by Licensor or its representatives of any of its and their representations and obligations hereunder.

23. **Representations and Warranties.**

a. Licensor represents and warrants to Licensee that (i) the Licensed Mark is available for use by Licensee upon the terms and subject to the conditions of this Agreement, (ii) the use of the Licensed Mark by Licensee in accordance with the provisions of this Agreement[, to Licensor's knowledge,] does not and shall not infringe on the trademark or other rights of any third party, (iii) Licensor has the full power and authority to enter into this Agreement and to grant the right and license provided for hereunder, and (iv) the grant of the license provided for herein, the execution and delivery of this Agreement and the performance of Licensor's obligations hereunder do not conflict with, nor will they cause Licensor, with or without the passage of time or the giving of notice, to be in default under, any agreement, contract, commitment, order, judgment or any obligation by which Licensor is bound.

b. Licensee represents and warrants that (i) it shall use its commercially reasonable efforts to promote, market, sell and distribute the Products in the Licensed Territory, (ii) Licensee has the full power and authority to enter into this Agreement and perform its obligations hereunder, (iii) Licensee has adequate capital to finance and adequate resources to fulfill the obligations contemplated by this Agreement, and (iv) the execution and delivery of this Agreement and the performance of Licensee's obligations hereunder do not conflict with, nor will they cause

Licensee, with or without the passage of time or the giving of notice, to be in default under, any agreement, contract, commitment, order, judgment or any obligation by which Licensee is bound.

24. **Payments Solely to Licensor.** Licensor hereby agrees that the amounts payable by Licensee to Licensor pursuant to the terms of this Agreement are the sole consideration owed from Licensee to Licensor and in no event shall Licensee be responsible for payments to any third parties, including, without limitation, payments Licensor may owe to any agents or other representatives of Licensor.

25. **Governing Law, Jurisdiction and Venue.** This Agreement shall be governed by the laws of the State of [•] without reference to conflict of laws principles. The Parties hereby agree to submit to the exclusive personal jurisdiction of the courts of [•], which shall be the exclusive venue for the resolution of all disputes arising under this Agreement.

26. **Assignment.** Neither Party shall assign or sublicense any of its rights or obligations under this Agreement without the prior written consent of the other Party, except that: (i) without the consent of Licensee, Licensor may assign its rights and obligations under this Agreement to any party that becomes the owner of the Licensed Mark; (ii) Licensee may assign all or part of its rights or obligations to an Affiliate of Licensee without Licensor's consent by providing ten (10) days' prior written notice to Licensor of such assignment, provided that the Affiliate agrees in writing to be bound by Licensee's obligations hereunder and that Licensee shall remain responsible for the Affiliate's compliance with the terms and conditions of this Agreement; and (iii) Licensee shall be entitled to sublicense the manufacture, distribution, sale and promotion of the Products with the prior written consent of Licensor, with such consent not to be unreasonably withheld or delayed, provided that (a) Licensee requires that any such sublicensee also abides by all the relevant terms and conditions of this Agreement, (b) Licensee shall remain liable for the sublicensee's compliance with the terms and conditions of this Agreement, and (c) Licensee delivers to Licensor all of the information in its possession about such sublicensee and a copy of the most recent term sheet reflecting the terms of the proposed sublicense. Any assignment made in contravention of this Agreement shall be null and void.

27. **Consequential Damages.** Except for the Parties' confidentiality or indemnification obligations herein, neither Party shall be liable to the other for any consequential, indirect, exemplary or special damages, including loss of profit, arising out of or related to this Agreement.

28. **Entire Agreement and Modification.** This Agreement sets forth the entire understanding and agreement of the Parties as to the subject matter hereof. This Agreement may be modified only by a writing signed by the Parties.

29. **Severability.** If any provision of this Agreement is held by a court of competent jurisdiction to be invalid or unenforceable for any reason, the remaining provisions will continue in full force without being impaired or invalidated in any way. The Parties agree to replace any invalid provision with a valid provision that most closely approximates the intent and economic effect of the invalid provision.

30. **Headings.** Titles or headings to the sections of this Agreement are not part of the terms of this Agreement, but are inserted solely for convenience.

31. **Notices.** All notices, requests and other communications under this Agreement must be in writing, and may be sent by facsimile or electronic mail and mailed by registered or certified mail, postage prepaid and return receipt requested, or delivered by hand to the Party to whom such notice is required or permitted to be given as set forth below. If mailed, any such notice shall be considered to have been given two (2) business days after it was mailed, as evidenced by the postmark. If delivered by facsimile, electronic mail or by hand, any such notice shall be considered to have been given when received by the Party to whom notice is given.

[insert notice addresses]

[•]

[•]

[•]

Attention: [•]

[•]

[•]

[•]

Attention: [•]

32. **Insurance.** During the Term, Licensee shall obtain and maintain, at its own cost and expense, standard product liability insurance coverage naming Licensor as additional insured, with limits no less than [•] per occurrence and [•] in the aggregate. Such policy shall provide for at least thirty (30) days' written notice to the additional insureds in the event of modification, cancellation or termination thereof. Licensee shall provide the additional insureds with a certificate of insurance evidencing such coverage within thirty (30) days following the Effective Date. In no event shall Licensee manufacture, market, sell or distribute the Products prior to receipt of such certificate by the additional insureds.

33. **Survival.** Upon the expiration or termination of this Agreement, each Party's rights and obligations under this Agreement shall terminate, except the following provisions shall survive such expiration or termination: Section 1, Section 8, Section 12 (for a period of five (5) years after such expiration or termination), Section 16, Section 19, Section 22, and Section 25 through Section 34, and any payment obligations for amounts earned during the Term, but not yet paid.

34. **Counterparts.** This Agreement may be executed in any number of counterparts, each of which shall be deemed an original, but all such counterparts together shall constitute but one and the same instrument.

[SIGNATURE PAGE FOLLOWS]

IN WITNESS WHEREOF, the Parties have executed this Agreement as of the Effective Date.

By: ____________________ By: ____________________

Name: Name:

Title: Title:

With respect to the terms, conditions and obligations set forth in Section 9:

By: ____________________

Name:

SCHEDULE A

Minimum Net Sales

Contract Year	Period	Minimum Net Sales
Contract Year 1	[date]–[date]	[amount]
Contract Year 2	[date]–[date]	[amount]
Contract Year 3	[date]–[date]	[amount]
Contract Year 4	[date]–[date]	[amount]

After the Contract Years listed above, Minimum Net Sales for each subsequent Contract Year shall be equal to [•] percent of the forecasted annual Net Sales for Products for such Contract Year as set forth in the Business Plan for such Contract Year.

Chapter 11

Retail Sales

§ 11:1 Introduction
- § 11:1.1 Department Stores
- § 11:1.2 Specialty Stores
- § 11:1.3 Discount Department Stores
- § 11:1.4 Off-Price Stores
  - [A] Factory Outlets
  - [B] Off-Price Retailers
  - [C] Retailer-Owned Off-Price Stores
- § 11:1.5 Boutiques
- § 11:1.6 Pop-Up Shops
- § 11:1.7 Internet Retailers
- § 11:1.8 Mail-Order (Catalog) Retailers and Television Retailers
- § 11:1.9 Transition to Brick-and-Mortar Stores and the Growth of Omni-Channel Retailing
- § 11:1.10 Shopping for the Experience

§ 11:2 Arrangements Between Retailers and Vendors
- § 11:2.1 Vendor Standards
- § 11:2.2 Selecting Products; Discounts and Markdown Allowances
- § 11:2.3 Purchase Orders
- § 11:2.4 Shipping, Delivery and Risk of Loss
- § 11:2.5 Acceptance and Terms of Payment
- § 11:2.6 Chargebacks
- § 11:2.7 Consignments

§ 11:3 Distribution Agreements

§ 11:4 Conclusion

§ 11:1 Introduction

Retailers represent the final stage in the journey of apparel from its point of origin to the ultimate consumer. In the United States, the retail apparel industry is large, mature (slow-growing), and, despite significant consolidation in recent years, fragmented and highly competitive.[1] The retail apparel industry includes the sale of womenswear, menswear, and childrenswear. In 2017, the U.S. retail apparel industry generated total revenues of approximately $327 billion, with womenswear representing the largest segment of the industry.[2] Apparel retailers offer merchandise in various styles (such as contemporary, casual, professional, and formal), for various occasions (such as special occasion, resort, and athletic), and at various price tiers.[3] Retailers often sell both apparel and accessories (such as footwear and handbags), as the consumer dynamics of both product categories are similar. Demand for apparel and accessories is largely driven by general economic trends (consumer confidence, personal disposable income, and consumer spending), population growth and demographic trends, and changes in consumer tastes and preferences.[4]

Prior to 1995, apparel retailers primarily used a single distribution channel: brick-and-mortar retail stores. But due to greater household access to the Internet and the rapid growth of mobile device usage, the retail apparel industry in the United States started to experience a strategic shift in the mid 1990s.[5] Increasingly, retailers have adopted e-commerce and mobile commerce platforms, either exclusively or as part of an omni-channel retail strategy that combines a physical presence with an online and mobile presence to deliver a seamless customer experience.[6] For example, some retailers have integrated mobile payment systems, such as Apple Pay, into brick-and-mortar retail stores.[7] In addition, the growth of the Internet has allowed apparel brands to directly access their customers through e-commerce and mobile commerce sites, mobile applications ("apps"), email distribution lists, and social media platforms. As a consequence of the visual and tactile nature of apparel, and the consumer's desire to try on apparel products for proper sizing and fit, brick-and-mortar stores

---

1. CAMILLA YANUSHEVSKY & XIONG JUN GOON, CFRA EQUITY RESEARCH, INDUSTRY SURVEYS, TEXTILES, APPAREL & LUXURY GOODS (JULY 31, 2018) [hereinafter YANUSHEVSKY, TEXTILES, APPAREL & LUXURY GOODS], at 17, 30.
2. *Apparel Retail in the U.S.*, MARKETLINE (MAR. 22, 2018), http://www.marketresearch.com/MarketLine-v3883/Apparel-Retail-United-States-11562224/.
3. DUN & BRADSTREET, FIRST RES., CLOTHING STORES (FEB. 5, 2018) [hereinafter CLOTHING STORES], at 2.
4. YANUSHEVSKY, TEXTILES, APPAREL & LUXURY GOODS, *supra* note 1, at 30.
5. PWC/KANTAR RETAIL, RETAILING 2020: WINNINGINA POLARIZED WORLD at 16 (2012), http://www.pwc.com/en_US/us/retail-consumer/publications/assets/pwc-retailing-2020.pdf.
6. *Id.* at 31.
7. YANUSHEVSKY, TEXTILES, APPAREL & LUXURY GOODS, *supra* note 1, at 26.

continue to be the primary source of retail apparel sales.[8] But online sales are on the rise. In 2017, online retail sales growth outpaced that of overall retail sales—a trend that is projected to continue through 2019—and, for the first time, more "Black Friday" sales were conducted online than in brick-and-mortar stores.[9] And this strategic shift towards e-commerce has been accompanied by the development of new technologies aimed at enhancing the online shopping consumer experience so that it more closely resembles the in-store experience. Some retailers are even using digital technology to mimic the process of trying products on, allowing customers to select a size and assess the fit without leaving their homes or waiting for the item to arrive in the mail. Nike, for example, acquired a company that is developing technology to enable shoppers to scan their feet and send the data to Nike for sizing purposes using their mobile phones.[10]

On the other hand, the continued growth of the Internet and advancement of technology has not rendered brick-and-mortar stores obsolete. Certain retailers previously operating exclusively through e-commerce and mobile commerce platforms have begun opening brick-and-mortar retail stores, in addition to their existing platforms, in an effort to increase awareness and exposure, gain new customers, better market their products, develop closer and more personalized customer relations, and boost sales and online traffic.[11] Such retailers include Warby Parker, Everlane, and Untuckit, Carbon 38, and Bonobos.[12] This is a further example of the growth and trend of an omni-channel retail strategy, "where merchants aim to provide customers with a seamless experience whether shopping online via desktop or mobile device or at a traditional retail store."[13] Customers are increasingly stepping away from the traditional in-store experience in favor of "shopping for the experience," in the form of retail ambiance, technology-infused experiences, personal engagement, social impact, fashion customization, and experience-based interactions.

---

8. Stephanie Clifford, *Once Proudly Web Only, Shopping Sites Hang Out Real Shingles*, N.Y. TIMES (Dec. 18, 2012), https://www.nytimes.com/2012/12/19/business/shopping-sites-open-brick-and-mortar-stores.html?_r=0.
9. YANUSHEVSKY, TEXTILES, APPAREL & LUXURY GOODS, *supra* note 1, at 27.
10. *Id.*
11. Mark Walsh, *The Future of E-Commerce: Bricks and Mortar*, GUARDIAN (Jan. 30, 2016), https://www.theguardian.com/business/2016/jan/30/future-of-e-commerce-bricks-and-mortar [hereinafter Walsh]; *Warby Parker Aims to Run Nearly 100 Stores this Year, as Other Web Shops Follow*, CNBC (Feb. 15, 2018), https://www.cnbc.com/2018/02/15/as-warby-parker-approaches-100-stores-other-internet-brands-follow.html.
12. *See id.*
13. Walsh, *supra* note 11.

Apparel retailers also have been impacted by the growth of "fast fashion" companies, principally the Inditex Group (known for its fast fashion brands including Zara and Massimo Dutti), the Arcadia Group Ltd. (which owns Topshop), H&M, Uniqlo, and Mango. These companies (typically manufacturers as well as retailers) feature a rapidly changing assortment of merchandise reflecting the latest fashion trends, sold at affordable prices, in attractively designed stores. The speed at which fast fashion companies can get a product from concept to shelves (generally around five weeks[14]) has induced more traditional retailers to shorten their delivery, or lead, times in order to remain competitive.[15] The high turnover by fast fashion brands, and their ability to quickly replicate runway designs, also led luxury brands to transition to a "four to six collections" per year model instead of the traditional "two collections" per year model.[16] Some luxury brands, such as Burberry, Ralph Lauren, and Tom Ford also now offer merchandise for sale immediately after runway shows instead of making customers wait months for merchandise to arrive in stores.[17]

But, ironically, even "fast fashion" originators now find themselves subject to the same pressure that they once exercised on traditional retailers and luxury brands. Even the fastest of the original fast fashion companies, like Zara, find themselves struggling to keep up with online-only retailers that also specialize in trendy, affordable clothing, such as Boohoo, ASOS, and Missguided.[18] Like the original fast fashion retailers, these online stores primarily target the young adult market, and are able to constantly refresh product offerings due to a lightning-fast, one- to four-week turnaround from concept

---

14. Mary Hanbury, *Zara is Facing a Massive Threat That Could Jeopardize the Business*, BUS. INSIDER (May 23, 2017), https://www.businessinsider.com/fast-fashion-is-getting-faster-2017-5 [hereinafter Hanbury].
15. Suzy Hansen, *How Zara Grew Into the World's Largest Fashion Retailer*, N.Y. TIMES (Nov. 9, 2012), https://www.nytimes.com/2012/11/11/magazine/how-zara-grew-into-the-worlds-largest-fashion-retailer.html?pagewanted=all&_r=0.
16. *Id.* (discussing how rapidly Inditex has increased its overall sales, despite using anonymous designers and little advertising).
17. Lydia Dishman, *In the Trenches With Burberry's Christopher Bailey*, FAST CO. (Aug. 31, 2012), http://www.fastcompany.com/3000941/trenches-burberrys-christopher-bailey; Elizabeth Baton, *Fashion Shows Adopted a See-Now, Buy-Now Model. Has It Worked?*, N.Y. TIMES (Feb. 7, 2017), https://www.nytimes.com/2017/02/07/fashion/see-now-buy-now-business-fashion-week.html.
18. Hanbury, *supra* note 14.

to sale.[19] In addition to offering a massive selection of ever-changing products, online-only retailers typically offer free shipping and returns, which allows customers to essentially try clothes on at home like they would in a dressing room.[20]

This section focuses on the major retail distribution channels for apparel in the United States, and the trends that continue to reshape the retail industry.

§ 11:1.1 Department Stores

Department stores are large retailers that stock a wide variety of fashion-oriented merchandise (typically tens of thousands of stock keeping units), which is separated into departments and offered to consumers at full price, traditionally, with seasonal markdowns.[21] Department stores, however, have come to rely more heavily on promotional pricing and sales to remain competitive.[22] Department stores generally can be divided into market segments, with differing levels of customer service, merchandise selection, and store layout dictated by the target market.[23] These market segments include: higher tier department stores (such as Saks Fifth Avenue and Neiman Marcus), which target affluent consumers and the lucrative "aspirational shopper"; upper moderate department stores (such as Macy's and Dillard's), which target mid-range households; and moderate department stores (such as Sears and J.C. Penney), which target more value-oriented consumers.[24] Department stores also can be divided by the assortment of merchandise they carry: full-line department stores (such as Macy's and J.C. Penney), which carry not only apparel and accessories, but also housewares and furniture; and specialty department stores (such as Barney's, Neiman Marcus, and Nordstrom), which focus on men's and women's apparel, footwear, and other accessories.[25] However, even among companies that offer,

---

19. *Id.*
20. CLOTHING STORES, *supra* note 3, at 6.
21. LESLIE DAVIS BURNS, ET AL., BUS. OF FASHION: DESIGNING, MANUFACTURING & MARKETING, 323 (5TH ED. 2016) [hereinafter BURNS].
22. DUN & BRADSTREET, FIRST RESEARCH, DEPARTMENT STORES (JUNE 4, 2018) [hereinafter DEPARTMENT STORES], at 4.
23. *Id.* at 2.
24. JASON ASAEDA, STANDARD & POOR'S, INDUSTRY SURVEYS, RETAILING: GENERAL (May 24, 2012) [hereinafter ASAEDA, RETAILING]; Tina Mulqueen, *Luxury Retail Is Making a Comeback Thanks to China, Millennials, and Men*, FORBES (June 29, 2018), https://www.forbes.com/sites/tinamulqueen/2018/06/29/luxury-retail-is-making-a-comeback-thanks-to-china-millennials-and-men/#49d6b3c382ec.
25. CAMILLA YANUSHEVSKY & XIONG JUN GOON, CFRA EQUITY RESEARCH, INDUSTRY SURVEYS, RETAIL (SEPT. 24, 2018) [hereinafter YANUSHEVSKY, RETAIL], at 10.

or previously offered, housewares and furniture, most companies have either eliminated or reduced selling space for "hard goods," which include appliances, furniture, and tools, due to a proliferation of retailers that specialize in those segments.[26] Apparel merchandise typically accounts for more than half of department store sales revenues.[27] This typically includes three main categories: (1) *fashion merchandise*, which has a relatively long lead time but a short selling season and is dependent on shifting customer preferences; (2) *basic merchandise*, which is relatively stable in style and demand (such as t-shirts and underwear); and (3) *fashion-basic merchandise*, which has fashion elements added to otherwise basic items and therefore requires longer lead times than basic merchandise (such as t-shirts with special trimming).[28] The size of department stores varies, but some department store chains have flagship stores that exceed 250,000 square feet.[29] Typically, the first floor of a department store, which is high traffic, carries cosmetics, jewelry, hosiery, and other accessories, which are higher margin merchandise.

A department store often serves as the "anchor tenant" in a large mall in order to attract consumer foot traffic to other smaller stores within the mall.[30] However, this relationship between department stores and malls is not as important as it once was. As department stores have become less popular, successful malls that once relied on four or five department stores as anchor tenants now typically need only one or two, opting to use movie theaters, restaurants, and off-price retail chains, such as TJ Maxx, as anchor tenants instead.[31] Additionally, as traditional shopping malls draw fewer customers, some department store chains, such as J.C. Penny and Nordstrom Local (as described in greater detail below), are looking to expand off-mall locations, finding that sales in their stand-alone stores outpace that of their mall-based stores.[32] The U.S. department store industry, which is comprised primarily of national and regional chains, has become increasingly consolidated, with the top four companies generating approximately 80% of the industry's total revenues.[33] Department store sales in the United States have experienced a significant decline since 2000, largely as a result of increasing competition from other

---

26. DEPARTMENT STORES, *supra* note 22, at 3.
27. *Id.* at 2.
28. YANUSHEVSKY, RETAIL, *supra* note 25, at 13.
29. DEPARTMENT STORES, *supra* note 22, at 2.
30. *Id.* at 3.
31. Sapna Maheshwari, *Department Stores, Once Anchors at Malls, Become Millstones*, N.Y. TIMES (Jan. 5, 2017), https://www.nytimes.com/2017/01/05/business/department-stores-macys-sears.html [hereinafter Maheshwari].
32. DEPARTMENT STORES, *supra* note 22, at 7.
33. *Id.* at 2.

retail channels—particularly online retailers—and changing shopping preferences.[34] Between 2005 and 2015, clothing store sales in general increased 29%, but during that same time period, clothing sales at conventional department stores decreased 31%.[35] As a result, many department store companies have laid off thousands of employees and closed stores.[36] For example, Macy's, the largest department store chain in the United States, closed 200 stores between 2010 and 2017, and announced the closure of 100 more of its 730 remaining stores in 2017.[37] And Sears, once the largest retailer in the United States, filed for bankruptcy protection in 2018,[38] although in February 2019, the U.S. Bankruptcy Court judge approved a plan for the purchase of Sears, which would allow the company to keep over 400 stores open and preserve up to 45,000 jobs.[39]

Accordingly, department stores have invested in various strategies to drive growth.[40] Some department store retailers have refocused their expansion strategies to emerging markets, such as Indonesia, India, and the Philippines, which have growing middle class populations.[41] Additionally, investment in technology has become essential for department store chains to remain competitive. Most companies now offer retail websites, which allow the stores to offer a wider variety of products and to reach consumers beyond local markets.[42] And some department store companies are investing in omni-channel sales capabilities, which integrate brick-and-mortar stores with websites and mobile operations (such as apps, mobile sites, and mobile payments).[43] For example, Macy's launched mobile wallets to allow customers to access coupons on their phones while shopping in stores and started accepting mobile payments, including Apple Pay,

---

34. *Id.*
35. CLOTHING STORES, *supra* note 3, at 8.
36. *Id.* at 1.
37. *Id.*; Maheshwari, *supra* note 31.
38. DEPARTMENT STORES, *supra* note 22, at 1; Tiffany Hsu, *Sears Went from Gilded-Age Boom to Digital-Age Bankruptcy*, N.Y. TIMES (Oct. 15, 2018), https://www.nytimes.com/2018/10/15/business/sears-bankrupt-history-timeline.html.
39. Lilian Rizzo, *Bankruptcy Judge Says He Will Approve Lampert Purchase of Sears*, WALL ST. J. (Feb. 7, 2019), https://www.wsj.com/articles/bankruptcy-judge-approves-lampert-purchase-of-sears-11549573078.
40. DEPARTMENT STORES, *supra* note 22, at 9.
41. *Id.* at 3.
42. *Id.*
43. *Id.*

in stores and online.[44] Macy's is also investing in improvements to its "Buy Online Pickup in Store" service to both encourage online spending and increase foot traffic in stores.[45]

In addition to facing competitive pressures, department store sales are subject to seasonal fluctuations.[46] The fourth quarter of the calendar year, which includes winter holiday shopping as well as some back-to-school shopping, can generate up to a third of a company's sales for the year.[47] Sales generally peak during winter holiday shopping, so holiday sales can significantly affect the entire fiscal year.[48] In the last decade, consumers have increasingly timed their purchases, particularly of luxury goods, to coincide with anticipated seasonal discounts or other promotions offered by department stores as they seek to clear excess inventory.[49] As a result, some department stores have reduced their inventory levels to prompt customers to make their purchases at the beginning of a season, rather than waiting for future price reductions.[50]

As their focus is attracting and retaining a broad base of customers, department stores often offer attractive rewards programs. These rewards may be offered through proprietary credit cards (where the retailer grants the credit), private label credit cards (where a third party grants the credit but the retailer's name goes on the card), and/or loyalty programs. For example, as members of Bloomingdale's "Loyallist" program, customers receive periodic "Friends & Family" discounts of up to 25% off merchandise in stores or online.[51] Neiman Marcus "InCircle" members receive special promotions or receive "triple points" for in-store purchases on designated days.[52] These proprietary and private label credit card programs provide a competitive advantage to department stores as compared to smaller specialty retailers, which often do not have the ability to offer similar benefits to attract customers. But as loyalty programs have come to play a larger role among retailers in general (households typically carry about thirty membership cards, less than half of which are actively used), it is a challenge for department store retailers to make their

---

44. *Id.*
45. Kate Taylor, *Macy's Is Copying Amazon in Its Latest Attempt to Lure Customers Back to Its Stores*, BUS. INSIDER (Mar. 29, 2018), https://www.businessinsider.com/macys-amazon-lockers-online-orders-pick-up-in-store-2018-3.
46. DEPARTMENT STORES, *supra* note 22, at 3.
47. *Id.*
48. *Id* at 7.
49. ASAEDA, RETAILING, *supra* note 24, at 2.
50. *Id.* at 16.
51. BLOOMINGDALE'S, https://www.bloomingdales.com/b/loyallist/benefits/.
52. NEIMAN MARCUS, http://www.incircle.com/.

loyalty programs stand out to customers.[53] Some retailers are offering more reward incentives beyond discounts, such as Nordstrom, which offers free alterations to customers enrolled in its loyalty program.[54]

Department store retailers typically use elaborate systems to manage their inventory from initial purchase to eventual sale to the consumer. They also utilize sophisticated information systems to manage their operations. These information systems include: point-of-sale systems to record and process transactions; merchandise planning systems to forecast and allocate merchandise; inventory management systems to monitor inventory levels; and electronic data interchange to process orders.[55] Department store retailers may use multiple warehouse and distribution centers that ship products to stores, but the latest growing trend is the use of retail stores themselves as distribution hubs in order to expedite shipping and thereby better compete with Amazon.[56] As of June 2018, one-third of department store companies currently use brick-and-mortar stores as fulfillment centers for online orders, and another quarter of retailers plan to implement the practice.[57]

Department stores typically purchase their inventory from a combination of manufacturers, distributers, and importers. Although department stores often have long-term relationships with particular suppliers, they seldom have formal long-term supply contracts.[58] Department store buyers may use historical sales levels and fashion trends to make inventory purchasing decisions. In addition to carrying a variety of recognized name brand merchandise, many department stores have sought to distinguish themselves by developing their own private label brands carried exclusively in their department stores.[59] Private label products give retailers more control over product design and quality and typically have higher margins.[60] Consumers have increasingly come to trust the quality of private labels at least as much as nationally recognized brands, and many consumers see private label brands as a better value for their money.[61] And, as a result, private label sales have been on the rise in department stores—a trend that is expected to continue. In 2017, for example, Macy's private apparel labels accounted for roughly 20% of revenues, and by 2020,

---

53. DEPARTMENT STORES, *supra* note 22, at 8.
54. *Id.*
55. *Id.* at 3.
56. *Id.* at 8.
57. *Id.*
58. *Id.* at 3.
59. BURNS, *supra* note 21, at 324.
60. DEPARTMENT STORES, *supra* note 22, at 8.
61. YANUSHEVSKY, RETAIL, *supra* note 25, at 8.

that number is projected to reach 40%.[62] A department store retailer may also differentiate its merchandise by negotiating arrangements with certain nationally recognized brands to supply its retail stores with limited distribution products or specific pieces each season that are available exclusively in its stores.[63]

Although department stores often sell merchandise from different brands under one section, such as women's shoes or men's apparel, department stores also may have "in-store shops," or separate shops within the larger department store, for certain recognized fashion brands. A few luxury fashion brands staff their "in-store shops" with their own sales associates, use their own distinctive marketing concepts and display formats, and sell their products directly to customers. These luxury brands prefer "in-store shops" for their products in order to offer higher levels of knowledgeable service, and to control pricing and discounting strategies. Other recognized fashion brands have separate shops that are more of a collaboration with the department store retailer. In such cases, the brand and the retailer negotiate an arrangement in which the brand may share the costs of special fixtures, and the brand may select the retailer's sales associates who will staff the shop (and may pay some or all of their compensation), but the products are sold by the brand to the retailer, which then resells them to the consumer. These arrangements offer the opportunity for increased sales for the fashion brand and retailer because dedicated sales associates may more effectively monitor inventory levels, display products more appropriately, and offer better customer service. Some department store retailers also use the "in-store shop" concept for their online stores by creating virtual "designer shops." The real estate issues associated with creating "in-store shops" are discussed in chapter 13.

§ 11:1.2 *Specialty Stores*

Specialty stores include retail stores that focus on stocking merchandise "for a well-defined target market," and/or that "carry the merchandise of one manufacturer or brand."[64] One of the largest specialty retailers in the United States is Gap Inc., which sells men's, women's, and children's clothing, and operates over 3,000 stores worldwide.[65] Gap Inc. owns Gap, Banana Republic, Old Navy (although it is slated to be spun off), and Athleta brands, each of which carries its

---

62. *Id.*
63. DEPARTMENT STORES, *supra* note 22, at 3, 8.
64. BURNS, *supra* note 21, at 325.
65. GAP INC., http://www.gapinc.com.

own private-label merchandise and targets a distinct market.[66] For example, Old Navy targets "value-oriented customers," while Banana Republic targets "sophisticated customers."[67] Athleta, Gap Inc.'s fitness and lifestyle brand, targets "active women."[68]

Specialty retailers are the most significant sales channel for apparel, particularly women's apparel.[69] Some specialty stores offer "a limited but deep assortment of merchandise," generally in one or two price zones.[70] Since these specialty stores are focused on a limited range of merchandise, they are expected to provide higher levels of service and knowledge with respect to the range of merchandise offered. For example, Sunglass Hut and Solstice each carry primarily sunglasses; they provide customers with a deep selection, from high-end designer sunglasses to lower priced merchandise, and from casual models to models geared towards sports or active lifestyles.[71] Due to this heavy concentration in a narrow category of products, these types of specialty stores often are less sensitive to broad macroeconomic conditions and retail trends than general merchandisers; but, on the other hand, they are more susceptible to shifts in narrowly defined consumer preferences or demographics.[72] Fashion fads and trends significantly affect clothing sales, so stores that compete in more trend-driven segments may experience wide fluctuations.[73] High-end stores that rely on a particular image are particularly likely to suffer as a result of changes in consumer tastes.[74]

§ 11:1.3 Discount Department Stores

Discount department stores are large, high-traffic stores offering value-oriented pricing on a variety of merchandise such as apparel, personal care products, electronics, household furnishings, and groceries.[75] Discount department stores typically occupy large spaces (averaging 100,000 square feet), either as stand-alone stores or as anchors in strip malls.[76] Discount department stores are able to

---

66. CLOTHING STORES, *supra* note 3, at 2.
67. *Id.*
68. *Id.*
69. YANUSHEVSKY, TEXTILES, APPAREL & LUXURY GOODS, *supra* note 1, at 36.
70. BURNS, *supra* note 21, at 325.
71. SUNGLASS HUT, https://www.sunglasshut.com/; SOLSTICE, https://www.solsticesunglasses.com/.
72. VICTOR AHLUWALIA & XIONG JUN GOON, CFRA EQUITY RESEARCH, INDUSTRY SURVEYS, SPECIALTY RETAIL (Apr. 16, 2018) [hereinafter AHLUWALIA, SPECIALTY RETAIL], at 25.
73. CLOTHING STORES, *supra* note 3, at 8.
74. *Id.*
75. DUN & BRADSTREET, FIRST RES., DISCOUNT DEPARTMENT STORES, at 1 (June 18, 2018).
76. *Id.*

maintain competitive prices through a combination of supply chain management systems, quantity discounts obtained from manufacturers, high turnover rates on products, and lower overhead.[77] In the United States, the discount department store industry is highly concentrated (the eight largest companies account for almost 100% of industry revenue) and includes such major participants as Walmart Inc. and Target Corporation.[78] According to some studies, over 80% of American households have shopped at either a Walmart or a Target store.[79] Traditionally, the grocery offerings at discount department stores did not include fresh, perishable foods, but, because consumers buy food more frequently than most other goods, Walmart and Target are increasingly offering a full selection of groceries to increase foot traffic at both new and existing locations.[80]

Some discount department stores have collaborated successfully with luxury fashion designers to reach a broader range of customers and compete with the fast fashion companies. In a typical collaboration, the fashion designer produces a new branded line of apparel or accessories, at lower price points, specifically for a particular discount department store retailer that sells the line exclusively for a limited period of time. These collaborations have been beneficial to retailers by attracting new customers, and have benefitted fashion designers by increasing their revenues and broadening their customer base, at least temporarily, without negatively affecting their brand image.[81] For example, since 2006, Target Corporation has collaborated with international designers and high-end brands such as Missoni, Alexander McQueen, Proenza Schouler, Lilly Pulitzer, and Victoria Beckham to offer limited-edition apparel and accessory collections. The Missoni collection, launched in September 2011, included apparel, luggage, home furnishings, and beauty products priced at between $2.99 and $599 (Missoni items at Bergdorf Goodman cost up to $12,000 at the time), and sold out within a few days.[82]

Most discount department stores also sell private label products that are intended to offer near brand-name quality at lower prices, while also providing better margins for retailers than the sale of

---

77. *Id.*
78. *Id.*
79. *Id.* at 2.
80. *Id.* at 7.
81. Catherine Valenti, *Designers Flock to Mass-Market Retailers*, ABC NEWS (May 1, 2002); Abha Bhattarai, *Upscale, Downscale: Target Draws Customers With Collaborations With High-End Brands*, WASH. POST (Apr. 13, 2018), https://wapo.st/2qup7yc?tid=ss_mail&utm_term=.4d6df9c32efd.
82. Stephanie Clifford, *Demand at Target for Fashion Line Crashes Web Site*, N.Y. TIMES (Sept. 13, 2011), https://nyti.ms/2JgFZBv.

third-party goods.[83] And with the stigma of "generic" goods becoming increasingly outdated, the private-label market share is growing.[84] For example, Target announced plans to launch twelve new private label brands, ranging from apparel to home goods, following the massive success ($2 billion in revenue in 2017) of its private-label childswear line, Cat & Jack, which launched in 2016.[85] Some industry experts now refer to the stylish, low-price, private-label clothing sold at discount department stores like Walmart and Target as its own clothing category: "cheap chic."[86]

§ 11:1.4 *Off-Price Stores*

Off-price stores sell brand-name merchandise at discounted prices.[87] Off-price apparel retail has been a rapidly growing sales channel, particularly among younger women.[88] Off-price stores generally belong to one of the following three categories, described below: factory outlets, off-price retailers, and retailer-owned off-price stores.

[A] Factory Outlets

Factory outlet stores have evolved considerably from their historical origins. Initially, brand manufacturers opened factory outlet stores to sell their own branded merchandise that either deviated from technical production specifications or remained unsold at the end of a season. These company factory outlets were located near the company's manufacturing facilities, and the products were sold only to company employees at discounted prices.[89] Although company factory outlets began to offer their merchandise for sale to the general public, they remained single-store locations throughout the 1970s.[90] The first enclosed factory outlet center opened in 1980 and was not intended to compete directly with traditional retail malls.[91] As malls comprised entirely of factory outlets began to proliferate in the United States and Europe, manufacturers needed to increase the amount and variety of merchandise available for factory outlet sale. In a significant

---

83. AHLUWALIA, SPECIALTY RETAIL, *supra* note 72, at 23.
84. *Id.*
85. *Id.*
86. CLOTHING STORES, *supra* note 3, at 8.
87. BURNS, *supra* note 21, at 327.
88. CLOTHING STORES, *supra* note 3, at 1.
89. COUGHLAN, A. & SOBERMAN, D., A SURVEY OF OUTLET MALL RETAILING: PAST, PRESENT AND FUTURE 2 (Insead 2004), http://flora.insead.edu/fichiersti_wp/inseadwp2004/2004-36.pdf.
90. *Id.*
91. *Id.*

shift, companies began to produce merchandise styled similarly to their full-price offerings, but with a slightly lower quality, specifically for sale at lower prices in their factory stores.[92] Outlet stores, and malls comprised of outlets, are generally located in more remote locations than other shopping centers.[93]

[B] Off-Price Retailers

In contrast to factory outlet stores, off-price retailers typically buy imperfect merchandise and excess inventory from a variety of full-price retailers and sell them at discounted prices in their own stores. Off-price retailers include Ross Stores and TJX stores (for example, Marshall's and T.J. Maxx). Off-price retailers are able to maintain discounted prices on merchandise because their business model and buying cycles operate differently than those of full-price retail stores. Rather than buying from manufacturers for each seasonal cycle, off-price retail buyers continually look for merchandise to carry in their stores. As a result of the timing of their purchases, buyers are able to get merchandise that was not purchased on the standard cycle by full-priced department stores or boutiques.

Although some exclusively online off-price retailers such as Overstock.com and 6pm have entered the market, traditional brick-and-mortar off-price retailers have managed to thrive without a significant online presence.[94] TJX stores have limited online e-commerce offerings, while Ross Stores have none.[95] These retailers have been referred to as "Amazon-proof" because they provide customers a "treasure-hunt" shopping experience that is difficult to replicate online.[96] Additionally, because value-focused retailers target lower income families, who may have more limited online access, off-price stores have more brick-and-mortar growth opportunities than some other categories of retailers.[97] New store expansion is currently expected to drive

---

92. Andria Cheng, *Coach Profit Rises 26%, but Margin Falls Short*, MARKET WATCH, WALL ST. J. (Jan. 25, 2011), https://www.marketwatch.com/story/coach-plans-buyback-as-profit-rises-26-2011-01-25.
93. CLOTHING STORES, *supra* note 3, at 1.
94. Mary Hanbury, *We Shopped at TJ Maxx and Ross to See Which Was a Better Discount Store—and the Winner Was Clear*, BUS. INSIDER (May 17, 2018), https://www.businessinsider.com/ross-stores-and-tj-maxx-compared-pictures-details-2018-5.
95. *Id.*
96. Elaine Low, *Department Stores, Malls in 2018: Amazon Will Let You Live—For Now*, INV'R'S BUS. DAILY (Jan. 6, 2018), https://www.nasdaq.com/article/department-stores-malls-in-2018-amazon-will-let-you-live-for-now-cm901372 [hereinafter Low].
97. AHLUWALIA, SPECIALTY RETAIL, *supra* note 72, at 19.

revenues for both TJX and Ross Stores.[98] However, some experts predict that these off-price retailers' lack of meaningful online presence will eventually take a toll if those retailers do not invest in e-commerce.[99]

[C] Retailer-Owned Off-Price Stores

Some department store retailers have opened their own off-price outlet stores. These retailers operate outlet stores as a separate distribution channel to sell excess merchandise from their regular stores or special orders purchased specifically for the off-price store at discounted prices.[100] These off-price outlets include Saks Fifth Avenue's OFF 5th, Nordstrom Rack, and Neiman Marcus Last Call.[101] In addition to carrying merchandise from their respective full-price retail stores, these off-price outlet stores often also carry private-label brands.

§ 11:1.5 Boutiques

Boutiques, which are smaller retail stores (and may even occupy less than 2,000 square feet[102]), target a specific niche market or sell unique products. Traditionally, the term "boutique" was used to describe an independent, "one-of-a-kind" brick-and-mortar store that specialized in fashionable apparel or accessories for a local market. The term "boutique" has been used to describe chains of smaller stores, such as Francesca's Collections, which target fashion-forward women in their twenties and thirties,[103] and online retailers that offer unique products. Boutiques typically buy a limited amount of pieces from the collections of several different brands, and curate their merchandise to reflect their image or style. Boutiques operate on a smaller scale than department stores, appealing to customers seeking a more personalized shopping experience. At a boutique, a customer may have the ability to develop a relationship with the

98. *Id.*
99. Low, *supra* note 96.
100. BURNS, *supra* note 21, at 328.
101. ASAEDA, RETAILING, *supra* note 24, at 17.
102. CLOTHING STORES, *supra* note 3, at 1.
103. James Brumley, *Why Francesca's Is Thriving When It Shouldn't Be*, SEEKING ALPHA (Apr. 22, 2017), https://seekingalpha.com/article/4064295-francescas-thriving.

boutique's owners.[104] The prominence of luxury fashion boutiques has continued to rise over time, and certain commentators have predicted that, by 2025, luxury fashion e-commerce will have a quarter of the industry's market share.[105] As an example of such growth, Farfetch Limited, a global luxury fashion platform with a network of more than 1,000 luxury brand and boutique partners, announced an expansion of its strategic partnership with JD.com, China's largest retailer, in February 2019.[106]

§ 11:1.6 Pop-Up Shops

Pop-up stores are temporary retail locations set up by brands or retailers to offer selected merchandise for sale for a limited time period.[107] Pop-up stores are generally intended to raise brand awareness and to attract consumer interest rather than to generate significant revenues.[108] The pop-up store concept has been used both by high-end and mainstream brands. High-end brands may gravitate towards temporary concept stores to reach a broader audience, even if visitors are only entering the store to browse,[109] while mainstream brands may use pop-up stores to offer more limited and exclusive items. Online retailers also sometimes use pop-up stores as a test prior to opening a full brick-and-mortar store. Amazon, for example, experimented

---

104. See the *Vogue* article on Ikram Goldman, owner of the Chicago boutique Ikram; *see* Lynn Yaeger, *Ikram Goldman: On Timeless Style and Her New Flagship Store*, VOGUE MAG. (Aug. 2, 2011, 4:47 PM), https://www.vogue.com/article/ikram-goldman-time-well-spent.

105. Andria Cheng, *What Farfetch's IPO Filing Says about the $300 Billion Luxury Fashion Industry*, FORBES (Aug. 21, 2018), https://www.forbes.com/sites/andriacheng/2018/08/21/what-farfetchs-ipo-filing-says-about-the-300-billion-luxury-fashion-industry/#67ab157ebb1f.

106. Press Release, Business Wire, Farfetch and JD.com Expand Strategic Partnership to Build the Premier Luxury Gateway to China (Feb. 28, 2019), https://www.apnews.com/58a37854d9904a49bcd2a0c65b0c2ca0.

107. Pop-up store leases usually last between six weeks and a year, with tenants commonly willing to sign month-to-month leases. Nellie Day, *Pop-Up Shops: A Short-Term Solution to Vacancies*, THE BALANCE (Jan. 13, 2019), https://www.thebalancesmb.com/pop-up-shops-a-short-term-solution-to-vacancies-2866555.

108. Steven Johnson, *Why There Are Pop-Ups for Everything Now*, ATLANTIC (Nov. 8, 2017), https://www.theatlantic.com/business/archive/2017/11/popup-shop-corporate/545054/ [hereinafter Johnson].

109. For example, Agent Provacateur launched a destination pop-up shop for Valentine's Day in Dublin, open only from January 24 to February 14 2019. Marie Kelly, *Luxury Lingerie Brand Agent Provocateur Opens in House of Fraser, Dundrum Today*, IMAGE (Jan. 24, 2019), https://www.image.ie/fashion/luxury-lingerie-brand-agent-provocateur-opens-in-house-of-fraser-dundrum-today-140264.

with pop-up stores before opening its first permanent store.[110] And one-time online-only lingerie retailer Adore Me decided to establish brick-and-mortar stores based on the feedback it received at pop-up locations.[111]

§ 11:1.7 *Internet Retailers*

Although most brick-and-mortar retailers now have an online presence, there are some retailers that use the Internet as their exclusive or primary retail sales channel. The impact of such retailers on the industry has continued to expand over the last year; according to the U.S. Census Bureau, e-commerce sales in the first quarter of 2018 totaled $123.7 billion, which represented a 3.9% increase over the fourth quarter in 2017.[112] In addition to this financial impact, e-commerce has had significant social impact by introducing customers to a more convenient and accessible shopping process with near immediate results, termed the "Amazon Effect," with Amazon as the most recognizable face of such developments.[113]

Online apparel retailers face certain marketing challenges that are not faced by brick-and-mortar retailers. Customers cannot physically feel the texture of the clothing or try on garments for proper size, styling, or fit. Accordingly, customers rely more heavily on visual images, detailed product specifications, and customer reviews located on the online retailers' website pages. Online retailers are increasingly providing customers with improved ways to view their products online, including by utilizing photographs from different angles, zooming features, and videos in which customers can see the apparel or accessories on models in movement. They are also offering consumers more personalized services, such as the "chat with a specialist" option available on many sites, and are tracking consumer preferences more closely than traditional retail stores.[114] Many online retailers offer fast and free shipping options, and have more lenient return policies than brick-and-mortar retailers to compensate for the customers'

---

110. Greg Bensinger, *What's That? An Amazon Store?*, WALL ST. J. (Nov. 29, 2013), https://blogs.wsj.com/digits/2013/11/29/whats-that-an-amazon-store/; Johnson, *supra* note 108.

111. Tom Coleman, *Here's How 5 E-Commerce Brands Used Pop-Up Stores to Get Ahead*, STOREFRONT MAG. (June 2018), https://blog.thestorefront.com/heres-how-5-e-commerce-brands-used-pop-ups-to-get-ahead/.

112. Kacen J. Bayless, *Analyzing the Amazon Effect*, COLUMBIA BUS. TIMES (Aug. 30, 2018), http://columbiabusinesstimes.com/2018/08/30/analyzing-amazon-effect/.

113. *Id.*

114. BURNS, *supra* note 21, at 332–33.

inability to try on apparel and accessories before making purchases. Some brick-and-mortar retailers are able to offer rapid same-day fulfillment options by filling online orders from their brick-and-mortar retail stores (either through in-store pickup options or by delivery from the store). Online retailers are pursuing various strategies to offer comparable delivery options, including partnering with brick-and-mortar retailers and using distribution centers and third-party delivery services.

Online flash sale sites, such as Gilt, Rue La La, and Ideeli, have attracted a broad customer base. Gilt, the first of these flash sale sites, offered manufacturers an outlet for excess designer goods, but with a higher profile, more fashionable image so the brands would not tarnish their high-end image by selling at deeply discounted prices.[115] Flash sale sites cater to urban sophisticates and largely gained popularity based on word of mouth marketing, building a loyal customer base.[116] By emphasizing limited supplies and a limited time to purchase the merchandise, Gilt prompted customers to make rapid purchasing decisions. Nearly 50% of the company's revenue was generated within one hour of a sale launching.[117] As more flash sale sites emerged, and the quality and quantity of available merchandise decreased, Gilt's growth slowed and it undertook a variety of initiatives to boost growth, such as adding sales for luxury vacations and restaurant meals and offering private-label brands manufactured in Los Angeles factories.[118] Eventually, Hudson's Bay purchased Gilt at a steep discount, however it later sold the company to competing flash sale site, Rue La La, after it was unable to improve performance.[119]

Other new e-commerce business models have emerged, including personal subscription retail services, such as ShoeDazzle, JustFab, and Stitch Fix; collaborative consumption online retailers, such as Rent the Runway and Bag Borrow or Steal; and retailers offering pre-owned or vintage fashion, such as The RealReal and ReFashioner. Personal subscription online retailers offer subscribers a selection of goods to

---

115. *The Rise, Stumble and Future of Gilt Groupe's Business Model*, BUS. OF FASHION (Dec. 15, 2011), https://www.businessoffashion.com/articles/fashion-tech/the-rise-stumble-and-future-of-gilt-groupes-business-model.

116. *Id.*

117. *Id.*

118. Isabel Vincent, *Fashion Web Site's Bogus Brands a "Gilt" Trip,"* N.Y. POST (July 1, 2012), https://nypost.com/2012/07/01/fashion-web-sites-bogus-brands-a-gilt-trip/.

119. Richard Kestenbaum, *Why Rue La La Is Acquiring Gilt Groupe*, FORBES (June 4, 2018), https://www.forbes.com/sites/richardkestenbaum/2018/06/04/why-rue-la-la-is-acquiring-gilt-groupe/#38e8bb627534.

purchase every month, based on style surveys, at a flat rate.[120] These personal subscription models may generate relatively steady revenue streams.[121] ShoeDazzle, which also benefits from endorsements and monthly style selections by celebrities, offers stylist-selected shoes at affordable prices.[122] Collaborative consumption online retailers, such as Rent the Runway, offer customers the ability to rent or "borrow" high-end and luxury merchandise, such as handbags and apparel, for a fraction of the full retail price for a limited time period.[123] This business model assumes that certain luxury items may be used only for a single occasion, or reflect the current trend only for a single season, and therefore renting such items may be more attractive than paying the full purchase price to own them.[124] Retailers of pre-owned fashion often target specific market segments (such as high-end designers) and may emphasize the eco-friendly nature of reselling pre-owned fashion products.[125] Online auction sites, such as eBay.com and Invaluable.com, also facilitate online sales of both new and pre-owned apparel and accessories. Several other retailers have begun to follow the lead of the subscription pioneers like Stitch Fix: Sephora, The Gap, Ann Taylor, J.C. Penney, Under Armor, and Amazon all began to experiment with the subscription box experience in 2017.[126] The benefits of tapping into the subscription model include establishing monthly recurring revenue through stronger relationships with customers—customers that are given a personalized sense of belonging through subscriptions are more likely to remain loyal to a given company.[127]

From its founding in 1994, when the company solely sold books, Amazon has grown to be the world's largest online retailer and one of the largest retailers of any kind in the United States.[128] Amazon's

---

120. *The Rise of New Business Models*, BUS. OF FASHION (Jan. 18, 2012), https://www.businessoffashion.com/articles/fashion-tech/e-commerce-week-the-rise-of-new-business-models.
121. *Id.*
122. SHOEDAZZLE, https://www.shoedazzle.com/howitworks.htm.
123. Helena Pike, *Will the 'Sharing Economy' Work for Fashion?*, BUS. OF FASHION (May 8, 2016), https://www.businessoffashion.com/articles/fashion-tech/will-the-sharing-economy-work-for-fashion-rent-the-runway-rental.
124. *Id.*
125. *See, e.g.*, KINDRED BLACK, https://www.kindredblack.com/pages/about.
126. George Ricter, *Think Tank: Why Established Retailers Will Continue Adopting Subscription Models*, WOMEN'S WEAR DAILY (Feb. 9, 2018), https://wwd.com/business-news/business-features/think-tank-subscriptions-1202545824/.
127. *Id.*
128. *From Bookstore to Superstore: The Evolution of Amazon*, CHANNEL ADVISOR (May 4, 2018), https://www.channeladvisor.com/blog/industry-trends/from-bookstore-to-superstore-the-evolution-of-amazon-com/.

growth can be attributed to its expansion into a variety of merchandise categories and by acting as both a business-to-business service provider (including cloud computing services and third-party marketplaces), and as a retail sales channel. The company's methods of disrupting the retail market have included free shipping for Amazon Prime members; two-day, one-day, and one-hour shipping for Amazon Prime members; transparency in price leadership; and unconventional return policies.[129] Amazon's success has significantly impacted the retail industry, as traditional retailers are investing heavily to improve their online operations and in-store customer experience in order to more effectively compete with Amazon.

One method brick-and-mortar stores have taken to counter the Amazon Effect is to rethink what the purpose of physical space is, such as the new retail store Nordstrom Local, a clothing store with no dedicated inventory, where customers can pick up and try on their online purchases at the store-front; beverages are also available.[130] Brick-and-mortar retailers have also come up with improved methods of customer analytics unavailable to e-commerce websites, such as the decision of candy retailer Lolli and Pops to track the paths of customers once they entered stores to see why certain inventory was not performing well at particular locations.[131] Finally, brick-and-mortar stores have also undertaken more efforts to leverage mobile technology in store—according to a study done by SOTI, 92% of shoppers prefer stores that offer mobile experiences, and 89% of retailers are expected to provide their employees with mobile technology by 2020.[132]

Not to be outdone, Amazon has continued to strive towards new innovations in its business model. Paralleling other companies that started online then moved to brick-and-mortar spaces, in June 2017, Amazon acquired Whole Foods for $13.7 billion, and launched a brick-and-mortar retail experience in Seattle called Amazon Go.[133] At this location, there is no store staff to help customers with their shopping, and customers are able to enter their payment into their mobile app and simply walk out of the store with their purchases.[134]

129. Trent Riter, *Amazon Changed the Face of Retail, Let Us Count the Ways*, SPSCOMMERCE (July 11, 2017), https://www.spscommerce.com/blog/ways-amazon-changed-retail-spsa/.

130. Lin Grosman, *What the Amazon Effect Means for Retailers*, FORBES (Feb. 22, 2018), https://www.forbes.com/sites/forbescommunicationscouncil/2018/02/22/what-the-amazon-effect-means-for-retailers/#563591502ded.

131. *Id.*

132. *Id.*

133. Caglar Bozkurt, *Amazon's Retail Expansion Strategy*, TWENTIFY (Apr. 20, 2018), http://www.twentify.com/blog/amazons-retail-expansion-strategy.

134. *Id.*

§ 11:1.8 Mail-Order (Catalog) Retailers and Television Retailers

Mail-order (or catalog) retail and television retail represent a small portion of global retail sales, but are important retail distribution channels. Mail-order retailers (such as L.L. Bean, Inc.) historically did not invest in stores or traditional forms of advertising, but marketed their merchandise to targeted customers through catalogs, from which customers could place orders by mail or over the telephone. Mail-order retailers typically maintain highly valued lists of customers who have purchased merchandise in the past and monitor their customers' purchasing behavior.[135] Mail-order retailers are able to reach a broad consumer base without investing capital in opening brick-and-mortar stores. The rising costs of printing and mailing, combined with the growth of the Internet have, however, reduced the number of catalogs that are mailed annually to consumers from nearly twenty billion in 2007 to less than half that amount in 2018.[136] Although many mail-order retailers have begun to devote more resources to online ordering, web-based advertising, and email messaging, successful sellers still rely on print catalogs to tell stories, inspire consumers, and cut through digital fatigue.[137] To combat rising print costs, retailers are using demographic and spending data to optimize catalog delivery to coincide with specific holidays and life events that are important to their targeted consumers.[138]

Home shopping retailers, such as evine (formerly ShopNBC and then ShopHQ), HSN, and QVC, use television shopping channels to sell a broad range of merchandise, including apparel, accessories, and cosmetics, which customers order over the telephone or online.[139] Home shopping channels typically sell exclusive products through daily broadcasts with a broad customer reach. QVC reaches 360 million households around the globe via seventeen television networks and

---

135. Matthew Hudson, *Catalog Retailers and Mail Order Sales*, THE BALANCE (Jan. 15, 2018), https://www.thebalancesmb.com/catalog-retailers-and-mail-order-sales-2890250.

136. Michael Stone, *Amazon Looks Back to the Future With a Retail Catalog*, FORBES (July 31, 2018), https://www.forbes.com/sites/michaelstone/2018/07/31/amazon-looks-back-to-the-future/#4b8b90fd4130.

137. *Id.*

138. Courtney Reagan, *Millennials Are More Interested in Catalogs Than Your Grandmother Is*, CNBC (Dec. 21, 2017), https://www.cnbc.com/2017/12/21/millennials-are-more-interested-in-catalogs-than-your-grandmother-is.html.

139. BURNS, *supra* note 21, at 474.

in 2017 purchased the Home Shopping Network to solidify its dominance in video and ecommerce.[140] Home shopping retailers may also have brick-and-mortar stores. For example, HSN encourages viewers who feel the products they see on television are too expensive to visit their outlet stores, which offer a variety of promotions and discounts.[141]

Channels like QVC have remained competitive by cultivating memorable host and guest personalities who inspire high customer retention rates and intensity levels.[142] This unique blend of entertainment and shopping to some degree complements traditional in-store shopping and e-commerce, as 74% of QVC customers report that they also shop on Amazon.[143] Still, QVC and HSN's parent company, Qurate, announced over 2,000 job cuts after the merger of QVC and HSN so it could dedicate more funds to "accelerate the business's digital transformation."[144] To remain competitive in the years ahead, the company plans to spend the savings on new facilities, warehouse automation, social and digital growth, and enhanced content.[145]

§ 11:1.9 *Transition to Brick-and-Mortar Stores and the Growth of Omni-Channel Retailing*

The past few years have witnessed a transition back to the roots of retail: from retailers operating purely through e-commerce and mobile commerce platforms, to retailers that originally only operated online opening brick-and-mortar stores.

Warby Parker, an eyeglass retailer founded online in 2010, was one of the first movers sparking the trend of e-commerce retailers opening brick-and-mortar stores—"'online moving offline.'"[146] In 2013, Warby Parker opened its first store in New York, where many

---

140. Press Release, QVC, HSN, Inc. Joins QVC Group as Liberty Interactive Completes Acquisition (Dec. 29, 2017), https://corporate.qvc.com/newsroom/pressrelease/hsn-inc-joins-qvc-group-liberty-interactive-completes-acquisition/.

141. HOME SHOPPING NETWORK, HSN OUTLET, https://www.hsn.com/content/HSN_Outlet/261.

142. 2017 INVESTOR DAY, QVC GROUP, at 13 (Nov. 16, 2017).

143. *Id.* at 19.

144. Gina Acosta, *Accelerating Transformation at QVC, HSN*, RETAIL LEADER (Oct. 10, 2018), https://retailleader.com/accelerating-transformation-qvc-hsn.

145. *Id.*

146. Lauren Thomas, *Warby Parker Aims to Run Nearly 100 Stores This Year, as Other Web Shops Follow*, CNBC (Feb. 15, 2018) [hereinafter Thomas], https://www.cnbc.com/2018/02/15/as-warby-parker-approaches-100-stores-other-internet-brands-follow.html.

shoppers were requesting a place to try their glasses on.[147] Warby Parker has grown its physical footprint over the past five years, using physical locations to "gain exposure, new customers, and insights into shopping behavior."[148] As of February 2018, Warby Parker operated sixty-four storefronts across the United States and was well on its way toward operating 100 storefronts by the end of the year.[149] Warby Parker has also experimented with pop-up shops, stores on wheels, and other methods to reach customers.[150]

Neil Blumenthal, CEO of Warby Parker, described the "'presentation by retail experts of either [online] or [offline]'" as a "'false choice.'"[151] Indeed, the lines between online and offline retailing are increasingly blurred, with other companies like Everlane and Untuckt developing a physical footprint as well.[152] Carbon38 began to expand offline in September 2018.[153] The RealReal opened its first physical location in Los Angeles on July 31, 2018, following the opening of a New York store in November 2017.[154] Reformation has fourteen stores across the United States as of March 2019.[155]

Many retailers begin with trial pop-up shops.[156] CNBC reported that some online retailers use their online databases, locate a segment of loyal customers, and initiate a physical store in that area,[157] while other online retailers determine physical store location based on the best available real estate and development of relationships with top

---

147. *Id.*
148. *Id.*
149. *Id.*
150. *Id.*
151. *Id.*
152. *Id.*; *see also* EVERLANE, https://www.everlane.com/visit-us; UNTUCKIT, https://www.untuckit.com/blogs/store-locations.
153. *Carbon38 to Open First Permanent Store*, SGBMEDIA (Mar. 29, 2108), https://sgbonline.com/carbon38-to-open-first-permanent-store/.
154. Ingrid Schmidt, *Luxe Consignment Brand the RealReal Opens L.A. Storefront Complete With Whiskey Bar*, HOLLYWOOD REPORTER (July 31, 2018) [hereinafter Schmidt], https://www.hollywoodreporter.com/news/thereal-real-la-store-opens-fashion-family-a-whiskey-bar-1130923.
155. REFORMATION, https://www.thereformation.com/pages/stores?utm_source=TnL5HPStwNw&utm_medium=10&utm_campaign=LinkShare&sid=LS298X102&ranMID=40090&ranEAID=2116208&ranSiteID=TnL5HPStwNw-1PoQ83y44DLXOs9XtZuXjQ.
156. Mark Walsh, *The Future of E-Commerce: Bricks and Mortar*, THE GUARDIAN (Jan. 30, 2016) [hereinafter Walsh], https://www.theguardian.com/business/2016/jan/30/future-of-e-commerce-bricks-and-mortar.
157. Thomas, *supra* note 146.

U.S. mall and shopping center owners.[158] Certain real estate developers are even offering flexible lease terms to up-and-coming retailers.[159] These flagship stores are a terrific marketing vehicle for the brand's online presence.[160] Warby Parker co-founder and co-chief executive Dave Gilboa said that there is a halo effect, "where stores themselves become a great generator of awareness for our brand and drive a lot of traffic to our website, as well and [stet] accelerate our e-commerce sales."[161] Rati Levesque, chief merchant for The RealReal, explained that "'[h]aving bricks-and-mortar space is really a growth accelerator by creating brand awareness and adding credibility; when customers come in to feel and touch and understand what quality means to us, it gives them a better understanding of our standards.'"[162]

While some stores sell products that the customer may take with them that day, other originally online-only retailers have opened what amount to showrooms, which allow customers to try on and sample products while keeping real estate and other traditional retail costs low.[163] One such example is Bonobos "guideshops," which let customers try on clothing, with orders placed online for home delivery.[164]

Notably, it is becoming increasingly hard to launch a brand only online, due to the crowded and competitive e-commerce environment.[165] By opening physical stores, retailers aim to increase awareness and "draw customers in a realm where the retail options aren't infinite or influenced by an all-powerful gatekeeper."[166]

Despite the resurgence of brick-and-mortar locations, it is critical to remember that the brick-and-mortar store is just *one* avenue for a consumer to shop in the modern world. Customers bounce between brick-and-mortar, online shopping, and mobile and social media platforms.[167] For example, a survey by Retail Dive revealed that two-thirds

---

158. *Id.*
159. *Id.*
160. Walsh, *supra* note 156.
161. *Id.*; *see also* Douglas MacMillan, *Warby Parker Adds Storefronts to Its Sales Strategy*, WALL ST. J. (Nov. 17, 2014), https://www.wsj.com/articles/warby-parker-adds-storefronts-to-its-sales-strategy-1416251866.
162. Schmidt, *supra* note 154.
163. Walsh, *supra* note 156.
164. *Id.*; *see also* Caroline Lane, *Online Retailers Shift to Brick-and-Mortar Stores: Here Is Why*, NATURAL INSIGHT (Aug. 16, 2017), https://www.naturalinsight.com/blog/retail-merchandising.
165. *Id.*
166. *Id.*
167. Caroline Lane, *The Future of Retail: Generation Z and Experiential Marketing*, NATURAL INSIGHT (Aug. 2, 2017) [hereinafter Lane], https://www.naturalinsight.com/blog/the-future-of-retail-generation-z-and-experiential-marketing.

of surveyed customers said they research products online (at least occasionally) before shopping for them in a store.[168] Consumers are therefore looking for a seamless experience that can fuse these avenues together.[169] Forward-thinking companies are conscious that the two channels (online and offline) work most effectively together,[170] representing omni-channel retailing. As Paul Martin, the UK Head of Retail for KPMG in the United Kingdom, said in KPMG's 2017 Global Online Consumer Report, "'[c]ompanies should be channel agnostic, meaning it does not matter if they start with online or offline, what matters is that all channels are interlinked to give consumers the convenience they need. Online plays a major part in the customer journey or ROPO (research online, purchase offline).'"[171] Sephora EVP of Omni Retail Mary Beth Laughton noted that it is up to retailers to make it as easy as possible for customers to switch back and forth between mediums.[172] Sephora even went so far as to merge its in-store and digital retail teams to create one omni-retail department in 2017.[173] Illustrative of the importance of omni-channel retailing, in 2016 the National Retail Federation's annual "Big Show" conference in New York featured several sessions that included "omni-channel retailing" in their titles.[174]

With the rise of Generation Z, or individuals born in the mid-1990s and beyond, the importance of an integrated online and offline presence will likely only increase. Sixty-seven percent of Generation Z prefers to shop in a brick-and-mortar store most of the time, with another 31% preferring to shop in-store sometimes.[175] Their preference

---

168. Sandy Skrovan, *Why Researching Online, Shopping Offline Is the New Norm*, RETAIL DIVE (May 17, 2017), https://www.retaildive.com/news/why-researching-online-shopping-offline-is-the-new-norm/442754/.
169. *Id.*
170. Lana Bandoim, *Can You Integrate Brick-And-Mortar Stores With Online Shopping?*, FORBES (May 30, 2019), https://www.forbes.com/sites/ lanabandoim/2019/05/30/can-you-integrate-brick-and-mortar-stores-with-online-shop ping#29f185f52aec.
171. KPMG, THE TRUTH ABOUT ONLINE CONSUMERS, 2017 GLOBAL ONLINE CONSUMER REPORT 13 (2017) [hereinafter KPMG], https://assets.kpmg.com/content/dam/kpmg/xx/pdf/2017/01/the-truth-about-online-consumers.pdf.
172. CB INSIGHTS, SEPHORA TAKEDOWN: HOW SEPHORA BUILT A BEAUTY EMPIRE TO SURVIVE THE RETAIL APOCALYPSE 6 (2018) [hereinafter CB INSIGHTS, SEPHORA], https://www.cbinsights.com/research/report/sephora-teardown/.
173. *Id.*
174. Walsh, *supra* note 156.
175. IBM INST. FOR BUS. VALUE, UNIQUELY GENERATION Z, WHAT BRANDS SHOULD KNOW ABOUT TODAY'S YOUNGEST CONSUMERS 14 (2017), https://www-935.ibm.com/services/us/gbs/thoughtleadership/uniquelygenz/.

for purchasing in stores doesn't mean that the "offline" has replaced the "online"; rather, Gen Z typically has conducted online research before even venturing into a brick-and-mortar store.[176] Gen Z wants to engage with their favorite brands across all channels.[177] As a result, retail companies need to strengthen both their in-store and online experiences "to serve this mobile-focused, high spending demographic."[178]

§ 11:1.10 *Shopping for the Experience*

In addition to the resurgence of brick-and-mortar stores, shoppers are turning to "innovative brands that are disrupting and revolutionizing the traditional in-store shopping experience."[179] Where customers want to shop and spend their money is no longer governed by brand messages, but is instead influenced by the experiences the customers receive from brands, which include customer service, digital experiences, and retail ambiance.[180] As e-commerce start-ups are expanding into the brick-and-mortar space, corporate retailers are also shaking up their store formats to focus on branding and customer experience.[181] As Sephora's SVP of Omni Experience & Innovation explained, "'[c]onsumers are looking for retail stores to be creative spaces. They are looking for experiences.'"[182] Retail stores are defining themselves as destinations and experiences, "offering discoveries, dining options, and human connections."[183]

The RealReal store in Los Angeles, for example, has a whiskey bar, partners with Hollywood names to clean out their closets (often for a cause), offers curbside pickups and drop-offs for consignment, and retains in-store experts (horologists, gemologists, tailors, and personal stylists) for its shoppers.[184] Reformation's crown jewel is its fitting room. There is only one of each item on display in the store; shoppers send an item to their fitting room by requesting it on a monitor or asking an employee to scan the barcode. The clothes then wait for the

---

176. Lane, *supra* note 167.
177. *Id.*
178. *Id.*
179. *Id.*
180. Daniel Newman, *Customer Experience Is the Future of Marketing*, FORBES (Oct. 13, 2015), https://www.forbes.com/sites/danielnewman/2015/10/13/customer-experience-is-the-future-of-marketing/#62ae5814193d.
181. CB INSIGHTS, SURVIVING THE RETAIL APOCALYPSE 49–50 (2018), http://mdcventures.vc/wp-content/uploads/2016/07/CB-Insights_Retail-Apocalypse-Briefing.pdf.
182. CB INSIGHTS, SEPHORA, *supra* note 172, at 10.
183. Christina Binkley, *At Luxury Stores, It Isn't Shopping, It's an Experience*, WALL ST. J. (Apr. 16, 2017), https://www.wsj.com/articles/at-luxury-stores-it-isnt-shopping-its-an-experience-1492394460; Lane, *supra* note 167.
184. Schmidt, *supra* note 154.

customer in their fitting room. Fitting rooms are equipped with phone chargers and speakers, and shoppers have the option to change the lighting. The displays also show the materials used in the products, including the item's "RefScale" (a measure of the garment's water usage, carbon emissions, and waste generated in manufacturing). Different sizes of garments can be requested through in-room tablets, and then appear in the "magic wardrobe" in the fitting room, with employees opening the other side and hanging new items.[185] Sephora has focused on in-store technologies for beauty enthusiasts, such as its beacon technology that allows Sephora's app to recognize when a user is in a Sephora store and then provide the user with an in-store map, daily promotions, and the user's online shopping cart and wish list.[186] Sephora is also experimenting with smaller store formats, dubbed "Sephora Studios," which are designed to blend into local neighborhoods and complement, rather than replace, the larger store formats.[187] These Sephora Studios aim to foster personalized connections between customers and beauty associates, providing a more intimate shopping experience.[188] The RealReal, Reformation, and Sephora all have created experiences that a shopper cannot find online.

Today's consumers "'are looking at personalization of services'" and are "'more similar to the 1920s consumer with a personal relationship with shopkeepers.'"[189] Consumers want to be treated as individuals.[190] Younger consumers desire personalized interactions, customized experiences, and one-on-one engagement, and want to feel like part of a community.[191] Retailers are using experiential marketing campaigns, experimenting with installations, showrooms, events, and so forth.[192] Broad cultural phenomena offer another platform for marketing by retailers and brands, with some customers contributing free air time via Instagram. Sephora even promoted its Sephora Collection at Coachella 2018 by offering free hair and makeup touch-ups and festival-inspired looks in a Wi-Fi-enabled and air-conditioned tent.[193]

---

185. Mella Robinson, *This Apparel Startup Fixed the Worst Part of Shopping for Clothes in Stores–and It Could Defy Retail's Curse*, BUS. INSIDER (Jan. 18, 2019), https://www.businessinsider.com/how-reformation-clothing-stores-beat-online-shopping-2018-1.
186. CB INSIGHTS, SEPHORA, *supra* note 172, at 10.
187. *Id.* at 37–38.
188. *Id.*
189. KPMG, *supra* note 171, at 18.
190. *Id.* at 18, 34.
191. *Id.* at 34; Lane, *supra* note 167.
192. Lane, *supra* note 167.
193. CB INSIGHTS, SEPHORA, *supra* note 172, at 25.

Certain brands (in addition to Reformation, which focuses on sustainable manufacturing) are distinguishing themselves by offering their customers the experience of making a social impact. There are various models of philanthropy employed in connection with fashion.[194] Some brands choose to aid developing countries by setting up "one-for-one" and "buy-one-donate-one" models to the needy or establishing manufacturing facilities to help people (usually women) gain control of their lives.[195] FEED, for example, was founded in 2007 with "the simple idea of creating products that would engage people in the fight against hunger in a tangible way."[196] Each product has a number stamped on it reflecting the number of meals or micronutrient packets provided with its purchase. Warby Parker also focuses on social responsibility, working with a handful of partners worldwide to ensure that for every pair of glasses sold, a pair is distributed to someone in need.[197] TOMS originally subscribed to the "buy-one-donate-one" model, providing one pair of shoes to impoverished children for each pair of shoes purchased; however, with the increasing concern that giving shoes hurts local shoemakers, TOMS has expanded its outreach to include the gifts of sight, water, safe birth, and kindness.[198] Other designers choose medical-based charities with personal meaning for them, perhaps selecting diseases that have affected them or their loved ones.[199] Still other companies cede control to the consumer, letting shoppers select a charity to receive a donation from a list of affiliated charities.[200] Designs That Donate is one such methodology through which consumers choose their charity—with over 200 affiliated charities, the consumer selects the charity that will receive the money Designs That Donate applies for each sale.[201]

Companies that promote their support for different causes have been gaining traction with the Millennial crowd.[202] According to Cone Communications research, 87% of millennials are more willing to

---

194. Lauren Parker, *Consumers Increasingly Embracing Brands That Give Back*, ACCESSORIES MAG. (Apr. 25, 2017) [hereinafter Parker], https://www.accessoriesmagazine.com/brands-moving-ahead-giving-back/.
195. *Id.*
196. *Id.*; *see also* FEED, ABOUT, https://www.feedprojects.com/about-feed.
197. WARBY PARKER, BUY A PAIR, GIVE A PAIR, https://www.warbyparker.com/buy-a-pair-give-a-pair.
198. Parker, *supra* note 194; TOMS, WHAT WE GIVE, https://www.toms.com/what-we-give.
199. Parker, *supra* note 194.
200. *Id.*
201. *Id.*; *see also* DESIGNS THAT DONATE, https://designsthatdonate.com/.
202. Danielle Sabrina, *Rising Trend: Social Responsibility Is High on Millennials' List*, HUFFINGTON POST (Feb. 3, 2017, 11:18 AM), https://www.huffingtonpost.com/danielle-sabrina/rising-trend-social-respo_b_14578380.html.

purchase a product with a social or environmental benefit (compared to the 83% U.S. average) and 70% of millennials are prepared to pay more for a product to make an impact on issues they care about (compared to the 66% U.S. average).[203]

Still other companies are offering their customers the experience of fashion customization, with made-to-order fashion. Ordering a custom piece was traditionally only an option for bespoke and couture customers.[204] But the recent rush of technological advances have created another option: "economical individualized clothing (call it mass customization) for the middle market."[205] Sizing algorithms and e-commerce enable companies to offer an assortment of designs and fits at similar price points to off-the-rack prices, thus enabling consumers to buy made-to-order clothing and shoes online.[206] Frilly is a made-to-order women's clothing site that lets shoppers customize each garment.[207] Frilly is the first fashion online platform delivering true customization, allowing customers to choose the color, hem length, neckline, sleeve style, and fabric, in addition to adding details like a scalloped hem or a belt.[208] Frilly's proprietary 3D rendering software shows each option as the customer builds and adjusts their piece.[209] Frilly's goal is to bring made-to-measure luxury to the masses, with prices from $58 to $2,000.[210] Frilly also boasts a commitment to sustainability, with chemical-free pieces, a cut-to-order model to minimize waste, and in-house wear and cleaning tests.[211]

§ 11:2 Arrangements Between Retailers and Vendors

The line between fashion brands and fashion retailers is becoming increasingly indistinct. Many fashion brands sell their products

---

203. *New Cone Communications Research Confirms Millennials as America's Most Ardent CSR Supporters*, CONE (Sept. 23, 2015), http://www.conecomm.com/news-blog/new-cone-communications-research-confirms-millennials-as-americas-most-ardent-csr-supporters.
204. Deborah L. Jacobs, *Made-To-Order Fashion Goes Mainstream*, FORBES (July 1, 2013), https://www.forbes.com/sites/deborahljacobs/2013/07/01/made-to-order-fashion-goes-mainstream/#4ec2e926195d.
205. *Id.*
206. *Id.*
207. Celia Shatzman, *New Site Frilly Makes Customizable Made-To-Order Fashion With Just a Few Clicks*, FORBES (Aug. 29, 2017, 11:00 AM), https://www.forbes.com/sites/celiashatzman/2017/08/29/new-site-frilly-makes-customizable-made-to-order-fashion-with-just-a-few-clicks/#725f29664ba8.
208. *Id.*
209. *Id.*
210. *Id.*
211. *Id.*

directly to consumers through owned or licensed retail stores, catalogs, and their own e-commerce platforms.[212] Through direct-to-consumer sales, a brand owner can offer its entire product line and create a "showcase" for the brand.[213] Furthermore, streamlined relationships allow brands to engage directly with consumers on social media, gather data on trends and spending habits, and build digital communities that enhance product exposure.[214] Many brand owners, however, continue to distribute their products by selling them at wholesale prices to retailers, such as department stores and Internet retailers, who in turn resell them at retail prices to the ultimate consumer. This strategy can significantly expand the geographic consumer base for the brand.[215] A company may engage in either "open distribution," in which it sells its products to any type of retailer, or "selected distribution," in which it sells only to select retailers based on their geographic or customer profile.[216]

The arrangements that govern the relationship between the company, as vendor, and the retailer, as buyer, include a combination of standard terms and conditions, individual purchase orders, and oral agreements. The Model Uniform Commercial Code, which forms the basis of uniform commercial codes adopted in all fifty states,[217] provides a framework for interpreting agreements between the vendor and the retailer, and also provides default rules for matters where the agreements are silent or unclear.[218] In particular, Article 2 of the Model Uniform Commercial Code, relating to sales, "applies to transactions in goods," but not services.[219] For the purposes of this section,

---

212. Eilene Zimmerman, *Designers and Manufacturers Bypass Department Stores; Frustrated With Giant Retailers, Small Brands Open Their Own Local Outposts*, CRAIN'S N.Y. BUS., Dec. 17, 2012, at 16.

213. Suman Bhattacharyya, *'A Lovely Irony': DTC Brands Are Flocking Toward Multibrand Physical Retail Spaces*, DIGIDAY (Oct. 24, 2018), https://digiday.com/retail/dtc-multi-brand-retail-spaces/.

214. Katherine Hays, *How Direct-to-Consumer Brands Are Tearing Down and Rebuilding the Marketing Scene*, ADWEEK (Mar. 26, 2018), https://www.adweek.com/brand-marketing/how-direct-to-consumer-brands-are-tearing-down-and-rebuilding-the-marketing-scene/.

215. Michael Elmgreen, *Selling Wholesale to Retailers: How to Choose Retail Partners*, HANDSHAKE (June 25, 2015), https://www.handshake.com/blog/selling-wholesale-how-to-qualify-retailers-to-stock-your-products.

216. BURNS, *supra* note 21, at 444–45.

217. States Adopting the UCC, U.S. LEGAL [hereinafter U.S. LEGAL], https://uniformcommercialcode.uslegal.com/states-adopting-the-ucc/.

218. The United Nations Convention on Contracts for the International Sale of Goods (CISG) applies to international product sales. The buyer and seller may agree to opt out of parts of or the entire CISG. *See* CISG, I.I.(6).

219. U.C.C. § 2-102.

all references to the "UCC" are to the Uniform Commercial Code as in effect in the State of New York.[220]

This section describes the principal elements of the arrangements between vendors and retailers.

§ 11:2.1 Vendor Standards

When an apparel or accessory vendor and a retailer form a relationship, they typically agree to a set of terms and conditions that will govern purchases and sales between the parties. In many cases, the retailer (particularly a large retailer) possesses more of the leverage in this negotiation, as there are often numerous vendors competing for space in the stores (physical or virtual) of a limited pool of retailers.[221] Retailers prefer that vendors accept the retailer's terms and conditions because they tend to be both retailer-friendly in substance and comprehensive in the issues they address. Having standard terms and conditions that apply to all vendors with which the retailer does business also eases the administrative and operational burden on a retailer that manages relationships with numerous vendors.

A retailer often posts its extensive terms and conditions, sometimes called a "vendor standards" or "vendor compliance" manual, on a website for potential vendors to review.[222] Vendors often can access these documents after logging into a secure site. The vendor manual cover the retailer's policies, procedures, and standards, including technology for transmitting orders, labels (including Universal Product Code, or "UPC" requirements), packing and presentation of products, audits, shipping (typically the vendor pays all freight and handling), routing, returns, terms of payment, and insurance.[223] The vendor standards also include company policies regarding safety and sustainability, and compliance with labor standards.[224] The retailer may also have supplemental vendor standards depending on the type of product.[225] The vendor must sign a legal compliance form (a short

---

220. N.Y. U.C.C. Law § 2-102 (McKinney 2018).

221. GUILLERMO JIMENEZ & BARBARA KOLSUN, FASHION LAW: A GUIDE FOR DESIGNERS, FASHION EXECUTIVES, AND ATTORNEYS 200 (2009) [hereinafter JIMENEZ, FASHION LAW].

222. *Id.*

223. Curt Barry, *How to Make Vendor Compliance Programs Work for You*, F. CURTIS BARRY & CO. (2018), https://www.fcbco.com/articles-and-white papers/articles/bid/129567/how-to-make-vendor-compliance-programs-work-for-you.

224. *E.g.*, NORDSTROM DIRECT SUPPLIER COMPLIANCE MANUAL 10-12 (2015), http://www.nordstromsupplier.com/content/sc_manual/ndirect/ndirect_manual.pdf.

225. *See id.* at 20.

document indicating it agrees to the vendor standards) as a prerequisite to a business relationship with the retailer.[226]

Certain vendors, particularly luxury fashion brands that have more exclusive distribution strategies, may have the leverage to negotiate individual agreements with retailers that have different terms than the retailer's vendor standards.[227] Similarly, a retailer may be willing to consider specific deviations from its vendor standards in order to maintain an important vendor relationship.

A vendor may request copies of the financial statements of a retailer or other assurances that the retailer can pay for the items that it orders.[228] This is more common where the retailer is a small-volume specialty boutique rather than a large department store chain with publicly available financial statements. A vendor's factoring firm also may require certain credit checks of retailers before accepting invoices.

As part of the vendor standards, particularly for department stores, a vendor may agree to invest in electronic data interchange (EDI) technology systems that link the vendor and the retailer through interconnected computer terminals.[229] The retailer uses electronic point-of-sale scanners to read the bar code on each product that is sold, and then relays information to the vendor as to the color, size, and sale price of such product.[230] This exchange of data allows vendors to tailor their production to more closely fit consumer demand and makes shipping and distribution more efficient.[231]

Moreover, EDI enables retailers to maximize efficiency by automatic replenishment (the "just in time" reordering of certain merchandise) based on changing inventory levels and projected requirements. Automatic replenishment is most commonly used for basic items, which are easier and faster to produce than seasonal or fashion

---

226. *See* JIMENEZ, FASHION LAW, *supra* note 221.

227. *See* Kelsey Lindsey, *Why the Relationship Between Department Stores and Luxury Brands Is Changing*, RETAIL DIVE (Nov. 10, 2015), https://www.retaildive.com/news/why-the-relationship-between-department-stores-and-luxury-brands-is-changin/408703/ (detailing tension between luxury brands and retailers as brands open their own stores and expand further into ecommerce).

228. *See* U.C.C. § 2-609.

229. *E.g.* MACY'S, VENDOR STANDARDS at 9–16 (2017), https://macysnet.com/MDOCWeb/documents.aspx?document=Vendor%20Standards.

230. *See* YANUSHEVSKY, RETAIL, *supra* note 25, at 24.

231. Shahrooz Kohan, *Why an Integrated ERP & EDI Solution Is Essential for Growing Fashion Companies*, AIMS 360 (Sept. 5, 2017), https://www.aims360.com/aims360-sps-outreach-innovative-edi-customers/.

apparel, and are increasingly being manufactured in automated factories.[232] A stock keeping unit (SKU) is a unique identifier assigned to each product that a retailer sells. The retailer will perform a bulk projection for each SKU at the beginning of each season. Thereafter, based on sales data that the retailer generates and transmits to the vendor through EDI, additional products are automatically reordered as necessary, depending upon which sizes and colors the retailer sells to customers. The retailer might require special standards for vendors to participate in automatic replenishment, such as consistently being able to fill purchase orders at a certain percentage.[233] Research consistently indicates that when retailers and vendors collaborate, such as sharing point-of-sale data, both parties can benefit.[234]

§ 11:2.2 Selecting Products; Discounts and Markdown Allowances

Retailers may arrange for the purchase of products from vendors as many as six to nine months before the products will arrive in retail stores (though this lead time continues to shorten).[235] For major retailers, management may set overall annual financial objectives for the company; thereafter, each of the retailer's buyers may develop a merchandise plan, consistent with these objectives, based on historic sales data and more recent trends.[236] Buyers may go "to market" and meet with individual vendors in their showrooms to review the set of product samples in the vendor's line for each season. The vendors may give the retailers product catalogs or line sheets (documents that contain renderings of the styles (with size, color, and price information)) available for production, to aid them in placing their orders.[237]

---

232. YANUSHEVSKY, RETAIL, *supra* note 25, at 24.

233. *See, e.g.*, SAKS FIFTH AVENUE, VENDOR STANDARDS MANUAL (June 3, 2019) [hereinafter SAKS VENDOR STANDARDS], at 10, https://hbcediextranet.hbc.com/main.aspx?site=EdiExtranet&langid=en&d=116&p=/116/cps__documents_EN.cps.

234. *The Impact of Retail Collaboration in an Evolving Space*, SKU LOCAL (Mar. 20, 2018), http://www.skulocal.com/insights/the-impact-of-retail-collaboration-in-an-evolving-space/; *see also* YANUSHEVSKY, RETAIL, *supra* note 25, at 24. Although a vendor gives up some bargaining power when it depends on key retail accounts for a large portion of its total revenues, the vendor's performance also improves as the retailer gains a greater market share. Thus, collaborative behavior between vendors and suppliers, such as sharing point-of-sale data and coordinating planning, will result in competitive advantages for both parties.

235. *See* YANUSHEVSKY, RETAIL, *supra* note 25, at 22.

236. *Id.* at 14.

237. *See generally* BURNS, *supra* note 21, at 265–66.

New technology is impacting the market experience by allowing retailers and vendors to perform more transactions online. For example, companies like Joor, Ordre, and Farfetch create digital wholesale marketplaces with intuitive user interfaces, high resolution imagery, and virtual reality technology to connect fashion brands with retailers; brands upload their line sheets and retail buyers digitally browse and order merchandise.[238] These companies are also increasingly using their technology to sell directly to consumers, offering partners higher margins and control over brand experience.[239]

A retailer may agree to purchase from a vendor specific quantities of particular SKUs, broken down by color and size. Because the products have not yet been produced, this agreement is tentative. Orders could be canceled by the vendor for a variety of reasons; for example, the vendor might not have received enough orders from its retail accounts to make production of a certain style or color cost-effective, or there could be a delay in production caused by circumstances outside of the vendor's control.[240] The retailer and the vendor typically will communicate throughout the production process in order to address any such issues in advance of scheduled delivery of the products.

Retailers rarely carry a vendor's complete line and, instead, choose styles that they expect to sell well, given their customer profiles. Retailers may also negotiate exclusivity arrangements, under which the vendor agrees not to sell certain SKUs to any other retailers. Often, a vendor and a retailer will negotiate a front-end discount (for example, 10% off the wholesale price of a vendor's product). The front-end discount is often only a verbal understanding, without written documentation; in some cases, it may be a long-standing arrangement that applies to all products sold by the vendor to the retailer.

Markdown allowances (MDAs) are a form of support that a vendor may provide to a retailer at the end of a season if the vendor's products fail to sell at the full retail price (and therefore must be discounted).[241] The rationale for MDAs is that vendors should be required to absorb part of the cost if their products do not sell well in the retail stores.[242] The retailer may also benefit from terms that allow it to return to

---

238. *See* Sarah Shannon, *Alibaba Snaps up Stake in Ordre*, BUS. OF FASHION (May 18, 2018), https://www.businessoffashion.com/articles/news-bites/alibaba-snaps-up-stake-in-ordre.

239. *Id.*

240. *See* BURNS, *supra* note 21, at 306–07.

241. *See generally* MARY GAHLHAR, THE FASHION DESIGNER SURVIVAL GUIDE: START AND RUN YOUR OWN FASHION BUSINESS 140–41 (2008).

242. *See* Vanessa O'Connell, *Saks Settles Vendor Lawsuits*, WALL ST. J. (Nov. 23, 2007), http://online.wsj.com/article/SB119567367880700863.html.

the vendor products that do not sell during the season and deduct a corresponding amount from the vendor's account.

The level of MDAs depends on the vendor's business strategy and industry standards. A vendor is often willing to bear or pay MDAs to encourage a retailer to continue to buy its products. Vendors will reduce markdown allowances when their profits and image suffer from over-promotion by retailers at discount prices. Brands such as Ralph Lauren and Coach have made notable MDA reductions in response to department retailers' attempts to appeal to price-conscious consumers.[243] Similar to front-end discounts, MDAs are rarely documented in a written agreement and are typically a verbal understanding. This is consistent with UCC § 2-202, which provides that parties' written agreements may also be interpreted or supplemented by course of dealing, usage of trade, or course of performance.

The New York Supreme Court, in a 2007 decision, found that a course of performance between a vendor and a retailer could supplement the retailer's vendor standards manual.[244] Where performance takes place in repeated occurrences, acceptance of past practices is relevant in interpreting the parties' agreement. Thus, the court declined to dismiss the vendor's claim alleging improper markdown allowances, noting that:

> Where the contract for sale involves repeated occasions for performance by either party with knowledge of the nature of the performance and opportunity for objection to it by the other, *any course of performance accepted or acquiesced in without objection shall be relevant* to determine the meaning of the agreement.[245]

§ 11:2.3 Purchase Orders

The UCC broadly defines the concept of a contract, providing that "a contract for the sale of goods may be made in any manner sufficient to show agreement, including offer and acceptance, [and] conduct by both parties which recognizes the existence of a contract . . . ."[246] As long as there is agreement between the parties, a contract may be found

---

243. Mary Hanbury, *Michael Kors, Gap, and Ralph Lauren Are Trying a New Strategy to Survive the Retail Apocalypse – and Customers Are Going to Hate It*, BUS. INSIDER (Jan. 23, 2019), https://www.businessinsider.com/michael-kors-gap-and-ralph-lauren-cut-discounts-2018-1.

244. Feinberg v. Federated Dep't Stores, Inc., 832 N.Y.S.2d 760, 763 (Sup. Ct. 2007) (citing U.C.C. § 2-202(1)(a)).

245. *Id.* at 763–64 (citing U.C.C. § 2-208) (emphasis added).

246. N.Y. U.C.C. Law § 2-204 (2018).

notwithstanding that it cannot be determined when the contract was made, or if specific terms are missing from the contract.[247]

The retailer's vendor standards may expressly specify that the transmission of the purchase order constitutes an offer.[248] The UCC provides that unless otherwise indicated, an offer may be accepted "in any manner and by any medium reasonable in the circumstances."[249] However, the vendor standards might specify that a vendor's acceptance may be indicated by written confirmation, shipment of goods, participation in an inventory replenishment program, or other performance consistent with acceptance.[250] The UCC provides that, between merchants, if an offeree includes additional or different terms in its acceptance, such additional or different terms would become part of the contract unless the offer expressly limits acceptance to the terms of the offer.[251] Therefore, vendor standards often provide that acceptance of the offer constitutes the vendor's acceptance of all terms and conditions therein, and that the retailer's prior written consent is required for any different or additional terms in the seller's acceptance.[252]

§ 11:2.4 *Shipping, Delivery and Risk of Loss*

To facilitate the purchasing process, the retailer and the vendor need to agree on the shipping and delivery terms for the purchased products. For large retailers, a vendor may ship goods to the retailer's distribution center (DC). Items are then regrouped and shipped from a centralized DC to the retailer's individual stores. The retailer and the vendor must also agree on which party bears the cost and risk of loss for each part of the shipping and delivery process.

The International Chamber of Commerce developed a set of shorthand shipping and delivery terms called "International Commercial terms" or "Incoterms" to be used in international commerce (though

---

247. *See id.* § 2-305 ("The parties if they so intend may conclude a contract for sale even if the price is not settled.").

248. *See, e.g.*, MACY'S—MACYS.COM—MASTER PURCHASING AGREEMENT (May 2019) [hereinafter MACY'S PURCHASING AGREEMENT], § 1 (utilizing "Offer and Acceptance" as the header of the section discussing the vendor's acceptance of the agreement), https://macysnet.com/MDOCWeb/documents.aspx?document=Vendor%20Standards%20-%20Master%20Purchasing%20A.

249. N.Y. U.C.C. LAW § 2-206 (2018).

250. *See, e.g.*, MACY'S PURCHASING AGREEMENT, *supra* note 248, § 1.

251. N.Y. U.C.C. Law § 2-207 (2018).

252. *See, e.g.*, MACY'S PURCHASING AGREEMENT, *supra* note 248, § 3; NORDSTROM TERMS AND CONDITIONS OF PURCHASE ORDER [hereinafter NORDSTROM PURCHASE ORDER TERMS], https://www.nordstromsupplier.com/Content/sc_manual/POTermsAndConditions.pdf.

the latest version of Incoterms recognizes the application of Incoterms to both international and domestic transactions).[253] Parties that wish to incorporate these standard shipping and delivery terms into their agreements must specify that the Incoterms definitions apply.[254]

In the absence of such specification, the relevant state law will apply. The Model Uniform Commercial Code historically contains a set of default shipping and delivery terms governing domestic transactions.[255] These definitions are similar to the Incoterms, however, they have several notable differences. For example, the UCC's definitions of "FOB" and "FAS" (described below) require the seller to take additional steps during delivery before the risk is transferred to the seller.[256] As a result, these distinctions may create ambiguities when a U.S. company ships goods internationally.[257] To mitigate these issues, the code's authors repealed its shipping and delivery definitions in 2001, citing "inconsisten[cy] with modern commercial practices."[258] However, no states ever adopted the changes and the ALI reinstated the definitions in 2011.[259] Today, most states follow a set of guidelines similar to those proposed in the UCC to govern domestic transactions.[260]

Commonly used UCC shipping and delivery terms include the following:

- ***F.O.B. (free on board)*** means that the risk passes from sender to receiver at the specified location.[261] Thus, for orders that are shipped "FOB DC," the vendor is responsible for delivering the goods to the DC, and the risk of loss of the goods does not pass to the retailer until the goods arrive at the DC. In contrast, if an order is shipped "FOB factory," title passes to the retailer and the retailer assumes responsibility when the

---

253. INCOTERMS 2010, INT'L CHAMBER OF COMMERCE (2010), https://www.iccwbo.org/WorkArea/DownloadAsset.aspx?id=2147497569.
254. DAVID ZARFES & MICHAEL BLOOM, CONTRACTS & COMMERCIAL TRANSACTIONS 286 (2014).
255. U.C.C. § 2-319-24 (2018).
256. Manal Bensafi et al., *Incoterms: Too Simple?*, ASS'N OF CORP. COUNSEL (Jan. 31, 2017), https://www.acc.com/resource-library/incoterms-too-simple.
257. *Id.*
258. Amendments to Uniform Commercial Code Art. 2—Sales, AM. LAW INST., 81–84 (2001).
259. *Recommendation of the Permanent Editorial Board for the Uniform Commercial Code to withdraw the 2003 Amendments to UCC Articles 2 and 2A from the Official Text of the Uniform Commercial Code*, 65 CONSUMER FIN. L. Q. REP. 150, 160 (2011).
260. U.S. LEGAL, *supra* note 217.
261. N.Y. U.C.C. Law § 2-319(1) (2018).

goods are loaded onto the transport vehicle at the vendor's factory. Returned goods are generally shipped by the retailer "FOB origin," which means the retailer has a duty to ship the goods from the origin at the retailer's premises, not to deliver the goods to the vendor at its warehouse.[262] The risk of loss does not pass until the goods are loaded onboard the carrier at the origin.[263]

- ***F.A.S. (free alongside ship)*** means the risk passes from seller to buyer when the goods are brought alongside the vessel at a designated location.[264]
- ***C.F.*** or ***C. & F. (cost and freight)*** indicates which party bears the freight costs, when a different party bears the risk of loss. For example, if goods are shipped "C.F. DC," the vendor pays for the freight to the DC, but the risk of loss passes upon shipment at the vendor's warehouse.[265]
- ***C.I.F. (cost, insurance, and freight)*** is similar to C.F. except that the costs required to be borne also include insurance.[266]

§ 11:2.5 Acceptance and Terms of Payment

Under the UCC, the buyer has a right to reject goods that do not conform to the parties' agreement.[267] In addition, under the UCC, the buyer has a right to inspect goods before payment or acceptance.[268] The UCC provides that goods are deemed to be accepted when, after a reasonable opportunity to inspect, the buyer accepts the goods, fails to reject the goods, or takes actions inconsistent with the seller's ownership of the goods.[269] Acceptance precludes the buyer's rejection of the goods.[270]

Once the goods are accepted, the retailer becomes obligated to pay the vendor. Where a contract requires payment before inspection of the goods, such payment does not impair the buyer's right to inspect the goods.[271] A retailer's vendor standards may further provide that

262. *See, e.g.*, SAKS VENDOR STANDARDS, *supra* note 233, at 29, 38.
263. N.Y. U.C.C. Law § 2-319(1)(c) (2018).
264. *Id.* § 2-319(2).
265. *Id.* § 2-320.
266. *Id.*
267. *Id.* § 2-601.
268. *Id.* § 2-513.
269. *Id.* § 2-606.
270. *Id.* § 2-607(2).
271. *Id.* § 2-512.

the retailer reserves the right to hold for the vendor or return to the vendor any rejected merchandise.[272]

Because of the frequency of transactions, a vendor normally maintains an ongoing trial balance with the retailer, reflecting the numerous payments and adjustments between them. The vendor has a strong interest in receiving payment promptly, to increase its cash flow and maximize its ability to produce additional products.

§ 11:2.6 Chargebacks

Although the retailer has a right to inspect the goods before they are deemed accepted, in practice it is logistically impossible for the retailer to inspect immediately the thousands of SKUs it receives. Many retailers provide in their vendor standards that acceptance of non-conforming goods is not a waiver of the retailer's right to recover damages.[273] Therefore, the retailer typically recovers damages after acceptance, in the form of "chargebacks."

Chargebacks are deductions from a vendor's account for any failures to comply with the vendor standards. Vendor standards typically specify that the vendor must ship in exact conformity with the purchase order.[274] The retailer will assess chargebacks if the vendor ships fewer units (a "shortage"), more units (an "overage"), or different units than as stated on the purchase order ("distortion"). Chargebacks are assessed at different rates depending on the type of noncompliance. For example, chargebacks may range from $25 per receipt, plus a per unit cost, for missing hangers, to $250 per receipt, plus a per carton cost and freight, for shipping to the wrong distribution center, to 100% of the purchase price plus all expenses incurred by the retailer for shipping problematic goods, such as prohibited furs.[275] These chargebacks are reflected in offsets against amounts payable by the retailer to the vendor. Occasionally, the retailer will choose not to deduct chargebacks owed for the sake of preserving a relationship with the vendor if, for example, it receives only a few damaged goods out of an otherwise acceptable shipment.

Deficiencies in product shipments are not always discovered immediately; often, they are not discovered until the retailer conducts its next periodic inventory, which can sometimes be up to a year later. Some retailers require or encourage their vendors to utilize radio frequency identification (RFID), a system that uses radio frequency electromagnetic fields to transmit information wirelessly

---

272. *See, e.g.*, NORDSTROM PURCHASE ORDER TERMS, *supra* note 252, § 5.
273. *See, e.g.*, SAKS VENDOR STANDARDS, *supra* note 233, at 27.
274. *See id.*
275. *See, e.g.*, MACY'S—MACYS.COM—MACY'S VENDOR STANDARDS (Oct. 2017), at 39, Appendix I.

and automatically identify a product that is labeled with such a tag.[276] This enables retailers to take inventory of their stock by waving a detector wand over multiple items rather than scanning each item's bar code individually.[277] Although the fashion industry has been slow to adopt RFID systems, promising case studies at retailers such as Macy's indicate the technology has the potential to significantly increase inventory accuracy and reduce unforeseen defects.[278]

It is not uncommon for vendors to dispute chargebacks and other retailer deductions through legal action.[279] From the viewpoint of retailers, however, chargebacks create incentives for vendors to adhere to their agreements with retailers and allow retailers to process items more efficiently. One vendor standards manual states: "The purpose is not to chargeback your company, but to achieve compliance so we can move merchandise to the selling floor quickly."[280] In 2017 Target and Walmart announced tighter vendor requirements and increased penalties for non-compliance in an effort to improve their supply chains.[281] In response, many vendors complained that the retailers intended to use these tools as new profit centers and urged them to instead focus on improving communication regarding their delivery expectations.[282] It remains to be seen whether changes in chargeback policies will ultimately enhance or disrupt collaboration between retailers and vendors.

---

276. *See* EFFICIENT CONSUMER RESPONSE, MEASURING THE IMPACT OF RFID IN RETAILING 4 (Feb. 2018), http://ecr.pl/wp-content/uploads/2018/03/Measuring-the-Impact-of-RFID-in-Retailing.pdf.
277. *See* BURNS, *supra* note 21, at 32–33.
278. Barbara Thau, *Is the 'RFID Retail Revolution' Finally Here? A Macy's Case Study*, FORBES (May 15, 2017), https://www.forbes.com/sites/barbarathau/2017/05/15/is-the-rfid-retail-revolution-finally-here-a-macys-case-study/#47d21f443294.
279. *See, e.g.*, Lanfear v. Home Depot, 718 F. Supp. 2d 1364, 1370 (N.D. Ga. 2010); Int'l Design Concepts, LLC v. Saks Inc., 486 F. Supp. 2d 229, 237 (S.D.N.Y. 2007); Complaint at 14, *id.*, (No. 05 Civ. 4754); *see also* Saks Inc., Annual Report (Form 10-K), at 15–16 (May 26, 2008); *see also* Saks Inc., Current Report (Form 8-K), at 1 (Sept. 5, 2007); *see also* Michael Barbaro, *Saks Settles With S.E.C. on Overpayments*, N.Y. TIMES, Sept. 6, 2007, https://www.nytimes.com/2007/09/06/business/06saks.html.
280. *See, e.g.*, SAKS VENDOR STANDARDS, *supra* note 233, at 37.
281. Chris Caouette, *New Year's Resolution for Suppliers: Get in Charge of Chargebacks*, MULTI-CHANNEL MERCHANT (Jan. 3, 2018), https://multichannelmerchant.com/blog/new-years-resolution-suppliers-get-charge-chargebacks/.
282. *Id.*

Retailers typically do not assess chargebacks on late or unfilled shipments; instead the retailer has a right to cancel these orders. Recognizing that most apparel sold in the United States is manufactured abroad, the parties typically try to work together in the event of a delay in the supply chain.[283] However, late shipments may impair a vendor's eligibility to participate in an automatic replenishment program,[284] and repeated late shipments may cause the retailer to terminate its relationship with the vendor.

§ 11:2.7 Consignments

Another form of contractual relationship between a vendor and a retailer is a consignment transaction, in which the retailer pays the vendor for the product only *after* the retailer has actually sold the product to the ultimate consumer. This arrangement shifts to the vendor the risk that products will not sell in the retail stores. The retailers, in turn, can generate profits from any consigned products that are sold in its stores, without incurring any losses for unsold stock. Consignment arrangements permit retailers to carry and sell more products, resulting in a larger variety of merchandise for customers.

New or small vendors may agree to a consignment arrangement with a retailer for a trial period. If a vendor can demonstrate that its products have high sales volume, high margin, and "turn" (the ability to sell the entire quantity initially shipped to stores), then the retailer may be more likely to form a long-term relationship with the vendor. Although consignment still only comprises a small percentage of the overall apparel market, it has expanded into a $50 billion sector in the last decade.[285] Much of the growth has been in the sale of secondhand or hobbyist designer goods online as ecommerce retailers look to capitalize on swiftly changing trends while minimizing risk.[286]

A more detailed narrative regarding consignments in the retail industry can be found in chapter 23, section 23:4.5.

---

283. Bradley Blackburn, *Clothing 'Made in America': Should U.S. Manufacture More Clothes?*, ABC NEWS (Mar. 10, 2011), http://abcnews.go.com/Business/MadeInAmerica/made-america-clothes-clothing-made-usa/story?id=13108258#.UMocBeT7J8E.

284. *See, e.g.*, SAKS VENDOR STANDARDS, *supra* note 233, at 10.

285. FUNG BUS. INTELLIGENCE CENTRE, ONLINE CONSIGNMENT MARKET 3 (Jan. 11, 2016), https://www.fbicgroup.com/sites/default/files/Online%20Consignment%20report%20by%20FBIC%20Global%20Retail%20Tech%20Jan.%2011%202016.pdf.

286. *Id.* at 5–8.

§ 11:3 Distribution Agreements

Brands seeking to expand the sale of their products into new territories may use distributors to sell to retailers in such territories, rather than using their own sales personnel or independent sales agents. A distribution agreement is an agreement between a brand and a distributor pursuant to which the distributor purchases specified products from the brand at an agreed price and resells them to retailers in the territory covered by the agreement. Distributors typically resell the products at a higher price, but in some cases may take a percentage of sales as compensation. In a typical distribution arrangement, the distributor holds inventory in the territory, undertakes marketing and promotion in the territory, performs after-sales service and takes the credit risk for sales of the products in the territory. A distribution agreement can be a cost-effective way for a brand to develop a consumer base for its products in a territory where it previously had only a minimal presence.

There are, however, disadvantages to using distributors. The distributor, rather than the brand, will have control over the marketing and sales process; accordingly, inappropriate conduct by the distributor could negatively impact the image of the brand. In addition, the amount of the distributor's mark-up may make the products less competitive with comparable brands sold directly by the manufacturer in the territory. Furthermore, the brand will not have a direct relationship with the retailers of its product, which may impair the ability of the brand to move to direct sales in the territory in the future. Some industry analysts predict that distribution advantages will diminish as brands expand into new markets through digital presence.[287] By cultivating relationships with consumers online, brands can retain control over their image and experiences and rely on distributors solely for physical delivery.[288]

§ 11:4 Conclusion

As the "Amazon Effect" continues to drive the changing face of the retail apparel industry, retailers have increasingly adopted e-commerce and mobile commerce platforms, either exclusively or as part of an omni-channel retail strategy, to deliver a seamless customer experience. Still, the continued growth of the Internet presence of retailers has not rendered brick-and-mortar stores obsolete, with distribution channels ranging from department stores, to boutiques, to pop-up shops continuing to change and adapt to appeal to customers seeking more personalized shopping experiences.

---

287. BUS. OF FASHION & MCKINSEY & CO., THE STATE OF FASHION 2018, 32–33 (2017), https://cdn.businessoffashion.com/reports/The_State_of_Fashion_2018_v2.pdf.

288. *Id.*

Chapter 12

Antitrust

§ 12:1 Introduction
§ 12:2 Basics of Antitrust Claims
§ 12:3 Horizontal Relationships
§ 12:4 Vertical Relationships
§ 12:4.1 Vertical Price Restraints
[A] Resale Price Maintenance
[B] Suggested Retail Prices
[C] Persuasion and Refusals to Deal
[D] Consignment
[E] Promotional Programs and Direct Rebates
[F] Cooperative Advertising
§ 12:4.2 Non-Price Vertical Agreements
[A] Exclusive Dealing and Exclusive Distribution
[B] Territorial and Customer Restrictions
[C] Tying
§ 12:5 Price Discrimination—The Robinson-Patman Act
§ 12:6 Antitrust Review

§ 12:1 Introduction

Many discussions of fashion law give short shrift to the subject of antitrust law. The popular conception of antitrust law is that it is only relevant to the risk of monopolies. And because there is robust competition in the retail and apparel space, there is a tendency to leap to the conclusion that antitrust law is irrelevant to the world of fashion. However, the scope of the antitrust laws of the United States and the various states is broad and the consequences of violation can be severe.

In general, it is correct that antitrust laws seek to protect competition, based on the view that competition will tend to promote innovation, put downward pressure on prices, drive firms to be more efficient, lead to the best allocation of resources, and otherwise benefit consumers. In the United States, the major federal antitrust laws are the Sherman Antitrust Act (the "Sherman Act"),[1] the Clayton Antitrust Act,[2] and the Federal Trade Commission Act.[3] In addition, each state has its own antitrust laws, which often (but not always) parallel the federal antitrust laws. The federal government enforces the U.S. antitrust laws through two agencies—the Antitrust Division of the U.S. Department of Justice (DOJ) and the Federal Trade Commission (FTC).[4] While the DOJ has the exclusive right to file criminal antitrust lawsuits, which are generally brought only under Section 1 of the Sherman Act ("Section 1"), both the DOJ and the FTC investigate civil antitrust matters. Private parties may also bring civil lawsuits under the antitrust laws, and are entitled to treble damages if they are successful. Accordingly, violations, or suspected violations, of the antitrust laws can result in government investigations and criminal prosecutions, as well as private actions seeking large damage awards.

The conduct of business in the fashion industry poses particular antitrust risks because of the structure of the industry, which is heavily dependent on supply chains, because the industry is highly competitive, and because there can be tension between intellectual property laws that give exclusive rights to specific market players, and the antitrust laws that ensure competition. Activities in the fashion industry have been subject to antitrust scrutiny in the United States for many years. For example, in 1941, the FTC was successful in ending an agreement between fashion manufacturers to use a boycott mechanism to penalize merchants that dealt in copies of the manufacturers' fashion designs.[5]

This chapter highlights the principal antitrust issues that may be applicable to brands and retailers in the fashion industry.

§ 12:2 Basics of Antitrust Claims

Like other types of legal claims, an antitrust plaintiff must establish the basic elements of a cause of action. There are certain elements,

---

1. 15 U.S.C. §§ 1–7.
2. 15 U.S.C. §§ 12–27, 29 U.S.C. §§ 52–53.
3. 15 U.S.C. §§ 41–58. Foreign jurisdictions also have antitrust laws that should be considered when conducting business outside of the United States. A discussion of these statutes is beyond the scope of this chapter. Broadly speaking, foreign antitrust laws roughly parallel the U.S. antitrust laws discussed in this section.
4. State governments may also enforce federal antitrust laws through their respective Attorneys General.
5. Fashion Originators' Guild of Am., Inc. v. Fed. Trade Comm'n, 312 U.S. 457 (1941). *See also supra* chapter 4 (discussing the role of antitrust in the development of copyright law in the fashion industry).

however, that are especially basic to antitrust claims. First, Section 1 of the Sherman Act holds that "[e]very contract, combination . . . or conspiracy, in restraint of trade . . . is declared to be illegal."[6] Courts have held that in order to make a civil claim under Section 1, a plaintiff must establish (i) that there was an agreement among two or more separate entities (ii) that unreasonably restrains trade.

In the fashion industry, however, competitors often engage in what is described as "parallel conduct," that is, actions that are taken by companies that are ostensibly in competition with one another but that might be seen as implying some agreement to work together. For example, fashion companies may be well aware that if they make a pricing or sourcing decision, then familiar competitors are likely to follow suit. It is black-letter law, though, that parallel conduct alone is insufficient to establish an agreement to restrain trade for purposes of Section 1, even where competitors are engaging in "consciously parallel" conduct. Put differently, fashion companies may take action based on an expectation that competitors will have an interest in matching the conduct, which results in parallel conduct even without a preexisting agreement to restrain trade.[7] The key question is whether the actors are making *unilateral* business decisions (which are not subject to prohibition under Section 1) or whether they have established "a conscious commitment to a common scheme designed to achieve an unlawful objective."[8]

An agreement for purposes of Section 1 need not be a formal contract or agreement, but rather can be established through a wink-and-a-nod, or any form of offer and acceptance that results in a conscious commitment to a common scheme. Furthermore, an agreement can be proven through "direct or circumstantial evidence that reasonably tends to prove" the existence of an agreement.[9] In applying antitrust laws, however, courts have placed limits on the inferences that can be made from ambiguous evidence, to prevent mistakes where evidence of competitive behavior (such as parallel pricing by competitors) may look similar to the evidence one might see in a conspiracy. In particular, "[t]o survive a motion for summary judgment or for a directed verdict, a plaintiff seeking damages . . . must present evidence that tends to exclude the possibility that the alleged conspirators acted independently . . . ."[10] The plaintiff must then

---

6. 15 U.S.C. § 1.
7. *See, e.g.*, Brooke Grp. Ltd. v. Brown & Williamson Tobacco Corp., 509 U.S. 209, 227 (1993).
8. Monsanto Co. v. Spray-Rite Serv. Corp., 465 U.S. 752, 768 (1984).
9. *Id.*
10. Matsushita Elec. Indus. Co. v. Zenith Radio Corp., 475 U.S. 574, 588 (1986) (citations omitted).

also establish that the agreement between conspirators is an illegal restraint of trade. Although the issue is discussed in more depth in the following sections, generally, a court's inquiry with respect to a potential restraint will be "whether or not the challenged restraint enhances competition."[11]

Section 2 of the Sherman Act provides that a person shall not "monopolize, or attempt to monopolize, or conspire with any other person or persons to monopolize, any part of the trade or commerce among the several States."[12] In order to make a monopolization claim under section 2, a plaintiff must first establish that a defendant (or defendants) engaged in anticompetitive conduct and, second, that through such conduct, the defendant or defendants either acquired or maintained a monopoly in a properly defined relevant market.[13] For an attempt to monopolize claim, courts have indicated that such conduct needs to create a dangerous probability of monopolization in a given market and reflect a specific intent by the defendant to monopolize such market.[14]

For many antitrust claims, a plaintiff will have to properly establish the definition of a relevant market, consisting both of a relevant

---

11. NCAA v. Bd. of Regents, 468 U.S. 85, 104 (1984). The plaintiff must also establish that the agreement impacted interstate or foreign commerce. *See, e.g.*, McLain v. Real Estate Bd. of New Orleans, 444 U.S. 232, 241–42 (1980).
12. 15 U.S.C. § 2.
13. *See, e.g.*, Verizon Comms. Inc. v. Law Offices of Curtis V. Trinko LLP, 540 U.S. 398, 407 (2004); United States v. Grinnell Corp., 384 U.S. 563, 570–71 (1966). Certain types of behavior have been held, as a matter of law, to be not unlawful under section 2, including aggressive pursuit of legitimate business objectives (*see, e.g.*, USFL v. NFL, 842 F.2d 1335, 1361 (2d Cir. 1988)) and—when standing alone—claims that a party desired to defeat competitors or was openly hostile toward competitors. *See, e.g.*, Brooke Grp. Ltd. v. Brown & Williamson Tobacco Corp., 509 U.S. 209, 225 (1993). Further, a person's actions designed to influence governmental action are protected by the First Amendment, and thus generally cannot violate the antitrust laws (subject to certain exceptions) even where they are designed to harm competitors or competition through government action. *See, e.g.*, E. R.R. Presidents Conference v. Noerr Motor Freight, 365 U.S. 127 (1961).
14. *See* Ass'n for Intercollegiate Athletics for Women v. NCAA, 735 F.2d 577, 585–86 (D.C. Cir. 1984) (failure to prove "[defendant's] conduct derived from a specific intent to monopolize suffices to dispose of [plaintiff's] conclusory charge of a conspiracy to monopolize"); Spectrum Sports, Inc. v. McQuillan, 506 U.S. 447, 456-60 (1993) (no liability for attempted monopolization "absent proof of a dangerous probability that they would monopolize a particular market").

product market and a relevant geographic market.[15] In attempting to establish a relevant market, courts generally look to products that are reasonably substitutable for one another. The U.S. Supreme Court has noted that in defining a relevant market, "[t]he circle must be drawn narrowly to exclude any other product to which, within reasonable variations in price, only a limited number of buyers will turn."[16] And in making a claim, plaintiffs in many cases will have to establish that the defendant or defendants have (or have a likelihood of attaining) "monopoly power," which means the power to raise prices and exclude competition.

Monopoly power can be established directly through evidence of control or exclusion, or indirectly through evidence of high concentrations in a relevant market, evidence relating to "barriers to entry," and evidence of other characteristics of a market and its participants.[17] Private plaintiffs must also establish that, in addition to suffering injuries as a result of defendant's actions, plaintiff also suffered "antitrust injury," meaning an injury "of the type the antitrust laws were intended to prevent and that flows from that which makes the defendant's acts unlawful."[18] Accordingly, injuries suffered by a plaintiff as a result of a competitor's pro-competitive activities, or lost profits to a competitor that are not associated with harm to competition, will not allow that plaintiff to sustain a claim under the antitrust laws.

---

15. *See, e.g.*, United States v. Marine Bancorp., 418 U.S. 602, 618 (1974); Brown Shoe Co. v. United States, 370 U.S. 294, 324 (1962).
16. Times-Picayune Publ'g v. United States, 345 U.S. 594, 612 n.31 (1953). The Antitrust Division and F.T.C. have also published guidelines to how they seek to establish relevant markets, *See* U.S. DEP'T OF JUSTICE & FED. TRADE COMM'N, HORIZONTAL MERGER GUIDELINES (2010), https://www.ftc.gov/os/2010/08/100819hmg.pdf.
17. *See, e.g.*, United States v. Aluminum Co. of Am., 148 F.2d 416 (2d Cir. 1945) (finding that 90% market share constitutes a monopoly); Bailey v. Allgas, Inc., 284 F.3d 1237, 1250 (11th Cir. 2002) (less than 50% share insufficient to establish market power); AD/SAT v. Associated Press, 181 F.3d 216, 229 (2d Cir. 1999) ("[A] 33 percent market share does not approach the level required for a showing of dangerous probability of monopoly power.").
18. *See* Atl. Richfield Co. v. USA Petroleum Co., 495 U.S. 328, 334 (1990) ("ARCO"); Brunswick Corp. v. Pueblo Bowl-O-Mat, Inc., 429 U.S. 477, 489 (1977). In *ARCO*, the Supreme Court explained that the rationale behind this was to ensure "that a plaintiff can recover only if the loss stems from a competition-*reducing* aspect of the defendant's behavior." *ARCO*, 495 U.S. at 344 (emphasis added).

§ 12:3 Horizontal Relationships

The federal antitrust law that has the most direct effect on activities in the fashion industry is Section 1 of the Sherman Act. Section 1 prohibits unreasonable restraints of trade and impacts both vertical restraints (those up and down the supply chain) and horizontal restraints (between competitors). The antitrust laws are the most severe with respect to horizontal agreements, which can be evaluated not only under the rule of reason analysis (described below), but also as *per se* illegal arrangements.

Certain agreements between *competing* companies may be considered so harmful under the federal antitrust laws that they are prohibited outright. A court may deem such an agreement "*per se*" or automatically illegal, with no opportunity to offer justifications or show procompetitive effects. All other agreements are evaluated under the "rule of reason," under which an agreement is unlawful only if its anticompetitive effects substantially outweigh any procompetitive benefits.

The most serious antitrust violations are agreements among horizontal competitors to fix prices, allocate markets, rig bids, or suppress output. These agreements are deemed *per se* unlawful and are pursued as criminal violations by the Department of Justice. An agreement between competitors will be found to constitute price fixing not only when a particular price is agreed upon, but also when competitors agree to raise, lower, or otherwise stabilize price, rebates, discounts, surcharges, or other terms of competition between them.[19] Accordingly, an oral or written agreement between competitors to fix prices or warranty terms on products they sell will be deemed *per se* illegal.[20] If, however, each competitor decides independently to charge the same price as the other, or to have the same warranty terms on its products as the other, that is merely parallel conduct without an agreement, and would not be illegal.

Agreements between competitors or potential competitors designed to allocate customers or geographic areas to one or the other company also are considered *per se* illegal.[21] Similarly, agreements among competitors to boycott a third party can be *per se* illegal.[22]

---

19. *See, e.g.*, F.T.C. v. Super. Ct. Trial Lawyers Ass'n, 493 U.S. 411, 421–23 (1990).
20. United States v. Trenton Potteries Co., 273 U.S. 392 (1927).
21. *See, e.g.*, Blue Cross & Blue Shield United v. Marshfield Clinic, 65 F.3d 1406, 1415 (7th Cir. 1995).
22. Tying arrangements can also be considered *per se* illegal. However, these arrangements are vertical and are discussed in the next section, *infra* section 12:4.

In addition, agreements among competitors to fix or suppress the wages of employees, including agreements among competitors not to poach each other's employees, are deemed *per se* unlawful, and have become a target of criminal antitrust enforcement by the DOJ.[23] Specifically in the fashion industry, there have been investigations in several countries and fines imposed based on alleged wage-fixing in the modeling industry.[24]

When the Antitrust Division of the DOJ prosecutes violations of Section 1, the DOJ places an emphasis on seeking lengthy prison sentences for individuals who are responsible for the offense. In addition, the DOJ seeks financial penalties of up to $100 million for corporations and $1 million for individuals, or if it is higher, twice the gain or loss.[25]

§ 12:4 Vertical Relationships

Companies operating in the fashion industry typically are not fully vertically integrated; they rarely design, source, manufacture, distribute and sell all of their own products. As a result, brands and retailers typically enter into contractual arrangements with third parties both up and down the supply chain. These vertical relationships may raise potential price-related and non-price-related antitrust issues under Section 1 of the Sherman Act. Section 1 only applies, however, when conduct is between separate and different firms; it does not apply to unilateral conduct, including conduct between parent and subsidiary.

---

23. *See* U.S. DEP'T OF JUSTICE, ANTITRUST DIV. & FED. TRADE COMM'N, ANTITRUST GUIDANCE FOR HUMAN RESOURCE PROFESSIONALS (Oct. 2016), https://www.justice.gov/atr/file/903511/download.

24. In 2016, the French competition authority imposed fines totaling €2.38 million on the main professional union of modeling agencies and thirty-seven individual modeling agencies for wage-fixing conduct. Press Release, L'Autorité de la Concurrence, The Autorité Fines for Anticompetitive Agreement the Modelling Sector's Main Professional Union and 37 Modelling Agencies (Sept. 29, 2016), http://www.autoritedelaconcurrence.fr/user/standard.php?lang=en&id_rub=630&id_article=2870. Similarly, in 2016, the UK competition authority imposed fines totaling £1.5 million on five modeling agencies and a trade association for the exchange of confidential and sensitive information regarding models' wages. *See* Press Release, Competition & Mkts. Auth., Model Agencies Fined £1.5 Million for Price Collusion (Dec. 16, 2016), https://www.gov.uk/government/news/model-agencies-fined-15-million-for-price-collusion.

25. 15 U.S.C. § 1.

§ 12:4.1 Vertical Price Restraints

[A] Resale Price Maintenance

Resale Price Maintenance (RPM) is an arrangement between a brand or manufacturer and a distributor or retailer in which the brand or manufacturer specifies the price, or a minimum price, for which a product may be resold. Federal antitrust laws and state antitrust laws view RPM arrangements differently. Under federal law, agreements that may constitute an RPM are analyzed by courts under a "rule of reason" analysis. This is a detailed, fact-intensive, antitrust analysis that balances procompetitive and anticompetitive effects, and holds the agreement unlawful only if the anticompetitive effects outweigh any procompetitive benefits. For example, a firm may restrain intrabrand competition (that is, competition among dealers of a single brand of products) in order to improve the firm's positioning in the interbrand competitive marketplace (that is, in competition with other suppliers). These effects are particularly likely in the fashion industry, in which price discounting by retailers can siphon off and deteriorate the brand value of the supplier. RPM is a tool that can be effective in protecting the supplier's brand and competitive positioning in the larger marketplace, which increases competition and benefits consumers.[26] Because there are potential procompetitive effects from RPM agreements, in 2007 the U.S. Supreme Court held in *Leegin v. PSKS, Inc.* that RPM agreements should be evaluated under the rule of reason, overturning a century-old rule that had deemed such agreements *per se* unlawful.[27] The Court in *Leegin* outlined general analytical principles applicable to a determination of whether a particular instance of RPM is illegal. RPM agreements will be viewed favorably if they promote competition between competitors. This is called interbrand competition (or competition between brands), even if it is at the expense of competition between retailers in selling the same brand. The Court explained that protecting this interbrand

---

26. Historically, courts considered it *per se* (or presumptively) illegal under the Sherman Act for manufacturers of a product to mandate minimum or maximum retail prices. In 1987, the U.S. Supreme Court in State Oil Co. v. Khan, 522 U.S. 3 (1997), held that maximum RPM was no longer *per se* illegal under federal law. The Court's decision in *Leegin* held that minimum RPM agreements would also be judged under the rule of reason.

27. Leegin Creative Leather Prods., Inc. v. PSKS, Inc., 551 U.S. 877 (2007) (*Leegin* involved a leather apparel manufacturer that sought to maintain a uniform minimum price for its products and, when it discovered that a boutique retailer was discounting below the minimum price, stopped selling to the retailer.).

competition is "the primary purpose of the antitrust laws"[28] and that competition is promoted by RPM because it both encourages retailers to invest in "tangible or intangible services or promotional efforts that aid the manufacturer's position against rival[s]" and "has the potential to give consumers more options so that they can choose among low-price, low-service brands; high-price, high-service brands; and brands that fall in between."[29]

Further, the Court explained that RPM allows a manufacturer to protect its retailers because it eliminates free riding. Retailer margins can be maintained as discounters that do not follow the company's pricing can be terminated. This has a positive competitive effect as retailers are encouraged to invest in the sales of a manufacturer's products knowing that they will not be undercut by discounters.[30] The Court also explained that RPM can be used by new market entrants to "induce competent and aggressive retailers to make the kind of investment of capital and labor that is often required in the distribution of products unknown to the consumer"[31] While the Court's decision in *Leegin* meant that the *"per se"* designation has been removed from RPM agreements under federal law, such agreements are still subject to a rule of reason analysis under Section 1, and thus still may be found to be illegal if the anticompetitive effects outweigh the procompetitive effects. Courts analyzing such agreements typically focus on the market share and market power of the entity seeking to impose an RPM agreement, the number of manufacturers in the market that have RPM agreements, and whether the driving force behind the agreement was the manufacturer or the retailer. The Supreme Court indicated that where there are few competitors using RPM agreements, the manufacturer is the cause of the agreements, and the manufacturer lacks market power, such arrangements are more likely to be upheld.[32] If a company does not have market power, and its RPM has the purpose and effect of encouraging interbrand competition, the arrangement is likely to be upheld.[33]

The impact of *Leegin*, however, has been muted by the activity of a number of state attorneys general, who have pursued RPM agreements aggressively under state laws—which in many cases still held RPM

28. *Id.* at 887 (quoting *State Oil Co.*, 522 U.S. at 15).
29. *Id.*
30. 551 U.S. at 887–89.
31. *Id.* at 888 (quoting Cont'l T.V., Inc. v. GTE Sylvania Inc., 433 U.S. 36, 55 (1977)).
32. 551 U.S. at 897–98.
33. *Id.* at 889–90. These include cartel-like behavior among manufacturers seeking to maintain monopoly pricing or discouraging price cutting, rather than facilitating competition.

agreements to be *per se* unlawful. As a result, most suppliers in the United States continue to avoid entering into RPM agreements with their retailers, to avoid triggering action from state attorneys general under unfavorable state laws. Instead, suppliers use other tools to achieve the procompetitive effects of RPM agreements, such as minimum advertised pricing (MAP) policies, or unilaterally announced suggested retail prices, which are discussed below.

[B] Suggested Retail Prices

Under both federal and state antitrust law, it has been well settled in the courts that manufacturers may suggest retail prices to retailers and use suggested retail prices in advertising aimed at the ultimate consumers, and that retailers may use the manufacturer's suggested prices so long as their choice to do so has been made independently.[34] If retailers are making such pricing decisions independently and the parties have no agreements regarding price, Section 1 of the Sherman Act cannot apply.

Further, manufacturers may print suggested retail prices on the product itself or on a price tag (which is also called "pre-ticketing") without triggering antitrust scrutiny under Section 1 of the Sherman Act.[35] Government guidance indicates that manufacturers seeking to pre-ticket items should identify the retail prices as suggested.[36]

[C] Persuasion and Refusals to Deal

Companies can seek to persuade retailers to charge certain prices. They are permitted to firmly explain the benefits of following their suggested retail pricing and can refuse to deal with retailers who do not use their suggested resale prices. Specifically, the U.S. Supreme Court has held that it is *not* concerted action—and therefore beyond the scope of Section 1—when a manufacturer unilaterally announces a pricing policy and refuses to do business with those who do not adhere to the policy.[37] A manufacturer will not be in violation of Section 1 if it only engages in "exposition, persuasion and argument"

---

34. *See* United States v. Parke, Davis & Co., 362 U.S. 29, 44 (1960) (no agreement when a dealer "independently decides to observe specified resale prices"); Monsanto Co. v. Spray-Rite Serv. Corp., 465 U.S. 752, 761 (1984) (dealers may independently decide to acquiesce to suggested resale prices set in advance).
35. *See, e.g.*, Mesirow v. Pepperidge Farm, 703 F.2d 339, 344 (9th Cir.), *cert. denied*, 464 U.S. 820 (1983); Malone v. Crown Cent. Petroleum Corp., 474 F. Supp. 306, 310-11 (D. Md. 1979).
36. *See* Advisory Op. to Nat'l Outerwear& Sportswear Ass'n, 88 F.T.C. 1016, 1017 (1976).
37. *See Monsanto*, 465 U.S. at 761.

with a retailer in regard to suggested prices.[38] Before Section 1 can be implicated, it must be demonstrated that there is an agreement between two separate parties or entities, and a unilateral refusal to deal, by definition, is unilateral. There is a limit, however, to what can be done under the guise of unilateral activity. Even though unilateral activity is implicated when a company decides to terminate a retailer that does not follow its pricing, that otherwise unilateral conduct can be transformed into an illegal agreement when the company subsequently agrees to take back the terminated retailer if the retailer also agrees to prices that the company dictates.[39] Courts have also found that certain actions are so aggressive with respect to "encouraging" distributors or retailers to adhere to suggested retail prices that they also cross the line from unilateral to concerted conduct. Instead of being considered unilateral conduct (the retailer deciding unilaterally to charge the company's price), the conduct becomes an RPM agreement under the antitrust laws between the company and the retailer.[40] Because the line between proper unilateral conduct and concerted conduct may be difficult to determine, manufacturers using suggested retail prices should consult with their antitrust counsel in order to develop a clear policy to minimize the potential antitrust risks.

[D] Consignment

A consignment agreement, in which a manufacturer consigns merchandise to a distributor or retailer and sets its own price for the product, will not raise antitrust issues so long as the manufacturer is unilaterally setting the price through bona fide consignment. Courts have found that certain types of purported consignment arrangements are not bona fide consignment, but instead are vertical price fixing between the manufacturer and distributor. In *Simpson v. Union Oil Co.*, the U.S. Supreme Court found an arrangement was illegal where a major oil company had "consigned" gasoline to a vast network of distributors in an situation that also included evidence that distributors had been coerced into the arrangement by the defendant, and that the distributors carried the risk of loss and exhibited indicators of ownership over what was supposed to

---

38. *See* Acquaire v. Canada Dry Bottling Co., 24 F.3d 401, 410 (2d Cir. 1994) ("[e]vidence of pricing suggestions, persuasion, conversations, arguments, exposition, or pressure is not sufficient to establish the coercion necessary to transgress § 1 of the Sherman Act").
39. *See* United States v. Colgate & Co., 250 U.S. 300 (1919); *Monsanto*, 465 U.S. 752; United States v. Parke, Davis & Co., 362 U.S. 29, 44 (1960).
40. *See Monsanto*, 465 U.S. at 766.

be a consigned product.[41] A company, especially one that may have economic leverage over distributors or retailers, that seeks to utilize a consignment arrangement should take care to ensure that the distributor or retailer agreement does not transfer the company's control or the risk of loss associated with the product, and that the consignment agreement is entered into for a good, non-price, business reason.[42]

[E] Promotional Programs and Direct Rebates

Rebates issued directly by manufacturers to consumers, even where the retailer actually pays the rebate to the customer on behalf of the manufacturer and is reimbursed, have not been held to represent concerted action triggering Section 1 scrutiny, so long as the retailer remains free to set its own prices on the underlying products.[43] Similarly, as long as the retailer is free to set the ultimate prices, a manufacturer's promotional allowance that reduces wholesale prices is also not considered to be concerted action for Section 1 purposes.[44]

Promotional programs that *do* require that wholesale discounts granted to retailers by manufacturers be "passed through" to consumers are agreements between the parties for Section 1 purposes; however, courts will likely analyze such arrangements under the rule of reason.[45] Courts have generally held that such programs are justifiable for certain reasons, such as when manufacturers have "a legitimate interest in making sure the retailer receiving the discount 'is not pocketing the price support instead of passing it on to consumers'" and when such programs can lower retail prices and increase interbrand competition.[46] Courts have also indicated that such arrangements are more likely to be regarded favorably where retailers

41. Simpson v. Union Oil Co., 377 U.S. 13 (1964).

42. *See* United States v. GE, 272 U.S. 476, 488 (1926); Day v. Taylor, 400 F.3d 1272, 1277-78 (11th Cir. 2005); Hardwick v. Nu-Way Oil Co., 589 F.2d 806 (5th Cir. 1979).

43. *See, e.g.*, Checkers Motors Corp. v. Chrysler Corp., 283 F. Supp. 876 (S.D.N.Y. 1968) (upheld plan that offered cash rebate for taxi purchasers from authorized dealers where dealers determined retail price), *aff'd*, 405 F.2d 319 (2d Cir. 1969).

44. *See, e.g.*, Santa Clara Valley Distrib. Co. v. Pabst Brewing Co., 556 F.2d 942, 945 (9th Cir. 1977); FLM Collision Parts, Inc. v. Ford Motor Co., 543 F.2d 1019, 1029–30 (2d Cir. 1976).

45. AAA Liquors, Inc. v. Joseph E. Seagram & Sons, Inc., 705 F.2d 1203 (10th Cir. 1982) (quoting Lehrman v. Gulf Oil Corp., 464 F.2d 26, 40 (5th Cir. 1972)). *See also* Acquaire v. Canada Dry Bottling Co., 24 F.3d 401, 411 (2d Cir. 1994).

46. *AAA Liquors*, 705 F.2d at 1206.

are free to act independently in offering even greater discounts or simply not agreeing to the promotional program in the first place.[47]

[F] Cooperative Advertising

Cooperative advertising arrangements can be indirect constraints on price if they impact how a distributor or retailer advertises and promotes products. For example, cooperative advertising programs can entail making advertising funds available only if the retailer advertises a certain price (or no price at all) or if the retailer otherwise follows the advertising criteria set by the company. Such programs generally involve a manufacturer requiring distributors or retailers to contribute to a cooperative advertising fund from which the distributors or retailers could be reimbursed as long as they run advertisements in accordance with price maintenance terms given by the manufacturer. These advertising programs also often require the retailer to present a particular look and feel mandated by the manufacturer. Cooperative advertising programs have been upheld under both federal and state antitrust laws. In recent decades, such agreements have not been successfully challenged, as long as the distributors or retailers were free to decline to participate and were able to set their own retail prices.[48]

§ 12:4.2 Non-Price Vertical Agreements

Vertical agreements concerning non-price terms generally have not been subject to the same level of judicial scrutiny as RPM agreements, and the U.S. Supreme Court has held that vertical non-price restraints have "real potential to stimulate interbrand competition."[49] Non-price vertical restraints include exclusive dealing or distribution arrangements as well as territorial and customer restrictions. As explained in more detail below, courts have also held that such agreements merit different treatment than agreements as to price. In non-price vertical restraints, state antitrust law generally follows federal law, but care should be taken to review the laws of all applicable jurisdictions.

---

47. *Id.*
48. *See, e.g.*, *In re* Nissan Antitrust Litig., 577 F.2d 910 (5th Cir. 1978); Lake Hill Motors v. Jim Bennett Yacht Sales, Inc., 246 F.3d 752, 757 (5th Cir. 2001); *In re* Sony Music Entm't, 2000 FTC LEXIS 95 (2000) (consent order where distributors agreed to stop requiring dealers to use the distributors' pricing scheme in order to obtain refunds related to advertising).
49. Bus. Elecs. Corp. v. Sharp Elecs. Corp., 485 U.S. 717, 724 (1988) (quoting Cont'l T.V., Inc. v. GTE Sylvania Inc., 433 U.S. 36, 52 n.19 (1977)).

[A] Exclusive Dealing and Exclusive Distribution

Exclusive dealing includes arrangements in which a company prohibits a particular retailer from selling products that compete with the company's products as a condition of selling such company's products. Such arrangements can also include requirements for a retailer to purchase all of its requirements of a certain product from the manufacturer, require the retailer to purchase the entirety of the manufacturer's output, or include incentives for the retailer to follow such patterns.[50]

Courts have analyzed exclusive dealing arrangements under the rule of reason,[51] or some form of it, and have focused on the potential of the agreements to foreclose competitors from the marketplace–an inquiry that will depend on the duration of the agreement, the market power of the companies at issue, and the potential for competitive harm in the given situation.[52] For example, plaintiff competitors have generally failed in cases where manufacturers form agreements with retailers in order to have the retailer give preferential treatment to the manufacturer's products over its competitors, but where such competitor's products are still available from the retailer.[53] Similarly, where other distribution channels into a given market are available for rival manufacturers, exclusive dealing arrangements are less likely to be found unlawful.[54]

Exclusive distribution includes arrangements in which a company agrees to distribute its products through a single retailer, usually in a specific geographic area. Such arrangements also have the effect of prohibiting the company itself from distributing its product in the given territory. Because such agreements generally promote interbrand competition, they are evaluated under the rule of reason. Courts analyze such agreements by considering the strength of interbrand

---

50. *See* Omega Envtl., Inc. v. Gilbarco, Inc., 127 F.3d 1157, 1162–65 (9th Cir. 1997); Taggart v. Rutledge, 657 F. Supp. 1420, 1443–45 (D. Mont. 1987), *aff'd mem.*, 852 F.2d 1290 (9th Cir. 1988); Ryko Mfg. Co. v. Eden Servs., 823 F.2d 1215, 1234 (8th Cir. 1987); Concord Boat Corp. v. Brunswick Corp., 207 F.3d 1039, 1162–63 (8th Cir. 2000).
51. Section 1 or 2 of the Sherman Act may apply, as well as section 5 of the FTC Act or section 3 of the Clayton Act. *See, e.g.*, Standard Oil Co. v. United States, 337 U.S. 293, 306–07 (1949); Tampa Elec. Co. v. Nashville Coal Co., 365 U.S. 320, 329 (1961); Luria Bros. & Co. v. F.T.C., 389 F.2d 847, 861 (3d Cir. 1968); United States v. Dentsply Int'l, 399 F.3d 181, 191 (3d Cir. 2005).
52. *See Omega Envtl.*, 127 F.3d at 1162; *Dentsply*, 399 F.3d 181; *In re* Interco, Inc., 108 F.T.C. 133, 134 (1986) (lack of market power).
53. *See, e.g.*, El Aguila Food Prods. v. Gruma Corp., 301 F. Supp. 2d 612, 620–21 (S.D. Tex. 2003).
54. *See Dentsply*, 399 F.3d at 189.

competition in the relevant market, the duration of the exclusivity, and the geographic or customer scope of the agreement.[55] For example, if a company agrees to make an exclusive item for a particular retailer, such as a special product in an apparel line, a court may consider the effects on intrabrand competition (only one retailer will be selling the product) and interbrand competition (how that exclusive product will affect competition against other manufacturer's products) when deciding if the arrangement is an unreasonable restraint of trade.

[B] Territorial and Customer Restrictions

Territorial and customer restrictions include agreements between manufacturers and distributors whereby a distributor is only given the right to sell the manufacturer's product in a specific area or to a specific type of customer. The U.S. Supreme Court has held that such restrictions are to be judged under the rule of reason.[56]

Territorial and customer restrictions have been considered to be acceptable, with courts generally finding that such arrangements stimulate interbrand competition and are therefore legal.[57] It is important to note, however, that the procompetitive impact of these types of arrangements still must outweigh any anticompetitive impacts.[58]

"Dual distribution" situations present a different set of considerations. Here, the manufacturer operates as a distributor in competition with the manufacturer's other distributors. In dual distribution situations, the company is in both a horizontal and vertical relationship with its distributor, which raises the issue of whether the more severe restrictions that apply to horizontal relationships apply in these circumstances. Courts tend to resolve the issue by deciding whether the company's action is the type a company typically engages in when attempting to control its distribution channel by vertical restraints, or whether it is more akin to actions taken by horizontal competitors to limit competition.[59]

---

55. *See, e.g.*, Orson, Inc. v. Miramax Film Corp., 79 F.3d 1358, 1368–72 (3d Cir. 1996); Ralph C. Wilson Indus. v. Chronicle Broad. Co., 1982 U.S. Dist. LEXIS 17689, at *5 (N.D. Cal. 1982).
56. Cont'l T.V., Inc. v. GTE Sylvania Inc., 433 U.S. 36, 51–54 (1977).
57. *See, e.g.*, E. Sci. Co. v. Wild Heerbrugg Instruments, Inc., 572 F.2d 883, 885–86 (1st Cir. 1978) (citing *Sylvania*, 433 U.S. 36).
58. *See* Toys "R" Us, Inc. v. F.T.C., 221 F.3d 928 (7th Cir. 2000).
59. *See* PSKS, Inc. v. Leegin Creative Leather Prods., 615 F.3d 412, 420–21 (5th Cir. 2010).

[C] Tying

Tying agreements are arrangements where a supplier will sell one product only on condition that the customer also purchases a second product. They may be found to be illegal, either under the *per se* rule or under a rule of reason analysis, if the supplier has market power; the products are in fact separate products (rather than components of a single product); and the purchase of the "tied" item is required in order to also acquire the "tying" item.[60] The competitive harm that may be presented by tying arrangements is the limitation that it may impose on the freedom to purchase products from other sources.[61]

A critical issue in determining whether a tying arrangement is *per se* illegal is whether the supplier has market power in the tying (desired) product. This is not a simple determination. Typically, if a company has less than a 30% market share in the tying product, it will be held not to have the requisite market power.[62]

Unlike other *per se* offenses, there are defenses to claims of illegal tie-ins. Tying arrangements will generally not be condemned as unreasonable if they are used for new products that are being introduced into the marketplace or if products are technical in nature.[63] Also, there can be no illegal tying arrangement if the company also offers both the tying and tied product on an unbundled basis.[64] This is true even if the price of the two products together is less than the price of each separately. If a company requires a buyer to purchase the products of a separate entity (other than the company) in order to get the desired product from the company, it will not constitute a tying arrangement because both the tying and tied product have to be sold by the same entity, unless the company has an economic interest in the "separate" entity.[65]

---

60. *See* Jefferson Parish Hosp. No. 2 v. Hyde, 466 U.S. 2 (1984); Ill. Tool Works v. Indep. Ink, Inc., 547 U.S. 28 (2006).
61. *See* N. Pac. Ry. Co. v. United States, 356 U.S. 1, 5–6 (1958).
62. *See Jefferson Parish Hosp.*, 466 U.S. at 26-29; Dickson v. Microsoft Corp., 309 F.3d 193, 210 n.20 (4th Cir. 2002); Sheridan v. Marathon Petroleum Co., 530 F.3d 590, 595 (7th Cir. 2008).
63. *See, e.g.*, United States v. Jerrold Elecs. Corp., 187 F. Supp. 545 (E.D. Pa. 1960), *aff'd per curiam*, 365 U.S. 567 (1961).
64. *See, e.g.*, *N. Pac. Ry. Co.*, 356 U.S. at 6 n.4; Monsanto Co. v. Scruggs, 459 F.3d 1328, 1340–41 (Fed. Cir. 2006).
65. *See, e.g.*, Ohio-Sealy Mattress Mfg. Co. v. Sealy, Inc., 585 F.2d 821, 834–35 (7th Cir. 1978); Venzie Corp. v. U.S. Mineral Prods. Co., 521 F.2d 1309, 1317 (3d Cir. 1975); County of Tuolumne v. Sonora Cmty. Hosp., 236 F.3d 1148, 1158 (9th Cir. 2001).

§ 12:5 Price Discrimination—The Robinson-Patman Act

The antitrust laws also prohibit a company from discriminating in price between competing customers. The Robinson-Patman Act restricts certain types of price discrimination.[66] Although both the Antitrust Division of the DOJ and the FTC have enforcement authority under the law, in practice, the Antitrust Division does not enforce either the civil or criminal provisions, and the FTC has not brought an enforcement action since 2000.[67] The vast majority of lawsuits brought under the Robinson-Patman Act are brought by private parties that may receive treble damages if they are successful. However, just as the DOJ has ceased active enforcement of the Robinson-Patman Act, private plaintiffs have also had a more difficult time successfully litigating cases under the Robinson-Patman Act due to changing interpretations of the law's requirements by courts.[68]

There are two major types of price discrimination covered by the Robinson-Patman Act—"primary line" and "secondary line" discrimination.[69] A primary line situation involves a type of predatory pricing, such as where a company sells a product of similar grade and quality[70] as a competitor, but sells its product at a price below its own costs, and with a reasonable prospect of recouping its "investment" in its below-cost pricing by chasing competitors from the market with the scheme.[71] A secondary line violation, on the other hand, involves a company selling the same products to distributors or retailers (as opposed to consumers), but at different prices.[72] An example of a secondary line violation would include a company selling the same products to a retail chain at different prices than it charges a smaller, independent retailer.

---

66. 15 U.S.C. § 13. No criminal prosecution has been brought under the Robinson-Patman Act for over forty years.
67. In the Matter of McCormick & Co., 2000 F.T.C. LEXIS 19 (2000).
68. Robert J. Toth, *A Powerful Law Has Been Losing a Lot of Its Punch*, WALL ST. J., May 21, 2012.
69. *See* FED. TRADE COMM'N, FTC GUIDE TO THE ANTITRUST LAWS, PRICE DISCRIMINATION AMONG BUYERS: ROBINSON-PATMAN VIOLATIONS [hereinafter FTC GUIDE], https://www.ftc.gov/bc/antitrust/price_discrimination.shtm.
70. Products sold need to be tangible and not incidental to the sale of something intangible, such as a service. *See, e.g.*, Windsor Auctions, Inc. v. eBay, Inc., No. C-08-05409 RMW, 2008 U.S. Dist. LEXIS 66305 (N.D. Cal. June 15, 2009) (holding that eBay's auction services, even when accounting for the presence of underlying goods, did not qualify as a commodity under the Robinson-Patman Act).
71. *Id.*
72. *Id.*

For actionable price discrimination, one company must sell the same product to competing customers at different prices. When determining the price at which a product is sold, courts look to the net price after all discounts and rebates are taken into consideration. In addition, actionable price discrimination does not arise when the disfavored distributor or retailer has a discount functionally available to it but chooses not to take advantage of the discount.[73]

Generally speaking, it is a defense to these discrimination claims either that prices were lowered by a company in a given instance in order to meet, but not beat, a competitor's pricing,[74] or that sales to different parties entail different costs[75] or changing conditions. The last defense has particular applicability to the fashion industry as it permits a company to discriminate in prices between competing parties when, for example, at the end of a season the company seeks to sell that season's merchandise quickly.

In addition to the types of price discrimination discussed above, the Robinson-Patman Act also prohibits other behavior that may impact companies in the fashion industry. If a company offers promotional materials to one retailer but does not offer them to other retailers, or provides payments for promotional materials to some retailers but not all retailers, such practices can violate the Robinson-Patman Act. Any promotional or advertising services offered to some must be offered on a nondiscriminatory basis.[76] However, if a company treats all competing parties in a proportionately equal manner, a violation does not arise.[77] Finally, retailers may also be found liable

---

73. *See* F.T.C. v. Anheuser-Busch, Inc., 363 U.S. 536 (1960); Toledo Mack Sales & Serv., Inc. v. Mack Trucks, Inc., 530 F.3d 204, 209–10 (3d Cir. 2008); Conoco Inc. v. Inman Oil Co., 774 F.2d 895, 901–02 (8th Cir. 1985); Raynor Mfg. Co. v. Raynor Door Co., 2009 U.S. Dist. LEXIS 6159, at *27 (D. Kan. 2009).

74. *See id. See also* Standard Oil Co. v. Fed. Trade Comm'n, 340 U.S. 231, 251 (1951) (meeting competition defense is an absolute defense to Robinson-Patman Act price discrimination claims); Falls City Indus. v. Vanco Beverage, 460 U.S. 428 (1983) (seller may lower prices on an area-wide basis rather than on a customer-by-customer basis); Sun Oil Co., 55 F.T.C. 955, 965 (1959), *set aside*, 294 F.2d 465 (5th Cir. 1961), *rev'd*, 371 U.S. 505, 512 (1963) (explaining that defense may be available when prices are lowered in order to allow downstream distributor to better compete with its competition in certain instances).

75. *See id.* Defendants generally have more difficulty meeting the requirements of the "cost justification" defense. *See, e.g.*, Texaco Inc. v. Hasbrouck, 496 U.S. 543, 561 n.18 (1990).

76. *See, e.g.*, Hinkleman v. Shell Oil Co., 962 F.2d 372, 381 (4th Cir. 1992); Motive Parts Warehouse v. Facet Enters., 774 F.2d 380, 395 (10th Cir. 1985); In the Matter of Foremost-McKesson, Inc., 109 F.T.C. 127 (1987).

77. *See* FTC GUIDE, *supra* note 69.

for Robinson-Patman Act violations where they "induce" the relevant price discrimination.[78]

§ 12:6 Antitrust Review

This chapter provides an overview of the primary antitrust issues that may arise for brands and retailers in the fashion industry. There are additional antitrust laws and issues that can impact the fashion industry. Importantly, because of the intensely factual nature of most antitrust issues, it is advisable to seek the advice of experienced antitrust legal counsel before engaging in conduct that could potentially raise concerns under federal or state antitrust laws.

---

78. *See* Feesers, Inc. v. Michael Foods, 591 F.3d 191, 208–09 (3d Cir.), *cert. denied*, 131 S. Ct. 160 (2010).

Chapter 13

Real Estate

§ 13:1 Introduction
§ 13:2 A Brick-and-Mortar Presence: Initial Considerations
§ 13:2.1 Finding a Suitable Space
§ 13:2.2 Forms of Real Property Interests
§ 13:2.3 Holding Real Property Interests; Guaranties and Security Deposits
§ 13:3 Drafting Lease Provisions
§ 13:3.1 Space
§ 13:3.2 Term
§ 13:3.3 Use Provisions
§ 13:3.4 Exclusive Use and Use Restrictions
§ 13:3.5 Rent
§ 13:3.6 Rent Abatements
§ 13:3.7 Visibility and Signage
§ 13:3.8 Practical Considerations; Alterations
§ 13:3.9 Assignments and Subleases
§ 13:3.10 Other Provisions
§ 13:4 Special Considerations With Respect to Fashion Shows

§ 13:1 Introduction*

The development of the fashion industry has been inextricably linked to real estate. Apparel and accessories are produced in manufacturing facilities, stored in warehouses and distribution centers, displayed at trade and fashion shows, and sold in brick-and-mortar stores. Since the 1970s, however, and with seemingly even greater

* The authors would like to acknowledge the work of Andrew Lance and Ben Imdieke in preparing this chapter. Mr. Lance is a partner in the New York office, and Mr. Imdieke is an associate in the San Francisco office, of Gibson, Dunn & Crutcher LLP.

speed, U.S. fashion companies have become less reliant on real estate[1] with iconic brands such as Ralph Lauren, Lord & Taylor, Calvin Klein, Henri Bendel, and Gap abandoning flagships in Midtown Manhattan to focus on digital strategies and seek lower rents, among other things.[2] Despite some notable standouts bucking the trend by re-shoring some of their manufacturing,[3] many apparel and accessory designers today outsource manufacturing to contract factories outside the United States, some have experimented with digital trade and fashion shows, and nearly all use e-commerce and mobile commerce retail sales and delivery platforms.[4]

Fashion companies continue to utilize real estate in both traditional and innovative ways. Despite the increasing pressure from online sales, most retail sales are still transacted in brick-and-mortar stores.[5] Although department stores appear to be on the decline,[6] other areas of the market, fast-fashion, for example, have seen considerable growth in site visits.[7] Fashion companies are also experimenting with new and inventive uses of physical space to gain public exposure, attract customers, and sell products. Temporary installations commonly referred to as "pop-up" shops and co-retail locations[8] have become a popular way for emerging brands and e-commerce sites to test the potential and feasibility of a more significant brick-and-mortar

---

1. Derek Thompson, *What in the World Is Causing the Retail Meltdown of 2017*, ATLANTIC (Apr. 10, 2017), https://www.theatlantic.com/business/archive/2017/04/retail-meltdown-of-2017/522384/.
2. Nathaniel Meyersohn, *Why Retailers Are Fleeing Fifth Avenue*, CNN (Jan. 12, 2019, 7:55 AM), https://www.cnn.com/2019/01/12/business/calvin-klein-store-gap-nike-new-york/index.html.
3. *See, e.g.*, Harry Moser & Sandy Montalbano, *Why Made-in-USA Fashion Is Turning Heads*, INDUS. WK. (Jan. 18, 2018), https://www.industryweek.com/economy/why-made-usa-fashion-turning-heads.
4. *See* Arnold J. Karr, *U.S. E-commerce Grows 14.3% in Q4*, WOMEN'S WEAR DAILY (Feb. 10, 2013), https://www.wwd.com/retail-news/financial/us-e-commerce-grows-143-in-q4-6711305; Kristiano Ang, *Study Offers Closer Look at Online Shopping*, WOMEN'S WEAR DAILY (Oct. 22, 2012), https://www.wwd.com/retail-news/direct-internet-catalogue/study-offers-closer-look-at-online-shopping-6436453.
5. Krista Garcia, *The State of U.S. Apparel Shopping in Five Charts*, EMARKETER (Apr. 26, 2018), https://retail.emarketer.com/article/state-of-us-apparel-shopping-five-charts/5ae2106bebd4000b78fe1517.
6. *Id.*
7. Krista Garcia, *Why Fast Fashion Is Experiencing Rapid Growth*, EMARKETER (Sept. 10, 2018), https://retail.emarketer.com/article/why-fast-fashion-experiencing-rapid-growth/5b980b94b0e5e604903ba03a.
8. Sally Herships, *You've Heard of Co-Working, Now There's Co-Retailing*, MARKETPLACE (May 30, 2017), https://www.marketplace.org/2017/05/30/business/youve-heard-of-coworking-now-theres-coretailing.

presence,[9] and e-commerce brands are opening showrooms at which consumers can view and try-on merchandise before ordering it online.[10] Co-working locations also appear eager to get in on the action, both in terms of operations and retail.[11] A study from Jones Lang LaSalle predicts co-working space in malls, street fronts, and other retail properties will grow at an annual rate of 25% through 2023 to reach about 3.4 million square feet.[12]

The persistence of brick-and-mortar retail stores (whether full-scale or otherwise) can be attributed to the desire of the fashion consumer to physically engage with the products—to feel the fabrics, to view the construction, to test the drape and fit. Fashion consumers also may gain a sense of enrichment and engagement with a particular fashion brand, and with the broader fashion community, by shopping in a physical store that they cannot gain by shopping online.[13] The physical presence of retail stores for elite brands also continues to be a key ingredient in maintenance of the brand's luxury status and competitive magnetism in the eyes of consumers, even more so at a time when an increasing portion of the interaction with consumers is digital.

This chapter explores certain significant real estate law issues that commonly arise in the fashion industry. While the discussion is not intended to be location-specific or exhaustive, many of the issues present themselves most vividly in a dense urban environment, such as New York City.

---

9. *See* Mary Billard, *A Chicer, Cheaper New Outlook*, N.Y. TIMES (Jan. 4, 2012), http://travel.nytimes.com/2012/01/05/fashion/warby-parkers-pop-up-store-offers-eyeglass-frames.html.

10. *See* Stephanie Clifford, *E-Commerce, With Bricks and Mortar, Too*, ON THE RUNWAY BLOG, N.Y. TIMES (Dec. 19, 2012, 10:39 AM), http://runway.blogs.nytimes.com/2012/12/19/e-commerce-with-bricks-and-mortar-too/; Caroline Tell, *Selling Jewelry and a Lifestyle, a Snapshot at a Time*, N.Y. TIMES (Feb. 6, 2013), https://www.nytimes.com/2013/02/07/fashion/dannijo-sells-jewelry-and-a-lifestyle-a-picture-at-a-time.html.

11. *See* Laura Ewen, *Is Co-working the Next Hot Retail Concept*, RETAIL DIVE (June 13, 2018), https://www.retaildive.com/news/is-co-working-the-next-hot-retail-concept/524843/.

12. *See* Andria Cheng, *One Big Potential Beneficiary of the Coworking Space Trend: Brick-and-Mortar Retailers*, FORBES (Aug. 10, 2018, 10:00 AM), https://www.forbes.com/sites/andriacheng/2018/08/10/retail-coworking-spaces/#11e829b86d6f.

13. *See* Gardiner Morse, *Retail Isn't Broken, Stores Are*, HARV. BUS. REV. (Dec. 2011), http://hbr.org/2011/12/retail-isnt-broken-stores-are/ar/1.

§ 13:2 A Brick-and-Mortar Presence: Initial Considerations

§ 13:2.1 *Finding a Suitable Space*

Once a fashion company has decided to establish a brick-and-mortar presence, it must locate an appropriate physical space. In many cases, a fashion company will engage the services of a real estate broker who is knowledgeable about the local real estate market. An experienced broker can advise the company on the neighborhoods that are best suited to the company's brand and price point, and are consistent with the company's design profile (for instance, edgy versus traditional, exclusive versus mass market), marketing strategy (destination store versus drawing on street traffic in an area populated by other fashion retailers), and distribution constraints. A broker can be most effective when the company has clearly defined objectives, as well as financial parameters for an economically viable location, and communicates these objectives and parameters clearly to the broker.

Often a company will conduct a "beauty contest" among several real estate brokerage firms seeking to represent the company, based on an initial request by the company for proposals from the brokers. Such a process can generate, at minimal expense, an initial spectrum of useful ideas and insights about the market under consideration and the viability of the company's objectives and financial parameters. A beauty contest also provides the company's internal team with exposure to the personalities and working style of various brokers so that the company is able to select a real estate brokerage team that is a good match. Retailers with recurring real estate needs or a large portfolio of real estate assets often will hire in-house brokerage professionals or enter into exclusive arrangements with one or more brokerage firms in order to have resources dedicated to their real estate requirements.

Once a real estate broker has been engaged, the broker conducts a series of discussions with the company and walking tours of various sub-markets, seeking to refine the non-economic objectives of the company based on options for locations in the market, to confirm that the economic expectations are realistic for the market, and to identify potential locations based on the presence (or absence) of similar and competing retail presences.[14] This process usually results in the broker generating a book of suitable spaces, projected (or actual) asking economic terms for the lease or purchase of space, projected

14. *See* Julie Satow, *Homework Trumps Gut Instinct in Retail Brokering*, N.Y. TIMES (Mar. 13, 2012), https://www.nytimes.com/2012/03/14/realestate/commercial/data-trumps-gut-instinct-in-retail-brokering.html.

build-out issues and costs, and rental and operating expense projections for the term of the proposed lease or ownership.

Upon locating one or more suitable spaces, the broker assists the company in the negotiation of the business terms for lease or purchase, hopefully resulting in a term sheet or letter of intent (collectively, "term sheet"). Although term sheets rarely are binding, a tenant is not likely to get more favorable terms in the binding agreement (lease or purchase) than those that appear in the term sheet. Accordingly the company should seriously consider involving legal counsel in the discussions before the term sheet is signed to ensure that the key issues are thoroughly addressed at this stage. The negotiation often involves the exchange of one or more draft term sheets, as well as diligence concerning the suitability of the space. This evaluation may require the company to engage internal or external resources that may include land use, design, and engineering professionals. Often a project management firm is engaged to assist in evaluating the feasibility, timing, and expense of the build-out. Assuming a deal is reached for appropriate space, the project manager also can supervise or oversee bidding of contracts for the performance of the build-out of the space and, if desired, the actual construction of the space.

Upon reaching agreement on the business terms of the transaction, the broker and legal counsel can assist the company in negotiating the lease or purchase agreement.

It is rare that a fashion company will need to pay a broker for brokerage services. Real estate brokers typically are compensated by the landlord (for a lease) or by the seller (for a purchase) pursuant to a separate commission agreement. It is important, however, that the amount and manner of compensating the brokers be resolved and documented before or at the time they are hired, because the law in many states provides that the broker is entitled to a commission even absent a written agreement if the broker is engaged and is the procuring cause of a transaction.[15]

§ 13:2.2 Forms of Real Property Interests

Fashion companies typically hold retail real property interests in the form of either a (i) lease, pursuant to which the company, as tenant, leases space from an owner, as landlord; or (ii) license, pursuant to which the company, as licensee, obtains a right to use space from a licensor. A fashion company may also hold an ownership interest (known as a "fee estate") in real property; however, because ownership requires the commitment of capital that instead could

15. *See* Greendlinger v. Marilyn A. Donahue Real Estate, Inc., 2004 NY Slip Op. 50913 (2004).

be applied to the company's operations, and because real estate is illiquid, ownership of real property interests is relatively uncommon for most fashion companies, with the exception of irreplaceable retail locations. For these reasons, this chapter will not address ownership of real estate specifically, and will focus on leases and licenses.

There are a number of significant differences between leases and licenses.[16] Under a lease, the landlord grants exclusive possession of the applicable real property to the tenant for an agreed-upon term;[17] under a license, the licensor grants the licensee the right to use the applicable real property, rather than a possessory interest in such real property.[18] The term (or time period) of a lease tends to be fixed and is usually longer than that of a license.[19] In many jurisdictions, statutory protections are available to a tenant under a lease that are not available to a licensee under a license.[20]

A fashion company should consider the following factors in determining whether to pursue a lease or a license for retail space:

- The amount of space required (including any possible expansion space);
- The intended length of the term (including any possible extension options and early termination strategies);
- The intended current and potential future use of the space (including whether the use will require significant capital investment by the tenant);
- The desire for exclusive rights to the location and/or restrictions on competitive uses in the project where the space is located; and
- The importance of the space to the strategic plan of the company.

If a fashion company requires a small amount of retail space for a short amount of time and a less formal use, such as a temporary "pop-up" shop or kiosk, a license may be preferable to a lease. If, however, a fashion company requires a large amount of retail space

---

16. *See* MILTON R. FRIEDMAN, FRIEDMAN ON LEASES (Andrew R. Berman ed., 6th ed. 2017) [hereinafter FRIEDMAN], § 37:1.1 (Supp. July 2018).
17. *Id.* § 1:2.2 ("A lease creates a possessory interest in land. . . . It is safe to say that leases are both transfers of property interests and contracts.").
18. *Id.*
19. *Id.*
20. *Id.*; *see also* N.Y. REAL PROP. ACTS. LAW § 733 (notice relating to a proceeding for non-payment of rent must be given at least five days prior to the hearing with respect thereto).

for a longer term and a formal use, such as a retail store or a boutique, a lease may be preferable. In particular, if the space is intended to be a flagship store or the primary source of revenue for the company, then the company may prefer a lease in order to have the broadest range of contractual rights, statutory protections, and legal remedies. Pop-up locations usually are documented as licenses, whereas a presence for a longer term, and/or that involves considerable capital investment by the tenant or by the landlord in reliance on the tenant's continued occupancy, usually are documented as leaseholds.

An alternative arrangement that can take the form of a lease or a license (or a sublease or sublicense) is the "shop within a shop" or "in-store shop."[21] In this arrangement, traditionally seen in department stores but beginning to be seen in other locations, such as co-working spaces, individual retailers are permitted to use space within a larger retail department store or other location where people are likely to be present, often in close proximity to one another. Retailers benefit from this arrangement because it minimizes their real property-related concerns, such as build-out and maintenance obligations, allowing them to focus on their core operations, and the department store or other location benefits from this arrangement because it attracts customers interested in the retailer and the concept of one-stop shopping, or one-stop living and working.[22] In the traditional department store context, to focus customers while emphasizing variety, a department store will usually group individual retailers by product category, such as handbags, causing competing brands, such as Chanel and Louis Vuitton, to be adjacent to one another.[23] For this reason "shop within a shop" arrangements traditionally have been most beneficial to brand-driven retailers with low substitutability, such as those with a strong brand identity and loyal customer base.[24] Brand-driven retailers are attractive to a department store primarily because they offer an established customer base that can provide a dependable source of foot traffic. A department store often structures these arrangements as licenses or short-term leases (or sublicenses or short-term subleases, if the store leases its space) in order to preserve flexibility in its business and marketing plans, but a well-known, successful brand may be able to secure a longer-term lease based on

---

21. FRIEDMAN, *supra* note 16, § 37:4 (Supp. July 2018).
22. SPECIALTY RETAIL REPORT, FEATURE: STORE WITHIN A STORE OFFERS ONE-STOP SHOPPING FOR CONSUMERS.
23. *Id.*
24. KNOWLEDGE @ WHARTON, THE ECONOMIC INCENTIVES OF THE 'STORE-WITHIN-A-STORE' RETAIL MODEL (Sept. 2, 2009), http://knowledge.wharton.upenn.edu/article.cfm?articleid=2333.

its reputation and ability to attract customers (and, of course, the rent it is willing to pay).

Fashion companies may also need space for office use, warehousing, and distribution. Facilities for these uses historically have been less unique than retail premises, although they may still need to be strategically located. An emerging generation of light manufacturing spaces may take on more retail-like or co-working aspects, as smaller domestic makers operate in turn-key builds as part of repurposed or new construction developments involving gathering spaces, bocce courts, and microbreweries.[25] Further consideration could be given to the determination about whether to arrange for self-operated fulfillment operations or using a third-party provider, particularly if the business model will include an online sales presence.[26] In addition, while many issues discussed regarding retail leases apply to leases for other purposes, the most significant issues may not be applicable, and the overall business risk may be lower, since leases for office, warehouse, or distribution space usually have a lower rent and carrying costs; are more readily deployed for different users; and are less visible to the public. For these reasons the discussion below will focus principally on leases of retail space. For the sake of simplicity the remainder of this chapter will refer to "leases," "landlords," and "tenants," but many of the issues discussed apply equally to "licenses," "licensors," and "licensees," respectively.

§ 13:2.3 Holding Real Property Interests; Guaranties and Security Deposits

Prior to entering into a legal arrangement to acquire an interest in real property, a company should determine which legal entity will hold the interest and, in particular, whether the real property interest should be held by a different entity than that which holds other assets of the business. Some companies endeavor to protect the company's non-real estate assets by creating a separate entity to enter into a real property lease. This entity is often a wholly owned, direct or indirect subsidiary of the parent company, and its sole purpose is to enter into and hold the lease or the company's portfolio of real estate assets. Such single-purpose subsidiaries do not generally hold assets other than the applicable leasehold interest(s). In the case of companies that have more than one brick-and-mortar presence, there may

---

25. *See, e.g.*, Adam Robinson, *Creative Industrial Workspaces*, DEV. MAG. (Spring 2017), https://www.naiop.org/Magazine/2017/Spring-2017/Business-Trends/Creative-Industrial-Workspaces.

26. *See, e.g.*, Aden Andrus, *Amazon Fulfillment, Is Amazon FBA Worth the Cost*, DISRUPTIVE ADVERT. (June 28, 2018), https://www.disruptiveadvertising.com/ppc/ecommerce/amazon-fulfillment/.

be a separate subsidiary entity that serves as the tenant under each lease. This multi-subsidiary structure is used primarily to segregate liability under each lease and to shelter the assets of the parent company, since a landlord's contractual recourse under a lease is typically limited to the tenant entity itself.[27]

Some landlords require that the parent company, or another entity that holds operating assets of the company, sign the lease as tenant. Many landlords, however, will accept a single-purpose subsidiary as tenant if a security deposit in the form of cash or a letter of credit and/or a guaranty from a creditworthy entity or individual is provided to support the lease payments.[28] In addition, landlords of tenants that are closely held may require a "good guy" guaranty pursuant to which a creditworthy entity or individual guaranties the obligations of the tenant under the lease, but only until the leased premises are returned in the condition required by the lease.[29] The primary intention of a "good guy" guaranty is to motivate a struggling tenant to surrender its premises to the landlord quickly so that the premises can be re-leased. "Good guy" guaranties are most common in retail spaces where the landlord carefully curates the tenant mix, such as Chelsea Market in Manhattan, and in those areas where a dark store window can adversely affect the retail traffic for other tenants and damage a landlord's ability to attract and keep tenants at landlord-favorable rents, such as a shopping mall.

Tax considerations should also be taken into account when structuring ownership of an interest in real property, as more particularly discussed in chapter 1.

§ 13:3 Drafting Lease Provisions

§ 13:3.1 Space

A lease for brick-and-mortar space should clearly and accurately describe the relevant space. This is usually best accomplished by attaching an exhibit depicting the space to the lease itself. It can also be helpful to specify the exact rentable square footage of the space, as agreed upon by the landlord and the tenant, since this number is frequently used in rent calculations, and to specify whether the premises is subject to remeasurement during the lease term. In addition,

---

27. Landlord's recourse under a lease may also be limited to the tenant entity itself by applicable law. *See, e.g.*, OMV Assocs., L.P. v. Clearway Acquisition, Inc., 82 Mass. App. Ct. 561 (2012).
28. *See* FRIEDMAN, *supra* note 16, § 35:1 (Supp. July 2019) (guaranties).
29. Andrew A. Lance, *Lease Assignments and Assumptions*, *in* COMMERCIAL LEASING (Joshua Stein ed., 3d ed. 2017) [hereinafter Lance]; *see also* FRIEDMAN, *supra* note 16, § 35:2.1 (Supp. July 2019).

the lease should specify the delivery condition of the space, including any work that the landlord is required to perform and any tenant improvement allowance that the landlord is required to provide, as discussed below.

In the event a fashion company foresees the potential for expanding its brick-and-mortar presence within the same building, it may want to negotiate for expansion options in the lease. Expansion options are usually in one of three forms: (1) a right to take on additional space, (2) a right of first offer with respect to additional space, or (3) a right of first refusal with respect to additional space.[30] In each circumstance, the lease should specify the exact space to which the right is applicable, any rights to such space that are superior to those of the fashion company (such as the right of an existing tenant to extend the term of its lease or a right available to another tenant in the building), and any requirements for the delivery condition of the space, such as landlord work or tenant improvement allowances.

If the expansion option is in the form of a right to take on additional space, then the fashion company will typically have the option to expand into the specified space as of a specified date or, more frequently, the date on which such space becomes available for leasing, subject to the exercise of any superior rights. In this circumstance, rent is typically established in advance and set forth in the lease, or is based on the market rates at the time of the expansion, and exactly how such "market rate" will be determined. If the option is in the form of a right of first offer, then when such space becomes available for leasing, the landlord must offer such space to the fashion company before it can offer it to anyone else, subject to superior rights. In this circumstance, rent is also based on market rates at the time of the expansion. And if the option is in the form of a right of first refusal, then if the landlord receives a bona fide proposal for the lease of such space from a prospective tenant, it must first offer the applicable space to the fashion company, subject to superior rights. In this circumstance, rent and other lease terms are based on those included in the prospective tenant's proposal.

Conversely, a fashion company may wish to mitigate risks with respect to holding a real property interest by negotiating for the option to surrender space in certain circumstances. If surrender options are available, then they are usually limited to specified space and exercisable at a specified time, and they are often conditioned upon the company's failure to meet certain sales targets by such time and/or the payment of a fee to the landlord, which may be specified in the lease or based on a calculation set forth in the lease.

30. *See* FRIEDMAN, *supra* note 16, § 3:3 (Supp. Apr. 2018) (tenant's option for more space).

In addition, especially in the case of small spaces, a landlord may ask for the right to relocate a fashion company in order to accommodate its own leasing activities.[31] A fashion company will usually be hesitant to agree to such a relocation right unless it is appropriately qualified, such that the new space will have comparable size, configuration, light, and street or concourse frontage, and will satisfy the fashion company with respect to use concerns, as discussed below. In addition, any relocation should be performed at landlord's cost (including both demising and build-out of the new space, as needed, and moving of inventory and other items to the new space, which should also include the reasonable costs of advertising) and should not result in an increased rental burden under the lease.

§ 13:3.2 Term

Another important provision in a lease for retail space is its duration, or, the term. Historically, a new fashion company may prefer a lease with a relatively short term (under five years), while a more established fashion company may prefer a long-term lease (ten or more years), especially at flagship locations, which longer term was traditionally preferred to hedge against increasing rents and operating costs. However, given the current state of retail leasing, a fashion company should think carefully about whether a longer term is likely to result in a better deal (for example, better concessions), or whether it may simply lock the company into space at a higher rate than the market is likely to require in the future. *Hic Sunt Leones*. The lease should be clear about when the term commences and expires, and under what conditions. Often the term of a lease commences upon the substantial completion of the work that a landlord is required to perform in order to prepare space for a fashion company, as discussed below, or on a fixed date specified in the lease.[32] The expiration date is usually the last day of a fixed period after the commencement date or a fixed date specified in the lease.

In the event the term of a lease commences upon the substantial completion of any landlord work, a fashion company may seek to include provisions to ensure that the landlord work is substantially completed and possession of the space is delivered to the fashion company by a fixed date that is consistent with the fashion company's plans for opening and operating the space. Similarly, in the event the term of a lease commences by a fixed date specified in the lease, a fashion company may want the lease to include provisions to ensure that any landlord work is substantially completed by such date. The

---

31. *See id.* (landlord's right to relocate a tenant).
32. *Id.* § 4:2.2 (Supp. Apr. 2018).

two most common provisions used to accomplish this goal are (1) a rent abatement and (2) a termination right.[33] One or both of these provisions can be used, such as in the following example:

> *Landlord shall use commercially reasonable efforts to cause Landlord's Work to be Substantially Completed on or before January 1, 2020, subject to Tenant Delay and Force Majeure. If Landlord fails to Substantially Complete Landlord's Work and to deliver possession of the Demised Premises to Tenant in the condition required by this Lease on or before January 1, 2020, subject to Tenant Delay and Force Majeure, then all Fixed Rent and Additional Rent shall be abated one (1) day for each day thereafter until Landlord's Work has been Substantially Completed and possession of the Demised Premises has been delivered to Tenant in the condition required by this Lease. If Landlord fails to Substantially Complete Landlord's Work and to deliver possession of the Demised Premises to Tenant in the condition required by this Lease on or before February 1, 2020, subject to Tenant Delay and Force Majeure, then Tenant shall have the right to terminate this Lease upon written notice to Landlord. Upon Tenant's exercise of such right in accordance with the immediately preceding sentence, this Lease shall terminate and shall be of no further force or effect, and Landlord shall return any amounts paid on account of the first month's rent hereunder and any security deposit to Tenant within five (5) days of Landlord's receipt of such notice. For purposes of this Lease, "Landlord's Work" shall mean the alterations shown on the plans and specifications attached hereto as Exhibit A; "Substantially Complete" and similar terms shall mean the state of progress of Landlord's Work at which Landlord is ready to deliver exclusive possession of the Demised Premises to Tenant with Landlord's Work, including all aspects thereof necessary for the commencement and completion of any initial alterations to be performed by Tenant; completed except for punch list items, meaning minor details of construction, decoration or mechanical adjustment which do not materially interfere with Tenant's access to the Demised Premises or the commencement and completion of any initial alterations to be performed by Tenant; "Tenant Delay" means any delay which Landlord may encounter in the performance of Landlord's Work by reason of any act or omission of Tenant, its employees, agents, contractors, architects, consultants, mechanics and/or laborers; and "Force Majeure" means an "Act of God," strike, lockout, labor dispute, civil commotion, or any other event or cause beyond the reasonable control of Landlord or Tenant, as applicable, provided that a lack of financing or funds is expressly excluded from the definition of "Force Majeure."*

33. *See* Young v. Kaplan, 288 N.E.2d 698 (Ill. App. Ct. 1972).

Other factors that may influence the commencement date of the lease are seasonal requirements of the company. The holiday season from "Black Friday" (the day after Thanksgiving) through the end of the calendar year is a particularly busy time for many fashion companies, and some companies are busy at the beginning of spring and fall when new product lines arrive. If a company's business depends in large part on revenue brought in during a specific period, the company may want to ensure that the commencement date occurs early enough for the company to be able to operate during such period, and if there is a delay, the company may seek to defer taking possession (and the payment of rent) until after such period has ended. A fashion company should also consider whether any delay in the commencement date will similarly delay the expiration date or whether the expiration date will remain fixed regardless of possible delays.

Two additional lease provisions that may affect the duration of the term of a lease are cancellation provisions and extension provisions. If the term of a lease is longer than a fashion company would prefer, it may be able to negotiate a cancellation option exercisable after a specified period of time.[34] Similar to a surrender option, the company's ability to exercise a cancellation option may be based on whether it is able to meet certain sales targets by a specified date. In other circumstances, the option is exercisable as of a specified date and is not subject to additional conditions, but if it is exercised, the company may be required to pay a fee to the landlord. Note that if all or a portion of the rent payable under the lease is based on sales, the landlord may also want the right to cancel the lease if certain sales targets are not met by a specified date.

An extension option can be useful to a fashion company because it allows the company to defer making a decision about extending the term of the lease until it has been operating in the relevant space for a period of time, as landlords are typically prohibited from offering the space to other parties until the date by which the company must exercise the option has passed. In addition, extension option provisions frequently specify the fixed rent payable during the extension term(s) in advance or provide that it is discounted from then-market rates by five or ten percent (often with a floor tied to the rent payable during the last month or year of the initial term of the lease).[35] It is best if the lease includes specific terms with respect to any extension options, including how market rates are calculated, how disputes regarding market rates are resolved, and whether the landlord must perform any

34. *See* FRIEDMAN, *supra* note 16, ch. 22 (Apr. 2019).
35. *See id.* § 14:1.3 (Supp. Apr. 2019) (recomputing rent upon renewal).

work or pay any tenant improvement allowance to tenant in connection therewith.

§ 13:3.3 Use Provisions

In negotiating a lease, particular attention should be paid to those terms that could impact the objectives and profitability of the company in both obvious and subtle ways. The principal lease provision that must fit the company's business strategy is the "use" provision.

For a women's apparel company, for example, the use provision should clearly permit the sale of women's apparel as follows:

> *Tenant shall be permitted to use the Demised Premises for the retail sale of women's apparel.*

However, it is important to consider ancillary uses of the space that the company may require, such as office or storage use, hosting events that may involve the serving of alcoholic beverages, showroom use, and personal consultations or shopping services that attract walk-in traffic, as well as modifications to the use that may be necessary as a result of changes in the company's business plan or the need to pursue exit strategies.[36] A women's apparel company may expand to sell accessories, a men's line, or a children's line. It may be acquired by a company that sells additional product lines. Or, it may determine to transfer the lease to a new tenant (an assignment) or to allow another company to utilize the space (a sublease). Ideally, the fashion company should negotiate a broad use provision that gives it the flexibility to make these types of changes, such as the following:

> *Tenant shall be permitted to use the Demised Premises for the retail sale of apparel, accessories, and related items, and for uses ancillary thereto (including, without limitation, storage, light manufacturing, related special events involving food and beverage service (including serving of alcoholic beverages to the extent permitted by law) and office use), for other lawful retail uses, and for no other purposes.*

A fashion company should also be cautious of subtle restrictions in use provisions. Consider the following:

36. *See* S.H. Spencer Compton & Joshua Stein, *Tenant's Checklist of Silent Lease Issues (Third Edition)* (Sept. 2012) [hereinafter Compton & Stein], https://www.joshuastein.com/PDF/Tenant_s_Checklist_of_Silent_Lease_Issues_(3rd_Ed)_35.pdf (exit strategies).

> *Tenant shall be permitted to use the Demised Premises for the operation of Tenant's business and for uses ancillary thereto, and for no other purpose.*

The lack of specificity regarding the business that the tenant is permitted to operate makes this provision seem broad. However, a landlord could argue that the inclusion of the word "Tenant's" to modify the business that can be operated restricts the permitted use to the business of the tenant originally named in the lease. This interpretation could hinder the tenant's ability to assign or sublease the lease to a different tenant entity, and could even be interpreted to prevent the evolution of the Tenant's business into new product areas. A requirement that tenant operate the leased premises under a specified trade name could have a similar effect.

In most jurisdictions, the use of real property is regulated by applicable laws, and a government-issued license, permit, and/or certificate (such as a certificate of occupancy) may be required for a fashion company to operate its brick-and-mortar business. Landlords and tenants often negotiate which party is responsible for obtaining and maintaining such licenses, permits, and/or certificates. A fashion company should understand the legal requirements to renovate and operate leased premises, and the effort, delay, and expense that may be required, suffered, or incurred, to satisfy such requirements in order to reach an acceptable business resolution of this issue.

§ 13:3.4 Exclusive Use and Use Restrictions

If a fashion company leases space in a building with multiple tenants in close proximity (such as a shopping mall), then it may seek to limit direct competition from nearby tenants. In this circumstance, a fashion company might negotiate for an exclusive use provision pursuant to which the landlord agrees not to lease nearby spaces for the same or similar uses, and gives the company the exclusive right to use the leased premises for specified uses. A fashion company may also seek to preclude the landlord's ability to lease space to direct competitors of the company. Note that a landlord generally prefers narrow exclusive use provisions to preserve the greatest latitude in its own leasing efforts. For instance, a landlord may attempt to limit exclusive use provisions to certain portions of the market (for example, "upscale" or "discount") or demographics (sex, age, etc.). Many shopping mall leases contain a covenant that a tenant shall not violate exclusive use provisions in other leases in that mall. Any such requirement should include a specific description of the applicable exclusive use provisions that the fashion company cannot violate and ideally would be limited to provisions existing as of the date of the lease.

Conversely, a fashion company may wish to be included in a cluster of stores dedicated to similar product categories. For example, a company selling women's jewelry may wish to be included in the portion of a shopping mall dedicated to accessories. In this case, a fashion company may seek a landlord covenant to lease spaces in the applicable area only for uses consistent with the desired product category, a termination right if this covenant is breached, and/or a provision making the fashion company's lease obligations contingent on the continued use of such spaces in a manner consistent with the desired product category. In addition, small retailers whose business depends on foot traffic from a nearby larger store, such as shops near a department store "anchor tenant" in a shopping mall, may want similar terms and conditions in their leases, including a termination right if the larger store ceases operations and/or a provision making the lease obligations contingent on the continued operation of the larger store. Requirements regarding the quality of adjacent stores in a cluster or nearby anchor tenants may also be desirable.[37]

A landlord also may seek to limit a fashion company's ability to lease additional space within a given geographic area so as to not draw business away from the leased premises, in particular if payments to the landlord are based on revenues from the leased premises, as discussed below. This provision is typically called a "radius restriction," as it often restricts a company from opening another store within a specified radius or within a bounded area, such as "below 14th Street in Manhattan."[38] The fashion company should endeavor to narrow any radius restriction both as to geographic area and scope, and it should be clear in the lease that the radius restriction does not prohibit any sales through other means of distribution, such as online sales and sales through department stores or other merchants, or any sales not specific to the brand(s) and/or line(s) sold at the leased premises.

§ 13:3.5 Rent

The type of rent payable to a landlord under a fashion company lease usually takes one of three forms:

- *Fixed rent*, consisting of a fixed amount per square foot of space leased by the fashion company, which is payable monthly, in advance, and which may escalate during the term in accordance with pre-agreed fixed dollar amounts, a pre-agreed fixed percentage, or a formula tied to an objective, publicly reported index;

---

37. *See* FRIEDMAN, *supra* note 16, §§ 27:6, 27:7 (Supp. July 2019).
38. *See id.* § 28:1 (Supp. July 2019) (radius restrictions).

- *Percentage rent*, consisting of a percentage of gross revenues generated from sales at the leased premises, which is payable on a monthly, quarterly, or annual basis, in arrears; and
- *Additional rent*, consisting of other payments that may be due to the landlord under the lease, which may be payable on dates that are specified in advance or within a certain period of time after the landlord's demand.

The amount of fixed rent payments is typically determined prior to entering into the lease based on market conditions in the local market and deal-specific factors. Percentage rent payments are typically determined by the use of a formula set forth in the lease, such as the following:

> *In addition to Fixed Rent, Tenant shall pay to Landlord percentage rent in an amount equal to 2% of Gross Revenues over $500,000 up to (and including) $1,000,000 and 3% of Gross Revenues above $1,000,000.*

Fashion companies may prefer to pay a share of their revenues as percentage rent, in lieu of paying only a fixed rent, for a number of reasons. A start-up fashion company may negotiate for a percentage rent provision to limit its front-end lease expenses while it is building its customer base and revenue stream. A percentage rent component may allow a company to negotiate lower fixed rent payments premised upon the possibility of a high upside for the landlord when the business succeeds. And percentage rent provisions encourage cooperation and alignment of the objectives between landlord and tenant by giving the landlord a financial interest in the success of the tenant's business.

In negotiating a percentage rent provision, it is important to carefully define the method for calculating revenues.[39] A landlord typically prefers a general percentage rent provision that includes all gross revenues generated from the sale of apparel or other items at the leased premises, but a fashion company should request that certain expenses be excluded from the calculation, such as taxes, insurance proceeds, refunds, discounts, credit card fees, and, if applicable, commissions, sales incentives, and gratuities payable to employees.[40] A landlord may also seek to include revenues from the company's other points-of-sale, such as online sales. When deciding whether to pay landlord a portion of such other revenues, a fashion company should carefully consider its business objectives and future plans; if such revenues are to be included, the applicable points-of-sale should

---

39. *See id.* ch. 6 (Supp. Nov. 2018) (percentage rent).
40. Compton & Stein, *supra* note 36.

be appropriately defined. A sample definition of gross revenues for a percentage rent provision is as follows:

> *"Gross Revenues" shall include, without limitation, all funds received by Tenant, without deduction and/or set-off of any kind (except as otherwise expressly set forth in this definition), from the sale of all goods, merchandise, and services of any kind or nature from the Demised Premises and from Internet sales that are either originated at terminals in the Demised Premises or picked up by customers at the Demised Premises during each Lease Year; provided, however, Gross Revenues shall exclude the amount of any federal, state or city taxes (including assessments such as municipal or business improvement district assessments) that may now or hereafter be imposed upon or be required to be collected and paid, and that in fact are paid in full, by Tenant against its sales or in respect of the Demised Premises, any insurance proceeds received by Tenant, all refunds, chargebacks, or credits issued by Tenant against its sales, the value of any discounts actually given by Tenant in accordance with this Lease, the actual amount of all commissions, sales incentives, and gratuities actually paid to and retained by individual employees and truthfully reported as such in the form required by law for the payment of same (as evidenced by documentation reasonably satisfactory to Landlord to prove that such commissions, sales incentives, or gratuities were paid to employees in addition to their regular salaries), and any other pass-through expenses actually paid by Tenant against its sales. Gross Revenues shall include sales made for cash or credit, provided that credit card, interchange, or merchant fees actually paid by Tenant in connection with credit sales shall be excluded from Gross Revenues.*

A landlord typically verifies a fashion company's compliance with the percentage rent provisions of the lease by requiring delivery of reports of sales on a monthly, quarterly, and/or annual basis. Such sales reports may need to be audited annually by an independent certified public accountant in accordance with generally accepted accounting principles. A landlord may also request the right to audit a fashion company's records and books of account, including daily sales and receipt records, in order to confirm that the landlord is receiving the full amount to which it is entitled under the percentage rent provision.

The final form of rent payable by fashion companies, additional rent, can be divided into two categories: (1) regularly recurring payments, and (2) non-recurring expenses payable by the tenant under the lease.

Two items that are typically included in regularly recurring payments of additional rent are real estate taxes and operating expense payments. In some markets, such as New York City, a tenant pays its share of increases in the landlord's expenses for these items each year as compared to the landlord's similar expenses in a base year (which base year correlates roughly with the first year of the lease term). In other markets, a tenant pays its share of the landlord's expenses for these items on a pass-through basis. In either case, a tenant's share is typically expressed as the ratio of the amount of space leased by such tenant over the total amount of space in the building, although sometimes a building's retail and office (or other use) components are considered separately for this calculation to account for cost differences attributable to differing uses. For instance, a ground floor retail tenant in an office tower may object to contributing to the expense of repairing and maintaining elevators in the building. Landlords and tenants typically heavily negotiate which expense items are included and excluded in operating expenses and, to a lesser extent, real estate taxes, and there are a number of practice guides that consider this topic in detail.[41] Some landlords choose to simplify the negotiation process and administrative burden related to the determination of operating expenses by increasing fixed rent by a specified percentage each year in lieu of charging a tenant for operating expenses.[42] A landlord of a multi-tenanted retail space also may require tenants to contribute toward a marketing budget for the space as a whole, either as a part of operating expenses or as a separate fixed payment.

Non-recurring payments of additional rent can include overtime charges for heating, ventilation, and air-conditioning; charges for a tenant's use of the freight elevator or loading dock; and late fees for a tenant's failure to make payments on time, among other items. A fashion company may be able to predict some of these expenses based upon its business plan and operating history, but other expenses, such as late fees, can be unpredictable.

§ 13:3.6 Rent Abatements

A fashion company's ability to pay rent for a brick-and-mortar retail location depends upon its ability to generate revenue through the operation of its business in the leased premises. A fashion company often also negotiates for abatements of rent payments that may be due and payable during periods when the company cannot operate its business in the leased premises, such as during the initial build-out of the space and in other circumstances discussed below.[43] Landlords are typically hesitant to provide rent abatements other than those

41. *See, e.g.*, FRIEDMAN, *supra* note 16, §§ 5:4, 5:5 (Supp. Nov. 2018).
42. *Id.*
43. *Id.* §§ 5:1.3, 5:1.5 (Supp. Nov. 2017).

during an initial build-out, as they result in a loss of rent revenue, which may disrupt the landlords' cash flow, their ability to service any debt secured by the building, and their ability to obtain and maintain financing for the same reason. When landlords agree to rent abatement provisions, they are typically limited in one or more of the following ways:

- Some landlords will only provide rent abatements to a tenant when the cause of such tenant's inability to operate is the landlord's gross negligence or willful misconduct. From a tenant's perspective, the cause of its inability to operate should be irrelevant as long as it is not the tenant's own actions; however, if a landlord is unwilling to agree to a rent abatement provision so broad in scope, a tenant should seek to expand the list to include circumstances such as a landlord's failure to perform its obligations under the lease, unavailability of utilities, and force majeure.[44] In any event, tenants are not typically given rent abatements for circumstances that are within the tenant's control. Note that rent abatements resulting from a casualty to or taking of the leased premises are typically handled in a separate casualty and condemnation provision.
- A landlord typically requires at least one notice of the cause of a tenant's inability to operate its business prior to providing a rent abatement, and most landlords also require the tenant's inability to operate to have been continuing for a specified number of consecutive days, or business days, before the tenant is entitled to an abatement.
- Landlords may also seek to narrowly define what constitutes a tenant's inability to operate its business. In addition, landlords may limit rent abatements to only those portions of the leased premises within which a tenant cannot generate revenue.
- Some landlords require a tenant to utilize its business interruption insurance (which tenants are often required to maintain) prior to receiving a rent abatement.

Since a landlord's success is often dependent on its ability to generate a steady stream of rental income and a tenant's success is often dependent on its ability to generate revenue, rent abatement provisions tend to be highly negotiated and carefully drafted. A sample rent abatement provision is as follows:

---

44. Mark A. Senn, COMMERCIAL REAL ESTATE LEASES: PREPARATION, NEGOTIATION, AND FORMS § 17 (5th ed., 2012).

If at any time there is an Abatement Event with respect to all or any substantial portion of the Demised Premises, then Tenant shall receive an abatement of all Rent otherwise due hereunder with respect to the Demised Premises, or the portion thereof affected by the Abatement Event. For purposes hereof, "Abatement Event" means a cessation or interruption in the provision of the repairs, maintenance, and/or services required to be provided by Landlord under this Lease or in access to the Demised Premises (other than as a result of a casualty, or of the negligent or willful acts or omissions of Tenant or any occupant of the Demised Premises, or as a result of a breach by Tenant of this Lease), which failure renders the Demised Premises, or substantial portion thereof, Untenantable for more than two (2) consecutive days (or, in the event such cessation or interruption is the result of Force Majeure, for more than thirty (30) consecutive days). Such rent abatement shall commence on the date such Abatement Event begins (or, in the event such cessation or interruption is the result of Force Majeure, on the thirty-first (31st) day of such Abatement Event) and shall continue until such Abatement Event ceases or such earlier date on which Tenant resumes occupancy of the Demised Premises for purposes of operating its business therein. For purposes of this Lease, "Untenantable" means that Tenant (or any occupant claiming by, through or under Tenant) shall be unable to occupy, and shall not be occupying, the Demised Premises or the applicable portion thereof for the purposes for which Tenant (or such occupant) was using the Demised Premises or such portion thereof (as permitted pursuant to this Lease). Tenant shall give Landlord prompt notice of the occurrence of any such condition, but Tenant's failure to give such notice shall not affect its rights under this Section unless Landlord could not otherwise have reasonably known of the existence of such condition.

A clearly drafted rent abatement provision is particularly important if the fashion company's primary source of revenue is its brick-and-mortar retail store.

§ 13:3.7 Visibility and Signage

An important consideration for a fashion company entering into a lease is the visibility of the retail store to potential customers. A fashion company should consider visibility-related factors such as street frontage, window space, lighting, and signage when selecting a brick-and-mortar location. It is equally important that the fashion company's rights with respect to visibility are protected under the lease, for instance by limiting the landlord's right to later relocation of the tenant.

Several considerations can impact the visibility of a fashion company's leased premises, including local laws, zoning requirements, building codes, applicable landmark designations, and the requirements of the landlord as set forth in the lease. All but the last category may vary by jurisdiction and should be carefully reviewed by a fashion company prior to entering into a lease. For example, the Zoning Resolution of the City of New York requires signage in parts of Times Square to be illuminated at all times, while a landmark designation could completely prevent the use of exterior signage.[45]

Landlords of retail spaces typically are concerned about items that can be seen from the outside of leased premises (such as a street or concourse). A landlord may have established a uniform aesthetic for the building or may be concerned with maintaining the reputation and quality of the building. Fashion companies may need to reconcile their signage and visibility needs with these landlord concerns.

Retail leases often contain several provisions that restrict a fashion company's ability to maximize visibility.[46] In the most restrictive circumstance, a landlord designates a "control zone" consisting of all or specific portions of the leased premises that are visible from outside of the leased premises. Within the "control zone" the landlord typically has continuous control and sole discretion over appearance and presentation, including control and discretion over lighting, signage, awnings, banners, flags, and displays. A landlord exercises this control by means of an approval right over any modification to the appearance and presentation of the "control zone," and this approval can be given or withheld in the landlord's sole discretion.

Since the fashion business is seasonal and trend-driven, a fashion company may need to frequently change its window displays. Therefore, a "control zone" provision may be too restrictive on a fashion company's ability to successfully operate its business, as well as being burdensome as an administrative matter. Accordingly, the "control zone" provision might be qualified in the following ways:

- The landlord's approval of the appearance of the "control zone" and modifications thereto may not be unreasonably withheld, conditioned, or delayed and shall be deemed granted if the landlord does not respond to a request for approval within a specified number of days of its receipt thereof;

- The landlord must pre-approve the initial appearance of the "control zone," as reflected in documentation that is attached to the lease, and the tenant has the ability to make modifications thereto so long as the modifications are consistent with the quality standards and business plan

45. CITY OF NEW YORK, ZONING RESOLUTION OF THE CITY OF NEW YORK, https://www1.nyc.gov/site/planning/zoning/access-text.page.
46. FRIEDMAN, *supra* note 16, § 33:1 (July 2019).

reflected in the documentation that is attached to the lease; and/or

- The landlord's approval is not required for the appearance of the "control zone" and modifications thereto so long as the appearance of the "control zone" complies with the landlord's narrowly defined criteria that are expressly set forth in the lease.

Furthermore, any aspects of visibility and signage that are essential to the operation of the fashion company's business, such as lighting during operating hours and directional signage, should be specifically permitted under the lease.

In addition to general "control zone" provisions, a retail lease often contains specific provisions with respect to a tenant's signage. Although a fashion company may need to make changes to its signage less frequently than to its window displays, signage is an important component of the company's overall visibility to its potential customers.

Lease restrictions with respect to signage are not always limited to the appearance or design of signage, but may also include restrictions with respect to the size of signage, the location of signage, and how signage is attached to the wall or building.[47] The issue of approval over the appearance or design of signage can generally be resolved in the same manner as set forth above with respect to "control zone" approvals. To the extent that the maximum size of signage, the permissible locations for signage, and the method of attachment of signage can be agreed upon prior to lease execution, the agreements should be expressly set forth in the lease, and illustrative diagrams should be attached to the lease. In addition, the landlord and tenant should discuss which party is responsible for obtaining any necessary governmental approvals or permits with respect to signage; which party is responsible for maintaining, repairing, replacing, and, if required, removing signage; and which party is responsible for the costs associated with these activities.[48]

A fashion company may also seek to impose restrictions on the landlord with respect to signage in the areas surrounding the leased premises. This concern is particularly relevant if the landlord sells or leases signage to third parties that do not lease space in the building, but it also applies to the signage of competing tenants and signage that could aesthetically harm the appearance of the leased premises. In addition, a fashion company will want to ensure that it is included on certain of landlord's signage, including monuments, pylons, and

47. *Id.*
48. *Id.*

billboards, and that the location and size of such signage is appropriate for the tenant's position within the building's overall tenant mix. Fashion company tenants may also seek the right to install displays in vitrines located in the building.

Another consideration that can affect both "control zone" displays and signage in urban settings is the possibility that the landlord or other parties may need to erect temporary structures, such as scaffolding and sidewalk bridges, from time to time to perform maintenance, repairs, and replacements, and to comply with law.[49] Scaffolding and sidewalk bridges can obscure retail storefronts on the lower floors of a building, thereby interfering with the visibility of leased premises. Lease provisions with respect to scaffolding and sidewalk bridges must balance the landlord's need to utilize such scaffolding and sidewalk bridges against the resulting interference caused to the tenant's business. Typically, a landlord is required to exercise commercially reasonable efforts to avoid interference with the tenant's business—which may require the landlord to utilize double-height scaffolding, to place temporary signage identifying the tenant's business on such scaffolding, and/or to schedule work that requires scaffolding at times when the tenant's business tends to be slow. In addition, a landlord may be required to provide a rent abatement if the scaffolding or sidewalk bridges obscure the leased premises in violation of the foregoing requirements or for an extended period of time. A sample lease provision with respect to scaffolding and sidewalk bridges is as follows:

> *Landlord and persons authorized by Landlord shall have the right, upon at least ten (10) Business Days' prior written notice to Tenant, to erect and maintain sidewalk bridges and/or scaffolding on or about the Demised Premises and/or the Building that are required to be maintained pursuant to applicable laws in connection with the operation of the Building or any repairs, improvements, or other work performed at the Building, in which event Landlord shall, at Landlord's cost, place identifying signage provided to Landlord by Tenant on such sidewalk bridges and/or scaffolding in front of the Demised Premises, provided that such signage shall comply with applicable laws. Landlord shall use commercially reasonable efforts to minimize the time during which such sidewalk bridges and/or scaffolding remains in place and shall reasonably cooperate with Tenant to schedule the use of sidewalk bridges and/or scaffolding during times when they will least interfere with the operation of business in the Demised*

49. For example, landlords must perform maintenance of a building façade at least once every five years. CITY OF NEW YORK, LOCAL LAW NO. 11 (1998).

> *Premises as determined by Tenant, provided that Landlord shall not be obligated to incur overtime or premium charges in connection therewith. Landlord's violation of this Section or the presence of sidewalk bridges and/or scaffolding in front of the Demised Premises for more than thirty (30) days or during the months of September, November, December, and February shall be deemed an Abatement Event and shall entitle Tenant to a rent abatement in accordance with the provisions of this Lease without the need for the delivery of any notice to Landlord or the passage of any additional amount of time.*

A fashion company should take the possibility of changes in its business plan into account when negotiating visibility-related lease provisions. The broader the fashion company's rights, the better, and any restriction of the tenant's rights to the tenant originally named in the lease should be avoided, if possible.

§ 13:3.8 Practical Considerations; Alterations

A fashion company should ensure that the leased premises are built out to suit the company's needs and that terms of the lease are consistent with the company's operational requirements.

Retail spaces that are leased to fashion companies are often built out to suit the company's specific needs. The initial build-out of the space can be performed by contractors engaged by the landlord or the tenant, and in each case there are unique concerns. If the landlord is building out the fashion company's space, it is best for the company to provide plans and specifications or work with the landlord in the preparation thereof to ensure that the space is customized to the company's needs. In addition, as discussed above, specific lease provisions should be included to ensure that the landlord's work is completed in a timely manner.

If the fashion company is building out its own space, it may be able to obtain a tenant improvement allowance from the landlord. Such allowances are typically provided by landlords as an inducement for the tenant to enter into the lease. The primary considerations for a fashion company that is constructing improvements using a tenant improvement allowance are access to funds and avoiding circumstances in which the company has to advance payments to third parties. The lease should provide for regular disbursements of tenant improvement funds and contain minimal conditions to each disbursement, and the company should be able to pay its contractors and materialmen directly from the funds rather than receiving them on a reimbursement basis. The company may also be able to pay certain "soft" costs, such as architect's invoices and permitting fees, from a tenant improvement allowance, although these expenses are typically capped at a specified percentage of the total amount of the allowance.

Alterations performed by a fashion company tenant are usually subject to the landlord's prior written approval. However, it is typical for the landlord to pre-approve preliminary drawings, or more developed plans and specifications, for the tenant's initial build-out prior to lease execution, and such plans should be attached to the lease to minimize the risk of disputes, if possible.[50] In addition, a tenant can often obtain exceptions to the approval requirement for certain types of work. A landlord typically seeks approval rights over any work that could affect the structural integrity of the building or the functioning of building systems, and alterations in a "control zone" that will be visible from outside the leased premises are subject to the considerations discussed above. Landlords may also insist that alterations conform to a certain quality standard, and they may seek to restrict a tenant's right to perform alterations that would not be considered standard for a retail apparel or accessories store.

A tenant is typically able to obtain the right to perform non-structural alterations that do not affect building systems, are not visible from outside the leased premises, and are standard without obtaining the landlord's prior approval, provided that such alterations comply with the quality standards set forth in the lease and applicable law.[51] A tenant may also seek the right to make purely decorative changes, such as painting, without obtaining the landlord's prior approval, although this right could be limited by "control zone" provisions.

Many landlords require the right to pre-approve architects, contractors, and others who may be involved with alterations in the building. Landlords may have preferred providers, in which case the fashion company should request that the identity of such providers be scheduled in the lease.[52] It may be important for a fashion company to obtain pre-approval, in the lease, for certain of its providers, in particular for those that are integral to the project, such as a famous architect who may be designing the space.[53]

In some circumstances alterations to leased premises may be funded and/or performed by the landlord. In the former circumstance, it is important for a tenant to limit requisition requirements so that it is able to access the funds easily and timely pay its contractors and materialmen. Ideally, funds should be disbursed up front rather than on a reimbursement basis so that the company does not have to use

---

50. FRIEDMAN, *supra* note 16, § 23:7 (Supp. Apr. 2019).
51. Compton & Stein, *supra* note 36.
52. *Id.*
53. *Id.*

its own funds for the alterations. In the latter circumstance, the lease should expressly provide for the landlord's obligations and include detailed plans. Even if a landlord is not required to perform alterations under the lease, it should reasonably cooperate with the tenant's alterations process, including opening and closing out permits and obtaining any necessary governmental approvals.

A fashion company also should consider compliance with the Americans with Disabilities Act (ADA).[54] Since a retail store is a "place of public accommodation" under the ADA,[55] any alterations within the leased premises will need to be ADA-compliant, and the ADA may also require modifications to the leased premises' existing condition. ADA compliance can be expensive, so the lease should specify the party responsible for ADA compliance.

Another practical consideration is access to building systems and facilities. A fashion company may need access to electricity and heating, ventilation, and air conditioning (HVAC). Electricity is either obtained directly from the utility company, in which case the fashion company should pay the bill directly, or from the landlord, in which case the fashion company should pay on a submetered basis. Other means of payment for electricity such as rent inclusion tend to be more expensive.[56] HVAC can be obtained in a number of different ways depending on the building and the fashion company's requirements. Even if a fashion company utilizes HVAC provided by the landlord, it may need to install, maintain, and use supplemental systems, which can impose a significant additional cost. A fashion company should ensure that sufficient HVAC capacity and/or supplemental sources to maintain the temperature of the leased premises is available from the landlord when it is crowded with customers, and that its rights to use any necessary condenser water, roof space, and other HVAC-related items are clearly stated in the lease. A fashion company should also be aware of any after-hours charges and requirements, in particular because the space may require services on evenings and weekends.[57]

A fashion company may need to access the loading dock. The lease should clearly permit access through the building to the loading dock at times and in circumstances consistent with the company's

---

54. Americans with Disabilities Act of 1990, Pub. Law No. 101-336, 104 Stat. 327 (July 26, 1990).

55. 28 C.F.R. pt. 36 (2012).

56. *See* Empire State Bldg. Co. v. Joseph Scott Props., Inc., 2011 N.Y. Slip Op. 50248 (2011) (holding that landlord's profit from an electricity rent inclusion factor is not an illegal windfall).

57. In particular, a fashion company may seek the inclusion of a lease provision splitting the cost among all tenants requesting after-hours service for any given period of time.

requirements. If the leased premises are on a floor other than the ground floor, this access path will likely include a freight elevator. The company should be aware of charges and requirements associated with the use of the loading dock and, if applicable, the freight elevator, and it should attempt to negotiate for free or discounted after-hours usage, at least in connection with its move-in and initial alterations.[58]

Another practical consideration for fashion companies is their future interactions with other tenants in the building. A fashion company may seek the right to engage in activities that could potentially create problems for its neighbors, such as playing music, and its neighbors may create issues for the company. This is a particular concern if the leased premises are adjacent to a restaurant, which may emit odors and smoke, and attract rodents and insects. Most leases contain restrictions on a tenant's ability to engage in activities that might interfere with the rights of other tenants, so a fashion company should ensure that the lease contains appropriate carve-outs for desired activities within its leased premises, and that the company has the right to cause the landlord to enforce the non-interference provisions of its neighbors' leases.[59]

A final practical consideration for fashion companies is the scope of any operational requirements that are set forth in the lease. Landlords may require a fashion company tenant to keep the store open and operating continuously during specified hours. A fashion company should negotiate for the right to remain closed or "go dark" during certain periods, such as during inventory review periods or for renovations, and for the lease to provide that the company is not in breach of a continuous operating requirement unless it has been non-operational continuously for a specified period of time.[60] In addition, a fashion company may seek the ability to modify its operating hours as it acquires more information on consumer shopping habits during the course of operations.

A lease also may require the tenant to operate in accordance with certain standards, which may be defined by reference to other locations operated by the same company, by reference to neighboring tenants or the general quality of the building, or by reference to some other objective or subjective standard. A fashion company should seek to avoid giving the landlord detailed approval rights over the operating standards for its retail stores, sticking to general benchmarks like cleanliness, and operating standards that are specific enough to be

58. Compton & Stein, *supra* note 36.
59. *See id.* (competitors).
60. Marc C. Singer, *"Going Dark" Provisions: Making Clients See the Light*, 179 N.J. L.J 980 (2005).

clear but vague enough to provide the fashion company with sufficient flexibility in its operations. The concerns that apply to use provisions, as discussed above, apply equally in the context of quality standards.

§ 13:3.9 Assignments and Subleases

As discussed above, in negotiating the terms of a lease, a fashion company should consider potential changes to its strategic plan. If the business is very successful, the fashion company may need to expand into a bigger space or may seek to sell the company. If the business is struggling, the company may need to reduce or eliminate its rent obligations. The fashion industry can be unpredictable, so it is important that a lease provides sufficient flexibility to address the opportunities and challenges that may arise over the duration of the lease.

The assignment and sublease provisions of a lease can significantly impact a fashion company's ability to effectuate strategic change. A lease typically contains a provision prohibiting assignment and subletting without the landlord's prior written consent. In light of the public policy considerations that disfavor restraints on alienation,[61] courts have narrowly construed this restriction to apply only to transactions at the tenant-entity level, unless the lease expressly states otherwise.[62] However, many leases contain specific language limiting upper tier transactions such as transfers of direct or indirect interests in the tenant entity, changes in control, and sales of all or substantially all of a tenant's assets. Landlords may also limit a tenant's ability to engage in transfers by requiring a specific "key" employee to be involved in the operation of the business at all times.

In order to preserve the necessary flexibility, a fashion company may consider the following strategies:

- Obtain the landlord's pre-approval of assignments and/or subleases to certain specified entities affiliated with the tenant entity and/or entities that are controlling, controlled by, and/or under common control with the tenant entity;[63]
- Obtain the landlord's pre-approval of mergers and consolidations, transfers of direct or indirect interests in the tenant entity, changes in control of the tenant entity, growth investments associated with raising capital, employee ownership or sales

61. *See* Riggs v. Pursell, 66 N.Y. 193, 201 (1878).
62. Lance, *supra* note 29.
63. Note that "control" is usually defined by a specified percentage of ownership, the power to control the day-to-day management of the company, or both.

of all or substantially all of the tenant entity's assets; landlords often condition pre-approval of such transactions on the satisfaction of certain requirements, including a net worth and/or liquidity test;[64]

- Obtain the ability to change the identity of the key person, being sure to provide that the death or incapacity of any key person is not a default under the lease unless a reasonably acceptable replacement key person is not appointed within a specified period of time; and
- Obtain the landlord's covenant to not unreasonably withhold, delay, or condition its consent to any assignment or subletting.[65]

Landlords may agree to one or more of these proposals, but they often impose conditions and requirements, such as a notice requirement, a requirement that the tenant not be in default at the time of the proposed transaction, and requirements that must be satisfied before the landlord can be challenged for being unreasonable. The following is a sample permitted transfer provision that includes some of these requirements:

> *Notwithstanding the foregoing, provided that Tenant is not in monetary or material non-monetary default after any applicable notice and the expiration of any applicable cure period hereunder, Landlord's consent shall not be required for (i) the merger or consolidation of Tenant into or with another entity, or the assignment of this Lease in connection with such a merger or consolidation, (ii) the assignment of Tenant's entire interest under this Lease, or the sublease of substantially all of the Premises for substantially all of the Term, in connection with the sale of all or substantially all of the assets of Tenant (excluding cash or cash equivalents), or (iii) the assignment of Tenant's entire interest under this Lease, or the sublease of substantially all of the Premises for substantially all of the Term, to an Affiliate of Tenant or of Guarantor (but only so long as such assignee or subtenant remains*

64. Lance, *supra* note 29. Considering the growing popularity of private equity investment in fashion companies, a company also may seek transfer provisions which would allow investment and exit by serial private equity investors without requiring the consent of the landlord at each transaction. Similarly, it also may be desirable to have the flexibility to undertake an initial public offering or a going private transaction without the consent of the landlord.

65. *See id.* (discussing the "nebulous nature of the reasonableness standard" and standards for determining reasonableness used and followed by New York courts).

an Affiliate of Tenant or Guarantor) provided that in each case: (A) such transaction must be for a valid business purpose and not principally for the purpose of transferring Tenant's interest in this Lease or to circumvent Tenant's obligations under this Lease, (B) Tenant shall have notified Landlord in writing of such transaction, (C) the Guaranty shall remain in full force and effect, and Guarantor shall have ratified the Guaranty in writing, (D) control of the operations of the business in the Premises shall remain continuous and shall not change as a result of such transaction, and (E) reasonable evidence of all of the foregoing requirements shall have been provided to Landlord prior to such transaction. In addition, Landlord's consent shall not be required for the direct or indirect transfer of shares or equity interests in Tenant (including, without limitation, the issuance of equity securities, treasury stock or a new class of stock) on a public exchange. Furthermore, the "conversion" from one form of business entity to another pursuant to applicable provisions of state law which provide for the continuity of such converted entity (such as conversion from corporation to a limited liability company) shall not in and of itself constitute an assignment or transfer. The term "Affiliate" means, as to any designated person or entity, any other person or entity which controls, is controlled by, or is under common control with, such designated person or entity. The term "control" (and with correlative meaning, "controlled by" and "under common control with") means ownership or voting control, directly or indirectly, of 50% or more of the voting stock, partnership interests or other beneficial ownership interests of the entity in question.

A fashion company also should consider whether it will remain liable under the lease after the assignment transaction has been consummated. This concern also applies to any guarantor who has provided a guaranty in connection with a lease. Most leases contain a provision stating that the tenant remains liable under the lease notwithstanding any assignment or deemed assignment, and a guaranty usually remains in place until all of the obligations of the tenant under the lease have been satisfied.[66] However, a fashion company may be able to negotiate the right for the release of the tenant and/or a guarantor if certain requirements are met such as providing a replacement guarantor that satisfies a net worth and/or liquidity test.

§ 13:3.10 Other Provisions

There are a number of other issues that a fashion company must consider when entering into a lease. As discussed elsewhere, intellectual property is an important and valuable aspect of a fashion

66. Lance, *supra* note 29.

company's business, and a fashion company should ensure that its intellectual property is protected under the lease. Inventory can be valuable, so it may be necessary to address building security in the terms of the lease. If there is debt financing secured by a mortgage lien on the building, a fashion company should obtain an agreement that will permit the lease to continue even if the lender forecloses.[67]

§ 13:4 Special Considerations With Respect to Fashion Shows

Some of the most creative uses of real property can be seen at fashion shows. While the goal of a fashion show is to showcase a designer's line for the upcoming season, the physical location of the fashion show has come to play an important role in the presentation of that line. In Louis Vuitton's show during Paris Fashion Week (Fall/Winter 2013), the runway was set in a grand hotel, accentuating the "louche implications" of designer Marc Jacobs's lingerie-like lace dresses and 1950s style coats.[68] Similarly, during New York Fashion Week (Fall/Winter 2013), Tommy Hilfiger chose a library set on Park Avenue to emphasize his "Americanized, hyper-preppy version of English style."[69] This can cut both ways, as the 2018 New York Fashion Week closed out with a dramatic event at an exclusive Upper East Side townhouse on the market for $14.35 million.[70]

There are a number of special considerations that a fashion company should take into account when planning a fashion show, including the following:

- Since fashion shows are short-term events, the form of real property interest granted to the fashion company is typically a license. As discussed above, a licensee does not have the same statutory protections afforded to a tenant,[71] so it is important for the fashion company to carefully consider and incorporate

---

67. Such agreements are typically called subordination, non-disturbance and attornment agreements. FRIEDMAN, *supra* note 16, § 8:1 (Nov. 2018).

68. Lisa Armstrong, *Paris Fashion Week: Louis Vuitton Autumn/Winter 2013*, TELEGRAPH (Mar. 6, 2013) (quoting Marc Jacobs), http://fashion.telegraph.co.uk/news-features/TMG9913201/Paris-Fashion-Week-Louis-Vuitton-autumnwinter-2013.html.

69. Eric Wilson, *Preppy Style and Joe Flacco at the Tommy Hilfiger Show*, ON THE RUNWAY BLOG, N.Y. TIMES (Feb. 8, 2013, 8:48 PM), http://runway.blogs.nytimes.com/2013/02/08/preppy-style-and-joe-flacco-at-the-tommy-hilfiger-show/.

70. *Fashion Fuses With Real Estate to Close Out NYFW 2018*, ASPIRE METRO (Feb. 27, 2018), https://aspiremetro.com/fashion-fuses-real-estate-close-nyfw-2018/.

71. FRIEDMAN, *supra* note 16, § 37:1.1 (Supp. July 2018).

remedies if the company is not able to hold the show for reasons outside of its control.[72]

- Fashion shows are increasingly held at novel locations, such as abandoned warehouses and unusual loft spaces. In many circumstances, there may be legal restrictions on the use of such spaces for fashion shows based, for example, on the certificate of occupancy and zoning requirements. A fashion company must consider the legality of its use of the applicable space and provide sufficient time to obtain any necessary governmental permits or approvals. The license agreement should address whether the licensor or licensee is responsible for the effort and cost of obtaining such permits and approvals. It is prudent for a fashion company to negotiate for a termination right if they cannot be obtained.

- Most fashion shows involve music, often played loudly to establish a tone for the show. Depending on the location and time of day, the use of loud music could create practical and legal problems. Practical problems such as complaints from neighbors could generate negative publicity and administrative burdens.[73] Legal problems, such as violations of air and noise ordinances, could cause the termination of the show. A fashion company should consider these issues and should seek to address them in advance by obtaining any related permits, utilizing noise attenuation techniques, and scheduling the show so as to minimize conflict regarding noise levels.

- In some circumstances, a fashion company may serve food and/or beverages at a fashion show or fashion show-related event. In such circumstances, there are often additional legal requirements that must be addressed. Local health department regulations will likely apply, and a licensor may wish to address issues relating to food service, such as odors, refuse, and extermination requirements, in the license agreement. In addition, it is likely that the fashion company will need to obtain a special permit or license in order to serve alcoholic beverages.

---

72. Remedies may include a refund of the license payment or a portion thereof and/or the opportunity to change the date of the show if the show cannot be held on the date specified.

73. Mireya Navarro, *Is Fashion Week Smoking?*, GREEN BLOG, N.Y. TIMES (Feb. 18, 2011, 7:41 AM), http://green.blogs.nytimes.com/2011/02/18/is-fashion-week-smoking/.

Chapter 14

E-Commerce and Mobile Commerce

§ 14:1 Introduction
§ 14:2 Developing E-Commerce and Mobile Commerce Platforms
§ 14:2.1 E-Commerce Stores
§ 14:2.2 Mobile Commerce
§ 14:3 Legal Issues Affecting E-Commerce and Mobile Commerce
§ 14:3.1 Contract Issues
§ 14:3.2 Data Privacy and Security Issues
[A] Regulatory Privacy Issues
[B] Private Privacy Litigation
§ 14:3.3 State Taxation and *South Dakota v. Wayfair*
§ 14:3.4 Other E-Commerce Issues
§ 14:4 Payment Methods

§ 14:1 Introduction

Beginning in the mid-1990s, e-commerce (the purchase and sale of goods over the Internet) emerged as a viable retail sales channel in the United States. E-commerce offers retailers the advantages of lower operational costs, a 24/7 sales platform, and an expansive customer reach. By the second quarter of 2018, e-commerce represented 9.6% of total retail sales.[1] It is projected to make up 17% of United States retail sales by 2022.[2] Mobile commerce (the purchase of goods using mobile devices such as smartphones and tablets), which developed

---

1. U.S. CENSUS, QUARTERLY RETAIL E-COMMERCE SALES 2ND QUARTER 2018 (Aug. 17, 2018), https://www.census.gov/retail/mrts/www/data/pdf/ec_current.pdf.
2. Daniel Keyes, *E-Commerce Will Make up 17% of all US Retail Sales by 2022—and One Company Is the Main Reason*, BUS. INSIDER

more recently, accounted for 34.5% of U.S. e-commerce retail sales in 2017 and is expected to account for 53.9% of U.S. e-commerce retail sales in 2021.[3] Most significantly, as Americans increasingly adopt a digital- and mobile-centric lifestyle, consumers are using the Internet and their mobile devices as a part of their entire product research, browsing, and purchasing experience.[4] Studies have shown that 82% percent of smartphone users consult their phones before making in-store purchases.[5]

E-commerce sales of apparel make up a large and growing share of domestic apparel sales.[6] Online apparel sales accounted for 27.4% of U.S. apparel sales in 2017, up from 23.5% in 2016 and 20.7% in 2015.[7] Amazon has contributed to the growth of e-commerce in apparel both through expanding its private label lines and by providing a platform for sales by specialty retailers that traditionally sell through brick-and-mortar stores.[8] Gap, American Eagle, and Abercrombie & Fitch are investing in digital sales, while Macy's plans to redesign

---

(Aug. 11, 2017), http://www.businessinsider.com/e-commerce-retail-sales-2022-amazon-2017-8.

3. *U.S. Mobile Retail Commerce Sales as Percentage of Retail E-Commerce Sales from 2017 to 2021*, STATISTA, https://www.statista.com/statistics/249863/us-mobile-retail-commerce-sales-as-percentage-of-e-commerce-sales/.
4. Andrew Meola, *The Rise of M-Commerce: Mobile Shopping Stats & Trends*, BUS. INSIDER (Dec. 21, 2016), http://www.businessinsider.com/mobile-commerce-shopping-trends-stats-2016-10.
5. John Ellett, *New Research Shows Growing Impact of Online Research on In-Store Purchases*, FORBES (Feb. 8, 2018), https://www.forbes.com/sites/johnellett/2018/02/08/new-research-shows-growing-impact-of-online-research-on-in-store-purchases/.
6. James Melton, *E-Commerce Is Transforming the Apparel Business and Gaining Market Share in the Process*, DIGITAL COMMERCE 360 (June 27, 2018), https://www.digitalcommerce360.com/2018/06/27/e-commerce-is-transforming-the-apparel-business-and-gaining-market-share-in-the-process/.
7. *Id.*
8. Daphne Howland, *27% of Apparel Sales Are Now Online*, RETAIL DIVE (July 2, 2018), https://www.retaildive.com/news/27-of-apparel-sales-are-now-online/526941/; Kali Hays, *Amazon Poised to Become Largest Apparel Retailer as It Tackles Heath Care*, WOMEN'S WEAR DAILY (Jan. 20, 2018), https://wwd.com/business-news/financial/amazon-becomes-largest-apparel-retailer-healthcare-venture-warrent-buffet-jamie-diamond-1113 2556/; Lauren Thomas, *Amazon's 100 Million Prime Members Will Help It Become the No. 1 Apparel Retailer in the US*, CNBC (Apr. 19, 2018), https://www.cnbc.com/2018/04/19/amazon-to-be-the-no-1-apparel-retailer-in-the-us-morgan-stanley.html.

its online and mobile shopping interface in 2018.[9] Mobile platforms, in particular, provide fashion companies with a continuing point of contact with consumers.[10] There are three main categories of mobile apps: Discovery Apps, which allow users to browse apparel from a wide range of retailers; Personal Shopping Apps, facilitating direct customer communication with an in-store personal shopper; and Fashion Aggregator Apps, which enable customers to purchase items from multiple brands with a single click.[11] Many retailers and brands recognize the importance of connecting with consumers through mobile devices, in addition to more traditional websites and brick-and-mortar stores.[12]

The retail industry has increasingly experienced the practice of "showrooming" in brick-and-mortar stores.[13] Showrooming occurs when a consumer visits a brick-and-mortar store to view, examine, or compare products, but then chooses to purchase the product online, either from that retailer or another retailer, typically because of more favorable pricing.[14] According to some estimates, approximately 46% of shoppers showroom.[15] However, the opposite phenomenon, called "webrooming" (browsing online but purchasing in-store), is even more pervasive: 69% of shoppers webroom.[16] The increase in webrooming is a result of retailers adopting e-commerce, focusing on in-store customer experience, offering discounts to customers who buy in-store

---

9. *Id.*
10. Neenu Jacob, *Fashion Apps Are a Major Sales Opportunity for Fashion Brands*, SMART INSIGHTS (June 28, 2017), https://www.smartinsights.com/mobile-marketing/app-marketing/fashion-apps-major-sales-opportunity-fashion-brands/.
11. *Id.*
12. *5 Reasons Fashion Needs Mobile Shopping Apps*, INSIDE FMM (Dec. 5, 2011); Cate Trotter, *How Retailers Use In-Store Apps to Increase Sales*, INSIDER TRENDS (Apr. 8, 2016) (identifying Hointer, Rebecca Minkoff, American Apparel, and Belk as particularly focused on mobile app development), https://www.insider-trends.com/how-retailers-use-in-store-apps-to-increase-sales/.
13. Humayun Khan, *Consumers Are Showrooming and Webrooming Your Business, Here's What That Means and What You Can Do About It*, SHOPIFY (June 7, 2018), https://www.shopify.com/retail/119920451-consumers-are-showrooming-and-webrooming-your-business-heres-what-that-means-and-what-you-can-do-about-it; Bryan Pearson, *Whatever Happened to Showrooming? How Big Retail Is Taking Back the Shopping Trip*, FORBES (Aug. 16, 2017), https://www.forbes.com/sites/bryanpearson/2017/08/16/whatever-happened-to-showrooming-how-big-retail-is-taking-back-the-shopping-trip/#4bfe5c6779cb.
14. *Id.*
15. *Id.*
16. *Id.*

or agreeing to match any price the customer finds online, and offering in-store perks such as special events and readily available Wi-Fi.[17]

As e-commerce expands domestically, retailers and brands are also building their online presence internationally.[18] In 2017, global e-commerce sales totaled US$2.3 trillion.[19] These sales are expected to reach 4.9 trillion dollars by 2021.[20] As of 2017, China is the largest e-commerce market in the world, with total sales of 672 billion dollars.[21] The other largest e-commerce markets include: the United States, the United Kingdom, Japan, Germany, and France.[22] Retailers in the United States increasingly turn to online distribution channels to enter new markets and build their customer base, without having to invest significant resources in establishing a brick-and-mortar presence.[23] On all but one continent (North America), purchases from overseas made up the majority of purchases in the second half of 2015.[24]

U.S. retailers tend to prioritize certain countries for e-commerce expansion.[25] They begin by expanding into top-tier markets that already have a developed e-commerce presence, such as the United Kingdom, China, Japan, and South Korea.[26] They next expand into those countries that are in the early stages of e-commerce development, have complex domestic regulations, or are digitally advanced but have only a small market (for example, India, Mexico, Saudi Arabia, and Sweden).[27] Retailers tend to avoid countries, such as Russia and Argentina, that have uncertain political climates or challenging infrastructures.[28] Moreover, U.S. retailers face significant inventory

---

17. *Id.*
18. Shachar Baryamin, *E-Commerce and the Global Expansion Trend*, MARKETBEYOND (Feb. 20, 2018), https://themarketbeyond.com/e-commerce-global-expansion-trend/.
19. *Retail E-Commerce Sales Worldwide from 2014 to 2021*, STATISTA, https://www.statista.com/statistics/379046/worldwide-retail-e-commerce-sales/.
20. *Id.*
21. Richie Edquid, *10 of the Largest Ecommerce Markets in the World by Country*, BUS. (Feb. 22, 2017), https://www.business.com/articles/10-of-the-largest-ecommerce-markets-in-the-world-b/; *see also id.* at 7–8, 10.
22. *Id.*
23. *See* Aaron Orendorff, *Global Ecommerce: Statistics and International Growth Trends*, SHOPIFY (Sept. 1, 2017), https://www.shopify.com/enterprise/global-ecommerce-statistics.
24. *Id.*
25. *Id.*; *Key Findings from the 2018 E-Retailer Global Expansion Report*, INTERNET RETAILER (Aug. 2018), https://www.eshopworld.com/wp-content/uploads/2018/08/Aug2018_IR_GlobalExpansion_KFR_eShopWorld-2.pdf.
26. *Id.*
27. *Id.*
28. *Id.*

management issues in fulfilling international e-commerce orders.[29] These challenges can be addressed by finding a trustworthy international provider of warehousing and delivery services.[30] In managing international mobile sales platforms, brands and retailers also must be conscious of the need to account for pricing policies developed to control against the risk of antitrust liability (see chapter 12) and reimported gray market goods that can undermine a brand's U.S. pricing strategy (see chapter 8).[31]

§ 14:2 Developing E-Commerce and Mobile Commerce Platforms

§ 14:2.1 E-Commerce Stores

The most common way that retailers establish an e-commerce presence is by creating a website that serves as an e-commerce store. In an e-commerce store, the customer browses the product offerings, selects an item for purchase, places the item in an electronic shopping cart, enters billing, shipping, and payment information, and then makes the purchase, generally followed by an electronic receipt. The customer may interface directly with the retailer's e-commerce store, or may initially view a third-party website or an ad, and then click through to the e-commerce store.

A retailer either locates the e-commerce store on its existing website, or identifies and registers a unique domain name for a new e-commerce website. Domain names bring Internet users to a particular website because the registrant of a domain name targets it to a specific numerical Internet Protocol address that identifies the server or servers that host the owner's website.[32] Domain names consist of several parts that are separated by dots: first, the set of letters or numbers specifically chosen by the registrant, known as the "second-level domain," followed by the suffix that identifies the Internet registry that the domain has been registered in, known as the TLD, or top-level domain (for example, "com" or "org"). After the TLD, the website host can set up subdirectories for additional

---

29. *Id.*
30. Nathan Resnick, *International Warehouses in Global Ecommerce: A Guide*, SHOPIFY (Aug. 16, 2017), https://www.shopify.com/enterprise/international-warehouses-ecommerce-guide.
31. COUNTRY COMMERCIAL GUIDES, INTERNATIONAL TRADE ADMINISTRATION, https://www.export.gov/ccg.
32. Howard S. Hogan & Stephen Feingold, *Domain Name Registration, Maintenance and Protection*, *in* INTELLECTUAL PROPERTY LAW IN CYBERSPACE, 463–64 (G. Peter Albert, Jr., ed., BNA Books 2011) (internal citation omitted).

"pages" of the website, identified by letters or numbers that follow a backslash (\). The Internet Corporation for Assigned Names and Numbers (ICANN), a non-profit organization that coordinates the Domain Name System and Internet Protocol addresses, accredits a domain name registrar for each TLD, which then assigns domain names to registrants.[33] The registrar for each TLD maintains the official registry, which is the central database of names registered to that TLD.

Domain names for an e-commerce website traditionally reflected the name of the company selling products or services on the website (such as Burberry.com). In early days of the web, courts asserted that "[w]eb users often assume, as a rule of thumb, that the domain name of a particular company will be the company name followed by '.com'" and that users often attempt to find websites "by hazarding a guess at the domain name."[34] This is less true today: the typical web user types the name of the company into a search engine rather than guessing the domain name.[35] Nevertheless, the domain name chosen for an e-commerce portal should be an easy to remember name. If an unauthorized third party registers a domain name that incorporates a famous mark or something confusingly similar, the trademark owner may have remedies either under U.S. trademark law or under the Uniform Domain-Name Dispute-Resolution Policy (UDRP), which governs the terms of domain name registrations for popular TLDs. For a more thorough discussion of these remedies, see chapter 2, sections 2:2, 2:9.4, and 2:15.1, and chapter 7, section 7:3.3.

It is important to remember that, in addition to the TLD's that are most widely used in the United States (for example .com, .org, and .edu), most countries have appointed authorities to manage separate, nation-specific country code TLDs ("ccTLDs"). Among the most popular are .uk for the United Kingdom, .ca for Canada, .de for Germany, .jp for Japan, .ru for the Russian Federation, and .cn for China. As a result, a company that has reserved its name as a .com should also consider whether to register the same name as one or more ccTLDs. In particular, companies should consider the popularity, acceptance, and usage of ccTLDs in important markets, and the protections that national authorities give to trademark owners whose marks are registered by third parties. Some national ccTLD authorities, for example, do not recognize the remedies set forth in

---

33. *Id.* at 466.

34. *See, e.g.*, Brookfield Commc'ns, Inc. v. West Coast Entm't Corp., 174 F.3d 1036, 1045 (9th Cir. 1999); MARK LEMLEY, PETER MENELL, & ROBERT MERGES, 2 INTELLECTUAL PROPERTY IN THE NEW TECHNOLOGICAL AGE § V.D.4 (2016) (ebook).

35. *Id.*

the UDRP that apply to .com or .org domains. Companies that are frequent victims of counterfeiting may especially want to head off the misuse of their marks by registering available ccTLDs domain names that are most likely to be exploited by unauthorized third parties. There are currently about 1,500 TLDs in existence,[36] which includes around 300 ccTLDs.[37] Other types of top-level domains include generic (gTLD—for example, fashion or .gap (the latter is more specifically referred to as a brand TLD)), generic-restricted (grTLD), sponsored (sTLD), and test (tTLD) top-level domains.[38]

A retailer might internally develop a full e-commerce website, including a point-of-sale retail platform (such as the shopping chart, and order and payment processing systems).[39] Alternatively, a retailer might purchase an off-the-shelf website design and development package, or enter into a design and development agreement with a software developer.[40] If the website design and development arrangement does not include development of a shopping cart platform, the retailer might obtain such services from a third-party service provider.[41]

An e-commerce platform services agreement with a third-party service provider might include the provision of the following services: warehousing of physical inventory, order taking and processing, payment and sales tax calculation and collection, order fulfillment (including shipment of goods to purchasers, customer service, handling of returns, providing sales reports and consumer and data usage reports for transactions and traffic on the website), and setting up procedures to comply with privacy and data security policies and legal requirements.[42] These providers typically charge a monthly fee for their services (which increases based on the type and extent of services provided). The electronic shopping cart integrates with numerous gateways to accept credit cards, PayPal payments, and other forms of payment. E-commerce platform service providers include Shopify, Magneto, YoKart, BigCommerce, VTEX, WooCommerce, and Tictail.[43] The choice of a service provider and the type of platform used (such as an enterprise cloud platform or an open source

---

36. IANA, ROOT ZONE DATABASE, https://www.iana.org/domains/root/db.
37. *Id.*
38. *Id.*
39. *Launching a Retail E-Commerce Website for the Sale of Goods Checklist*, PRACTICAL L. CO., http://us.practicallaw.com/4-520-4924?q=e-commerce.
40. *Id.*
41. *Id.*
42. *Id.*
43. Bill Carmody, *Top Seven E-Commerce Platforms in 2018*, INC. (Jan. 14, 2018), https://www.inc.com/bill-carmody/top-seven-ecommerce-platforms-in-2018.html.

technology), may have implications for the portability of the system and whether it can be moved in-house or transferred.

A retail e-commerce website should contain appropriate legal notices addressing the retailer's policies and practices with respect to consumers. Websites should contain the retailer's Terms of Sale, covering such matters as payment and order processing, and shipping, return, and exchange policies. The website should also contain the retailer's Terms of Use, covering such matters as website access, dispute resolution, forum selection, limitation of liability, and indemnification. Importantly, websites should contain the retailer's privacy policies, which typically cover the following matters: security (describing the retailer's encryption technology, as well as the physical, electronic, and administrative measures taken by the retailer to maintain the security of personally identifiable data); data collection (describing the types of personally identifiable data and computer hardware and software data that the retailer collects when the customer uses the website); use of customer data (describing how the retailer uses personally identifiable data internally, including showing customers targeted advertisements and sending emails to the customer, and the extent to which the retailer shares personally identifiable data with third parties); use of cookies; links to third-party websites (including disclaimers about such websites); opt-out policies (for example, with respect to online behavioral advertising); the protection of children's privacy; and, perhaps, suggestions as to how the consumer can reduce privacy risks. Websites also disclose the retailer's copyright and trademark policies. Many retailers use the "FAQ" format to provide concise descriptions of some of their most important terms and policies.

§ 14:2.2 Mobile Commerce

In addition to an e-commerce website, many retailers create a mobile commerce website and/or a mobile commerce application, or "app," for smartphones or tablets. In the fourth quarter of 2017, e-commerce retailers saw more than half of their sales come from mobile devices.[44] Thirty-three percent of sales came from PC websites, while 23% came from mobile websites and 44% came from mobile apps.[45] Mobile websites and/or apps allow consumers to perform multiple

44. Greg Sterling, *Retailers With Shopping Apps Now See Majority of E-Commerce Sales From Mobile*, MKTG. LAND (Feb. 21, 2018), https://marketingland.com/retailers-shopping-apps-now-see-majority-e-commerce-sales-mobile-234931. *See* ACQUITY GRP. LLC, 2012 BRAND ECOMMERCE AUDIT, at 14 (Nov. 29, 2012).

45. *Id.*

shopping functions through their mobile smartphone or tablet, including reviewing product descriptions, product images, and product price information; checking customer product ratings and reviews; redeeming store coupons; scanning barcodes in stores; and completing a product purchase. A mobile website is similar to a desktop or laptop computer website, but is designed for a mobile device's smaller display screen and touch user interface. Retailers often use "responsive web design," or RWD, techniques to provide an optimal viewing and navigation experience across a range of devices.[46] RWD uses flexible images and grids which convert to fit the size of the screen, obviating the need to create different designs for different devices.[47]

In contrast, a mobile app is a software program that is downloaded and installed on a specific mobile device. An app can pull content from the Internet (similar to a website), but can also download content so that the content can be accessed without use of the Internet. A mobile app, unlike a website, runs locally on a device and so must be designed for a specific operating system. Two of the most widely used operating systems are Apple's iOS, which is carried exclusively on Apple products, and Google's Android OS, which has been adopted by many manufacturers. Consumers can purchase particular apps for their mobile device through the relevant app store (such as the Apple App Store and Google Play). Before it begins the design and development process for a mobile app, a retailer should set up an account with the applicable app store.[48] In addition, the retailer must enter into a developer agreement with the operator of the app store, and, if different, the technology provider. These agreements are usually entered into online through a clickwrap process (described more fully below). App store developer agreements should be reviewed carefully because they typically cover the following matters: revenue sharing between the developer and the platform, in-app advertising, security and technical requirements for the app, nondisclosure of the app store operator's confidential information, conditions resulting in possible suspension and termination of distribution of the app, indemnification of the app store, forum selection and choice of law, and the requirements applicable to end users, such as privacy and licensing agreements. The app and any updates to the app are typically reviewed by the app store.

---

46. *See HTML Responsive Web Design*, W3SCHOOLS, https://www.w3schools.com/html/html_responsive.asp.
47. *Responsive Web Design*, KNOWLEDGE HUB, https://responsivedesign.is/.
48. *Apple Developer*, APPLE INC., https://developer.apple.com/account/; *Google Play Console*, GOOGLE INC., https://play.google.com/apps/publish/signup/.

The retailer may either internally design and develop the mobile app, or outsource the design and development (programing) of the app to a third party pursuant to a design and development agreement. The design and development of an app includes organizing the content, the user interaction and the visual appearance, and tailoring the app to a particular device.[49] An app design and development agreement typically addresses such matters as the ownership of the software code and the other intellectual property associated with the app, the developer's specific responsibilities and payment terms, the extent of the ongoing support for the app, and confidentiality.

§ 14:3 Legal Issues Affecting E-Commerce and Mobile Commerce

Retail e-commerce and mobile commerce transactions for the sale of goods are subject to many of the same statutes and legal principles that are applicable to physical transactions in goods. E-commerce and mobile commerce transactions also raise certain new legal issues.

§ 14:3.1 *Contract Issues*

Despite the differences between traditional paper retail transactions and online retail sales, many traditional state law contract principles (such as offer and acceptance) still apply to e-commerce and mobile commerce transactions. Transactions involving the sale of goods over the Internet in the United States are subject to the provisions of the Uniform Commercial Code as adopted in the applicable state. However, e-commerce also necessitated new legislation to facilitate online transactions. All fifty states have enacted electronic signature and records laws, such as the Electronic Signatures and Records Act in New York, to recognize the validity of electronic signatures and records.[50] The Electronic Signatures in Global and National Commerce Act, a federal statute, recognizes the validity of electronic signatures and electronic records in interstate and foreign commerce.[51]

Retailers typically use either "clickwrap" or "browsewrap" agreements contained on their website to contractually bind users to the website's terms. A "clickwrap" requires an express, affirmative acceptance of the website terms through the "click" of an "I accept" or "I agree" button, whereas a "browsewrap" is simply a posting of website terms, typically through a hyperlink on the home page, which

---

49. *See, e.g.*, Nick Babich, *Mobile UX Design: Key Principles*, UX PLANET (July 12, 2016), https://uxplanet.org/mobile-ux-design-key-principles-dee1a632f9e6.
50. N.Y. STATE TECH. LAW §§ 301–309.
51. 15 U.S.C. §§ 7001 *et seq.*

states that use of the website signifies acceptance of an agreement with the retailer. Courts have considered the issue of whether "clickwraps" and "browsewraps" create enforceable contracts.

In general, "clickwraps" have been held to create enforceable contracts, unless the terms are unconscionable.[52] However, to be enforceable the layout and the language of the website must still give the user reasonable notice that a click will manifest assent to the agreement.[53] For example, in *Hancock v. American Telephone and Telegraph Co.*, the Tenth Circuit Court of Appeals, applying Florida and Oklahoma law, upheld a clickwrap agreement where customers were required to complete a registration process to access the Internet.[54] During registration, customers were presented with a screen displaying the seller's terms of service and were not be able to proceed without clicking the "I Agree" button.[55] Subsequently customers were emailed updates to the terms of service in which they were notified that continued use of the service signified continued agreement to the terms of service.[56] The court stated that under the basic contract law principles of Florida and Oklahoma, a consumer is bound by the terms of a clickwrap agreement if the clickwrap agreement gives a consumer reasonable notice of its terms and the consumer affirmatively manifests assent to its terms.[57] The court also noted a consensus had developed among earlier cases that notice of the terms of an agreement must be reasonably conspicuous and there must be unambiguous manifestation of assent to those terms for an online

---

52. *See, e.g.*, Hancock v. Am. Tel. & Tel. Co., 701 F.3d 1248, 1256 (10th Cir. 2012); Applebaum v. Lyft, Inc., 263 F. Supp. 3d 454, 470 (S.D.N.Y. 2017) (upholding a clickwrap agreement because users were required to scroll through a clearly labeled terms of service agreement and click on a conspicuous bar labeled "I Accept" before proceeding); Kai Peng v. Uber Techs., Inc., 237 F. Supp. 3d 36, 49 (E.D.N.Y. 2017) (upholding a clickwrap agreement because the users were asked to confirm twice that they had reviewed all the documents and agreed to all the contracts, first in a webpage with a clickable button and subsequently in a popup); Cordas v. Uber Techs., Inc., 228 F. Supp. 3d 985, 991 (N.D. Cal. 2017) (upholding a terms of service agreement because the user was instructed in a statement adjacent to a button with the word "Done" that, by creating an account, the user agreed to the terms and conditions); *In re* Online Travel Co., 953 F. Supp. 2d 713, 719 (N.D. Tex. 2013) (finding a clickwrap agreement valid because the user agreement was conspicuously presented and the plaintiffs assented by clicking the accept button).
53. Sgouros v. TransUnion Corp., 817 F.3d 1029, 1034 (7th Cir. 2016).
54. *Hancock*, 701 F.3d at 1258.
55. *Id.* at 1257.
56. *Id.* at 1254.
57. *Id.* at 1256.

agreement to be upheld.[58] The *Hancock* court concluded that the defendant's presentation of the terms of service complied with these principles and found no reason why the agreement would not be valid and enforceable under Florida and Oklahoma contract law.[59]

In contrast, in *Sgouros v. TransUnion Corp.*, the Seventh Circuit Court of Appeals, applying Illinois state law, did not uphold a clickwrap terms of service agreement after finding that the website did not provide users reasonable notice that their click on a button constituted assent to the website's terms of service.[60] The terms of service were presented in a scrollbox with the title "Service Agreement," and users were required to click a button stating "I Accept and Continue to Step 3" to access the services provided by the website.[61] The court, however, determined that any notice that may have existed was undone by bold misleading text directly above the button stating that a click on the button constituted assent for TransUnion to obtain access to the purchaser's personal information, with no mention of the service agreement.[62] Finding that no reasonable person would have interpreted the disclosure to indicate that clicking the button also constituted acceptance of the service agreement,[63] the court held that no agreement arose between the parties.[64]

"Browsewrap" agreements do not require affirmative action by the website user to indicate assent, and therefore, the validity of a "browsewrap" agreement depends on a factual analysis of whether the user has actual or constructive knowledge of the terms and conditions of the applicable website.[65] Courts consistently enforce browsewrap agreements where the user has actual knowledge of an agreement.[66] Where there is no evidence that the website's user had actual knowledge of the terms and conditions, a browsewrap agreement is valid if the website put a reasonably prudent user on notice that the terms of the contract apply.[67] To make this determination, courts examine the design and content of the website and agreement's webpage, often

58. *Id.* at 1257 (citing *Specht*, 306 F.3d at 35).
59. *Id.* at 1258.
60. Sgouros v. TransUnion Corp., 817 F.3d 1029, 1036 (7th Cir. 2016).
61. *Id.* at 1033.
62. *Id.* at 1035.
63. *Id.*
64. *Id.* at 1036.
65. *See* Nicosia v. Amazon.com, Inc., 834 F.3d 220, 233 (2d Cir. 2016); Nguyen v. Barnes & Noble Inc., 763 F.3d 1171, 1176 (9th Cir. 2014).
66. *See Nguyen*, 763 F.3d at 1176 (collecting cases).
67. Specht v. Netscape Commc'n Corp., 306 F.3d 17, 35 (2d Cir. 2002).

finding inquiry notice if the webpage design renders the reference to the agreement reasonably conspicuous.[68]

The seminal "browsewrap" case is *Specht v. Netscape Communications Corp.*,[69] where the U.S. Court of Appeals for the Second Circuit, applying California law, addressed the issue of whether persons who downloaded software from Netscape's webpage had agreed to be bound by the arbitration clause found in the software's license terms; such terms were only visible to users by scrolling down the webpage to a screen located below the download button.[70] The court explained that a contract requires a mutual manifestation of assent between the parties, and there cannot be a manifestation of consent where there is no reasonable notice of the terms of the contract.[71] The court held that since there was no requirement to unambiguously manifest assent, such as clicking an "I agree" button, and the reference to the existence of the license terms was on a lower screen, a "reasonably prudent" user of the website "would not have known or learned, prior to acting on the invitation to download, of the reference to [the] license terms hidden below the 'Download' button on the next screen."[72] The sole act of using the website did not manifest assent to its terms and conditions.

Courts generally find that use of a website manifests assent to an agreement only where the agreement is visually conspicuous and the user is instructed, or given some additional indication, that use of the website constitutes assent.[73] In *Nguyen v. Barnes & Noble Inc.*, the Ninth Circuit Court of Appeals, applying New York law, held that "where a website makes its terms of use available via a conspicuous hyperlink on every page of the website but otherwise provides no notice to users nor prompts them to take any affirmative action to demonstrate assent, even close proximity of the hyperlink to relevant buttons users must click on—without more—is insufficient to give rise to constructive notice."[74] In *Nguyen*, the website displayed a prominent hyperlink to the terms of service in the bottom left-hand corner of every page on the site near buttons relevant to the user such that the hyperlink would enter the user's visual field if the user were

---

68. James v. Glob. TelLink Corp., 852 F.3d 262, 267 (3d Cir. 2017); *Nicosia*, 834 F.3d at 232; *Specht*, 306 F.3d at 30.
69. *See Specht*, 306 F.3d 17.
70. *Id.* at 20.
71. *Id.* at 29–30.
72. *Id.* at 35.
73. *See* Cullinane v. Uber Techs., Inc., 893 F.3d 53, 64 (1st Cir. 2018); James v. Glob. TelLink Corp., 852 F.3d 262, 267 (3d Cir. 2017); Nguyen v. Barnes & Noble Inc., 763 F.3d 1171, 1179 (9th Cir. 2014).
74. *See Nguyen*, 763 F.3d at 1179.

completing an order.[75] The court determined that this was insufficient to give rise to constructive notice.[76]

Even if the user is given additional indication that they will be bound by an agreement through the use of a website, if the terms of the agreement or the additional notice is not reasonably conspicuous, such notice will also not give rise to constructive notice of the terms.[77] For example, in *Cullinane v. Uber Technologies, Inc.*, the First Circuit Court of Appeals, applying Massachusetts state law, found that Uber's terms of service were not communicated reasonably and, therefore, the user had not assented to the terms.[78] The court came to this decision, even though Uber provided a visually conspicuous hyperlink to the terms of service and additional text stating that by creating an account the user agrees to the terms of service and privacy policy, because other conspicuous terms on the webpage diminished the conspicuousness of the terms of service hyperlink and the notice of being bound.[79]

Similarly, in *Hines v. Overstock.com, Inc.*,[80] the U.S. District Court for the Eastern District of New York refused to enforce an online retailer's website Terms and Conditions. The court, applying New York law, denied Overstock.com's motion to compel arbitration, finding there was no valid agreement to arbitrate because there was no meeting of the minds sufficient to form a contract. Overstock.com's "Terms and Conditions" stated that "[e]ntering this site will constitute your acceptance of these Terms and Conditions." However, the Terms and Conditions were only referenced in a hyperlink at the bottom of the page of Overstock's website.[81] The court found that the user had neither actual nor constructive notice of the Terms and Conditions because the user was not prompted to review the Terms and Conditions upon entering the website, and the hyperlink at the bottom of the page was not prominently displayed.[82]

Another case testing the enforceability of a website's terms of use in the fashion industry was *In re Zappos.com Inc., Customer Data Security Breach Litigation*,[83] a class action lawsuit brought by Zappos customers. Zappos moved to compel arbitration based on an arbitration clause in its website's Terms of Use. The U.S. District Court for

75. *Id.* at 1177.
76. *Id.* at 1179.
77. *Cullinane*, 893 F.3d at 64.
78. *Id.*
79. *Id.*
80. *See* Hines v. Overstock.com, Inc., 668 F. Supp. 2d 362 (E.D.N.Y. 2009).
81. *Id.* at 365.
82. *Id.*
83. *In re* Zappos, MDL No. 235, 2012 WL 4466660 (D. Nev. Sept. 27, 2012).

Nevada, while noting the federal policy favoring arbitration, applied Nevada contract law to deny Zappos' motion to compel arbitration on the grounds that Zappos and its users had not entered into an enforceable contract to arbitrate. The court noted that, although the Terms of Use were located on every Zappos webpage, users were required to scroll down to the bottom of the webpage to locate the Terms of Use; the Terms were inconspicuous as they were in the same size, font, and color as other insignificant links; and the website did not direct a user to the Terms when creating an account or making a purchase.[84] The court held that under the circumstances, "[n]o reasonable user would have reason to click on the Terms of Use. . . ."[85] Moreover, the court found that any agreement would be unenforceable because Zappos retained the unilateral right to change its Terms of Use at any time without notice to the consumer.

In contrast, where a website gives users explicit textual notice that continued use will act as a manifestation of the users assent and the terms or hyperlink to the terms are reasonably conspicuous, courts are more likely to enforce a browsewrap agreement.[86] For example, the Illinois Supreme Court, in *Hubbert v. Dell Corp.*,[87] applying Texas law, upheld a "browsewrap" agreement where a reasonable person would have been on notice that making purchases online meant consenting to the Terms and Conditions of Sale. Unlike the agreements in *Specht* and *Hines*, the Terms and Conditions of Sale were visible at several points throughout the online order process, including blue hyperlinks on each of the five online forms whose completion was necessary for users to make a purchase.[88] Moreover, the last three forms contained the statement that "[a]ll sales are subject to Dell's Term[s] and Conditions of Sale."[89] The court concluded that this statement, combined with making the Terms and Conditions visible and accessible online through blue hyperlinks, was sufficient notice to users that purchasing products online would bind them to the Terms and Conditions of Sale.[90] Similarly, in *Meyer v. Uber Technologies, Inc.*, the Second Circuit Court of Appeals, applying California contract law, found that Uber provided reasonably conspicuous notice of their Terms of Service because the webpage was uncluttered and had a warning directly under the registration button that stated, "By

---

84. *Id.* at *4.
85. *Id.* (citing *Hines*, 668 F. Supp. 2d at 367).
86. *See* James v. Glob. TelLink Corp., 852 F.3d 262, 267 (3d Cir. 2017); Nguyen v. Barnes & Noble Inc., 763 F.3d 1171, 1177 (9th Cir. 2014).
87. Hubbert v. Dell Corp., 835 N.E.2d 113 (Ill. 2005).
88. *Id.* at 118.
89. *Id.*
90. *Id.* at 122.

creating an Uber account, you agree to the TERMS OF SERVICE AND PRIVACY POLICY" with the relevant hyperlinks.[91] Likewise, in *Wiseley v. Amazon.com, Inc.*, the Ninth Circuit Court of Appeals, applying Washington state law, determined that there was sufficient notice to create a valid contract where the checkout page of a website alerted the user that by clicking the checkout button the user was agreeing to the hyperlinked Conditions of Use.[92]

These cases indicate that the more conspicuous a website's terms, and the greater the evidence that a user has consciously elected to accept the terms, the more likely that the terms will be enforceable. In contrast, if a website is designed in such a way that a user is unlikely to see the terms and understand their significance, the less likely it is that a court will enforce the terms.

§ 14:3.2 Data Privacy and Security Issues

The most significant new legal issues in e-commerce transactions relate to consumer privacy and data security. E-commerce transactions typically involve the collection of personally identifiable consumer data (data that can identify a person or a mobile device), such as consumer names and addresses, and financial and payment information. This data is often shared with third parties, other than the retailer, which deliver content, display ads, or perform data analyses in connection with online transactions. Although this data allows merchants to provide consumers with a richer experience, more tailored to their interests, critics have expressed concerns about the potential for privacy-related harms based on the unauthorized sharing of this data, including the unexpected revelation of previously private and sensitive information, unwanted intrusions, and possible economic injury stemming from identity theft.

Privacy issues are magnified by the widespread use of mobile devices. Smartphones are generally "on" and carried by a consumer throughout the consumer's waking hours. Moreover, some retailers have replaced cash registers with mobile devices, often operated by sales associates. Mobile devices and mobile apps collect, store, and use personal data in more complex ways than Internet browser software, and consequently may pose a greater security risk. Mobile apps may use hardware IDS (permanent identification numbers associated with a device) to promote functions and track users, may collect geo-location information through GPS and other methods, and may

---

91. Meyer v. Uber Techs., Inc., 868 F.3d 66, 79 (2d Cir. 2017).
92. Wiseley v. Amazon.com, Inc., 709 F. App'x 862, 864 (9th Cir. 2017).

be able to access certain files (such as contacts and call logs) stored on a mobile device.[93]

[A] Regulatory Privacy Issues

In the United States, there is no comprehensive federal law that regulates the collection, use, and disclosure of personally identifiable data. There is, however, a patchwork of federal and state laws and regulations that regulate aspects of consumer privacy and data security, and federal and state agencies have developed certain privacy guidelines and recommendations, and continue to pursue enforcement actions.

1. ***Federal Regulation.*** The most important of these federal regulatory agencies is the Federal Trade Commission (FTC), which has wide-ranging authority to protect consumers against unfair methods of competition and unfair or deceptive acts involving commerce and false advertising.[94] In particular, the FTC interprets its authority under section 5 of the Federal Trade Commission Act (15 U.S.C. § 45) to prevent "unfair or deceptive acts or practices" as empowering it to deter uses of personal data that are unfair or deceptive. For example, the FTC regularly commences enforcement actions against companies, including retailers, which misrepresent, fail to disclose, or do not comply with, their own privacy policies.[95]

   In March 2012, the FTC issued a report on consumer privacy, entitled Protecting Consumer Privacy in an Era of Rapid Change: Recommendations for Businesses and Policymakers (the "FTC Privacy Report") that applies to all commercial entities that collect or use consumer data that can be reasonably linked to a specific consumer or device, unless the entity collects only non-sensitive data from fewer than 5,000 consumers annually and does not share such data.[96] The FTC Privacy Report urges companies that collect and use consumer data to implement

93. See the discussion of mobile app privacy risks in CHRISTOPHER G. CWALINA, RICHARD RAYSMAN & STEVEN B. ROOSA, HOLLAND & KNIGHT LLP, PLC INTELLECTUAL PROPERTY & TECHNOLOGY, MOBILE APP PRIVACY: THE HIDDEN RISKS (PRACTICAL LAW COMPANY 2013).

94. 15 U.S.C. §§ 41–58. *See also infra* chapter 15 (discussing the FTC's role in preventing false advertising).

95. 15 U.S.C. § 46; *see also* FTC privacy policy enforcement cases, https://www.ftc.gov/opa/reporter/privacy/privacypromises.shtml.

96. FED. TRADE COMM'N, FTC REPORT, PROTECTING CONSUMER PRIVACY IN AN ERA OF RAPID CHANGE: RECOMMENDATIONS FOR BUSINESSES AND POLICYMAKERS (Mar. 2012), https://www.ftc.gov/reports/protecting-consumer-privacy-era-rapid-change-recommendations-businesses-policymakers.

"best practices" for handling consumers' personal information.[97] In broad terms, the FTC Privacy Report makes the following recommendations:

(a) It exhorts companies to implement a "privacy by design" approach throughout their organizations and at every phase of product development, by incorporating substantive privacy protections into their practices (such as data security, reasonable collection limits, sound retention and disposal practices, and efforts to ensure data accuracy), and by maintaining comprehensive data management procedures through the life cycle of a product.

(b) It recommends that companies take steps to simplify consumer choice by offering choices at a time and in a context in which the consumer is making a decision about his or her data. The FTC Privacy Report acknowledges that there will be some instances in which the need to collect and use data is understood based on the context of the transaction or the relationship, but it asks that companies obtain affirmative express consent before using customer data in a materially different manner than claimed when the data was collected or before collecting particularly sensitive data (such as information about children, financial and health information, and precise geolocation data).

(c) It also asks companies to make their data practices more transparent by creating shorter, clearer, and more standardized privacy practices, by providing reasonable access to the consumer data they maintain (proportionate to the sensitivity of the data and nature of its use) and by taking steps to educate consumers about the companies' privacy practices.[98]

The FTC Privacy Report also encouraged Congress to enact baseline privacy legislation, and in particular recommended creation of a system by which consumers can elect to force companies not to collect data about them, using a "Do Not Track" mechanism inspired by anti-telemarketing "Do Not Call" state and federal regulations.[99]

In addition, the FTC issued two other publications in 2012 specifically directed at developers of mobile apps. The first,

---

97. *Id.* at i–iii, 1.
98. *Id.* at 24–30, 48–50, 60–61, 64.
99. *Id.* at i–iv, viii, 1.

Marketing Your Mobile App: Get it Right from the Start, is a guide directed at mobile app developers that promotes compliance with truth-in-advertising and privacy principles.[100] The second, *Mobile Apps for Kids: Disclosure Still Not Making the Grade*, addresses disclosure issues in the privacy polices of some mobile apps.[101] The FTC recommends that companies provide parents with greater transparency and basic information, such as what data will be collected, how that data is used, and with whom the data is shared.[102]

The FTC, moreover, is specifically empowered to address issues related to the data privacy rights of children pursuant to the Children's Online Privacy Protection Act of 1998 (COPPA), and it has promulgated the specific "COPPA Rule" pursuant to that authority, to address privacy protections for children under the age of thirteen (13).[103] Under these provisions, operators of websites or online services that are either directed to children under age thirteen (13) or have actual knowledge that they are collecting personal information (such as name, address, phone number, and social security number) from such children, must give notice to parents and obtain their verifiable consent before collecting, using, or disclosing such information, and must keep such information secure.[104] Such operators are also prohibited from conditioning children's participation in activities on the collection of more personally identifiable information than is necessary for such participation.[105]

In 2010, the FTC initiated a review of the COPPA Rule to address evolving technology and changes in Internet and social media

100. FED. TRADE COMM'N, FTC STAFF REPORT, MOBILE APPS FOR KIDS: DISCLOSURES STILL NOT MAKING THE GRADE (Dec. 2012) [hereinafter MOBILE APPS FOR KIDS], https://www.ftc.gov/sites/default/files/documents/reports/mobile-apps-kids-disclosures-still-not-making-grade/121210mobilekidsappreport.pdf. The FTC revisited this publication with a survey three years later and found "an increase in easy-to-locate privacy policies." Kristin Cohen & Christina Yeung, *Kids' App Disclosures Revisited*, FTC BUS. BLOG (Sept. 3, 2015, 11:04 AM), https://www.ftc.gov/news-events/blogs/business-blog/2015/09/kids-apps-disclosures-revisited.

101. FED. TRADE COMM'N, MARKETING YOUR MOBILE APP: GET IT RIGHT FROM THE START (Aug. 2012) [hereinafter MARKETING YOUR MOBILE APP], https://www.ftc.gov/system/files/documents/plain-language/pdf-0140_marketing-your-mobile-app.pdf.

102. MOBILE APPS FOR KIDS, *supra* note 100, n.80.

103. Children's Online Privacy Protection Rule, 16 C.F.R. pts. 312 *et seq.* (1999) (issued pursuant to 15 U.S.C. § 6502(b)(1) (1998)).

104. *Id.* at pts. 312.4–312.5.

105. *Id.* at pt. 312.7.

usage. It then adopted formal amendments to the COPPA Rule in December 2012. These significant amendments expanded the types of entities covered by COPPA (such as general audience plug-ins and ad networks that have actual knowledge that they are collecting personal information from websites directed to children). The amendments also further detailed the types of information that are considered to be subject to the statute (including photographs, and video and audio files that contain a child's image or voice, and geolocation information, as well as certain persistent identifiers). And the amendments provided further guidance on approved means for marketers to obtain verifiable consent from parents to collect data about their children, as well as new data retention and deletion requirements.[106] The FTC enforces COPPA vigorously.

2. ***State Regulation.*** Many states have also implemented laws and regulations, and taken policy positions, affecting e-commerce and mobile commerce.

In particular, California has taken significant steps to address consumer privacy issues. In 2003, California passed the California Online Privacy Protection Act, which regulated privacy policies and other disclosures to consumers for any websites that collected and maintained personally identifiable data from California residents, even if the company was located outside of California.[107] More recently, California enacted the California Consumer Privacy Act of 2018, which would broadly apply to any entity that either (a) has annual gross revenues in excess of $25 million; (b) possesses the personal information of 50,000 or more consumers, households, or devices; or (c) earns more than

---

106. Children's Online Privacy Protection Rule, 78 Fed. Reg. 3972, 3975, 3978–83, 3986–92 (Jan. 17, 2013). The Commission has announced that it will not take an enforcement action against operators that collect a child's voice only to convert the words to text and then delete the recording. Enforcement Policy Statement Regard the Applicability of the COPPA Rule to the Collection and Use of Voice Recordings, 82 Fed. Reg. 58,076, 58,076–77 (Dec. 8, 2017). The Commission regularly evaluates new methods of obtaining verifiable parental consent through the COPPA safe harbor provision. *See, e.g.*, Press Release, Fed. Trade Comm'n, FTC Approves iKeepSafe COPPA "Safe Harbor" Oversight Program (Aug. 6, 2014), https://www.ftc.gov/news-events/press-releases/2014/08/ftc-approves-ikeepsafe-coppa-safe-harbor-oversight-program; Press Release, Fed. Trade Comm'n, FTC Approves kidSAFE Safe Harbor Program (Feb. 12, 2014), https://www.ftc.gov/news-events/press-releases/2014/02/ftc-approves-kidsafe-safe-harbor-program.

107. CAL. BUS. & PROF. CODE §§ 22575–79.

half of its annual revenue from selling consumers' personal information.[108] Although it may be amended before it goes into effect in January 2020, as passed, the law would require businesses collecting information about California consumers to:

(a) disclose what personal information is collected about a consumer and the purposes for which that personal information is used;[109]

(b) delete a consumer's personal information if requested to do so, unless it is necessary for the business to maintain that information for certain purposes;[110]

(c) disclose what personal information is sold or shared for a business purpose, and to whom;[111]

(d) stop selling a consumer's information if requested to do so (the "right to opt out"), unless the consumer is under 16 years of age, in which case the business is required to obtain affirmative authorization to sell the consumer's data (the "right to opt in");[112] and

(e) not discriminate against a consumer for exercising any of the aforementioned rights, including by denying goods or services, charging different prices, or providing a different level or quality of goods or services, subject to certain exceptions.

In comparison, in March 2010, the Massachusetts Office of Consumer Affairs and Business Regulation promulgated regulations requiring entities that own or license personal information about a resident of Massachusetts to develop and implement a comprehensive written information security program. Among other provisions, covered entities must:

(a) assess the reasonably foreseeable internal and external risks to the security of data containing personal information;

(b) implement procedures for preventing terminated employees from accessing physical and electronic records containing personal information; and

108. CAL. CIV. CODE § 1798.140(c)(1).
109. CAL. CIV. CODE § 1798.100 & 1798.110.
110. CAL. CIV. CODE § 1798.105(D).
111. CAL. CIV. CODE § 1798.115.
112. CAL. CIV. CODE § 1798.120(D); CAL. CIV. CODE § 1798.135.

(c) take reasonable steps to verify that any third-party service provider with access to personal information has the capacity to protect such personal information.[113]

These Massachusetts regulations also establish computer security system requirements for entities that own or license personal information about a resident of Massachusetts and electronically store or transmit this information. Covered entities are required, to the extent technically feasible, to:

(a) control user IDs and other identifiers;

(b) restrict access to company computer systems to active user accounts only;

(c) control data security passwords to ensure that such passwords are kept in a location and/or format that does not compromise the security of the data they protect;

(d) encrypt transmitted records and files containing personal information that will travel across public networks, and encrypt all data containing personal information to be transmitted wirelessly; and

(e) encrypt all personal information stored on laptops or other portable devices.[114]

The Massachusetts data security regulations attempt to take into account the particular business's size, scope of business, amount of resources, and the need for security.

State attorneys general, moreover, are also very active in policing these and other privacy protections. For example, in May 2017, the Target Corporation reached an $18.5 million settlement—the largest state data breach settlement in history—with forty-seven states and the District of Columbia. Under the terms of the agreement, Target will be required to develop, implement, and maintain a comprehensive information security program, to hire a third party to conduct a security assessment, and implement additional administrative safeguards to further strengthen the company's data security.[115]

---

113. 201 MASS. CODE REGS. 17.00 *et seq.*

114. 201 MASS. CODE REGS. 17.04.

115. Press Release, State of Cal. Dep't of Justice, Attorney General Becerra: Target Settles Record $18.5 Million Credit Card Data Breach Case (May 23, 2017), https://oag.ca.gov/news/press-releases/attorney-general-becerra-target-settles-record-185-million-credit-card-data; Press Release, N.Y. State Office of the Att'y Gen., A.G. Schneiderman Announces

In early 2017, the New York Attorney General reached a settlement with two mobile app developers for failures to disclose their data collection practices in a privacy policy. The New York Attorney General's Office investigated app developers, headquartered in Michigan and California, for deceptive trade practice violations rather than misusing customer data or disclosing data to third parties.[116] In 2016, the New York Attorney General reached a settlement with Uber Technologies stemming from an investigation into Uber's collection, maintenance, and disclosure of user information, such as names, email addresses, payment details, and real-time geo-location data. As part of the settlement, Uber agreed to adopt protective technologies for user data and limit employee access to user location information.[117]

In 2012, the New Jersey Attorney General entered into a consent order with an app developer that it had alleged had violated COPPA by transmitting names and device identification numbers of mobile devices used by children, without providing notification of this policy on their website and without obtaining parental consent. The consent decree requires the developer to stop collecting and transmitting the personal data of children without parental consent, destroy all previously collected and transmitted data, and more broadly, remove data analytics from its apps.[118]

The California Department of Justice released a report titled "Privacy on the Go: Recommendations for the Mobile Ecosystem," to help educate the mobile app industry and promote privacy best practices.[119] The Privacy on the Go report recommends

---

$18.5 Million Multi-State Settlement With Target Corporation Over 2013 Data Breach (May 23, 2017), https://ag.ny.gov/press-release/ag-schneiderman-announces-185-million-multi-state-settlement-target-corporation-over.

116. Press Release, N.Y. State Office of the Att'y Gen., A.G. Schneiderman Announces Settlements With Mobile App Developers For Failure To Disclose Data Collection Practices (Feb. 9, 2017), https://ag.ny.gov/press-release/ag-schneiderman-announces-settlements-mobile-app-developers-failure-disclose-data.

117. Press Release, N.Y. State Office of the Att'y Gen., A.G. Schneiderman Announces Settlement with Uber to Enhance Rider Privacy (Jan 6, 2016), https://ag.ny.gov/press-release/ag-schneiderman-announces-settlement-uber-enhance-rider-privacy.

118. Consent Decree, *Chiesa v. 24 X 7 Digital Media, LLC*, No. 12-03402 (D.N.J. June 26, 2012).

119. CAL. DEP'T OF JUSTICE, PRIVACY ON THE GO: RECOMMENDATIONS FOR THE MOBILE ECOSYSTEM (Jan. 2013), http://oag.ca.gov/sites/all/files/pdfs/privacy/privacy_on_the_go.pdf.

a higher degree of consumer protection than is currently afforded by existing law, and focuses on the principles of transparency about data practices, limitations on the collection and retention of data, meaningful consumer choices, security, and accountability.[120] The report also sets forth specific recommendations for: app developers (such as developing a privacy policy that is clear, accurate, and conspicuously accessible); app platform providers (such as making app privacy policies accessible from the app platform so they can be reviewed before the app is downloaded); mobile ad networks (such as providing a privacy policy to the app developers who will enable the delivery of targeted ads through the network, and transitioning to app-specific or temporary device identifiers); operating systems developers (such as developing global privacy settings and overrides that consumers can use to set controls); and mobile carriers (such as educating mobile customers on mobile privacy).

In the event that personal information about a company's customers is lost or stolen, the company must address the requirements of the relevant states' data breach statutes. All fifty states, as well as the District of Columbia, Guam, Puerto Rico, the Virgin Islands, and some localities have enacted differing privacy breach notification laws.[121] Although there is some variation, many of these statutes follow the lead set by California and share certain key elements. California's data breach statute, for example, applies to "[a]ny person or business that conducts business in California, and that owns or licenses computerized data that includes personal information."[122] Personal information includes an individual's name in combination with that individual's social security number or credit card number and security code; it also includes an individual's user name or email address associate with a password or security question and answer that would permit access to the individual's account.[123]

---

120. *Id.* at 4.

121. NAT'L CONFERENCE OF STATE LEGISLATURES, STATE SECURITY BREACH NOTIFICATION LAWS, https://www.ncsl.org/issues-research/telecom/security-breach-notification-laws.aspx.

122. CAL. CIV. CODE § 1798.82(a). The California Consumer Privacy Act also updated California's laws governing breaches of consumer information to strengthen protections for consumers. Like the rest of the statute, these provisions will not go into effect in 2020, and are expected to be amended again before then. CAL. CIV. CODE §§ 1798.150, 1798.81.5(D)(1)(A).

123. CAL. CIV. CODE § 1798.82(h). Other states also continue to update their laws related to data breaches, including different definitions of personal information, exemptions for encrypted data.

The statute requires that holders of personal information notify the individuals affected upon "unauthorized acquisition of computerized data that compromises the security, confidentiality, or integrity of personal information maintained by the person or business."[124]

The California data breach statute provides for a wide range of penalties and enforcement procedures in the event of a violation, but also provides that "a person or business that maintains its own notification procedures as part of an information security policy for the treatment of personal information and is otherwise consistent with the timing requirements . . . shall be deemed to be in compliance with the notification requirements . . . if the person or business notifies subject persons in accordance with its policies in the event of a breach of security of the system."[125] The notice must be provided in either written form or electronic form—if the recipients have consented to receive notifications electronically in advance—unless over 500,000 individuals have been affected or the cost of notice would exceed $250,000.[126] The notice must be written in plain language and must set forth the circumstances of the breach, such as the types of personal information compromised, the relevant dates of the breach, and, if possible to determine, a general description of the breach incident.[127] Additionally, if the notifying business was the source of the breach, the business also must provide free identity theft prevention and mitigation services for no less than twelve (12) months for all individuals whose information may have been breached.[128] This creates incentives for a company that collects personal data to promulgate—and adhere to—a reasonable information security notification procedure.

3. ***International Regulation.*** It is also important to note that advances in technology and the globalization of the economy have increased the volume of electronic data that flows among and between different nations. The fashion industry, which has long been global in scope, is increasingly transmitting data across borders in connection with the movement of products through the supply and distribution chains. As a result, it is important for industry participants to monitor developments as

---

124. CAL. CIV. CODE § 1798.82(g).
125. CAL. CIV. CODE § 1798.82(*l*).
126. CAL. CIV. CODE § 1798.82(j).
127. CAL. CIV. CODE § 1798.82(gd).
128. CAL. CIV. CODE § 1798.82(d)(2)(G).

many countries continue to adopt and refine their own laws on privacy and data collection.

For example, on January 25, 2012, the European Commission proposed a comprehensive reform of its 1995 data protection rules to create a single set of rules on data protection across the European Union, which would strengthen online privacy rights, and address the enforcement issues created by the differing implementation of the 1995 rules by its member states.[129] The resulting General Data Protection Regulation (GDPR) went into effect on May 25, 2018, and had a significant impact on companies globally due to its breadth and increased obligations on companies holding personal information. The GDPR applied EU privacy regulations on all companies that have data subjects in the European Union, regardless of where the company itself was located.[130] The GDPR also relied on a broader definition of personal data of "information relating to an identified or identifiable natural person," which included information like name, device number, contact information, location information, IP address, age, or even a photo.[131] The GDPR also significantly increased potential penalties, including allowing for administrative fines of the greater of €20 million or up to 4% of total worldwide annual revenue.[132]

The GDPR also required companies (those that were "data controllers") to provide greater transparency and accountability to both data subjects and EU regulators regarding how the controllers collected, used, disclosed, and stored information about data subjects.[133] In addition, data subjects (individual consumers) also were given additional rights, including:

(a) the right to access the company has about them;[134]

(b) the right to correct information about them;[135]

(c) the right to have information about them deleted;[136]

---

129. Press Release, European Comm'n, Commission Proposes a Comprehensive Reform of Data Protection Rules to Increase Users' Control of Their Data and to Cut Costs for Businesses (Jan. 25, 2012), http://europa.eu/rapid/press-release_IP-12-46_en.htm?locale=en.
130. GDPR art. 3.
131. GDPR art. 4.
132. GDPR art. 83.
133. GDPR arts. 5–11, 24–43,
134. GDPR art. 15.
135. GDPR art. 16.
136. GDPR art. 17.

(d) the right to receive all data they provided to the company in a commonly used format;[137]

(e) the right to have processing of their data stopped if the accuracy of the data was contested, if the processing was unlawful, or if the data processing was no longer necessary;[138]

(f) the right to object to the processing of their data;[139] and

(g) the right not to be subject to automated decision making.[140]

The GDPR also raised breach disclosure requirements, both by broadening the definition of what constituted a break to essentially any security incident that has affected the confidentiality, integrity, or availability of personal data, and by shortening the reporting time frame to within seventy-two (72) hours of becoming aware of the breach (at least for certain types of breaches).[141]

Similarly, on May 1, 2018, the *Information Security Technology—Personal Information Security Specification* (the "Specification") went into effect in China.[142] Although the Specification is not binding and cannot be used as the legal basis for enforcement, enforcement agencies in China can still use the Specification as a reference or guideline in their administration and enforcement activities.[143] The specification was modeled on GDPR, but there are key differences.[144] The Specification applies to entities in China using information systems to process personal data (including public institutions and private companies).[145] Foreign companies likely will need to comply, although the extent to which it is binding on any companies

---

137. GDPR art. 20.
138. GDPR art. 18.
139. GDPR art. 21.
140. GDPR art. 22.
141. GDPR arts. 32–34.
142. Galaad Delval, *Old Rules, New Specification for Data Protection in Mainland China*, INT'L ASS'N OF PRIVACY PROF'LS (May 3, 2018), https://iapp.org/news/a/old-rules-new-specification-for-data-protection-in-mainland-china/ [hereinafter Delval]; Samm Sacks, *New China Data Privacy Standard Looks More Far-Reaching than GDPR*, CTR. FOR STRATEGIC & INT'L STUDIES (Jan. 29, 2018), https://www.csis.org/analysis/new-china-data-privacy-standard-looks-more-far-reaching-gdpr. [hereinafter *New China Data Privacy Standard*].
143. *Id.*
144. Samm Sacks, *China's Emerging Data Privacy System and GDPR*, CTR. FOR STRATEGIC & INT'L STUDIES (Mar. 9, 2018), https://www.csis.org/analysis/chinas-emerging-data-privacy-system-and-gdpr.
145. *Id.*

is still unclear.[146] Like GDPR, the specification governs the all processing of personal data from collection, use, disclosure, and storage.[147] Personal data is broadly defined to include (a) data that can be used to identify a natural person, such as name, address, personal ID number, bank account number, fingerprints, retina, etc.; (b) data that contains personal private information, such as health or medical records, electronic communications (email, text messages), and contacts; (c) data that reflects personal use of services, such as purchase or operating records, software or hardware data, or geographic location; and (d) data that may lead to bodily harm, property damage, reputational harm, harm to personal health, or discriminative treatment of an individual if such data were disclosed, leaked, or abused.[148]

The considerable differences among the data privacy laws of various international jurisdictions pose issues and risks for both consumers and global businesses. These differences in approach to data privacy issues significantly increase compliance burdens for U.S. businesses that operate in multiple foreign jurisdictions.

[B] Private Privacy Litigation

Class action suits involving data security breaches continue to be filed, asserting claims based on unfair competition, negligence, or the violation of consumer privacy laws.

One of the most hotly contested issues in these lawsuits is the standards that should govern whether plaintiffs have standing to bring claims over real or perceived threats to the security of their personal data. For example, in 2011, a series of cases held that the alleged unauthorized collection of a plaintiff's "personal information" does not constitute an injury in fact under Article III of the U.S. Constitution.[149] Courts have differed, however, on the question of whether a violation of a privacy statute can itself confer Article III standing.[150] Many courts have rejected more speculative theories of

146. *Id.*
147. *New China Data Privacy Standard*, *supra* note 142.
148. Delval, *supra* note 142.
149. *See, e.g.*, *In re* Specific Media Flash Cookies Litig., No. 10-CV-1256-GW, 2011 WL 1661532 (C.D. Cal. Apr. 28, 2011); *In re* iPhone Application Litig., No. 11-MD-02250-LHK, 2011 WL 4403963 (N.D. Cal. Sept. 20, 2011); Low v. LinkedIn, No. 11-CV-01468-LHK, 2011 WL 5509848 (N.D. Cal. Nov. 11, 2011).
150. *Compare In re* iPhone Application Litig., 844 F. Supp. 2d 1040, 1055 (N.D. Cal. 2012) (concluding that a violation of Stored Communications Act does confer standing), *with In re* Google, Inc. Privacy Policy Litig.,

injury as sufficient to establish Article III standing—these theories include lost benefit of bargain, diminution of value of personally identifiable information, and increased risk of future identity theft.[151] And in one case, a district court in the Western District of Washington granted a motion to dismiss a proposed privacy class action finding that in light of the potential exorbitant costs of discovery, a "complex, large-scale case such as a class action should naturally have a higher plausibility threshold," but the plaintiffs' conclusory allegations of harm did not meet their burden to show an injury in fact.[152] In other instances, courts have determined that in assessing injury-in-fact, plaintiffs need not "suffer any particular type of harm to have standing . . . [c]onsequently . . . a plaintiff need not show actual monetary loss for purposes of injury in fact."[153] The plaintiff may meet the injury requirement "by virtue of statutes creating legal rights, the invasion of which creates standing."[154]

Plaintiffs have had an easier time establishing injuries when retailers collect unnecessary information about them under specific state statutes designed to protect their privacy. For example, California courts have applied the state's Song-Beverly Credit Card Act[155] to prohibit retailers from requesting any type of personal identification information about a consumer that is unnecessary to complete a credit card transaction, including zip codes.[156] In 2013, the Massachusetts Supreme Court reached a similar conclusion with respect to that state's comparable statute,[157] finding a Massachusetts resident may

---

No. C 12-01382 PSG, 2012 U.S. Dist. LEXIS 183041 (N.D. Cal. Dec. 28, 2012) (finding no standing even though plaintiffs had asserted a claim under Wiretap Act).

151. *See, e.g.*, Provost v. Aptos, Inc., No. 1:17-CV-02120-ELR, 2018 WL 1465766, at *6 (N.D. Ga. Mar. 12, 2018).

152. Grigsby v. Valve Corp., No. C12-0553JLR, 2012 U.S. Dist. LEXIS 179096, at *10–13 (W.D. Wash. Nov. 14, 2012). *But see In re* Sony Gaming Networks & Customer Data Sec. Breach Litig., 2012 U.S. Dist. LEXIS 146971, at *50 (S.D. Cal. Oct. 11, 2012) (finding that plaintiffs had "articulated sufficient particularized and concrete harm to sustain a finding of injury-in-fact at this stage in the pleadings" because they had alleged "that their sensitive Personal Information was wrongfully disseminated, thereby increasing the risk of future harm" but not enough to sustain a negligence claim under California law).

153. *In re* Google Inc. Cookie Placement Consumer Privacy Litig., 806 F.3d 125, 134 (3d Cir. 2015).

154. *Id.*

155. CAL. CIV. CODE §§ 1747 *et seq.*

156. Pineda v. Williams-Sonoma Stores, Inc., 51 Cal. 4th 524 (2011).

157. MASS. GEN. LAWS ch. 93, § 105 (a).

bring an action even absent a showing of identity fraud, because "the principal purpose of" the statute "is to guard consumer privacy in credit card transactions, not to protect against credit card identity fraud."[158] Even if a consumer did not experience any economic damages from violation of a privacy statute, Massachusetts courts have ruled that this is sufficient to pursue injunctive relief for an alleged violation.[159]

In 2019, the U.S. Supreme Court stepped into the debate in *Frank v. Gaos*.[160] Plaintiffs, on behalf of a putative class of 129 million users of Google's search engine, alleged that Google violated users' privacy under the Stored Communications Act, 18 U.S.C. § 2701 *et seq.*, by disclosing the search terms they used to third-party websites. The parties agreed to an $8.5 million class action settlement consisting of $2 million in attorneys' fees and costs and $6.5 million distributed as a *cy pres* award to various institutions studying Internet privacy and information sharing. Under the proposed settlement, class members would receive no money. The district court approved the settlement, concluding that it would not be feasible to distribute the $6.5 million portion of the settlement to class members. The Ninth Circuit affirmed. The Supreme Court, in response to an argument raised by the Solicitor General in an amicus brief, ordered supplemental briefing on whether any named plaintiff had Article III standing. The Court ultimately accepted the Solicitor General's view that the case should be remanded for the lower courts to address that question in the first instance. The outcome of that remand—and any subsequent reconsideration of the standing issue by the Supreme Court—is likely to have far-reaching implications fo the future of private data privacy litigation.

An example of a data privacy lawsuit that arose in the specific context of the fashion industry is the case *In re Zappos.com Inc., Customer Data Security Breach Litigation*, discussed above.[161] There, plaintiffs sued for damages allegedly arising from a data security breach at the Zappos.com website. In line with the recent trend of many courts in data privacy breach cases, the *Zappos* court ultimately held that neither diminution of personal information nor increased threat of future harm, without allegations of actual identity theft or fraud, constituted an injury-in-fact to confer standing.[162]

---

158. Tyler v. Michaels Stores, Inc., 464 Mass. 492 (2013).

159. *See, e.g.*, Diviacchi v. Speedway LLC, 109 F. Supp. 3d 379, 386 (D. Mass. 2015).

160. Frank v. Gaos, __ U.S. __, No. 17-961, slip op. (Mar. 20, 2019).

161. *In re* Zappos, MDL No. 235, 2012 WL 4466660 (D. Nev. Sept. 27, 2012).

162. *See In re* Zappos.com, Inc., Customer Data Sec. Breach Litig., No. 312CV00325RCJVPC, 2015 WL 10892034, at *7 (D. Nev. June 1, 2015).

§ 14:3.3 *State Taxation and* South Dakota v. Wayfair

Increasingly, e-commerce transactions by out-of-state sellers with in-state customers may be subject to the sales tax of that state. In *South Dakota v. Wayfair,*[163] the U.S. Supreme Court overruled more than fifty years of case law denying states the ability to impose sales tax collection obligations on out-of-state sellers with respect to sales to in-state customers. The Supreme Court had previously held in *Quill Corp. v. North Dakota* that the Dormant Commerce Clause forbids states from imposing sales tax collection obligations on sellers that did not have a physical presence in the state.[164]

In general, a state sales tax is valid if the tax (1) is applied to an activity with a substantial nexus with the taxing state, as required by the Dormant Commerce Clause, (2) is fairly apportioned, (3) does not discriminate against interstate commerce, and (4) is fairly related to the services provided by the State.[165] In *Quill*, the Supreme Court had found that, with respect to state sales and use taxes, an out-of-state seller had a "substantial nexus" with a state only if the seller had a physical presence in that state.[166] In *Quill*, the Supreme Court focused on how the administrative cost of compliance with a state's tax scheme on an out-of-state seller with only a handful of in-state customers could easily result in an undue burden on interstate commerce.[167]

Beginning in 2015, some states began passing so-called "kill *Quill*" legislation, imposing sales tax collection obligations on out-of-state sellers that did not have a physical presence in the state.[168] This movement was in reaction to lost tax revenue due to the growth of e-commerce, and encouraged by a 2015 concurrence by Justice Kennedy calling for revisiting *Quill* in light of "dramatic technological and social changes" to an "increasingly interconnected economy[,]" primarily due to the meteoric rise of e-commerce since *Quill* was decided.[169] South Dakota was one such state that passed "kill *Quill*" legislation by enacting Senate Bill 106 ("the Act"). The South Dakota legislature had found that the inability to collect sales tax from remote sellers

163. South Dakota v. Wayfair, 138 S. Ct. 2080 (2018).

164. Quill Corp. v. North Dakota, 504 U.S. 298 (1992).

165. *See* Complete Auto Transit, Inc. v. Brady, 430 U.S. 274, 279 (1977).

166. *Quill*, 504 U.S. at 317–18.

167. *See id.* at 313, n.6.

168. *Nexus Considerations: Navigating the "Kill* Quill*" Revolt*, THOMPSON REUTERS (Jan. 22, 2018), https://tax.thomsonreuters.com/blog/checkpoint/nexus-considerations-navigating-the-kill-quill-revolt.

169. *See* Direct Mktg. Ass'n v. Brohl, 135 S. Ct. 1124, 1134–35 (Kennedy, J., concurring).

was "seriously eroding the sales tax base" and "causing revenue losses and imminent harm through the loss of critical funding for state and local services"—the South Dakota Department of Revenue estimated revenue lost from the inability to tax e-commerce at between $48 million and $58 million annually.[170] Under the Act, South Dakota required out-of-state sellers to collect and remit sales tax "as if the seller had a physical presence in the state," provided that the seller delivered $100,000 of goods or engaged in 200 separate transactions within South Dakota annually.[171] The Act was explicit that it did not apply retroactively.[172] Wayfair, Inc., a leading online retailer with no physical presence or employees in South Dakota, sought to challenge the Act as invalid under *Quill*, and the U.S. Supreme Court eventually granted certiorari.[173]

In *Wayfair*, the Supreme Court agreed with South Dakota, finding that "*Quill* [was] flawed on its own terms" and abolishing the physical presence requirement.[174] The physical presence rule was no longer "a necessary interpretation of the substantial nexus requirement," because it *created* market distortions rather than resolving them, and ultimately imposed the type of "arbitrary and formalistic distinctions that the [C]ourt's modern Commerce Clause precedents disavow."[175] First, the Supreme Court found that *Quill*'s focus on administrative compliance costs was misplaced in the age of e-commerce, where "the physical presence rule is a poor proxy for the compliance costs faced by companies that do business in multiple States."[176] For instance, a small business with a diverse physical presence would be more burdened, under *Quill*, than national corporations centralized in a single state but selling goods in every other state over the Internet. Second, the Supreme Court found that application of the physical presence rule led to arbitrary taxation, as the physical presence rule "treat[ed] economically-identical actors differently, and for arbitrary reasons."[177] A business with a single warehouse in South Dakota could be compelled to collect sales taxes, even though a national corporation with dramatically larger in-state sales volume would be exempt if it sold exclusively online. Finally, the Supreme Court focused on the actual loss to tax revenue suffered by states as a result of this arbitrary application. The Supreme Court noted that "the real

---

170. *Wayfair*, 138 S. Ct. at 2088–89.
171. *Id.*
172. *Id.* at 2089.
173. *Id.*
174. *Id.* at 2092.
175. *Id.*
176. *Id.* at 2093.
177. *Id.* at 2094.

world implementation of Commerce Clause doctrines now makes it manifest that the physical presence rule as defined by *Quill* must give way to the far-reaching systemic and structural changes in the economy and many other social dimensions caused by the Cyber Age."[178]

Nevertheless, not every state sales tax may necessarily pass constitutional muster after *Wayfair*. The *Wayfair* decision was limited to whether physical presence was required to establish substantial nexus—the basis of the South Dakota Supreme Court's decision below—and the Supreme Court did not directly resolve whether the Commerce Clause barred South Dakota's sales tax scheme on separate grounds. Without *Quill*, the guiding principle of the constitutionality of an out-of-state sales tax scheme is the four-prong test of *Complete Auto Transit v. Brady*,[179] and the Supreme Court did not directly address any element of that test other than substantial nexus, electing instead to remand the decision back to the South Dakota Supreme Court. Furthermore, sales tax schemes that can or will apply retroactively may remain invalid. The Supreme Court in *Wayfair* was clear that South Dakota's Act was unlikely to cause undue burden to interstate commerce because it was explicitly non-retroactive—meaning that South Dakota could not hold out-of-state sellers liable for sales tax not collected after the Act was passed, but before *Wayfair* was decided. Similar schemes that do not specifically provide for non-retroactivity could present a more difficult problem, as permitting states to hold out-of-state sellers retroactively liable for sales taxes could entail enormous compliance costs that themselves may cause an undue burden on interstate commerce.[180] In addition, the prevalence of consumer-submitted use taxes in the pre-*Wayfair* era could render state efforts to retroactively collect sales tax from out-of-state sellers unconstitutional as double-taxation.[181]

---

178. *Id.* at 2097 (internal quotations omitted).

179. 430 U.S. 274 (1977).

180. *See* Daniel Hemel, *There Is No Retroactivity Concern With Overruling* Quill, MEDIUM (Jan. 28, 2018), https://medium.com/whatever-source-derived/there-is-no-retroactivity-concern-with-overruling-quill-f6623da6a2d7; David A. Sausen & Gus Weinkam, *In* Wayfair, *Supreme Court Overturns* Quill *"Physical Presence Sales Tax Rule*, MONDAQ (July 10, 2018), http://www.mondaq.com/unitedstates/x/717680/sales+taxes+VAT+GST/In+Wayfair+Supreme+Court+Overturns+Quill+Physical+Presence+Sales+Tax+Rule.

181. *See* Zach Gladney, "Wayfair": *What Are the Practical Retroactivity Concerns?*, BLOOMBERG BNA (July 19, 2018).

§ 14:3.4 Other E-Commerce Issues

Other federal statutes and regulations affecting e-commerce and mobile commerce that may be applicable in the fashion industry include:

- The Controlling the Assault of Non-Solicited Pornography and Marketing ("CAN-SPAM") Act of 2003[182] establishes national requirements for the use and transmission of commercial email. CAN-SPAM does not prohibit the use of spam emails, but does prohibit deceptive or misleading practices (such as misleading subject headers) in commercial email messages. The statute also requires the implementation of procedures for recipients to "optout" of future mailings and prohibits sending emails to recipients who have in fact opted out. CAN-SPAM provides criminal and civil penalties for non-compliance.
- The Computer Fraud and Abuse Act (CFAA)[183] establishes federal criminal penalties and a civil cause of action for unauthorized computer access with an intent to defraud.[184] Although courts have differed as to the circumstances under which CFAA applies to employees who take advantage of access to their employers' computers, there is no doubt that it prohibits companies from obtaining unauthorized access to the computer systems of competitors, business partners, or consumers.
- In February 2013, President Obama signed an executive order for "Improving Critical Infrastructure Cybersecurity."[185] The executive order seeks to promote the sharing of information between private companies and the government regarding cyber threats, and directs certain federal agencies to develop and implement voluntary cybersecurity standards for private critical infrastructure companies, with the goal of reducing cyber risk.[186]

---

182. 15 U.S.C. §§ 7701–7713.
183. 18 U.S.C. § 1030.
184. 18 U.S.C. § 1030(c), (g).
185. Exec. Order, Improving Critical Infrastructure Cybersecurity (Feb. 12, 2013), https://www.whitehouse.gov/the-press-office/2013/02/12/executive-order-improving-critical-infrastructure-cybersecurity.
186. *Id.*

§ 14:4 Payment Methods

The growth of e-commerce, and particularly mobile commerce, continues to impact the payment methods adopted by retailers and used by consumers. In the United States, credit card and debit card payments have been the most common form of payment for e-commerce transactions.[187] Some retailers and some consumers, however, now use online payment systems, such as PayPal or Google Checkout, which facilitate online transactions through the electronic transfer of funds.[188] These payment systems permit a consumer to create an account with the payment service provider (for example, PayPal) which can then be linked to the consumer's bank account, credit card account, or debit card account. The payment service provider can transfer funds from the consumer's account with the provider directly to the vendor, without sharing the consumer's financial information with the vendor.

In addition, consumers are increasingly using their mobile devices to initiate a transfer of funds to pay for goods and services that are purchased online, purchased in a brick-and-mortar store through a point of sale payment, or purchased directly from another person.[189] Mobile proximity payments are payments in which a consumer's mobile device uses embedded or attached technology to interface directly with a vendor's point of sale equipment in a brick-and-mortar location.[190] Mobile wallets, such as Apple Pay, which can be linked to credit cards or bank accounts, have become a common method of making mobile proximity payments. Mobile payments and mobile wallets, however, raise security issues as to the possible loss or theft

---

187. FED. RESERVE BANK OF BOSTON, 2016 AND 2017 SURVEYS OF CONSUMER PAYMENT CHOICE: SUMMARY RESULTS (2018); FED. RESERVE, CONSUMERS AND MOBILE FINANCIAL SERVICES (Mar. 2012) [hereinafter CONSUMERS & MOBILE FIN. SERVS.], https://www.federalreserve.gov/econresdata/mobile-device-report-201203.pdf. *See also* FED. RESERVE, FEDERAL RESERVE PAYMENTS STUDY 2016, https://www.federalreserve.gov/paymentsystems/files/2016-payments-study-20161222.pdf.

188. MARIANNE CROWE, ELISA TAVILLA & BREFFNI MCGUIRE, FED. RESERVE BANK OF BOSTON, MOBILE BANKING AND PAYMENT PRACTICES OF U.S. FINANCIAL INSTITUTIONS: 2016 MOBILE FINANCIAL SERVICES SURVEY RESULTS FROM FIS IN SEVEN FEDERAL RESERVE DISTRICTS (Dec. 2017) [hereinafter MOBILE FIN. SERV. SURVEY], https://www.bostonfed.org/publications/mobile-banking-and-payment-surveys/mobile-banking-and-payment-practices-of-us-financial-institutions.aspx.

189. MOBILE FIN. SERV. SURVEY, *supra* note 188 (Mobile commerce was 20% of commerce in 2016 compared to 11.7% in 2014). *See also* CONSUMERS & MOBILE FIN. SERVS., *supra* note 187, Exec. Summary at 1.

190. PwC, MOBILE PROXIMITY PAYMENT: 5 THINGS RETAILERS SHOULD KNOW (2016), https://www.pwc.com/it/it/publications/assets/docs/mobile-proximity.pdf; FED. FIN. INSTS. EXAMINATION COUNCIL, CONTACTLESS PAYMENT

of the mobile device, as well as the security of the transmission of information from the consumer to the vendor.[191]

In the United States, the federal regulatory framework for mobile payments is complex and often dependent upon the type of activity and the funding source.[192] U.S. regulators continue to struggle to determine the extent to which new methods of mobile payment are subject to existing laws. Mobile payments may be subject to the Electronic Funds Transfer Act,[193] the Truth in Lending Act,[194] the Dodd-Frank Act,[195] the Gramm-Leach-Bliley Act,[196] and the Economic Growth, Regulatory Relief and Consumer Protection Act[197] (which rolled back some of the regulations imposed by Dodd-Frank),[198] among other laws and regulations.[199]

Neverthless, credit card payments are currently the most commonly used form of payment in the United States for consumer e-commerce

---

CARDS, PROXIMITY PAYMENTS AND OTHER DEVICES, https://ithandbook.ffiec.gov/it-booklets/retail-payment-systems/payment-instruments,-clearing,-and-settlement/emerging-retail-payment-technologies/contactless-payment-cards,-proximity-payments-and-other-devices.aspx.

191. SUSAN PANDY & MARIANNE CROWE, FED. RESERVE BANK OF BOSTON, MULTI-FACETED EVOLUTION OF MOBILE PAYMENT STRATEGY, AUTHENTICATION, AND TECHNOLOGY (Oct. 30, 2017), https://www.bostonfed.org/publications/mobile-payments-industry-workgroup/multi-faceted-evolution-of-mobile-payment-strategy-authentication-and-technology.aspx; CONSUMERS & MOBILE FIN. SERVS., *supra* note 188.

192. MARK E. BUDNITZ, PEW CHARITABLE TRS., THE LEGAL FRAMEWORK OF MOBILE PAYMENTS: GAPS, AMBIGUITIES, AND OVERLAP (Feb. 10, 2016), https://www.pewtrusts.org/en/research-and-analysis/white-papers/2016/02/the-legal-framework-of-mobile-payments; FED. DEPOSIT INS. CORP., MOBILE PAYMENTS: AN EVOLVING LANDSCAPE (Winter 2012), https://www.fdic.gov/regulations/examinations/supervisory/insights/siwin12/siwinter12-article1.pdf [hereinafter FDIC MOBILE PAYMENTS].

193. Electronic Funds Transfer Act, 15 U.S.C. § 1693.

194. Truth in Lending Act, Pub. L. No. 90-321, 82 Stat. 146 (1968) (codified at 15 U.S.C. §§ 1601–13, 1616).

195. Dodd-Frank Wall Street Reform and Consumer Protection Act, Pub. L. No. 111-203, 124 Stat. 1376-2223 (2010).

196. Financial Services Modernization Act of 1999 (also known as the "Gramm-Leach-Bliley Act"), Pub. L. No. 106-102, 113 Stat. 1338 (1999) (codified at 15 U.S.C. §§ 6801–10, 6821–27).

197. Consumer Protection Act, Pub. L. No. 115-174 (2018)

198. Samuel R. Woodall III, Mitchell S. Eitel, Michael T. Escue, C. Andrew Gerlach, Camille L. Orme, Benjamin H. Weiner, & Michael A. Wiseman, *"Economic Growth, Regulatory Relief, and Consumer Protection Act" Is Enacted*, N.Y.U. COMPLIANCE & ENFORCEMENT BLOG (June 5, 2018), https://wp.nyu.edu/compliance_enforcement/2018/06/05/economic-growth-regulatory-relief-and-consumer-protection-act-is-enacted/#_edn1.

199. FDIC MOBILE PAYMENTS, *supra* note 192.

transactions, so retailers must remain cognizant of the laws that seek to protect the security of consumers' credit card transactions and records. On the federal level, these laws include the following:

- The Restore Online Shoppers' Confidence Act of 2011 (ROSCA),[200] which provides limits on a retailer's ability to add charges to a consumer's financial account after the transaction, and specifically prohibits a post-transaction third party from charging a consumer's financial account for any goods or services sold online unless such third party has clearly disclosed to the consumer the price and other material terms of the transaction.

- The Electronic Funds Transfer Act of 1978 and Regulation E thereunder,[201] which regulates electronic funds transfers to or from the account of a consumer held by a financial institution, as well as store gift cards.

- The Fair and Accurate Credit Transactions Act of 2003,[202] which focuses on combatting identity theft, prohibits the printing of a credit card receipt showing more than the last five digits of the card, but does not apply to electronically displayed confirmations.

For example, on March 23, 2017, the FTC filed suit against six entities and four individuals alleging violations of ROSCA based on sales of products through a "negative option" where a consumer's silence is taken as an acceptance of the offer.[203] The defendants settled the lawsuit, paying more than $2.5 million and requirements to change marketing practices.[204]

The Payment Card Industry (PCI) Standards Council, launched in 2006, is responsible for the development, management, education, and awareness of the PCI Security Standards for merchants that accept credit card payments and store or transmit cardholder data. The PCI Standards Council was founded by five global payment

---

200. Restore Online Shoppers' Confidence Act of 2011, Pub. L. No. 111-345, 124 Stat. 3618 (2011).

201. Electronic Funds Transfer Act of 1978, 15 U.S.C. §§ 1693, 1693a–1693r.

202. Fair and Accurate Credit Transactions Act of 2003, Pub. L. No. 108-159, 117 Stat. 1952 (2003) (codified at 15 U.S.C. § 1681).

203. Fed. Trade Comm'n v. AAFE Prods. Corp., Case No. 3:17CV575 AJB JMA (S.D. Cal. Mar. 23, 2017), https://www.ftc.gov/system/files/documents/cases/bnri_complaint.pdf.

204. Press Release, Fed. Trade Comm'n, Online Marketers Banned from Deceiving Shoppers (Sept. 13, 2017), https://www.ftc.gov/news-events/press-releases/2017/09/online-marketers-banned-deceiving-shoppers.

brands (including American Express, MasterCard Worldwide, and Visa Inc.), each of which has agreed to incorporate the PCI Security Standards as the technical requirements of their security programs and which individually enforce compliance with such standards.[205] The PCI Security Standards include technical and operational requirements for building and maintaining a secure network, and protecting cardholder data. The key standard is the PCI Data Security Standard, which addresses vulnerability assessments, remediation, and reporting requirements.[206]

205. PCI SECURITY STANDARDS COUNCIL, https://www.pcisecuritystandards.org/.

206. PCI SSC DATA SECURITY STANDARDS OVERVIEW, https://www.pcisecuritystandards.org/security_standards/index.php.

Chapter 15

False Advertising

§ 15:1 Introduction
§ 15:2 What Constitutes Actionable "False or Misleading" Advertising?
§ 15:2.1 Commercial Speech Versus Non-Commercial Speech
§ 15:2.2 "Advertising" Defined
§ 15:2.3 Non-Actionable Statements of Opinion Versus Actionable Statements of Fact
§ 15:2.4 Material Versus Immaterial False and Misleading Statements
§ 15:2.5 Literally False Advertisements Versus Ambiguous But Misleading Advertisements
§ 15:2.6 Specific Claims (or Disclaimers) Must Be Considered Within the Context of the Larger Advertisement
§ 15:3 Historical Regulation of False Advertising
§ 15:4 Federal Regulation of False Advertising Today
§ 15:4.1 Private Litigation Under the Lanham Act
[A] Establishing Standing to Sue Under Section 43(a)
[B] Prima Facie Elements of a Section 43(a) Claim for False Advertising
[C] "Establishment Claims": A Special Case
[D] Remedies for False Advertising Available Under the Lanham Act
[E] Common Defenses to a Section 43(a) Claim
§ 15:4.2 Administrative Regulation: FTC Oversight of "Unfair or Deceptive Acts of Practices"
[A] The FTC's Mandate and Structure
[B] Broad Scope of the FTC's Investigative and Prosecutorial Powers
[C] FTC Administrative Proceedings
[D] FTC Prosecutions in Federal Court
[E] FTC Enforcement of Labeling Regulations
[F] "Made in the USA" Labeling

§ 15:4.3 Administrative Regulation: Concurrent FDA Oversight of Cosmetic Products
[A] FDA and "Misbranding and Mislabeling" of "Cosmetic" Products
[B] FDA Administrative Proceedings and Prosecutions in Federal Court
§ 15:5 State Regulation of False Advertising
§ 15:5.1 "Little FTC Act" Jurisdictions
§ 15:5.2 "Little UDTP Act" Jurisdictions
§ 15:5.3 California's Approach to Regulation
§ 15:5.4 Cosmetics Consumer Class Actions
§ 15:6 Private Self-Regulation of False Advertising
§ 15:7 "The New Horizon": False Advertising on Social Media Platforms
§ 15:7.1 Section 43(a) Suits Involving Digital Communications
§ 15:7.2 FTC Oversight of Social Media Advertisements
§ 15:7.3 Communications Decency Act
Appendix 15A Examples of Effective and Ineffective Disclosures in Digital Advertising

§ 15:1 Introduction

The age-old motto *caveat emptor*, or "let the buyer beware," may be sound advice for consumers, but if a merchant disseminates false or misleading advertisements, an equally applicable rule may be *caveat venditor*, or "let the seller beware." The fashion industry relies on a continual stream of marketing and advertising to connect with consumers. This chapter describes the modern substantive law that protects consumers and businesses against false or misleading advertising; surveys the historical development of this body of law; and provides an overview of the national, state, and intra-industry bodies that regulate advertising practices. Finally, this chapter briefly highlights some emerging trends in the regulation of false and misleading advertising on an increasingly important platform for commercial communication: social media.

§ 15:2 What Constitutes Actionable "False or Misleading" Advertising?

The threshold question of what constitutes actionable "false or misleading" advertising has been heavily litigated, and over the years courts have identified several factors that can be important in evaluating what kinds of advertisements may be actionable as a matter of law, and which cannot.

§ 15:2.1 Commercial Speech Versus Non-Commercial Speech

In determining the degree to which communications are protected by the First Amendment of the U.S. Constitution, courts have long drawn an important distinction between commercial speech (that is, speech that "propose[s] a commercial transaction," or that "relate[s] solely to the economic interests of the speaker or its audience") and non-commercial speech.[1] In general, courts will subject a regulation of non-commercial speech to the strictest of scrutiny, but will use the more deferential, "intermediate scrutiny" standard for regulation of commercial speech.[2] Against this backdrop, courts have consistently found regulations that proscribe false and misleading advertisements to reach only commercial speech, thereby sidestepping constitutional concerns.[3]

Drawing the line between commercial and non-commercial speech is not always an easy task, however. In *Kasky v. Nike, Inc.*,[4] the California Supreme Court reversed a finding by a trial court (affirmed by an intermediate appellate court) that an advertising campaign undertaken by Nike to rebut allegations of child labor abuse constituted non-commercial speech. In classifying the campaign as "non-commercial," the lower courts focused on the fact that the advertisements addressed an important matter of public concern.[5] The California Supreme Court disagreed, finding that the subject of the speech in question was not dispositive, but rather whether Nike had spoken in its commercial capacity and directed its speech at a commercial audience.[6] When Nike appealed the issue to the U.S. Supreme Court, the Court initially agreed to take the case, but later dismissed the appeal without reaching the merits.[7]

§ 15:2.2 "Advertising" Defined

"Advertising"—in the context of a "false advertising" claim brought as a matter of federal law—is a legal term of art, denoting a specific type of commercial speech. Courts have narrowly defined advertising as commercial speech that is also (1) broadly disseminated to a target

---

1. United States v. United Foods, Inc., 533 U.S. 405, 409 (2001); Cent. Hudson Gas & Elec. Corp. v. Pub. Serv. Comm'n of N.Y., 447 U.S. 557, 562 (1980).
2. *Cent. Hudson*, 447 U.S. 557.
3. *See, e.g.*, Gordon & Breach Sci. Publishers v. Am. Inst. of Physics, 859 F. Supp. 1521, 1535–36 (S.D.N.Y. 1994).
4. Kasky v. Nike, Inc., 45 P.3d 243, 247–48 (Cal. 2002).
5. *Id.* at 249.
6. *Id.*
7. Nike, Inc. v. Kasky, 539 U.S. 654 (2003).

audience of potential consumers (2) for the purpose of influencing their present or future buying decisions.[8] Under this definition, "advertising" need not be traditional mass print or broadcast advertising as long as the communications at issue are part of a concerted effort to reach a sufficiently large segment of the relevant purchasing public. For example, in *Dow Corning Corp. v. Xiao*, the court held that a "handful of e-mail communications" could give rise to "false advertising" liability where there were only 128 potential targets for the services that the defendant was offering.[9]

At the same time, claims made about a product to third parties who do not fall within the relevant class of targeted consumers generally do not constitute advertising.[10] Similarly, a letter containing claims about the sender's product would be unlikely to constitute advertising if it were only mailed to a single customer within a larger class.[11] And a claim about a product that was printed on the inside of the product's opaque packaging (thus rendering it invisible to all consumers prior to purchase) would also be unlikely to qualify as an advertisement.[12]

In *Fashion Boutique of Short Hills, Inc. v. Fendi USA, Inc.*,[13] the Second Circuit held that where a plaintiff fashion boutique could only establish that employees at a defendant boutique had made "approximately 30" false or misleading disparaging remarks to individual consumers over a two-year period, it had failed to meet its burden of proving that defendant was engaging in "commercial advertising or promotion" under federal law. The court noted that "[t]he touchstone of whether a defendant's actions may be considered . . . advertising or promotion . . . is that the contested representations are part of an organized campaign to penetrate the relevant markets. Proof of widespread dissemination . . . is normally concomitant of meeting this requirement. Thus, businesses harmed by isolated disparaging statements do not have redress . . . ."[14]

---

8. *Gordon & Breach Sci. Publishers*, 859 F. Supp. at 1535–36.
9. Dow Corning Corp. v. Xiao, No. 11-10008-BC, 2011 WL 2015517 (E.D. Mich. May 20, 2011). *See also* Nat'l Artists Mgmt. Co. v. Weaving, 769 F. Supp. 1224, 1235–36 (S.D.N.Y. 1991) (finding that claims expressed to ten individuals constituted advertising where the consumer class in question was particularly small and insular).
10. Guardian Life Ins. Co. v. Am. Guardian Life Ins. Co., No. 95-3997, 1995 WL 723186 (E.D. Pa. Nov. 14, 1995).
11. Ultra-Temp. Corp. v. Advanced Vacuum Sys., Inc., 27 F. Supp. 2d 86, 92–93 (D. Mass. 1998).
12. Gillette Co. v. Norelco Consumer Prods. Co., 946 F. Supp. 115, 134 (D. Mass. 1996).
13. Fashion Boutique of Short Hills, Inc. v. Fendi USA, Inc., 314 F.3d 48 (2d Cir. 2002).
14. *Id.* at 56.

§ 15:2.3 Non-Actionable Statements of Opinion Versus Actionable Statements of Fact

The law further distinguishes between statements of mere *opinion,* which are not actionable under either state or federal law,[15] and statements of *fact*, which can be actionable if false.[16] Indeed, while the Supreme Court has held that "there is no constitutional value in false statements of fact," even demonstrably "pernicious" opinions will not give rise to liability.[17]

At times, though, the line between statements of fact and statements of opinion can be a blurry one. Courts draw this distinction pragmatically, keeping the characteristics of the consumer class in mind. For example, "puffing"—or disseminating non-falsifiable claims that are couched in broad, vague, or hyperbolic language—is generally non-actionable, even where the claim might seem to be somewhat factual in nature. This is because courts assume that reasonable consumers are unlikely to rely on obvious puffery when making purchasing decisions.[18] But where a court finds that an advertisement's target audience would be likely to interpret a statement as communicating a falsifiable factual claim that consumers might rely on, that claim may be legally classified as a statement of fact—even if the advertiser actually presented it as a "mere opinion."[19]

The court's parsing of advertising claims in *TYR Sport Inc. v. Warnaco Swimwear, Inc.*[20] provides a useful demonstration of the approach that courts take to evaluating this sometimes slippery

---

15. Groden v. Random House, 61 F.3d 1045, 1051 (2d Cir. 1995).
16. Pizza Hut, Inc. v. Papa John's Int'l, Inc., 227 F.3d 489, 495–96 (5th Cir. 2000).
17. Gertz v. Robert Welch, Inc., 418 U.S. 323, 339–40 (1974).
18. For examples of statements that have been found to constitute puffery, see Gillette Co. v. Norelco Consumer Prods. Co., 946 F. Supp. 115, 131 (D. Mass. 1996) ("Anything Closer Could Be Too Close For Comfort"); Avon Prods., Inc. v. S.C. Johnson & Son, Inc., 32 U.S.P.Q.2d 1001, 1994 WL 267836, at *7 (S.D.N.Y. 1994) (claim that an insect repellant was "100 times better" than a competing product); Bologna v. Allstate Ins. Co., 138 F. Supp. 2d 310, 323 (E.D.N.Y. 2001) ("You're in good hands with Allstate"); Tylka v. Gerber Prods. Co., No. 96 C 1647, 1999 WL 495126, at *8 (N.D. Ill. July 1, 1999) (claim that a baby food was the "most nutritious"); Marcyan v. Nissen Corp., 578 F. Supp. 485, 507 (N.D. Ind. 1982), *aff'd sub nom.* Marcyan v. Marcy Gymnasium Equip. Co., 725 F.2d 687 (7th. Cir. 1983) (claim that a line of health products were "the best exercising machines of their type").
19. Fed. Trade Comm'n, Policy Statement on Deception, 103 F.T.C. 174, 182–83, *appended to* Cliffdale Assocs., 103 F.T.C. 110 (Oct. 14, 1983) [hereinafter FTC, Policy Statement on Deception], § III.
20. TYR Sport Inc. v. Warnaco Swimwear, Inc., 679 F. Supp. 2d 1120 (C.D. Cal. 2009).

distinction. In *TYR Sport*, a swimwear manufacturer sued a competitor for allegedly making false or misleading statements about the superiority of its own products relative to those sold by the plaintiff.[21] The defendant manufacturer asserted that the statements in question were non-actionable puffery and filed a motion to dismiss the suit.[22] Engaging in a statement-by-statement analysis, the court agreed that the defendant's stated intention to "recommend [that] every American wear [its product] at the Olympic trials in June" was a matter of pure opinion, and labeled the defendant's assertion that it was "far ahead of its competitors in swimsuit technology" as "the most innocuous form of puffery." But the court held that defendant's claim that its swimsuits gave swimmers "a 2% advantage over the suits of competitors" did constitute an actionable claim of fact that reasonable consumers might rely upon.[23] Accordingly, the motion to dismiss was granted as to the first two statements, but not as to the last.[24]

The court's parsing of advertising claims in *Gasser v. Kiss My Face, LLC*[25] provides a useful demonstration of the approach that courts take to evaluating this sometimes slippery distinction. In *Gasser*, a class of consumers sued cosmetic company Kiss My Face alleging it misled consumers by labeling products as "natural" when they allegedly include unnatural ingredients.[26] Kiss My Face asserted that the statements in question were non-actionable puffery and filed a motion to dismiss the suit.[27] Engaging in a statement-by-statement analysis, the court held that defendant's statements that its sunscreens provided "100% natural mineral advanced protection" and "100% natural mineral hydrating defense" statements" were actionable because they "could confuse a reasonable consumer in regards to whether the 'natural mineral' content of the products is the only part that is 100% natural, or whether the entire product is 100% natural."[28] The court, however, found that the phrases "nourish naturally with our botanical blends" and "obsessively natural kids" were not actionable as a matter of law because no "reasonable consumer" could interpret these phrases as conveying a false message because the product indisputably did contain *some* natural ingredients, and the ad did not promise to make the "kids" natural.[29] Accordingly, the court denied

21. *Id.* at 1127.
22. *Id.*
23. *Id.* at 1137–38.
24. *Id.*
25. Gasser v. Kiss My Face, LLC, No. 17-CV-01675-JSC, 2017 WL 4773426, at *1 (N.D. Cal. Oct. 23, 2017).
26. *Id.*
27. *Id.* at *2.
28. *Id.* at *5.
29. *Id.* at *5.

the motion to dismiss as to the first two statements, and granted the motion as to the latter two phrases.[30]

§ 15:2.4 Material Versus Immaterial False and Misleading Statements

Further, because "not all deceptions affect consumer decisions,"[31] only false or misleading factual advertising claims that are material to the consumer decision-making process are actionable. A claim is "material" to consumer decision-making when it speaks to an "inherent quality or characteristic" of the product in question that would likely be important from the perspective of the relevant consumer class.[32] Product qualities or characteristics that have been consistently found to be material to consumer decision-making include:

- Claims regarding the purpose of the product;
- Claims concerning the safety of the product;
- Claims concerning the quality or efficacy of the product;
- Claims concerning the cost of the product;
- Claims regarding the domestic origins of a product (for example, "Made in the USA"); and
- Findings made by another agency or a third party regarding the product.[33]

The court's decision in *Buetow v. A.L.S. Enterprises*[34] provides a helpful illustration of this materiality analysis. In *Buetow*, the defendant clothing manufacturer sold "Scent Lok" brand hunting gear—a form of "carbon-impregnated" clothing that allegedly eliminated human odor and gave hunters an advantage against their four-legged quarries. Presumably following a particularly unlucky hunting trip, five hunters filed suit against the manufacturer for false advertising. A Minnesota federal district court initially sided with the hunters and found that Scent Lok's advertising claims didn't pass the smell test. On appeal, however, the Court of Appeals for the Eighth Circuit reversed, concluding that because "the plaintiffs [we]re consumers who ha[d] proved no future harm," it was "an error of law to *assume*

30. *Id.* at *11.
31. Johnson & Johnson Vision Care, Inc. v. 1-800 Contacts, Inc., 299 F.3d 1242, 1250 (11th Cir. 2002).
32. *Id.* at 1251.
33. FTC, Policy Statement on Deception, *supra* note 19.
34. Buetow v. A.L.S. Enters., 713 F. Supp. 2d 832 (D. Minn. 2010).

that a false statement materially deceived and injured the plaintiffs."[35] The Court of Appeals then remanded the case back to the district court for further evaluation of the question as to whether Scent Lok had actually materially misled the hunters.

§ 15:2.5 Literally False Advertisements Versus Ambiguous But Misleading Advertisements

Importantly, the law protects against both "false" advertisements and "misleading" advertisements. A "false advertisement" is any advertisement that is either grammatically clear and literally false, or grammatically unclear but false under all reasonable interpretations. An example of a clear falsity would be an advertisement claiming that a pain reliever "stops pain immediately" when in fact the pain reliever only reduces pain quickly.[36]

An example of an unclear statement that is false under alternate interpretations would be an advertisement that calls a line of dental equipment "polysapphire" to imply that sapphires are present in some form, and in doing so, uses a term that is susceptible to several different reasonable interpretations, all of which are false because no sapphires are used.[37]

By contrast, a "misleading advertisement" is any advertisement that has the tendency to deceive or confuse a substantial number of targeted consumers, even if it is either (a) grammatically clear and literally true, or (b) grammatically unclear and of ambiguous truth value (that is, subject to multiple reasonable interpretations, at least one of which is literally true). An example of a literally true but misleading advertisement would be one that correctly claims that a pain reliever "can reduce inflammation that comes with most pain" better than a competitor product, but misleads a substantial number of target consumers into incorrectly believing that the former product is *generally superior at providing pain relief*.[38] An example of an advertisement that is unclear but misleading would be one that claims a product is the "1st Choice of Doctors"—a claim that could be literally false if read to imply that more than 50% of all polled doctors favored the product, literally true if read to imply that the largest non-majority plurality

35. Buetow v. A.L.S. Enters., 650 F.3d 1178 (8th Cir. 2011) (emphasis added).
36. Am. Home Prods. Corp. v. Abbott Labs., 522 F. Supp. 1035, 1042 (S.D.N.Y. 1981).
37. Johnson & Johnson v. GAC Int'l, Inc., 862 F.2d 975 (2d Cir. 1988).
38. Am. Home Prods. Corp. v. Johnson & Johnson, 577 F.2d 160, 164 (2d Cir. 1978).

of polled doctors favored the product, and factually misleading either way if more doctors actually endorse a competitive product.[39]

Because false and misleading advertisements deceive consumers and place competitors at an unfair disadvantage, both practices are proscribed at the federal and state level. Yet as a practical matter, it is far easier to prove a claim based on an advertisement that is literally false. Courts and government regulatory bodies generally feel comfortable resolving the issue of literal falsity on their own. When an advertisement is alleged to be literally false, the claim can usually be resolved expediently, and at relatively little cost to the parties. Where an advertisement is only alleged to be misleading, however, a number of thorny evidentiary issues arise. For example: What consumer base was the advertiser targeting?[40] Do consumers falling within that class tend to be credulous, sophisticated, or somewhere in between?[41] And what percentage of that consumer class would *actually* be deceived by the advertisement if they encountered it?[42] Consequently, a party arguing that an advertisement is misleading must offer some evidence of actual consumer reaction to the advertisement—evidence that usually takes the form of consumer surveys, which must be carefully designed and properly executed in a statistically sound manner.[43]

Showing that a "substantial"[44] or "not insubstantial"[45] number of properly surveyed consumers were actually confused by an advertisement is usually sufficient to establish that the advertisement is actionably misleading. While rules of thumb do exist to quantify these standards—confusion among 20% of consumers or more has often be found to constitute substantial deception; confusion among 10–15% of consumers have been found to constitute substantial deception only under appropriate circumstances; confusion among less than 10% of consumers has generally been found to be insubstantial—courts

---

39. Mead Johnson & Co. v. Abbott Labs., 201 F.3d 883, 883–84 (7th Cir. 2000).

40. FTC, Policy Statement on Deception, *supra* note 19.

41. *Id.*

42. *See, e.g.*, Proctor & Gamble Co. v. Ultreo, Inc., 574 F. Supp. 2d 339, 345 (S.D.N.Y. 2008).

43. *See generally* Shari Seidman Diamond, *Reference Guide on Survey Research, in* REFERENCE MANUAL ON SCIENTIFIC Evidence 359–424 (3d ed. 2011).

44. FTC, Policy Statement on Deception, *supra* note 19.

45. Johnson & Johnson-Merck Co. Pharm.Co. v. Smithkline Beecham Corp., 960 F.2d 294, 298 (2d Cir. 1992) (establishing the standard under the Lanham Act).

have also stressed that this inquiry into confusion is fundamentally "qualitative, not quantitative."[46]

§ 15:2.6 Specific Claims (or Disclaimers) Must Be Considered Within the Context of the Larger Advertisement

Further, in evaluating a false or misleading advertising claim, it is critical to evaluate the context in which the allegedly misleading message is featured. When determining whether an advertisement is actionably false or misleading, courts and regulatory agencies take into account all avenues of communication: written text, spoken words, sound, images, and the general atmosphere that is created by combining these disparate elements.[47] A single claim that would not be false or misleading when considered in isolation might be found to be impliedly false or misleading when considered contextually.[48]

Disclaimers or disclosures are factored into this holistic evaluation, but courts and regulatory bodies often cast a wary eye on such provisions. Effective communication of a disclaimer or disclosure requires that it be made prior to purchase, and provided in close physical or temporal proximity to the primary advertising message.[49] Written disclaimers must be clearly worded, conspicuously placed, and printed in a reasonably large font.[50] Oral disclaimers must be delivered at a reasonable pace in the same tone and volume as the sales offer.[51] And all disclaimers must communicate their message using language appropriate for the target audience: lengthy or nuanced disclaimers may be acceptable when the target audience is a sophisticated consumer class, but clearer and shorter statements must be offered if the class tends to be more credulous.[52]

---

46. Coca-Cola Co. v. Tropicana Prods., Inc., 538 F. Supp. 1091, 1096 (S.D.N.Y. 1982).

47. *Id.*

48. *See, e.g.*, Pizza Hut, Inc. v. Papa John's Int'l, Inc., 227 F.3d 489, 499–501 (5th Cir. 2000) (noting that the claim "Better Ingredients. Better Pizza." might constitute mere puffery were it considered in isolation, but finding that it became a falsifiable statement of fact when it was considered in the context of an advertisement that also featured specific claims about the quality of the advertiser's sauce and dough).

49. FTC, Policy Statement on Deception, *supra* note 19.

50. FED. TRADE COMM'N, COMPLYING WITH THE TELEMARKETING SALES RULE, http://business.ftc.gov/documents/bus27-complying-telemarketing-sales-rule.

51. *Id.*

52. Koch v. Greenberg, No. 07 Civ. 9600 (BSJ)(DF), 2008 WL 4778813, at *3 (S.D.N.Y. Oct. 31, 2008).

The National Advertising Division of the Better Business Bureau (NAD), a self-regulatory body within the advertising industry, illustrated how a fashion advertisement might be contextually false or misleading in a 2011 decision recommending the discontinuation of a print advertisement for NatureLuxe Mousse mascara. The advertisement, which claimed that the product could make users' lashes appear twice as full as bare lashes, featured a large headshot of pop singer Taylor Swift with eyelashes that had been digitally enhanced to appear longer and fuller.[53] Although a disclaimer in fine-print at the bottom right corner noted that that Swift's eyelashes had been subjected to post-production manipulation, the NAD found that the use of the image was likely to mislead consumers into believing that NatureLuxe would provide similar results. In response to the NAD's finding, Proctor & Gamble voluntarily terminated the campaign.

Similarly, in 2017, the NAD recommended the discontinuation of advertisements for Benefit Cosmetics' They're Real! mascara. The advertisements claimed the product was the "#1 best-selling Prestige Mascara in the U.S." and "#1 best-selling Prestige Mascara in the U.S. for 3 years," subject to disclosures in fine-print with citations to out-of-date studies by a market research group. The NAD found that the disclosures were not clear and conspicuous, and that the sales data on which Benefit relied was too outdated to support its "#1 selling" claim.[54] In response to the NAD's finding, Benefit voluntarily agreed to discontinue use of the advertising materials containing the claims.[55]

Importantly, advertisers cannot use a disclaimer to avoid liability for an otherwise false advertisement. For example, the NAD has opined that a disclaimer cannot stand in contradiction to the primary message conveyed by the advertisement.[56] And courts have held that a disclaimer cannot be used to correct a literally false claim that is made elsewhere in the advertisement.[57] Indeed, courts have

53. Sarah Anne Hughes, *CoverGirl Ad Featuring Taylor Swift Nixed Over 'Enhanced' Eyelashes*, CELEBRITORY BLOG WASH. POST (Dec. 22, 2011, 1:12 PM), https://www.washingtonpost.com/blogs/celebritology/post/cover girl-ad-featuring-taylor-swift-nixed-over-enhanced-eyelashes/2011/12/22/gIQAEIlgBP_blog.html?utm_term=.752fc7d9941a.

54. *See* Press Release, Advertising Self-Regulatory Council, NAD Recommends Benefit Cosmetics Discontinue Promoting its 'they're Real! Mascara' Product with '#1 Best-Selling' Claims (Sept. 13, 2017), http://www.asrcreviews.org/nad-recommends-benefit-cosmetics-discontinue-promoting-its-theyre-real-mascara-product-with-1-best-selling-claims.

55. *Id.*

56. *In re* Citicorp Credit Servs., Inc., NAD Case No. 3235 (Sept. 14, 1995).

57. JR Tobacco v. Davidoff of Geneva (CT), Inc., 957 F. Supp. 426, 437 (S.D.N.Y. 1997).

even pointed to the inclusion of egregiously ineffective disclaimers as evidence that advertisers were acting strategically and trying to deceive their target audience.[58]

Under other circumstances, authorities have also sometimes affirmatively required advertisers to include disclosures and disclaimers. Those involved in the fashion industry should familiarize themselves with the complex web of federal statutes and regulations that govern textile and clothing labeling.[59] Most notably, these regulations include the Textile Fiber Products Identification Act (the "Textile Act"),[60] the Wool Products Labeling Act (the "Wool Act"),[61] the Leather and Imitation Leather Guide,[62] and the Fur Products Labeling Act (the "Fur Act"),[63] which establish labeling requirements for apparel, including requirements with respect to fiber content, country of origin, and manufacturer identification. The Rule on Care Labeling of Textile Wearing Apparel and Certain Piece Goods[64] contains requirements for care instructions (washing or dry-cleaning) on apparel, and these instructions must be permanently attached to the garment. Apparel products that contain fur, leather, wool or "faux fur" are required to comply with additional guidelines. The Federal Trade Commission, discussed below, also enforces certain of these federal apparel labeling regulations.[65]

Additional federal laws (and the regulations promulgated thereunder) that regulate the use of certain chemicals or substances, and may impact the textile and apparel industry, include the Federal Hazardous Substances Act (which imposes certain requirements on the use of hazardous substances in household products), the Flammable Fabrics Act (which sets flammability and testing standards), and the Toxic Substance Control Act (which imposes testing, record keeping requirements and restrictions relating to certain chemicals).[66]

---

58. McNeil-P.P.C., Inc. v. Guardian Drug Co., 984 F. Supp. 1066, 1072 (E.D. Mich. 1997).
59. A complete survey of these statutes and regulations, compiled by the Federal Trade Commission can be found at FED. TRADE COMM'N, TEXTILE, WOOL, FUR, APPARELAND LEATHER MATTERS, https://www.ftc.gov/news-events/media-resources/tools-consumers/apparel-and-labeling.
60. Textile Fiber Products Identification Act, 15 U.S.C. § 70 (2011).
61. Wool Products Labeling Act of 1939, 15 U.S.C. § 68 (2011).
62. Leather and Imitation Leather Guide, 16 C.F.R. § 24.
63. Fur Products Labeling Act, 15 U.S.C. § 69 (2011).
64. Trade Regulation Rule On Care Labeling of Textile Wearing Apparel and Certain Piece Goods, 16 C.F.R. § 423.6 (2000).
65. *See infra* section 15:4.2[E].
66. Federal Hazardous Substances Act, 16 C.F.R. § 1500 (2011); Flammable Fabrics Act of 1953, 15 U.S.C. §§ 1191–1204 (2008); Toxic Substances Control Act of 1976, 15 U.S.C. § 53 (2012).

For a more thorough discussion of design and manufacturing issues, see chapter 9.

§ 15:3 Historical Regulation of False Advertising

Although the use of false or misleading advertisements is as old as the use of advertisements themselves, it was not until the rise of a national American mass media in the late nineteenth century that the harm inflicted by commercial deception began to attract widespread attention.[67] In the first decade of the twentieth century, a series of high-profile investigative articles detailing the dangers posed by fraudulent medicines made national headlines.[68] Public outcry was immediate, but existing prohibitions against fraud proved to be ineffective on several counts. For example, plaintiffs faced a difficult hurdle in proving the culpable mental state of the advertisers. In addition, the common requirement that both reliance and actual injury be shown meant that even when false or misleading advertisements were actionable, they could not be enjoined until after they had already caused considerable harm.[69]

In 1911, the trade association journal of the publishing industry responded by drafting and distributing a model statute that made the publication of a "misleading, deceptive of untrue" advertisement an actionable offense in its own right.[70] State legislatures across the country took note of this proposal, and a version of this model statute was ultimately enacted in forty-six states.[71] Congress was somewhat slower to respond, but in 1914 the passage of the Federal Trade Commission Act established the Federal Trade Commission (FTC), which was charged with investigating and preventing deceptive interstate trade practices.[72] The passage of the Trademark Act in 1920 also created a private right of action against false or misleading

---

67. CHERYL LEE JOHNSON, CALIFORNIA ANTITRUST AND UNFAIR COMPETITION LAW § 17.02 (LEXISNEXIS PRESS, REV. 2012 ED.) [hereinafter JOHNSON].

68. Samuel Hopkins Adams, *The Great American Fraud*, COLLIER'S MAG. (1905) (11-part series) (later reprinted and republished, in its entirety, by the American Medical Association). This landmark series of articles spurred Congress to pass the first Pure Food and Drug Act (1906), which was a precursor to the modern Food, Drug, and Cosmetic Act that continues to be enforced today.

69. Gary S. Marx, *Section 43(a) of the Lanham Act: A Statutory Cause of Action for False Advertising*, 40 W&L L. REV. 383, 385–86 (1983).

70. JOHNSON, *supra* note 67, § 17.02.

71. *Id. See also generally* Note, *The Regulation of Advertising*, 56 COLUM. L. REV. 1018 (1956).

72. ECON. HISTORY ASS'N, ADVERTISING BANS IN THE UNITED STATES, http://eh.net/encyclopedia/article/Nelson.AdBans.

advertisements in limited circumstances.[73] In 1946, this provision of the Trademark Act was superseded (and greatly expanded) by section 43(a) of the Lanham Act,[74] which recognizes a much broader private right of action.[75]

The burgeoning consumer-rights movement of the 1960s and 1970s prompted still greater regulation of false and misleading advertisement at all levels, as Congress increased the scope and strength of the FTC's regulatory authority.[76] At the same time, state and local legislatures responded by passing similar—and in some cases stronger—state law remedies.[77] The advertising industry itself reacted to this intensifying scrutiny by establishing internal regulatory bodies intended to promote intra-industry governance and forestalling additional external oversight.[78]

§ 15:4 Federal Regulation of False Advertising Today

The Trademark Act of 1946—better known as the "Lanham Act"—is the only federal statute that permits private litigants to sue over the distribution of false or misleading advertisements that affect interstate commerce.[79] Most other regulation of false or misleading advertisements at the federal level is left to the discretion of two government agencies: the FTC (which is vested with broad authority to regulate any "unfair or deceptive acts of practices" affecting interstate commerce)[80] and the Food and Drug Administration (FDA) (which is vested, for purposes relevant to this treatise, with the authority to regulate the advertisement of "cosmetic products" affecting interstate commerce).[81]

---

73. Trademark Act, ch. 104, § 3, 41 Stat. 533 (1920), subsequently repealed by the Lanham Act.
74. Lanham Act § 43(a) (codified at 15 U.S.C. § 1125(a)).
75. *Id.*
76. J. THOMAS MCCARTHY, MCCARTHY ON TRADEMARKS AND UNFAIR COMPETITION [hereinafter MCCARTHY], § 27:118.
77. *See, e.g.*, JOHNSON, *supra* note 67, § 17.02 (discussing the evolution of California consumer protection statutes during this period).
78. Hugh Latimer & John Kuzin, *The NAD: A Primary Forum for Resolving Advertising Disputes*, METRO. CORP. COUNSEL (Jan. 2009).
79. Lanham Act § 43(a) (codified at 15 U.S.C. § 1125(a)).
80. Federal Trade Commission Act § 5 (codified at 15 U.S.C. § 45).
81. Federal Food, Drug and Cosmetic Act § 201(i) (codified at 21 U.S.C. § 362).

§ 15:4.1 *Private Litigation Under the Lanham Act*

[A] Establishing Standing to Sue Under Section 43(a)

Section 43(a) of the Lanham Act provides, in part, that:

> Any person who . . . in commercial advertising or promotion, misrepresents the nature, characteristics, qualities, or geographic origin of his or her or another person's goods, services, or commercial activities, shall be liable in a civil action by any person who believes that he or she is likely to be damaged by such act.[82]

Although consumers might seem to fall within the sweeping parameters of this provision, courts have consistently limited standing under Section 43(a) to businesses that hold a reasonable belief that their commercial interests are likely to be damaged by the allegedly false or misleading advertisement.[83]

For many years, the circuits were divided on the appropriate test for determining whether a particular business qualifies under this rubric. On one end of the spectrum, the Seventh, Ninth, and Tenth Circuits strictly limited standing to only those plaintiffs who were in direct competition, or could otherwise point to some likely "competitive" injury.[84] On the other end, the Third, Fifth, and Eleventh Circuits had adopted a flexible five-factor test derived from the Supreme Court's antitrust jurisprudence.[85] The Second Circuit charted a middle course, advocating a "reasonable interest" test under which standing was presumed where the plaintiff and defendant were direct competitors, but which allowed non-competitors to rebut the presumption against standing by demonstrating that they harbored a reasonable concern about likely commercial injury.[86]

---

82. 15 U.S.C. § 1125(a).
83. *See, e.g.*, PDK Labs, Inc. v. Friedlander, 103 F.3d 1105, 1112 (2d Cir. 1997).
84. Jack Russell Terrier Network of N. Cal. v. Am. Kennel Club, Inc., 407 F.3d 1027, 1037 (9th Cir. 2005); B. Sanfield, Inc. v. Finlay Fine Jewelry Corp., 258 F.3d 578, 581–82 (7th Cir. 2001); Stanfield v. Osborne Indus., Inc., 52 F.3d 867, 873 (10th Cir. 1995).
85. Phoenix of Broward, Inc. v. McDonald's Corp., 489 F.3d 1156, 1162–64 (11th Cir. 2007); Proctor & Gamble Corp. v. Amway Co., 242 F.3d 539, 562–63 (5th Cir. 2001); Conte Bros. Auto, Inc. v. Quaker State-Slick 50, Inc., 165 F.3d 221, 234 (3d Cir. 1988).
86. Famous Horse, Inc. v. 5th Ave. Photo, Inc., 624 F.3d 106, 113 (2d Cir. 2010).

The Supreme Court resolved this circuit split in 2014, and articulated a new test in *Lexmark International, Inc. v. Static Control Components, Inc.*[87] In *Lexmark*, the Court held that standing to bring a false advertising claim under the Lanham Act requires a two-step analysis: a zone of interests test and a proximate cause analysis. The Court rejected all of the pre-existing legal tests, and instead announced a new test, requiring a Lanham Act plaintiff to allege "an injury to a commercial interest in reputation or sales . . . flowing directly from the deception wrought by the defendant's advertising; and that that occurs when deception of consumers causes them to withhold trade from the plaintiff."[88] The decision provides consistency across jurisdictions, and expands the number of claims that can be brought in the circuits that had previously used a more restrictive test.

[B] Prima Facie Elements of a Section 43(a) Claim for False Advertising

In order to prevail on a section 43(a) claim under the Lanham Act, a plaintiff bears the burden of establishing the following *prima facie* elements[89] by a preponderance of the evidence:[90]

(1) The defendant made a false statement of fact in commercial advertising or promotion about their own or a competitor's goods or services;

(2) The statement either actually deceived, or is likely to deceive, a substantial segment of the intended audience;

(3) The deception was "material" in that it is likely to influence purchasing decisions;

(4) The defendant caused the statement to enter interstate commerce; and

(5) The statement results in actual or probable injury to the plaintiff (for example, loss of sales, loss of goodwill, creating consumer confusion).

---

87. Lexmark Int'l, Inc. v. Static Control Components, Inc., 572 U.S. 118 (2014).

88. *Id.* at 133.

89. *See* Zenith Elec. Corp. v. Exzec, Inc., 182 F.3d 1340, 1347–48 (Fed. Cir. 1999).

90. It is worth noting that some jurisdictions also require plaintiffs to satisfy the heightened pleading requirements imposed by Federal Rule of Civil Procedure 9(b), and allege with "particularity" those facts which support a claim of falsity. *See, e.g.*, RPost Holdings v. Trustifi Corp., No. CV 11-2118 PSG (SHx), 2011 WL 4802372, at *3–4 (C.D. Cal. Oct. 11, 2011).

It is important to note that while many federal and state regulations place a burden on advertisers to show that they had "prior substantiation" to support their claims at the time they were disseminated,[91] the Lanham Act does not. Consequently, the mere assertion that a defendant lacked proof of a claim at the time that it was made is insufficient to create liability under the Lanham Act. In most circumstances, a plaintiff bringing a section 43(a) claim must *affirmatively prove* that the claim itself is in fact false or misleading.[92] The exception to this rule occurs in the case of so-called "establishment claims"—claims that are expressly predicated on some underlying test, study, or survey.[93]

[C] "Establishment Claims": A Special Case

When an advertiser predicates an advertising claim on an underlying test, study, or survey,[94] a plaintiff can prevail on a section 43(a) claim by showing that this predicate does not actually "establish the proposition for which [it is] cited"[95]—a showing that implicitly establishes that the claim itself was literally false as it was conveyed to consumers.[96]

A plaintiff can attack predicate tests, studies, or surveys in two distinct ways.

First, the plaintiff can show that the methodology and/or the execution of that methodology was so fatally flawed as to render the

91. *See, e.g.*, Fed. Trade Comm'n, Policy Statement Regarding Advertising Substantiation, appended to Thompson Med. Co., 104 F.T.C. 648, 839 (1984), *aff'd*, 791 F.2d 189 (D.C. Cir. 1986), *cert. denied*, 479 U.S. 1086 (1987).

92. *See, e.g.*, Sandoz Pharms. Corp. v. Richardson-Vicks, Inc., 902 F.2d 222, 228 (3d Cir. 1990) ("a Lanham Act plaintiff bears the burden of showing that a challenged advertisement is false or misleading, not merely that it is unsubstantiated by acceptable tests or other proof").

93. Castrol, Inc. v. Quaker State Corp., 977 F.2d 57, 63 (2d Cir. 1992).

94. For illustrative examples of language that has been found to create establishment claims, see Gillette Co. v. Norelco Consumer Prods. Co., 946 F. Supp. 115, 119 (D. Mass. 1996) ("[Defendant's electric razor] is clinically proven to shave with less irritation than wet shavers"); S.C. Johnson & Son, Inc. v. Clorox Co., 930 F. Supp. 753, 780 (E.D.N.Y. 1996) ("Testing proves [Defendant's inset bait] kills up to 98% [of insects]. The other guys, no more than 60%."); McNeil-P.C.C., Inc. v. Bristol-Myers Squibb Co., 938 F.2d 154, 1544 (2d Cir. 1991) ("[I]n doctor supervised clinical studies . . . [Defendant's pain reliever] was shown to provide greater headache relief than [Plaintiff's pain reliever]."); *In re* Visa USA, 28 NAD Case Rep. No. 3506NFY (Dec. 7, 1998) ("[T]ravel agencies surveyed estimated they've lost more than $5.1 billion in sales to American Express Travel Offices").

95. *Castrol, Inc.*, 977 F.2d at 63.

96. *Id.*

results fundamentally unreliable.[97] Issues that plaintiffs might seize upon to satisfy this burden include:[98]

- Whether industry (or government) testing standards exist, and if so, whether the test in question is in compliance with these standards;
- Whether superior testing procedures exist, and if so, whether those procedures would have been feasible;
- Whether the testing procedures that were adopted appropriately mimic expected consumer use of the product in question;
- Whether the test, study, or survey was conducted in an objective manner, and by skilled and experienced individuals;
- Whether the results that were achieved were statistically significant; and
- Whether other tests, studies, or surveys exist that either support or contradict the results that were achieved.

For example, a high-profile 2012 FTC settlement involving Skechers USA Inc. revolved around establishment claims that allegedly suffered from several of these flaws. Over a period of two years, Skechers widely disseminated a series of video advertisements that featured prominent celebrities like former quarterback Joe Montana and reality television star Kim Kardashian. In these advertisements, Skechers claimed that wearing shoes that incorporated its "rocker-bottom" technology could improve muscle tone and facilitate greater weight loss when compared with wearing competitors' shoes.[99] In support of these claims, the advertisements featured a certified chiropractor who cited an "independent clinical study" that he claimed to have conducted.[100] A subsequent complaint filed by the FTC and joined by forty-four state attorneys-general alleged that Skechers had failed to disclose that this supposedly "independent" expert was in fact paid for his endorsement, and was actually married to a Skechers marketing executive at the time that he appeared in the advertisement.[101] In

---

97. S.C. Johnson & Son, Inc. v. Clorox Co., 930 F. Supp. 753, 780 (E.D.N.Y. 1996).

98. *See, e.g.*, Charles J. Walsh & Marc S. Klein, *From Dog Food to Prescription Drug Advertising: Litigating False Scientific Establishment Claims Under the Lanham Act*, 22 SETON HALL L. REV. 329, 419–37 (1992).

99. Jim Puzzanghera, *Skechers Agrees to Pay $50 Million to Settle Toning-Shoe Cases*, L.A. TIMES (May 7, 2012) [hereinafter Puzzanghera], http://articles.latimes.com/2012/may/17/business/la-fi-ftc-skechers-20120517.

100. *Id.*

101. *Id.*

addition, the complaint cast doubts on the methodological soundness of the study, noting that it suffered from glaring design defects as well as wildly inaccurate result reporting (to the extent that some individuals who were recorded as having lost weight actually gained it).[102] Skechers ultimately settled the suit for $50 million.[103]

Second, a plaintiff can argue that the advertiser's interpretation of testing or survey results unduly overstates the conclusions that can be fairly drawn from them.[104]

In meeting either of these burdens, however, relatively minor methodological flaws or mild overstatements will not suffice.[105] The flaws and/or overstatements that a plaintiff highlights must be so substantial that they fundamentally undermine the legitimacy of the claim at issue.[106]

[D] Remedies for False Advertising Available Under the Lanham Act

The Lanham Act affords two main types of remedies: (1) equitable relief in the form of temporary restraining orders, preliminary injunctions, permanent injunctions, orders mandating corrective advertising, and/or recalls and destruction of offending materials;[107] and (2) monetary relief in the form of actual damages, litigation costs and attorneys' fees, costs to cover corrective advertising, and disgorged profits traceable to the offending materials. Under appropriate circumstances, courts have the authority to enhance these monetary damages for the purpose of future deterrence.[108]

A plaintiff who prevails in a section 43(a) claim will typically be granted a specific permanent injunction against the offending advertisement, and, depending on the circumstances, a court may also order the losing party to affirmatively correct misperceptions that have developed in the market through additional advertising.[109] In other instances, a court may go so far as to order the recall and destruction of existing advertising materials when the deception is

---

102. *Id.*
103. *Id.*
104. Castrol, Inc. v. Quaker State Corp., 977 F.2d 57, 63 (2d Cir. 1992).
105. S.C. Johnson & Son, Inc. v. Clorox Co., 930 F. Supp. 753, 780 (E.D.N.Y. 1996).
106. *Id.*
107. The Lanham Act authorizes a wide range of equitable relief. *See* 15 U.S.C. § 1116.
108. *See* 15 U.S.C. § 1117.
109. Abbott Labs v. Mead Johnson & Co., 971 F.2d 6, 19 (7th Cir. 1992).

shown to be willful,[110] or where the advertisement creates a serious public safety hazard.[111]

Federal litigation is a time-consuming process, and because advertisements typically run on a relatively short cycle, plaintiffs often seek a temporary restraining order or a preliminary injunction to prevent ongoing circulation of the advertisement while a suit is pending. The standards that a plaintiff must meet to qualify for either of these provisional orders vary slightly by jurisdiction, but generally require a showing of (1) likely irreparable harm stemming from the alleged violation and (2) a likelihood of ultimate success on the merits.[112]

Prevailing plaintiffs can also seek money damages, although courts often require an additional showing of either actual consumer deception and attending injuries (that is, loss of sales, loss of goodwill, etc.) or willfulness on the part of the advertiser.[113] Money damages can be awarded under many guises. The Lanham Act enumerates at least three distinct forms—actual damages, profit disgorgement, and litigation costs[114]—any of which can be trebled if the court deems it necessary for deterrence purposes or to fully compensate a plaintiff.[115] The Lanham Act also authorizes courts to award additional damages where they deem it appropriate, although purely punitive damages are not permitted.[116]

In "exceptional cases" where a plaintiff succeeds in proving that a defendant acted willfully, maliciously, fraudulently, deliberately, or otherwise in bad faith, a court may also award attorneys' fees.[117] This provision is a doubled-edged sword, however: courts have also awarded attorneys' fees to prevailing *defendants* in "exceptional cases" where plaintiffs have brought claims or made motions in bad faith[118] or with fraudulent intent.[119] Courts have held that "an 'exceptional' case is simply one that stands out from others with respect to the substantive strength of a party's litigating position (considering both the

---

110. Perfect Fit Indus. v. Acme Quilting Co., 646 F.2d 800, 803 (2d Cir. 1981).
111. Playskool, Inc. v. Product Dev. Grp., Inc., 699 F. Supp. 1056, 1063 (E.D.N.Y. 1988).
112. *Id.*
113. Seat Sack, Inc. v. Childcraft Educ. Corp., 417 F. App'x 931, 933 (Fed. Cir. 2011).
114. 15 U.S.C. § 1117(a).
115. Note, however, that such enhanced damages "shall . . . not [constitute] a penalty." *Id.*
116. Burger King Corp. v. Mason, 855 F.2d 779, 780–81 (11th Cir. 1988).
117. 15 U.S.C. § 1117(a).
118. Tire Kingdom, Inc. v. Morgan Tire & Auto, Inc., 253 F.3d 1332, 1336 (11th Cir. 2001).
119. Patsy's Brand, Inc. v. I.O.B. Realty, Inc., 317 F.3d 209, 222 (2d Cir. 2003).

governing law and the facts of the case) or the unreasonable manner in which the case was litigated."[120]

[E] Common Defenses to a Section 43(a) Claim

In addition to rebutting any of the *prima facie* elements of a false advertising claim, defendants can raise a host of affirmative defenses to a section 43(a) claim. These defenses include—but are not limited to—unreasonable delay/laches,[121] acquiescence,[122] mootness,[123] and unclean hands.[124] The precise elements of these affirmative defenses vary by jurisdiction.

§ 15:4.2 Administrative Regulation: FTC Oversight of "Unfair or Deceptive Acts of Practices"

[A] The FTC's Mandate and Structure

Under the Federal Trade Commission Act (the "FTC Act"), the FTC is identified as the primary federal agency charged with regulating false or misleading advertisements. Pursuant to the FTC Act, the FTC is empowered to enforce all consumer protection laws enacted by Congress,[125] as well as to enforce any trade regulations that it promulgates under its freestanding rulemaking authority.[126] Within the FTC, the Division of Advertising Practices and the Division of Enforcement—both subdivisions of the Bureau of Consumer Protection—are specifically charged with "protect[ing] consumers from deceptive and unsubstantiated advertising."[127]

---

120. Louis Vuitton Malletier, S.A. v. My Other Bag, Inc., No. 18-293-cv (2d Cir. Mar. 15, 2019) (citing Octane Fitness, LLC v. Icon Health & Fitness, Inc., 134 S. Ct. 1749 (2014)), *aff'g* No. 14-CV-3419 (JMF), 2018 WL 317850 (Jan. 8, 2018).
121. Jarrow Formulas, Inc. v. Nutrition Now, Inc., 304 F.3d 829, 839 (9th Cir. 2002).
122. Angel Flight of Ga., Inc. v. Angel Flight Am., Inc., 522 F.3d 1200 (11th Cir. 2008).
123. Am. Express Travel Related Servs. Co. v. Mastercard Int'l Inc., 776 F. Supp. 787, 791 (S.D.N.Y. 1991).
124. Hot Wax, Inc. v. Turtle Wax, Inc., 191 F.3d 813, 814 (7th Cir. 1999).
125. FTC Act § 5 (codified at 15 U.S.C. § 45).
126. *See* 15 U.S.C. § 57a (vesting the FTC with the power to "prescribe . . . rules which define with specificity acts or practices which are unfair or deceptive acts or practices in or affecting commerce.").
127. FED. TRADE COMM'N, DIV. OF ADVERT. PRACTICES, https://www.ftc.gov/about-ftc/bureaus-offices/bureau-consumer-protection/our-divisions/division-advertising-practices.

[B] Broad Scope of the FTC's Investigative and Prosecutorial Powers

The FTC can use its subpoena power to investigate allegedly false or misleading advertisement at both the micro level (that is, individuals or companies) and the macro level (that is, entire industries). An FTC investigation can be opened as a result of a request originating from within the federal government (that is, coming from the President, the Attorney General, or an official within another federal agency)[128] or from a private entity (that is, a competitor or a private self-regulatory body such as the NAD).[129]

As detailed below, the FTC is also empowered to initiate administrative proceedings based on any information that it uncovers, and any resulting cease-and-desist orders are enforceable in federal court.[130] Where the FTC has "reason to believe" that an entity is currently violating, or will imminently violate, a federal consumer protection statute, it may also elect to bypass these administrative channels and seek an injunction directly from a federal district court.[131]

If the FTC concludes that a party has violated one of its own internally promulgated rules, it has the authority to levy a civil penalty of up to $10,000 per violation.[132] The FTC can also impose additional forms of liability where doing so will vindicate consumer or market interests; examples include awarding actual damages, rescinding contracts, and disgorging profits.[133] The FTC takes particular interest in companies that seek to bolster sales by falsely or misleadingly claiming that their products offer ancillary health benefits.[134]

[C] FTC Administrative Proceedings

If the FTC has "reason to believe" that an advertising practice is violative of federal consumer protection laws or FTC rules,[135] the FTC may file a formal administrative complaint against the offending party.[136] This complaint must contain "a clear and concise factual statement sufficient to inform each respondent with reasonable

---

128. *See, e.g.*, 16 C.F.R. § 2.1.
129. Press Release, Fed. Trade Comm'n, Dietary Supplement Advertiser Settles FTC Charges of Deceptive Health Claims (May 12, 1998), https://www.ftc.gov/news-events/press-releases/1998/05/dietary-supplement-advertiser-settle-ftc-charges-deceptive-health.
130. 5 U.S.C. § 45(b).
131. 15 U.S.C. § 53(b).
132. 15 U.S.C. § 45(m)(1)(A).
133. *Id.*
134. *See, e.g.*, Puzzanghera, *supra* note 99.
135. 15 U.S.C. § 45(b).
136. 16 C.F.R. § 3.11(a).

definiteness of the types of acts or practices alleged to be in violation of the law."[137]

A respondent has fourteen days to file an answer after being served with an FTC complaint.[138] Unlike in federal court, filing a motion to dismiss does *not* toll this deadline,[139] and the respondent's answer *must* specifically admit or deny each fact alleged in the complaint, as well as detail all facts that support each defense that the respondent raises in its answer.[140] If the respondent chooses to contest the charges, the FTC will appoint a "complaint counsel" from within the staff of the Bureau of Consumer Protection and the matter will be adjudicated before an administrative law judge (ALJ).

Within five days of the FTC's receipt of the respondent's answer, both parties have a duty to disclose all extant material relevant to the allegations raised in either the complaint or the response.[141] Material that is "not reasonably accessible" to a party because of undue burden or cost may be excluded from this mandatory discovery process.[142] Additional discovery—including depositions, interrogatories, requests for production, and requests for admission—may subsequently be sought by either party. The ALJ will rule on any discovery disputes or motions that arise prior to the hearing, and the ALJ will also preside at the hearing if the dispute is not resolved at an earlier stage. Procedures associated with witness and evidentiary designations generally mirror the parallel procedures in federal court.[143] Because the hearing itself is not governed by the Federal Rules of Evidence, however, all "relevant, material and reliable evidence" may be admitted subject to the discretion of the ALJ.[144]

Both parties have the right to file proposed findings of fact and/or proposed conclusions of law, along with a proposed order, within twenty-one days after the close of the hearing.[145] The ALJ is obligated to issue a written decision within seventy days of the last such filing,[146] or, if neither party chooses to exercise this right, within eighty-five days of the closing of the hearing itself.[147]

After the ALJ issues an initial decision, either the FTC or the respondent may appeal that decision to the full FTC Commission

137. 16 C.F.R. § 3.11(b)(2).
138. 16 C.F.R. § 3.12(a).
139. FTC Rules of Practice, 74 Fed. Reg. 1808 (Jan. 13, 2009).
140. 16 C.F.R. § 3.11(b)(1).
141. 16 C.F.R. § 3.31(b).
142. 16 C.F.R. § 3.31(c)(3).
143. 16 C.F.R. § 3.21(b).
144. 16 C.F.R. § 3.43(b).
145. 16 C.F.R. § 3.46.
146. 16 C.F.R. § 3.51.
147. *Id.*

("Commission") within ten days.[148] An order of the Commission becomes final and enforceable sixty days after it has been served unless the order is stayed by the Commission or by a reviewing court. After all administrative avenues have been exhausted,as a matter of right a respondent who remains dissatisfied with the outcome of the proceedings may appeal a final administrative ruling to any circuit court of competent jurisdiction.[149] If any party still remains dissatisfied with the outcome after circuit court review, they may then petition the U.S. Supreme Court for discretionary review.

[D] FTC Prosecutions in Federal Court

Alternatively, under section 13(b) of the FTC Act, the FTC is authorized to seek injunctive relief directly from a federal district court where it has "reason to believe" that a party is currently violating, or will soon violate, a federal consumer protection statute.[150] In some instances, courts have even granted ancillary FTC requests for monetary relief.[151] The FTC is also empowered to bring an enforcement proceeding in federal court if a respondent is violating a previously issued FTC order.[152] All FTC proceedings in federal court are procedurally governed by the Federal Rules of Civil Procedure.

[E] FTC Enforcement of Labeling Regulations

As noted earlier, the FTC is also empowered to enforce federal labeling regulations.[153] In a 2012–2013 enforcement action, the FTC announced that four retailers (Amazon.com, Inc.; Leon Max Inc.; Macy's Inc.; and Sears, Roebuck & Co.) had agreed to pay penalties totaling $1.26 million to settle the FTC's charges that they violated the Textile Act, and the related rules, by labeling and advertising products sold in stores and online as made of bamboo when such products were actually made of rayon.[154] The penalties reflected the amount of products sold, as well as how long the companies continued to sell mislabeled textiles after a warning from the FTC. In a subsequent action, the FTC announced that three clothing retailers (The Neiman Marcus Group, Inc.; DrJays.com; and Eminent Inc.) violated

148. 16 C.F.R. § 3.52(a); 16 C.F.R. § 3.53(b).
149. 15 U.S.C. § 45(c).
150. 5 U.S.C. § 706(2)(E).
151. FTC v. Bronson Partners, LLC, 654 F.3d 359, 365–67 (2d Cir. 2011).
152. 5 U.S.C. § 45(b).
153. *See supra* section 15:2.6.
154. Press Release, Fed. Trade Comm'n, Four National Retailers Agree to Pay Penalties Totaling $1.26 Million for Allegedly Falsely Labeling Textiles as Made of Bamboo, While They Actually Were Rayon (Jan. 3, 2013), https://www.ftc.gov/opa/2013/01/bamboo.shtm.

the FTC Act and the Fur Act by falsely claiming that some products had "faux" fur and by not naming the animal that produced the fur.[155] No penalties were assessed.

On January 3, 2013, the FTC announced an Enforcement Policy Statement applicable to retailers that directly import textile, wool, and fur products. The Textile Act, Wool Act, and Fur Act allow retailers to avoid liability for mislabeling if they rely in good faith on a "guaranty" from a U.S. supplier that certifies its products are not falsely labeled. Importantly, the statutes do not permit retailers to obtain a "guaranty" from a foreign supplier. But the 2013 Enforcement Policy Statement provides that the FTC will not commence an enforcement action if a retailer: (i) cannot legally obtain a guaranty (that is, because the supplier is foreign), (ii) does not misrepresent claims provided by the supplier, and (iii) does not market the product as a private label product. The policy does not apply, however, if the retailer knew or should have known that the marketing claim was false.[156]

The FTC also pursues claims against companies that are alleged to disseminate false claims that their products are "all natural" or "100% natural" despite containing synthetic ingredients.[157] To settle these claims, companies have entered into consent orders that require the companies to refrain from making similar misrepresentations in the future and to have competent and reliable evidence to substantiate any ingredient-related, environmental, or health claims made.

[F] "Made in the USA" Labeling

On a subject that is closely related to labeling, the FTC has promulgated standards to help determine when claims that a product is "Made in the USA" are truthful or false. In particular, the Commission advises that textile, wool, and fur products advertised as "Made in the USA" must be "all or virtually all" made in the United States, "meaning that all significant parts and processing that go into the product must be of U.S. origin."[158] The FTC frequently brings enforcement

---

155. Press Release, Fed. Trade Comm'n, Retailers Agree to Settle FTC Charges They Marketed Real Fur Products as Fake Fur (Mar. 19, 2013), https://www.ftc.gov/opa/2013/03/neiman.shtm.

156. Press Release, Fed. Trade Comm'n, FTC Announces Enforcement Policy Statement for Retailers that Directly Import Textile, Wool, and Fur Products (Jan. 3, 2013), https://www.ftc.gov/opa/2013/01/eps.shtm.

157. Press Release, Fed. Trade Comm'n, FTC Approves Four Final Orders Barring Companies from Making False All-Natural Claims (July 13, 2016), https://www.ftc.gov/news-events/press-releases/2016/07/ftc-approves-four-final-orders-barring-companies-making-false-all.

158. FED. TRADE COMM'N, COMPLYING WITH THE MADE IN THE USA STANDARD, https://www.ftc.gov/tips-advice/business-center/guidance/complying-made-usa-standard.

actions against false "Made in the USA" claims. For example, in 2018, the Commission announced two settlements and a final order arising from allegedly deceptive claims by a hockey puck seller, a mattress company, and a backpack business that their products were "Made in the USA," when in reality the products were imported from foreign countries such as China.[159]

California law is even more restrictive, making it illegal to mark a product "Made in the USA" unless 95% of the product had been made in the United States.[160] Congress has considered legislation to federalize this question.[161]

Private litigants also pursue "Made in the USA" claims. For example, in *Dashnaw v. New Balance Athletics, Inc.*,[162] a class of consumers alleged that shoe maker New Balance mischaracterized its line of "Made in USA" sneakers and violated both California law and the FTC guidelines because, allegedly, only 70% of its products were made with domestic components or labor.

§ 15:4.3 Administrative Regulation: Concurrent FDA Oversight of Cosmetic Products

[A] FDA and "Misbranding and Mislabeling" of "Cosmetic" Products

Pursuant to section 201(i) of the federal Food, Drug, and Cosmetic Act (the "FD&C Act"),[163] the FDA technically shares concurrent jurisdiction with the FTC to regulate false and misleading claims made about "cosmetic" products in interstate commerce. "Cosmetic" products are defined under the FD&C Act as any "articles intended to be rubbed, poured, sprinkled, or sprayed on, introduced into, or otherwise applied to the human body or any part thereof for cleansing, beautifying, promoting attractiveness, or altering the appearance, [excluding soap]."[164] Examples of common cosmetics include—but are by no means limited to—perfumes, lipsticks, fingernail polishes,

159. Press Release, Fed. Trade Comm'n, FTC, Puck Seller, and Backpack Company Face Off on Made in USA Claims (Sept. 12, 2018), https://www.ftc.gov/news-events/blogs/business-blog/2018/09/ftc-puck-seller-backpack-company-face-made-usa-claims.

160. CAL. BUS. & PROF. CODE § 17533.1.

161. Reinforcing American-Made Products Act of 2017, S. 118, 115th Cong., § 2 (2017).

162. Dashnaw v. New Balance Athletics, Inc., No. 3:17-cv-00159 (S.D. Cal. filed Jan. 26, 2017).

163. Codified at 21 U.S.C. § 362.

164. 21 U.S.C. § 321(i).

makeup, and hair dyes.[165] Under the terms of a 1971 inter-agency agreement between the FTC and the FDA, however, the FDA focuses its efforts solely on addressing packaging issues—that is, misbranding and mislabeling that occurs on the packaging itself.[166]

The two primary federal laws that establish cosmetic packaging requirements are the FD&C Act, and the Fair Packaging and Labeling Act (the "FP&L Act").[167] The FD&C Act generally prohibits the marketing of adulterated or misbranded cosmetics in interstate commerce.[168] Under the FD&C Act, a cosmetic product is considered "adulterated" if:[169]

- "It bears or contains any poisonous or deleterious substance which may render it injurious to users under the conditions of use prescribed in the labeling thereof, or under conditions of use as are customary and usual" (excluding hair dyes);
- "It consists in whole or in part of any filthy, putrid or decomposed substance";
- "It has been prepared, packed, or held under insanitary conditions whereby it may have become contaminated with filth, or whereby it may have been rendered injurious to health";
- "Its container is composed, in whole or in part, of any poisonous or deleterious substance which may render the contents injurious to health"; or
- "It bears or contains a color additive which is unsafe" (excluding hair dyes).

Similarly, under the FD&C Act, a product is considered "misbranded" if:[170]

- "Its labeling is false or misleading in any particular";
- "Its container is so made, formed, or filled as to be misleading";

---

165. U.S. FOOD & DRUG ADMIN., IS IT A COSMETIC, A DRUG, OR BOTH? (OR IS IT SOAP?) (July 8, 2002, updated Apr. 30, 2012) [hereinafter FDA, IS IT A COSMETIC, A DRUG, OR BOTH?], https://www.fda.gov/Cosmetics/GuidanceRegulation/LawsRegulations/ucm074201.htm.
166. *See* "Working Agreement Between the FTC and FDA," 1971–1973 Trade Reg. Rep. (CCH) ¶ 9851 (1971).
167. 15 U.S.C. §§ 1451 *et seq.*
168. 21 U.S.C. § 362.
169. FD&C Act § 601.
170. FD&C Act § 602.

- "Its packaging or labeling is in violation of an applicable regulation issued pursuant to section 3 or 4 of the Poison Prevention Packaging Act of 1970"; or
- The label does not prominently and conspicuously include all disclosures required under other federal provisions.

Additionally, the FP&L Act requires all cosmetic packaging to include label disclosures prominently identifying the product; listing the name and place of business of the manufacturer, packer, or distributor; and noting the net quantity of the contents in both metric and U.S. customary units.[171] Failure to include all of these disclosures on the packaging constitutes a violation of the FP&L Act (and, by extension, the FD&C Act as well).[172]

As a practical matter, advertisers should take special care not to make any claims about cosmetic products that, if true, might render them "drugs" under federal law. In particular, the FD&C Act defines drugs as "articles intended for use in the diagnosis, cure, mitigation, treatment or prevention of disease" or otherwise "intended to affect the structure or any function" of a human or animal body.[173] To the extent that cosmetic products make such claims, they will be subjected to the far more rigorous advertising/packaging regulations associated with drugs, and failure to comply with those heightened regulations could lead to additional liability.[174]

In the first decade of the twenty-first century, the FDA issued only a handful of warning letters to cosmetics manufacturers, but the FDA has increasingly focused on this market. For example, in September 2012, the FDA issued a formal notice to Lancôme USA, Inc., noting that some of the "anti-aging" claims Lancôme was making about various lines of its cosmetic products were more consistent with claims commonly associated with drugs. The FDA warned Lancôme that unless they were prepared to submit their products to the FDA for testing to verify these claims, they could be subject to administrative action if they continued to disseminate them.[175] In 2014, the FTC brought a similar complaint against L'Oréal alleging that the company made false and unsubstantiated claims that its

---

171. 15 U.S.C. § 1453.

172. *See, e.g.*, U.S. FOOD & DRUG ADMIN., FDA AUTHORITY OVER COSMETICS (Mar. 3, 2005), https://www.fda.gov/Cosmetics/GuidanceRegulation/LawsRegulations/ucm074162.htm.

173. FDA, IS IT A COSMETIC, A DRUG, OR BOTH?, *supra* note 165 (quoting FD&C Act § 201(g)(1)).

174. 21 C.F.R. § 101.

175. Alene Dawson, *Clamping Down on Beauty Product Claims*, L.A. TIMES (Oct. 28, 2012), https://www.latimes.com/features/image/la-ig-beauty-crackdown-20121028,0,4282901.story.

Lancôme Génifique and L'Oréal Paris Youth Code skincare products provided anti-aging benefits by targeting users' genes in national advertising campaigns.[176] L'Oréal later agreed to a consent order that prohibited the company from making these claims without reliable scientific evidence substantiating such claims.[177]

The FDA is not alone in regulating this space, however. In a 2010 decision, a district court in the Northern District of California concluded that the U.S. Department of Agriculture (USDA) also has jurisdiction over personal care products, under the federal Organic Foods Production Act of 1990 (OFPA), which was designed to establish national standards governing the marketing of certain agricultural products as organically produced products.[178] Pursuant to OFPA, the USDA has promulgated regulations governing the use of the term "organic" in the labeling and marketing of agricultural products.[179] In a subsequent case, another court noted that although the USDA had, for a time, disclaimed the ability to regulate cosmetic products under OFPA, it changed its position, and confirmed in 2011 that the USDA's National Organic Program would coordinate with the FTC and the FDA regarding the use of the term "organic" in the marketing of personal care products in order to achieve a "comprehensive approach" across agencies.[180]

[B] FDA Administrative Proceedings and Prosecutions in Federal Court

Much like the FTC, the FDA is authorized to investigate allegations concerning the adulteration or misbranding of cosmetics, and, at its discretion, the FDA may institute administrative proceedings against parties who it believes are operating in violation of relevant federal laws. Although it often opens investigations on its own accord, FDA regulations also specify a procedure whereby private parties—including aggrieved competitors—can petition for an FDA investigation.[181]

---

176. Press Release, Fed. Trade Comm'n, FTC Approves Final Order Settling Charges that L'Oréal USA, Inc. Made Deceptive Advertising Claims for its Anti-Aging Cosmetics (Sept. 26, 2014), https://www.ftc.gov/news-events/press-releases/2014/09/ftc-approves-final-order-settling-charges-loreal-usa-inc-made.
177. *Id.*
178. 7 U.S.C. § 6501; All One God Faith, Inc. v. Hain Celestial Grp., Inc., No. C 09-03517 JF (HRL), 2011 WL 4433817, at *3 (N.D. Cal. Sept. 22, 2011).
179. 7 C.F.R. § 205.300.
180. Brown v. Hain Celestial Grp., Inc., No. C 11-03082 LB, 2012 WL 3138013, at *4–5 (N.D. Cal. Aug. 1, 2012).
181. 21 C.F.R. § 10.30.

Once it has determined that an administrative proceeding is justified, the FDA usually begins by sending the accused party a notice letter requesting that they voluntarily take steps to remedy the issue. If the issue is not satisfactorily resolved in a timely manner, the FDA may escalate by issuing a formal warning letter demanding that immediate corrective action be taken.[182] If the issue still remains unaddressed, much like the FTC, the FDA is empowered to file suit in federal court seeking injunctive relief, civil and criminal penalties, and/or seizure and destruction of the offending packaging.[183]

§ 15:5 State Regulation of False Advertising

Importantly, neither the Lanham Act nor the FTC Act, nor the FD&C Act, confers exclusive jurisdiction over advertising issues in either federal agencies or the federal courts. States, accordingly, take a variety of approaches when it comes to regulating the dissemination of false or misleading advertising.[184] By far the two largest camps are those states that have enacted statutes modeled on the Uniform Deceptive Trade Practices Act (the "UDTP Act"), and those that have enacted statutes modeled on the Federal FTC Act. Collectively, nearly two-thirds of the states have adopted one or both of these approaches.[185] California has taken a particularly aggressive stance: not only has it enacted both a "Little FTC Act"[186] and a "Little UDTP Act,"[187] it has also enacted additional legislation that creates a statutory vehicle for pursuing state class actions based on false or misleading advertisements.[188]

§ 15:5.1 *"Little FTC Act" Jurisdictions*

Just short of half of the states have enacted a "Little FTC Act" that closely mirrors the substance and language of the Federal FTC Act.[189] Although interpretations of the Federal FTC Act are not technically binding at the state level, most state legislatures have directed state courts to consider FTC regulations and judicial opinions interpreting

---

182. *See, e.g.*, U.S. FOOD & DRUG ADMIN., WARNING LETTERS AND NOTICE OF VIOLATION LETTERS TO PHARMACEUTICAL COMPANIES, https://www.fda.gov/drugs/enforcement-activities-fda/warning-letters-and-notice-violation-letters-pharmaceutical-companies.
183. 21 U.S.C. §§ 331–334.
184. *See generally* MCCARTHY, *supra* note 76, §§ 27:113–27:116.
185. *Id.* § 27:114–27:115.
186. CAL. BUS. & PROF. CODE §§ 17203 *et seq.*
187. CAL. CIV. CODE § 3369.
188. CAL. CIV. CODE §§ 1750–1784.
189. MCCARTHY, *supra* note 76, § 27:115.

the Federal FTC Act as compelling persuasive authority when interpreting these parallel state provisions.[190]

For example, in New York, this admonition has led to an interpretation of the New York "Little FTC Act"[191] that creates a particularly high bar for would-be plaintiffs: although both consumers and competitors have standing to bring suit for false or misleading advertisements, only those offenses that so severely impact the public interest that the FTC itself is likely to intervene are deemed actionable.[192]

§ 15:5.2 "Little UDTP Act" Jurisdictions

Drafted by the National Conference of Commissioners on Uniform State Laws, the UDTP Act was designed to serve as a model for future state legislation in the area of false and misleading advertising.[193] As such, it generally prohibits deceptive commercial conduct, and specifically prohibits misleading advertising.[194] Over the ensuing decades, slightly more than one-fifth of the states have enacted "little UDTP Acts."[195]

Standing under the UDTP Act is broadly conferred on any person who is likely to be damaged by a deceptive trade practice—but under the various "Little UDTP Acts" enacted by respective states, parties are largely restricted to seeking equitable relief.[196] While the UDTP Act does not provide for monetary damages, it does authorize an award of attorneys' fees upon a showing of willfulness or frivolousness by a prevailing party.[197]

In 2019, Lululemon was sued by a Florida customer under Florida's Deceptive and Unfair Trade Practices Act, alleging that the retailer deliberately misled customers about the percentage of Pima Cotton that can be found in its products.[198] The plaintiffs cited to FTC guidance that apparel manufacturers should accurately reflect the fiber

---

190. *See, e.g.*, MASS. ANN. LAWS ch. 93A, § 2(b) (directing Massachusetts courts to consider parallel federal law when interpreting the Massachusetts Consumer Protection Act).
191. N.Y. GEN. BUS. LAW §§ 349, 350.
192. Boule v. Hutton, 320 F. Supp. 2d 132 (S.D.N.Y. 2004).
193. HANDBOOK OF THE NATIONAL CONFERENCE OF COMMISSIONS ON UNIFORM STATE LAWS, 131–32 (1964), revised at 306–15 (1966), reproduced as revised at 94 U.L.A.
194. Unif. Deceptive Practices Act § 2(a)(2).
195. MCCARTHY, *supra* note 76, § 27:114.
196. *See, e.g.*, Glazewski v. Coronet Ins. Co., 483 N.E.2d 1263 (Ill. 1985) (interpreting the Illinois Little UDTP Act).
197. Unif. Deceptive Practices Act §§ 3(a), 3(b).
198. Kiara Cruz v. Lululemon Athletica Inc., No. 9:19-cv-80296-KAM (S.D. Fla. filed Mar. 4, 2019).

content on product labels, including percentages of cotton types such as Pima cotton.[199]

§ 15:5.3 California's Approach to Regulation

In addition to adopting both a Little FTC Act [200] and a Little UDTP Act,[201] California has also enacted the Consumers Legal Remedies Act (the "CLR Act").[202] Along with proscribing a wide range of deceptive commercial activities,[203] the CLR Act broadly confers standing on all consumers who reasonably believe that they have suffered damages as a result of the deceptive practice in question,[204] and authorizes equitable relief, monetary damages, and even punitive damages under limited circumstances.[205] Remedies under the CLR Act may be sought in addition to any other remedies that are otherwise provided under California law.[206] Perhaps most notable, however, is the fact that the CLR Act creates a special vehicle for pursuing state consumer class actions against offending advertisers.[207] As a practical matter, plaintiffs often allege violations of multiple California state law provisions.[208]

§ 15:5.4 Cosmetics Consumer Class Actions

As discussed earlier in section 15:4.3, the FDA has jurisdiction to investigate false or misleading advertising claims within the cosmetics industry under the FD&C Act. Historically, when other industries have drawn scrutiny from the FDA, those industries have also faced copycat consumer class action litigation from the plaintiffs' class action bar. These private suits typically allege state law false

---

199. FED. TRADE COMM'N, CALLING IT COTTON: LABELING AND ADVERTISING COTTON PRODUCTS, https://www.ftc.gov/tips-advice/business-center/guidance/calling-it-cotton-labeling-advertising-cotton-products.
200. CAL. BUS.& PROF. CODE §§ 17200 *et seq.*
201. CAL. CIV. CODE § 3369.
202. CAL. CIV. CODE §§ 1750–1784.
203. CAL. CIV. CODE § 1770.
204. Meyer v. Sprint Spectrum L.P., 200 P.3d 295 (Cal. 2009).
205. CAL. CIV. CODE § 1780.
206. CAL. CIV. CODE § 1752.
207. CAL. CIV. CODE § 1781.
208. *See, e.g.*, Rosales v. Fitflop USA, LLC, No. 11cv0973-W(KSC), 2012 WL 664187 (S.D. Cal. Dec. 20, 2012) (resolving discovery dispute in a consumer class action suit alleging violations of both the California "Little FTC" Act and the CLR Act stemming from health claims made by a footwear manufacturer).

advertising claims, piggybacking directly off of publicly available warning letters issued by the FDA.[209]

There is mounting evidence to suggest that the cosmetics industry is increasingly a target for this type of derivative private litigation; indeed, Neutrogena Corporation, L'Oreal USA, Inc., Lancôme USA, Inc., Avon Products Inc., and Coty, Inc. are just some of the most high-profile cosmetics manufacturers who have been sued under state consumer protection laws in the wake of an FDA warning letter.[210] In 2018, plaintiffs' counsel filed a class action against Tarte, Inc. on behalf of consumers, alleging that a line of "high performance naturals" beauty products was falsely advertised because they contain synthetic ingredients.[211]

Importantly, in 2012, the Court of Appeals for the Ninth Circuit held that the FD&C Act "and its regulations bar pursuit of" federal false advertising claims related to "matters of . . . labeling" that are "entrust[ed]" to the FDA and "the FDA's comprehensive regulation of that labeling."[212] Accordingly, the court held that private Lanham Act false advertising claims that depend on interpretation of federal labeling regulations, or that require the application of standards that could conflict with federal regulations, are preempted.[213] On June 12, 2014, the Supreme Court reversed this decision, holding that the FD&C Act does *not* preclude a private party from bringing a Lanham Act claim challenging as misleading a food label that is regulated by the FDCA.[214] As a result, companies that market cosmetic goods should take care to make sure that the claims that they make about their products are consistent with federal regulations in order to avoid litigation by both the FDA and private parties.

---

209. For example, the food industry has been a frequent target for private class action litigation that follows on FDA regulatory activity. *See, e.g.*, Mason v. Coca-Cola Co., 774 F. Supp. 2d 699 (D.N.J. 2011) (asserting state law claims for false and misleading advertising predicated on the same issues raised in a 2011 FDA warning letter); Dennis v. Kellogg, 697 F.3d 858 (9th Cir. 2012) (same).

210. *See, e.g.*, *In re* Avon Anti-Aging Skincare Creams & Prod. Mktg. & Sales Practices Litig., No. 2:12-cv-09084-GW-JC (C.D. Cal. filed Jan 10, 2013); Algarin v. Coty, Inc., No. 12CV2868 (S.D. Cal. Dec. 3, 2012); Trujillo v. Avon Prods., Inc., No. 2:12-cv-09084 (C.D. Cal. filed Oct. 23, 2012); Nino v. L'Oreal USA, Inc., No 1:12-cv-23462 (S.D. Fla. Sept. 21, 2012); Chow v. Neutrogena Corp., No. 2:12-cv-04624 (C.D. Cal. May 25, 2012).

211. Patora v. Tarte Inc., Case No. 7:18-cv-11760 (S.D.N.Y. filed Dec. 14, 2018].

212. Pom Wonderful LLC v. Coca-Cola Co., 679 F.3d 1170, 1176, 1178 (9th Cir. 2012).

213. *Id.* at 1179.

214. POM Wonderful LLC v. Coca-Cola Co., 573 U.S. 102, 106 (2014).

§ 15:6 Private Self-Regulation of False Advertising

The Better Business Bureau's National Advertising Division, or "NAD," is a self-regulatory body that was collectively founded by the advertising industry in 1971.[215] Much like the Motion Picture Association of America, the NAD was created during a period when the industry faced particularly acute government scrutiny. The NAD was organized to promote *intra*-industry regulation, in the hope that better self-policing might forestall the imposition of additional external oversight.[216]

The NAD broadly investigates "complaints or questions from any source involving the truth or accuracy of national advertising."[217] Because the NAD is a private regulatory body, any findings or recommendations made by the NAD are exhortative and compliance is purely voluntary. Nevertheless, the NAD has long exerted a powerful influence over the advertising industry, because industry actors recognize the NAD's usefulness on both the macro level (reducing the need for intrusive government regulation) and the micro level (providing a neutral and expedient framework for resolving industry disputes).[218] And although compliance with NAD findings is technically voluntary, the NAD can also refer disputes to the FTC or FDA for official enforcement proceedings when parties refuse to abide by its decisions.[219]

As a private regulatory body, the NAD retains complete discretion in deciding whether or not to pursue a complaint. Complaints typically originate from competitors and other intra-industry actors. The NAD usually chooses not to pursue complaints in which:

---

215. Although NAD is the oldest and most prominent self-regulatory body within the advertising industry, it is not the only such organization. Additional organizations with a more narrow focus include the Electronic Retailing Self-Regulation Program (focused on regulating online advertising) and the Children's Advertising Review Unit (focused on regulating advertising aimed at minors).

216. Hugh Latimer & John Kuzin, *The NAD: A Primary Forum For Resolving Advertising Disputes*, METRO. CORP. COUNSEL (Jan. 2009).

217. NAT'L ADVERT. REVIEW COUNSEL, THE ADVERTISING INDUSTRY'S PROCESS OF VOLUNTARY SELF-REGULATION, § 2.1A, http://www.asrcreviews.org/wp-content/uploads/2012/04/NAD-CARU-NARB-Procedures-Effective-2-1-16.pdf.

218. *See, e.g.*, *A Day in the Life of the National Advertising Division*, BRANDWEEK (Nov. 2, 2009).

219. *See, e.g.*, Andrew McDougall, *NAD Refers Ad Case to FTC Following Nail Polish Claim Concerns*, COSMETICSDESIGN.COM USA (July 15, 2013) (describing request that FTC evaluate claims that Fiore Rx had become the preferred antifungal nail polish after the company failed to respond to an NAD complaint), https://www.cosmeticsdesign.com/Regulation-Safety/NAD-refers-ad-case-to-FTC-following-nail-polish-claim-concerns.

- The advertisement in question is merely local or has limited reach;
- Resolution of the dispute requires sophisticated or unique legal analysis;
- The issue in question is the subject of pending litigation or legislative or regulatory investigation; or
- The issue is moot because the advertisements in question are no longer in circulation.

After determining that it is appropriate to act on a complaint, the NAD formally initiates a "challenge" by mailing a copy of the complaint to the advertiser, who then has fifteen business days to respond.[220] The advertiser may not raise counterclaims against a challenging party in this response, but may file a separate complaint and thereby initiate a separate "challenge" if appropriate.[221] If the advertiser fails to respond, the NAD typically alerts the FTC.[222] If the advertiser responds, a further round of briefing (set on a ten business day schedule) typically occurs.[223] Discovery is not otherwise permitted,[224] and an NAD attorney will generally make his or her own determination, in consultation with the NAD Director, as to whether a challenged advertisement is misleading.[225]

After briefing has been submitted and reviewed, both the challenger and the respondent may arrange to meet with the NAD attorney assigned to the dispute, either jointly or *ex parte*.[226] The NAD will then promulgate a written decision within fifteen days of this final contact, to be published in a press release also issued by the NAD.[227] Prior to publication, the respondent will be given the opportunity to draft a short "Advertiser's Statement" in which the respondent may indicate whether (and why) it agrees or disagrees with the NAD's decision, and whether it intends to appeal the decision to the National Advertising Review Board (NARB).[228] A respondent's failure to indicate both disagreement and intent to appeal may waive its right

---

220. NAD Procedures §§ 2.2.B, 2.5.
221. *Id.*
222. NAD Procedures § 2.10B.
223. NAD Procedures §§ 2.6, 2.7.
224. John E. Villafranco, *Challenging a Competitor's Advertising Claims*, THE ANTITRUST SOURCE (May 2005).
225. *Guidance for Food Advertising Self-Regulation*, at 44 (Nat'l Advertising Review Council, White Paper, 2004).
226. NAD Procedures § 2.8B.
227. NAD Procedures § 2.9A.
228. NAD Procedures § 2.9B.

to appeal; a complainant has no such right, but may request an appeal at the discretion of the NAD.[229]

A 2018 battle between toothbrush manufacturers Philips Oral Healthcare, Inc. and Proctor & Gamble, maker of Oral-B products, illustrates this process. In response to a series of advertisements touting that the Philips Sonicare DiamondClean gives consumers "Up to 82% more plaque removal than Oral-B's best brush head" and "Improved gum health up to 70% more than Oral-B's best brush head," Proctor & Gamble filed a complaint with the NAD challenging these claims.[230] Following an investigation, the NAD determined that Philip's claims were not sufficiently tailored to the data in its supporting study, and recommended that the challenged claims be expressly modified to make clear that the claimed benefits are limited to individuals with moderate gingivitis.[231] The NAD also recommended that Philips modify its commercial voiceovers to incorporate the models compared, and modify its website advertising based on the study in the same manner.[232] Philips and Proctor & Gamble, both unsatisfied with the NAD's decision, each announced plans to appeal the decision.[233]

As a practical matter, appeals to the NARB are extremely uncommon.[234] When they do occur, however, the appeal is heard by a five-person panel of NARB members. Unlike cross-complaints—which are not permitted before the NAD—cross-appeals are permitted before the NARB.[235] Following the submission of written briefs by both appellant and appellee,[236] both parties typically appear before the NARB panel to present oral arguments at a formal hearing. Following these oral arguments, the panel deliberates before ultimately issuing a written decision.

229. NAD Procedures § 3.1A.

230. ADVERT. SELF-REGULATORY COUNCIL, NAD RECOMMENDS PHILIPS ORAL HEALTHCARE MODIFY CERTAIN CLAIMS FOR 'SONICARE DIAMOND CLEAN' TOOTHBRUSH, https://asrcreviews.org/nad-recommends-philips-oral-health care-modify-certain-claims-for-sonicare-diamondclean-toothbrush/.

231. *Id.*

232. *Id.*

233. *Id.*

234. *See, e.g.*, NARB CASE REPORTS (showing only 44 NARB cases from 2012 to 2018), http://case-report.bbb.org/Search/LatestCases.

235. NAD Procedures § 3.1D.

236. NAD Procedures § 3.1C.

§ 15:7 "The New Horizon": False Advertising on Social Media Platforms

It would hardly be an overstatement to say that the so-called "digital revolution" has had a profound impact on the way that businesses attract and interact with consumers.[237] As of 2012, according to surveys of business professionals, 90% of respondents who reported using marketing in their professional capacity also reported using social media as an advertising platform—and 93% of those users identified their use of social media as "important to their business."[238] In the fashion industry, 80% of luxury brands now have a platform on either Instagram, Pinterest, or both.[239] Indeed, major transnational corporations of all types are increasingly dedicating entire divisions to developing and disseminating digital advertising content through social media portals such as Facebook, Twitter, and YouTube.[240]

It's not hard to understand the powerful lure of a digital billboard that can be viewed by millions of people around the world simultaneously. But with power comes responsibility—and just as the development of social media is creating new advertising opportunities that would have been unfathomable only a few years ago, social media advertising practices are increasingly being subjected to regulatory scrutiny.

Generally speaking, this new frontier is governed by the same rules that are outlined above. Indeed, in most cases, the only novel element is the mode by which the challenged claims are transmitted from advertiser to consumer. The primary exception is the Communications Decency Act of 1996 (CDA),[241] which shields "service providers" from liability stemming from content generated by other users under certain circumstances.

---

237. *See generally* W. Glynn Mangold & David J. Faulds, *Social Media: The New Hybrid Element of Promotion Mix*, 52 BUS. HORIZONS 357, 359–61 (2009).

238. Kylie Jane Wakefield, *Charting the Rise of Social Media Marketing*, THE CONTENT STRATEGIST (May 2012), https://contently.com/2012/05/02/charting-the-rise-of-social-media-marketing/; *see also* Michael Stelzner, *2011 Social Media Marketing Industry Report*, SOCIAL MEDIA EXAMINER (Apr. 2011), https://www.socialmediaexaminer.com/social-media-marketing-industry-report-2011/.

239. Scott Galloway, L2 Digital IQ Index: Fashion (Excerpt) (Oct. 4, 2012), https://www.rankingthebrands.com/PDF/Digital%20IQ%20Index%20Fashion%202012,%20L2%20ThinkTank.pdf.

240. Drew Hendricks, *The Rise of Social Media Marketing*, TECHI, Aug. 2012.

241. 47 U.S.C. § 230(c).

§ 15:7.1 Section 43(a) Suits Involving Digital Communications

Courts have already shown themselves amenable to private civil suits brought against advertisers who are spreading false or misleading messages in a digital format.

In *Proctor & Gamble Co. v. Haughen*,[242] an employee of Amway Corporation sent an email to Amway's network of distributors and customers suggesting that the President of Proctor & Gamble ("P&G") was an active member of the Church of Satan who was funneling a large percentage of P&G's profits to Church. The Court of Appeals for the Tenth Circuit affirmed a finding of liability against the Amway employee under the Lanham Act, confirming that a mass email message could constitute commercial advertising under the Lanham Act.[243]

A decade later, in *Doctor's Associates, Inc. v. QIP Holders, LLC*,[244] a district court extended this precedent beyond email communications and into the modern "social media" era. The company that franchises the Subway fast food chain sued the company behind the competing Quiznos fast food franchise chain after Quiznos sponsored a nationwide contest called "Quiznos v. Subway TV Ad Challenge," in which consumers were encouraged to submit user-generated videos to an online portal hosted by Quiznos (located at "www.meatornotmeat.com") in which they compared Subway sandwiches with Quiznos sandwiches.[245] Several of the resulting videos allegedly contained false and misleading information in violation of section 43(a) of the Lanham Act.[246] In denying a motion for summary judgment brought by Quiznos, the court held that the videos in question constituted commercial speech that was intended to influence consumer purchasing decisions, and on that basis found that genuine issues of material fact existed as to the strength of Subway's case.[247] Quiznos subsequently settled out of court under undisclosed terms.

While the case law addressing false and misleading advertisements distributed through social media outlets still remains relatively underdeveloped, given the ubiquity of social media in modern life, it is not difficult to imagine that more and more cases will arise that require judges and juries to evaluate false advertising principles in the context of social media marketing campaigns. The underlying rules and

---

242. Proctor & Gamble Co. v. Haughen, 222 F.3d 1262 (10th Cir. 2000).
243. *Id.* at 1275–76.
244. Doctor's Assocs., Inc. v. QIP Holders, LLC, No. 3:06-cv-1710(VLB), 2010 WL 669870 (D. Conn. Feb. 19, 2010).
245. *Id.* at *2, *6–8.
246. *Id.* at *1.
247. *Id.* at *22–25.

regulations may remain largely the same, but their application to the brave new world of cyber-communication promises a host of practical and substantive legal challenges to come.

§ 15:7.2 FTC Oversight of Social Media Advertisements

In 2000, the FTC helped to usher in the age of online advertising regulation by releasing the first guide to online advertising, entitled "Dot.Com Disclosures."[248] In this inaugural guide, the FTC stressed that because "[t]he same consumer protection laws that apply to commercial activities in other media apply online . . . [m]any of the general principles of advertising law apply to Internet ads"[249]—and indeed, the guide is in large part a restatement of the advertising principles outlined above, simply reframed in a digital context. For example, after restating the long-settled rule that clear and adequate disclosures must be provided in close proximity to advertising claims when qualification is called for, the guide identified warning signs that a webpage may not be providing users with adequate disclosure, such as when an advertisement requires readers to scroll down on a webpage to see a disclaimer, and there are no "texts or visual cues" to prompt users of the need to scroll down.[250] The FTC also presciently noted that "new issues arise almost as fast as technology develops," leaving ample room for future refinement and elaboration.[251]

In 2009, the FTC issued a new guide targeted at false advertising in a social media context. In discussing product endorsements that are disseminated through social media platforms, the FTC established that:

(1) Where a social media figure (for example, a blogger) is being materially compensated by an advertiser for his or her endorsement, such compensation must be disclosed;[252]

(2) Where a popular figure (for example, a celebrity) is being materially compensated by an advertiser to endorse a product using a social media outlet, such compensation must be disclosed

---

248. FED. TRADE COMM'N, DOT.COM DISCLOSURES INFORMATION ABOUT ONLINE ADVERTISING (May 2000), https://www.ftc.gov/sites/default/files/attachments/press-releases/ftc-staff-issues-guidelines-internet-advertising/0005dotcomstaffreport.pdf.

249. *Id.* at 1.

250. *See id.* at 6–7.

251. *Id.* at 1.

252. Julie Brill, Comm'r, Fed. Trade Comm'n, Keynote Address at the University of North Carolina Law Review Symposium: Privacy and Consumer Protection in Social Media (Nov. 18, 2011).

(unless consumers would be likely to understand that they were being compensated without any disclosure);[253]

(3) In the event of inadequate disclosure, both advertisers and endorsers may be subject to an enforcement action;[254] and

(4) Where consumers themselves are paid to endorse a product in an advertisement disseminated through a social media outlet, and that advertisement suggests that the consumer's reported experience is "typical," the general experience that consumers can actually expect from the product must be clearly disclosed—a mere "results not typical" disclaimer is insufficient.[255]

The FTC elaborated on its views of these issues in 2010, when it brought an enforcement action against a public relations agency that was promoting video games by having its employees post positive reviews on iTunes without disclosing that they were being paid to do so. The FTC determined that this omission was material and actionable. [256] In 2011, the FTC brought another enforcement action against an educational company that was recruiting paid affiliates to promote music education courses through blog posts without revealing that they were being compensated for their endorsements.[257] The company ultimately settled for $250,000.[258]

Then, in March of 2013, the FTC updated the original "Dot.Com Disclosures" guide to address some of the most important technological developments that have come to pass in the last decade.[259] In light of the growing importance of social media platforms, the updated guide addresses some of the practical issues confronting modern advertisers who are crafting advertisements designed to be viewed on relatively small modern mobile devices. While the legal principles that undergird the FTC's latest guidance are familiar, the key (as always) lies in the execution—for example, the FTC warns that

---

253. *Id.*
254. *Id.*
255. *Id.*
256. In the Matter of Reverb Commc'ns, Inc., 75 Fed. Reg. 53,968 (Fed. Trade Comm'n Sept. 2, 2010) (consent decree).
257. In the Matter of Legacy Learning Sys., Inc., 76 Fed. Reg. 15,311 (Fed. Trade Comm'n Mar. 21, 2011) (consent decree).
258. Press Release, Fed. Trade Comm'n, Firm to Pay FTC $250,000 to Settle Charges That It Used Misleading Online 'Consumer' and 'Independent' Reviews (Mar. 5, 2011), http://ftc.gov/opa/2011/03/legacy.shtm.
259. FED. TRADE COMM'N, DOT.COM DISCLOSURES: HOW TO MAKE EFFECTIVE DISCLOSURES IN DIGITAL ADVERTISING (MAR. 2013) [hereinafter DOT.COM DISCLOSURES], https://www.ftc.gov/os/2013/03/130312dotcomdisclosures.pdf.

because "[d]isclosures must be effectively communicated to consumers before they make a purchase or incur a financial obligation . . . [w]hen a product advertised online can be purchased from brick and mortar stores or from online retailers other than the advertiser itself, necessary disclosures should be made in the ad."[260]

The FTC can institute both administrative proceedings and also bring claims in federal court to address false advertising online. For example, the FTC initiated proceedings, and then entered in to a 2019 consent order with online student loan refinancer SoFi over such allegedly deceptive claims as "Refinancing student loans saves $22,359 on average," and "Start saving on your student loans. Average monthly savings $292."[261] The final consent order, approved by the Commission, prohibits the company from misrepresenting to consumers how much money consumers will save or have saved using its products unless the claims are supported by reliable evidence.[262]

The social media site and mobile app Twitter—one of the most popular modern social media outlets—provides a useful illustration of the challenges that advertisers face in making use of social media and mobile forms of communication. Twitter had traditionally imposed a strict 140-character limit on all messages (or "tweets") that users post (later expanded to 280 characters). Given these hard space constraints, advertisers may find it difficult to fully disclaim or qualify statements made in tweets. For example, in 2011, the Department of Transportation fined Spirit Airlines, Inc., for failing to note that additional surcharges apply in a tweet that promised "fares from just $9* each way!" [263]

The FTC's "Dot.Com Disclosures" guide suggests that in the realm of social media communication, when an advertisement cannot be modified so that it does not necessitate a disclosure and where adequate disclosure is precluded by space limitations, "the space-constrained ad [simply] should not be used."[264]

The FTC has taken the position that its Endorsement Guides apply to all social media sites, and, in particular, reach individual influencers on forums like Instagram. The Endorsement Guides provide that if there is a "material connection" between an endorser and an

---

260. *Id.* at 15.

261. Press Release, Fed. Trade Comm'n, FTC Approves Final Order with SoFi (Feb. 25, 2019), https://www.ftc.gov/news-events/press-releases/2019/02/ftc-approves-final-order-sofi?utm_source=govdelivery.

262. *Id.*

263. *See* Spirit Airlines, Inc., Violations of 49 U.S.C. § 41712 and 14 C.F.R. § 399.84, Order 2011-11-23 (Nov. 21, 2011) (consent order), https://www.regulations.gov/#!documentDetail;D=DOT-OST-2011-0003-0062.

264. DOT.COM DISCLOSURES, *supra* note 259, at 7.

advertiser that might affect the weight or credibility that consumers give the endorsement, that connection should be clearly and conspicuously disclosed.[265]

The FTC has taken steps to enforce these guidelines. In 2016, national retailer Lord & Taylor agreed to settle FTC charges that it deceived consumers by paying fifty fashion influencers to post Instagram pictures, without disclosing that compensation.[266] In 2017, after reviewing numerous Instagram posts by celebrities, athletes, and other influencers, the FTC sent out more than ninety letters reminding influencers that they should clearly and conspicuously disclose their relationships to brands when promoting or endorsing products through social media.[267] Later that year, the FTC approved a final consent order in its first-ever case against individual social media influencers,[268] illustrating that companies seeking endorsements and individual influencers must both be careful to comply with the FTC's guidelines.

The FTC can be expected to remain active as online and mobile advertisers continue to experiment with new forms of advertising. To assist advertisers in negotiating these waters, the 2013 Dot.Com Disclosures report includes an appendix of illustrations, demonstrating in graphical terms examples of disclosures that the FTC considers to be problematic and those that the FTC considers to be acceptable.

§ 15:7.3 Communications Decency Act

The Communications Decency Act of 1996 (CDA) provides, in relevant part, that "[n]o provider or user of an interactive computer service shall be treated as the publisher or speaker of any information provided by another information content provider."[269] In the context

---

265. FED. TRADE COMM'N, THE FTC'S ENDORSEMENT GUIDES: WHAT PEOPLE ARE ASKING, https://www.ftc.gov/tips-advice/business-center/guidance/ftcs-endorsement-guides-what-people-are-asking.

266. Press Release, Fed. Trade Comm'n, Lord & Taylor Settles FTC Charges It Deceived Consumers Through Paid Article in an Online Fashion Magazine and Paid Instagram Posts by 50 "Fashion Influencers" (Mar. 15, 2016), https://www.ftc.gov/news-events/press-releases/2016/03/lord-taylor-settles-ftc-charges-it-deceived-consumers-through.

267. Press Release, Fed. Trade Comm'n, FTC Staff Reminds Influencers and Brands to Clearly Disclose Relationship (Apr. 19, 2017), https://www.ftc.gov/news-events/press-releases/2017/04/ftc-staff-reminds-influencers-brands-clearly-disclose.

268. Press Release, Fed. Trade Comm'n, FTC Approves Final Consent Order against Owners of CSGO Lotto Website (Nov. 29, 2017), https://www.ftc.gov/news-events/press-releases/2017/11/ftc-approves-final-consent-order-against-owners-csgo-lotto.

269. 47 U.S.C. § 230(c).

of false and misleading advertisements, this provision functions as a statutory safe harbor that shields the "providers" and third-party "users" of "interactive computer services" from liability for false and misleading statements disseminated through those interactive computer services by others.

Since 1996, courts have found that this protection excludes defendants who, while they may not have been directly responsible for creating or posting the advertisement, nevertheless facilitated its creation or transformed it in some meaningful way. For example, in *MCW v. Badbusinessbureau.com*,[270] a district court rejected a CDA defense where the defendants operated a website that both served as a consumer complaint forum and sold services. Faced with claims that the defendants had violated section 43(a) by providing consumers with specific guidance on how to create complaints targeted at the plaintiff, allowed the resulting complaints to be posted on their website, and actually edited some of the complaints themselves, the court noted "[t]he distinction between merely publishing information provided by a third-party as an interactive computer service and actually creating or developing any of the information posted as an information content provider is critical."[271]

The *Doctor's Associates* decision (discussed above) is similarly instructive on the scope of the CDA defense: In rejecting defendant's motion for summary judgment, the court held that because defendants had played an active role in the creation of the product-to-product comparison videos in question—first by providing sample videos to consumers, and then by expressly soliciting users to post similar videos on their website—they could not be heard to argue that they were protected as a mere "service provider" under the terms of the CDA.[272]

There are, of course, numerous websites and other new media forums that allow third parties to post content related to the fashion industry. To the extent that these sites merely provide a neutral environment for users to comment, it is likely that CDA immunity will continue to apply. To the extent that sites play either an active or even a passive role in the creation of content, however, it is less certain that the CDA will immunize them from liability.

---

270. MCW v. Badbusinessbureau.com, No. 3:02-CV-2727-G, 2004 WL 833595 (N.D. Tex. Apr. 19, 2004).

271. *But cf.* Barnes v. Yahoo, 570 F.3d 1096 (9th Cir. 2009), suggesting, in dicta, that for the purposes of establishing CDA immunity, "publication [might] involve[] reviewing, editing, and deciding whether to publish or to withdraw from publication third party content."

272. Doctor's Assocs., Inc. v. QIP Holders, LLC, No. 3:06-cv-1710(VLB), 2010 WL 669870 , at *22–24 (D. Conn. Feb. 19, 2010).

Appendix 15A

Examples of Effective and Ineffective Disclosures in Digital Advertising*

Appendix: Examples

* From .COM DISCLOSURES, a report of the Federal Trade Commission (Mar. 2013).

Example 1

The disclosure “imitation” needs to accompany the triggering term “pearl,” so that consumers are not misled about the type of pearls being sold. The disclosure would not be as effective if it was separated from the word “pearl” or placed on a different page. The FTC’s Guides for the Jewelry, Precious Metals, and Pewter Industries, 16 C.F.R. § 23.19, recognize this and advise that the disclosure “imitation” immediately precede the word pearl. In this situation, there is no reason to evaluate proximity differently in online ads than other types of ads.

Example 2

This ad must disclose that the diamond weights are not exact and that a 3/4 carat diamond may weigh between .72 and .78 carats. Here, though, because of the blank space between the textual description of the product and the disclosure, even consumers who scroll down to the end of the text (see second screen) will probably think that there is no more information to view and are likely to miss the disclosure.

Example 3

Advertisers should take into consideration the variety of devices and platforms that consumers can use to view their ads and ensure that necessary disclosures are clear and conspicuous on any device or platform that is capable of displaying their message.

In this example, consumers might not expect a monthly service fee for cameras used to monitor their homes over the Internet, so a disclosure is necessary to prevent the ad from being misleading. Placing the disclosure in a different column than the camera price it qualifies, as in this example, rather than directly under the price information, makes it less likely that consumers viewing this webpage on a desktop computer would notice the disclosure here.

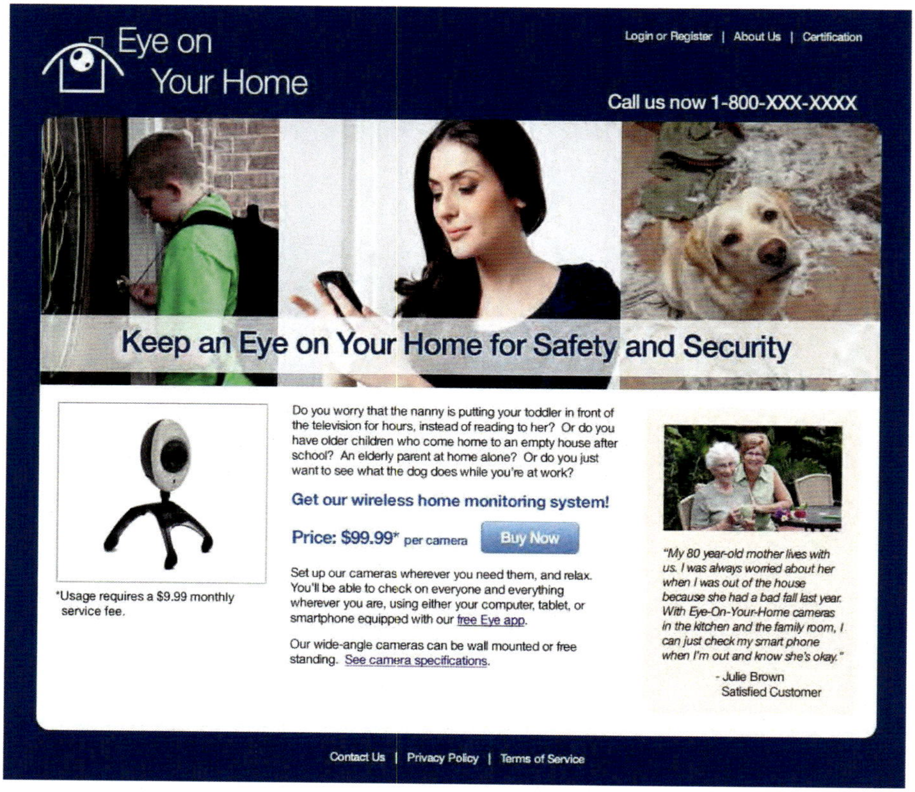

Webpage on a desktop

(continued on next page)

Example 3 (cont'd)

Consumers viewing this webpage on a smartphone or other device with a small screen, however, would likely find it too small to read (see mobile screen without zooming, below), requiring them to zoom in on the part or parts that they wish to read.

They are likely to zoom in on the center column (see zoomed-in mobile screen, below), which contains the main information on the page and might not scroll left to see the disclosure in the left column. As a result, consumers who use a smart phone to view this website, which has not been optimized for mobile devices, might easily miss the monthly monitoring fee disclosure.

Mobile screen (no zooming)

Mobile screen (zoomed-in)

A-5

Example 4

Hyperlinks should not be used to communicate disclosures that are an integral part of a claim or inseparable from it, including important health and safety information. In this example, the hyperlink "Important Health Information" leads to a disclosure, "Frost-a-tron may not keep perishable food items cold enough to prevent the growth of bacteria when the temperature is over 80°F, such as in a hot car. Use in these conditions could lead to food-borne illness." The fact that the cooler might not keep food cold enough to prevent the growth of dangerous bacteria should not be hidden behind a hyperlink, even one labeled "Important Health Information." This is especially true when the cooler is promoted for keeping perishable food fresh and cold on road trips. Moreover, any disclosure that is integral to the primary claim should be immediately adjacent to that claim.

Example 5

Although hyperlinks generally should not be used to disclose information integral to the claim — such as the existence and nature of additional fees consumers might not expect — a hyperlink can be used to disclose the details if they are too complex to describe next to the basic price information. Here the hyperlink leads to the disclosure, "Monitoring plan price: $15.95 per month with one camera, $9.95 per month/per camera with two cameras, $7.95 per month/ per camera with three or more cameras. Save 10% with a 12-month commitment, 20% with a 24-month commitment. Additional 5% discount for seniors and families of active duty military personnel."

This information about the monitoring plan's prices is likely is too complex to appear adjacent to the price per camera claim, and thus can be placed behind a properly labeled hyperlink. The statement "Service plan required" and the hyperlink are next to the price per camera; and together, the statement and the hyperlink's label communicate to consumers the specific nature and importance of the information to which the hyperlink leads.

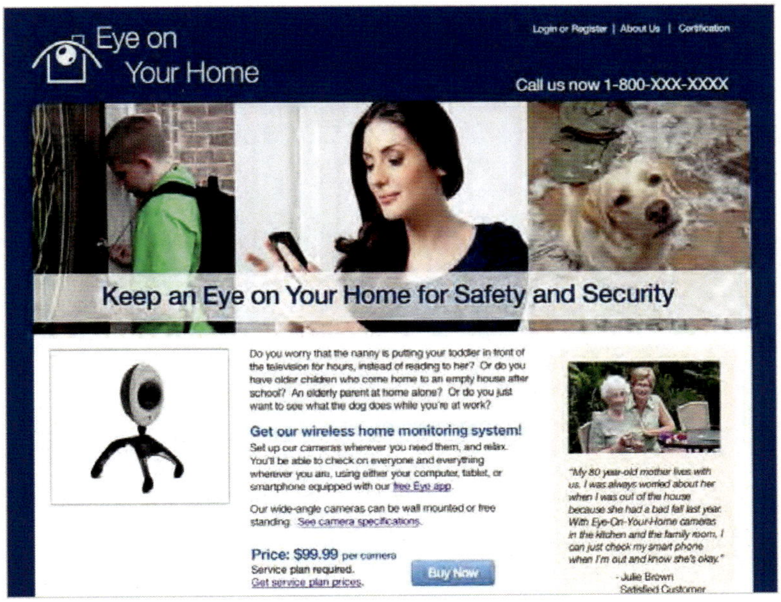

Moreover, all cost information, including any such fees, should be presented clearly and conspicuously to consumers prior to purchase.

A-7

Example 6

Because the advertiser's assertion that "Satisfaction is guaranteed" implies that dissatisfied consumers can get a full refund of the purchase price, the advertiser should clearly and conspicuously disclose any restocking fees.

The hyperlink "Restocking fee applies to all returns." leads to the disclosure, "If you return the Frost-a-tron within 30 days there is a restocking fee of $19.95. After 30 days and before 90 days, the restocking fee is $29.95. After 90 days, the restocking fee is $49.95. Shipping and handling fees are non-refundable. No COD on returns." The details in this return policy are likely too complex to disclose next to the guarantee. The label of the hyperlink adequately conveys the nature and relevance of the information to which it leads.

Example 7

This ad must disclose that the diamond weights are not exact and that a 3/4 carat diamond may weigh between .72 and .78 carats. Even if the hyperlink "3/4 Ct." clicks through to a page that lists the weight range for every size diamond sold by the advertiser, this disclosure is not clear and conspicuous.

Underlining "3/4 Ct." may or may not indicate to consumers that this is a hyperlink. Even if consumers recognize it as a hyperlink, the label here does not communicate the relevance of the information to which that link leads — in this case, to a disclosure that diamond weights are not exact, that the diamonds sold by this merchant may vary in weight, and that the advertised ¾ carat diamonds might each actually weight less than 0.75 carats. Consumers might expect to find additional general information about "carats" or diamond weights generally, but not necessarily information that qualifies the claim that they are purchasing diamonds of a specific weight.

Example 8

Because the advertiser's assertion that "Satisfaction is guaranteed" implies that dissatisfied consumers can get a full refund of the purchase price, the advertiser should disclose any restocking fees. The hyperlink "Disclaimer" leads to the disclosure, "If you return the Frost-a-tron within 30 days there is a restocking fee of $19.95. After 30 days and before 90 days, the restocking fee is $29.95. After 90 days, the restocking fee is $49.95. Shipping and handling fees are non-refundable. No COD on returns."

The hyperlink label "Disclaimer" does not adequately convey that the information to which this hyperlink leads concerns significant restocking fees applied to all product returns; nor would hyperlinks labeled "Disclosure," "Details," or even "Return Information."

In contrast, the hyperlink in Example 6, "Restocking fee applies to all returns," does convey the nature and importance of the information in question.

Example 9

This ad must disclose that the diamond weights are not exact and that a 3/4 carat diamond may weigh between .72 and .78 carats. Even if the hyperlink clicks through to a page that lists the weight range for every size diamond sold by the advertiser, this disclosure is not clear and conspicuous because the hyperlink's label does not indicate the importance of the information to which the link leads so that consumers understand why they should click on it. Although the label does indicate that more information about the earrings is available if the consumer clicks through, it does not indicate that it is related to the weight of the diamonds being advertised. Consumers could expect, for example, that this link takes them to shipping and ordering information, rather than information about the diamond weights.

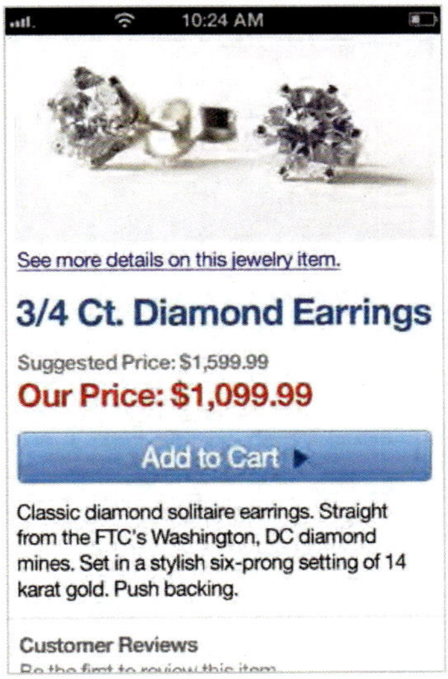

Example 10

Julie Brown's endorsement is followed by a symbol consisting of the letters "FS" in a circle that is intended to disclose that she received a free sample (in this case, a free camera) in exchange for providing her endorsement.

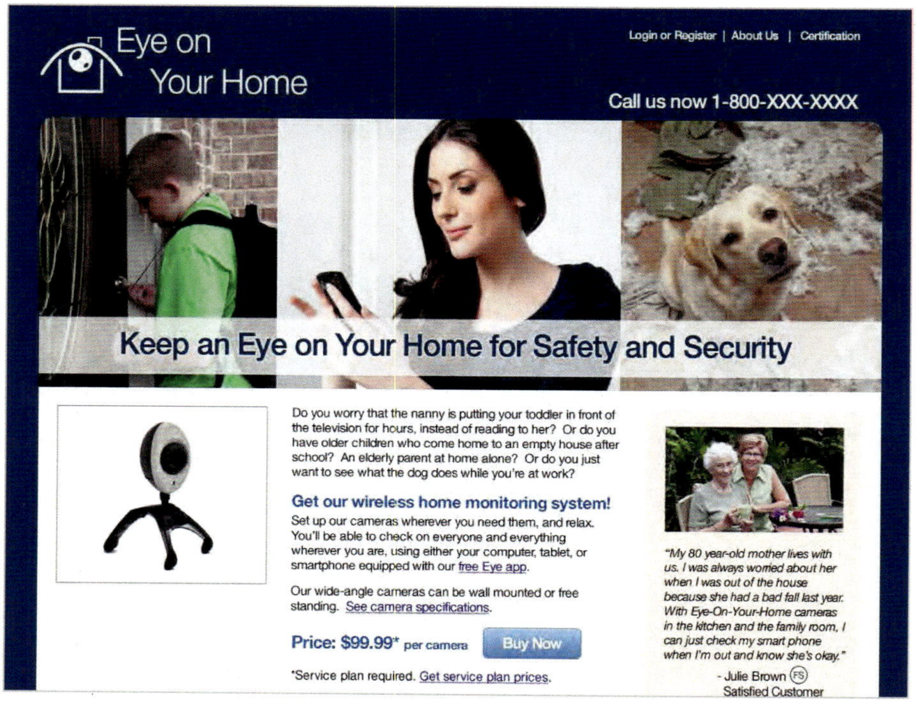

Icons, abbreviations, and symbols such as this are not adequate to prevent a claim from being misleading if they do not provide sufficient clues about why a claim is qualified or about the nature of the disclosure, or if consumers simply do not understand their meaning. The fact that the icon or symbol also functions as a hyperlink to an explanation of its meaning would not be sufficient to make the disclosure clear and conspicuous.

Example 11

Hyperlinks should be adjacent to the claims to which they relate, in order to increase the likelihood that consumers will see them and understand their relevance.

In this example, the hyperlink about restocking fees is right next to the claim that triggers the need for this qualifying information — that satisfaction is guaranteed.

Example 12

Hyperlinks should be adjacent to the claim to which they relate, in order to increase the likelihood that consumers will see them and understand their relevance.

In this example, the substantial gap between the end of the webpage's main text and the hyperlink makes it unlikely that consumers will notice the hyperlink. In addition, as noted in Example 9, the hyperlink is inadequately labeled.

Example 13

If the purchase or use of the advertised product entails significant additional charges beyond the basic price of the product and consumers reasonably might not expect those charges, they should be disclosed prominently on the same page as, and immediately adjacent to, statements of the product's basic cost.

In this example, disclosure of the existence and amount of a monthly monitoring fee only on the check-out page (see next page) would likely be deemed insufficiently clear and conspicuous; this fee should be clearly stated next to the price of the cameras on the preceding website pages that provide that price information.

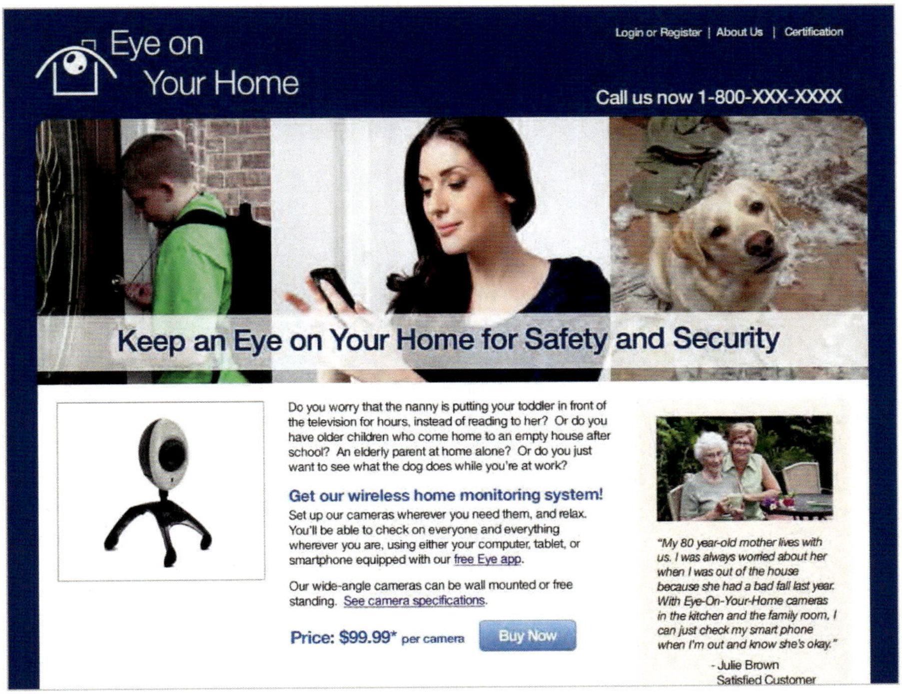

(continue on next page)

Example 13 (continued)

However, disclosure on the check-out page of the sales tax the consumer owes on this purchase, as well as reasonable shipping and handling charges, would not be problematic, because consumers expect these charges.

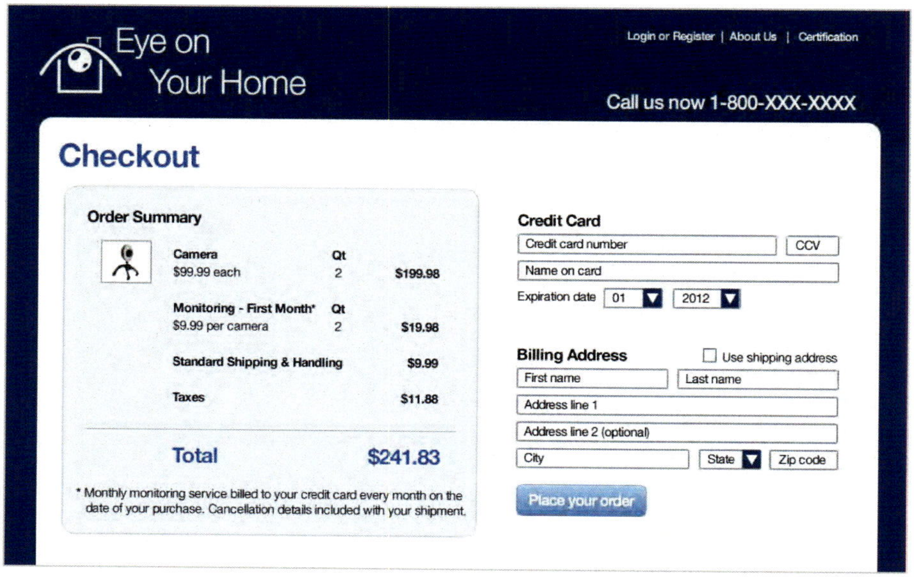

Example 14

This space-constrained message requires two disclosures: (1) that JuliStarz is a paid endorser for Fat-away; and (2) the amount of weight that consumers who use Fat-away can generally expect to lose in the depicted circumstances, which is much less than the 30 pounds Juli says she lost in 6 weeks. See Guides Concerning the Use of Endorsements and Testimonials in Advertising, 16 CFR Part 255.

Even if the link in the message led directly to those disclosures on the Fat-away website, those disclosures would not be adequate if consumers could purchase Fat-away at a brick and mortar store or from a third-party online retailer (a retailer that is not affiliated with the advertiser). In either case, they might not click through to the Fat-away website, and thus would not see these disclosures.

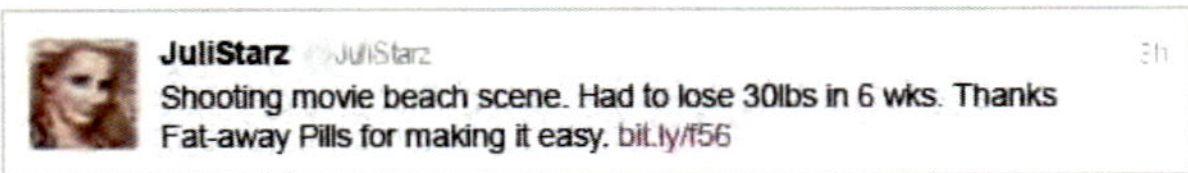

Example 15

In some cases, required disclosures can easily be incorporated into a space-constrained ad. This space-constrained message requires two disclosures: (1) that JuliStarz is a paid endorser for Fat-away; and (2) the amount of weight that consumers who use Fat-away can generally expect to lose in the depicted circumstances, which is much less than the 30 pounds Juli says she lost in 6 weeks. This space-constrained ad signals that Juli is a paid endorser by beginning with "Ad:" which only takes up four characters. It also succinctly discloses, "Typical loss: 1lb/wk."

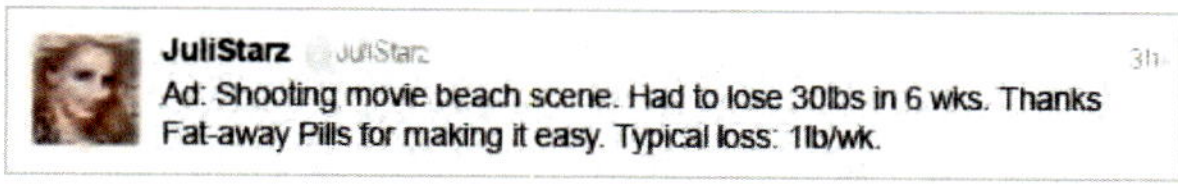

Example 16

The initial space-constrained message requires two disclosures: (1) that Juli is a paid endorser for Fat-away; and (2) the amount of weight that consumers who use Fat-away can generally expect to lose in the depicted circumstances, which is much less than the 30 pounds Juli says she lost in 6 weeks. Putting that information in a subsequent message is problematic, because unrelated messages may arrive in the interim. By the time Juli's disclosures arrive, consumers might no longer be reading these messages, or they simply might not realize that those disclosures pertain to the original message.

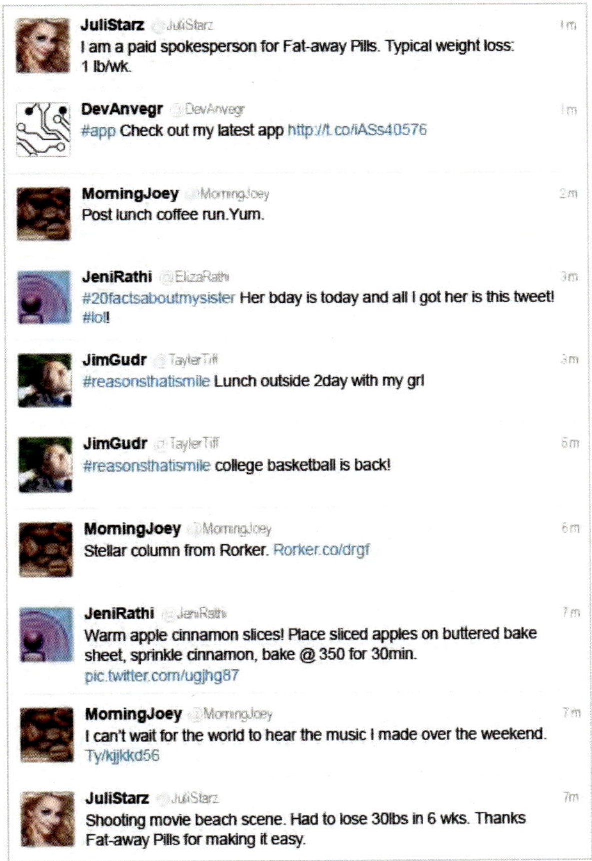

Example 17

These space-constrained messages all require the following disclosures: (1) that JuliStarz is a paid endorser for Fat-away; and (2) the amount of weight that consumers who use Fat-away can generally expect to lose in the depicted circumstances which is much less than the 30 pounds Juli says she lost in 6 weeks. Although each of these messages includes an abbreviation or link that leads to disclosure of the relevant information, each of them may be inadequate to prevent consumers from being misled.

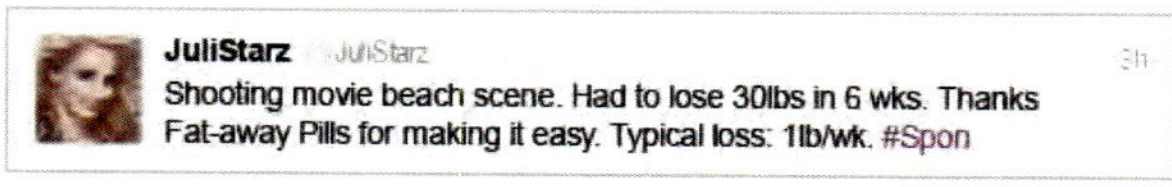

Consumers might not understand that "#spon" means that the message was sponsored by an advertiser. If a significant proportion of reasonable viewers would not, then the ad would be deceptive.

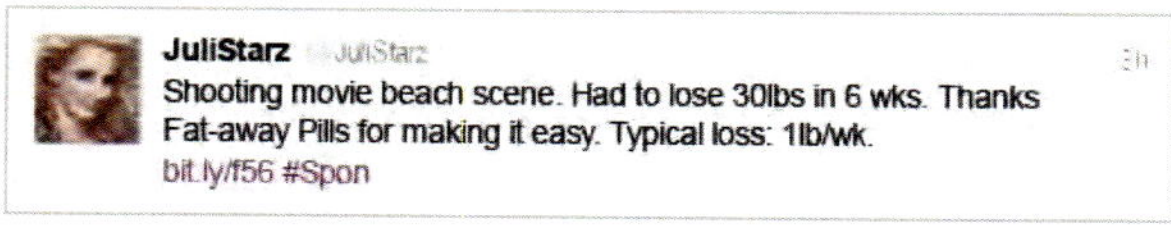

Putting #spon directly after the link might confuse consumers and make it less likely that they would understand that it is a disclosure.

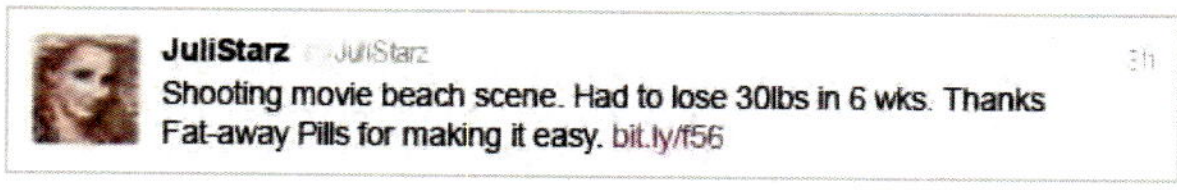

Consumers viewing "bit.ly/f56," which links to the advertiser's official website for the product, might not realize the nature and relevance of the information that could be found by clicking on it. Moreover, if consumers can buy Fat-away in brick and mortar stores, at third-party online retailers, or in any way other than by clicking on the link, consumers who do not click on the link would be misled.

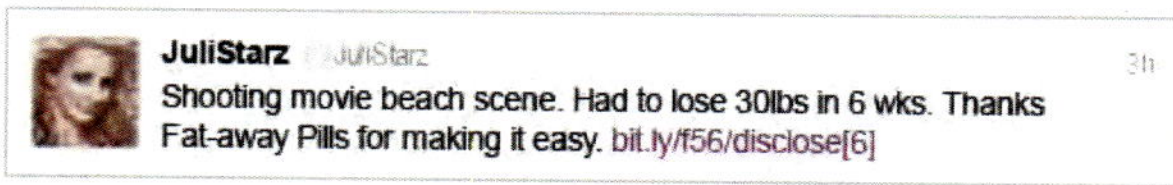

Similarly, consumers viewing "bit.ly/f56/disclose[6]," which leads to a third-party website with disclosures, would not necessarily understand what they will find at that website, or why they should click on that link.

Example 18

Both disclosures in this ad appear in text that contrasts poorly with the background of the page and they therefore are both easy to miss. Because the disclosures are not prominent, they are not clear and conspicuous.

Example 19

Most webpages viewable on desktop devices may also be viewable on smartphones, but, as discussed earlier, consumers may miss disclosures on mobile devices because of the need to zoom in on text and to scroll horizontally as well as vertically.

Disclosures are more likely to be clear and conspicuous on websites that are optimized for mobile devices or created using responsive design, which automatically detects the kind of device the consumer is using to access the site and arranges the content on the site so it makes sense for that device.

In this example, the website is optimized for mobile devices, and both the information about the service plan requirement and the hyperlink to the plan's prices are immediately adjacent to the camera price they qualify.

Example 20

Because the negative option in this example (enrollment in a recipe club) addresses a different subject than the main offer (cookware), the advertiser should take special care to ensure that the disclosure of the negative option is clear and conspicuous. In this case, requiring consumers to affirmatively acknowledge the disclosure by clicking on one of the two boxes on the second page — neither of which has been preselected — before they can proceed to checkout, should achieve that goal.

(continue on next page)

Example 20 (continued)

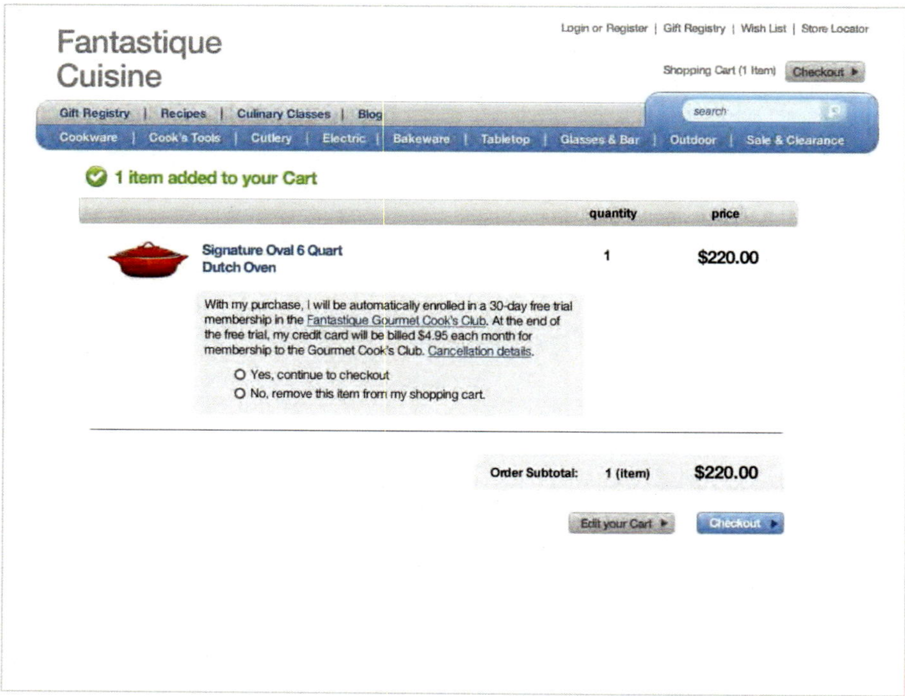

Example 21

The blogger in this example obtained the paint she is reviewing for free and must disclose that fact. Although she does so at the end of her blog post, there are several hyperlinks before that disclosure that could distract readers and cause them to click away before they get to the end of the post. Given these distractions, the disclosure likely is not clear and conspicuous.

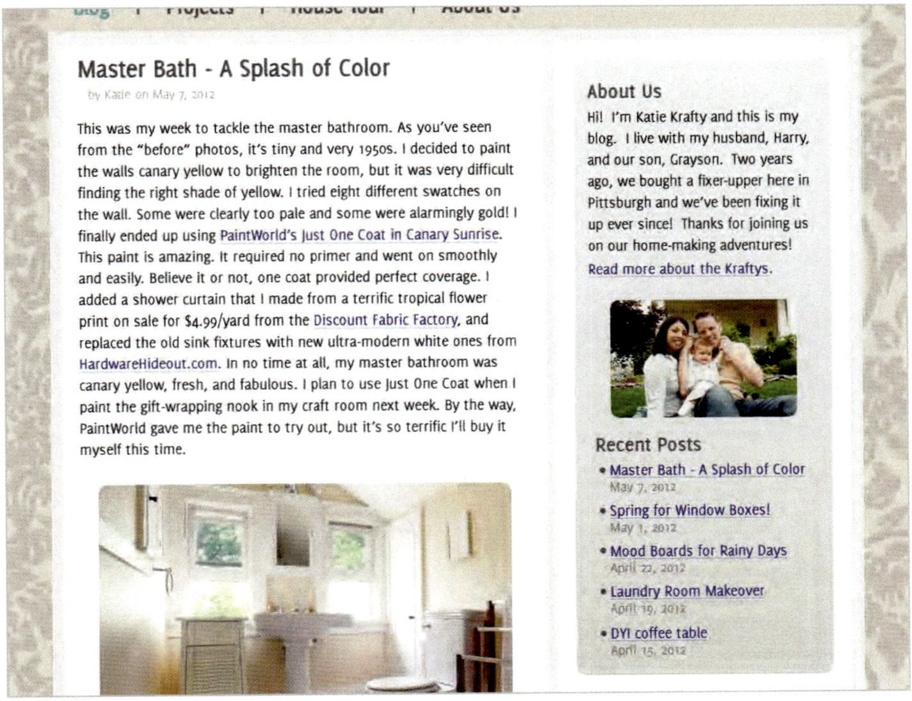

Example 22

All of the elements of an ad should be considered in assessing whether a disclosure is clear and conspicuous. In some cases, elements that the advertiser might think make an ad more eye-catching could actually distract consumers from important disclosures.

In this example, an animated spokesperson moving around and discussing the benefits of the Eye on Your Home monitoring cameras might distract consumers from the disclosure of the monthly monitoring fee.

Chapter 16

Labor and Employment

§ 16:1 Introduction
§ 16:2 Wages and Hours
§ 16:2.1 Overview
§ 16:2.2 Overtime Exemptions
[A] Executive Exemption
[B] Administrative Exemption
[C] Learned Professional Exemption
[D] Creative Professional Exemption
[E] Computer Professional Exemption
[F] Outside Sales Exemption
[G] Combination Exemption
[H] Highly Compensated Employee Exemption
§ 16:2.3 Unpaid Trainees or Interns
§ 16:2.4 Restrictions on Home Workers
§ 16:2.5 "Hot Goods" and Combating Unfair Labor Practices
§ 16:3 Child Labor Laws and Sweatshop Practices
§ 16:3.1 Federal Child Labor Law
[A] Employer-Employee Relationship
[B] Age of the Minor
[C] Wages
[D] Work Prohibitions
[E] Enforcement, Penalties and Contesting Penalties
§ 16:3.2 State Child Labor Laws
§ 16:3.3 Concerns Over Sweatshop Practices
§ 16:3.4 Addressing Labor Problems Through Self-Regulation: Corporate Codes of Conduct
§ 16:4 Anti-Discrimination Laws
§ 16:4.1 Role of the EEOC
§ 16:4.2 Defense to Sex and Age Claims: Bona Fide Occupational Qualifications
§ 16:4.3 Pregnancy Discrimination
§ 16:4.4 Family and Medical Leave Act

§ 16:5 Health Issues in the Fashion Industry and Implications for Employers
§ 16:6 Use of Sales Representatives
§ 16:7 Bargaining Units
§ 16:8 Social Media Usage

§ 16:1 Introduction

The fashion industry is highly dependent on the skills and talents of the industry's human resources, including production workers, retail sales associates, fashion designers, and models. The intricate relationships between these individuals and their employers are governed by, and subject to, federal and state laws, industry standards, individual employment agreements, and, in some cases, collective bargaining agreements. This chapter will address the principal labor and employment issues encountered by companies in the fashion industry.

The general economic and market trends impacting the fashion industry (which are discussed in detail in other chapters) directly affect those individuals that work in the industry. In particular, as a consequence of the high labor content of apparel, many apparel manufacturers have shifted production out of the United States to countries with lower labor costs.[1] The apparel production jobs that remain in the United States tend to be more highly skilled specialty manufacturing, with the lower-skilled and lower-paying jobs moving principally to Asia.[2] Nonetheless, the average hourly wages of production workers in apparel manufacturing in the United States are significantly lower than the national average.[3] Similarly, as the retail environment becomes increasingly competitive, many retailers have found it cost-effective to hire part-time and seasonal workers to satisfy their staffing needs, particularly during the busiest shopping seasons, rather than hiring additional full-time employees who would be entitled to higher wages and benefits.[4] This creates both a reduction in full-time employment opportunities and a challenge for the management and training of employees. Not surprisingly, companies in the fashion industry frequently confront disputes over the wages, hours, and working conditions of their employees.

---

1. *See* FIRST RESEARCH INDUS. PROFILE, APPAREL MANUFACTURING (Mar. 4, 2013).
2. *Id.* at 5.
3. *Id.*
4. *See* FIRST RESEARCH INDUS. PROFILE, CLOTHING STORES (Sept. 3, 2012).

§ 16:2 Wages and Hours

The Fair Labor Standards Act (FLSA) prescribes minimum wage and overtime requirements on a national level. Wage-and-hour lawsuits have become increasingly common, especially lawsuits for unpaid overtime brought by employees who claim they were improperly classified as "exempt" under the FLSA or not paid for "off the clock" work. These cases are attractive for plaintiffs' attorneys in part because the FLSA provides a mechanism for a large class of employees to bring a "collective action" challenging an employer's overtime practices in a single lawsuit.[5]

An employee does not have an automatic right to represent other employees. Rather, the employee must show that he or she is "similarly situated" to the other employees to be represented.[6] Nevertheless, FLSA collective actions are frequently approved, or "certified," often in conjunction with state-law class actions raising similar claims under state wage-and-hour laws. This can create substantial exposure for employers. In one recent case, a large, nationwide retailer settled company-wide federal and state wage-and-hour claims for up to $640 million.[7]

---

5. 29 U.S.C. § 216(b). The FLSA "collective action" device is unusual in that no employee may join a collective action unless he or she affirmatively "opts in" to the lawsuit. By contrast, in class actions that proceed under Rule 23(b)(3) of the Federal Rules of Civil Procedure, all plaintiffs covered by the class definition automatically become members of the certified class unless they affirmatively "opt out" of the lawsuit.
6. *Id.* In determining whether employees are "similarly situated," courts typically undertake a two-step process. At the outset of a case, a court will apply a fairly lenient standard, and will permit other employees to "opt in" to the lawsuit as long as the employees present some evidence (such as signed declarations) attesting that they perform similar job duties. *See, e.g.*, Lusardi v. Xerox Corp., 118 F.R.D. 351 (D.N.J. 1987). Then, at the close of discovery, after both parties have had an opportunity to develop the evidence, courts will determine whether the conditionally certified class should be "decertified." In conducting that analysis, courts consider such factors as (1) the similarity of the employees' job duties and employment settings, (2) whether the employer's defenses may be asserted collectively or are individual to each employee, and (3) fairness and procedural considerations. *See, e.g.*, Morgan v. Family Dollar, 551 F.3d 1233, 1261 (11th Cir. 2008); Thiessen v. Gen. Elec. Capital Corp., 267 F.3d 1095, 1103 (10th Cir. 2001).
7. Steven Greenhouse & Stephanie Rosenbloom, *Wal-Mart Settles 63 Lawsuits Over Wages*, N.Y. TIMES (Dec. 23, 2008), https://www.nytimes.com/2008/12/24/business/worldbusiness/24iht-24walmart.18903928.html.

§ 16:2.1 Overview

The FLSA applies to most employers: Any enterprise that employs two or more employees who are engaged in commerce and has at least $500,000 in "annual gross volume of sales made or business done" is covered.[8] Employees of enterprises that have fewer than $500,000 in business are still covered if they, in any given workweek, engage in interstate commerce.[9] Examples of interstate commerce include producing goods that will be shipped out of state, making telephone calls out of state, traveling out of state, and even performing janitorial services in a building where goods are produced for out-of-state sales.[10] Coverage under the FLSA is broad, and companies should be cautious before concluding that they, or their employees, fall outside of its scope.

Effective July 24, 2009, the federal minimum wage is $7.25 per hour.[11] Employers may pay employees under twenty years of age a lower wage of not less than $4.25 an hour for *only* the first ninety consecutive calendar days of employment.[12] If an employee customarily and regularly receives more than $30 per month in tips, the employer may consider such tips as part of his or her wages, but must nevertheless pay a direct wage of at least $2.13 per hour to the employee if the employer claims a tip credit.[13] The FLSA permits employment at wages lower than the minimum wage in the following narrow categories if the employer applies for, and receives, a certificate from the Department of Labor: (a) student learners; (b) full-time students in retail or service establishments; and (c) individuals whose "earning or productive capacities for the work to be performed are impaired by physical or mental disabilities, including those related to age or injury."[14]

The FLSA does not limit the number of hours or days in a week that an employee may work, as long as the employee is at least sixteen years of age.[15] However, the FLSA requires employers to pay covered

---

8. 29 U.S.C. § 203(s).
9. 29 U.S.C. § 206.
10. *See* DEP'T OF LABOR, WAGE AND HOUR DIVISION, FACT SHEET #14: COVERAGE UNDER THE FAIR LABOR STANDARDS ACT (FLSA), https://www.dol.gov/whd/regs/compliance/whdfs14.htm#.UM3dmuR1GSo.
11. 29 U.S.C. § 206.
12. *Id.*
13. 29 U.S.C. § 203(m); *see also* DEP'T OF LABOR, WAGE AND HOUR DIVISION, FACT SHEET #15: TIPPED EMPLOYEES UNDER THE FAIR LABOR STANDARDS ACT (FLSA), https://www.dol.gov/whd/regs/compliance/whdfs15.htm#.UM3isuR1GSo.
14. *See* DEP'T OF LABOR, WAGES AND HOURS WORKED: MINIMUM WAGE AND OVERTIME PAY, https://www.dol.gov/compliance/guide/minwage.htm.
15. 29 U.S.C. §§ 203, 207.

employees not less than one and one-half times their regular rate of pay for all hours worked in excess of forty in a workweek, unless the employees qualify for a specified exemption from the overtime requirements as described below.[16]

The FLSA specifically provides that states may set higher minimum wages or more generous overtime requirements than that provided under federal law.[17] Twenty-nine states and the District of Columbia have done so.[18] For example, in California, the minimum wage is $11.00 per hour.[19] California law also requires that employers pay (1) one and one-half times an employee's regular rate of pay if the employee works more than eight hours in a day, and (2) double time if an employee works more than twelve hours in a particular day or more than eight hours on the seventh workday of any given week.[20] Moreover, California requires employers to provide meal and rest breaks during the workday to nonexempt employees.[21] Meal requirements entitle an employee to a thirty-minute break for workdays lasting more than five hours, and two such breaks for workdays lasting more than ten hours, during which the employee must be relieved of all duty and free to leave the premises.[22] Rest requirements entitle an employee to a ten-minute break for shifts lasting between three and one-half to six hours, twenty minutes for six to ten hours, and so forth.[23]

Importantly, the FLSA does not alter, or relieve employers from complying with, the terms of any collective bargaining agreement whose terms are more generous than those of the FLSA.[24]

---

16. 29 U.S.C. § 207.
17. *See* 29 U.S.C. § 218(a) ("No provision of this chapter or of any order thereunder shall excuse noncompliance with any Federal or State law or municipal ordinance establishing a minimum wage higher than the minimum wage established under this chapter or a maximum work week lower than the maximum workweek established under this chapter . . . .").
18. The Department of Labor's website has a chart that provides an overview of the minimum-wage and overtime requirements of all 50 states; *see* DEP'T OF LABOR, WAGE AND HOUR DIVISION, WAGE AND HOUR DIVISION (WHD), MINIMUM WAGE LAWS IN THE STATES (Mar. 29, 2019), https://www.dol.gov/whd/minwage/america.htm#content.
19. *See id.*
20. *See id.*
21. Brinker Rest. Corp. v. Super. Ct., 273 P.3d 513, 521 (Cal. 2012).
22. *Id.* at 532–34.
23. *Id.* at 529.
24. *See* DEP'T OF LABOR, WAGE AND HOUR DIVISION, FACT SHEET #17A: EXEMPTION FOR EXECUTIVE, ADMINISTRATIVE, PROFESSIONAL, COMPUTER & OUTSIDE SALES EMPLOYEES UNDER THE FAIR LABOR STANDARDS ACT (FLSA), https://www.dol.gov/whd/overtime/fs17a_overview.htm.

California imposes specific requirements for commission-based employees beyond those imposed by the FLSA. California recently amended its Labor Code to require companies to enter into written agreements with any employee that is paid on a commission basis.[25] The company must provide the signed agreement to each covered employee and obtain a signed receipt in return.[26] California law further requires that the written agreement must "set forth the method by which the commissions shall be computed and paid."[27] And, if the agreement expires but the parties continue to work under its terms, the statute provides that the agreement terms will continue to apply until a new agreement is entered into or the employment terminates.[28] The California law reflects a recent state-law trend. In commenting on the amendment, the California legislature noted it was "follow[ing] the lead" of other states with similar written requirements.[29]

Several state laws also obligate employers to disclose wage information to employees. For example, the New York Wage Theft Prevention Act requires private-sector employers to provide a written notice regarding wages to all employees annually, and to newly hired employees on point of hire. This notice must explain (1) the basis for and rate of the employee's wage, including the overtime rate of pay, if applicable; (2) what allowances, if any, the employer will claim against the minimum wage; (3) the employee's regular pay day; (4) the employer's official name and any "doing business as" names; and (5) the address and telephone number of the employer's main office.[30] The employee must sign and date an acknowledgment of the notice.[31] The notice should be in English and, if different, in the employee's primary language.[32] The employer must keep the notice and acknowledgment, as well as payroll records, for six years.[33] If an employer fails to comply with the act's requirements, it may be subject to fines and even criminal prosecution.[34]

---

25. CAL. LAB. CODE § 2751(a) (2012).
26. CAL. LAB. CODE § 2751(b).
27. CAL. LAB. CODE § 2751(a).
28. CAL. LAB. CODE § 2751(b).
29. *Hearing on AB 1396 Before the S. Comm. on Labor and Industrial Relations*, 2011–2012 Sess. (Cal. 2011).
30. N.Y. LAB. LAW § 195.
31. *Id.*
32. *Id.*
33. *Id.*
34. N.Y. LAB. LAW §§ 198, 198-a, 215.

§ 16:2.2 Overtime Exemptions

Certain categories of employment are exempt from the overtime provisions of the FLSA, typically because the employees have specialized skills that would remedy any inequality of bargaining power between employer and employee. This section provides an overview of the more common exemptions that may apply in the fashion industry. To qualify for these exemptions, employees generally must be compensated on a salaried basis at a rate not less than $913 per week.[35] They must also show that their "primary duty" consists of exempt work, as defined by the applicable exemption.

In determining an employee's "primary duty," courts consider a variety of factors, including: the relative importance of the employee's exempt duties in comparison with other tasks; the amount of time the employee spends on exempt work; whether the employee works free from direct supervision; and the relationship between the employee's salary and the wages paid to nonexempt employees with similar responsibilities.[36] While the amount of time the employee spends performing exempt work is not dispositive, employees who spend more than 50% of their time on exempt tasks will generally satisfy the "primary duty" requirement.[37]

In the event of litigation, the employer bears the burden of proving that an employee or category of employees qualifies for the relevant exemption. Therefore, employers should document the duties of exempt employees to evidence that those employees perform the work required to qualify for the exemption. For example, employers might specifically emphasize exempt duties on job applications, job descriptions, and performance reviews. If the employer claims that an employee performs exempt work, but in fact, the employee does not perform those duties nor is expected to, the employee will be deemed nonexempt.

Employers who fail to comply with the overtime requirements of the FLSA incur liability to affected employees for back pay for two years from the date the lawsuit is filed.[38] However, in cases where an employee can prove a "willful violation," the FLSA provides for three years of damages.[39] Affected employees are also entitled to liquidated damages unless the employer shows that it acted "in good faith" in classifying the employee as exempt and had "reasonable grounds" for believing that it was acting consistently with the FLSA.[40] In practice,

---

35. 29 C.F.R. § 541.600.
36. 29 C.F.R. § 541.700.
37. *Id.*
38. 29 U.S.C. § 255(a).
39. *Id.*
40. 29 U.S.C. § 260.

the "willful violation" and "good faith" inquiries tend to merge; if an employer found liable under the statute can show that it acted in good faith, and thus is exempt from paying liquidated damages, a court will be unlikely to impose three years' back pay rather than two. An employer that documents the duties of exempt employees and holds employees accountable if they do not perform exempt duties will be less likely to be held liable for liquidated damages or for additional back pay.

[A] Executive Exemption

Company executives and many lower-level managers and supervisors may qualify for the "executive" exemption to the FLSA. To qualify for this exemption, (1) an employee's primary duty must be the management of the company or a recognized department or subdivision thereof; (2) the employee must customarily and regularly direct the work of two or more employees; and (3) the employee must have the authority to hire or fire other employees or to make suggestions on personnel decisions (such as hiring, firing, advancement, or promotion) that are given particular weight.[41] Exempt management work includes activities such as: interviewing and training employees; setting their pay or their hours; directing their work; handling employee complaints; disciplining employees; determining the techniques the employees use; determining the materials, supplies, machinery, equipment or tools to be used; and determining the merchandise purchased, stocked, or sold.[42]

In determining whether a manager supervises the work of two or more employees, managers can be classified as exempt if they supervise the "equivalent" of two full-time employees—for example, four half-time employees.[43] An important limitation, however, is that each supervised employee may only be counted once.[44] For example, if Manager 1 supervises Manager 2, who in turn supervises Employee 1 and Employee 2, either Manager may be deemed exempt based on supervision of Employees 1 and 2. But if Manager 2 takes credit for supervising those employees, Manager 1 cannot also take credit for the same employees, even if they share supervisory authority.

[B] Administrative Exemption

The administrative exemption is reserved for employees who perform a company's "back office" support functions, as opposed to "front

---

41. 29 C.F.R. § 541.100.
42. 29 C.F.R. § 541.102.
43. 29 C.F.R. § 541.104.
44. *Id.*

office" work such as retail sales. To qualify as exempt, an employee's primary duty must be the "performance of office or non-manual work directly related to the management or general business operations of the employer or [its] customers," and the employee must "exercise . . . discretion and independent judgment with respect to matters of significance."[45]

Exempt administrative tasks include, but are not limited to, work in such areas as: tax; finance; accounting; insurance; quality control; purchasing; procurement; advertising; marketing; research; safety and health; personnel management; human resources; employee benefits; labor relations; public relations; government relations; computer network, Internet, and database administration; and legal and regulatory compliance.[46] Examples of employees who will generally meet the test for the administrative exemption include: executive assistants of top management; human resources managers who develop or interpret a company's employment policies; and buyers who evaluate reports on competitor pricing to determine a product's appropriate retail price.[47]

As noted above, an employee must exercise discretion or independent judgment in performing exempt duties. If an employee works in advertising, for example, and is responsible for developing the content of advertisements and negotiating contracts for advertising space, he or she likely would qualify for the exemption. If the employee performs only routine clerical work, such as laying out an advertisement pursuant to someone else's specifications, or recording the prices paid for advertisements in a company database, he or she likely would not qualify for the exemption.

[C] Learned Professional Exemption

The FLSA also exempts employees whose primary duty consists of work that requires advanced knowledge in a field of science or learning customarily acquired by a prolonged course of specialized intellectual instruction.[48] This exemption is reserved for employees who work in fields such as law; medicine; accounting; engineering; architecture; or the physical, chemical, and biological sciences.[49] To qualify for this exemption, an employee's job duties must require work that is predominantly intellectual in character, as distinguished from routine manual, mechanical or physical work.[50] For example, an

---

45. 29 C.F.R. § 541.200.
46. 29 C.F.R. § 541.201.
47. 29 C.F.R. § 541.203.
48. 29 C.F.R. § 541.300.
49. 29 C.F.R. § 541.301.
50. *Id.*

engineer responsible for designing or refining an assembly-line process for manufacturing textiles is likely an exempt professional, but an employee who works on that assembly line placing buttons on apparel most likely is not.

Most employees who satisfy this exemption will have an advanced professional degree in the relevant field. But the exemption may still be available to employees who lack an advanced degree if they obtain the requisite knowledge through a combination of work experience and intellectual instruction.[51] To take advantage of this "combination" exception, employees should possess at least a high-school diploma (or its equivalent) and some college-level work (for example, an associates' degree or its equivalent), plus several years of relevant job experience. Mere "on-the-job training" does not suffice to meet this exception without some academic credentials in the relevant field. This exception to the degree requirement should be used sparingly; employers who classify primarily non-degreed engineers or accountants as exempt professionals may find it difficult to defend the exemption.

[D] Creative Professional Exemption

In addition to the learned professionals, the FLSA also recognizes an exemption for professionals whose primary duty consists of work requiring invention, imagination, originality or talent in a recognized field of artistic or creative endeavor.[52] This exemption includes employees who work in fields such as music, writing, acting, and the graphic arts.[53] Examples of exempt creative professionals include actors, musicians, composers, conductors, and soloists. The exemption also covers painters, cartoonists, novelists, short-story writers, screenplay writers, and creative staff in an advertising department, as long as such employees exercise independent creative thinking in their work.[54] For example, if a fashion designer is responsible for creating new designs for a seasonal collection, that person is likely an exempt creative professional. But if a person is responsible for copying or illustrating a concept conceived and designed by someone else, then the case for an exemption will become much more difficult.

[E] Computer Professional Exemption

Computer systems analysts, computer programmers, software engineers, or other similarly skilled workers in the computer field are

---

51. *Id.*
52. 29 C.F.R. § 541.302.
53. *Id.*
54. *Id.*

eligible for exemption as professionals under the FLSA.[55] To qualify for this exemption, an employee's primary duty must include systems analysis or the design, development, documentation, analysis, creation, testing, or modification of computer systems or programs.[56] This exemption is generally reserved for actual computer programmers. Employees who are merely adept at using common computer applications (such as PowerPoint or Publisher), or even industry-specific computer programs (such as design or graphics applications programmed by someone else), typically do not qualify for this exemption. (They may, however, qualify as exempt administrative professionals if they exercise sufficient independent judgment on matters of significance when performing their work.) In addition, employees who only engage in the manufacture or repair of computer hardware do not qualify for this exemption.[57]

[F] Outside Sales Exemption

The FLSA also provides an exemption for employees whose primary duty is making sales or obtaining orders or contracts for services or for the use of facilities, as long as the employees are customarily and regularly engaged away from the employer's place or places of business in performing such sales work.[58] For outside sales employees, exempt work includes not only the time spent actually making sales, but also any time spent performing tasks "incidental" to sales, such as writing sales reports, updating or revising a sales or display catalogue, planning itineraries, or attending sales conferences.[59] Merely displaying an employer's merchandise at a runway or trade show, however, without actually selling it, is not considered exempt outside sales activity.[60] Similarly, promotional work, including work involving the arrangement of merchandise on shelves or the replenishment of stock, is not exempt work unless it is performed to promote the employee's own outside sales work.[61]

[G] Combination Exemption

In some circumstances, an employee will perform a combination of exempt executive, administrative, and professional work. For example, a manager who works for a large apparel design firm may spend part of his or her day supervising a team of employees, and part

---

55. 29 C.F.R. § 541.400.
56. *Id.*
57. 29 C.F.R. § 541.401.
58. 29 C.F.R. § 541.500.
59. *Id.*
60. 29 C.F.R. § 541.502.
61. 29 C.F.R. § 541.503.

of his or her day using creative skills to develop new designs. Under the FLSA, an employee whose primary duty consists of a combination of the exempt executive, administrative, and professional tasks described above may be classified as exempt, even if time spent on any one of those tasks in isolation would be insufficient.[62]

[H] Highly Compensated Employee Exemption

Of particular note, it is much easier for an employer to make the case that an employee qualifies for a particular exemption if the employee is highly compensated (that is, earns over $134,004 per year).[63] Such employees will be deemed exempt as long as they customarily and regularly perform at least one of the duties performed by exempt executive, administrative, or professional employees.[64] The ordinary criteria for the exemptions are relaxed in the case of highly compensated employees, because such employees are presumed to have sufficient bargaining power to obviate any need for the protection of federal law.

Some states have stricter criteria than the FLSA for exempting an employee from overtime requirements. For example, California's administrative, executive, and professional exemptions, although similar to the FLSA's, specifically require the employee to spend more than 50% of his or her time performing the duties applicable to the exemption.[65] Pennsylvania does not provide any exemption at all for computer employees.[66]

§ 16:2.3 *Unpaid Trainees or Interns*

The fashion industry has traditionally relied on internships as both a low-cost source of labor and as a training technique. The FLSA requires that employers pay the minimum wage and any applicable overtime premium to every person that they "employ"—that is, anyone the employer "suffer[s] or permit[s]" to work.[67] This definition is intentionally broad, but there are exceptions for trainees and for participants in certain internship programs.[68] These exceptions are narrow, however, and trainee and internship programs should be structured to ensure that they comply with the FLSA.

The Labor Department's Wage and Hour Division has developed a six-factor test for evaluating the legality of unpaid trainee or internship

62. 29 C.F.R. § 541.708.
63. 29 C.F.R. § 541.601.
64. *Id.*
65. CAL. LAB. CODE § 515.
66. 43 PA. CONS. STAT. ANN. § 333.105.
67. 29 U.S.C. § 203(g).
68. As discussed, special rules also apply to independent contractors.

programs. To be unpaid, an internship or trainee program must meet these criteria:

1. The program, even though it takes place within the employer's facilities, should be similar to the training that would be given in an educational environment;
2. The experience should be for the benefit of the intern or trainee;
3. The intern/trainee must not displace regular employees, but must work under close supervision of existing staff;
4. The employer that provides the training should derive no immediate advantage from the activities of the intern/trainee, and on occasion its operations may actually be impeded;
5. The intern/trainee should not necessarily be entitled to a job at the conclusion of the internship; and
6. The employer and the intern/trainee must understand that the intern/trainee is not entitled to wages for the time spent in the internship.[69]

The paradigmatic example of an exempt internship is an assignment for which the intern will receive class credit, and may even be required to submit a paper or take an exam for a grade. Unpaid internships are appropriate when they are an extension of the classroom experience. Employers structuring unpaid internship programs might schedule events that resemble the classroom environment, such as lectures by special guests, opportunities to "shadow" top executives for a day, tours of the worksite, or outside excursions to fashion shows. Interns might be assigned to mentors who might provide constructive feedback to them or provide a written evaluation at the end of the internship.

Employers should avoid hiring unpaid interns simply to fill an immediate short-term business need of the company, such as preparing necessary paperwork to assist designers with the launch of a new product line. While such opportunities can provide interns with a meaningful experience, the interns are performing work that the employer would otherwise need to hire paid workers to perform.

One criterion identified by the Department of Labor that may prove difficult in practice for employers to implement is the requirement that the employer "derive[] no immediate advantage" from the

---

69. *See* DEP'T OF LABOR, WAGE AND HOUR DIVISION, FACT SHEET #71: INTERNSHIP PROGRAMS UNDER THE FAIR LABOR STANDARDS ACT, https://www.dol.gov/whd/regs/compliance/whdfs71.htm#.UMzun-R1GSo.

intern's or trainee's activities. In many cases, internships provide students with work that will also incidentally benefit the employer. This criterion is apparently intended to motivate companies to invest time and resources into an internship program for the students' primary benefit (and at times at a net loss to the company), such as lectures, tours, or the mentorship opportunities described above.

Further, it is natural for employers to seek to maintain relationships with talented students who they identify as top prospects for employment after graduation. If the internship is unpaid, however, no promise of future employment should be made at the conclusion of the program. It would be appropriate, however, to provide the intern with information about how to apply for a full-time position at the conclusion of his or her education, and to consider the intern for a position at that time.

In sum, employers should view unpaid internships as a way to support their local communities and provide students with skills they can use when they enter the job market. To the extent that these internships become a free source of labor for a company to perform necessary business-related tasks, they carry significant litigation risks. For example, unpaid interns of the Hearst Corporation brought suit against Hearst alleging that the company "used interns at 19 magazines to complete tasks necessary to its operations such as to answer phones, make deliveries, and organize clothing and accessories."[70] The plaintiffs alleged that this work fell outside the narrow guidelines for unpaid interns under the FLSA, and that Hearst thus violated the minimum wage and overtime provisions of the FLSA and the New York labor law.[71] The district court conditionally certified a class under the FLSA, based on declarations submitted by the interns suggesting that Hearst "used interns to perform entry-level work with little supervision."[72] The court subsequently denied class certification on the state law wage claims. The court found that the plaintiffs failed to show commonality because they had not "show[n] anything more than a uniform policy of unpaid internship[s]."[73] After the Second Circuit affirmed the district court's denial of class certification, Hearst filed a motion for summary judgment on the claims of the individual defendants.[74] The district court granted Hearst's

---

70. Xuedan Wang v. Hearst Corp., 2012 U.S. Dist. LEXIS 97043, at *2 (S.D.N.Y. July 12, 2012).
71. *See id.*
72. *Id.* at 6.
73. Xuedan Wang v. Hearst Corp., No. CV-00793, Dkt. 149, at 9 (S.D.N.Y. May 8, 2013).
74. *Id.*, Dkt. 172 (S.D.N.Y. Oct. 29, 2015), Dkt. 180 (S.D.N.Y. Jan. 29, 2016).

motion and the Second Circuit affirmed.[75] This case suggests that employers in the fashion industry should proactively review their internship practices in order to reduce the likelihood of successful litigation against them.

§ 16:2.4 Restrictions on Home Workers

The FLSA places restrictions on certain types of work that an employee can perform in his or her home without prior approval from the Department of Labor. For example, employers who wish to employ home workers to manufacture knitted outerwear, gloves and mittens, buttons and buckles, handkerchiefs, embroideries, or jewelry (in non-hazardous working conditions) must provide the Department of Labor with written assurance that they will comply with the FLSA's wage-and-hour requirements, among other things.[76] The FLSA also generally prohibits home workers from manufacturing women's apparel or jewelry in hazardous working conditions unless the employee is unable to work in a factory due to age or disability (physical or mental), or is a caretaker for a disabled person in the home.[77]

§ 16:2.5 "Hot Goods" and Combating Unfair Labor Practices

One purpose of the FLSA is to eliminate unfair competition arising from "goods produced under substandard conditions."[78] To that end, the FLSA prohibits "any person"—which would include employers in the fashion industry—from the shipment, transportation, offer to ship or transport, or sale in interstate commerce, of any goods that were produced in violation of the FLSA's requirements concerning minimum wage, overtime pay, or child labor.[79] The two exceptions to this prohibition are (i) common carriers and (ii) "innocent," or good-faith, purchasers who received "written assurance from the producer that the goods were produced in compliance with the requirements of this chapter, and who acquired such goods for value without notice of any such violation."[80] This prohibition, known as the "hot goods" clause, reduces an employer's economic incentive to violate the FLSA.

---

75. *Id.*, Dkt. 193 (S.D.N.Y. Aug. 24, 2016), Dkt. 196 (S.D.N.Y. Jan. 2, 2018).
76. 29 C.F.R. §§ 530.1–530.2.
77. *See* DEP'T OF LABOR, WAGES AND HOURS WORKED: MINIMUM WAGE AND OVERTIME PAY, https://www.dol.gov/compliance/guide/minwage.htm.
78. Citigroup Indus. Credit v. Brock, 483 U.S. 27, 36 (1987).
79. 29 U.S.C. § 215(a)(1); *see also Citigroup Indus. Credit*, 483 U.S. at 33 (explaining the broad application of "any person").
80. *Id.*

A 2012 federal Executive Order on human trafficking strengthened existing prohibitions on the use of trafficking by federal contractors and subcontractors.[81] The Executive Order directed the Federal Acquisition Regulatory Council to amend the Federal Acquisition Regulations to clarify anti-trafficking requirements and expectations among government contractors and subcontractors.[82] The requested amendments included a prohibition on misleading recruitment practices, a requirement to maintain compliance plans for contracts exceeding $500,000 performed abroad, and a process to identify industries or sectors with a history of human trafficking.[83]

§ 16:3 Child Labor Laws and Sweatshop Practices

The FLSA imposes limitations on employers' use of child labor, and many state laws supplement the federal regime. Child labor laws serve an important role in ensuring that both the fashion industry and youth working in that industry have a mutually positive relationship in a demanding field. This section provides an overview of child labor laws at the federal and state level, and then addresses a child labor issue particularly pertinent to the fashion industry—namely, sweatshop practices.

§ 16:3.1 Federal Child Labor Law

The FLSA provides broadly that "[n]o [covered] employer shall employ any oppressive child labor . . . ."[84] Thus, to determine whether youth workers in the fashion industry are covered by the FLSA, two main prerequisites must be met: (1) the existence of an employer-employee relationship and (2) the minor must be of a qualifying age. After it is determined that the FLSA applies, the child labor provisions must be complied with, including the wages and type of work assigned. If a company violates a child labor law, the Wage and Hour Division of the U.S. Department of Labor has the authority to impose civil and criminal sanctions.

[A] Employer-Employee Relationship

The FLSA applies only to employer-employee relationships. Independent contractors are exempt from FLSA coverage. It is not easy to determine, however, whether a working relationship is that of employer-employee.

---

81. Exec. Order No. 13627, 77 Fed. Reg. 60,029 (Sept. 25, 2012).
82. *Id.*
83. *Id.*
84. 29 U.S.C. § 212(c).

The FLSA's language as to who is an "employer" and who is an "employee" is unclear. The FLSA defines "employer" as "any person acting directly or indirectly in the interest of an employer in relation to an employee."[85] And the FLSA defines an "employee," circularly, as "any individual employed by an employer."[86] "Employ" is defined as "to suffer or permit to work."[87] In an effort to give guidance to courts deciphering the FLSA language, and thus whether the FLSA applies to a working relationship, the U.S. Supreme Court has set forth several factors to consider, none of which is dispositive. These factors include: (1) the degree of control exercised by the employer over the worker; (2) a worker's opportunities for profit or loss; (3) the degree of skill and independent initiative required to perform the work; and (4) the permanence or duration of the working relationship.[88] Generally, a court looks to "whether the individual is, as a matter of economic reality, in business for himself" or, instead, "economically dependent upon the business to which he renders his services."[89] Accordingly, because the circumstantial nature of the test makes it difficult to predict whether an individual court will agree with the employer's labeling of its workers as employees or independent contractors, fashion companies should be cautious in deeming their hired minors to be "independent contractors."[90]

[B] Age of the Minor

For non-agricultural employment, the FLSA's child labor provisions apply only if the minor is between fourteen and seventeen years of age.[91] Accordingly, these provisions do not apply to a person eighteen years or older, and the FLSA generally prohibits the employment of a minor younger than fourteen years old.[92] Exceptions exist to the latter, but none is likely to apply to the fashion industry.[93]

---

85. 29 U.S.C. § 203(d).
86. 29 U.S.C. § 203(e)(1).
87. 29 U.S.C. § 203(g).
88. *See* Nationwide Mut. Ins. Co. v. Darden, 503 U.S. 318, 323–24 (1992); Rutherford Food Corp. v. McComb, 331 U.S. 722, 730 (1947).
89. Carrell v. Sunland Const., Inc., 998 F.2d 330, 332 (5th Cir. 1993).
90. Fashion companies should confirm that they are a covered "enterprise" under the FLSA. This is because the FLSA's coverage extends only to a qualified enterprise, as defined in the FLSA. Fashion companies likely fall under the definition for "[e]nterprise engaged in commerce or in the production of goods for commerce," found in section 203 of the FLSA. *See* 29 U.S.C. § 203(s).
91. 29 U.S.C. § 213; 29 C.F.R. § 570.2(a).
92. *Id.*
93. For example, the FLSA exempts from coverage any child, regardless of age, who performs as an actor in television or movie productions, as well as any child who delivers newspapers. 29 U.S.C. § 213(c)(3), (d).

The FLSA distinguishes between minors aged fourteen and fifteen years old ("young minors"), and those between sixteen and seventeen years old ("older minors"). As might be expected, more stringent regulations apply to those who are fourteen and fifteen years old. Although the following sections address the various distinctions more fully, companies in the fashion industry should be particularly aware of the general principles governing hours of work.

This hours distinction limits the number of hours that younger minors may work, including how many hours each day (no more than three hours per day when school is in session) and each week (no more than eighteen hours per week when school is in session).[94] In addition, those minors must work outside of school hours.[95] And even then, the hours are restricted: the FLSA prohibits fourteen- and fifteen-year-old minors from working before 7 a.m. or after 7 p.m.[96] The FLSA relaxes the hours requirement only during the summer months.[97] Further, the FLSA provides some general exceptions to the hours standards, including if the minor is enrolled in a qualifying work-study program[98] or if the minor has graduated from high school.[99]

Once a minor reaches sixteen years of age, the FLSA's regulation of hours worked terminates. At that point, the minor may be employed for any number of hours at any time—including during school hours.[100]

[C] Wages

Employers in the fashion industry must pay their minor employees wages that are compliant with the FLSA. The child labor provisions of the FLSA do not themselves prescribe standard wages.[101] Rather, workers who are minors must be paid wages calculated pursuant to the general wage-and-hours provisions of the FLSA, which are discussed above.[102] It should be noted that the FLSA provides only two

94. 29 C.F.R. § 570.35(a)(3), (5).
95. 29 C.F.R. § 570.35(a)(1).
96. 29 C.F.R. § 570.35(a)(6).
97. 29 C.F.R. § 570.35(a).
98. 29 C.F.R. §§ 570.35(c)(4), 570.37.
99. 29 C.F.R. § 570.35(c)(1)(i).
100. As noted above, state law may restrict hours for minors between 16 and 17 years of age, unlike federal law.
101. 29 C.F.R. § 570.103(a).
102. *Id.*

exemptions from the minimum wage or overtime provisions for child labor, neither of which applies to workers in the fashion industry.[103]

[D] Work Prohibitions

The FLSA proscribes certain types of work that minors may not perform. The FLSA divides the type of work permitted to be performed into the same two categories of younger and older minors. For the younger category, those workers may perform, among other things, "[w]ork of an intellectual or artistically creative nature" and "[c]ashiering, selling, modeling, art work, work in advertising departments, window trimming, and comparative shopping."[104] Workers aged sixteen or seventeen may perform most work, except for that deemed particularly hazardous under the regulations, such as coal mining and roofing operations.[105]

[E] Enforcement, Penalties and Contesting Penalties

The Wage and Hour Division of the U.S. Department of Labor is authorized to enforce the FLSA. Pursuant to that authority, the Wage and Hour Division ("Division") may conduct investigations of employers to determine whether the federal child labor laws are being violated. Employers should be prepared to provide information to the Division as to the age of their workers and the hours of their work.

Violation of the federal child labor laws is a serious matter. Employers risk significant penalties, both civil and criminal, for each violation. Civil monetary penalties may be assessed in amounts up to $11,000 for each worker whose employment violates the FLSA or its regulations.[106] Further, employers may be subject to criminal penalties, from a monetary fine of up to $10,000, to imprisonment for up to six months.[107]

If a violation is found, the Division must issue and serve a written notice of the penalty to the employer.[108] The notice must explain the reason for the penalty and the process for contesting the penalty.[109] If the employer desires to take exception to the penalty, the employer must, within fifteen days after receiving the notice, request an

---

103. Those exceptions are for minors who deliver newspapers and for minors who work at home in the making of evergreen wreaths. 29 C.F.R. § 570.103(c).

104. 29 C.F.R. § 570.34(b), (d).

105. 29 C.F.R. §§ 570.50, 570.53, 570.67.

106. 29 U.S.C. § 216(e)(1)(A)(i).

107. 29 U.S.C. § 216(a).

108. 29 C.F.R. § 580.3.

109. 29 C.F.R. § 580.4.

administrative hearing.[110] Otherwise, the assessed penalty amount is not subject to administrative or judicial review.[111]

§ 16:3.2 *State Child Labor Laws*

Fashion companies must not only comply with federal child labor law, but any applicable state laws as well. Many states have additional requirements governing the hiring of minors, such as the requirement that employers obtain "working papers" or "work permits" for any minors hired. Employers must abide by the most stringent standard applicable to them.

New York, for example, has extensive child labor laws. Fashion companies operating in New York must obtain an employment certificate for any employee eighteen years of age or younger. In addition, companies should be aware of New York's rules on child models, which were significantly tightened in 2014. New York expanded the definition of child performers to include runway and print models, and, in addition to restrictive hour standards, require employers of underage models to (1) arrange for an adult chaperone to accompany models under the age of sixteen (16) at all times; (2) set aside time and a dedicated space (and in some instances, provide teachers) for instruction of underage models; (3) obtain a Certificate of Eligibility and require all underage models to provide a Child Performer Permit; and (4) set aside at least 15% of the underage model's gross earnings in a trust account in the model's name established by his or her parent or guardian.[112] Companies may be subject to state sanctions for any violation of the New York child labor laws. The New York Division of Labor Standards, which is charged with enforcing the New York child labor laws, may impose civil or criminal penalties, including imprisonment.

§ 16:3.3 *Concerns Over Sweatshop Practices*

Apparel and accessory manufacturers have a strong interest in ensuring that their products are not manufactured under sweatshop conditions. A "sweatshop," as defined by the U.S. government, is a "business that regularly violates BOTH safety or health AND wage or child labor laws."[113] Although sweatshop practices are not permitted under U.S. federal law and many state laws, the foreign countries

---

110. 29 C.F.R. § 580.5.
111. *Id.*
112. N.Y. LAB. LAW § 186.
113. U.S. GEN. ACCOUNTING OFFICE, "SWEATSHOPS" IN THE U.S.: OPINIONS ON THEIR EXTENT AND POSSIBLE ENFORCEMENT OPTIONS 16 (1988), http://archive.gao.gov/d17t6/136973.pdf.

where most apparel and accessory products are manufactured may have less rigorous, or less rigorously enforced, labor laws. As several fashion companies have discovered, sweatshop labor practices create the risk of both legal liability in the United States and negative publicity.

Legal liability may result from both governmental and private action, although the reach of U.S. law generally stops at the domestic border.[114] As previously discussed, the Wage and Hour Division may impose penalties for sweatshop conditions. And private plaintiffs have brought suit against companies under various theories of liability for alleged sweatshop conditions. In one sweatshop case asserting violations of the Racketeer Influenced and Corrupt Organizations Act, fashion retailers settled with the factory worker plaintiffs for approximately $20 million.[115]

Fashion companies also risk damaging negative media coverage if their products are manufactured under sweatshop conditions. Negative media coverage can harm a brand, even if no legal liability results. In 1996, Kathie Lee Gifford's "sweetheart" image was tarnished when it was revealed during congressional testimony that her clothing designs were made by child laborers in Honduran sweatshops.[116] Such revelations can create lasting and costly damage to a fashion brand, as consumers and investors often measure a brand's success against its positive coverage in the public media.[117]

§ 16:3.4 Addressing Labor Problems Through Self-Regulation: Corporate Codes of Conduct

Many apparel and accessory manufacturers have adopted formal codes of conduct to self-regulate the use of child labor and other labor practices in their production processes. Typical codes of conduct outline the company's commitment to safe and healthy working environments and provide specific guidelines for the company's suppliers

---

114. EEOC v. Arabian Am. Oil Co., 499 U.S. 244, 248 (1991) ("[The] long-standing principle of American law that legislation of Congress, unless a contrary intent appears, is meant to apply only within the territorial jurisdiction of the United States." (internal quotation marks omitted)).

115. GLOBAL EXCHANGE, THE SAIPAN VICTORY, https://globalexchange.org/campaigns/legacy-campaigns/fair-trade/#saipan; *see also* Does I v. Gap, Inc., 2003 WL 22997250, at *1 (D. N. Mar. I. Sept. 11, 2003).

116. Lynne Duke, *The Man Who Made Kathie Lee Cry*, WASH. POST, July 31, 2005.

117. *See* Ian Phau, Min Teah & Joe Chuah, *Consumer Attitudes Towards Luxury Fashion Apparel Made in Sweatshops*, J. FASHION MKTG. & MGMT., vol. 19, issue 2 (2015), https://doi.org/10.1108/JFMM-01-2014-0008.

and contract manufacturers.[118] The U.S. Department of Labor has studied corporate codes of conduct and identified the following common provisions:

> (1) prohibitions on child labor; (2) prohibitions on forced labor; (3) prohibitions on discrimination based on race, religion, or ethnic origin; (4) requirements to ensure the health and safety of the workplace; (5) provisions on wages, usually based on local laws regarding minimum wage or prevailing wage levels in the local industry; (6) provisions regarding limits on working hours, including forced overtime, in accordance with local laws; and (7) support for freedom of association and the right to organize and bargain collectively.[119]

By adopting and enforcing such a code of conduct, fashion companies can minimize the likelihood of costly external regulation and litigation over alleged child labor and sweatshop violations.[120] Further, corporate codes of conduct promote a company's "socially responsible" image in the public mind.[121]

§ 16:4 Anti-Discrimination Laws

It is rare that a company's management makes a corporate decision to actively discriminate in the selection or termination of employees on the basis of race, sex, age, disability or some other protected

118. *See, e.g.*, GAP INC., CODE OF VENDOR CONDUCT, http://www.accessfacility.org/sites/default/files/Gap%20Code%20of%20Vendor%20Conduct_0.pdf; LEVI STRAUSS & CO., GLOBAL SOURCING AND OPERATING GUIDELINES, http://www.levistrauss.com/wp-content/uploads/2014/01/Global-Sourcing-and-Operating-Guidelines.pdf; NIKE, INC., THE NIKE CODE OF ETHICS, https://s1.q4cdn.com/806093406/files/doc_downloads/2011-Inside-the-Lines-online-booklet-FINAL-11-10-26.pdf.

119. BUREAU OF INT'L LABOR AFFAIRS, U.S. DEP'T OF LABOR, THE APPAREL INDUSTRY AND CODES OF CONDUCT: A SOLUTION TO THE INTERNATIONAL CHILD LABOR PROBLEM? iv (1996), https://www.dol.gov/ilab/reports/pdf/apparel.pdf.

120. J. Thomas Rosch, Comm'r, Fed. Trade Comm'n, Remarks at the NAD Annual Conference 2008: Self-Regulation and Consumer Protection: A Complement to Federal Law Enforcement, 1, 12 (Sept. 23, 2008), https://www.ftc.gov/speeches/rosch/080923Rosch-NADSpeech.pdf ("Self-regulatory initiatives also make good business sense. The more energy an industry puts into regulating itself, the less chance the government will get involved in trying to legislate the same results.").

121. *See* Douglas A. Kysar, *Preferences for Processes: The Process/Product Distinction and the Regulation of Consumer Choice*, 118 HARV. L. REV. 525, 640–41 (2004) ("[M]any consumers have come to view themselves as purchasing . . . not only products, but also shares of responsibility in the moral and ecological economy that produces them.").

characteristic. Rather, companies typically face liability under the anti-discrimination laws in two circumstances: (a) where an employee colorably claims that his or her immediate supervisor terminated (or failed to hire or promote) him or her for an impermissible reason, usually by pointing to statements made by the supervisor at or around the time the employment decision occurred; or (b) where the company institutes a particular policy or practice that has the effect of systematically disadvantaging a particular group.

The first scenario is referred to as "disparate treatment" liability. Based on agency principles, an employer will be held liable for the discriminatory acts of its supervisory employees who have authority to make employment decisions, even if higher-level managers were unaware of the discriminatory intent behind the decision.[122] The second scenario is called "disparate impact" liability. This form of liability does not require discriminatory intent; it merely requires that a particular employment practice disproportionately affect members of a protected group.[123]

To minimize the risk of liability under the anti-discrimination laws, employers might develop formal equal employment policies that memorialize the employer's commitment to make hiring, firing, promotion, pay, and other employment decisions without regard to race, religion, sex, age, disability, sexual orientation, national origin or veteran's status. When hiring or promoting employees, employers should be cautious in administering employment tests and background checks, as such procedures may expose employers to disparate impact claims.[124] Employers might also institute regular internal training programs that advise managers about their legal obligation not to discriminate. Such training programs should emphasize that managers can only make employment decisions for business-related reasons. For example, managers should avoid making comments on performance reviews that could be viewed as criticism of a person's disability (for example, "not productive due to extended medical leave"). Companies are advised to have clear lines of communication so that employees know whom to contact in case they believe they are victims of discrimination. Any complaints of discrimination must be investigated and resolved promptly, and there should be specific human resources representatives tasked with responding to such complaints.

Companies should pay particular attention to new requirements regarding sexual harassment prevention policies and training, as many states have recently enacted laws #MeToo laws aimed at preventing sexual harassment. In October 2018, for instance, a law

---

122. *See, e.g.*, Staub v. Proctor Hosp., 131 S. Ct. 1186 (2011).
123. *See, e.g.*, Lewis v. City of Chi., 130 S. Ct. 2191 (2010).
124. *E.g.*, Ricci v. DeStefano, 129 S. Ct. 2658 (2009).

came into effect requiring employers in New York State to circulate a policy prohibiting sexual harassment that complies with state requirements and to conduct annual sexual harassment training for all employees.[125]

§ 16:4.1 Role of the EEOC

The U.S. Equal Employment Opportunity Commission (EEOC) is the federal agency responsible for enforcing compliance with numerous federal employment statutes, including Title VII of the Civil Rights Act of 1964 ("Title VII"), which prohibits employment discrimination based on race, color, religion, sex, or national origin; the Age Discrimination in Employment Act (ADEA); the Equal Pay Act; and Title I of the Americans with Disabilities Act (ADA), which prohibits discrimination against people with disabilities in the private sector and state and local governments.[126]

The EEOC exercises its enforcement authority in two principal ways. Under each of Title VII, the ADEA, and the ADA, employees who believe that their employer has discriminated against them based on any legally protected characteristic (race, sex, age, disability, etc.) must file a "charge" of discrimination with the EEOC and any state anti-discrimination agency within 180 days of the alleged adverse employment action—such as termination, failure to hire, or demotion.[127] The EEOC will then investigate the "charge" and determine whether or not to institute an enforcement action against the employer. During the investigation period, the EEOC may seek additional information from the employer, such as by conducting interviews with key employees, or analyzing documents or answers to written questions.

If the EEOC decides against instituting an enforcement action, it will issue a "no-action" letter to the employee. Upon receipt of this letter, the employee has up to ninety days to decide whether to file a lawsuit against the employer.[128] If the employee files a lawsuit after this time period, the lawsuit will generally be deemed untimely and dismissed. In the lawsuit, an employee typically may raise only claims that were first described in the EEOC "charge"; the employee

---

125. N.Y. LAB. LAW § 201-G.

126. *See* U.S. EQUAL EMP'T OPPORTUNITY COMM'N (EEOC), OVERVIEW, https://www.eeoc.gov/eeoc/.

127. *See* 42 U.S.C. § 2000e-5(e). The employee has 300 days to file the "charge" in states that have a local agency that enforces a state anti-discrimination law. *Id.*

128. *See* 42 U.S.C. § 2000e-5(f).

may not raise claims for the first time in court.[129] The EEOC may determine to bring its own enforcement action based on the information in the employee's charge, in which case the government agency would itself proceed as plaintiff, and the employee may or may not join the lawsuit.[130]

The EEOC can also initiate investigations and take enforcement action on its own, without the assistance of an employee-initiated charge. This form of "directed investigation" by the EEOC is becoming increasingly common, and provides more flexibility to the agency, as it can engage in a more freestanding investigation of a company's employment practices than might be possible in the context of a specific employee charge.[131]

In recent years, both the EEOC and private plaintiffs have brought employment discrimination cases against employers in the fashion industry. For example, in 2004, Abercrombie & Fitch Stores, Inc. was sued by both the EEOC and private plaintiffs in two putative class actions.[132] The lawsuits alleged that Abercrombie & Fitch, a nationwide apparel retailer, violated Title VII by maintaining recruiting and hiring practices that excluded minorities and women, and that limited minority and female employment through restrictive marketing and other practices. The lawsuits were resolved by a consent decree approved by the federal district court under which Abercrombie & Fitch paid $50 million to affected employees, and consented to an injunction that prohibited Abercrombie & Fitch from discriminating against applicants based upon race, color, or national origin (with specific emphasis on African Americans, Asian Americans, and Latinos); discriminating against women based on their sex; or denying promotional opportunities to women and minorities.

In particular, Abercrombie & Fitch agreed to implement new hiring and recruiting procedures to ensure that qualified female and minority applicants were considered for employment. The company also agreed to ensure that minorities and women were promoted into manager-in-training and manager positions without discrimination. The company agreed to hire a Vice President of Diversity and up to twenty-five diversity recruiters, post a notice of the consent decree on a website and distribute it periodically to employees, provide equal

---

129. *See, e.g.*, Whalen v. W.R. Grace & Co., 56 F.3d 504, 506 (3d Cir. 1995); Evans v. Techs. Applications & Serv. Co., 80 F.3d 954, 963 (4th Cir. 1996).

130. *See* 42 U.S.C. § 2000e-5(f).

131. *See, e.g.*, SYSTEMIC TASK FORCE REPORT TO THE CHAIR OF THE EQUAL EMPLOYMENT OPPORTUNITY COMMISSION.

132. *See* EEOC v. Abercrombie & Fitch Stores, Inc., No. CV-04-4731 SI (N.D. Cal. Mar. 8, 2006).

employment training to all managers, and ensure that any marketing materials would reflect the company's commitment to diversity. Finally, the court appointed a monitor to help ensure Abercrombie & Fitch's compliance with the consent decree.[133]

GAP Inc. successfully defended a disability discrimination suit brought by the EEOC under the ADA when it was revealed during the discovery phase of the case that the EEOC had withheld relevant evidence about the terminated employee's medical condition. In that lawsuit, the EEOC alleged that the employee was terminated because he suffered from glomerulonephritis, a kidney disease that impairs bowel function.[134] Three years after the EEOC started its investigation and nearly a year after the complaint against the GAP was filed, the EEOC sought leave to amend its complaint, based on testimony from a medical expert, to allege that the employee's symptoms were instead caused by HIV medication.[135] A magistrate judge denied the EEOC's motion to amend, because documents reviewed by the judge (that the EEOC initially sought to withhold as privileged) revealed that the agency had known from the outset that this was an HIV-related case.[136] The judge held that the EEOC could not amend at this late stage, because it would prejudice GAP to alter the lawsuit in such a fundamental way: "HIV is not just another medical condition," the judge reasoned, but "carries social and political, as well as medical connotations," and "the GAP is commercially sensitive to the GLBT market."[137] Because defending the case would have involved fundamental changes to the GAP's litigation strategy, the court denied leave to amend, and the EEOC voluntarily dismissed.[138]

In 2018, a group of female former employees sued Nike, alleging that it systematically discriminated against women in pay and promotions, and fostered a hostile work environment.[139] In response to the lawsuit, Nike restructured its corporate leadership, including

133. During the monitoring phase of the lawsuit, a dispute arose regarding whether Abercrombie's in-store marketing material violated the terms of the consent decree by allegedly featuring predominantly white, male models. Plaintiffs and the EEOC brought a motion to enforce the consent decree, arguing that the marketing material effectively served as a "hiring guide" and deterred non-white applicants and/or encouraged managers to give preference to white applicants in hiring and promoting employees. The Special Master and the district court denied the motion.

134. EEOC v. Gap, Inc., 2011 U.S. Dist. LEXIS 148348 (E.D. Mich. Dec. 27, 2011).

135. *See id.* at *1–2.

136. *See id.* at *4–5.

137. *See id.* at *7.

138. *See id.*

139. Cahill v. Nike, Inc., 18-cv-01477 (D. Or. Aug. 9, 2018).

ousting at least eleven executives, admitted it failed in hiring and promoting women, and announced raises for 7,000 employees after conducting an internal review of its pay practices.[140]

§ 16:4.2 Defense to Sex and Age Claims: Bona Fide Occupational Qualifications

Of particular applicability to the fashion industry, Title VII contains a bona fide occupational qualifications defense (BFOQ), which permits employers to make distinctions among applicants "on the basis of . . . religion, sex, or national origin in those certain instances where religion, sex, or national origin is a bona fide occupational qualification reasonably necessary to the normal operation of th[e] particular business or enterprise."[141] The ADEA contains a similar provision that permits employers to distinguish between employees based on age where age is a "bona fide occupational qualification reasonably necessary to the normal operation of the particular business."[142] Under no circumstances can race be considered a bona fide occupational qualification.

The EEOC has taken the position that the BFOQ defense should be construed narrowly.[143] Men and women cannot be denied employment based on stereotypes about the comparative skill sets or competencies of the genders—for example, the stereotype that women are less aggressive than men and, therefore, would not make good sales associates.[144] Likewise, the preferences of customers or clients for sales associates of a particular gender, or a mere desire to increase competitiveness by hiring more attractive people of a particular gender, are insufficient reasons to use gender as a hiring criterion.[145] However, in cases where selection based on gender is necessary for the purpose of "authenticity or genuineness," the EEOC will consider the BFOQ defense to be met.[146] For example, employers may take gender into account when selecting actors, actresses, or fashion models who must wear gender-appropriate clothes in advertisements.[147]

---

140. Jessica Golden, *Nike Accused of Fostering Hostile Workplace in New Gender Discrimination Lawsuit*, CNBC (Aug. 10, 2018), https://www.cnbc.com/2018/08/10/ex-nike-employees-sue-over-gender-discrimination-hostile-workplace.html.
141. 42 U.S.C. § 2000e-2(e)(1).
142. 29 U.S.C. § 623(f)(1).
143. 29 C.F.R. § 1604.2(a).
144. *Id.*
145. *See* Gerdom v Cont'l Airlines, 692 F.2d 602 (9th Cir. 1982); Diaz v. Pan Am. World Airways, Inc., 442 F.2d 385 (5th Cir. 1971).
146. Phillips v. Martin Marietta Corp., 400 U.S. 542, 547 (1971).
147. *Id.*

§ 16:4.3 Pregnancy Discrimination

The Pregnancy Discrimination Act has a simple mandate: employers may not discriminate against women on the basis of pregnancy, childbirth, or complications from pregnancy.[148] Rather, women who are pregnant must be treated the same as other applicants or employees with similar capacities or limitations.[149] If, for example, a pregnant employee is unable to work as a result of the pregnancy, an employer must treat her in the same way as any other employee on temporary disability (for example, provide her with the same benefits or paid or unpaid leave as other disabled employees).[150] The EEOC brought an enforcement action for pregnancy discrimination against dELiA*s Inc., a specialty clothing store that targets teenage girls and young women.[151] According to the complaint, company officials repeatedly subjected store managers to harassment, for example, by repeatedly questioning their ability to do their jobs.[152] The company ultimately agreed to pay $75,000 to settle the claims, and further agreed to institute discrimination training for managers.[153]

§ 16:4.4 Family and Medical Leave Act

The Family and Medical Leave Act (FMLA) requires employers to provide covered employees with unpaid leave for certain family and medical reasons. The FMLA requires that employers provide at least twelve workweeks of leave during any twelve-month period for the following qualifying reasons: (a) a serious health condition that makes the employee unable to perform the essential functions of his or her job; (b) birth of a child or care for a newborn baby (one year or younger); (c) placement of a child with the employee for adoption or foster care and subsequent child care (within a year of placement); (d) care for a spouse, child, or parent who has a serious health condition; and (e) an exigency related to a spouse, child or parent who is on covered active duty in the military.[154] Ordinarily, if the leave is foreseeable (as in the case of birth of a child), the employee must provide the employer with at least thirty days' notice of intent to take the

148. 42 U.S.C. § 2000e(k).

149. *See* EEOC, FACTS ABOUT PREGNANCY DISCRIMINATION, https://www.eeoc.gov/facts/fs-preg.html.

150. *See id.*

151. *See* Press Release, EEOC, dELiA*s Will Pay $75,000 to Settle EEOC Pregnancy Discrimination Lawsuit (Aug 2, 2012), https://www.eeoc.gov/eeoc/newsroom/release/8-2-12.cfm.

152. *Id.*

153. *Id.*

154. 29 U.S.C. § 2612.

leave.[155] However, if medically necessary, employees may take intermittent leave (up to twelve weeks), but may be required to document the need for such leave.[156] In addition to these FMLA requirements, employers should ensure that they comply with more generous state requirements, where applicable.[157]

§ 16:5 Health Issues in the Fashion Industry and Implications for Employers

In recent years, the fashion industry and the general public have become increasingly concerned with the prevalence of severely underweight fashion models. This has led to both governmental and private actions.

Recent legislation in Israel is one of the most prominent examples of a governmental response to the problem. In March 2012, Israel's Knesset enacted a law that forbids underweight models from working in Israel's fashion market.[158] To determine whether a model is underweight, the Israeli law adopts the World Health Organization (WHO) standard of a "malnourished" person. Under the WHO standard, malnourishment is determined by calculating a person's body-mass index (BMI). The Israeli law further requires models to provide medical documentation showing that they have healthy BMIs, but no criminal liability attaches for failure to comply with the law.[159] Similarly, in 2015, France's National Assembly passed a law requiring models to have a medical certificate deeming them fit to work, including certifying that they have a healthy BMI.[160] Hiring models without obtaining a medical certificate can result in six months imprisonment and a fine of €75,000.[161] The United States does not have a similar law.

In the United States, health concerns about models have been addressed primarily through the fashion industry itself. *Vogue* announced in May 2012 that, for all of its nineteen magazines, it would "not knowingly work with models under the age of sixteen

---

155. *Id.*

156. *Id.*

157. *See, e.g.*, District of Columbia Family and Medical Leave Act of 1990, D.C. CODE ANN. §§ 32-501 to 32-517.

158. Erin Skarda, *Israel Bans "Underweight" Models*, TIME (Mar. 21, 2012), http://newsfeed.time.com/2012/03/21/israel-bans-underweight-models/.

159. *Id.*

160. Vanessa Friedman, *A New Age in French—Modeling*, N.Y. TIMES (May 8, 2017), https://www.nytimes.com/2017/05/08/fashion/france-laws-thin-models.html.

161. *Id.*

or who appear to have an eating disorder."[162] On a broader scale, the Council of Fashion Designers of America (CFDA) created a Health Initiative ("Initiative") in 2007 that is targeted at underweight and young models. The CFDA introduced the Initiative as a means to "protect women, and very young girls in particular, within the business, sending the message that beauty is health."[163] The Initiative provides the following five recommendations centered on encouraging healthy weight and behavior in models:

- Educate the industry to identify the early warning signs in an individual at risk of developing an eating disorder.
- Models who are identified as having an eating disorder should be required to seek professional help, and models who are receiving professional help for an eating disorder should not continue modeling without that professional's approval.
- Develop workshops for the industry (including designers, agents, editors, and models and their families) on the nature of eating disorders, how they arise, how we identify and treat them, and complications that may arise if left untreated.
- Support the well-being of younger individuals by not hiring models under the age of sixteen for runway shows; not allowing models under the age of eighteen to work past midnight at fittings or shoots; and providing regular breaks and rest . . . .
- Supply healthy meals, snacks, and water backstage and at shoots, and provide nutrition and fitness education.[164]

The Initiative does not have the force of law, nor does the CFDA attempt to enforce the Initiative's recommendations. The CFDA explicitly states that its Initiative is "about awareness and education, not policing."[165] To that end, the CFDA includes a recommendation that models be permitted to work without undergoing a physical examination to determine their health or BMI.[166]

---

162. Samantha Critchell, *Vogue Bans Too-Skinny Models from Its Pages*, NBC N.Y. (May 3, 2012), https://www.nbcnewyork.com/news/local/Vogue-Bans-Too-Skinny-Models-Eating-Disorders-Conde-Nast-Announcement-150077795.html.
163. COUNCIL OF FASHION DESIGNERS OF AM., ABOUT, CFDA HEALTH INITIATIVE, https://cfda.com/philanthropy/initiative/initiative-for-health-safety-and-diversity.
164. *Id.*
165. *Id.*
166. *Id.*

§ 16:6 Use of Sales Representatives

Fashion brands may use sales representatives to market and sell their products to retailers. In hiring a sales representative, a company should consider the general employment issues discussed above, as well as the specific issue of whether the person's employment status will be that of "independent contractor" or "employee." This classification may affect, among other things, the company's liability for taxes, liability under Title VII as an "employer," liability under state laws addressing independent contractor misclassification,[167] or even liability for breach of contract.

In determining how to classify a sales representative, a company should consider the common-law factors typically used to assess whether a worker is an independent contractor or employee. These factors include "the source of the instrumentalities and tools," "the location of the work," "whether the hiring party is in business," and "the tax treatment of the hired party."[168] One particularly important factor is the degree of control the company exerts over the sales representative's work. For example, a company may require the representative, as an independent contractor, to report sales results on a daily basis or to make only certain statements to customers.[169] But if the company imposes requirements concerning the "methods, details, and particulars" of how the sales representative does his or her work, the relationship may become one of employer and employee.[170]

Companies concerned about inadvertently entering into employment relationships with sales representatives should consider entering into a written agreement stating that the sales representative is an "independent contractor." Although courts look to the substance of the employment relationship, not its form, courts may weigh the agreement as important evidence that the sales representative is an independent contractor.[171] One court has observed that an employment agreement that stated the sales representative was an "independent contractor" was "not dispositive," but nonetheless "strong evidence" of independent contractor status.[172]

A company experiences several legal benefits by hiring a sales representative as an independent contractor rather than an employee. First, the company may not be liable for taxes ordinarily owed for

---

167. *E.g.*, MASS. GEN. LAWS ch. 149, § 148B.
168. *See* Nationwide Mut. Ins. Co. v. Darden, 503 U.S. 318, 323–24 (1992); *see also supra* note 69 and accompanying text.
169. *See* Fesler v. Whelen Eng'g Co., 688 F.3d 439, 443 (8th Cir. 2012); Brown v. J. Kaz, Inc., 581 F.3d 175, 180–81 (3d Cir. 2009).
170. *Fesler*, 688 F.3d at 443.
171. *See, e.g.*, *Brown*, 581 F.3d at 181.
172. *Id.*

employees, such as unemployment tax.[173] In addition, the company may not be held liable for the payment of certain employee benefits under state law.[174] An independent contractor also cannot pursue discrimination claims against the hiring company under Title VII or other federal anti-discrimination laws.[175] Nonetheless, several federal circuit courts have concluded that "independent contractors" may still bring discrimination claims under 42 U.S.C. § 1981, and thus companies should not view "independent contractor" status as a shield against all liability.[176] A company should monitor whether it is in fact treating its sales representatives as "independent contractors," given the potential exposure if a court determines that the sales representatives are *de facto* "employees." Moreover, if such a determination is made, an employer loses the protection afforded under state laws that make a contractor's workers' compensation coverage his or her exclusive remedy for work-related injuries.[177]

If a company enters into a written independent contractor agreement with a sales representative, such agreement would typically provide for the payment of commissions. The commissions may vary based on the type (for example, specialty stores or department stores) and location of the retailer, and the type of product.[178] The commission may be based on a percentage of "net sales," which may be defined as the invoiced price of goods actually shipped (rather than ordered), with deductions for such items as freight, insurance, discounts, returns, and chargebacks.[179]

A sales representative agreement may also contain other substantive provisions addressing the respective rights of the parties. For example, a company may prohibit a sales representative from representing competing brands, or a sales representative may seek to serve

---

173. *See, e.g.*, Avanti Press, Inc. v. Emp't Dep't Tax Section, 274 P.3d 190, 190–91 (Or. Ct. App. 2012).

174. *See, e.g.*, Arnold v. Mut. of Omaha Ins. Co., 135 Cal. Rptr. 3d 213, 215 (Ct. App. 2011).

175. *Brown*, 581 F.3d at 181, 185.

176. *See, e.g.*, *id.*; Taylor v. ADS, Inc., 327 F.3d 579, 581 (7th Cir. 2003); Webster v. Fulton Cty., 283 F.3d 1254, 1257 (11th Cir. 2002); Danco, Inc. v. Wal-Mart Stores, Inc., 178 F.3d 8, 13–14 (1st Cir. 1999).

177. *See, e.g.*, TEX. LAB. CODE ANN. §§ 408.001(a), 406.123(a) (making workers' compensation statute the sole source for the independent contractor's personal injury-related rights and remedies); Garza v. Zachry Constr. Corp., 373 S.W.3d 715, 717–18 (Tex. App. 2012) (explaining exclusivity of workers' compensation statute).

178. *See* TOBY MEADOWS, HOW TO SET UP & RUN A FASHION LABEL 137 (6th ed. 2012).

179. *See* Donald L. Kreindler, *Selling and Buying: Commercial Agreements in the Fashion Sector, in* FASHION LAW: A GUIDE FOR DESIGNERS, FASHION EXECUTIVES, AND ATTORNEYS 160, 173–74 (2010).

as the company's sole sales representative in a specified geographic area. If a company has sales representatives for multiple jurisdictions, a sales representative agreement might address the situation in which orders are placed through one sales representative and shipped to another sales representative's territory, or in which sales are made to multiple territories. For example, the sales representative agreement might provide for "split commissions," in which the commission is divided between the sales representatives from both territories.[180]

Although the sales representative negotiates the sale of merchandise to retailers, the company is the party that must ultimately accept the purchase order. If the sales representative does not have the authority to bind the company, the sales representative agreement should clearly so provide.[181]

§ 16:7 Bargaining Units

Employers in the fashion industry may encounter issues relating to the unionization of their workforce. Recently, the National Labor Relations Board (NLRB) has reversed its position regarding the size of appropriate bargaining units.

Before 2011, when an employer challenged the appropriateness of a bargaining unit, the NLRB applied a "community of interest" test, which involved weighing several factors, including (1) whether the employees are organized into a separate department; (2) have distinct skills and training; (3) have distinct job functions and perform distinct work; (4) are functionally integrated with the employer's other employees; (5) have frequent contact with other employees; (6) interchange with other employees; (7) have distinct terms and conditions of employment; and (8) are separately supervised.[182] Based on these factors, the Board determined on a case-by-case basis "whether the petitioned-for employees share[d] a community of interest sufficiently distinct from employees excluded from the proposed unit to warrant a separate appropriate unit."[183]

---

180. *See, e.g.*, Liszt v. Karen Kane, Inc., No. Civ.A.3:97-CV-3200-L, 2001 WL 739076 (N.D. Tex. June 26, 2001).

181. *See, e.g.*, Am. Div. of Engineered Apparel, Inc. v. Bloomingdale's, Div. of Federated Dep't Stores Inc., No. 83 Civ. 6935 (IBC), 1986 WL 1447 (S.D.N.Y. Jan. 28, 1986) (holding that when a sales representative was designated by an employment contract as president of a vendor, the representative had authority to bind the vendor to discounts, returns to vendor and markdowns orally promised by the representative to a department store).

182. United Operations, Inc., 338 N.L.R.B. No. 123 (2002).

183. PCC Structurals, Inc., 365 N.L.R.B. No. 160 (2017).

In 2011, the NLRB decided *Specialty Healthcare & Rehabilitation Center of Mobile*, in which it held that as long as a proposed union consisted of an identifiable group of employees, the unit would be presumed appropriate.[184] Under *Specialty Healthcare*, if an employer believed that the proposed unit should contain additional employees, it was required to demonstrate that those employees shared an "overwhelming" community of interest with those in the requested unit.[185] In practice, the "overwhelming" community of interest standard proved difficult for employers to meet and increased the ability of small segments of a retailer's workforce to successfully petition to form "micro-units" of unionized employees.

In 2017, the NLRB overturned *Specialty Healthcare*, abandoning the "overwhelming" community of interest standard and reinstating the Board's prior standard for determining the appropriateness of a petitioned-for bargaining unit.[186] The standard in *PCC Structurals* lessens the burden on employers challenging the scope of a union's bargaining unit and decreases the risk of "micro-units." This area of law continues to evolve and it remains to be seen how circuit courts will respond to the *PCC Structurals* decision.

§ 16:8 Social Media Usage

The use of social media has increased dramatically. Facebook alone has over two billion monthly active users.[187] It is now commonplace for employees to use social media to network with colleagues and interact with friends. Social media presents potential legal pitfalls, however, as companies attempt to adapt their existing policies to online activities. On one hand, employers should be aware that activity otherwise protected under the labor and employment laws—such as discussions about wages or working conditions—does not cease to be protected simply because it occurs online. On the other hand, employees should understand that conduct otherwise prohibited by an employer's policies, such as harassing coworkers or disclosing confidential information, does not become permissible because it occurs on social media. Employers should stay informed about developments in this evolving area of the law, and should consider adopting a standalone "social media policy" to address these important issues.

---

184. *See* Specialty Healthcare, 357 N.L.R.B. No. 83 (2011).
185. *See id.*
186. PCC Structurals, Inc., 365 N.L.R.B. No. 160 (2017).
187. FACEBOOK, FACEBOOK REPORTS FOURTH QUARTER AND FULL YEAR 2018 RESULTS (Jan. 30, 2019), https://investor.fb.com/investor-news/press-release-details/2019/Facebook-Reports-Fourth-Quarter-and-Full-Year-2018-Results/default.aspx.

Social media usage implicates a number of labor and employment laws. Of particular note, the National Labor Relations Act (NLRA) provides protection to both union and non-union employees "to engage in [ ] concerted activities for the purpose of collective bargaining or other mutual aid or protection."[188] Under section 7 of the NLRA, protected activity encompasses a wide range of work-related activity, such as discussing employees' wages or work conditions.[189] Section 8, in turn, makes it an unfair labor practice for any employer to discipline, terminate, or otherwise take any adverse employment action against an individual for engaging in protected activity.[190] The NLRB has recently issued several decisions holding companies liable for violating the NLRA when they fire employees because of work-related Facebook posts. In *Design Technology Group, LLC d/b/a Bettie Page Clothing*, for example, the NLRB determined that a fashion boutique was required to reinstate three employees who had been fired because of Facebook posts criticizing a manager and discussing an employee-rights handbook.[191] The NLRB concluded that the employees' activity was a "classic concerted protected activity."[192] Similarly, in *Hispanics United of Buffalo Inc.*, the NLRB also ordered reinstatement of employees who were fired because of Facebook posts discussing how they felt about a manager's criticism of their work.[193]

On the other hand, the Acting General Counsel of the NLRB has taken the position that, in the case of an employer who terminated an employee "for writing inappropriate and offensive Twitter postings," despite a warning not to do so, the employee was not engaging in protected activity under the NLRA.[194] Thus, if the content of an employee's posts is egregious and amounts to harassment or intimidation of coworkers, then an employer should be able to discipline even if the employee's posts arguably relate to the terms and conditions of employment. Of course, these cases are likely to be fact-specific, and therefore an employer must exercise judgment, and consult with legal

188. 29 U.S.C. § 157.
189. *Id.*
190. 29 U.S.C. § 158.
191. Design Tech. Grp., LLC d/b/a Bettie Page Clothing & DTG Cal. Mgmt., LLC d/b/a Bettie Page Clothing and Vanessa Morris, No. 20-CA-035511, slip op. at 3 (N.L.R.B. Apr. 19, 2013).
192. *Id.* at 1.
193. Hispanics United of Buffalo, Inc. and Carlos Ortiz, No. 03-CA-02872, slip op. at 1 (N.L.R.B. Dec. 14, 2012).
194. *See* Memorandum, Office of the General Counsel, Report of the Acting General Counsel Concerning Social Media Cases (Aug. 18, 2011); *see also* Google Inc., Case No. 32-CA-205351, NLRB Advice Memorandum (Jan. 16, 2018).

counsel, before disciplining or terminating an employee for social media usage.

Employees may also bring employment-discrimination suits under Title VII or other federal and state laws, claiming that they were harassed by coworkers on social networking sites and that the employer did not do enough to prevent or remedy the harassment. For example, in *Blakey v. Continental Airlines*, a Title VII employment-discrimination case, the New Jersey Supreme Court held that the employer could be held liable for postings on work-related message forums that constitute harassment.[195] The lesson of *Blakey* is that employers have a duty to take all necessary steps to stop harassment if the employer learns or has reason to know that it is occurring. To that end, companies should consider adopting policies that make clear to employees that use of social media to harass coworkers will not be tolerated, and that emails and Internet usage on company computers may be monitored. Companies should also promptly investigate any allegations of improper conduct on social media sites.

Employers should also consider implementing procedures to govern the use of social media in making hiring decisions. In one recent case that ultimately settled, an employer was sued by a job applicant who claimed the employer refused to hire him based on a Google search that revealed the applicant's religious views.[196] To protect against such liability, companies should consider separating the ultimate decision-maker from the person who performs background research on a candidate. That is, ideally, a neutral party should conduct the Internet search, using only public information, and prepare a summary report that focuses exclusively on job-related criteria. Companies should also be aware of any applicable state laws that restrict the practices that employers can use when evaluating potential applicants. For example, at least 26 states have enacted laws barring employers from seeking access to applicants' social media accounts.[197] Other states have similar laws pending.

Many companies have adopted social media policies as an effective method to assist employees in conducting appropriate online activity. One online database, http://socialmediagovernance.com/policies/, has collected over 250 social media policies adopted by a wide range of companies. A company's social media policy may include provisions

---

195. Blakey v. Continental Airlines, 164 N.J. 38, 45–46 (2000).

196. Complaint, Gaskell v. Univ. of Ky., No. 09-cv-00244-KSF-REW (E.D. Ky. Aug. 28, 2009).

197. NAT'L CONFERENCE OF STATE LEGISLATURES, STATE SOCIAL MEDIA PRIVACY LAWS (Nov. 6, 2018), http://www.ncsl.org/research/telecommunications-and-information-technology/state-laws-prohibiting-access-to-social-media-usernames-and-passwords.aspx.

instructing employees on such topics as (1) indicating whether their online activity is in their personal or corporate capacity; (2) particular websites that employees are expected or encouraged to avoid; (3) whether employees are permitted to access social media sites on company property; and (4) whether and how employees will be disciplined for violating the policy. Employers should also consider including appropriate disclaimers in these policies to the effect that they are not intended to prevent employees from discussing the terms or conditions of their employment, or otherwise engaging in activity protected by section 7 of the NLRA. These disclaimers may help protect against, if not completely eliminate, the likelihood that the NLRB could bring a successful employment action against a company.

Chapter 17

Employment Agreements

§ 17:1 Introduction
§ 17:2 Basic Employment Terms
§ 17:2.1 Title and Scope
§ 17:2.2 Term
§ 17:2.3 Compensation
§ 17:2.4 Ownership of Creations
§ 17:2.5 Other Matters
§ 17:3 Confidentiality Covenants
§ 17:3.1 Confidentiality in the Fashion Industry
§ 17:3.2 Drafting Confidentiality Agreements
§ 17:4 Covenants Not to Compete and Related Restrictive Covenants
§ 17:4.1 Covenants Not to Compete
§ 17:4.2 Related Restrictive Covenants

§ 17:1 Introduction

In the United States, most employees perform services for their employer without a formal written employment agreement. Almost all employment relationships in the United States are "at-will" relationships, because they can be ended by either party at any time and for any legal reason. However, "at-will" employees are subject to general company policies relating to working conditions, including such matters as severance, vacations, and participation in benefit plans. Moreover, employees may owe certain duties to their employers (such as good faith and fair dealing) under the common law of the applicable state, even in the absence of a specific written agreement.[1] And, as discussed in chapter 16, employers are required to comply with

1. See, for example, the discussion of fiduciary duties of officers and directors under Delaware law in *supra* section 1:2.4.

applicable federal, state, and local laws regarding labor and employment when dealing with their employees.

A company in the fashion industry, however, may find it necessary or desirable to enter into employment agreements with certain of its employees, particularly those who provide unique or otherwise important services to the company or can significantly harm the company if they leave for a competitor. A prospective employee may request an employment agreement as a pre-condition to accepting an offer of employment, or the company may seek to bind an employee to certain obligations during and after the termination of, the employee's employment with the company. The specific terms of employment agreements vary with the circumstances and are often subject to significant negotiations.

Many companies enter into employment agreements with their most senior executive officers. Fashion brands also may enter into formal employment agreements (or more informal offer letters) with their important creative talent. Large companies may have a creative director who leads separate design teams for particular categories of products (for example, apparel, footwear, and accessories), while smaller companies may have a single head designer for all product categories. In general, employment agreements for creative talent, such as creative directors or head designers, typically address the basic terms of employment discussed below.

§ 17:2 Basic Employment Terms

§ 17:2.1 Title and Scope

An essential purpose of an employment agreement is to set out the nature and scope of the employee's roles and responsibilities at the company. The employment agreement may confer upon the employee a specific title, such as "Creative Director" or "Head Accessory Designer," either for the entire company, a division of the company, or a particular brand. If the employee will have a specific title, the agreement might simply require the employee to perform the customary duties of a person employed in such capacity. Alternatively, the agreement might set forth in detail the specific duties of the employee. For example, the agreement might indicate the employee's specific areas of responsibility, such as determining the theme for each collection, developing designs, selecting fabrics, and the number of collections per year to be designed. It also might specify the employee's reporting relationships and supervisory roles, if any. The agreement may provide that the employee will devote all of his or her business time to the company, or may specify a minimum number of hours or days per week to be worked, and the number (and perhaps timing) of vacation days. If the company has multiple locations, the agreement may specify the particular locations where the employee's services are to be performed.

A creative director also may be responsible for the image-related aspects of the brand. Accordingly, he or she may be required to be available for meetings with retail customers of the brand, for tradeshows, and for press appearances. In addition, a creative director may be required to maintain an active social media presence promoting the brand.

§ 17:2.2 Term

An employment agreement should specify its precise duration. Typically, this includes the commencement date of employment, the term of employment (for example, three years from the date of commencement) and, if applicable, any renewal options. For example, a three-year employment agreement might automatically renew for two successive one-year periods, unless one party delivers written notice to the other party of its intent not to renew within a specific time period (such as ninety days) prior to the expiration of the then-current term. In other cases, an employment may not have a specified term, but rather just state it applies until either the employee or the company terminates the employee's employment.

The agreement should also specify the circumstances in which the employer may terminate the employee's employment prior to the expiration of the term. Typically, an employer may terminate an employee either with or without "Cause," with each type of termination having different economic consequences for the employer and the employee. Although the definition of "Cause" is subject to negotiation, it typically includes some or all of the following concepts (sometimes with specific notice and cure periods): continuing failure to perform assigned duties; material breach by the employee of the employment agreement or company policies; engaging in willful conduct ; conviction of, or a plea of nolo contendere to, a felony or another crime involving moral turpitude; or willful commission of any act or omission involving dishonesty, disloyalty, or fraud. Typically, if an employee is terminated for "Cause," the employee will not be entitled to further compensation (other than accrued but unpaid base salary and, depending on company policy and applicable state law, unused vacation days). In many employment agreements, the long-term physical or mental disability or death, of the employee is treated in the same manner as a termination for "Cause" for compensation purposes. It may be helpful, however, to include a provision defining "long-term disability," and creating a process for determining whether it has occurred (such as an evaluation by a physician selected by the company in accordance with specified procedures).

An employer may terminate an employee without "Cause," sometimes (but not usually) subject to providing a specified period of notice to the employee. In such event, the employee is typically eligible for specified severance benefits, ranging from a few weeks of salary (for example, under a company-wide severance policy) to payment of salary and other compensation for a specified term (for example, six or twelve months) or the remaining unexpired term of the employment agreement. In addition, an employee may receive accelerated vesting of certain outstanding, but unvested, equity-based awards, as well as a continuation of group health benefits, for a specified time after termination. Any severance benefits should be contingent on the employee executing a release of claims; otherwise, the employee could take the severance benefits and still bring a discrimination or other claim.

Employment agreements also may permit the employee to resign for "Good Reason." This protection typically is limited to high-level executives. Again, the definition of "Good Reason" is subject to negotiation, but typically includes the following concepts (sometimes with specific notice and cure periods): material reduction in salary; material adverse change in assigned duties; loss of a designated title; material breach of the employment agreement by the company; or relocation outside of a designated geographic area. If an employee resigns with "Good Reason," the employee is often treated similarly to a termination by the company without "Cause." If an employee resigns without "Good Reason," perhaps after providing a specified period of notice, the employee usually will be treated similarly to a termination by the company for "Cause."

Since the rationale for a company termination or employee resignation is fact-dependent and often subjective, it may be difficult to determine in a particular instance whether "Cause" or "Good Reason" exists. Accordingly, the party who ends the employment relationship in the belief that "Cause" or "Good Reason" exists takes a risk that a court (or, if provided in the agreement, an arbitrator) may conclude otherwise.[2] In such event, an employer may be compelled

---

2. *See, e.g.*, Musman v. Modern Deb, Inc., 377 N.Y.S.2d 17 (App. Div. 1975), which concerned the interpretation of an employment agreement in connection with a termination of employment. A general manager and designer for the apparel business of Modern Deb, Inc. had an employment agreement that provided for a five-year term with a salary of $40,000 per year, plus an annual bonus. The agreement provided that if the employee were to be discharged without cause, Modern Deb would pay him his full compensation and bonus for the remainder of the five-year term. The employee was discharged before the term expired. The employee successfully argued that the termination was without cause, and his lost salary

to provide additional compensation to the terminated employee, or an employee may not receive compensation that he or she expected to receive when resigning. Thus, precise definitions are desirable for both parties' sakes.

Employment agreements for senior executive officers, particularly in public companies, may contain a "change in control" provision, also known as a "golden parachute." These provisions specify that the executive will receive certain additional compensation in the event of a change in control of the company, as defined in the employment agreement (usually including mergers, liquidations, certain changes in the composition of the company's board of directors, and acquisitions of a specified percentage of the company's equity securities). Typically, the change in control must be followed within a specified period of time by a termination of the executive's employment without Cause or for Good Reason (which is known as a "double trigger" provision because both the change in control and the subsequent termination must occur in order for the executive to receive the payments). In most cases, the protection is more generous severance than terminations outside the applicable window (*e.g.*, twenty-four instead of twelve months of continued base salary). Change of control provisions provide some economic protection to the executive in a change of control situation, and also provide some assurance to the company that the executive will remain with the company at least until a transaction can be completed and a transition effectuated. Although a full discussion of these provisions is beyond the scope of this chapter, change in control provisions must be carefully structured to avoid adverse tax consequences to both the executive and the company.[3]

§ 17:2.3 Compensation

An employment agreement typically sets forth a "package" of compensation to be paid by the company to the employee. Companies may obtain and use comparative industry data, obtained from publicly available sources or compensation experts, to determine the appropriate amount and types of compensation to offer a particular

---

was calculated at $108,333.50. The trial court reduced this amount to $59,187.03, deducting the wages that the employee had earned after finding new employment. The Appellate Division modified the judgment and held that the employment agreement did not require the employee to mitigate damages. Accordingly, the employee was awarded the entire $108,333.50 plus interest.

3. For a fuller discussion of change in control provisions, including the federal tax implications of these provisions, see Jonathan M. Ocker & Gregory C. Schick, EXECUTIVE EMPLOYMENT AGREEMENTS, A-15–A-19 (Corporate Practice Series Portfolio 88-1st, BNA 2012).

employee. At a minimum, a compensation package typically includes an annual base salary, payable in cash. Increases in base salary during the term of the employment agreement usually are discretionary. Alternatively, although fairly uncommon, base salary may be subject to automatic cost of living increases or specified incremental increases over the term of the agreement. In some cases, the employee may be granted a one-time signing or retention payment (or a relocation allowance), which may be contingent on continuation of employment for a specified period of time or which may be subject to repayment if the employee resigns or is fired for "Cause" before a specified date.

The compensation package also may include annual bonuses in the form of cash or equity-based securities (such as stock options, restricted stock, stock appreciation rights, or "phantom" equity). Bonuses sometimes are guaranteed, but more typically are discretionary or are tied to achievement of individual and/or company performance targets. Equity-based compensation may vest in installments over a specified period of time, in order to provide ongoing incentives to the employee. Federal and state securities laws relating to the issuance of securities need to be considered in connection with any equity-based compensation (as discussed in chapter 1).

In some cases, a designer might request compensation tied directly to his or her work product. For example, a designer might request a percentage of revenues or profits from sales of one or more products or lines that he or she designs over a specified period of time. Such compensation provisions are uncommon because they can be complicated to negotiate, draft, and monitor, particularly if they require a determination of the company's profits. Moreover, the designer would need to have access to certain financial information of the company, which might otherwise be confidential, in order to verify the amount of the required payments.

Typically, the employee is entitled to participate in company-wide benefit plans (such as health insurance and retirement plans) and is subject to company-wide policies (such as prohibitions on sexual harassment and discrimination). The employee should be reimbursed for reasonable and pre-approved company travel, entertainment, and other expenses (perhaps at a designated level such as "first class"), subject to standard documentation requirements, and may be issued company mobile devices or computers.

The employment agreement should also address any applicable tax issues, in particular issues under section 409A of the Internal Revenue Code.[4] Section 409A provides that all non-qualified deferred compensation must comply with certain rules regarding the payment

4. 26 U.S.C. § 409A.

of deferred compensation (in general, compensation that "vests" in one year but may not be payable until a later year). Great care is required in designing deferred compensation arrangements, because failure to comply may result in immediate tax inclusion of deferred amounts, plus a 20% additional tax and interest assessed against the employee. Subject to certain exceptions, an amount generally constitutes deferred compensation unless, by its terms, it must be paid out no later than two-and-a-half months after the end of the year in which it "vests." Exceptions to section 409A coverage can include certain types of equity awards and certain types of severance benefits. A tax expert should review employment agreements to ensure that section 409A is not violated. The employment agreement should include boilerplate language that the parties intend that all amounts payable to the employee will be paid in compliance with section 409A such that there will be no adverse tax consequences, penalties, or interest for the employee, and, accordingly, the agreement will be modified to the extent necessary to comply with, and to the extent permissible under, section 409A.

§ 17:2.4 Ownership of Creations

The employment agreement should address the issue of ownership of the intellectual property developed by the employee, or under the employee's direction, during the term of the agreement. This is particularly important where the employee performs a creative or design role at the company. For some forms of intellectual property, the default rule is that an employer generally owns the works that are prepared by an employee within the scope of his or her employment, as under the "work made for hire" provisions of the Copyright Act (17 U.S.C. § 101). To avoid any dispute, however, an employment agreement will typically specify that all work performed by the employee, and all ideas, designs, materials, and processes conceived or developed by the employee, during the term of the agreement must be disclosed and delivered to the company and become the property of the company. Accordingly, the company will have the right to obtain and hold in its own name all trademarks, patents, copyrights, and other applicable protections covering such intellectual property.

§ 17:2.5 Other Matters

Employment agreements should also contain a range of standard but important provisions that relate to the operation and construction of the agreement itself. An employment agreement should specify the governing law that is intended to apply to the interpretation of the agreement (which, however, may not necessarily be controlling).

In addition, it should specify any relevant dispute resolution mechanism, such as the submission of disputes to arbitration.

Since certain employees may have access to confidential information of the company, and relationships with customers and suppliers of the company, employment agreements generally also include certain restrictive covenants imposing obligations on the employee for the benefit of the employer. Certain of the most common restrictive covenants are described below.

§ 17:3 Confidentiality Covenants

§ 17:3.1 *Confidentiality in the Fashion Industry*

Companies in the fashion industry, like most companies, typically seek to preserve the confidentiality of certain proprietary and non-public information concerning their business. Employees of a fashion company may have access to this information in the course of their employment. Under the common law of many states, an employee may have a fiduciary duty to his or her employer not to use confidential information obtained in the course of employment to compete against the employer, even after the termination of employment.[5] This fiduciary duty may arise out of the employee's general common law duties of good faith, fair dealing, and loyalty to the employer.[6] Moreover, certain confidential information may be classified as trade secrets (secrets that provide a commercial advantage) and may be entitled to additional protections under applicable state and federal trade secret laws.[7] Notwithstanding these common law or statutory remedies, it is advisable for a company to require its employees to contractually agree to maintain confidentiality, either as a covenant in a full employment agreement or in a separate confidentiality agreement, in order to clarify the scope and terms of the employee's obligations and to provide a contractual remedy if the employee breaches its obligations.

Confidentiality covenants generally prohibit an employee from disclosing the company's confidential information to third parties and the public during a specified time period, except as specifically directed by the company or as required by law. Confidentiality covenants also can prohibit employees from disclosing confidential or

5. *See, e.g.*, Thin Film Lab, Inc. v. Comito, 218 F. Supp. 2d 513, 520 (S.D.N.Y. 2002) (citing N. Atl. Instruments, Inc. v. Haber, 188 F.3d 38, 47 (2d Cir. 1999)).

6. *See* Paz Sys., Inc. v. Dakota Grp. Corp., 514 F. Supp. 2d 402, 409 (E.D.N.Y. 2007) (citing Anacop, Inc. v. Shell Knob Servs., Inc., 1994 WL 9681, at *12 (S.D.N.Y. Jan. 10, 1994).

7. *See generally supra* chapter 6.

proprietary information belonging to third parties with whom the company has a relationship, such as suppliers or customers. (Similarly, companies may also enter into confidentiality agreements with third parties, such as suppliers and independent contractors that may have access to confidential or proprietary information of the company in the course of their business relationships.)

Confidentiality agreements are of particular importance in the fashion industry because of the high-profile nature of the business and the creative elements involved in fashion design. Confidential or proprietary information for a fashion company could include, among other matters: financial data; customer and supplier data; product designs, processes, and materials; and marketing strategy. If a fashion designer is a well-known celebrity, confidential information might also include information about the designer's personal life and social activities.

Confidentiality agreements are also frequently used in connection with particular fashion events, to prevent premature public disclosure of novel ideas or new designs. It has been reported that Saint Laurent required certain of its models to enter into confidentiality agreements in advance of a highly anticipated runway show.[8] It also has been reported that Tom Ford required journalists and guests viewing a presentation in London to enter into confidentiality agreements prohibiting them from disclosing details of a womenswear collection until it became available in stores several months later.[9] Sarah Burton, a designer for Alexander McQueen, reportedly signed a confidentiality agreement with Buckingham Palace regarding the design of the Duchess of Cambridge's wedding dress.[10]

§ 17:3.2 Drafting Confidentiality Agreements

In general, confidentiality covenants are enforceable under the laws of most states, absent circumstances that would typically render a contract unenforceable, such as fraud or duress. The discussion

8. *See* Charlotte Cowles, *Saint Laurent Model Louise Parker on Hedi Slimane, Her Exclusive Contract, and Those High Heels*, THE CUT BLOG, N.Y. MAG. (Oct. 22, 2012, 10:25 AM), http://nymag.com/thecut/2012/10/saint-laurent-model-louise-parker-talks-slimane.html.

9. *See* Tamara Abraham, *It Leaves a Bad Taste in Our Mouths: Bloggers' Backlash Over Tom Ford's Secretive Fashion Week Presentations*, DAILY MAIL (Feb. 22, 2011), https://www.dailymail.co.uk/femail/article-1359570/It-leaves-bad-taste-mouths-Bloggers-backlash-Tom-Fords-secretive-fashion-week-presentations.html.

10. *See* Anita Singh, *Sarah Burton: How I Kept Kate Middleton's Wedding Dress Secret*, TELEGRAPH (Nov. 2, 2011), http://fashion.telegraph.co.uk/news-features/TMG8862555/Sarah-Burton-how-I-kept-Kate-Middletons-wedding-dress-secret.html.

below assumes that the confidentiality covenant is contained in a separate agreement between the employer and the employee or independent contractor, and that New York law applies, unless another state law is specifically indicated

Courts applying New York law have held that confidentiality covenants, like other covenants restricting employees, are enforceable to the extent that they are "reasonable in time and area, necessary to protect the employer's legitimate interests, not harmful to the general public and not unreasonably burdensome to the employee."[11] Therefore, confidentiality agreements and other restrictive covenants should be drafted with care.

Confidentiality agreements are contracts between the party (the "Disclosing Party") in possession of the confidential information (for example, the fashion company) and the party (the "Receiving Party") that will receive access to the confidential information (for example, the employee or independent contractor).

In some cases, the Disclosing Party and/or the Receiving Party will encompass multiple entities and individuals. For example, the Disclosing Party may include the company and its subsidiaries, and the Receiving Party may include an independent contractor, its employees and its representatives. In addition, a well-known fashion designer working for the company could either be made a party to the agreement, or a third-party beneficiary of the agreement, to the extent confidential information relates to the designer, so that he or she would have enforcement rights in the event the Receiving Party violates the agreement.

For example, if an employee or independent contractor is granted access to a fashion designer's home or personal studio in the course of employment, the confidentiality agreement should protect sensitive personal information of the designer, including details about the designer's home and personal activities.

A confidentiality agreement should initially set forth the business purpose for the agreement, such as the employee's commencement of employment with the company, and note the critical importance of the confidential information to the company. Moreover, the agreement should recite the consideration for the confidentiality covenants. New employment is sufficient consideration for confidentiality obligations in most states, including New York. In New York, initial or continued employment may also be sufficient consideration for an

11. Ashland Mgmt. Inc. v. Altair Invs. NA, LLC, 59 A.D.3d 97, 102 (N.Y. App. Div. 2008) (quoting Reed, Roberts Assocs. Inc. v. Strauman, 40 N.Y.2d 303 (1976)).

enforceable confidentiality agreement.[12] Consideration could also be a promotion and accompanying salary increase or a bonus. Ideally, companies should require their employees to enter into a confidentiality agreement prior to the start of their employment, before they are exposed to any confidential information.

The core of a confidentiality agreement is the definition of the confidential information that is intended to be protected by the agreement. The definition should cover the scope of the protected information, how such information may be identified, and the forms it may take. It should not be overly broad, but should be tailored to the company's business and the specific role of the employee or independent contractor in that business. A sample definition of confidential information is set forth below:

> *"Confidential Information" will be broadly construed to mean any information directly or indirectly concerning the Disclosing Party that is obtained by the Receiving Party during the course of its services to the Disclosing Party or access to the Disclosing Party's premises and properties, both prior to and after the date of this Agreement (other than such information that is readily available to the public or is already public knowledge other than through an act or omission of the Receiving Party), including, but not limited to, any oral or written, tangible or intangible, information, in any medium, relating to or derived from:*
>
> - *the business processes or finances of the Disclosing Party;*
> - *the distributors, licensees, suppliers, and customers of the Disclosing Party;*
> - *the products, materials, fabrics, designs, sketches, drawings, photographs, inventions, trade secrets, concepts or ideas created by the Disclosing Party;*
> - *the marketing, advertising, and pricing strategy of the Disclosing Party;*
> - *personal information regarding any individual designers employed by the Disclosing Party (including, but not limited to, (i) any information regarding the designer's premises, (ii) the existence and terms of the relationship, whether personal, business, or otherwise, between the designer and any other person or party, and (iii) any image, likeness, photograph, video, audio, or graphic depiction of the designer or his or her premises and properties); and*

12. *See Ashland Mgmt. Inc.*, 59 A.D.3d at 106 (denying motion for summary judgment dismissing complaint alleging violation of confidentiality agreement, noting that one defendant signed a confidentiality agreement after being employed by the employer for fourteen years).

- *any discussions and oral or written communications between the Disclosing Party and any other parties relating to any pending business negotiations or transactions.*

Confidential information may also include notes or summaries that the Receiving Party makes that contain or are derived from the information described above.

The confidentiality agreement should prohibit the employee or independent contractor from disclosing confidential information to third parties, or using confidential information for purposes other than those agreed to by the parties. The employee or independent contractor should also be prohibited from duplicating, photographing, or removing from the company's premises any tangible confidential information. When an employee or an independent contractor terminates his or her relationship with the company, such person or party should be required to return to the company or destroy all confidential information of the company in his or her possession.

Many fashion companies and their designers have public profiles, and are the subject of articles in the media and mentions in social media. Accordingly, in order to control the flow of information to the press, the confidentiality agreement might contain a provision requiring the employee to decline interviews with the media or bloggers regarding the company or its designers, report any media inquiries to the company, and comply with the company's policy on using social media.

Confidentiality agreements typically cover the period during which a party has a relationship with the company and a specified period of time thereafter. Courts will generally enforce confidentiality obligations of a long or unlimited duration because they do not limit free competition in the same manner as non-compete agreements as discussed below.[13] If the duration should be found unreasonable, courts can often simply modify a confidentiality agreement's duration to one that is reasonable as discussed below.[14]

A company bringing a breach of contract claim for violation of a confidentiality agreement may be awarded monetary damages.[15] In

---

13. *Id.* at 105 (noting that "there is no reason to suppose that an unlimited durational limitation on the use of confidential information will prevent defendants from pursuing their livelihood or that it will have the effect of precluding them from operating a successful competing business").
14. *See id.* at 106.
15. *See, e.g.*, Dolgoff Holophase, Inc. v. E.I. Du Pont de Nemours & Co., 212 A.D.2d 661 (N.Y. App. Div. 1995) (also noting that such a cause of action accrues on the date the confidential information is first disclosed, and does not further accrue upon subsequent disclosures of the confidential information).

addition, injunctive relief may be available to prevent the employee from using the confidential information to compete against the employer if such use would result in irreparable harm to the employer, so long as the restrictions are "temporally and geographically reasonable and necessary to protect [the employer's] legitimate business interests."[16] The employee's mere possession of confidential information, absent proof that the employee has actually breached the confidentiality agreement, generally is not a sufficient basis for injunctive relief.[17] Although a contractual provision that monetary damages would be an inadequate remedy may be helpful, it may not control whether a court will decide that injunctive relief is appropriate.[18]

Confidentiality agreements (and other restrictive covenant agreements) should have carefully crafted severability and assignment provisions in order to maximize the likelihood that the agreements will be effective. A severability provision provides that if one portion of the agreement is held to be unenforceable by a court, the other provisions of the agreement will remain in effect. The severability provision should require the court to modify the affected portion so as to effectuate the intent of the parties. This is important because courts applying New York law may partially enforce an employee restrictive covenant, such as a confidentiality provision.[19] The confidentiality agreement also should be expressly assignable by the company in connection with a sale or transfer of the business, in order to protect the confidential information in such circumstance.

§ 17:4 Covenants Not to Compete and Related Restrictive Covenants

§ 17:4.1 Covenants Not to Compete

A covenant not to compete (also called a "non-competition agreement" or a "non-compete") is a provision that restricts an employee from competing with his or her employer, typically during the term of employment and for a specified period of time after the employment

---

16. Delta Enter. Corp. v. Cohen, 93 A.D.3d 411, 412 (N.Y. App. Div. 2012). *See also* Sylmark Holdings Ltd. v. Silicone Zone Int'l Ltd., 5 Misc. 3d 285, 295 (N.Y. Sup. Ct. 2004) (noting that "[a] contract to retain the confidentiality of certain matters which should be kept in confidence will be enforced by injunction").
17. *See* U.S. Re Cos. v. Scheerer, 41 A.D.3d 152, 155 (N.Y. App. Div. 2007).
18. *See, e.g.*, Art Capital Grp. LLC v. Getty Images, Inc., 24 Misc. 3d 1247(A) (Sup. Ct. N.Y. Cty. 2009).
19. *See* BDO Seidman v. Hirshberg, 93 N.Y.2d 382, 394 (1999).

relationship ends.[20] A traditional covenant not to compete provides that the employee will not enter into an employment or similar relationship with a competitor of the employer, or offer services of a competitive nature, for a specific period of time in a designated geographic area.[21] Variants of the traditional covenant not to compete that are less commonly used in the United States include "forfeiture for competition" provisions and "garden leave" provisions. A forfeiture for competition provision does not prohibit an employee from competing with his or her former employer after the employment relationship ends; however, if the employee chooses to compete, he or she will forfeit certain compensation. A garden leave provision, commonly used in the United Kingdom, requires the employee to provide a period of advance notice to the employer prior to resigning; during this period, the employee is not permitted to work for another company, but may not be obligated to provide services to the employer, and continues to receive his or her salary and benefits. The employer typically can waive all or part of the garden leave period. The rationale for these competition-related provisions is that an employee should not be able to use valuable trade secrets and other confidential information about the employer's business gained during the course of employment to immediately compete with the employer.

The validity and enforcement of covenants not to compete are governed by state law, which varies considerably from state to state.[22] For example, California law takes a particularly harsh view of non-competes by generally prohibiting employment-based non-competes.[23] The following discussion of traditional covenants not to compete is based on New York law, unless another state law is specifically indicated.

Covenants not to compete invoke significant public policy concerns, and thereafter are subject to judicial scrutiny. One court noted: "No restrictions should fetter an employee's right to apply to his own best advantage the skills and knowledge acquired by the overall experience of his previous employment."[24] Courts are often motivated by "powerful considerations of public policy which militate against

---

20. *See generally* Harlan M. Blake, *Employee Agreements Not to Compete*, 73 HARV. L. REV. 625 (1960) [hereinafter Blake].
21. *See id.* at 626.
22. For a state-by-state analysis of non-competes, see BRIAN M. MALSBERGER, COVENANTS NOT TO COMPETE: A STATE-BY-STATE SURVEY (BNA 8th ed. 2012).
23. California has rendered employee non-competition covenants void, subject to narrow exceptions, "[E]very contract by which anyone is restrained from engaging in a lawful profession, trade, or business of any kind is to that extent void." CAL. BUS. & PROF. CODE § 16600 (West 2012).
24. Reed, Roberts Assocs., Inc. v. Strauman, 40 N.Y.2d 303, 307 (1976).

sanctioning the loss of a man's livelihood."[25] Another important policy often noted by courts is the "general public policy favoring robust and uninhibited competition."[26] Thus, the enforceability of a convent not to compete after an employment relationship ends is more limited than that of confidentiality agreements because courts weigh these strong public policy concerns against the employer's interest in protecting its property.[27] In particular, courts applying New York law have adopted the view that traditional covenants not to compete may be unenforceable in instances where the employee has been terminated without cause and does not receive severance benefits in connection therewith.[28]

In general, New York law applies a common law reasonableness test to determine whether a given covenant not to compete is enforceable. "New York law subjects contractual non-compete provisions to an overriding limitation of reasonableness."[29] A covenant not to compete that is reasonable "(1) is no greater than is required for the protection of the legitimate interest of the employer, (2) does not impose undue hardship on the employee, and (3) is not injurious to the public."[30] Whether a particular covenant not to compete is reasonable depends largely on the nature of the employer's interest and the restrictions imposed in the specific context of the case.[31] Courts may hold the entire covenant to be unenforceable in a particular context, or may narrow the scope of the covenant in light of the circumstances.

As a threshold matter, an employer seeking to enforce a covenant not to compete must provide sufficient evidence that the covenant protects a legitimate interest of the employer (such as trade secrets or

---

25. Purchasing Assocs., Inc. v. Weitz, 13 N.Y.2d 267, 272 (1963).
26. Ashland Mgmt. Inc. v. Altair Invs. NA, LLC, 59 A.D.3d 97, 104 (N.Y. App. Div. 2008).
27. Johnson Controls, Inc. v. A.P.T. Critical Sys., Inc., 323 F. Supp. 2d 525, 533–34 (S.D.N.Y. 2004) (noting that "New York courts have endeavored to balance public policy concerns relating to the benefits of competition and the unfettered flow of talent and ideas in our economy with employers' legitimate right to protect the fruits of their labor"); Am. Broad. Cos. v. Wolf, 52 N.Y.2d 394, 404 (1981) (noting that "[t]here is, in short, general judicial disfavor of anticompetitive covenants contained in employment contracts").
28. SIFCO Indus. Inc. v. Advanced Plating Techs., Inc., 867 F. Supp. 155 (S.D.N.Y. 1994).
29. Pure Power Boot Camp, Inc. v. Warrior Fitness Boot Camp, LLC, 813 F. Supp. 2d 489, 506 (S.D.N.Y. 2011).
30. BDO Seidman v. Hirshberg, 93 N.Y.2d 382, 388–89 (1999).
31. *See* Reed, Roberts Assocs., Inc. v. Strauman, 40 N.Y.2d 303, 307 (1976); *BDO Seidman*, 93 N.Y.2d at 858 (stating that "the application of the test of reasonableness of employee restrictive covenants focuses on the particular facts and circumstances giving context to the agreement").

customer lists).[32] Courts then consider a number of factors, including the duration of the non-compete and its geographic scope, in determining reasonableness. Unlike confidentiality agreements, covenants not to compete of unlimited duration are unenforceable. In addition, courts often require the covenant not to compete to be in force only in a limited geographic area.[33] However, given the global nature of many companies in the fashion industry, courts have indicated that restrictions with a larger geographic scope may sometimes be acceptable.[34] In particular, covenants that bar an employee from competing while still receiving payments from the company are afforded more flexibility because the employee obtains additional consideration in exchange for the restriction on his or her activities.[35] For example, a court applying New York law granted a preliminary injunction enforcing a worldwide non-compete restricting a senior executive of Estee Lauder from working for a direct competitor, notwithstanding a lack of geographic limitation.[36] The court noted that factors such as the magnitude of the executive's responsibilities while in the company's employ, the "international scope of Estee Lauder's business and the cosmetics industry in general," and that the executive would continue to receive his salary during the period of restriction contributed to its determination that the non-compete was not overly broad geographically; however, the court reduced the duration of the non-compete from twelve to five months.[37]

Covenants not to compete that accompany the sale of a business are also more liberally enforced on the rationale that competition by the seller could erode the goodwill for which the buyer has bargained and paid.[38]

---

32. *See* Renaissance Nutrition, Inc. v. Jarrett, No. 08-CV-800S, 2012 WL 42171 (W.D.N.Y. Jan. 9, 2012).
33. *See Pure Power Boot Camp*, 813 F. Supp. 2d at 507.
34. *See, e.g.*, Bus. Intelligence Serv., Inc. v. Hudson, 580 F. Supp. 1068, 1073 (S.D.N.Y. 1984) (upholding a non-competition clause with a worldwide geographic scope "given the international nature of [the employer's] business"); Misys Int'l Banking Sys., Inc. v. TwoFour Sys., LLC, 6 Misc. 3d 1004(A) (N.Y. Sup. Ct. 2004) ("The determination of reasonableness requires that the geographic scope be analyzed in light of the evidence . . . which here established the international nature of the business.").
35. *See, e.g.*, Bradford v. N.Y. Times Co., 501 F.2d 51, 57–58 (2d Cir. 1974) (upholding a non-competition agreement spanning ten years with no geographic limitation where the employee was to receive annual installments of stock as long as he did not compete).
36. *See* Estee Lauder Cos. v. Batra, 430 F. Supp. 2d 158, 181 (S.D.N.Y. 2006).
37. *Id.*
38. *See* Shearson Lehman Bros. Holdings, Inc. v. Schmertzler, 500 N.Y.S.2d 512, 516 (App. Div. 1986) (stating that employee restrictive covenants

If an employee's services are deemed "special, unique or extraordinary," a non-compete may be more likely to be enforceable.[39] An employee's services are considered unique or extraordinary if it "appear[s] that his services are of such character as to make his replacement impossible or that the loss of such services would cause the employer irreparable injury."[40] The scope of the employee's involvement in the business is another relevant factor in determining uniqueness: "[I]t is not necessary that the employee should be the only 'star' of his employer or that the business will grind to a halt if the employee leaves . . . in determining uniqueness, the inquiry now focuses more on the employee's relationship to the employer's business than on the individual person of the employee."[41]

Fashion designers and fashion executives often move to several different companies over the course of their careers, seeking greater responsibility and higher compensation.[42] Because of the nature of the industry, a fashion professional who leaves one company will often seek new employment at a competing company. Yet, this may pose the greatest risk to the former employer. For example, when a director of sales in Nike's Jordan division resigned to take a position as Vice President of U.S. footwear sales and manufacturing at Reebok, Nike sought and obtained a preliminary injunction to bar the employee from working for Reebok for one year, invoking a non-compete he signed in connection with a prior promotion by Nike.[43] The court, applying Oregon law, found that Nike had a legitimate business interest in enforcing the non-compete because there was a substantial risk

---

in connection with the sale of a business are more liberally enforced, the sole limitation being "that the restraint . . . is . . . not more extensive . . . than is reasonably necessary to the buyer for the protection of his legitimate interest in the enjoyment of the asset bought" (punctuation omitted); *see also* Capital One Fin. Corp. v. Kanas, 871 F. Supp. 2d 520, 527 (E.D. Va. 2012) ("greater latitude is allowed in determining the reasonableness of a restrictive covenant when the covenant relates to the sale of a business"). Non-competition agreements accompanying the sale or dissolution of a business are excepted from California's general voiding of employee non-compete agreements. CAL. BUS. & PROF. CODE §§ 16601–16602.

39. Purchasing Assocs., Inc. v. Weitz, 13 N.Y.2d 267, 270 (1963).

40. *Id.* at 274.

41. Ticor Title Ins. Co. v. Cohen, 173 F.3d 63, 71 (2d Cir. 1999).

42. *See* David Jolly, *Season of Personnel Changes Shakes up the Fashion World*, N.Y. TIMES (Feb. 27, 2012), http://www.nytimes.com/2012/02/28/business/global/ysl-looking-for-new-creative-director.html (noting that fashion designers are "the rock stars of the fashion world, paid enormous salaries for the excitement and marketing firepower they bring to luxury conglomerates").

43. *See* Nike, Inc. v. McCarthy, 379 F.3d 576 (9th Cir. 2004).

that the employee, in shaping Reebok's product allocation, sales, and pricing strategies, could enable Reebok to divert a significant amount of Nike's footwear sales given the highly confidential information he acquired at Nike.[44]

Courts addressing the enforceability of a non-compete in a particular context often focus closely on the issue of whether the former employer and new employer are in fact competitors. For example, a court applying Missouri law determined that Victoria's Secret Stores, Inc. and May Department Stores Company were not in "material competition, and therefore the executive did not breach the non-compete in his employment agreement."[45] The executive left May Department Stores for a position as chief operating officer of Victoria's Secret, notwithstanding an employment agreement with May prohibiting him from being employed by a "competing business" for two years following his departure from May. The definition of "competing business" included any retail business that sold products or merchandise of the types sold in May's stores or that competed with May for customers. The court determined that May and Victoria's Secret were not competing businesses because, among other reasons, May's sold a range of products produced by others and focused its marketing strategy on competitive pricing not brand loyalty, while Victoria's Secret was vertically integrated, and targeted customers that were brand loyal and seeking specific items of intimate apparel.[46]

From an employee's perspective, in negotiating a non-compete provision, it is important to define the prohibited competitive activities specifically and narrowly in light of the circumstances. For example, a designer might be prohibited from engaging in only those activities that compete with the specific division, brand, or product lines that he or she actually designed for, rather than all of the divisions, brands, and products of his or her employer (which may be quite comprehensive). Alternatively, a designer might be prohibited from future employment with a division of a company that competes with his or her current employer, but not with other divisions of such company. The less broad the restriction, the more likely it will be upheld by a court.

---

44. *Id.* at 578. *See also* Nike, Inc. v. Dekovic, No. 14 Cv. 18876 (Or. Cir. Ct. Multnomah Cty. filed Dec. 8, 2014). Nike obtained a prelimiminary injunction preventing three former Nike designers from disclosing misappropriated trade secrets, working for Adidas or any Nike competitor, or publicly associating themselves with Adidas on social media. Gibson Dunn represented Nike in the lawsuit.

45. Victoria's Secret Stores, Inc. v. May Dep't Stores Co., 157 S.W.3d 256, 262 (Mo. Ct. App. 2004).

46. *Id.*

From an employer's perspective, non-compete provisions should be drafted to provide sufficient protection to the employer's legitimate business interests while not unduly restraining the ability of the employee to work. A court may be more likely to enforce a covenant not to compete if the employer is able to demonstrate it was negotiated in good faith and not motivated by a desire to restrict the employee's movement or gain a bargaining advantage.[47] The best time for a company to enter into a non-compete with an employee is in connection with the commencement of employment or a promotion. It is advisable to include in a non-compete provision a recitation of the importance of the confidential information or client relationships the employee will gain access to in the course of his or her employment, the competitive nature of the industry, the position of responsibility held by the employee, and the reasonableness of the restriction. To facilitate a remedy of specific performance, the provision also might include a statement in which the employee acknowledges the uniqueness of his or her services, and that breach of the covenant would result in irreparable harm to the employer. Language supporting the reasonableness of the restriction may support the employer's demonstration of an absence of overreaching.[48]

§ 17:4.2 *Related Restrictive Covenants*

The most common restrictive covenants that are used in connection with non-competes are non-solicitation, non-interference, and non-disparagement covenants. These restrictive covenants are similar to non-competes in that they are intended to prevent competitive harm to the employer, but they may be less burdensome to the employee.

A non-solicitation (or "anti-raid") covenant prohibits the employee from inducing to leave, and hiring, other employees of his or her employer during the term of employment and for a specified period of time after termination of employment. A sample non-solicitation provision is set forth below:

> *For the duration of the employment period, and for twelve (12) months thereafter, other than in the course of performing her duties, the Employee shall not directly or indirectly through another person (i) induce or attempt to induce, any employee of the Company or any of its subsidiaries to leave the employ of the Company or such subsidiary, or in any way interfere with the relationship between the Company or any of its subsidiaries and any employee thereof,*

---

47. *See* Blake, *supra* note 20, at 687.
48. BDO Seidman v. Hirshberg, 93 N.Y.2d 382 (1999).

> *or (ii) hire, within ninety days of such person's termination of employment with the Company or any of its affiliates, any person who was an employee of the Company or any subsidiary at any time while the Employee was employed by the Company.*

From an employee's perspective, non-solicitation provisions should be negotiated to shorten their duration or narrow their scope in order to reduce the future burdens on the employee. For example, the restriction may be limited to cover only senior employees or fashion designers of the company, or may specifically exclude persons hired through general advertisements that are not specifically targeting employees of the company. The provision also may be limited to only prohibit the actual act of hiring certain employees, rather than prohibiting inducement activities (which may be more subjective).

A non-interference covenant prohibits the employee from interfering with the company's business relationships with third parties such as suppliers and customers, during the term of employment and for a specified period of time after the termination of employment. A sample non-interference provision is set forth below:

> *For the duration of the employment period, and for a period of twelve (12) months thereafter, the Employee shall not induce, or attempt to induce, any wholesale or retail customer of the Company or any subsidiary, or any supplier, licensee, licensor, franchisee, or other business partner of the Company or any subsidiary to cease doing business with the Company or such subsidiary, or in any material way interfere with the relationship of any such customer, supplier, licensee, licensor, franchisee, or business partner and the Company or any subsidiary.*

Non-solicitation and non-interference covenants are generally evaluated pursuant to a reasonableness analysis similar to the analysis used for covenants not to compete.[49] Because they do not prohibit all competition with the employer, however, non-solicitation and non-interference covenants are narrower than non-competes and may be more likely to be found reasonable.[50]

---

49. *See* Reed, Roberts Assocs., Inc. v. Strauman, 40 N.Y.2d 303, 307 (1976); Investor Access Corp. v. Doremus & Co., 186 A.D.2d 401, 403 (N.Y. App. Div. 1992) (stating "[w]e can discern no qualitative difference between a mere nonsolicitation covenant and a limited noncompetition covenant which warrants inconsistent treatment").

50. As more limited clauses, non-interference and non-solicitation provisions are also more likely to be upheld. *See, e.g.*, Renaissance Nutrition, Inc. v. Jarrett, No. 08-CV-800S, 2012 WL 42171 (W.D.N.Y. Jan. 9, 2012).

A non-disparagement covenant prohibits the employee from making any public statements or taking any action to disparage the employer. In some cases, non-disparagement covenants may be mutual, particularly where the employee is a senior executive or is well known to the public. A sample mutual non–disparagement provision is set forth below:

> *For the duration of the employment period, and for a period of twelve (12) months thereafter (i) the Employee shall not take any action (or make any public statements) to disparage or criticize the Company, its subsidiaries, or its employees, officers, directors, or owners, and (ii) neither the Company nor its subsidiaries, nor any of their respective directors or senior executives, shall take any action (or make any public statements) to disparage or criticize the Employee. Nothing contained in this Section shall preclude either the Company or the Employee from enforcing their respective rights under this Agreement or responding truthfully to legal process or governmental inquiry.*

Non-disparagement covenants may be hard to successfully enforce because of the difficulty of determining whether the statements at issue actually damaged the other party and the extent of any such damage. These covenants, however, may serve a valuable deterrent function. Most commonly, nondisparagement clauses run only in favor of the company; however, especially for senior executives, they may be mutual. Mutuality can raise serious concerns for employers, who cannot control what every employee says. Thus, it is prudent for an employer to limit its nondisparagement obligations to instructing board members and senior executives not to disparage the employee.

Restrictive covenants, particularly non-competes, that are overly broad and continue for substantial periods after the termination of employment can be particularly burdensome to an employee, and may not be fully enforceable by the employer. They can negatively impact an employee's ability to gain meaningful future employment or may impair an employee's ability to function fully in a future position. Moreover, insisting on broad restrictive covenants may adversely impact the employer's ability to recruit and retain talented employees. Accordingly, restrictive covenants should be carefully tailored to protect legitimate interests of the employer while not unduly burdening the employee.

If an employer believes that an employee has violated, or intends to violate, a restrictive covenant, the employer should act quickly so as to maximize the effectiveness of a response. Although a full analysis of litigation strategy is beyond the scope of this chapter, there are a few general matters that an employer should consider in determining the most appropriate course of action to pursue. These considerations include the following:

- Does the employer have clear evidence of the suspected conduct or does it need to undertake an investigation to develop such evidence? What is the extent and cost of such an investigation?
- Has the employer collected and reviewed with legal counsel all relevant agreements and other documents that apply to the employee and the suspected conduct?
- Is the employer prepared to commit the necessary time and resources to litigate the issue?
- Is the employer prepared for the impact of a negative result in the litigation on its other employees?

Although an employer's initial reaction to a suspected violation of a restrictive covenant may be to consider instituting legal proceedings against the employee, such a course of action should only be undertaken if, after careful analysis of the relevant factors, litigation is warranted.

Chapter 18

Rights of Publicity

§ 18:1 Introduction
§ 18:2 Overview of Right of Publicity Law
§ 18:3 History of the Right of Publicity
§ 18:4 Leading Examples of State Right of Publicity Law
§ 18:4.1 California
§ 18:4.2 New York
§ 18:4.3 Indiana
§ 18:5 Practical Implications for the Fashion Industry

§ 18:1 Introduction

The use of models and celebrities in marketing fashion products is ubiquitous. Charles Frederick Worth, a British fashion designer working in Paris (considered to be the father of *haute couture*), first recognized the importance of linking celebrities to fashion in the early nineteenth century. To promote his fashion house La Maison Worth, Worth sought out an endorsement from the highly regarded Princess Pauline von Metternich, wife of Austria's ambassador to France and close friend of Napoleon's wife Empress Eugenie.[1] Her resulting connection to Worth's fashion house contributed immensely to the designer's success and status.[2]

Models and celebrities continue to serve a vital role in the fashion industry. Indeed, many models and celebrities earn a significant portion of their income from endorsement contracts with fashion companies. Fashion companies, eager to associate popular celebrities with their brands, may attempt to use a celebrity's identity to obtain commercial advantage over their competition, sometimes without

1. *See* UCHE OKONKWO, LUXURY FASHION BRANDING: TRENDS, TACTICS, TECHNIQUES, at 53–54 (Palgrave MacMillan 2007).
2. *Id.*

paying the celebrity for use of his or her likeness. A growing body of law—known as "right of publicity law"—has, in turn, recognized the proprietary right that all individuals, even non-celebrities, have in the commercial use of their own likeness. Fashion companies must therefore be careful to obtain appropriate permissions from individuals displayed or otherwise utilized in promotional and advertising materials.

§ 18:2 Overview of Right of Publicity Law

The so-called "right of publicity" is a philosophical relative of the right to privacy.[3] A violation of the right of publicity is generally considered a tort, akin to infringing an individual's property right.[4] In broad terms, the doctrine asserts that an individual whose likeness has commercial value has the exclusive right to control and realize the profits from the commercial use of that likeness, as well as the right to prevent the use of his or her personality publicly without permission.[5] A paradigmatic violation of the right occurs when a company uses the name or likeness of a celebrity to increase the attractiveness of its product in the eyes of the public. For example, fashion model Christie Brinkley asserted claims under the right of publicity after a publisher printed and distributed posters of her image without her consent.[6]

Although the right is often confused with the more commonly recognized copyright and trademark causes of action, the right of publicity constitutes a distinct intellectual property policy with differing rationales and resulting protections.

---

3. *See generally* Samuel D. Warren & Louis D. Brandeis, *The Right to Privacy*, 4 HARV. L. REV. 193 (1890) (responding to media trend of publishing private information about citizens' lives) [hereinafter WARREN & BRANDEIS]; *see also* J. THOMAS MCCARTHY, THE RIGHTS OF PUBLICITY AND PRIVACY, §§ 1:2, 1:7–1:8 (2d ed. 2011) [hereinafter MCCARTHY ON PUBLICITY AND PRIVACY] (explaining relationship of right of publicity to privacy law).
4. *See* MCCARTHY ON PUBLICITY AND PRIVACY, *supra* note 3, § 1.3 (outlining right of publicity).
5. *See* J. Thomas McCarthy, *The Human Persona as Commercial Property: The Right of Publicity*, 19 COLUM.-VLA J.L. & ARTS 129, 130–31 (1995) (describing purpose and limitations of right of publicity); *see also* Zacchini v. Scripps-Howard Broad. Co., 433 U.S. 562, 576–79 (1977) (outlining the right and determining that individual had right to publicity of "human cannonball" performance despite news stations' First and Fourteenth Amendment defenses).
6. *See* Brinkley v. Casablancas, 438 N.Y.S.2d 1004 (App. Div. 1981).

Copyright, for instance, applies to a work of authorship itself, rather than to the individual whose likeness is depicted in such a work.[7] As such, an advertisement featuring a celebrity could implicate both copyright and right of publicity causes of action, with the photographer who created the advertisement possessing a copyright claim, and the celebrity depicted in the advertisement possessing a right of publicity claim. As the two claims are wholly distinct from one another with standing granted to independent parties, federal copyright laws generally do not preempt state-based right of publicity claims.[8] At the same time, right of publicity law shares some important similarities with copyright law. For example, various courts have addressed the same kinds of concerns that underpin the statutory copyright defense of "fair use" in right of publicity actions even though the fair use concept is less developed for right of publicity claims.[9]

Parallels to trademark law are more readily apparent. Much like a business would seek to protect its mark from unfair use by third

---

7. *See* 17 U.S.C. § 102(a) (copyright applies to the rights one acquires in "original works of authorship fixed in any tangible medium of expression"); *see also supra* chapter 4.

8. *See* Jonathan Faber, *Indiana: A Celebrity-Friendly Jurisdiction*, RES GESTAE, vol. 45, no. 9 (Mar. 2000) (summarizing how the right of publicity is distinguished from traditional copyright and trademark law). State law right of publicity actions are preempted by federal copyright law, however, where the conduct alleged to violate the right consists solely of distributing a work in which the plaintiff claims a copyright. *See, e.g.*, Maloney v. T3Media, Inc., 853 F.3d 1004 (9th Cir. 2017) (claim preempted); Fleet v. CBS, Inc., 50 Cal. App. 4th 1911 (Ct. App. 1996) (claim preempted); Downing v. Abercrombie & Fitch, Inc., 265 F.3d 994 (9th Cir. 2001) (claim not preempted where publicity claim based on defendant's advertising use of a photo of plaintiffs taken after surf competition); Toney v. L'Oreal USA, Inc., 406 F.3d 905 (7th Cir. 2005) (claim not preempted where publicity claim based on likeness used in connection with packaging and promotion of product). To avoid preemption, the right of publicity claim must contain elements that can be differentiated from the elements of a copyright infringement claim. *See, e.g.*, KNB Enters. v. Matthews, 78 Cal. App. 4th 362, 364–65 (Ct. App. 2000) (finding that models' right of publicity claims in distribution of erotic photographs were not preempted where photos had been posted on a website for profit without models' consent, and noting that "a human likeness is not copyrightable, even if captured in a copyrightable photograph").

9. *See, e.g.*, *Zacchini*, 433 U.S. at 569–78 (balancing the First Amendment interest in the right to comment on another's work against the owner's right to exploit that work commercially); White v. Samsung Elecs., Inc., 989 F.2d 1512, 1516 (9th Cir. 1993) (Kozinski, J., dissenting) (describing the importance of the fair use defense in a right of publicity case); *see also* David Leichtman, Yakub Hazzard, David Martinez & Jordan S. Paul, *Transformative Use Comes of Age in Right of Publicity Litigation*, LANDSLIDE (Sept./Oct. 2011), https://www.robinskaplan.com/~/media/

parties,[10] individuals with right of publicity claims seek to prevent others from benefitting from the use of their fame. Indeed, the two causes of action could overlap in appropriate circumstances. In *Motown Record Corp. v. Hormel & Co.*, for example, the music group "The Supremes," in asserting a claim under section 43(a) of the Lanham Act (15 U.S.C. § 1125(a)), argued that the group had a right to protect "the 'persona' or the likeness, style and image of [the group]."[11] The court, in denying defendant's motion for summary judgment on the trademark claim, held that "plaintiffs may be able to show some kind of protectable interest in the persona of 'The Supremes.'"[12]

§ 18:3 History of the Right of Publicity

The modern-day right to publicity finds its roots in the right to privacy. In their seminal 1890 law review article *The Right to Privacy*, Samuel Warren and Louis Brandeis famously responded to the development of intrusive journalism, noting that the press was "overstepping in every direction the obvious bounds of proprietary and of decency," and thus invading certain "sacred precincts of private and domestic life."[13] They argued that common law must recognize a right of privacy in order to protect the individual's "right to be let alone."[14]

In 1903, the New York Legislature moved swiftly to overturn a New York Court of Appeals ruling refusing to recognize a common law right of privacy[15] by enacting sections 50 and 51 of the New York Civil Rights Law, making it a tort to use an individual's "name, picture or photograph" in advertising or trade without his or her consent.[16]

The right of publicity continued its development in the 1950s, as the increase in film and television consumption molded the concept

---

A6974642423042EDA0695C61BE471AF5.ashx; Thomas E. Kadin, *Fumbling the First Amendment: The Right of Publicity Goes 2-0 Against Freedom of Expression*, 112 MICH. L. REV. 8 (2014) (discussing application of "transformative use" test in right of publicity cases).

10. *See supra* chapter 2.
11. Motown Record Corp. v. Hormel & Co., 657 F. Supp. 1236, 1241 (C.D. Cal. 1987) (citing MCCARTHY ON PUBLICITY AND PRIVACY, *supra* note 3).
12. *Id.*
13. *See* WARREN & BRANDEIS, *supra* note 3, at 195–96.
14. *See id.* at 193.
15. *See* Roberson v. Rochester Folding Box Co., 64 N.E. 442, 443 (N.Y. 1902) (refusing to recognize a common law right of privacy for fear it would "result not only in a vast amount of litigation, but in litigation bordering upon the absurd").
16. *See* Seth A. Dymond, *So Many Entertainers, So Little Protection: New York, the Right of Publicity, and the Need for Reciprocity*, 47 N.Y.L. SCH. L. REV. 447, 451 (2003) (describing the state legislature enactment of New York Civil Rights Law §§ 50–51 after *Roberson* was decided).

of "celebrity" as we know it today.[17] The pervasiveness of magazines and newspaper gossip columns increased the public's appetite for information about the private lives of their favorite celebrities, and the public began to look to the famous for cues on what they should wear and buy.[18] Recognizing the opportunity to profit from this phenomenon, companies began exploiting the immense marketing power of celebrities, and celebrity product testimonials became widespread.[19] Soon, the names and faces of movie stars, musicians, and professional athletes were being used to sell numerous consumer goods, including fashion.[20]

It was during this time that courts began to recognize a property-based cause of action in the impermissible use of one's identity.[21] Judge Jerome Frank, in the seminal Second Circuit case *Haelan Laboratories, Inc. v. Topps Chewing Gum, Inc.*, was the first to coin the phrase "right of publicity" and recognize it as a property-based cause of action.[22] In *Haelan*, a baseball card company brought suit after a competitor induced a baseball player to use his likeness on its baseball cards, even though it was aware the player had already signed a contract with the plaintiffs granting them the exclusive rights to use his likeness on their own baseball cards.[23] The court recognized that the injury suffered by plaintiffs—the loss of value of the exclusive rights to use the player's likeness on its baseball cards—could be deemed a cognizable harm only if the right to use a person's likeness were assignable to another party.[24] And, for such a right to be assignable, the court determined that the right must be recognized as a form of property.[25] The court held that an individual has a quasi-property right to control the use of his likeness, as well as the right to assign the commercial use of his likeness to another, the so-called "right of publicity."[26]

Many early decisions considering the right of privacy failed to establish the range of protected interests, instead debating whether or

---

17. *See generally* Michael Madow, *Private Ownership of Public Image: Popular Culture and Publicity Rights*, 81 CAL. L. REV. 127 (1993) [hereinafter Madow].
18. *Id.* at 162–63.
19. *Id.* at 164.
20. *Id.* at 165–66.
21. Steven M. Fleischer, *The Right of Publicity: Preventing an Identity Crisis*, 27 N. KY. L. REV. 985, 989 (2000).
22. Haelan Labs., Inc. v. Topps Chewing Gum, Inc., 202 F.2d 866 (2d Cir. 1953).
23. *Id.* at 867.
24. *Id.* at 868.
25. *Id.*
26. *Id.*

not to recognize the right of privacy at all. Professor William Prosser, best known for his seminal works in the field of torts, authored a 1960 article titled "Privacy," that described a personal right of privacy, protected in four categories:

(1) Protection against intrusion into one's private affairs;

(2) Avoidance of disclosure of one's embarrassing private facts;

(3) Protection against publicity placing one in a false light in the public eye; and

(4) Remedies for appropriation, usually for commercial advantage, of one's name or likeness.[27]

As to the fourth category, he noted that "[t]he interest protected is not so much a mental as a proprietary one, in the exclusive use of the plaintiff's name and likeness as an aspect of his identity."[28]

Although courts were initially reluctant to embrace the right of publicity,[29] the U.S. Supreme Court upheld the right as a valid cause of action nearly twenty-five years later in *Zacchini v. Scripps-Howard Broadcasting Co.*[30] Zacchini, a performer of a famous "human cannonball" act, sued when a local news station aired his entire fifteen-second act on the nightly news. The value of his act, he claimed, depended on the public's desire to pay to witness the event, a desire that would be diminished by allowing the news station to air the entirety of his performance. The Court recognized that Zacchini possessed a protectable interest in his image, and denied the news station's First Amendment defenses. In granting Zacchini such protection, the Court held that it meant to provide "an economic incentive for him to make the investment required to produce a performance of interest to the public."[31]

In the decades following *Haelen* and *Zacchini*, the right of publicity has developed into an established doctrine recognized in most jurisdictions, either through state statutory law or common law.[32] It is important to note that, unlike trademark and copyright law, the right of publicity has not been granted federal statutory protection in the United States. Thirty-three states recognize the right of publicity

27. *See* William L. Prosser, *Privacy*, 48 CALIF. L. REV. 383, 389 (1960).

28. *Id.* at 406. Years later, Judge Montgomery Oliver Koelsch would note this difference between the interests in Professor Prosser's four privacy torts in Motschenbacher v. R.J. Reynolds Tobacco Co., 498 F.2d 821, 823–24 (9th Cir. 1974).

29. *See* Madow, *supra* note 17, at 176.

30. Zacchini v. Scripps-Howard Broad. Co., 433 U.S. 562 (1977).

31. *Id.* at 576.

32. *See* MCCARTHY ON PUBLICITY AND PRIVACY, *supra* note 3, § 6:3.

either by statute or common law, with twenty-one of those states recognizing a common-law right of publicity. Some state statutes explicitly recognize a right of publicity, while others have enacted privacy statutes that encompass the right of publicity.[33] Only two states, Nebraska and New York, have explicitly rejected a common law right of publicity.[34] In Nebraska, the state court's ruling was overruled by statute;[35] New York, the very state in which *Haelan* was decided, does not recognize a common law right of publicity, instead relying on the right as codified in New York's privacy statute.[36]

Although the extent to which each state has recognized and applied the right of publicity tends to vary, the current majority view extends the right to every individual, not just those who are famous.[37] In practice, however, celebrities are far more likely to possess sufficient commercial value in their likeness to justify expensive litigation.[38] Of the states that recognize the right, the vast majority hold that only natural, human persons possess it, excluding corporations and other institutions from asserting the right.[39] In many states, the

---

33. *See id.* § 6:2–6:3; *see also* JENNIFER E. ROTHMAN, ROTHMAN'S ROADMAP TO THE RIGHT OF PUBLICITY (2018), https://www.rightofpublicityroadmap.com/ (analysis of the right to publicity on a state-by-state basis) [hereinafter ROTHMAN].

34. *See* MCCARTHY ON PUBLICITY AND PRIVACY, *supra* note 3, § 6:2 (noting that in both states "a court expressly rejected the concept and held that a common law right of publicity does not exist in that state"); *see also* Carson v. Nat'l Bank of Commerce Tr. & Sav., 501 F.2d 1082, 1085–86 (8th Cir. 1974) (rejecting right of publicity in Nebraska).

35. *See* NEB. REV. STAT. § 20-201.

36. *See* MCCARTHY ON PUBLICITY AND PRIVACY, *supra* note 3, § 6:76 (noting the adoption of New York's privacy statute and continued rejection of common law right of publicity).

37. *See id.* § 4.16. Neither celebrity hubs New York nor California require the commercialization of identity for an individual to possess a protectable right of privacy. As one California Court of Appeals has observed, "California's appropriation statute is not limited to celebrity plaintiffs." KNB Enters. v. Matthews, 78 Cal. App. 4th 362, 367 (Ct. App. 2000).

38. *See* Sheldon W. Halpern, *The Right of Publicity: Maturation of an Independent Right Protecting the Associative Value of Personality*, 46 HASTINGS L.J. 853, 854, 856–58 (1995) (discussing celebrity personality commercial value); Sara J. Crasson, *The Limited Protections of Intellectual Property Law for the Variety Arts: Protecting Zacchini, Houdini, and Cirque Du Soleil*, 19 VILL. SPORTS & ENT. L.J. 73, 105 (2012) ("few variety artists have approached Vanna White's level of celebrity or notoriety, so it is unlikely many would achieve her level of protection" in a right of publicity claim).

39. *See* MCCARTHY ON PUBLICITY AND PRIVACY, *supra* note 3, § 4:40. Courts have found that musical groups have publicity rights. *See id.* § 4:41;

right survives the death of the individual for some number of years, although the precise length that such a right remains valid depends on which state's law applies. For example, Tennessee recognizes the right for ten years after death; Virginia for twenty years; Florida for forty years; Kentucky, Nevada, and Texas for fifty years; California for seventy years; Washington for seventy-five years; and Oklahoma for one-hundred years.[40]

The right of publicity first came into its own in the 1950s, during the golden age of film and television. Now, in the twenty-first century, as the use of social media (both by consumers and marketers) continues to expand and develop, one can predict that new layers of complexity will be added to right of publicity law. In particular, as technology advances, it is likely that society's definition of "celebrity" will continue to evolve as brands develop new ways to use celebrity and other personal likenesses to endorse goods and services, whether via Twitter handle, YouTube channel, or Pinterest "pin." As a result, it continues to be extremely important to consider the different ways that a company could run afoul of a state's right of publicity law.

The three states with the most developed body of right of publicity law are California, New York, and Indiana. A brief outline of each state's developments in right of publicity follows.

§ 18:4 Leading Examples of State Right of Publicity Law

§ 18:4.1 California

California, home to numerous celebrities and the lion's share of U.S. television and movie production, has long served as an aggressive advocate of the right of publicity. In 1971, California codified the right of publicity in California Civil Code section 3344:

> Any person who knowingly uses another's name, voice, signature, photograph, or likeness, in any manner, on or in products, merchandise, or goods, or for purposes of advertising or selling, or soliciting purchases of, products, merchandise, goods or services, without such person's prior consent, or, in the case of a minor, the prior consent of his parent or legal guardian, shall be liable for any damages sustained by the person or persons injured as a result thereof . . . .

---

see also, e.g., Brockum Co., a Div. of Krimson Corp. v. Blaylock, 729 F. Supp. 438, 446 (E.D. Pa. 1990).

40. *See generally* MCCARTHY ON PUBLICITY AND PRIVACY, *supra* note 3, § 9.

> As used in this section, "photograph" means any photograph or photographic reproduction, still or moving, or any videotape or live television transmission, of any person, such that the person is readily identifiable.[41]

California extended the right to deceased personalities via the enactment of section 990 of the California Civil Code in 1995. This provides heirs the right to protect the publicity value of a deceased individual for fifty years following that person's death. In 1999, section 990 was renamed section 3344.1 to immediately follow the state's right of publicity statute.[42]

The California Supreme Court recognized an additional common law right of publicity in 1979.[43] Prior to that addition, the plaintiff could establish a right of publicity claim under California common law by alleging "(1) the defendant's use of the plaintiff's identity; (2) the appropriation of plaintiff's name or likeness to defendant's advantage, commercially or otherwise; (3) lack of consent; and (4) resulting injury."[44] The statutory right of publicity contained in section 3344 of the California Civil Code, in contrast, requires two additional elements: knowing use of the plaintiff's identity for advertising or solicitation of purchases; and direct connection between the use and the commercial purpose.[45] This dual statutory and common law protection makes the right of publicity afforded to residents of California broader than that offered by the laws of most states.

---

41. CAL. CIV. CODE § 3344.
42. CAL. CIV. CODE § 3344.1.
43. *See* companion cases Lugosi v. Universal Pictures, 603 P.2d 425, 428 n.6 (Cal. 1979); Guglielmi v. Spelling-Goldberg Prods., 603 P.2d 454, 454 (Cal. 1979).
44. Eastwood v. Super. Ct., 149 Cal. App. 3d 409, 417–18 (Ct. App. 1983).
45. *See* CAL. CIV. CODE § 3344(a) (outlining knowledge requirements); CAL. CIV. CODE § 3344(e) (requiring commercial use for claim to be actionable); *see also Eastwood*, 149 Cal. App. 3d at 417 (noting additional elements of statutory right); Michaels v. Internet Entm't Grp., Inc., 5 F. Supp. 2d 823, 837 (C.D. Cal. 1998). In *Eastwood*, the court held that the second element was "[t]he appropriation of the plaintiff's name or likeness for the defendant's advantage." *Eastwood*, 149 Cal. App. 3d at 417. Further, the second element at common law affords broader protection than the California statute because the former requires appropriation of the plaintiff's identity for the defendant's "advantage," whether commercial or otherwise, whereas § 3344(a) requires appropriation for commercial purposes only, that is, for the purposes of advertising or selling, or soliciting purchases of products, merchandise, goods or services. *See id.* (discussing scope of common law right of publicity).

The common view in California is that the right of publicity is assignable, and one appellate court has directly held that the right is assignable.[46]

Although the right has traditionally been understood to apply only to the use of a person's name or likeness, California courts have interpreted the state's right of publicity also to apply to uses of an individual's overall identity, beyond the simple use of a person's name or likeness, under appropriate circumstances.[47]

For example, in *Motschenbacher v. R.J. Reynolds Tobacco Co.*,[48] a famous race car driver sued R.J. Reynolds for misappropriation of his name, likeness, personality, and endorsement after the company used a picture of Motschenbacher's distinctively decorated race car in an advertisement for cigarettes.[49] Although Motschenbacher was not identifiable in the photograph, and the car's number had been changed, the Ninth Circuit held that Motschenbacher created at least an issue of fact as to whether his "likeness" was identifiable to consumers through the use of the markings on his car.[50] Arguably, such reasoning could be applied to items sold in the fashion industry whose work may be identifiable to consumers even when the names or images of specific designers are not used.

Another example of the extensive application of California's right of publicity law can be found in *Midler v. Ford Motor Co.*[51] In *Midler*, an advertiser sought Bette Midler's voice for a car advertisement. After she declined, Ford hired an impersonator to duplicate Midler's vocal style.[52] The Ninth Circuit held that an identifiable voice, much like a name or likeness, constitutes part of a celebrity's commercial identity and is thus protected within the purview of the right of publicity.[53]

In *White v. Samsung Electronics America, Inc.*,[54] Samsung created a 1992 ad campaign projecting the continued viability of their products in the future. In one scene, a robot was portrayed turning letters on a large light board while wearing a ball gown in an imitation of

---

46. *See* Timed Out, LLC v. Youabian, Inc., 229 Cal. App. 4th 1001, 1008 (Ct. App. 2014).
47. *See, e.g.*, White v. Samsung Elecs. Am., Inc., 971 F.2d 1395, 1397–99 (9th Cir. 1992), *cert. denied*, 508 U.S. 951 (1993).
48. Motschenbacher v. R.J. Reynolds Tobacco Co., 498 F.2d 821 (9th Cir. 1974).
49. *Id.* at 822.
50. *Id.* at 827.
51. Midler v. Ford Motor Co., 849 F.2d 460 (9th Cir. 1988).
52. *Id.*
53. *Id.*; *see also* Waits v. Frito-Lay, Inc., 978 F.2d 1093 (9th Cir. 1992) (holding that Frito-Lay violated the publicity rights of singer Tom Waits by hiring a voice impersonator to record a commercial for tortilla chips).
54. White v. Samsung Elecs. Am., Inc., 971 F.2d 1395 (9th Cir. 1992).

Vanna White's role on the popular game show "Wheel of Fortune." While the Ninth Circuit dismissed White's statutory claims, determining that the mechanical features of the robot did not equal White's "likeness" within the meaning of section 3344,[55] it found that White had created an actionable issue of fact as to whether Samsung had violated her common law right of publicity.[56] Determining that the common law right of publicity extended beyond section 3344's definition of "likeness," the Ninth Circuit held that White was entitled to argue to a jury that her common law right of publicity had been violated.[57] The Ninth Circuit refused to rehear the case *en banc*, but Judge Alex Kozinski authored a strongly worded dissent, arguing that the majority approach did not give sufficient credit to the defenses of fair use and parody, applicable in the trademark and copyright context.[58] Judge Kozinski's dissent continues to influence the debate on the appropriate extent of California's common law right of publicity.[59]

On top of this debate on the extent of California's right of publicity, courts often struggle with the factual inquiry into the value of right of publicity claims under California law. Indeed, relatively few right of publicity cases have reached a final adjudication as to damages, because so many of these cases settle under undisclosed terms long before reaching trial. In 2011, for example, reality television star Kim Kardashian filed suit in California against Old Navy's parent company, The Gap, Inc., alleging that Old Navy had deliberately infringed upon her public persona by using a look-alike model to deceive consumers into thinking that Kardashian had appeared in their commercials.[60] Kardashian brought claims under California's common law and statutory law, seeking $20 million in damages.[61] But the claims were settled in 2012 pursuant to a confidential settlement agreement.[62]

§ 18:4.2 New York

Although New York was an early frontrunner in the establishment of publicity rights, the state's current recognition of the right

---

55. *Id.* at 1397.
56. *Id.* at 1399.
57. *Id.* The court noted that "[i]t is not important *how* the defendant has appropriated the plaintiff's identity, but *whether* the defendant has done so." *Id.* at 1398 (emphases in original).
58. White v. Samsung Elecs. Am., Inc., 989 F.2d 1512 (9th Cir. 1993).
59. *See, e.g.*, MCCARTHY ON PUBLICITY AND PRIVACY, *supra* note 3, at app. A.
60. Kardashian v. The Gap, Inc., No. 2:11-cv-06568 (C.D. Cal. filed Aug. 10, 2011).
61. *Id.*
62. *Id.*

of publicity is anchored to the state's privacy statute rather than a separate cause of action.[63]

In 1903, New York was the first state to provide statutory protection for the right of privacy.[64] Unlike a majority of jurisdictions, New York does not recognize a distinct common law right of privacy[65] or publicity;[66] nor has it created a separate statutory right of publicity.[67] The New York privacy statute, codified at sections 50 and 51 of New York Civil Rights Law, provides the only commercial protection for the name and likeness of a living person.[68]

Section 50 of the Civil Rights Law provides:

> A person, firm or corporation that uses for advertising purposes, or for the purposes of trade, the name, portrait or picture of any living person without having first obtained the written consent of such person, or if a minor of his or her parent or guardian, is guilty of a misdemeanor.[69]

---

63. *See, e.g.*, John C. Fuller, *Like a Candle in the Wind:* Shaw Family Archives, Ltd. v. CMG Worldwide, Inc. *and the Flickering Recognition of Marilyn Monroe's Right of Publicity in New York*, 15 VILL. SPORTS & ENT. L.J. 299, 312 (2008) [hereinafter Fuller].

64. N.Y. CIV. RIGHTS LAW §§ 50–51.

65. *See* Roberson v. Rochester Folding Box Co., 171 N.Y. 538, 536 (1902).

66. *See* Stephano v. News Grp. Publ'ns, Inc., 474 N.E.2d 580, 583–84 (N.Y. 1984). Although the Second Circuit first coined the phrase "right of publicity," New York's recognition of a separate right of publicity ended in 1984 with *Stephano*. In *Stephano*, the court of appeals rejected the notion that a separate right of publicity exists, holding that such right is "encompassed under the Civil Rights Law as an aspect of the right of privacy." *Id.* at 584.

67. *See* MCCARTHY ON PUBLICITY AND PRIVACY, *supra* note 3, § 6:76 (noting the adoption of New York's privacy statute and continued rejection of common law right of publicity); *see also* Ryan v. Volpone Stamp Co., 107 F. Supp. 2d 369, 391 (S.D.N.Y. 2000) (stating that New York has not created a statutory right of publicity); *but see* Andrew Denney, *"Right To Publicity" Bills in NY Legislature Stir Free Speech, Liability Concerns*, N.Y. L.J. (Mar. 22, 2018) [hereinafter Denney], https://www.law.com/newyork lawjournal/2018/03/22/right-to-publicity-bills-in-ny-legislature-stir-free-speech-liability-concerns/ (stating that bills pending in both the state Assembly and the state Senate would create a statutory right to publicity if passed).

68. *See* Pirone v. MacMillan, Inc., 894 F.2d 579, 585–86 (2d Cir. 1990) (affirming that "the state statutory provisions concerning a right of publicity are exclusive," and thus the Civil Rights Law clearly "preempts any common law right of publicity action").

69. N.Y. CIV. RIGHTS LAW § 50.

Section 51 of the statute "consists of only two elements: the commercial use of a person's name or photograph and the failure to procure the person's written consent for such use."[70] Section 51 provides:

> Any person whose name, portrait, picture or voice is used within this state for advertising purposes or for the purposes of trade without the written consent first obtained as above provided may maintain an equitable action in the supreme court of this state against the person, form or corporation so using his name, portrait, picture or voice, to prevent and restrain the use thereof; and may also sue and recover damages for any injuries sustained by reason of such use and if the defendant shall have knowingly used such person's name, portrait, picture or voice in such manner as is forbidden or declared to be unlawful by section fifty of this article, the jury, in its discretion, may award exemplary damages.[71]

New York's statutes apply "to any use of a person's picture or portrait for advertising or trade purposes" without prior authorization.[72] Unlike California, Indiana, and numerous other jurisdictions, New York does not recognize a post-mortem right of publicity, meaning that the right does not survive the death of an individual and cannot be assigned to pass on after the death of that individual.[73] It is

---

70. Shamsky v. Garan, Inc., 167 Misc. 2d 149, 154 (Sup. Ct. N.Y. Cty. 1995).

71. N.Y. Civ. Rights Law § 51.

72. Stephano v. News Grp. Publ'ns, Inc., 474 N.E.2d 580, 584 (N.Y. 1984). While the court in *Stephano* recognized that such a violated privacy right may "more accurately be described as a right of publicity," the court held that such right falls under the right of privacy and preempts any cause of action under an "independent common-law right of publicity." *Id.*

73. *See* Shaw Family Archives Ltd. v. CMG Worldwide, Inc., 486 F. Supp. 2d 309, 314 (S.D.N.Y. 2007). *Shaw* concerned the estate of deceased actress Marilyn Monroe, who died in California in 1962. The court held that, because Monroe died before California enacted its Celebrity Rights Act in 1985 and New York did not recognize a descendible right of publicity, Monroe's name, image, and voice were in the public domain in California and New York. *Id.* Thus, by implication, her name, image, and voice would also be in the public domain in any state that, at the time of Monroe's death, did not recognize a descendible right of publicity. *Id.* Following the court's ruling, California passed legislation that created descendible rights of publicity for 70 years after death of the celebrity. *See* Cal. Civ. Code § 3344.1; McCarthy on Publicity and Privacy, *supra* note 3, § 9:22 (tracing the history of California's publicity statute). A similar bill in the New York state legislature failed. *See* Fuller, *supra* note 63, at 331. However, pending bills in the New York state legislature would create a descendible right of publicity if they are passed. *See* Denney, *supra* note 67.

generally understood, however, that individuals in New York may assign their publicity rights to another individual during their life.[74]

Similarly, New York also has not been as assertive as states like California in expanding the protections to characteristics that may identify an individual above and beyond his or her name, likeness, and voice.

For example, in the 1920 case *Pfaudler v. Pfaudler Co.*, the Appellate Division of the New York Supreme Court held that "name" for purposes of the statute means a person's full legal name.[75] Traditionally, New York courts in similar cases had found that a "name" does not encompass an individual's nickname, stage name, or any unique name belonging to a plaintiff.[76] The current consensus of New York courts, however, is that the right of publicity *can*, in appropriate circumstances, apply to nicknames and phonetically similar names. In 1978, Muhammad Ali successfully showed that a caricature of an African-American boxer with the phrase "the Greatest" in *Playgirl Magazine* evoked his identity, even though the image did not use his name.[77]

If a likeness gets close enough to an actual celebrity image, New York courts may also find a violation of the statute.[78] For example, in

---

74. *See* Haelan Labs., Inc. v. Topps Chewing Gum, Inc., 202 F.2d 866, 868 (2d Cir. 1953) ("[the] right of publicity would usually yield [the holder] no money unless it could be made the subject of an exclusive grant"); Cory v. Nintendo of Am., Inc., 592 N.Y.S.2d 6, 8 (App. Div. 1993) (denying model's right of publicity claim because his publicity rights had been assigned to his agent, who authorized use of his image in challenged video game); Ippolito v. Ono-Lennon, 526 N.Y.S.2d 877, 879 (Sup. Ct. 1988) (suggesting that rights under N.Y. Civil Rights Law §§ 50–51 can be "assigned" or "sold").

75. *See* Pfaudler v. Pfaudler Co., 186 N.Y.S. 725, 726 (App. Div. 1920) (interpreting definition of "name" in N.Y. CIV. RIGHTS LAW §§ 50–51).

76. *See* Davis v. R.K.O. Pictures, 16 F. Supp. 195, 196 (S.D.N.Y. 1936) (holding that §§ 50–51 "do not apply to any assumed or 'stage name' of the plaintiff"); Geisel v. Poynter Prods., 295 F. Supp. 331, 356 (S.D.N.Y. 1968) (holding that "the name 'Dr. Seuss' is an assumed name or pseudonym rather than a surname and is, therefore, not a protectable 'name' within the meaning of Section 51 of the New York Civil Rights Law"); Nebb v. Bell Syndicate, 41 F. Supp. 929, 930 (S.D.N.Y. 1941) (concluding that defendant comic strip publishers who called a fictitious characters "Rudy Nebb" had never heard of plaintiff Rudy Nebb, had no intention of referencing plaintiff, and holding that use of the same name as plaintiff, without knowledge or intent, was not sufficient to violate sections 50 and 51).

77. *See* Ali v. Playgirl, Inc., 447 F. Supp. 723, 726–27 (S.D.N.Y. 1978).

78. *See* Young v. Greneker Studios, Inc., 26 N.Y.S.2d 357, 358 (App. Div. 1941) (holding the use of a mannequin made in the plaintiff's likeness may constitute a "portrait" or "picture" for purposes of sections 50 and 51).

2018, the Court of Appeals of New York held that a video game avatar may qualify as a "portrait" for purposes of the statute.[79] A use of a "look-alike" can similarly violate the statute.[80] In *Onassis v. Christian Dior-New York, Inc.*,[81] Jacqueline Kennedy-Onassis sued the fashion house for infringement of sections 50 and 51 after defendant ran an advertisement featuring a model with a striking resemblance to the former First Lady, causing her to be identified with the brand. The New York Supreme Court held that a look-alike can constitute a "portrait" or "picture" where the overall impression created clearly was the plaintiff had herself appeared in the advertisement.[82]

Celebrities have also brought "right of publicity" actions in New York courts based on even more unusual and tenuous interpretations of the concept of their respective "likenesses," often settling for undisclosed amounts before the cases reach trial. In 2010, Lindsay Lohan settled with E-Trade Financial Corporation after the actress, who had been the subject of sustained news coverage related to allegations of drug use and driving under the influence, claimed that E-Trade was referencing her in a Super Bowl ad in which babies discuss a "milkaholic" named Lindsay.[83] While it is uncertain whether Ms. Lohan would have prevailed at trial, her case nonetheless serves as a reminder to companies of the risks of litigation when making a reference that may be attributable to a celebrity likeness.

§ 18:4.3 Indiana

Although not as large of a center for the entertainment industry as California and New York, Indiana has what is considered one of the most protective right of publicity statutes in the country.[84]

---

79. *See* Lohan v. Take-Two Interactive Software, Inc., 73 N.Y.S.3d 780, 785–86 (2018) (holding that "a graphical representation in a video game or like media may constitute a 'portrait' within the meaning of [sections 50 and 51]").

80. *See* Allen v. Nat'l Video, Inc., 610 F. Supp. 612, 626 (S.D.N.Y. 1985); *see also* Ali v. Playgirl, Inc., 447 F. Supp. 723, 726 (S.D.N.Y. 1978) (holding that "portrait" or "picture" extends beyond photographs to "representations which are recognizable as likenesses").

81. Onassis v. Christian Dior-N.Y., Inc., 472 N.Y.S.2d 254 (Sup. Ct. 1983).

82. *Id.* at 261–62.

83. *See Lohan Satisfied After Settling NYC E-Trade Lawsuit*, WASH. TIMES, Sept. 21, 2010.

84. *See* Erik W. Kahn, *"Delebs" and Postmortem Right of Publicity*, LANDSLIDE (Jan./Feb. 2016), https://www.americanbar.org/groups/intellectual_property_law/publications/landslide/2015-16/january-february/delebs_and_postmortem_right_publicity/ [hereinafter Kahn].

In 1994, the Indiana state legislature enacted Indiana's Right of Publicity law,[85] which broadly protects "name; voice; signature; photograph; image; likeness; distinctive appearance; gestures; or mannerisms"[86] and states that "[t]he rights recognized under this chapter are property rights, freely transferable and descendible, in whole or in part . . . ."[87] Transfer of these rights may occur "by contract, license, gift, trust, testamentary document and [by] operation of the laws of in testate succession applicable to the state administering the estate and property of an intestate deceased personality, regardless of whether the state recognizes the property rights set forth under this chapter."[88] Further, Indiana's statute is "supplemental to any other rights and remedies provided by law,"[89] meaning that the statute supplements, rather than replaces, any common law right of publicity that may exist in the state.[90] Indiana's statute also provides for the longest post-mortem publicity rights in the country, extending one-hundred years after the date of the individual's death.[91]

On its face, moreover, Indiana's statute applies to acts within the state "regardless of a personality's domicile, residence, or citizenship."[92] This provision has an inherent tension with the general rule that the law of the state in which the deceased was domiciled at the time of death controls whether a descendible right of publicity exists in the deceased's estate. But the full effect of the Indiana provision on this general rule has not been determined.[93]

Notably, Indiana is home to CMG Worldwide, a company that has represented the estates of popular deceased celebrities in the entertainment, sports, cultural, and musical fields, including Jackie Robinson, Amelia Earhart, Jerry Garcia, Aaliyah, and James Dean.[94] CMG Worldwide's presence in Indiana has led to notable cases interpreting Indiana's statute.

In 2005, for example, Marilyn Monroe, LLC (MMLLC), a Delaware company established to control the intellectual property assets of the residuary beneficiaries of Monroe's will, and its licensing agent, CMG Worldwide, filed suit against the Shaw Family Archives Ltd. (SFA) in

---

85. IND. CODE ANN. §§ 32-36-1-1 through 32-36-1-20.
86. IND. CODE ANN. § 32-36-1-6.
87. IND. CODE ANN. § 32-36-1-16.
88. *Id.*
89. IND. CODE ANN. § 32-36-1-20.
90. *See* ROTHMAN, *supra* note 33.
91. IND. CODE ANN. § 32-36-1-8.
92. IND. CODE ANN. § 32-36-1-1(a).
93. *See* Shaw Family Archives Ltd. v. CMG Worldwide, Inc., 486 F. Supp. 2d 309, 318 (S.D.N.Y. 2007); *see also* Kahn, *supra* note 84.
94. *See* CMG WORLDWIDE, CLIENTS, https://www.cmgworldwide.com/clients/.

the United States District Court for the Southern District of Indiana, claiming that SFA violated the Indiana Right of Publicity Act by using Monroe's "name, image, and likeness for commercial purposes without consent."[95] SFA, before being served in Indiana, filed a separate suit against MMLLC and CMG in the Southern District of New York, seeking a declaratory action regarding the post-mortem publicity rights of Monroe.[96] The two cases were consolidated in the Southern District of New York.[97] The federal court in New York applied Indiana law and held that an individual could not devise by will a property right that did not exist at the time of death; as such, the Indiana statute did not apply.[98] An Indiana court subsequently reached the same result, holding that Indiana's right of publicity law did not apply to individuals who died prior to its enactment in 1994.[99]

§ 18:5 Practical Implications for the Fashion Industry

The right of publicity arises most often in the fashion and retail industry in the context of models, celebrities, or fashion designers who believe a company has attempted to link their likeness to the company's brand without their permission. The failure to obtain appropriate permission can lead to lengthy and expensive litigation.

For example, the heirs of Humphrey Bogart threatened to bring suit against Burberry, Ltd. after the London-based fashion company licensed an image of Bogart wearing a Burberry trench coat in the final scene of "Casablanca."[100] Although Burberry had received a copyright license from the photo agency before using the photo, it had not received a license from Bogart's heirs, who held his right of publicity.[101] Burberry used the photo on its Facebook page in a timeline showing the influence of the brand in history, and included a caption explaining that the image was from the iconic 1940s film.[102] Rather

---

95. Shaw Family Archives Ltd. v. CMG Worldwide, Inc., 486 F. Supp. 2d 309, 310, 312 (S.D.N.Y. 2007).
96. *Id.* at 310.
97. *Id.* at 311. The court followed Indiana's "first-to-file" rule, which gave priority to the first-filed Indiana lawsuit. *Id.*
98. *Id.* at 319. The same decision was made as to the California post-mortem right of publicity statute. *Id.*
99. Dillinger, LLC v. Elec. Arts Inc., 795 F. Supp. 2d 829 (S.D. Ind. 2011) (holding that the Indiana Right of Publicity statute did not create a post-mortem right of publicity in the likeness of John Dillinger, an American gangster who died in 1934).
100. *See Bogart Heirs and Burberry at Odds Over Trench Coat Image*, L.A. TIMES, May 4, 2012, http://articles.latimes.com/2012/may/04/business/la-fi-burberry-bogart-20120504.
101. *Id.*
102. *Id.*

than wait to be sued, Burberry filed its own declaratory judgment action first in New York, alleging that Bogart's heirs were "attempting to exert and assert against Burberry rights which [they do] not possess" and asking the court to declare that Burberry's use of Bogart's name and image in social media didn't infringe Bogart Corp.'s trademark or rights of publicity.[103] Bogart's heirs then brought their own suit in California, alleging violation of Bogart's right of publicity and other intellectual property rights.[104] The cases were was settled under undisclosed terms in August 2012,[105] but they could have resulted in not only costly motion practice to determine the correct venue, but also extensive litigation, even if Burberry's view of the heir's rights was correct.[106]

It is also risky to put a celebrity's image or name on a piece of apparel itself without that celebrity's permission. For example, in 1990, the exclusive licensee of "The Rolling Stones" obtained a permanent injunction against a manufacturer who had used the musical group's name on T-shirts without a license, with the court finding in part that the manufacturer had infringed on the licensee's right of publicity.[107] And in 2013, actor Peter Fonda sued Dolce & Gabbana USA Inc. and Nordstrom Inc. in California, alleging that the companies

---

103. Burberry Ltd. v. Bogart LLC, No. 12-cv-03491 (complaint filed May 5, 2012, S.D.N.Y.).

104. Bogart LLC v. Burberry Grp. PLC, No. BC483967 (complaint filed May 7, 2012, Superior Court of California, Los Angeles County).

105. *See* Bill Doahue, *Burberry Makes Peace in Humphrey Bogart Image Battle* LAW360 (Aug. 1, 2012).

106. In another high-profile case involving right of publicity issues, Jemella Group Ltd. sued singer Katy Perry and her licensing company, Killer Queen, LLC, in 2013, after Perry had served as a paid endorser of Jemella's line of hair products. Jemella initially sought declaratory judgment that they had not violated an oral agreement to extend Perry's endorsement deal. Perry and Killer Queen filed counterclaims seeking more than $6.5 million in damages, alleging that Jemella had continued to use Perry's right of publicity without compensating her. *See* Aaron Taube, *Katy Perry Wants $6.5M From Hair Products Co. for Ad Deal*, LAW360 (Apr. 24, 2013); Jemella Grp. Ltd. v. Killer Queen, LLC, Complaint, No. 2:13-cv-02562-RGK-JCG (C.D. Cal. Apr. 11, 2013). The case settled under undisclosed terms months later, but the website TMZ reported that Ms. Perry received "a significant amount of money." *Katy Perry Scores Payday from Hair Company . . . Because She Deserves It*, TMZ.COM (July 8, 2013), http://www.tmz.com/2013/07/08/katy-perry-hair-company-lawsuit/.

107. Brockum Co., a Div. of Krimson Corp. v. Blaylock, 729 F. Supp. 438, 446 (E.D. Pa. 1990).

violated his right of publicity by selling men's T-shirts bearing his image.[108]

Because of these risks, it is undoubtedly important that companies try to acquire appropriate permissions from models, celebrities, and fashion designers before utilizing their likeness in any advertising, promotional, or apparel material. As Burberry's experience illustrates, moreover, when licensing a copyright to use a particular image, clearance of the appropriate right of publicity of any individuals depicted may be as important as the copyright itself, because copyright and right of publicity are independent causes of action. The most conservative course of action is to obtain right of publicity releases for *all individuals* appearing in *any* sort of media for the fashion brand, even if that individual is not a celebrity. There may, however, be circumstances where a person's participation in an event that is clearly and openly for promotional purposes may be held to imply consent for that person's image to be used in a subsequent promotional campaign.

Because right of publicity law varies from state to state, it is important for advertisers who publish or broadcast advertisements nationally across the United States to ensure that they have complied with the laws of states that afford the broadest protection to the right of publicity, such as California and Indiana.[109] Further, companies who plan to use celebrity images should ensure that their insurance carriers sufficiently cover right of publicity claims.[110]

---

108. Kira Lerner, *'Easy Rider' Star Sues D&G, Nordstrom for $3M Over T-Shirts*, LAW360 (July 22, 2013). Peter Fonda subsequently dismissed the lawsuit. Eriq Gardner, *Hollywood Docket: Peter Fonda Withdraws Lawsuit Against Dolce & Gabbana*, HOLLYWOOD REPORTER (July 3, 2014), https://www.hollywoodreporter.com/thr-esq/hollywood-docket-peter-fonda-withdraws-716698. More recently, a court in the United Kingdom found that the apparel store Topshop committed the tort of "passing off"—a common-law doctrine in the United Kingdom preventing a merchant from "passing off" its goods or services as those of another—by selling unauthorized T-shirts bearing singer Rihanna's image. Fenty v. Arcadia Grp. Brands Ltd., [2015] EWCA Civ 3, Case No. A3/2013/2087 & A3/2013/2955, decided Jan. 22, 2015.

109. *See generally* MCCARTHY ON PUBLICITY AND PRIVACY, *supra* note 3, § 6.

110. *See, e.g.*, OneBeacon Am. Ins. Co. v. Digital Projections, Inc., No. 13-cv-00559 (complaint filed Feb. 21, 2013, N.D. Ga.). In this insurance coverage dispute, Digital Projections sought insurance protection from OneBeacon after actors George Clooney and Julia Roberts brought a right of publicity claim based on alleged use of the celebrities' likenesses in advertising campaigns without their permission. OneBeacon argued that its insurance policies contained exclusions for personal and advertising injury arising out of the infringement of copyright, patent, trademark, secret or other intellectual property rights. *Id.* (The parties eventually stipulated to dismiss the case.)

The use of images in Internet, mobile communications, and social media campaigns, moreover, give these issues new salience. When fashion brands and retailers develop plans for utilizing social media, it is important to account for right of publicity issues. In *Cohen v. Facebook, Inc.*, Facebook defeated claims that its use of its users' profile images in the company's "Friend Finder" service violated the users' rights, because the plaintiffs could not show that the use had caused them any injury.[111] But under a different set of facts, a company that attempts to use social media users' images in a more blatantly commercial way may not be so fortunate.[112]

Fashion designers, in fact, may find right of publicity law to be a fertile area to explore in protecting their overall persona from being exploited by others, particularly where the consuming public identifies designers not by their image, but by the attributes of their original, recognizable designs or celebrity creators. As discussed in previous chapters, intellectual property protection that has been readily granted to painters, composers, musicians, and inventors in the context of copyrights and patents has been less well-developed, or even held to be unavailable, in the context of certain types of fashion designs. But it can be argued that, much like a singer's voice can be closely linked to her identity,[113] aspects of certain fashion designer's creations are identifiable as being the work of that particular designer. Although there is not a large body of case law recognizing causes of

---

111. Cohen v. Facebook, Inc., 798 F. Supp. 2d 1090, 1097 (N.D. Cal. 2011).

112. *See, e.g.*, Fraley v. Facebook, Inc., 830 F. Supp. 2d 785, 791–93, 803 (N.D. Cal. 2011) (refusing to dismiss right of publicity claims on an initial motion to dismiss where plaintiffs clicked the "Like" button on a company's Facebook page, and then each plaintiff's name and profile photograph bearing his likeness were subsequently featured, without his consent, in a Sponsored Story advertisement displayed to his Facebook friends). More recently, celebrities have been asserting right of publicity claims related to images they post of themselves on social media, where those images originally were taken by the paparazzi. Generally, these right of publicity claims follow copyright infringement claims that a paparazzo has threatened against the celebrity, and the celebrity responds by asserting their right of publicity in the paparazzo's image. *See, e.g.*, *Lawsuits Over Paparazzi Images on Instagram Raise Celebrity Questions Over Right of Publicity*, FASHION L. (Oct. 19, 2018), http://www.thefashionlaw.com/home/lawsuits-over-instagram-images-raise-celebrity-questions-over-right-of-publicity; Odell Beckham, Jr. v. Splash News & Picture Agency, LLC, No. 2:18-cv-01001 (E.D. La. filed Feb. 1, 2018).

113. *See* Midler v. Ford Motor Co., 849 F.2d 460, 463–64 (9th Cir. 1988).

action based on the misappropriation of a designer's right of publicity, companies would be wise to consider right of publicity issues before marketing products that arguably appropriate a famous designer's overall professional identity.

Moreover, if a fashion designer's name is used as a fashion brand, and the related trademarks that identify the brand to the public are owned by a company, issues may arise from the company's use of the fashion designer's likeness. The designer's likeness may be an important part of the company's marketing campaign for the brand. During the period that the fashion designer is employed by the company, the company's use of the designer's likeness is typically covered in the designer's employment agreement (and is typically subject to the designer's pre-approval). If the designer leaves the company and is no longer associated with it, however, the company should carefully consider the best way to address these issues in light of applicable state law.

Finally, even where there is no alleged infringement of a celebrity's right of publicity, companies should be careful to consider the practical risks of making even an approved use of a celebrity's right of publicity. For example, companies have frequently suffered public relations crises when a paid spokesperson is embroiled in scandal or altercations with the law.[114] In many cases, these risks may be mitigated by a so-called "morals clause" that allows the company to extricate itself from financial commitments and publicly disassociate itself from a celebrity in the event that he or she commits an act that attracts moral opprobrium. But because the company may nonetheless suffer continuing reputational damage, the preferred course is to use available sources of information to try in the first place to choose celebrity spokespeople unlikely to engage in behavior that the

---

114. For example, several fashion brands, including Burberry and H&M, dropped Kate Moss from their advertising campaigns after a U.K. tabloid ran photos of her using cocaine. *See* Guy Trebay & Eric Wilson, *Kate Moss Is Dismissed by H&M After a Furor Over Cocaine*, N.Y. TIMES (Sept. 21, 2005), https://www.nytimes.com/2005/09/21/business/media/kate-moss-is-dismissed-by-hm-after-a-furor-over-cocaine.html. More recently, sports brand Reebok dropped rapper Rick Ross after he released a song with controversial lyrics about women. *See* Lawrence Crook III, *Reebok Drops Rick Ross Over Lyric Apology Fallout*, CNN (Apr. 13, 2012), https://www.cnn.com/2013/04/11/showbiz/reebok-drops-rick-ross/index.html. And, in 2016, Nike dropped Manny Pacquiao after he made homophobic remarks. *See* Kurt Badenhausen, *Nike Drops Manny Pacquiao for a Second Time After Anti-Gay Remarks*, FORBES (Feb. 17, 2016), https://www.forbes.com/sites/kurtbadenhausen/2016/02/17/nike-drops-manny-pacquiao-for-a-second-time-after-anti-gay-comments.

company's customers may find distasteful. It is also important to thoroughly investigate the celebrity's other endorsement and design deals before launching an expensive campaign featuring that celebrity in order to make sure that the celebrity has no other commitments that could be inconsistent with the image the company wishes to project or otherwise lead to legal disputes.[115]

115. For example, see the discussion of the Macy's, Inc. dispute with J.C. Penney Company, Inc. over the interpretation of Martha Stewart's licensing agreements, discussed in *supra* chapter 10.

Chapter 19

Customs and International Trade Issues

§ 19:1 Introduction
§ 19:2 Importer Responsibilities
§ 19:2.1 Reasonable Care
[A] Generally
[B] Forced Labor
[C] Intellectual Property Rights
§ 19:2.2 Recordkeeping Requirements
§ 19:3 Entry of Merchandise
§ 19:4 Classification
§ 19:5 Valuation
§ 19:5.1 Assists
§ 19:5.2 Royalties
§ 19:5.3 Buying Agents
§ 19:5.4 Related Parties
§ 19:5.5 Alternative Means of Valuation
§ 19:5.6 Reconciliation
§ 19:6 Country of Origin Rules and Marking
§ 19:6.1 Non-Preferential Rules of Origin
§ 19:6.2 Textile and Apparel Rules of Origin
§ 19:6.3 Preferential Rules of Origin
§ 19:6.4 Country of Origin Marking
§ 19:7 Administrative Process
§ 19:8 Penalties and Enforcement of the Customs Laws
§ 19:8.1 Seizure and Forfeiture
§ 19:8.2 Monetary Penalties
Table 19-1 U.S. Customs and Border Protection Mitigation Guidelines Mitigation

§ 19:9 Exporting From the United States
§ 19:9.1 Economic Sanctions
§ 19:9.2 Export Controls
Appendix 19A Department of Homeland Security U.S. Customs and Border Protection: Entry Summary
Appendix 19B Sample Page from Harmonized Tariff Schedule of the United States (2013)

§ 19:1 Introduction

International trade in the fashion industry involves a complex web of connections among suppliers, agents, shippers, brokers, and buyers to facilitate the flow of goods across borders and around the world. Imports of textiles and apparel into the United States alone totaled approximately $106 billion in 2017.[1] For many fashion industry businesses, working effectively with foreign suppliers and managing legally compliant importing activities are critical elements of success.

Businesses operating in the fashion industry have long had to navigate an intricate network of laws and regulations associated with importing textiles or apparel products into the United States. For many years, the United States and many other countries negotiated and enforced bilateral quotas on imports of textile and apparel products. These quotas were governed by the rules of the Multifibre Arrangement (MFA).[2] The MFA represented a significant departure from the normal principle of non-discrimination among trading partners who were signatories to the General Agreement on Tariffs and Trade (GATT). After GATT was replaced by the World Trade Organization (WTO) in 1994, the MFA was replaced by a transitional WTO Agreement on Textiles and Clothing (ATC).[3] The ATC provided for a gradual elimination of import quotas on textile and apparel imports over a ten-year period ending in 2005. The ATC created special "safeguard" rules to deal with import surges and established a Textile Monitoring Body at the WTO to supervise and enforce the terms of the ATC. While imports of textile and apparel products

---

1. Annual data on imports of all textile and apparel products into the United States, as well as breakouts by country and product category, are available on the website of the Office of Textiles and Apparel (OTEXA), a unit of the International Trade Administration in the U.S. Department of Commerce. *See* OTEXA, TRADE DATA U.S. IMPORTS AND EXPORTS OF TEXTILES AND APPAREL, http://otexa.trade.gov/msrpoint.htm.
2. GATT, ARRANGEMENT REGARDING INTERNATIONAL TRADE IN TEXTILES, DEC. 20, 1973 (BISD 21st Supp. 1975).
3. Agreement on Textiles and Clothing, Marrakesh Agreement Establishing the World Trade Organization, Annex 1A, Apr. 15, 1994, 1868 U.N.T.S. 14.

into the United States are no longer subject to quota restrictions, the import duty rates applied to these items often remain significantly higher than those applied to other types of merchandise.

This chapter will introduce the basic requirements and obligations of U.S. fashion businesses with respect to importing goods into the United States. The chapter starts with an overview of the responsibilities placed on importers under the Customs Modernization Act. It then moves to a discussion of key customs issues involving declarations to the U.S. government of classification, valuation, and country of origin of imported goods, with a focus on issues of special importance to textile and apparel importers. Finally, the chapter concludes with a discussion of administrative processes and penalties for violations of U.S. customs laws, and a short introduction to the laws and regulations governing exports from the United States.

§ 19:2 Importer Responsibilities

U.S. import laws and regulations are administered by U.S. Customs and Border Protection ("CBP" or "Customs"), an agency within the Department of Homeland Security. CBP has a broad mandate to safeguard U.S. borders, and anti-terrorism and immigration law enforcement efforts are at the forefront of CBP's responsibilities. With respect to commercial trade, CBP regulates and facilitates the movement of commodities between the United States and its trading partners, and assesses and collects duties, taxes, and fees on imported merchandise. CBP operates twenty field offices that provide managerial oversight and communicate CBP policies and guidance to 328 different ports of entry into the United States.[4] The ports of entry are responsible for daily operations to process imports, collect duties, and inspect items arriving from overseas.

CBP orders its relationship with the importing community based on the two concepts of "shared responsibility" and "informed compliance." Under this model, CBP proactively communicates its requirements to importers, who in turn are responsible for ensuring that their activities are in compliance with customs laws and regulations. CBP conducts frequent seminars and other programs to provide information to the importing community, and also makes available a wide range of Informed Compliance publications on its website for guidance in specific importing areas.[5] CBP also maintains a publicly

---

4. U.S. Customs & Border Prot., Office of Field Operations Contact Numbers, https://www.cbp.gov/contact/cbp-hq/office-field-operations-contact-numbers.
5. These publications are maintained on the CBP website, https://www.cbp.gov/trade/rulings/informed-compliance-publications.

accessible database of ruling decisions on classification, valuation, and other issues relating to importing goods into the United States.[6]

§ 19:2.1 Reasonable Care

The Customs Modernization Act[7] places a fundamental duty on importers to exercise "reasonable care" in their importing operations. Specifically, under section 484 of the Tariff Act,[8] importers must use reasonable care to enter, classify, and determine the value of their imported merchandise, and to provide CBP with any other information necessary to enable CBP to properly assess duties, collect accurate statistics, and determine whether other applicable legal requirement, if any, have been met. The concept of reasonable care is not susceptible to a fixed definition. What activities will satisfy the obligation to exercise reasonable care will vary depending on the circumstances of particular import transactions.[9] At the heart of the reasonable care obligation, however, is that the importer must seek out the relevant facts relating to its imported merchandise so as to be able to make an accurate declaration to CBP. Turning a blind eye to the activities of foreign suppliers, even those outside the direct control of the importer, is inconsistent with the exercise of reasonable care.

[A] Generally

For a business involved in importing apparel from a foreign supplier, the exercise of reasonable care requires taking steps to ensure that accurate information is provided for key aspects of the import transaction—specifically, importers should ensure imports are properly described, classified, valued, and marked. The following list includes a number of basic questions that should be confirmed by an importer prior to the merchandise arriving in the United States:[10]

- Do you know how your merchandise was produced, from raw materials to finished goods, by whom and where?

---

6. The CBP database of ruling decisions is known as CROSS (Customs Rulings Online Search System), http://rulings.cbp.gov/.
7. Title VI of the North American Free Trade Area Implementation Act, Pub. L. No. 103-182, §§ 601-92, 107 Stat. 2057, 2170–2295 (1993).
8. Tariff Act of 1930, ch. 467, § 484, 46 Stat. 590, 722–24 (codified as amended at 19 U.S.C. § 1484).
9. U.S. CUSTOMS & BORDER PROT., WHAT EVERY MEMBER OF THE TRADE COMMUNITY SHOULD KNOW: REASONABLE CARE (AN INFORMED COMPLIANCE PUBLICATION) 7 (Sept. 2017), https://www.cbp.gov/sites/default/files/assets/documents/2018-Mar/icprescare2017revision.pdf [hereinafter CPB, WHAT EVERY MEMBER OF THE TRADE COMMUNITY SHOULD KNOW].
10. *Id.* at 8–12.

- Do you have an accurate description of the merchandise that can be used for customs entry documents?
- Have steps been taken to ensure that the merchandise is properly classified, including seeking a ruling from CBP in complex cases?
- Is the merchandise properly marked to show the country of origin?
- Do you have a full understanding of all costs and payments associated with the imported merchandise, including commissions, indirect payments, royalties, etc.?
- If the transaction is with a related party, is the invoice price "acceptable" for customs value?
- If the merchandise is entered under a conditionally free or reduced tariff rate program, do you have full supporting documentation to support the claim?

[B] Forced Labor

As a part of the fundamental duty of "reasonable care," importers are required to take reliable measures to ensure imports are not the product of forced labor.[11] Specifically, importers should establish reliable procedures to ensure they are not violating federal law prohibiting the importation into the United States of any goods "mined, produced, or manufactured wholly or in part in any foreign country" by either convict labor, forced labor, or indentured labor.[12] "Forced labor" is defined as "all work or service which is exacted from any person under the menace of penalty for its nonperformance and for which the worker does not offer himself voluntarily" including forced child labor.[13] The following list includes a number of questions that should be confirmed by an importer prior to the merchandise arriving in the United States to ensure they are not violating this law:[14]

- Do you know how your goods are made, from raw materials to finished goods, by whom, where, and under what conditions?
- Do you vet new suppliers/vendors for forced labor risks through questionnaires or some other means?
- Do your contracts with suppliers include terms prohibiting the use of forced labor?

---

11. *Id.* at 14–15.
12. 19 U.S.C. § 1307.
13. *Id.*
14. CPB, WHAT EVERY MEMBER OF THE TRADE COMMUNITY SHOULD KNOW, *supra* note 9, at 14–15.

- Have you established a reliable procedure of having a third-party auditor familiar with evaluating forced labor risks conduct periodic, unannounced audits of your supply chain for forced labor?

Although the forced labor import prohibition has been in place since 1930, it was rarely enforced because, prior to March 10, 2016, the prohibition did not apply to importation of goods made by forced labor if they were not produced in sufficient quantities domestically to meet U.S. consumptive demand.[15] Since the repeal of the consumptive demand exception, CBP has made forced labor import prohibition a top priority.[16] Thus, it is increasingly important that importers ensure they are taking reasonable care to ensure they are not importing goods produced by forced labor as part of the overall reasonable care obligation.[17]

[C] Intellectual Property Rights

Furthermore, importers are required to take reliable measures to determine whether imports are subject to trademark, copyright, or patent, and if so, to ensure imports are not violating intellectual property rights.[18] The following list includes a number of questions that should be confirmed by an importer prior to the merchandise arriving in the United States to ensure they are not violating intellectual property rights:

- If imports or packaging bears a trademark registered in the United States, have you established a reliable procedure to ensure that it is genuine and not restricted from importation

15. Tariff Act of 1930, ch. 497, § 509, 46 Stat. 590, 698, *repealed by* Trade Facilitation and Trade Enforcement Act of 2015, Pub. L. No. 114-125, 130 Stat. 122, 910. ("[I]n no case shall such provisions be applicable to goods, wares, articles, or merchandise so mined, produced, or manufactured which are not mined, produced, or manufactured in such quantities in the United States as to meet the consumptive demands of the United States.")
16. U.S. CUSTOMS & BORDER PROT., FORCED LABOR, https://www.cbp.gov/trade/trade-community/programs-outreach/convict-importations ("Repeal of the consumptive demand exception should enhance CBP's ability to prevent products made with forced labor from being imported into the United States.")
17. *Id.*
18. CPB, WHAT EVERY MEMBER OF THE TRADE COMMUNITY SHOULD KNOW, *supra* note 9, at 13.

under the gray-market or parallel import requirements of U.S. law[19] or that you have permission from the trademark holder to import such requirements?

- If imports or packaging consists of registered copyrighted material, have you established a reliable procedure to ensure that it is authorized and genuine?[20]
- If you are importing goods that have been refurbished or remanufactured, do you have documentation detailing the remanufacturing process?
- Have you established a reliable procedure to determine if the merchandise is subject to a U.S. International Trade Commission or court ordered exclusion?[21]

As these illustrative questions suggest, exercising reasonable care in importing requires a thorough understanding of the supply chain used to produce and deliver the merchandise. CBP has also noted that consultation with experts, such as legal counsel or customs brokers or consultants, is one way in which an importer can demonstrate fulfillment of his or her reasonable care obligation.

§ 19:2.2 Recordkeeping Requirements

Importers are required to maintain certain records relating to their entries of merchandise, which must be supplied to CBP upon demand. CBP has created a list of the required records (known as the "(a)(1)(A) list" after the paragraph of section 509 of the Tariff Act[22] referring to such records), which includes:

---

19. *See* 19 C.F.R. § 133.23 (2018) defining "gray-market articles" as those "bearing a genuine trademark or trade name identical with or substantially indistinguishable from one owned and recorded by a citizen of the United States . . . and imported without the authorization of the U.S. owner."
20. I 19 C.F.R. § 133.42 (2018) prohibiting the importation of "infringing copies" defined as "piratical articles" such that they are "copies . . . unlawfully made (without the authorization of the copyright owner)" and granting CBP enforcement authority.
21. *See* 19 U.S.C. §§ 1337(d) and (g) authorizing the International Trade Commission to issue exclusion orders directing CBP to prevent the infringing goods from entering the United States; for further discussion of the authority of the International Trade Commission to enforce trademark rights see *supra* section 2:9.5.
22. Tariff Act of 1930, ch. 497, § 509, 46 Stat. 590, 733 (codified as amended at 19 U.S.C. § 1509(a)(1)(A)).

1. General list of records required for most entries (including bill of lading or airway bill, declaration of entry, packing list, and bond information);
2. Records or information required (by 19 C.F.R. § 141.61) for completion of entry or entry summary documentation;
3. Records or information required for the entry of merchandise and required to be produced at the time the Customs Form 7501 is filed;
4. Documents/records or information required for entry of special categories of merchandise, including textile certificates of origin;
5. Other Federal and State agency or government documents;
6. Licenses, authorizations, and permits; and
7. Foreign Trade Zone documents.

The full (a)(1)(A) list of documents is included as an appendix to Part 163 of the CBP Regulations.[23] There are additional recordkeeping requirements that pertain to customs brokers and to any person who completes and signs a Certificate of Origin for goods exported to Canada or Mexico pursuant to the North American Free Trade Agreement (NAFTA).[24] In general, these records must be kept for five years from the date of entry, although certain exceptions apply.[25] Records must be kept in their original format unless the recordkeeper has adopted an alternative storage method that is commonly used in standard business practice (such as machine readable data or CD-ROM) and has notified CBP of its plans.[26]

The consequences of failing to maintain required entry records can be severe if a recordkeeper is unable to produce records in response to a demand from CBP. If the failure to produce is due to negligence, CBP

23. 19 C.F.R. pt. 163, app. (2018).
24. 19 C.F.R. § 163.2 (2018). Recordkeeping requirements for brokers are listed in 19 C.F.R. part 111, and NAFTA recordkeeping requirements in 19 C.F.R. part 181. In September 2018, the U.S., Mexican, and Canadian governments concluded an agreement to create a successor to NAFTA known as the United States—Mexico—Canada Agreement (USMCA). *See* OFFICE OF THE U.S. TRADE REP., NORTH AMERICAN FREE TRADE AGREEMENT (NAFTA), https://ustr.gov/trade-agreements/free-trade-agreements/united-states-mexico-canada-agreement. If Congress passes a bill to implement the USMCA, it will go into effect in 2020.
25. 19 C.F.R. § 163.4 (2018).
26. 19 C.F.R. § 163.5 (2018).

may assess an administrative penalty for each release of merchandise, not to exceed the lesser of 40% of the appraised value of the merchandise or $10,000.[27] In the case of a failure to produce records resulting from a willful failure to maintain, store, or retrieve a demanded record, the penalty is increased to an amount not to exceed $100,000 or 75% of the appraised value of the merchandise.[28] These penalties can be reduced or eliminated pursuant to CBP's mitigation authority. Penalties will not be assessed for a failure to turn over records that (i) have been destroyed through no fault of the recordkeeper (for example, in a natural disaster); (ii) have previously been supplied to CBP; (iii) if the recordkeeper is a participant in CBP's Recordkeeping Compliance Program and the failure is a first, non-intentional violation; or (iv) if the recordkeeper is otherwise able to substantially comply with the request.[29]

§ 19:3 Entry of Merchandise

Merchandise imported to the United States must be "entered" by filing paper or electronic documents with CBP. The first step in a formal entry[30] is to submit documentation showing that the merchandise can be released from CBP custody into the United States. These records typically include:

- a Customs Form 3461;
- a commercial (or pro forma) invoice;
- packing lists; and
- evidence of the right to make entry, such as a bill of lading.[31]

The entry must also show evidence that a bond has been posted with CBP to cover any potential duties or charges.[32] An importer may arrange for a bond with a U.S. surety company, or, if a customs broker is used to make entry, the broker may allow use of its bond to provide coverage. These documents to determine admissibility into the United States must be filed within fifteen calendar days of the date

---

27. 19 C.F.R. § 163.6(b)(1)(ii) (2018).
28. 19 C.F.R. § 163.6(b)(1)(i) (2018).
29. 19 C.F.R. § 163.6(b)(3) (2018).
30. Imports of merchandise valued at less than $2500 can usually be entered through informal entries, but the maximum value for informal entries is limited to $250 for textile and apparel products. 19 C.F.R. § 143.23 (2018).
31. 19 C.F.R. § 142.3(a) (2018).
32. 19 C.F.R. § 142.4 (2018).

that a shipment arrives at a U.S. port of entry.[33] If no entry documentation is filed within fifteen days, the merchandise may be placed in a warehouse at the importer's risk and expense, and is subject to sale at public auction (or destruction) after six months.[34]

After presentation of entry documents, a follow-up entry summary (Customs Form 7501, included as Appendix 19A) must be submitted within ten working days.[35] The entry summary contains the information necessary for CBP to assess duties and collect statistics, and must be submitted with a deposit of estimated duties.[36] After the entry summary is filed, CBP appraises and determines the classification of the merchandise.

CBP has broad authority to examine imported merchandise and documents to determine compliance with U.S. customs laws, including whether the value of goods has been properly declared, whether goods have been correctly invoiced, and whether the goods comply with country of origin labeling requirements. CBP also enforces a wide range of laws for other governmental agencies with respect to imported goods, such as flammability standards and labeling requirements for apparel for the Consumer Products Safety Commission, labeling requirements for textile fiber products, and "Made in America" marking requirements for the Federal Trade Commission.[37] For a further discussion of labeling requirements, see chapters 9 and 15.

Textile and apparel goods are considered "trade-sensitive" merchandise by CBP, so they are often subject to a higher percentage of examinations and audits than other types of goods. In addition, as discussed further above in chapters 2 and 3, CBP also enforces intellectual property laws and general exclusion orders of the International Trade Commission.

If CBP decides to examine merchandise, it must issue a notice of detention.[38] After the notice, CBP has thirty days to decide whether to release, seize, or deny entry of the merchandise. Imports of textiles and textile products entered into the United States are additionally subject to a 180-day "conditional release" period.[39] This means that

---

33. 19 C.F.R. §§ 141.5, 142.2(a) (2018).
34. 19 C.F.R. §§ 127.14(a)(2), 127.29 (2018). Port directors may require an importer to file an entry summary at the time of entry if there is a record of late or delinquent filing of entry summaries, or a record of unpaid customs bills. 19 C.F.R. § 142.13 (2018).
35. 19 C.F.R. § 142.12(b) (2018).
36. 19 C.F.R. § 142.12(c) (2018).
37. *See, e.g.*, U.S. CUSTOMS & BORDER PROT., SUMMARY OF LAWS ENFORCED BY CBP, https://www.cbp.gov/trade/rulings/summary-laws-enforced/us-code.
38. 19 C.F.R. § 151.16(c) (2018).
39. 19 C.F.R. § 141.113(b) (2018).

if CBP finds that the country of origin of the textile product was not accurately represented at entry, CBP may issue a notice for immediate redelivery of the merchandise to CBP custody. A failure to comply with this demand can result in the assessment of damages equal to the value of the merchandise involved.[40]

A CBP redelivery notice can create significant problems for importers of apparel, particularly if the demand arrives months after the import of the merchandise. By this time, the merchandise is likely to have already been sold and the importer may have no realistic means to regain custody of the merchandise. This circumstance is detailed at some length in *Essex Manufacturing, Inc. v. United States*,[41] which the U.S. Court of International Trade described as a "saga that highlights the risks and dangers that attend the many opportunities inherent in doing business in today's global economy." Essex imported a shipment of women's jackets allegedly produced in Mongolia. At the time, Mongolian jackets were not subject to import quotas in the United States, but Chinese-produced jackets were subject to quotas. CBP reviewed Essex's entry documentation, determined that the Mongolian certificate of origin supplied with the entry was not valid, and demanded that Essex redeliver the jackets into CBP's custody. By that time, however, Essex had already shipped the jackets to its customer, a major retailer, and had no means of complying with the demand. In rejecting Essex's challenges to CBP's redelivery notice, the Court observed that Essex "may indeed be the unwitting victim of deceit perpetrated by others somewhere 'upstream' in the supply chain." Because the regulation requiring redelivery is a "strict liability" provision, however, the result was that Essex was ordered to pay liquidated damages equal to the value of the imported merchandise despite having exercised reasonable care in its import operations.

§ 19:4 Classification

All merchandise that is entered into the United States must be "classified" in one of the provisions of the Harmonized Tariff Schedule of the United States (HTSUS).[42] The HTSUS is a comprehensive system of product classification consisting of ninety-nine chapters grouped into twenty-two different sections, with the two final chapters (chapters 98 and 99) used for special tariff programs and temporary duty provisions. Within each chapter, there are multiple product

---

40. *Id.*
41. Essex Mfg. v. United States, 27 C.I.T. 630 (Ct. Int'l Trade 2003).
42. The HTSUS is updated annually. The current version can be found on the website of the U.S. International Trade Commission, https://www.usitc.gov/tata/hts/index.htm.

headings and subheadings that provide increasingly specific descriptions of goods.

The HTSUS is organized by increasing degrees of complexity among chapters, beginning with crude and natural products, and continuing through advanced manufactured goods. Similarly, the product subheadings within individual chapters progress from more basic to more refined articles. The section of the HTSUS of greatest relevance to importers in the fashion industry is Section XI (including chapters 50 to 63), which covers "Textiles and Textile Articles." Within Section XI, two chapters are reserved for apparel and related goods: chapter 61 covers articles of apparel or clothing accessories that are knitted or crocheted, while chapter 62 covers apparel and clothing accessories that are not knitted or crocheted.

Individual product categories in the HTSUS are designated at increasing levels of specificity by four-digit, six-digit, and eight-digit code numbers. For example, a typical progression from a four-digit heading to an eight-digit subheading is as follows:

> 6105: Men's or boys' shirts, knitted or crocheted;
>
> 6105.20: Of man-made fibers;
>
> 6105.20.10: Containing 23 percent or more by weight of wool or fine animal hair.

The HTSUS also includes even more specific ten-digit codes, which are used for collection of statistical data, but are not considered part of the legal HTSUS classification. The HTSUS classification determines the duty rate to be applied to the imported merchandise. The rates of duty for each HTSUS subheading are listed in two columns, with Column 2 currently applicable only to imports from Cuba and North Korea. The Column 1 duty rates are divided into "General" rates reflecting normal duties, and "Special" lower rates reflecting the effect of bilateral trade agreements or other special duty programs. A sample HTSUS page is included as Appendix 19B. The importer has primary responsibility for correctly classifying his or her imported merchandise, which is subject to the "reasonable care" requirement described above.

The HTSUS is consistent with the Harmonized System, an agreed-upon framework adopted by most major trading nations for an internationally consistent system of classifying goods.[43] Under the

---

43. The Harmonized Commodity Description and Coding System (HS or "Harmonized System") is used by more than 200 countries as a framework for customs duties and for collection of trade statistics. *See* OFFICE OF U.S. TRADE REP., TARIFF SCHEDULES, https://ustr.gov/issue-areas/industry-manufacturing/industrial-tariffs/tariff-schedules.

Harmonized System, the tariff systems of participating countries are consistent through the six-digit classification level. This harmonized approach to tariff classification facilitates trade by minimizing the extent to which importers are confronted with multiple different systems for identifying and classifying merchandise in different countries. The Harmonized System is overseen by the World Customs Organization (WCO), which also publishes reference decisions interpreting the scope of the subheadings of the Harmonized System and the classification of particular merchandise.[44]

Needless to say, identifying the correct tariff provision for imported merchandise in the HTSUS can be extremely complex. This is particularly true for imported clothing and apparel, in which classification often turns on technical characteristics of the imported merchandise and for which the differences in duty rates between individual HTSUS provisions can be significant. One case litigated at the Court of International Trade, for example, involved the tariff classification of one style of UGG boots.[45] CBP successfully argued for classification in HTSUS 6404.19.35 as "footwear of the slip-on type, that is held to the foot without the use of laces or buckles or other fasteners," which carried a duty rate of 37%.[46] By contrast, the importer's proposed HTSUS classification of 6404.19.90, covering "other footwear" valued at more than $12 per pair, was dutiable at only a 9% rate.[47]

CBP has issued a publication that describes general principles for classifying apparel under the HTSUS and provides a glossary of commonly used terms.[48] In addition, there are a number of explanatory materials available that aid in interpreting the scope of particular HTSUS provisions. These materials include:

---

44. These activities are carried out by the WCO's Harmonized System Committee. Published decisions can be purchased at the following link: http://wcoomdpublications.org/.

45. Deckers Outdoor Corp. v. United States, 844 F. Supp. 2d 1324 (Ct. Int'l Trade 2012), *aff'd*, No. 2012-1411, 2013 U.S. App. LEXIS 9322 (Fed. Cir. May 8, 2013). In another case litigated at the Court of International Trade, CBP successfully argued for classification of children's clogs in HTSUS 6402.99.31 as "other footwear with outer soles and uppers of rubber or plastics," which carried a duty rate of 6%. By contrast, the importer's proposed HTSUS classification of 6402.99.80 as "waterproof footwear with outer soles and uppers of rubber or plastics," was duty free. LF USA, Inc. v. United States, 290 F. Supp. 3d 1339 (Ct. Int'l Trade 2017).

46. *Id.* at 1325.

47. *Id.* at 1326.

48. U.S. CUSTOMS & BORDER PROT., CLASSIFICATION: APPAREL TERMINOLOGY UNDER THE HTSUS (June 2008), https://www.cbp.gov/sites/default/files/assets/documents/2016-Apr/icp057_3.pdf [hereinafter CBP, CLASSIFICATION: APPAREL TERMINOLOGY].

- The General Notes to the HTSUS;
- The General Rules of Interpretation;
- The Additional U.S. Rules of Interpretation;
- Section and Chapter Notes to the HTSUS; and
- Additional U.S. Notes, which provide definitions or information on the scope of provisions.

In addition, the WCO publishes Explanatory Notes regarding the scope of each heading of the harmonized system at the international level.[49] These Explanatory Notes are not binding under U.S. law, but CBP considers them to be useful sources of guidance and as persuasive authority in interpreting the Harmonized System.[50]

§ 19:5 Valuation

All merchandise imported into the United States is appraised by CBP after the importer has declared the value of the goods in its entry documentation. The preferred means of appraisement is the transaction value of the goods, which is defined as the "price actually paid or payable" for merchandise sold for export to the United States, plus certain additions.[51] The price actually paid or payable is the total payment from the buyer to the seller for the imported merchandise, excluding international freight and insurance charges.[52] Payments may be either direct (that is, to the seller) or indirect (that is, to a third party on behalf of the seller). CBP takes the view that all payments from a buyer to a seller are presumptively part of the price actually paid or payable, unless the importer can show that the payments are "completely unrelated" to the imported merchandise.[53]

If not already included in the price, the following items must be added to the price actually paid or payable to determine transaction value: (i) packing costs incurred by the buyer; (ii) any selling commission paid by the buyer; (iii) the value of any "assist" provided directly or indirectly by the buyer, (iv) any royalty or license fee that the buyer

---

49. WORLD CUSTOMS ORG., EXPLANATORY NOTES TO THE HARMONIZED SYSTEM (6th ed. 2017).
50. CBP, CLASSIFICATION: APPAREL TERMINOLOGY, *supra* note 48.
51. 19 C.F.R. § 152.103(a) (2018).
52. CPB, WHAT EVERY MEMBER OF THE TRADE COMMUNITY SHOULD KNOW, *supra* note 9, at 8.
53. Generra Sportwear Co. v. United States, 905 F.2d 377 (Fed. Cir. 1990); Chrysler Corp. v. United States, 17 C.I.T. 1049 (Ct. Int'l Trade 1993).

is required to pay as a condition of the sale; and (v) the proceeds of any subsequent resale, disposal, or use of the imported merchandise that accrue to the seller.[54] Assists and royalties, in particular, are a recurring source of customs valuation issues for apparel importers.

§ 19:5.1 Assists

If a buyer provides a foreign assembler with bolts of fabric free of charge to produce clothing for importation to the United States, the value of that material is treated as an "assist" that must be included in the transaction value declared to Customs. Assists are defined to include (i) any materials, components, or parts included in the imported merchandise; (ii) tools, dies, or molds used to produce imported merchandise; or (iii) items consumed in producing the imported merchandise, when supplied directly or indirectly by the buyer, free of charge or at a reduced cost.[55] Drawings, sketches, and the like may also be treated as assists if performed outside of the United States and if necessary to production of the imported merchandise.[56] In the case of drawings, CBP does not generally consider "specification-type" drawings reflecting minor alterations of existing styles to be assists. In cases where a drawing reflects a unique style that could not otherwise be produced by the manufacturer, however, CBP has found the drawings to constitute assists.[57]

An assist can generally be valued at the cost of acquisition (if purchased) or the cost of production (if produced by the buyer or a related party), and reasonably apportioned over the production benefiting from the assist.[58] Assist valuation can also take into account normal depreciation and wear. For example, if used industrial sewing machines are provided to a supplier, the assist would be valued at the book value of the sewing machines rather than the cost of a new machine. In the context of apparel manufacturing, CBP also has determined that the value of bolts of fabric supplied as an assist includes the value of waste or scrap fabric because the waste fabric is "consumed in the production" of the imported merchandise despite not being physically incorporated in the final product.[59]

---

54. 19 C.F.R. § 152.103(b) (2018).
55. 19 C.F.R. § 152.102(a) (2018).
56. 19 C.F.R. § 52.102(a)(iv) (2018).
57. *See, e.g.*, HQ 548566 (Oct. 19, 2004) (explaining CBP approach to determining whether patterns provided to a foreign apparel manufacturer are dutiable assists).
58. 19 C.F.R. § 152.103(d)–(e) (2018).
59. *See, e.g.*, HQ 545909 (Nov. 30, 1995).

§ 19:5.2 Royalties

License fees or royalty payments relating to imported merchandise are dutiable (and must be included in transaction value) if the buyer must pay the license fee or royalty "as a condition of the sale of the imported merchandise for exportation to the United States."[60] Whether specific royalty payments are dutiable or not is assessed on a case-by-case basis. Over time, CBP has developed a three-part test for determining whether royalty payments or license fees are dutiable.[61] The test involves asking the following three questions:

1. Was the imported merchandise manufactured under patent?
2. Was the royalty involved in the production or sale of the imported merchandise?
3. Could the importer buy the product without paying the fee?

CBP views affirmative answers to the first two questions and a negative response to the third question as indicating that the royalty or license fee is a condition of sale and, therefore, dutiable. Of particular importance for the fashion industry, royalty payments or license fees for use of trademarks and copyrights in the United States typically are considered to be non-dutiable expenses of sale.[62] Conversely, royalties or license fees for patented manufacturing processes used to make the imported merchandise are generally treated as dutiable.[63]

§ 19:5.3 Buying Agents

Sourcing of apparel items from foreign countries often involves the use of buying agents, who provide services such as assisting in identifying manufacturers capable of meeting the importer's requirements, placing orders, negotiating prices, arranging for production and shipment of the merchandise, and assisting with returns of damaged or defective merchandise. Commissions paid to buying agents are not dutiable as long as the facts clearly show that the principal exercises control over the activities of the agent.[64] The factors that courts and CBP have considered in assessing the dutiability of commissions paid to alleged buying agents include:

---

60. 19 U.S.C. § 1401a(b)(1)(D).
61. 27 Cust. B. & Dec. No. 6, 1993 CUSBUL LEXIS 133, at *23–27 (Jan. 21, 1993) (*"Hasbro II"*).
62. 19 C.F.R. § 152.103(f) (2018).
63. *Id.*
64. *See, e.g.*, J.C. Penney Purchasing Corp. v. United States, 80 Cust. Ct. 84, 95, 451 F. Supp. 973, 983 (Cust. Ct. 1978).

- whether the principal has knowledge of the agent's activities and directs the agent;
- whether the buyer and foreign manufacturer are aware of each other (as opposed to communicating solely with the agent); and
- whether the agent has any financial interest in the manufacturer.[65]

To ensure that commissions paid to a buying agent will not be treated as dutiable, it is important to draft any agreement to demonstrate a *bona fide* agency agreement, making clear that the principal has the right to control the agent with respect to entrusted matters.[66]

§ 19:5.4 Related Parties

When a sale for exportation occurs between related parties, such as between parent and subsidiary corporations, the use of transaction value is subject to additional conditions to ensure that the value is "acceptable" for appraisement purposes.[67] Acceptability in this context turns on a showing that the relationship between the buyer and seller did not influence the price actually paid or payable, either through an examination of the circumstances of the sale or by a comparison to a "test value," such as the transaction value of identical or similar merchandise exported to the United States at around the same time as the imported merchandise.[68] If the transaction value cannot be shown as "acceptable," then an alternate valuation method must be used.

One leading case dealing with related party valuation issues is *VWP of America v. United States*,[69] which involved the appropriate transaction value for exports of woolen fabric for men's suits by a Canadian manufacturer, Victor Woolen Products, Ltd. (VWPC), to its U.S. sales subsidiary, Victor Woolen Products of America, Inc. (VWPA). CBP determined that the sale between VWPC and VWPA could not be

---

65. *See, e.g.*, HQ H125835 (May 18, 2011); HQ H098419 (Oct. 26, 2010); HQ 545422 (Mar. 13, 1995).
66. *See, e.g.*, Moss Mfg. Co. v. United States, 896 F.2d 535 (Fed. Cir. 1990) (emphasizing that buying agent has the burden of proving existence of a bona fide agency and that the charges paid were in fact bona fide buying commissions).
67. 19 C.F.R. § 152.103(j)(2) (2018).
68. CPB, WHAT EVERY MEMBER OF THE TRADE COMMUNITY SHOULD KNOW, *supra* note 9, at 10.
69. VWP of Am., Inc. v. United States, 175 F.3d 1327 (Fed. Cir. 1999).

used as transaction value, and instead valued the imported merchandise based on VWPA's resale price of the fabric to unrelated U.S. customers. VWPA protested CBP's decision, claiming that it had demonstrated that the sales price between the VWP companies "closely approximated" the transaction value of similar suits imported into the United States. The Court of Appeals for the Federal Circuit found that the sale between VWPC and VWPA was a *bona fide* sale that could be used as transaction value if the price closely approximated the transaction of similar merchandise imported around the same time, a factual question on which the Court expressed no opinion.[70] Following additional factual findings on remand, CBP ultimately determined that the sale price between VWPC and VWPA was not sufficiently close to the price of other similar, imported merchandise to be used as transaction value. CBP again determined to value the imported fabric based on the resale price between VWPA and its U.S. customers.[71] The case was ultimately settled after a subsequent appeal.[72]

§ 19:5.5 *Alternative Means of Valuation*

When the transaction value of imported merchandise cannot be determined for any reason, the valuation statute lists a number of alternative bases for valuing imported merchandise. The next basis for valuation is the transaction value of identical or similar merchandise imported to the United States at or about the same time as the merchandise being appraised.[73] The transaction value of identical or similar merchandise must be an appraised value previously accepted by Customs. The identical or similar merchandise must be produced in the same country and must be commercially interchangeable with the merchandise being appraised. Small differences in quantity, or sales at a different commercial level, can be used as long as adjustments are made to take account of any relevant differences.

The next alternative basis for valuation is called "deductive value," which is essentially the resale price of the merchandise in the United States after importation, with deductions for certain items.[74] Deductive value is generally calculated by starting with the selling price of the merchandise in the United States and making deductions to that price for items such as customs duties, selling expenses (for

---

70. *Id.*
71. VWP of Am., Inc. v. United States, 27 C.I.T. 434 (Ct. Int'l Trade 2003).
72. VWP of Am., Inc. v. United States, 30 C.I.T. 614 (Ct. Int'l Trade 2006).
73. 19 U.S.C. § 1401a(a)(1)(B)-(C); 19 C.F.R. § 152.104 (2013).
74. 19 U.S.C. § 1401a(a)(1)(D).

example, advertising costs), transportation, warehousing, and profit and general expenses.[75]

If neither transaction value nor deductive value can be used, the next alternative method of valuation is computed value.[76] Computed value is a cost-based valuation of the imported merchandise, consisting of the cost of materials, fabrication, and other processing used to produce the merchandise, with an addition for profit and general expenses.[77] Assists and packing costs must also be included in computed value. The cost amounts for materials, fabrication, and processing used to determine computed value are based on the regular business records of the producer of the merchandise, assuming that they are kept in conformance with generally accepted accounting standards. Similarly, the amount for profit and general expenses will be based on the producer's records so long as those amounts are consistent with those of other producers in the same country in producing goods of the same class or kind for export to the United States.[78]

If none of the preceding methods of valuation can be used to appraise the imported merchandise, the statute provides for use of a "fall back" method of valuation that must be derived from one of the other methods, adjusted as necessary.[79]

§ 19:5.6 Reconciliation

The information needed to appraise imported merchandise may not always be available at the time of importation. For example, the final price between the buyer and seller may still be under negotiation when the merchandise is imported, or in the case of deductive or computer value, the necessary records for valuation may not be available until some later time. CBP has developed a process called reconciliation, which allows importers to identify imported merchandise for which final information on valuation is not available at the time of import and to provide that information to CBP at a later date.[80] Importers must submit an application to CBP to participate in the

---

75. 19 C.F.R. § 152.105 (2018).
76. 19 U.S.C. § 1401a(a)(1)(E). The valuation statute also provides that importers may elect to reverse the normal order of priority to use computed value rather than deductive value as a basis for valuation. 19 U.S.C. § 1401a(a)(2).
77. 19 C.F.R. § 152.106 (2018).
78. 19 C.F.R. § 152.106(b)(2) (2018).
79. 19 U.S.C. § 1401a(f).
80. The CBP website maintains updated information on the operation of the reconciliation program. *See* U.S. CUSTOMS & BORDER PROT., WHAT IS RECONCILIATION?, https://www.cbp.gov/trade/entry-summary/reconciliation/reconciliation.

reconciliation program. When entries of imported merchandise are flagged for value reconciliation, the final valuation data must be submitted to CBP within twenty-one months.[81]

§ 19:6 Country of Origin Rules and Marking

Importers are required to declare the country of origin of merchandise they import into the United States. When an import supply chain involves multi-country sourcing of materials, or manufacturing activities taking place in different countries to produce an imported product, determining the correct country of origin for imported merchandise can be highly complex. Further complicating matters is that the United States does not use a single system for determining the country of origin of imported merchandise. Instead, there are (i) *non-preferential* rules of origin[82] applying to imported merchandise (other than textiles and apparel items) from countries with whom the United States maintains most-favored-nation trading status; (ii) a special set of non-preferential rules of origin applying exclusively to imports of *textile and apparel* products;[83] and (iii) *preferential* rules of origin used to determine eligibility under bilateral or regional free trade agreements or other special trade programs.[84] Additional complexity results from the fact that these different systems often apply widely divergent legal principles and rules for determining the origin of merchandise. In sum, rules of origin pose an unusual number of potential pitfalls for importers, particularly in the case of textile and apparel imports.

The determination of a product's country of origin can be significant because the United States is a party to several unilateral and multilateral free trade agreements, including but not limited to NAFTA and its planned successor agreement, the United States-Mexico-Canada Agreement (USMCA),[85] the Chile-United States Free

---

81. *See id.*
82. 19 C.F.R. § 102.11 (2018).
83. 19 U.S.C. § 3592.
84. VIVIAN JONES & MICHAEL MARTIN, CONG. RESEARCH SERV., INTERNATIONAL TRADE: RULES OF ORIGIN [hereinafter INT'L TRADE: RULES OF ORIGIN], at 4–5, https://digitalcommons.ilr.cornell.edu/cgi/viewcontent.cgi?article=1885&context=key_workplace.
85. *See* OFFICE OF THE U.S. TRADE REP., NORTH AMERICAN FREE TRADE AGREEMENT (NAFTA), https://ustr.gov/trade-agreements/free-trade-agreements/north-american-free-trade-agreement-nafta; OFFICE OF THE U.S. TRADE REP., UNITED STATES-MEXICO-CANADA AGREEMENT (USMCA), https://ustr.gov/trade-agreements/free-trade-agreements/united-states-mexico-canada-agreement. As of the date of this writing, the USMCA had not been ratified by the U.S. Congress.

Trade Agreement, and many others. Additional free trade agreements are almost always under consideration, if not subject to active negotiations. Depending on the terms of the particular free trade agreement, tariffs, quotas, and preferences on fashion-related goods may be eliminated or substantially reduced.[86]

As of 2019, the U.S. administration has signaled a preference for bilateral trade agreements over multilateral agreements.[87] Changes in these fair trade agreements have significant implications for the apparel and textile industry in particular. As the CBP notes on their website, the enforcement of Free Trade Agreements makes textiles a "politically sensitive industry" as the "average duty rate for textiles is 16% and more than $21.1 billion of entered textiles and wearing apparel claim preferential tariff treatment."[88] Thus, this evolving area continues to be watched closely by stakeholders due to the high-risks associated with renegotiated agreements and non-compliance enforcement.

§ 19:6.1 *Non-Preferential Rules of Origin*

The non-preferential rules of origin apply two major principles to determine the country of origin of imported merchandise. The first rule is straightforward: goods that are wholly the growth, product, or manufacture of a single country are attributed to that country.[89] In many cases, however, the "wholly obtained" rule will not be sufficient to determine the country of origin. In cases where the imported merchandise includes components from multiple countries, the country of origin is determined by identifying the last country in which the merchandise was "substantially transformed" into a new and different article of commerce from its constituent parts.[90] Application of the "substantial transformation" test is fact-specific and can be complex. Among the factors that CBP has relied upon in judging whether a substantial transformation has occurred are (i) whether the change in the article confers a new character, name, or use; (ii) the nature of the manufacturing process involved; (iii) the value added in the manufacturing process; and (iv) whether the essential character of the

---

86. *See* OFFICE OF THE U.S. TRADE REP., FREE TRADE AGREEMENTS, https://www.ustr.gov/trade-agreements/free-trade-agreements.

87. *See, e.g.*, Geoffrey Gertz, *What Will Trump's Embrace of Bilateralism Mean for America's Trade Partners*, BROOKINGS (Feb. 8, 2017), https://www.brookings.edu/blog/future-development/2017/02/08/what-will-trumps-embrace-of-bilateralism-mean-for-americas-trade-partners/.

88. U.S. CUSTOMS & BORDER PROT., PRIORITY TRADE ISSUES: TEXTILES, https://www.cbp.gov/trade/priority-issues/textiles.

89. 19 C.F.R. § 102.11 (2018).

90. 19 C.F.R. § 134.1(b) (2018).

imported merchandise is established by the manufacturing process or by the parts or materials used to make the article.[91]

§ 19:6.2 Textile and Apparel Rules of Origin

Special rules of origin apply principally to textile and apparel products classified in chapters 50 through 63 of the Harmonized Tariff System.[92] These rules generally determine the country of origin of textile and apparel items based on the location in which particular manufacturing or processing steps occur. Although the specific rules of origin are lengthy and complex, there are several general principles that are reflected in the rules:

- If a textile or apparel product is wholly obtained or produced in one country, that country will be the country of origin;[93]
- The country of origin of yarn, thread, and the like is the country in which the fibers are spun or extruded;[94]
- The country of origin of fabric is the country in which the fabric is formed by weaving, knitting, or any other fabric-making process;[95] and
- For most other textile and apparel products, where the article is assembled in a single country, that country is the country of origin.[96] This rule is subject to exceptions for knit-to-shape articles, in which the country of origin is the country in which major parts are knitted or crocheted to the shape used in the final product, and for a number of non-apparel textile items that are governed by special rules.[97]

There is also a special "multi-country rule" applicable to textile or apparel products created from processing in two or more countries where the country of origin cannot be determined from the preceding rules.[98] Under the multi-country rule, the country of origin is

91. U.S. INT'L TRADE COMM'N, COUNTRY OF ORIGIN MARKING: REVIEW OF LAWS, REGULATIONS, AND PRACTICES, USITC Pub. 2975, at 2-4, 2-5 (July 1996), https://www.usitc.gov/publications/332/pub2975.pdf.
92. 19 C.F.R. § 102.21 (2018).
93. 19 U.S.C. § 3592(b)(1)(A).
94. 19 U.S.C. § 3592(b)(1)(B).
95. 19 U.S.C. § 3592(b)(1)(C).
96. 19 U.S.C. § 3592(b)(1)(D).
97. 19 U.S.C. § 3592(b)(2).
98. U.S. CUSTOMS & BORDER PROT., WHAT EVERY MEMBER OF THE TRADE COMMUNITY SHOULD KNOW ABOUT: TEXTILE AND APPAREL RULES OF ORIGIN 12–13 (Apr. 2004), https://www.cbp.gov/sites/default/files/assets/documents/2016-Apr/icp006r3_3.pdf.

the country in which the most important assembly or manufacturing process occurs.[99] If the "most important" assembly or manufacturing process cannot be determined, then the country of origin is the last country in which an important manufacturing or assembly step occurred.[100]

§ 19:6.3 Preferential Rules of Origin

As discussed earlier, free trade agreements and a variety of other special trade programs include preferential rules of origin to determine whether imported goods qualify for entry into the United States at free or reduced rates of duty. The specific rules of origin vary by agreement, but typically are more difficult to satisfy than non-preferential rules of origin. For example, the NAFTA and its planned successor agreement, the USMCA,[101] rules of origin require that a product undergo a specified tariff shift (from one Harmonized Tariff Schedule heading to another) and may also require the product to meet a regional value content requirement in order to qualify for preferential treatment.[102] Most free trade agreements and special trade programs also include special rules of origin for textile and apparel products. While the terms of individual agreements vary, the United States generally has applied a "yarn forward" standard for the country of origin for textiles and apparel.[103] Under this standard, fibers may be produced in any country, but the yarn used to make the textiles or apparel must be formed within the free trade area in order to qualify for preferential treatment. With respect to special trade programs, duty-free treatment is available for certain textile and apparel products that meet the detailed rules set forth in the African Growth and Opportunity Act,[104] the Andean Trade Promotion and Drug Eradication Act,[105] the Caribbean Basin Trade Partnership Act,[106]

---

99. 19 U.S.C. § 3592(b)(3)(A).
100. 19 U.S.C. § 3592(b)(3)(B).
101. *See* United States-Mexico-Canada Agreement, annex 4-B, https://ustr.gov/trade-agreements/free-trade-agreements/united-states-mexico-canada-agreement/united-states-mexico.
102. 19 C.F.R. pt. 181, app. (2018).
103. INT'L TRADE: RULES OF ORIGIN, *supra* note 84, at 5.
104. African Growth and Opportunity Act, Title I of Trade and Development Act of 2000, Pub. L. No. 106-200, §§ 101-31, 114 Stat. 251, 252-75.
105. Andean Trade Promotion and Drug Eradication Act, Title XXXI of the Trade Act of 2002, Pub. L. No. 107-210, §§ 3101-108, 116 Stat. 933, 1023-38.
106. United States-Caribbean Basin Trade Partnership Act, Title II of the Trade and Development Act of 2000, Pub. L. No. 106-200, §§ 201-13, 114 Stat, 251, 275-88.

and the Haitian Hemispheric Opportunity Through Partnership Encouragement Act.[107]

§ 19:6.4 Country of Origin Marking

Goods imported into the United States must be "marked" with the English name of the country of origin, unless an exception applies.[108] The marking must be "as legibly, indelibly, and permanently as the nature of the article (or container) will permit,"[109] and must be in a conspicuous location that a purchaser can easily locate. The purpose of the marking laws is to ensure that the "ultimate purchaser" in the United States will be informed as to the country of origin of imported goods prior to purchase.[110]

The requirement that marking be "conspicuous" has a special meaning in the context of apparel products. Customs has determined, for example, that shirts, blouses, and sweaters must be marked with a fabric label that is sewn "on the inside center of the neck midway between the shoulder seams or in that immediate area."[111] In some cases, CBP has accepted screen printed labels or heat seal labels on garments as sufficiently conspicuous.[112] Jeans, slacks, skirts, and similar items "must be marked by means of a permanent label affixed in a conspicuous location on the garment, such as the inside of the waistband."[113] Reversible garments are exempt from the standard neck marking requirement and may instead be marked using other means, such as a sewn-in label on the lower inside seam.[114] Accessory articles, such as ties, scarves, and mufflers, may also be marked using a sewn-in label.[115]

Special marking requirements are triggered when an imported article is marked with a country or locality name of a place other than

---

107. Haitian Hemispheric Opportunity Through Partnership Encouragement Act of 2006, Title V of the Tax Relief and Health Care Act of 2006, Pub. L. No. 109-432, §§ 5001-06, 120 Stat. 2922, 3181-90.

108. 19 U.S.C. § 1304. When an imported article is exempt from the marking requirement, the container or holder in which the article reaches the ultimate purchaser in the United States generally must still be marked. *See* 19 C.F.R. § 134.22 (2018).

109. *Id.*

110. United States v. Friedlaender & Co., 27 C.C.P.A. 297, 302 (1940).

111. TD 54640(6) (1958).

112. *See, e.g.*, HQ 562700 (June 10, 2003); NY N045657 (Dec. 24, 2008).

113. TD 71-264(3).

114. *See, e.g.*, HQ 733890 (Dec. 31, 1990).

115. *See, e.g.*, HQ 559620 (May 17, 1996). There is a statutory exception to the marking requirements for imported silk scarves and silk fabric. 19 U.S.C. § 1304.

the country of origin. If the country or locality name has the potential to mislead the purchaser about the true country of origin of the article, then the actual country of origin name must appear in close proximity, preceded by "Made in," "Product of," or similar wording.[116] For example, CBP has held that a label for a Chinese-origin garment containing the words "New York," must also be marked "Made in China" on the same side of the label in approximately the same size font.[117] There are a large number of rulings in which CBP has recognized that country or place names that are "used as symbols or decorations" or "as an integral part of the design" of a garment are not likely to confuse the ultimate purchaser as to the country of origin of the article and thus do not trigger the special marking requirements.[118]

Textile and apparel articles are also subject to special marking requirements administered by the Federal Trade Commission under the Textile Fiber Products Identification Act,[119] the Wool Products Labeling Act, and similar laws.[120] These laws generally require that imported garments include specified information, such as fiber names; fiber content by percentage; country of origin; and the name of the importer, distributor, retailer, or foreign manufacturer.[121]

§ 19:7 Administrative Process

Because of the complexities associated with importing textile and apparel items, it is often advisable to consult with CBP about the proper classification, valuation, or country of origin of the merchandise to be imported. CBP regulations provide that any person with "a demonstrable interest" in a transaction (such as the importer or exporter) may seek a binding ruling under Part 177 of the Customs regulations prior to importation of the merchandise.[122] The form of the ruling request is a letter that must provide all relevant facts relating to the transaction and describe the proposed transaction in sufficient detail to permit proper application of the customs laws and

---

116. 19 C.F.R. § 134.46 (2018).
117. HQ 735233 (Jan. 28, 1994).
118. *See, e.g.*, HQ 733795 (Feb. 15, 1991) (American flag and Statue of Liberty prints on garments were integral part of design and were not likely to confuse as to country of origin); HQ 723604 (Nov. 3, 1983) ("USA" displayed on women's apparel used as symbol or decoration rather than as country of origin indicator).
119. 15 U.S.C. § 70.
120. 15 U.S.C. § 68.
121. For a more detailed discussion of apparel labeling requirements, see *supra* chapters 9 and 15.
122. 19 C.F.R. § 177.1 (2018).

regulations.[123] For example, a request for a classification ruling should include a complete description of the merchandise and information on its commercial designation and use. Photographs and/or samples of the merchandise to be classified are often supplied with ruling requests.[124] CBP will usually act on ruling requests within thirty days of receipt.[125] Importers often engage experts such as lawyers or customs brokers to assist in preparing binding ruling requests.

Administrative decisions by CBP with respect to imported merchandise, such as classification or value, can be protested by importers. A protest is commenced by filing, within 180 days of liquidation, a CBP Form 19 with the port director whose decision is protested. The protest must specifically describe the merchandise at issue and explain the nature of the objection to CBP's decision. The protest may also seek further review by CBP's Office of Regulations and Rulings in lieu of review by the port director if certain criteria are satisfied. CBP must allow or deny a protest within two years from the date of filing.

If the importer disagrees with CBP's decision on a protest, it may commence litigation in the Court of International Trade. The Court of International Trade is an Article III court (that is, a court established under Article III of the U.S. Constitution), located in New York City, but with authority to hold trials at federal courthouses throughout the United States to accommodate the needs of parties not located in New York. The court has exclusive jurisdiction over several types of international trade litigation including protests from CBP decisions. Rulings of the Court of International Trade may be appealed to the Court of Appeals for the Federal Circuit.[126]

§ 19:8 Penalties and Enforcement of the Customs Laws

Textile and apparel imports are considered a "priority trade issue" for enforcement of the customs laws by CBP. Importers of textile and apparel articles are more likely to be the subject of customs examinations and audits than other importers. CBP's enforcement efforts in textiles and apparel are directed principally at improper or misleading country of origin marking, duty evasion, and illegal transshipments. In 2017, for example, CBP seized more than 17,000 import shipments involving apparel and accessories, watches and jewelry, footwear and

123. 19 C.F.R. § 177.2 (2018).
124. 19 C.F.R. § 177.2(b)(3) (2013).
125. U.S. CUSTOMS & BORDER PROT., BINDING RULING REQUESTS, https://help.cbp.gov/app/answers/detail/a_id/280/~/binding-ruling-requests.
126. *See generally* U.S. COURT OF INT'L TRADE, ABOUT THE COURT, https://www.cit.uscourts.gov/AboutTheCourt.html.

handbags and wallets valued at nearly $811 million for violations of intellectual property rights and smuggling.[127]

§ 19:8.1 Seizure and Forfeiture

CBP has both mandatory and discretionary authority to seize imports in certain circumstances. Of these circumstances, those most relevant to textile and apparel importation include the following:

- CBP is required to seize imports that:
    - Are "stolen, smuggled, or clandestinely imported or introduced."[128]
    - Are found to be the product of forced labor in violation of 19 U.S.C. § 1307 (after following CBP procedures).[129]
- CBP has discretionary authority to seize imports that:
    - Fail to comply with relevant importation laws and regulations relating to health, safety, or conservation.[130]
    - Fail to comply with licensing or permit requirements.[131]
    - Violate intellectual property rights.[132]
    - Are marked intentionally in violation of country of origin marking requirements or the importer has received written notices that previous importations of identical merchandise from the same supplier were found to be marked in violation of the country origin marking requirements.[133]
    - Fail to comply with quantitative restrictions.[134]
    - The CBP has "reasonable cause to believe" violate 19 U.S.C. 1592 (the civil fraud statute).[135]

---

127. U.S. CUSTOMS & BORDER PROT., INTELLECTUAL PROPERTY RIGHTS SEIZURE STATISTICS, FY 2017, https://www.cbp.gov/document/stats/fy-2017-ipr-seizure-statistics.
128. 19 U.S.C. § 1595a(c)(1)(A).
129. *See* 19 C.F.R. §§ 12.42 to 12.45.
130. 19 U.S.C. § 1595a(c)(2)(A).
131. 19 U.S.C. § 1595a(c)(2)(B).
132. 19 U.S.C. § 1595a(c)(2)(C) (violations of intellectual property rights "including, but not limited to" 15 U.S.C. §§ 1124, 1125, 1127; 17 U.S.C. § 506; and 18 U.S.C. §§ 2318, 2320). *See supra* section 2:9.5.
133. 19 U.S.C. §§ 1595a(c)(2)(E) and (F). *See supra* section 19:6.
134. 19 U.S.C. § 1595a(c)(3).
135. 19 U.S.C. § 1592(c)(14). For further discussion of violation of section 1592, see *infra* section 19:8.2.

In addition, CBP is required to seize goods that are exported, or attempted to be exported, from the United States contrary to law.[136]

For merchandise seized through administrative or judicial forfeitures, CBP sends a Notice of Seizure to the importer.[137] The most common process for importers to contest a seizure is through a petition for administrative relief. The petition must be filed within thirty (30) days of the notice of seizure, unless an agreement is reached with CBP on an extension of the period.[138] CBP has broad discretion over the disposition of petitions for administrative relief, including the ability to release the merchandise to the importer upon payment of a negotiated penalty.

As discussed earlier in this chapter, the number of seizures for violations of the forced labor import prohibition has greatly increased. Prior to the repeal of the consumptive demand exception, CBP had not issued a detention order or finding barring the entry of goods on the basis of the forced labor import prohibition since 2000.[139] However, from March 10, 2016 to the date of this publication, CBP has issued six detention orders.[140] For example, on May 18, 2018, CBP issued a detention order detaining "all Turkmenistan Cotton or products produced in whole or in part with Turkmenistan cotton."[141] In addition to the risks associated with increased enforcement, applicable regulations allow CBP to issue detention orders if CBP finds "that information available reasonably but not conclusively indicates that merchandise" violates the forced labor prohibition.[142] Once a detention order is issued, importers must submit, within three (3) months following the importation, a certificate of origin and a detailed statement demonstrating that the subject merchandise was not produced with forced labor to obtain release of the shipments.[143] If the proof submitted does not establish the admissibility of the merchandise, or if none is provided, CBP will exclude the shipment.[144] Furthermore, if CBP is provided with information sufficient to make

---

136. 19 U.S.C. § 1595a(d). *See infra* section 19:9.

137. 19 C.F.R. § 162.75(c) (20138). In cases where a seizure appears related to a possible crime, Customs is required to report the matter to the U.S. Attorney for possible criminal proceedings.

138. 19 C.F.R. § 171.2(b) (20138).

139. U.S. CUSTOMS & BORDER PROT., DETENTION ORDERS (WITHHOLD RELEASE ORDERS), https://www.cbp.gov/trade/trade-community/programs-outreach/convict-importations/detention-orders.

140. *Id.* CBP issued five detention orders against merchandise imported from China and one against merchandise imported from Turkmenistan.

141. *Id.*

142. 19 C.F.R. § 12.42(e) (2018).

143. 19 C.F.R. § 12.43 (2018).

144. 19 C.F.R. § 12.44(a) (2018).

a determination that the imports in question violate the forced labor import prohibition, then CBP will publish a formal finding to that effect in the Customs Bulletin and in the Federal Register.[145] Imports subject to a formal finding will be seized if the importer fails to provide proof establishing the admissibility of the imports.[146] Thus, increased enforcement resulting from the repeal of the consumptive demand exception and the ability of CBP to detain imports based on a reasonable belief of a violation, heighten the risks associated with non-compliance of the forced labor prohibition.

Furthermore, in 2017, CBP seized a record number of import shipments for violations of intellectual property rights with textile and apparel imports comprising the largest percentage of all intellectual property rights seizures at 15%.[147] This trend has continued into 2018. For example, on June 28, 2018, CBP seized four shipments of counterfeit Mexican national team soccer jerseys with an estimated retail value of $66,390 originating in Hong Kong.[148] On June 4, 2017, CBP seized over 2,000 pieces of counterfeit apparel with an estimated retail value of $289,130 also originating in Hong Kong.[149] Therefore, to avoid being subject to seizure and forfeiture, importers should be familiar with intellectual property rights and follow the reasonable care guidance discussed earlier in this chapter.[150]

§ 19:8.2 Monetary Penalties

In addition, CBP can assess monetary penalties against importers for violations of applicable laws and regulations. Monetary penalties may be in addition to, or in place of, a seizure enforcement

---

145. 19 C.F.R. § 12.42(f) (2018).
146. 19 C.F.R. § 12.44(b) (2018).
147. Press Release, U.S. Customs & Border Prot., Record Number of IPR Seizures in FY17 for CBP, ICE (Mar. 5, 2018), https://www.cbp.gov/newsroom/national-media-release/record-number-ipr-seizures-fy17-cbp-ice.
148. Press Release, U.S. Customs & Border Prot., CBP Seizes Hundreds of Counterfeit World Cup Soccer Jerseys (July 2, 2018), https://www.cbp.gov/newsroom/local-media-release/cbp-seizes-hundreds-counterfeit-world-cup-soccer-jerseys.
149. Press Release, U.S. Customs & Border Prot., Philadelphia CBP Seizes $289,130 Shipment of Counterfeit Apparel from Hong Kong (June 25, 2018), https://www.cbp.gov/newsroom/local-media-release/philadelphia-cbp-seizes-289130-shipment-counterfeit-apparel-hong-kong.
150. *See also* U.S. CUSTOMS & BORDER PROT., WHAT EVERY MEMBER OF THE TRADE COMMUNITY SHOULD KNOW ABOUT: CBP ENFORCEMENT OF INTELLECTUAL PROPERTY RIGHTS (Aug. 2012), https://www.cbp.gov/sites/default/files/assets/documents/2017-Feb/enforce_ipr_3_0.pdf.

mechanism. For example, under 19 U.S.C. § 1509(g) CBP may impose penalties for failure to comply with a lawful for demand for recordkeeping information.[151]

However, the principal statutory basis for administrative penalties in importing is section 592 of the Tariff Act of 1930.[152] This provision gives CBP the authority to issue penalties for material and false statements (or omissions) made in connection with the entry or attempted entry of merchandise into the United States. CBP takes a broad view of what constitutes a "material" false statement or omission. In general, any information an importer provides that may be relevant to classification, appraisement, admissibility, or origin of the merchandise, as well as information tending to conceal unfair trade practices, will be considered to be material.

Section 592 provides for differing levels of penalties based on whether the violation is determined to result from negligence, gross negligence, or fraud. Negligence results from a failure to exercise reasonable care in ensuring that information provided in connection with imported merchandise is accurate and complete.[153] Gross negligence involves acts that are committed with actual knowledge or disregard of the relevant facts and the importer's obligations under the statute.[154] The highest level of culpability, which is fraud, is reserved for material false statements or acts that are committed knowingly, that is, voluntarily and intentionally.[155]

Penalties assessed under section 1592 can be very substantial. In one case, *United States v. Inn Foods, Inc.*,[156] for example, CBP alleged that an importer of frozen produce had committed fraud or alternatively, had been negligent or grossly negligent in undervaluing its imports. In addition to the actual revenue loss of approximately $625,000 in unpaid duties, CBP sought penalties in excess of $15 million based on fraud.[157] Ultimately, the Federal Circuit affirmed the judgment of the Court of International Trade awarding CBP $7.5 million based on a finding of fraud. In another high-profile section 1592 penalty action, Pentax ultimately agreed to pay $20 million

151. 19 U.S.C. § 1509(g). For recordkeeping requirements, see *supra* section 19:2.2.

152. 19 U.S.C § 1592.

153. 19 C.F.R. pt. 171, app. B, at (C)(1) (2018).

154. *Id.* at (C)(2).

155. *Id.* at (C)(3).

156. United States v. Inn Foods, Inc., 515 F. Supp. 2d 1347 (Ct. Int'l Trade 2007) *aff'd*, 560 F.3d 1338 (Fed. Cir. 2009).

157. *Id.* at 1361.

in penalties to the Department of Justice for false country of origin marking on imported cameras.[158]

Section 1592 specifies a potential maximum penalty for each degree of culpability, depending on whether the violation at issue resulted in the loss of duties or whether it is a "non-revenue loss" violation. CBP has also published mitigation guidelines that indicate the extent of the reduction in penalties that CBP will often grant in section 592 cases.[159]

Table 19-1
U.S. Customs and Border Protection Mitigation Guidelines Mitigation

Culpability Level	Statutory Maximum Penalty	Mitigation Guidelines (Revenue Loss Violation)	Mitigation Guidelines (Non-Revenue Loss Violation)
Fraud	Domestic value of merchandise	5 times to 8 times total loss of duty	50% to 80% of dutiable value
Gross Negligence	Four times total loss of duties or 40% of dutiable value	2.5 times to 4 times total loss of duty	25% to 40% of dutiable value
Negligence	Two times total loss of duties or 20% of dutiable value	0.5 times to 2 times total loss of duty	5% to 20% of dutiable value

An importer's potential liability for section 1592 penalties can be substantially reduced by filing a "prior disclosure" of a violation with CBP.[160] A prior disclosure must identify the circumstances of a violation and must be filed before the importer has knowledge of a pending Customs investigation. If a valid prior disclosure is filed with CBP, the maximum penalty for fraudulent violations is reduced to

158. *See* Press Release, U.S. Dep't of Justice, Pentax Corporation Agrees to Pay $20 Million for Violating Country of Origin Marking Laws (Nov, 8, 1999), https://www.justice.gov/opa/pr/1999/November/537civ.htm.
159. 19 C.F.R. § 162.73(a) (2018); 19 C.F.R. pt. 171, app. B, at F(2) (2018).
160. 19 C.F.R. § 162.74 (2018).

one times the total loss of duties, or 10% of the dutiable value of the merchandise (in the case of a non-duty loss violation).[161] The penalties for negligent and grossly negligent violations are limited to interest owed on any unpaid duties and fees.[162] This significant reduction in potential liability reflects CBP's policy of encouraging self-disclosure of violations and is a strong incentive to importers to quickly investigate and self-report any compliance issues that are discovered in their importing operations.

Judicial review of section 1592 penalties is available only through a suit by the United States in the Court of International Trade to recover unpaid penalties. An importer wishing to challenge a penalty assessment under section 1592 must refuse to tender the penalty amount and await the institution of a suit by the United States to recover the penalty. When proceedings are brought under section 1592, all issues including liability and the amount of the penalty are reviewed by the Court of International Trade without deference to CBP's findings. The government's burden of proof with respect to the penalty claim differs according to whether the penalty is based on allegations of fraud, gross negligence, or negligence.

§ 19:9 Exporting From the United States

Although this chapter focuses principally on issues involved in importing goods into the United States, many fashion companies are increasingly active in export markets. Exporting from the United States offers the opportunity to access new consumer markets, particularly in emerging market economies.

The Trade Information Center at the U.S. Commerce Department offers extensive resources to assist U.S. businesses in developing export markets. Commerce publishes a fairly comprehensive and well-regarded *Basic Guide to Exporting*, which is keyed to the needs of small-to-medium businesses and new exporters.[163] Commerce also organizes trade shows in the United States to match U.S. businesses with foreign buyers, and also arranges for foreign trade missions where U.S. companies can make contacts with potential business partners. Other services include market research, statistics, and trade leads; introduction to public and private export financing sources; and counseling on the business environment in particular markets.

---

161. 19 C.F.R. § 162.73(b) (2018).

162. The reduced penalties applicable in prior disclosure circumstances are listed in Appendix B to Part 171 of the Customs Regulations, 19 C.F.R. pt. 171, app. B, at F(2)(f) (2018).

163. *See* EXPORT.GOV, A BASIC GUIDE TO EXPORTING (July 25, 2018), https://www.export.gov/article?id=Why-Companies-should-export.

While the U.S. government actively promotes exporting U.S.-made goods in most instances, exporters must be aware of sanctions and export control measures that exist with respect to certain governments, regions, and individuals. The United States sometimes employs economic sanctions as a means of exerting pressure on foreign governments to change policies and/or to express political opposition against such policies. These sanctions restrict or prohibit trade with the specified targets. U.S. export controls protect against the transfer of certain goods, technologies and information to foreign countries or foreign nationals for national security or foreign policy reasons. Although many exporting activities undertaken by fashion companies will not involve either U.S. sanctions or export control issues, it is prudent to have a basic understanding of these regimes so as to avoid the substantial fines and penalties that can be assessed for even inadvertent violations.

§ 19:9.1 *Economic Sanctions*

As is the case with free trade agreements, discussed earlier in this chapter, the implementation and enforcement of economic sanctions is a highly politically sensitive area. Recently, sanction measures have been strengthened with respect to Syria, re-implemented with respect to Iran, and newly implemented with respect to the Crimea Region of Ukraine; conversely, longstanding restrictions on trade with other governments, such as Myanmar (Burma) and Sudan, have been revoked to reflect political developments.[164] Sanctions may be comprehensive, prohibiting most or all unlicensed dealings with the target, or may be limited to a specific set of activities. The embargo on trade with Cuba is an example of comprehensive sanctions, while measures prohibiting trade in African "blood diamonds" are a type of limited sanctions applicable only to specific goods.

Economic sanctions are administered by the Office of Foreign Assets Control (OFAC) in the Treasury Department. OFAC provides advice to exporters, issues licenses for activities that would otherwise be prohibited by sanctions, and has an active enforcement division. OFAC also maintains a list of "Specially Designated Nationals and Blocked Persons" who are targeted by specific sanctions programs. Key sanctions programs administered by OFAC include Cuba, Iran, North Korea, Russia, and Syria sanctions, and various nonproliferation and counter-terrorism sanctions.

---

164. For a complete list of sanctions programs and country information, see the U.S. DEP'T OF TREASURY, RESOURCE CENTER, https://www.treasury.gov/resource-center/sanctions/Programs/Pages/Programs.aspx.

Changes to economic sanctions resulting from administrative changes and political developments can have significant impacts on importers of textiles and apparel. For example, following the Trump Administration's decision to re-implement sanctions with respect to Iran, Nike announced that it would not provide cleats to the Iranian soccer team for the 2018 World Cup.[165]

§ 19:9.2 Export Controls

Exports from the United States may also be subject to export controls administered by the Bureau of Industry and Security (BIS) in the Commerce Department. BIS is responsible for implementing and enforcing the Export Administration Regulations (EAR), which govern the export and re-export of most commercial items from the United States. Although the scope of BIS's authority to regulate exports is broad, in practice only a relatively small percentage of exports require a license from BIS. These items are so-called "dual-use" items that have both commercial and military applications, some military items, and some short supply items.[166]

The first step in determining whether a license is required is to consult the Commerce Control List (CCL) maintained by BIS to see whether the item has a specific five-digit Export Classification Control Number.[167] If the item is not listed on the CCL, then typically no export license will be required unless the export is to an embargoed country to an end-user of concern, or in support of a prohibited end use. If the item is classifiable under an ECCN, then licensing requirements are dictated by the country of ultimate destination and the reason for control of the item. If an export license is required, applications may be submitted to BIS pursuant to an online application system. License approvals are generally valid for four (4) years.

---

165. Jacob Bogage, *Nike Will Not Outfit Iranian World Cup Team Due to Sanctions*, WASH. POST (June 9, 2018), https://www.washingtonpost.com/news/early-lead/wp/2018/06/09/nike-will-not-outfit-iranian-world-cup-team-due-to-sanctions/?noredirect=on&utm_term=.ee7a2ab5ca1e.

166. Exports of defense or military-related items or technologies are subject to the International Traffic in Arms Regulations (ITAR), which are administered by the Department of State.

167. The Commerce Control List is published in part 774, Supplement No. 1 of the Export Administration Regulations, 15 C.F.R. pt. 774 (2013), https://www.bis.doc.gov/index.php/regulations/commerce-control-list-ccl.

Appendix 19A

Department of Homeland Security U.S. Customs and Border Protection: Entry Summary

DEPARTMENT OF HOMELAND SECURITY
U.S. Customs and Border Protection

ENTRY SUMMARY

OMB APPROVAL NO. 1651-0022
EXPIRATION DATE 01/31/2021
ESTIMATED BURDEN 10 MIN

1. Filer Code/Entry No.		2. Entry Type	3. Summary Date
4. Surety No.	5. Bond Type	6. Port Code	7. Entry Date

8. Importing Carrier	9. Mode of Transport	10. Country of Origin	11. Import Date
12. B/L or AWB No.	13. Manufacturer ID	14. Exporting Country	15. Export Date

16. I.T. No.	17. I.T. Date	18. Missing Docs	19. Foreign Port of Lading	20. U.S. Port of Unlading
21. Location of Goods/G.O. No.	22. Consignee No.		23. Importer No.	24. Reference No.

25. Ultimate Consignee Name and Address City State Zip	26. Importer of Record Name and Address City State Zip

27.	28. Description of Merchandise			32.	33.	34.
Line No.	29. A. HTSUS No. B. ADA/CVD No.	30. A. Grossweight B. Manifest Qty.	31. Net Quantity in HTSUS Units	A. Entered Value B. CHGS C. Relationship	A. HTSUS Rate B. ADA/CVD Rate C. IRC Rate D. Visa No.	Duty and I.R. Tax Dollars Cents

		CBP USE ONLY		**TOTALS**
Other Fee Summary for Block 39	35. Total Entered Value $	A. LIQ CODE	B. Ascertained Duty	37. Duty
	Total Other Fees $	REASON CODE	C. Ascertained Tax	38. Tax
36. DECLARATION OF IMPORTER OF RECORD (OWNER OR PURCHASER) OR AUTHORIZED AGENT			D. Ascertained Other	39. Other
			E. Ascertained Total	40. Total

I declare that I am the ☐ Importer of record and that the actual owner, purchaser, or consignee for CBP purposes is as shown above, **OR** ☐ owner or purchaser or agent thereof. I further declare that the merchandise ☐ was obtained pursuant to a purchase or agreement to purchase and that the prices set forth in the invoices are true, **OR** ☐ was not obtained pursuant to a purchase or agreement to purchase and the statements in the invoices as to value or price are true to the best of my knowledge and belief. I also declare that the statements in the documents herein filed fully disclose to the best of my knowledge and belief the true prices, values, quantities, rebates, drawbacks, fees, commissions, and royalties and are true and correct, and that all goods or services provided to the seller of the merchandise either free or at reduced cost are fully disclosed.
I will immediately furnish to the appropriate CBP officer any information showing a different statement of facts.

41. DECLARANT NAME	TITLE	SIGNATURE	DATE

42. Broker/Filer Information (Name, address, phone number)	43. Broker/Importer File No.

CBP Form 7501 (2/18) **Page 1 of 5**

Appendix 19B

Sample Page from Harmonized Tariff Schedule of the United States (2013)

Harmonized Tariff Schedule of the United States (2019) Revision 4

Annotated for Statistical Reporting Purposes

VIII
42-20

Heading/ Subheading	Stat. Suf-fix	Article Description	Unit of Quantity	Rates of Duty 1 General	Rates of Duty 1 Special	Rates of Duty 2
4203		Articles of apparel and clothing accessories, of leather or of composition leather:				
4203.10		Articles of apparel:				
4203.10.20	00	Of reptile leather	No.	4.7%[1/]	Free (A*, AU, BH, CA, CL, CO, D, E, IL, JO, KR, MA, MX, OM, P, PA, PE, SG)	35%
4203.10.40		Other		6%[8/]	Free (AU, BH, CA, CL, CO, D, IL, JO, KR, MA, MX, OM, P, PA, PE, R, SG) 4.8% (E)	35%
		Coats and jackets:				
	10	Anoraks	No.			
		Other:				
	30	Men's and boys'	No.			
	60	Women's, girls' and infants'	No.			
		Other:				
	85	Men's and boys'	No.			
	95	Women's, girls' and infants'	No.			
		Gloves, mittens and mitts:				
4203.21		Specially designed for use in sports:				
		Baseball and softball gloves and mitts (including batting gloves):				
4203.21.20	00	Batting gloves	No.	3%[9/]	Free (A, AU, BH, CA, CL, CO, D, E, IL, JO, KR, MA, MX, OM, P, PA, PE, SG)	30%
4203.21.40	00	Other	No.	Free[1/]		30%
		Ski or snowmobile gloves, mittens and mitts:				
4203.21.55	00	Cross-country ski gloves, mittens and mitts	prs.	3.5%[1/]	Free (A, AU, BH, CA, CL, CO, D, E, IL, JO, KR, MA, MX, OM, P, PA, PE, SG)	45%
4203.21.60	00	Other	prs.	5.5%[1/]	Free (A, AU, BH, CA, CL, CO, D, E, IL, JO, KR, MA, MX, OM, P, PA, PE, SG)	45%
4203.21.70	00	Ice hockey gloves	prs.	Free[1/]		30%
4203.21.80		Other		4.9%[10/]	Free (A*, AU, BH, CA, CL, CO, D, E, IL, JO, KR, MA, MX, OM, P, PA, PE, SG)	30%
	30	Golf gloves	doz.			
	60	Other	No.			

Chapter 20

Foreign Corrupt Practices Act

§ 20:1 Introduction
§ 20:2 Foreign Corrupt Practices Act: Origins
§ 20:3 Foreign Corrupt Practices Act: Central Provisions
  § 20:3.1 Anti-Bribery Provisions
    [A] Who Is Covered?
    [B] What Conduct Is Covered?
    [C] Affirmative Defenses and Statutory Exception
  § 20:3.2 Accounting Provisions
    [A] Books and Records Provision
    [B] Internal Controls Provision
§ 20:4 FCPA Enforcement
  § 20:4.1 Case Study: Ralph Lauren
  § 20:4.2 Case Study: Avon
    [A] History of the Avon Investigation
    [B] Ramifications of the Avon Investigation
  § 20:4.3 Case Study: Nu Skin
  § 20:4.4 Supply Chain Risks
    [A] Third-Party Manufacturers
    [B] Transportation Service Providers
    [C] Distributors
§ 20:5 Issue-Spotting in FCPA Enforcement
  § 20:5.1 Issuers vs. Non-Issuers
  § 20:5.2 Third-Party Payments
  § 20:5.3 Successor Liability
  § 20:5.4 Foreign Officials
  § 20:5.5 Gifts and Entertainment
  § 20:5.6 Crafting an Effective Compliance Program
  § 20:5.7 Responding to a Potential Violation

§ 20:1 Introduction

The apparel industry is characterized both by its global breadth, and by the complexity of the supply chain that fuels it. In the context of the international fashion industry—where even small companies often employ international suppliers or maintain overseas manufacturing operations—it is essential to have an understanding of the potential jurisdictional reach of U.S. laws governing corporate conduct. The United States has become a leading force in combating international corruption by aggressively enforcing the Foreign Corrupt Practices Act (FCPA) against corporations doing business in a wide variety of industries. Even those companies that implement corporate social responsibility measures and comprehensive compliance programs designed to identify unsafe practices at overseas production facilities can end up being held responsible for local compliance failures. Given the dynamic nature of anti-corruption enforcement, it is essential for every company with international operations or supply chains to have a firm grasp on its compliance responsibilities and potential liabilities. The fashion industry is no exception.

§ 20:2 Foreign Corrupt Practices Act: Origins

The FCPA was enacted in 1977, in response to widespread concern about pervasive international corruption involving U.S.-based companies. Often motivated by a desire to secure favorable treatment by a foreign government—but in some cases precipitated simply by a business culture in which "facilitating payments" were necessary to ensure the performance of basic ministerial or clerical functions—U.S. companies were using corporate funds to pay foreign officials.

The problem of corrupt corporate foreign payments attracted particular attention in the wake of the Watergate investigation, when several corporations and executive officers were charged with using corporate funds to make illegal political contributions domestically.[1] In 1974, the Securities and Exchange Commission (SEC) conducted an investigation into the circumstances of those contributions, and discovered that companies were falsifying their financial records to conceal the source and misuse of corporate funds

1. *Hearing Concerning H.R. 4353, The International Anti-Bribery and Fair Competition Act of 1998, Before the H. Subcomm. on Finance & Hazardous Materials of the H. Comm. on Commerce*, 105th Cong. (Sept. 10, 1998) (statement of Paul V. Gerlach, Associate Director, Division of Enforcement, U.S. Sec. & Exch. Comm'n), www.sec.gov/news/testimony/testarchive/1998/tsty1198.txt.

for illegal purposes—including questionable foreign payments.[2] Public companies were creating "slush funds" and using the cash to make illegal campaign contributions at home and illegal bribes abroad.[3] The SEC administered an amnesty program under which some 400 U.S. companies—including more than one hundred members of the Fortune 500—admitted to making more than $300 million in improper payments to various foreign officials.[4]

Between 1975 and 1977, Congress held a variety of hearings regarding the problem of foreign corporate payments, exploring their implications for both domestic legal liability and foreign policy.[5] Ultimately, the FCPA was enacted in 1977, making it unlawful for certain classes of persons and entities to bribe foreign government officials for the purpose of obtaining or retaining business. The FCPA was amended twice: first in 1988, to clarify the terms of the statute in adherence with the original congressional intent; and again in 1998, to ensure compliance with the Convention on Combating Bribery of Foreign Public Officials in International Business Transactions, an international instrument promulgated by the Organisation for Economic Cooperation and Development to combat corruption in international business.

§ 20:3 Foreign Corrupt Practices Act: Central Provisions

The FCPA has two complementary sets of provisions: the anti-bribery provisions and the accounting provisions. Among other things, the anti-bribery provisions directly prohibit companies that list their securities on any U.S. stock exchange, as well as U.S. persons or entities (or any foreign persons or entities acting within U.S. territory), from bribing foreign government officials in order "to obtain or retain business." The accounting provisions require that business entities subject to SEC regulation must maintain (1) accurate books and records, and (2) a system of internal controls that reasonably assures that corporate assets are used only for authorized corporate purposes. Each of these sets of provisions has both criminal and civil applications, and is subject to dual enforcement, with prosecution of the criminal elements falling within the exclusive jurisdiction of

---

2. U.S. SEC. & EXCH. COMM'N, REPORT OF THE SECURITIES AND EXCHANGE COMMISSION ON QUESTIONABLE AND ILLEGAL CORPORATE PAYMENTS AND PRACTICES 3 (1976).
3. U.S. DEP'T OF JUSTICE, PROPOSED LEGISLATIVE HISTORY, INTERNATIONAL ANTI-BRIBERY ACT OF 1998, https://www.justice.gov/criminal/fraud/fcpa/docs/leghistory.pdf.
4. H.R. REP. NO.95-640, at 4 (1977).
5. *See* Mike Koehler, *The Story of the Foreign Corrupt Practices Act*, 73 OHIO ST. L.J. 929 (2012).

the U.S. Department of Justice (DOJ), and civil enforcement lying primarily (but not exclusively) within the purview of the SEC.

§ 20:3.1 Anti-Bribery Provisions

Broadly, the FCPA's anti-bribery provisions prohibit certain entities from corruptly paying, or even merely offering or promising to pay, money or anything of value to a foreign official in order to influence that official to exercise his discretion or perform his duties in a manner that would assist the payor in obtaining or retaining business.[6] In particular, 15 U.S.C. §§ 78dd-1(a) and 78dd-2(a) prohibit:

(i) U.S. companies or U.S.-listed companies (or their directors, officers, employees, agents, or stockholders), as well as U.S. citizens, nationals, or residents (or any agents thereof),

(ii) from the "use of the mails or any means or instrumentality of interstate commerce,"

(iii) corruptly,

(iv) "in furtherance of an offer, payment, promise to pay, or authorization of the payment of any money, or offer, gift, promise to give, or authorization of the giving of anything of value,"

(v) to "any foreign official,"

(vi) for purposes of influencing an act or decision of the foreign official in his official capacity—including inducing such foreign official to influence or affect an act of a foreign government or instrumentality—or securing any other improper advantage,

(vii) in order "to assist [the payor] in obtaining or retaining business for or with, or directing business to, any person."

The FCPA also prohibits the same U.S. persons or entities listed above from engaging in *"any act outside the United States"* that is "in furtherance" of a violative act, "irrespective of whether such United States person [or company] makes use of the mails or any means or instrumentality of interstate commerce."[7] Moreover, "any person," while *within* U.S. territory, is prohibited from using the mails or any instrumentality of interstate commerce "in furtherance of" a violative act.[8] Each of these provisions is discussed below in further detail.

---

6. 15 U.S.C. §§ 78dd-1(a), (g); 78dd-2(a), (i); 78dd-3(a).
7. 15 U.S.C. § 78dd-1(g) (emphasis added).
8. 15 U.S.C. § 78dd-3(a).

[A] Who Is Covered?

The anti-bribery provisions of the FCPA apply broadly to corporations and individuals, including not only directors and officers, but also any employees, agents, or stockholders acting on behalf of a subject entity.[9] Punishable conduct includes ordering, authorizing, or assisting in violations of the anti-bribery provisions.[10] The concepts of conspiracy[11] and aiding and abetting[12] apply equally to FCPA violations, and the SEC and DOJ have filed such charges in FCPA enforcement actions.[13]

Under the FCPA's core anti-bribery provisions, the corporate violator must be an "issuer" (or agent thereof), a "domestic concern" (or agent thereof), or a foreign business or person carrying out an act "in furtherance" of this type of payment while in the United States.[14] An "issuer" is any corporation that has a class of securities registered under section 12 of the Securities Exchange Act of 1934 (the "Exchange Act"), or one that is required under section 15(d) of the Exchange Act to file periodic and other reports with the SEC.[15] Under this definition, a foreign company may qualify as an "issuer" if it lists American Depositary Receipts (ADRs) on a national securities exchange in the United States,[16] or has a class of securities that is

---

9. 15 U.S.C. § 78dd-1(a).
10. *Id.*
11. 18 U.S.C. § 371; OFFICES OF THE U.S. ATT'YS, U.S. DEP'T OF JUSTICE U.S. ATTORNEYS' CRIM. RESOURCE MANUAL, at 9-923 (1997) [hereinafter U.S. ATTORNEYS' CRIM. RESOURCE MANUAL]. To establish conspiracy to violate the FCPA, the government must prove (1) agreement to commit a corrupt offer or payment, (2) criminal intent, and (3) an act in furtherance of that corrupt offer or payment.
12. 18 U.S.C. § 2; U.S. ATTORNEYS' CRIM. RESOURCE MANUAL, *supra* note 11, at 9-2474. To establish aiding and abetting liability under the FCPA, the government must show that the accused (1) had specific intent to facilitate the commission of a corrupt offer or payment by another; (2) had the requisite intent of the underlying offense; (3) assisted or participated in the commission of the underlying offense; and that (4) someone committed the underlying offense.
13. *See* U.S. DEP'T OF JUSTICE & U.S. SEC. & EXCH. COMM'N, A RESOURCE GUIDE TO THE U.S. FOREIGN CORRUPT PRACTICES ACT, at 12 (Nov. 2012), https://www.sec.gov/spotlight/fcpa/fcpa-resource-guide.pdf [hereinafter RESOURCE GUIDE] (asserting that a "foreign national or company may also be liable under the FCPA if it aids and abets, conspires with, or acts as an agent of an issuer or domestic concern, regardless of whether the foreign national or company itself takes any action in the United States").
14. RESOURCE GUIDE, *supra* note 13, at 10.
15. 15 U.S.C. § 78c(a)(8); RESOURCE GUIDE, *supra* note 13, at 10–11.
16. As of December 31, 2011, 965 foreign companies were registered with the RESOURCE GUIDE, *supra* note 13, at 11.

quoted in U.S. over-the-counter markets,[17] if such company is required to file periodic reports with the SEC. Thus, a company need not be a U.S. company to be subject to FCPA jurisdiction and enforcement. A "domestic concern" includes any individual who is a U.S. citizen, national, or resident, as well as any corporate entity (corporation, partnership, association, joint-stock company, unincorporated organization, business trust, sole proprietorship, etc.) that has its principal place of business in the United States and that is organized under the laws of the United States or any of its states, territories, possessions, or commonwealths.[18]

Issuers and domestic concerns are subject to prosecution under the FCPA's anti-bribery provisions when they employ any means or instrumentality of interstate commerce in furtherance of making a corrupt payment to a foreign official. The FCPA defines "interstate commerce" to include communication, trade, commerce, and transportation among states or between any state and any foreign country.[19]

In 1998, the FCPA was amended to include so-called "alternative jurisdiction" provisions, designed to expand the reach of the law to cover actions undertaken *outside* the United States by any U.S. person or entity—even absent "use of the mails or any means or instrumentality of interstate commerce."[20] These provisions are based on a principle of nationality jurisdiction, and prohibit violative conduct by any "United States person"—a term defined to include "a national of the United States" as well as "any corporation, partnership, association, joint-stock company, business trust, unincorporated organization, or sole proprietorship organized under the laws of the United States or any State, territory, possession, or commonwealth of the United States, or any political subdivision thereof."[21]

On the face of the text, the FCPA's anti-bribery provisions generally do not apply directly to the foreign subsidiaries of issuers or domestic concerns, even if wholly or majority-owned. Rather, the FCPA covers foreign companies and persons that "either directly or through an agent, engage in *any* act in furtherance of a corrupt payment (or an offer, promise, or authorization to pay) while in the territory of the United States."[22] However, enforcement authorities have construed

17. RESOURCE GUIDE, *supra* note 13, at 11; *see also* F. Joseph Warin, Charles Falconer, & Michael S. Diamant, *The British Are Coming!: Britain Changes Its Law on Foreign Bribery and Joins the International Fight Against Corruption*, 46 TEX. INT'L L.J. 1, 9 (2010) [hereinafter Warin, Falconer & Diamant].

18. 15 U.S.C. § 78dd-2(h)(1); RESOURCE GUIDE, *supra* note 13, at 11.

19. RESOURCE GUIDE, *supra* note 13, at 11.

20. 15 U.S.C. §§ 78dd-1(g), 78dd-2(i).

21. 15 U.S.C. §§ 78dd-1(g)(2), 78dd-2(i)(2).

22. RESOURCE GUIDE, *supra* note 13, at 11 (emphasis added).

this provision broadly, so that even relatively minor acts—such as routing a payment through a U.S. bank account[23] or engaging in certain email traffic with the parent company in the U.S.[24]—may qualify as "acts in furtherance" sufficient to trigger FCPA jurisdiction.[25] But the sole federal court to consider this issue has thrown cold water on DOJ's expansive interpretation of the law, rejecting out of hand that the use of U.S. mails from outside of the United States could possibly constitute being "in the territory of the United States."[26] Foreign subsidiaries may also be subject to agency liability for the actions of a parent company that qualifies as an issuer or domestic concern. Conversely, the conduct of a subsidiary abroad may incur liability for a parent issuer that knew or consciously disregarded the risk of the subsidiary making illicit payments. Foreign subsidiaries can also subject a U.S. parent to liability by violating the FCPA's accounting provisions—discussed further below.

[B] What Conduct Is Covered?

The anti-bribery provisions of the FCPA prohibit "offering to pay, paying, promising to pay, or authorizing the payment of money or anything of value to a foreign official in order to influence any act or decision of the foreign official in his or her official capacity or to secure any other improper advantage in order to obtain or retain business."[27]

In practice, this broad prohibition means that an FCPA violation may occur even if the offer of payment is rejected, and even if there is no actual payment made or benefit bestowed. Moreover, "anything of value" includes any item with economic value—not just cash, but also travel expenses and lavish gifts. Past enforcement practice suggests

---

23. *See, e.g.*, Information, United States v. DaimlerChrysler Auto. Russia SAO, No. 1:10-CR-00064 (D.D.C. 2010); Information, United States v. DaimlerChrysler China Ltd., No. 1:10-CR-00066 (D.D.C. 2010); Information, United States v. SSI Int'l Far E., Ltd., No. 06-CR-398 (D. Or. 2006).
24. *See, e.g.*, Information, United States v. Syncor Taiwan, Inc., No. 1:02-CR-1244 (C.D. Cal. 2002).
25. RESOURCE GUIDE, *supra* note 13, at 11; Warin, Falconer & Diamant, *supra* note 17, at 10.
26. *See* Transcript of Oral Argument on June 6, 2011, United States v. Patel, No. 1:09-cr-335 (D.D.C.); *Significant dd-3 Development in Africa Sting Case*, FCPA PROFESSOR (June 9, 2011), http://fcpaprofessor.com/significant-dd-3-development-in-africa-sting-case/.
27. RESOURCE GUIDE, *supra* note 13, at 10.

that "anything of value" may also encompass more idiosyncratic benefits, such as education,[28] medical expenses,[29] and internships.[30]

Regardless of the form or magnitude of the bribe (or attempted or promised bribe), in order to violate the FCPA, the payor must have corrupt intent—the desire to induce the recipient to misuse his or her official position.[31] The bribe must also meet the business purpose test—it must be made in order to obtain or retain business. This test has been broadly construed to include bribes made to obtain business advantages of many kinds—not only winning government contracts, but also ensuring favorable tax treatment, obtaining (or circumventing the requirement of obtaining) a license or permit, or securing government action to prevent a competitor from entering the market.[32] The core precedent for this approach to "business purpose" is *United States v. Kay,* in which the U.S. Court of Appeals for the Fifth Circuit in 2004 held that bribes paid to obtain favorable tax treatment, in the form of reduced customs duties and sales taxes, qualified as payments made to "obtain or retain" business—in violation of the FCPA.[33]

The anti-bribery provisions apply only to corrupt payments made to: (1) "foreign officials"; (2) foreign political parties or officials thereof; (3) any candidates for foreign political office; or (4) any person at all, when the payor "knows" that all or part of the payment will be offered, promised, or transmitted to an individual who falls in one of the other three categories.[34]

In keeping with the sweeping reach of the FCPA's anti-bribery provisions, many of the key terms in these statutory provisions are defined quite broadly.

The FCPA defines "knowing" to include not only being "aware that such person is engaging in such conduct, that such circumstance exists, or that such result is substantially certain to occur," but also

---

28. Lucent Technologies Inc., Non-Prosecution Agreement, Appendix A, ¶ 20 (Nov. 14, 2007), https://www.justice.gov/criminal/fraud/fcpa/cases/lucent-tech.html.

29. Indictment ¶ 23, United States v. Kozeny, No. 05-cr-00518 (S.D.N.Y. 2008), https://www.justice.gov/criminal/fraud/fcpa/cases/kozenyv.html.

30. Non-Pros. Agreement between JPMorgan Securities (Asia Pacific) Limited and U.S. Dep't of Justice, Criminal Div., Fraud Section, Nov. 17, 2016, https://www.justice.gov/opa/press-release/file/911206/download. *See also infra* at section 20:5.5.

31. 15 U.S.C. §§ 78dd-1(a), 78dd-1(g), 78dd-2(a), 78dd-2(i), 78dd-3(a); *see also* H.R. REP. NO. 95-640, at 7 (1977); RESOURCE GUIDE, *supra* note 13, at 14.

32. RESOURCE GUIDE, *supra* note 13, at 12–13.

33. United States v. Kay, 359 F.3d 738 (5th Cir. 2004).

34. 15 U.S.C. §§ 78dd-1(a)(1)–(3), 78dd-2(a)(1)–(3), 78dd-3(a)(1)–(3).

being "aware of a high probability of the existence of such circumstance."[35] Past enforcement practice demonstrates that prosecutors will impute knowledge to persons or companies that consciously disregard or deliberately ignore facts that reasonably alert them to highly probable violations. In *United States v. King*, for example, the Eighth Circuit affirmed a jury instruction in an FCPA prosecution that construed "knowledge" to include "deliberate ignorance," allowing the jury to impute knowledge to the defendant if it finds, beyond a reasonable doubt, a conscious intention to avoid knowledge.[36]

Similarly, the term "foreign officials" is defined expansively to include both high- and low-ranking officials and employees of foreign governments, departments, agencies, and instrumentalities—or anyone acting for or on behalf of such government or government entity.[37] "Foreign officials" also include officers and employees of "public international organizations," designated by the President, a category currently including—among others—the United Nations, the World Trade Organization, the International Committee of the Red Cross, and the International Monetary Fund.[38]

Because the term "instrumentality" is not defined in the statute, litigation over the scope of the "foreign official" definition has challenged whether employees of state-owned entities (SOEs) are covered by the term. The *Resource Guide to the U.S. Foreign Corrupt Practices Act* (the "Resource Guide"), issued jointly by the SEC and DOJ in November 2012, states the government's position that an agency or instrumentality of a foreign government *may* include an entity owned or controlled by the state—even if it is not wholly owned or explicitly controlled[39]–but that the determination "requires a fact-specific analysis of an entity's ownership, control, status, and function."[40]

---

35. 15 U.S.C. §§ 78dd-1(f)(2), 78dd-2(h)(3), 78dd-3(f)(3).
36. *See* United States v. King, 351 F.3d 859, 866 (8th Cir. 2003).
37. 15 U.S.C. §§ 78dd-1(f)(1)(a), 78dd-2(h)(2)(A), 78dd-3(f)(2)(A).
38. 15 U.S.C. §§ 78dd-1(f)(1), 78dd-2(h)(2), 78dd-3(f)(2); 22 U.S.C. § 288; Implementing the Agreement Establishing the World Trade Organization Concerning Legal Capacity and Privilege and Immunities, 62 Fed. Reg. 18,017 (Apr. 9, 1997); International Committee of the Red Cross, 12 Fed. Reg. 24,247 (June 23, 1988); Designating Public International Organization Entitled to Enjoy Certain Privileges, Exemptions, and Immunities, 11 Fed. Reg. 7713 (July 11, 1946); Designating Public International Organizations Entitled to Enjoy Certain Privileges, Exemptions, and Immunities, 11 Fed. Reg. 1809 (Feb 19, 1946) (United Nations).
39. RESOURCE GUIDE, *supra* note 13, at 20–21.
40. *Id.* at 20.

In 2014, in *United States v. Esquenazi*, the Eleventh Circuit considered the breadth of the FCPA definition of "foreign official," largely affirming the government's more expansive interpretation.[41] Defendants Joel Esquenazi and Carlos Rodriguez were convicted in 2011 of violating the FCPA,[42] and sentenced to fifteen and seven years' imprisonment, respectively.[43] On appeal, the defendants challenged the district court's jury instructions regarding whether a Haitian telecommunications company can be considered an "instrumentality" of the Haitian government under the FCPA.[44] The court held that the company was an instrumentality, and provided a complex, multi-factored test to determine when a government controls an entity, which is discussed in further detail below in section 20:5.6.[45]

Since then, DOJ and the SEC have continued to push the boundary of who constitutes a "foreign official" for purposes of the FCPA. The SEC levied FCPA charges against Alere, Inc., for payments to the manager of a privately incorporated health insurance company that the SEC alleged Colombia's Ministry of Health took control of following allegations of mismanagement.[46] In addition, DOJ treated an employee of a commercial company who received allegedly corrupt payments from SBM Offshore as a "foreign official" for the purposes of the FCPA due to the company's license to operate on behalf of a state-owned entity.[47]

---

41. United States v. Esquenazi, 752 F.3d 912 (11th Cir. 2014).
42. Press Release, U.S. Dep't of Justice, Two Telecommunications Executives Convicted by Miami Jury on All Counts for Their Involvement in Scheme to Bribe Officials at State-Owned Telecommunications Company in Haiti (Aug. 5, 2011), https://www.justice.gov/opa/pr/2011/August/11-crm-1020.html.
43. Press Release, U.S. Dep't of Justice, Executive Sentenced to 15 Years in Prison for Scheme to Bribe Officials at State-Owned Telecommunications Company in Haiti (Oct. 25, 2011), https://www.justice.gov/opa/pr/2011/October/11-crm-1407.html.
44. *Esquenazi*, 752 F.3d at 920.
45. *Id.* at 925–26.
46. Order Instituting Cease-and-Desist Proceedings Pursuant to Section 8A of the Securities Exchange Act of 1934, Making Findings, and Imposing a Cease-and-Desist Order, SEC Administrative Penalty No. 3-18228 (Sept. 28, 2017), https://www.sec.gov/litigation/admin/2017/33-10417.pdf.
47. *See* Press Release, U.S. Dep't of Justice, SBM Offshore N.V. and United States-Based Subsidiary Resolve Foreign Corrupt Practices Act Case Involving Bribes in Five Countries (Nov. 29, 2017), https://www.justice.gov/opa/pr/sbm-offshore-nv-and-united-states-based-subsidiary-resolve-foreign-corrupt-practices-act-case.

[C] Affirmative Defenses and Statutory Exception

There are two affirmative defenses and one statutory exception built into the FCPA's anti-bribery provisions. First, the local law defense is available in the unusual circumstance when a defendant can establish that a corrupt payment under the FCPA was actually *lawful* under the written laws and regulations of the country in which the payment was made.[48] Second, the so-called "reasonable and bona fide expenditures" defense is available when the questionable expenses disbursed are directly related either to the execution or performance of a contract between the defendant and the foreign official's employing government or agency, or to the promotion and/or demonstration of the defendant's products and services.[49]

The FCPA's anti-bribery provisions also contain a narrow statutory exception for "facilitating payments" that are made simply to "expedite or to secure the performance of a routine government action."[50] According to the SEC and DOJ, such payments must be made for the sole purpose of ensuring completion of a non-discretionary, usually ministerial action—for example, processing paperwork, issuing visas, establishing police protection, or supplying utilities and services such as power, water, phone, or mail.[51] In practice, however, there may be reasons not to rely too heavily on this exception. Some courts have suggested that this exception only applies to a very narrow category of small dollar, nondiscretionary activities by lower-level officials,[52] and even in some situations that would seem to fit within that narrow category the DOJ has declined to apply it.[53]

§ 20:3.2 Accounting Provisions

The FCPA's accounting provisions complement the anti-bribery provisions by requiring that public companies accurately account for their assets and liabilities—effectively preventing issuers from concealing evidence of illicit payments. Companies whose securities are listed in the United States must (a) make and keep books and records that accurately and fairly reflect the transactions of the

48. 15 U.S.C. §§ 78dd-1(c), 78dd-3(c).
49. *Id.*
50. 15 U.S.C. §§ 78dd-1(b), 78dd-2(b), 78dd-3(b).
51. RESOURCE GUIDE, *supra* note 13, at 25.
52. *See Kay*, 359 F.3d at 751; United States v. Duperval, 777 F.3d 1324, 1334–35 (11th Cir. 2015).
53. *See* Press Release, U.S. Dep't of Justice, Westinghouse Air Brake Technologies Corporation Agrees to Pay $300,000 Penalty to Resolve Foreign Bribery Violations in India (Feb. 14, 2008), https://www.justice.gov/archive/opa/pr/2008/February/08_crm_116.html.

corporation and (b) devise and maintain an adequate system of internal accounting controls.

The accounting provisions apply to "issuers"—any company that has a class of securities registered pursuant to section 12 of the Exchange Act, or that is required to file annual or other periodic reports with the SEC. As such, these provisions extend to any company with securities traded on a U.S. national securities exchange, including foreign issuers of exchange-traded Level 1 and Level 2 ADRs, and those companies with stock traded over-the-counter in the United States that are also required to file periodic reports with the SEC.[54] In contrast to the anti-bribery provisions, however, the accounting provisions of the FCPA do not explicitly cover private companies.[55] (Private companies may still be subject to liability if they violate the FCPA when acting on behalf of an issuer, as agent or stockholder; if they engage in some conduct that causes an issuer to commit an FCPA violation; or if they conspire with an issuer to violate the FCPA.)

These accounting provisions effectively expand the jurisdictional reach of the FCPA, because an issuer's books and records are understood to include the books and records of any consolidated subsidiaries and affiliates. Thus, according to U.S. authorities, an issuer is obligated to ensure that its foreign subsidiaries and joint ventures comply with the FCPA's accounting provisions.[56] However, for subsidiaries in which the parent issuer owns a minority stake (50% or less), a safe-harbor provision protects the parent as long as it in "good faith" uses its influence, to the extent reasonable under the circumstances, to cause the minority-owned subsidiary or affiliate to devise and maintain an FCPA-compliant system of internal accounting controls.[57] The relevant circumstances that will be taken into account when assessing a parent's "good faith" efforts include: the parent's relative degree of ownership of the domestic or foreign firm, and the business laws and practices of the country where the firm is located.

The parent issuer faces a mosaic of potential liability concerns under the accounting provisions. First, there is potential direct criminal liability for the parent itself if it "knowingly" fails to comply with the accounting provisions, even if the most immediate impact was at the subsidiary level.[58] Second, a parent company may be subject to civil liability for any subsidiary's failure to comply with the accounting provisions—regardless of whether the parent had any knowledge

---

54. *Id.* at 42–43.
55. *Id.* at 43.
56. RESOURCE GUIDE, *supra* note 13, at 43.
57. 15 U.S.C. § 78m(b)(6).
58. 15 U.S.C. § 78m(b)(5).

of the problem.[59] Conspiring in, or aiding and abetting, violations of the accounting provisions may also result in criminal or civil liability.[60] And it is not only companies—parents and subsidiaries alike—that face FCPA liability; individuals can also be held criminally or civilly liable for a variety of conduct, such as aiding and abetting (or causing) an issuer to violate the accounting provisions, making materially false statements in violation of the Exchange Act, or evading accounting controls.[61]

[A] Books and Records Provision

The first of the FCPA's accounting provisions, the so-called "books and records" provision, requires issuers to "make and keep books, records, and accounts, which, in reasonable detail, accurately and fairly reflect the transactions and dispositions of the assets of the issuer."[62] "Reasonable detail" is defined in the statute to consist of "such level of detail . . . as would satisfy prudent officials in the conduct of their own affairs."[63] The provision is designed to make it more difficult for a company to disguise improper payments, but it applies equally to the recording of all the company's transactions. Notably, questionable payments that do not meet the elements of an FCPA bribery offense may nonetheless violate the books and records provision if they are improperly recorded.[64]

[B] Internal Controls Provision

The internal controls provision of the FCPA requires issuers to "devise and maintain a system of internal accounting controls sufficient to provide reasonable assurances that":

(i) transactions are executed in accordance with management's general or specific authorization;

(ii) transactions are recorded as necessary (I) to permit preparation of financial statements in conformity with generally accepted accounting principles or any other criteria applicable to such statements, and (II) to maintain accountability for assets;

(iii) access to assets is permitted only in accordance with management's general or specific authorization; and

---

59. 15 U.S.C. § 78m(b)(2), (6).
60. *See* RESOURCE GUIDE, *supra* note 13, at 43–45.
61. *See id.*
62. 15 U.S.C. § 78m(b)(2)(A).
63. 15 U.S.C. § 78m(b)(7).
64. RESOURCE GUIDE, *supra* note 13, at 39.

(iv) the recorded accountability for assets is compared with the existing assets at reasonable intervals and appropriate action is taken with respect to any differences . . . .[65]

Just as in the books and records provision, which requires records to be kept in "reasonable detail," the internal controls provision defines "reasonable assurances" according to a "prudent person" standard: they consist of "such level of detail and degree of assurance as would satisfy prudent officials in the conduct of their own affairs."[66] The statute does not, however, impose specific requirements for the internal controls that issuers must implement; each company may create a system that is tailored to its specific needs and circumstances.[67]

§ 20:4 FCPA Enforcement

In the past, SEC and DOJ enforcement actions have tended to focus on natural resource developers (especially in the oil and gas industries); government contractors; and military, energy, and infrastructure suppliers. In April 2013, however, U.S. authorities conducted the first-ever FCPA enforcement action in the fashion industry, with the SEC and DOJ each entering into a non-prosecution agreement (NPA) with New York-based apparel retailer Ralph Lauren Corporation, discussed in further detail below in section 20:4.1. In addition, other investigations seem to signal that DOJ and the SEC may also be paying attention to other related industries—including cosmetics and the retail industry generally, as highlighted in the Avon case discussed below in section 20:4.2.[68] Indeed, makers and retailers of apparel face many of the same challenges as other multinational companies that engage in overseas manufacture, cross-border procurement, and import for sale. Section 20:4.4 outlines some of the common supply-chain issues that have implications for potential FCPA exposure in the fashion and retail apparel industry.

§ 20:4.1 *Case Study: Ralph Lauren*

On April 22, 2013, Ralph Lauren Corporation ("Ralph Lauren") entered into separate NPAs with both the SEC and DOJ to resolve FCPA allegations relating to payments made to government officials

---

65. 15 U.S.C. § 78m(b)(2)(B).
66. 15 U.S.C. § 78m(b)(7).
67. RESOURCE GUIDE, *supra* note 13, at 40.
68. In 2012, the *New York Times* reported that global retail giant Wal-Mart Stores Inc. had been investigating potential FCPA violations within the company. Because Wal-Mart is a client of the authors' law firm, this chapter will not comment on those reports.

in Argentina to obtain customs clearance of merchandise.[69] As part of the resolutions, the company agreed to pay $882,000 in penalties[70] and to disgorge $734,846 in profits and interest.[71] In addition, the NPA with DOJ obligates the company to continue to enhance its compliance policies and to submit annual, written reports on these efforts.[72] Ralph Lauren's NPA with the SEC is unusual in that it is the first the SEC has entered into for FCPA-related misconduct.[73]

According to the NPAs, from 2005 through 2009, the General Manager (described as a "dual U.S. and Argentine citizen"[74]) and others at Ralph Lauren's indirect, wholly owned subsidiary in Argentina ("RLC Argentina") approved payments to Argentine customs officials through a customs broker "to assist in improperly obtaining paperwork necessary for RLC products to clear customs, to permit clearance of items without the necessary paperwork, to permit the clearance of prohibited goods, and to avoid inspection of products by Argentine customs officials."[75] The NPA with DOJ explicitly states that these payments "were not for routine government action" for purposes of the FCPA's facilitation payments exception.[76] The broker obtained money for the payments by submitting invoices to RLC Argentina for line items such as "Loading and Delivery Expenses" and "Stamp Tax/Label Tax."[77] During this period, RLC Argentina paid the broker almost $600,000 to make improper payments to Argentine customs

---

69. *See* Press Release, U.S. Dep't of Justice, Ralph Lauren Corp. Resolves Foreign Corrupt Practices Act Investigation and Agrees to Pay $882,000 Monetary Penalty (Apr. 22, 2013), https://www.justice.gov/opa/pr/2013/April/13-crm-456.html [hereinafter DOJ Ralph Lauren Press Release]; Press Release, U.S. Sec. & Exch. Comm'n, SEC Announces Non-Prosecution Agreement with Ralph Lauren Corp. Involving FCPA Misconduct (Apr. 22, 2013), https://www.sec.gov/news/press/2013/2013-65.htm [hereinafter SEC Ralph Lauren Press Release].
70. Non-Pros. Agreement between Ralph Lauren Corp. and U.S. Dep't of Justice, Criminal Div., Fraud Section, at 2, Apr. 22, 2013, https://www.justice.gov/criminal/fraud/fcpa/cases/ralph-lauren/Ralph-Lauren.-NPA-Executed.pdf [hereinafter DOJ Ralph Lauren NPA].
71. Non-Pros. Agreement between Ralph Lauren Corp. and Sec. & Exch. Comm'n Div. of Enforcement, at 2, Apr. 22, 2013, https://www.sec.gov/news/press/2013/2013-65-npa.pdf [hereinafter SEC Ralph Lauren NPA].
72. DOJ Ralph Lauren NPA, *supra* note 70, at 3.
73. SEC Ralph Lauren Press Release, *supra* note 69.
74. DOJ Ralph Lauren NPA, *supra* note 70, at A-1; SEC Ralph Lauren NPA, *supra* note 71, at ex. A ¶ 3.
75. SEC Ralph Lauren NPA, *supra* note 71, at ex. A ¶ 5; *see also* DOJ Ralph Lauren NPA, *supra* note 70, at A-2.
76. DOJ Ralph Lauren NPA, *supra* note 70, at A-2.
77. *Id.* at A-3; SEC Ralph Lauren NPA, *supra* note 71, at ex. A ¶ 6.

officials.[78] The NPA with the SEC contains an additional paragraph explaining that the General Manager also provided or authorized several gifts to government officials to secure the importation of products into Argentina, including perfume, dresses, and handbags valued at between $400 and $14,000 each.[79]

The conduct was discovered during an internal investigation, which was initiated after RLC Argentina employees raised concerns about the customs broker in 2010.[80] Within two weeks of uncovering the payments and gifts, Ralph Lauren self-reported its preliminary findings to DOJ and the SEC.[81] On discovering the misconduct, the company ended its relationship with the customs broker and undertook several remedial measures, including:

- amending its anti-corruption policy and translating it into eight languages;
- enhancing its third-party due diligence procedures;
- enhancing its commissions policy;
- amending its gift policy; and
- conducting in-person anti-corruption training for certain employees.[82]

The NPAs also describe the company's extensive cooperation with DOJ and the SEC, which included:

- promptly reporting its findings;
- voluntarily producing documents and information;
- providing accurate translations of documents;
- making witnesses available for interviews; and
- reviewing certain other global operations, including those in Italy, Hong Kong, and Japan.[83]

According to DOJ's press release, the NPA "acknowledges RLC's extensive, thorough, and timely cooperation," and its "early and

78. DOJ Ralph Lauren NPA, *supra* note 70, at A-4; SEC Ralph Lauren NPA, *supra* note 71, at ex.A ¶ 7.
79. SEC Ralph Lauren NPA, *supra* note 71, at ex. A ¶ 8.
80. *Id.* at ex. A ¶ 11.
81. *Id.*
82. *Id.* at ex. A. ¶12; DOJ Ralph Lauren NPA, *supra* note 70, at 1.
83. DOJ Ralph Lauren NPA, *supra* note 70, at 1; SEC Ralph Lauren NPA, *supra* note 71, at ex. A ¶ 12.

extensive remediation."[84] According to the SEC's press release, the NPA was "due to the company's prompt reporting of the violations on its own initiative, the completeness of the information it provided, and its extensive, thorough, and real-time cooperation with the SEC's investigation," as well as "the significant remedial measures."[85]

Notably, there is no suggestion that the company was aware of or approved this conduct or that there was a U.S. nexus. Rather, the NPAs recite that the General Manager of the subsidiary was an "agent" of Ralph Lauren, an issuer, for purposes of the FCPA;[86] that Ralph Lauren failed to implement adequate internal controls, including an anti-corruption program and training, at RLC Argentina;[87] and that, with respect to the NPA with the SEC, the payments were inaccurately recorded in RLC Argentina's books and records, which were then consolidated into Ralph Lauren's books and records.[88]

§ 20:4.2 Case Study: Avon

Another illustration of the potential for FCPA compliance issues in the fashion industry is the investigation of Avon Products, Inc. ("Avon"), a global manufacturer and marketer of beauty products and related items. On December 17, 2014, Avon entered into a deferred-prosecution agreement (DPA) with DOJ and a civil settlement with the SEC to resolve FCPA allegations that Avon Products (China) Co. Ltd. ("Avon China"), a wholly owned subsidiary of Avon, gave Chinese officials meals, travel, and entertainment to obtain the necessary direct selling licenses and avoid fines and bad press.[89] Avon agreed to pay a penalty of $67,648,000[90] and to disgorge $67,365,013 in profits

---

84. DOJ Ralph Lauren Press Release, *supra* note 69.
85. SEC Ralph Lauren Press Release, *supra* note 69.
86. DOJ Ralph Lauren NPA, *supra* note 70, at A-1; SEC Ralph Lauren NPA, *supra* note 71, at ex. A ¶ 3.
87. DOJ Ralph Lauren NPA, *supra* note 70, at A-3; SEC Ralph Lauren NPA, *supra note* 71, at ex. A ¶ 9.
88. *Id.* at ex. A; SEC Ralph Lauren NPA, *supra* note 71, at ex. A ¶ 10.
89. *See* Press Release, U.S. Dep't of Justice, Avon China Pleads Guilty to Violating the FCPA by Concealing More Than $8 Million in Gifts to Chinese Officials (Dec. 17, 2014), https://www.justice.gov/opa/pr/avon-china-pleads-guilty-violating-fcpa-concealing-more-8-million-gifts-chinese-officials [hereinafter DOJ Avon Press Release]; Press Release, U.S. Sec. & Exch. Comm'n, SEC Charges Avon with FCPA Violations (Dec. 22, 2014), https://www.sec.gov/news/pressrelease/2014-285.html [hereinafter SEC Avon Press Release].
90. Deferred Prosecution Agreement, United States v. Avon Prods., Inc., No. 14-00828 (S.D.N.Y. Dec. 17, 2014) [hereinafter DOJ Avon DPA], at 7.

and interest,[91] a total of approximately $135 million. In addition, the DPA with DOJ obligates the company to retain an independent compliance monitor to oversee its FCPA compliance program for eighteen (18) months, after which it must self-report its compliance efforts for another eighteen (18) months.[92] Concurrently, Avon China pleaded guilty to distributing more than $8 million in gifts, cash, and travel, and to attempting to disguise these actions.[93]

[A] History of the Avon Investigation

In 2006, Avon made headlines when it secured the first license to make door-to-door sales in China.[94] But in June 2008, a whistleblower informed the company that Avon employees were using meals and gifts to influence Chinese officials.[95] The company moved quickly to initiate an internal probe led by the audit committee, hiring outside counsel to conduct an investigation and compliance review; Avon voluntarily disclosed its internal investigation to DOJ and the SEC in October 2008.[96]

Avon's internal probe reportedly expanded in 2011 to include reviews of FCPA compliance in additional countries, including Brazil, Mexico, Argentina, India, and Japan.[97] The conduct under scrutiny spanned a time period from as early as 2004 to as recently as 2010.[98] In its 2011 annual report filed with the SEC, the company reported

91. SEC Avon Press Release, *supra* note 89; Complaint, SEC v. Avon Prods., Inc., No. 14-cv-9956 (S.D.N.Y. Dec. 17, 2014), https://www.sec.gov/litigation/complaints/2014/comp-pr2014-285.pdf.

92. DOJ Avon Press Release, *supra* note 89.

93. Plea Agreement, United States v. Avon Prods. (China) Co., No. 14-cr-00828 (S.D.N.Y. Dec. 17, 2014), https://www.justice.gov/sites/default/files/criminal-fraud/legacy/2014/12/30/avon-china-plea-agt-file-stamped.pdf.

94. Phil Wahba, *Avon Sales Slide as Door-to-Door Reps Leave*, REUTERS (Feb. 14, 2012), https://www.reuters.com/article/2012/02/14/us-avon-idUSTRE81D0N920120214 ("In 2006, Avon became the first Western company to win a license from China to sell products door-to-door, which was viewed as a coup for [then CEO Andrea] Jung.").

95. Press Release, Avon Products Inc., Avon Statement on Voluntary Disclosure (Oct. 20, 2008), http://phx.corporate-ir.net/phoenix.zhtml?c=90402&p=irol-newsArticle&ID=1581421&highlight=.

96. Samuel Rubenfeld, *Avon Warns of Further Firings Amid FCPA Probe*, CORRUPTION CURRENTS BLOG, WALL ST. J. (Nov. 1, 2012 5:57 PM), http://blogs.wsj.com/corruption-currents/2012/11/01/avon-warns-of-further-firings-amid-fcpa-probe/.

97. Ellen Byron, *Avon Bribe Investigation Widens*, WALL ST. J. (May 5, 2011), http://online.wsj.com/article/SB10001424052748704322804576303302214411400.html.

98. *Id.*

that the investigation had broadened in scope to include a variety of different kinds of potential FCPA violations:

> The internal investigation and compliance reviews are focused on reviewing certain expenses and books and records processes, including, but not limited to, travel, entertainment, gifts, use of third-party vendors and consultants and related due diligence, joint ventures and acquisitions, and payments to third-party agents and others, in connection with our business dealings, directly or indirectly, with foreign governments and their employees.[99]

In October 2011, Avon disclosed to investors a formal SEC order of investigation into potential FCPA violations.[100] In early 2012, press reports indicated that federal prosecutors were also formally investigating Avon, focusing on "a 2005 internal audit report by the company that concluded Avon employees in China may have been bribing officials in violation of the Foreign Corrupt Practices Act," at a magnitude of several hundreds of thousands of dollars paid to Chinese officials and third-party consultants.[101]

The *Wall Street Journal* reported that Avon's internal probe uncovered an email summary of a 2008 sales strategy meeting, discussing potentially increasing the company's spending on gifts and travel for Chinese officials, in order to match competitors' efforts.[102] In the expanded probe, Avon also reportedly discovered millions of dollars in payments made to Brazilian and French consultants who assisted the company with its tax bills in those countries.[103] Prosecutors were also reportedly interested in 2005 audit reports reportedly showing hundreds of thousands of dollars in payments made in China.[104]

In July 2012, federal prosecutors reportedly sought an interview with Avon's former CEO and then-full-time chairman, Andrea Jung—even though "it is rare," in FCPA investigations, "for chief executives

---

99. AVON PRODS. INC., ANNUAL REPORT (FORM 10-K), at 12 (Feb. 29, 2012), https://www.sec.gov/Archives/edgar/data/8868/000000886812000010/d10k.htm.

100. AVON PRODS. INC., QUARTERLY REPORT (FORM 10-Q), at 11 (Oct. 27, 2011), https://www.sec.gov/Archives/edgar/data/8868/000000886811000016/a2011930-10q.htm.

101. Joe Palazzolo & Emily Glazer, *Foreign Bribe Case at Avon Presented to Grand Jury*, WALL ST. J. (Feb. 13, 2012), http://online.wsj.com/article/SB10001424052970203315804577209443264460570.html.

102. Joe Palazzolo, Emily Glazer, & Joann S. Lublin, *Prosecutors Ask to Meet Jung in Avon Bribe Probe*, WALL ST. J. (July 29, 2012), http://online.wsj.com/article/SB10000872396390444840104577553683406542666.html.

103. *Id.*

104. *Id.*

of large corporations to be asked in for questioning."[105] In August 2012, Avon reported in its quarterly filing that the company was "in discussions with the SEC and DOJ regarding mutually resolving the government investigations."[106]

Since disclosure of the FCPA investigation, Avon has made notable changes in its leadership and management. In May 2011, Avon terminated several senior executives, including its chief financial officer; the former general manager of its Chinese unit; the former head of corporate affairs for China; and the former head of global internal audit and security. In addition, a senior vice president responsible for many of the company's global operations retired in February 2012 after being placed on leave in connection with the investigation.[107] Avon's vice chairman of developed markets and former chief financial officer was terminated at year-end 2011 in connection with the bribery investigation.[108] In April 2012, another senior Group VP resigned, reportedly in connection with conduct during her time as head of internal audit from 2003 to 2005.[109] The General Counsel was also replaced in September 2012.[110] Most visibly, Andrea Jung–though she is not accused of any wrongdoing in the context of the FCPA investigation—stepped down early from her position as Executive Chairman at year-end 2012.[111]

[B] Ramifications of the Avon Investigation

The Avon investigation sets a benchmark for the high cost of internal FCPA probes: reports indicate that the company expended more

---

105. Joe Palazzolo & Emily Glazer, *Foreign Bribe Case at Avon Presented to Grand Jury*, WALL ST. J. (Feb. 13, 2012), http://online.wsj.com/article/SB10001424052970203315804577209443264460570.html.

106. AVON PRODS. INC., QUARTERLY REPORT (FORM 10-Q), at 12 (Aug. 1, 2012), http://www.sec.gov/Archives/edgar/data/8868/000000886812000063/a201263010q.htm.

107. Joe Palazzolo & Joann S. Lublin, *Avon Fires Vice Chairman*, WALL ST. J., Jan. 31, 2012, http://online.wsj.com/article/SB10001424052970204652904577193550538605694.html.

108. *Id.*

109. Samuel Rubenfeld, *Another Avon Exec Resigns Amid Bribery Probe*, CORRUPTION CURRENTS BLOG, WALL ST. J. (Apr. 26, 2012 2:26 PM), http://blogs.wsj.com/corruption-currents/2012/04/26/another-avon-exec-resigns-amid-bribery-probe/.

110. Kristin Jones, *Avon Names General Counsel*, WALL ST. J. (Sept. 10, 2012), http://online.wsj.com/article/SB10000872396390444554704577644002911291744.html.

111. Emily Glazer, *Avon Chairman Andrea Jung to Resign; Fred Hassan to Take Over*, WALL ST. J. (Oct. 5, 2012), http://online.wsj.com/article/SB10000872396390443635404578038203052881038.html.

than $300 million on outside counsel and other expenses related to the investigation.[112]

In addition, Avon faced other legal ramifications arising from the FCPA investigation. Starting in July and August 2010, several derivative actions were filed against Avon alleging breach of fiduciary duty, abuse of control, waste of corporate assets, and/or unjust enrichment in connection with failures in FCPA compliance and internal controls.[113] In 2015, Avon agreed to pay $62 million to settle a shareholder class action claiming that it inflated stock prices by hiding FCPA violations.[114] In 2016, the company reached settlements in three derivative lawsuits that required it to pay $4 million in legal fees and implement an extensive FCPA compliance program.[115] Between the investigation, DOJ and SEC penalties, and shareholder litigation, Avon has paid more than half a billion dollars to resolve the alleged FCPA violations.

§ 20:4.3 Case Study: Nu Skin

Another FCPA enforcement action in the fashion industry became public in 2016. The subject of the investigation was Nu Skin, a skincare and dietary supplement company. On September 20, 2016, the SEC instituted cease-and-desist proceedings, and Nu Skin settled to resolve FCPA allegations that a $150,000 payment identified as a donation, was in fact a bribe to a Chinese official to intervene in an investigation into Nu Skin's compliance with direct selling laws.[116] The company paid $300,000 in penalties, and disgorged $465,688 in profits and interest.[117]

---

112. *See* Peter J. Henning, *Foreign Bribery Cases That Can Drag On and On*, DEALBOOK BLOG, N.Y. TIMES (Dec. 22, 2014 12:29 PM), https://dealbook.nytimes.com/2014/12/22/foreign-bribery-cases-that-can-drag-on-and-on/.
113. AVON PRODS. INC., ANNUAL REPORT (FORM 10-K) at F-40 to F-41 (Feb. 24, 2011).
114. Carmen Germaine, *Avon Pays $62M to End Investors' FCPA Suit*, LAW360 (Aug. 18, 2015 4:45 PM), https://www.law360.com/articles/692407/avon-pays-62m-to-end-investors-fcpa-suit.
115. Stephen Dockery, *Avon Settles Bribery Suits, Agrees to Major Compliance Overhaul*, WALL ST. J. (Apr. 14, 2016 5:47 PM), https://blogs.wsj.com/riskandcompliance/2016/04/14/avon-settles-bribery-suits-agrees-major-compliance-overhaul/.
116. In the Matter of Nu Skin Enters., Inc., Order Instituting Cease-and-Desist Proceedings Pursuant to Section 21C of the Securities and Exchange Act of 1934, Making Findings, and Imposing a Cease-and-Desist Order, SEC Administrative Proceeding No. 3-17556 (Sept. 20, 2016), https://www.sec.gov/litigation/admin/2016/34-78884.pdf.
117. *Id.*

According to the cease-and-desist order, Nu Skin's wholly owned subsidiary in China ("Nu Skin China") held a promotional meeting in a city where it was not licensed to operate, which was discovered by a provincial agency.[118] Nu Skin China responded to the agency that it would like to "donate some money instead of a fine," and decided to ask a party official to intervene in the investigation in return for a donation to his charity[119] Nu Skin China sought approval from Nu Skin US for the donation, and was informed of the FCPA risk and encouraged to include anti-corruption language in the donation letter, but moved ahead with the donation and omitted the recommended language.[120] Two days after the donation, the agency informed Nu Skin China it would not be charged or fined.[121]

The cease-and-desist order states that Nu Skin US did not create or ensure compliance with a reasonable system of internal accounting controls to ensure that transactions were recorded accurately.[122] Beyond the substantial FCPA risk in fashion industry supply chains, this demonstrates that regulators are sometimes as aggressive as to initiate an enforcement action based on a single incorrectly designated donation.

§ 20:4.4 Supply Chain Risks

Apparel brands and retailers inevitably have multiple layers of direct and indirect business partners both domestically and abroad, constituting a complex supply chain that traverses national borders. Under the third-party-payment provisions of the FCPA, a company may face liability for improper payments made by its business or joint venture partners.[123] Any third party that receives payment (or any other thing of value) from a company, and subsequently makes an improper payment with that company's "knowledge," could potentially expose the company to liability under the FCPA's third-party-payment provisions (discussed in greater detail below).[124] Key categories of overseas third parties could include the following: (1) vendors and factories; (2) transport companies and customs clearance agents; (3) travel agencies; (4) immigration and visa agents; (5) real estate agents; (6) tax agents; (7) accountants; and (8) lawyers. This section analyzes in detail three of the most common overseas

118. *Id.*
119. *Id.*
120. *Id.*
121. *Id.*
122. *Id.*
123. 15 U.S.C. § 78dd-1(a)(3); 15 U.S.C. § 78dd-2(a)(3); 15 U.S.C. § 78dd-3(a)(3).
124. 15 U.S.C. § 78dd-2(h)(3)(A)(i), (ii).

partners for apparel brands and retailers: third-party manufacturers, transportation service providers, and distributors.

[A] Third-Party Manufacturers

A company's liability for the conduct of a third party turns on the nature of their relationship. In general, for example, a retailer should not incur FCPA liability for unlawful conduct by the manufacturers of products sold by the retailers, absent any joint venture or agency relationship between the entities. However, the more that a third party can reasonably be seen to be speaking for or acting as an agent on behalf of a retailer, the greater the risk that regulators will attribute the acts of the third party to that retailer. To date, no FCPA enforcement action has alleged that a retailer knowingly enabled a vendor to make improper payments in order to facilitate the manufacture and transport of products to the retailer. But as a company's level of control over its vendors increases, so do the associated risks that unlawful conduct by the vendors could be attributed to the company.

[B] Transportation Service Providers

Transportation service providers may similarly have more or less interaction with a particular retailer. For example, a retailer may purchase goods from a manufacturer pursuant to an agreement under which the manufacturer arranges transportation and customs clearing services, and any losses occurring during such transport and customs processes are the responsibility of the manufacturer. This attenuated relationship makes it hard to envision a circumstance under which a retailer could be held liable under the FCPA for the unlawful conduct of a transporter or customs broker.

On the other hand, a retailer may hire the transportation services, and direct the transport vendors' activities, including scheduling shipments and resolving any issues with the customs-clearance process (even if the manufacturer is ultimately responsible for ensuring that the goods clear customs). This direct engagement with and oversight of such relatively high-risk business partners increases the risk that the retailer may be held liable for the transport vendors' unlawful activities. Moreover, given the FCPA's expansive third-party-payment provisions, there is also a risk that the retailer may be held responsible for unlawful conduct by customs clearance agents, due to the retailer's greater involvement in the transport and customs clearance process.

Indeed, in recent years the government has brought more than fifteen enforcement actions in cases involving improper payments to customs officials.[125] For example, in March 2011, the Colorado-based Ball Corporation—manufacturer of metal packaging for food, beverages, and household products—paid a $300,000 civil penalty to settle SEC charges of violating the FCPA books-and-records and internal control provisions.[126] Ball allegedly paid bribes totaling more than $100,000 to Argentine customs officials in order "to secure the importation of prohibited used machinery and the exportation of raw materials at reduced tariffs."[127] The improper payments were made by Ball's Argentine subsidiary, Formametal, whose senior officers approved payments to be funneled through the company's third-party non-governmental customs agent. The payments were invoiced as "customs advisory services" or "fees for customs assistance."[128] In addition to Formametal's violations of the FCPA, Ball was held liable for failing to "devise and maintain an effective system of internal controls to prevent and detect violations of the FCPA at Formametal," even after Ball officers had notice of Formametal's questionable practices.[129]

[C] Distributors

Enforcement authorities have brought a series of FCPA enforcement actions against companies for unlawful activity by their distributors, alleging that the companies knowingly lowered product sales prices so that the distributors would have a sufficient margin to pay government officials in order to win sales contracts.[130] For example, in 2011, Diageo—the London-based maker of top liquor brands such as Johnnie Walker and Windsor Scotch whiskeys, among others—paid $16 million to settle SEC charges that the company, through its subsidiaries and third-party distributors, spent more than $2.7 million

---

125. *See, e.g.*, actions against ABB Vetco Gray, American Rice, Avery Dennison, Baker Hughes, Ball Corporation, BJ Services, Chiquita, Con-Way, Diageo, Dow, Helmerich & Payne, Nature's Sunshine Products, Noble Corporation, Panalpina, Pride International, Royal Dutch Shell, Tidewater, and Transocean Inc.

126. *See* In the Matter of Ball Corp., Order Instituting Cease-and-Desist Proceedings Pursuant to Section 21C of the Securities Exchange Act of 1934, Making Findings, Imposing a Cease-and-Desist Order and a Civil Money Penalty, SEC Administrative Proceeding No. 3-14305 (Mar. 24, 2011), https://www.sec.gov/litigation/admin/2011/34-64123.pdf.

127. *Id.*

128. *Id.*

129. *Id.*

130. *See, e.g.*, enforcement actions against Smith & Nephew (2012), Johnson & Johnson (2011), Diageo (2011), Daimler (2010), Fiat (2008), Faro Technologies (2008), AGA Medical (2008), AB Volvo (2008), Ingersoll Rand (2007), and InVision (2005).

on illicit payments to foreign government officials in India, South Korea, and Thailand.[131] In India, according to the SEC, Diageo "engaged in a pervasive practice of making illicit direct and indirect payments to government officials throughout India to obtain and retain liquor sales," resulting in more than $11 million in unjustly obtained sales.[132] Diageo reimbursed cash payments made by its third-party distributors to various employees of government liquor stores and the Indian military's Canteen Stores Department.[133] The payments were made with Diageo's knowledge and authorization, with the intent of increasing government sales orders.[134] Diageo then violated the accounting provisions of the FCPA by failing to account properly for the payments—disguising them as "promotion" or "special incentive" expenses.[135] This level of involvement in the improper payments, nominally made by third-party distributors, but clearly authorized and supervised by Diageo employees, was sufficient to expose Diageo to FCPA liability.

§ 20:5 Issue-Spotting in FCPA Enforcement

The preceding discussion illustrates the potentially sweeping reach of the FCPA, and demonstrates the risks that multinational corporations face when seeking to conduct business abroad within the bounds of the law. The following section outlines some of the specific issues that prudent managers and directors in the fashion industry should take into account when contemplating how to anticipate and respond to potential FCPA issues.

§ 20:5.1 Issuers vs. Non-Issuers

A key threshold determination in evaluating potential FCPA exposure is whether a corporation meets the statutory definition of an "issuer." Issuers are subject to additional provisions of law that do not affect non-issuers—namely, the accounting provisions[136] and the

131. Press Release, U.S. Sec. & Exch. Comm'n, SEC Charges Liquor Giant Diageo with FCPA Violations (July 27, 2011), https://www.sec.gov/news/press/2011/2011-158.htm.
132. Order Instituting Cease-and-Desist Proceedings Pursuant to Section 21C of the Securities Exchange Act of 1934, Making Findings and Imposing a Cease-and-Desist Order and a Civil Penalty, SEC Administrative Proceeding No. 3-14490 (July 27, 2011), https://www.sec.gov/litigation/admin/2011/34-64978.pdf.
133. *Id.*
134. *Id.*
135. *Id.*
136. 15 U.S.C. § 78m(b)(2)(A)–(B).

first of the three anti-bribery provisions of the FCPA.[137] The distinction is particularly important because the accounting provisions are more easily and frequently prosecuted by U.S. enforcement agencies. Indeed, issuers that have committed no violation of the FCPA's anti-bribery provisions may nonetheless be held liable for the inaccurate recording of any payment, whether ultimately determined to be improper or not, as well as any inadequate internal controls or the circumvention of relevant controls.[138]

As discussed above, an "issuer" is any corporation with a class of securities registered under section 12 of the 1934 Securities Exchange Act (the "Exchange Act"), or one that is required under section 15(d) of the Exchange Act to file periodic and other reports with the SEC.[139] A "domestic concern," on the other hand, is any individual who is a U.S. citizen, national, or resident, or any corporate entity with its principal place of business in the United States that is organized under the laws of the United States (or of a state, territory, possession, or commonwealth).[140] Both issuers and domestic concerns may be held liable for violating the FCPA's anti-bribery provisions, regardless of whether they took any action within the United States that furthered the corrupt payment.[141]

In contrast, under 15 U.S.C. § 78dd-3, persons and entities that are not issuers or domestic concerns are prohibited—while within U.S. territory—from using any "means or instrumentality of interstate commerce" to take any action in furtherance of transmitting an improper payment to a foreign official for the purpose of obtaining or retaining business.

---

137. 15 U.S.C. § 78dd-1, which codifies section 30A of the Securities Exchange Act of 1934, contains the anti-bribery provision governing issuers; § 78dd-2 is the parallel provision governing "domestic concerns." The third anti-bribery provision, 15 U.S.C. § 78dd-3, is based on territorial jurisdiction over certain foreign nationals or entities that are neither issuers nor domestic concerns.

138. RESOURCE GUIDE, *supra* note 13, at 39 ("In instances where all the elements of a violation of the anti-bribery provisions are not met—where, for example, there was no use of interstate commerce—companies nonetheless may be liable if the improper payments are inaccurately recorded.").

139. 15 U.S.C. § 78c(a)(8); RESOURCE GUIDE, *supra* note 13, at 10–11.

140. 15 U.S.C. § 78dd-2(h)(1); RESOURCE GUIDE, *supra* note 13, at 11.

141. Note, however, that non-U.S.-based issuers would not be subject to liability unless they employed a means or instrumentality of interstate commerce, as they are not covered by the alternative jurisdiction provisions at 15 U.S.C. §§ 78dd-1(g) & 78dd-2(i). *See supra* section 20:3.1.

§ 20:5.2 Third-Party Payments

The FCPA's third-party payment provisions generally prohibit making corrupt payments through intermediaries.[142] This prohibition encompasses the practice of making a payment to any third party with the knowledge that all or part of that payment will be transmitted to a foreign official. The "knowledge" standard is defined to include conscious disregard and deliberate ignorance: A person's state of mind is "knowing" with respect to conduct, a circumstance, or a result if he is either "aware" of such conduct or result or the substantial certainty of such result, or if he "has a firm belief that such circumstance exists or that such result is substantially certain to occur."[143] Moreover, knowledge can be "established if a person is aware of a high probability of the existence of such circumstance, unless the person actually believes that such circumstance does not exist."[144] Accordingly, prosecutors will impute knowledge to persons or companies that consciously disregard or deliberately ignore facts that reasonably alert them to highly probable violations.[145] Courts have recognized this expansive definition, construing knowledge to include willful blindness or conscious avoidance of certain circumstances.[146]

The "Resource Guide highlights a number of "red flags" commonly associated with third parties, such as excessive commissions for third-party consultants and agents, or excessive discounts for third-party distributors.[147] In selecting third-party partners, companies should beware of vague "consulting agreements," overly close relationships between the third party and any foreign officials, and the use of offshore bank accounts, among other warning signs.[148] The best way to minimize the risk associated with the use of third-party agents is to conduct appropriate due diligence before entering into any agreement with a prospective consultant, distributor, or other outside agent.

Past prosecutions have targeted, for example, global freight forwarding company Panalpina and several of its oil-and-gas industry customers. Panalpina admitted to paying $27 million to foreign officials in several countries, including Azerbaijan, Brazil, and Russia,

---

142. 15 U.S.C. §§ 78dd-1(a)(3); 78dd-2(a)(3); 78dd-3(a)(3).
143. 15 U.S.C. § 78dd-1(f)(2)(A)(i)–(ii).
144. 15 U.S.C. § 78dd-1(f)(2)(B).
145. U.S. DEP'T OF JUSTICE, LAY-PERSON'S GUIDE TO THE FCPA STATUTE, at n.42 (June 2001).
146. *See, e.g.*, United States v. King, 351 F.3d 859, 866 (8th Cir. 2003); United States v. Kozeny, 664 F. Supp. 2d 369, 389 (S.D.N.Y. 2009).
147. RESOURCE GUIDE, *supra* note 13, at 22.
148. *Id.* at 22–23.

for the purpose of expediting its customers' imports and reducing their customs burdens.[149] The Switzerland-based parent company entered into a deferred prosecution agreement related to charges of violating and conspiring to violate the FCPA's anti-bribery provisions, while the U.S. subsidiary Panalpina Inc. pleaded guilty to violating the books and records provisions.[150] Panalpina's clients—including Royal Dutch Shell, Transocean, and Noble—paid criminal fines and disgorgement in varying amounts in the millions of dollars.[151]

In late 2010, a joint DOJ-SEC enforcement proceeding was brought against RAE Systems Inc., a California-based company with shares traded on the New York Stock Exchange, based on conduct that took place at its two Chinese joint-venture entities, RAE-KLH (Beijing) Co. and RAE Coal Mine Safety Instruments (Fushun) Co.[152] Chinese sales personnel employed by the joint ventures allegedly made more than $400,000 in improper payments to foreign officials in order to obtain business in China; the payments were concealed in the accounts by being falsely recorded as "business fees" or "travel and entertainment" expenditures.[153] Although the illicit payments were made by Chinese employees of a China-based joint venture, and the conduct took place exclusively in China, RAE Systems was prosecuted for its failure to implement adequate internal controls, despite knowing of a number of red flags indicating that its Chinese affiliates were engaging in

149. Press Release, U.S. Dep't of Justice, Oil Services Companies and a Freight Forwarding Company Agree to Resolve Foreign Bribery Investigations and to Pay More Than $156 Million in Criminal Penalties (Nov. 4, 2010), https://www.justice.gov/opa/pr/2010/November/10-crm-1251.html; Press Release, U.S. Sec. & Exch. Comm'n, SEC Charges Seven Oil Services and Freight Forwarding Companies for Widespread Bribery of Customs Officials (Nov. 4, 2010), https://www.sec.gov/news/press/2010/2010-214.htm.

150. Samuel Rubenfeld & Joseph Palazzolo, *Panalpina Settlements Announced, With $236.5 Million in Penalties*, CORRUPTION CURRENTS BLOG, WALL ST. J. (Nov. 4, 2010, 3:28 PM), http://blogs.wsj.com/corruption-currents/2010/11/04/panalpina-settlements-announced-with-2365-million-in-penalties/.

151. Press Release, U.S. Dep't of Justice, Oil Services Companies and a Freight Forwarding Company Agree to Resolve Foreign Bribery Investigations and to Pay More Than $156 Million in Criminal Penalties (Nov. 4, 2010), https://www.justice.gov/opa/pr/2010/November/10-crm-1251.html.

152. Complaint, SEC v. RAE Sys. Inc., No. 10-cv-2093 (D.D.C. Dec. 10, 2010), https://www.sec.gov/litigation/complaints/2010/comp21770.pdf; Non-Prosecution Agreement, *In re* RAE Sys. Inc. (D.D.C. Dec. 10, 2010), https://www.justice.gov/criminal/fraud/fcpa/cases/rae-systems/12-10-10rae-systems.pdf.

153. Press Release, U.S. Sec. & Exch. Comm'n, SEC Charges RAE Sys. for Illegal Payments Made Through Joint Ventures to Win Chinese Government Contracts (Dec. 10, 2010), https://www.sec.gov/news/press/2010/2010-242.htm.

bribery.[154] RAE paid $1.15 million in civil disgorgement and a criminal monetary penalty of $1.7 million.[155]

§ 20:5.3 Successor Liability

The FCPA has implications for all forms of international business transactions—not merely the sale of goods and services to foreign governments, but also purely private transactions such as mergers, acquisitions, and joint ventures. Successor criminal liability is an increasingly well-established feature of corporate law: it is the common-law doctrine under which successor corporations—following a merger, consolidation, or, in some cases, an asset purchase—may be held derivatively liable for the criminal conduct of a predecessor entity.[156] The doctrine of successor liability is now a recognized exception to the traditional rule that purchasing the assets of another company does not cause the purchaser to inherit the seller's liabilities.[157] In fact, a substantial number of FCPA prosecutions have arisen in the merger and acquisition context,[158] highlighting the need for companies to undertake extensive due diligence in advance of any such acquisition.

In the Resource Guide, the SEC and DOJ emphasize the importance of due diligence, prompt remediation, and voluntary disclosure in mitigating the risk of successor liability. The first step is "to conduct thorough risk-based FCPA and anticorruption due diligence on potential new business acquisitions."[159] This process includes reviewing the target company's sales and financial data; auditing selected transactions; reviewing contracts with customers and third-party agents and distributors; and engaging in discussions with the target's

---

154. Press Release, U.S. Dep't of Justice, RAE Systems Agrees to Pay $1.7 Million Criminal Penalty to Resolve Violations of the Foreign Corrupt Practices Act (Dec. 10, 2010), https://www.justice.gov/opa/pr/2010/December/10-crm-1428.html.

155. *See* Complaint, SEC v. RAE Sys. Inc., No. 10-cv-2093 (D.D.C. Dec. 10, 2010), https://www.sec.gov/litigation/complaints/2010/comp21770.pdf; Non-Prosecution Agreement, *In re* RAE Sys. Inc. (D.D.C. Dec. 10, 2010), https://www.justice.gov/criminal/fraud/fcpa/cases/rae-systems/12-10-10rae-systems.pdf.

156. *See generally* H. Lowell Brown, *Successor Corporate Criminal Liability: The Emerging Federal Common Law*, 49 ARK. L. REV. 469 (1996).

157. *See* Daniel J. Grimm, *The Foreign Corrupt Practices Act in Merger and Acquisition Transactions: Successor Liability and its Consequences*, 7 N.Y.U. J. L. & BUS. 247, 281–87 (2010).

158. Carolyn Lindsey, *More Than You Bargained For: Successor Liability Under the U.S. Foreign Corrupt Practices Act*, 35 OHIO N.U. L. REV. 959, 965–68 (2009).

159. RESOURCE GUIDE, *supra* note 13, at 28.

senior management regarding compliance issues and local corruption risks.[160]

The Resource Guide states that "[i]n a significant number of instances, DOJ and SEC have declined to take action against companies that voluntarily disclosed and remediated conduct and cooperated with DOJ and SEC in the merger and acquisition context."[161] For example, in December 2002, DOJ and the SEC disposed of an enforcement action against radiopharmaceutical company Syncor International and its Taiwanese subsidiary. The subsidiary's alleged bribery of foreign officials in Taiwan came to light in the course of due diligence performed by Ohio-based Cardinal Health Inc. as it pursued the acquisition of Syncor. Cardinal disclosed the misconduct to DOJ and the SEC before the merger was completed. Syncor Taiwan pleaded guilty and paid a $200 million criminal fine;[162] Syncor International paid a $500,000 civil penalty in the course of settling with the SEC;[163] and Cardinal Health was not subjected to any successor liability.[164]

Nonetheless, another case illustrates the manner in which DOJ and the SEC are pushing at the boundaries of the doctrine of successor liability in the FCPA arena. Lockheed Martin announced its intention to acquire Titan Corporation, a defense contractor based in California. Pre-acquisition due diligence revealed, however, that Titan had committed several potential FCPA violations, which the two companies jointly disclosed to the SEC and DOJ in February 2004. During the pendency of the investigation, the companies twice extended the deadline for the acquisition—but when Titan failed to reach a settlement with the Justice Department, Lockheed exercised its option to terminate the merger agreement.[165] In March 2005, the investigation of Titan was successfully concluded, with the company pleading guilty to violating the FCPA's anti-bribery and accounting provisions, paying a $13 million criminal fine, and disgorging an additional $15.5 million in a parallel civil settlement with the SEC.[166] The *Titan* case sent a strong signal of the SEC's and DOJ's commitment

---

160. *Id.* at 31.
161. *Id.* at 28.
162. Criminal Information, United States v. Syncor Taiwan, Inc., No. 02-cr-1244 (C.D. Cal. Dec. 5, 2002), https://www.justice.gov/criminal/fraud/fcpa/cases/syncor-taiwan/12-05-02syncor-taiwan-info.pdf.
163. Complaint, SEC v. Syncor Int'l Corp., No. 02-cv-2421 (D.D.C. Dec. 10, 2002), https://www.sec.gov/litigation/complaints/comp17887.htm.
164. RESOURCE GUIDE, *supra* note 13, at 29.
165. Renae Merle, *Lockheed Martin Declines to Extend Titan Deadline*, WASH. POST, June 25, 2004, at E01.
166. Plea Agreement, United States v. Titan Corp., No. 05-cr-0314 (S.D. Cal. Mar. 1, 2005), https://www.justice.gov/criminal/fraud/fcpa/cases/titan-corp/03-01-05titan-plea.pdf; Complaint, SEC v. Titan Corp., No. 05-cv-0411

to the aggressive enforcement of the FCPA; at the time, the combined civil and criminal penalty of $28.5 million was the largest-ever penalty imposed for an FCPA violation.[167]

§ 20:5.4 Foreign Officials

Multinational companies must be vigilant in conducting business with a wide range of foreign entities and individuals. The FCPA prohibits unlawful payments to foreign officials, foreign political parties, foreign party officials, and candidates for foreign political office.[168] The FCPA defines a "foreign official" as:

> any officer or employee of a foreign government or any department, agency, or instrumentality thereof, or of a public international organization, or any person acting in an official capacity for or on behalf of any such government or department, agency, or instrumentality, or for or on behalf of any such public international organization.[169]

The term "foreign official" clearly encompasses employees of any foreign government's executive, legislative, and judicial branches, including ministries and cabinets—from the most senior officials to the lowest-level bureaucrats. But the definition goes further, to include "any person acting in an official capacity for or on behalf of" any such "government or department, agency, or instrumentality." In this way, the statute reaches individuals who may not be traditional government employees, but who are still acting for or on behalf of a foreign government.

Perhaps more controversially, the statute also refers to employees of any "instrumentality" of the foreign government—without defining the term "instrumentality." The definition of an agency or instrumentality of a foreign government has been the subject of contentious litigation. The Eleventh Circuit's decision in *United States v. Esquenazi* was the first appellate-level decision to interpret "foreign official,[170] as noted above in section 20:3.1. The Eleventh Circuit articulated a two-part test for whether an entity is an instrumentality: whether it is (1) controlled by the government of a foreign country

---

(D.D.C. Mar. 1, 2005), https://www.sec.gov/litigation/litreleases/lr19107.htm.

167. F. Joseph Warin & Jason A. Monahan, *Foreign Corrupt Practices Act Due Diligence and Voluntary Disclosure*, J. PAYMENT SYSTEMS L. 426, 429 (Aug.–Sept. 2005).

168. 15 U.S.C. §§ 78dd-1(a)(1)-(2), 78dd-2(a)(1)-(2), 78dd-3(a)(1)–(2).

169. 15 U.S.C. §§ 78dd-1(f)(1)(A), 78dd-2(h)(2)(A), 78dd-3(f)(2)(A).

170. United States v. Esquenazi, 752 F.3d 912, 925 (11th Cir. 2014).

and (2) performs a function the government treats as its own.[171] The considerations for whether a government "controls" an entity include:

(1) the foreign government's formal designation of that entity;

(2) whether the government has a majority interest;

(3) the government's ability to hire and fire the entity's principals;

(4) the extent to which the entity's profits, if any, go directly to the government;

(5) the extent to which the government funds the entity if it fails to break even; and

(6) the length of time these indicia have existed.[172]

To determine whether an entity performs a function the government "treats as its own," consider:

(1) whether the entity has a monopoly over the function it exists to carry out;

(2) whether the government subsidizes the costs associated with the entity providing services;

(3) whether the entity provides services to the public at large in the foreign country; and

(4) whether the public and the government of the foreign country generally perceive the entity to be preforming a governmental function.[173]

A number of federal district courts have also considered the meaning of an "instrumentality" of a foreign government. In three prominent cases, the *Lindsey Manufacturing* case,[174] the *Control Components Inc.* case,[175] and the *O'Shea* case,[176] the defendants argued that their indictments should be dismissed because the employees of state-owned enterprises (SOEs) to whom payments were allegedly made were not "foreign officials" within the FCPA's definition of the term.

---

171. *Id.* at 925.
172. *Id.* at 925–26.
173. *Id.* at 926–27.
174. United States v. Noriega, No. 10-cr-1031 (C.D. Cal. filed Sept. 15, 2010).
175. United States v. Carson, No. 08:2009-cr-00077 (C.D. Cal. filed Apr. 8, 2009).
176. United States v. O'Shea, No. 4:2009-cr-00629 (S.D. Tex. filed Nov. 16, 2011).

The *Lindsey Manufacturing* case involved allegedly corrupt payments to a Mexican state-owned electric utility called the Comisión Federal de Electricidad (CFE). In April 2011, Judge A. Howard Matz of the U.S. District court for the Central District California denied the defendants' motion to dismiss, ruling that "a state-owned corporation having the attributes of CFE may be an 'instrumentality' of a foreign government within the meaning of the FCPA, and officers of such a state-owned corporation . . . may therefore be 'foreign officials' within the meaning of the FCPA."[177] In addition, Judge Matz set forth a non-exhaustive list of factors to consider in determining whether a particular state-owned enterprise qualifies as an "instrumentality" of a foreign government. These factors include whether the entity:

(1) provides a service to citizens;

(2) has officers and directors that are or are appointed by government officials;

(3) is financed through governmental appropriations or revenues obtained from "government-mandated taxes, licenses, fees or royalties";

(4) is vested with and exercises "exclusive or controlling power to administer its designated functions"; and

(5) is widely perceived to be performing official functions.[178]

The *Control Components Inc.* (CCI) case involved allegedly corrupt payments to commercial energy companies owned in whole or in part by foreign governments. In May 2011, Judge James V. Selna—also of the Central District of California—denied the CCI defendants' motion to dismiss, reasoning that the question of whether an entity is a government instrumentality is one of fact that cannot be separated from the evidence to be presented at trial.[179] Judge Selna, like Judge Matz, provided a non-exhaustive list of factors to guide this factual determination, including.

(1) The foreign state's characterization of the entity and its employees;

(2) The foreign state's degree of control over the entity;

(3) The purpose of the entity's activities;

---

177. United States v. Aguilar, 783 F. Supp. 2d 1108 (C.D. Cal. 2011).

178. *Id.*

179. Order, United States v. Carson, No. 8:09-cr-00077 (C.D. Cal. May 18, 2011).

(4) The entity's obligations and privileges under the foreign state's law, including whether the entity exercises exclusive or controlling power to administer its designated functions;

(5) The circumstances surrounding the entity's creation; and

(6) The foreign state's extent of ownership of the entity, including the level of financial support by the state (for example, subsidies, special tax treatment, and loans)."[180]

In contrast to the *Lindsey* and *CCI* cases, the district court in the *O'Shea* case denied the defendant's motion to dismiss the indictment before trial without issuing a written opinion.[181]

The Resource Guide issued by the SEC and DOJ in November 2012 facially endorses a multifactor, fact-based approach to determining whether a particular entity is an "instrumentality" of a foreign government. Citing a combination of the factors listed in the *Lindsey* and *CCI* cases, the Resource Guide states that "[w]hile no one factor is dispositive or necessarily more important than another, as a practical matter, an entity is unlikely to qualify as an instrumentality if a government does not own or control a majority of its shares."[182] Some reported enforcement actions, however, seem to conflict somewhat with this interpretation. Notably, in its 2010 settlement with the global telecommunications equipment giant Alcatel-Lucent, DOJ characterized a Malaysian telecommunications provider as "state-owned and controlled" because the ministry of finance held 43% of its shares.[183] According to the Resource Guide, U.S. enforcement authorities determined that the Malaysian government had "substantial control over the company" because the finance ministry "held the status of a 'special shareholder' had veto power over all major expenditures, and controlled important operational decisions."[184] This enforcement action and related federal court rulings make it clear that there is no bright-line rule for what will qualify an entity as an "instrumentality" of a government.

180. *Id.*

181. Management Order, United States v. O'Shea, No. 4:09-cr-00629 (S.D. Tex. 2012).

182. RESOURCE GUIDE, *supra* note 13, at 21.

183. Deferred Prosecution Agreement, Statement of Facts ¶ 21, United States v. Alcatel-Lucent, S.A., No. 10-20907 (S.D. Fla. Dec. 20, 2010).

184. RESOURCE GUIDE, *supra* note 13, at 21.

§ 20:5.5 Gifts and Entertainment

The FCPA broadly prohibits the corrupt "offer, payment, promise to pay, or authorization of the payment of any money, or offer, gift, promise to give, or authorization of the giving of *anything of value*" to a foreign official.[185] The statutory language is crafted to encompass many kinds of improper benefits—not only cash payments, but also gifts, travel, entertainment, and other "things of value." The scope of this prohibition can be difficult to define, especially because it is a common business practice in many countries to exchange gifts as tokens of respect or of thanks. For example, the Chinese concept of *guanxi* encompasses the exchange of gifts, favors, and banquets as a traditional and deeply entrenched way of building business relationships. In Brazil, the *jeito* or *jeitinho* ("little way") is a flexible principle that entails finding a way around red tape—which can mean something as innocent as deftly navigating bureaucracy, or relying on personal connections to clear the way for an appropriate governmental action, but may also encompass conduct that is unacceptable under the FCPA.

The Resource Guide provides some helpful parameters. While emphasizing the fact-dependent nature of the assessment of the propriety of a payment or gift, the Resource Guide lists the following "hallmarks of appropriate gift-giving":

- "[T]he gift is given openly and transparently";
- It is recorded accurately in the books and records of the giver;
- It is given for the sole purpose of demonstrating "esteem or gratitude"; and
- It is permitted under local law.[186]

In addition, the Resource Guide states that gifts of "nominal value, such as cab fare, reasonable meals and entertainment expenditures, or company promotional items" are generally not subject to enforcement action"; small tokens or nominal payments are ordinarily not targeted unless "they comprise part of a systemic or long-standing course of conduct that evidences a scheme" to bribe foreign officials.[187] On the other hand, the Resource Guide highlights a number of problematic cases involving more extravagant gifts, such as luxury items or improperly lavish trips, or a series of smaller gifts adding up to a pattern of

185. 15 U.S.C. §§ 78dd-1(a), 78dd-2(a), 78dd-3(a) (emphasis added).
186. RESOURCE GUIDE, *supra* note 13, at 15.
187. *Id.*

bribery—cases where enforcement action was deemed appropriate due to "clear indicia of corrupt intent" or improper purpose.[188]

Companies should consider promulgating a gift and entertainment policy, which should include clear guidelines and processes for gift-giving by executives, employees, and agents. Depending on the scope of international operations, larger enterprises could set monetary thresholds for categories of gifts, and annual caps on the amount set aside for corporate gift-giving.[189]

§ 20:5.6 *Crafting an Effective Compliance Program*

Perhaps the most important step that an international business should consider is the implementation of an effective corporate compliance program. Such a compliance program should be designed with an eye toward cultivating a culture of compliance within the company, and identifying and addressing potential FCPA violations and other forms of misconduct. In addition to the clear prudential value, a compliance program's adequacy is one of the factors that may be taken into consideration by U.S. enforcement authorities when deciding whether and how to take action against a company.[190]

There is no one-size-fits-all approach to crafting a compliance program; each company must take into account the particular characteristics and risks associated with its business. Factors to consider include—but are not limited to—the company's countries of operation and their reputation for business corruption; the extent to which third-party consultants, agents, distributors, partners, or resellers are involved in the business; and the dynamic market for the company's goods and services.[191]

The Resource Guide, while declining to outline any hard-and-fast rules for an adequate compliance program, enumerates some "hallmarks of effect compliance programs," including—but not limited to—the following:

- A clear commitment by senior management to a zero-tolerance policy for corrupt conduct;
- A foundational code of conduct and set of compliance procedures that are clearly laid out and effectively disseminated;
- An autonomous and effective oversight mechanism, including a means of confidential reporting and a means for conducting internal investigations;

188. *Id.* at 15–16.
189. *Id.* at 16.
190. *Id.* at 56.
191. *Id.*

- The use of training programs, incentives, and disciplinary measures to ensure employee adherence to the compliance program and policies; and
- Due diligence, both pre- and post-acquisition.[192]

§ 20:5.7 Responding to a Potential Violation

The SEC and DOJ both resolve potential FCPA violations through one of four types of resolutions: (1) declination (declining to bring an enforcement action); (2) non-prosecution agreement (NPA); (3) deferred prosecution agreement (DPA); and (4) trial. DOJ also has the option of entering into plea agreements, and the SEC uses cease-and-desist orders and civil injunctions.[193]

The Resource Guide includes several factors that increase the likelihood DOJ or the SEC will issue a declination, including full and voluntary disclosure of potential misconduct by the corporation and good-faith implementation of a robust compliance program.[194] To incentivize voluntary self-disclosure, in 2016, DOJ launched a pilot program, which has now been enhanced and made permanent, under which companies would be eligible for a 50% reduction of any fine if, among other factors, they disclosed FCPA violations and cooperated fully with the government.[195]

When weighing options after discovering a potential violation, there is not just the risk of a DOJ or SEC enforcement action, but also risk of action by other U.S. government agencies and foreign anti-corruption agencies. Multi-jurisdictional enforcement actions are becoming more common, with U.S. and foreign agencies coordinating their investigations and companies paying penalties to both.[196] In 2018, the

---

192. *Id.* at 57–62.

193. *Id.* at 74–77.

194. *Id.* at 75–77.

195. *See* Rod Rosenstein, Deputy Att'y Gen., Remarks at the 34th Int'l Conference on the Foreign Corrupt Practices Act (Nov. 29, 2017), https://www.justice.gov/opa/speech/deputy-attorney-general-rosenstein-delivers-remarks-34th-international-conference-foreign [hereinafter Rosenstein, Remarks at 34th Int'l Conference on the FCPA].

196. *See, e.g.*, Press Release, U.S. Dep't of Justice, Keppel Offshore & Marine Ltd. and U.S. Based Subsidiary Agree to Pay $422 Million in Global Penalties to Resolve Foreign Bribery Case (Dec. 22, 2017), https://www.justice.gov/opa/pr/keppel-offshore-marine-ltd-and-us-based-subsidiary-agree-pay-422-million-global-penalties; Press Release, U.S. Dep't of Justice, SBM Offshore N.V. and United States-Based Subsidiary Resolve Foreign Corrupt Practices Act Case Involving Bribes in Five Countries (Nov. 29, 2017), https://www.justice.gov/opa/pr/sbm-offshore-nv-and-united-states-based-subsidiary-resolve-foreign-corrupt-practices-act-case.

DOJ announced a policy to attempt to avoid "piling on" of duplicative penalties by multiple U.S. and foreign government agencies for the same violation.[197] It remains to be seen how this policy will be put into practice.

For corporate violations, civil penalties for anti-bribery violations are up to $16,000, while civil penalties for accounting violations are up to the amount of the financial gain attributable to the violation or up to $150,000 for an individual or $725,000 for a company.[198] Criminal penalties are up to $2 million for each violation of the anti-bribery provisions and $25 million for each violation of the accounting provisions.[199] In addition, under the Alternative Fines Act, the fine can be up to twice the earnings obtained due to the violation.[200] Finally, the SEC frequently obtains the monetary component of its resolutions in the form of the equitable relief of disgorgement of gains obtained due to the violation and pre-judgment interest.[201]

Violation of the FCPA can result not only in large financial penalties, but increasingly, also in jail time for culpable individuals. The shift over the past decade toward focusing on prosecuting individual actors for corporate misconduct was memorialized in the 2015 "Yates Memo."[202] Even after the change in administrations, Deputy Attorney General Rosenstein reaffirmed DOJ's commitment to continuing this policy, stating, "Effective deterrence of corporate corruption requires prosecution of culpable individuals."[203]

---

197. *See* Rod Rosenstein, Deputy Att'y Gen., Remarks at the American Conference Institute's 20th Anniversary New York Conference on the Foreign Corrupt Practices Act (May 9, 2018), https://www.justice.gov/opa/speech/deputy-attorney-general-rod-j-rosenstein-delivers-remarks-american- conference-institute-0.
198. RESOURCE GUIDE, *supra* note 13, at 69.
199. *Id.* at 68.
200. *Id.* at 68–69.
201. *Id.* at 76.
202. U.S. Dep't of Justice Memo, Individual Accountability for Corporate Wrongdoing, Sally Yates, Deputy Attorney General (Sept. 9, 2015), https://www.justice.gov/archives/dag/file/769036/download.
203. Rosenstein, Remarks at 34th Int'l Conference on the FCPA, *supra* note 195.

Chapter 21

Going Public

§ 21:1 Introduction
§ 21:2 Preparing for an IPO
§ 21:2.1 The Underwriters
§ 21:2.2 The Trading Market
§ 21:2.3 Work Streams
§ 21:3 IPO Process and Timeline
§ 21:3.1 The Registration Statement and SEC Review
§ 21:3.2 The Road Show and Pricing
§ 21:3.3 Gun Jumping
§ 21:4 Drafting the Prospectus
§ 21:4.1 Prospectus Summary
§ 21:4.2 Risk Factors
§ 21:4.3 Use of Proceeds
§ 21:4.4 Capitalization, Dilution and Selected Financial Data
§ 21:4.5 Management's Discussion & Analysis of Financial Condition and Results of Operations
§ 21:4.6 Business
§ 21:4.7 Management and Compensation
§ 21:4.8 Principal Stockholders and Transactions with Related Parties
§ 21:4.9 Description of Securities
§ 21:4.10 Underwriting
§ 21:4.11 Financial Statements and Other Data
§ 21:5 Conducting the Road Show
§ 21:6 Additional Documentation
§ 21:6.1 The Underwriting Agreement
§ 21:6.2 Lock-Up Agreements
§ 21:6.3 Additional Filings
§ 21:7 Life after an IPO
Appendix 21A Sample Risk Factors

§ 21:1 Introduction

When a company in the fashion industry has achieved a certain level of growth and development, it may consider "going public." "Going public" is a process in which a company registers its securities with the Securities and Exchange Commission (SEC), lists its securities on a stock exchange, and then sells some of those securities to the public in an underwritten initial public offering (IPO). Companies that "go public" typically, but not always, have an experienced management team that is familiar with the company and the broader industry, and either (i) a track record of high growth, or (ii) strong and sustained revenues and profits.

The determination to go public may be motivated by capital requirements, business opportunities or the liquidity needs of company insiders or private equity sponsors. A company in the fashion industry may seek to raise capital in the public markets to repay existing indebtedness or to fund expansion plans (such as entering into new consumer markets.[1] A company may desire having publicly traded securities in order to facilitate strategic acquisitions or attract, retain, and motivate key employees. Private equity sponsors and other early investors in a company may encourage the company to go public in order to create a market for sales of their equity and realize a return on their investment. If a company is privately held by a family, the decision to go public may be motivated by the family's desire to have a liquid market for their shares for personal financial and estate planning purposes or as a result of generational turnover. Accordingly, an IPO may include the sale of shares offered by the company ("primary shares") and shares offered by existing stockholders ("secondary shares").

Many successful brands and retailers have become public companies. One of the most iconic names in clothing, Levi Strauss, had one of the largest public offerings in any industry year-to-date in March 2019, with the company valued at $6.6 billion and shares trading above the initial offering price.[2] Online retail subscription business, Stitch Fix, Inc., raised $120 million in a 2017 IPO with a $1.63 billion valuation.[3] J. Jill, Inc., the women's apparel brand

---

1. Kayla Hutzler, *Going Public Key for Luxury Brands to Grow on a Global Scale*, LUXURY DAILY (Jan.13, 2012).
2. Joshua Franklin & Uday Sampath Kumar, *Levi Strauss Valued at $6.6 Billion as IPO Prices Above Target*, REUTERS (Mar. 20, 2019), https://www.reuters.com/article/us-levi-strauss-ipo/levi-strauss-valued-at-66-billion-as-ipo-prices-above-target-idUSKCN1R12U5.
3. Lauren Thomas, *Stitch Fix Shares Retreat After IPO Pop, Close at $15.15*, CNBC (Nov. 17, 2017), https://www.cnbc.com/2017/11/17/stitch-fix-ipo-opening-trade.html.

returned to the public markets in 2017, after previously going public in the 1990s (and subsequently being taken private in 2006).[4] In its second IPO, which consisted entirely of secondary shares, J. Jill was valued at $553 million after its first day of trading.[5] The global outerwear brand Canada Goose Holdings Inc. went public in 2017 raising $255 million.[6] Farfetch Limited, the London-based luxury online marketplace, went public in 2018, with a valuation of approximately $5 billion. Although Farfetch's shares have traded down from the initial public offering price, the valuation represents a successful luxury fashion IPO.[7] A lower priced but highly touted multi-brand fashion retailer, Revolve, also filed for an initial public offering in 2018, but has not gone public as of March 2019.[8] Revolve represents the phenomenon of rapidly evolving consumer tastes and the use of "influencers" to market goods through Internet retail.[9]

Although there are significant advantages for a brand or retailer in being a public company, there are also significant challenges in going public and subsequently operating as a public company. The IPO process itself is arduous, time consuming, and expensive. Senior management of the company must devote considerable time and attention to preparation for an IPO, as well as to consulting with the company's legal, accounting, and financial advisors for months in advance of going public. Similarly, senior management must review disclosure documents and market the securities to potential investors. The company may need to hire additional experienced personnel to perform such public company functions as legal, risk,

---

4. Megan Woolhouse, *J.Jill's IPO Doesn't Excite Investors*, BOSTON GLOBE (Mar. 9, 2017), https://www.bostonglobe.com/business/2017/03/09/jill-ipo-doesn-excite-investors/GDwMHW01SwL6lbtePS8dtM/story.html.
5. *Id.*
6. Lauren Gensler, *Canada Goose Shares Fly Higher in $250 Million IPO*, FORBES (Mar. 16, 2017), https://www.forbes.com/sites/laurengensler/2017/03/16/canada-goose-ipo/#2ff4863833a3.
7. *Luxury Online Fashion Site Farfetch Sets Terms for $600 Million US IPO*, NASDAQ (Sep. 5, 2018), https://www.nasdaq.com/article/luxury-online-fashion-site-farfetch-sets-terms-for-600-million-us-ipo-cm1018310; Jelena Sokolova, *Farfetch Well Placed as Online Luxury Takes Off*, MORNINGSTAR (Feb. 4, 2019), https://www.morningstar.com/articles/910808/farfetch-well-placed-as-online-luxury-takes-off.html.
8. Donovan Jones, *Revolve Group Files for $100 Million IPO*, SEEKING ALPHA (Oct. 16, 2018), https://seekingalpha.com/article/4211987-revolve-group-files-100-million-ipo.
9. Marc Bain, *The Word "Influencer" Appears 79 Times in Revolve's IPO Filing*, QUARTZY (Oct. 1, 2018), https://qz.com/quartzy/1408391/revolves-ipo-filing-mentions-the-word-influencer-79-times/.

internal auditing, and investor relations. The out-of-pocket costs of going public, including compensating the underwriters, legal counsel, accountants, and financial printers, as well as SEC and listing exchange fees, can be substantial. Moreover, there are significant ongoing compliance obligations, and related costs, imposed on public companies.[10]

The Jumpstart Our Business Startups Act (the "JOBS Act"), enacted in 2012, and the Fixing America's Surface Transportation Act (the "FAST Act"), enacted in 2015, streamlined the IPO process, particularly for companies with less than $1 billion in gross annual revenues known as "emerging growth company's" (EGCs).[11] The JOBS Act, among other things, allows EGCs to initially submit registration statements confidentially and reduces the disclosures required regarding executive compensation. Currently, EGCs can submit all draft registration statements to the SEC confidentially until fifteen (15) days before the beginning of an IPO road show.[12] EGCs may also omit the earliest year of audited financial statements that a non-EGC company would be required to include in the registration statement. Other scaled disclosure obligations serve to lessen the burden on EGCs as they go public in in their first few years of public company life. A company ceases to be an emerging growth company at the end of the year of the fifth anniversary of going public (or sooner upon the occurrence of certain events).[13]

While a successful IPO can be a positive strategic move, the IPO process and public company status place a fashion company in the spotlight, which presents opportunities and challenges. Public companies are subject to continuing disclosure requirements under the federal securities laws such that many aspects of the company's

10. Significant compliance requirements are imposed on public companies under the Securities Exchange Act of 1934, as amended; the Sarbanes-Oxley Act of 2002; and the Dodd-Frank Wall Street Reform and Consumer Protection Act of 2010, among others.

11. *Update on Emerging Growth Companies and the JOBS Act*, EY (Nov. 2016), https://www.ey.com/Publication/vwLUAssets/ey-update-on-emerging-growth-companies-and-the-jobs-act-november-2016/%24FILE/ey-update-on-emerging-growth-companies-and-the-jobs-act-november-2016.pdf.

12. At the time of the first public filing of the registration statement, the earlier confidentially submitted registration statements will be visible publicly as well.

13. An issuer may lose EGC status earlier than the five year deadline if one of the following criteria are met: (1) the issuer has annual revenues in excess of $1 billion, (2) over a rolling thirty-six- (36-) month period, the company issues more than $1 billion in nonconvertible debt securities, or (3) the company becomes a large accelerated filer, meaning the issuer has a public float of $700 million or more.

financial, business, product, and compensation information become widely available to industry competitors, business partners, and employees and are required to be publicly updated regularly. Investors and industry analysts focus attention on a public company's financial performance and, in particular, on management's guidance with respect to future earnings often on a quarterly basis. The challenge of meeting or exceeding the analysts' quarterly earnings estimates raises particular concerns for brands and retailers, which depend on discretionary consumer spending and are subject to rapidly shifting consumer preferences and broader economic trends. If a public company fails to meet earnings estimates, or otherwise experiences weak financial results, the market price of the company's shares may decline, sometimes significantly. In such circumstances, the company can face significant difficulties, including employee retention problems, stockholder litigation, threats from activist stockholders seeking to change the strategic direction of the company, or unwanted acquisition offers. For these and other reasons, a number of public companies in the fashion industry have chosen to cease being public companies and "go private."

§ 21:2 Preparing for an IPO

The IPO process requires significant planning and preparation, which may begin as early as twenty-four months before the IPO is formally commenced. Initially, the company should assemble a team of experienced outside legal advisors, qualified independent accountants, and other experts (such as tax advisors, compensation consultants, public relations firms and independent IPO advisory firms to guide it through the IPO process. It is important to engage advisors who have significant IPO experience, because going public involves compliance with numerous technical legal and accounting requirements. Failure to comply with these requirements can lead to delays, penalties, litigation and the potential failure of the IPO to launch or close.

§ 21:2.1 *The Underwriters*

A critical part of IPO preparation is selecting experienced investment banks to serve as underwriters of the offering. The underwriters will undertake to advise the company as to the appropriate time to conduct the IPO, based on an analysis of the company's preparedness for public company status and an assessment of external market conditions for IPOs generally and the capital markets landscape for the company's industry. Companies select specific investment banks to serve as lead underwriters for a variety of reasons, including their reputation and relevant experience, the strength of the relevant industry group at the particular investment bank relationships with key bankers at the investment bank, and the strength of the equity research analysts at the investment bank.[14] The underwriters, with the assistance of their own legal counsel, perform due diligence, assist the company in the preparation of the marketing and legal documentation for the offering, and advise the company on matters relating to the marketability of the offering (such as the size of the offering and the mix of primary shares and secondary shares to be offered) and the valuation of the company. In a classic underwritten offering, once the "road show" is successfully completed and they have received orders for the shares, the underwriters purchase the shares from the company and resell them to the public. Underwriters are typically compensated for their services by way of the discount (or "spread") between the two prices, which constitutes the underwriting commission (typically ranging from 3% to 7%, which generally decreases on a percentage basis as the size of the offering increases). Underwriters also typically request an over-allotment option, also known as a "green shoe," which allows them to purchase additional shares from the company or the selling stockholders (generally sized at 15% of the base offering size) at the same price per share as the shares purchased in the base deal.

§ 21:2.2 The Trading Market

The company must make certain determinations regarding the trading of its securities after the IPO. In particular, it must determine which stock exchange to select for the listing of its shares. This decision is typically made in consultation with the underwriters, based on the applicable listing requirements and the needs of the company. Most companies in the fashion industry list their shares on stock exchanges located in the country in which their business is based. For example, Ralph Lauren Corporation and Farfetch are listed on the New York Stock Exchange; Stitch Fix is listed on the Nadsaq Stock Exchange; Hudson's Bay Co., the Canadian retailer, is listed on the Toronto Stock Exchange; ASOS plc, the U.K.-based online fashion and beauty retailer, was admitted to AIM on the London Stock Exchange; and, Salvatore Ferragamo S.p.A. is listed on the Milan Stock Exchange.

The company must also select a transfer agent and registrar to perform stock recordation and transfer services, since public companies

14. Equity research analysts publish research and projections about companies in a specific industry sector. These analysts are ranked by third-party publications on the basis of the accuracy of their projections and the following they command by investors, industry commentators and finance professionals.

have a wide stockholder base and large numbers of shares. The company also selects a financial printer to print copies of the prospectus and to file the registration statement and other required materials electronically with the SEC, through the SEC's Electronic Data Gathering, Analysis and Retrieval system (EDGAR). After a document is publicly filed on EDGAR, it becomes available to the public, including stockholders, analysts and the media.

§ 21:2.3 Work Streams

As a company begins the IPO process, it typically undertakes several significant and time consuming work streams, which are necessary to position the company for the IPO. These work streams include (i) compiling the documents requested by legal counsel and the underwriters for review as part of the due diligence process; (ii) reviewing the company's historical financial statements to ensure compliance with applicable accounting principles, auditor independence standards and federal securities law requirements; and (iii) reviewing the company's internal governance, compensation, capital, and organizational structures in light of its anticipated status as a public company.

The due diligence process involves an in-depth analysis and examination of the company through meetings with management of the company and a document review. In the course of due diligence, the following areas, among others, are reviewed: the company's business and operations, historical financial statements, accounting policies, acquisition history (including accounting treatment for any predecessors), internal controls,[15] historical executive compensation and proposed employee compensation programs, related party transactions, pending litigation, and environmental and other regulatory compliance issues. Diligence on companies in the fashion industry often focuses more specifically on their supply chain, license arrangements, retail store leases, intellectual property, and cybersecurity. The company's documents that are responsive to due diligence requests are generally posted in a secure electronic data room to allow legal counsel and other professionals to review them remotely. A company also typically sends a questionnaire to its directors and officers to confirm

15. Section 404 of the Sarbanes-Oxley Act of 2002 (15 U.S.C. § 7262) and the rules promulgated thereunder, require that the management of a public company perform a formal assessment of the company's internal controls for financial reporting and include in the company's annual report an assessment of the effectiveness of such controls (identifying any "material weaknesses"). Further, the company's independent accountants must report on management's assessment.

certain compensation, related party transaction and related information that must be disclosed in the registration statement.

The due diligence process seeks to ensure the accuracy and completeness of the material factual disclosures in the registration statement. Section 11 of the Securities Act of 1933 imposes civil liability for material misstatements or omissions in a registration statement on: (i) the issuer of the securities, (ii) every director of the issuer, (iii) every person who signs the registration statement, (iv) every person who has consented to be named as an expert with respect to a portion of the registration statement, and (v) the underwriters.[16] This liability is broad, as the plaintiffs alleging liability under section 11 in a civil suit need not prove either scienter or, subject to certain exceptions, reliance.[17] Persons *other than the issuer*, however, may assert a "due diligence defense"[18] to liability, if, after reasonable investigation, they had reasonable ground to believe, and did believe, at the time the registration statement became effective, that the statements therein were true and that there was no omission to state a material fact required to be stated therein or necessary to make the statements therein not misleading. The company, with the assistance of its counsel and other advisors, will often prepare a file consisting of information supporting the factual statements made about the company and its industry in the registration statement.

During the IPO preparation period, the company typically undertakes a corporate governance review. In particular, it should evaluate the qualifications of the members of its existing Board of Directors. A public company will face new challenges, and a well rounded Board with diverse backgrounds and relevant experience will be an invaluable asset. The company will also be concerned with ensuring that it has the appropriate number of independent directors as well as those with specific skill sets (such as financial expertise) for purposes of complying with federal securities laws and stock exchange requirements for public companies. Similarly, the company will need to review its Board committee structure, committee composition, and committee charters, particularly with respect to the audit committee, compensation committee, and governance committee.

---

16. Securities Act § 11 (codified as amended at 15 U.S.C. § 77k). Note that section 12 of the Securities Act of 1933 (codified as amended at 15 U.S.C. § 77*l*) imposes liability when a security is sold in violation of section 5 (codified as amended at 15 U.S.C. § 77e) or when a security is sold by means of a prospectus or oral communication that contains a material misstatement or omission. A section 12 claim, however, requires privity (*i.e.*, is limited to claims against a seller).
17. *Id.*
18. *Id.*

The stock exchanges have specific standards relating to governance matters, including independence, board structure, board committee composition and charters, and executive sessions. For example, both the New York Stock Exchange and NASDAQ require that the majority of the members of a public company's board of directors be deemed independent (pursuant to a specified definition) within one year after an IPO, with at least one director being independent at the time of the IPO, pursuant to their independence phase-in rules.[19]

Typically, a company will also review and revise its director and management compensation arrangements to be more appropriate for a public company of its size and type. A company often engages the services of an independent compensation consultant to advise it as to appropriate compensation levels. The company may enter into, or amend, formal employment agreements with key employees and adopt equity-based compensation plans (such as restricted stock plans or option plans) for directors and officers. Companies that are going public generally purchase new director and officer liability insurance policies (if they have not previously done so) or enhance their existing policies to reflect their new public company status.

A company may also consider simplifying or modifying its capital and organizational structure. For example, outstanding preferred stock of the newly public company is usually converted to common stock or redeemed, and subsidiaries may be created or liquidated. The company's organizational documents (charter and bylaws) typically need to be amended to remove provisions that are not typical or suitable for a public company (such as pre-emptive rights) and to add provisions that are important for a public company (such as limitations on director and officer liability and indemnification provisions) or that may be desirable for a public company (such as a supermajority voting requirement for certain stockholder actions). Although it is generally easier to change a company's charter prior to going public (because charter amendments typically require a stockholder vote and there are generally substantially fewer stockholders before the IPO), any changes should be carefully reviewed by the underwriters to determine their possible effect on the marketing of the stock.

§ 21:3 IPO Process and Timeline

§ 21:3.1 The Registration Statement and SEC Review

In an IPO, a U.S. company typically files with the SEC a registration statement on Form S-1, which is the long-form registration statement that is used when no other form is authorized or prescribed; it requires

19. *See* NASDAQ Rule 5605(b)(1) and NYSE Rule 303A.01.

extensive disclosure about the company's business, management, and financial statements.[20] The Form S-1 registration statement consists of: (i) a facing page, which sets forth the name of the company, the securities being registered, and the calculation of the SEC filing fee; (ii) Part I, the information contained in the prospectus, which is the substantive information that is conveyed to prospective investors (including the financial statements); (iii) Part II, which sets forth the expenses of the offering, the terms of the indemnification of the company's officers and directors, recent sales of unregistered securities, the exhibits to the registration statement (including the company's charter and bylaws, material contracts, and consents), the company's financial statement schedules, and the company's undertakings; and (iv) the signature page (the registration statement must be signed by the company, its principal executive officer, its principal financial officer, its controller or principal accounting officer, and by at least a majority of the company's Board of Directors).

The preparation and drafting of the registration statement can take several months. The first draft of most sections is generally prepared by the company and its legal counsel and accountants, while the investment bankers generally take the lead on the marketing-focused aspects of the Business section. Thereafter, group drafting sessions conducted in person to facilitate the exchange of views among the company, the underwriters, their respective legal counsel and the accountants. After the registration statement is drafted, it is submitted to the SEC. A majority of these submissions are made by EGCs and are therefore submitted to the SEC confidentially. It takes at least thirty (30) days for the SEC to review the registration statement and provide comments to the company. Once the comments are received, the company and its advisors prepare a response letter to the SEC's comments and an amended registration statement, responding to those comments that required a change in the company's disclosure. These documents are filed, and an iterative process of comments by the SEC and responses by the company (and revised registration statements) continues for approximately one to three months. Although, early submissions of the registration statement to the SEC by EGCs may be made confidentially, all draft registration statements must be filed publicly at least fifteen (15) days prior to the commencement of the company's road show with respect to the offering, which is often the first public acknowledgement by the company of its contemplated IPO.

---

20. *See* Form S-1 Registration Statement under the Securities Act of 1933. Foreign private issuers, which are generally companies organized outside of the United States, typically file a registration statement on Form F-1.

§ 21:3.2 The Road Show and Pricing

After the company has addressed all of the SEC's comments, and the SEC has provided informal clearance of the registration statement, the company and the underwriters typically commence a "road show," which is comprised of meetings attended by senior company management in several cities, to meet over lunches, dinners, and other sessions with potential investors in the IPO, as discussed in more detail below later in this chapter. Printed copies of the preliminary prospectus are produced, and these printed copies are delivered to potential investors. Under Item 501 of Regulation S-K (discussed below), the preliminary prospectus for an IPO is required to contain a *bona fide* estimate of the range of the maximum offering price for the shares to be offered in the IPO. For an IPO, a price range in excess of $2 per share for offerings of up to $10 per share, or in excess of 20% of the high end of the range for offerings over $10 per share, generally will not be considered a *bona fide* estimate of the range of the maximum offering price. At the conclusion of the road show, which generally lasts approximately eight to ten business days, the company and the underwriters set the price for the securities to be sold in the offering. The underwriters base their price recommendations on the estimate set forth in the preliminary prospectus and the feedback received from potential investors during the road show. The registration statement must be declared effective by the SEC before the securities may be sold to the public; this is generally done immediately prior to pricing the securities. Once the offering has "priced," the trading of the security on a stock exchange begins the next morning, the final prospectus containing the offering price is filed with the SEC, and the offering is closed several business days thereafter.

§ 21:3.3 Gun Jumping

During the IPO process, companies must adhere to the rules designed to prevent issuers from "gun jumping." Gun jumping is an oral or written external communication outside of the prospectus (and outside of specific exemptions) that is reasonably calculated to generate interest in purchasing the company's securities.[21] For brands and

21. *See* Securities Act § 5, as amended. There are various exemptions from the section 5(c) prohibitions, including Securities Act Rules 134, 135, 163A and 169 (codified at 17 C.F.R. §§ 230.134, 230.135, 230.163A, and 230.169). Note that the JOBS Act, *supra* section 21:1, also permits certain pre-filing communications by emerging growth companies and persons authorized to act on their behalf, which is known as testing the waters.

retailers, this presents a unique challenge because of the importance of continuous advertising in print media, on television and online (including through blogs, Instagram accounts, partnerships with influencers, and other social media). As a practical matter, ensuring that communications and advertisements focus on the products of the company (such as a new line of footwear), rather than on the company and its IPO (such as the growth of the company or the contemplated timing of the IPO), generally minimizes a company's risk of violating these rules. In addition, to the extent any information about the company's business is released, it is important to ensure that it relates to historical, factual information and the substance, timing and presentation of the information is consistent with past company practices. Once the IPO process has formally commenced (generally considered to occur upon the first organizational meeting of the company, the underwriters and their respective counsel), all public communications about the company or the IPO should be reviewed by legal counsel because violations of the gun jumping rules can delay the IPO or result in civil liability for the company.[22]

§ 21:4 Drafting the Prospectus

The prospectus is the principal document used by the company and the underwriters to present the company to potential investors, and is the basis for the road show presentation that management delivers to potential institutional investors in meetings during road show. The content of the prospectus is dictated by the specific requirements of the federal securities laws (principally the requirements of Form S-1 and Regulation S-K (non-financial disclosure) and Regulation S-X (financial disclosure)), by the need to protect the company and its directors, officers, and underwriters from liability under the federal securities laws, by industry custom, and by the desire to market the securities of the company to potential investors. The prospectus cover pages include certain basic information about the offering and may also include photographs of the company's products or retail spaces.

Although the organization of the prospectus can vary depending on the company and industry in which it operates, prospectuses for fashion companies generally contain the following principal sections:

---

22. *Id.* For example, the Salesforce.com IPO was famously postponed to avoid a "gun jumping" issue arising from a press interview with the company's CEO. *See* Steve Gelesi, *Salesforce.com's IPO Delay*, MKT. WATCH (June 4, 2004), https://www.marketwatch.com/story/salesforcecom-sees-gun-jumping-risk.

§ 21:4.1 Prospectus Summary

This section is also referred to as "the box." The Prospectus Summary contains a concise review of the company's business and the principal terms of the offering. It typically includes a brief discussion of the company's market opportunity, the company's competitive strengths (such as owning a portfolio of strong, well-recognized brands) and its strategy (such as diversifying its geographic presence or growing its online presence). The Prospectus Summary also includes certain summary financial information about the company. The underwriters devote considerable attention to crafting a Prospectus Summary that both appropriately reflects the company's business and effectively markets the company's prospects to potential investors.

§ 21:4.2 Risk Factors

This section contains a discussion of the most significant risks facing the company and their potential effect on the company's business, operations and financial results. These risk factors should be concise, well-organized, written in "plain English" and tailored to the company's risk profile at the time of the offering. These risks are designed to present investors with a comprehensive understanding of the challenges a company may or will face, so that they can make an informed decision whether to invest in its stock.

Companies generally disclose three categories of risk factors: industry risks, risks that are unique to the company, and risks that relate specifically to the securities being offered. Brands and retailers typically include industry and company risk factors addressing the following areas: economic uncertainties; fashion trends and consumer preferences; competition; growth and expansion; the global supply chain; wholesale customers; retail stores; intellectual property; e-commerce, cybersecurity, and data privacy risks.

The risk factors disclosed by Revolve (which had not completed an initial public offering as of March 8, 2019, but had made a filing in 2018 to pursue an IPO that may yet be consummated) in Appendix 21A provide a timely example of the risk factors faced by an e-commerce based retailer. The extract below summarizes a number of these risks concisely:

> Customer complaints or negative publicity about our sites, products, product delivery times, customer data handling and security practices or customer support, especially on blogs, social media websites and our sites, could rapidly and severely diminish consumer use of our sites and consumer and supplier confidence in us and result in harm to our brands. We believe that much of the growth in our customer base to date has originated from social

> media and influencer-driven marketing strategy. If we are not able to develop and maintain positive relationships with our network of over 2,500 of influencers, our ability to promote and maintain awareness of our sites and brands and leverage social media platforms to drive visits to our sites may be adversely affected.

§ 21:4.3 *Use of Proceeds*

This section contains information with respect to the intended use of the net proceeds from the sale of securities by the company in the IPO. A typical use of proceeds for a company may include working capital, acquisitions and refinancings.

§ 21:4.4 *Capitalization, Dilution and Selected Financial Data*

The Capitalization section contains a table depicting the capital structure of the company, both before and after the offering. If there is substantial dilution to the new purchasers in the offering, a Dilution section will compare the prices paid by existing stockholders and by purchasers in the offering and the net book value of the company's stock. The Selected Financial Data section presents important items from the balance sheet and income statement.

§ 21:4.5 *Management's Discussion & Analysis of Financial Condition and Results of Operations*

The "MD&A" provides a detailed, narrative analysis of the company's recent historical financial performance and its current financial condition (as reflected in the company's financial statements included in the registration statement). It also describes significant financial trends and uncertainties. The MD&A provides information with respect to the company's business segments, accounting policies, liquidity, capital resources, stock-based compensation practices, contractual obligations and off-balance sheet obligations. It also includes separate quantitative and qualitative disclosure on market risk, which addresses such issues as interest rate, commodity and foreign currency exchange risks applicable to the company.

§ 21:4.6 *Business*

The Business section describes the company's business in narrative form. It typically includes a discussion of the company's history, strategy, products, supply and distribution chain, properties, customers, backlog, competitors, intellectual property and so forth. For a company in the fashion industry, the Business section should address such matters as whether the company owns manufacturing facilities or uses third-party factories, the extent and nature of the company's licensing arrangements, whether the company owns or leases retail stores, and the extent and nature of e-commerce and marketing activities. In addition, the Business section will address regulatory and intellectual property matters, including regulation by the U.S. Food & Drug Administration pursuant to the Federal Food, Drug and Cosmetic Act.

For a brand or retailer, the Business section also presents an opportunity for the company to define itself and its products within the broader industry. The company and the underwriters typically work with counsel to draft a section that appropriately conveys the company's distinctive identity and prospects for growth.

§ 21:4.7 Management and Compensation

The Management section provides general information (including name, age, term of office, business experience, qualifications, and involvement in certain legal proceedings) about the directors and executive officers of the company. The Compensation section includes disclosure of the plan and non-plan compensation awarded to, earned by, or paid to the company's directors and certain "named executive officers," for services to the company for specified periods. An emerging growth company may elect to comply with more limited executive compensation disclosure requirements (such as providing compensation information for three, instead of five, "named executive officers") and, most significantly, need not present a Compensation Discussion and Analysis section (which is a comprehensive review of the company's executive compensation practices).

§ 21:4.8 Principal Stockholders and Transactions with Related Parties

These sections identify the company's principal stockholders, indicate the amount (and percentage) of securities of the company owned by each of the principal stockholders, the directors and executive officers, and describe any related party transactions (transactions in excess of $120,000 between the company and its principal stockholders, directors, or executive officers). For example, these sections might describe any stockholders' agreements or registration rights agreements and are designed to provide potential investors with information about constraints on future actions by the company as well as certain rights that some affiliates may hold.

§ 21:4.9 Description of Securities

This section describes the principal terms of the securities being offered in the IPO. The terms of securities typically include their voting rights, dividend rights, par value, and any preferences. This section also identifies any provisions in the company's organizational documents that may hinder a change in control of the company.

§ 21:4.10 Underwriting

The underwriting section describes the plan of distribution of the securities and the underwriters' compensation. Typically, it is drafted by the underwriters. This section also includes a description of any lock-up arrangements with stockholders of the company, as described below, and any material relationships between the company and the underwriters, including indemnification rights and the right of underwriters to exercise their overallotment option in the company's stock.

§ 21:4.11 Financial Statements and Other Data

U.S. companies are generally required to include in the registration statement three years of annual financial statements (two years for emerging growth companies) prepared in accordance with U.S. Generally Accepted Accounting Principles, as well as interim financial statements for the period subsequent to the end of the company's fiscal year. Some interim financial statements that are not reasonably expected to be included in the preliminary prospectus used to market the deal may be omitted in certain situations from early drafts of the registration statement. Annual financial statements are required to be audited by an independent certified public accountant registered with the Public Company Accounting Oversight Board.

Additional financial data, such as pro forma financial statements reflecting a recent or contemplated acquisition, may also be required. Projections of future financial performance typically are not included in a registration statement.

§ 21:5 Conducting the Road Show

As noted above, the company and the underwriters conduct a road show to meet with potential investors in the IPO and market the securities. As part of this process, the company will print the preliminary prospectus and deliver it to potential investors. The preliminary prospectus is known as the "red herring" because it must bear a legend in red ink stating that the securities may not be sold prior to the effectiveness of the registration statement. The road show is organized by the underwriters and consists of a series of meetings in selected cities in the United States, and sometimes internationally, among senior management (typically the Chief Executive Officer and the Chief Financial Officer) of the company and potential institutional investors. The road show presentation itself typically consists of twenty to thirty slides that are presented by senior management. The information contained in the road show presentation must be derived from information in the registration statement and should not contain any other material information.

The road show gives potential institutional investors the opportunity to meet the company's management and learn about the company's business and strategy. It also gives investors the chance to ask questions about the company's business model. The road show is also used by the underwriters to solicit interest in the company's offering and determine the offering price. Although a preliminary pricing range is included in the preliminary prospectus, as discussed above, feedback during the road show from potential investors can cause the underwriters to reevaluate the appropriate pricing for the securities. In some cases, an IPO may be delayed or cancelled if investors are unwilling to purchase the securities at a price deemed acceptable by the company, its key stockholders and/or the selling stockholders.[23]

Brands and retailers, especially luxury fashion brands, offer a unique product and overall customer experience that may be difficult to convey to investors in the typical thirty-minute road show meetings. In an effort to address this challenge, fashion brands may adopt unique strategies.[24] For example, Brunello Cucinelli S.p.A., the luxury Italian apparel and cashmere company, notably began an investor education process one year ahead of its IPO by flying analysts and potential investors from around the world to the company headquarters in Solomeo, Italy.[25] Guests were treated to town celebrations and informal meals, and visited Mr. Cucinelli's home where he produces his own olive oil in small quantities.[26] This tailored, unique approach

---

23. For example, Graff Diamonds Corp. postponed its Hong Kong IPO in 2012 after its road show due to adverse market conditions. *See* Vicki M. Young, *Graff Cancels IPO Over Market Fears*, WOMEN'S WEAR DAILY (May 31, 2012), https://pmcwwd.files.wordpress.com/2012/05/wwd0531web.pdf.

24. A classic example was Donna Karan's personal demonstration of her favorite pieces from her latest collection during the marketing process of the IPO. Steve Salerno, *How Donna Beat the Street*, WORTH (Dec.1998–Jan. 1999, reprinted Feb. 17, 2017), https://www.worth.com/from-the-archives-donna-karan-beat-the-street/.

25. Evan Clark & Luisa Zargani, *Fashion and the Art of the IPO*, WOMEN'S WEAR DAILY (Dec. 27, 2012), https://pmcwwd.files.wordpress.com/2012/12/wwd1227web.pdf.

26. *Id.*

allowed analysts and potential investors to get to know the company's Chief Executive Officer on a personal level and to understand the company's unique brand and image. In April 2012, the IPO was reportedly seventeen times oversubscribed.[27] In some circumstances, samples of the company's most popular or iconic products may be made available for viewing during the road show or provided to potential investors so that they may become more familiar with the company's business and products.

§ 21:6 Additional Documentation

In addition to the registration statement (as initially submitted and subsequently amended), there are other documents that need to be prepared, and in some cases negotiated or filed, in order to complete the IPO process. The principal additional documents are:

§ 21:6.1 *The Underwriting Agreement*

The underwriting agreement among the company, any selling stockholders and the underwriters is the principal contractual arrangement governing an IPO contains the key economic terms of the agreement between the company and the investment banker. This agreement also includes company representations, such as representations by the company with respect to its formation, operations, financial statements, compliance with law, and other general and industry-specific matters. The underwriting agreement also includes indemnification provisions relating principally to the accuracy of the company's disclosures in the registration statement.

§ 21:6.2 *Lock-Up Agreements*

Lock-up agreements typically are signed by all or most of the company's existing stockholders. Such agreements are intended to reduce the downward pressure on the company's stock and negative media attention that might result from insiders or significant stockholders selling the company's stock in the open market soon after the IPO. These agreements prohibit those stockholders from selling their shares, typically for a period of 180 days after the pricing of the IPO.

§ 21:6.3 *Additional Filings*

In addition to filing a registration statement with the SEC, the company, key shareholders and underwriters typically make certain other important filings in connection with an IPO, which include

---

27. *Id.*

filings by directors and officers to indicate their personal ownership of stock. The company also prepares and files a registration statement on Form 8-A to register the company's securities under the Securities Exchange Act of 1934 (the "Exchange Act") as well as documentation to be listed for the trading of its securities on a stock exchange, as described above.

§ 21:7 Life after an IPO

After the IPO, the company will be a public company, and faces a range of compliance and governance matters. In particular, the company will need to develop internal processes for identifying and timely disclosing material public information, and for preparing and filing periodic reports (such as Forms 10-K, 10-Q, and 8-K) with the SEC under the Exchange Act.[28] The company also will have to comply with corporate governance requirements under the federal securities laws, applicable state law and the rules of the applicable securities exchange. In conjunction with its IPO, companies generally adopt a number of internal policies, such as corporate codes of conduct, securities trading policies, social media policies and whistleblower policies to support ongoing compliance efforts.

As indicated above, the company's directors, certain officers, and ten percent stockholders must file reports with the SEC detailing their ownership and trading activities in securities of the company.[29] Typically, the company assists it directors and officers with this process in order to ensure that these filings are timely made.

The company will need to schedule regular and special meetings of its Board of Directors and Board committees, particularly the audit, governance, and compensation committees. The company also will need to schedule annual stockholders' meetings, and prepare and file proxy materials with the SEC in connection with such meetings.[30] Proxy materials include a proxy statement, which describes the matters to be voted on at the stockholders meeting and contains additional information about the company's principal stockholders, Board of Directors, and management. The proxy statement is sent to stockholders in advance of the meeting.

---

28. Securities Exchange Act § 13, codified as amended at 15 U.S.C. § 78m, and related regulations.
29. Securities Exchange Act § 16, codified as amended at 15 U.S.C. § 78p, and related regulations.
30. Securities Exchange Act § 14, codified as amended at 15 U.S.C. § 78n, and related regulations.

In addition, the company will launch its investor relations program, often with the support of an outside consultant. Most public companies hold a conference call to which investors and analysts are invited, at the time that the company's performance for the previous quarter is announced. In addition to these "earnings" related conference calls, companies will send representatives to industry analyst events and maintain regular contacts with the company's principal stockholders. In addition, the company may wish to monitor changes in its stock ownership, through a review of public filings and public disclosures, and perhaps by engaging a stock surveillance firm. Companies should be attentive to possible investments by known stockholder activists who may seek a change in the company's Board of Directors and its strategic direction, particularly in the event the company's stock is trading below its typical range. These investor relations activities are particularly important for public companies that have a widespread stockholder base.

Appendix 21A

Sample Risk Factors

As filed with the Securities and Exchange Commission on May 28, 2019
Registration No. 333-227614

SECURITIES AND EXCHANGE COMMISSION
Washington, D.C. 20549

AMENDMENT NO. 5 TO FORM S-1

REGISTRATION STATEMENT
Under
The Securities Act of 1933

REVOLVE GROUP, LLC

to be converted as described herein into a corporation named

REVOLVE GROUP, INC.

(Exact Name of Registrant as Specified in its Charter)

Delaware	5961	46-1640160
(State or other Jurisdiction of Incorporation or Organization)	(Primary Standard Industrial Classification Code Number)	(I.R.S. Employer Identification Number)

16800 Edwards Road
Cerritos, California 90703
(562) 677-9480
(Address, including zip code, and telephone number, including area code, of registrant's principal executive offices)

Michael Karanikolas
Michael Mente
16800 Edwards Road
Cerritos, California 90703
(562) 677-9480
(Name, address, including zip code, and telephone number, including area code, of agent for service)

Copies to:

Michael Nordtvedt Katherine H. Ku Wilson Sonsini Goodrich & Rosati Professional Corporation 633 West Fifth Street, Suite 1550 Los Angeles, California 90071 (323) 210-2900	Jesse Timmermans Jodi Lumsdaine Chapin Revolve Group, Inc. 16800 Edwards Road Cerritos, California 90703 (562) 677-9480	Thomas Holden Ropes & Gray LLP Three Embarcadero Center San Francisco, California 94111 (415) 315-6300

Approximate date of commencement of proposed sale of the securities to the public: As soon as practicable after the effective date of this Registration Statement.

If any of the securities being registered on this Form are to be offered on a delayed or continuous basis pursuant to Rule 415 under the Securities Act of 1933, check the following box. ☐

If this Form is filed to register additional securities for an offering pursuant to Rule 462(b) under the Securities Act, please check the following box and list the Securities Act registration statement number of the earlier effective registration statement for the same offering. ☐

If this Form is a post-effective amendment filed pursuant to Rule 462(c) under the Securities Act, check the following box and list the Securities Act registration statement number of the earlier effective registration statement for the same offering. ☐

If this Form is a post-effective amendment filed pursuant to Rule 462(d) under the Securities Act, check the following box and list the Securities Act registration statement number of the earlier effective registration statement for the same offering. ☐

Indicate by check mark whether the registrant is a large accelerated filer, an accelerated filer, a non-accelerated filer, smaller reporting company, or an emerging growth company. See the definitions of "large accelerated filer," "accelerated filer," "smaller reporting company," and "emerging growth company" in Rule 12b-2 of the Exchange Act. (Check one):

Large accelerated filer	☐	Accelerated filer	☐
Non-accelerated filer	☒	Smaller reporting company	☐
		Emerging growth company	☒

If an emerging growth company, indicate by check mark if the registrant has elected not to use the extended transition period for complying with any new or revised financial accounting standards provided pursuant to Section 7(a)(2)(B) of the Securities Act. ☐

CALCULATION OF REGISTRATION FEE

Title of Each Class of Securities to be Registered	Amount to be Registered(1)	Proposed Maximum Offering Price per Share	Proposed Maximum Aggregate Offering Price(1)	Amount of Registration Fee(2)
Class A Common Stock, par value $0.001	13,529,411	$18.00	$243,529,398	$29,516

(1) Estimated solely for the purpose of calculating the registration fee in accordance with Rule 457(a) under the Securities Act of 1933, as amended. Includes the offering price of any additional shares that the underwriters have the option to purchase.

(2) The Registrant previously paid $12,450 of this amount in connection with the prior filings of this registration statement.

The registrant hereby amends this registration statement on such date or dates as may be necessary to delay its effective date until the registrant shall file a further amendment which specifically states that this registration statement shall thereafter become effective in accordance with Section 8(a) of the Securities Act of 1933 or until the registration statement shall become effective on such date as the U.S. Securities and Exchange Commission, acting pursuant to said Section 8(a), may determine.

RISK FACTORS

Investing in our Class A common stock involves a high degree of risk. Before making an investment decision, you should carefully consider the risks and uncertainties described below, which we believe are material risks of our business and this offering. Our business, financial condition, operating results or growth prospects could be harmed by any of these risks. In such an event, the trading price of our Class A common stock could decline, and you may lose all or part of your investment. In assessing these risks, you should also refer to all of the other information contained in this prospectus, including our consolidated financial statements and related notes. Please also see "Cautionary Note Regarding Forward-Looking Statements."

Risks Related to Our Business and Industry

If we fail to effectively manage our growth, our business, financial condition and operating results could be harmed.

We have grown rapidly, with our net sales increasing from $399.6 million for 2017 to $498.7 million for 2018. To effectively manage our growth, we must continue to implement our operational plans and strategies, improve and expand our infrastructure of people and information systems, and expand, train and manage our employee base. Since our inception, we have rapidly increased our employee headcount to support the growth of our business. The number of our employees increased from 742 as of December 31, 2017 to 983 as of December 31, 2018. We have expanded across all areas of our business. To support continued growth, we must effectively integrate, develop and motivate a large number of new employees while maintaining our corporate culture. We face significant competition for personnel. To attract top talent, we have had to offer, and expect to continue to offer, competitive compensation and benefits packages before we can validate the productivity of new employees. We may also need to increase our employee compensation levels to remain competitive in attracting and retaining talented employees. The risks associated with a rapidly growing workforce will be particularly acute if we choose to expand into new merchandise categories and internationally. Additionally, we may not be able to hire new employees quickly enough to meet our needs. If we fail to effectively manage our hiring needs or successfully integrate new hires, our efficiency, our ability to meet forecasts and our employee morale, productivity and retention could suffer, which may have an adverse effect on our business, financial condition and operating results.

We are also required to manage numerous relationships with various vendors and other third parties. Further growth of our operations, vendor base, fulfillment centers, information technology systems or internal controls and procedures may not be adequate to support our operations. If we are unable to manage the growth of our organization effectively, our business, financial condition and operating results may be adversely affected.

If we are unable to anticipate and respond to changing customer preferences and shifts in fashion and industry trends in a timely manner, our business, financial condition and operating results could be harmed.

Our success largely depends on our ability to consistently gauge tastes and trends and provide a balanced assortment of merchandise that satisfies customer demands in a timely manner. We typically enter into agreements to manufacture and purchase our merchandise in advance of the applicable selling season and our failure to anticipate, identify or react appropriately, or in a timely manner to changes in customer preferences, tastes and trends or economic conditions could lead to, among other things, missed opportunities, excess inventory or inventory shortages, markdowns and write-offs, all of which could negatively impact our profitability and have a material adverse effect on our business, financial condition and operating results. Failure to respond to changing customer preferences and fashion trends could also negatively impact our brand image with our customers and result in diminished brand loyalty.

Our business depends on our ability to maintain a strong community of brands, engaged customers and influencers. We may not be able to maintain and enhance our existing brand community if we receive customer complaints, negative publicity or otherwise fail to live up to consumers' expectations, which could materially adversely affect our business, operating results and growth prospects.

Over the course of 2018, we offered over 850 emerging and established brands through REVOLVE, including 21 brands developed and owned by us, which we refer to as owned brands, and over 250 brands through FORWARD, but we have a limited operating history with many of these brands. Our ability to identify new brands and maintain and enhance our relationships with our existing brands is critical to expanding our base of customers. A significant portion of our customers' experience depends on third parties outside of our control, including vendors, suppliers and logistics providers such as FedEx, UPS and the U.S. Postal Service. If these third parties do not meet our or our customers' expectations or if they increase their rates, our business may suffer irreparable damage or our costs may increase. In addition, maintaining and enhancing relationships with third-party brands may require us to make substantial investments, and these investments may not be successful. Also, if we fail to promote and maintain our brands, or if we incur excessive expenses in this effort, our business, operating results and financial condition may be materially adversely affected. We anticipate that, as our market becomes increasingly competitive, maintaining and enhancing our brands may become increasingly difficult and expensive. Maintaining and enhancing our brands will depend largely on our ability to provide high quality products to our customers and a reliable, trustworthy and profitable sales channel to our vendors, which we may not do successfully.

Customer complaints or negative publicity about our sites, products, product delivery times, customer data handling and security practices or customer support, especially on blogs, social media websites and our sites, could rapidly and severely diminish consumer use of our sites and consumer and supplier confidence in us and result in harm to our brands. We believe that much of the growth in our customer base to date has originated from social media and influencer-driven marketing strategy. If we are not able to develop and maintain positive relationships with our network of over 3,500 of influencers, our ability to promote and maintain awareness of our sites and brands and leverage social media platforms to drive visits to our sites may be adversely affected.

Our industry is highly competitive and if we do not compete effectively our operating results could be adversely affected.

The retail industry is highly competitive. We compete with department stores, specialty retailers, independent retail stores, the online offerings of these traditional retail competitors and eCommerce companies that market merchandise similar to the merchandise we offer. We believe our ability to compete depends on many factors within and beyond our control, including:

- attracting new customers and engaging with existing customers;
- cultivating our relationships with our customers;
- further developing our data analytics capabilities;
- maintaining favorable brand recognition and effectively marketing our services to customers;
- the amount, diversity and quality of brands and merchandise that we or our competitors offer;
- expanding and maintaining appealing owned brands and merchandise;

- the price at which we are able to offer our merchandise;
- maintaining and growing our market share;
- price fluctuations or demand disruptions of our third-party vendors;
- the speed and cost at which we can deliver merchandise to our customers and the ease with which they can use our services to return merchandise; and
- anticipating and quickly responding to changing apparel trends and consumer shopping preferences.

We expect competition to increase as other established and emerging companies enter the markets in which we compete, as customer requirements evolve and as new products and technologies are introduced.

Many of our current competitors have, and potential competitors may have, longer operating histories, larger fulfillment infrastructures, greater technical capabilities, faster shipping times, lower-cost shipping, larger databases, greater financial, marketing, institutional and other resources and larger customer bases than we do. These factors may allow our competitors to derive greater revenue and profits from their existing customer bases, acquire customers at lower costs or respond more quickly than we can to new or emerging technologies and changes in apparel trends and consumer shopping behavior. These competitors may engage in more extensive research and development efforts, enter or expand their presence in the personalized retail market, undertake more far-reaching marketing campaigns, and adopt more aggressive pricing policies, which may allow them to build larger customer bases or generate revenue from their existing customer bases more effectively than we do. If we fail to execute on any of the above better than our competitors, our operating results may be adversely affected.

Competition, along with other factors such as consolidation within the retail industry and changes in consumer spending patterns, could also result in significant pricing pressure. These factors may cause us to reduce prices to our customers, which could cause our gross margins to decline if we are unable to appropriately manage inventory levels and/or otherwise offset price reductions with comparable reductions in our operating costs. If our prices decline and we fail to sufficiently reduce our product costs or operating expenses, our profitability may decline, which could have a material adverse effect on our business, financial condition and operating results.

We may be unable to accurately forecast net sales and appropriately plan our expenses in the future.

We base our current and future expense levels on our operating forecasts and estimates of future net sales and gross margins. Net sales and operating results are difficult to forecast because they generally depend on the volume, timing, value and type of the orders we receive, all of which are uncertain. In addition, we cannot be sure the same growth rates, trends and other key performance metrics are meaningful predictors of future growth. Our business is affected by general economic and business conditions in the United States, and we anticipate that it will be increasingly affected by conditions in international markets. In addition, we experience seasonal trends in our business, and our mix of product offerings is highly variable from day-to-day and quarter-to-quarter. This variability makes it difficult to predict sales and could result in significant fluctuations in our net sales, margins and profitability from period-to-period. A significant portion of our expenses is fixed, and as a result, we may be unable to adjust our spending in a timely manner to compensate for any unexpected shortfall in net sales. Any failure to accurately predict net sales or gross margins could cause our operating results to be lower than expected, which could materially adversely affect our financial condition and stock price.

Our recent growth rates may not be sustainable or indicative of our future growth.

Although our net sales and profitability have grown rapidly, this should not be considered as indicative of our future performance. We may not be successful in executing our growth strategy, and even if we achieve our strategic plan, we may not be able to sustain profitability. In future periods, our net sales could decline or grow more slowly than we expect.

We believe that our continued revenue growth will depend upon, among other factors, our ability to:

- identify new and emerging brands, maintain relationships with emerging and established brands, and develop and grow existing owned brands or develop new owned brands;
- acquire new customers and retain existing customers;
- develop new features to enhance the consumer experience on our sites;
- increase the frequency with which new and repeat customers purchase products on our sites through merchandising, data analytics and technology;

- add new suppliers and deepen our relationships with our existing suppliers;
- enhance and scale the systems our consumers use to interact with our sites and invest in our infrastructure platform;
- target additional categories and price points beyond premium apparel for Millennials, such as luxury, beauty, men's apparel and lower price points;
- expand internationally; and
- pursue strategic acquisitions.

We cannot assure you we will be able to achieve any of the foregoing. Our customer base may not continue to grow or may decline as a result of increased competition and the maturation of our business. Failure to continue our revenue growth rates could have a material adverse effect on our financial condition and operating results. You should not rely on our historical rate of revenue growth as an indication of our future performance or the rate of growth we may experience in any new category or internationally. International markets have historically grown, and we expect will continue to grow, at a slower rate at least until we have more infrastructure in place in those markets.

Use of social media and influencers may materially and adversely affect our reputation or subject us to fines or other penalties.

We use third-party social media platforms as, among other things, marketing tools. For example, we maintain Instagram, Snapchat, Facebook, Twitter, Pinterest, YouTube and Google+ accounts. We also maintain relationships with thousands of social media influencers and engage in sponsorship initiatives. As existing eCommerce and social media platforms continue to rapidly evolve and new platforms develop, we must continue to maintain a presence on these platforms and establish presences on new or emerging popular social media platforms. If we are unable to cost-effectively use social media platforms as marketing tools or if the social media platforms we use do not evolve quickly enough for us to fully optimize such platforms, our ability to acquire new consumers and our financial condition may suffer. Furthermore, as laws and regulations rapidly evolve to govern the use of these platforms and devices, the failure by us, our employees, our network of social media influencers, our sponsors or third parties acting at our direction to abide by applicable laws and regulations in the use of these platforms and devices or otherwise could subject us to regulatory investigations, class action lawsuits, liability, fines or other penalties and have a material adverse effect on our business, financial condition and operating results.

In addition, an increase in the use of social media for product promotion and marketing may cause an increase in the burden on us to monitor compliance of such materials, and increase the risk that such materials could contain problematic product or marketing claims in violation of applicable regulations. For example, in some cases, the FTC has sought enforcement action where an endorsement has failed to clearly and conspicuously disclose a financial relationship or material connection between an influencer and an advertiser. We do not prescribe what our influencers post, and if we were held responsible for the content of their posts or their actions, we could be forced to alter our practices, which could have an adverse impact on our business.

Negative commentary regarding us, our products or influencers and other third parties who are affiliated with us may also be posted on social media platforms and may be adverse to our reputation or business. Influencers with whom we maintain relationships could engage in behavior or use their platforms to communicate directly with our customers in a manner that reflects poorly on our brand and may be attributed to us or otherwise adversely affect us. It is not possible to prevent such behavior, and the precautions we take to detect this activity may not be effective in all cases. Our target consumers often value readily available information and often act on such information without further investigation and without regard to its accuracy. The harm may be immediate, without affording us an opportunity for redress or correction.

Our quarterly operating results may fluctuate, which could cause our stock price to decline.

Our quarterly operating results may fluctuate for a variety of reasons, many of which are beyond our control. These reasons include those described in these risk factors as well as the following:

- fluctuations in net sales generated from the brands on our sites, including as a result of seasonality and the timing and success of events that we host, such as our annual #REVOLVEfestival in the Coachella Valley;
- fluctuations in product mix between sites and between owned and non-owned brands;
- our ability to effectively launch and manage new sites and brands;

- fluctuations in the levels or quality of inventory;
- fluctuations in capacity as we expand our operations;
- our success in engaging existing customers and attracting new customers;
- the amount and timing of our operating expenses;
- the timing and success of new products and brands we introduce;
- the impact of competitive developments and our response to those developments;
- our ability to manage our existing business and future growth;
- disruptions or defects in our sites, such as privacy or data security breaches; and
- economic and market conditions, particularly those affecting our industry.

Fluctuations in our quarterly operating results may cause those results to fall below the expectations of analysts or investors, which could cause the price of our Class A common stock to decline. Fluctuations in our results could also cause a number of other problems. For example, analysts or investors might change their models for valuing our Class A common stock, we could experience short-term liquidity issues, our ability to retain or attract key personnel may diminish and other unanticipated issues may arise.

In addition, we believe that our quarterly operating results may vary in the future and that period-to-period comparisons of our operating results may not be meaningful. For example, our historical growth may have overshadowed the seasonal effects on our historical operating results. These seasonal effects may become more pronounced over time, which could also cause our operating results to fluctuate. You should not rely on the results of one quarter as an indication of future performance.

If we fail to acquire new customers, or fail to do so in a cost-effective manner, we may not be able to increase net sales or maintain profitability.

Our success depends on our ability to acquire customers in a cost-effective manner. In order to expand our customer base, we must appeal to and acquire customers who have historically used other means of commerce in shopping for apparel and may prefer alternatives to our offerings, such as traditional brick-and-mortar retailers and the websites of our competitors. We have made significant investments related to customer acquisition and expect to continue to spend significant amounts to acquire additional customers. For example, we engage in social media marketing campaigns and maintain relationships with thousands of social media and celebrity influencers. Such campaigns are expensive and may not result in the cost-effective acquisition of customers. In addition, the competition for relationships with influencers is increasing, and the cost of maintaining such relationships will likely increase. We cannot assure you that the net profit from new customers we acquire will ultimately exceed the cost of acquiring those customers. If we fail to deliver a quality shopping experience, or if consumers do not perceive the products we offer to be of high value and quality, we may not be able to acquire new customers. If we are unable to acquire new customers who purchase products in numbers sufficient to grow our business, we may not be able to generate the scale necessary to drive beneficial network effects with our suppliers, our net sales may decrease, and our business, financial condition and operating results may be materially adversely affected.

We also seek to engage with our customers and build awareness of our brands through sponsoring unique events and experiences such as #REVOLVEfestival," #REVOLVEaroundtheworld," and #REVOLVEAwards," as well as short-term pop-up retail experiences. We anticipate that our marketing initiatives may become increasingly expensive as competition increases, and generating a meaningful return on those initiatives may be difficult. If our marketing efforts are not successful in promoting awareness of our brands and products, driving customer engagement or attracting new customers, or if we are not able to cost-effectively manage our marketing expenses, our operating results will be adversely affected.

We obtain a significant amount of traffic via social networking websites or other channels used by our current and prospective customers. As eCommerce and social networking continue to rapidly evolve, we must continue to establish relationships with these channels and may be unable to develop or maintain these relationships on acceptable terms. We also use paid and non-paid advertising. We acquire and retain customers through retargeting, paid search/product listing ads, affiliate marketing, paid social, personalized email marketing and mobile "push" communications through our mobile apps. If we are unable to cost-effectively drive traffic to our sites, our ability to acquire new customers and our financial condition would suffer.

If we fail to retain existing customers, or fail to maintain average order value levels, we may not be able to maintain our revenue base and margins, which would have a material adverse effect on our business and operating results.

A significant portion of our net sales are generated from sales to existing customers, particularly those existing customers who are highly engaged and make frequent and/or large purchases of the merchandise we offer. If existing customers no longer find our offerings appealing, or if we are unable to timely update our offerings to meet current trends and customer demands, our existing customers may make fewer or smaller purchases in the future. A decrease in the number of our customers who make repeat purchases or a decrease in their spending on the merchandise we offer could negatively impact our operating results. Further, we believe that our future success will depend in part on our ability to increase sales to our existing customers over time, and if we are unable to do so, our business may suffer. If we fail to generate repeat purchases or maintain high levels of customer engagement and average order value, our growth prospects, operating results and financial condition could be materially adversely affected.

We purchase inventory in anticipation of sales, and if we are unable to manage our inventory effectively, our operating results could be adversely affected.

Our business requires us to manage a large volume of inventory effectively. We add a total of over 1,000 new apparel, footwear, accessories and beauty styles to our sites in a typical week, and we depend on our forecasts of demand for and popularity of various products to make purchase decisions and to manage our inventory of stock-keeping units, or SKUs. Demand for products, however, can change significantly between the time inventory is ordered and the date of sale. Demand may be affected by seasonality, new product launches, rapid changes in product cycles and pricing, product defects, promotions, changes in consumer spending patterns, changes in consumer tastes with respect to our products and other factors, and our consumers may not purchase products in the quantities that we expect.

Seasonality in our business does not follow that of traditional retailers, such as typical concentration of net sales in the holiday quarter. We believe our results are impacted by a pattern of increased sales leading up to #REVOLVEfestival in April and during the early summer months, which results in increased sales during the second quarter of each fiscal year. We also believe that we have experienced slower growth in orders placed and active customers during the first quarter. We expect this seasonality to continue in future years.

It may be difficult to accurately forecast demand and determine appropriate levels of product. We generally do not have the right to return unsold products to our suppliers. If we fail to manage our inventory effectively or negotiate favorable credit terms with third-party suppliers, we may be subject to a heightened risk of inventory obsolescence, a decline in inventory values, and significant inventory write-downs or write-offs. In addition, if we are required to lower sale prices in order to reduce inventory level or to pay higher prices to our suppliers, our profit margins might be negatively affected. Any of the above may materially and adversely affect our business, financial condition and operating results.

Merchandise returns could harm our business.

We allow our customers to return products, subject to our return policy. If the rate of merchandise returns increases significantly or if merchandise return economics become less efficient, our business, financial condition and operating results could be harmed. Further, we modify our policies relating to returns from time to time, which may result in customer dissatisfaction or an increase in the number of product returns. From time to time our products are damaged in transit, which can increase return rates and harm our brand.

We rely on consumer discretionary spending, which may be adversely affected by economic downturns and other macroeconomic conditions or trends.

Our business and operating results are subject to global economic conditions and their impact on consumer discretionary spending. Some of the factors that may negatively influence consumer spending include high levels of unemployment, higher consumer debt levels, reductions in net worth, declines in asset values and related market uncertainty, home foreclosures and reductions in home values, fluctuating interest rates and credit availability, fluctuating fuel and other energy costs, fluctuating commodity prices and general uncertainty regarding the overall future political and economic environment. Economic conditions in certain regions may also be affected by natural disasters, such as earthquakes, hurricanes, tropical storms and wildfires. Consumer purchases of discretionary items, including the merchandise that we offer, generally decline during periods of economic uncertainty, when disposable income is reduced or when there is a reduction in consumer confidence. For example, our business was adversely affected by the Great Recession in 2008.

Adverse economic changes could reduce consumer confidence, and thereby could negatively affect our operating results. In challenging and uncertain economic environments, we cannot predict when macroeconomic uncertainty may arise, whether or when such circumstances may improve or worsen or what impact such circumstances could have on our business.

Our inability to identify, develop and introduce new merchandise offerings in a timely and cost-effective manner may damage our business, financial condition and operating results.

The retail industry is driven in part by fashion and beauty trends, which may shift quickly. Our continued success depends on our ability to anticipate, gauge and react in a timely and cost-effective manner to changes in consumer preferences for products, consumer attitudes toward our industry and brand and where and how consumers shop for those products. We must continually work to develop, produce and market new products, maintain and enhance the recognition of our brands, maintain a favorable mix of products and develop our approach as to how and where we market and sell our products.

We have an established process for the identification, development, evaluation and validation of our new products. Nonetheless, each new product launch involves risks, as well as the possibility of unexpected consequences. For example, sales of our new products may not be as high as we anticipate, due to lack of acceptance of the products themselves or their price, or limited effectiveness of our marketing strategies. In addition, our ability to launch new products may be limited by delays or difficulties affecting the ability of our suppliers or manufacturers to timely manufacture, distribute and ship new products. Sales of new products may also be affected by inventory management. We may also experience a decrease in sales of certain existing products as a result of newly-launched products. Any of these occurrences could delay or impede our ability to achieve our sales objectives, which could have a material adverse effect on our business, financial condition and operating results.

As part of our ongoing business strategy we expect we will need to continue to introduce new products in our traditional product categories of clothing, shoes and accessories, while also expanding our product launches into adjacent categories in which we may have little to no operating experience. For example, in December 2016, we launched REVOLVE Beauty, which now includes over 225 brands in skincare, cosmetics and haircare. In addition, we launched a lower price point offering in March 2019, which may cannibalize sales from our other sites and adversely affect customer lifetime value and our operating results. The success of product launches in adjacent categories could be hampered by our relative inexperience operating in such categories, the strength of our competitors or any of the other risks referred to above. Furthermore, any expansion into new product categories may prove to be an operational and financial constraint which inhibits our ability to successfully accomplish such expansion. Our inability to introduce successful products in our traditional categories or in adjacent categories could limit our future growth and have a material adverse effect on our business, financial condition and operating results.

There is no assurance that consumers will continue to purchase our products in the future. Customers may consider our offerings to be premium products and purchase fewer or lower-priced products if their discretionary income decreases. During periods of economic uncertainty, we may need to reduce prices in response to competitive pressures or otherwise, to maintain sales, which may adversely affect margins and profitability.

Our business, including our costs and supply chain, is subject to risks associated with sourcing, manufacturing and warehousing.

A majority of the merchandise we offer on our sites is sourced from third-party vendors, and as a result we may be subject to price fluctuations or demand disruptions. Our operating results would be negatively impacted by increases in the prices of our merchandise, and we have no guarantees that prices will not rise. In addition, as we expand into new categories and product types, we expect that we may not have strong purchasing power in these new areas, which could lead to higher prices than we have historically seen in our current categories. We may not be able to pass increased prices on to customers, which could adversely affect our operating results. Moreover, in the event of a significant disruption in the supply of the fabrics or raw materials used in the manufacture of the merchandise we offer, we and the vendors that we work with might not be able to locate alternative suppliers of materials of comparable quality at an acceptable price.

In addition, merchandise and materials we receive from vendors and suppliers may not be of sufficient quality or free from damage, or such merchandise may be damaged during shipping, while stored in one of our fulfillment centers or when returned by customers. We may incur additional expenses and our reputation could be harmed if customers and potential customers believe that our merchandise does not meet their expectations, is not properly labeled or is damaged.

If we do not successfully optimize, operate and manage the expansion of capacity of our fulfillment centers, our business, financial condition and operating results could be harmed.

If we do not optimize and operate our fulfillment centers successfully and efficiently, it could result in excess or insufficient fulfillment capacity, an increase in costs or impairment charges or harm our business in other ways. If we do not have sufficient fulfillment capacity or experience a problem fulfilling orders in a timely manner, our customers may experience delays in receiving their purchases, which could harm our reputation and our relationship with our customers.

We have designed and built our own fulfillment center infrastructure, including customizing third-party inventory and package handling software systems, which is tailored to meet the specific needs of our business. If we continue to add fulfillment and warehouse capabilities, add new businesses or categories with different fulfillment requirements or change the mix in products that we sell, our fulfillment network will become increasingly complex and operating it will become more challenging. Failure to successfully address such challenges in a cost-effective and timely manner could impair our ability to timely deliver our customers' purchases and could harm our reputation and ultimately, our business, financial condition and operating results.

In September 2018, we entered into a five-year lease for approximately 281,000 square feet of fulfillment and office space. In the first quarter of 2019, we consolidated substantially all of our fulfillment activities into this centralized facility and have terminated the lease of our existing distribution facility. Beginning in May 2019, we will sublet one of our existing fulfillment centers through its remaining lease term. We are still in the process of consolidating certain other facilities, which may include subleasing or terminating additional existing facilities. The transition has, and will continue to put near-term pressure on our managerial, financial, operational and other resources. We expect that our current capacity will support our near-term growth plans. Over the long term, we cannot assure you that we will be able to locate suitable facilities on commercially acceptable terms in accordance with our expansion plans, nor can we assure you that we will be able to recruit qualified managerial and operational personnel to support our expansion plans. If we are unable to secure new facilities for the expansion of our fulfillment operations or to effectively control expansion-related expenses, our business, prospects, financial condition and operating results could be materially and adversely affected. If we grow faster than we anticipate, we may exceed our fulfillment center capacity sooner than we anticipate, we may experience problems fulfilling orders in a timely manner or our customers may experience delays in receiving their purchases, which could harm our reputation and our relationship with our customers, and we would need to increase our capital expenditures more than anticipated. Many of the expenses and investments with respect to our fulfillment centers are fixed, and any expansion of such fulfillment centers will require additional investment of capital. We expect to incur higher capital expenditures in the future for our fulfillment center operations. We may incur such expenses or make such investments in advance of expected sales, and such expected sales may not occur.

We rely on third-party suppliers, manufacturers, distributors and other vendors, and they may not continue to produce products or provide services that are consistent with our standards or applicable regulatory requirements, which could harm our brand, cause consumer dissatisfaction, and require us to find alternative suppliers of our products or services.

We do not own or operate any manufacturing facilities. We use multiple third-party suppliers and manufacturers based primarily in China and, to a lesser extent, the United States and India to source and manufacture all of our products under our owned brands. We engage our third-party suppliers and manufacturers on a purchase order basis and are not party to long-term contracts with any of them. The ability of these third parties to supply and manufacture our products may be affected by competing orders placed by other customers and the demands of those customers. If we experience significant increases in demand, or need to replace a significant number of existing suppliers or manufacturers, there can be no assurance that additional supply and manufacturing capacity will be available when required on terms that are acceptable to us, or at all, or that any supplier or manufacturer will allocate sufficient capacity to us in order to meet our requirements.

In addition, quality control problems, such as the use of materials and delivery of products that do not meet our quality control standards and specifications or comply with applicable laws or regulations, could harm our business. In the past, we have experienced negative press and government enforcement actions as a result of our vendors' failure to comply with certain applicable laws and regulations, and may experience similar negative press as a result of any future non-compliance by our vendors. We do not regularly inspect these vendors and quality control problems could result in regulatory action, such as restrictions on importation, products of inferior quality or product stock outages or shortages, harming our sales and creating inventory write-downs for unusable products.

We have also outsourced portions of our distribution process, as well as certain technology-related functions, to third-party service providers. Specifically, we rely on third parties in a number of foreign countries and territories, we are dependent on third-party vendors for credit card processing, and we use third-party hosting and networking providers to host our sites. The failure of one or more of these entities to provide the expected services on a timely basis, or at all, or at the prices we expect, or the costs and disruption incurred in changing these outsourced functions to being performed under our management and direct control or that of a third party, may have a material adverse effect on our business, financial condition and results of operations. We are not party to long-term contracts with some of our distributors, and upon expiration of these existing agreements, we may not be able to renegotiate the terms on a commercially reasonable basis, or at all.

Further, our third-party manufacturers, suppliers and distributors may:

- have economic or business interests or goals that are inconsistent with ours;
- take actions contrary to our instructions, requests, policies or objectives;
- be unable or unwilling to fulfill their obligations under relevant purchase orders, including obligations to meet our production deadlines, quality standards, pricing guidelines and product specifications, and to comply with applicable regulations, including those regarding the safety and quality of products;
- have financial difficulties;
- encounter raw material or labor shortages;
- encounter increases in raw material or labor costs which may affect our procurement costs;
- disclose our confidential information or intellectual property to competitors or third parties;
- engage in activities or employ practices that may harm our reputation; and
- work with, be acquired by, or come under control of, our competitors.

Shipping is a critical part of our business and any changes in our shipping arrangements or any interruptions in shipping could adversely affect our operating results.

We primarily rely on two major vendors for our shipping. If we are not able to negotiate acceptable pricing and other terms with these entities or they experience performance problems or other difficulties, it could negatively impact our operating results and our customer experience. In addition, our ability to receive inbound inventory efficiently and ship merchandise to customers may be negatively affected by inclement weather, fire, flood, power loss, earthquakes, labor disputes, acts of war or terrorism, trade embargoes and similar factors. For example, strikes at major international shipping ports have in the past impacted our supply of inventory from our vendors, and the escalating trade dispute between the United States and China could lead to increased tariffs on our goods and restrict the flow of the goods between the United States and China. We are also subject to risks of damage or loss during delivery by our shipping vendors. If our merchandise is not delivered in a timely fashion or is damaged or lost during the delivery process, our customers could become dissatisfied and cease shopping on our sites, which would adversely affect our business and operating results.

Our failure to adequately and effectively staff our fulfillment centers, through third parties or with our own employees, could adversely affect our customer experience and operating results.

We currently receive and distribute merchandise at fulfillment centers in the United States, none of which are operated by a third party. If we are unable to adequately staff our fulfillment centers to meet demand or if the cost of such staffing is higher than historical or projected costs due to mandated wage increases, regulatory changes, international expansion or other factors, our operating results could be harmed. In addition, operating fulfillment centers comes with potential risks, such as workplace safety issues and employment claims for the failure or alleged failure to comply with labor laws or laws respecting union organizing activities. Any such issues may result in delays in shipping times or packing quality, and our reputation and operating results may be harmed.

Any failure by us or our vendors to comply with product safety, labor or other laws, or to provide safe conditions for our or their workers may damage our reputation and brand and harm our business.

The merchandise we sell to our customers is subject to regulation by the Federal Consumer Product Safety Commission, the Federal Trade

Commission and similar state and international regulatory authorities. As a result, such merchandise could be in the future subject to recalls and other remedial actions. Product safety, labeling and licensing concerns, including consumer disclosure and warning regarding chemical exposure, may require us to voluntarily remove selected merchandise from our inventory. Such recalls or voluntary removal of merchandise can result in, among other things, lost sales, diverted resources, potential harm to our reputation and increased customer service costs and legal expenses, which could have a material adverse effect on our operating results.

We purchase our merchandise from numerous domestic and international vendors. Failure of our vendors to comply with applicable laws and regulations and contractual requirements could lead to litigation against us, resulting in increased legal expenses and costs. In addition, the failure of any such vendors to provide safe and humane factory conditions and oversight at their facilities could damage our reputation with customers or result in legal claims against us.

If our suppliers fail to use ethical business practices and fail to comply with changing laws and regulations, our brand image could be harmed due to negative publicity.

Our core values, which include developing the highest quality products while operating with integrity, are an important component of our brand image, which makes our reputation sensitive to allegations of unethical or improper business practices, whether real or perceived. We do not control our suppliers and manufacturers or their business, and they may not comply with our guidelines or the law. A lack of compliance could lead to reduced sales or recalls or damage to our brand or cause us to seek alternative suppliers, which could increase our costs and result in delayed delivery of our products, product shortages or other disruptions of our operations. In addition, we rely on our manufacturers' and suppliers' compliance reporting in order to comply with regulations applicable to our products. This is further complicated by the fact that expectations of ethical business practices continually evolve and may be substantially more demanding than applicable legal requirements. Ethical business practices are also driven in part by legal developments and by diverse groups active in publicizing and organizing public responses to perceived ethical shortcomings. Accordingly, we cannot predict how such regulations or expectations might develop in the future and cannot be certain that our guidelines or current practices would satisfy all parties who are active in monitoring our products or other business practices worldwide.

Certain of our key operating metrics are subject to inherent challenges in measurement, and real or perceived inaccuracies in such metrics may harm our reputation and negatively affect our business.

We track certain key operating metrics using internal data analytics tools, which have certain limitations. In addition, we rely on data received from third parties, including third-party platforms, to track certain performance indicators. Data from both such sources may include information relating to fraudulent accounts and interactions with our sites or the social media accounts of our influencers (including as a result of the use of bots, or other automated or manual mechanisms to generate false impressions that are delivered through our sites or their accounts). We have only a limited ability to verify data from our sites or third parties, and perpetrators of fraudulent impressions may change their tactics and may become more sophisticated, which would make it still more difficult to detect such activity.

Our methodologies for tracking metrics may also change over time, which could result in changes to the metrics we report. If we undercount or overcount performance due to the internal data analytics tools we use or issues with the data received from third parties, or if our internal data analytics tools contain algorithmic or other technical errors, the data we report may not be accurate or comparable with prior periods. In addition, limitations, changes or errors with respect to how we measure data may affect our understanding of certain details of our business, which could affect our longer-term strategies.

If our performance metrics are not accurate representations of the reach or monetization of our network, if we discover material inaccuracies in our metrics or the data on which such metrics are based, or if we can no longer calculate any of our key performance metrics with a sufficient degree of accuracy and cannot find an adequate replacement for the metric, our business, financial condition and operating results could be adversely affected.

Increases in labor costs, including wages, could adversely affect our business, financial condition and results of operations.

Labor is a significant portion of our cost structure and is subject to many external factors, including unemployment levels, prevailing wage rates, minimum wage laws, potential collective bargaining arrangements, health insurance costs and other insurance costs and changes in employment and labor legislation or other workplace regulation. From time to time, legislative proposals are made to increase the federal minimum wage in the United States, as well as the minimum wage in California and a number of other states and municipalities, and to reform entitlement programs, such as health insurance and paid leave programs. As minimum wage rates increase or related laws and regulations change, we may need to increase not only the wage rates of our minimum wage employees, but also the wages paid to our other hourly or salaried employees. Any increase in the cost of our labor could have an adverse effect on our business, financial condition and results of operations or if we fail to pay such higher wages we could suffer increased employee turnover. Increases in labor costs could force us to increase prices, which could adversely impact our sales. If competitive pressures or other factors prevent us from offsetting increased labor costs by increases in prices, our profitability may decline and could have a material adverse effect on our business, financial condition and results of operations. In particular, the job market in Southern California, where our principal offices and fulfillment centers as well as the majority of our employees are located, is very competitive.

Developments in labor and employment law and any unionizing efforts by employees could have a material adverse effect on our results of operations.

We face the risk that Congress, federal agencies or one or more states could approve legislation or regulations significantly affecting our businesses and our relationship with our employees, such as the previously proposed federal legislation referred to as the Employee Free Choice Act, which would have substantially liberalized the procedures for union organization. None of our domestic employees are currently covered by a collective bargaining agreement, but any attempt by our employees to organize a labor union could result in increased legal and other associated costs. Additionally, given the National Labor Relations Board's "speedy election" rule, our ability to timely and effectively address any unionizing efforts would be difficult. If we enter into a collective bargaining agreement with our domestic employees, the terms could materially adversely affect our costs, efficiency and ability to generate acceptable returns on the affected operations.

Additionally, the Department of Labor issued a final rule in 2016 raising the minimum salary basis exemption from overtime payments for executive, administrative and professional employees. The rule increases the minimum salary from the current amount of $23,660 to $47,476 and up to 10% of non-discretionary bonus, commission and other incentive payments can be counted towards the minimum salary requirement. The rule was scheduled to go into effect on December 1, 2016. The rule was temporarily enjoined from going into effect in November 2016, and later invalidated in August 2017, after several states and business groups filed separate lawsuits against the Department of Labor challenging the rule. However, any future rule similar to this rule that impacts the way we classify certain positions, increases our payment of overtime wages or increases the salaries we are required to pay to currently exempt employees to maintain their exempt status may have a material adverse effect on our business, financial condition and results of operations.

If sensitive information about our customers is disclosed, or if we or our third-party providers are subject to real or perceived cyber-attacks, our customers may curtail use of our platform, we may be exposed to liability and our reputation would suffer.

We collect, transmit and store personal and financial information provided by our customers, such as names, email addresses, the details of transactions and credit card and other financial information. Some of our third-party service providers, such as identity verification and payment processing providers, also regularly have access to customer data. In an effort to protect sensitive information, we rely on a variety of security measures, including encryption and authentication technology licensed from third parties. However, advances in computer capabilities, increasingly sophisticated tools and methods used by hackers and cyber terrorists, new discoveries in the field of cryptography or other developments may result in our failure or inability to adequately protect sensitive information.

Like other online services, we are also vulnerable to computer viruses, unauthorized access, phishing or social engineering attacks, ransomware attacks, denial-of-service attacks and other real or perceived cyber-attacks. Any of these incidents could lead to interruptions or shutdowns of our platform, loss or corruption of data, or unauthorized access to or disclosure of personal data or other sensitive information. Cyberattacks could also result in the theft of our intellectual property. We have been subject to attempted cyber, phishing or social engineering attacks in the past and may continue to be subject to such attacks in the future. If we gain greater visibility, we may face a higher risk of being targeted by cyberattacks. Advances in computer capabilities, new technological discoveries or other developments may result in cyber-attacks becoming more sophisticated and more difficult to detect. We and our third-party service providers may not have the resources or technical sophistication to anticipate or prevent all such cyberattacks. Moreover, techniques used to obtain unauthorized access to systems change frequently and may not be known until launched against us or our third-party service providers. Security breaches can also occur as a result of non-technical issues, including intentional or inadvertent actions by our employees, our third-party service providers, or their personnel.

We and our third-party service providers regularly experience cyber-attacks aimed at disrupting our and their services. If we or our third-party service providers experience, or are believed to have experienced, security breaches that result in marketplace performance or availability problems or the loss or corruption of, or unauthorized access to or disclosure of, personal data or confidential information, people may become unwilling to provide us the information necessary make purchases on our sites. Existing customers may also decrease their purchases or close their accounts altogether. We could also face potential liability and litigation, which may not be adequately covered by insurance. Any of these results could harm our growth prospects, our business and our reputation.

Failure to comply with federal, state and international laws and regulations and our contractual obligations relating to privacy, data protection and consumer protection, or the expansion of current or the enactment of new laws or regulations relating to privacy, data protection and consumer protection, could adversely affect our business and our financial condition.

We collect and maintain significant amounts of personal data and other data relating to our customers and employees. A variety of federal, state and international laws and regulations, and certain industry standards, govern or apply to our collection, use, retention, sharing and security of consumer data. We are subject to certain laws, regulations, contractual obligations and industry standards (including, for example, the Payment Card Industry Data Security Standard, or PCI-DSS) relating to privacy, data protection, information security and consumer protection, including California's Consumer Legal Remedies Act and unfair competition and false advertising laws, which are evolving and subject to potentially differing interpretations. These requirements may be interpreted and applied in a manner that is inconsistent from one jurisdiction to another or may conflict with other rules or our practices. As a result, our practices likely have not complied or may not comply in the future with all such laws, regulations, requirements and obligations. Any failure, or perceived failure, by us to comply with our privacy policies or with any federal, state or international laws, regulations, industry self-regulatory principles, industry standards or codes of conduct, regulatory guidance, orders to which we may be subject or other legal or contractual obligations relating to privacy, data protection, information security or consumer protection could adversely affect our reputation, brand and business, and may result in claims, proceedings or actions against us by governmental entities or others or other liabilities or require us to change our operations and/or cease or modify our use of certain data sets. Any such claim, proceeding or action could hurt our reputation, brand and business, force us to incur significant expenses in defense of such proceedings, distract our management, increase our costs of doing business, result in a loss of customers and suppliers or an inability to process credit card payments and may result in the imposition of monetary penalties. We may also be contractually required to indemnify and hold harmless third parties from the costs or consequences of non-compliance with any laws, regulations or other legal obligations relating to privacy or consumer protection or any inadvertent or unauthorized use or disclosure of data that we store or handle as part of operating our business.

Federal, state and international governmental authorities continue to evaluate the privacy implications inherent in the use of third-party "cookies" and other methods of online tracking for behavioral advertising and other purposes. U.S. and foreign governments have enacted, have considered or are considering legislation or regulations that could significantly restrict the ability of companies and individuals to engage in these activities, such as by regulating the level of consumer notice and consent required before a company can employ cookies or other electronic tracking tools or the use of data gathered with such tools. Additionally, some providers of consumer devices and web browsers have implemented, or announced plans to implement, means to make it easier for Internet users to prevent the placement of cookies or to block other tracking technologies, which could if widely adopted result in the use of third-party cookies and other methods of online tracking becoming significantly less effective. Regulation of the use of these cookies and other online tracking and advertising practices, or a loss in our ability to make effective use of services that employ such technologies, could increase our costs of operations and limit our ability to track trends, optimize our product assortment or acquire new customers on cost-effective terms and consequently, materially adversely affect our business, financial condition and operating results.

Foreign laws and regulations relating to privacy, data protection, information security, and consumer protection often are more restrictive than those in the United States. The European Union, for example, traditionally has imposed stricter obligations under its laws and regulations relating to privacy, data protection and consumer protection than the United States. In May 2018 the European Union's new regulation governing data practices and privacy called the General Data Protection Regulation, or GDPR, became effective and substantially replaced the data protection laws of the individual European Union member states. The law requires companies to meet more stringent requirements regarding the handling of personal data of individuals in the EU than were required under predecessor EU requirements. In the United Kingdom, a Data Protection Bill that substantially implements the GDPR also became law in May 2018. The law also increases the penalties for non-compliance, which may result in monetary penalties of up to 20.0 million Euros or 4% of a company's worldwide turnover, whichever is higher. The GDPR and other similar regulations require companies to give specific types of notice and in some cases seek consent from consumers and other data subjects before collecting or using their data for certain purposes, including some marketing activities. Outside of the European Union, many countries and territories have laws, regulations, or other requirements relating to privacy, data protection, information security, and consumer protection, and new countries and territories are adopting such legislation or other obligations with increasing frequency. Many of these laws may require consent from consumers for the use of data for various purposes, including marketing, which may reduce our ability to market our products. There is no harmonized approach to these laws and regulations globally. Consequently, we would increase our risk of non-compliance with applicable foreign data protection laws by expanding internationally. We may need to change and limit the way we use personal information in operating our business and may have difficulty maintaining a single operating model that is compliant. In addition, various federal, state and foreign legislative and regulatory bodies, or self-regulatory organizations, may expand current laws or regulations, enact new laws or regulations or issue revised rules or guidance regarding privacy, data protection, information security and consumer protection. For example, California recently enacted the California Consumer Privacy Act, or CCPA, which will, among other things, require new disclosures to California consumers and afford such consumers new abilities to opt out of certain sales of personal information, when it goes into effect on January 1, 2020. Legislators have stated that they intend to propose amendments to the CCPA before it goes into effect, and it remains unclear what, if any, modifications will be made to this legislation or how it will be interpreted. The effects of the CCPA potentially are significant, however, and may require us to modify our data processing practices and policies and to incur substantial costs and expenses in an effort to comply. As a general matter, compliance with laws, regulations, and any applicable rules or guidance from self-regulatory organizations relating to privacy, data protection, information security and consumer protection, may result in substantial costs and may necessitate changes to our business practices, which may compromise our growth strategy, adversely affect our ability to acquire customers, and otherwise adversely affect our business, financial condition and operating results.

System interruptions that impair customer access to our sites or other performance failures in our technology infrastructure could damage our business, reputation and brand and substantially harm our business and results of operations.

The satisfactory performance, reliability and availability of our sites, transaction-processing systems and technology infrastructure are critical to our reputation and our ability to acquire and retain customers, as well as maintain adequate customer service levels.

We currently use two redundant third-party data center hosting facilities in Los Angeles County, California. If the facilities where the computer and communications hardware are located fail, or if we suffer an interruption or degradation of services at our main facility, we could lose customer data and miss order fulfillment deadlines, which could harm our business. Our systems and operations are vulnerable to damage or interruption from fire, flood, power loss, telecommunications failure, terrorist attacks, cyberattacks, data loss, acts of war, break-ins, earthquake and similar events. For example, in September 2018 a distributed denial of service, or DDoS, attack caused our sites to be down for several hours, and we could be the subject of similar attacks in the future. In the event of a failure of our main facility, the failover to our back-up facility could take substantial time, during which time our sites could be completely shut down. Our back-up facility is designed to support transaction volume at a level slightly above our average daily sales, but is not adequate to support spikes in demand. The back-up facility may not process effectively during time of higher traffic to our sites and may process transactions more slowly and may not support all of our sites' functionality.

We use complex custom-built proprietary software in our technology infrastructure, which we seek to continually update and improve. We may not always be successful in executing these upgrades and improvements, and the operation of our systems may be subject to failure. In particular, we have in the past and may in the future experience slowdowns or interruptions in some or all of our sites when we are updating them, and new technologies or infrastructures may not be fully integrated with existing systems on a timely basis, or at all. Additionally, if we expand our use of third-party services, including cloud-based services, our technology infrastructure may be subject to increased risk of slowdown or interruption as a result of integration with such services and/or failures by such third parties, which are out of our control. Our net sales depend on the number of visitors who shop on our sites and the volume of orders we can handle. Unavailability of our sites or reduced order fulfillment performance would reduce the volume of goods sold and could also materially adversely affect consumer perception of our brand. We may experience periodic system interruptions from time to time. In addition, continued growth in our transaction volume, as well as surges in online traffic and orders associated with promotional activities or seasonal trends in our business, place additional demands on our technology platform and could cause or exacerbate slowdowns or interruptions. If there is a substantial increase in the volume of traffic on our sites or the number of orders placed by customers, we will be required to further expand, scale and upgrade our technology, transaction processing systems and network infrastructure. There can be no assurance that we will be able to accurately project the rate or timing of increases, if any, in the use of our sites or expand, scale and upgrade our technology, systems and infrastructure to accommodate such increases on a timely basis. In order to remain competitive, we must continue to enhance and improve the responsiveness, functionality and features of our sites, which is particularly challenging given the rapid rate at which new technologies, customer preferences and expectations and industry standards and practices are evolving in the eCommerce industry. Accordingly, we redesign and enhance various functions on our sites on a regular basis, and we may experience instability and performance issues as a result of these changes.

Any slowdown or failure of our sites and the underlying technology infrastructure could harm our business, reputation and our ability to acquire, retain and serve our customers, which could materially adversely affect our results of operations and our business interruption insurance may not be sufficient to compensate us for the losses that could occur.

We are increasingly dependent on information technology, and if we are unable to protect against service interruptions, data corruption, cyber-based attacks or network security breaches, our operations could be disrupted.

We rely on information technology networks and systems to market and sell our products, to process, transmit and store electronic and financial information, to manage a variety of business processes and activities and to comply with regulatory, legal and tax requirements. We are increasingly dependent on a variety of information systems to effectively process customer orders. We depend on our information technology infrastructure for digital marketing activities and for electronic communications among our personnel, customers, manufacturers and suppliers around the world. These information technology systems, some of which are managed by third parties, may be susceptible to damage, disruptions or shutdowns due to failures during the process of upgrading or replacing software, databases or components, power outages, hardware failures, computer viruses, attacks by computer hackers, telecommunication failures, user errors or catastrophic events. Any material disruption of our systems, or the systems of our third-party service providers, could disrupt our ability to track, record and analyze the products that we sell and could negatively impact our operations, shipment of goods, ability to process financial information and transactions, and our ability to receive and process retail customers and eCommerce orders or engage in normal business activities. If our information technology systems suffer damage, disruption or shutdown and we do not effectively resolve the issues in a timely manner, our business, financial condition and results of operations may be materially and adversely affected, and we could experience delays in reporting our financial results.

Our eCommerce operations are important to our business. Our website serves as an effective extension of our marketing strategies by exposing potential new consumers to our brand, product offerings and enhanced content. Due to the importance of our website and eCommerce operations, we are vulnerable to website downtime and other technical failures. Our failure to successfully respond to these risks could reduce eCommerce sales and damage our brand's reputation.

We must successfully maintain, scale and upgrade our information technology systems, and our failure to do so could have a material adverse effect on our business, financial condition and results of operations.

We have identified the need to significantly expand, scale and improve our information technology systems and personnel to support recent and expected future growth. As such, we are in process of implementing, and will continue to invest in and implement, significant modifications and upgrades to our information technology systems and procedures, including replacing legacy systems with successor systems, making changes to legacy systems or acquiring new systems with new functionality, hiring employees with information technology expertise and building new policies, procedures, training programs and monitoring tools. These types of activities subject us to inherent costs and risks associated with replacing and changing these systems, including impairment of our ability to leverage our eCommerce channels, fulfill customer orders, potential disruption of our internal control structure, substantial capital expenditures, additional administration and operating expenses, acquisition and retention of sufficiently skilled personnel to implement and operate the new systems, demands on management time, the introduction of errors or vulnerabilities and other risks and costs of delays or difficulties in transitioning to or integrating new systems into our current systems. These implementations, modifications and upgrades may not result in productivity improvements at a level that outweighs the costs of implementation, or at all. Additionally, difficulties with implementing new technology systems, delays in our timeline for planned improvements, significant system failures, or our inability to successfully modify our information systems to respond to changes in our business needs may cause disruptions in our business operations and have a material adverse effect on our business, financial condition and results of operations.

Some of our software and systems contain open source software, which may pose particular risks to our proprietary applications.

We use open source software in the applications we have developed to operate our business and will use open source software in the future. We may face claims from third parties demanding the release or license of the open source software or derivative works that we developed from such software (which could include our proprietary source code) or otherwise seeking to enforce the terms of the applicable open source license. These claims could result in litigation and could require us to purchase a costly license, publicly release the affected portions of our source code, or cease offering the implicated solutions unless and until we can re-engineer them to avoid infringement. In addition, our use of open source software may present additional security risks because the source code for open source software is publicly available, which may make it easier for hackers and other third parties to determine how to breach our website and systems that rely on open source software. Any of these risks could be difficult to eliminate or manage and, if not addressed, could have an adverse effect on our business and operating results.

Our software is highly complex and may contain undetected errors.

The software underlying our sites is highly complex and may contain undetected errors or vulnerabilities, some of which may only be discovered after the code has been released. We rely heavily on a software engineering practice known as "continuous deployment," meaning that we typically release software code multiple times per day. This practice may result in the more frequent introduction of errors or vulnerabilities into the software underlying our platform. Any errors or vulnerabilities discovered in our code after release could result in damage to our reputation, loss of customers, disruption to our eCommerce channels, loss of revenue or liability for damages, any of which could adversely affect our growth prospects and our business.

Our business may be adversely affected if we are unable to provide our customers a cost-effective shopping platform that is able to respond and adapt to rapid changes in technology.

The number of people who access the Internet through devices other than personal computers, including mobile phones, smartphones, handheld computers such as notebooks and tablets, video game consoles, and television set-top devices, has increased dramatically in the past few years. The smaller screen size, functionality, and memory associated with some alternative devices may make the use of our sites and purchasing our products more difficult. The versions of our sites developed for these devices may not be compelling to consumers. In addition, it is time consuming and costly to keep pace with rapidly changing and continuously evolving technology. We launched our mobile applications for REVOLVE and FORWARD in 2013, and all of our North American sites and a majority of our international sites are mobile-optimized. In 2018, 49.3% of orders were placed from a mobile device. However, we cannot be certain that our mobile applications or our mobile-optimized sites will be successful in the future.

As existing mobile devices and platforms evolve and new mobile devices and platforms are released, it is difficult to predict the problems we may encounter in adjusting and developing applications for changed and alternative devices and platforms, and we may need to devote significant resources to the creation, support and maintenance of such applications. If we are unable to attract consumers to our websites through these devices or are slow to develop a version of our websites that is more compatible with alternative devices or a mobile application, we may fail to capture a significant share of consumers in the fashion retail market, which could materially and adversely affect our business.

Further, we continually upgrade existing technologies and business applications, and we may be required to implement new technologies or business applications in the future. The implementation of upgrades and changes requires significant investments. Our results of operations may be affected by the timing, effectiveness and costs associated with the successful implementation of any upgrades or changes to our systems and infrastructure. In the event that it is more difficult for our customers to buy products from us on their mobile devices, or if our customers choose not to buy products from us on their mobile devices or to use mobile products that do not offer access to our websites, our customer growth could be harmed and our business, financial condition and operating results may be materially adversely affected.

Government regulation of the Internet and eCommerce is evolving, and unfavorable changes or failure by us to comply with these regulations could substantially harm our business and results of operations.

We are subject to general business regulations and laws as well as regulations and laws specifically governing the Internet and eCommerce. Existing and future regulations and laws could impede the growth of the Internet, eCommerce or mobile commerce. These regulations and laws may involve taxes, tariffs, privacy, data protection, data security, anti-spam, content protection, electronic contracts and communications, consumer protection, website accessibility, Internet neutrality and gift cards. It is not clear how existing laws governing issues such as property ownership, sales and other taxes and consumer privacy apply to the Internet as many of these laws were adopted prior to the advent of the Internet and do not contemplate or address the unique issues raised by the Internet or eCommerce. It is possible that general business regulations and laws, or those specifically governing the Internet or eCommerce, may be interpreted and applied in a manner that is inconsistent from one jurisdiction to another and may conflict with other rules or our practices. We cannot be sure that our practices have complied, comply or will comply fully with all such laws and regulations. Any failure, or perceived failure, by us to comply with any of these laws or regulations could result in damage to our reputation, a loss in business and proceedings or actions against us by governmental entities or others. Any such proceeding or action could hurt our reputation, force us to spend significant amounts in defense of these proceedings, distract our management, increase our costs of doing business, decrease the use of our sites by consumers and suppliers and may result in the imposition of monetary liability. We may also be contractually liable to indemnify and hold harmless third parties from the costs or consequences of non-compliance with any such laws or regulations. In addition, it is possible that governments of one or more countries or territories may seek to censor content available on our sites or may even attempt to completely block access to our sites. Adverse legal or regulatory developments could substantially harm our business. In particular, in the event that we are restricted, in whole or in part, from operating in one or more countries or territories, our ability to retain or increase our customer base may be adversely affected, and we may not be able to maintain or grow our net sales and expand our business as anticipated.

If we cannot successfully protect our intellectual property, our business would suffer.

We rely on trademark, copyright, trade secrets, confidentiality agreements and other practices to protect our brands, designs, proprietary information, technologies and processes. Our principal trademark assets include the registered trademarks "REVOLVE," "FORWARD BY ELYSE WALKER" and multiple owned brand names and our logos and taglines. Our trademarks are valuable assets that support our brand and consumers' perception of our services and merchandise. We also hold the rights to the "revolve.com" and "fwrd.com" Internet domain names and various other related domain names, which are subject to Internet regulatory bodies and trademark and other related laws of each applicable jurisdiction. We have copyrights and other proprietary rights associated with our owned brands' apparel and other products.

If we are unable to protect our trademarks or domain names in the United States or in other jurisdictions in which we may ultimately operate, our brand recognition and reputation would suffer, we would incur significant expense establishing new brands and our operating results would be adversely impacted. We expend substantial resources in the development of new high-quality products but are susceptible to counterfeiting, which may harm our reputation for producing such products and force us to incur expenses in enforcing our intellectual property rights. Counterfeiting of our products may be difficult or costly to detect and any related claims or lawsuits to enforce our rights can be expensive to resolve, require management time and resources, and may not provide a satisfactory or timely result. Despite our efforts to enforce our intellectual property rights, counterfeiters may continue to violate our intellectual property rights by using our trademarks or imitating or copying our products, which could harm our brand, reputation and financial condition. Since our products are sold internationally, we are also dependent on the laws of a range of countries and territories to protect and enforce our intellectual property rights.

We currently have no registered copyrights, applications for copyright registrations, patents issued or applications pending in the United States or internationally. Any registered copyrights or patents that may be issued in the future may not provide us with any competitive advantages or may be challenged by third parties, and future registered copyrights or patent applications may never be granted. Even if issued, there can be no assurance that these registered copyrights or patents will adequately protect our intellectual property or survive a legal challenge, as the legal standards relating to the validity, enforceability and scope of protection of registered copyright, patent and other intellectual property rights are uncertain. Our limited registered copyright and patent protection may restrict our ability to protect our technologies and processes from competition. We primarily rely on unregistered copyrights to protect our designs and products and on trade secret laws to protect our technologies and processes, including the algorithms we use throughout our business. Others may independently develop the same or similar designs, products, technologies and processes, or may improperly acquire and use information about our technologies and processes, which may allow them to provide products or services similar to ours, which could harm our competitive position.

We may be required to spend significant resources to monitor and protect our intellectual property rights, and the efforts we take to protect our proprietary rights may not be sufficient.

The inability to acquire, use or maintain our marks and domain names for our sites could substantially harm our business, financial condition and operating results.

We currently are the registrant of marks for our brands in numerous jurisdictions and are the registrant of the Internet domain name for the websites of revolve.com and fwrd.com and our other sites, as well as various related domain names. However, we have not registered our marks or domain names in all major international jurisdictions. Domain names generally are regulated by Internet regulatory bodies. As our business grows we may incur material costs in connection with the registration, maintenance, and protection of our marks. If we do not have or cannot obtain on reasonable terms the ability to use our marks in a particular country, or to use or register our domain name, we could be forced either to incur significant additional expenses to market our products within that country, including the development of a new brand and the creation of new promotional materials and packaging, or to elect not to sell products in that country. Either result could materially adversely affect our business, financial condition and operating results.

Furthermore, the regulations governing domain names and laws protecting marks and similar proprietary rights could change in ways that block or interfere with our ability to use relevant domains or our current brand. Also, we might not be able to prevent third parties from registering, using or retaining domain names that interfere with our consumer communications or infringe or otherwise decrease the value of our marks, domain names and other proprietary rights. Regulatory bodies also may establish additional generic or country-code top-level domains or may allow modifications of the requirements for registering, holding or using domain names. As a result, we might not be able to register, use or maintain the domain names that use the name REVOLVE, FORWARD, superdown or our brands in all of the countries and territories in which we currently or intend to conduct business.

We may be accused of infringing intellectual property or other proprietary rights of third parties.

We are also at risk of claims by others that we have infringed their copyrights, trademarks or patents, or improperly used or disclosed their trade secrets, or otherwise infringed or violated their proprietary rights, such as the right of publicity. The costs of supporting any litigation or disputes related to these claims can be considerable, and we cannot assure you that we will achieve a favorable outcome of any such claim. If any such claim is valid, we may be compelled to cease our use of such intellectual property or other proprietary rights and pay damages, which could adversely affect our business. Even if such claims were not valid, defending them could be expensive and distracting, adversely affecting our operating results.

We are subject to payment-related risks.

We accept payments using a variety of methods, including credit card, gift cards, debit card, PayPal and other third-party payment vendors, which subjects us to certain regulations and the risk of fraud, and we may in the future offer new payment options to customers that would be subject to additional regulations and risks. We pay interchange and other fees in connection with credit card payments, which may increase over time and adversely affect our operating results. While we use a third party to process payments, we are subject to payment card association operating rules and certification requirements, including the PCI-DSS and rules governing electronic funds transfers. If we fail to comply with applicable rules and regulations, we may be subject to fines or higher transaction fees and may lose our ability to accept online payments or other payment card transactions. If any of these events were to occur, our business, financial condition and operating results could be adversely affected.

We may incur significant losses from fraud.

We have in the past incurred and may in the future incur losses from various types of fraud, including stolen credit card numbers, claims that a customer did not authorize a purchase, merchant fraud and customers who have closed bank accounts or have insufficient funds in open bank accounts to satisfy payments. Although we have measures in place to detect and reduce the occurrence of fraudulent activity in our marketplace, those measures may not always be effective. In addition to the direct costs of such losses, if the fraud is related to credit card transactions and becomes excessive, it could potentially result in us paying higher fees or losing the right to accept credit cards for payment. In addition, under current credit card practices, we are liable for fraudulent credit card transactions because we do not obtain a cardholder's signature. Our failure to adequately prevent fraudulent transactions could damage our reputation, result in litigation or regulatory action and lead to expenses that could substantially impact our operating results.

We have identified a material weakness in our internal control over financial reporting and if we have failed to remediate this weakness and maintain proper and effective internal controls, our ability to produce accurate and timely consolidated financial statements could be impaired, which could harm our operating results, our ability to operate our business and investors' views of us.

Ensuring that we have adequate internal financial and accounting controls and procedures in place so that we can produce accurate consolidated financial statements on a timely basis is a costly and time-consuming effort that needs to be evaluated frequently. As a private company, we have not historically prepared public company financial statements. In connection with the audit of our 2017 consolidated financial statements, we have identified a material weakness in our internal control over financial reporting. A material weakness is a deficiency, or a combination of deficiencies, in internal control over financial reporting, such that there is a reasonable possibility that a material misstatement of the company's annual or interim consolidated financial statements will not be prevented or detected on a timely basis.

In connection with the audit of our 2017 consolidated financial statements, we and our independent registered public accounting firm identified a material weakness in our internal controls in 2017 related to the lack of resources necessary to perform adequate review of our financial information. To remediate such material weakness, we hired additional personnel with requisite skills in both technical accounting and internal control over financial reporting. In addition, we engaged external advisors that provided financial accounting assistance and evaluated and documented the design and operating effectiveness of our internal controls and assisted with the remediation and implementation of our internal controls as required. We will continue to evaluate the longer-term resource needs of our various financial functions. While we have fully implemented our remediation plan with respect to this material weakness, we cannot assure you we will have addressed the underlying causes of the material weakness or that we will not identify other control deficiencies in the future.

Implementing any appropriate changes to our internal controls and continuing to update and maintain our internal controls may distract our officers and employees, entail substantial costs to implement new processes and modify our existing processes and take significant time to complete. If we fail to enhance our internal control over financial reporting to meet the demands that will be placed upon us as a public company, including the requirements of the Sarbanes-Oxley Act of 2002 or the Sarbanes-Oxley Act, we may be unable to report our financial results accurately or in a timely manner, which could increase operating costs and harm our business, including our investors' perception of our business and our share price. The actions we plan to take are subject to continued management review supported by confirmation and testing, as well as audit committee oversight. While we expect to fully remediate the material weakness, we cannot assure you that we will be able to do so in a timely manner, which could impair our ability to report our financial position.

If our internal control over financial reporting or our disclosure controls and procedures are not effective, we may not be able to accurately report our financial results, prevent fraud or file our periodic reports in a timely manner, which may cause investors to lose confidence in our reported financial information and may lead to a decline in our stock price.

We have been a private company for 16 years, and as such, we have not had the internal control and financial reporting requirements that are required of a publicly traded company. We are required to comply with the requirements of the Sarbanes-Oxley Act, following the later of the date we are deemed to be an "accelerated filer" or a "large accelerated filer," each as defined in the Securities Exchange Act of 1934, as amended, or the Exchange Act, or the date we are no longer an "emerging growth company," as defined in the JOBS Act, which could be as early as our first fiscal year beginning after the effective date of this offering. The Sarbanes-Oxley Act requires that we maintain effective internal control over financial reporting and disclosure controls and procedures. In particular, we must perform system and process evaluation, document our controls and perform testing of our key controls over financial reporting to allow management and our independent registered public accounting firm to report on the effectiveness of our internal control over financial reporting, as required by Section 404 of the Sarbanes-Oxley Act. Our testing, or the subsequent testing by our independent registered public accounting firm, may reveal deficiencies in our internal control over financial reporting that are deemed to be material weaknesses. If we are not able to comply with the requirements of Section 404 in a timely manner, or if we or our independent registered public accounting firm identify deficiencies in our internal control over financial reporting that are deemed to be material weaknesses, the market price of our stock would likely decline and we could be subject to lawsuits, sanctions or investigations by regulatory authorities, which would require additional financial and management resources.

We continue to invest in more robust technology and in more resources in order to manage those reporting requirements. Implementing the appropriate changes to our internal controls and remediating our material weakness may distract our officers and employees, result in substantial costs to implement new processes or modify our existing processes and require significant time to complete. Any difficulties or delays in implementing the system could impact our ability to timely report our financial results. In addition, we currently rely on a manual process in some areas which increases our exposure to human error or intervention in reporting our financial results. For these reasons, we may encounter difficulties in the timely and accurate reporting of our financial results, which would impact our ability to provide our investors with information in a timely manner. As a result, our investors could lose confidence in our reported consolidated financial information, and our stock price could decline.

In addition, any such changes do not guarantee that we will be effective in maintaining the adequacy of our internal controls, and any failure to maintain that adequacy could prevent us from accurately reporting our financial results.

Customer growth and activity on mobile devices depends upon effective use of mobile operating systems, networks and standards that we do not control.

Purchases using mobile devices by consumers generally, and by our customers specifically, have increased significantly, and we expect this trend to continue. To optimize the mobile shopping experience, we are dependent on our customers downloading our specific mobile applications for their particular device or accessing our sites from an Internet browser on their mobile device. As new mobile devices and platforms are released, it is difficult to predict the problems we may encounter in developing applications for these alternative devices and platforms, and we may need to devote significant resources to the creation, support and maintenance of such applications. In addition, our future growth and our results of operations could suffer if we experience difficulties in the future in integrating our mobile applications into mobile devices, if problems arise with our relationships with providers of mobile operating systems or mobile application download stores, such as those of Apple Inc. or Google Inc., if our applications receive unfavorable treatment compared to competing applications, such as the order of our products in the Apple App Store, or if we face increased costs to distribute or have customers use our mobile applications. We are further dependent on the interoperability of our sites with popular mobile operating systems that we do not control, such as iOS and Android, and any changes in such systems that degrade the functionality of our sites or give preferential treatment to competitive products could adversely affect the usage of our sites on mobile devices. In the event that it is more difficult for our customers to access and use our sites on their mobile devices, or if our customers choose not to access or to use our sites on their mobile devices or to use mobile products that do not offer access to our sites, our customer growth could be harmed and our business, financial condition and operating results may be materially and adversely affected.

We may expand our business through acquisitions of other businesses, which may divert management's attention and/or prove to be unsuccessful.

We acquired Alliance, Inc. in 2014 and may acquire additional businesses or technologies in the future. Acquisitions may divert management's time and focus from operating our business. Acquisitions also may require us to spend a substantial portion of our available cash, incur debt or other liabilities, amortize expenses related to intangible assets or incur write-offs of goodwill or other assets. In addition, integrating an acquired business or technology is risky. Completed and future acquisitions may result in unforeseen operational difficulties and expenditures associated with:

- incorporating new businesses and technologies into our infrastructure;
- consolidating operational and administrative functions;
- coordinating outreach to our community;
- maintaining morale and culture and retaining and integrating key employees;
- maintaining or developing controls, procedures and policies (including effective internal control over financial reporting and disclosure controls and procedures); and

- identifying assuming liabilities related to the activities of the acquired business before the acquisition, including liabilities for violations of laws and regulations, intellectual property issues, commercial disputes, taxes and other matters.

Moreover, we may not benefit from our acquisitions as we expect, or in the time frame we expect. We also may issue additional equity securities in connection with an acquisition, which could cause dilution to our stockholders. Finally, acquisitions could be viewed negatively by analysts, investors or our customers.

If we fail to attract and retain key personnel, or effectively manage succession, our business, financial condition and operating results could be adversely affected.

Our success, including our ability to anticipate and effectively respond to changing style trends, depends in part on our ability to attract and retain key personnel on our executive team, particularly our co-chief executive officers, and in our merchandising, data science, engineering, marketing, design and other organizations. Competition for key personnel is strong, and we cannot be sure that we will be able to attract and retain a sufficient number of qualified personnel in the future, or that the compensation costs of doing so will not adversely affect our operating results. We do not have long-term employment or non-competition agreements with any of our personnel. If we are unable to retain, attract and motivate talented employees with the appropriate skills at cost-effective compensation levels, or if changes to our business adversely affect morale or retention, we may not achieve our objectives and our business and operating results could be adversely affected. In addition, the loss of one or more of our key personnel or the inability to promptly identify a suitable successor to a key role could have an adverse effect on our business. In particular, our co-chief executive officers have unique and valuable experiences leading our company from its inception through today. If either of them were to depart or otherwise reduce their focus on our company, our business may be disrupted. We do not currently maintain key-person life insurance policies on any member of our senior management team or other key employees.

Adverse litigation judgments or settlements resulting from legal proceedings in which we may be involved could expose us to monetary damages or limit our ability to operate our business.

We have in the past and may in the future become involved in private actions, collective actions, investigations and various other legal proceedings by customers, employees, suppliers, competitors, government agencies or others. The results of any such litigation, investigations and other legal proceedings are inherently unpredictable and expensive. Any claims against us, whether meritorious or not, could be time-consuming, result in costly litigation, damage our reputation, require significant amounts of management time and divert significant resources. If any of these legal proceedings were to be determined adversely to us, or we were to enter into a settlement arrangement, we could be exposed to monetary damages or limits on our ability to operate our business, which could have an adverse effect on our business, financial condition and operating results.

Expansion of our operations internationally will require management attention and resources, involves additional risks and may be unsuccessful.

Notwithstanding that 17.9% of our total net sales in 2018 was derived from customers outside of the United States, we have limited experience with operating internationally and selling our merchandise outside of the United States and do not have physical operations outside of the United States. If we choose to expand internationally we would need to adapt to different local cultures, standards and policies. The business model we employ and the merchandise we currently offer may not have the same appeal to consumers outside of the United States. Furthermore, to succeed with customers in international locations, it likely will be necessary to locate fulfillment centers in foreign markets and hire local employees in those international centers, and we may have to invest in these facilities before proving we can successfully run foreign operations. We may not be successful in expanding into international markets or in generating revenue from foreign operations for a variety of reasons, including:

- localization of our merchandise offerings, including translation into foreign languages and adaptation for local practices;
- navigating shipping and returns in a more fragmented geography, particularly if the European Union were to lose members or change its policies regarding the flow of goods across country borders;
- different consumer demand dynamics, which may make our model and the merchandise we offer less successful compared to the United States;
- competition from local incumbents that understand the local market and may operate more effectively;

- regulatory requirements, taxes, trade laws, trade sanctions and economic embargoes, tariffs, export quotas, custom duties or other trade restrictions or any unexpected changes thereto;
- laws and regulations regarding anti-bribery and anti-corruption compliance;
- differing labor regulations where labor laws may be more advantageous to employees as compared to the United States and increased labor costs;
- more stringent regulations relating to privacy and data security and access to, or use of, commercial and personal information, particularly in Europe;
- changes in a specific country's or region's political or economic conditions; and
- risks resulting from changes in currency exchange rates.

If we invest substantial time and resources to establish and expand our operations internationally and are unable to do so successfully and in a timely manner, our operating results would suffer.

We have operations in China, which exposes us to risks inherent in doing business there.

We use multiple third-party suppliers and manufacturers based primarily in China. With the rapid development of the Chinese economy, the cost of labor has increased and may continue to increase in the future. Furthermore, pursuant to Chinese labor laws, employers in China are subject to various requirements when signing labor contracts, paying remuneration, determining the term of employees' probation and unilaterally terminating labor contracts. Our results of operations will be materially and adversely affected if the labor costs of our third-party suppliers and manufacturers increase significantly. In addition, we and our manufacturers and suppliers may not be able to find a sufficient number of qualified workers due to the intensely competitive and fluid market for skilled labor in China.

Operating in China exposes us to political, legal and economic risks. In particular, the political, legal and economic climate in China, both nationally and regionally, is fluid and unpredictable. Our ability to operate in China may be adversely affected by changes in U.S. and Chinese laws and regulations such as those related to, among other things, taxation, import and export tariffs, environmental regulations, land use rights, intellectual property, currency controls, network security, employee benefits, hygiene supervision and other matters. In addition, we may not obtain or retain the requisite legal permits to continue to operate in China, and costs or operational limitations may be imposed in connection with obtaining and complying with such permits. In addition, Chinese trade regulations are in a state of flux, and we may become subject to other forms of taxation, tariffs and duties in China. Furthermore, the third parties we rely on in China may disclose our confidential information or intellectual property to competitors or third parties, which could result in the illegal distribution and sale of counterfeit versions of our products. If any of these events occur, our business, financial condition and results of operations could be materially and adversely affected. See also "—Recent and potential tariffs imposed by the U.S. government or a global trade war could increase the cost of our products, which could have a material adverse effect on our business, financial condition and results of operations."

Our reliance on overseas manufacturing and supply partners, including vendors located in jurisdictions presenting an increased risk of bribery and corruption, exposes us to legal, reputational, and supply chain risk through the potential for violations of federal and international anti-corruption law.

We derive a significant portion of our merchandise for our owned brands from third-party manufacturing and supply partners in foreign countries and territories, including countries and territories perceived to carry an increased risk of corrupt business practices. The U.S. Foreign Corrupt Practices Act, or the FCPA, prohibits U.S. corporations and their representatives from offering, promising, authorizing or making payments to any foreign government official, government staff member, political party or political candidate in an attempt to obtain or retain business abroad. Notwithstanding our efforts to conduct our operations in material compliance with the FCPA, our international vendors could be determined to be our "representatives" under the FCPA, which could expose us to potential liability for the actions of these vendors under the FCPA. If we or our vendors were determined to have violated the FCPA, the U.K. Bribery Act of 2010, or any of the anti-corruption and anti-bribery laws in the countries and territories where we and our vendors do business, we could suffer severe fines and penalties, profit disgorgement, injunctions on future conduct, securities litigation, bans on transacting certain business, and other consequences that may have a material adverse effect on our business, financial condition and results of operations. In addition, the costs we may incur in defending against any anti-corruption investigations stemming from our or our vendors' actions could be significant. Moreover, any actual or alleged corruption in our supply chain could carry significant reputational harms, including negative publicity, loss of good will, and decline in share price.

Recent and potential tariffs imposed by the U.S. government or a global trade war could increase the cost of our products, which could have a material adverse effect on our business, financial condition and results of operations.

The U.S. government has recently imposed increased tariffs on certain imports from China. While the current tariffs only affect a small portion of the products that we currently import from China, specifically handbags and makeup, the current U.S. administration has increased the tariff rate from 10% to 25% and indicated that the higher tariffs may be imposed on additional imports from China, including finished goods apparel and shoes, which, if imposed, would include a predominant portion of the products that we import from China. In retaliation for the current and proposed tariffs, China has already implemented, and announced a plan to impose additional tariffs on a wide range of American products. There is also a concern that the imposition of additional tariffs by the United States could result in the adoption of tariffs by other countries as well, leading to a global trade war. Such tariffs could have a significant impact on our business, particularly the REVOLVE segment and owned brands. While we may attempt to renegotiate prices with suppliers or diversify our supply chain in response to tariffs, such efforts may not yield immediate results or may be ineffective. We might also consider increasing prices to the end consumer; however, this could reduce the competitiveness of our products and adversely affect net sales. If we fail to manage these dynamics successfully, gross margins and profitability could be adversely affected. As of the date of this prospectus, tariffs have not had a material impact on our business, but increased tariffs or trade restrictions implemented by the United States or other countries in connection with a global trade war could have a material adverse effect on our business, financial condition and results of operations.

We may experience fluctuations in our tax obligations and effective tax rate, which could adversely affect our operating results.

We are subject to taxes in the United States and the United Kingdom. We record tax expense based on current tax liabilities and our estimates of future tax liabilities, which may include reserves for estimates of probable settlements of tax audits. At any one time, multiple tax years are subject to audit by various taxing jurisdictions. The results of these audits and negotiations with taxing authorities may affect the ultimate settlement of these issues. As a result, we expect that throughout the year there could be ongoing variability in our quarterly tax rates as taxable events occur and exposures are reevaluated. Further, our effective tax rate in a given financial statement period may be materially impacted by changes in tax laws, changes in the mix and level of earnings by taxing jurisdictions, or changes to existing accounting rules or regulations. An example is the recently enacted legislation referred to as the Tax Cuts and Jobs Act, or the 2017 Tax Act. Foreign governments may enact tax laws in response to the 2017 Tax Act that could result in further changes to global taxation. There are numerous factors that could affect our tax rate. These may include, among other factors, intercompany transactions, losses incurred in jurisdictions for which we are not able to realize the related tax benefits, and entry into new businesses and geographies. Fluctuations in our tax obligations and effective tax rate could adversely affect our business, financial condition and operating results.

The enactment of tax reform legislation, including legislation implementing changes in taxation of international business activities, could materially impact our financial position and results of operations.

Legislation or other changes in tax laws could increase our liability and adversely affect our after-tax profitability. For example, the Tax Cuts and Jobs Act, or the Tax Act, was enacted in the United States on December 22, 2017. The Tax Act could have a significant impact on our effective tax rate, cash tax expenses and net deferred tax assets. The Tax Act reduces the U.S. corporate statutory tax rate, eliminates or limits the deduction of several expenses that were previously deductible, imposes a mandatory deemed repatriation tax on undistributed historic earnings of foreign subsidiaries, requires a minimum tax on earnings generated by foreign subsidiaries and permits a tax-free repatriation of foreign earnings through a dividends received deduction (subject to certain exceptions). We have completed our evaluation of the overall impact of the Tax Act on our effective tax rate and balance sheet through fiscal year 2018 and reflected the amounts in our financial statements. The Tax Act may have significant impacts in future periods.

We could be required to collect additional sales taxes or be subject to other tax liabilities that may increase the costs our customers would have to pay for our offering and adversely affect our operating results.

On June 21, 2018, the U.S. Supreme Court held in *South Dakota v. Wayfair, Inc.* that states could impose sales tax collection obligations on out-of-state retailers even if those retailers lack any physical presence within the states imposing sales taxes. Under *Wayfair*, a person requires only a "substantial nexus" with the taxing state before the state may subject the person to sales tax collection obligations therein. An increasing number of states, both before and after the

Supreme Court's ruling, have considered or adopted laws that attempt to impose sales tax collection obligations on out-of-state retailers. The Supreme Court's *Wayfair* decision has removed a significant impediment to the enactment of these laws, and it is possible that states may seek to tax out-of-state retailers, including for prior tax years. Although we believe that we currently collect sales taxes in all states that have adopted laws imposing sales tax collection obligations on out-of-state retailers since *Wayfair* was decided, a successful assertion by one or more states requiring us to collect sales taxes where we presently do not do so, or to collect more taxes in a jurisdiction in which we currently do collect some sales taxes, could result in substantial tax liabilities, including taxes on past sales, as well as penalties and interest. The imposition by state governments of sales tax collection obligations on out-of-state retailers in jurisdictions where we do not currently collect sales taxes, whether for prior years or prospectively, could also create additional administrative burdens for us, put us at a competitive disadvantage if they do not impose similar obligations on our competitors and decrease our future sales, which could have a material adverse impact on our business and operating results.

We may require additional capital to support business growth, and this capital might not be available or may be available only by diluting existing stockholders.

We intend to continue making investments to support our business growth and may require additional funds to support this growth and respond to business challenges, including the need to develop our services, expand our inventory, enhance our operating infrastructure, expand the markets in which we operate and potentially acquire complementary businesses and technologies. Accordingly, we may need to engage in equity or debt financings to secure additional funds. If we raise additional funds through further issuances of equity or convertible debt securities, our existing stockholders could suffer significant dilution, and any new equity securities we issue could have rights, preferences and privileges superior to those of holders of our Class A common stock. Any debt financing secured by us in the future could involve restrictive covenants relating to our capital-raising activities and other financial and operational matters, which may make it more difficult for us to obtain additional capital and to pursue business opportunities. In addition, we may not be able to obtain additional financing on terms favorable to us, if at all. If we are unable to obtain adequate financing or financing on terms satisfactory to us, when we require it, our ability to continue to support our business growth and to respond to business challenges could be significantly limited, and our business and prospects could fail or be adversely affected.

Operating as a public company will require us to incur substantial costs and will require substantial management attention. In addition, our management team has limited experience managing a public company.

As a public company, we will incur substantial legal, accounting and other expenses that we did not incur as a private company. For example, we will be subject to the reporting requirements of the Exchange Act, the applicable requirements of the Sarbanes-Oxley Act and the Dodd-Frank Wall Street Reform and Consumer Protection Act, or the Dodd-Frank Act, and the rules and regulations of the Securities and Exchange Commission, or the SEC. The rules and regulations of NYSE will also apply to us following this offering. As part of these new requirements, we will need to establish and maintain effective disclosure and financial controls and make changes to our corporate governance practices. We expect that compliance with these requirements will increase our legal and financial compliance costs and will make some activities more time-consuming.

Most of our management and other personnel have little experience managing a public company and preparing public filings. In addition, we expect that our management and other personnel will need to divert attention from other business matters to devote substantial time to the reporting and other requirements of being a public company. In particular, we expect to incur significant expense and devote substantial management effort to complying with the requirements of Section 404 of the Sarbanes-Oxley Act. We may need to hire additional accounting and financial staff with appropriate public company experience and technical accounting knowledge.

Our credit facility contains restrictive covenants that may limit our operating flexibility.

Our credit facility contains restrictive covenants that limit our ability to transfer or dispose of assets, merge with other companies or consummate certain changes of control, acquire other companies, incur additional indebtedness and liens and enter into new businesses. We therefore may not be able to engage in any of the foregoing transactions unless we obtain the consent of the lender or terminate the credit facility, which may limit our operating flexibility. In addition, our credit facility is secured by all of our assets, including our intellectual property, and requires us to satisfy certain financial covenants. There is no guarantee that we will be able to generate sufficient cash flow or sales to meet these financial covenants or pay the principal and interest on any debt under our facility. Furthermore, there is no guarantee that future working capital, borrowings or equity financing will be available to repay or refinance any such debt. Any inability to make scheduled payments or meet the financial covenants on our credit facility would adversely affect our business.

Our operating results could be adversely affected by natural disasters, public health crises, political crises or other catastrophic events.

Our principal offices, data centers and our fulfillment centers are located in Southern California, an area which has a history of earthquakes, and are thus vulnerable to damage. Natural disasters, such as earthquakes, wildfires, hurricanes, tornadoes, floods and other adverse weather and climate conditions; unforeseen public health crises, such as pandemics and epidemics; political crises, such as terrorist attacks, war and other political instability; or other catastrophic events, whether occurring in the United States or internationally, could disrupt our operations in any of our offices and fulfillment centers or the operations of one or more of our third-party providers or vendors. In particular, these types of events could impact our merchandise supply chain, including our ability to ship merchandise to customers from or to the impacted region, and could impact our ability or the ability of third parties to operate our sites and ship merchandise. In addition, these types of events could negatively impact consumer spending in the impacted regions. To the extent any of these events occur, our business and operating results could be adversely affected.

Risks Relating to Our Class A Common Stock and this Offering

The market price of our Class A common stock may be volatile or may decline steeply or suddenly regardless of our operating performance, and we may not be able to meet investor or analyst expectations. You may not be able to resell your shares at or above the initial public offering price and may lose all or part of your investment.

The initial public offering price for our Class A common stock was determined through negotiations between the underwriters and us, and may vary from the market price of our Class A common stock following this offering. If you purchase shares of our Class A common stock in this offering, you may not be able to resell those shares at or above the initial public offering price. We cannot assure you that the market price following this offering will equal or exceed prices in privately negotiated transactions of our shares that have occurred from time to time before this offering. The market price of our Class A common stock may fluctuate or decline significantly in response to numerous factors, many of which are beyond our control, including:

- actual or anticipated fluctuations in our customer base, the level of customer engagement, net sales or other operating results;
- variations between our actual operating results and the expectations of securities analysts, investors and the financial community;
- any forward-looking financial or operating information we may provide to the public or securities analysts, any changes in this information or our failure to meet expectations based on this information;
- actions of securities analysts who initiate or maintain coverage of us, changes in financial estimates by any securities analysts who follow our company or our failure to meet these estimates or the expectations of investors;
- whether investors or securities analysts view our stock structure unfavorably, particularly our dual-class structure and the significant voting control of our executive officers, directors and their affiliates;
- additional shares of our Class A common stock being sold into the market by us or our existing stockholders, or the anticipation of such sales, including if existing stockholders sell shares into the market when applicable "lock-up" periods end;
- announcements by us or our competitors of significant products or features, technical innovations, acquisitions, strategic partnerships, joint ventures or capital commitments;
- changes in operating performance and stock market valuations of companies in our industry, including our vendors and competitors;
- price and volume fluctuations in the overall stock market, including as a result of trends in the economy as a whole;
- lawsuits threatened or filed against us;
- developments in new legislation and pending lawsuits or regulatory actions, including interim or final rulings by judicial or regulatory bodies; and
- other events or factors, including those resulting from war or incidents of terrorism, or responses to these events.

In addition, extreme price and volume fluctuations in the stock markets have affected and continue to affect many eCommerce and other technology companies' stock prices. Often, their stock prices have fluctuated in ways unrelated or disproportionate to the companies' operating performance. In the past, stockholders have filed securities class action litigation following periods of market volatility. If we were to become involved in securities litigation, it could subject us to substantial costs, divert resources and the attention of management from our business and seriously harm our business.

Moreover, because of these fluctuations, comparing our operating results on a period-to-period basis may not be meaningful. You should not rely on our past results as an indication of our future performance. This variability and unpredictability could also result in our failing to meet the expectations of industry or financial analysts or investors for any period. If our revenue or operating results fall below the expectations of analysts or investors or below any forecasts we may provide to the market, or if the forecasts we provide to the market are below the expectations of analysts or investors, the price of our Class A common stock could decline substantially. Such a stock price decline could occur even when we have met any previously publicly stated revenue or earnings forecasts that we may provide.

An active trading market for our Class A common stock may never develop or be sustained.

We have been approved to list our Class A common stock on the New York Stock Exchange, or NYSE, under the symbol "RVLV." However, we cannot assure you that an active trading market for our Class A common stock will develop on that exchange or elsewhere or, if developed, that any market will be sustained. Accordingly, we cannot assure you of the likelihood that an active trading market for our Class A common stock will develop or be maintained, the liquidity of any trading market, your ability to sell your shares of our Class A common stock when desired, or the prices that you may obtain for your shares. Further, our directors, executive officers and employees, as well as friends and family members of our executive officers and certain members of senior management, and persons with whom we have a business relationship, have the opportunity to purchase up to 588,235 shares of our Class A common stock, or 5% of the shares offered by this prospectus, at the initial public offering price through a directed share program. To the extent any of our executive officers, directors or employees purchase shares in this offering, fewer shares may be actively traded in the public market because these stockholders will be restricted from selling the shares by a 180-day lock-up restriction, which would reduce the liquidity of the market for our Class A common stock.

Future sales of shares by existing stockholders could cause our stock price to decline.

If our existing stockholders, including employees and service providers who obtain equity, sell or indicate an intention to sell, substantial amounts of our Class A common stock in the public market after the lock-up and legal restrictions on resale discussed in this prospectus lapse, the trading price of our Class A common stock could decline. Based on shares outstanding as of March 31, 2019, upon the completion of this offering, we will have outstanding a total of 11,764,706 shares of Class A common stock and 56,664,523 shares of Class B common stock. This assumes no exercise of outstanding options and gives effect to the Corporate Conversion, the repurchase of an aggregate of 2,400,960 shares of Class B common stock from TSG and Capretto, and the issuance of 11,764,706 shares of Class A common stock on the completion of this offering. Of these shares, only the shares of Class A common stock sold in this offering will be freely tradable, without restriction, in the public market immediately after the offering. Each of our directors, executive officers and other holders of substantially all our outstanding shares have entered into lock-up agreements with the underwriters that restrict their ability to sell or transfer their shares for a period of 180 days after the date of this prospectus. However, Morgan Stanley & Co. LLC and Credit Suisse Securities (USA) LLC may, in their sole discretion, waive the contractual lock-up before the lock-up agreements expire. After the lock-up agreements expire, 56,664,523 shares outstanding as of March 31, 2019 (assuming the closing of the offering) will be eligible for sale in the public market, of which 54,803,633 shares are held by directors, executive officers and other affiliates and will be subject to volume limitations under Rule 144 of the Securities Act of 1933, as amended, or the Securities Act, and various vesting agreements. Sales of a substantial number of such shares upon expiration of the lock-up and market stand-off agreements, the perception that such sales may occur or early release of these agreements, could cause our market price to fall or make it more difficult for you to sell your Class A common stock at a time and price that you deem appropriate.

In addition, after giving effect to the Corporate Conversion, 5,130,502 shares of Class B common stock were subject to outstanding stock options as of March 31, 2019. These shares will become eligible for sale in the public market to the extent permitted by the provisions of various vesting agreements, the lock-up agreements and Rules 144 and 701 of the Securities Act. We intend to file a registration statement on Form S-8 under the Securities Act covering all the shares of Class A common stock subject to stock options outstanding and reserved for issuance under our stock plans. That registration statement will become effective immediately on filing, and shares covered by that registration statement will be eligible for sale in the public markets, subject to Rule 144 limitations applicable to affiliates and the lock-up agreements described above. If these additional shares are sold, or if it is perceived that they will be sold in the public market, the trading price of our Class A common stock could decline.

The dual class structure of our common stock will have the effect of concentrating voting control with our executive officers, directors and their affiliates, and it may depress the trading price of our Class A common stock.

Our Class B common stock has ten votes per share and our Class A common stock, which is the stock we are offering in this offering, has one vote per share. Our existing stockholders, all of which hold shares of Class B common stock, will collectively own shares representing approximately 98% of the voting power of our outstanding capital stock following the completion of this offering. MMMK Development, Inc., an entity controlled by our co-chief executive officers, will control approximately 67% of the voting power of our outstanding capital stock following the completion of this offering and therefore will be able to control all matters submitted to our stockholders for approval, including the election of directors and approval of significant corporate transactions, such as a merger or other sale of our company or our assets, even if their stock holdings represent less than 50% of the outstanding shares of our capital stock. Our co-chief executive officers may have interests that differ from yours and may vote in a way with which you disagree and which may be adverse to your interests. This concentration of ownership will limit the ability of other stockholders to influence corporate matters and may cause us to make strategic decisions that could involve risks to you or that may not be aligned with your interests.

This control may also adversely affect the market price of our Class A common stock. In July 2017, FTSE Russell and Standard & Poor's announced that they would cease to allow most newly public companies utilizing dual or multi-class capital structures to be included in their indices. Affected indices include the Russell 2000 and the S&P 500, S&P MidCap 400 and S&P SmallCap 600, which together make up the S&P Composite 1500. Under the announced policies, our dual class capital structure would make us ineligible for inclusion in any of these indices, and as a result, mutual funds, exchange-traded funds and other investment vehicles that attempt to passively track these indices will not be investing in our stock. These policies are new and it is unclear what effect, if any, they will have on the valuations of publicly traded companies excluded from the indices, but it is possible that they may depress these valuations compared to those of other similar companies that are included in the indices.

We may invest or spend the proceeds of this offering in ways with which you may not agree or in ways that may not yield a return.

We currently intend to use $40.8 million of the net proceeds to us from this offering to repurchase an aggregate of 2,400,960 shares of Class B common stock from TSG and Capretto, and the remainder of the net proceeds to us from this offering primarily for general corporate purposes. We may also use a portion of the net proceeds from this offering for the acquisition of, or investment in, brands or businesses that complement our business, although we have no present commitments or agreements to enter into any such acquisition or investment. Our management will have considerable discretion in the application of the net proceeds, and you will not have the opportunity, as part of your investment decision, to assess whether the proceeds are being used appropriately. The net proceeds may be used for purposes that do not increase the value of our business or increase the risks to you, which could cause the price of our Class A common stock to decline. Until net proceeds are used, they may be placed in investments that do not produce significant income or that may lose value.

If securities or industry analysts either do not publish research about us or publish inaccurate or unfavorable research about us, our business or our market, or if they adversely change their recommendations regarding our Class A common stock, the trading price or trading volume of our Class A common stock could decline.

The trading market for our Class A common stock will be influenced in part by the research and reports that securities or industry analysts may publish about us, our business, our market or our competitors. If one or more of the analysts initiate research with an unfavorable rating or downgrade our Class A common stock, provide a more favorable recommendation about our competitors or publish inaccurate or unfavorable research about our business, our Class A common stock price would likely decline. If any analyst who may cover us were to cease coverage of us or fail to regularly publish reports on us, we could lose visibility in the financial markets, which in turn could cause the trading price or trading volume of our Class A common stock to decline.

We are an emerging growth company, and any decision on our part to comply only with certain reduced reporting and disclosure requirements applicable to emerging growth companies could make our Class A common stock less attractive to investors.

We are an emerging growth company, and for as long as we continue to be an emerging growth company, we may choose to take advantage of exemptions from various reporting requirements applicable to other public companies but not to "emerging growth companies," including:

- not being required to have our independent registered public accounting firm audit our internal control over financial reporting under Section 404 of the Sarbanes-Oxley Act;
- reduced disclosure obligations regarding executive compensation in our periodic reports and annual report on Form 10-K; and
- exemptions from the requirements of holding non-binding advisory votes on executive compensation and stockholder approval of any golden parachute payments not previously approved.

We could be an emerging growth company for up to five years following the completion of this offering, although we expect to not be an emerging growth company sooner. Our status as an emerging growth company will end as soon as any of the following takes place:

- the last day of the fiscal year in which we have more than $1.07 billion in annual revenue;
- the date we qualify as a "large accelerated filer," with at least $700.0 million of equity securities held by non-affiliates;
- the date on which we have issued, in any three-year period, more than $1.0 billion in non-convertible debt securities; or
- the last day of the fiscal year ending after the fifth anniversary of the completion of this offering.

We cannot predict if investors will find our Class A common stock less attractive if we choose to rely on any of the exemptions afforded emerging growth companies. If some investors find our Class A common stock less attractive because we rely on any of these exemptions, there may be a less active trading market for our Class A common stock and the market price of our Class A common stock may be more volatile.

Under the JOBS Act, emerging growth companies can also delay adopting new or revised accounting standards until such time as those standards apply to private companies. We have elected to take advantage of this extended transition period, and as a result, our financial statements may not be comparable with similarly situated public companies.

We have elected to take advantage of the "controlled company" exemption to the corporate governance rules for NYSE-listed companies, which could make our Class A common stock less attractive to some investors or otherwise harm our stock price.

Because we qualify as a "controlled company" under the corporate governance rules for NYSE-listed companies, we are not required to have a majority of our board of directors be independent, nor are we required to have a compensation committee or an independent nominating function. In light of our status as a controlled company, in the future we could elect not to have a majority of our board of directors be independent or not to have a compensation committee or nominating and corporate governance committee. Accordingly, should the interests of our management and MMMK Development, Inc., an entity controlled by our co-chief executive officers, differ from those of other stockholders, the other stockholders may not have the same protections afforded to stockholders of companies that are subject to all of the corporate governance rules for NYSE-listed companies. Our status as a controlled company could make our Class A common stock less attractive to some investors or otherwise harm our stock price.

Future securities issuances could result in significant dilution to our stockholders and impair the market price of our Class A common stock.

Future issuances of shares of our Class A common stock or the conversion of a substantial number of shares of our Class B common stock, or the perception that these sales or conversions may occur, could depress the market price of our Class A common stock and result in dilution to existing holders of our Class A common stock. Also, to the extent outstanding options and warrants to purchase our shares of our Class A or Class B common stock are exercised or options or other equity-based awards are issued or become vested, there will be further dilution. The amount of dilution could be substantial depending upon the size of the issuances or exercises. Furthermore, we may issue additional equity securities that could have rights senior to those of our Class A common stock. As a result, purchasers of our Class A common stock in this offering bear the risk that future issuances of debt or equity securities may reduce the value of our Class A common stock and further dilute their ownership interest.

As of March 31, 2019, there were 5,130,502 shares of Class B common stock subject to outstanding options, after giving effect to the Corporate Conversion. In connection with this offering, all of the shares of Class A common stock issuable upon the conversion of shares of Class B common stock subject to outstanding options will be registered for public resale under the Securities Act. Accordingly, these shares will be able to be freely sold in the public market upon issuance as permitted by any applicable vesting requirements, and subject to compliance with applicable securities laws.

In addition, following the closing of this offering, the holders of all of our Class B common stock will have rights, subject to certain conditions, to require us to file registration statements for the public resale of the shares of Class A common stock issuable upon conversion of their shares of Class B common stock, or to include such shares in registration statements that we may file.

The requirements of being a public company may strain our resources, result in more litigation and divert management's attention.

As a public company, we will be subject to the reporting requirements of the Exchange Act, the Sarbanes-Oxley Act, the Dodd-Frank Act, the listing requirements of the NYSE and other applicable securities rules and regulations. Complying with these rules and regulations has increased and will increase our legal and financial compliance costs, make some activities more difficult, time consuming or costly and increase demand on our systems and resources. To address these challenges, we recently expanded our finance and accounting teams. The Exchange Act requires, among other things, that we file annual, quarterly and current reports with respect to our business and operating results. The Sarbanes-Oxley Act requires, among other things, that we maintain effective disclosure controls and procedures and internal control over financial reporting. We are required to disclose changes made in our internal control and procedures on a quarterly basis. In order to maintain and, if required, improve our disclosure controls and procedures and internal control over financial reporting to meet this standard, significant resources and management oversight may be required. As a result, management's attention may be diverted from other business concerns, which could adversely affect our business and operating results. We may need to hire additional employees or engage outside consultants to comply with these requirements, which will increase our costs and expenses.

In addition, changing laws, regulations and standards relating to corporate governance and public disclosure are creating uncertainty for public companies, increasing legal and financial compliance costs and making some activities more time consuming. These laws, regulations and standards are subject to varying interpretations, in many cases due to their lack of specificity, and, as a result, their application in practice may evolve over time as new guidance is provided by regulatory and governing bodies. This could result in continuing uncertainty regarding compliance matters and higher costs necessitated by ongoing revisions to disclosure and governance practices. We intend to invest resources to comply with evolving laws, regulations and standards, and this investment may result in increased general and administrative expenses and a diversion of management's time and attention from revenue-generating activities to compliance activities. If our efforts to comply with new laws, regulations and standards differ from the activities intended by regulatory or governing bodies due to ambiguities related to their application and practice, regulatory authorities may initiate legal proceedings against us and our business may be adversely affected.

These new rules and regulations may make it more expensive for us to obtain director and officer liability insurance, and in the future, we may be required to accept reduced coverage or incur substantially higher costs to obtain coverage. These factors could also make it more difficult for us to attract and retain qualified members of our board of directors, particularly to serve on our audit committee and compensation committee, and qualified executive officers.

By disclosing information in this prospectus and in filings required of a public company, our business and financial condition will become more visible, which we believe may result in threatened or actual litigation, including by competitors and other third parties. If those claims are successful, our business could be seriously harmed. Even if the claims do not result in litigation or are resolved in our favor, the time and resources needed to resolve them could divert our management's resources and seriously harm our business.

Delaware law and provisions in our certificate of incorporation and bylaws that will be in effect on the completion of this offering could make a merger, tender offer or proxy contest difficult, thereby depressing the trading price of our Class A common stock.

Our certificate of incorporation and bylaws that will be in effect on the completion of this offering contain provisions that could depress the trading price of our Class A common stock by acting to discourage, delay or prevent a change of control of our company or changes in our management that the stockholders of our company may deem advantageous. These provisions include the following:

- permit the board of directors to establish the number of directors and fill any vacancies and newly created directorships;
- require super-majority voting to amend some provisions in our certificate of incorporation and bylaws;
- authorize the issuance of "blank check" preferred stock that our board of directors could use to implement a stockholder rights plan;
- eliminate the ability of our stockholders to call special meetings of stockholders;
- prohibit stockholder action by written consent, which requires all stockholder actions to be taken at a meeting of our stockholders;
- provide that the board of directors is expressly authorized to make, alter or repeal our bylaws;
- restrict the forum for certain litigation against us to Delaware;
- reflect the dual class structure of our common stock; and
- establish advance notice requirements for nominations for election to our board of directors or for proposing matters that can be acted upon by stockholders at annual stockholder meetings.

Any provision of our certificate of incorporation or bylaws, that will be in effect on the completion of this offering or Delaware law that has the effect of delaying or deterring a change in control could limit the opportunity for our stockholders to receive a premium for their shares of our common stock, and could also affect the price that some investors are willing to pay for our Class A common stock. For information regarding these and other provisions, see the section captioned "Description of Capital Stock—Anti-Takeover Provisions."

Our bylaws that will be in effect on the completion of this offering will provide that the Court of Chancery of the State of Delaware (or, if the Court of Chancery does not have jurisdiction, the federal district court for the District of Delaware) will be the exclusive forums for substantially all disputes between us and our stockholders, which could limit our stockholders' ability to obtain a favorable judicial forum for disputes with us or our directors, officers or employees.

Our bylaws that will be in effect on the completion of this offering will provide that the Court of Chancery of the State of Delaware (or, if the Court of Chancery does not have jurisdiction, the federal district court for the District of Delaware) is the exclusive forum for:

- any derivative action or proceeding brought on our behalf;
- any action asserting a breach of fiduciary duty;
- any action asserting a claim against us arising under the Delaware General Corporation Law, our certificate of incorporation or our bylaws; and
- any action asserting a claim against us that is governed by the internal-affairs doctrine.

These exclusive-forum provisions may limit a stockholder's ability to bring a claim in a judicial forum that it finds favorable for disputes with us or our directors, officers or other employees, which may discourage lawsuits against us and our directors, officers and other employees. If a court were to find the exclusive-forum provision in our bylaws that will be in effect on the completion of this offering to be inapplicable or unenforceable in an action, we may incur additional costs associated with resolving the dispute in other jurisdictions, which could seriously harm our business. These exclusive-forum provisions do not apply to claims under the Securities Act or the Exchange Act.

Chapter 22

Selling a Fashion Company or Fashion Brand

§ 22:1 Introduction
§ 22:2 The Sale Process
  § 22:2.1 Potential Buyers
  § 22:2.2 Due Diligence
  § 22:2.3 Confidentiality and Standstill Agreements
§ 22:3 The Transaction Structure
  § 22:3.1 Form of Transaction
  § 22:3.2 Purchase Price
    [A] Cash
    [B] Equity Securities of the Buyer
    [C] Buyer Promissory Notes
  § 22:3.3 Purchase Price Adjustment Mechanisms
  § 22:3.4 Contingent Payment Mechanisms
    [A] Earn-Outs
    [B] Sale of Brand or Royalty Rights
§ 22:4 Ancillary Agreements
§ 22:5 Risk Allocation
  § 22:5.1 Representations and Warranties
  § 22:5.2 Covenants
  § 22:5.3 Indemnities
  § 22:5.4 Escrow Arrangements
§ 22:6 Closing Conditions and Termination Rights
§ 22:7 Illustrative Acquisitions in the Fashion Industry
  § 22:7.1 Classic Stock Purchase Agreement
  § 22:7.2 Public Company Tender Offer
Appendix 22A Sample Earn-Out Provision
Appendix 22B Sample Fashion Industry Representations and Warranties

§ 22:1 Introduction

One of the most significant and difficult strategic decisions for a company is the determination to sell the whole company or certain of its brands. The decision to engage in a sale transaction may be motivated by a variety of factors, including liquidity issues, strategic objectives, attaining the targeted investment holding period or exit value, other market opportunities, or any combination of the foregoing. A growing company may require significant additional resources or economies of scale to continue its expansion. A midsized U.S. fashion brand or retailer may seek to combine with a larger company that has international operations.[1] A multi-brand company might determine to divest certain of its brands in order to focus on other brands that align with its overall strategic plan.[2] A public company might combine with another public company to achieve business synergies. Alternatively, a public company might seek to become a private company ("go private"), through a sale to a private equity firm, and thereby reduce the reporting requirements and public market pressures applicable to public companies. Increasingly, public companies are facing pressures from "activist" investors who challenge management to increase perceived shareholder value, potentially by selling the company, and fashion companies are no exception. Activists have addressed such companies as the Jones Group and Men's Wearhouse.[3] In 2018, Perry Ellis addressed a strategic buyer's takeover proposal,[4] which it rejected due to the opposition of a key licensing partner.[5]

The fashion industry has experienced a range of sale transactions that illustrate many of these business objectives. The strategic

---

1. Adreianne Pasquarelli, *Gap Buy Signals Growth in Retail M&A Market; Intermix Purchase Comes as Industry Seeks Ways to Boost Customer Base*, CRAIN'S N.Y BUS., Jan. 13, 2013.
2. Jason Asaeda, *Industry Surveys, Apparel & Footwear: Retailers & Brands*, STANDARD & POOR'S, Oct. 25, 2012, at 4.
3. *A Look at Shareholder Activism in the Retail Sector*, LAW 360 (Feb. 10, 2014), https://www.gibsondunn.com/wp-content/uploads/documents/publications/HerzecaGallardoShareholder.pdf. Some commentators have even suggested that activists should address brand fatigue. *See New Activist Investors at Burberry Should Push for Creative Overhaul*, BUS. OF FASHION (Mar. 1, 2017), https://www.businessoffashion.com/articles/opinion/activists-giving-makeovers-thats-what-burberry-needs.
4. *Randa Responds to Perry Ellis International, Inc.'s Special Committee*, PR NEWSWIRE (July 9, 2018), https://www.prnewswire.com/news-releases/randa-responds-to-perry-ellis-international-incs-special-committee-300677047.html.
5. Kimberly Chin, *Perry Ellis Ends Takeover Talks With Randa*, WALL ST. J. (Aug. 14, 2018), https://www.wsj.com/articles/perry-ellis-ends-takeover-talks-with-randa-1534255517?ns=prod/accounts-wsj.

acquisition of Versace by Michael Kors, announced in late 2018 for just over $2 billion (mostly in cash), is one of the largest transactions. The acquisition represents a continuing strategy on the part of Kors to become a luxury conglomerate, which it hinted at in 2017 through its acquisition of Jimmy Choo. Coach pursued a similar series of acquisitions, including Kate Spade and Stuart Weitzman. These transactions reflect the continuing challenges of the retail sector and may represent defensive diversification as an existential necessity that may hold fresh challenges of its own.[6]

The goal of many designers and investors in start-up fashion companies is to eventually sell the company at a premium price to a corporate entity that can sustain and grow the company. However, the conglomeratization trend may represent a narrow phenomenon in a landscape of decreasing opportunities for sales of entire fashion companies. Successful deals have become increasingly rare in the United States, as sales routinely entail complex challenges, and many companies have cut crucial marketing and design resources from their budgets.[7] In 2017, Abercrombie and American Apparel unsuccessfully attempted to sell themselves, with American Apparel eventually filing for bankruptcy. Additionally, the 2015 purchase by Ascena Retail Group of the holding company of Ann Taylor for just over $2 billion was valued at almost 85% less in 2017.[8] Diversification by fast fashion powerhouses has focused more on organic brand diversification (such as the buildout of H&M's brand portfolio with its "& Other Stories" design and concept stores). Similar diversification by way of investment is illustrated by Forever 21's purchase of a minority stake in online subscription and styling company Dailylook, announced in 2018.[9] Despite the diminished size and frequency of these deals, fashion companies will continue to be purchased and sold.

For these types of transactions, the preparation and planning process is similar in certain respects to the preparation and planning process for an initial public offering, as described in chapter 21. Indeed, the process of pursuing a "parallel track" with both an IPO and a sale process as potential outcomes has become common in many parts

---

6. Pamela N. Danziger, *Luxury Brand Mergers and Acquisitions Set to Explode*, FORBES (Aug. 16, 2017), https://www.forbes.com/sites/pamdanziger/2017/08/16/luxury-brand-mergers-and-acquisitions-set-to-explode/#699a673e9c0.
7. Lauren Hirsch, *RPT-Fashion M&A, Like a Crop Top, Is Hard to Pull Off*, REUTERS (July 11, 2017), https://www.reuters.com/article/usa-ma-fashion/rpt-fashion-ma-like-a-crop-top-is-hard-to-pull-off-idUSL1N1K11QT.
8. *Id.*
9. Daphne Howland, *Forever 21 Invests in Online Styling Service DailyLook*, RETAIL DIVE (Oct. 1, 2018), https://www.retaildive.com/news/forever-21-invests-in-online-styling-service-dailylook/538504/.

of the market, including retail generally.[10] Potential buyers will seek to conduct business, financial and legal due diligence on the company or business to be acquired, and the company will need to prepare and organize the due diligence process, including establishing an electronic data room. The company will need legal advisors and will often hire financial advisors to assist in valuing, negotiating, and executing the transaction. In fact, some companies undertake a dual track process in which they simultaneously prepare for an IPO and attempt to sell the company. The prospect of a successful IPO process may provide additional leverage to the company in negotiating with potential buyers, but a dual track requires a significant commitment of time and resources.

There are aspects of a sale transaction, however, that differ markedly from an initial public offering, principally the nature of the process and the governing agreements. This chapter discusses the sale transaction process and the relevant agreements applicable to a private fashion company that is for sale in its entirety, or a public or private company that is selling or disposing of only certain of its fashion brands. The discussion will not focus in detail on the sale of a public company in its entirety, since the agreements for such transactions tend to have fewer fashion-industry-specific provisions. The sale of a public company also raises additional non-industry specific legal considerations under state fiduciary duty law and the federal securities laws that are noted, but not considered in depth.[11]

A fashion company may elect to sell or dispose of only a portion of its brands, or a buyer may purchase only one of several brands on offer. For example, in late 2013, Liz Claiborne reportedly sold Lucky Brand Apparel to Leonard Green & Partners for $225 million.[12] Fashion brands are not always sold as stand-alone operating businesses like Lucky, they are sometimes sold primarily for their name and license potential, to groups such Iconix Brand Group, Inc. (Nasdaq: Icon) and Authentic Brands Group, a private company. These transactions may take many forms, including a classic sale of stock or assets, or the

10. For example, Petco was both preparing an IPO and auctioned at the same time in 2015, and was ultimately sold for a reported $4.5 billion. *See* Dana Mattioli & Telis Demos, *Petco Reaches $4.6 Billion Deal to Be Sold to Private-Equity Firm CVC, Pension Fund*, WALL ST. J. (Nov. 23, 2015), https://www.wsj.com/articles/cvc-cppib-near-roughly-4-5-billion-buyout-of-petco-1448228764.

11. For a fuller discussion of these issues, see STEPHEN I. GLOVER, ET AL., M&A PRACTICE GUIDE (LexisNexis 2012) [hereinafter GLOVER], §§ 3.04, 16.

12. Michael J. de la Merced, *Lucky Brand Apparel Sold to Leonard Green for $225 Million*, N.Y. TIMES (Dec. 10, 2013), https://dealbook.nytimes.com/2013/12/10/leonard-green-to-buy-lucky-brand-jeans-for-225-million/.

transfer of a portfolio of license agreements relating to the brand in question.

§ 22:2 The Sale Process

In a sale process, the seller may be either the equity owners of the company or the company itself, depending on the form of the transaction. In either case, the seller should consider how to conduct the sale process to achieve the most favorable result for the company and its owners. There are three principal ways to conduct a sale process: (i) enter into discussions with only one potential buyer, (ii) contact a limited number of potential buyers, or (iii) engage in a full-blown auction process and contact a wide range of potential buyers. Numerous factors, including the attractiveness of the company or the brand, particular timing constraints (such as a need to close by the end of a calendar year), and specific business objectives (such as the desire to combine with a global company), all may impact the choice of a sale strategy. As discussed in chapter 23, many fashion brands and retailers are also the subject of a restructuring under bankruptcy laws, which can in turn entail a range of sale processes and structures that are discussed in that chapter.

To determine the most suitable process, the seller typically considers the universe of possible strategic and financial buyers that might be interested in acquiring the company or brand and that have the financial capacity to consummate a transaction. Strategic buyers are companies in a similar or related business that focus on the strategic and synergistic value of an acquisition. Financial buyers are typically private equity firms that focus on growing the company and then exiting their investment though a public offering or sale within four to seven years. Strategic buyers may be able to use their own equity securities or available cash for the purchase price (but may also use debt), while financial buyers typically use a more highly leveraged combination of equity and debt financing.

§ 22:2.1 *Potential Buyers*

Many acquisitions of private companies or brands in the fashion industry occur through negotiations between a seller and a single potential buyer (or group of buyers working together in a consortium), often where the parties have a preexisting relationship. In such cases, a potential buyer may insist upon entering into an exclusivity agreement with the seller, providing for a period of exclusive negotiations (for example, thirty to ninety days) during which the seller cannot negotiate with other parties, as a precondition for investing the time and expense in the negotiation and due diligence process. The exclusivity agreement may also include a term sheet setting forth the expected deal terms, such as price, acquisition structure, and form of consideration. Generally, the exclusivity provisions of the agreement are binding on the parties, while the deal term provisions typically are not binding, but serve as a guide for the negotiation of the definitive agreement.

If the company or brand is particularly attractive to multiple potential buyers, however, the seller might consider informally contacting potential buyers or conducting a formal auction process. In a formal auction process, the seller typically retains an investment banking firm and legal counsel to conduct and manage the process. The seller and its investment bankers begin by contacting potential strategic and/or financial buyers to determine which parties are interested in participating in the auction process. The investment bankers typically require that potential bidders execute a nondisclosure agreement and upon obtaining this agreement, proceed to deliver to interested parties a detailed confidential memorandum, describing the acquisition opportunity. The auction process itself typically consists of several rounds in which prospective buyers provide initial indications of interest, perform increasingly detailed due diligence, refine their valuations, and, if they remain interested and are suitable candidates, submit final bids. A final bid package generally includes a bid letter outlining the financial and other important terms of the proposed transaction, the amount and source of any third-party equity or debt financing, and any items of due diligence that remain to be completed, as well as a draft acquisition agreement that the bidder is prepared to sign (typically, this will be a revised version of the draft acquisition agreement presented by the seller to each of the bidders). The seller, in consultation with its advisors, reviews the final bid packages and determines which bidder offers the most attractive combination of financial and contractual terms, with a particular focus on price and certainty of closing. If more than one bidder offers a compelling bid, the seller and its banker may institute a further round of bidding to determine a clear winner. At the end of the process, the seller and the winning bidder negotiate to reach agreement on definitive documentation for the transaction. In the case of a publicly traded company, additional legal considerations must be factored in by the company's board of directors and others, and a clear business strategy must be developed and articulated to the market. An excellent example of a strategic acquisition by a public company is Michael Kors's acquisition of Versace, after which the company changed its name and rebranded itself as a luxury conglomerate called Capri Holdings.[13]

---

13. Declan Eytan, *Michael Kors Holdings Finalizes Versace Acquisition, Changes Name to Capri Holdings*, FORBES (Dec. 31, 2018), https://www.forbes.

Although multiple reasons are given for the deal, including the strong heritage and brand recognition of Versace, most important may have been the goal to claim a bigger chunk of luxury sales.[14] There are clear advantages to an auction process, principally greater certainty that the seller is achieving the most favorable economic outcome. There are, however, notable disadvantages. An auction process involving multiple bidders can be time-consuming and difficult to manage. The company's management will need to respond to multiple requests for due diligence and prepare management presentations for each of the bidders, who may have varying degrees of familiarity with the company and its business. In addition, a large auction process with multiple bidders, and their teams of financial, legal, and accounting advisors, can lead to inadvertent early public disclosure of the sale process that may cause disruption and uncertainty among both employees and customers of the company. In particular, if the details of an auction process are "leaked" to the public, but a sale is not consummated, the reputation of the company and the brand can be damaged and key employees and customers may leave.

§ 22:2.2 Due Diligence

During either exclusive negotiations or an auction process, potential buyers typically perform business, financial, and legal due diligence on the company or brand that is being sold. Due diligence in a sale context is conducted for several reasons: to refine a valuation analysis; to identify any potential legal or business impediments to consummating the acquisition (such as the need to obtain third-party consents to material contracts); to determine if there are matters that need to be specifically addressed in the acquisition agreement; and to learn in detail about the operations of the business. Of particular interest to buyers of a fashion company are topics such as compliance with domestic and foreign labor, manufacturing and environmental laws, compliance of subcontractors and suppliers with such laws, leases and other long-term commitments, and intellectual property matters. For a discussion of the regulatory framework for manufacturing underlying these important due diligence concerns, see chapter 9.

---

com/sites/declaneytan/2018/12/31/michael-kors-holdings-finalizes-versace-acquisition-changes-name-to-capri-holdings/#45fef6e02de9.

14. Cathaleen Chen & Lauren Sherman, *Game On: Michael Kors Acquires Versace for $2.1 Billion*, BUS. OF FASHION (Sept. 25, 2018), https://www.businessoffashion.com/articles/news-analysis/game-on-michael-kors-acquires-versace-for-2-billion.

Potential strategic buyers also typically focus on how the company's business, operational systems, and employees can be integrated into the buyer's business. If a potential buyer is a competitor of the seller, it may be necessary or desirable to institute special due diligence procedures both to comply with applicable antitrust laws and to preserve the confidentiality of competitively sensitive information. Such procedures might often include having certain sensitive information reviewed only by a "clean team" comprised of mutually identified professionals who are cordoned off from "insiders" such as officers and employees of the buyer.

§ 22:2.3 *Confidentiality and Standstill Agreements*

As indicated above, the seller and its advisors should require each potential bidder to execute an appropriate confidentiality agreement as a precondition to receiving a confidential memorandum or performing due diligence on the company. For a discussion of the principal provisions in a confidentiality agreement, see chapter 17. If the seller is a public company, it may be desirable to include a standstill provision in the confidentiality agreement. A standstill provision prevents the potential buyer from taking certain enumerated actions, including acquiring shares of the company's securities, making a "hostile offer" for the company (that is, an offer that has not been consented to by the company's board of directors), or engaging in a proxy contest with respect to the company, for a specified period of time (typically six months to two years). A standstill provision acts to prevent a potential buyer from disrupting an existing or potential auction or negotiation process.

§ 22:3 The Transaction Structure

§ 22:3.1 *Form of Transaction*

The acquisition of a company can be structured in a variety of ways. It can be structured as a purchase of equity interests (pursuant to a stock purchase agreement), a purchase of specified assets subject to certain specified liabilities (pursuant to an asset purchase agreement), or a merger (pursuant to a merger agreement). The seller's and the buyer's preferences as to the form of the acquisition will depend on many factors, including the nature of the business and the assets being sold, the type and extent of the company's liabilities, the number of equity holders of the company, the need to obtain third-party consents, the laws of the company's jurisdiction of organization, and the tax implications of the transaction. In an asset purchase transaction, for example, the buyer can select which assets to purchase and which liabilities to assume, subject to negotiations with the seller.

This may be desirable in cases where the buyer seeks to purchase only a particular brand or a division of a company, or is concerned about assuming certain outstanding or contingent liabilities of the company. An acquisition of the stock or other equity interests in a company may be preferable if the assets are too numerous or difficult to transfer. The tax implications of the transaction will differ depending upon how the company is structured, and will impact the buyer's and seller's preferences for either an asset purchase or an equity purchase. A discussion of the tax considerations applicable to different ownership structures is set forth in chapter 1.

Acquisitions of public companies are typically effected either through a merger of the target company with a wholly owned subsidiary of the buyer (a "triangular merger"), or through a tender offer by the buyer for the equity securities of the target company, followed by a second-step triangular merger. A far less common disposition structure, which is currently in vogue with some public companies that are under pressure to increase shareholder value, is a "spinoff" of a division or subsidiary of a company to the shareholders of its owner. Due to their limited use, they will not be discussed in depth here. For U.S. federal income tax purposes, a reverse triangular merger, where the buyer's subsidiary merges into the target company, is generally treated as a stock acquisition.[15] A transaction involving a public company also can be structured so that the target company is merged directly into the buyer or so that both the target company and the buyer are merged into a new entity in a consolidation, but these structures are less commonly used.

§ 22:3.2 Purchase Price

The purchase price for a company may include one or more types of consideration. The most common forms of consideration include: cash; equity securities of the buyer; notes of the buyer; or other properties of the buyer.

[A] Cash

A buyer offering a cash purchase price may obtain the funds entirely from its own operations or may need to raise external financing for all or a portion of such funds. A buyer using internally generated funds may be able to close a transaction more quickly, absent regulatory or stockholder approval issues. A buyer that is dependent on raising funds from external sources creates additional uncertainty and potential delays for the seller. As described below, each party may seek

15. Rev. Rul. 73-427, 1973-2 C.B. 301; Rev. Rul. 79-273, 1979-2 C.B. 125; Rev. Rul. 90-95, 1990-2 C.B. 67.

to impose obligations on the other party in respect of such financing to mitigate those concerns and to increase the certainty of closing.

Cash consideration, in the currency of the seller, can be advantageous because it does not need to be "valued" and does not change in value (other than in respect of inflation) over the interval between the execution and the closing of the acquisition agreement. However, if the consideration for an acquisition is all cash, the seller will not have a continuing interest in the business after the acquisition closes.

[B] Equity Securities of the Buyer

If the purchase price for an acquisition includes equity securities of the buyer, the parties will need to address the valuation of such securities. The seller typically will perform due diligence on the buyer and consult with its financial advisors to determine its view of valuation. The parties will then negotiate for the manner in which the buyer's securities will be valued and issued to the sellers.

When equity securities are being issued to the seller, such issuances must comply with applicable state and federal securities laws. If such shares are unregistered, the seller may seek demand or piggyback registration rights to permit those shares to be freely tradable.[16] For U.S. federal income tax purposes, if the purchase price is paid solely in cash, the transaction should be a taxable transaction for the seller. If all or a portion of the consideration consists of stock of an acquiring corporation, however, the transaction may be tax free to the seller with respect to the stock portion of the consideration received.

[C] Buyer Promissory Notes

If the purchase price includes a buyer promissory note, the parties will need to negotiate the terms of the note. The key terms of a note include the principal amount, the interest rate and the maturity of the note, and whether the note will be guaranteed by a third party (such as a larger parent company) or secured by the buyer's assets. Typically, a buyer will insist that notes issued as consideration for an acquisition should not be negotiable instruments in order to preserve the ability of the buyer to set off interest and principal payments against amounts owed by the seller to the buyer as a result of indemnification provisions in the acquisition agreement, discussed below, or otherwise. For U.S. federal income tax purposes, the receipt of notes as consideration may qualify as an installment sale, which would allow the seller to defer recognizing a portion of its gain until it actually receives a cash payment.[17] If the notes bear interest at less than the

---

16. For a discussion of these registration rights, see *supra* chapter 1.
17. 26 U.S.C. § 453 (2012).

applicable federal rate or AFR (a minimum rate published monthly by the Internal Revenue Service that is generally less than a market rate), a portion of their principal amount will be treated as interest for income tax purposes (paid by the buyer and received by the seller) rather than as purchase price, resulting in ordinary income to the seller and potential interest deductions for the buyer.[18]

§ 22:3.3 Purchase Price Adjustment Mechanisms

If a buyer is acquiring a privately held company or a brand owned by a multi-brand public or private company, it may seek an adjustment to the purchase price paid at closing through a post-closing purchase price adjustment mechanism. Such provisions protect the buyer against certain losses between the date of the most recently available financial statements and the date of the closing of the transaction, as well as possible seller manipulation of payables and receivables during such period. Post-closing adjustment mechanisms are generally structured to adjust the purchase price to reflect any increase or decrease in certain balance sheet items at closing as compared to target amounts. These items typically include: working capital (current assets minus current liabilities, subject to certain agreed adjustments), net assets, and/or net debt. Post-closing working capital adjustment provisions, the most common adjustments, may operate as follows. Initially, the parties agree on a target amount of working capital that the company should have as of the closing. Prior to closing, the seller prepares an estimate of working capital as of the closing, and the purchase price paid at closing is increased or decreased on a dollar for dollar basis by the amount by which the estimate varies from the target amount. After the closing, the buyer prepares an actual calculation of working capital as of the closing; if the actual working capital at closing exceeds the estimated working capital, then the buyer pays the seller the difference, and if the actual working capital is less than the estimated working capital, then the seller pays the buyer the difference.

Most post-closing purchase price adjustment provisions provide detailed guidance for making the computations, and some (particularly for retailers) may require that the company complete a physical inventory at closing. These provisions also may provide a dispute resolution mechanism to resolve any issues between the parties as to the calculation of the adjustment. Disputes are typically referred to independent accountants, who are authorized to review the disputed matters and make a final determination.

---

18. 26 U.S.C. §§ 1271–75; 26 U.S.C. § 483.

§ 22:3.4 Contingent Payment Mechanisms

A prospective buyer and seller may be interested in consummating a transaction, but there may be a significant gap between the price that the buyer is willing to pay and the price that the seller is willing to accept because of conflicting views as to the value of the business. This may occur, for example, where the business has a short operating history or has a new patent or product with an uncertain future commercial potential. This gap often can be addressed through the use of certain mechanisms, such as an "earn-out," a royalty right, or another contingent payment mechanism that could deliver additional future consideration to the seller based on the company's future performance. These mechanisms are discussed in more detail below.

[A] Earn-Outs

In an earn-out, the seller typically receives additional consideration (often cash) if the company's business, as operated by the buyer after the closing, achieves certain agreed benchmarks during a specified period of time. The earn-out provision should specify the specific accounting principles to be used in the calculation of the relevant financial benchmark. Moreover, the provision should specify the scope of the business that will be subject to the earn-out. For example, the provision should indicate whether the earn-out will apply to new product lines that are developed or acquired by the business subsequent to the closing.

The seller may seek to impose certain obligations on the buyer to increase the likelihood that the benchmarks will be achieved and that the earn-out will be paid.[19] For example, the seller may require a commitment of the buyer to invest specified amounts in the business over the term of the earn-out. Similarly, the seller may request certain post-closing operational covenants so that the seller can better monitor achievement of the benchmarks. Such covenants might include maintenance of separate books and records for the business, prohibitions on integrating the business with other businesses of the buyer, and certain veto rights over specified actions of the buyer.

While earn-outs can be advantageous in addressing value uncertainty, they have significant disadvantages for both parties. They can be complex, and difficult to negotiate and then monitor effectively during the earn-out period. From a practical perspective, the seller's ability to realize value from an earn-out is largely dependent

---

19. *See* Christine Lagurio, *How to Structure an Earn-out*, INC. (Mar. 11, 2010), https://www.inc.com/guides/earn-out-structuring.html.

on the buyer's financial investment in, and skill in operating, the business. Accordingly, earn-outs may be most desirable for a seller that will have a continuing role in the operation of the business after the closing and during the earn-out period. From a buyer's perspective, earn-out provisions may be undesirable to the extent that they impose burdensome restrictions on the buyer's operation of the business. Moreover, the operation of these provisions frequently leads to a dispute between the buyer and the seller.[20] As such, these provisions should be approached with care and caution.

The use of earn-outs may also create tax and accounting issues that need to be considered by the parties. For U.S. federal income tax purposes, an earn-out will be treated as an installment obligation similar to a note, unless the seller elects a different treatment. If the seller does not elect to treat the earn-out as an installment obligation, the seller must generally recognize gain at the time of the sale, taking into account the estimated value of the earn-out. The gain recognized is subsequently adjusted to reflect differences between the estimated value and what turns out to be the actual value. In certain limited circumstances, a seller may apply the "open transaction doctrine" to an earn-out and defer the recognition of gain in a manner more favorable than that applicable to an installment obligation.

[B] Sale of Brand or Royalty Rights

If the company has valuable intellectual property rights, such as trademarks for a well-recognized brand, it may be possible to structure an acquisition so that the seller receives a continuing royalty on sales of the branded products after the closing. Such an acquisition could be structured through the creation of a joint venture company, and might operate in the following way: (i) all of the non-intellectual property assets and liabilities of the company would be transferred to the buyer; (ii) all of the intellectual property rights (for example, the trademarks for the brands) of the company would be transferred to a new joint venture company, owned jointly by the buyer and the seller; and (iii) the joint venture company would license the intellectual property to the buyer and/or third parties in return for a royalty. Through this structure, the buyer can use, and will have an equity interest (perhaps a controlling equity interest) in, the company's intellectual property. At the same time, the seller will retain an equity interest (perhaps

20. GAIL WEINSTEIN, ET AL., THE ENDURING ALLURE AND PERENNIAL PITFALLS OF EARNOUTS, HARV. L. SCH. FORUM ON CORP. GOVERNANCE & FIN. REG. (Feb. 10, 2018), https://corpgov.law.harvard.edu/2018/02/10/the-enduring-allure-and-perennial-pitfalls-of-earnouts/.

a minority interest) in a future royalty stream from the intellectual property after the closing. Since the joint venture company merely holds and licenses intellectual property rights, and does not otherwise operate a business, it should not have significant management or infrastructure requirements or expenses.

The joint venture agreement between the buyer and the seller, however, would have to address certain fundamental issues regarding control of the joint venture and transfers of interests in the joint venture entity. The joint venture might operate through a board of directors or a manager, and certain enumerated actions might require the vote or consent of both parties. In particular, the joint venture agreement should set forth a specific process with respect to amending, terminating, or replacing the joint venture's licensing arrangements and other agreements with the buyer or seller, or their respective affiliates. The joint venture agreement should also address transfers of interests in the joint venture, both between the parties and to third parties. Consideration should be given to prohibiting all transfers for a specified period of time (other than to affiliates or by operation of law) in order to solidify the foundation of the joint venture. Thereafter, the parties might have rights of first refusal or first offer, and drag (forced sale) and tag (participation) rights, with respect to third-party sales, in order to protect each party's interest, yet facilitate a possible future sale of the company.[21] The parties might also consider including buy-out rights between the parties after a specified time or at specified intervals. The buy-out pricing might be based on a stated formula (such as a multiple of current EBITDA at the time of the buy-out) or might be determined by an independent third-party expert, as more fully discussed in chapter 10. A buy-out right might be particularly desirable for the original brand owner who would like the ability to regain control of its brand in the event that the joint venture arrangement is not successful.

A similar structure was used by Bebe Stores, Inc., which formed a joint venture company in 2016 with Bluestar Alliance, LLC. In this transaction, Bluestar Alliance contributed $35 million to a newly created entity, BB Brand Management LLC, to acquire Bebe's trademarks and other intellectual property, and the resulting entity became owned 50/50 by the parties. BB Brand Management then granted Bebe an exclusive license to operate its retail stores and websites, and a non-exclusive license to conduct its business,

---

21. Rights of first refusal and first offer are described more fully in *supra* chapter 10, and drag-along and tag-along rights are described in more detail in *supra* chapter 1.

including the design, manufacture, advertisement, and promotion of Bebe-branded apparel.[22]

§ 22:4 Ancillary Agreements

In many sale transactions, the acquisition agreement will be supplemented by certain important ancillary agreements, either between the parties or between one of the parties and a third party, that create additional value or are necessary or desirable for the buyer to operate the company's business after the closing. In the case of a company that uses or includes the name of a living person as its trademark, the buyer may seek a separate agreement with that person. For example, in the sale of Versace to Kors, it was a closing requirement to have the previously negotiated employment agreement with Donatella Versace and the consulting agreement with Allegra Versace Beck both be in effect.[23] The buyer may seek to acquire such person's publicity rights (for example, likeness, voice, and signature) for commercial purposes, and/or his or her rights to business related social media accounts (such as Facebook, Twitter and Pinterest accounts).[24] The buyer also may seek to impose certain restrictions on such person's future use of his or her name in connection with the sale of goods or services. This in turn can lead to the awkward situation experienced by "designers from Halston through to Roland Mouret [who] have lost control of their companies, then suffered the ignominy of seeing designs that they would never have approved of executed in their name."[25] As the quoted article also notes, in many cases the financial rewards for incurring this risk are nevertheless compelling.[26] For a discussion of what could result if there is not a sufficient meeting of the minds on post sale activities, see chapter 2.

In addition to important agreements with founders, if the buyer is acquiring a brand from a larger multi-brand company, the buyer may enter into a transition services agreement with the seller. If the seller historically provided certain services (such as financial,

---

22. BEBE STORES, INC., CURRENT REPORT (Form 8-K) (June 8, 2016).
23. *See* Stock Purchase Agreement filed as an exhibit to MICHAEL KORS HOLDINGS LTD., CURRENT REPORT (Form 8-K) (Sept. 24, 2018).
24. For a further discussion of the legal issues associated with rights of publicity, see *supra* chapter 18.
25. Alexander Fury, *Donna Karan: Your Name May be on the Label, But It Doesn't Mean a Job for Life* (July 5, 2015), https://www.independent.co.uk/life-style/fashion/features/donna-karan-your-name-may-be-on-the-label-but-it-doesn-t-mean-a-job-for-life-10367320.html.
26. *See id.*

accounting, human resource, or sourcing services) to the brand, it may be desirable for the seller to continue to provide such services to the brand after the closing until the buyer is able to perform those services directly. Transition services agreements typically specify the particular services to be provided by the seller, the payment terms for such services, and the period of time during which such services will be provided (which may differ depending upon the service).

As part of the sale negotiations, the parties typically discuss whether, and to what extent, the senior management, and other employees, of the company will be retained by the buyer after the closing. In situations where the company has a key senior executive, creative director, or head designer, the buyer may condition consummation of the transaction on entering into an employment agreement with such person. For a discussion of the principal terms of employment agreements, see chapter 16.

If the buyer is issuing equity securities to the seller as part or all of the consideration, the buyer may insist on entering into an agreement with the seller imposing restrictions on the seller's ability to transfer such shares for a specified period of time or to specified parties, such as competitors of the buyer. On the other hand, as discussed above, the seller may seek registration rights with respect to such shares so that they can become freely transferable. If the seller is receiving equity securities that represent a significant percentage of the buyer's outstanding shares, the seller may seek a contractual right to representation on the buyer's board of directors for a specified period of time after the closing (subject to any applicable stockholder approval requirements).

§ 22:5 Risk Allocation

§ 22:5.1 Representations and Warranties

Acquisition agreements typically contain representations and warranties about each of the buyer, the seller, and the company (or, in the case of a merger, the merging parties and the parent acquiror). These representations and warranties typically speak as of the date of the agreement (or, in certain cases, as of a specified date), and are subsequently brought down to (or reaffirmed as of) the closing date. Representations and warranties serve the dual purposes of confirming the buyer's due diligence review of the company (and, in some case, the seller's due diligence review of the buyer) and allocating risk among the parties. Representations and warranties are typically far more extensive for private companies than for public companies. Public companies are subject to the ongoing disclosure requirements of the federal securities laws and file periodic reports (such as a Form 10-K) with the SEC containing material information about the company.[27] Accordingly, a public company typically makes representations about its public filings with the SEC and its financial statements rather than extensive representations and warranties about each aspect of its business. If a particular brand or business line of a public company is being sold, the representations and warranties typically are more similar to those in a private company acquisition agreement, because the company's SEC filings may not disclose all of the information that is material to that brand or business line.

Representations and warranties typically are more extensive for sellers than for buyers, unless the buyer is issuing its securities to the seller as all or part of the consideration for the transaction. In such a case, the representations and warranties of the buyer may mirror the seller's or, if the buyer is a public company, may reference its public filings.

Each party to an acquisition agreement typically makes certain basic representations and warranties about itself and the agreement. These representations include that such party is duly organized and has the power to enter into the agreement; and, that the agreement has been duly authorized, executed, and delivered, and is enforceable against it in accordance with its terms. The buyer typically requires the seller (or the company itself) to make more detailed representations about such matters as the company's capitalization, financial statements, accounts receivable, taxes, material contracts, liabilities, litigation, real and personal properties, intellectual property, labor and employee benefits, environmental matters, and compliance with law. In addition to the representations and warranties applicable to businesses generally, some of the more specific representations and warranties that a buyer may request from a company in the fashion industry (depending upon the specific type of business being conducted) relate to:

- Intellectual property rights;
- Principal customers and suppliers;
- Dealers and distributors;
- Inventory;
- Purchase commitments;
- Product warranties and product liabilities;

---

27. See the periodic reporting requirements under section 13 of the Securities Exchange Act of 1934 and the related regulations (codified as amended at 15 U.S.C. § 78m, and related regulations).

- Discount and promotional programs;
- Retail store leases;
- Privacy policies;
- Data usage and security; and
- Customs duties.

Appendix 22B contains sample representations and warranties (including a definition of "material adverse effect") covering these fashion industry specific matters.

Representations and warranties may be subject to important qualifications. They may be qualified by materiality, the absence of a material adverse effect on the company, or the knowledge of the seller, and the use and extent of such qualifications are often heavily negotiated. For example, a representation as to product liability claims against the company might be phrased in one of the following formulations: (i) the company has not had any product liability claims asserted against it in the last five fiscal years; (ii) the company has not had any material product liability claims asserted against it in the last five years; (iii) the company has not had any product liability claims asserted against it in the last five years that, individually or in the aggregate, are reasonably likely to have a material adverse effect on the company; or (iv) to the seller's knowledge, the company has not had any product liability claims asserted against it in the last five years. These qualifications shift the risk, in varying degrees, to the buyer from the seller, with respect to product liability claims. Representations and warranties also may be qualified by reference to disclosure schedules that are attached to the agreement; these schedules either set forth information called for by the representations or provide exclusions from the representations. Buyers and sellers often negotiate whether, and the extent to which, schedules may be updated between the signing and the closing of the agreement, as well as the impact of such updates on the respective termination and indemnification rights of the parties. Representations and warranties may terminate at closing or may survive for specified periods of time thereafter, as negotiated by the parties.

The buyer or the seller may consider obtaining an insurance policy covering losses from a breach of some or all of the seller's representations and warranties in the acquisition agreement. These policies may be useful to a seller in minimizing potential liability from certain identifiable contingent risks, such as tax risks, which may be remote but could have substantial economic consequences. They may also be useful to a buyer that is concerned with the creditworthiness of the seller and the seller's ability to fund its future indemnification obligations. Representation and warranty insurance is typically priced in a manner that reflects not only the underlying risk, but the extent of due diligence and the terms of the agreement, and typically includes a meaningful retention or deductible. The insurance carrier may also require the payment of an initial fee to cover the expenses of its due diligence review. In the past few years, the market has increasingly accepted these policies, which have become more competitive in both price and availability.[28]

§ 22:5.2 Covenants

Acquisition agreements that do not have simultaneous signings and closings also typically contain affirmative and negative covenants of each party that apply during the period between signing and closing. These covenants serve to protect the interests of each party in the transaction pending the closing. Affirmative covenants of the seller might include a commitment to operate the business of the company in the ordinary course consistent with past practice; to obtain required third-party consents and, if applicable, stockholder approval for the transaction; and to assist the buyer in obtaining financing for the transaction. Negative covenants of the seller might include restrictions on making any distributions or dividends, hiring new senior employees, entering into material contracts, settling legal proceedings, or engaging in material acquisitions or dispositions, without the consent of the buyer. Affirmative covenants of the buyer might include a commitment to obtain regulatory approvals and, if applicable, stockholder approval for the transaction and a commitment to use commercially reasonable efforts to obtain financing for the transaction within a specified time period. Acquisition agreements may also have post-closing covenants, such as agreements by the seller not to compete with, or solicit employees of, the buyer after the closing; for a discussion of such covenants, see chapter 16.

§ 22:5.3 Indemnities

Buyers of private companies generally seek protection from breaches of representations and warranties, either in the form of post-closing indemnities from the seller or by purchasing insurance as described above. The seller might seek a reciprocal indemnity from the buyer covering a breach of the buyer's representations and warranties and

28. JEFFREY CHAPMAN, ET AL., M&A REPORT–HOW REPRESENTATIONS AND WARRANTIES INSURANCE IS TRANSFORMING RISK ALLOCATION IN M&A TRANSACTIONS (Nov. 27, 2017), https://www.gibsondunn.com/ma-report-how-representations-and-warranties-insurance-is-transforming-risk-allocation-in-ma-transactions/ [hereinafter Chapman].

covenants, and third-party claims relating to liabilities assumed by the buyer or the conduct of the business after the closing. The seller, in particular, should seek to impose a deductible or a threshold that must be satisfied before the buyer can make an indemnification claim, in order to avoid small claims. A deductible is an amount that reduces the indemnification obligation of the seller, while a threshold merely sets a reference point that, when met, requires the seller to indemnify the buyer for the full amount of the indemnification obligation. An insurer will also require a retention or deductible. In addition to a deductible or a threshold, the seller also should seek to impose a cap on the total amount of its indemnification obligation, typically subject to an exception for fraud, so that it can determine the maximum extent of its potential liability in connection with the sale. Of course, insurance coverage is also always subject to a maximum amount.

Acquisition agreements for the sale of a public company typically do not provide for the survival of representations and warranties or for indemnities, because the sellers are public shareholders and the mechanics of indemnification would be too complex. Therefore, in acquisitions of public companies, buyer due diligence becomes even more critical.

§ 22:5.4 Escrow Arrangements

A buyer of a private company may seek to retain a portion of the purchase price and hold it in escrow for a specified period of time to fund possible future indemnification obligations of the seller. This is particularly important if the seller is an individual or group of individuals or if there are concerns as to the future ability of the seller to perform its indemnification obligations. An escrow arrangement shifts the leverage to the buyer in a post-closing dispute over indemnification. For example, the purchase of Versace by Capri entailed a €100 million escrow.[29] Accordingly, the seller should protect its interest in the escrow by having the escrowed funds held by an independent escrow agent in an interest bearing account pursuant to specific guidelines. For U.S. federal income tax purposes, the escrowed amount is generally treated as additional purchase price received by the seller. If all or a portion of the escrowed funds is released to the buyer, the purchase price is generally reduced by that amount.

---

29. Section 3.1 of the Stock Purchase Agreement filed under CAPRI HOLDINGS LTD., CURRENT REPORT (Form 8-K) (Dec. 31, 2018). Note that representation and warranty insurance, if available for the transaction, would likely have cost approximately €4 million for such coverage; an expense which the parties may have preferred not to incur. *See* Chapman, *supra* note 28.

§ 22:6 Closing Conditions and Termination Rights

As discussed above, in many cases there will be an interval between signing and closing a transaction. For example, the buyer may be required to obtain regulatory approvals for the transaction or make a pre-merger notification filing under the Hart-Scott-Rodino Antitrust Improvements Act of 1976;[30] the seller may need to obtain third-party consents or stockholder approval; and/or the buyer may need to obtain financing for the acquisition. In such cases, the acquisition agreement will specify those specific conditions that are required to occur, or be waived, before the parties are obligated to close the transaction. Most acquisition agreements include the following general conditions to each party's obligation to close: the continued accuracy (often qualified by materiality) of the representations and warranties of the other party; the performance (often qualified by materiality) by the other party of all covenants to be performed by it; the absence of any law or governmental order preventing the closing; and the receipt of all specified consents or approvals. Buyers also typically seek a closing condition to the effect that between signing and closing, the company has not suffered a "material adverse change," as such term is negotiated and defined in the agreement. Further, if a transaction is structured as a "tender offer," the buyer must obtain a sufficient percentage of the outstanding shares of the target (generally just over 50%) in order to effectuate a merger under applicable state law, and accordingly, the buyer will condition the closing upon obtaining that level of ownership.

A buyer that is funding an acquisition using external financing may seek to condition its obligation to close the transaction on obtaining such financing. From a seller's perspective, such a financing condition makes the likelihood of closing the transaction more uncertain. In many cases, in lieu of a financing condition, the parties negotiate a specific termination fee (as described below) to be paid by the buyer to the seller if the buyer fails to obtain the financing and therefore cannot consummate the transaction. Such an arrangement caps the liability of the buyer for a financing failure (absent bad faith, fraud, or similar issues), and at the same time provides a negotiated amount of compensation to the seller. Whenever a buyer is using external financing, however, the seller should require the buyer to adhere to certain performance standards (such as using commercially reasonable efforts) to obtain the financing, and should review the buyer's commitment letters from its external financing sources to confirm the status and terms of such financing. Importantly, the conditions to the

30. 15 U.S.C. § 18a (2012).

closing of the financing should mirror the conditions to the closing of the acquisition, in order to minimize the risk that the acquisition will not close solely because of a financing failure.

The acquisition agreement typically provides a list of circumstances that will permit one or both parties to terminate the agreement prior to closing. Such events typically include: the mutual consent of the parties; failure to close the transaction by a specified date; breach by either party of its representations and warranties; and issuance of a governmental order restraining or prohibiting the transaction. Some buyers also insist on a closing condition or termination right in the event that the company fails to meet or achieve certain benchmarks. The benchmarks may be specific financial metrics, an operational milestone (such as a new product launch or retail store opening), or a third-party event (such as the renewal of a long-term third-party license agreement).

If the company to be acquired is a public company, the target company typically seeks additional termination rights. The most important termination right is a "fiduciary duty out" that allows the company to terminate the acquisition agreement if the company's board of directors deems it appropriate in the exercise of its fiduciary duties (typically because it has received a superior acquisition offer from another bidder). In certain circumstances, termination of the agreement will obligate one party to a pay a termination fee to the other party. A termination fee paid by a company to a buyer for a failure to close for specified reasons (typically receipt of a superior acquisition offer) is known as a "break-up fee" and a termination fee paid by a buyer to a company for failure to close for specified reasons (typically failure to obtain financing or regulatory approval) is known as a "reverse break-up fee." The precise terms of fiduciary-out provisions and the amount of termination fees, and their relationship to specific performance rights, are typically subject to extensive negotiation between the parties.[31]

§ 22:7 Illustrative Acquisitions in the Fashion Industry

The following summary of two transactions illustrates the operation of some of the provisions described above.

31. For a more complete discussion of these provisions, see GLOVER, *supra* note 11, §§ 8.12, 13.05.

§ 22:7.1 Classic Stock Purchase Agreement

The 2014 stock purchase agreement whereby Steve Madden Ltd. acquired the privately owned footwear company Dolce Vita Holdings, Inc. for $60 million provides an example of a transaction with almost all of the features discussed above, including typical purchase price adjustment provisions, an earn-out and a post-closing indemnification secured by an escrow agreement.[32]

§ 22:7.2 Public Company Tender Offer

An example of a transaction involving two public fashion companies and the use of the "tender offer" technique can be found in the 2017 all-cash acquisition by Coach, Inc. (which subsequently changed its name to Tapestry, Inc.) of Kate Spade & Co. Under the terms of the transaction, Kate Spade shareholders received $18.50 per share in cash for a total transaction value of $2.4 billion. According to Coach's press release dated May 8, 2017, the transaction represented a 27.5% percent premium "to the unaffected closing price of Kate Spade's shares as of December 27, 2016, the last trading day prior to media speculation of a transaction."[33] As discussed above in this chapter, the risk of leaks in the sale process of a public company is serious, and in this case, such leaks or rumors may have caused the stocks of Kate Spade to trade at an increased price due to speculation that the company would be sold.

---

32. *See* STEVEN MADDEN, LTD., ANNUAL REPORT (Form 10-K) (Dec. 31, 2014).
33. *See* COACH, INC., CURRENT REPORT (Form 8-K) (July 10, 2017).

Appendix 22A

Sample Earn-Out Provision

1. Certain Definitions.

"Company Business" means the business of the Company as acquired by Buyer at the closing and as such business may develop during the Fiscal Years (as defined below) during which Earnout Payments (as defined below) accrue in accordance with the provisions of this Agreement, whether through marketing to existing or future customers (including, without limitation, customers of Buyer's parent company and other Affiliates of Buyer's parent company), the development of new products or services or otherwise. In furtherance of the foregoing, the Company Business shall include all of the following:

(a) the sale, license or other disposition of any part of the Company Business (including a transfer of any parts of the Company Business to Buyer or an Affiliate of Buyer for use other than in connection with the Company Business); and

(b) the sale, license or other disposition of any (i) product or service of the Company Business or (ii) any product or service derived from, or containing as a material component, any product or service of the Company Business.

For the avoidance of doubt, "Company Business" shall not include (1) any business (or related revenue) currently conducted by Buyer's parent company or its Affiliates or (2) any future business (or related revenue) conducted by Buyer's parent company or its Affiliates (other than Buyer).

"Company Revenues" means gross revenues (including royalties and other license fees) of the Company Business as determined in accordance with Section 2(c); provided, that if Buyer or any of its Affiliates bundles any product or service of the Company Business with any other product or service, the proportional revenue associated with the product or service of the Company Business shall be included as gross revenues of the Company Business, using the standard wholesale or retail price, as applicable, that would be charged by the Company

Business for such product or service if such product or service were not bundled and were sold to similarly situated unaffiliated third parties by the Company Business.

"Fiscal Year" means a fiscal year of the Company Business beginning on January 1 and ending on December 31.

Terms not specifically defined herein shall have the meanings set forth in the Acquisition Agreement.

2. Payments.

(a) For each of the [ ] Fiscal Years, Buyer shall pay to Seller an amount ("Earnout Payment") equal to [ ]% of the annual Company Revenues for such Fiscal Year in excess of $[ ], subject to a maximum annual Earnout Payment of $[ ].

(b) Company Revenues and resulting Earnout Payments, if any, shall be calculated by Buyer on a monthly basis during each of the applicable Fiscal Years. Within thirty (30) days after the end of any month that occurs during an applicable Fiscal Year, Buyer shall pay to Seller the amount of Earnout Payments, if any, earned in such month by a wire transfer payment to an account specified by Seller and shall contemporaneously deliver to Seller a statement showing Buyer's good faith calculation of (i) the Company Revenues for such month, (ii) the aggregate Company Revenues year-to-date through the end of such month, (iii) the Earnout Payments, if any, earned during such month, and (iv) the aggregate Earnout Payments, if any, earned year-to-date through the end of such month, together with the components and supporting information therefor (all in reasonable detail). Buyer's calculations of the Company Revenues and Earnout Payments are subject to an annual verification as set forth in Section 4.

(c) For purposes of calculating the Company Revenues and Earnout Payments, all revenues shall be recognized in accordance with U.S. GAAP as applied consistently with the Company's Financial Statements; provided, however, that if, as to any particular customer, Company Revenues are recognized in accordance with the foregoing prior to the time that payment from such customer is received, the payment of the associated Earnout Payment, if any, shall be deferred until such time as payment from such customer is actually received (with payments being applied to the oldest accounts first). The parties acknowledge and agree that, in accordance with the foregoing, Company Revenues may arise from agreements or other arrangements entered into before, on or after the closing.

3. Certain Agreements Regarding the Company Business.

During the Fiscal Years for which Earnout Payments may be made, and after the closing:

(a) Buyer shall operate the Company Business as a separate business unit within its parent company. The Company Business shall not be combined (by acquisition, merger, consolidation, reorganization, joint venture or other means) with, nor shall any material portion thereof be sold to, any other business or entity, without the prior written consent of Seller; provided, that this sentence shall not prohibit a change in control of Buyer's parent company.

(b) Buyer shall maintain separate financial books and records for the Company Business sufficient to permit an audit thereof in accordance with U.S. GAAP. Seller shall have reasonable access to the financial books and records of the Company Business during normal business hours with reasonable prior notice to Buyer.

(c) Buyer shall use commercially reasonable efforts consistent with sound business practice, and the past practice of the Company Business, to maximize the Company Revenues and the Earnout Payments.

(d) Buyer may provide products or services to, or obtain products or services from, other business units of Buyer's parent company and Affiliates of Buyer's parent company, and engage in other transactions with other business units of Buyer's parent company and Affiliates of Buyer's parent company, on terms (1) no less favorable than those on which it would engage in such transactions with third parties, or (2) as otherwise agreed by Seller and Buyer.

(e) Neither Buyer nor its Affiliates shall compete directly or indirectly with the Company Business (as it is currently conducted or as it may be conducted during any of the Fiscal Years for which Earnout Payments may be made), whether through existing companies, business units or divisions, or through the acquisition of a company that engages in business in direct or indirect competition with the Company, or otherwise appropriate the business opportunities available to the Company Business.

(f) Subject to the foregoing, Buyer shall be free to determine, in good faith, the wholesale and retail prices, and royalty rates, of its products and services as it believes is reasonable under the circumstances and shall not be required to adopt any particular pricing model; provided, however, that Buyer shall not engage in any promotional, discount or other activity with its customers, including, without limitation, the bundling of its products and services with those of Buyer's parent company or other Affiliates of Buyer, with the purpose or effect of delaying or reducing Company Revenues for any applicable Fiscal Year that would otherwise in the ordinary course of business consistent with past practice be reasonably expected to be recognized in such Fiscal Year.

4. Verification of Earnout Payments.

(a) Company Revenues shall be verified promptly after the end of each of the applicable Fiscal Years by an audit conducted by Buyer's independent accountants. Copies of such accountants' report setting forth the computation of Company Revenues, together with the components and supporting information therefor (all in reasonable detail), shall be submitted in writing to Seller and Buyer and, unless either Seller or Buyer notifies the other within forty-five (45) days after the receipt of the report that it objects to the computation of Company Revenues set forth therein or the components and supporting information therefor, the report shall be binding and conclusive on bother Seller and Buyer for the purposes of the Acquisition Agreement. Seller shall have reasonable access to the books and records of the Company Business and to Buyer's independent accountants' work papers during regular business hours with reasonable prior notice to verify the computation of Company Revenues made by such accountants and the components and supporting information therefor.

(b) If either Seller or Buyer notifies the other in writing within forty-five (45) days after receipt of such accountants' report that it objects to the computation of Company Revenues set forth therein (or any component or supporting information therefor), the amount of Company Revenues for the Fiscal Year to which such report relates shall be determined by negotiation between Seller and Buyer. If Seller and Buyer are unable to reach agreement within thirty (30) days after such notification, the determination of the amount of Company Revenues for the period in question shall be submitted to a mutually agreeable third-party firm of independent certified public accountants ("Special Accountants") for determination, whose determination shall be binding and conclusive on the parties. If the Special Accountants determine that Company Revenues have been understated by Buyer's independent accountants by five percent (5%) or more, then Buyer shall pay the Special Accountants' fees, costs and expenses. If Company Revenues have not been understated by Buyer's independent accountants, or have been understated by Buyer's independent accountants by less than five percent (5%), then Seller shall pay the Special Accountants' fees, costs and expenses.

(c) Within three (3) business days after the calculation of Company Revenues for the applicable Fiscal Year becomes binding and conclusive on the Parties (i) if the amount of Company Revenues so determined results in a lesser amount of Earnout Payments owed than has previously been paid by Buyer pursuant to Section 2(b), then Seller shall make a wire transfer payment in the amount of the difference to an account specified by Buyer, and (ii) if the amount of Company Revenues so determined results in a greater amount of Earnout Payments owed than has previously been paid by Buyer pursuant to Section 2(b), then Buyer shall make a wire transfer payment in the amount of the difference to an account specified by Seller.

Appendix 22B

Sample Fashion Industry Representations and Warranties[1]

A. Defined Terms

B. "Company Entities" means the Company and its Subsidiaries (each, individually, a "Company Entity").

"Company Intellectual Property" means any Intellectual Property owned (in whole or in part), licensed to any extent or used in the conduct of a Company Entity's business, whether in the name of such company, any employee, another company or otherwise.

"Company's Knowledge," or words to similar effect, means the facts and circumstances that are known by [ ], after reasonable inquiry and investigation.

"Contract" means any contract, indenture, mortgage, deed of trust, note, instrument, lease, license, arrangement, undertaking or other agreement (whether written or oral).

"Copyrights" means all United States and foreign copyrights, whether registered or not, copyright registrations and applications to register the same.

"Encumbrance" means any charge, claim, community property interest, equitable interest, lien, hypothecation, option, pledge, mortgage, security interest, right of first refusal, or restriction of any kind, including any restrictions on use, voting, transfer, receipt of income, or exercise of any other attribute of ownership, or other encumbrance of any kind, whether voluntarily incurred or given, or arising by operation of Law.

"Governmental Authority" means any supranational, national, state, municipal, local or foreign government, any instrumentality, subdivision, court, administrative agency

1. These representations and warranties are extensive and are subject to negotiation by the parties. They do not include materiality qualifiers; however, there is a definition of "Material Adverse Effect" that may be used as a qualifier.

or commission or other authority thereof, or any quasi-governmental or private body exercising any regulatory, taxing, importing or other governmental or quasi-governmental authority or any judicial authority (or any department, bureau or division thereof).

"Hazardous Materials" means any substance, material or waste that is regulated by any Governmental Authority, including any material, substance or waste that is defined as a "hazardous waste," "hazardous material," "hazardous substance," "extremely hazardous substance," "restricted hazardous waste," "contaminant," "toxic waste" or "toxic substance" under any provision of any Law, including petroleum, petroleum products (including crude oil and any fraction thereof), asbestos, asbestos-containing materials, urea formaldehyde and polychlorinated biphenyls.

"Intellectual Property" means all of the following in any domestic or foreign jurisdiction: (a) all inventions (whether patentable or unpatentable and whether or not reduced to practice), all improvements thereto, and all Patents; (b) all Trademarks; (c) all Copyrights and all moral rights, and applications, registrations, and renewals in connection therewith; (d) all mask works and all applications, registrations, and renewals in connection therewith; (e) all trade secrets, technical knowledge and confidential business information (including confidential ideas, research and development, know-how, formulas, compositions, manufacturing and production processes and techniques, technical data, designs, drawings, patterns and prototypes), customer and supplier lists, pricing and cost information, and business and marketing plans and proposals); (f) all Software; (g) all URLs and Domains; (h) all rights of publicity (including names, likeness, voices and images); and (i) any other confidential or proprietary information.

"Law" means all laws, statutes, rules, ordinances, codes, regulations, judgments, decrees, injunctions, writs or orders of any Governmental Authority.

"Material Adverse Effect" means any change, circumstance or effect, or combination thereof, that is material and adverse, or would reasonably be expected to be material and adverse, to (a) the business, assets, properties, results of operations or condition (financial or otherwise) [and prospects] of the Company Entities, taken as a whole, or (b) the ability of the Company to consummate the transactions contemplated by this Agreement; provided, however, that Material Adverse Effect shall not include any adverse change, event, development or effect arising from or relating to (i) the transactions contemplated by this Agreement; (ii) general business or economic conditions, or conditions (such as the price of raw materials) that relate to the business of designing, manufacturing, marketing and selling women's apparel and accessories, other than conditions that adversely affect the Company Entities in a disproportionate manner to other entities engaged in a business similar to that of the Company Entities; (iii) financial, banking or securities markets; (iv) any applicable Law, or U.S. GAAP or interpretations thereof, other than any such changes that adversely affect the Company Entities in a disproportionate manner to other entities engaged in a business similar to that of the Company Entities; or (v) any acts of terrorism, war or natural disaster or calamities.

"Patents" means all United States and foreign inventions, patents, letters patents and applications therefore (including provisional applications), and all improvements, reissues, divisions, renewals, continuations, continuations in part, reexaminations, provisionals and extensions thereof, and all invention disclosures, patent disclosures and design rights, and all documentation relating to any of the foregoing.

"Person" means any individual, corporation, partnership, limited partnership, limited liability company, trust, association or other entity or Governmental Authority.

"Permitted Encumbrances" means (a) Encumbrances for taxes not yet due and payable or the validity or amount of which is being contested in good faith by appropriate proceedings, and where adequate reserves are established and maintained in accordance with U.S. GAAP; (b) immaterial Encumbrances of carriers, warehousemen, mechanics, materialmen, repairmen and other similar liens arising or incurred in the ordinary course of business and not yet in default or delinquent; (c) in the case of any leased real property, zoning, building, or other restrictions, variances, covenants, rights of way, Encumbrances, easements and other minor irregularities in title that do not interfere in any material respect with the present use or occupancy of such leased real property by the Company Entities; and (d) all exceptions, restrictions, easements, imperfections of title, charges, rights-of-way and other Encumbrances that do not interfere in any material respect with the present use of the affected assets of the Company Entities, taken as a whole.

"Proprietary Rights Agreement" means any Contract relating to Intellectual Property to which any Company Entity is a party or by which the business of the Company Entities is bound, including, without limitation, any license agreement, design agreement, manufacturing agreement, agreement for software acquisition, development agreement, publishing agreement, private label agreement and/or any other distribution agreement.

"Software" means computer software, whether in the form of Source Code, object code, executable code, firmware or otherwise, and whether tangible or intangible, together with all related engineering and product specifications; schematics; logic diagrams; flow charts; designs; routines; sub-routines; program and system logic; program architecture; program structure; sequence and organization; programmer's notes; program documentation; operating instructions; technical and user manuals and training materials; all updates, upgrades, modifications, enhancements, improvements and derivatives of the foregoing; and all other information and technical data related to the ownership, use, design, development, testing, enhancement, support and/or maintenance of the Software.

"Source Code" means human-readable computer programming code and related technical information and documentation sufficient to enable a reasonably skilled programmer to understand the design, logic, structure and functionality of the Software and to modify, enhance, support, maintain and diagnose errors in the Software.

"Subsidiaries" means the entities listed on Schedule [ ].

"Trademark" means any name, title, slogan, trademark, trade name, trade dress, service mark, logo, insignia, or other form of device, design, format, designation used to communicate the source of a good or service, any trademark registrations, renewals and applications therefor; and service mark registrations, renewals and applications therefor, together with all translations, adaptations, derivations, and combinations thereof and including all goodwill associated therewith.

"URLs and Domains" shall mean any and all universal locators ("URLs") and domain names in which any of the Company Entities possesses any rights and/or ownership interests or which have heretofore been used by the Company Entities, along with all websites, home pages, social networking pages and designations (whether on Twitter, Facebook or otherwise) that have heretofore been used in or for the Company Entities' business, together with the goodwill of the business symbolized therein, and to any and all related HTML code, Javascript, CGI, pdf/jpg/gif files, IP addresses, AS number registrations and all other supporting files and directories created by or for or used by any Company Entity for the websites directly accessed through any such URLs, social networking pages and designations and domain names.

C. Representations and Warranties.

1. Intellectual Property.

(i) Schedule [ ] contains an accurate and complete list of all items of Intellectual Property of the type described in clauses (a), (b), (f) and (g) of the definition of Intellectual Property owned (in whole or in part), licensed to any extent, or used in the conduct of any Company Entity's business, whether in the name of such company, any employee, another company, or otherwise (collectively, the "Specified Company Intellectual Property"), showing in each case the registered or other owner, expiration date and registration and application number, if any, and with respect to each website, home page, URL, social networking page and designation listed on Schedule [ ] (collectively, the "Web Sites"), the registrar, registrant and expiration date. Except as set forth in Schedule [ ], all registered Specified Company Intellectual Property is valid and enforceable and no claim by any Person contesting the validity, enforceability, use or ownership of any of the same has been made, is currently outstanding or, to the Company's Knowledge, is threatened.

(ii) Except as disclosed in Schedule [ ], with respect to each item constituting part of the Specified Company Intellectual Property that has been registered with, filed in or issued by, as the case may be, the United States Patent and Trademark Office or such other Governmental Authorities as indicated in Schedule [ ], all such registrations remain in full force and effect, and all applications and filings and/or issuances are pending and in good standing, all without challenges of any kind.

(iii) Each Company Entity owns, or has the valid right to use pursuant to a Contract set forth in Schedule [ ], all Specified Company Intellectual Property and, to the Company's Knowledge, owns, or has the valid right to use pursuant to a Contract set forth in Schedule [ ], all other Company Intellectual Property that is necessary to or used in the operation of its business as currently operated. Except as disclosed in Schedule [ ], the Company Entities have the perpetual, royalty-free and unrestricted right to use, market, sell, assign and transfer the Specified Company Intellectual Property and, to the Company's Knowledge, all other Company Intellectual Property, anywhere in the world, in each case free and clear of any Encumbrances other than Permitted Encumbrances. The Company Entities have the sole and exclusive right to bring actions for infringement or unauthorized use of any of the Specified Company Intellectual Property and, to the Company's Knowledge, all other Company Intellectual Property owned by them, and, to the Company's Knowledge, there is no basis for any such action. Except as specifically disclosed in Schedule [ ], no part of the Intellectual Property, including, without limitation, any Source Code, is subject to or held in, or required to be held in, escrow or in any third party's possession, and no transaction heretofore engaged in by any Company Entity has required any Company Entity to provide, sell, license, assign or transfer any Source Code or any Software to any Person.

(iv) Except as set forth in Schedule [ ], to the Company's Knowledge, the Company Entities, the Company Intellectual Property and/or the operation of the business as currently operated by the Company Entities, do not infringe, misappropriate or otherwise violate any Intellectual Property, or rights thereto, of any Person. Except as set forth in Schedule [ ], (A) no claim, written or oral, that the Company Entities, the Company Intellectual Property and/or the operation of the business as currently operated by the Company Entities infringe, misappropriate or otherwise violate the Intellectual Property, or rights thereto, of any Person has been asserted or, to the Company's Knowledge, could reasonably be expected to be asserted, and (B) no claim, written or oral, that threatens the use of the Company's Intellectual Property by any of the Company Entities, has been asserted or, to the Company's Knowledge, could reasonably be expected to be asserted. Except as set forth in Schedule [ ], to the Company's Knowledge, no Person is engaging in any activity that infringes, misappropriates or otherwise violates any of the Company Intellectual Property.

(v) The Company has never conducted its business under any corporate, trade or fictitious name other than its name.

(vi) Except as set forth in Schedule [ ], the Software, computer hardware (whether general purpose or special purpose), and other similar or related items of automated, computerized and/or software system(s) that are used or relied on by the Company Entities in the conduct of their business is sufficient for the operation of the business as currently operated by the Company Entities.

(vii) Except as disclosed in Schedule [ ], each Company Entity (A) directly, or through contractors, operates and manages each website, as applicable, (B) has the right to modify each website, accept and place advertising thereon, and to make links and hyperlinks therefrom to other internet sites, and (C) to the Company's Knowledge, owns or possesses the perpetual, world-wide, royalty-free, fully assignable right to operate each website as presently conducted, including, without limitation, the fully assignable right to operate such website with its current host on its current server as presently operated and to use, enhance, create derivative works of or from and maintain all Source Code and other Intellectual Property necessary to operate, develop, modify, make derivative works of or from, support and maintain each website.

(viii) Except as set forth in Schedule [ ], no Person who has performed services in connection with the development and/or enhancement of any of the Intellectual Property, whether as employee, consultant or as independent contractor, nor any other past or present employee of any Company

Entity, holds any proprietary or other ownership rights with respect to any such Intellectual Property. Except as disclosed in Schedule [ ], each past or present employee, agent, consultant or contractor who has contributed to or participated in the creation or development of any Intellectual Property on behalf of any Company Entity or any predecessor in interest thereto either: (A) is a party to a "work-for-hire" agreement under which a Company Entity is deemed to be the original owner/author of all property rights therein; or (B) has executed an enforceable assignment in favor of a Company Entity (or such predecessor in interest, as applicable) of all right, title and interest in all of the same.

(ix) The business of the Company Entities does not utilize any inventions, trade secrets or proprietary information of any Company Entity employee or independent contractor made prior to such employee's employment or independent contractor's engagement by such Company Entity, except for inventions, trade secrets, or proprietary information that has been assigned to a Company Entity pursuant to a Proprietary Rights Agreement.

(x) Except as set forth in Schedule [ ], each of the Company Entities has taken all commercially reasonable measures to protect the confidentiality of the assets of the Company Entities in its possession, including, without limitation, requiring all current and former employees, consultants, contractors and other Persons with access to such assets of the Company Entities to execute binding confidentiality agreements and, to the Company's Knowledge, no such employee, consultant, contractor or other Person is in breach of or has violated any term of any such confidentiality agreements.

2. Material Contracts.

(i) Schedule [ ] contains a complete and correct list of all Contracts of the types described below to which any Company Entity is a party or by which its respective assets, business or properties are bound (collectively, the "Material Contracts"): (A) any distributor, sales agent, sales representative, sales consultant, marketing, dealer, supply or similar

Contract; (B) any Contract providing for the purchase from a supplier of all or substantially all of the requirements of any Company Entity for any raw material, product or service; (C) any lease, license, permit, franchise, insurance policy or other Contract concerning or relating to any real or personal property used for the conduct and operation of any Company Entity; (D)(x) any employment, consulting, agency, collective bargaining, independent contractor or other similar Contract, (y) any retention Contract, severance Contract, change of control Contract or other similar Contract, and (z) any non-competition, non-disclosure or non-solicitation Contract or any Contract relating to Intellectual Property, in each case with any stockholder, director, officer, employee, sales representative, distributor, dealer, agent or independent contractor of any Company Entity; (E) any Contract that prohibits any Company Entity from engaging in any business or line of business, selling any product(s) or otherwise competing anywhere in the world; (F) any Contract providing in whole or in part for the use of, or limiting the use of, any Intellectual Property; (G) any license agreement to which any Company Entity is a party and as to which a Company Entity has granted a license to a Person to manufacture, distribute or sell apparel accessories, and/or other goods under, or otherwise utilize, any Trademark owned or licensed by a Company Entity; (H) any proposed license agreements that are currently in active negotiation; (I) any franchise agreement; (J) any loan agreement, indenture, letter of credit, mortgage, security agreement, pledge agreement, deed of trust, bond, note, guaranty, and other agreement or instrument relating to indebtedness or obtaining of or extension of credit; (K) any Contract providing for any surety, indemnification or contribution by a Company Entity; (L) any brokerage or finder's Contract; (M) any joint venture, partnership or similar Contract involving a sharing of profits or expenses (including joint research and development and joint marketing Contracts); (N) any asset purchase Contract, stock purchase Contract, merger Contract or other acquisition or divestiture Contract, including any Contract relating to the sale, lease or disposal of any material assets of any Company Entity (other than sales of goods or services of a Company Entity in the ordinary course of business); (O) any Contract with respect to which the aggregate amount that could reasonably be expected to be paid or received thereunder in the future exceeds [ ] per year, other than purchase orders for the purchase and sale of Inventory entered into in the ordinary course of business; (P) any purchase order or commitment for the sale of Inventory of any Company Entity not entered into in the ordinary course of business; (Q) any Contract with any affiliate or any stockholder, director or officer of any Company Entity; (R) any Contract relating to the acquisition by any Company Entity of any capital stock of, or other equity interest in, any other Person; (S) any Contract requiring any Company Entity to indemnify or hold harmless any Person; (T) any other Proprietary Rights Agreement; or (U) any other Contract that is material to the business of any Company Entity (whether or not made in the ordinary course of the business).

(ii) The Company has delivered to Buyer complete and correct copies of each of the Material Contracts that is in writing and a summary of any oral Material Contract.

(iii) There does not exist under any Material Contract any event of default or event or condition that, after notice or lapse of time or both, would constitute a violation, breach or event of default thereunder by any Company Entity or, to the Company's Knowledge, any other party to any Material Contract. Each Material Contract is in full force and effect and constitutes a legal, valid, binding and enforceable obligation of the Company Entity party thereto, subject in each case to bankruptcy, insolvency or other laws affecting creditor's rights or general principles of equity. Except as set forth in Schedule [ ], no Company Entity has received notice from any party to a Material Contract to the effect that such party (A) currently intends not to continue its relationship with the Company Entity party to such Material Contract upon the expiration of such

Material Contract, (B) has breached or intends to breach such Material Contract or intends not to perform in such a manner as would prejudice the rights of the Company Entity party to such Material Contract, (C) claims that such Material Contract has been breached by any other party thereto in a manner which would prejudice the rights of the Company Entity party to such Material Contract, (D) currently intends to exercise its right, if any, to terminate such Material Contract, or (E) as related to a license agreement that is a Material Contract, currently intends to exercise its right, if any, to "buyout" such license agreement.

3. Suppliers and Customers.

(i) Set forth in Schedule [ ] is a list of names and addresses of the twenty (20) largest customers and the twenty (20) largest suppliers (measured by dollar volume of purchases or sales in each case) of each Company Entity, and the dollar amount of the business done by such Company Entity with each such customer or supplier, during the calendar years ended December 31, [ ] and December 31, [ ].

(ii) Except as set forth on Schedule [ ], to the Company's Knowledge, the relationships of each Company Entity with its suppliers and customers are reasonably good commercial working relationships, and no (A) supplier to any Company Entity that supplied more than [ ] of products or services (excluding, for the avoidance of doubt, employees of any Company Entity) to any Company Entity during the year ended December 31, [ ] or (B) customer who accounted for more than [ ] of the sales of products or services of any Company Entity during the year ended December 31, [ ] has cancelled or otherwise terminated, or, to the Company's Knowledge, threatened to cancel or otherwise terminate, its relationship with any Company Entity.

4. Real Property Leases.

(i) Schedule [ ] contains a complete and correct list of all oral or written leases, subleases, licenses and other use and occupancy agreements (including all amendments and modifications thereto) relating to real property used or occupied by any Company Entity (collectively, the "Real Property Leases"). The Company has delivered to Buyer complete and correct copies of each of the Real Property Leases.

(ii) Subject to the terms of the respective Real Property Leases, each of the Company Entities has a valid and subsisting leasehold or subleasehold estate in the applicable leased property. To the Company's Knowledge, no Company Entity's occupation, possession or use of its leased real property has been disturbed and no claim has been asserted or threatened in writing adverse to the rights of such Company Entity to the continued occupation, possession and use of any such leased real property. To the Company's Knowledge, there are no material defaults (or events that, with notice or lapse of time or both, would constitute a material default) by any Company Entity under any of the Real Property Leases. No Company Entity has assigned, transferred, conveyed, leased or otherwise transferred any of its interest in any of its leased real property. No Company Entity has been notified in writing by any other party to any Real Property Lease that a Company Entity is in default under any of the Real Property Leases.

(iii) To the Company's Knowledge, all of the Company Entities' leased real property is (A) in commercially reasonable operating condition and repair and not in need of maintenance or repairs other than ordinary maintenance and repairs, (B) usable in the ordinary course of the Company Entity's business, and (C) adequate and suitable for the use to which it is being put. No Company Entity has received written notice of any condemnation, fire, health, safety, building, environmental, Hazardous Materials, pollution control, zoning or other land use regulatory proceedings.

5. Products.

(i) All of the products sold by any Company Entity have been manufactured for such Company Entity in accordance with the Company's specification and performance standards and the Company

Entities do not have any warranty liability with respect thereto in excess of the reserves established in the Company's most recent audited financial statements. There are no outstanding claims, actions or proceedings asserted by any third party alleging that any product sold by any Company Entity is defective or in any way caused any injury to any third party and, to the Company's Knowledge, there are no fundamental design flaws or fundamental manufacturing defects that could reasonably be expected to give rise to product liability or product recall or major repair.

(ii) All of the products sold by any Company Entity, and the labels and packaging thereof, comply with all applicable Laws including, without limitation, those that (A) relate to textile, wool or fur products, (B) address product safety or flammability, or (C) ban, require the labeling or reporting of, or restrict the type and/or concentration of, potentially Hazardous Materials therein.

6. Dealers and Distributions.

Schedule [ ] contains complete and correct list by product line of all sales representatives, dealers, distributors and franchisees of the Company Entities. The Company Entities have provided to Buyer complete and correct copies of all Contracts with all sales representatives, dealers, distributors and franchisees of the Company Entities and a description of all material modifications and exceptions (whether oral or written) to such Contracts. The Company Entities have timely paid when due all commissions and other amounts owed by them under such Contracts.

7. Discounts and Promotions.

Schedule [ ] sets forth the terms of all discounts, returns, markdowns, promotions, co-op advertising and other similar programs and allowances currently offered by the Company Entities to any of their respective customers.

8. Customs Duties.

Each Company Entity has, since December 31, [ ], complied with all Laws relating to customs duties and has fully paid all customs duties that were due.

9. Purchase Commitments.

The future purchase commitments of the Company Entities with respect to the brands identified on Schedule [ ] do not exceed [ ] months of anticipated requirements for the retail stores of the Company Entities in the ordinary course of business (giving effect to anticipated store openings and closings).

10. Inventory.

(i) To the Company's Knowledge, the inventory, wherever located, owned by the Company Entities as of the closing (including, without limitation, all finished goods, work in process, raw materials, parts and all other materials and supplies that could be used or consumed in the production of goods, collectively "Inventory") consists only of items of a quality and quantity usable or saleable in the ordinary course of business of the Company Entities within a reasonable period of time, with excess and obsolete Inventory accounting for no more than [ ] percent of the Company Entities' total Inventory as reflected in the Company's consolidated balance sheet as of closing. The Company Entities have good and marketable title to the Inventory free and clear of all Encumbrances, except Permitted Encumbrances.

(ii) The Inventory does not include any items held on consignment or that are discontinued or subject to product recalls.

(iii) The Company Entities are not under any obligation with respect to accepting items of Inventory or merchandise that are in the possession of its customers other than in the ordinary course of business.

(iv) The Company Entities will have, as of the closing, such quantities and types of Inventory as are reasonably required to conduct the business of the Company after closing, consistent with past practice.

11. Privacy Statements and Policies.

(i) A privacy statement regarding the collection, retention, use and distribution of the personally identifiable information of individuals visiting the websites of the Company Entities is posted and accessible to such individuals on such websites.

(ii) The privacy statements currently in use by the Company Entities are, and all privacy statements used by the Company Entities since December 31, [ ] were at all times when in effect, accurate and consistent in all material respects with the Company Entities' actual practices with respect to the collection, retention, use and disclosure of individual personally identifiable information.

(iii) The Company Entities do not knowingly collect information from children under the age of 13.

12. Data Usage and Security.

(i) All data that has been collected, stored, maintained or otherwise used by the Company Entities has been collected, stored, maintained and used in compliance with all applicable Laws.

(ii) The Company Entities have implemented commercially reasonable practices to ensure the protection of their information technology systems from unauthorized access. Except as set forth on Schedule [ ], to the Company's Knowledge, there has been no breach of security involving such information technology systems.

Chapter 23

Distressed Fashion Businesses, Restructuring, and Bankruptcy

§ 23:1 Introduction
§ 23:2 Preparation for a Bankruptcy Case
§ 23:2.1 Fiduciary Duties
[A] Insolvency and the Standing of Creditors
[B] Determining Solvency
[C] Special Considerations for Private Equity Portfolio Companies
§ 23:2.2 D&O Coverage
§ 23:2.3 Liquidity Needs
[A] Typical Financing Arrangements
[A][1] Asset-Backed Lending (ABL) Financing
[A][2] Term Loan Financing
[A][3] Factoring Arrangements
[B] Cash Collateral
[C] DIP Financing
§ 23:2.4 Venue Considerations
[A] Third-Party Releases
[B] Stub Rent Obligations Under Section 365(d)(3)
[C] Assumption of Intellectual Property Licenses
§ 23:3 Filing a Bankruptcy Case
§ 23:3.1 Automatic Stay
§ 23:3.2 First Day Relief
[A] Employee Wages and Benefits
[B] Insurance
[C] Shippers, Warehousemen, and Goods in Transit
[D] Reclamation and Section 503(b)(9) Claims
§ 23:4 Issues in a Bankruptcy Case
§ 23:4.1 First Day Relief
[A] Property of the Estate

[B] Post-Petition Value Creation
[B][1] Source of Revenue and Prepetition Liens
[B][2] Oversecured Creditors' Right to Postpetition Interest
§ 23:4.2 Treatment of Non-Residential Real Property Leases
[A] Deadline to Assume or Reject
[B] Assumption
[B][1] Cure & Compensation
[B][1][a] Defaults Under Ipso Facto Clauses
[B][1][b] Defaults for Non-Monetary Breaches
[B][2] Adequate Assurance
[C] Assignment
[C][1] Adequate Assurance
[C][2] Non-Assignability of Leases
[C][3] Special Rules for Shopping Center Leases
[C][4] Designation Rights
[D] Rejection and Damages Cap
[E] Rent Obligations and Stub Rent
[F] Special Rules if Debtor Is Landlord
§ 23:4.3 Treatment of Executory Contracts
§ 23:4.4 Intellectual Property
[A] Limitations on Assignment
[A][1] Whether an Intellectual Property License is an Executory Contract
[A][2] Applicable Law Exception
[B] Limitations on Assumption
[C] Special Rules if Debtor Is Licensor
[C][1] Non-Trademark Licensees
[C][2] Trademark Licensees
§ 23:4.5 Treatment of Consignments in Bankruptcy
[A] Consignments Governed by Article 9 of the U.C.C.
[A][1] Definition of Article 9 Consignment
[A][2] Consignor's Right to Obtain Senior Security Interest in Consigned Goods
[A][3] If a Consignor Does Not Obtain a PMSI in Consigned Goods
[B] Consignments Not Governed by Article 9 of the U.C.C.
§ 23:5 Bankruptcy Outcomes
§ 23:5.1 Reorganization or Liquidation Under Chapter 11
§ 23:5.2 Sales Authorized by Section 363
[A] The Basics of a Section 363 Sale
[B] Advantages of a 363 Sale to Buyers and Sellers
[B][1] Going Out of Business Sales
[B][1][a] Compliance with Federal and State Law
[B][1][b] Merchandise Augmentation
[B][1][c] Duration
[B][1][d] Lease Restrictions

§ 23:1 Introduction

The fashion industry thrives on innovation and competition, which inevitably leads to financial successes as well as financial hardships throughout the supply chain. Retail channels continue to evolve as brick-and-mortar establishments face both normal risks of operating a business and evolving consumer shopping behaviors.

An example of a meteoric rise and fall of a trendy fashion line originated by an online tastemaker who achieved personal fame is the boom-and-bust brand "Nasty Gal." Nasty Gal was founded in 2006 by the author of *#GIRLBOSS*,[1] Sophia Amoruso, a then 22-year-old woman whose first business was buying, restyling, and selling vintage clothing on eBay before launching her own website.[2] The company grew rapidly online, with sales leap-frogging to nearly $100 million in just six years before experiencing a steady but fatal decline.[3] Ultimately, in 2016, Nasty Gal filed for bankruptcy protection—with almost 200 employees and two brick-and-mortar locations—and became yet another casualty of rapid growth, overestimated demand, and other pressures typically experienced by fashion companies.[4]

Retailers nationwide have been facing their own pressures from changing tastes and purchasing patterns, driven in large part by competition from online and mobile sales, resulting in a series of high-profile bankruptcy filings among even well-established retailers such as Sears, Payless Shoes, and Sports Authority, with many more brands predicted to fail.[5]

---

1. SOPHIA AMORUSO, #GIRLBOSS (2015).
2. *See* Andrea Chang, *Nasty Gal Clothing Company—As Red-Hot as Its Founder's Lipstick*, L.A. TIMES (Aug. 26, 2012), https://www.latimes.com/style/la-xpm-2012-aug-26-la-fi-nasty-gal-20120826-story.html; Clare O'Connor, *Nasty Gal's Sophia Amoruso Hits Richest Self-Made Women List With $280 Million Fortune*, FORBES (June 1, 2016), https://www.forbes.com/sites/clareoconnor/2016/06/01/nasty-gal-sophia-amoruso-richest-women-net-worth/#807b0e5774b6.
3. *See* Shan Li, *Nasty Gal, Once a Fashion World Darling, Is Now Bankrupt. What Went Wrong?*, L.A. TIMES (Feb. 24, 2017), https://www.latimes.com/business/la-fi-nasty-gal-20170224-story.html.
4. *See* Clare O'Connor, *As Nasty Gal Files Bankruptcy, Founder Sophia Amoruso's Fortune Decimated*, FORBES (Nov. 11, 2016), https://www.forbes.com/sites/clareoconnor/2016/11/11/as-nasty-gal-files-bankruptcy-founder-sophia-amorusos-fortune-decimated/#137ab7506da8; *In re* Nasty Gal, Inc., Declaration of Joe Scirocco in Support of Emergency First Day Motions for Relief, Docket No. 4 (Nov. 10, 2016), http://omnimgt.com/CMSVol2/pub_47154/597869_4-0.pdf.
5. *See* Hayley Peterson, *Retailers Are Filing for Bankruptcy at a Staggering Rate—and these 17 Companies Could Be the Next to Default*, BUS. INSIDER (Feb. 25, 2019), https://www.businessinsider.com/retail-bankruptcies-expected-this-year-2019-2; Lauren Thomas, *Sears, Mattress Firm and More:*

This chapter focuses on the common challenges facing fashion companies in a distressed situation arising from real estate holdings, intellectual property assets, vendor relationships, and asset dispositions.

§ 23:2 Preparation for a Bankruptcy Case

This section summarizes issues commonly encountered by companies evaluating a bankruptcy filing, including fiduciary duties owed to stakeholders, the potential need for expanded director and officer insurance coverage, pre- and post-bankruptcy liquidity, and factors relevant to strategic venue selection. These considerations are informative for both distressed companies as well as customers, vendors, and investors doing business with these companies.

§ 23:2.1 *Fiduciary Duties*

The directors and officers of fashion-industry corporations owe fiduciary duties to their corporations.[6] Directors serve as agents of the corporation and are ultimately responsible for management of the business. They are obligated to remain informed about the business and make major decisions for the corporation regarding significant transactions or the scope of the corporation's operations.[7] Officers of the corporation are subject to the same duties as directors. These principles generally apply to other corporate structures, such as partnerships and limited liability companies.[8]

Here Are the Retailers That Went Bankrupt in 2018, CNBC (Dec. 31, 2018), https://www.cnbc.com/2018/12/31/here-are-the-retailers-including-sears-that-went-bankrupt-in-2018.html; Phil Wahba & John Kell, *These Are the 10 Biggest Retail Bankruptcies of the Last Decade*, FORTUNE (Mar. 2, 2016), http://fortune.com/2016/03/02/biggest-retail-bankruptcies/.

6. *See, e.g.*, Guth v. Loft, Inc., 5 A.2d 503, 510 (Del. 1939) ("Corporate officers and directors are not permitted to use their position of trust and confidence to further their private interests. While technically not trustees, they stand in a fiduciary relation to the corporation and its stockholders.").

7. *See, e.g.*, Smith v. Van Gorkom, 488 A.2d 858, 872 (Del. 1985) (duty of care requires that directors inform themselves "prior to making a business decision, of all material information reasonably available to them").

8. In general, state law provides that fiduciary duties apply by default to other business forms, including partnerships and limited liability companies. *See, e.g.*, DEL. CODE ANN. tit. 6, § 15-404 (providing that partners owe fiduciary duties of care and loyalty to other partners and to the partnership); Auriga Capital Corp. v. Gatz Props., 40 A.3d 839, 849–51 (Del. Ch. 2012) (holding that the Delaware LLC Act "starts with the default that

When a corporation is insolvent, directors and officers may be held accountable by a broader group of stakeholders, including the corporation's creditors. Because insolvency is difficult to determine with precision, directors and officers of corporations facing financial distress must take account of certain special considerations to protect against potential liability.

[A] Insolvency and the Standing of Creditors

The rule in the majority of jurisdictions—including Delaware, the most common jurisdiction of incorporation and the state with the most extensively developed body of corporate law—is that while ordinarily fiduciary duties owed to the corporation are enforceable by shareholders, once a corporation becomes insolvent, fiduciary duties are also enforceable by creditors.[9] The duties owed do not change; rather, the identity of the ultimate beneficiaries for whom the fiduciary duties are exercised expands to include creditors.[10] The rationale is that at the point of insolvency, creditors become the true economic stakeholders of the enterprise and thus should be granted standing to pursue derivative claims (that is, claims belonging to the corporation) based on directors' and officers' breaches of fiduciary duties owed to the corporation.

---

managers of LLCs owe enforceable fiduciary duties"). However, certain states (including Delaware) allow these default rules to be overridden through clear and unambiguous language in the organizational documents that modifies or eliminates the traditional fiduciary duties. *See, e.g.*, DEL. CODE ANN. tit. 6, § 18-1101(c); Miller v. Am. Real Estate Partners, L.P., No. CIV.A.16788, 2001 WL 1045643 (Del. Ch. Sept. 6, 2001) (finding that language in a partnership agreement failed to clearly preclude the application of default fiduciary duties); Related Westpac LLC v. JER Snowmass LLC, C.A. No. 5001-VCS, 2010 WL 2929708 (Del. Ch. July 23, 2010) (dismissing breach of fiduciary duty claims brought by an operating member of two limited liability companies against another member because the alleged fiduciary duties were inconsistent with the operating agreement).

9. N. Am. Catholic Educ. Programming Found., Inc. v. Gheewalla, 930 A.2d 92, 101 (Del. 2007) ("It is well settled that directors owe fiduciary duties to the corporation. When a corporation is solvent, those duties may be enforced by its shareholders, who have standing to bring derivative actions on behalf of corporations because they are the ultimate beneficiaries of the corporation's growth and increased value. When a corporation is insolvent, however, its creditors take the place of shareholders as the residual beneficiaries of any increase in value.").

10. *Id.* ("When a solvent corporation is navigating in the zone of insolvency, the focus for Delaware directors does not change: directors must continue to discharge their fiduciary duties to the corporation and its shareholders by exercising their business judgment in the best interests of the corporation for the benefit of its shareholder owners.").

In this context, actions and strategies that would not ordinarily raise concerns if undertaken by a solvent company could support a breach of fiduciary duty claim in the context of an insolvent corporation. For example, implementing a new business initiative that has a small chance of generating significant returns for a controlling shareholder and a high risk of failure could incentivize certain creditors to bring a breach of fiduciary duty claim on behalf of the corporation against its officers and directors if the initiative fails. As is often the case, if the initiative fails, the question of when the corporation became insolvent will be answered in hindsight.

[B] Determining Solvency

Determining whether and when a corporation becomes insolvent is a difficult, fact-intensive inquiry. No uniform, clear definition of what constitutes insolvency is shared among the courts. Instead, courts have developed several different analytical approaches to determining solvency. Most commonly, courts apply the "balance sheet test" (a calculation of an entity's assets and liabilities), the "cash flow test" (a calculation of an entity's ability to pay its debts as they become due), or a hybrid of the two tests.[11] Further, in evaluating solvency on an after-the-fact basis, complex valuation disputes frequently arise. For example, the parties to a valuation dispute may disagree as to whether the distressed company's assets should be valued on a going-concern or liquidation basis—a distinction that can dramatically shift valuation to an extent that may resolve the question of balance-sheet insolvency.

The complexity of the solvency inquiry means that directors and officers cannot know whether a court will later determine the corporation to have been insolvent. Furthermore, a bankruptcy filing will involve extensive scrutiny and examination of pre-filing decision-making by the company's creditors, an official committee of unsecured creditors,[12] the bankruptcy court, and other interested parties.

---

11. *See, e.g.*, M. Sheinfeld & J. Pippitt, *Fiduciary Duties of Directors of a Corporation in the Vicinity of Insolvency and After Initiation of a Bankruptcy Case*, 60 BUS. LAW. 79, 90–92 (2004) (describing the different tests for insolvency); 11 U.S.C. § 101(32)(A) (Bankruptcy Code definition of insolvency for corporations as the "financial condition such that the sum of such entity's debts is greater than all of such entity's property, at fair valuation."); *In re* Iridium Operating LLC, 373 B.R. 283, 344 (Bankr. S.D.N.Y. 2007) (noting that the Court of Appeals for the Second Circuit "has adopted a flexible approach to insolvency analysis").

12. *See* 11 U.S.C. § 1102. It is common for a committee of between three and seven unsecured creditors to be formed by the Office of the U.S. Trustee to serve as a "watchdog" over a Chapter 11 debtor in possession. This official committee's professionals are paid out of the bankruptcy estate.

Directors and officers of distressed fashion companies must therefore exercise a high degree of caution in business decisions, and take steps to protect themselves from potential liability.[13]

[C] Special Considerations for Private Equity Portfolio Companies

In the context of a private equity portfolio company in which investment firm professionals serve as directors of a distressed portfolio company, additional considerations must be taken into account. Such professionals may owe fiduciary duties to two distinct sets of constituents: the investment firm's investors and limited partners, and the portfolio company. Conflicts of interest between the two sets of duties like these can arise in many contexts, including in connection with acquisition decisions, executive compensation, management or monitoring fees payable by the portfolio company, and debt or equity financing being provided to the portfolio company by the investment firm sponsor.[14]

§ 23:2.2 *D&O Coverage*

Because the restructuring of a financially distressed retailer entails difficult decisions, extensive scrutiny of pre-restructuring decisions,

---

13. Such steps would include the acquisition of expanded director and officer insurance coverage, observing corporate formalities, keeping detailed records of informed decision-making, ensuring that the board of directors has independent directors and committees to deal with any potentially conflicted transactions, and taking account of the interests of all of the corporation's stakeholders (including creditors) rather than primarily focusing on shareholder interests.
14. These issues arose in Miller v. McCown De Leeuw & Co. (*In re* The Brown Schools), 386 B.R. 37 (Bankr. D. Del. 2008). There, a private equity firm acquired a controlling interest in a portfolio company and also, through an affiliate, entered into a financial and advisory agreement with the company through which the firm was entitled to receive up to $800,000 in annual fees. Despite a substantial existing debt load, the company borrowed additional money from an affiliate of the private equity firm and another lender, and ultimately field for bankruptcy. The bankruptcy trustee filed suit against the private equity firm and its appointed directors on the portfolio company's board, alleging among other things that the firm engaged in self-dealing and breached its fiduciary duties of good faith and loyalty by wrongfully prolonging the company's existence so that the private equity firm could profit, and engaged in corporate waste by accepting management fees from the company. The bankruptcy court denied a motion to dismiss, finding that because the private equity defendants stood on both sides of transactions to the detriment of the portfolio company's creditors, the burden shifted to the private equity defendants to prove that the transactions were entirely fair.

and substantial risks of litigation, it is essential to ensure (and ideally such matters are addressed far earlier in a company's existence) that steps are taken to appropriately protect directors and officers from liability both throughout and after the restructuring process. Such protection is necessary to allow management to focus on implementing restructuring plans without distraction, and to facilitate the retention of critical personnel throughout the process. Accordingly, a review of existing director and officer insurance policies should be undertaken early in the process to account for the potential impact of a restructuring and, if necessary and feasible, to obtain supplemental coverage addressing any potential gaps or previously unanticipated contingencies. While the specific requirements of any particular fashion company depend on its financial circumstances and the nature of contemplated restructuring options, certain best practices are generally applicable.

First, the scope of coverage should be evaluated. While typical director and officer ("D&O") insurance policies cover claims made while the policies are in place—that is, before the policies have expired—the purchase of additional "tail coverage" can extend coverage for claims based on pre-expiration events that may not be asserted until after the policy expiration date. Also known as "runoff coverage," tail coverage extends the noticing period for claims under a policy and allows management to preserve its ability to notice claims under a policy after that policy's coverage period has expired. Such supplemental coverage is particularly important in the context of bankruptcy, where an official creditor committee and other interested parties will often undertake a detailed investigation of the pre-bankruptcy conduct of directors and officers.

Another frequent consideration in evaluating existing D&O coverage in connection with a restructuring is the language of any "change in control" provisions in the policies. Such provisions are intended to protect the insurer against a change in the insured risk resulting from significant changes to the management structure of the enterprise. In general, a "change in control" occurs under a D&O policy when a person, entity, or group of persons or entities acquires 50% or more of the voting power to select a majority of the board of directors of the insured company. A change-of-control provision can be triggered in a wide range of scenarios through an in- or out-of-court restructuring. For example, a Chapter 11 plan of reorganization frequently involves a change of company ownership when company-creditors' holdings are converted to equity stakes in the reorganized entity on the effective date of a confirmed plan. A sale of substantially all of a debtor's assets under section 363 of the Bankruptcy Code also may trigger a change-in-control provision as assets of the debtor are transferred to a purchaser or remain in place as part of a liquidation trust. In any restructuring scenario, management should consult restructuring experts and confer with existing and potential replacement insurance providers to ensure that restructuring alternatives do not give rise to unexpected gaps in coverage.

§ 23:2.3 *Liquidity Needs*

[A] Typical Financing Arrangements

As discussed in chapter 1, substantial fashion companies typically finance their operations through asset-based financing, term financing, or a combination of both. Asset-based lending financing is financing secured by a first lien on the company's current assets including inventory and accounts receivable, where loan draws are often made available based on a "revolving" line of credit under a borrowing-base formula tied to inventory and accounts receivable. Term loan financing is financing secured by a first lien on the company's fixed assets, including any real estate and intellectual property rights; or a combination thereof.

[A][1] Asset-Backed Lending (ABL) Financing

In a typical asset-based financing arrangement, the amount of loans available for the borrower at a given point in time is closely tied to the borrower's revolving or non-fixed assets.[15] The borrowing capacity under an asset-based facility is a function of the "borrowing base" of the borrower. The borrowing base is calculated based on the total value of certain types of the borrower's assets (most commonly, inventory and accounts receivable) deemed eligible pursuant to the credit agreement.[16] For each type of asset, the lender agrees to a specific advance rate—that is, it specifies the percentage of the value of

---

15. Asset-backed financing is typically provided on a revolving basis, where the borrower is free to repay and reborrow loans from time to time, provided that certain conditions precedent (typically including an officer certification that no default has occurred and a re-verification, or "bring-down," of representations and warranties made at closing) are satisfied. This contrasts to term financing, discussed in *infra* section 23:2.3[A][2], where a fixed loan amount is provided to the borrower and, once amounts thereunder have been repaid, they cannot be re-borrowed under the terms of the credit agreement.

16. Asset-based loan credit agreements typically define eligible assets through a broad defined term with a specific list of exceptions (that is, ineligible assets). For example, the definition of "eligible receivables" may exclude all receivables that remain outstanding ninety (90) or more days past their due date.

eligible borrowing base assets against which it is willing to lend. The amount available for borrowing is determined by applying advance rates to the total borrowing base value of each type of asset.

Many fashion companies' inventories fluctuate significantly on a seasonal basis, with most companies holding peak inventory shortly before and through the year-end holiday season, with a substantial decline shortly thereafter. Correspondingly, availability under an asset-backed loan facility will decline at the same time that the borrower's need to finance inventory accumulation decreases. In the context of a healthy company, this results in a cyclical draw down and partial repayment of loans under the asset-backed loan facility. However, in the context of a distressed business considering a bankruptcy filing in the near-term, an imminent reduction in the borrowing base may precipitate a liquidity crisis. For this reason, borrowers on the verge of an imminent bankruptcy filing may choose to draw down all available loans under a revolving asset-based loan facility immediately before an upcoming recalculation of the borrowing base.[17] ABL lenders hold substantial leverage over distressed fashion companies and may take steps to protect themselves, such as by seeking a reduction in the maximum facility borrowing amount, reducing advance rates, or requiring the borrower to pursue a sale of some or all of its assets to pay down outstanding principal.

[A][2] Term Loan Financing

In addition to revolving credit facilities, retail companies typically rely on term loan financing in the form of a secured term loan. Where, as is common in retail capital structures, the borrower has both a term loan facility and an asset-backed revolving loan credit facility, the credit documents typically provide for a "collateral split" that divides current assets—such as inventory and accounts receivable—into one pool and fixed assets—including property, plant, and equipment and intellectual property assets—into another. The obligations under the asset-backed revolving credit facility are secured by a first-priority lien on current assets and a second-priority lien on

17. This technique is also common in the oil and gas industry, where borrowing base calculations may be less frequent and assets may be subject to more dramatic fluctuations in value. *See, e.g.*, Max Frumes, *Draw First, Ask Questions Later: Why Oil and Gas Companies Are Fully Tapping Their Revolvers Before Restructuring*, FORBES (Feb. 16, 2016), https://www.forbes.com/sites/maxfrumes/2016/02/16/draw-first-ask-questions-later-why-oil-and-gas-companies-are-fully-tapping-their-revolvers-before-restructuring/#c8f4bdd697b6.

fixed assets, while the reverse is true for the obligations under the term loans. The relative rights of lenders under the two facilities, including the rights of each lender in the event of a bankruptcy filing, are typically set forth in an intercreditor agreement. Understanding intercreditor rights is critical to assessing options for an in- or out-of-court capital structure solution to financing issues, including addressing near-term maturities.

For fashion businesses, the company brand is typically a crucial asset and may constitute a substantial portion of the enterprise's value. Accordingly, it is essential to fully understand how intellectual property rights relating to the brand interact with any restrictions set forth in the retailer's credit documents. Financing documents may have a substantial degree of flexibility in allowing the use of a portion of the intellectual property to support a refinancing of existing debt.

Such a strategy was the focal point of high-profile litigation between J. Crew and the lenders under its secured term loan facility.[18] The obligations under the term loan facility were secured by, among other things, the company's intellectual property, including its J. Crew trademarks. In order to address a near-term maturity for debt issued by J. Crew's holding company, the company contributed a substantial portion of its intellectual property to a newly formed unrestricted subsidiary that was not an obligor on the term loan, effectively moving the assets "out of the system" of subsidiaries holding term loan collateral. J. Crew argued that this maneuver was permitted under the investment and affiliate-transactions covenants of the credit agreement. Shortly after the transfer, the company commenced a declaratory-judgment action seeking a declaration that the transaction was permitted under the applicable term loan credit agreement covenants. The litigation was resolved when a consent solicitation undertaken by J. Crew was approved by over 80% of term loan lenders that amended their credit agreement on terms favorable to the company.[19]

---

18. A similar exchange undertaken by Claire's Stores, Inc. appears to constitute the first prominent example of the strategy of transferring a portion of intellectual property to an unrestricted subsidiary to support a refinancing or exchange of existing debt. Press Release, Claire's Stores, Inc., Claire's Stores, Inc. Announces Offer to Exchange (Aug. 12, 2016), http://www.clairestores.com/static-files/bb467caa-e6af-402c-89a5-0888e9d3dffd.

19. A group of "holdout" lenders led by Eaton Vance and Highland have continued to litigate the original causes of action in New York state court; while the trial court dismissed the lenders' complaint in April 2018, an appeal of the dismissal remains pending.

[A][3] *Factoring Arrangements*

Factoring arrangements are another significant source of financing for fashion businesses. Factoring typically involves three parties: a factor, which purchases accounts receivable and performs other services related to the accounts, the party that seeks to convert its accounts receivable into working capital, and customers (also known as account debtors), whose purchases of goods and services generate the accounts receivable. In exchange for a factoring commission, current accounts receivable owed by customers are sold to the factor. Depending on the terms of a particular arrangement, the factor may make cash advances before its purchase of the accounts.

While, on the surface, factoring arrangements may appear to constitute a sale of receivables to the factor, in the context of a bankruptcy, a court may recharacterize this arrangement as a secured loan, or a "disguised financing" rather than a "true sale." Bankruptcy courts often focus on whether the risk of loss has been transferred to the factor to determine whether the arrangement is a true sale or disguised financing. If the factoring arrangement is characterized as a financing, rather than having the factor continue to collect the transferred accounts upon the bankruptcy of the transferor retailer, the factor is instead placed in the position of a prepetition lender with a security interest in the ostensibly transferred accounts and their proceeds, which are deemed property of the bankrupt's estate. Such proceeds would constitute cash collateral in bankruptcy that the debtor can use to fund its cash needs, subject to court approval and adequate protection of the transferee/lender's interest in the accounts.[20]

Where a distressed fashion businesses face a liquidity crisis as a result of suppliers contracting trade terms, such crises may be exacerbated when factoring arrangements are jeopardized by a sudden restriction in trade terms. This was the case in the Chapter 11 bankruptcy case of Rue21, a national retailer of youth fashion accessories. Rue21's Chapter 11 filing was triggered in substantial part by a contraction in trade terms from its suppliers, including a substantial factoring community that Rue21 vendors relied on for their own

20. *See, e.g.*, Dryden Advisory Grp., LLC v. Beneficial Mut. Sav. Bank (*In re* Dryden Advisory Grp., LLC), 534 B.R. 612 (Bankr. M.D. Pa. 2015) (sustaining a factor's objection to the debtor's use of cash collateral to the extent that cash consisted of proceeds of accounts receivable that the debtor had factored prepetition; the court rejected the debtor's argument that the factoring arrangement should be recharacterized as a secured financing agreement, such that the accounts passed from the debtor prepetition and were not deemed to be property of the debtor's estate).

liquidity.[21] The company's plan of reorganization involved a debt-for-equity conversion, and general unsecured creditors (including factoring claimants) received a limited recovery primarily consisting of 4% of equity in the reorganized company. The Chapter 11 plan included a coercive provision to encourage factors to provide go-forward financing despite their significant losses; specifically, any factoring party that "cease[d] to provide financing support to the Debtors' vendors . . . on terms substantially similar to those provided by such . . . factoring party" within the year prior to the petition date would immediately lose the benefit of certain release and injunction provisions provided by the Chapter 11 plan.[22] The *Rue21* case and case law recognizing factoring arrangements as "disguised financings" illustrate that while factors may appear to have leverage over a distressed retail factoring counterparty, bankruptcy provides debtors with certain tools to reduce or eliminate any such leverage and coerce factors into continuing to provide liquidity during or after the bankruptcy case.

[B] Cash Collateral

The filing of a petition for relief under Chapter 11 of the Bankruptcy Code creates an estate consisting of all property owned by the debtor as of the petition date, including any cash.[23] To the extent that the debtor's cash (including cash proceeds of its assets) is encumbered by liens held by its prepetition secured creditors, the debtor's ability to use such cash to fund its operations during the bankruptcy case will require either the secured creditors' consent or a court order authorizing the use of cash collateral on a nonconsensual basis.[24] Given the immediate need for liquidity at the outset of a Chapter 11 case, debtors commonly file an emergency motion seeking authorization to use cash collateral contemporaneously with the petition.[25] In considering a cash collateral motion, the court seeks to balance the competing

---

21. *See* Daphne Howland, *Teen Apparel Retailer Rue21 Files for Chapter 11 Bankruptcy*, RETAIL DIVE (May 16, 2017), https://www.retaildive.com/news/teen-apparel-retailer-rue21-files-for-chapter-11-bankruptcy/442800/.
22. *In re* Rue21, Inc., Debtors' Joint Plan of Reorganization Pursuant to Chapter 11 of the Bankruptcy Code, Dkt. No. 316 at 45.
23. 11 U.S.C. § 541.
24. The Bankruptcy Code defines cash collateral to include "cash, negotiable instruments, documents of title, securities, deposit accounts or other cash equivalents" subject to a creditor's liens. 11 U.S.C. § 363(a).
25. In order to balance a debtor's immediate need for cash with the requirement of providing interested parties (including the secured creditor and any creditors committees) with notice and an opportunity to object, bankruptcy courts frequently consider an interim request at the initial hearing, which provides sufficient access to cash collateral to bridge the debtor to the date of a final hearing on the motion.

goals of ensuring fair treatment of secured creditors and other parties in interest with affording the debtor an opportunity to reorganize.

In order to use a secured creditor's cash collateral, the debtor must demonstrate that the secured creditor's interest in that collateral is adequately protected against a decline, or diminution, in value.[26] The concept of adequate protection provides a means for the debtor to access much-needed liquidity while protecting the prepetition secured creditor's interest in cash collateral through the provision of an alternative means.

Critically, the secured creditor is only entitled to adequate protection to the extent of any diminution in its interest in collateral. The extent of any such diminution depends on the court's determination of the value of the secured creditor's interest in property of the debtor's estate, including but not limited to cash collateral. Adequate protection may be provided in the form of cash payments to the secured creditor (including payment of the creditor's attorneys' fees and expenses), replacement liens (including liens on non-encumbered assets and junior liens on encumbered assets), and other protection that can provide "the indubitable equivalent" of the secured creditor's interest in the property.[27]

[C] DIP Financing

To the extent that existing sources of liquidity (including unencumbered assets and any available cash collateral) are insufficient to fund a debtor's operations through a Chapter 11 case, the debtor will need to obtain debtor in possession (DIP) financing at the outset of the bankruptcy case. Section 364 of the Bankruptcy Code provides a mechanism for a debtor in possession to obtain post-petition financing, subject to court approval. The Bankruptcy Code includes these special protections to encourage prospective DIP lenders to extend credit to a Chapter 11 debtor so that the debtor has a reasonable opportunity to reorganize or prepare for an orderly liquidation.

The Bankruptcy Code allows for four types of DIP financing: (1) unsecured financing supported by a superpriority administrative expense claim that must be paid ahead of all other unsecured claims; (2) financing secured by liens on unencumbered assets; (3) financing secured by junior liens on encumbered assets; and (4) financing secured by senior "priming" liens on encumbered assets. The first three types are "non-priming" forms of DIP financing: they do not involve the creation of a senior or "priming" lien on existing collateral. The fourth type is only available as a last resort when a debtor is

---

26. 11 U.S.C. § 361.
27. *Id.*

unable to obtain any other type of financing. Similar to the use of a lender's cash collateral, a priming DIP may only be approved with either the consent of the prepetition secured lender whose liens are primed, or through court approval if the debtor can demonstrate that the secured lender is adequately protected from a diminution in the value of its collateral resulting from the priming lien.

DIP financing loans are typically negotiated in the weeks leading up to a bankruptcy filing, although in some cases DIP financing is obtained post-petition. DIP financing is frequently (though not always) provided by the debtor's existing secured lenders, who are already familiar with the collateral package and may prefer to extend further credit to the debtor in order to protect their prepetition position and gain influence over the Chapter 11 case. DIP credit agreements typically include highly restrictive negative covenants that, for example, prevent the debtor from incurring further indebtedness, paying dividends to shareholders, or making any investments out of the ordinary course of business, in each case with very limited exceptions. Other common covenants include setting deadlines for the debtors to achieve certain "milestones," such as obtaining approval of a disclosure statement or confirmation of a plan of reorganization, and budget covenants requiring the debtor to report its projected cash flows (generally over a thirteen- (13-)week period) and forbidding the debtor from deviating from the projections by more than a certain variance percentage. While in practice it is relatively rare for a DIP lender to call a default and force the debtor into liquidation, these covenants provide the secured lender with substantial leverage over the debtor and enable the lender to influence both the timing of the Chapter 11 case and the debtor's operations.

A motion seeking approval of the DIP financing is usually filed as a "first-day" motion to be heard at the debtor's initial hearing; in most cases, the debtor seeks emergency approval of an interim DIP loan in the amount necessary to bridge the debtor to a final hearing on the DIP motion. This arrangement allows the debtor to obtain necessary financing immediately while preserving the rights of all parties in interest to object to the proposed financing (or to offer alternative financing on better terms).

§ 23:2.4 Venue Considerations

A debtor's choice of forum for its bankruptcy case is a critical pre-filing strategic consideration. While historically the bankruptcy courts of Delaware (Wilmington) and New York (Manhattan) have been the preferred venues for large corporate bankruptcy filings, this trend has declined over time with other venues including bankruptcy courts in Texas and Virginia seeing an increase in corporate filings.

The venue statute governing bankruptcy cases provides that a Chapter 11 case may be commenced in any district "in which the domicile, residence, principal place of business in the United States, or principal assets in the United States" of the filing entity have been located for the 180 days immediately preceding the filing (or for a majority of such period than they were located in any other district during the period).[28] An entity's domicile is generally held to be its state of incorporation. In many cases, more than one venue may satisfy the statutory requirements, affording the debtor a choice of jurisdiction for its bankruptcy case.

While general considerations such as the convenience of the parties and the relative experience and expertise of the bankruptcy courts are taken into account, in many cases a debtor's venue decision is driven by differing precedents applicable in different jurisdictions on issues that may be critical to the debtor's restructuring efforts. Three such issues—the permissibility of nonconsensual third-party releases, the treatment of so-called "stub rent" lease obligations in bankruptcy, and the assumption of intellectual property licenses—are discussed below.

[A] Third-Party Releases

A Chapter 11 plan of reorganization, upon its confirmation, provides the debtor with a discharge of its pre-confirmation debts, subject to certain exceptions.[29] This statutory discharge is available only to the debtor and not to third parties including its directors, officers, or shareholders. In fact, section 524(e) of the Bankruptcy Code specifically provides that the "discharge of a debt of a debtor does not affect the liability of any other entity on, or the property of any other entity for, such debt."[30]

Despite this apparent prohibition, debtors commonly seek and obtain broad releases (including releases of the claims of non-debtor third parties) to affiliated third parties, including officers, directors, lenders, shareholders, non-debtor guarantors, or insurance carriers. These releases are generally provided through provisions included in a debtor's plan of reorganization and implemented through the plan's injunction provision. Such releases are pursued to facilitate a successful reorganization, generally where the third parties would otherwise be able to assert indemnification claims against the estate based on the released claims, or where the releases serve as an inducement for

---

28. 28 U.S.C. § 1408(1). The statute also provides that venue is appropriate in any district "in which there is pending a case under title 11 concerning [the filer's] affiliate, general partner, or partnership." 28 U.S.C. § 1408(2).
29. 11 U.S.C. § 1141(d).
30. 11 U.S.C. § 524(e).

the third parties to provide funding or other essential support for the reorganization. In effect, these third-party releases provide the equivalent of the Bankruptcy Code's discharge to non-debtor entities. Such releases are most controversial when asserted on a "nonconsensual" basis—that is, where a release provision purports to grant releases of claims against non-debtor entities on behalf of certain third parties that have not affirmatively consented to the release.

The debate over the permissibility of this practice and the scope of acceptable third-party releases (including whether and under what circumstances nonconsensual releases are allowed) has divided courts across circuits.[31] The minority of circuits adopting a strict prohibition on nonconsensual third-party releases read section 524(e) as a definitive limitation on section 105(a).[32]

By contrast, the majority of circuits applying a relatively less restrictive view on third-party releases hold that section 524(e) is not an explicit limitation on bankruptcy courts' equitable powers under section 105(a).[33] However, even in these less restrictive circuits, courts

---

31. While section 524(e) of the Bankruptcy Code appears to facially prohibit third-party releases, section 105(a) recognizes bankruptcy courts' broad equitable powers and allows those courts to "issue any order, process, or judgment that is necessary or appropriate to carry out the provisions of [title 11 of the United States Code]," though it does not permit bankruptcy courts "to create substantive rights unavailable under applicable law." 11 U.S.C. § 105(a). Courts' disagreements arise out of differing interpretations of the interplay between sections 105(a) and 524(e) of the Bankruptcy Code.

32. *In re* Pac. Lumber Co., 584 F.3d 229, 253 (5th Cir. 2009); *see also In re* Vitro S.A.B. de C.V., 701 F.3d 1031, 1061 (5th Cir. 2012) (citing *Pac. Lumber* and other cases, and noting that prior rulings in the Fifth Circuit "seem broadly to foreclose non-consensual non-debtor releases and permanent injunctions."); Resorts Int'l, Inc. v. Lowenschuss (*In re* Lowenschuss), 67 F.3d 1394, 1401 (9th Cir. 1995) ("This court has repeatedly held, without exception, that § 524(e) precludes bankruptcy courts from discharging the liabilities of non-debtors."); *In re* Am. Hardwoods, Inc., 885 F.2d 621, 626 (9th Cir. 1989) (holding that section 524(e) of the Bankruptcy Code "limits the court's equitable power under section 105 to order the discharge of the liabilities of nondebtors"); *In re* W. Real Estate Fund, Inc., 922 F.2d 592, 600 (10th Cir. 1990) (discussing section 524(e) and stating that "[o]bviously, it is the debtor, who has invoked and submitted to the bankruptcy process, that is entitled to its protections; Congress did not intend to extend such benefits to third-party bystanders.").

33. Kaine v. Johns-Manville Corp. (*In re* Johns-Manville Corp.), 843 F.2d 636, 640, 649 (2d Cir. 1988) (approving nonconsensual third-party releases of the debtor asbestos manufacturing company's insurers); *In re* Drexel Burnham Lambert Grp., Inc., 960 F.2d 285, 293 (2d Cir. 1992) (approving a release enjoining future actions by securities class action claimants against the debtors' directors and officers); *In re* Continental Airlines,

have scrutinized nonconsensual third-party release provisions and have required specific factual findings and evidence supporting the appropriateness of plan releases.[34]

---

203 F.3d 203, 214–15 (3d Cir. 2000) (declining to rule on the propriety of third-party release, but implying that the releases might have been permissible had the bankruptcy court made specific findings that the releases were fair and necessary to the reorganization); Menard-Sanford v. Mabey (*In re* A.H. Robins Co.), 880 F.2d 694, 701–02 (4th Cir. 1989) (approving a third-party release pursuant to section 105(a) of the Bankruptcy Code); *In re* Dow Corning Corp., 280 F.3d 648 (6th Cir. 2002) (adopting a seven-factor test for approving nonconsensual third-party releases and declining to approve a proposed release); *In re* Airadigm Commc'ns, Inc., 519 F.3d 640, 657 (7th Cir. 2008) (approving a third-party release through an exculpation clause where the third party obtaining the release had contributed approximately $221 million to support the debtor's plan); *In re* Seaside Eng'g & Surveying, Inc., 780 F.3d 1070, 1079 (11th Cir. 2015) (affirming the confirmation of a plan of reorganization, including third-party releases in favor of former principals of the debtor who would act as key employees of the reorganized debtor).

34. *See, e.g.*, *In re* Metromedia Fiber Network, Inc., 416 F.3d 136 (2d Cir. 2005) (holding that the bankruptcy court's findings were insufficient to support the validity of a confirmed plan's nonconsensual third-party release provision but dismissing the appeal as equitably moot); *In re* Washington Mut., Inc., 442 B.R. 314, 349 (Bankr. D. Del. 2011) (declining to approve third-party releases in favor of noncontributing directors and officers and engaging in a separate analysis for each group of separately situated third parties for which releases are proposed). In determining whether to approve nonconsensual third-party releases, courts frequently apply a form of the seven-factor test set forth by the Sixth Circuit in *In re* Dow Corning Corp. Under this test, a court may enjoin a nonconsenting creditor's claims against a non-debtor when the following seven factors are present: "(1) There is an identity of interests between the debtor and the third party, usually an indemnity relationship, such that a suit against the non-debtor is, in essence, a suit against the debtor or will deplete the assets of the estate; (2) The non-debtor has contributed substantial assets to the reorganization; (3) The injunction is essential to reorganization, namely, the reorganization hinges on the debtor being free from indirect suits against parties who would have indemnity or contribution claims against the debtor; (4) The impacted class, or classes, has overwhelmingly voted to accept the plan; (5) The plan provides a mechanism to pay for all, or substantially all, of the class or classes affected by the injunction; (6) The plan provides an opportunity for those claimants who choose not to settle to recover in full and; (7) The bankruptcy court made a record of specific factual findings that support its conclusions." 280 F.3d at 658. *See, e.g.*, Nat'l Heritage Found., Inc. v. Highbourne Found., 760 F.3d 344, 351 (4th Cir. 2014) (denying third-party releases that would enjoin claims against the debtor's directors and officers where only one of the *Dow Corning* factors was satisfied); *In re* Metromedia, 416 F.3d at 143 (citing *Dow Corning* in finding the bankruptcy court's findings insufficient to approve the proposed release).

Thus, where the ability to provide nonconsensual third-party releases is anticipated to be critical to a successful reorganization—for example, where financial support from a sponsor or contributions by incumbent directors and officers during and after the bankruptcy case are necessary—a company will probably consider filing in one of the less restrictive circuits. Even in these circuits, as courts increasingly scrutinize the appropriateness of such releases, it will be essential for a debtor to establish a clear factual record to support proposed releases as part of a plan of reorganization.

[B] Stub Rent Obligations Under Section 365(d)(3)

For the majority of fashion companies that lease all or nearly all of their retail locations, rent payments can constitute a substantial ongoing cost. Reorganization efforts for any retailer will entail a comprehensive review of store locations that will likely encompass the closure of underperforming stores. As a means of preserving limited liquidity, companies may opt to skip one or more rent payments in certain locations in the weeks or months leading up to a bankruptcy filing. A circuit split on the treatment of so-called "stub rent" obligations constitutes another significant strategic consideration for the venue decision. Stub rent is the amount due to a landlord for the period of use and occupancy between the petition date and the first postpetition rent payment date. Under commercial leases, rent is usually paid in advance, most commonly on a monthly basis. When a tenant fails to make a rent payment shortly before a bankruptcy filing, the critical issue is whether the resulting obligation constitutes a priority unsecured claim (which may get paid in full at the end of a case, but is vulnerable to potential administrative insolvency years after a bankruptcy is filed) or a post-petition obligation (which a debtor is required to pay in full as the obligation arises pursuant to section 365(d)(3) of the Bankruptcy Code).[35]

Courts have generally followed one of two approaches in determining the classification of stub rent claims. Generally, courts in the Third, Sixth, Seventh, and Eight Circuits follow the "billing date" approach.[36] Courts in the Second, Fourth, Ninth, and Tenth Circuits

35. 11 U.S.C. § 365(d)(3) ("The trustee shall timely perform all the obligations of the debtor . . . arising from and after the order for relief under any unexpired lease of nonresidential real property, until such lease is assumed or rejected, notwithstanding section 503(b)(1) of this title.").

36. *See In re* Goody's Family Clothing Inc., 610 F.3d 812, 816–17 (3d Cir. 2010) (adopting the billing date approach held applicable to tax claims in *In re* Montgomery Ward Holding Corp., 268 F.3d 205, 209–10 (3d Cir. 2001) to the context of stub rent); *In re* Koenig Sporting Goods, Inc., 203 F.3d 986, 987 (6th Cir. 2000) (adopting the billing date approach based

follow the "proration" approach.[37] Under the billing date approach, whether rent constitutes an obligation under section 365(d)(3) of the Bankruptcy Code depends on the date on which rent becomes due and payable under the lease. If that date is prior to the petition date, then stub rent is deemed an administrative claim that can be paid at the end of a bankruptcy case, rather than an obligation that must be performed currently pursuant to section 365(d)(3). In contrast, the proration approach divides the stub rent obligation into two portions: the debtor is obligated to pay stub rent currently pursuant to section 365(d)(3) for the period between the petition date and the first post-petition rental payment due date, regardless of when the monthly payment giving rise to the stub rent was due.

To the extent that a company has flexibility in the timing of its bankruptcy filing and its choice of venue, filing in a "billing date" jurisdiction can result in substantial savings to the estate by avoiding the necessity of paying outstanding rent obligations as current post-petition expenses.

[C] Assumption of Intellectual Property Licenses

A third issue on which circuit courts are divided is the issue of whether intellectual property licenses can be assumed by the debtor

---

on the language of section 365(d)(3) and terms of the lease indicating that rent was paid in advance on the first day of each month); HA-LO Indus. v. CenterPoint Props. Tr., 342 F.3d 794, 799 (7th Cir. 2003) (citing *Koenig* and adopting the billing date approach); *In re* Burival, 406 B.R. 548, 550–51 (B.A.P. 8th Cir. 2009) (adopting an extreme form of the billing date approach in the context of a semi-annual crop land lease).

37. *See In re* Stone Barn Manhattan LLC, 398 B.R. 359, 361 (Bankr. S.D.N.Y. 2008) (collecting cases following both billing date and proration approach and adopting the proration approach); *In re* NETtel Corp., 289 B.R. 486, 488 (Bankr. D.D.C. 2002) (adopting the proration approach and holding that rent "arises" for purposes of section 365(d)(3) in an accrual sense, meaning during the corresponding period of occupancy, such that rent owed by virtue of section 365(d)(3) must be fixed by prorating monthly rent to the number of days during the period of pendency of the bankruptcy proceeding and date of rejection of the lease); *In re* Treesource Indus., Inc., 363 F.3d 994, 996 (9th Cir. 2004) (implicitly adopting the proration approach by holding that a creditor's claim on the debtor's obligation to remove fixtures, equipment, and improvements from the premises on termination of the lease did not qualify as an administrative expense claim because the obligation arose on the lease's rejection rather than during the post-petition/pre-rejection period); *In re* Furr's Supermarkets, Inc., 283 B.R. 60, 70 (B.A.P. 10th Cir. 2002) (adopting the proration approach and reasoning that it was more consistent with the legislative purpose underlying section 365(d)(3)).

pursuant to section 365 of the Bankruptcy Code. This issue is discussed in detail below in section 23:4.4[B].

§ 23:3 Filing a Bankruptcy Case

§ 23:3.1 *Automatic Stay*

A primary benefit for a company seeking relief under Chapter 11 of the Bankruptcy Code is the commencement of a bankruptcy case provides "breathing room" for the debtor by halting most creditor actions against the debtor. Section 362 of the Bankruptcy Code provides that an automatic stay is immediately triggered by the filing of a bankruptcy petition without the need for a court order.[38] Notably, the stay only applies to entities that file a bankruptcy petition; other entities, such as non-debtor affiliates, officers, and owners are not protected.

The automatic stay prevents an extensive list of collection and enforcement actions by creditors, collection agencies, or governmental entities against the debtor or property of the debtor's estate, which actions are based on prepetition claims or circumstances.[39] Among other things, the stay halts the commencement or continuation of a judicial, administrative, or other action or proceeding against the debtor that was or could have been commenced before the bankruptcy filing; the enforcement of a judgment obtained prepetition against the debtor or its property, any acts to obtain possession of or exercise control over property of the estate, and any act to create, perfect, or enforce against property of the estate.[40] The automatic stay prevents landlords from commencing or continuing eviction proceedings against debtor tenants; the protection of the automatic stay combined with the debtor's ability to assume or reject unexpired commercial leases shift negotiating leverage in favor of the debtor. Similarly, entities are typically barred from terminating contracts on account of prepetition defaults.

Section 362 also includes a long list of exceptions to the automatic stay.[41] Commonly invoked exceptions include actions by parties to securities contracts to close out open positions, actions by taxing authorities in connection with conducting audits, and the right of governmental units to enforce their police and regulatory powers.

---

38. 11 U.S.C. § 362(a) ("[A] petition filed under [the Bankruptcy Code] . . . operates as a stay, applicable to all entities . . . .")
39. The stay does not apply to suits against a debtor that are based entirely on postpetition conduct.
40. 11 U.S.C. § 362(a).
41. 11 U.S.C. § 362(b).

If a creditor wishes to take actions against the debtor that are prohibited by the automatic stay, it must first obtain relief from the stay from the bankruptcy court. A court may grant relief from the stay "for cause" on request of a party in interest, after notice and a hearing. While "cause" is not defined, the statute provides that it includes "the lack of adequate protection of an interest in property of the relevant party in interest.[42] Absent relief, a creditor or interested party who willfully violates the automatic stay may be liable for not only actual damages, including costs and attorneys' fees, but also punitive damages.[43]

§ 23:3.2 *First Day Relief*

When a company commences a bankruptcy case, the new "debtor" subjects itself to immediate supervision by the bankruptcy court. While the company may continue to operate in the ordinary course of business, typically the court's permission is required to facilitate most of its usual business practices. Absent court approval, a debtor may not pay any prepetition claims—including, for instance, employee wages earned prior to the bankruptcy filing, insurance premiums that came due prior to the petition date, and unpaid trade debt from vendors the debtor may rely upon during this critical time. To minimize disruption of the business and provide reassurance to affected constituencies, Chapter 11 debtors usually file a set of so-called "first-day motions" concurrently with, or shortly after, the filing of their bankruptcy petitions.

While the particular first-day motions filed vary from case to case based on a debtor's unique needs, these motions generally establish procedures or obtain court authority to provide for certain post-petition payments of pre-petition claims or provide for other special treatment of certain critical constituencies. These motions are usually heard on an emergency interim basis at the initial hearing in the bankruptcy case, with a final hearing set after a longer notice period.[44] In addition to the common first-day motions described below, other common motions include requests to continue use of a centralized cash management system, where absent court approval a company would be

---

42. 11 U.S.C. § 362(d)(1).
43. 11 U.S.C. § 362(k)(1).
44. These "second-day" hearings are scheduled for after the formation of an official committee of unsecured creditors, in order to ensure that general unsecured creditors' interests are represented. *See* 11 U.S.C. § 1102(a)(1) (requiring the United States Trustee, "as soon as practicable after [the petition date]," to "appoint a committee of creditors holding unsecured claims . . . .").

required to disrupt cash flow by closing bank accounts and opening new ones, and to continue honoring customer and vendor programs to maintain goodwill with customers and vendors.

[A] Employee Wages and Benefits

Employees are often described as the "lifeblood" of fashion and retail companies. Following a bankruptcy filing, a debtor must act quickly to maintain morale and provide assurances to encourage employees to remain with the company and work to preserve its going-concern value while minimizing disruptions to the business. Because employee wages are typically paid in arrears, a debtor lacks authority to pay its employees for prepetition wage and benefit claims absent court authorization. To address this issue, debtors file a first-day motion seeking authority to pay prepetition employee wage and benefit claims (including wages and salaries, business expenses, benefits (including medical, dental, and insurance programs), retirement program expenses, and vacation, sick days, and other paid leave benefits) not to exceed the cap of $12,850 per employee prescribed by the Bankruptcy Code.[45] Because most employees' wage and benefit claims fall under the limits imposed by the statutory cap, and because a plan of reorganization cannot be confirmed without providing for payment in full of these "priority" unsecured claims, allowing immediate payment of these claims is justifiable in furtherance of a successful reorganization.[46]

[B] Insurance

Fashion companies typically maintain a wide range of insurance policies and workers' compensation programs in the ordinary course of their business. Their insurance policies may cover general liability, products liability, excess liability, directors' and officers' liability, fiduciary liability, foreign liability, criminal liability, automobile, personal accident, and many other potential risks. The ability to maintain uninterrupted coverage under insurance policies is essential to risk management and, therefore, to preserving the value of the estate of a company operating in bankruptcy. The maintenance of certain insurance coverage is also frequently required by applicable law as a precondition of operating the business. Accordingly, courts almost

45. 11 U.S.C. § 507(a)(4)–(5). Amounts in excess of the cap are treated as general unsecured claims. The dollar amount of the cap is adjusted every three (3) years to account for inflation based on the Consumer Price Index for All Urban Consumers, published by the Department of Labor. 11 U.S.C. § 104.

46. 11 U.S.C. § 1129(a)(9)(B).

always grant debtors' first-day motion seeking authorization to pay essential insurance premiums as they come due in the ordinary course of business, whether they arise prepetition or postpetition.

[C] Shippers, Warehousemen, and Goods in Transit

Fashion companies have complex supply and distribution chains. The efficient and timely delivery of goods is critical to profitability; inventories turn over frequently and fluctuate as to product mix and overall volume on a seasonal basis. In connection with a Chapter 11 filing, ensuring that existing processes for shipping and distributing goods remain intact with minimal disruption is an essential component of maintaining a retailer's going concern value. Because most suppliers provide goods on an advance, invoiced basis, in a bankruptcy, suppliers could be left with prepetition claims against the estate and, by operation of the automatic stay, be precluded from pursuing recovery of these claims. This risk causes suppliers to become wary of continuing to do business, particularly where news has leaked indicating that a company is considering a bankruptcy filing. In turn, suppliers may restrict trade terms, contract the invoicing period, or require cash up front in exchange for goods. Shipping providers may delay or withhold deliveries. This may precipitate a liquidity crisis and drive the timing of a bankruptcy filing. Delays in product delivery can undermine the ability to execute a business strategy, and damage customer relationships and brand perception. Further, third parties such as shippers and warehousemen in possession of goods may be able to assert possessory liens against the goods under applicable law.

To mitigate these risks and reassure vendors, debtors may file a first-day motion seeking authority to allow payment of their shippers, warehousemen, and other key supply chain vendors. These motions seek to establish a mechanism for the payment of all or a portion of such vendors' prepetition claims, as well as for ongoing payments in the ordinary course of business.[47] In exchange for receiving this relief, vendors often agree to comply with certain procedures set forth in the proposed order. Such procedures typically require vendors to continue to provide services to the debtor on customary trade terms consistent with those provided to the debtor during a given period (for example,

47. In lieu of immediate payment, these motions may also seek to treat vendors' claims as administrative priority claims under section 503(b) of the Bankruptcy Code. Such claims must be repaid in full as a condition of confirming any plan of reorganization and are further discussed in *infra* section 23:3.2[D].

one year) prior to the bankruptcy filing, and to agree to release any possessory liens.

[D] Reclamation and Section 503(b)(9) Claims

In addition to or in lieu of seeking money damages for unpaid bills, vendors providing goods to a fashion company may seek to recover possession of their goods by pursuing a reclamation claim. Once a retailer has commenced a bankruptcy case, reclamation is the exclusive remedy for reclaiming possession of goods from the debtor. While reclamation is historically a remedy available under state common law, section 546(c) of the Bankruptcy Code recognizes the remedy subject to the satisfaction of certain statutory elements that apply in addition to common law requirements.[48] Should a seller fail to establish a valid reclamation claim, it may pursue an administrative expense priority claim under section 503(b)(9) of the Bankruptcy Code for the value of any goods sold to the debtor within twenty (20) days of the bankruptcy filing.[49] Failing that, the seller will be left with a general unsecured claim for the value of the goods sold.

Because fashion retailers typically have a high volume of inventory and relatively quick turnover rate, they may receive a large volume of section 503(b)(9) claims following a bankruptcy filing. This can create significant liquidity concerns for a debtor and may constitute a constraint on the debtor's flexibility in developing a plan of reorganization. Accordingly, in addition to regular pre-bankruptcy diligence, many fashion debtors will file a first-day motion seeking to identify reclamation and section 503(b)(9) claims, and to establish procedures for expeditiously resolving all such claims. These procedures vary from case to case, but generally govern the timing and substance of claims and demands.

---

48. 11 U.S.C. § 546(c).

49. The Bankruptcy Code does not define the term "value," and courts are divided on the appropriate way to determine the value of goods in connection with a section 503(b)(9) claim. A Delaware bankruptcy court has held that the invoiced price for the goods is presumptively the best determinant of value, unless the presumption can be rebutted by evidence of the specific facts and circumstances of the case. *In re* SemCrude, L.P., 416 B.R. 399, 405 (Bankr. D. Del. 2009). By contrast, a Texas bankruptcy court has held that the value of goods should be determined by replacement cost, that is, the value that it would cost the debtor to acquire similar goods. *In re* Pilgrim's Pride Corp., 421 B.R. 231, 242–43 (Bankr. N.D. Tex. 2009). Further, where goods are resold by the debtor, there is a plausible argument that the retail price should determine the value of the goods.

§ 23:4 Issues in a Bankruptcy Case

§ 23:4.1 *First Day Relief*

[A] Property of the Estate

As mentioned previously, when a case is commenced under the Bankruptcy Code, an "estate" of the debtor is automatically created containing virtually all of the debtor's assets.[50] The "property of the estate" is subject to the jurisdiction of the bankruptcy court[51] and is afforded certain protections, including the automatic stay[52] and turnover requirements.[53] The use and sale of estate property is subject to the limitations of section 363 of the Bankruptcy Code.[54] In fashion bankruptcy cases, whether property is included in the estate is of particular importance in regard to the sale of inventory held pursuant to consignment relationships, which is discussed below in section 23:4.5.

Section 541(a) of the Bankruptcy Code provides that the estate is comprised of the following property "wherever located and by whomever held":[55]

---

50. 11 U.S.C. § 541 ("The commencement of a case under section 301, 302, or 303 of this title creates an estate.").
51. 28 U.S.C. § 1334(e)(1) ("The district court in which a case under title 11 is commenced or is pending shall have exclusive jurisdiction . . . of all the property, wherever located, of the debtor as of the commencement of such case, and of property of the estate").
52. The automatic stay applies to "the enforcement, against the debtor or against property of the estate, of a judgment obtained before the commencement of the case," 11 U.S.C. § 362(a)(2), "any act to obtain possession of property of the estate or of property from the estate or to exercise control over property of the estate," 11 U.S.C. § 362(a)(3), and "any act to create, perfect, or enforce any lien against property of the estate." 11 U.S.C. § 362(a)(4).
53. 11 U.S.C. § 542(a) ("Except as provided in subsection (c) or (d) of this section, an entity, other than a custodian, in possession, custody, or control, during the case, of property that the trustee may use, sell, or lease under section 363 of this title, or that the debtor may exempt under section 522 of this title, shall deliver to the trustee, and account for, such property or the value of such property, unless such property is of inconsequential value or benefit to the estate.").
54. 11 U.S.C. § 363(b).
55. 11 U.S.C. § 541(a).

- "all legal or equitable interests of the debtor in property as of the commencement of the case,"[56] including tangible and intangible property and causes of action;[57]
- "any interest in property that the trustee recovers"[58] under certain sections of the Bankruptcy Code, including property recovered on account of avoidable transfers[59] such as the avoidance of a statutory lien on the property of the debtor,[60] a preference,[61] a fraudulent transfer,[62] or a postpetition transfer;[63]
- "any interest in property preserved for the benefit of . . . the estate" under section 551 of the Bankruptcy Code,[64] which provides for the automatic preservation of any avoided transfer;
- "any interest in property . . . ordered transferred to the estate" under section 510(c) of the Bankruptcy Code,[65] which provides for the transfer to the estate of liens securing an equitably subordinated claim;
- "proceeds, products, offspring, rents, or profits of or from property of the estate";[66] and
- "any interest in property that the estate acquires after the commencement of the case."[67]

Section 541(b) sets forth certain interests that are excluded from the property of the estate,[68] including "any interest of the debtor as a lessee under a lease of nonresidential real property that has terminated at the expiration of the stated term of such lease before the

---

56. 11 U.S.C. § 541(a)(1).
57. United States v. Whiting Pools, Inc., 462 U.S. 198, 205, n.9 (1983). *See also* 4 NORTON BANKR. L. & PRAC. 3d, § 61:4. Legal or Equitable Interest Generally (Code § 541(a)(1)) ("Code § 541(a)(1) includes every conceivable interest of the debtor in the estate; all forms of property whether tangible or intangible, personal or real, contingent or fixed, causes of action, leasehold interests, or possessory interests are encompassed.").
58. 11 U.S.C. § 541(a)(3).
59. 11 U.S.C. § 550.
60. 11 U.S.C. § 545.
61. 11 U.S.C. § 547(b).
62. 11 U.S.C. § 548(a).
63. 11 U.S.C. § 549.
64. 11 U.S.C. § 541(a)(4).
65. *Id.*
66. 11 U.S.C. § 541(a)(6).
67. 11 U.S.C. § 541(a)(7).
68. 11 U.S.C. § 541(b).

commencement of the case."[69] Courts broadly interpret inclusions within property of the estate.[70] The extent of the estate's interest in property is the same as the extent of the debtor's interest in property existing at the time of the bankruptcy filing.[71] While bankruptcy law determines whether an interest is property of the estate, state law creates a debtor's interest in property and defines the nature and extent of such property.[72]

[B] Post-Petition Value Creation

Issues regarding value creation can arise in connection with (1) determining the property to which a secured creditor's lien extends and (2) whether a secured creditor is entitled to postpetition interest.

[B][1] Source of Revenue and Prepetition Liens

As a general rule, in bankruptcy, liens resulting from security agreements entered into prepetition ("prepetition liens") that extend to property acquired by the debtor after the debtor and the creditor entered into the security agreement ("after-acquired property") are invalid as to after-acquired property acquired by the debtor postpetition ("postpetition property").[73] However, an important exception to the general rule is that a secured lender retains its prepetition liens in postpetition property that is the proceeds, products, offspring, profits, or rents of any collateral owned by the debtor prepetition ("prepetition collateral proceeds"), subject to certain exceptions.[74] Therefore, a key question that arises is whether a debtor's cash that is generated postpetition (which is postpetition property) is prepetition collateral proceeds (and therefore subject to a creditor prepetition lien) or was generated from sources other than the secured creditor's collateral.

Courts look to the definition of "proceeds" under state or federal law to determine whether the manner in which the revenue was generated fits the definition of proceeds. Because the definition of proceeds often requires that such proceeds are generated by an act of disposition, courts have found that where revenue was not generated

---

69. 11 U.S.C. § 541(b)(2).
70. United States v. Whiting Pools, Inc., 462 U.S. 198, 204–05 (1983) ("The House and Senate Reports on the Bankruptcy Code indicate that § 541(a)(1)'s scope is broad.").
71. 11 U.S.C. § 541(d).
72. Butner v. United States, 440 U.S. 48, 54–55 (1979).
73. 11 U.S.C. § 552(a) ("Except as provided in subsection (b) of this section, property acquired by the estate or by the debtor after the commencement of the case is not subject to any lien resulting from any security agreement entered into by the debtor before the commencement of the case.").
74. 11 U.S.C. § 552(b).

by a sale of collateral, but rather by the use of collateral or the labor of the debtor, the revenue is not proceeds.[75] In the context of restaurant bankruptcy cases, courts have distinguished between the portions of revenue received by a restaurant in exchange for food inventory and the portion of revenue received in return for services, finding that the former is proceeds of inventory subject to prepetition liens and that the latter is not.[76] At least one court has suggested that retailers such as fashion businesses may be similar to restaurants in the contribution of services to revenue.[77] However, other courts have noted that grocery stores, which may be more akin to a clothing retail store, do not entail the same level of services.[78] In at least one case, a court has

---

75. Fed. Deposit Ins. Corp. v. Hastie (*In re* Hastie), 2 F.3d 1042, 1045–46 (10th Cir. 1993) (looking to the state law definition of "proceeds" and finding that cash dividends were not subject to the creditor's prepetition lien because "proceeds" arise from an "act of disposition" and receipt of cash dividends is not an act of disposition); *In re* Strick Chex Columbus Two, LLC, 542 B.R. 914, 918–20 (Bankr. N.D. Ga. 2015) (looking to the definition of proceeds under federal law to determine that only the portion of revenue received by a restaurant in exchange for food inventory constituted proceeds of that inventory and the portion of revenue received in return for services was not proceeds of inventory); *In re* Cafeteria Operators, L.P., 299 B.R. 400, 409 (Bankr. N.D. Tex. 2003) (looking to the definition of proceeds under state law to determine that only the portion of revenue received by a restaurant in exchange for food inventory constituted proceeds of that inventory and the portion of revenue received in return for services was not proceeds of inventory); *In re* S & J Holding Corp., 42 B.R. 249, 250 (Bankr. S.D. Fla. 1984) (looking to the state law definition of "proceeds" and finding that postpetition revenue from a debtor's video and vending machines were not proceeds of the video game equipment because the cash was not received from the sale of the collateral, but through the use of it); Wolinsky v. Vermont Fed. Bank, FSB (*In re* Vermont Knitting Co.), 111 B.R. 464, 469 (Bankr. D. Vt. 1990) (looking to the state law definition of "proceeds" and finding that a postpetition deposit forfeited by a bidder in a sale of collateral was not proceeds of the debtor's equipment and machinery because the collateral was not "sold, exchanged, collected, or otherwise disposed of").
76. *In re* Strick Chex Columbus Two, LLC, 542 B.R. at 918–20; *In re* Cafeteria Operators, 299 B.R. at 409.
77. *In re* S.F. Drake Hotel Assoc., 131 B.R. 156, 159 (Bankr. N.D. Cal. 1991), *aff'd*, 147 B.R. 538 (N.D. Cal. 1992) ("A hotel operation is unlike a racetrack, restaurant, or retail store, where the primary objective of the customer is to receive a service.").
78. *In re* Cafeteria Operators, 299 B.R. at 407 (distinguishing between a grocery store where "consumers were solely purchasing the food component" and restaurants where "customers are paying some premium to have the food prepared prior to consumption and served to them").

assumed without discussion that the proceeds of clothing inventory are subject to a prepetition lien.[79]

[B][2] Oversecured Creditors' Right to Postpetition Interest

As a general rule, postpetition interest on prepetition debt is not an allowed claim in a bankruptcy case, which can provide a distressed company significant leverage in negotiations with its lenders to avoid bankruptcy.[80] However, an important exception to this rule is that oversecured creditors are entitled to accrue postpetition interest from the date of the filing of the bankruptcy petition until the effective date of a plan of reorganization.[81] Therefore, it is necessary to determine the value of the creditor's collateral in order to determine if the creditor is oversecured and entitled to postpetition interest. However, the Bankruptcy Code does not specify when collateral should be valued nor what standard of valuation should be applied in a Chapter 11 case—only that value should be "determined in light of the purpose of the valuation and of the proposed disposition or use of such property."[82]

Because the value of a secured creditor's collateral can fluctuate over the course of a case (for example, a fashion business may have seasonal variations in the amount of inventory), the date of valuation may be important to determining whether a secured creditor is oversecured or undersecured. Courts have split over whether to use a single valuation date or a more flexible approach.[83] Some courts have adopted a flexible approach under which postpetition interest and fees can begin accruing from the date a creditor's claim becomes

79. *In re* Tom McCormick Enters., Inc., 26 B.R. 437, 440–41 (Bankr. M.D. Tenn. 1983) (recognizing a that a bank claimed a security interest in the proceeds of its collateral deposited to the account, but finding that the bank was precluded by the automatic stay from to unilaterally appropriating such proceeds to partially satisfy its prepetition debt and must either apply for court permission to move against the collateral or await final disposition of the estate).

80. 11 U.S.C. § 502(b)(2).

81. 11 U.S.C. § 506(b). A creditor is considered to be oversecured when the value of its collateral exceeds the amount of the creditor's allowed claim. *See* United States v. Ron Pair Enters., Inc., 489 U.S. 235, 239 (1989).

82. 11 U.S.C. § 506(a)(1).

83. *See In re* SW Hotel Venture, LLC, 460 B.R. 4, 26–31 (Bankr. D. Mass. 2011), *aff'd in part, rev'd in part and remanded sub nom.*, 479 B.R. 210 (B.A.P. 1st Cir. 2012), *vacated*, 748 F.3d 393 (1st Cir. 2014) (describing the disagreement among courts on the issue of what is the appropriate date for determining entitlement to postpetition, preconfirmation interest and charges under § 506(b)).

oversecured and stop accruing when the collateral value is used up.[84] Other courts have adopted a "single-valuation approach" under which collateral is always valued on a specific date (such as the date of the bankruptcy filing[85] or the confirmation date[86]) to determine if the creditor is oversecured.

As noted above, there is no proscribed method for valuing collateral in the Bankruptcy Code, which provides for a case-by-case analysis. In 1997, the U.S. Supreme Court ruled, in the context of a Chapter 13 case (for individuals to discharge debts through a payment plan), that replacement value ("the price a willing buyer in the debtor's trade, business, or situation would pay a willing seller to obtain property of like age and condition"[87]) is the proper standard for the valuation of collateral where the debtor is retaining the collateral in a cram-down situation.[88] The Supreme Court left "to bankruptcy courts, as triers of

---

84. Prudential Ins. Co. of Am. v. SW Boston Hotel Venture, LLC (*In re* SW Boston Hotel Venture, LLC), 748 F.3d 393, 405–08 (1st Cir. 2014); *In re* Heritage Highgate, Inc., 679 F.3d 132, 142 n.7 (3d Cir. 2012) (recognizing that "the appropriate time as of which to value collateral may differ depending on the facts presented"); Fin. Sec. Assurance Inc. v. T-H New Orleans Ltd. P'ship (*In re* T-H New Orleans Ltd. P'ship), 116 F.3d 790, 798 (5th Cir. 1997) ("[F]or purposes of determining whether a creditor is entitled to accrue interest under § 506(b) in the circumstance where the collateral's value is increasing and/or the creditor's allowed claim has been or is being reduced by cash collateral payments, such that at some point in time prior to confirmation of the debtor's plan the creditor may become oversecured, valuation of the collateral and the creditor's claim should be flexible and not limited to a single point in time, such as the petition date or confirmation date."); *In re* Urban Communicators PCS Ltd. P'ship, 379 B.R. 232 (Bankr. S.D.N.Y.), *aff'd in part, rev'd in part on other grounds*, 394 B.R. 325 (S.D.N.Y. 2008).

85. Orix Credit Alliance, Inc. v. Delta Res., Inc. (*In re* Delta Res., Inc.), 54 F.3d 722, 729 (11th Cir. 1995) (per curiam) ("[T]he oversecured creditor's allowed secured claim for postpetition interest is limited to the amount that a creditor was oversecured at the time of filing.").

86. *In re* Addison Props. Ltd. P'ship, 185 B.R. 766, 784 (Bankr. N.D. Ill. 1995) (finding that value is set for the purposes of adequate protection at the date of petition and set for confirmation purposes on the date of the confirmation hearing).

87. Assocs. Commercial Corp. v. Rash, 520 U.S. 953, 959 n.2 (1997). Replacement value is considered to be synonymous with fair market value. *In re* Heritage Highgate, Inc., 679 F.3d 132, 141 (3d Cir. 2012) ("[T]he Rash Court considered its 'use of the term replacement value . . . consistent with . . . the meaning of fair-market value' because both reflect 'the price a willing buyer in the debtor's trade, business, or situation would pay a willing seller to obtain property of like age and condition.'" (quoting *Rash*, 520 U.S. at 959 n.2)).

88. *Rash*, 520 U.S. at 962.

fact, identification of the best way of ascertaining replacement value on the basis of the evidence presented."[89] The Bankruptcy Abuse Prevention and Consumer Protection Act of 2005 (BAPCPA) codified the replacement value approach for the valuation of personal property in individual debtor cases under Chapter 7 or 13.[90] The BAPCPA amendment did not address Chapter 11, although some courts have applied the replacement value approach in Chapter 11 cases where the collateral is retained by the debtor.[91] Where the collateral in question is sold for a fair sale price in a non-collusive, arm's-length transaction, courts have generally found that the actual sale price should be used to determine the value of the collateral.[92]

§ 23:4.2 Treatment of Non-Residential Real Property Leases

Given market shifts away from brick-and-mortar stores and toward online retail, a key issue for many fashion debtors is to identify and close underperforming store locations that are a strain on the debtors' operations. In bankruptcy, a debtor may reject burdensome store

---

89. *Id.* at 965 n.6, 117.

90. Bankruptcy Abuse Prevention and Consumer Protection Act (BAPCPA), Pub. L. No. 109–8, 119 Stat. 23 (Apr. 20, 2005); 11 U.S.C. § 506(a)(2) ("If the debtor is an individual in a case under chapter 7 or 13, such value with respect to personal property securing an allowed claim shall be determined based on the replacement value of such property as of the date of the filing of the petition without deduction for costs of sale or marketing.")

91. *In re* Heritage Highgate, 679 F.3d at 141; *In re* Nat'l Truck Funding LLC, No. 17-51243-KMS, 2018 WL 2670498, at *3 (Bankr. S.D. Miss. June 1, 2018) ("Although *Rash* was decided in the context of chapter 13, its emphasis on 'actual use' of the property as the guide to valuation also applies in chapter 11."); *In re* Lucero, No. 13-14-10406 TA, 2014 WL 2159553, at *4 (Bankr. D.N.M. May 23, 2014); CRE/ADC Venture 2013, LLC v. Rocky Mountain Land Co. (*In re* Rocky Mountain Land Co.), No. 12-21643 HRT, 2014 WL 1338292, at *5 (Bankr. D. Colo. Apr. 3, 2014); *In re* Mayslake Village–Plainfield Campus, Inc., 441 B.R. 309, 320 n.2 (Bankr. N.D. Ill. 2010) ("The same [replacement] value can be used in this matter, even though a Chapter 11 cram down plan is involved.").

92. Ford Motor Credit Co. v. Dobbins, 35 F.3d 860, 870–71 (4th Cir. 1994); *In re* Two S Corp., 875 F.2d 240, 243 (9th Cir. 1989) (finding that "the cases state that the price paid at a commercially reasonable sale is the best evidence of value); *In re* Urban Communicators PCS Ltd. P'ship, 379 B.R. 232 (Bankr. S.D.N.Y.), *aff'd in part, rev'd in part on other grounds*, 394 B.R. 325 (S.D.N.Y. 2008) (finding that, where a sale of collateral has occurred, the sale price is the value of the collateral).

leases,[93] whereby a landlord will have a damage claim against the debtor, which is often significantly capped under the Bankruptcy Code.[94] Alternatively, a debtor may assume store leases and assign such leases to third parties to generate revenue, provided that the debtor cures existing defaults under the lease and the assignee provides adequate assurance of future performance.[95] For profitable store locations, a debtor may assume the leases by curing existing defaults.[96] As discussed below, a debtor must continue to meet its postpetition rent obligations until the debtor has rejected a lease.

As discussed below, a fashion debtor will generally need to decide whether to assume or reject its leases within 210 days from the date the debtor files its bankruptcy petition. A debtor may assume, assume and assign, or reject a lease by filing a motion with the court[97] or as part of a plan of reorganization.[98] The decision to assume, assume and assign, or reject an unexpired lease is generally within the business judgment of the debtor; the business judgment standard only requires that the debtor demonstrate that its decision is in the best interest of the company and courts are generally reluctant to second-guess the debtor's business judgment.[99]

[A] Deadline to Assume or Reject

An important time requirement for fashion debtors is that leases of non-residential real property must be assumed or rejected within 120 days of the filing of the bankruptcy petition.[100] The time period may be extended by an additional ninety (90) days on motion of the debtor or landlord, for a maximum period of 210 days, and may only be

---

93. 11 U.S.C. § 365(a).
94. 11 U.S.C. § 502(b)(6).
95. 11 U.S.C. § 365(a).
96. *Id.*
97. Fed. R. Bankr. P. 6006(a), 9014.
98. 11 U.S.C. § 1123(b)(2).
99. Richmond Leasing Co. v. Capital Bank, N.A., 762 F.2d 1303, 1309 (5th Cir. 1985) ("It is well established that 'the question whether a lease should be rejected . . . is one of business judgment.'"); *see also In re* Orion Pictures Corp., 4 F.3d 1095, 1098 (2d Cir. 1993) ("At heart, a motion to assume should be considered a summary proceeding, intended to efficiently review the trustee's or debtor's decision to adhere to or reject a particular contract in the course of the swift administration of the bankruptcy estate."); Sharon Steel Corp. v. Nat'l Fuel Gas Distribution Corp., 872 F.2d 36, 39 (3d Cir. 1989) (finding the bankruptcy court properly granted a motion to reject the agreement upon finding that the rejection would benefit the estate).
100. 11 U.S.C. § 365(d)(4)(A).

extended further with the consent of the landlord.[101] If leases are not assumed within this time, they are deemed rejected and the debtor must vacate the leased premises.[102]

In deciding whether sufficient cause exists to warrant the ninety- (90-)day extension, courts may consider:

- whether the debtor was paying for the use of the property;
- whether the debtor's continued occupation could damage the lessor beyond the compensation available under the Bankruptcy Code;
- whether the lease is the debtor's primary asset;
- whether the debtor has had sufficient time to formulate a plan of reorganization;
- the complexity of the case facing the debtor;
- the number of leases that the debtor must evaluate; and
- the need for judicial determination of whether a lease exists.[103]

A fashion debtor with a large numbers of leases will generally be able to demonstrate cause exists for the ninety- (90-)day extension. However, the Bankruptcy Code protects landlords from further lease extension without their consent.[104] The 210-day time limit may make it difficult for a fashion debtor to restructure in bankruptcy, particularly because a DIP financing lender may require a debtor to make decisions about its leases as early as 120 to 150 days after the petition date.[105] Given the short timeline, a debtor may spend a significant amount of time prior to the filing of its bankruptcy case analyzing store locations and may choose to file a rejection motion for certain locations as part of its first-day motions.[106]

---

101. 11 U.S.C. § 365(d)(4)(B).
102. 11 U.S.C. § 365(d)(4)(A).
103. *See* S. St. Seaport L.P. v. Burger Boys, Inc., 94 F.3d 755, 761 (2d Cir. 1996).
104. 11 U.S.C. § 365(d)(4)(B)(ii).
105. AM. BANKR. INST., COMMISSION TO STUDY THE REFORM OF CHAPTER 11, at 131–34 (2014), http://commission.abi.org/full-report.
106. *See* TSA WD Holdings, Inc., et al. (f/k/a Sports Authority Holdings, Inc.), Debtors' First Omnibus Motion for Order, Pursuant to Sections 105(a), 365(a), and 554 of the Bankruptcy Code, and Bankruptcy Rule 6004, Authorizing (A) Rejection of Certain Unexpired Leases and Subleases of Non-Residential Real Property *Nunc Pro Tunc* to the Petition Date, and (B) Abandonment of Any Remaining Property Located at Store Locations Covered by Such Leases and Subleases, Docket No. 104, Case No. 16-10527 (filed Mar. 2, 2016).

[B] Assumption

If there has been a default in a non-residential lease, the debtor cannot assume the lease unless the debtor (1) "cures, or provides adequate assurance that the trustee will promptly cure, such default";[107] (2) "compensates, or provides adequate assurance that the trustee will promptly compensate," the other party to the lease, "for any actual pecuniary loss to such party resulting from such default";[108] and (3) "provides adequate assurance of future performance" under the lease.[109]

[B][1] Cure & Compensation

In order to assume a lease, a debtor generally must (1) cure existing defaults,[110] such as paying outstanding rent, tax, operating expense payments, and other sums due under the lease and curing non-monetary defaults; and (2) compensate the landlord for any actual pecuniary loss of the landlord resulting from the default.[111] However, as discussed below, breaches resulting from *ipso facto* clauses are exempted from the cure and compensation requirements, and incurable non-monetary breaches will not prevent assumption if the debtor cures the breach on a go-forward basis.

[B][1][a] Defaults Under Ipso Facto Clauses

The cure and compensation requirements do not apply to a default that is a breach of a provision relating to:

- "the insolvency or financial condition of the debtor at any time before the closing of the case";[112]
- the commencement of the bankruptcy case;[113]
- the appointment of a trustee in bankruptcy or a receiver under state law;[114] or
- the satisfaction of any penalty rate (such as a default rate of interest) or penalty provisions (such as a liquidated damages clause) for failure to perform a non-monetary obligation under the lease.[115]

---

107. 11 U.S.C. § 365(b)(1)(A).
108. 11 U.S.C. § 365(b)(1)(B).
109. 11 U.S.C. § 365(b)(1)(C).
110. 11 U.S.C. § 365(b)(1)(A).
111. 11 U.S.C. § 365(b)(1)(B).
112. 11 U.S.C. § 365(b)(2)(A).
113. 11 U.S.C. § 365(b)(2)(B).
114. 11 U.S.C. § 365(b)(2)(C).
115. 11 U.S.C. § 365(b)(2)(D).

A lease that terminates or is modified upon the above terms are known as *ipso facto* clauses and are generally unenforceable in bankruptcy.[116]

[B][1][b] Defaults for Non-Monetary Breaches

For non-monetary breaches, such as the debtor's failure to obtain insurance, a debtor must cure the breach at or after the time of assumption and must compensate the landlord for any pecuniary losses resulting from the default.[117] Non-monetary breaches incapable of cure are typically exempt from this requirement,[118] such as a prepetition breach of a "going dark" clause.[119] However, a debtor must operate in accordance with these lease provisions on a go-forward basis after assumption.[120]

[B][2] Adequate Assurance

If the debtor is in default on a lease, in order to assume a lease, the debtor must provide adequate assurance of future performance under such lease.[121] No adequate assurance of future performance is required of the debtor if it is not in default under the lease.

The Bankruptcy Code does not define "adequate assurance of future performance" and the assessment of whether such assurance has been provided is determined by the bankruptcy court under the facts and circumstances of each case.[122] Factors courts have used in assessing

---

116. 11 U.S.C. § 365(e)(1).

117. 11 U.S.C. § 365(b)(1)(A) ("[I]f such default arises from a failure to operate in accordance with a nonresidential real property lease, then such default shall be cured by performance at and after the time of assumption in accordance with such lease, and pecuniary losses resulting from such default shall be compensated.").

118. The cure requirement does not apply to a default that is "a breach of a provision relating to the satisfaction of any provision (other than a penalty rate or penalty provision) relating to a default arising from any failure to perform nonmonetary obligations under an unexpired lease of real property, if it is impossible for the trustee to cure such default by performing nonmonetary acts at and after the time of assumption." 11 U.S.C. § 365(b)(1)(A).

119. *In re* Claremont Acquisition Corp., Inc., 113 F.3d 1029 (9th Cir. 1997), held that an earlier version of the statute precluded cure of a "going dark" provision. Congress legislatively overruled *Claremont Acquisition* in enacting the current version of Section 365(b)(1)(A).

120. 11 U.S.C. § 365(b)(1)(A).

121. 11 U.S.C. § 365(b)(1)(C).

122. *In re* Filene's Basement, LLC, No. 11-13511 (KJC), 2014 WL 1713416, at *11 (Bankr. D. Del. Apr. 29, 2014) ("The term 'adequate assurance

whether a debtor has provided adequate assurance of future performance under a lease include:

- whether the debtor's financial data indicates its ability to generate an income stream sufficient to meet its obligations;
- the general economic outlook in the debtor's industry;
- the presence of a guarantee;
- the debtor's payment history;
- the extent and history of defaults;
- the presence of a security deposit;
- evidence of profitability;
- plan that would earmark money exclusively for the landlord; and
- whether the unexpired lease is at, or below, the prevailing rate.[123]

Adequate assurance of future performance does not require absolute certainty of future performance.[124]

[C] Assignment

A debtor may assign a lease if (A) the debtor assumes such lease in accordance with the Bankruptcy Code, which requires cure and compensation; and (B) provides adequate assurance of future performance by the assignee of such lease, which must be provided whether or not there has been a default in the lease.[125]

---

of future performance' is not statutorily defined, but courts have determined that '[w]hether "adequate assurance of future performance" has been provided is determined by the facts and circumstances of each case.'"); *In re* Great Atl. & Pac. Tea Co., 472 B.R. 666, 674 (S.D.N.Y. 2012).

123. *In re* Filene's Basement, 2014 WL 1713416, at *11; *In re* Patriot Place, Ltd., 486 B.R. 773, 801 (Bankr. W.D. Tex. 2013); *In re* Great Atl. & Pac. Tea Co., 472 B.R. at 674–75.

124. *In re* Patriot Place, Ltd., 486 B.R. 773, 801 (Bankr. W.D. Tex. 2013) (courts have held that a debtor need not prove that it will "thrive and make a profit" or provide an "absolute guarantee of performance" to meet the adequate assurance requirement of § 365(b)(1)(C); instead, it must appear that the rent will be paid and other lease obligations will be met by the debtor."); *see also In re* Filene's Basement, LLC, 2014 WL 1713416, at *11; *In re* Great Atl. & Pac. Tea Co., 472 B.R. at 674–75.

125. 11 U.S.C. § 365(f)(2).

[C][1] Adequate Assurance

In order to assign a lease, the debtor must provide adequate assurance of future performance under such lease by the proposed assignee.[126] This requirement provides needed protection to the landlord because the assignment relieves the debtor and the bankruptcy estate from liability for breaches arising after the assignment.[127]

As discussed above, the Bankruptcy Code does not define "adequate assurance of future performance" and the assessment of whether such assurance has been provided is determined by the bankruptcy court under the facts and circumstances of each case.[128] For an assignee, the primary focus of the inquiry centers on the assignee's ability to satisfy the financial obligations imposed by the lease, though non-monetary factors, such as use provisions, may also be considerations.[129]

[C][2] Non-Assignability of Leases

The Bankruptcy Code generally invalidates anti-assignment provisions in leases.[130] Courts sometimes look beyond the literal wording of a contractual provision to invalidate clauses that in reality operate to prohibit assignment.[131] Also, a debtor may not assume or assign an

---

126. 11 U.S.C. § 365(f)(2)(B).

127. 11 U.S.C. § 365(k); Cinicola v. Scharffenberger, 248 F.3d 110, 120 (3d Cir. 2001).

128. *In re* Fleming Cos., 499 F.3d 300, 307 (3d Cir. 2007) ("'Adequate assurance of future performance' are not words of art; the legislative history of the [Bankruptcy] Code shows that they were intended to be given a practical, pragmatic construction. . . . What constitutes 'adequate assurance of future performance' must be determined by consideration of the facts of the proposed assumption."); Cinicola v. Scharffenberger, 248 F.3d 110, n.10, 120 (3d Cir. 2001) ("Section 365(b) requires adequate assurance of future performance of an executory contract when a debtor seeks to assume an executory contract on which it has defaulted. This protection is also required when a debtor seeks to assign an executory contract under § 365(f). Under either section, the definition of the term "should be generally the same.").

129. *In re* Evelyn Byrnes, Inc., 32 B.R. 825, 829 (Bankr. S.D.N.Y. 1983).

130. 11 U.S.C. § 365(f)(1).

131. *See, e.g.*, Antone Corp. v. Haggen Holdings, LLC (*In re* Haggen Holdings, LLC), Bankr. No. 15-11874 (KG), Civ. No. 15-1136 (GMS), 2017 WL 3730527, at *4 (D. Del. Aug. 30, 2017) ("Importantly, § 365(f)(1) is not only concerned with anti-assignment provisions that prohibit assignment. It also addresses any such clause that 'restricts, or conditions,' assignment. . . . [T]he offending provision may not necessarily be one that directly prohibits assignment of a contract, but may be one that indirectly interferes with a debtor's ability to realize the value of its assets. De facto anti-assignment provisions may be found in a variety of forms including lease provisions that limit the permitted use of the leased premises,

unexpired lease of nonresidential real property if the lease has been terminated under applicable nonbankruptcy law prior to the order for relief.[132]

[C][3] Special Rules for Shopping Center Leases

If the lease a debtor seeks to assume or assume and assign is located in a shopping center, the Bankruptcy Code contains additional adequate assurance requirements (more favorable to the landlords) that the debtor or assignee must meet:

- The financial condition of the entity assuming the lease is adequate to ensure its ability to pay rent and fulfill other considerations due under the lease.
- Any percentage rent due under the lease will not substantially decline.
- Assumption or assignment is subject to all the existing provisions in the lease and will not breach any provision, other lease, financing agreement, or master lease relating to the shopping center.
- Assumption or assignment will not disrupt any tenant mix or balance in the shopping center.[133]

The Bankruptcy Code does not define the term "shopping center" and leaves the determination of whether a group of properties is a shopping center to the bankruptcy courts. Factors a court may consider in determining whether a group of properties should be considered a shopping center, include:

- a combination of leases;
- all leases held by a single landlord;
- all tenants engaged in the commercial retail distribution of goods;
- the presence of a common parking area;
- the purposeful development of the premises as a shopping center;
- the existence of a master lease;

---

lease provisions that require payment of some portion of the proceeds or profit realized upon assignment, and cross-default provisions.").

132. 11 U.S.C. § 365(c)(3).
133. 11 U.S.C. § 365(b)(3).

- the existence of fixed hours during which all stores are open;
- the existence of joint advertising;
- contractual interdependence of the tenants as evidenced by restrictive use provisions in their leases;
- the existence of percentage rent provisions in the leases;
- the right of the tenants to terminate their leases if the anchor tenant terminates its lease;
- joint participation by tenants in trash removal and other maintenance;
- the existence of a tenant mix; and
- the contiguity of the stores.[134]

No single factor determines whether a property qualifies as a shopping center, and a bankruptcy court should examine the presence or absence of the relevant factors.[135]

[C][4] Designation Rights

The sale by a debtor of its "designation rights" allows the debtor to quickly realize value from its leases. "Designation rights" are generally defined as "the right to direct the debtors to assume and assign . . . unexpired leases . . . to third parties qualifying under the Bankruptcy Code."[136] One author has written that, "[t]he permissibility of the sale of designation rights is essentially settled law."[137]

A sale of designation rights typically involves a motion for a sale of the right of a third-party lease purchaser, often chosen through an auction process, to acquire an interest in certain leases, to then market the space to prospective tenants, and later, to seek assumption and assignment of the leases. The process can involve three discrete steps: a bidding procedures motion; a sale hearing; and later, an assumption and assignment hearing.[138] The second hearing, after notice to the landlords of the relevant locations, to consider and rule

---

134. *In re* Joshua Slocum Ltd., 922 F.2d 1081, 1087–88 (3d Cir. 1990).

135. *Id.* at 1088 ("Because the bankruptcy court did not adequately consider each of the factors enumerated above its reading of the Act was overly restrictive.").

136. Robert N.H. Christmas, *Designation Rights—A New, Post-BAPCPA World*, 25 AM. BANKR. INST. J. 10 (Feb. 2006).

137. *Id.* at 10. *See also* Concurrent Session: Everything-Must-Go Sale: The Ins and Outs of Retail Bankruptcies, 031116 ABI-CLE 133 (2016) [hereinafter ABI-CLE, Concurrent Session: Everything-Must-Go Sale].

138. ABI-CLE, Concurrent Session: Everything-Must-Go Sale, *supra* note 137.

upon the motion to assume and assign, is an important step in the designation process as it provides protections to landlords by giving the landlord a right to object to the assumption and assignment.[139] The designation buyer will be limited in how much time it has to find a new tenant by the 210-day limit (discussed above).

[D] Rejection and Damages Cap

The rejection of a lease generally constitutes a breach of such lease (rather than an automatic termination of the lease), which breach is deemed to occur immediately before the filing of the bankruptcy petition.[140] A non-debtor landlord under a lease of non-residential real property is entitled to the immediate surrender of the premises,[141] and has a general unsecured claim for money damages usually subject to customary state law defenses such as the landlord's duty to mitigate. The landlord's unsecured claim is also subject to a statutory cap set forth in section 502(b)(6) of Bankruptcy Code, which limits the landlord's damages to:

(1) the greater of (i) one year of rent under the lease or (ii) "15 percent, not to exceed three years, of the remaining term of such lease" calculated from the earlier of (a) the petition date or (b) the date on which the landlord repossessed or the debtor surrendered the leased property; plus

(2) any unpaid rent due under such lease, without acceleration, calculated from the earlier of (a) the petition date or (b) the date on which the landlord repossessed or the debtor surrendered the leased property."[142]

Fundamentally, landlords and tenants should be mindful that this statutory cap only limits what would otherwise be a legitimate damage claim, so first determine if the damage resulting from rejection would exceed the cap. Also, courts have split as to how to interpret the phrase "15 percent, not to exceed three years, of the remaining term of such lease" (the "15% option") in calculating the damages cap. The majority of courts apply the "rent approach" under which the 15% option is calculated as 15% of the remaining rent due under the lease.[143] Other courts apply the "time approach" under which the 15%

139. *In re* Ames Dep't Stores, Inc., 287 B.R. 112 (Bankr. S.D.N.Y. 2002).

140. 11 U.S.C. §§ 365(g)(1), 502(g).

141. 11 U.S.C. § 365(d)(4).

142. 11 U.S.C. § 502(b)(6).

143. *In re* Highland Superstores, Inc., 154 F.3d 573, 577 (6th Cir. 1998); *In re* Andover Togs, Inc., 231 B.R. 521, 545–47 (Bankr. S.D.N.Y. 1999); *In re* Gantos, Inc., 176 B.R. 793, 796 (Bankr. W.D. Mich. 1995).

option is calculated as the amount of rent due for the first 15% of the time remaining under the lease.[144] Under either the rent approach or the time approach, the 15% option cannot exceed three years' rent.

Courts are also divided on how to determine which claims result from the termination of a lease and whether the cap applies to all lease-related damages, only to future rent, or only to claims that directly arise from the termination of the lease.[145]

[E] Rent Obligations and Stub Rent

A debtor must pay rent due under its leases during the pendency of a bankruptcy case until the date the debtor rejects a lease, or continues payment and cures by assumption of a lease. Unpaid obligations that were incurred prepetition are treated as general unsecured claims (unless paid in full if the lease is assumed), which are not paid until distributions are made under the debtor's plan of reorganization and usually are not paid in full. Unpaid obligations incurred postpetition are administrative expenses, which are immediately payable and are entitled to priority over unsecured claims. Courts have split in determining whether to treat rent for the month in which a debtor's bankruptcy petition was filed as an unsecured claim or administrative claim.

In a majority of circuits, including in the Second, Fourth, and Ninth Circuits, courts use an "accrual method" to account for rent obligations.[146] Under the accrual method, prorated rent for the days of the month falling before the petition date is an unsecured claim, and prorated rent for the days of the month occurring after the petition date ("stub rent") is an administrative expense. In other circuits, including in the Third and Eighth Circuits, courts use a "billing method" to determine the treatment of rent obligations.[147] Under the billing method, the court looks to the date of the rent bill and, if the bill for the month came due prepetition, the post-petition obligations for occupancy for that month are treated as administrative expense

---

144. *In re* Filene's Basement, LLC, No. 11-13511 (KJC), 2015 WL 1806347, at *7 (Bankr. D. Del. Apr. 16, 2015); *In re* Iron-Oak Supply Corp., 169 B.R. 414, 420 (Bankr. E.D. Cal. 1994) ("The correct interpretation, however, is that the Congress intended that the phrase 'remaining term' be a measure of time, not rent."); Sunbeam Oster Co. v. Lincoln Liberty Ave., Inc. (*In re* Allegheny Intern., Inc.), 145 B.R. 823, 828 (W.D. Pa. 1992).

145. *See, e.g.*, *In re* Foamex Int'l, Inc., 368 B.R. 383, 391–92 (Bankr. D. Del. 2007) (finding that maintenance and repair damages are not "rent reserved" and accordingly are not subject to the statutory cap).

146. *See In re* Stone Barn Manhattan LLC, 398 B.R. 359, 362–65 (Bankr. S.D.N.Y. 2008).

147. *See In re* Montgomery Ward Holding Corp., 268 F.3d 205, 209–10 (3d Cir. 2001).

claims, which can be paid at the end of the bankruptcy, rather than as current obligations, which shifts the burden of administrative insolvency on to the landlord. When debtors file for bankruptcy after the rent due date, debtors' have argued that section 365(d)(3) does not apply to stub rent because it cannot be paid timely.

As noted above, the treatment of stub rent may influence a debtor's decision as to when and where to file its bankruptcy case. If a debtor files after its rent bills are due, filing in a venue that utilizes the billing method increases the cash available to the debtor because the debtor does not have to pay stub rent currently, which in an accrual-method jurisdiction would be immediately payable.

[F] Special Rules if Debtor Is Landlord

If the debtor is the lessor under an unexpired lease of real property and decides to reject the lease, the non-debtor lessee can elect to either (a) treat the rejection of the lease as a termination of the lease[148] or (b) "retain its rights under such lease (including rights such as those relating to the amount and timing of payment of rent and other amounts payable by the lessee and any right of use, possession, quiet enjoyment, subletting, assignment, or hypothecation)" and thereby remain in possession of the property.[149]

If the non-debtor lessee elects to retain its rights, the debtor is only able to reject its obligation to provide future services to the non-debtor lessee under the lease and the lessee can offset against the rent it owes to the debtor any damages caused by the debtor's non-performance of the lease.[150] If the lease is in a shopping center, the non-debtor lessee's election to retain its rights "does not affect the enforceability under applicable nonbankruptcy law of any provision in the lease pertaining to radius, location, use, exclusivity, or tenant mix or balance."[151]

§ 23:4.3 Treatment of Executory Contracts

Real property leases are a certain type of "executory contract" generally understood to be a contract where the obligations of both parties "are so far unperformed that the failure of either to complete performance would constitute a material breach excusing the performance of the other."[152] Similar to leases, in bankruptcy a debtor may

---

148. 11 U.S.C. § 365(h)(1)(A)(i).
149. 11 U.S.C. § 365(h)(1)(A)(ii).
150. 11 U.S.C. § 365(h)(1)(B).
151. 11 U.S.C. § 365(h)(1)(C).
152. *In re* Interstate Bakeries Corp., 751 F.3d 955, 962 (8th Cir. 2014) (quoting Vern Countryman, *Executory Contracts in Bankruptcy: Part I*, 57 MINN. L. REV. 439, 460 (1973)); *see also In re* Exide Techs., 607 F.3d 957, 962 (3d Cir. 2010); Everex Sys, Inc. v. Cadtrak Corp. (*In re* CFLC, Inc.), 89 F.3d 673, 677 (9th Cir. 1996).

reject burdensome executory contracts,[153] which creates a prepetition damage claim for the counterparty.[154] Alternatively, a debtor may assume executory contracts and assign them to third parties to generate revenue, provided that the debtor cures existing defaults under the executory contract and the assignee provides adequate assurance of future performance.[155] For profitable contracts, a debtor may assume the executory contracts by curing existing defaults.[156] Unlike leases, there is no deadline for rejecting an executory contract. If the debtor elects not to assume, assign, or reject, then the agreement will be unaffected by the bankruptcy filing. It will "ride through" the bankruptcy and be binding on the reorganized debtor.

A debtor may assume, assign, or reject an executory contract by filing a motion with the court[157] or through a provision in a plan of reorganization.[158] The decision to assume, assume and assign, or reject an executory contract is within the reasonable business judgment of the debtor. The reasonable business judgment standard only requires that the debtor demonstrate that its decision is in the best interest of the company, and courts are generally reluctant to second-guess the debtor's business judgment.

§ 23:4.4 *Intellectual Property*

An issue of particular importance in fashion bankruptcies is the treatment of intellectual property, particularly the ability of a debtor to assume and assign any intellectual property licenses to which it is a party. Most forms of intellectual property meet the definition of an "executory contract," so the Bankruptcy Code's framework for performance, assumption, assignment, and rejection apply.

[A] Limitations on Assignment

The general requirements for assignment of an executory contract are described above. This section provides a brief overview of two issues specific to intellectual property licenses: (1) whether an intellectual property license is an executory contract capable of assignment, and (2) whether the assignment of an intellectual property license requires consent under the applicable-law exception.

153. 11 U.S.C. § 365(a).
154. 11 U.S.C. § 502(b)(6).
155. 11 U.S.C. § 365(a).
156. *Id.*
157. *Id.*
158. 11 U.S.C. § 1123(b)(2).

[A][1] Whether an Intellectual Property License is an Executory Contract

Intellectual property licenses are generally considered executory contracts under the Countryman test[159] because both the licensor and licensee have significant ongoing obligations.[160] A licensor's obligations may include:

- refraining from suing the licensee for infringement;
- protecting the licensed intellectual property against infringement by third parties;
- defending claims that the licensed intellectual property infringes a third-party's rights;
- maintaining its rights in the licensed intellectual property;
- not license the intellectual property to third parties (if the license is exclusive); and
- monitoring the quality of goods or services the licensee offers under a licensed trademark.

A licensee's obligations may include:

- marking all products made under the license with the proper statutory patent notice;
- reporting and account for sales of licensed products;
- complying with restrictions on the scope of its use of the licensed intellectual property;
- maintaining confidentiality of licensed trade secrets; and
- maintaining the quality of goods or services offered under a licensed trademark.

However, the Third and Eighth Circuits have held that a perpetual, royalty-free exclusive trademark license agreement is not an executory contract where the parties have substantially performed all material obligations under the purchase agreement, including full payment of the purchase price and transfer of the purchased assets, and a failure by the parties to perform their remaining obligations under the ancillary

159. *See supra* note 152.

160. *In re* CFLC, Inc., 89 F.3d 673, 677 (9th Cir. 1996) (finding a patent license to be executory).

license agreement would not be a material breach of the transaction documents taken as a single, integrated agreement.[161]

[A][2] Applicable Law Exception

Although the Bankruptcy Code generally invalidates anti-assignment provisions in executory contracts,[162] one exception is that a debtor may not "assume or assign" an executory contract (even if the contract does not contain an anti-assignment provision) if (1) "applicable law" excuses the counterparty "from accepting performance from or rendering performance to an entity other than the debtor" and (2) the counterparty does not consent to assumption or assignment.[163] This "applicable law" exception is particularly important to the assignability of intellectual property licenses because most bankruptcy courts have recognized that "applicable law" includes federal common law.[164]

Whether the applicable law exception applies to prohibit assignment without the licensor's consent may depend on (1) whether the rights granted to the licensee are non-exclusive or exclusive, and (2) the type of intellectual property and how applicable federal law distinguishes between assignments and licenses. The following describes the general views regarding different types of intellectual property:

- Non-exclusive patent licenses generally have been found to require consent for assignment under applicable non-bankruptcy law.
- Exclusive patent licenses generally have been found to require consent for assignment because federal patent jurisprudence distinguishes between patent licenses and assignments.[165]
- Non-exclusive copyright licenses generally have been found to require consent for assignment under applicable non-bankruptcy law.
- Exclusive copyright licenses generally have been found to be assignable without consent because the Copyright Act defines an exclusive copyright license as a "transfer of copyright

---

161. *See In re* Interstate Bakeries Corp., 751 F.3d 955, 962–64 (8th Cir. 2014); *In re* Exide Tech., 607 F.3d 957 (3d Cir. 2010).
162. 11 U.S.C. § 365(f)(1).
163. 11 U.S.C. § 365(c)(1).
164. *See* Unarco Indus. Inc. v. Kelley Co., 465 F.2d 1303, 1306 (7th Cir. 1972), *cert. denied*, 410 U.S. 929 (1979).
165. *In re* Hernandez, 285 B.R. 435, 438–40 (Bankr. D. Ariz. 2002).

ownership"[166] and courts have found that the "protections and remedies" of a copyright owner include the right to transfer.[167]

- Trademark licenses generally have been found to require consent for assignment, and courts generally have not distinguished between exclusive and non-exclusive trademark licenses as a trademark owner would have the same concerns regarding the identity of its licensees and the quality of products bearing its trademark in both instances.[168]

[B] Limitations on Assumption

Because the applicable law exception uses the phrase "assume or assign,"[169] there is a split among courts as to whether the provision prohibits both assumption and assignment, or only assignment of executory contracts without the consent of the non-debtor party.

The Third, Fourth, Ninth, and Eleventh Circuits have adopted a "hypothetical test" that prohibits a debtor from assuming an executory contract without counterparty's consent if applicable law excuses the counterparty from accepting performance from or rendering performance to a third party.[170]

The First and Fifth Circuits have adopted an "actual test" that allows assumption without assignment.[171] The actual test looks at whether the non-debtor contract party was compelled to accept performance from or provide service to a third party (not the debtor with

---

166. 17 U.S.C. §§ 101, 201(d)(2).

167. *See, e.g., In re* Golden Books Family Entm't, Inc., 269 B.R. 311, 317 (Bankr. D. Del. 2001); Traicoff v. Digital Media, Inc., 439 F. Supp. 2d 872, 877 (S.D. Ind. 2006); *but see* Gardner v. Nike, Inc., 279 F.3d 774 (9th Cir. 2002) (reaching the opposite conclusion based on legislative history, policy considerations, and statutory construction).

168. *See In re* Trump Entm't Resorts, Inc., 526 B.R. 116, 127 (Bankr. D. Del. 2015).

169. 11 U.S.C. § 365(c)(1).

170. RCI Tech. Corp. v. Sunterra Corp. (*In re* Sunterra Corp.), 361 F.3d 257 (4th Cir. 2004); Cinicola v. Scharffenberger, 248 F.3d 110 (3d Cir. 2001); Perlman v. Catapult Entm't, Inc. (*In re* Catapult Entm't, Inc.), 165 F.3d 747, 750 (9th Cir. 1999); Jamestown v. James Cable Partners, L.P. (*In re* James Cable Partners, L.P.), 27 F.3d 534, 537 (11th Cir. 1994); *In re* W. Elecs., Inc., 852 F.2d 79, 83 (3d Cir. 1988).

171. Bonneville Power Admin. v. Mirant Corp. (*In re* Mirant Corp.), 440 F.3d 238, 249–51 (5th Cir. 2006)) (adopting the actual test in connection with section 365(e) of the Bankruptcy Code); Institut Pasteur v. Cambridge Biotech Corp., 104 F.3d 489, 493 (1st Cir.), *cert. denied*, 521 U.S. 1120 (1997); Summit Inv. & Dev. Corp. v. Leroux, 69 F.3d 608, 612–13 (1st Cir. 1995).

which it originally contracted). The actual test is also followed by certain bankruptcy courts in the Second and Eighth Circuits.

As many circuit courts have not addressed the issue, a district or bankruptcy court may have adopted or indicated a preference for one of the tests or an alternative analysis.[172] In a jurisdiction where the circuit court has not yet adopted any of these approaches, the parties face substantial litigation risk. The actual test is generally more debtor-friendly as it allows a debtor to continue to access valuable intellectual property in running its business, whereas the application of the hypothetical test prevents access to such intellectual property.

[C] Special Rules if Debtor Is Licensor

[C][1] Non-Trademark Licensees

Where the debtor is a licensor under an intellectual property license and decides to reject the license (other than a trademark license), the non-debtor licensee can elect to either (a) treat the license agreement as terminated;[173] or (b) retain its rights under such license to the intellectual property, including a right to enforce any exclusivity provision, "as such rights existed immediately before the case commenced" for the duration of such contract and any extension period under the license.[174]

If the non-debtor licensee elects to retain its rights under the license, the licensee must continue to make royalty payments due under the contract.[175] The debtor must allow the license to exercise its rights under the license,[176] and, on the written request of the licensee, the debtor must provide to the licensee (to the extent provided in the license) any intellectual property (including such embodiment) held by the debtor and not interfere with the rights of the licensee to the intellectual property (including such embodiment) as provided in the

---

172. *See In re* Footstar, Inc., 323 B.R. 566, 570–72 (Bankr. S.D.N.Y. 2005). The *Footstar* analysis was adopted in *In re* Adelphia Commc'ns Corp., 359 B.R. 65, 72 (Bankr. S.D.N.Y. 2007), and in *In re* Aerobox Composite Structures, LLC, 373 B.R. 135, 141–42 (Bankr. N.M. 2007). *See also In re* Kazi Foods of Mich., Inc., 473 B.R. 887 (Bankr. E.D. Mich. 2011) (adopting hypothetical test in addressing undecided issue in the Sixth Circuit).

173. 11 U.S.C. § 365(n)(1)(A).

174. 11 U.S.C. § 365(n)(1)(B).

175. 11 U.S.C. § 365(n)(2)(B).

176. 11 U.S.C. § 365(n)(2)(A).

license contract.[177] The retained license only applies to licensed intellectual property as it exists at the petition date.[178]

Unless and until the debtor rejects the license contract, on the written request of the licensee, the debtor must perform the license, provide to the licensee (to the extent provided in the license) any intellectual property held by the debtor and not interfere with the rights of the licensee as provided in the license contract.[179]

[C][2] Trademark Licensees

Because the Bankruptcy Code's definition of intellectual property does not include trademarks or similar rights,[180] some courts have found that Bankruptcy Code's protections for non-debtor licensees are not available to trademark licensees.[181] In this instance, a non-debtor trademark licensee would not have the option to retain its rights under a license rejected by the debtor and would have only have an unsecured claim for damages. Other courts have held that, while the Bankruptcy Code protections do not expressly apply to trademark licenses, a trademark licensee may still be protected on equitable grounds[182] or under other provisions of the Bankruptcy Code.[183]

---

177. 11 U.S.C. § 365(n)(3).

178. *In re* Lakewood Eng'g & Mfg. Co., 459 B.R. 306, 342–43 (Bankr. N.D. Ill. 2011) (licensee not entitled to any postpetition improvements or updates made by the licensor); Mission Prod. Holdings, Inc. v. Tempnology, LLC (*In re* Tempnology, LLC), No. 16-9016, 2018 WL 387621, at *7 (1st Cir. Jan. 12, 2018) (citing S. Rep. No. 100-505, at 12 (1988) (section 365(n) legislative history) (limiting access to physical embodiments of the licensed intellectual property to embodiments existing on the petition date that are reasonably sufficient to enable the licensee to exploit the underlying intellectual property).

179. 11 U.S.C. § 365(n)(4).

180. 11 U.S.C. § 101(35A) ("The term 'intellectual property' means (A) trade secret; (B) invention, process, design, or plant protected under title 35; (C) patent application; (D) plant variety; (E) work of authorship protected under title 17; or (F) mask work protected under chapter 9 of title 17; to the extent protected by applicable nonbankruptcy law."). A mask work is a series of related images used in the manufacture of semi-conductor chip products.

181. *See, e.g.*, *Tempnology*, 2018 WL 387621, at *9–11; *In re* Old Carco LLC, 406 B.R. 180, 211 (Bankr. S.D.N.Y. 2009); *In re* HQ Glob. Holdings, Inc., 290 B.R. 507, 513 (Bankr. D. Del. 2003); *In re* Centura Software Corp., 281 B.R. 660, 674–75 (Bankr. N.D. Cal. 2002).

182. *In re* Crumbs Bake Shop, Inc. 522 B.R. 766 (Bankr. D.N.J. 2014).

183. Sunbeam Prods., Inc. v. Chicago Am. Mfg., LLC, 686 F.3d 372, 377–78 (7th Cir. 2012) (holding that rejection of a trademark license constitutes a breach of the license agreement and, under applicable law, a licensor's breach does not terminate a licensee's right to use intellectual property).

On May 23, 2019, the U.S. Supreme Court ruled that a debtor-licensor's rejection of a trademark license does not prevent a non-debtor licensee from continuing to operate under the license.[184]

§ 23:4.5 Treatment of Consignments in Bankruptcy

It is not uncommon for some fashion businesses, such as department stores, to obtain some portion of their inventory pursuant to so-called consignment agreements, as opposed to simple sales agreements. If a fashion retailer who is in possession of consigned inventory files for bankruptcy protection, analyzing all potential consignment transactions is necessary to determine which parties will have interests in the consigned inventory in the aftermath of the bankruptcy filing.

[A] Consignments Governed by Article 9 of the U.C.C.

If a transaction is a "consignment" as defined in Uniform Commercial Code (U.C.C.) section 9-102(2), then Article 9 of the U.C.C. governs the security interests in the consigned goods that are the subject of such consignment transaction.

[A][1] Definition of Article 9 Consignment

In order for a transaction to be deemed an Article 9 consignment, each of the following elements of the Article 9 definition of "consignment" must be satisfied:

> "Consignment" means a transaction, regardless of its form, in which a person delivers goods to a merchant for the purpose of sale and:
>
> (A) the merchant:
>
> (i) deals in goods of that kind under a name other than the name of the person making delivery;
>
> (ii) is not an auctioneer; and
>
> (iii) is not generally known by its creditors to be substantially engaged in selling the goods of others;
>
> (B) with respect to each delivery, the aggregate value of the goods is $1,000 or more at the time of delivery;

But see Tempnology, 2018 WL 387621, at *11 (rejecting the Seventh Circuit's application of section 365(g) to trademark licenses).

184. Mission Prod. Holdings v. Tempnology, LLC, No. 17-1657, slip op. (May 23, 2019).

(C) the goods are not consumer goods immediately before delivery; and

(D) the transaction does not create a security interest that secures an obligation.[185]

As a threshold matter, an Article 9 consignment requires the delivery of goods to a merchant.[186] Such goods must be delivered for the primary purpose of selling such goods, as opposed to another purpose, such as storing the goods.[187] The merchant must deal in goods of the same kind that are delivered to the merchant by the consignor and such merchant must not sell such goods under the name of the party making the delivery (that is, consignor).[188] A merchant who sells its goods under its own name, which is typical of most fashion retailers, would satisfy this element of the statutory definition. Additionally, the merchant cannot be an auctioneer, which is often understood to mean that the merchant acts exclusively as an auctioneer.[189]

Moreover, a merchant must not be generally known by its creditors to be substantially engaged in selling the goods of others. First, to establish that a merchant is "generally known by its creditors" to be engaged in the sale of consigned goods requires a showing that a majority of the merchant's creditors are aware of such consignment

---

185. U.C.C. § 9-102(a)(20) (2010).

186. The U.C.C. defines "merchant" as "a person who deals in goods of the kind or otherwise by his occupation holds himself out as having knowledge or skill peculiar to the practices or goods involved in the transaction or to whom such knowledge or skill may be attributed by his employment of an agent or broker or other intermediary who by his occupation holds himself out as having such knowledge or skill." U.C.C. § 2-104(1).

187. *Compare In re* Georgetown Steel Co., 318 B.R. 352, 357–58 (Bankr. D.S.C. 2004) (court found that supplier delivered hot briquetted iron to debtor for the purpose of sale even though debtor incorporated such raw material into its steel products and sold such products to its customers), *with In re* Greenline Equip., Inc., 390 B.R. 576, 581 (Bankr. N.D. Miss. 2008) (court found that farm equipment delivered to merchant primarily for temporary storage was not delivered for sale even if such equipment was incidentally sold).

188. In *In re* G.S. Distribution, Inc., 331 B.R. 552, 561–62 (Bankr. S.D.N.Y. 2005), the court found that a jeweler who dealt exclusively in jewelry of one manufacturer and sold its jewelry under such manufacturer's name did not meet the requirement of selling "under a name other than the name of the person making delivery."

189. *In re* Morgansen's LTD, 302 B.R. 784, 788 (Bankr. E.D.N.Y. 2003) ("It is surely the case that the debtor did not exclusively act as an auctioneer.").

sales.[190] Whether a majority of creditors is aware of the consignment sales is determined based on the number of creditors, not the amount of their claims.[191] Notably, some courts have found that the "general knowledge" requirement is not satisfied as to a specific creditor seeking to invoke the statutory definition if such creditor is shown to have actual knowledge of the consignment arrangement at issue.[192] Second, to establish that a merchant is "substantially engaged" in consignment sales generally requires a showing that at least 20% of the merchant's inventory is held on a consignment basis.[193]

Additionally, an Article 9 consignment requires that the aggregate value of goods that are delivered in each delivery is equal or greater than $1,000. Furthermore, such goods must not be "consumer goods," which are defined in the U.C.C. as "goods that are used or bought for use primarily for personal, family, or household purposes."[194] Inventory for sale in a business are not "consumer goods."[195]

Finally, a secured transaction cannot be the basis for an Article 9 consignment. Put another way, the consigned goods cannot serve as a security interest held by the consignor for the purpose of securing payment by the buyer (that is, debtor) of an underlying obligation.[196] This interpretation of the last element of an Article 9 consignment is

---

190. *See, e.g., In re* Downey Creations, LLC, 414 B.R. 463, 471 (Bankr. S.D. Ind. 2009); *In re* Valley Media, Inc., 279 B.R. 105, 124–25 (Bankr. D. Del. 2002); Rayfield Inv. Co. v. Kreps, 35 So. 3d 63, 66 (Fla. Dist. Ct. App. 4th Dist. 2010).

191. *See In re* Valley Media, 279 B.R. at 126; *In re* Wicaco Mach. Corp., 49 B.R. 340, 344 (E.D. Pa. 1984) (court held that knowledge of consignment relationship by 20% creditors, which represented 63% of claims against debtor, did not satisfy the general knowledge requirement).

192. *See* Fariba v. Dealer Servs. Corp., 178 Cal. App. 4th 156, 169 (Ct. App. 2009) (court held that lender could not take advantage of Article 9 "consignment" definition because it had actual knowledge of merchant's substantial engagement in the sale of consigned goods).

193. *See, e.g., In re* Valley Media, 279 B.R. at 125; *Rayfield*, 35 So. 3d at 66.

194. U.C.C. § 9-102(a)(23).

195. *See, e.g.,* Auto. Fin. Corp. v. Humberto Cornejo, No. D044553, 2005 WL 1349904, at *7 (Cal. Ct. App. June 8, 2005) (holding that "the same property cannot simultaneously be both a consumer good and inventory").

196. *See, e.g., In re* Aaura, Inc., No. 06 B 01853, 2006 WL 2568048, at *3 (Bankr. N.D. Ill. Sept. 1, 2006) (holding that "a situation in which goods are transferred to a 'consignee' while the 'consignor' retains title only to secure payment of an obligation—an arrangement in which the nominal consignment is in effect a security arrangement" fails to satisfy the Article 9 definition of consignment); *In re* Georgetown Steel Co., 318 B.R. 352, 360 (Bankr. D.S.C. 2004) ("Whether an interest 'secures an obligation' has been described as dependent upon whether there is a duty to pay for unsold goods.").

consistent with the U.C.C.'s broad definition of a "security interest," which includes "any interest of a consignor."[197]

The U.C.C. is silent as to which party has the burden of proof with respect to establishing that a particular transaction does—or does not—satisfy the statutory definition of an Article 9 consignment. In practice, courts generally place the burden of proof on the party that seeks to either invoke or avoid the consequences of an Article 9 consignment to its benefit.[198] On the one hand, a debtor seeking to sell consigned inventory not subject to a senior perfected security interest may have the burden of showing that such inventory is the subject of a "consignment" as defined in section 9-102(a)(20). On the other hand, a consignor who failed to obtain a senior perfected security interest (discussed below) in certain goods may have the burden of showing that such goods are not the subject to a "consignment" as defined in section 9-102(a)(20).

[A][2] Consignor's Right to Obtain Senior Security Interest in Consigned Goods

If a transaction meets the criteria of an Article 9 consignment, then the party that is making the delivery of goods (that is, consignor)[199] to the merchant (that is, consignee/debtor)[200] is deemed to have a purchase-money security interest (PMSI) in such goods (that is, consigned goods).[201] However, the senior priority of the consignor's PMSI is not a foregone conclusion. The consignor must take certain steps required by Article 9 to perfect its PMSI and to ensure that its PMSI is senior to all other preexisting perfected security interests.[202]

---

197. U.C.C. § 1-201(b)(35).

198. *See In re* Downey Creations, LLC, 414 B.R. 463, 471 (Bankr. S.D. Ind. 2009) (placing burden of proof on consignor provides some incentive for consignor to file UCC-1 financing statement to protect its interest simply out of an abundance of caution); *In re* G.S. Distribution, Inc., 331 B.R. 552, 561 (Bankr. S.D.N.Y. 2005) (court held that debtor had burden of proving applicability of Article 9 because it was seeking to sell goods at issue); *In re* Valley Media, 279 B.R. at 124 (same).

199. The U.C.C. defines "consignor" as "a person that delivers goods to a consignee in a consignment." U.C.C. § 9-102(a)(21).

200. The U.C.C. defines "consignee" as "a merchant to which goods are delivered in a consignment." U.C.C. § 9-102(a)(19).

201. Section 9-103(d) of Article 9 of the U.C.C. provides: "The security interest of a consignor in goods that are the subject of a consignment is a purchase-money security interest in inventory." U.C.C. § 9-103(d).

202. The Official Comments to section 9-103 of Article 9 of the U.C.C. explain that "the priority of the consignor's interest as against the rights of lien creditors of the consignee, competing secured parties, and purchasers of the goods from the consignee can be determined by reference to the

Specifically, section 9-324(b) requires that a consignor take the following steps to obtain a senior security interest in the consigned inventory at issue:

(1) the purchase-money security interest is perfected when the debtor receives possession of the inventory;

(2) the purchase-money secured party sends an authenticated notification to the holder of the conflicting security interest;

(3) the holder of the conflicting security interest receives the notification within five (5) years before the debtor receives possession of the inventory; and

(4) the notification states that the person sending the notification has or expects to acquire a purchase-money security interest in inventory of the debtor and describes the inventory.[203]

In summary, to take advantage of the benefits of an Article 9 "consignment," a consignor must (1) perfect the PMSI before the consignee (that is, debtor) receives possession of the inventory by filing a UCC-1 financing statement;[204] (2) send an authenticated notice to all holders of conflicting security interests in the debtor's inventory;[205] (3) ensure that all holders of conflicting security interests receive such notice within five (5) years before the consignee (that is, debtor) receives possession of the inventory; and (4) state in such notice that the consignor has or expects to acquire a PMSI in certain inventory that will be in the consignee's (that is, debtor's) possession, and adequately describe such inventory.[206]

If the consignor has fulfilled each of these requirements, then its PMSI in the consigned goods and the proceeds thereof will take priority over all conflicting and prior perfected security interests in such

---

priority rules generally applicable to inventory, such as sections 9-317, 9-320, 9-322, and 9-324 [of the U.C.C.]." U.C.C. § 9-103, cmt. 6.

203. U.C.C. § 9-324(b).

204. Section 9-310(a) of Article 9 of the U.C.C. provides that "a financing statement must be filed to perfect all security interests," and the exceptions to this rule do not apply to consigned goods. U.C.C. § 9-310(a). The Official Comments to this section explain that "Subsection (a) establishes a central Article 9 principle: Filing a financing statement is necessary for perfection of security interests . . . ." U.C.C. § 9-310, cmt. 2.

205. A U.C.C. state search in the consignee's jurisdiction will reveal all conflicting security interest holders. Only lien holders that have filed financing statements covering the same type of inventory that covers the consigned inventory (or inventory in general if no type is specified) require such notice. U.C.C. § 9-324(c).

206. U.C.C. § 9-324(b).

inventory and proceeds.[207] In other words, the PMSI will take priority over all otherwise senior security interests. Typically, these prior perfected security interests include liens held by the consignee's lenders on all of the consignee's assets, including all inventory (that is, blanket liens). Therefore, a consignor has the right to avoid the default rule regarding perfection—first in time, first in right[208]—and gain senior priority for its PMSI notwithstanding prior perfected security interests that would otherwise be senior to subsequently perfected security interests.

[A][3] If a Consignor Does Not Obtain a PMSI in Consigned Goods

It is conceivable, and in practice can be quite common, for a consignor to fail to obtain a senior PMSI in the consigned inventory held by a consignee (that is, debtor). This can happen for any of the following reasons: (1) the consignor failed to perfect its PMSI by not filing a UCC-1 financing statement; (2) the consignor failed to timely perfect its PMSI before the consignee (that is, debtor) received possession of the consigned inventory; (3) the consignor failed to notify the debtor's existing lien holders with liens on inventory of the consignor's PMSI; (4) the consignor failed to timely notify the debtor's existing lien holders before the consignee (that is, debtor) received possession of the consigned inventory; or (5) the consignor failed to provide the requisite information in its notice to the debtor's existing lien holders (for example, notice of a PMSI in inventory as opposed to just a security interest; description of specific consigned inventory). As a result, the consignor may have any of the following: (i) an unperfected PMSI; (ii) a perfected PMSI without senior priority over existing senior liens; or (iii) a senior PMSI with respect to certain, but not all, consigned inventory held by the debtor.[209]

In that case, the default rules regarding perfection and priority in Article 9 of the U.C.C. apply. First, a perfected security interest has priority over an unperfected security interest.[210] Second, a prior

---

207. *Id.*

208. *See* U.C.C. § 9-322(a)(1) ("Conflicting perfected security interests and agricultural liens rank according to priority in time of filing or perfection.").

209. For example, if a consignor fails to fulfill each of the requirements set forth in section 324(b) of Article 9 of the U.C.C. before the debtor receives possession of the first shipment of consigned inventory, but then satisfies these requirements before the debtor receives possession of the second shipment of consigned inventory, then the consignor will have a senior PMSI in the second shipment of consigned inventory even though it does not have a senior PMSI in the first shipment.

210. U.C.C. § 9-322(a)(2).

perfected security interest has priority over a subsequently perfected security interest.[211] Therefore, any prior perfected liens on the debtor's inventory will remain senior to the consignor's unperfected or subsequently perfected PMSI, with respect to all or a portion of the consigned inventory. The fact that the collateral at issue is consigned inventory does not prevent the debtor's creditors from taking or maintaining a security interest in such goods because section 9-319 of the U.C.C. specifically permits the consignee's (that is, debtor's) creditors to take security interests in consigned inventory so long as the consignor does not have a senior perfected PMSI in such consigned inventory.[212]

The Bankruptcy Code provides a debtor in possession with the rights of a hypothetical judicial lien creditor that is perfected with respect to all of the debtor's property as of the petition date.[213] Notably, the debtor's knowledge or the knowledge of any creditor does not affect this right.[214] Section 9-317(a) of the U.C.C. provides that an unperfected security interest is subordinate to the security interest of a lien creditor.[215] As such, pursuant to the state law (that is, applicable U.C.C. provisions adopted in debtor's jurisdiction), the debtor can avoid any liens that are unperfected as of the petition date and would therefore be junior to the debtor's judicial lien. Therefore, if as of the petition date, a consignor failed to obtain a senior PMSI in any or all of the consigned inventory, with respect to such inventory, a debtor can avoid the rights of the consignor in such consigned inventory. In practice, courts have generally applied these provisions to allow a debtor to retain possession and control over consigned inventory that

---

211. U.C.C. § 9-322(a)(1).

212. Section 9-319(a) of Article 9 of the U.C.C. provides: "(a) Except as otherwise provided in subsection (b), for purposes of determining the rights of creditors of, and purchasers for value of goods from, a consignee, while the goods are in the possession of the consignee, the consignee is deemed to have rights and title to the goods identical to those the consignor had or had power to transfer." Subsection (b) of section 9-319 provides: "For purposes of determining the rights of a creditor of a consignee, law other than this article determines the rights and title of a consignee while goods are in the consignee's possession if, under this part, a perfected security interest held by the consignor would have priority over the rights of the creditor."

213. 11 U.S.C. § 544(a)(1).

214. 11 U.S.C. § 544(a).

215. Specifically, section 9-317(a) of Article 9 of the U.C.C. provides, in relevant part: "A security interest . . . is subordinate to the rights of: . . . a person that becomes a lien creditor before the earlier of the time: (A) the security interest . . . is perfected." U.C.C. § 9-317(a).

is not subject to a senior PMSI and to sell such consigned inventory in the debtor's bankruptcy case.[216]

In Sports Authority's bankruptcy case, a consignment dispute became the show-stopper for the sporting goods retail chain. Within just a couple weeks of filing for bankruptcy protection, the retailer had to commence lawsuits against approximately 160 of its consignment vendors, thereby destroying its relationships with these vendors.[217] According to the company, the purpose of these lawsuits was to establish that each of these 160 vendors failed to follow the required procedures, as described above, for retaining a first-priority security interest in the consigned goods (or at least a portion of the goods) that they delivered to Sports Authority pre-bankruptcy.[218] However, the bankruptcy court delayed ruling on this issue, and instead required

---

216. *In re In re* Downey Creations, LLC, 414 B.R. 463, 473 (Bankr. S.D. Ind. 2009) (court held that debtor was entitled to avoid consignor's unperfected security interest in consigned inventory and retain possession of such inventory); *In re* Niblett, 441 B.R. 490, 493 (Bankr. E.D. Va. 2009) (court held that trustee had the right to sell consigned property that was not subject to a perfected security interest); *In re* Valley Media, Inc., 279 B.R. 105, 133 (Bankr. D. Del. 2002) (court held that debtor had priority over consignors' unperfected security interests in inventory and could sell such inventory at auction pursuant to a court-approved sale process). *But see* Order, *In re* TSAWD Holdings, Inc. (f/k/a/ Sports Auth. Holdings, Inc.), No. 16-10527 (MFW) (May 3, 2016) (court disregarded applicable U.C.C. provisions and only permitted debtors to continue to sell consigned inventory pursuant to applicable consignment agreements, subject to disgorgement against consignors if debtors prevailed in pending adversary proceedings against consignors).

217. *See* Peg Brickley, *Sports Authority Plays Hardball in Suits Against Suppliers*, WALL ST. J. (Mar. 16, 2016), https://www.wsj.com/articles/sports-authority-plays-hardball-in-suits-against-suppliers-1458141293.

218. *See In re* TSAWD Holdings, Inc., Debtors' Omnibus Reply in Support of Entry of Final Orders on (I) Debtors' Motion for Interim and Final Orders (A) Authorizing the Debtors to (I) Continue to Sell Consigned Goods in the Ordinary Course of Business Free and Clear of All Liens, Claims and Encumbrances and (II) Grant Administrative Expense Priority to Consignment Vendors for Consigned Goods Delivered Postpetition; and (B) Grant Replacement Liens to Consignment Vendors with Perfected Security Interests in Consigned Goods and/or Remit the Consignment Sale Price Arising from Sale of Consigned Goods to Putative Consignment Vendors; and (II) Debtors' Emergency Motion for Interim and Final Orders (A) Authorizing the Debtors to Assume the Closing Store Agreement, (B) Authorizing and Approving Store Closing Sales Free and Clear of All Liens, Claims and Encumbrances, (C) Authorizing the Implementation of Customary Employee Bonus Program and Payments to Non-Insiders Thereunder, (D) Approving Dispute Resolution Procedures, and (E) Approving the Debtors' Store Closing Plan, Docket No. 991 (Apr. 4, 2016), http://www.kccllc.net/sportsauthority/document/list/4201.

that while these lawsuits were pending, the retailer had to comply with its consignment agreements in order to continue to sell its consigned inventory.[219] Ultimately, the company settled its lawsuits with the vast majority of its consignment vendors in the fall of 2016,[220] but it took almost three years for the bankruptcy court to finally resolve the last of the consignment disputes (against the vendor).[221]

[B] Consignments Not Governed by Article 9 of the U.C.C.

Where a transaction is found to be a "consignment" under section 9-102(a)(20), the rights of the debtor (standing in the shoes of a hypothetical judicial lien creditor), the consignor, and the debtor's secured creditors in consigned inventory are reasonably well defined with reference to Article 9 of the U.C.C. and section 544 of the Bankruptcy Code. But what happens in a retailer's bankruptcy case when the goods at issue are not proven to be the subject to a "consignment" transaction as defined in Article 9 of the U.C.C.? In short, the result is generally no different if the transaction at issue results from a commercial relationship between a retailer and vendor (usually wholesaler) where the vendor delivers goods for resale by the retailer.

As revised in 2001, Article 9 of the U.C.C. is intended to capture all "consignments," including those previously addressed in section 2-326 of the U.C.C.[222] However, a consignment that falls outside the statutory definition set forth in Article 9 is necessarily governed by non-Article 9 law.[223] Fortunately, the options are limited.

---

219. *See In re* TSAWD Holdings, Inc., Final Order Authorizing the Debtors to Sell Prepetition Consigned Goods Docket No. 1704 (May 3, 2016), http://www.kccllc.net/sportsauthority/document/1610527160503000000000024.

220. *See* Matt Chiappardi, *Sports Authority Gets Nod for 'Perfect' Vendor Settlement*, LAW360 (July 7, 2016), https://www.law360.com/articles/814732/sports-authority-gets-nod-for-perfect-vendor-settlement; *In re* TSAWD Holdings, Inc., Order, Pursuant to Bankruptcy Code Section 105(A) and Bankruptcy Rule 9019, Approving the Settlement Agreement By and Among the Debtors, Term Loan Agent, and Certain Consignment Vendors Party Thereto, Docket No. 2434 (July 7, 2016), http://www.kccllc.net/sportsauthority/document/1610527160707000000000049.

221. *See* TSA Stores, Inc. v. Sport Dimension Inc. (*In re* TSAWD, Inc.), No. 16-10527 (MFW), Adv. No. 16-50368 (MFW) (Apr. 12, 2019) (holding that vendor did not obtain priority security interest in consigned goods because it failed to timely file a UCC-1 financing statement and provide notice of its interest).

222. U.C.C. § 2-326, cmt. 4 ("Certain true consignment transactions were dealt with in former Sections 2-326(3) and 9-114. These provisions have been deleted and have been replaced by new provisions in Article 9.").

223. U.C.C. § 9-102, cmt. 14 ("A consignment excluded from the application of this Article by one of those subparagraphs may still be a true consignment; however, it is governed by non-Article 9 law.").

One possibility is the application of the common law of bailments and consignments. A common law consignment is an agency or bailment relationship between the consignor and the consignee.[224] The consignor acts as the principal, while the consignee is merely its agent.[225] As one court explained, a common law (that is, "true") consignment "exists where one party—usually a wholesaler—transfers possession of goods to another—usually a retailer—who in turn resells the goods to third-party consumers."[226] A true consignment is distinguishable from a sale because a consignment relationship has the following hallmarks: title and risk of loss remain in the consignor, the consignor sets the price of the goods and the terms of the sale, and the consignee (that is, debtor) receives only a commission for the goods sold.[227] However, in the context of a fashion retailer—or any retailer—where the retailer rather than its vendors, controls the sale terms of its inventory (including consigned inventory) and pays vendors for the cost of such inventory, such that few, if any, of the hallmarks of a true consignment are present, it is unlikely that a court would find that such a relationship constitutes a common law consignment. This is particularly true given the commercial nature of the consignment relationship between the retailer and its vendors.[228]

The other possibility is the application of section 2-326 of Article 2 of the U.C.C., which governs sales.[229] Section 2-326 distinguishes

---

224. United States v. Nektalov, 440 F. Supp. 2d 287, 298 (S.D.N.Y. 2006), *aff'd sub nom.* E.J.D. Diamond Mfr. v. United States, 273 F. App'x 65 (2d Cir. 2008); Consol. Accessories Corp. v. Franchise Tax Bd., 161 Cal. App. 3d 1036, 1040 (Ct. App. 1984).

225. *Id.*

226. *Nektalov*, 440 F. Supp. 2d at 298.

227. *Id.* at 298–99. *See also* Johnson v. Hallett, No. 14 Civ. 1922 (DAB), 2015 WL 1516661, at *7 (S.D.N.Y. Mar. 31, 2015) (court held that requirement of consignee to consult with consignor regarding price is a hallmark of common law consignment); *Consol. Accessories*, 161 Cal. App. 3d at 1040–41 (court found common law consignment because consignee received 20% of sale price as commission and had no obligation to pay for unsold goods).

228. In *In re* Haley & Steele, Inc., 20 Mass. L. Rptr. 204 (Sup. Ct. Nov. 14, 2005), the court distinguished between "consumer consignors" and "commercial consignors" and noted that commercial consignors should be subject to Article 9 of the U.C.C.

229. *See, e.g., In re* G.S. Distribution, Inc., 331 B.R. 552, 562 (Bankr. S.D.N.Y. 2005) ("Because the consignment arrangement falls outside the definition of consignment in § 9–102(a)(2), the analysis must proceed to § 2–326 of the U.C.C. to determine the respective rights of the Debtor (acting for its general creditors) and [the consignment vendor]."); *In re* Morgansen's LTD, 302 B.R. 784, 787 (Bankr. E.D.N.Y. 2003) ("The standard approach is first to go to section 9–102(a)(20), and if the transaction does not fit under this section, then to go next to section 2–326; if the transaction

between a "sale on approval" and a "sale or return."[230] A "sale on approval" exists if the goods at issue are delivered to the buyer (that is, debtor) primarily for use; a "sale or return" exists if the goods at issue are delivered to the buyer (that is, debtor) primarily for resale.[231] This distinction is significant because goods that are held by the buyer (that is, debtor) on "sale or return" are immediately subject to the claims of the buyer's (that is, debtor's) creditors, while goods that are held on approval are not.[232]

In the context of a fashion retailer, it is expected that vendors deliver goods to the retailer (that is, debtor) primarily for the purpose of resale by the retailer (that is, on "sale or return"). Such goods are subject to the claims of the retailer's (that is, debtor's) creditors, which are governed by Article 9.[233] Therefore, the same Article 9 rules regarding perfection and priority discussed above are applicable. With respect to goods that are held by a buyer (that is, debtor) on "sale or return," a consignor can protect its interests in such goods by perfecting a security interest in such goods pursuant to Article 9 of the U.C.C. In the absence of such a protective measure, the existing senior security interests in inventory held by the retailer's (that is, debtor's) creditors will prevail over the unperfected interests of the consignor; and in bankruptcy, the rights of the retailer (that is, debtor) as a judicial lien creditor, will prevail over the unperfected interests of the consignor.[234]

§ 23:5 Bankruptcy Outcomes

Fashion company bankruptcies will often follow the trend set in the retail industry. This means the company will often choose to liquidate certain assets and shut down some retail locations in order to maximize the company's value. A fashion company will have several options available to it and may choose to either reorganize or liquidate through a Chapter 11 plan, or conduct a sale of its assets as authorized by section 363 of the Bankruptcy Code.

---

does not fit under section 2–236, then the transaction falls entirely outside the Uniform Commercial Code, and the Court must then fall back on the common law of bailments and other traditional practices.").

230. U.C.C. § 2-326(1).
231. *Id.*
232. U.C.C. § 2-326(2).
233. Article 9 governs all secured transactions and therefore all claims of the buyer's (that is, debtor's) creditors. *See* U.C.C. § 9-101.
234. *See In re* Valley Media, Inc., 279 B.R. 105, 132 (Bankr. D. Del. 2002).

§ 23:5.1 Reorganization or Liquidation Under Chapter 11

A fashion company facing financial difficulty may choose to exit bankruptcy pursuant to a reorganization plan or a liquidation plan, or a combination of the two. While a liquidation is expressly contemplated under Chapter 11, the primary purpose of Chapter 11 is to enable the successful reorganization of the debtor on the theory that such reorganization will allow creditors to receive greater value than what they would receive in a liquidation. Furthermore, a reorganized debtor preserves jobs for employees, produces returns, and overall benefits the community. A company executing a liquidation plan, by contrast, ceases to continue after the execution of the plan. Instead, its assets are sold and those proceeds are distributed to creditors in an orderly manner. Whether a company should seek to implement a liquidation plan or reorganization plan depends on a variety of business and legal factors that are specific to that company's objectives and circumstances. In order to facilitate the foregoing, the Bankruptcy Code requires that a Chapter 11 plan must address, at minimum, the following:

1. Designation of classes of similarly situated creditors;
2. Specification and treatment of unimpaired classes (that is, creditors that will be paid in full through implementation of the plan);
3. Specification and treatment of impaired classes (that is, creditors that will not be paid in full through implementation of the plan);
4. Provide similar treatment for each claim and interest within each class;
5. Adequate means of plan implementation;
6. Inclusion of certain equity securities restrictions in the organizational documents of the debtor; and
7. Contain provisions regarding the selection of officers and directors that are consistent with interests of creditors, security holders and public policy.[235]

An important principal of a Chapter 11 reorganization is the "absolute priority rule." This rule is found in section 1129(b)(2)(B) of the Bankruptcy Code and comes into play when a class of similarly situated creditors do not agree with the plan. It requires that either (1) the dissenting creditors be paid in full or (2) creditors holding claims

---

235. 11 U.S.C. § 1123.

or interests that are junior to the dissenting creditors receive nothing under the plan.[236] The ability of a creditor to confirm the plan over dissenting creditors, per section 1129(b)(2)(B)(ii), is called a "cram-down" whereby a plan can be confirmed if it provides fair and equitable treatment to each class of creditors and at least one impaired class of creditors votes to accept the plan.

Another important rule is the "best interests of creditors test." This rule requires that for any given class of claims, each creditor in such class must either (1) accept the plan or (2) receive an amount that such creditor would receive or retain in a hypothetical liquidation.[237] This ensures that creditors receive at least as much in a reorganization plan as they would in a Chapter 7 liquidation.

§ 23:5.2 Sales Authorized by Section 363

Because the traditional practice of reorganization under Chapter 11 is very time consuming and expensive, it has given rise to unique challenges in the fashion industry. It has therefore become increasingly common for bankrupt fashion companies to forego this process. Instead, many fashion companies choose to petition the court to allow a sale of all or substantially all assets, or a going-out-of-business sale (each commonly referred to as a "363 sale" because of its authorization under section 363 of the Bankruptcy Code).[238] The ability to quickly organize a sale of assets in bulk as a going concern is favorable to many fashion debtors because it reduces the cost of administering the debtor's estate, provides an alternative to what can be an expensive and time consuming plan confirmation process, and preserves going-concern value.[239] The primary goal of a 363 sale is to create value for the business "so that it may continue to operate, provide its employees with jobs, pay its creditors, and produce a return for its stockholders."[240] In order to take advantage of this expedited process and obtain authority to sell its assets or conducting a going out of business sale, a fashion debtor must comply with the requirements under 11 U.S.C. § 363.

---

236. 11 U.S.C. § 1129(b)(2)(B)(i).
237. 11 U.S.C. § 1129(a)(7).
238. Jacob A. Kling, *Rethinking 363 Sales*, 17 STAN. J.L. BUS. & FIN. 258, 260 (2012).
239. George W. Kuney, *Let's Make It Official: Adding an Explicit Preplan Sale Process as an Alternative Exit from Bankruptcy*, 40 HOUS. L. REV. 1265, 1270 (2004).
240. *See* H.R. Rep. No. 95-595, at 220 (1977).

[A] The Basics of a Section 363 Sale

As a general rule of thumb, a fashion company that has filed for Chapter 11 protection cannot conduct transactions outside the ordinary course of business unless it obtains court approval (for example, it may continue to sell clothing to customers in a retail location, but cannot sell off its intellectual property such as a fashion label). Section 363, however, grants companies in bankruptcy a mechanism that allows them to conduct sales outside the normal course of business. In order to exercise this right, the fashion debtor must first satisfy certain legal requirements, which are (1) providing sufficient notice (usually at least twenty-one (21) days) to parties in interest; (2) obtaining the highest and best price; and (3) conducting the sale in good faith.

The required notice must, at minimum, include (1) the time and place of any public sale; (2) the terms and conditions of any private sale; and (3) the time fixed for filing objections.[241] If the sale involves all or substantially all of the company's assets, the court may impose stricter notice requirements.

The requirement that the company choose the highest and best offer is tied to the company's duty to maximize value from an asset sale. It is also open to some interpretation depending on the circumstances. "In deciding whether to approve a purchase offer or in choosing which is the better offer when competing offers have been made, courts generally consider factors in addition to a higher dollar amount."[242]

Finally, the sale must be conducted in good faith so the winning bidder can take the assets free and clear of other interests and to be protected against the sale being overturned on appeal.[243]

Overall, the company must show there is a sound business purpose to conduct the sale.[244] Courts will analyze various non-exclusive

---

241. Fed. R. Bankr. P. 2002(c)(1).

242. *In re* Landscape Props., Inc., 100 B.R. 445, 447 (Bankr. E.D. Ark. 1988).

243. Jared A. Wilkerson, *Defending the Current State of Section 363 Sales*, 86 AM. BANKR. L.J. 591, 626 n.147 (2012).

244. *In re* Lionel Corp., 722 F.2d 1063, 1071 (2d Cir. 1983); *see also* Jared A. Wilkerson, *Defending the Current State of Section 363 Sales*, 86 AM. BANKR. L.J. 591, 620 (2012) ("Sound business judgment is a malleable standard at best, so the modern and widely-used version of the test generally requires the judge to make four objective findings: (1) whether a sound business reason exists for the proposed transaction; (2) whether fair and reasonable consideration is provided—often determined by shopping the assets to potential bidders; (3) whether the transaction has been

factors in determining whether a sale has a sound business purpose.[245] The Second Circuit gives the following guidance:

> In fashioning its findings, a bankruptcy judge must not blindly follow the hue and cry of the most vocal special interest groups; rather, he should consider all salient factors pertaining to the proceeding and, accordingly, act to further the diverse interests of the debtor, creditors and equity holders, alike. He might, for example, look to such relevant factors as the proportionate value of the asset to the estate as a whole, the amount of elapsed time since the filing, the likelihood that a plan of reorganization will be proposed and confirmed in the near future, the effect of the proposed disposition on future plans of reorganization, the proceeds to be obtained from the disposition vis-a-vis any appraisals of the property, which of the alternatives of use, sale or lease the proposal envisions and, most importantly perhaps, whether the asset is increasing or decreasing in value. This list is not intended to be exclusive, but merely to provide guidance to the bankruptcy judge.[246]

[B] Advantages of a 363 Sale to Buyers and Sellers

A 363 sale provides several advantages to companies and buyers in an asset sale. As noted earlier, a 363 sale is beneficial to the company because it can reduce the costs and time associated with administering the debtor's estate, preserving value for creditor and company alike. While these considerations are important, the primary advantage of a 363 sale is that the company can sell and the buyer can take the property free and clear of any interests provided that one of the following five conditions must be satisfied:

(1) nonbankruptcy law permits a sale free and clear of interests;

(2) the parties holding the interests consent to the sale;

(3) the interest is a lien and the price obtained for the property exceeds the aggregate value of all liens on the property;

---

proposed and negotiated in good faith; and (4) whether adequate and reasonable notice is provided to all interested parties, including the United States Trustee, the creditors' committee(s), etc. In other words, the judge ensures procedural protections and gives creditors a chance to protect themselves.")

245. Some courts use the "Gulf Oil Standard," which is an alternative test to whether a section 363 sale should be approved. The Gulf Oil Standard eschews the sounds business purpose test and gives greater deference to judges and creditors. *See, e.g., In re* Cont'l Air Lines, Inc., 780 F.2d 1223, 1227 (5th Cir. 1986).

246. *In re* Lionel Corp., 722 F.2d 1063, 1071 (2d Cir. 1983).

(4) there is a good faith dispute regarding the validity of the interest; or

(5) the interest can be satisfied by money.[247]

Furthermore, under Section 363(m), the buyer can take the assets knowing that the sale should not be reversed on appeal if the buyer acted in good faith.

A 363 sale can also be advantageous because section 363(k) allows secured creditors to bid up to the face value of their allowed secured claims for the assets at auction, typically known as credit bidding. Credit bidding "is a tool well-calibrated to maximize the value of a bankruptcy estate for several reasons. First, credit bidding increases the often small pool of bidders sufficiently familiar with the debtor's assets to buy them on a truncated timetable. Second, it constrains debtors from favoring 'white knight' buyers who do not offer the highest purchase price. Third, credit bidding reduces the cost to submit a bid and minimizes transaction costs in general."[248]

[B][1] Going Out of Business Sales

A fashion debtor may also choose to maximize asset values for creditors by selling off certain assets and inventory, and even shutting down retail locations in a "going out of business" sale ("GOB sale"). This option is attractive to certain fashion debtors because liquidating inventory and assets at underperforming store locations will allow it to streamline its operations and give it a better chance to successfully emerge from Chapter 11. The debtor's primary duty is to maximize the value of its assets for the benefit of creditors, however, because the assets of a fashion company may consist of inventory and leases, the duty to maximize asset values will often clash with the rights of landlords and the landlord's obligations to other tenants.[249] Depending on how the sale is conducted, GOB sales can also conflict with federal, state, and local regulations and requirements. Notwithstanding the diverse interests involved in a GOB sale, most courts have interpreted the Bankruptcy Code to allow debtors to circumvent certain legal, regulatory, and contractual restrictions to GOB sales.[250]

---

247. 11 U.S.C. § 363(f).

248. Vincent S. J. Buccola & Ashley C. Keller, *Credit Bidding and the Design of Bankruptcy Auctions*, 18 GEO. MASON L. REV. 99, 100 (2010).

249. *See generally* Paul Traub & Susan F. Balaschak, *Going Out of Business Sales: Balancing the Interests of Landlords, Creditors, Regulatory Agencies and the Public in Chapter 11 Retail Cases*, 9 J. BANKR. L. & PRAC. 91 (1999) [hereinafter Traub & Balaschak].

250. *See id.* at 9 and n.1. ("Given that the language implementing the majority of GOB Sales and assumptions and assignments of leases are contained in court orders and non-published decisions, and given that

GOB sales are governed by section 363 of the Bankruptcy Code and follow a procedure (and requirements) similar to that of a typical 363 sale, with a chief difference being that GOB sales have a limited window in which they must occur because the Bankruptcy Code gives a debtor only up to 210 days (discussed above) to decide whether to assume or reject an executory contract or unexpired lease.[251] Due to the limited time frame, debtors will usually seek approval for a GOB sale as soon as possible after the bankruptcy petition has been filed.[252]

[B][1][a] Compliance with Federal and State Law

Without the protections and benefits of bankruptcy law, a debtor who operates in various states and wishes to conduct a GOB sale would need to comply with state and local regulations. A minority of courts have held that 28 U.S.C. § 959(b) requires that a trustee and debtor manage property in accordance with the state and local laws in which the property sits.[253] This means that certain jurisdictions may apply state or local law to GOB sales, which, in some cases, can frustrate the sale process. A state law, for example, may place strict limits on the type of advertising that is allowed for a GOB sale or require that the debtor obtain various permits. The larger the debtor, the more difficult it becomes for them to comply with various state and local regulations, and compliance with those laws and regulations could be prohibitive. Instead, Debtors who face these types of restrictions will often negotiate with the interested parties in order to balance the competing interests and obtain some relief from such restriction. The majority of courts find that bankruptcy law grants broad discretion to the court in advancing the policies of bankruptcy and allows bankruptcy law to preempt certain state laws that may prove prohibitive to the GOB sale process, which means many courts allow debtors to skirt state and local laws and regulations when conducting a GOB sale.[254]

---

the vast majority of objections raised by landlords to debtors' motions for approval of GOB Sales and assumptions and assignments of leases are resolved outside the courtroom, many resolutions of the issues discussed . . . are not found in published cases but instead through the practical experiences of landlords, attorneys, and the like, involved in numerous liquidation sales and assumptions and assignments of leases.").

251. Section 365(d)(4)(B)(i) of the Bankruptcy Code. This 120-day time period may be extended for up to ninety (90) days if the debtor shows sufficient cause for such extension. Any additional extensions are allowed only with approval by the landlord.

252. The Retail Business is Booming (in Bankruptcy), 22nd Annual Southeast Bankruptcy Workshop, 072717 ABI-CLE 133 (2017).

253. *See id. generally*.

254. Traub & Balaschak, *supra* note 249, at 92.

[B][1][b] Merchandise Augmentation

Merchandise augmentation is the practice of selling items that are not part of the GOB store's inventory (for example, the liquidator may seek to sell candy bars or water bottles in addition to the GOB store's inventory) with the inventory of the GOB store. In some cases, where the debtor is not closing all of its stores, the debtor may seek to sell inventory from a non-GOB store at a GOB store to liquidate old inventory. This practice of augmenting a GOB store's inventory is prohibited by many states and local governments. Some courts, however, have allowed merchandise augmentation. New York, for example, has allowed a debtor to transfer inventory between its stores and distribution centers whether they were closed or not.[255] Other courts have allowed transfers of inventory between GOB stores.[256] Delaware allows the very debtor friendly practice of allowing the liquidator to augment a GOB store's inventory with the inventory of liquidators or third parties on the theory that the GOB inventory's value will be enhanced by allowing this type of merchandise augmentation.[257] If a court allows merchandise augmentation to occur, it will often require certain consumer protections to be in place, such as signage, to alert consumers that certain items are not part of the debtor's inventory.[258]

[B][1][c] Duration

The duration of a GOB sale will often be contested. Arguments against a lengthy GOB sale may arise due to state or local regulations, or because of certain lease provisions. Landlords generally seek to limit the length of GOB sales on the argument that lengthy sales "[erode] the image of their malls, [take] business away from other tenants, and [reduce] the percentage rents the landlord would otherwise recover."[259] Despite the potential conflicts with state or local regulations and protests by landlords, however, debtors often seek to extend the duration of a GOB sale beyond what is normally permitted, and courts have regularly permitted such extensions.[260]

---

255. *See, e.g., In re* NYEC, Inc. f/k/a The Wiz, Inc., 97 B 48257(CB) (Bankr. S.D.N.Y. Dec. 18, 1997).
256. *See, e.g., In re* Rose's Stores, Inc., 93 B 0316 (Bankr. E.D.N.C. Dec. 23, 1993).
257. Traub & Balaschak, *supra* note 249, at 96.
258. *Id.*
259. *Id.* at 97.
260. *Id.* at 97–98.

[B][1][d] Lease Restrictions

A GOB sale may also give rise to numerous issues with respect to a lease between the fashion debtor and the landlord. Signage and advertising, for example, can be a hotly contested issue. Because leases often contain language that will restrict the appearance and placement of signage and advertising, a fashion debtor who wishes to advertise the GOB sale or erect signage to inform consumers of GOB sale may run afoul of such lease restrictions. Landlords, debtors and the third-party liquidators, however, generally come to some form of agreement on acceptable signage and advertising.[261]

Landlords may also seek to enforce "going dark" or "continuous use" provisions in a lease. These provisions restrict the lessee from closing down the store for a period of time, which can be problematic to a party who assumes a lease under the bankruptcy code, because such party will often seek to temporarily shut down a location in order to revamp or restock it for future use. Landlords argue that these restrictions are bargained for rights, and not enforcing these provisions may prevent them from getting percentage rents.[262] Nevertheless, the provisions are generally found unenforceable as anti-assignment clauses that violate section 365(f).[263] Landlords in shopping centers, however, do receive an exception to this general rule because the effects of not enforcing these types of provision can be magnified in a shopping center context.[264]

---

261. *Id.* at 98.
262. *Id.* at 100.
263. *See In re* Goody's, LLC, No. 09-10124 CSS, 2009 WL 7812260, at *6 (Bankr. D. Del. Jan. 15, 2009).
264. *See* 11 U.S.C. § 365(b)(3)(C).

Table of Authorities

(References are to pages.)

CASES

1-800 Contacts, Inc. v. Lens.com, Inc. 2-100, 7-21
4 Pillar Dynasty LLC v. New York & Co. 7-31, 7-32

A

A.V. by Versace, Inc. v. Gianni Versace, S.p.A. 2-73
A&H Sportswear, Inc. v. Victoria's Secret Stores, Inc. 2-29, 2-37
AAA Liquors, Inc. v. Joseph E. Seagram & Sons, Inc. 12-12, 12-13
Aaura, Inc., *In re* 23-52
Abbott Labs v. Mead Johnson & Co. 15-19
Abercrombie & Fitch Co. v. Hunting World, Inc. 2-38
Abercrombie & Fitch Co. v. Moose Creek, Inc. 2-40
Abercrombie & Fitch Stores, Inc. v.
Am. Eagle Outfitters, Inc. 2-14
Abercrombie & Fitch v. Fashion Shops of Ky., Inc. 8-12, 8-18
Acquaire v. Canada Dry Bottling Co. 12-11, 12-12
ActiveVideo Networks v. Verizon Commc'ns 3-15
AD/SAT v. Associated Press 12-5
Addison Props. Ltd. P'ship, *In re* 23-31
Adelphia Commc'ns Corp., *In re* 23-48
Adidas Am., Inc. v. Skechers USA, Inc. 2-63, 4-44, 7-10
adidas-America, Inc. v. Payless Shoesource, Inc. 2-33, 2-34,
.... 2-36, 2-41, 2-42,
.... 2-45, 2-47, 2-51, 2-54
Aerobox Composite Structures, LLC, *In re* 23-48
Airadigm Commc'ns, Inc., *In re* 23-18
AK Metals L.L.C. v. Norman Indus. Materials Inc. 2-100
Alfred Bell & Co. v. Catalda Fine Arts 4-6
Alfred Dunhill of London, Inc. v.
Kasser Distillers Prods. Corp. 2-103

Alfred Dunhill, Ltd. v. Interstate Cigar Co. 6-14
Algarin v. Coty, Inc. 15-33
Ali v. Playgirl, Inc. 18-14, 18-15
Alice Corp. v. CLS Bank, Int'l 3-5, 3-6
All One God Faith, Inc. v. Hain Celestial Grp., Inc. 15-29
Allen v. Nat'l Video, Inc. 18-15
Alliance Metals, Inc. v. Hinely Indus., Inc. 2-30
ALPO Petfoods, Inc. v. Ralston Purina Co. 2-66
Already LLC v. Nike, Inc. 2-75
Am. Airlines, Inc. v. Google Inc. 2-97, 2-98
Am. Airlines, Inc. v. Yahoo! Inc. 2-97
Am. Bridal & Prom Indus. Assoc., Inc. v. The P'ships & Unincorp. Assocs. Identified on Sched. A. 7-7
Am. Broad. Cos. v. Wolf 17-15
Am. Div. of Engineered Apparel, Inc. v. Bloomingdale's, Div. of Federated Dep't Stores Inc. 16-33
Am. Express Travel Related Servs. Co. v. Mastercard Int'l Inc. 15-21
Am. Hardwoods, Inc., *In re* 23-17
Am. Home Prods. Corp. v. Abbott Labs 15-8
Am. Home Prods. Corp. v. Johnson & Johnson 15-8
Am. Int'l Pictures, Inc. v. Foreman 8-6
Am. Online, Inc. v. Huang 7-29
Am., Inc. v. Skechers USA, Inc. 2-63, 4-44, 7-10
Amazon.com, Inc. v. ToysNet 7-35
Amazon.com, Inc. v. Wong 7-35
Ames Dep't Stores, Inc., *In re* 23-41
AMF, Inc. v. Sleekcraft Boats 2-30, 2-31, 2-41, 2-45
Anacop, Inc. v. Shell Knob Servs., Inc. 17-8
Andover Togs, Inc., *In re* 23-41
Angel Flight of Gea., Inc. v. Angel Flight Am., Inc. 15-21
Anheuser-Busch, Inc. v. VIP Prods., LLC 2-85, 2-86, 7-11
Animale Grp. Inc. v. Sunny's Perfume Inc. 2-69
Anthony's Pizza Hldg. Co. v. Anthony's Pizza & Pasta Int'l, Inc. 2-105, 2-106
Antone Corp. v. Haggen Holdings, LLC (*In re* Haggen Holdings, LLC) 23-38
Apple, Inc. v. Samsung Elecs. Co 3-20, 3-21
Applebaum v. Lyft, Inc. 14-11
Archie MD, Inc. v. Elsevier, Inc. 6-18
Arnold v. Mut. of Omaha Ins. Co. 16-32
AroChen Int'l, Inc v. Buirkle 7-35
Aronson v. Lewis 1-21
Arrow Fastener Co. v. Stanley Works 7-9

Art Attacks Ink, LLC v. MGA Entm't Inc. 4-31, 4-32
Art Capital Grp. LLC v. Getty Images, Inc. 17-13
Ashland Mgmt. Inc. v. Altair Invs. NA, LLC 17-10, 17-11, 17-15
Aspex Eyewear Inc. v. Clariti Eyewear, Inc. 3-39, 3-40
Ass'n for Intercollegiate Athletics for Women v. NCAA.............. 12-4
Assocs. Commercial Corp. v. Rash.. 23-31
Atl. Monthly Co. v. Frederick Ungar Publ'g Co. 2-11
Atl. Richfield Co. v. USA Petroleum Co.................................... 12-5
Auriga Capital Corp. v. Gatz Props, LLC 1-27, 23-4
Australian Gold, Inc. v. Hatfield.................................. 2-94, 2-99
Auto. Fin. Corp. v. Humberto Cornejo 23-52
Autoskill, Inc. v. Nat'l Educ. Support Sys., Inc. 4-39
Avanti Press, Inc. v. Emp't Dep't Tax Section 16-32
Avery Dennison Corp. v. Sumpton.. 2-54
Avon Anti-Aging Skincare Creams & Prod. Mktg. &
Sales Practices Litig., *In re* 15-33
Avon Prods., Inc. v. S.C. Johnson & Son, Inc. 15-5

B

B. Sanfield, Inc. v. Finlay Fine Jewelry Corp. 15-15
Bachellerie v. Z. Cavaricci, Inc. 2-102
Baidu, Inc. v. Register.com, Inc... 7-26
Bailey v. Allgas, Inc. 12-5
Balenciaga Am., Inc. v. Dollinger 7-7, 7-12, 7-14,
.... 7-15, 7-16, 7-32
Balenciaga v. liu zhixian, zhixian liu 2-109
Ball Corp., In the Matter of.. 20-24
Baltimore Orioles, Inc. v.
Major League Baseball Players Assoc....................................... 4-24
Bambu Sales, Inc. v. Ozak Trading Inc. 7-30
Bandag, Inc. v. Al Bolster's Tire Stores, Inc. 8-7
Banff, Ltd. v. Federated Dep't Stores, Inc..................................... 2-37
Banjo Buddies, Inc. v. Renosky 2-65, 2-67, 2-69
Barnes v. Yahoo 15-43
Basile, S.p.A. v. Basile.. 2-30
Bata Indus. Ltd. v. Warrington Inc... 5-15
Bauer Bros. LLC v. Nike, Inc. 2-27, 2-28, 2-74,
.... 2-75, 2-76, 2-77
Bausch & Lomb, Inc. v. Allergan, Inc. 2-65
Baxter v. MCA, Inc.. 4-31
Bayer Corp. v. Custom Sch. Frames, LLC.................................... 2-93

Bd. of Supers. for La. St. Univ. Ag. &
Mech. College v. Smack Apparel Co. 2-19, 2-79, 2-89
Bd. of Supervisors for Louisiana St. Univ. v.
Smack Apparel Co. 2-19, 2-89
BDO Seidman v. Hirshberg 17-13, 17-15, 17-19
Beacon Mut. Ins. Co. v. OneBeacon Ins. Grp. 2-36
Berman v. Sugo LLC 6-11, 6-12, 6-13
Best Lock Corp. v. Ilco Unican Corp. 3-9
Big O Tire Dealers, Inc. v. Goodyear Tire & Rubber Co. 2-36
Bill Diodato Photography, LLC v. Kate Spade, LLC 4-19
Bilski v. Kappos 3-5
Binder v. Disability Grp., Inc. 2-98
Bird v. Parsons 7-29
Blakey v. Continental Airlines 16-36
Blisscraft of Hollywood v. United Plastics Co. 3-8
Blockowicz v. Williams 7-13
Bloor v. Falstaff Brewing Co. 10-16
Blue Cross & Blue Shield United v. Marshfield Clinic 12-6
BMG Music v. Perez 8-10, 8-14
Bobbs-Merrill Co. v. Straus 8-5
Bodum USA Inc. v. Trudeau Corp. 5-15
Bogart LLC v. Burberry Grp. PLC 18-18
Bologna v. Allstate Ins. Co. 15-5
Bonito Boats Inc. v. Thunder Craft Boats Inc. 3-8
Bonneville Power Admin. v.
Mirant Corp. (*In re* Mirant Corp.) 23-47
Boston Celtics Ltd. P'ship S'holders Litig., *In re* 1-30
Bouchat v. Balt. Ravens, Inc. 4-31
Boule v. Hutton 15-31
Bowman v. Monsanto Co. 8-3, 8-8
Boxer v. Husky Oil Co. 1-30
Bradford v. N.Y. Times Co. 17-16
Branded LLC, *In re* 2-12
Brandir Int'l, Inc. v. Cascade Pac. Lumber Co. 4-14
Brignoli v. Balch Hardy & Scheinman, Inc. 6-15
Brilliance Audio, Inc. v. Haights Cross Commc'ns, Inc. 8-4
Brinker Rest. Corp. v. Super. Ct. 16-5
Brinkley v. Casablancas 18-2
Brockum Co., a Div. of Krimson Corp. v. Blaylock 18-8, 18-18
Brooke Grp. Ltd. v. Brown & Williamson Tobacco Corp. 12-3, 12-4
Brooke Hollow Inc. v. Antebi Footwear Grp. LLC 3-32
Brookfield Commc'ns Inc. v.
W. Coast Entm't Corp. 2-37, 2-93, 2-94, 14-6
Brown Shoe Co. v. United States 12-5

Brown v. Hain Celestial Grp., Inc. 15-29
Brown v. J. Kaz, Inc. 16-31, 16-32
Brunswick Corp. v. Pueblo Bowl-O-Mat, Inc. 12-5
Buetow v. A.L.S. Enters. 15-7, 15-8
Burberry Ltd. v. Bogart LLC 18-18
Burberry Ltd. v. Euro Moda, Inc. 2-90, 7-9
Burberry Ltd. v. Target Corp. 6-9
Burberry v. Designers Imports, Inc. 6-9
Burch v. Burch 6-20, 6-21
Burger King Corp. v. Mason 15-20
Burival, *In re* 23-20
Bus. Elecs. Corp. v. Sharp Elecs. Corp. 12-13
Bus. Intelligence Serv., Inc. v. Hudson 17-16
Butner v. United States 23-28

C

Cadbury Beverages v. Cott Corp. 2-43
Cafeteria Operators, L.P., *In re* 23-29
Cahill v. Nike, Inc. 16-26
Cairns v. Franklin Mint Co. 2-10, 2-11
Californians for Disability Rights v. Mervyn's, LLC 6-7
Campbell v. Acuff-Rose Music, Inc. 4-41, 4-42
Capital One Fin. Corp. v. Kanas 17-17
Caremark Int'l Inc. Derivative Litig., *In re* 1-20
Carl Zeiss Stiftung v. V.E.B. Carl Zeiss, Jena 2-83
Carol Barnhart Inc. v. Economy Cover Corp. 4-9, 4-13, 4-14
Carrell v. Sunland Const., Inc. 16-17
Carson v. Nat'l Bank of Commerce Tr. & Sav. 18-7
Cartier Int'l B.V. v. Ben-Menachem 7-32
Castrol, Inc. v. Quaker State Corp. 15-17, 15-19
Cel-Tech Commc'ns, Inc. v. L.A. Cellular Tel. Co. 6-4, 6-5
Cent. Hudson Gas & Elec. Corp. v. Pub. Serv. Comm'n of N.Y. 15-3
Centura Software Corp., *In re* 23-49
Century 21 Real Estate Corp. v. Lendingtree, Inc. 2-79
Century 21 v. Lending Tree 2-79
Certain Handbags, *In re* 2-72, 2-73
Certain Handbags, Luggage, Accessories and Packaging Thereof, *In re* 2-72
CFLC, Inc., *In re* 23-45
Chanel, Inc. v. Suttner 2-9

Chanel, Inc. v. WGACA, LLC 2-102
Chattanoga Mfg., Inc. v. Nike, Inc. 2-80, 2-81
Checkers Motors Corp. v. Chrysler Corp. 12-12
Checkpoint Sys. Inc. v. Check Point Software Techs., Inc. 2-96
Chiesa v. 24 X 7 Digital Media, LLC 14-23
Chloé v. Queen Bee of Beverly Hills, LLC 7-7
Chloe v. Zarafshan 7-30
Chosun Int'l, Inc. v. Chrisha Creations, Ltd. 4-12
Chow v. Neutrogena Corp. 15-33
Christian Dior-N.Y., Inc. v. Koret, Inc. 10-18
Christian Louboutin S.A. v.
Yves Saint Laurent Am. Holding, Inc. 2-59, 2-88, 2-89, 2-90
Chrysler Corp. v. United States 19-14
Cinicola v. Scharffenberger 23-38, 23-47
Citicorp Credit Servs., Inc., *In re* 15-11
Citigroup Indus. Credit v. Brock 16-15
Citizens Fin. Grp., Inc. v.
Citizens Nat'l. Bank of Evans City 2-77
Claremont Acquisition Corp., Inc., *In re* 23-36
Clatworthy & Son Ltd v. Dale Display Fixtures Ltd 5-15
Cmty. for Creative Non-Violence v. Reid 4-22
Cmty. of Christ Copyright Corp. v. Devon Park Restoration
Branch of Jesus Christ's Church 4-44
Coach Leatherware Co. v. AnnTaylor, Inc. 2-52
Coach Servs., Inc. v. Triumph Learning LLC 2-17
Coach, Inc. v. Celco Customs Servs. Co. 7-30
Coach, Inc. v. Goodfellow 7-20
Coachella Music Festival, LLC v. Simms 2-98
Coca-Cola Co. v. Tropicana Prods., Inc. 15-10
Cohen v. Facebook, Inc. 18-20
College Network, Inc. v. Moore Educ. Publishers, Inc. 2-96, 2-100
CollegeSource, Inc. v. AcademyOne, Inc. 2-100
Company Doe v. Public Citizen 9-25
Company Doe v. Tenenbaum 9-24, 9-25
Complete Auto Transit, Inc. v. Brady 14-31, 14-33
Concord Boat Corp. v. Brunswick Corp. 12-14
Conoco Inc. v. Inman Oil Co. 12-18
Consol. Accessories Corp. v. Franchise Tax Bd. 23-59
Cont'l Air Lines, Inc., *In re* 23-64
Cont'l T.V., Inc. v. GTE Sylvania Inc. 12-9, 12-13, 12-15
Conte Bros. Auto, Inc. v. Quaker State-Slick 50, Inc. 15-15
Contessa Food Prods. v. Conagra, Inc. 3-17
Continental Airlines, *In re* 23-17
Converse Inc. v. ITC 2-15, 2-16, 2-74

Cordas v. Uber Techs., Inc. 14-11
Corning Glass Works v. Sumitomo Elec. USA, Inc. 3-11
Cortner v. Israel 4-22
Cory v. Nintendo of Am., Inc. 18-14
Cosmetic Ideas, Inc. v. IAC/Interactivecorp 4-30
Cosmos Jewelry v. Po Sun Hon Co. 2-14
Costco Wholesale Corp. v. Omega, S.A. 8-14
County of Tuolumne v. Sonora Cmty. Hosp. 12-16
CRE/ADC Venture 2013, LLC v. Rocky Mountain Land Co. (*In re* Rocky Mountain Land Co.) 23-32
Crocs, Inc. v. Cheng's Enters. 3-38
Crocs, Inc. v. CVS Caremark, Corp. 3-32, 3-38
Crocs, Inc. v. Effervescent, Inc. 3-32, 3-33
Crocs, Inc. v. Int'l Trade Comm'n 3-17, 3-18, 3-38
Crocs, Inc. v. Skechers U.S.A., Inc. 3-32
Crocs, Inc. v. Walgreen, Co. 3-32, 3-38
Crown Packaging Tech., Inc. v. Rexam Beverage Can Co. 3-15
Crumbs Bake Shop, Inc., *In re* 23-49
CSIRO v. Cisco Sys., Inc. 3-20
Cuban Cigar Brands N.V. v. Upmann Int'l, Inc. 2-80, 2-103
Cullinane v. Uber Techs., Inc. 14-13, 14-14
Cunnius, *In re* 7-6
CytoSport, Inc. v. Vital Pharm., Inc. 2-47

D

Daimler AG v. Bauman 7-17
Dallas Cowboys Cheerleaders, Inc. v. Pussycat Cinema, Ltd. 2-33, 2-46
Danco, Inc. v. Wal-Mart Stores, Inc. 16-32
Daou v. Huffington 6-12
Dashnaw v. New Balance Athletics, Inc. 15-26
Dastar Corp. v. Twentieth Century Fox Film Corp. 6-14, 6-15
David E. Watson, P.C. v. United States 1-25
Davidoff & CIE, S.A. v. PLD Int'l Corp. 8-7
Davis v. R.K.O. Pictures 18-14
Davis v. The Gap, Inc. 4-42, 4-43
Dawn Donut Co. v. Hart's Food Stores, Inc. 2-83
Day v. Taylor 12-12
Deckers Outdoor Corp. v. Ash Int'l Grp. 3-34
Deckers Outdoor Corp. v. Conscious Corp. 3-34
Deckers Outdoor Corp. v. Lamo Sheepskin Inc. 3-34

Deckers Outdoor Corp. v. Minnetonka Moccasin 3-34
Deckers Outdoor Corp. v. Ollie's Bargain Outlet, Inc. 3-34
Deckers Outdoor Corp. v. Sears Holding Corp. 3-34
Deckers Outdoor Corp. v. ShoesScandal.com LLC 3-34
Deckers Outdoor Corp. v. United States 19-13
Deckers Outdoor Corp. v. Walgreens Co. 3-34
Delta Enter. Corp. v. Cohen 17-13
Delville v. Firmenich Inc. 6-13
Dennis v. Kellogg 15-33
Dentsply Sirona Inc. v. L I K Supply, Corp. 7-16, 7-31
Depuy Spine, Inc. v. Medtronic Sofamor Danek, Inc. 3-19
Desco Vitro Glaze of Schenectady v. Mech. Constr. Corp. 10-17
Desny v. Wilder 6-7
Diane Von Furstenberg Studio, LP v.
    ID Beauty Int'l Distribution LTD. 10-6
Diaz v. Pan Am. World Airways, Inc. 16-27
Dickson v. Microsoft Corp. 12-16
Dictaphone Corp. v. Dictamatic Corp. 2-102
Dillinger, LLC v. Elec. Arts Inc. 18-17
Direct Mktg. Ass'n v. Brohl 14-31
Diviacchi v. Speedway LLC 14-30
Doctor's Assocs., Inc. v. QIP Holders, LLC 15-38, 15-43
Does I v. Gap, Inc. 16-21
Dolgoff Holophase, Inc. v. E.I. Du Pont de Nemours & Co. 17-12
Donald Bruce & Co. v. B.H. Multi Com Corp. 4-11
Door-Master Corp. v. Yorktown, Inc. 3-9
Dow Corning Corp. v. Xiao 15-4
Dow Corning Corp., *In re* 23-18
Downey Creations, LLC, *In re* 23-52, 23-53, 23-57
Downing v. Abercrombie & Fitch, Inc. 18-3
Drexel Burnham Lambert Grp., Inc., *In re* 23-17
Dryden Advisory Grp., LLC v. Beneficial Mut. Sav. Bank
    (*In re* Dryden Advisory Grp., LLC) 23-12
Du Pont de Nemours & Co. v. Yoshida Int'l, Inc. 2-102

E

E. & J. Gallo Winery v. Gallo Cattle Co. 2-10
E. I. Du Pont de Nemours & Co., *In re* 2-17, 2-30
E. R.R. Presidents Conference v. Noerr Motor Freight 12-4
E. Remy Martin & Co., S.A. v. Shaw-Ross Int'l Imports, Inc. 2-24
E. Sci. Co. v. Wild Heerbrugg Instruments, Inc. 12-15

E.J. Brooks Co. v. Cambridge Sec. Seals.. 6-12
E.J.D. Diamond Mfr. v. United States 23-59
Eastwood v. Super. Ct.. 18-9
eBay Inc. v. MercExchange, LLC 2-58, 2-59, 2-60, 2-62,
....2-63, 3-3, 3-22, 4-44
Edible Arrangements, LLC v. Provide Commerce, Inc............... 2-101
Edina Realty, Inc. v. TheMLSonline.com..................................... 2-101
EEOC v. Abercrombie & Fitch Stores, Inc. 16-25
EEOC v. Arabian Am. Oil Co... 16-21
EEOC v. Gap, Inc. 16-26
Egyptian Goddess, Inc. v. Swisa, Inc................................... 3-18, 3-31
El Aguila Food Prods. v. Gruma Corp... 12-14
El Greco Leather Prods. Co. v. ShoeWorld, Inc. 2-50
Elec. Comm'ns, Inc. v. Elec. Components for Indus. Co. 2-103
Elecs. Boutique Holdings Corp. v. Zuccarini 2-70
Electrolux Corp. v. Val-Worth, Inc. 6-9, 6-10
Eli Lilly & Co. v. Natural Answers, Inc. 2-93
Eliya, Inc. v. Steven Madden, Ltd. 2-90, 2-91
Elsevier, Inc. v. Siew Yee Chew 7-9
EMI Catalogue P'ship v.
Hill, Holliday, Connors, Cosmopulos Inc............................. 6-14
Emmpresa Cubana Del Tabaco v. Culbro Corp. 2-24
Empire State Bldg. Co. v. Joseph Scott Props., Inc. 13-27
Enfish LLC v. Microsoft Corp... 3-6
Entrepreneur Media, Inc. v. Smith 2-41
Ergo Baby Carrier, Inc. v. Tenenbaum... 9-24
Esquire v. Ringer 4-9
Essex Mfg. v. United States 19-11
Estee Lauder Cos. v. Batra 17-16
Estée Lauder, Inc. v. The Gap, Inc...........................2-29, 2-37, 2-39,
....2-41, 2-42, 2-43, 2-58
Ethicon, Inc. v. U.S. Surgical Corp. 3-12
Eva's Bridal Ltd. v. Halanick Enters., Inc................2-83, 2-84, 2-107
Evans v. Techs. Applications & Serv. Co...................................... 16-25
Eve of Milady v. Impression Bridal, Inc. 4-8, 4-12
Evelyn Byrnes, Inc., *In re* 23-38
Everex Sys, Inc. v. Cadtrak Corp. (*In re* CFLC, Inc.).................. 23-43
Exide Tech., *In re* 23-43, 23-46
Expert Reports in Am. Airlines, Inc. v. Google Inc. 2-97
Express, LLC v. Fetish Grp., Inc. 4-12, 4-36
Exxon Corp. v. Oxxford Clothes, Inc. 2-82, 2-83
Exxon Corp. v. Texas Motor Exch., Inc.. 2-41

F

F.T.C. v. Anheuser-Busch, Inc. 12-18
F.T.C. v. Super. Ct. Trial Lawyers Ass'n 12-6
Falls City Indus. v. Vanco Beverage 12-18
Famous Horse, Inc. v. 5th Ave. Photo Inc. 2-33, 15-15
Fariba v. Dealer Servs. Corp. 23-52
Fashion Boutique of Short Hills, Inc. v. Fendi USA, Inc. 15-4
Fashion Originator's Guild of Am. v. FTC 4-5, 4-10, 12-2
Fed. Deposit Ins. Corp. v. Hastie (*In re* Hastie) 23-29
Fed. Trade Comm'n v. AAFE Prods. Corp. 14-37
Feesers, Inc. v. Michael Foods 12-19
Feinberg v. Federated Dep't Stores, Inc. 11-35
Feist Publ'ns, Inc. v. Rural Tel. Serv. Co. 4-6, 4-7, 4-29, 4-32
Fekete v. GA Ins. Co. of N.Y. 6-14
Feldenkrais Guild of N. Am. v. Wildman 2-98
Fendi Adele S.R.L. v. Ashley Reed Trading, Inc. 7-30
FenF, LLC v. Smarthingz, Inc. 2-98
Fenty v. Arcadia Grp. Brands Ltd 18-19
Ferrari S.P.A. Esercizio v. Roberts 2-34
Fesler v. Whelen Eng'g Co. 16-31
Filene's Basement, LLC, *In re* 23-36, 23-37, 23-42
Fin. Express LLC v. Nowcom Corp. 2-94
Financial Sec. Assurance Inc. v. T-H New Orleans Ltd.
P'ship (*In re* T-H New Orleans Ltd. P'ship) 23-31
Fitbit, Inc. v. Aliphcom 3-6
Fleet v. CBS, Inc. 18-3
Fleming Cos., *In re* 23-38
Flexitized, Inc. v. Nat'l Flexitized Corp. 6-11
FLM Collision Parts, Inc. v. Ford Motor Co. 12-12
Foamex Int'l, Inc., *In re* 23-42
Folio Impressions, Inc. v. Byer Cal. 4-6, 4-8, 4-12,
.... 4-17, 4-33, 4-34
Fonovisa, Inc. v. Cherry Auction, Inc. 7-20, 7-21, 7-22, 7-28
Footstar, Inc., *In re* 23-48
Ford Motor Credit Co. v. Dobbins 23-32
Foremost-McKesson, Inc., In the Matter of 12-18
FormFactor Inc. v. Micro-Probe Inc. 6-8
Fortune Dynamic, Inc. v. Victoria's Secret Stores
Brand Mgmt., Inc. 2-35, 2-52
Fourth Est. Pub. Benefit Corp. v. Wall-Street.com, LLC 4-24, 4-30
Fraley v. Facebook, Inc. 18-20
Frank v. Gaos 14-30

Frisch's Rests., Inc. v. Elby's Big Boy 2-30
FTC v. Bronson Partners, LLC 15-24
Fujifilm Corp. v. Benun 8-8
Fun-Damental Too, Ltd. v. Gemmy Indus. Corp. 2-13
Furr's Supermarkets, Inc., *In re* 23-20

G

G.S. Distribution, Inc., *In re* 23-51, 23-53, 23-59
Gaiman v. McFarlane 4-39
Galiano v. Harrah's Operating Co. 4-14
Gantos, Inc., *In re* 23-41
Gardner v. Nike, Inc. 23-47
Garza v. Zachry Constr. Corp. 16-32
Gaskell v. Univ. of Ky. 16-36
Gasser Chair Co. v. Infanti Chair Mfg. Corp. 2-15
Gasser v. Kiss My Face, LLC 15-6, 15-7
Gatz Props., LLC v. Auriga Capital Corp. 1-27
Gayle Martz, Inc. v. Sherpa Pet Grp., LLC 2-62, 2-65
Geisel v. Poynter Prods. 18-14
Gen. Motors Corp. v. Devex Corp. 3-22
Gen. Motors Corp. v. Keystone Auto. Corp. 2-26, 2-34,
.... 2-35, 2-44, 2-104
General Steel Domestic Sales, LLC v. Chumley 2-100
Generra Sportwear Co. v. United States 19-14
Georgetown Steel Co., *In re* 23-51, 23-52
Georgia-Pac. Consumer Prods. LP v. Von Drehle Corp. 2-68
Gerdom v Cont'l Airlines 16-27
Gertz v. Robert Welch, Inc. 15-5
Gibson Guitar Corp. v. Paul Reed Smith Guitars 2-32
Gibson Tex, Inc. v. Sears Roebuck & Co. 4-29, 4-32, 4-33
Gibson v. World Sav. & Loan Ass'n 6-4
Gillette Co. v. Norelco Consumer Prods. Co. 15-4, 15-5, 15-17
Girl Scouts of U.S.A. v.
Bantam Doubleday Dell Publ'g Grp., Inc. 6-9
Glazewski v. Coronet Ins. Co. 15-31
Golden Books Family Entm't, Inc., *In re* 23-47
Goody's Family Clothing Inc., *In re* 23-19
Goody's, LLC, *In re* 23-68
Google Inc. Cookie Placement Consumer Privacy Litig., *In re* 14-29
Google Inc. v. Am. Blind & Wallpaper Factory, Inc. 2-101
Google, Inc. Privacy Policy Litig., *In re* 14-28

Gordon & Breach Sci. Publishers v.
Am. Inst. of Physics 15-3, 15-4
Gorham Mfg. Co. v. White.. 3-17
GoTo.com, Inc. v. Walt Disney Co. 2-14, 2-62, 2-96
Graham v. Allis-Chambers Mfg. Co. 1-20
Graham v. Eagle Distrib. Co. 6-14
Great Atl. & Pac. Tea Co., *In re* 23-37
Greendlinger v. Marilyn A. Donahue Real Estate, Inc. 13-5
Greenline Equip., Inc., *In re* 23-51
Grigsby v. Valve Corp. 14-29
Groden v. Random House 15-5
Grosso v. Miramax Film... 6-7
Grotrian, Helfferih, Schulz, Th. Steinweg Nachf. v.
Steinway & Sons 2-40
Gruner + Jahr USA Publ'g v. Meredith Corp. 2-27, 2-40
GTFM, Inc. v. Solid Clothing, Inc. 2-9, 2-27, 2-28,
....2-29, 2-44, 2-56, 2-57
Guardian Life Ins. Co. v.
Am. Guardian Life Ins. Co. 15-4
Guardian Pool Fence Sys. Inc. v. Sunwest Indus., Inc.............. 2-100
Gucci Am., Inc. v. Action Activewear................................ 2-37, 2-38,
....2-42, 2-44, 2-50
Gucci Am., Inc. v. Alibaba Grp. Holding Ltd.............................. 7-22
Gucci Am. Inc. v. Bagsmerchant, LLC................................ 7-9, 7-12
Gucci Am., Inc. v. Curveal Fashion......................... 7-12, 7-16, 7-17
Gucci Am., Inc. v. Daffy's, Inc. 2-69
Gucci Am., Inc. v. Frontline Processing Corp. 7-8, 7-25, 7-26
Gucci Am., Inc. v. Laurette Co. 7-12
Gucci Am., Inc. v. MyReplicaHandbag.com 7-31
Gucci Am., Inc. v. Weixing Li..................2-69, 7-14, 7-15, 7-17, 7-18
Gucci Shops, Inc. v. Dreyfoos & Assocs., Inc. 2-10, 2-39
Gucci Shops, Inc. v. R.H. Macy & Co. 2-60, 2-62
Gucci Timepieces Am. Inc. v. Yidah Watch Co. 2-14
Gucci v. Gucci Shops, Inc... 2-10
Guess?, Inc. v. Gold Ctr. Jewelry 2-68
Guglielmi v. Spelling-Goldberg Prods. 18-9
Guild of Am., Inc. v. Fed. Trade Comm'n. 12-2
Gunther-Wal Prods. v. Mattel, Inc. 6-7
Guth v. Loft, Inc... 1-21, 23-4

H

H. L. Hayden Co. of N.Y. v. Siemens Med. Sys., Inc. 8-7
H. M. Kolbe Co. v. Armgus Textile Co. 4-8
HA-LO Indus. v. CenterPoint Props. Tr. 23-20
Haelan Labs., Inc. v. Topps Chewing Gum, Inc. 18-5, 18-14
Haley & Steele, Inc., *In re* 23-59
Halo Elecs., Inc. v. Pulse Elecs., Inc. 3-19, 3-23
Hancock v. Am. Tel. & Tel. Co. 14-11, 14-12
Harco Nat. Ins. Co. v. Green Farms. Inc. 1-32
Hard Rock Café Licensing Corp. v.
    Concession Servs., Inc. 7-20, 7-21, 7-22
Hardwick v. Nu-Way Oil Co. 12-12
Harper & Row, Publishers, Inc. v. Nation Enters. 4-46
Hasbro, Inc. v. Lanard Toys, Ltd. 2-59
Health Indus. v. European Health Spas 2-83
Hearts on Fire Co. v. Blue Nile, Inc. 2-96
Helene Curtis Indus., Inc. v. Church & Dwight Co. 2-30
Herb Reed Enters., LLC v. Fla. Entm't Mgmt., Inc. 2-63
Heritage Highgate, Inc., *In re* 23-31, 23-32
Hermès Int'l v. John Doe 6-10
Hermès Int'l v.
    Lederer de Paris Fifth Ave., Inc. 2-14, 2-35, 2-64, 7-10
Hernandez, *In re* 23-46
Highland Superstores, Inc., *In re* 23-41
Highmark Inc. v. Allcare Health Mgmt. Sys., Inc. 3-22
Hines v. Overstock.com, Inc. 14-14
Hinkleman v. Shell Oil Co. 12-18
Hot Wax, Inc. v. Turtle Wax, Inc. 15-21
HQ Global Holdings, Inc., *In re* 23-49
Hubbert v. Dell Corp. 14-15
Hudson Hotels Corp. v. Choice Hotels Int'l 6-11
Hudson Ins. Co. v. Colony Ins. Co. 10-15
Hygiene Prods. Aktiebolag v. First Quality Baby Prods., LLC 3-16

I

I.P. Lund Trading ApS v. Kohler Co. 2-30
Imperial Laces v. Westchester Lace 4-12
Impression Prods., Inc. v. Lexmark Int'l, Inc. 8-8
In K Mart Corp. v. Cartier, Inc. 8-9
In re Aaura, Inc. 23-52

In re Addison Props. Ltd. P'ship 23-31
In re Adelphia Commc'ns Corp. 23-48
In re Aerobox Composite Structures, LLC 23-48
In re Airadigm Commc'ns, Inc. 23-18
In re Am. Hardwoods, Inc. 23-17
In re Ames Dep't Stores, Inc. 23-41
In re Andover Togs, Inc. 23-41
In re Avon Anti-Aging Skincare Creams & Prod. Mktg. & Sales Practices Litig. 15-33
In re Boston Celtics Ltd. P'ship S'holders Litig. 1-30
In re Branded LLC 2-12
In re Burival 23-20
In re Cafeteria Operators, L.P. 23-29
In re Caremark Int'l Inc. Derivative Litig. 1-20
In re Centura Software Corp. 23-49
In re CFLC, Inc. 23-45
In re Citicorp Credit Servs., Inc. 15-11
In re Claremont Acquisition Corp., Inc. 23-36
In re Cont'l Air Lines, Inc. 23-64
In re Continental Airlines 23-17
In re Crumbs Bake Shop, Inc. 23-49
In re Cunnius 7-6
In re Dow Corning Corp. 23-18
In re Downey Creations, LLC 23-52, 23-53, 23-57
In re Drexel Burnham Lambert Grp., Inc. 23-17
In re E. I. Du Pont de Nemours & Co. 2-17, 2-30
In re Evelyn Byrnes, Inc. 23-38
In re Exide Tech. 23-43, 23-46
In re Filene's Basement, LLC 23-36, 23-37, 23-42
In re Fleming Cos. 23-38
In re Foamex Int'l, Inc. 23-42
In re Footstar, Inc. 23-48
In re Furr's Supermarkets, Inc. 23-20
In re G.S. Distribution, Inc. 23-51, 23-53, 23-59
In re Gantos, Inc. 23-41
In re Georgetown Steel Co. 23-51, 23-52
In re Golden Books Family Entm't, Inc. 23-47
In re Goody's Family Clothing Inc. 23-19
In re Goody's, LLC 23-68
In re Google Inc. Cookie Placement Consumer Privacy Litig. 14-29
In re Google, Inc. Privacy Policy Litig. 14-28
In re Great Atl. & Pac. Tea Co. 23-37
In re Greenline Equip., Inc. 23-51
In re Haley & Steele, Inc. 23-59

In re Heritage Highgate, Inc. 23-31, 23-32
In re Hernandez 23-46
In re Highland Superstores, Inc. 23-41
In re HQ Global Holdings, Inc. 23-49
In re Interco, Inc. 12-14
In re Interstate Bakeries Corp. 23-43, 23-46
In re iPhone Application Litig. 14-28
In re Iridium Operating LLC 23-6
In re Iron-Oak Supply Corp. 23-42
In re Joshua Slocum Ltd. 23-40
In re Kazi Foods of Mich., Inc. 23-48
In re Koenig Sporting Goods, Inc. 23-19
In re Lakewood Eng'g & Mfg. Co. 23-49
In re Lamb-Grs, LLC 2-13
In re Landscape Props., Inc. 23-63
In re Lionel Corp. 23-63, 23-64
In re Lucero 23-32
In re Metromedia 23-18
In re Metromedia Fiber Network, Inc. 23-18
In re Montgomery Ward Holding Corp. 23-19, 23-42
In re Morgansen's LTD 23-51, 23-59
In re Nasty Gal, Inc. 23-3
In re Nat'l Truck Funding LLC 12-32
In re NETtel Corp., Inc. 23-20
In re Niblett 23-57
In re Nissan Antitrust Litig. 12-13
In re NYEC, Inc. f/k/a The Wiz, Inc. 23-67
In re Old Carco LLC 23-49
In re Online Travel Co. 14-11
In re Orion Pictures Corp. 23-33
In re Pac. Lumber Co. 23-17
In re Patriot Place, Ltd. 23-37
In re Peregrine Entm't, Ltd 4-27
In re Pilgrim's Pride Corp. 23-25
In re RAE Sys. Inc. 20-28, 20-29
In re Rose's Stores, Inc. 23-67
In re rue21, inc. 23-13
In re S & J Holding Corp. 23-29
In re S.F. Drake Hotel Assoc. 23-29
In re Seagate Tech., L.L.C. 3-23
In re Seaside Eng'g & Surveying, Inc. 23-18
In re SemCrude, L.P. 23-25
In re Sony Gaming Networks & Customer Data Sec. Breach Litig. 14-29

In re Sony Music Entm't 12-13
In re Specific Media Flash Cookies Litig. 14-28
In re Stella McCartney Ltd. 2-12
In re Stone Barn Manhattan LLC 23-20, 23-42
In re Strick Chex Columbus Two, LLC 23-29
In re SW Hotel Venture, LLC 23-30
In re Tom McCormick Enters., Inc. 23-30
In re Treesource Indus., Inc. 23-20
In re Trump Entm't Resorts, Inc. 23-47
In re TSAWD Holdings, Inc. 23-57, 23-58
In re Two S Corp. 23-32
In re Urban Communicators PCS Ltd. P'ship 23-31, 23-32
In re Valley Media, Inc. 23-52, 23-53, 23-57, 23-60
In re Vertex Grp. LLC 2-19
In re Visa USA 15-17
In re Vitro S.A.B. de C.V. 23-17
In re W. Real Estate Fund, Inc. 23-17
In re Wal-Mart Stores, Inc. 2-13
In re Washington Mut., Inc. 23-18
In re West Elecs., Inc. 23-47
In re Wicaco Mach. Corp. 23-52
In re Zahn 3-8
In re Zappos.com, Inc.,
Customer Data Sec. Breach Litig. 14-14, 14-30
In the Matter of Ball Corp. 20-24
In the Matter of Foremost-McKesson, Inc. 12-18
In the Matter of Legacy Learning Sys., Inc. 15-40
In the Matter of McCormick & Co. 12-17
In the Matter of Nu Skin Enters., Inc. 20-21
In the Matter of Reverb Commc'ns, Inc. 15-40
Indep. Nail & Packing Co. v. Stronghold Screw Prods., Inc. 2-81
Industria Arredamenti Fratelli Saporiti v.
Charles Craig, Ltd. 2-88
Infogroup, Inc. v. Database LLC 2-100
Institut Pasteur v. Cambridge Biotech Corp. 23-47
Int'l Design Concepts, LLC v. Saks Inc. 11-40
Int'l Diamond Imps., Inc. v. Oriental Gemco (N.Y.), Inc. 4-34
Int'l Info. Sys. Sec. Certification Consortium v.
Security Univ., LLC 2-79
Int'l Star Class Yacht Racing Ass'n v.
Tommy Hilfiger, U.S.A., Inc. 2-20, 2-67, 2-68
Interco, Inc., *In re* 12-14
Interpace Corp. v. Lapp, Inc. 2-30, 2-44
Interstate Bakeries Corp., *In re* 23-43, 23-46

Investor Access Corp. v. Doremus & Co. 17-20
Inwood Labs., Inc. v. Ives Labs., Inc. 2-7, 2-88, 7-20
iPhone Application Litig., *In re* 14-28
Ippolito v. Ono-Lennon 18-14
Iridium Operating LLC, *In re* 23-6
Iron-Oak Supply Corp., *In re* 23-42
Irwin & Leighton, Inc. v. W.M. Anderson Co. 1-33
ITC Ltd. v. Punchgini Inc. 6-2, 6-10

J

J. Choo (Jersey) Ltd. v. Towerstone Ltd. 5-4
J. Crew Grp., Inc. v. Fenton 6-19
J.C. Penney Purchasing Corp. v. United States 19-16
JA Apparel Corp. v. Abboud 2-10
Jack Russell Terrier Network of N. Cal. v.
Am. Kennel Club, Inc. 15-15
James v. Glob. TelLink Corp. 14-13, 14-15
Jamestown v. James Cable Partners, L.P.
(*In re* James Cable Partners, L.P.) 23-47
Jarrow Formulas, Inc. v. Nutrition Now, Inc. 15-21
Jay Franco & Sons, Inc. v. Franek 2-89
Jefferson Parish Hosp. No. 2 v. Hyde 12-16
Jeffrey Milstein, Inc. v. Greger, Lawlor, Roth, Inc. 2-13, 6-9
Jemella Grp. Ltd. v. Killer Queen, LLC 18-18
John Paul Mitchell Sys. v. Pete-n-Larry's Inc. 8-22
John Wiley & Sons, Inc. v. Kirtsaeng 8-14, 8-15
Johnson & Johnson v. GAC Int'l, Inc. 15-8
Johnson & Johnson Vision Care, Inc. v.
1-800 Contacts, Inc. 15-7
Johnson & Johnson-Merck Co. Pharm.Co. v.
Smithkline Beecham Corp. 15-9
Johnson Controls, Inc. v. A.P.T. Critical Sys., Inc. 17-15
Johnson v. Hallett 23-59
Jordache Enters., Inc. v. Hogg Wyld, Ltd. 2-40, 2-46, 2-47,
.... 2-48, 2-49, 2-84
Jordache Enters., Inc. v. Levi Strauss & Co. 2-47
Joshua Slocum Ltd., *In re* 23-40
Jovani Fashion v. Cinderella Divine Inc. 4-14
Jovani Fashion, Ltd. v. Fiesta Fashions 4-14
JR Tobacco v. Davidoff of Geneva (CT), Inc. 15-11
Juicy Couture, Inc. v. Bella Int'l, Ltd. 7-12
Julian Bakery, Inc. v. Healthsource Int'l, Inc. 2-99

K

K2 Advisors, LLC v. K2 Volatility Fund, LP 2-9
Kai Peng v. Uber Techs., Inc. 14-11
Kaine v. Johns-Manville Corp. (*In re* Johns-Manville Corp.)...... 23-17
Kalisch-Jarcho Inc. v. City of N.Y. 6-9
Kamen v. Kemper Fin. Servs.. 1-48
Kardashian v. The Gap, Inc.. 18-11
Karen Millen Ltd. v. Dunnes Stores.. 5-3
Kasky v. Nike, Inc. 15-3
Kason Indus., Inc. v. Component Hardware Grp., Inc................ 2-81
Kazi Foods of Mich., Inc., *In re* 23-48
Keds Corp. v. Renee Int'l Trading Corp. 2-34
Kellogg Co. v. Exxon Corp.. 2-81
Kellogg Co. v. Nat'l Biscuit Co. 2-3
Kenner Parker Toys Inc. v. Rose Art Indus., Inc. 2-7
Kentucky Fried Chicken Corp. v.
Diversified Packaging Corp... 2-83
Kevin M. Ehringer Enters., Inc. v. McData Servs. Corp.............. 10-16
Key W. Hand Print Fabrics, Inc. v. Serbin, Inc. 4-46
Keystone Driller Co. v. General Excavator Co. 2-77
Kiara Cruz v. Lululemon Athletica Inc. 15-31
Kieselstein-Cord v. Accessories by Pearl, Inc. 4-11, 4-13
Kirtsaeng v. John Wiley & Sons, Inc. 4-47, 4-48, 8-4,
.... 8-5, 8-11, 8-15, 8-23
Klauber Bros. v. Bon-Ton Stores, Inc. 4-34
KNB Enters. v. Matthews 18-3, 18-7
Knitwaves, Inc. v. Lollytogs Ltd. 4-8, 4-12
Koch v. Greenberg 15-10
Koenig Sporting Goods, Inc., *In re* 23-19
Kookai S.A. v. Shabo 2-52
Korn v. First Unim Life Ins. Co. 6-14
Kouf v. Walt Disney Pictures & Television................................ 4-16
KP Permanent Make-Up, Inc. v.
Lasting Impression I, Inc.................................. 2-12, 2-29, 2-30
Kraftco Corp. v. Kolbus 10-16
Kroboth v. Brent 10-16
Kroma Makeup EU LLC v.
Boldface Licensing + Branding Inc. 2-76, 10-15
Kuryakyn Holdings, LLC v. Ciro, LLC 4-23
Kyocera Wireless Corp. v. Int'l Trade Comm'n 2-72

L

L & L Wings, Inc. v. Marco-Destin Inc. 2-69
L.A. Gear v. Thom McAn Shoe Co. 2-14, 3-9
L.A. Printex Indus. Inc. v. Aeropostale, Inc. .... 4-17, 4-18, 4-30, ... 4-31, 4-32, 4-34, 4-35, 4-36
L.A. T-Shirt & Print, Inc. v. Rue 21, Inc. 4-16
L&A Designs v. Xtreme ATVs, Inc. 2-94
LaChapelle v. Fenty 4-19
Lake Hill Motors v. Jim Bennett Yacht Sales, Inc. 12-13
Lakewood Eng'g & Mfg. Co., *In re* 23-49
Lamb-Grs, LLC, *In re* 2-13
Landscape Props., Inc., *In re* 23-63
Lane Capital Mgmt., Inc. v. Lane Capital Mgmt., Inc. 2-27
Lanfear v. Home Depot 11-40
Langman Fabrics v. Graff Californiawear, Inc. 4-22
LaserDynamics, Inc. v. Quanta Comput., Inc. 3-20
Laukus v. Rio Brands, Inc. 2-67
Laureyssens v. Idea Grp., Inc. 4-30
Leegin Creative Leather Prods., Inc. v. PSKS, Inc. 12-8
Leegin v. PSKS, Inc. 12-8, 12-9
Legacy Learning Sys., Inc., In the Matter of 15-40
Lehrman v. Gulf Oil Corp. 12-12
Levi Strauss & Co. v. Abercrombie & Fitch Trading Co. 2-54
Levi Strauss & Co. v. Blue Bell, Inc. 2-7, 2-35
Levi Strauss & Co. v. Shilon 2-77
Levi Strauss & Co. v. Sunrise Int'l Trading Inc. 2-69
Levitt v. Yelp, Inc. 6-6
Lewinson v. Henry Holt & Co. 4-30
Lewis v. City of Chi. 16-23
Lexmark Int'l, Inc. v. Static Control Components, Inc. 15-16
LF USA, Inc. v. United States 19-13
Lionel Corp., *In re* 23-63, 23-64
Liszt v. Karen Kane, Inc. 16-33
Litton Sys., Inc. v. Whirlpool Corp. 3-18
Liz Claiborne, Inc. v. Mademoiselle Knitwear, Inc. 8-16, 8-17, 8-18
Lockheed Martin Corp. v. Network Sols., Inc. 7-24, 7-26, 7-27, 7-29
Lohan v. Take-Two Interactive Software, Inc. 18-15

Lois Sportswear U.S.A., Inc. v.
Levi Strauss & Co. 2-26, 2-32, 2-33, 2-34,
....2-35, 2-36, 2-37, 2-38, 2-42,
.... 2-44, 2-46, 2-47, 2-50, 2-52, 2-104
Londontown Mfg. Co. v. Cable Raincoat Co. 2-41
Louis Vuitton Malletier v.
Burlington Coat Factory Warehouse Corp. 2-40
Louis Vuitton Malletier v. WhenU.com.................................. 7-31
Louis Vuitton Malletier, S.A. v.
Akanoc Sols., Inc...7-27, 7-28, 7-30, 7-32
Louis Vuitton Malletier, S.A. v.
Dooney & Bourke, Inc.............................2-14, 2-29, 2-40, 2-47,
....2-48, 2-53, 2-56, 2-60, 2-90
Louis Vuitton Malletier S.A. v.
Haute Diggity Dog, LLC.................2-27, 2-41, 2-46, 2-51, 2-53,
.... 2-54, 2-55, 2-56, 2-85, 2-86, 7-11
Louis Vuitton Malletier S.A. v.
Hyundai Motor Am.........................2-51, 2-53, 2-54, 2-56, 7-11
Louis Vuitton Malletier S.A. v. Ly USA, Inc. 2-6, 7-10
Louis Vuitton Malletier, S.A. v.
My Other Bag, Inc.. 2-86, 4-48, 15-21
Louis Vuitton Malletier S.A. v. Sunny Merch. Corp. 7-10
Louis Vuitton N. Am. Inc. v. Joon Ma 6-17
Low v. LinkedIn.. 14-28
Lubrizol Enters., Inc. v. Richmond Metal Finishers, Inc. 10-17
Lucero, *In re* 23-32
Ludden v. Metro Weekly.. 4-23
Lugosi v. Universal Pictures 18-9
Lujan v. Defenders of Wildlife 2-76
Lulirama Ltd. v. Axcess Broad. Servs., Inc. 4-23
Luria Bros. & Co. v. F.T.C.. 12-14
Lusardi v. Xerox Corp... 16-3
Luxottica Grp. S.p.A. v. Hao Li 7-31
LVL XIII Brands, Inc. v. Louis Vuitton Malletier S.A................. 6-21

M

M2 Software, Inc. v. Madacy Entm't 2-37
Macy's Inc. v. Martha Stewart Living Omnimedia, Inc. 10-6, 10-7
Macy's, Inc. v. J.C. Penney Corp. 10-6, 10-7
Maharishi Hardy Blechman Ltd. v.
Abercrombie & Fitch Co. 2-14
Maidenform Brands Inc. v. Times Three Clothier LLC 3-30

Maker's Mark Distillery, Inc. v. Diageo N. Am., Inc. 2-89
Malone v. Crown Cent. Petroleum Corp. 12-10
Maloney v. T3Media, Inc. 18-3
Mannion v. Coors Brewing Co. 4-18
Marcyan v. Marcy Gymnasium Equip. Co. 15-5
Marcyan v. Nissen Corp. 15-5
Marimar Textiles, Inc. v. Jude Clothing & Accessories Corp. 6-17
Mars, Inc. v. Coin Acceptors, Inc. 3-20
Martin's Herend Imports, Inc. v.
Diamond & Gem Trading USA, Co. 8-22
Mary Kay, Inc. v. Michael Kors LLC 2-105
Mason v. Coca-Cola Co. 15-33
Masquerade Novelty, Inc. v. Unique Indus., Inc. 4-11, 4-13
Matsushita Elec. Indus. Co. v. Zenith Radio Corp. 12-3
Mattel, Inc. v. MGA Entm't, Inc. 4-37, 6-8
Mayo Collaborative Servs. v. Prometheus Labs., Inc. 3-5
Mazer v. Stein 4-9
McCormick & Co., In the Matter of 12-17
McLain v. Real Estate Bd. of New Orleans 12-4
McNeil-P.C.C., Inc. v. Bristol-Myers Squibb Co. 15-17
McNeil-P.P.C., Inc. v. Guardian Drug Co. 15-12
MCW v. Badbusinessbureau.com 15-43
Mead Johnson & Co. v. Abbott Labs. 15-9
Mead Johnson & Co. v. Baby's Formula Svc., Inc. 2-81
Menard-Sanford v. Mabey (*In re* A.H. Robins Co.) 23-18
Merck Eprova AG v. Gnosis S.p.A. 2-66
Mesirow v. Pepperidge Farm 12-10
Metcalf v. Bochco 4-16
Metro. Opera Ass'n v. Metro. Opera Ass'n of Chi. 2-11
Metromedia Fiber Network, Inc., *In re* 23-18
Meyer v. Sprint Spectrum L.P. 15-32
Meyer v. Uber Techs., Inc. 14-16
Michaels v. Internet Entm't. Grp., Inc. 18-9
Miche Bag, LLC v. Ayers 4-11, 4-44, 4-45, 4-47, 4-48
Microsoft Corp. v. AT&T Corp. 3-24
Microsoft Corp. v. Shah 7-27
Midler v. Ford Motor Co. 18-10, 18-20
Miller v. Am. Real Estate Partners, L.P. 23-5
Miller v. McCown De Leeuw & Co.
(*In re* The Brown Schools) 23-7
Millinery Creators' Guild v. FTC 4-5
Minn. Pet Breeders, Inc. v. Schell & Kampeter, Inc. 2-66
Mission Prod. Holdings, Inc. v. Tempnology, LLC
(*In re* Tempnology, LLC) 10-18, 23-49, 23-50

Misys Int'l Banking Sys., Inc. v. TwoFour Sys., LLC 17-16
Modern Appealing Clothing v. Ivanka Trump Marks, LLC............ 6-6
Mon Cheri Bridals, Inc. v. Wen Wu 4-7, 4-8
Monsanto Co. v. Scruggs 12-16
Monsanto Co. v. Spray-Rite Serv. Corp. 12-3, 12-10, 12-11, 12-16
Monster Energy Co. v. Wensheng 7-7
Montgomery v. Alcoa, Inc. 4-22
Montgomery Ward Holding Corp., *In re* 23-19, 23-42
Moran v. Household Int'l Inc. 1-20
Morgan v. Family Dollar 16-3
Morgansen's LTD, *In re* 23-51, 23-59
Morningside Grp. Ltd. v.
Morningside Capital Grp., L.L.C. 2-102
Morningware, Inc. v. Hearthware Home Prods., Inc. 2-101
Moseley v. V Secret Catalogue, Inc. 2-5, 2-52, 2-53, 2-57
Moss Mfg. Co. v. United States 19-17
Motion Picture Patents Co. v. Universal Film Mfg. Co. 8-3
Motive Parts Warehouse v. Facet Enters. 12-18
Motown Record Corp. v. Hormel & Co. 18-4
Motschenbacher v. R.J. Reynolds Tobacco Co. 18-6, 18-10
Multi Time Mach., Inc. v. Amazon.com, Inc. 2-31, 2-32
Munsingwear, Inc. v. Jockey Int'l, Inc. 2-34, 2-35, 2-51
Mushroom Makers, Inc. v. R.G. Barry Corp. 2-64
Musman v. Modern Deb, Inc. 17-4

N

N. Am. Catholic Educ. Programming Found., Inc. v.
Gheewalla 23-5
N. Atl. Instruments, Inc. v. Haber 17-8
N. Pac. Ry. Co. v United States 12-16
Nasty Gal, Inc., *In re* 23-3
Nat Lewis Purses v. Carole Bags 4-20
Nat'l Artists Mgmt. Co. v. Weaving 15-4
Nat'l Grange of the Order of Patrons of Husbandry v.
California Guild 2-98
Nat'l Heritage Found., Inc. v. Highbourne Found. 23-18
Nat'l Truck Funding LLC, *In re* 12-32
National Football League v. Sunmei 7-16
Nationwide Mut. Ins. Co. v. Darden 16-17, 16-31
NBA v. New World Creation Inc. of N.Y. 2-8
NCAA v. Bd. of Regents 12-4
Nebb v. Bell Syndicate 18-14

Nespresso USA, Inc. v. Africa Am. Coffee Trading Co. 2-93
Netnumina Sols., Inc. v. Dietrehab.com, Inc. 4-24
NETtel Corp., *In re* 23-20
Network Automation, Inc. v. Advanced Sys. Concepts, Inc. 2-96
New Kids on the Block v. News Am. Publ'g, Inc. 2-78
New York City Triathlon v. NYC Triathlon Club 2-60
Newport News Holdings Corp. v.
  Virtual City Vision, Inc. 2-6, 2-82
Nguyen v. Barnes & Noble Inc. 14-12, 14-13, 14-14, 14-15
Niblett, *In re* 23-57
Nicholas Labs. Ltd. v. Almay, Inc. 10-10
Nichols v. Universal Pictures Co. 4-38
Nicosia v. Amazon.com, Inc. 14-12
Nike v. Enter Play Sports, Inc. 6-16
Nike, Inc. v. Dekovic 6-18, 17-18
Nike, Inc. v. Enter Play Sports, Inc. 6-16, 6-17
Nike, Inc. v. Just Did It Enters. 2-68
Nike, Inc. v. Kasky 15-3
Nike, Inc. v. McCarthy 17-17, 17-18
NIKE, Inc. v. Superstar Int'l Inc. 3-32
Nike, Inc. v. Wu 7-9, 7-12, 7-14, 7-19
Nino v. L'Oreal USA, Inc. 15-33
Nintendo of Am. v. Ketchum 4-47
Nissan Antitrust Litig., *In re* 12-13
Nola Spice Designs, L.L.C. v. Haydel Enters., Inc. 4-18, 4-19
North Am. Med. Corp. v. Axiom Worldwide, Inc. 2-94
Nw. Nat'l Ins. Co. of Milwaukee, Wisc. v. Alberts 2-61
Novelty Textile Mills, Inc. v. Joan Fabrics Corp. 4-8, 4-32, 4-33
Nu Skin Enter., Inc., In the Matter of 20-21
N.Y. Stock Exch., Inc. v. N.Y., N.Y. Hotel, LLC 2-57
N.Y. Times Co. v. United States 4-16
N.Y.C. Triathlon, LLC v. N.Y.C. Triathlon Club, Inc. 2-70
NYEC, Inc. f/k/a The Wiz, Inc., *In re* 23-67

O

O. & W. Thum Co. v. Dickinson 2-81
O. A. Newton & Son Co. v. Horsey 1-17
Oakley, Inc. v. Mountain View Mktg., Inc. 3-35
Oakley, Inc. v. NY Eyewear Trading Co. 3-34
Oakley, Inc. v. Predator Outdoor Prods., LLC 3-40
Oakley, Inc. v. Talitor Far East Co. 3-40

Octane Fitness, LLC v.
ICON Health & Fitness, Inc. 2-68, 3-22, 15-21
OddzOn Prods., Inc. v. Just Toys, Inc. 3-17
Odell Beckham, Jr. v. Splash News & Picture Agency, LLC......... 18-20
Ohio-Sealy Mattress Mfg. Co. v. Sealy, Inc. 12-16
Old Carco LLC, *In re* 23-49
Olson v. Nat'l Broad. Co. 4-39
Omega Envtl., Inc. v. Gilbarco, Inc. 12-14
Omega S.A. v. Costco Wholesale Corp. 8-13, 8-14,
.... 8-15, 8-22, 8-23
OMV Assocs., L.P. v. Clearway Acquisition, Inc. 13-9
On Davis v. The Gap, Inc. 4-42, 4-43
Onassis v. Christian Dior-N.Y., Inc. 18-15
OneBeacon Am. Ins. Co. v. Digital Projections, Inc. 18-19
Online Travel Co., *In re* 14-11
Opticians Ass'n of Am. v. Indep. Opticians of Am. 2-59, 2-62
Optimum Techs., Inc. v. Home Depot U.S.A., Inc. 2-67
Oralabs, Inc. v. Kind Grp., LLC 7-10
Oriental Fin. Grp., Inc. v.
Cooperativa de Ahorro y Credito Oriental 2-81
Orion Pictures Corp., *In re* 23-33
Orix Credit Alliance, Inc. v. Delta Res., Inc.
(*In re* Delta Res., Inc.) 23-31
Orson, Inc. v. Miramax Film Corp. 12-15
Osawa & Co. v. B&H Photo 8-7
Out Fit 7 Ltd. v. Nanjing 3D Info. Tech., Co. 7-9

P

Pac. Lumber Co., *In re* 23-17
Paddington Corp. v. Attiki Importers & Distribs., Inc. 2-40
Pagliero v. Wallace China Co. 2-87
Panduit Corp. v. Stahlin Bros. Fibre Works, Inc. 3-19
Parfums Givenchy, Inc. v. Drug Emporium, Inc. 8-9, 8-10, 8-13
Partners for Health & Home, L.P. v. Yang 2-99
Patora v. Tarte Inc. 15-33
Patrick Collins Inc. v. Doe 4-30
Patriot Place, Ltd., *In re* 23-37
Patsy's Brand, Inc. v. I.O.B. Realty, Inc. 2-103, 15-20
Patsy's Italian Rest., Inc. v. Banas 2-83
Paul Frank Indus., Inc. v. Sunich 2-7
Paul v. Haley 6-12
Pauley Petroleum, Inc. v. Cont'l Oil Co. 1-33

Payless Shoesource, Inc. v. Reebok Int'l Ltd. 2-35, 2-45
Payless v. Reebok 2-45
Paz Sys., Inc. v. Dakota Grp. Corp. 17-8
PDK Labs, Inc. v. Friedlander 15-15
Pearson Edu., Inc. v. Liu 8-5
People v. Ningbo Beyond Home Textile Co. 6-5
People v. Pratibha Syntex Ltd. 6-5
Peregrine Entm't, Ltd, *In re* 4-27
Perfect 10 v. Visa Int'l Serv. Ass'n 7-24, 7-25
Perfect Fit Indus. v. Acme Quilting Co. 15-20
Perlman v. Catapult Entm't, Inc.
(*In re* Catapult Entm't, Inc.) 23-47
PETA v. Doughney 2-34, 2-97
Peter F. Gaito Architecture, LLC v. Simone Dev. Corp. 4-34
Peter Pan Fabrics, Inc. v. Martin Weiner Corp. 4-12
Petroliam Nasional Berhad v. GoDaddy.com, Inc. 7-26
Pfaff v. Wells Elecs., Inc. 3-10
Pfaudler v. Pfaudler Co. 18-14
Philip Morris U.S.A., Inc. v. Filizardo 6-9
Phillips v. Martin Marietta Corp. 16-27
Phoenix of Broward, Inc. v. McDonald's Corp. 15-15
Pilgrim's Pride Corp., *In re* 23-25
Pineda v. Williams-Sonoma Stores, Inc. 14-29
Pirone v. MacMillan, Inc. 18-12
Pivot Point Int'l Inc. v. Charlene Prods., Inc. 4-10, 4-11, 4-14
Pizza Hut, Inc. v. Papa John's Int'l, Inc. 15-5, 15-10
Pizzeria Uno Corp. v. Temple 2-30
Plasticware, LLC v. Flint Hills Res., LP 8-22
Playboy Enters., Inc. v. Netscape Commc'ns, Inc. 2-96
Playboy Enters., Inc. v. Welles 2-78
Playskool, Inc. v. Product Dev. Grp., Inc. 15-20
Poe v. Missing Persons 4-11
Polaroid Corp. v. Polarad Elecs. Corp. 2-30, 2-31,
.... 2-37, 2-38, 2-60
Polo Fashions, Inc. v. Craftex, Inc. 2-35, 2-36
Pom Wonderful LLC v. Coca-Cola Co. 15-33
Precision Instrument Mfg. Co. v.
Auto. Maint. Mach. Co. 2-77
Pretty Girl, Inc. v. Pretty Girl Fashions, Inc. 2-27, 2-60, 2-63
Proctor & Gamble Co. v. Haughen 15-38
Proctor & Gamble Co. v. Ultreo, Inc. 15-9
Proctor & Gamble Corp. v. Amway Co. 15-15
ProFitness Physical Therapy Ctr. v. Pro–Fit Orthopedic &
Sports Physical Therapy P.C. 2-81

Promatek Indus., Ltd. v. Equitrac Corp. 2-94
Provost v. Aptos, Inc. 14-29
Prudential Ins. Co. of Am. v. SW Boston Hotel Venture, LLC
(*In re* SW Boston Hotel Venture, LLC) 23-31
PSKS, Inc. v. Leegin Creative Leather Prods. 12-15
Puma SE v. Forever 21, Inc. 2-63, 2-91, 2-92
Purchasing Assocs., Inc. v. Weitz 17-15, 17-17
Pure Power Boot Camp, Inc. v.
Warrior Fitness Boot Camp, LLC 17-15, 17-16

Q

Qualitex Co. v. Jacobson Prods. Co. 2-87, 2-88, 2-90
Quality King Distributors, Inc. v.
L'anza Research Int'l, Inc. 8-2, 8-9, 8-11
Quanta Comput., Inc. v. LG Elecs., Inc. 8-8
Quick Techs., Inc. v. Sage Grp. PLC 2-65
Quidgeon v. Olsen 2-99
Quill Corp. v. North Dakota 14-31

R

RAE Sys. Inc., *In re* 20-28, 20-29
Ralph C. Wilson Indus. v. Chronicle Broad. Co. 12-15
Rayfield Inv. Co. v. Kreps 23-52
Raynor Mfg. Co. v. Raynor Door Co. 12-18
RCI Tech. Corp. v. Sunterra Corp. (*In re* Sunterra Corp.) 23-47
Reebok Int'l, Ltd. v. Marnatech Enters., Inc. 2-69
Reed, Roberts Assocs., Inc. v.
Strauman 17-10, 17-14, 17-15, 17-20
Related Westpac LLC v. JER Snowmass LLC 23-5
Renaissance Nutrition, Inc. v. Jarrett 17-16, 17-20
Republic Molding Corp. v. B.W. Photo Utils. 2-77
Rescuecom Corp. v. Google Inc. 2-27, 2-96
Resorts Int'l, Inc. v. Lowenschuss (*In re* Lowenschuss) 23-17
Reverb Commc'ns, Inc., In the Matter of 15-40
Review Aus. Pty Ltd v. Innovative Lifestyle Invs. 5-13
Ricci v. DeStefano 16-23
Richardson v. Stanley Works, Inc. 3-17
Richmond Leasing Co. v. Capital Bank, N.A. 23-33
Riggs v. Pursell 13-29

Ringgold v. Black Entm't TV 4-43
Rio Props., Inc. v. Rio Int'l Interlink........ 7-9
Roberson v. Rochester Folding Box Co........ 18-4, 18-12
Robi v. Five Platters, Inc. 2-77
Roederer v. J. Garcia Carrion, S.A. 2-81
Roger Cleveland Golf Co. v. Prince........ 7-28, 7-29, 7-32, 7-33
Rolex Watch U.S.A., Inc. v. Jones 7-10, 7-32
Rolex Watch U.S.A., Inc. v. Rolex Deli Corp. 2-41, 2-55, 2-60
Romag Fasteners, Inc. v. Fossil, Inc. 2-67
Rosales v. Fitflop USA, LLC 15-32
Rose's Stores, Inc., *In re* 23-67
Rosetta Stone Ltd. v. Google, Inc........ 2-57, 2-79, 2-97, 2-98, 2-101
Roto-Rooter Corp. v. O'Neal 2-30
Roulo v. Russ Berrie & Co. 2-67
Roy Export Co. v. CBS........ 6-11
RPost Holdings v. Trustifi Corp. 15-16
rue21, inc., *In re* 23-13
Rutherford Food Corp. v. McComb 16-17
Ryan v. Volpone Stamp Co. 18-12
Ryko Mfg. Co. v. Eden Servs........ 12-14

S

S & J Holding Corp., *In re*........ 23-29
S. St. Seaport L.P. v. Burger Boys, Inc........ 23-34
S.C. Johnson & Son, Inc. v. Clorox Co........ 15-17, 15-18, 15-19
S.F. Drake Hotel Assoc., *In re*........ 23-29
Saenger Org., Inc. v. Nationwide Ins. Licensing Assoc., Inc. 4-22
Saks & Co. v. Hill 2-41
Salinger v. Colting........ 2-59, 2-60, 2-62
Sally Beauty Co. v. Beautyco, Inc........ 2-30
Samara Bros. v. Wal-Mart Stores 4-8
Samsung Elecs. Co. v. Apple Inc........ 3-20
Sandoz Pharms. Corp. v. Richardson-Vicks, Inc. 15-17
Sands, Taylor & Wood Co. v. Quaker Oats Co. 2-36, 2-44
Sanson Hosiery Mills v. Warren Knitting Mills 3-17
Santa Clara Valley Distrib. Co. v. Pabst Brewing Co. 12-12
Sara Lee Corp. v. Bags of N.Y., Inc........ 2-82, 7-30
Sara Lee Corp. v. Kayser-Roth Corp. 2-82
Saratoga Vichy Spring Co. v. Lehman........ 6-9
Sasqua Grp., Inc. v. Courtney........ 6-11
SCA Hygiene Prods. Aktiebolag v.
First Quality Baby Prods., LLC 3-40

Scarves By Vera, Inc. v. Todo Imports, Ltd. 2-44
Scarves by Vera, Inc. v. United Merchants & Mfrs. Inc. 4-8, 4-10
Schreiber v. Dunabin 7-29
Scott-Macon Sec., Inc. v. Zoltek Cos. 10-17
Seagate Tech., L.L.C., *In re* 3-23
Sears, Roebuck & Co. v. Sears Fin. Network 2-49
Seaside Eng'g & Surveying, Inc., *In re* 23-18
Seat Sack, Inc. v. Childcraft Educ. Corp. 15-20
SEC v. Avon Prods., Inc. 20-18
SEC v. RAE Sys. Inc. 20-28, 20-29
SEC v. Syncor Int'l Corp. 20-30
SEC v. Titan Corp. 20-30
Secalt S.A. v. Wuxi Shenxi Constr. Mach. Co. 2-68
Seiko Epson Corp. v. Nu-Kote Int'l, Inc. 3-8
Self Directed Placement Corp. v. Control Data Corp. 6-7
Selle v. Gibb 4-31
SemCrude, L.P., *In re* 23-25
Sennheiser Elec. Corp. v. Eichler 7-32
Sgouros v. TransUnion Corp. 14-11, 14-12
Shamsky v. Garan, Inc. 18-13
Shark Tank 1-2
Sharon Steel Corp. v. Nat'l Fuel Gas Distribution Corp. 23-33
Shaw Family Archives, Ltd. v.
CMG Worldwide, Inc. 18-12, 18-13, 18-16, 18-17
Shearson Lehman Bros. Holdings, Inc. v. Schmertzler 17-16
Sheila's Shine Prods., Inc. v. Sheila Shine, Inc. 2-83
Sheldon v. Metro-Goldwyn Pictures Corp. 4-29
Sheridan v. Marathon Petroleum Co. 12-16
SIFCO Indus. Inc. v. Advanced Plating Techs., Inc. 17-15
Silverman v. CBS, Inc. 2-24
Silvertop Assocs., Inc. v. Kangaroo Mfg., Inc. 4-16
Simpson v. Union Oil Co. 12-11, 12-12
Skechers U.S.A., Inc. v. Anthony L & S LLC 3-33
Skechers U.S.A., Inc. v. DB Shoe Co. 3-33
Skechers U.S.A., Inc. v. Eliya Inc. 3-33
Skechers U.S.A., Inc. v. FILA U.S.A. Inc. 3-33
Skechers U.S.A., Inc. v. Reebok Int'l Ltd. 3-33
Skechers U.S.A., Inc. v. Sears Holding Corp. 3-33
Skechers U.S.A., Inc. v. Shoe Confession, LLC 3-33
Skechers U.S.A., Inc. v. Steve Madden, Ltd. 3-33
Skechers U.S.A., Inc. v.
The Children's Place Retail Stores, Inc. 3-33
Skydive Ariz., Inc. v. Quattrocchi 2-99

Sleepy's LLC v. Select Comfort Wholesale Corp. 2-68
Slep-Tone Entm't Corp. v. Karaoke Kandy Store, Inc. 2-68
Sly Magazine, LLC v. Weider Publ'ns L.L.C. 6-21
Smith v. Jackson 4-34
Smith v. Mikki More, LLC 4-23
Smith v. Van Gorkom 1-20, 23-4
Smith v. Whitman Saddle Co. 3-18
Société de Developments et D'Innovations des Marches
Agricoles et Alimentaires-Sodima-Union de
Cooperatives Agricoles v. Int'l Yogurt Co. 2-24
Société Nationale Industrielle Aérospatiale v.
U.S. Dist. Court for S. Dist. of Iowa 7-18
Societe Yves Saint Laurent Couture S.A. v.
Societe Louis Dreyfus Retail Mgmt. S.A. 5-7
Soilworks, LLC v. Midwest Indus. Supply, Inc. 2-94
Sokol Holdings, Inc. v. BMB Munai, Inc. 6-11
Sole Resort, S.A. de C.V. v. Allure Resorts Mgmt., LLC 7-6
Solid 21, Inc. v. Breitling USA, Inc. 2-27
Sons of Thunder, Inc. v. Borden, Inc. 10-17
Sony Corp. of Am. v. Universal City Studios, Inc. 4-42
Sony Gaming Networks & Customer Data Sec.
Breach Litig., *In re* 14-29
Sony Music Entm't, *In re* 12-13
Sophia & Chloe, Inc. v. Brighton Collectibles, LLC 4-37
Soptra Fabrics Corp. v. Stafford Knitting Mills, Inc. 4-12, 4-35
South Dakota v. Wayfair 14-31, 14-32, 14-33
Specht v. Netscape Commc'n Corp. 14-12, 14-13, 14-15
Specific Media Flash Cookies Litig., *In re* 14-28
Spectravest, Inc. v. Mervyn's Inc. 4-36, 4-37
Spectrum Sports, Inc. v. McQuillan 12-4
Sports Auth. v. Prime Hospitality Corp. 2-38, 2-40, 2-43,
.... 2-44, 2-47, 2-48, 2-50
Spotra Fabrics Corp. v. Stafford Knitting Mills, Inc. 4-35
Spotted Friend, LLC v. Vigme, Inc. 6-18
SquirtCo v. Seven-Up Co. 2-30
St George Exec. Shuttle, LLC v.
W. Trails Charters & Tours LLC 2-99
Staggers v. Real Authentic Sound 4-23
Standard Fabrics Int'l, Inc. v. Dress Barn, Inc. 4-38
Standard Oil Co. v. Fed. Trade Comm'n 12-18
Standard Oil Co. v. United States 12-14
Stanfield v. Osborne Indus., Inc. 15-15
Star Athletica, L.L.C. v. Varsity Brands, Inc. 4-2, 4-15, 4-16, 4-39
Star Fabrics, Inc. v. DKJY, Inc. 4-7

Starbucks Corp. v. Wolfe's Borough Coffee, Inc. 2-54, 2-55, 2-56, 2-57
State Farm Fire & Cas. Co. v. Super. Ct. 6-4
State Oil Co. v. Khan 12-8, 12-9
Staub v. Proctor Hosp. 16-23
Steele v. Bulova Watch Co. 2-73
Stella McCartney Ltd., *In re* 2-12
Stephano v. News Grp. Publ'ns, Inc. 18-12, 18-13
Sterling v. Mayflower Hotel Corp. 1-48
Stevens Linen Assocs., Inc. v. Mastercraft Corp. 4-46
Stone Barn Manhattan LLC, *In re* 23-20, 23-42
Stone Creek, Inc. v. Omnia Italian Design, Inc. 2-66
Storus Corp. v. Aroa Mktg., Inc. 2-99
Strick Chex Columbus Two, LLC, *In re* 23-29
Summit Inv. & Dev. Corp. v. Leroux 23-47
Sunbeam Oster Co. v. Lincoln Liberty Ave., Inc. (*In re* Allegheny Intern., Inc.) 23-42
Sunbeam Prods., Inc. v. Chi. Am. Mfg., LLC 10-17
SunEarth, Inc. v. Sun Earth Solar Power Co. 2-68
Superior Form Builders, Inc. v. Dan Chase Taxidermy Supply Co. 4-47
SW Hotel Venture, LLC, *In re* 23-30
Swarovski Aktiengesellschaft v. Bldg. No. 19 .... 2-29, 2-59, 2-60, 2-79
Sweetheart Plastics, Inc. v. Detroit Forming, Inc. 2-83
Sylmark Holdings Ltd. v. Silicone Zone Int'l Ltd. 17-13
Synergistic Int'l, LLC v. Korman 2-67

T

Taggart v. Rutledge 12-14
Tamko Roofing Prods., Inc. v. Ideal Roofing Co. 2-66
Tampa Elec. Co. v. Nashville Coal Co. 12-14
Taylor v. ADS, Inc. 16-32
TCPIP Holding Co. v. Hoar Comm'ns, Inc. 2-53
Teaching Co. Ltd. P'ship v. Unapix Entm't, Inc. 2-67
TechnoMarine SA v. Jacob Time, Inc. 8-22
Telecom Int'l Am., Ltd. v. AT & T Corp. 6-10, 6-13
Texaco Inc. v. Hasbrouck 12-18
The Gap, Inc. v. G.A.P. Adventures, Inc. 2-27, 2-38, 2-40, 2-43, 2-55, 2-59
The North Face Apparel Corp. v. Fujian Sharing Imp. & Exp. Ltd. 7-13

Therasense, Inc. v. Becton, Dickinson & Co. 3-12
Thiessen v. Gen. Elec. Capital Corp. 16-3
Thin Film Lab, Inc. v. Comito 17-8
Thomas Wilson & Co. v. Irving J. Dorfman Co. 4-8
Thomson v. Larson 4-22
Ticor Title Ins. Co. v. Cohen 17-17
Tie Tech, Inc. v. Kinedyne Corp. 2-27
Tierney v. Moschino S.p.A. 2-80, 6-5
Tiffany (NJ) LLC v. Andrew 7-12, 7-15
Tiffany (NJ) LLC v. Dong 7-9, 7-12, 7-14, 7-15, 7-17
Tiffany (NJ) LLC v. Forbse 7-15, 7-18
Tiffany (NJ) LLC v. Qi Andrew 7-15, 7-18
Tiffany (NJ), Inc. v. eBay, Inc. 2-54, 2-55, 2-56, 7-21, 7-22
Tiffany & Co. v. Costco Wholesale Corp. 2-11, 2-39
Tiffany v. eBay 7-25
Tillamook Country Smoker, Inc. v.
Tillamook Cty. Creamery Ass'n 2-81
Timed Out, LLC v. Youabian, Inc. 18-10
Times-Picayune Publ'g v. United States 12-5
Tire Kingdom, Inc. v. Morgan Tire & Auto, Inc. 15-20
Todd v. Montana Silversmiths, Inc. 4-7, 4-8, 4-18
Toledo Mack Sales & Serv., Inc. v. Mack Trucks, Inc. 12-18
Tom McCormick Enters., Inc., *In re* 23-30
Tommy Hilfiger Licensing, Inc. v. Nature Labs, LLC 2-41, 2-85
Toney v. L'Oreal USA, Inc. 18-3
Too, Inc. v. Kohl's Dep't Stores, Inc. 8-19, 8-20
Too, Inc. v. The TJX Cos. 8-17, 8-18
Tool Works v. Indep. Ink, Inc. 12-16
Tory Burch LLC v. Yong Sheng Int'l Trade Co. 7-12, 7-32
Tory Burch v. Chris Burch v. Judge Strine 6-20
Toys "R" Us, Inc. v. F.T.C. 12-15
TrafFix Devices, Inc. v. Mktg. Displays, Inc. 2-88
Traicoff v. Digital Media, Inc. 23-47
Trans Union LLC v. Credit Research, Inc. 2-96
Trans-World Mfg. Corp. v. Al Nyman & Sons, Inc. 3-22
Treesource Indus., Inc., *In re* 23-20
Triangl Grp. Ltd. v. Jiangmen City Xinhui Dist.
Lingzhi Garment Co. 4-16
Triple-A Baseball Club Assocs. v. Ne. Baseball, Inc. 10-16
Troublé v. Wet Seal, Inc. 2-65
Trujillo v. Avon Prods., Inc. 15-33
Trump Entm't Resorts, Inc., *In re* 23-47
TSA Stores, Inc. v. Sport Dimension Inc.
(*In re* TSAWD, Inc.) 23-58

TSAWD Holdings, Inc., *In re* 23-57, 23-58
Twentieth Century Music Corp. v. Aiken 8-5
Two Pesos, Inc. v. Taco Cabana, Inc. 2-27
Two S Corp., *In re* 23-32
Tyler v. Michaels Stores Inc. 14-30
Tylka v. Gerber Prods. Co. 15-5
TYR Sport Inc. v. Warnaco Swimwear, Inc. 15-5, 15-6

U

U.S. Polo Ass'n, Inc. v. PRL USA Holdings, Inc. .... 2-30, 2-40, ... 2-48, 2-58, 2-60, 2-61
U.S. Re Cos. v. Scheerer 17-13
Ultra-Temp. Corp. v. Advanced Vacuum Sys., Inc. 15-4
Unarco Indus. Inc. v. Kelley Co. 23-46
Unicolors, Inc. v. Unicolors, Inc., Urban Outfitters, Inc. 4-31, 4-36
Union Carbide Corp. v. Ever-Ready, Inc. 2-7, 2-48
United Merchants & Mfrs., Inc. v. Sarne Co. 4-30
United States v. Aguilar 20-33
United States v. Alcatel-Lucent 20-34
United States v. Aluminum Co. of Am. 12-5
United States v. Avon Prods. (China) Co. 20-17, 20-18
United States v. Carson 20-32, 20-33, 20-34
United States v. Colgate & Co. 12-11
United States v. DaimlerChrysler Auto. Russia SAO 20-7
United States v. DaimlerChrysler China Ltd. 20-7
United States v. Dentsply Int'l 12-14
United States v. Duperval 20-11
United States v. Esquenazi 20-10, 20-31, 20-32
United States v. First Nat'l City Bank 7-14
United States v. Friedlaender & Co. 19-14
United States v. GE 12-12
United States v. Golden Acres, Inc. 1-32
United States v. Grinnell Corp. 12-4
United States v. Inn Foods, Inc. 19-30
United States v. Jerrold Elecs. Corp. 12-16
United States v. Kay 20-8, 20-11
United States v. King 20-9, 20-27
United States v. Kozeny 20-8, 20-27
United States v. Marine Bancorp. 12-5
United States v. Nektalov 23-59

United States v. Noriega.. 20-32
United States v. O'Shea.. 20-32, 20-34
United States v. Parke, Davis & Co. 12-10, 12-11
United States v. Patel 20-7
United States v. Ron Pair Enters., Inc. 23-30
United States v. SSI Int'l Far E., Ltd. 20-7
United States v. Syncor Taiwan, Inc. 20-7, 20-30
United States v. Titan Corp. 20-30
United States v. Torkington 2-64
United States v. Trenton Potteries Co. 12-6
United States v. United Foods, Inc. 15-3
United States v. Univis Lens Co. 8-8
United States v. Whiting Pools, Inc. 23-27, 23-28
United States v. Zhao 7-4
Univ. of Pittsburgh v. Champion Prods., Inc. 2-8
Urban Communicators PCS Ltd. P'ship, *In re* 23-31, 23-32
Urban Outfitters, Inc. v.
BCBG Max Azria Grp., Inc. 2-27, 2-29, 2-38, 2-40,
....2-42, 2-45, 2-46, 2-49, 2-50,
.... 2-51, 2-52, 2-59, 2-61, 2-62, 2-64, 2-74
US Airways Grp., Inc. v. British Airways PLC 10-16
USFL v. NFL 12-4

V

Valley Media, Inc., *In re* 23-52, 23-53, 23-57, 23-60
Venture Tape Corp. v. McGills Glass Warehouse 2-65
Venzie Corp. v. U.S. Mineral Prods. Co. 12-16
Verified Complaint for Forfeiture In Rem, U.S. v.
All Funds in Indus. & Commercial Bank of
China Ltd. Interbank Accounts in the United States 7-4
Verizon Comms. Inc. v. Law Offices of Curtis V. Trinko LLP 12-4
Vertex Grp. LLC, *In re* 2-19
Victoria's Secret Stores, Inc. v. May Dep't Stores Co. 17-18
VirnetX, Inc. v. Cisco Sys., Inc. 3-20
Visa USA, *In re* 15-17
Vitabiotics, Ltd. v. Krupka 6-13
Vitro S.A.B. de C.V., *In re* 23-17
Voda v. Cordis Corp. 3-24
VWP of Am., Inc. v. United States 19-17, 19-18

W

W. Diversified Servs., Inc. v. Hyundai Motor Am., Inc. 2-66
W. Geophysical Co. of Am., Inc. v. Bolt Assocs., Inc. 10-17
W. Real Estate Fund, Inc., *In re* 23-17
W.W.W. Pharm. Co. v. Gillette Co. 2-49
Waffenschmidt v. Mackay.. 7-13
Wainwright Sec., Inc. v. Wall St. Transcript Corp. 4-41
Waits v. Frito-Lay, Inc.. 18-10
Wal-Mart Stores, Inc. v. Samara Bros., Inc. 2-14, 6-14
Wal-Mart Stores, Inc., *In re* 2-13
Warner Bros. Entm't v. X One X Prods. 4-39, 4-40
Washington Mut., Inc., *In re* 23-18
Webadviso v. Bank of Am. Corp. 2-70
Webster v. Fulton Cty. 16-32
Weiss v. Reebok Int'l, Ltd. 3-38
West Elecs., Inc., *In re* 23-47
WesternGeco LLC v. ION Geophysical Corp. 3-19, 3-24
Whalen v. W.R. Grace & Co. 16-25
Whimsicality, Inc. v. Rubie's Costume Co. 4-8, 4-10
White v. Leanore Frocks 4-20
White v. Samsung Elecs. Am., Inc. 18-10, 18-11
Wicaco Mach. Corp., *In re* 23-52
Windsor Auctions, Inc. v. eBay, Inc. 12-17
Winter v. NRDC 2-65
Wiseley v. Amazon.com, Inc. 14-16
Wolff v. Rare Medium, Inc. 8-22
Wolinsky v. Vermont Fed. Bank, FSB
(*In re* Vermont Knitting Co.) 23-29
Wolstenholme v. Hirst 4-7
World Entm't, Inc. v. Brown... 2-99
Wultz v. Bank of China Ltd. 7-18

X

Xuedan Wang v. Hearst Corp. 16-14
Xymogen, Inc. v. Digitalev, LLC 2-99

Y

Young v. Greneker Studios, Inc.. 18-14
Young v. Kaplan.. 13-12
Yurman Design v. PAJ, Inc. 2-14, 2-15

Z

Zacchini v. Scripps-Howard Broad. Co. 18-2, 18-3, 18-6, 18-7
Zahn, *In re* 3-8
Zappos.com, Inc., Customer Data Sec.
Breach Litig., *In re* 14-14, 14-30
Zelinski v. Columbia 300, Inc. 2-67
Zenith Elec. Corp. v. Exzec, Inc. 15-16
Zino Davidoff SA v. CVS Corp. 2-62

STATUTES

United States Code (U.S.C.)

Title 5

§ 45(b) 15-22, 15-24
§ 706(2)(E) 15-24

Title 7

§ 6501 15-29

Title 11
(Bankruptcy Code)

§ 101(32)(A) 23-6
§ 101(35A) 23-49
§ 104 23-23
§ 105 .... 23-17, 23-34
§ 105(a) 23-17,
.... 23-18, 23-34, 23-58
§ 105(A) 23-58
§ 361 23-14
§ 362 23-21
§ 362(a) 23-21
§ 362(a)(2) 23-26
§ 362(a)(3) 23-26
§ 362(a)(4) 23-26
§ 362(b) 23-21
§ 362(d)(1) 23-22
§ 362(k)(1) 23-22
§ 363 .... 23-8, 23-26,
.... 23-60, 23-62, 23-63,
.... 23-64, 23-65, 23-66
§ 363(a) 23-13
§ 363(b) 23-26
§ 363(f) 23-65
§ 363(k) 23-65
§ 363(m) 23-65
§ 364 23-14
§ 365 .... 10-17, 23-21
§ 365(a) 23-33, 23-34, 23-44
§ 365(b) 23-38
§ 365(b)(1)(A) 23-35, 23-36
§ 365(b)(1)(B) 23-35
§ 365(b)(1)(C) 23-35,
.... 23-36, 23-37
§ 365(b)(2)(A) 23-35
§ 365(b)(2)(B) 23-35
§ 365(b)(2)(C) 23-35
§ 365(b)(2)(D) 23-35
§ 365(b)(3) 23-39
§ 365(b)(3)(C) 23-68
§ 365(c)(1) 23-46, 23-47
§ 365(c)(3) 23-39
§ 365(d)(3) 23-19,
.... 23-20, 23-43
§ 365(d)(4) 23-41
§ 365(d)(4)(A) 23-33, 23-34
§ 365(d)(4)(B) 23-34
§ 365(d)(4)(B)(i) 23-66
§ 365(d)(4)(B)(ii) 23-34
§ 365(e) 23-47
§ 365(e)(1) 23-36
§ 365(f) 23-38, 23-68
§ 365(f)(1) 23-38, 23-46
§ 365(f)(2) 23-37
§ 365(f)(2)(B) 23-38
§ 365(g) 23-50
§ 365(g)(1) 23-41
§ 365(h)(1)(A)(i) 23-43
§ 365(h)(1)(A)(ii) 23-43
§ 365(h)(1)(B) 23-43
§ 365(h)(1)(C) 23-43
§ 365(k) 23-38
§ 365(n) 23-49
§ 365(n)(1)(A) 23-48
§ 365(n)(1)(B) 23-48
§ 365(n)(2)(A) 23-48
§ 365(n)(2)(B) 23-48
§ 365(n)(3) 23-49
§ 365(n)(4) 23-49
§ 502(b)(2) 23-30
§ 502(b)(6) 23-41

§ 502(b)(6) 23-33
§ 502(g) 23-41
§ 503(b)(1) 23-19
§ 503(b)(9) 23-25
§ 506(a)(1) 23-30
§ 506(a)(2) 23-32
§ 506(b) 23-30, 23-31
§ 507(a)(4)–(5) 23-23
§ 510(c) 23-27
§ 522 23-26
§ 524(e) 23-16, 23-17
§ 541 .... 23-13, 23-26
§ 541(a) 23-26
§ 541(a)(1) 23-27, 23-28
§ 541(a)(3) 23-27
§ 541(a)(4) 23-27
§ 541(a)(6) 23-27
§ 541(a)(7) 23-27
§ 541(b) 23-27
§ 541(b)(2) 23-28
§ 541(d) 23-28
§ 542(a) 23-26
§ 542(c) 23-26, 23-27
§ 542(d) 23-26
§ 544 23-58
§ 544(a) 23-56
§ 544(a)(1) 23-56
§ 545 23-27
§ 546(c) 23-25
§ 547(b) 23-27
§ 548(a) 23-27
§ 549 23-27
§ 550 23-27
§ 551 23-27
§ 552(a) 23-28
§ 552(b) 23-28
§ 1102 23-6
§ 1102(a)(1) 23-22
§ 1123 23-61
§ 1123(b)(2) 23-33, 23-44
§ 1129(a)(7) 23-62
§ 1129(a)(9)(B) 23-23
§ 1129(b)(2)(B) 23-61
§ 1129(b)(2)(B)(i) 23-62
§ 1129(b)(2)(B)(ii) 23-62
§ 1141(d) 23-16

Title 14

§ 1125(c)(3)(A) 2-54

Title 15

§ 1 12-3
§§ 1–7 12-2
§ 2 12-4
§§ 12–27 12-2
§ 13 12-17
§ 18a 22-21
§§ 41–58 .... 9-27, 12-2, 14-17
§ 45 .... 14-17, 15-14, 15-21
§ 45(b) 15-22
§ 45(c) 15-24
§ 45(m)(1)(A) 15-22
§ 46 14-17
§ 53 15-12
§ 53(b) 15-22
§ 57a 15-21
§ 68 .... 9-27, 15-12, 19-25
§ 69 .... 9-27, 15-12
§ 70 .... 9-27, 15-12, 19-25
§ 77b(a)(6) 1-64
§ 77c(b) 1-62
§ 77d 1-53
§ 77e 1-53, 1-62, 21-8
§ 77k 21-8
§ 77*l* 21-8
§ 78(g)(1) 1-43
§ 78c(a)(8) 20-5, 20-26
§ 78dd-1 20-26
§ 78dd-1(a) 20-4, 20-5, 20-8, 20-35
§ 78dd-1(a)(1)–(2) 20-31
§ 78dd-1(a)(1)–(3) 20-8
§ 78dd-1(a)(3) 20-22, 20-27
§ 78dd-1(b) 20-11
§ 78dd-1(c) 20-11
§ 78dd-1(f)(1) 20-9
§ 78dd-1(f)(1)(a) 20-9, 20-31
§ 78dd-1(f)(2) 20-9

§ 78dd-1(f)(2)(A)(i)–(ii)...... 20-27
§ 78dd-1(f)(2)(B)............... 20-27
§ 78dd-1(g)............. 20-4, 20-6,
.... 20-8, 20-26
§ 78dd-1(g)(2)..................... 20-6
§ 78dd-2(a)........................ 20-4,
.... 20-8, 20-35
§§ 78dd-2(a)(1)–(2)........... 20-31
§§ 78dd-2(a)(1)–(3)............. 20-8
§ 78dd-2(a)(3)........ 20-22, 20-27
§ 78dd-2(b)....................... 20-11
§ 78dd-2(h)(1)......... 20-6, 20-26
§ 78dd-2(h)(2)..................... 20-9
§ 78dd-2(h)(2)(A)..... 20-9, 20-31
§ 78dd-2(h)(3)..................... 20-9
§ 78dd-2(h)(3)(A)(i).......... 20-22
§ 78dd-2(h)(3)(A)(ii)......... 20-22
§ 78dd-2(i)............... 20-4, 20-6,
.... 20-8, 20-26
§ 78dd-2(i)(2)..................... 20-6
§ 78dd-3.......................... 20-26
§ 78dd-3(a)........................ 20-4,
.... 20-8, 20-35
§§ 78dd-3(a)(1)–(2)........... 20-31
§§ 78dd-3(a)(1)–(3)............. 20-8
§ 78dd-3(a)(3)........ 20-22, 20-27
§ 78dd-3(b)....................... 20-11
§ 78dd-3(c)....................... 20-11
§ 78dd-3(f)(2)..................... 20-9
§ 78dd-3(f)(2)(A)...... 20-9, 20-31
§ 78dd-3(f)(3)..................... 20-9
§ 78m................... 21-19, 22-17
§ 78m(b)(2)...................... 20-13
§ 78m(b)(2)(A).................. 20-13
§ 78m(b)(2)(A)–(B)........... 20-25
§ 78m(b)(2)(B).................. 20-14
§ 78m(b)(5)...................... 20-12
§ 78m(b)(6).......... 20-12, 20-13
§ 78m(b)(7).......... 20-13, 20-14
§ 78n............................... 21-19
§ 78p............................... 21-19
§§ 81 *et seq*........................... 2-4
§ 113................................. 3-11
§§ 1051 *et seq.*...................... 2-4
§ 1052(d)........................... 2-17
§ 1065................................ 2-74
§ 1114(1)................ 2-26, 2-104
§ 1114(2)(D)(iii)................. 7-26
§ 1115(b)(2)......................... 2-83
§ 1116............................... 15-19
§ 1116(a)............................. 2-58
§ 1116(d)............................. 7-16
§ 1117............................... 15-19
§ 1117(a)......... 2-65, 2-66, 2-68,
.... 7-14, 7-29, 15-20
§ 1117(a)(3)......................... 7-30
§ 1117(b)............................. 7-30
§ 1117(c).................... 2-6, 7-30,
.... 7-31, 7-32
§ 1117(d)............................. 2-70
§ 1124............................... 19-27
§ 1125............................... 19-27
§ 1125(a)................. 6-14, 6-15,
.... 15-14, 15-15, 18-4
§ 1125(a)(1)......................... 2-76
§ 1125(a)(1)(A)................... 2-26
§ 1125(c)............................. 2-52
§ 1125(c)(1)............ 2-52, 2-105
§ 1125(c)(1)–(2).................. 2-53
§ 1125(c)(2)(B)........... 2-54, 2-55
§ 1125(c)(3)(A).......... 2-54, 2-79
§ 1125(d)..................... 2-6, 2-69
§ 1125(d)(1)(B)(v)................ 2-6
§ 1127.........2-4, 2-7, 2-8, 2-18,
.... 2-24, 2-53, 19-27
§ 1127(c)(2)......................... 2-53
§ 1127(c)(2)(B)..................... 2-54
§§ 1191–1204.................. 15-12
§§ 1451 *et seq.*................. 15-27
§ 1453............................... 15-28
§§ 1601–13...................... 14-36
§ 1616............................... 14-36
§ 1681............................... 14-37
§ 1693.................. 14-36, 14-37
§§ 1693a–1693r............... 14-37
§§ 2051–2089..................... 9-19
§ 2055................................. 9-23
§ 2058................................. 9-21
§ 2063(a)(5)......................... 9-20
§ 2064................................. 9-22

§ 2064(a) 9-22
§ 2068(a)(1)........................ 9-23
§ 2068(a)(2)........................ 9-23
§ 2068(a)(4)........................ 9-22
§ 2069(a)(1)............. 9-22, 9-23
§ 2084(a) 9-22
§ 6502(b)(1)...................... 14-19
§§ 6801–10 14-36
§§ 6821–27 14-36
§§ 7001 *et seq.* 14-10
§ 7262............................... 21-7
§§ 7701–13 14-34

TITLE 17

§§ 1–216 4-9
§ 101.................. 4-3, 4-9, 4-10,
.... 4-11, 4-20, 4-22,
...... 4-23, 4-24, 17-7, 23-47
§ 102.................................. 4-5
§ 102(a)..................... 4-3, 18-3
§ 102(b)............................ 4-16
§ 106............... 4-29, 8-10, 8-11
§ 106(3)................ 8-3, 8-5, 8-6
§§ 107–122 8-5
§ 107................................ 4-41
§ 107(2)............................ 4-42
§ 107(3)............................ 4-42
§ 107(4)............................ 4-42
§ 109(a)................ 8-3, 8-5, 8-6,
.... 8-10, 8-14, 8-15
§ 201(d)(2)...................... 23-47
§ 205................................ 4-27
§ 410................................ 4-30
§ 410(c) 4-8
§ 411(a)............................ 4-30
§ 502................................ 4-44
§ 503........................ 4-44, 4-45
§ 504........................ 4-44, 4-45
§ 504(b)............................ 4-45
§ 504(c) 4-47
§ 504(c)(1)........................ 4-46
§ 504(c)(2)........................ 4-47
§ 505........................ 4-44, 4-47
§ 506.............................. 19-27
§ 602................................ 8-10
§ 602(a)............................ 8-11
§§ 1301 *et seq.* 4-20
§ 1301(a)(2)....................... 4-21

TITLE 18

§ 2.................................... 20-5
§ 371 20-5
§ 981(b)............................. 7-3
§ 981(k)............................. 7-3
§ 1030............................ 14-34
§ 1030(c) 14-34
§ 1030(g) 14-34
§ 1836.............................. 6-16
§ 1836(b)(1)...................... 6-16
§ 1836(b)(2)...................... 6-16
§ 1839(3).......................... 6-16
§ 1839(5) 6-16
§ 2318............................ 19-27
§ 2320............................ 19-27
§ 2323................................ 7-3
§§ 2701 *et seq.* 14-30

TITLE 19

§ 1304............................ 19-24
§ 1307.................... 19-5, 19-27
§ 1337............. 2-71, 3-24, 3-25
§ 1337(a)(1)(C) 2-71
§ 1337(a)(3)....................... 2-71
§ 1337(d).................. 2-71, 19-7
§ 1337(d)(2)(A) 2-72
§ 1337(d)(2)(B) 2-72
§ 1337(e)–(g) 2-71
§ 1337(e)(1).............. 2-71, 2-73
§ 1337(e)(2)....................... 2-71
§ 1337(f).................. 2-71, 2-73
§ 1337(g).................. 2-71, 19-7
§ 1401a(a)(1)(B)–(C) 19-18
§ 1401a(a)(1)(D) 19-18
§ 1401a(a)(1)(E)............... 19-19
§ 1401a(a)(2) 19-19
§ 1401a(b)(1)(D) 19-16
§ 1401a(f)........................ 19-19
§ 1484.............................. 19-4
§ 1509(g) 19-30
§ 1509(a)(1)(A) 19-7

§ 1592 .... 19-27, 19-30, 19-31, 19-32
§ 1592(a) 19-27
§ 1592(c)(14) 19-27
§ 1595a(c)(1)(A) 19-27
§ 1595a(c)(2)(A) 19-27
§ 1595a(c)(2)(B) 19-27
§ 1595a(c)(2)(C) 19-27
§ 1595a(c)(2)(E) 19-27
§ 1595a(c)(2)(F) 19-27
§ 1595a(c)(3) 19-27
§ 1595a(d) 19-28
§ 3592 19-20
§ 3592(b)(1)(A) 19-22
§ 3592(b)(1)(B) 19-22
§ 3592(b)(1)(C) 19-22
§ 3592(b)(1)(D) 19-22
§ 3592(b)(2) 19-22
§ 3592(b)(3)(A) 19-22
§ 3592(b)(3)(B) 19-22

TITLE 21

§ 321(i) 15-26
§§ 331–34 15-30
§ 362 .... 15-14, 15-26, 15-27

TITLE 22

§ 288 20-9

TITLE 26

§ 164(f) 1-14
§ 199A 1-14
§ 199A(i) 1-14
§ 301(a) 1-22
§ 302(a) 1-22
§ 409A 17-6, 17-7
§ 453 22-10
§ 483 22-11
§ 701 1-17
§ 702 1-17
§ 731 1-18
§ 751 1-18
§§ 1271–75 22-11
§ 1361 1-23
§ 1361(a)(2) 1-23
§ 1361(b) 1-23
§ 1361(c)(4) 1-23
§ 1362(a) 1-23
§ 1362(b)(1)(B) 1-23
§ 1362(b)(5) 1-23
§ 1372(a) 1-24
§ 1374(a) 1-24
§ 1375(a) 1-24
§§ 1401–1403 1-14

TITLE 28

§ 959(b) 23-66
§ 1331 3-24
§ 1334(e)(1) 23-26
§ 1338(a) 3-24
§ 1391 3-24
§ 1408(1) 23-16
§ 1408(2) 23-16
§ 1920 2-67

TITLE 29

§§ 52–53 12-2
§ 157 16-35
§ 158 16-35
§ 203 16-4
§ 203(d) 16-17
§ 203(e)(1) 16-17
§ 203(g) 16-12, 16-17
§ 203(m) 16-4
§ 203(s) 16-4, 16-17
§ 206 16-4
§ 207 .... 16-4, 16-5
§ 212(c) 16-16
§ 213 16-17
§ 213(c)(3) 16-17
§ 213(d) 16-17
§ 215(a)(1) 16-15
§ 216(a) 16-19
§ 216(b) 16-3
§ 216(e)(1)(A)(i) 16-19
§ 218(a) 16-5
§ 255(a) 16-7
§ 260 16-7
§ 623(f)(1) 16-27
§ 2612 .... 16-28, 16-29

TITLE 35

§ 41 3-12
§ 101 .... 3-4, 3-5
§ 102 3-5
§ 102(a) 3-5, 3-10
§ 102(b) 3-5, 3-10
§ 102(c) 3-5
§ 102(d) 3-5
§ 103 3-5
§ 112 3-10
§ 112(b) 3-11
§ 115 3-11
§ 120 3-14
§ 123 3-12
§ 132 3-14
§ 134 3-14
§ 141 3-14
§ 145 3-14
§ 154 3-14
§ 154(a)(1) 3-23
§ 171 3-7
§ 173 3-18
§ 271(a) 3-16, 3-24
§ 271(f) 3-24
§ 271(f)(2) 3-19
§ 271(g) 3-24
§ 282(b)(3)(A) 3-10
§ 283 .... 3-19, 3-21
§ 284 .... 3-18, 3-19, 3-23
§ 285 .... 2-68, 3-19, 3-22
§ 286 3-16
§ 287 3-15
§ 287(a) 3-15, 3-21
§ 289 3-18
§ 292(a) 3-16
§ 292(b) 3-16

TITLE 42

§ 1981 16-32
§ 2000e(k) 16-28
§ 2000e-5(e) 16-24
§ 2000e-2(e)(1) 16-27
§ 2000e-5(f) 16-24, 16-25

TITLE 47

§ 230(c) 15-37, 15-42

TITLE 49

§ 41712 15-41

Statutes by Name

1909 Copyright Act 4-3, 4-9, 8-5
1976 Copyright Act 4-3, 4-5, 4-10, 4-11, 4-27, 8-5
1988 Copyright, Designs and Patents Act (CDPA) 5-9
Act to Revise, Consolidate and Amend the Statutes Relating
    to Patents and Copyrights Act 2-4
African Growth and Opportunity Act 19-23
Age Discrimination in Employment Act (ADEA) 16-24, 16-27
Alternative Fines Act 20-38
America Invents Act (AIA) 3-10, 3-11, 3-26
Americans with Disabilities Act of 1990 .... 13-27, 16-24
Andean Trade Promotion and Drug Eradication Act 19-23
Anticounterfeiting Consumer Protection Act of 1996 2-6
    § 7 2-6
    § 1000(a) 2-6
Anticybersquatting Consumer Protection Act of
    1999 (ACPA) 2-6, 2-69, 2-70, 2-82
    § 1000(a) 2-6

Architectural Works Copyright Protection Act 4-20
Bankruptcy Abuse Prevention and
Consumer Protection Act of 2005 (BAPCPA) 23-32
Berne Convention Implementation Act 4-28
California Consumer Privacy Act of 2018.............................. 14-20
California Online Privacy Protection Act 14-20
California Trade Secrets Act (CUTSA) 6-8
Canada's Industrial Design Act (CIDA) 5-15
Caribbean Basin Trade Partnership Act 19-23
Celebrity Rights Act in 1985.. 18-13
Children's Online Privacy Protection Act of
1998 (COPPA).. 14-19, 14-20, 14-23
Civil Rights Act of 1964... 16-24
Clayton Act
§ 3... 12-14
Clayton Antitrust Act 12-2, 4-5
Communications Decency Act of 1996 (CDA) 15-37, 15-42
Computer Fraud and Abuse Act (CFAA)................................. 14-34
Confidence Act of 2011... 14-37
Consumer Product Safety Act
§ 6.. 9-23
§ 15(b).. 9-21
§ 37.. 9-22
Consumer Product Safety Improvement Act of 2008 (CPSIA)....... 9-19
§ 102.. 9-19
§ 108.. 9-19
Consumer Products Safety Act 1972.. 9-19
Consumers Legal Remedies Act ("CLR Act").......................... 15-32
Controlling the Assault of Non-Solicited Pornography and
Marketing ("CAN-SPAM") Act of 2003 14-34
Copyright Act............................... 4-2, 4-9, 4-19, 4-22, 4-26, 4-29,
.... 4-44, 4-45, 4-47, 4-48, 5-14, 8-11,
.... 8-12, 8-15, 8-16, 8-20, 8-22, 17-7, 23-46
§ 1301... 4-20
Copyright Act of 1793.. 5-6
Copyright Act of 1870.. 4-9
Copyright Act of 1968.. 5-13
Copyright Act, R.S.C. 1985, c. C-42 5-15
Copyright, Designs and Patents Act, 1988 5-8
§ 213(4) 5-8
§ 213(6) 5-8
§ 216.. 5-8
§ 226(2) 5-8
§ 229.. 5-9

§ 237 5-8
§ 269 5-8
§ 273 5-8
CPSC Reform Act 9-24
Customs Modernization Act 19-3, 19-4
Defend Trade Secrets Act 6-15, 6-16, 6-17, 6-18
Delaware Limited Liability Company Act (DLLCA) 1-12,
.... 1-26, 1-27, 23-4
§ 201 1-27
Delaware Revised Uniform Limited
Partnership Act (DRULPA) 1-16, 1-29
§ 201 1-29
§ 201(d) 1-29
§ 303(b) 1-29
§ 1107 1-30
§ 1109 1-30
§ 1101(d) 1-30
Delaware Revised Uniform Partnership Act (DRUPA) 1-16
§ 105 1-17
Designs Act 1953 5-13
Designs Act 1954 5-13
§ 5(2) 5-13
§ 11(1) 5-14
§ 12(1) 5-14
§ 12(2) 5-14
Designs Act of 2000 5-17
§ 2(d) 5-17
§ 11 5-17
§ 19 5-17
Designs Act of 2003 .... 5-12, 5-13, 5-16, 5-17
§ 15 5-12
§ 15(2) 5-12
§ 27 5-12
§ 46 5-12
§ 71 5-13
§ 73(3) 5-12
§ 75 5-13
Designs Amendment Act 2010 5-13
Development Act of 2000 19-23
District of Columbia Family and
Medical Leave Act of 1990 16-29
Dodd-Frank Wall Street Reform and
Consumer Protection Act of 2010 .... 14-36, 21-4
Economic Growth, Regulatory Relief and
Consumer Protection Act 14-36

Electronic Funds Transfer Act of 1978 .... 14-36, 14-37
Electronic Signatures and Records Act 14-10
Equal Pay Act 16-24
Fair and Accurate Credit Transactions Act of 2003 14-37
Fair Labor Standards Act (FLSA) 16-3, 16-4, 16-5,
.... 16-6, 16-7, 16-8, 16-9,
.... 16-10, 16-11, 16-12, 16-14,
.... 16-15, 16-16, 16-17, 16-18, 19-19
§ 203 16-17
Fair Packaging and Labeling Act (FP&L Act) 15-27, 15-28
Family and Medical Leave Act (FMLA) 16-28, 16-29
Federal Food, Drug and Cosmetic Act 15-13, 15-26,
.... 15-27, 15-28, 15-30,
.... 15-32, 15-33, 21-15
§ 201(g)(1) 15-28
§ 201(i) 15-14, 15-26
§ 601 15-27
§ 602 15-27
Federal Hazardous Substances Act 15-12
Federal Trade Commission Act (the "FTC Act") 9-27, 12-2,
.... 14-20, 15-13, 15-21,
.... 15-25, 15-30, 15-31, 15-32
§ 5 .... 12-14, 14-17, 15-14, 15-21
§ 13(b) 15-24
Federal Trademark Dilution Act (FTDA) 2-5, 2-52, 2-53, 2-55
Financial Services Modernization Act of 1999 14-36
Fixing America's Surface Transportation Act
(the "FAST Act") 21-4
Flammable Fabrics Act of 1953 .... 9-20, 15-12
Florida's Deceptive and Unfair Trade Practices Act 15-31
Foreign Corrupt Practices Act (FCPA) 20-2, 20-3,
.... 20-4, 20-5, 20-6, 20-7,
.... 20-8, 20-9, 20-10, 20-11,
.... 20-12, 20-13, 20-14, 20-15, 20-17,
.... 20-18, 20-19, 20-20, 20-21, 20-22, 20-23,
.... 20-24, 20-25, 20-26, 20-27, 20-28, 20-29, 20-30,
.... 20-31, 20-32, 20-33, 20-35, 20-36, 20-37, 20-38
Fur Products Labeling Act (the "Fur Act") 9-27, 15-12, 15-25
Geneva Act of the Hague Agreement Concerning
the International Registration of Industrial Designs 5-5, 5-6
Global and National Commerce Act 14-10
Gramm-Leach-Bliley Act 14-36
Haitian Hemispheric Opportunity Through Partnership
Encouragement Act of 2006 19-24

Hart-Scott-Rodino Antitrust Improvements Act of 1976.......... 22-21
Illinois Little UDTP Act.......... 15-31
Indiana Right of Publicity Act.......... 18-17
Industrial Design Act, R.S.C., 1985.......... 5-15, 5-16
Innovative Design Protection Act of 2012 (IDPA).......... 4-20, 4-21
§ 2(a).......... 4-21
Innovative Design Protection and Piracy Prevention Act (IDPPPA).......... 4-20
Intellectual Property Act of 2008.......... 7-32
International Anti-Bribery and Fair Competition Act of 1998.......... 20-2
Italian Copyright Act art. 2.......... 5-10
Jumpstart Our Business Startups Act ("JOBS Act").......... 1-63, 21-4, 21-11
Lanham Act.......... 2-5, 2-6, 2-14, 2-27, 2-28, 2-32, 2-33, 2-34, 2-35, 2-36, 2-37, 2-46, 2-49, 2-50, 2-52, 2-58, 2-62, 2-65, 2-66, 2-67, 2-68, 2-69, 2-70, 2-73, 2-76, 2-80, 2-88, 2-89, 2-90, 2-91, 2-93, 2-94, 2-96, 2-97, 2-99, 2-100, 2-102, 2-104, 6-14, 7-9, 7-12, 7-14, 7-15, 7-16, 7-17, 7-22, 7-26, 7-29, 7-30, 7-31, 8-7, 8-17, 8-18, 8-19, 8-22, 15-9, 15-14, 15-16, 15-17, 15-19, 15-20, 15-30, 15-33, 15-38
§ 1.......... 2-4
§ 2(d).......... 2-16, 2-24
§ 32(1).......... 2-26
§ 35(a).......... 2-65, 7-14
§ 43(a).......... 2-26, 6-14, 15-14, 15-15, 15-16, 15-17, 15-38, 18-4
§ 43(d).......... 2-70
§ 45.......... 2-7
Lanham Act of 1946.......... 2-4
Leahy-Smith America Invents Act.......... 3-26
Little FTC Act.......... 15-30, 15-31, 15-32
Little UDTP Act.......... 15-30, 15-31, 15-32
Madrid Protocol Implementation Act.......... 2-110
Massachusetts Consumer Protection Act.......... 15-31
National Labor Relations Act (NLRA).......... 16-33, 16-35
§ 7.......... 16-37
National Securities Markets Improvement Act of 1996.......... 1-63
New York Wage Theft Prevention Act.......... 16-6
North American Free Trade Area Implementation Act.......... 19-4
Occupational Safety and Health Act.......... 9-27
Organic Foods Production Act of 1990 (OFPA).......... 15-29

Poison Prevention Packaging Act of 1970 15-28
§ 3 15-28
§ 4 15-28
Pregnancy Discrimination Act 16-28
Pure Food and Drug Act (1906) 15-13
Racketeer Influenced and
Corrupt Organizations (RICO) Act 7-22, 16-21
Registered Design Act of 1949 (RDA) 5-7, 5-8
Registered Designs Act 2005 .... 5-8, 5-16
§ 2(1) 5-16
§ 5(1) 5-16
§ 5(2) 5-16
§ 21(1) 5-16
§ 21(2) 5-16
§ 30(2) 5-16
§ 36(2) 5-16
Reinforcing American-Made Products Act of 2017 15-26
Restore Online Shoppers' Confidence Act of 2011 (ROSCA) 14-37
Robinson-Patman Act 12-17, 12-18, 12-19
Sarbanes-Oxley Act of 2002 21-4
§ 404 21-7
Securities Act of 1933 21-10
§ 2(a)(6) 1-64
§ 3(b) 1-61, 1-62
§ 4(2) 1-53, 1-62
§ 4(a)(6) 1-64
§ 5 .... 1-53, 1-62, 21-11
§ 5(c) 21-11
§ 11 21-8
§ 12 21-8
Securities Exchange Act of 1934 .... 20-13, 21-4, 21-19
§ 8A 20-10
§ 12 .... 20-5, 20-12, 20-26
§ 13 .... 21-19, 22-17
§ 14 21-19
§ 15(d) 20-5, 20-26
§ 16 21-19
§ 21(C) 20-21, 20-24, 20-25
§ 30A 20-26
Sherman Antitrust Act 12-2, 12-3, 12-8, 12-10, 12-11
§ 1 .... 12-2, 12-3, 12-6,
.... 12-7, 12-10, 12-11, 12-14
§ 2 .... 12-2, 12-4, 12-14
Sherman and Clayton Act 4-5

Song-Beverly Credit Card Act 14-29
Stored Communications Act 14-28, 14-30
South Dakota's Act 14-33
Tariff Act of 1930 2-71
§ 337 2-71
§ 484 19-4
§ 509 .... 19-6, 19-7
§ 592 19-30
Tax Relief and Health Care Act of 2006 19-24
Textile Fiber Products Identification Act (the "Textile Act") 9-27, 15-12, 15-24, 15-25, 19-25
Trade Act of 2002, Title XXXI 19-23
Toxic Substances Control Act of 1976 15-12
Trade and Development Act of 2000 19-23
Trade Facilitation and Trade Enforcement Act of 2015 (TFTEA) 19-6
Trademark Act of 1881 2-4
Trademark Act of 1920 15-13
Trademark Act of 1946 15-14
Trademarks Act 5-16
Trademark Dilution Revision Act of 2006 (TDRA) 2-5, 2-52, 2-53, 2-54, 2-55, 2-56, 2-57, 2-79
Trademark Law Revision Act of 1988 (TLRA) 2-5
Truth in Lending Act 14-36
Uniform Deceptive Trade Practices Act (UDTP Act) 15-30, 15-31, 15-32
§ 2(a)(2) 15-31
§ 3(a) 15-31
§ 3(b) 15-31
Uniform Partnership Act 1-16, 1-17
§ 105 1-17
Uniform Trade Secrets Act (UTSA) 6-8, 6-11
United States-Caribbean Basin Trade Partnership Act 19-23
U.S. Foreign Corrupt Practices Act 20-9, 20-24, 20-27, 20-29, 20-30, 20-35, 20-36, 20-37
Uniting and Strengthening America by Providing Appropriate Tools Required to Intercept and Obstruct Terrorism Act (USA Patriot Act) of 2001 7-4
Vessel Hull Act 4-20
Wiretap Act 14-29
Wool Products Labeling Act of 1939 (the "Wool Act") 9-27, 15-12, 15-25, 19-25

Public Laws

90-321 14-36
100-667 2-5
101-336 13-27
103-182
    §§ 601–92 19-4
104-98 .... 2-5, 2-52
104-153 2-6
106-102 14-36
106-200
    §§ 101–31 19-23
    §§ 201–13 19-23
107-56 7-4
107-210
    §§ 3101–108 19-23
108-159 14-37
109-8 23-32
109-312 2-52
109-432
    §§ 5001–06 19-24
110-314 9-19
110-403
    § 104 7-32
111-203 14-36
111-345 14-37
114-125 19-6
115-174 14-36

State Codes

California

Cal. Bus. & Prof. Code
    § 16600 17-14
    §§ 16601–602 17-17
    § 17200 .... 6-3, 6-4, 6-5
    §§ 17200 *et seq.* 15-32
    §§ 17203 *et seq.* 15-30
    § 17533.1 15-26
    §§ 22575–79 14-20
Cal. Civ. Code
    § 990 18-9
    §§ 1747 *et seq.* 14-29
    §§ 1750–84 .... 15-30, 15-32

§ 1752 15-32
§ 1770 15-32
§ 1780 15-32
§ 1781 15-32
§ 1798.81.5(d)(1)(A) 14-24
§ 1798.82(a) 14-24
§ 1798.82(d)(2)(G) 14-25
§ 1798.82(g) 14-25
§ 1798.82(gd) 14-25
§ 1798.82(h) 14-24
§ 1798.82(j) 14-25
§ 1798.82(*l*) 14-25
§ 1798.100 14-21
§ 1798.110 14-21
§ 1798.105(d) 14-21
§ 1798.115 14-21
§ 1798.120(d) 14-21
§ 1798.135 14-21
§ 1798.140(c)(1) 14-21
§ 1798.150 14-24
§ 3344 .... 18-8, 18-9, 18-11
§ 3344(a) 18-9
§ 3344(e) 18-9
§ 3344.1 .... 18-9, 18-13
§ 3369 .... 15-30, 15-32
§ 3426.1 6-8
§ 3426.1–3426.11 6-8

Cal. Fish & Game
§§ 4030–43 1-14

Cal. Lab. Code
§ 515 16-12
§ 2670 9-28
§ 2751(a) 16-16
§ 2751(b) 16-16

Delaware

Del. Code Ann.
tit. 6, § 15 1-16
tit. 6, § 15-306(a) 1-16
tit. 6, § 15-308 1-16
tit. 6, § 15-403 1-17
tit. 6, § 15-404 23-4
tit. 6, § 15-1208 1-18
tit. 6, § 17 1-29

tit. 6, § 18 1-26
tit. 6, § 18-1101(c) 23-5
tit. 6, § 18-1107 1-28
tit. 8, § 108 1-21
tit. 8, § 211(b) 1-21
tit. 8, § 220 1-21
tit. 8, § 362(a) 1-25, 1-26
tit. 8, § 362(b) 1-26
tit. 8, § 365 1-26
tit. 8, § 366(b) 1-26
tit. 8, § 391 1-21
tit. 8, §§ 101–398 1-20
tit. 8, §§ 502–503 1-22

Del. Gen. Corp. Law
§ 109(b) 1-21
§ 141 1-20
§ 211(b) 1-20
§ 262 1-49
§ 327 1-48

District of Columbia

D.C. Code Ann.
§§ 32-501–32-517 16-29

Indiana

Ind. Code Ann.
§§ 32-36-1-1 through 32-36-1-20 18-16
§ 32-36-1-1(a) 18-16
§ 32-36-1-6 18-16
§ 32-36-1-8 18-16
§ 32-36-1-16 18-16
§ 32-36-1-20 18-16

Louisiana

La. Rev. Stat. Ann.
§ 51:1427 6-5

Massachusetts

Mass. Ann. Laws
ch. 93A, § 2(b) 15-31
Mass. Gen. Laws
ch. 93, § 105(a) 14-29
ch. 149, § 148B 16-31

Nebraska

Neb. Rev. Stat.
§ 20-201 18-7

New York

N.Y.C. Admin. Code
§ 11-603 1-22
N.Y. Civ. Rights Law
§ 50 18-12
§ 51 18-13
§§ 50–51 .... 18-4, 18-12, 18-14
N.Y. Comp. Codes R. & Regs.
§ 11-603 1-22
N.Y. Gen. Bus. Law
§ 349 .... 6-13, 6-14, 15-31
§ 350 15-31
art. 33, §§ 680–695 10-22
N.Y. Lab. Law
§ 186 16-20
§ 195 16-6
§ 198 16-6
§ 198-a 16-6
§ 201-G 16-24
§ 215 16-6
art. 12-A, § 341 9-28
N.Y. Ltd. Liab. Co. Law
§ 206 1-27
§ 417 1-27
N.Y. Real Prop. Acts. Law
§ 733 13-6
N.Y. State Tech. Law
§§ 301–309 14-10
N.Y. Tax Law
§ 209 1-22
§ 210(1) 1-22
§ 210(1)(d) 1-22
§ 660(a) 1-24

Pennsylvania

43 Pa. Cons. Stat. Ann.
§ 333.105 16-12

Texas

Tex. Lab. Code Ann.
§ 406.123(a) 16-32
§ 408.001(a) 16-32

Washington

Wash. Rev. Code
§§ 19.330 *et seq.* 6-5

REGULATIONS, RULES, UNIFORM ACTS, RESTATEMENTS

Code of Federal Regulations (C.F.R.)

TITLE 7

§ 205.300 15-29

TITLE 14

§ 399.84 15-41

TITLE 15

pt. 774 19-34

TITLE 16

pts. 312 *et seq.* 14-19
pts. 312.4–312.5 14-19
pt. 312.7 14-19
pts. 436–437 10-22
§ 2.1 15-22
§ 3.11(a) 15-22
§ 3.11(b)(1) 15-23
§ 3.11(b)(2) 15-23
§ 3.12(a) 15-23
§ 3.21(b) 15-23
§ 3.31(b) 15-23
§ 3.31(c)(3) 15-23
§ 3.43(b) 15-23
§ 3.46 15-23
§ 3.51 15-23
§ 3.52(a) 15-24
§ 3.53(b) 15-24
§ 12.42(e) 19-28
§ 12.42(f) 19-29
§ 12.43 19-28
§ 12.44(a) 19-28
§ 12.44(b) 19-29
§§ 12.42–12.45 19-27
§ 24 .... 9-27, 15-12
§ 423.6 .... 9-27, 15-12
§ 1031.1 9-21
§ 1031.2 9-21
§ 1102 9-24
§ 1102.10 9-24
§ 1102.20 9-24
§ 1102.24 9-24
§ 1102.26 9-24
§ 1115.20 9-22
§ 1115.21 9-22
§ 1116.3 9-22
§ 1203.5 9-21
§ 1120.3(b) 9-21
§ 1500 15-12
§ 1500.91 9-20
§ 1610.1 9-20
§ 1610.4 9-20
§§ 1615.4–1615.5 9-21
§ 1615.31 9-21

TITLE 17

§ 230 1-62
§ 230.134 21-11
§ 230.135 21-11
§ 230.163A 21-11
§ 230.169 21-11
§ 230.251 1-64
§§ 230.251 *et seq.* 1-64
§ 230.500 1-62
§ 230.501(a) 1-57
§ 230.502(a) 1-64
§ 230.502(b) 1-61, 1-62
§ 230.502(c) 1-56
§ 230.504 1-63
§ 230.505 1-63
§ 230.506 1-53
§ 230.506(a) 1-56
§ 230.506(b) 1-62
§ 230.506(b)(2) 1-61
§ 230.506(c) 1-63

Title 19

pt. 111 19-8
pt. 163, app. 19-8
pt. 171, app. B, at (C)(1)... 19-30
pt. 171, app. B, at F(2)...... 19-31
pt. 171, app. B, at F(2)(f)......19-32
pt. 181 .... 19-8, 19-23
§ 102.11 .... 19-20, 19-21
§ 102.21 19-22
§ 127.14(a)(2).................. 19-10
§ 127.29 19-10
§ 133.23 19-7
§§ 133.31 *et seq.* 4-25
§ 133.42 19-7
§ 134.1(b) 19-21
§ 134.22 19-24
§ 134.46 19-25
§ 141.5 19-10
§ 141.61 19-8
§ 141.113(b) 19-10
§ 142.2(a) 19-10
§ 142.3(a) 19-9
§ 142.4 19-9
§ 142.12(b) 19-10
§ 142.12(c) 19-10
§ 142.13 19-10
§ 143.23 19-9
§ 151.16(c) 19-10
§ 152.102(a) 19-15
§ 152.102(a)(iv) 19-15
§ 152.103(a) 19-14
§ 152.103(b) 19-15
§ 152.103(d)–(e) 19-15
§ 152.103(f) 19-16
§ 152.103(j)(2) 19-17
§ 152.104 19-18
§ 152.105 19-19
§ 152.106 19-19
§ 152.106(b)(2) 19-19
§ 162.73(a) 19-31
§ 162.73(b) 19-32
§ 162.74 19-31
§ 162.75(c) 19-28
§ 163.2 19-8
§ 163.4 19-8
§ 163.5 19-8
§ 163.6(b)(1)(i) 19-9
§ 163.6(b)(1)(ii) 19-9
§ 163.6(b)(3) 19-9
§ 171.2(b) 19-28
§ 177.1 19-25
§ 177.2 19-26
§ 177.2(b)(3) 19-26
§§ 210.1 *et seq.* 3-25

Title 21

§ 10.30 15-29
§ 101 15-28

Title 26

§ 301.6109-1 1-22
§ 301.6109-1(a)(1)(ii)(D) 1-15
§ 301.7701-3(a) 1-17,
.... 1-26, 1-27
§ 301.7701-3(b) 1-26

Title 28

pt. 36 13-27

Title 29

§§ 530.1–530.2 16-15
§ 541.100 16-8
§ 541.102 16-8
§ 541.104 16-8
§ 541.200 16-9
§ 541.201 16-9
§ 541.203 16-9
§ 541.300 16-9
§ 541.301 16-9
§ 541.302 16-10
§ 541.400 16-11
§ 541.401 16-11
§ 541.500 16-11
§ 541.502 16-11
§ 541.503 16-11
§ 541.600 16-7
§ 541.601 16-12
§ 541.700 16-7
§ 541.708 16-12
§ 570.2(a) 16-17, 16-18
§ 570.34(b) 16-19

§ 570.34(d)........................ 16-19
§ 570.35(a)........................ 16-18
§ 570.35(a)(1)..................... 16-18
§ 570.35(a)(3)..................... 16-18
§ 570.35(a)(5)..................... 16-18
§ 570.35(a)(6)..................... 16-18
§ 570.35(c)(1)(i).................. 16-18
§ 570.35(c)(4)..................... 16-18
§ 570.37........................... 16-18
§ 570.50........................... 16-19
§ 570.53........................... 16-19
§ 570.67........................... 16-19
§ 570.103(a)....................... 16-18
§ 570.103(c)....................... 16-18
§ 580.3............................ 16-19
§ 580.4............................ 16-19
§ 580.5............................ 16-20
§ 1604.2(a)........................ 16-27

TITLE 37

pt. 1 3-26
§ 1.27....................... 3-12, 3-13
§ 1.56............................. 3-12
§ 1.378............................ 3-15
§ 201.10(c)........................ 4-10
§ 201.20........................... 4-28
§ 207(a)........................... 4-9
§ 207.8(a)......................... 4-10

Uniform Commercial Code

§ 1-201(b)(35) 23-53
§ 2-102................... 11-30, 11-31
§ 2-104(1) 23-51
§ 2-202........................... 11-31
§ 2-202(1)(a)..................... 11-35
§ 2-204........................... 11-35
§ 2-206........................... 11-36
§ 2-207........................... 11-36
§ 2-208........................... 11-35
§ 2-236........................... 23-60
§ 2-305 11-36
§ 2-319–24........................ 11-37
§ 2-319(1) 11-37
§ 2-319(1)(c)..................... 11-38
§ 2-319(2) 11-38
§ 2-320........................... 11-38
§ 2-326 .... 23-58, 23-59
§ 2-326(1) 23-60
§ 2-326(2) 23-60
§ 2-326(3) 23-58
§ 2-512........................... 11-38
§ 2-513 11-38
§ 2-601 11-38
§ 2-606 11-38
§ 2-607(2) 11-38
§ 2-609........................... 11-32
§ 9-101........................... 23-60
§ 9-102........................... 23-58
§ 9-102(a)(2)..................... 23-59
§ 9-102(a)(19).................... 23-53
§ 9-102(a)(20)........ 23-51, 23-53, ... 23-58, 23-59
§ 9-102(a)(21).................... 23-53
§ 9-102(a)(23).................... 23-52
§ 9-102(2) 23-50, 23-59
§ 9-103................... 23-53, 23-54
§ 9-103(d)........................ 23-53
§ 9-114........................... 23-58
§ 9-310........................... 23-54
§ 9-310(a) 23-54
§ 9-317........................... 23-54
§ 9-317(a) 23-56
§ 9-319(a)........................ 23-56
§ 9-319(b)........................ 23-56
§ 9-320........................... 23-54
§ 9-322........................... 23-54
§ 9-322(a)(1)............. 23-55, 23-56
§ 9-322(a)(2)..................... 23-55
§ 9-324 23-54
§ 9-324(b)................ 23-54, 23-55
§ 9-324(c)........................ 23-54

Restatements

Restatement of Torts

generally.................... 2-30, 2-87
§ 729.................................. 2-30
§ 730.................................. 2-30
§ 731.................................. 2-30
§ 742.................................. 2-87
§ 742, cmt. a...................... 2-87

Restatement (Second) of Torts

§ 623A.............................. 6-15

Restatement (Third) of Unfair Competition

§ 17 cmt. c......................... 2-88
§ 20 cmt. b......................... 2-36
§ 21 cmt. a......................... 2-29
§ 24 cmt. b......................... 8-3
§ 24 cmt. c......................... 8-17
§ 33 cmt. a......................... 2-84
§ 36 cmt. i.......................... 2-67

TAX MATERIALS

Internal Revenue Code

Internal Revenue Code of 1986 1-23

Revenue Rulings

73-427 22-9
79-273 22-9
90-95 22-9

Revenue Procedures

2013-30 1-23
2013-36 1-23

Index

(References are to sections unless otherwise indicated.)

A

Abandoned trademarks, 2:10.7
Abatements, rent, 13:3.2, 13:3.6
    sample provision, 13:3.6
Abboud, Joseph, 2:4.2
Abercrombie & Fitch Stores, 16:4.1, 22:1
Abercrombie & Fitch v. Fashion Shops of Kentucky, Inc., 8:3.3, 8:4.1
Abstractions test, copyright infringement, 4:7.2[C]
Acceptance of goods, retailer-vendor arrangements, 11:2.5
Access, copyright infringement, 4:7.1
Accounting. *See* Foreign Corrupt Practices Act (FCPA)
Accounting of profits, trademark infringement, 2:9.3
Accounting provisions
    license agreements, 10:2.2[F]
Accredited angel investors, 1:4.6
ACPA. *See* Anticybersquatting Consumer Protection Act (ACPA)
Acquiescence defense
    generally, 2:10.6
    false advertising, 15:4.1[E]
Acquisition agreements. *See also* Sale transactions (fashion companies/brands acquisitions)
    ancillary agreements, 22:4
    closing conditions, 22:6
    covenants, 22:5.2
    draft, 22:2.1
    due diligence, 22:2.2
    earn-outs, 22:3.4[A], App. 22A
    indemnities, 22:5.3
    representations and warranties, 22:5.1, App. 22B
    termination rights, 22:6
    transition services agreements, 22:4

Acquisitions
agreements. *See* Acquisition agreements
strategic acquisitions, 22:1
unsuccessful acquisitions, 22:1
ADA. *See* Americans with Disabilities Act (ADA)
Additional rent, brick-and-mortar lease, 13:3.5
non-recurring payments of additional rent, 13:3.5
Additive manufacturing, 9:1
ADEA. *See* Age Discrimination in Employment Act (ADEA)
Adequate assurance
assignment of real property lease (non-residential) and bankruptcy, 23:4.2[C][1]
assumption of real property lease (non-residential) and bankruptcy, 23:4.2[B][2]
Adidas, 9:1
adidas America Inc. v. Skechers USA, Inc., 2:9.1[B]
Administrative overtime exemption, 16:2.2[B]
Adore Me
pop-up stores, 11:1.6
Advance ship notice (ASN), 9:3
Advertising. *See also* False advertising
cooperative advertising, antitrust, 12:4.1[F]
defined, 15:2.2
license agreements, 10:2.2[G]
NAD, 15:2.6, 15:4.2[B], 15:6
search engine and Internet advertising, trademark infringement, 2:11
suggested retail prices, 12:4.1[B]
Aesthetic functionality doctrine, 2:10.9
Affirmative covenants, 22:5.2
Age claims, BFOQ defense, 16:4.2
Age discrimination claims, defense to, 16:4.2
Age Discrimination in Employment Act (ADEA), 16:4.1, 16:4.2
Agreement on Textiles and Clothing, 19:1
AIA. *See* American Invents Act (AIA)
AirMag product line, 3:6.2[B]
Airwave smart ski and snowboard goggles, 3:6.2[C]
Akanoc Solutions, Inc.
Louis Vuitton v. Akanoc Solutions, Inc., 7:3.4[B][2]
Alexander Wang Inc., 2:4.2, 3:6.1
Ali, Muhammad, 18:4.2
Alibaba Group Holding, Ltd.
Gucci America, Inc. v. Alibaba Group Holding, Ltd., 7:3.4[B]
Alice Corp. v. CLS Bank, International, 3:2.1
All natural products, 15:2.3, 15:4.2[E]

Already LLC v. Nike, Inc., 2:10.1
Alterations, brick-and-mortar lease, 13:3.8
Alternative jurisdiction, FCPA, 20:3.1[A]
Alternative service of process, 7:3.1[C]
Amarige perfume, 8:3.1
Amazon Effect, 11:1.7
Amazon Go, 11:1.7
Amazon.com
  as market disrupter, 11:1.7
  contribution to growth of e-commerce apparel, 14:1
  counterfeiting, enforcement, 7:4.2
  enforcement of FTC labeling regulations, 15:4.2[E]
  manufacturing, 9:1
  Multi Time Machine, Inc. v. Amazon.com, 2:7.2[A]
  on-demand apparel manufacturing, 9:1
  pop-up stores, 11:1.6
  subscription box e-commerce business model, 11:1.7
  success of, 11:1.7
  Whole Foods, 11:1.7
American Airlines, 2:43
American Apparel, Inc., 9:3, 22:1
American Depositary Receipts, 20:3.1[A]
American Invents Act (AIA), 3:3.1
Americans with Disabilities Act (ADA), 13:3.8, 16:4.1
AMF, Incorporated v. Sleekcraft Boats, 2:7.2[A]
Amoruso, Sophia (#GIRLBOSS), 23:1
Anchor tenant, 11:1.1
Ancillary agreements, 22:4
  sale transactions (fashion companies/brands acquisitions), 22:4
Android OS, 14:2.2
Angel investors, 1:4.6, 1:4.7
Anheuser-Busch, Inc. v. VIP Products, LLC, 2:10.8
Ann Taylor, 11:1.7, 22:1
Anthony's Pizza Holding Co. v. Anthony's Pizza & Pasta Int'l, Inc., 2:13:1
Anti-bribery provisions. *See* Foreign Corrupt Practices Act (FCPA)
Anti-corruption enforcement. *See* Foreign Corrupt Practices Act (FCPA)
Anti-discrimination laws, 16:4
  #MeToo laws, 16:4
  age discrimination claims, defense to, 16:4.2
  Age Discrimination in Employment Act (ADEA), 16:4.1, 16:4.2
  Americans with Disabilities Act (ADA), 16:4.1
  bona fide occupational qualifications, 16:4.2
  Civil Rights Act of 1964, Title VII, 16:4.1, 16:4.2
  disparate impact liability, 16:4

Anti-discrimination laws (*cont'd*)
disparate treatment liability, 16:4
Equal Employment Opportunity Commission (EEOC), 16:4.1, 16:4.2
Equal Pay Act, 16:4.1
Family and Medical Leave Act (FMLA), 16:4.4
pregnancy discrimination, 16:4.3
sex discrimination claims, defense to, 16:4.2
Anti-raid agreement (non-solicitation agreement), 17:4.2
Anticounterfeiting Consumer Protection Act, 2:2
Anticybersquatting Consumer Protection Act (ACPA), 2:2, 2:9.4
Antitrust. *See also* Sherman Act
Clayton Antitrust Act, 4:2
Fashion Originator's Guild, 4:2
Antitrust Division, DOJ, 12:1, 12:3, 12:5
Antitrust law
generally, 12:1, 12:6
boycotts, 12:1
claims, basics, 12:2
Clayton Antitrust Act, 12:1
consignment, 12:4.1[D]
cooperative advertising, 12:4.1[F]
customer restrictions, 12:4.2[B]
exclusive dealing and exclusive distribution, 12:4.2[A]
horizontal relationships, 12:3
monopoly power, 12:2
per se illegal arrangements, 12:3, 12:4.2[C]
persuasion to deal, 12:4.1[C]
pre-ticketing, 12:4.1[B]
price discrimination-Robinson-Patman Act, 12:5
primary line, price discrimination, 12:5
promotional programs, 12:4.1[E]
reason analysis rule, 12:4.2[C]
rebates, direct, 12:4.1[E]
refusal to deal, 12:4.1[C]
resale price maintenance (RPM), 12:4.1[A]
Robinson-Patman Act, 12:5
scope of laws, 12:1
secondary line, price discrimination, 12:5
suggested retail prices, 12:4.1[B]
territorial restrictions, 12:4.2[B]
tying agreements, 12:4.2[C]

vertical price restraints, 12:4.1
vertical relationships, 12:4
non-price vertical agreements, 12:4.2
vertical price restraints, 12:4.1
vertically integrated manufacturers, 12:4
Apparel. *See specific entries*
Apparel and textiles, rules of origin, 19:6.2
Apparel manufacturing. *See* Manufacturing
Apparel merchandise in department stores, types of, 11:1.1
Apple
force sensing fabric-based devices patent, 3:6.2[C]
iOS, 14:2.2
Nike and, 3:6.2[C]
Nike + iPod Sports Kit, 3:6.2[C]
smartphone design battle with Samsung, 3:6.1
wearable technology, 3:6.2[C]
Apple Pay, 11:1, 14:4
Applicable law exception
intellectual property and bankruptcy, 23:4.4[A][2]
Appraisal rights, 1:3.2
Apps, mobile. *See* Mobile apps
Arbitration and Meditation Center, 2:15.1
Architectural works, copyright protection, 4:4
Argentina
Ball Corporation case, 20:4.4[B]
Ralph Lauren case, 20:4.1
Armor, 11:1.7
Art Attacks Ink, LLC v. MGA Entertainment, Inc., 4:7.1
Article 17 of U.S. Code, section 107, 4:8.1
Ascena Retail Group, 22:1
Ash Footwear USA, 3:6.1
Ashley Reed Trading, Inc.
Fendi Adele S.R.L. v. Ashley Reed Trading, Inc., 7:3.5[A]
Asia, consumer market, 9:2
ASN. *See* Advance ship notice (ASN)
ASOS plc, 11:1, 21:2.2
Aspirational customers, 9:2
search engine advertising, trademark infringement, 2:11.2
Asset-backed lending financing
liquidity, bankruptcy cases, 23:2.3[A][1]
Asset freeze, counterfeiters, 7:3.3[B]
Assignment limitations
intellectual property and bankruptcy, 23:4.4[A]

Assignment of real property lease (non-residential) and bankruptcy, 23:4.2[C]
adequate assurance, 23:4.2[C][1]
designation rights, 23:4.2[C][4]
nonassignability of leases, 23:4.2[C][2]
shopping center leases, 23:4.2[C][3]
Assignment/sublease provisions, brick-and-mortar lease, 13:3.9
Assists
valuation, imported merchandise, 19:5.1
Assumption limitations
intellectual property and bankruptcy, 23:4.4[B]
Assumption of real property lease (non-residential) and bankruptcy, 23:4.2[B]
adequate assurance, 23:4.2[B][2]
cure and compensation, 23:4.2[B][1]
deadline, 23:4.2[A]
defaults, 23:4.2[B][1]
extensions available, 23:4.2[A]
going dark clause, 23:4.2[B][1][b]
ipso facto clauses, 23:4.2[B][1][a]
non-monetary breaches, 23:4.2[B][1][b]
ASTM International, Consumer Product Safety for Children's Jewelry, 9:5.1
ASTM International Standard, AFTM F 2923-11, 9:5.1
Astro pant, 3:6.1
At-will employees, 17:1
Athletic apparel. *See also* Nike
Columbia Sportswear North America, Inc., 3:6.1
design patents, 3:6.1
jerseys, "05" and, 2:4.1
Lululemon Athletica Canada Inc., 3:6.1
utility patents, 3:6.2[A]
utility patents, fashion/technology integration, 3:6.2[C]
Athletic attire
patents, 3:6.2[A]
Attorneys' fees
copyright infringement, 4:9.4
patent infringement, 3:4.2[C]
trademark infringement, 2:9.2[C]
Atwood, Brian, 2:4.2
Auction process, sale transactions, 22:2
Auction sites, online, 7:3.4[B]. *See also* eBay
e-commerce business model, 11:1.7
Audiovisual works, copyright protection, 4:2

Australia
design law protections, 5:5.3
Australian Gold, Inc. v. Hatfield, 2:11.1
Authentic Brands Group, 22:1
Automatic stay and exceptions
bankruptcy cases, filing, 23:3.1
Avon case study, FCPA enforcement, 20:4.2
history of investigation, 20:4.2[A]
ramifications of investigation, 20:4.2[B]

B

Bad faith
cybersquatting, 2:2
domain name infringement, 2:9.4, 2:15.1
false advertising, 15:4.1[D]
New York common law unfair competition, 6:3.2
patent infringement, 3:4.2[E]
trademark search, 2:6.3[A]
Bag Borrow or Steal, 11:1.7
Balance of the hardships, 2:9.1[B]
Balance sheets, 1:1.2[G], 1:4.5
Balenciaga v. liu zhixian, zhixian liu, 2:15.1
Ball Corporation, 20:4.4[B]
Bamboo products, false or misleading advertising, 15:4.2[E]
Banana Republic, 11:1.2
Bandier, 1:4.1
Bangladesh
garment factory fires, 9:5.2
Worker Safety Initiative, 9:5.2
Bank financing, 1:4.5
Bankruptcy, generally, 23:1. *See also headings under Bankruptcy*
American Apparel, 22:1
consent rights, equity investor, 1:3.2
consignments, 23:4.5
debt financing, 1:3.3
executory contracts, 23:4.3
intellectual property, 23:4.4
real property leases, non-residential, 23:4.2
filing for, 23:3
first day relief, 23:3.2, 23:4.1
intellectual property, 23:4.4
license agreement termination, 10:2.2[I]

Bankruptcy, generally (*cont'd*)
    outcomes, 23:5
    preparation for, 23:2
    real property leases (non-residential), 23:4.2
    subsidiaries, 1:2.11
Bankruptcy Abuse Prevention and Consumer Protection Act of 2005 (BAPCPA), 23:4.1[B][2]
Bankruptcy cases, filing, 23:3
    automatic stay and exceptions, 23:3.1
    Bankruptcy Code section 503(b)(9) claims, 23:3.2[D]
    Chapter 11 relief, benefits of, 23:3.1
    cram-down situations, 23:4.1[B][2]
    debtor in possession financing, approval of, 23:2.3[C]
    employee wages and benefits, 23:3.2[A]
    first day relief, 23:3.2, 23:4.1
    goods in transit, 23:3.2[C]
    insurance policies, 23:3.2[B]
    oversecured creditors, right to post-petition interest, 23:4.1[B][2]
    post-petition value creation, 23:4.1[B]
    prepetition liens, 23:4.1[B][1]
    proceeds, defined, 23:4.1[B][1]
    property of the estate, 23:4.1[A]
    reclamation, 23:3.2[D]
    revenue source, 23:4.1[B][1]
    shippers, 23:3.2[C]
    warehousemen, 23:3.2[C]
    workers' compensation programs, 23:3.2[B]
Bankruptcy cases, preparation for, 23:2
    change in control provisions, 23:2.2
    Chapter 11 reorganization plans, change in control provisions, 23:2.2
    director and officer
        coverage, 23:2.2
        fiduciary duties, 23:2.1
    fiduciary duties, 23:2.1
        insolvency, 23:2.1[A]
        pre-filing decision making, 23:2.1[B]
        private equity portfolio companies, 23:2.1[C]
        solvency determination, 23:2.1[B]
        standing of creditors, 23:2.1[A]
    liquidity needs, 23:2.3
        asset-backed lending financing, 23:2.3[A][1]
        borrowing base, 23:2.3[A][1]
        cash collateral, 23:2.3[B]
        collateral split, 23:2.3[A][2]

debtor in possession financing, 23:2.3[C]
disguised financing, 23:2.3[A][3]
factoring arrangements, 23:2.3[A][3]
financing arrangements, 23:2.3[A]
non-priming debtor in possession financing, 23:2.3[C]
priming debtor in possession financing, 23:2.3[C]
term loan financing, 23:2.3[A][2]
true sales, 23:2.3[A][3]
runoff coverage, 23:2.2
venue considerations, 23:2.4
generally, 23:2.4
billing date jurisdictions, 23:2.4[B]
intellectual property licenses, assumption of, 23:2.4[C], 23:4.4[B]
stub rent obligations, Bankruptcy Code section 365(d)(3), 23:2.4[B]
third-party releases, 23:2.4[A]
Bankruptcy Code section 503(b)(9) claims
first day relief, bankruptcy cases, 23:3.2[D]
Bankruptcy outcomes
generally, 23:5
Chapter 11 liquidation, 23:5.1
Chapter 11 reorganization, 23:5.1
sales authorized by Bankruptcy Code, section 363, 23:5.2
advantages for buyers and sellers, 23:5.2[B]
conditions required, 23:5.2[B]
continuous use provisions, 23:5.2[B][1][d]
credit bidding, 23:5.2[B]
duration, 23:5.2[B][1][c]
federal law compliance, 23:5.2[B][1][a]
going dark provisions, 23:5.2[B][1][d]
going out of business sales (GOB sales), 23:5.2[B][1]
lease restrictions, 23:5.2[B][1][d]
merchandise augmentation, 23:5.2[B][1][b]
section 363 sales, basics, 23:5.2[A]
state law compliance, 23:5.2[B][1][a]
BAPCPA. *See* Bankruptcy Abuse Prevention and Consumer Protection Act of 2005 (BAPCPA)
Bar codes, 7:4.1, 11:2.1, 11:2.6. *See also* Radio Frequency Identification (RFID) tags
Barbed-wire jewelry, *Todd v. Montana Silversmiths,* 4:3.1
Bargaining units, labor and employment, 16:7
Bauer Bros. LLC v. Nike, Inc, 2:10.1
BB Brand Management LLC, 22:3.4[B]
Beauty contest, 13:2.1

Bebe Stores, Inc., 22:3.4[B]
Belt buckles
Kieselstein-Cord v. Accessories by Pearl, Inc., 4:3.2[D]
Benefit Cosmetics' They're Real! mascara, 15:2.6
Berne Convention for the Protection of Literary and Artistic Works, 4:6.3, 4:7, 5:1
Best efforts clause, license agreement termination, 10:2.2[I]
Best Lock Corp. v. Ilco Unican Corp., 3:2.2
Better Business Bureau, 15:2.6. *See also* National Advertising Division (NAD)
BFOQ. *See* Bona fide occupational qualifications defense (BFOQ)
Big Show conference, National Retail Federation's annual (New York, 2016), 11:1.9
Bill Diodato Photography, LLC v. Kate Spade, LLC, 4:3.3
Billing date jurisdictions
bankruptcy cases, preparation for, 23:2.4[B]
BIRPI, 2:15.1
Black Friday sales, 11:1
Black market, 8:1. *See also* Gray market
Blakely v. Continental Airlines, 16:8
Bling, 9:2
Bloomingdale's Loyalist program, 11:1.1
Blue box, Tiffany, 2:5, 2:6.2
Blue sky laws, 1:4.7
Bluestar Alliance, LLC, 22:3.4[B]
Bluetooth
smart ski and snowboard goggles, 3:6.2[C]
Blufin S.p.A. (Italy), 5:4.3
Blugirl trademark, 5:4.3
Blumarine trademark, 5:4.3
Blurring, trademark dilution, 2:8.1
BMG Music v. Perez, 8:3.1
Board observers, 1:3.2
Board of directors. *See also* Corporations
co-ops, 1:2.9
creative control rights, 1:3.2
fiduciary duties, 1:2.4, 1:2.8
LLCs, 1:2.7
meetings, 1:2.4, 1:2.11
representation on, 1:3.2, 1:4.7
subsidiaries, 1:2.11
Bogart, Humphrey, 18:5
Bona fide occupational qualifications defense (BFOQ), 16:4.2
Bonobos, Inc., 11:1, 11:1.9
J. Crew Group Inc. v. Fenton, 6:5.2

Boohoo, 11:1
Borrow or rent (collaborative consumption) e-commerce business model, 11:1.7
Borrowing, factoring and, 1:4.4
Borrowing base
  liquidity, bankruptcy cases, 23:2.3[A][1]
Bottega Veneta International S.A.R.L., 3:6.1
Boutiques, 11:1.5
Bow Slide, 2:10.9[C]
Boycotts, 12:1
Brand names. *See* Sale transactions (fashion companies/brands acquisitions); Trademarks
Brand Theory, 1:3.2
Branded LLC, 2:4.4
Brandeis, Louis, 18:3
Bratz dolls, 4:7.1
Break-up fee
  sale transactions, termination rights, 22:6
Brexit
  United Kingdom, design law protections, 5:4.2
Brian Atwood, 2:4.2
Bribery. *See* Foreign Corrupt Practices Act (FCPA)
Brick-and-mortar lease provisions, 13:2.1
  additional rent, 13:3.5
  after-hours charges or requirements, 13:3.8
  alterations, 13:3.8
  assignment/sublease provisions, 13:3.9
  drafting lease provisions, drafting, 13:3
  exclusive use, 13:3.4
  expansion of space, 13:3.1
  fixed rent, 13:3.5
  gross revenues, sample definition of, 13:3.5
  leased premises, alterations to, 13:3.8
  leases and licenses distinguished, 13:2.2
  loading docks, 13:3.8
  non-recurring payments of additional rent, 13:3.5
  operational requirements detailed in lease, 13:3.8
  other provisions, 13:3.10
  other tenants, future interactions with, 13:3.8
  percentage rent, 13:3.5
  practical considerations; alterations, 13:3.8
  rent, 13:3.5
  rent abatements, 13:3.2, 13:3.6
  signage, 13:3.7
  soft costs, 13:3.8

Brick-and-mortar lease provisions (*cont'd*)
space, 13:3.1
surrender space, 13:3.1
term, 13:3.2
termination right, 13:3.2
use provisions, 13:3.3
use restrictions, 13:3.4
visibility, 13:3.7
Brick-and-mortar retail stores. *See also* E-commerce
lease provisions, drafting, 13:3
persistence, 13:1
real estate brokers, 13:2.1
real property interests, 13:2.2
retail sales transitioning back to, 11:1.9
showrooming practice, 14:1
suitable space, 13:2.1
Bridal cases
Eva's Bridal Ltd. v. Halanick Enterprises, Inc., 2:10.7
Mon Cheri Bridals Inc. v. Wen Wu, 4:3.1
Bridge financing, 1:4.7
Bridge the gap, 2:7.2[C]
Brinkley, Christine, 18:2
Broad cultural phenomena, 11:1.10
Brokers, brick-and-mortar presence, 13:2.1
Brooke Hollow, Inc., 3:6.1
Brookfield Communications, Inc. v. West Coast Entertainment Corp., 2:11.1
Browsewrap agreements, 14:3.1
Brunello Cucinelli S.p.A., 21:5
Buetow v. A.L.S. Enterprises, 15:2.4
Bulgari Time, 3:6.1
Burberry
Designers Imports, Inc., 6:3.1
domain name, 14:2.1
fast fashion, 11:1
plaid color scheme, 2:8.2, 7:3.2
sales, after runway shows, 11:1.1
Burberry Ltd. v. Bogart LLC, 18:5
Burberry's Group
trademark tartan plaid, 7:3.2
Burch, Chris, 6:5.3
Burch, Tory, 2:4.2, 6:5.3. *See also* Tory Burch company
Burch v. Burch, 6:5.3
Bureau of Industry and Security, 19:9.2
Burlington Coat Factory, 9:5.1

Burma (now known as Myanmar)
economic sanctions, 19:9.1
Business/fashion courses, 1:1.1
Business plan. *See also* Fashion companies (new business ventures)
generally, 1:1.2
business description section, 1:1.2[B]
competition section, 1:1.2[D]
drafting, 1:1.2
executive summary, 1:1.2[A]
financial projections section, 1:1.2[G]
implementation section, 1:1.2[E]
industry and market analysis, 1:1.2[C]
length, 1:1.2
modifying, 1:1.2
organization and management section, 1:1.2[F]
Business section, IPO prospectus, 21:4.6
Business structure. *See* Organizational structure
Buttwiper squeaker toy, 2:10.8
Buy-out rights, license agreements, 10:2.2[J]
Buyer promissory notes, 22:3.2[C]
Buyers
section 363 of Bankruptcy Code, sales authorized by, 23:5.2[B]
Buying agents, imported merchandise, 19:5.3
Byer California, 4:3.3
Bylaws
generally, 1:2.4
IPOs, 21:3.1

C

C. Wonder, 6:5.3
C corporation, 1:2.4, 1:2.8
California
Business and Professions Code section 17200, 6:2.1
common law of misappropriation, 6:2.2
Consumers Legal Remedies (CLR) Act, 15:5.3
data breach statute, 14:3.2[A]
e-commerce and mobile e-commerce regulation, 14:3.2[A]
idea man, 6:2.2
manufacturing, 9:1
non-competition agreements, 17:4.1
OSHA-approved state plans, 9:5.1

California (*cont'd*)
  Privacy on the Go: Recommendations for the Mobile Ecosystem, 14:3.2[A]
  publicity rights, 18:4.1
    Civil Code section 3344, text of, 18:4.1
  Quality King Distributors, Inc. v. L'anza Research International, Inc., 8:3.2
  trade secrets, 6:2.3
  unfair competition, 6:2
    Cel-Tech Communications, Inc. v. L.A. Cellular Tel. Co., 6:2.1
  wages and hours, 16:2.1
California Consumer Privacy Act of 2018, 14:3.2[A]
California Trade Secrets Act (CUTSA), 6:2.3
Call options, 1:3.2
Calvin Klein, 2:4.2, 3:6.1, 10:1
Campbell v. Acuff-Rose Music, Inc., 4:8.1
CAN-SPAM. *See* Controlling the Assault of Non-Solicited Pornography and Marketing (CANSPAM) Act
Canada
  design law protections, 5:5.5
  IPR Center (National Intellectual Property Rights Coordination Center), 7:2
Canada Goose Holdings, Inc., 21:1
Canada's Industrial Design Act (CIDA), 5:5.5
Canali, 9:2
Cancellation, trademark registrations, 2:6.3[F]
Cannonball, human, 18:3
CANSPAM Act (Controlling the Assault of Non-Solicited Pornography and Marketing Act), 14:3.4
Canteen Stores Department, 20:4.4
Capital rounds, 1:4.1
Capital structure, 1:3.1, 1:3.3, 21:4.4
Capitalization, IPO prospectus, 21:4.4
Capri Holdings, 22:1, 22:2.1, 22:5.4
Carbon38, 11:1, 11:1.9
Cardinal Health, 20:5.3
Carnival Cruise Lines
  smart wearables, 3:6.2[C]
Carol Barnhart v. Economy Cover Corp., 4:3.2[D]
Cartoon characters, copyright infringement, 4:7.2[D]
Cash collateral
  liquidity, bankruptcy cases, 23:2.3[B]
Cash flow statements, 1:1.2[G], 1:4.5
Cash purchase price, 22:3.2[A]

Cat & Jack, 11:1.3
Catalog retailers, 11:1.8
Caveat emptor, 15:1
Caveat venditor, 15:1
CBP. *See* Customs and Border Protection (CBP)
CDA. *See* Communications Decency Act (CDA)
CDPA. *See* Copyright, Designs, and Patents Act (CDPA), United Kingdom
Cease-and-desist order
  trademarks, 2:13
Cel-Tech Communications, Inc. v. L.A. Cellular Tel. Co., 6:2.1
Celebrities. *See* Publicity rights
Century 21 v. Lending Tree, 2:10.5
Certificate of formation, LLC, 1:2.7
Certificate of incorporation, 1:2.4
Certificate of limited partnership, 1:2.8
Certification marks, 2:3. *See also* Trademarks
Certilogo Code, 7:4.1
Champion T-shirts, 2:3
Chanel, Inc. v. What Goes Around Comes Around (WGACA), 2:11.3
Chanel luxury brand, 9:2, 10:1
Chanel No. 5, 2:4.1
Change in control provisions
  bankruptcy cases, preparation for, 23:2.2
Chapter 11. *See also headings under Bankruptcy*
  bankruptcy cases, preparation for, 23:2.2
  cash collateral, 23:2.3[B]
  change in control provisions, 23:2.2
  debtor in possession financing, 23:2.3[C]
  factoring arrangements, 23:2.3[A][3]
  liquidation, 23:5.1
  relief under, benefits of, 23:3.1
  reorganization, 23:2.2, 23:5.1
Characters, copyright infringement, 4:7.2[D]
Chargebacks, retailer-vendor arrangements, 11:2.6
Charitable causes, fashion business model methodologies connected to, 11:1.10
Chat with a specialist customer service, 11:1.7
Chattanoga Manufacturing, Inc. v. Nike Inc., 2:10.6
Cheerleader uniforms
  Star Athletica LLC v. Varsity Brands, Inc., 4:1, 4:3.2[D]
Chelsea Market, 13:2.3
Chen, Steven, 7:3.4[B][2]
Chewy Vuiton dog toy, 2:10.8, 7:3.2

Child labor laws, 16:3
  addressing labor problems through self-regulation, 16:3.4
  corporate codes of conduct, 16:3.4
  federal child labor law, 16:3.1
    age of minor, 16:3.1[B]
    employer-employee relationship, 16:3.1[A]
    enforcement, 16:3.1[E]
    penalties and contesting penalties, 16:3.1[E]
    wages, 16:3.1[C]
    work prohibitions, 16:3.1[D]
  Federal Labor Standards Act (FLSA), 16:3
  forced labor, 19:2.1[B]
  importer responsibilities, 19:2.1[B]
  New York, 16:3.2
  state child labor laws, 16:3.2
  sweatshops, 16:3.3
Children. *See also* Child labor laws
  COPPA Rule, 14:3.2[A]
  Mobile App for Kids: Disclosure Still Not Making the Grade (FTC), 14:3.2
  product safety, CPSC, 9:5.1
Children's Online Privacy Protection Act (COPPA), 14:3.2[A]
Chile-United States Free Trade Agreement, 19:6
China
  apparel manufacturing industry, 9:1
  Avon case study, 20:4.2
  Daimler AG v. Bauman, 7:3.3[C]
  design law protections, 5:5.2
    e-commerce law, 5:5.2
  e-commerce market, statistics, 14:1
  Gucci America, Inc. v. Weixing Li, 7:3.3[B], 7:3.3[C]
  Internet data regulation, 14:3.2[A]
  JD.com, 11:1.5
  Juicy Couture, Inc. v. Bella International, Inc., 7:3.3
  litigation, Louis Vuitton, 2:9.5
  luxury consumers, 9:2
  luxury purchases, 9:2
  Operation In Our Sites, 7:2
  Operation In Our Sites VII, 7:2
  privacy, mobile commerce/e-commerce, 14:3.2[A]
  RAE Systems, Inc., 20:5.2
  unfair competition lawsuits, pirated software, 6:2.1
  U.S. e-commerce retailers expansion into, 14:1
Chloé v. Queen Bee of Beverly Hills, LLC, 7:3.1[A]
Choreographic works, copyright protection, 4:2

Chosun International, Inc. v. Chrisha Creations, Ltd., 4:3.2[C]
Christian Dior, 2:4.2, 3:6.1, 18:4.2
Christian Louboutin, 3:6.1
Christian Louboutin S.A. v. Yves Saint Laurent America Holding, Inc., 2:10.9[A]
Chuck Taylor, Converse
  All Star shoes, 2:9.5
  sneakers, 2:5
CIDA. *See* Canada's Industrial Design Act (CIDA)
Civil litigation, counterfeiting, 7:3
Civil Rights Act of 1964, Title VII, 16:4.1, 16:4.2
Civil Rights Law
  New York, sections 50 & 51, 18:3, 18:4.2
Clariti Eyewear, 3:6.2[B]
Class actions
  Abercrombie & Fitch Stores, 16:4.1
  cosmetics false advertising, 15:5.4
  Frank v. Gaos, 14:3.2[B]
  In re Zappos.com Inc., Customer Data Security Breach Litigation, 14:3.2[B]
  Target Corporation data breach settlement, 14:3.2[A]
Classification, imported merchandise, 19:4
Clayton Antitrust Act, 4:2, 12:1
Clean team
  sale transactions (fashion companies/brands acquisitions), 22:2.2
Clickwrap agreements, 14:3.1
Closely held companies, corporate veil, 1:2.10
Closing. *See also* Sale transactions (fashion companies/brands acquisitions)
  conditions, 22:6
  interval between signing and closing, 22:6
  post-closing indemnities, 22:5.3
  post-closing working capital adjustment provisions, 22:3.3
  simultaneous signing and closing, 22:5.2, 22:6
CLR. *See* Consumers Legal Remedies Act (CLR Act)
CMG Worldwide, 18:4.3
CMT. *See* Cut, make, trim (CMT) manufacturing
Co-existence agreements, private, 2:13:1
Co-sale rights, 1:3.2
Coach, Inc.
  Kate Spade & Co., acquisition of, 22:1, 22:7.2
  overpromotion by retailers at discount prices, 11:2.2
COACH mark, 2:6.1, 2:6.2
Coach Services, Inc. v. Triumph Learning LLC, 2:6.1

Coalition. *See* Sustainable Apparel Coalition
Coca-Cola bottle, 3:2.2
Cohen v. Facebook, Inc., 18:5
Collaborative consumption (rent or borrow) e-commerce business model, 11:1.7
Collateral, 1:3.3, 1:4.5
Collateral split
  liquidity, bankruptcy cases, 23:2.3[A][2]
Collective marks, 2:3. *See also* Trademarks
Colors. *See also* Trademarks
  Burberry plaid color scheme, 2:8.2, 7:3.2
  Louboutin case, 2:10.9[A]
Columbia Sportswear North America, Inc., 3:6.1
Combination overtime exemption, 16:2.2[G]
Commerce Clause Doctrine, 14:3.3
Commerce Control List, 19:9.2
Commercial bank financing, 1:4.5
Commercial loans, 1:4.5
Commercial speech, false advertising, 15:2.1
Commingling funds, corporate veil, 1:2.10
Commission-based employees, 16:2.1
Common law
  consignments and bankruptcy, 23:4.5[B]
  copyright protection, 4:2
  misappropriation, California, 6:2.2
  unfair competition, New York, 6:3.1
Common phrases, trademarks, 2:4.4
Common stock, 1:3.2, 1:3.3, 1:4.3, 1:4.7. *See also* Preferred stock
Communications Decency Act (CDA), 15:7, 15:7.3
Community Design System (European Union), 5:2
Company Doe v. Tenenbaum, 9:5.1
Compensation
  employment agreements, 17:2.3
  IPO prospectus, 21:4.7
Compensation package
  employment agreements, 17:2.3
Competition. *See* Non-competition agreements; Unfair competition
Competitive proximity of products, confusion analysis, 2:7.2[C]
Compilation, works for hire, 4:5
Components
  sourcing decisions, design process, 9:3
Computer Fraud and Abuse Act, 14:3.4
Computer professionals, overtime exemption, 16:2.2[E]
Cone Communications, research by, 11:1.10

Confidentiality agreements, 17:3, 22:2.3
- generally, 17:3.1
- assignment provision, 17:3.2
- breach of contract claims, 17:3.2
- confidential information, sample definition of, 17:3.2
- drafting, 17:3.2
- fashion events and, 17:3.1
- severabililty provision, 17:3.2
- term, 17:3.2
- third-party disclosure, 17:3.2
- violations of, 17:3.2

Confusion, likelihood of
- ACPA, 2:2
- actual confusion evidence, 2:7.2[C]
- analysis, 2:7.2[C]
- bridge the gap, 2:7.2[C]
- competitive proximity of products, 2:7.2[C]
- Confusion Factors, 2:7.2
- consumer sophistication, 2:7.2[C]
- counterfeiting, 7:3.2
- defendant's intent, 2:7.2[C]
- *Dupont* factors, 2:6.1
- *eBay Inc. v. MercExchange, LLC,* 2:9.1[A], 2:9.1[B], 3:1
- establishing, 2:7.2[C]
- evidence of actual confusion, 2:7.2[C]
- examination of trademark application, 2:6.3[D]
- forward confusion, 2:7.2[B]
- image of famous character, 4:7.2[D]
- initial interest confusion, 2:7.2[B]
- marketing channels factor, 2:7.2[C]
- multifactor test, 2:11.2
- nominative fair use doctrine, 2:10.5
- parody defense, 2:10.8, 7:3.2
- passing off, 6:3.1[A]
- personal names, 2:4.2
- point-of-sale confusion, 2:7.2[B]
- post-sale confusion doctrine, 2:7.2[B], 7:3.2
- private co-existence agreements, 2:13:1
- progressive encroachment doctrine, 2:10.6
- quality of defendant's product, 2:7.2[C]
- reverse confusion, 2:7.2[B]
- search engine advertising, 2:11
- similarity of marks, 2:7.2[C]
- source confusion, 2:7.2[B]
- strength of mark, 2:7.2[C]
- trade dress, 2:6.1

Confusion, likelihood of (*cont'd*)
trademark enforcement strategy, 2:13
trademark law, 2:2
trademark searching, 2:6.3[A]
Troika factors, trademark infringement, 2:11.2
Confusion Factors, 2:7.2, 8:4.1. *See also* Trademark infringement
Conglomeratization trend, 22:1
Consent rights, equity investors, 1:3.2
Consignments
antitrust, 12:4.1[D]
bankruptcy. *See* Consignments and bankruptcy
retailer-vendor arrangements, 11:2.7
Consignments and bankruptcy, 23:4.5
Article 9, Uniform Commercial Code, 23:4.5[A]
common law, 23:4.5[B]
consignment, defined, 23:4.5[A][1]
consignment agreement, 23:4.5
consignments not governed by Article 9, 23:4.5[B]
consignor does not obtain PMSI, 23:4.5[A][3]
purchase money security interest in goods (PMSI), 23:4.5[A][2], 23:4.5[A][3]
senior security interest in consigned goods, 23:4.5[A][2]
UCC-1 financing statement, 23:4.5[A][2]
Constitution, U.S. *See* U.S. Constitution
Construction specifications
preproduction process, 9:3
Constructive use, trademark registration, 2:2
Consumer Product Safety Act, section 37, 9:5.1
Consumer Product Safety Commission (CPSC), 9:5.1, 19:3
Consumer Product Safety for Children's Jewelry, 9:5.1
Consumer Product Safety Improvement Act (CPSIA), 9:5.1
Consumer reports, saferproducts.gov database, 9:5.1
Consumer-rights movement, 15:3
Consumer sophistication, confusion analysis, 2:7.2[C]
Consumers
Generation Z (Gen Z), 11:1.9
Millennials, 11:1.10
younger consumers, 11:1.10
Consumers Legal Remedies Act (CLR Act), 15:5.3
Contacts, network of, 1:1.1
Contingent payment mechanisms, 22:3.4
Continuous use provisions
going out of business sales (GOB sales), 23:5.2[B][1][d]
going out of business sales (GOB sales), lease restrictions, 23:5.2[B][1][d]

Contract issues, mobile commerce/e-commerce, 14:3.1
Contributory trademark infringement, 7:3.4
Control Components Inc. case, 20:5.4
Controlling stockholders, 1:3.2
Controlling the Assault of Non-Solicited Pornography and Marketing (CANSPAM) Act, 14:3.4
Convention Establishing the World Intellectual Property Organization, 2:15.1
Convention on Combating Bribery of Foreign Public Officials in International Business Transactions, 20:2
Converse
  Chuck Taylor, 2:5, 2:9.5
  Nike, 3:6.1
Converse Inc v. ITC, 2:9.5
Convertible debt, 1:3.3, 1:4.3, 1:4.6
Convertible preferred stock, 1:3.2, 1:3.3, 1:4.3, 1:4.6, 1:4.7
Cooperative advertising, antitrust, 12:4.1[F]
Cooperatives (co-ops), 1:2.9
COPPA (Children's Online Privacy Protection Act), 14:3.2[A]
COPPA Rule, 14:3.2[A]
CopyCatClubs.com, 7:3.4[B][2]
Copyright, Designs, and Patents Act (CDPA), United Kingdom, 5:4.2
Copyright, generally, 4:1 *et seq.*, 18:2. *See also headings under Copyright;* International design law protections
  generally, 4:1
  change of ownership, 4:6.2
  distinguished from publicity rights, 18:2
  first sale doctrine, 8:2.2
  international designs. *See* International design law protections
  joint ownership, 4:5
  length, 4:6.4
  ownership, 4:5
  works for hire, 4:5
Copyright Act
  1870, 4:3.2[A]
  1909, 4:3.2[A]
  1976, 4:2, 4:3.1, 4:3.2[A], 4:3.2[B], 4:3.2[C]
  failure to transfer ownership of goods, 8:4.2
  impounding and disposition, 4:9.2
  1990 amendment, 4:4
  section 1301, 4:4
Copyright Act of 1793 (France), 5:4.1
Copyright applications
  elements, 4:6.1
  poor man's copyright, 4:6

Copyright infringement, 4:7
abstractions test, 4:7.2[C]
access, 4:7.1
Article 17 of U.S. Code, section 107, 4:8.1
attorneys' fees, 4:9.4
cartoon characters, 4:7.2[D]
damages and profits, 4:9.3
de minimis doctrine, 4:8.2
defenses, 4:8
disposition, 4:9.2
extrinsic/intrinsic test, 4:7.2[B]
fair use doctrine, 4:8.1
first sale doctrine, 8:2.2
impoundment, 4:9.2
injunctive relief, 4:9.1
licensing, 4:7.2[D]
movie characters, 4:7.2[D]
ordinary observer test, 4:7.2[A]
remedies, 4:9
statutory damages, 4:9.3[B]
substantial similarity, 4:7.2
successive filtering approach, 4:7.2[C]
Copyright notice, 4:6.3
Copyright Office
copyright registration, 4:6
separability doctrine, 4:3.2
Copyright protection
Berne Convention, 4:6.3, 4:7
categories, 4:2
common law, 4:2
Constitutional grant, Article 1, section 8, 4:2
creativity level, 4:3.1
development, 4:2
elements, 4:3
extending, fashion industry, 4:4
fixed form, 4:1, 4:3, 4:3.3
idea and expression, 4:3.3
originality test, 4:3.1
prior works, 4:3.1
separability doctrine, 4:3.2
Copyright registrations
importance of, 4:6
procedures, 4:6
renewals, 4:6.2
Corporate veil, piercing, 1:2.3, 1:2.10

Corporations. *See also* Board of directors; Stockholders
C corporation, 1:2.4, 1:2.8
defined, 1:2.4
described, 1:2.4–1:2.5
S corporation, 1:2.5, 1:3.2
subsidiaries as, 1:2.11
Corruption. *See* Foreign Corrupt Practices Act (FCPA)
Cosmetic products, mislabeling/misbranding
administrative proceedings, 15:4.3[B]
adulterated or misbranded cosmetics, defined, 15:4.3[A]
consumer class actions, 15:5.4
disclaimers, 15:2.6
false advertising, 15:5.4
FDA, 15:4.3
prosecutions, 15:4.3[B]
Cost, insurance, and freight (C.I.F.)
shipping and delivery terms, retailer-vendor arrangements, 11:2.4
Cost and freight (C.F. or C. & F.)
shipping and delivery terms, retailer-vendor arrangements, 11:2.4
Costco
Omega S.A. v. Costco Wholesale Corp., 8:3.4, 8:3.5, 8:5
Tiffany & Co. v. Costco Wholesale Corp., 2:7.2[C]
Cottage industry manufacturing, 9:3
Council of Fashion Designers of America, 16:5
Counterfeit apparel, customs seizure and forfeiture, 19:8.1
Counterfeiting, 7:1 *et seq. See also* Trademark infringement
generally, 7:1
alternative service of process, 7:3.1[C]
Burberry plaid color scheme, 2:8.2, 7:3.2
civil litigation, 7:3
contributory trademark infringement, 7:3.4
credit card processors, 7:3.4[B]
e-commerce platforms, enforcement by, 7:4.2
ex parte temporary restraining order, 7:3.3
expedited discovery, 7:3.3[C]
Fakes Are Never In Fashion campaign, 7:4.3
federal law enforcement, 7:2
globalization, 7:1
holograms, 7:4.1
IACC, 7:4.2
Internet, 7:1
internet service providers (ISPs), 7:3.5[B]
Inwood decision and its progeny, 7:3.4[A]

Counterfeiting (*cont'd*)
likelihood of confusion, 7:3.2
Louis Vuitton Chinese litigations, 2:9.5
monetary remedies, 7:3.5
New York City Police Department, 7:2
personal jurisdiction, 7:3.1
profits, 7:3.5[A]
public education, 7:4.3
restraint of counterfeiters' assets, 7:3.3[B]
RFID tags, 7:4.1
software, unfair competition lawsuits, 6:2.1
statutory damages, 7:3.5[B]
unclean hands entrapment defense, 2:10.4
websites, 7:3.1[A]
Country of origin rules, 19:6
apparel and textiles, 19:6.2
markings requirements, 19:6.4
non-preferential rules, 19:6.1
preferential rules, 19:6.3
Countryman test
intellectual property and bankruptcy, 23:4.4[A][1]
Covenants/Agreements
acquisition agreements, 22:5.2
agreements not to compete. *See* Non-competition agreements
confidentiality agreements. *See* Confidentiality agreements
CPSC. *See* Consumer Product Safety Commission (CPSC)
CPSIA. *See* Consumer Product Safety Improvement Act (CPSIA)
Cram-down situations
post-petition value creation, bankruptcy cases, 23:4.1[B][2]
Creative control
provisions, 1:3.2, App. 1A
rights, 1:3.2
Creative professionals, overtime exemption, 16:2.2[D]
Creativity level, copyright protection, 4:3.1
Credit bidding
section 363 of Bankruptcy Code, sales authorized by, 23:5.2[B]
Credit card processors, counterfeiting, 7:3.4[B]
Crimea Region of the Ukraine
economic sanctions, 19:9.1
Crocs, 3:6.1, 3:6.2[B]
Crocs, Inc. v. International Trade Commission, 3:6.2[B]
Crowdfunding
Regulation Crowdfunding, SEC, 1:4.7
Cuba
economic sanctions, 19:9.1
HTSUS, classification of imported merchandise, 19:4

Cullinane v. Uber Technologies, Inc., 14:3.1
Customer analytics, retail sales, 11:1.7
Customer restrictions
  antitrust, 12:4.2[B]
Customer service
  chat with a specialist, 11:1.7
Customs and Border Protection (CBP)
  administrative process, 19:7
  detention orders, 19:8.1
  Entry Summary, Department of Homeland Security, App. 19A
  forfeiture, 19:8.1
  fraud, 19:8.2
  importer responsibilities, 19:2
  IPR Center, 7:2
  mitigation guidelines, 19:8.2
  monetary penalties, 19:8.2
  negligence, 19:8.2
  penalties, 19:8
  seizures, 19:8.1
  self-disclosure, 19:8.2
  statistics, 19:8, 19:8.1
Customs enforcement, ICE, 7:2
Customs Form 7501, 19:3
Customs laws, 19:1. *See also* Customs and Border Protection (CBP); Imported merchandise
  administrative process, 19:7
  country of origin rules, 19:6
  enforcement, 19:8
  entry of merchandise, 19:3
  exporting, 19:9
  HTSUS, 19:4, App. 19B
  importer responsibilities, 19:2
  penalties, 19:8
    detention orders, 19:8.1
    forfeitures, 19:8.1
    fraud, 19:8.2
    gross negligence, 19:8.2
    mitigation guidelines, 19:8.2
    monetary penalties, 19:8.2
    negligence, 19:8.2
    seizures, 19:8.1
    self-disclosure, 19:8.2
    statistics, 19:8, 19:8.1
  valuation, 19:5

Customs Modernization Act, 19:2.1
Cut, make, trim (CMT) manufacturing, 9:3
CUTSA. *See* California Trade Secrets Act (CUTSA)
CVS, 3:6.1
Cyber security, 14:3.4, 21:2.3, 21:4.2
Cybersquatting, ACPA and, 2:2, 2:9.4

D

Dailylook, 22:1
Daimler AG v. Bauman, 7:3.3[C]
Damages
    real property leases (non-residential) and bankruptcy, 23:4.2[D]
Damages and profits, copyright infringement, 4:9.3
Daou v. Huffington, 6:3.1[B]
Dashnaw v. New Balance Athletics, Inc., 15:4.2[F]
Dastar Corp. v. Twentieth Century Fox Film Corp, 6:4.1
Data breach settlements, 14:3.2[A]
Data privacy, mobile commerce/e-commerce, 14:3.2
Database, saferproducts.gov, 9:5.1
Davis Onoculii eyewear, 4:8.1
De minimis doctrine, 4:8.2
Debt financing
    convertible, 1:3.3, 1:4.3, 1:4.6
    described, 1:3.3
    equity financing versus, 1:3.2, 1:3.3
Debtor in possession financing, 23:2.3[C]
Deceptive words, trademarks, 2:4.5
Deckers Outdoor Corporation, 3:6.1
Declaration, patent applications, 3:3.1
Declaration of Incontestability, 2:10.1
Defaults
    assumption of real property lease (non-residential) and bankruptcy, 23:4.2[B][1]
Defend Trade Secrets Act (DTSA)
    generally, 6:4.2
    claims, illustrative cases, 6:5.1
    ex parte civil seizure provision, 6:4.2
Defendant's intent, confusion analysis, 2:7.2[C]
Defenses
    copyright infringement, 4:8
    false advertising, 15:4.1[E]
    trademark infringement, 2:10
        aesthetic functionality, 2:10.9
        invalidity of trademark, 2:10.1

laches, 2:10.6
lack of standing, 2:10.2
naked licensing, 2:10.7
nominative fair use, 2:10.5
parody, 2:10.8
procurement fraud, 2:10.3
unclean hands, 2:10.4
Delaware Court of Chancery, 1:2.8
Delaware General Corporation Law (DGCL), 1:2.4, 1:2.6, 1:3.2
Delaware Limited Liability Company Act (DLLCA), 1:2.7
Delaware Revised Uniform Limited Partnership Act (DRULPA), 1:2.8
Delaware Revised Uniform Partnership Act (DRUPA), 1:2.3
Delaware Secretary of State, 1:2.3, 1:2.4, 1:2.7, 1:2.8
Delivery terms, retailer-vendor arrangements, 11:2.4
Dell, 14:3.1
Deloitte & Touche LLP report, 8:1
Demand registration rights, 1:3.2
Department of Homeland Security, 7:2, 19:2. *See also* Customs and Border Protection (CBP)
Customs and Border Protection: Entry Summary, App. 19A
Department of Justice (DOJ)
Antitrust Division, 12:1, 12:3, 12:5
Avon case study, 20:4.2
FCPA enforcement, generally, 20:4
IPR Center, 7:2
Operation In Our Sites, 7:2
Operation In Our Sites VII, 7:2
Ralph Lauren case study, 20:4.1
Resource Guide, FCPA. *See* Resource Guide to the U.S. Foreign Corrupt Practices Act
Department stores, 11:1.1
anchor tenant, 11:1.1
apparel merchandise, types of, 11:1.1
classification of, 11:1.1
discount, 11:1.3
fashion influencers, 15:7.2
first floor items, 11:1.1
flag-ship store, 11:1.1, 11:1.9
in-store shop, 13:2.2
in-store shop concept, 11:1.1
Lord & Taylor, 15:7.2
Macy's, 4:2, 10:2.2[A], 11:1.1, 15:4.2[E]
market segments, 11:1.1
private label products, 11:1.1
revenue statistics, 11:1.1
shop within a shop, 13:2.2

Derivative suits, 1:3.2
Design, 9:1 *et seq. See also* Manufacturing
generally, 9:1
luxury, 9:2
preproduction processes, 9:3, 10:2.2[D]
production stage, 9:3
sourcing decisions, 9:3
tech packs, 9:3
Design patent applications
AIA, 3:3.1
costs and fees, 3:3.3
declaration, 3:3.1
drawings, 3:3.1, 3:3.5
early filing, 3:3.1
employers, 3:3.1
examination, PTO, 3:3.4
growth, 3:6.1
oath, 3:3.1
pendency, 3:3.5
requirements, 3:3.1
term, 3:3.5
written specification, 3:3.1
Design patents. *See also* Patents
generally, 3:7
Columbia Sportswear North America, Inc., 3:6.1
described, 3:2.2
examples, App. 3A–1, App. 3A–2
fashion companies holding, 3:6.1
growth of, 3:6.1
number of patents filed, statistics, 3:6.1
point of novelty test, 3:4.1, 3:6.1
requirements, 3:2.2
uses, 3:6.1
Design teams, 9:3
Design Technology Group, LLC d/b/a Bettie Page Clothing, 16:8
Designation rights
assignment of real property lease (non-residential) and bankruptcy, 23:4.2[C][4]
Designer jeans
finishing stage of production, 9:3
Designs That Donate, 11:1.10
Destinations and experiences
retail stores as, 11:1.10
DGCL. *See* Delaware General Corporation Law (DGCL)

Diageo, 20:4.4[C]
Diamond, Shari Siedman, 2:7.2[C]
Diffusion, stockholder, 1:3.2
Digital revolution, 15:7
Dilution. *See also* Trademark dilution
  convertible debt, 1:3.3, 1:4.3, 1:4.6
  convertible preferred stock, 1:3.2, 1:3.3, 1:4.3, 1:4.6, 1:4.7
  Federal Trademark Dilution Act, 2:8
  IPO prospectus, 21:4.4
  Trademark Dilution Revision Act (TDRA), 2:8, 2:10.5
Direct rebates, antitrust, 12:4.1[E]
Direct-to-consumer retail sales, 11:2
Director and officer. *See also* Board of directors
  bankruptcy cases, preparation for
    coverage, 23:2.2
    fiduciary duties, 23:2.1
  liability insurance, 21:2.3
Disabilities, ADA, 13:3.8, 16:4.1
Disclaimers, false advertising, 15:2.6
Discount department stores, 11:1.3
Discount factoring, 1:4.4
Discounts, retailer-vendor arrangements, 11:2.2
Discovery apps, 14:1
Discrimination
  ADA, 13:3.8
  anti-discrimination laws, 16:4
  price discrimination, 12:5
Disguised financing
  liquidity, bankruptcy cases, 23:2.3[A][3]
Disparate impact liability, 16:4
Disparate treatment liability, 16:4
Disposition, copyright infringement, 4:9.2
Distinctiveness
  brand names, 1:1.1
  trade dress, 2:5
  trademarks, 2:3
Distressed fashion businesses. *See headings under Bankruptcy*
Distressed jeans
  finishing stage of production, 9:3
Distribution
  exclusive distribution, retailer-vendor arrangements, 11:2.1
Distribution agreements, retail sales, 11:3
Distributors
  FCPA enforcement actions, 20:4.4[C]
  manufacturer's General Certificate of Conformity, 9:5.1

Division or subsidiary, spinoffs, 22:3.1
Divisions, organizational structure, 1:2.11
DLLCA. *See* Delaware Limited Liability Company Act (DLLCA)
DMX Series 2000 Cushioning Technology, Reebok, 3:6.2[B]
Do Not Call mechanism, 14:3.2[A]
Do Not Track mechanism, 14:3.2[A]
Doctor's Associates, Inc. v. QIP Holders, LLC, 15:7.1, 15:7.3
Doctrine of equivalents, 2:4.3
Dodd-Frank Act, 14:4
Doing business as names, 1:2.2, 16:2.1
DOJ. *See* Department of Justice (DOJ)
Dolce & Gabbana USA Inc., 18:5
Dolce Vita Holdings, Inc.,
  Steve Madden Ltd., acquired by, 22:7.1
Domain names. *See also* E-commerce; Internet; Websites
  Anticybersquatting Consumer Protection Act, 2:9.4
  Balenciaga v. liu zhixian, zhixian liu, 2:15.1
  e-commerce stores, 14:2.1
  ex parte temporary restraining order, 7:3.3[A]
  infringement, 2:9.4, 2:15.1
  Lockheed Martin Corp. v. Network Solutions, Inc, 7:3.4[B][2]
  Newport News Holdings Corp. v. Virtual City Vision, Inc., 2:10.6
  North Face Apparel Corp. v. Fujian Sharing Import & Export Ltd. Co., 7:3.3[A]
  Operation In Our Sites, 7:2
  Operation In Our Sites VII, 7:2
  Public Interest Registry, 7:3.3[A]
  TLDs, 2:15.1, 14:2.1
  UDRP, 2:15.1, 14:2.1
Domestic apparel sales
  e-commerce, 14:1
Domestic manufacturing, 9:3
  statistics, 9:1
Dot.Com Disclosures report, 15:7.2, App. 15A
  updates by FTC, 15:7.2
Double taxation, 1:2.4, 1:2.5
Dow Corning Corp. v. Xiao, 15:2.2
Drab, et al.
  utility patent, App. 3B–2
Drafting
  business plans, 1:1.2
  confidentiality agreements, 17:3.2
  IPO prospectus, 21:4
  real estate, lease provisions, 13:3
Drag-along rights, 1:3.2, 22:3.4[B]

Dramatic works, copyright protection, 4:2
Drawings
 patent application, 3:3.1, 3:3.5
 technical, preproduction process, 9:3
DRULPA. *See* Delaware Revised Uniform Limited Partnership Act (DRULPA)
DRUPA. *See* Delaware Revised Uniform Partnership Act (DRUPA)
DTSA. *See* Defend Trade Secrets Act (DTSA)
DuPont factors, 2:6.1

E

E-commerce. *See also* Mobile commerce
 generally, 14:1
 Amazon, contribution to growth of e-commerce apparel, 14:1
 Black Friday sales, 11:1
 borrow or rent (collaborative consumption), 11:1.7
 brick-and-mortar stores, 13:1
 browsewrap agreements, 14:3.1
 business models, 11:1.7
 CAN-SPAM, 14:3.4
 clickwrap agreements, 14:3.1
 collaborative consumption (rent or borrow), 11:1.7
 conditions of use, hyperlink, 14:3.1
 contract issues, 14:3.1
 counterfeiting, enforcement, 7:4.2
 counterfeiting, federal law enforcement, 7:2
 data privacy, 14:3.2
 domain names, 14:2.1
 expansion statistics, 14:1
 global e-commerces sales, statistics, 14:1
 growth of, 14:4
 I Agree button, 14:3.1
 implementation section, business plan, 1:1.2[E]
 international presence, 14:1
 international regulation, 14:3.2[A]
 legal issues, 14:3
 luxury brands, 9:2
 luxury fashion, 11:1.5
 Maker's Row, 9:1
 mobile wallets, 14:4
 online auctions fashion offerings, 11:1.7
 payment methods, 14:4
 personal subscription/subscription box model, 11:1.7

E-commerce. *See also* Mobile commerce (*cont'd*)
physical presence requirement, abolishment of, 14:3.3
platform service providers, 14:2.1
pre-owned or vintage fashion offerings, 11:1.7
private privacy litigation, 14:3.2[B]
security issues, 14:3.2
showrooming practice, 14:1
sole proprietorships, 1:2.2
state regulation, 14:3.2[A]
state taxation and *South Dakota v. Wayfair,* 14:3.3
stores, 14:2.1
tablets, 14:2.2
third-party platform service providers, 14:2.1
trademark infringement. *See* Search engine and Internet advertising, trademark infringement
U.S. retailers expansion into certain countries, 14:1
webrooming practice, 14:1
E-commerce law
China, design law protections, 5:5.2
E-Trade Financial Corporation, 18:4.2
Earn-outs, 22:3.4[A], App. 22A
Earnings before interest, taxes, depreciation and amortization (EBITDA), 22:3.4[B]
eBay, 11:1.7
eBay Inc. v. MercExchange, LLC, 2:9.1[A], 2:9.1[B], 3:1
John Wiley & Sons, Inc. v. Kirtsaeng, 8:3.5, 8:5
Tiffany (NJ) Inc. v. eBay, Inc., Tiffany & Co., 7:3.4[B], 7:3.4[B][2]
Verified Rights Owner (VeRO) Program, 7:3.4[B]
EBITDA. *See* Earnings before interest, taxes, depreciation and amortization (EBITDA)
Economic sanctions, 19:9.1
Economical individualized clothing, 11:1.10
EDI. *See* Electronic data interchange (EDI) technology systems
Education, counterfeiting, 7:4.3
EEOC. *See* Equal Employment Opportunity Commission (EEOC)
Efforts clauses, license agreement termination, 10:2.2[I]
Egyptian Goddess, Inc. v. Swisa, Inc., 3:6.1
In re E.I. DuPont DeNemours & Co., 2:6.2
Electronic Data Gathering, Analysis and Retrieval (EDGAR) System, SEC's, 21:2.2
Electronic data interchange (EDI) technology systems, 11:2.1
Electronic Funds Transfer Act, 14:4
Electronic shopping cart, 14:2.1
Electronic Signatures and Records Act (New York), 14:3.1
Electronic Signatures in Global and National Commerce Act, 14:3.1
Eliya, Inc. v. Steven Madden, Ltd., 2:10.9[B]

Embrace, smart watch, 3:6.2[C]
Emerging growth companies, 21:1
Empatica, 3:6.2[C]
Employee wages and benefits
  first day relief, bankruptcy cases, 23:3.2[A]
Employees. *See* Labor and employment
Employers
  copyright-eligible work, 4:5
  patent applications, 3:3.1
Employment. *See also* Employment agreements; Labor and employment
  at-will employees, 17:1
Employment agreements, 17:2.3
  generally, 17:1
  at-will employees, 17:1
  basic terms, 17:2
  compensation package, 17:2.3
  confidentiality agreements, 17:3, 22:2.3
  construction of agreement, 17:2.5
  health insurance plan participation, 17:2.3
  intellectual property developed by employee, 17:2.4
  non-competition agreements, 17:4.1
    enforcement, 17:4.1
    forfeiture for competition provisions, 17:4.1
    garden leave provisions, 17:4.1
    reasonableness of restriction, 17:4.1
    validity and enforcement under state law, 17:4.1
  non-disparagement agreement, 17:4.2
  non-interference agreement, 17:4.2
  non-solicitation agreement (anti-raid agreement), 17:4.2
  operation of agreement, 17:2.5
  ownership of creations, 17:2.4
  restrictive non-competition agreements, 17:4
  retirement plan participation, 17:2.3
  scope of roles and responsibilities, 17:2.1
  Section 409A non-qualified deferred compensation plans, compliance (Section 409A coverage), 17:2.3
  tax issues, 17:2.3
  term, 17:2.2
  termination
    change in control provision/golden parachute, 17:2.3
    for good reason, 17:2.2
    with or without cause, 17:2.2
  title, 17:2.1
  work made for hire provision, Copyright Act (17 U.S.C. § 101), 17:2.4

Employment and labor issues. *See also* Wages and hours
  Fair Labor Association, 9:5.2
Endorsement Guides (FTC), 15:7.2
Enforcement
  counterfeiting, 7:2
  customs laws, 19:8
  Department of Homeland Security, 7:2
  FCPA. *See* Foreign Corrupt Practices Act (FCPA) enforcement
  Homeland Security Investigations Border Enforcement and Security Task Force, 7:2
  Immigration and Customs Enforcement, 7:2
  trademarks, 2:13:1
Enhanced damages, willful patent infringement, 3:4.2[E]
Entertainment and gifts, FCPA enforcement actions, 20:5.5
Entrepreneurship. *See also* Fashion companies (new business ventures)
  flourishing, 1:1.1
Entry of merchandise, 19:3
Environmental benefit, fashion business model methodologies connected to, 11:1.10
Equal Employment Opportunity Commission (EEOC)
  compliance enforcement for
    Age Discrimination in Employment Act (ADEA), 16:4.1, 16:4.2
    Americans with Disabilities Act (ADA), 16:4.1
    Civil Rights Act of 1964, Title VII, 16:4.1, 16:4.2
    Equal Pay Act, 16:4.1
  role of, 16:4.1
Equal Pay Act, 16:4.1
Equitable estoppel
  patent infringement claim, 3:6.2[B]
Equities securities of buyer, 22:3.2[B]
Equity financing, 1:3.2
  debt financing versus, 1:3.2, 1:3.3
  equity investors, 1:3.2
  risk, 1:3.2
Equivalents, doctrine of, 2:4.3
Ergo Baby Carrier, Inc., 9:5.1
Escrow amounts, 22:5.4
Esquenazi, Joel, 20:3.1[B]
Essex Manufacturing, Inc. v. United States, 19:3
Establishment claims and false advertising, 15:4.1[C]
Estée Lauder, 2:7.2[C], 17:4.1
Estée Lauder, Inc. v. The Gap, Inc., 2:7.2[C]
Estoppel, 2:10.7
  patent infringement claim, 3:6.2[B]

Eugénie, Empress, 18:1
Eurazeo Brands, 1:4.8
European Commission
privacy, mobile commerce/e-commerce, 14:3.2[A]
European countries
design law protections, 5:4
European Union
privacy, mobile commerce/e-commerce, 14:3.2[A]
European Union Intellectual Property Office (EUIPO), synthesis report, 7:4.3
European Union member states
design law protections, 5:2
Brexit, 5:4.2
registered and unregistered designs, 5:2
Europol, 7:2
Eva's Bridal Ltd. v. Halanick Enterprises, Inc., 2:10.7
Everlane, 11:1
Ex parte temporary restraining order, 7:3.3
Exclusive dealing, antitrust, 12:4.2[A]
Exclusive distribution
antitrust, 12:4.2[A]
retailer-vendor arrangements, 11:2.1
Exclusive negotiations, 22:2.2
Exclusive use, brick-and-mortar lease provisions, 13:3.4
Exclusivity agreements, 22:2.1
Executives, overtime exemption, 16:2.2[A]
Executory contracts, 23:4.3
bankruptcy, 23:4.3
intellectual property, 23:4.4
real property leases, non-residential, 23:4.2
intellectual property
and bankruptcy, 23:4.4
determination of, 23:4.4[A][1]
real property leases, non-residential, 23:4.2
Exhaustion doctrine, patents, 8:1, 8:2.4
Expedited discovery, counterfeiting, 7:3.3[C]
Experienced assistance, new business ventures, 1:1.1
Experiences and destinations
retail stores as, 11:1.10
Export Administration Regulations, 19:9.2
Export Classification Control Number, 19:9.2
Exporting, 19:9. *See also* Imported merchandise
Expression and idea, copyright protection, 4:3.3
Extrinsic/intrinsic test, copyright infringement, 4:7.2[B]
Eye Tracker technology, 3:6.2[C]

Eyewear
  Aspex Eyewear Inc. v. Clariti Eyewear, Inc., 3:6.2[B]
  Davis Onoculii eyewear, 4:8.1
  Google, 3:6.2[C]
  Oakley, Inc., 3:6.1, 3:6.2[B], 3:6.2[C]
  patent infringements, 3:6.2[B]
  smart glasses, 3:6.2[C]
  smart ski and snowboard goggles, 3:6.2[C]

F

Fabric
  flammability standards for fabrics and textiles, 9:5.1
  Flammable Fabrics Act, 9:5.1, 15:2.6
  high-performance fabrics, 3:6.2[A]
  rose-patterned fabric, Folio Impressions, 4:3.3
  smart fabrics, 3:6.2[C]
  sourcing decisions, design process, 9:3
Facebook, 15:7, 16:8
  ancillary agreements, 22:4
  Cohen v. Facebook, Inc., 18:5
  labor and employment, social media usage, 16:8
Fact vs. opinion, false advertising, 15:2.3
Factoring arrangements, 1:4.4
  liquidity, bankruptcy cases, 23:2.3[A][3]
Factory outlets, 11:1.4[A]
Failure to transfer ownership of goods, 8:4.2
Fair and Accurate Credit Transactions Act, 14:4
Fair Labor Association, 9:5.2
  Workplace Code of Conduct, 9:5.2
Fair Labor Standards Act (FLSA)
  unfair labor practices, combating, 16:2.5
Fair Packaging and Labeling Act (FP&L Act), 15:4.3[A]
Fair use doctrine
  copyright infringement, 4:8.1
Fakes Are Never In Fashion campaign, 7:4.3
False advertising, 15:1 *et seq. See also* Misleading advertising
  generally, 15:1
  acquiescence defense, 15:4.1[E]
  commercial speech, 15:2.1
  defenses, 15:4.1[E]
  defined, 15:2.5
  digital communications, section 43(a) suits, 15:7.1

disclaimers, 15:2.6
fact versus opinion, 15:2.3
FTC, 15:4.2
FTC, historical regulation, 15:3
historical regulation, 15:3
jurisdiction over, 15:5
laches, 15:4.1[E]
Lanham Act, 15:4.1
digital communications, section 43(a) suits, 15:7.1
establishment claims, 15:4.1[C]
literally false vs. ambiguous but misleading, 15:2.5
misbranding/mislabeling cosmetic products, 15:4.3
NAD, 15:2.6, 15:6
non-commercial speech, 15:2.1
private self-regulation, 15:6
remedies, 15:4.1[D]
social media platforms, 15:7
state regulation of, 15:5
unclean hands defense, 15:4.1[E]
False marking, patents, 3:3.6
Family, financing source, 1:4.3
Family and Medical Leave Act (FMLA), 16:4.4
Farfetch Limited, 11:1.5, 21:1, 21:2.2
online discounts and markdowns, 11:2.2
Fashion Boutique of Short Hills, Inc. v. Fendi USA, Inc., 15:2.2
Fashion/business courses, 1:1.1
Fashion companies (new business ventures), 1:1 *et seq. See also* Sale transactions (fashion companies/brands acquisitions)
business description, 1:1.2[B]
business plan, drafting, 1:1.2
C corporation, 1:2.4
capital structure, 1:3.1
challenges, 1:1.1
co-ops, 1:2.9
competition section, 1:1.2[D]
divisions, 1:2.11
equity financing, 1:3.2
executive summary, 1:1.2[A]
failure rate, 1:1.1
financial projections section, 1:1.2[G]
financing, 1:3.2
financing sources, 1:1.1, 1:4
general partnership, 1:2.3
implementation section, 1:1.2[E]

Fashion companies (new business ventures) (*cont'd*)
  industry and market analysis, 1:1.2[C]
  LLC, 1:2.7
  LP, 1:2.8
  organization and management section, 1:1.2[F]
  organizational structure, 1:2
  piercing corporate veil, 1:2.3, 1:2.10
  planning, 1:1.1
  preparatory steps, 1:1.1
  problems, 1:1.1
  public benefit corporation, 1:2.6
  S corporation, 1:2.5
  sole proprietorship, 1:2.2
  subsidiaries, 1:2.11
Fashion design. *See* Design
Fashion industry
  health issues, 16:5
  opportunities, 1:1.1
Fashion influencers, 15:7.2, 21:1
Fashion Originator's Guild, 4:2
Fashion Shops of Kentucky, Inc., 8:3.3, 8:4.1
Fashion shows, 13:4
Fashion technology companies, 1:1.1, 1:2.1, 1:4.6
Fast fashion, 11:1, 13:1
FCPA. *See* Foreign Corrupt Practices Act (FCPA)
  generally. *See* Foreign Corrupt Practices Act (FCPA)
  enforcement. *See* Foreign Corrupt Practices Act (FCPA) enforcement
FD&C Act. *See* Food, Drug, and Cosmetic Act (FD&C Act)
Federal Acquisition Regulatory Council, 16:2.5
Federal Hazardous Substances Act, 15:2.6
Federal Labor Standards Act (FLSA), 16:2
  administrative exemption, 16:2.2[B]
  California, 16:2.1
  combination exemption, 16:2.2[G]
  computer professional exemption, 16:2.2[E]
  creative professional exemption, 16:2.2[D]
  executive exemption, 16:2.2[A]
  highly compensated employee exemption, 16:2.2[H]
  home worker restrictions, 16:2.4
  hot goods, 16:2.5
  interns, 16:2.3
  learned professional exemption, 16:2.2[C]
  minimum wage, 16:2.1
  minors, 16:3.1

New York, 16:2.1
overtime exemptions, 16:2.2
administrative exemption, 16:2.2[B]
combination exemption, 16:2.2[G]
computer professional exemption, 16:2.2[E]
creative professional exemption, 16:2.2[D]
executive exemption, 16:2.2[A]
highly compensated employee exemption, 16:2.2[H]
learned professional exemption, 16:2.2[C]
outside sales exemption, 16:2.2[F]
overview, 16:2.1
trafficking by federal contractors and subcontractors, 16:2.5
trainees or interns, unpaid, 16:2.3
unpaid trainees or interns, 16:2.3
wages and hours, 16:2
Federal law enforcement, counterfeiting, 7:2
Federal regulation
false advertising, 15:4
manufacturing process, 9:5.1
Federal Trade Commission (FTC)
antitrust laws, 12:1
deceptive practices regulations, 9:5.1
Dot.Com Disclosures report
generally, 15:7.2, App. 15A
updates to, 15:7.2
endorsement guides, 15:7.2
enforcement policy statement, 15:4.2[E]
false advertising, 15:4.2[A]
investigative and prosecutorial powers, 15:4.2[B]
labeling regulations enforcement of, 15:4.2[E]
mandate and structure, 15:4.2[A]
Marketing Your Mobile App: Get It Right from the Start (FTC), 14:3.2
Mobile App for Kids: Disclosure Still Not Making the Grade, 14:3.2
mobile app publications, 14:3.2
privacy, mobile commerce/e-commerce, 14:3.2[A]
privacy report, 14:3.2
prosecutions in federal court, 15:4.2[D]
scope of, 15:4.2[A]
social media advertisements, 15:7.2
unfair or deceptive acts or practices, 15:4.2
Federal Trademark Dilution Act (FTDA), 2:2, 2:8
Federal trademark statutes, 2:6.2. *See also* Lanham Act (Trademark Act of 1946); Trademarks

Federal Unemployment Tax Act taxes (FUTA), 1:2.3
Federal unfair competition, 6:4.1
Federated Department Stores, Inc. *See* Macy's
Fee estate, 13:2.2
FEED, 11:1.10
Feinberg v. Federated Department Stores, Inc., 11:2.2
Fendi Adele S.R.L. v. Ashley Reed Trading, Inc., 7:3.5[A]
Fenton, Dwight, 6:5.2
Fenty shoe collection, Rihanna's
    LaChapelle v. Fenty, 4:3.3
    Puma SE v. Forever 21, Inc., 2:10.9[C]
Fictitious name, 1:2.2
Fiduciary duties
    bankruptcy cases, preparation for, 23:2.1
        insolvency, 23:2.1[A]
        pre-filing decision making, 23:2.1[B]
        private equity portfolio companies, 23:2.1[C]
        solvency determination, 23:2.1[B]
        standing of creditors, 23:2.1[A]
    board observers, 1:3.2
    board of directors, 1:2.4, 1:2.8
    controlling stockholders, 1:3.2
    corporations, 1:2.4
    fiduciary duty out, termination right, 22:6
    LLCs, 1:2.7
    LPs, 1:2.8
    subsidiaries, 1:2.11
Final bid package
    sale transactions (fashion companies/brands acquisitions), 22:2.1
Financial buyers, 22:2
Financial information, prospectus, 21:4.4, 21:4.11
Financing, 1:3.2. *See also* Angel investors; Debt financing; Equity financing; Venture capital investors
    angel investors, 1:4.6
    bank, 1:4.5
    capital rounds, 1:4.1
    commercial bank, 1:4.5
    factoring arrangements, 1:4.4
    friends and family, 1:4.3
    personal funds, 1:4.2
    private equity financing, 1:4.8
    sources, 1:1.1, 1:4
    stages/rounds, 1:4.1
    start-ups, 1:4
    venture capital investors, 1:4.7

Financing arrangements
liquidity, bankruptcy cases, 23:2.3[A]
Finishing stage of production, 9:3
First Amendment, 2:10.8, 4:8.1
publicity rights, 18:3
First Amendment of U.S. Constitution, 15:2.1
First day relief, bankruptcy cases, 23:3.2, 23:4.1
Bankruptcy Code section 503(b)(9) claims, 23:3.2[D]
cram-down situations, 23:4.1[B][2]
debtor in possession financing, approval of, 23:2.3[C]
employee wages and benefits, 23:3.2[A]
goods in transit, 23:3.2[C]
insurance policies, 23:3.2[B]
oversecured creditors, right to post-petition interest, 23:4.1[B][2]
post-petition value creation, 23:4.1[B]
prepetition liens, 23:4.1[B][1]
proceeds, defined, 23:4.1[B][1]
property of the estate, 23:4.1[A]
reclamation, 23:3.2[D]
revenue source, 23:4.1[B][1]
shippers, 23:3.2[C]
warehousemen, 23:3.2[C]
workers' compensation programs, 23:3.2[B]
First floor items, department stores, 11:1.1
First negotiation rights, 10:2.2[B]
First offer rights, 1:3.2, 10:2.2[B], 22:3.4[B]
First refusal rights, 1:3.2, 10:2.2[B], 13:3.1, 22:3.4[B]
First sale doctrine, 8:1 *et seq. See also* Gray market
Abercrombie & Fitch v. Fashion Shops of Kentucky, Inc., 8:3.3, 8:4.1
copyright law, 8:2.2
failure to transfer ownership of goods, 8:4.2
fashion/apparel context, 8:4
genuine goods doctrine, 8:4.1
gray market case law, 8:3
introduction, 8:1
John Wiley & Sons, Inc. v. Kirtsaeng, 8:3.5, 8:5
Liz Claiborne, Inc. v. Mademoiselle Knitwear, Inc., 8:4.1
Omega S.A. v. Costco Wholesale Corp., 8:3.4, 8:3.5, 8:5
overview, 8:2
Parfums Givenchy, Inc. v. Drug Emporium, Inc., 8:3.1
patent exhaustion doctrine, 8:1, 8:2.4
patent law, 8:2.4
purpose, 8:2.1
Quality King Distributors, Inc. v. L'anza Research International, Inc., 8:3.2

First sale doctrine *(cont'd)*
  Too, Inc. v. The TJX Cos., Inc., 8:4.1
  trademark law, 8:2.3
Fitbit, Inc. v. Aliphcom, 3:2.1
Fitting rooms
  shopping for the experience, 11:1.10
Fixed form, copyright protection, 4:1, 4:3, 4:3.3
Fixed rent, brick-and-mortar lease, 13:3.5
Fixing America's Surface Transportation Act (FAST Act), 21:1
Flag-ship store, 11:1.1, 11:1.9
Flammability standards for fabrics and textiles, 9:5.1
Flammable Fabrics Act, 9:5.1, 15:2.6
Flash sale sites, 11:1.7
FLSA. *See* Fair Labor Standards Act (FLSA)
FMLA. *See* Family and Medical Leave Act (FMLA)
Folio Impressions, Inc. v. Byer California, 4:3.3, 4:7.2[A]
Fonda, Peter, 18:5
Fonovisa, Inc. v. Cherry Auction, Inc., 7:3.4[A], 7:3.4[B][2]
Food, Drug, and Cosmetic Act (FD&C Act), 15:4.3[A]
Footwear. *See also* Nike
  Adidas, 9:1
  Ash Footwear USA, 3:6.1
  Chuck Taylor, Converse, 2:5, 2:9.5
  Crocs, 3:6.1, 3:6.2[B]
  Dashnaw v. New Balance Athletics, Inc., 15:4.2[F]
  Eliya, Inc. v. Steven Madden, Ltd., 2:10.9[B]
  Louboutin case, 2:10.9[A]
  Made in USA labeling, 15:4.2[F]
  patent infringements, 3:6.1, 3:6.2[B]
  patent protection, 3:6.1
  Puma SE v. Forever 21, Inc., 2:10.9[C]
  Reebok, 3:6.2[B], 17:4.1
  Section 337 Investigation, 2:9.5
  Skechers U.S.A., Inc., 3:6.1, 15:4.1[C]
  TOMS, 1:2.6
Force sensing fabric-based devices patent, Apple's, 3:6.2[C]
Foreign corporate payments, 20:2
Foreign Corrupt Practices Act (FCPA). *See also* Foreign Corrupt Practices Act (FCPA) enforcement
  generally, 20:1
  accounting provisions, 20:3.2
    books and records provision, 20:3.2[A]
    internal controls provision, 20:3.2[B]
    issuers and parent issuers, 20:3.2
    jurisdictional reach of FCPA, 20:3.2

alternative jurisdiction, 20:3.1[A]
anti-bribery provisions, 20:3.1
affirmative defenses, 20:3.1[C]
alternative jurisdiction provisions, 20:3.1[A]
business purpose test, 20:3.1[B]
corrupt intent, 20:3.1[B]
domestic concern, 20:3.1[A]
foreign business or person, 20:3.1[A]
foreign officials defined, 20:3.1[B]
instrumentality not defined, 20:3.1[B]
issuers, 20:3.1[A]
knowing defined, 20:3.1[B]
statutory exception, 20:3.1[C]
what conduct is covered, 20:3.1[B]
who is covered, 20:3.1[A]
books and records provision, 20:3.2[A]
central provisions, 20:3
accounting provisions, 20:3.2
anti-bribery provisions, 20:3.1
compliance program, crafting, 20:5.6
foreign officials, 20:3.1[B], 20:5.4
internal controls provision, 20:3.2[B]
issuers
accounting provisions, 20:3.2
anti-bribery provisions, 20:3.1[A]
issuers vs. non-issuers, 20:5.1
parent issuer, 20:3.2
origins of, 20:2
Resource Guide to the FCPA
generally, 20:3.1[B]
crafting an effective compliance program, 20:5.6
enforcement, issue spotting, 20:5
entertainment, 20:5.5
foreign officials, 20:5.4
gifts, 20:5.5
responding to a potential violation, 20:5.7
successor liability, 20:5.3
third-party payments, 20:5.2
Foreign Corrupt Practices Act (FCPA) enforcement, 20:4–20:5
generally, 20:4
Avon case study, 20:4.2
history of investigation, 20:4.2[A]
ramifications of investigation, 20:4.2[B]
compliance program, crafting, 20:5.6

Foreign Corrupt Practices Act (FCPA) enforcement (*cont'd*)
foreign officials
issue-spotting, 20:5.4
Resource Guide to the FCPA, 20:5.4
issue-spotting, 20:5
crafting an effective compliance program, 20:5.6
entertainment, 20:5.5
foreign officials, 20:5.4
gifts, 20:5.5
issuers vs. non-issuers, 20:5.1
Resource Guide, 20:5
responding to a potential violation, 20:5.7
successor liability, 20:5.3
third-party payments, 20:5.2
issuers vs. non-issuers, 20:5.1
non-prosecution agreements (NPAs), 20:4
Nu Skin case study, 20:4.3
Ralph Lauren case study, 20:4.1
Resource Guide to the FCPA
crafting an effective compliance program, 20:5.6
enforcement, issue spotting, 20:5
entertainment, 20:5.5
foreign officials, 20:5.4
gifts, 20:5.5
responding to a potential violation, 20:5.7
successor liability, 20:5.3
third-party payments, 20:5.2
supply chain risks, 20:4.4
distributors, 20:4.4[C]
third-party manufacturers, 20:4.4[A]
transportation service providers, 20:4.4[B]
Foreign officials, 20:3.1[B]
Resource Guide to the U.S. Foreign Corrupt Practices Act, 20:5.4
Foreign words, trademarks, 2:43
Forever 21, 22:1
Puma SE v. Forever 21, Inc., 2:10.9[C]
Forfeiture, CBP, 19:8.1
Forfeiture for competition provisions, 17:4.1
Form 10-K (SEC)
sale transactions, disclosure requirements for public companies, 22:5.1
Form 1040, 1:2.2, 1:2.5
Form 1065, 1:2.3
Form 1120, 1:2.4

Form 2553, 1:2.5
Form 8832, 1:2.7
Formametal, 20:4.4
Formation certificate, LLC, 1:2.7
Forward confusion, 2:7.2[B]
Founders. *See also* Organizational structure
  creative control rights, 1:3.2
  initial considerations, 1:2.1
  loans from friends/family, 1:4.3
  personal funds, 1:4.2
  piercing corporate veil, 1:2.3, 1:2.10
4 Pillar Dynasty LLC v. New York & Company, Inc., 7:3.5[B]
FP&L Act. *See* Fair Packaging and Labeling Act (FP&L Act)
France. *See also* Louis Vuitton
  design law protections, 5:4.1
  eighteenth century Paris, 9:2
  Paris Convention for the Protection of Industrial Property, 3:5.2
  Paris Fashion Week, 13:4
Francesca's Collections, 11:1.5
Frank v. Gaos, 14:3.2[B]
Fraud. *See also* False advertising
  Computer Fraud and Abuse Act, 14:3.4
  piercing corporate veil, 1:2.10
  trademark registration, 2:10.3
Free alongside ship (F.A.S.)
  shipping and delivery terms, retailer-vendor arrangements, 11:2.4
Free on board (F.O.B.)
  shipping and delivery terms, retailer-vendor arrangements, 11:2.4
Free People mark, 2:7.2[C]
Free shipping option, 11:1.7
Freeman, Debra, 7:3.3[C]
French Intellectual Property Code, 5:4.1
Friends, financing source, 1:4.3
Frilly, 11:1.10
FTC. *See* Federal Trade Commission (FTC)
FTC Act, 9:5.1, 15:4.2[A], 15:5
  Little FTC Act jurisdictions, 15:5.1
FTDA. *See* Federal Trademark Dilution Act (FTDA)
Full package manufacturing, 9:3
Funding. *See* Financing
FUR FREE FUR, 2:4.4
Fur Products Labeling Act, 9:5.1, 15:2.6
Fur Slide, 2:10.9[C]
FUTA (Federal Unemployment Tax Act taxes), 1:2.3

G

Gap, Inc., 11:1.7
  Banana Republic, 11:1.2
  Bangladesh Worker Safety Initiative, 9:5.2
  disability discrimination, 16:4.1
  domain names, 14:2.1
  Estée Lauder, Inc. v. The Gap, Inc., 2:7.2[C]
  Old Navy, 2:7.2[C], 11:1.2, 18:4.1
  On Davis v. The Gap, Inc., 4:8.1, 4:8.2
  specialty store, 11:1.2
Garden leave provisions, 17:4.1
Garment factory fires, Bangladesh, 9:5.2
Gasser v. Kiss My Face, LLC, 15:2.3
GATT. *See* General Agreement on Tariffs and Trade (GATT)
GDPR. *See* General Data Protection Regulation (GDPR)
General Agreement on Tariffs and Trade (GATT), 19:1
General Business Law, section 349, 6:3.2
General Certificate of Conformity, 9:5.1
General Data Protection Regulation (GDPR), 14:3.2[A]
General partnerships
  described, 1:2.3
  equity investor negotiations, 1:3.2
  LPs compared to, 1:2.8
  sole proprietorships compared to, 1:2.3
  subsidiaries as, 1:2.11
Generation Z (Gen Z), 11:1.9
Generic goods, 11:1.3
Generic terms, trademarks, 2:4.4
Geneva Act of the Hague Agreement Concerning the International Registration of Industrial Designs, 5:3
Genuine goods doctrine, 8:4.1
Geographic locations, trademarks, 2:4.3, 2:43
Gibson Tex, Inc. v. Sears Roebuck & Co., 4:7.2[A]
Gift tax, 1:4.3
Gifts
  FCPA enforcement, 20:5.5
Gifts and entertainment, FCPA enforcement actions, 20:5.5
Gildan Activewear Inc., 9:3
Gilt, 11:1.7
#GIRLBOSS (Sophia Amoruso), 23:1
Givenchy
  Parfums Givenchy, Inc. v. Drug Emporium, Inc., 8:3.1
Glasses. *See* Eyewear

Global apparel manufacturing industry, 9:1. *See also* Manufacturing
Global e-commerces sales, statistics, 14:1
Global Online Consumer Report, KPMG's 2017, 11:1.9
Globalization
  counterfeiting, 7:1
  international regulation of e-commerce, 14:3.2[A]
  luxury sector, 9:2
Go private, 21:1
GOB sales. *See* Going out of business sales (GOB sales)
Going dark provisions
  assumption of real property lease (non-residential) and bankruptcy, 23:4.2[B][1][b]
  going out of business sales (GOB sales), lease restrictions, 23:5.2[B][1][d]
Going out of business sales (GOB sales), 23:5.2[B][1]
  generally, 23:5.2[B][1]
  continuous use provisions, 23:5.2[B][1][d]
  duration, 23:5.2[B][1][c]
  federal law compliance, 23:5.2[B][1][a]
  going dark provisions, 23:5.2[B][1][d]
  lease restrictions, 23:5.2[B][1][d]
  merchandise augmentation, 23:5.2[B][1][b]
  state law compliance, 23:5.2[B][1][a]
Going public. *See* IPO (initial public offering); Prospectus, IPO
Golden Seeds, 1:4.6
Good guy guaranties, 13:2.3
Goodlatte, Bob, 4:4
Goods and services. *See also* Trademarks
  classification, PTO, 2:6.3[B], App. 2A
Goods in transit
  first day relief, bankruptcy cases, 23:3.2[C]
Google
  Android OS, 14:2.2
  Checkout, 14:4
  interactive cord, 3:6.2[C]
  Rosetta Stone Ltd. v. Google Inc., 2:11.2
  smart fabric, 3:6.2[C]
  smart glasses, 3:6.2[C]
  Stored Communications Act, violations under, 14:3.2[B]
Google AdWords
  broad match algorithm, 2:11.2
  search engine advertising, 2:11.2

Google Checkout
  e-commerce, 14:4
Google Glass, 3:6.2[C]
Google search engine users
  Frank v. Gaos, 14:3.2[B]
Gore-Tex, 3:6.2[A]
Goyard, 9:2
GPS, 3:6.2[C], 14:3.2
  smart ski and snowboard goggles, 3:6.2[C]
Gramm-Leach-Bliley Act, 14:4
Grape scent, motor oil, 2:6.2
Graphic works, copyright protection, 4:2
Gray market, 8:1 *et seq. See also* First sale doctrine
  generally, 8:1
  Abercrombie & Fitch v. Fashion Shops of Kentucky, Inc., 8:3.3, 8:4.1
  black market, 8:1
  case law, first sale doctrine, 8:3
  combat strategies, 8:5
  defined, 8:1
  e-commerce, 14:1
  John Wiley & Sons, Inc. v. Kirtsaeng, 8:3.5, 8:5
  materially different goods, 8:5
  Omega S.A. v. Costco Wholesale Corp., 8:3.4, 8:3.5, 8:5
  Parfums Givenchy, Inc. v. Drug Emporium, Inc., 8:3.1
  Quality King Distributors, Inc. v. L'anza Research International, Inc., 8:3.2
Green-red-green stripes, 2:6.2
GTFM, Inc. v. Solid Clothing, Inc, 2:7.1
Guaranties, real property interests, 13:2.3
Gucci
  Chinese e-commerce websites, 9:2
  green-red-green stripes, 2:6.2
  trademark, 2:4.2
Gucci, Paolo, 2:4.2
Gucci America, Inc. v. Alibaba Group Holding, Ltd., 7:3.4[B]
Gucci America, Inc. v. Curveal Fashion, 7:3.3[C]
Gucci America, Inc. v. Frontline Processing Corp., 7:3.1[B], 7:3.4[B][2]
Gucci America, Inc. v. Weixing Li, 7:3.3[B], 7:3.3[C]
Gucci Shops, Inc., 2:4.2
Guess? Inc., 3:6.1
Gun jumping, IPO, 21:3.3

H

Haelan Laboratories, Inc. v. Topps Chewing Gum, 18:3
Hague Agreement Concerning the International Registration of Industrial Designs, 5:3
  Geneva Act, 5:3
Hague Convention, 7:3.3[C]
Hair care products
  Quality King Distributors, Inc. v. L'anza Research International, Inc., 8:3.2
Haiti
  Télécommunications d'Haiti S.A., 20:3.1
Halo effect, 11:1.9
Hancock v. American Telephone and Telegraph Co., 14:3.1
Hand, Judge Learned, 4:7.2[C]
Hard luxury, 9:2
Hard Rock Café Licensing Corp. v. Concession Services, Inc., 7:3.4[A]
Harmonized Tariff Schedule of the United States (HTSUS), 19:4, App. 19B
  classification of imported merchandise, 19:4
Harper's Bazaar, 7:4.3
Hart-Scott-Rodino Antitrust Improvements Act, 22:6
Hashtags, use of trademarks in, 2:11.3
Haute Diggity Dog, LLC
  Louis Vuitton Malletier S.A. v. Haute Diggity Dog, LLC, 2:10.8
Health insurance plan participation
  employment agreements, 17:2.3
Health issues, fashion industry, 16:5
Hearst Corporation, 16:2.3
Heating, ventilation, and air conditioning (HVAC), 13:3.8
Hermes, 9:2, 14:2.1
Hermès Int'l v. Lederer de Paris Fifth Ave., Inc., 7:3.2
Higg Index, 9:5.2
High-performance fabrics, 3:6.2[A]
Highly compensated employee, overtime exemption, 16:2.2[H]
Hines v. Overstock.com Inc., 14:3.1
Hispanics United of Buffalo Inc., 16:8
H&M & Other Stories, design and concept stores, 22:1
Holding real property interests, 13:2.3
Holograms, 7:4.1, 8:5
Home Shopping Network (HSN), 11:1.8
Home shopping (television) retailers, 11:1.8
Home worker restrictions, 16:2.4

Homeland Security Department. *See* Department of Homeland Security
Homeland Security Investigations Border Enforcement and Security Task Force (ICE), 7:2
Hong Kong
  counterfeit apparel, customs seizure and forfeiture, 19:8.1
  Juicy Couture, Inc. v. Bella International, Inc., 7:3.3
  Stock Exchange, 9:2
Horizontal relationships, antitrust, 12:3
Hot goods, 16:2.5
Hours. *See* Wages and hours
HTSUS. *See* Harmonized Tariff Schedule of the United States (HTSUS)
Hubbert v. Dell Corp., 14:3.1
Hudson's Bay, 11:1.7
The Huffington Post, 6:3.1[B]
Human cannonball, 18:3
Human Rights Watch, 9:5.2
Hyper text markup language (HTML) code, 2:11.1
Hyundai
  Louis Vuitton Malletier S.A. v. Hyundai Motor America, 2:8

I

I Agree button
  e-commerce, 14:3.1
IACC. *See* International Anti-Counterfeiting Coalition (IACC)
Iamartino, sample design patent, App. 3A–2
ICANN. *See* Internet Corporation for Assigned Names and Numbers (ICANN)
ICE. *See* Immigration and Customs Enforcement (ICE)
Iconix Brand Group, Inc., 22:1
Idea and expression, copyright protection, 4:3.3
Idea man, 6:2.2
Ideeli, 11:1.7
IDS (permanent identification markers), 14:3.2
Immigration and Customs Enforcement (ICE), 7:2
  Homeland Security Investigations Border Enforcement and Security Task Force, 7:2
Implied-in-fact contract theory, 6:2.2
Imported merchandise. *See also* Customs laws
  classification, 19:4
  country of origin rules, 19:6
  entry, 19:3

reconciliation, 19:5.6
valuation, 19:5
Importer responsibilities, 19:2
reasonable care, 19:2.1
recordkeeping requirements, 19:2.2
Impoundment, copyright infringement, 4:9.2
Improving Critical Infrastructure Cybersecurity executive order, 14:3.4
In-house manufacturing, 9:3
In re E.I. DuPont DeNemours & Co., 2:6.2
In re Zappos.com Inc., Customer Data Security Breach Litigation, 14:3.2[B]
In-store shop concept, 11:1.1, 13:2.2
InCircle members, Nieman Marcus, 11:1.1
Income statements, 1:4.5
Incongruous phrases, trademarks, 2:4.4
Incontestable status, trademarks, 2:7.1, 2:10.1
Incorporation, certificate of, 1:2.4
Indemnification, license agreements, 10:2.2[L]
Indemnities
sale transactions (fashion companies/brands acquisitions), 22:5.3
Independent contractors
FLSA coverage, 16:2.5
sales representatives, 16:6
India
apparel manufacturers, unfair competition lawsuits, 6:2.1
design law protections, 5:5.7
luxury goods, 9:2
Indiana, right of publicity law, 18:4.3
Inditex Group, 9:3, 11:1
Industrial robotics, 9:1, 18:4.1
Sewbots, 9:1
Industry initiatives, manufacturing process, 9:5.2
Influencers, fashion, 15:7.2, 21:1
Information access, equity investors, 1:3.2
Information Security Technology—Personal Information Security Specification (the Specification, China), 14:3.2[A]
Infringement complaints, trademarks, 2:13:1
Initial interest confusion, 2:7.2[B]
Initial public offering. *See* IPO (initial public offering)
Injunctive relief
copyright infringement, 4:9.1
ex parte temporary restraining order, 7:3.3
patent infringement, 3:4.2[B]
trademark infringement, 2:9.1

Innovative brands, 11:1.10
Innovative Design Protection and Piracy Prevention Act, 4:4
Inspection rights, 1:3.2
Instagram, 1:1.1, 1:4.3, 15:7
Instructional text, works for hire, 4:5
Insurance, license agreements, 10:2.2[L]
Insurance policies
  first day relief, bankruptcy cases, 23:3.2[B]
  losses from breach, sale transactions, 22:5.1
Intellectual property. *See also* Trademarks
  bankruptcy. *See* Intellectual property and bankruptcy
  business description section, business plan, 1:1.2[B]
  French Intellectual Property Code, 5:4.1
  ownership, employee agreements, 17:2.4
  personal names, 1:1.1
  rights
    license agreements, 10:2.2[H]
    National Intellectual Property Rights Coordination Center, 7:2
    reasonable care, importer responsibilities, 19:2.1[C]
  trademarks, 2:2
  United International Bureaux for the Protection of Intellectual Property, 2:15.1
  WIPO, 2:6.3[G], 2:15.1, 5:3
Intellectual property and bankruptcy, 23:4.4
  generally, 23:4.4
  applicable law exception, 23:4.4[A][2]
  assignment limitations, 23:4.4[A]
  assumption limitations, 23:4.4[B]
  assumption of license, 23:2.4[C], 23:4.4[B]
  Countryman test, 23:4.4[A][1]
  executory contract, 23:4.4
  executory contract, determination, 23:4.4[A][1]
  licensor is debtor, 23:4.4[C]
    non-trademark licensees, 23:4.4[C][1]
    trademark licensees, 23:4.4[C][2]
  preparation for bankruptcy, 23:2.4[C]
Intent-to-use trademark applications, 2:6.3[C]
Internal Revenue Code Section 409A
  non-qualified deferred compensation plans, compliance, 17:2.3
International Anti-Counterfeiting Coalition (IACC), 7:4.2
International Bureau of World Intellectual Property Organization (WIPO), 2:6.3[G], 2:15.1, 5:3
International classification of goods and services, PTO, 2:6.3[B], App. 2A

International commercial terms or inco terms
    shipping terms, retailer-vendor arrangements, 11:2.4
International corruption. *See* Foreign Corrupt Practices Act (FCPA)
International design law protections
    generally, 5:1, 5:6
    Australia, 5:5.3
    Canada, 5:5.5
    China, 5:5.2
        e-commerce law, 5:5.2
    Community Design System, 5:2
    European countries individually, 5:4
    European Union member states, 5:2
    France, 5:4.1
    Geneva Act of the Hague Agreement Concerning the International Registration of Industrial Designs, 5:3
    India, 5:5.7
    International Bureau of World Intellectual Property Organization (WIPO), 2:6.3[G], 2:15.1, 5:3
    Italy, 5:4.3
    Japan, 5:5.1
    New Zealand, 5:5.4
    non-European countries, 5:5
    registered and unregistered designs, European Union member states, 5:2
    Singapore, 5:5.6
    United Arab emirates, 5:5.8
    United Kingdom
        generally, 5:4.2
        as European Union member state, 5:2
        Brexit, 5:4.2
    U.S.
        Geneva Act of the Hague Agreement Concerning the International Registration of Industrial Designs, 5:3
        protections in U.S. vs. international protections, 5:1, 5:2
International designers
    Target Corporation, collaboration with, 11:1.3
International regulation, mobile commerce/e-commerce, 14:1, 14:3.2[A]
International shipping, retailer-vendor arrangements
    international commercial terms or inco terms, 11:2.4
International trade. *See also* Customs laws; Imported merchandise
    United States Court of International Trade, 19:3, 19:4, 19:7
International Trade Commission (ITC)
    Crocs, Inc. v. International Trade Commission, 3:6.2[B]
    Section 337 Investigations, 2:9.5, 3:5.1
    trademark infringement, 2:9.5

International Trademark Association, 7:4.3
International trademark registration, 2:6.3[G], 2:15, App. 2B
Internet. *See also* Counterfeiting; Domain names; E-commerce; Social media platforms; Websites
 alternative service of process, 7:3.1[C]
 Anticybersquatting Consumer Protection Act, 2:9.4
 auction sites, counterfeiting, 7:3.4[B]
 contribution to globalization, 9:2
 COPPA Rule, 14:3.2[A]
 counterfeiting, 7:1
 cyber security, 14:3.4, 21:2.3, 21:4.2
 data regulation, China, 14:3.2[A]
 Improving Critical Infrastructure Cybersecurity executive order, 14:3.4
 saferproducts.gov database, 9:5.1
 search engine advertising, trademark infringement, 2:11
 secondary liability, trademark infringement, 7:3.4[B]
 tablets, 14:2.2
 trademark infringement. *See* Search engine and Internet advertising, trademark infringement
 trademark searching, 2:6.3[A]
Internet Corporation for Assigned Names and Numbers (ICANN), 14:2.1
Internet retailers, 11:1.7
 chat with a specialist customer service, 11:1.7
 e-commerce business models, 11:1.7
 expansion of, statistics, 11:1.7
 free shipping option, 11:1.7
 marketing challenges, 11:1.7
 online flash sale sites, 11:1.7
Internet service providers (ISPs)
 contributory liability, 7:3.4[B][2]
 counterfeiting, statutory damages, 7:3.5[B]
Interns or trainees, unpaid, 16:2.3
Intrinsic/extrinsic test, copyright infringement, 4:7.2[B]
Inventions. *See* Patents
Inventory management issues, international e-commerce, 14:1
INVESTING IN AMERICAN JOBS, 2:4.4
Inwood Laboratories, Inc. v. Ives Laboratories, Inc., 7:3.4[A]
iOS, 14:2.2
IPO (initial public offering). *See also* Prospectus, IPO
 generally, 21:1
 business section, 21:4.6
 capitalization, 21:4.4
 compensation, 21:4.7

dilution, 21:4.4
documentation, 21:6
drafting, 21:4
due diligence, 21:2.2
financial information, 21:4.4, 21:4.11
gun jumping, 21:3.3
lock-up agreements, 21:6.2
management section, 21:4.7
MD&A, 21:4.5
plain English, 21:4.2
post-IPO matters, 21:7
preparing, 21:2
principal requirements, 21:4
process, 21:3
prospectus, drafting, 21:4
registration statement, 21:3.1
risk factors, 21:4.2
road show, 21:3.2, 21:5
SEC Form 8-A, 21:6.2
securities section, 21:4.9
selling company, 22:1
stockholders section, 21:4.8
summary, 21:4.1
timeline, 21:3
trading market, 21:2.2
underwriters & underwriting, 21:4.10
underwriting agreement, 21:6.1
use of proceeds, 21:4.3
work streams, 21:2.3
IPR Center (National Intellectual Property Rights Coordination Center), 7:2
Ipso facto clauses
assumption of real property lease (non-residential) and bankruptcy, 23:4.2[B][1][a]
Iran
economic sanctions, 19:9.1
NIke, 19:9.1
Israel, underweight models, 16:5
Issuers, FCPA enforcement. *See* Foreign Corrupt Practices Act (FCPA)
Italy
design law protections, 5:4.3
ITC. *See* International Trade Commission (ITC)
iTunes, 15:7.2

J

J. Crew, 23:2.3[A][2]
J. Crew Group Inc. v. Fenton, 6:5.2
J. Jill, Inc., 21:1
JA Apparel, 2:4.2
Japan
    design law protections, 5:5.1
    U.S. e-commerce retailers expansion into, 14:1
Jawbone, 3:2.1
J.C. Penny, 11:1.7
    license agreement dispute, 10:2.2[A]
JD.com (China), 11:1.5
Jeans
    finishing stage of production, 9:3
Jewelry
    unfair competition lawsuits, replicated method of design, 6:2.1
Jimmy Choo, 3:6.1, 22:1
JOBS Act, 1:4.7, 21:1
Jockey
    Munsingwear, Inc. v. Jockey International, Inc., 2:7.2[B]
John Wiley & Sons, Inc. v. Kirtsaeng, 8:3.5, 8:5
Joint ownership, copyrights, 4:5
Joint venture agreement, 22:3.4[B]
Jones Group, Inc., 22:1
Joor, 11:2.2
Jordache Enterprises, Inc. v. Hogg Wyld, Ltd., 2:7.2[C]
JORDACHE mark, 2:10.8
Jordan, Michael, 2:10.6, 17:2.4
JORDAN trademark, 2:10.6
Joseph Abboud trademark, 2:4.2
Joseph Tierney (a.k.a. Rime) v. Moschino SpA, 2:10.5
Jovani Fashion v. Cinderella Divine Inc., 4:3.2[D]
Juicy Couture, Inc. v. Bella International, Inc., 7:3.3
Jumpstart Our Business Startups Act (JOBS Act), 1:4.7, 21:1
Jung, Andrea, 20:4.2[A]
Just Do It slogan, 2:3
JustFab, 11:1.7

K

Kardashian, Kim, 18:4.1
Kardashian sisters, 2:10.2, 10:2.2[H]
Kasky v. Nike, Inc., 15:2.1
Kate Spade & Co., 4:3.3, 22:1, 22:7.2
Key word search
  search engine advertising, 2:11.2
Kieselstein-Cord v. Accessories by Pearl, Inc., 4:3.2[D]
Kill *Quill* legislation, 14:3.3
Kiosks, 4:7.1, 13:2.2
Kirtsaeng, 8:3.5, 8:5
Kirtsaeng v. John Wiley & Sons, Inc., 4:9.4
Kiva Systems, 9:1
Kmart, 3:6.1
Knitwaves, Inc. v. Lollytogs Ltd., 4:3.2[C]
Kohl's, 8:4.2
Kozinski, Alex, 18:4.1
KPMG's 2017 Global Online Consumer Report, 11:1.9
Kroma Makeup EU LLC v. Boldface Licensing + Branding, Inc., 2:10.2, 10:2.2[H]
KROMA trademark, 2:10.2, 10:2.2[H]

L

L.A. Printex Industries Inc., v. Aeropostale, Inc., 4:3.3, 4:7.1, 4:7.2[B]
La Haute Maroquinerie salons, 9:2
La Maison Worth, 18:1
Labeling
  cosmetic products, misleading/misbranding, 15:4.3
    disclaimers, 15:2.6
  Made in USA labeling, 15:4.2[F]
  regulations, FTC, 15:4.2, 15:5
  requirements, apparel, 9:5.1, 15:2.6
Labor. *See* Employment and labor issues; Fair Labor Standards Act (FLSA); Labor and employment
Labor and employment
  generally, 16:1
  anti-discrimination laws, 16:4
    #MeToo laws, 16:4
    age discrimination claims, defense to, 16:4.2
    Age Discrimination in Employment Act (ADEA), 16:4.1, 16:4.2

Labor and employment, anti-discrimination laws (*cont'd*)
Americans with Disabilities Act (ADA), 16:4.1
bona fide occupational qualifications, 16:4.2
Civil Rights Act of 1964, Title VII, 16:4.1, 16:4.2
compliance enforcement, 16:4.1, 16:4.2
disparate impact liability, 16:4
disparate treatment liability, 16:4
Equal Employment Opportunity Commission (EEOC), 16:4.1, 16:4.2
Equal Pay Act, 16:4.1
Family and Medical Leave Act (FMLA), 16:4.4
pregnancy discrimination, 16:4.3
sex discrimination claims, defense to, 16:4.2
bargaining units, 16:7
child labor laws, 16:3
addressing labor problems through self-regulation, 16:3.4
corporate codes of conduct, 16:3.4
federal child labor law, 16:3.1
age of minor, 16:3.1[B]
employer-employee relationship, 16:3.1[A]
enforcement, 16:3.1[E]
penalties and contesting penalties, 16:3.1[E]
wages, 16:3.1[C]
work prohibitions, 16:3.1[D]
Federal Labor Standards Act (FLSA), 16:3
forced labor, 19:2.1[B]
New York, 16:3.2
reasonable care, importer responsibilities, 19:2.1[B]
state child labor laws, 16:3.2
sweatshops, 16:3.3
Civil Rights Act of 1964, Title VII, 16:8
Council of Fashion Designers of America (CFDA) Health Initiative, 16:5
eating disorders, 16:5
employee policies to conduct appropriate online activity, 16:8
Facebook, 16:8
forced labor, 19:2.1[B]
health issues in the fashion industry and implications for employers, 16:5
National Labor Relations Act (NLRA), 16:8
National Labor Relations Board (NLRB), 16:7, 16:8
New York, wages and hours, 16:2.1
reasonable care, importer responsibilities, 19:2.1[B]
sales representatives, classification of, 16:6

sales representatives as independent contractors, 16:6
social media usage, 16:8
sweatshops, 16:3.3
underweight models, prevalance of severely, 16:5
unions, 16:7
wages and hours, 16:2
California, 16:2.1
combating unfair labor practices, 16:2.5
Federal Labor Standards Act (FLSA), 16:2 *et seq.*
home worker restrictions, 16:2.4
hot goods, 16:2.5
minimum wage, 16:2.1
New York, 16:2.1
overtime exemptions, 16:2.2
administrative exemption, 16:2.2[B]
combination exemption, 16:2.2[G]
computer professional exemption, 16:2.2[E]
creative professional exemption, 16:2.2[D]
executive exemption, 16:2.2[A]
highly compensated employee exemption, 16:2.2[H]
learned professional exemption, 16:2.2[C]
outside sales exemption, 16:2.2[F]
overview, 16:2.1
trafficking by federal contractors and subcontractors, 16:2.5
unpaid trainees or interns, 16:2.3
World Health Organization (WHO), 16:5
Labor costs, manufacturing, 9:1
Labor Department, Wage and Hour Division, 16:2.3
LaChapelle v. Fenty, 4:3.3
Laches defense, 2:10.6, 15:4.1[E]
L.A.M.B., 2:4.5
Lancôme USA, Inc., 15:4.3[A]
Landlord as debtor
real property leases (non-residential) and bankruptcy, 23:4.2[F]
Landlords. *See* Brick-and-mortar lease provisions
Lanham Act (Trademark Act of 1946)
amendments, 2:2
Anticybersquatting Consumer Protection Act, 2:9.4
Confusion factors, 2:7.2
counterfeiting, monetary remedies, 7:3.5
domain name infringement, 2:9.4
false advertising, 15:4.1
digital communications, section 43(a) suits, 15:7.1
establishment claims, 15:4.1[C]
historical regulation, 15:3

Lanham Act (Trademark Act of 1946) (*cont'd*)
  injunctive relief for trademark infringement, 2:9.1
  lack of standing, trademark infringement defense, 2:10.2
  monetary relief for trademark infringement, 2:9.2
    attorneys' fees, 2:9.2[C]
    costs of action, 2:9.2[C]
    defendant's profits, 2:9.2[A]
    plaintiff's damages, 2:9.2[B]
  passage, 2:2
  search engine advertising, trademark infringement, 2:11.3
  section 32(1), text of, 2:7
  section 35(a), 2:9.2, 7:3.3[B]
  section 43(a), 6:4.1, 15:4.1
    Dastar Corp. v. Twentieth Century Fox Film Corp, 6:4.1
    defenses, 15:4.1[E]
    establishing standing, 15:4.1[A]
    establishment claims, 15:4.1[C]
    origin, defined under, 6:4.1
    prima facie elements, false adversing claims, 15:4.1[B]
    remedies, 15:4.1[D]
    text of, 2:7, 6:4.1, 15:4.1[A]
  TLRA, 2:2
  trade dress, 2:6, 6:4.1
  trademark dilution, 2:8
  trademark infringement, 2:7
  trademark protection, 2:2
  trademark registration, 2:6
L'anza, *Quality King Distributors, Inc. v. L'anza Research International, Inc.*, 8:3.2
LARDASHE mark, 2:10.8
Laredo, Texas
  e-commerce counterfeiting, federal law enforcement, 7:2
Learned professional, overtime exemption, 16:2.2[C]
Lease provisions. *See* Brick-and-mortar lease provisions
Lease restrictions
  going out of business sales (GOB sales), 23:5.2[B][1][d]
    continuous use provisions, 23:5.2[B][1][d]
    going dark provisions, 23:5.2[B][1][d]
Leather and Imitation Leather Guide, 9:5.1, 15:2.6
Leegin v. PSKS, Inc., 12:4.1[A]
Leon Max Inc.
  enforcement of FTC labeling regulations, 15:4.2[E]
Leonard Green & Partners, 22:1
Letters, in trademarks, 2:4.1
Levi Strauss & Company, 2:6.2, 3:6.1, 3:6.2[B], 21:1
  digital process for finishing stage, 9:3

Levi Strauss & Company v. Shilon, 2:10.4
Lexmark International, Inc. v. Static Control Components, Inc., 15:4.1[A]
Liability
- limited personal liability, 1:2.4, 1:2.7, 1:2.8
- unlimited personal liability, 1:2.2, 1:2.3, 1:2.8

Liability insurance
- director and officer liability insurance, 21:2.3
- product liability insurance, 10:2.2[L]
- sole proprietors, 1:2.2

License agreements
- generally, 10:1
- accounting provisions, 10:2.2[F]
- advertising, 10:2.2[G]
- automatic renewals, 10:2.2[I]
- buy-out rights, 10:2.2[J]
- first negotiation rights, 10:2.2[B]
- first offer rights, 10:2.2[B]
- first refusal rights, 10:2.2[B]
- indemnification, 10:2.2[L]
- insurance, 10:2.2[L]
- intellectual property rights, 10:2.2[H]
- manufacture/sale of products, 10:2
- nature, 10:2.2[A]
- new arrangements, considerations for, 10:1
- non-automatic renewals, 10:2.2[C]
- other provisions, 10:2.2[M]
- production development, 10:2.2[D]
- production process, 10:2.2[D]
- quality control, 2:10.7, 2:14, 10:2.2[D]
- renewals, 10:2.2[C]
- reporting provisions, 10:2.2[F]
- retail stores, 10:3
- royalties, 10:2.2[E]
- sample, App. 10A
- scope, 10:2.2[A]
- sublicensing, 10:2.2[A]
- term, 10:2.2[C]
- termination, 10:2.2[I]
- trademark requirements, 2:14

Licenses/leases, retail space, 13:2.2. *See also* Brick-and-mortar lease provisions
Licensing, 4:7.2[D]
- publicity rights, 18:5

Licensor is debtor
    intellectual property and bankruptcy, 23:4.4[C]
    non-trademark licensees, 23:4.4[C][1]
    trademark licensees, 23:4.4[C][2]
Likelihood of confusion. *See* Confusion, likelihood of
Likelihood of irreparable harm, 2:9.1[B]
Likelihood of success on the merits, 2:9.1[B]. *See also* Trademark infringement
Limco, Inc., 8:4.1
Limited liability companies (LLCs)
    described, 1:2.7
    equity investor negotiations, 1:3.2
Limited partnerships (LPs), 1:2.8
Limited personal liability, 1:2.4, 1:2.7, 1:2.8
Limited Too
    Too, Inc. v. Kohl's Department Stores, Inc., 8:4.2
    Too, Inc. v. The TJX Cos., 8:4.1
Lindsey Manufacturing case, 20:5.4
Line of credit, revolving, 1:4.5
Liquidation, Chapter 11, 23:5.1
Liquidity, preparation for bankruptcy cases, 23:2.3
    asset-backed lending financing, 23:2.3[A][1]
    borrowing base, 23:2.3[A][1]
    cash collateral, 23:2.3[B]
    collateral split, 23:2.3[A][2]
    debtor in possession financing, 23:2.3[C]
    disguised financing, 23:2.3[A][3]
    factoring arrangements, 23:2.3[A][3]
    financing arrangements, 23:2.3[A]
    non-priming debtor in possession financing, 23:2.3[C]
    priming debtor in possession financing, 23:2.3[C]
    term loan financing, 23:2.3[A][2]
    true sales, 23:2.3[A][3]
Literary works, copyright protection, 4:2
Little FTC Act, 15:5.1
Little UDTP Act jurisdictions, 15:5.2
Liz Claiborne, 22:1
Liz Claiborne, Inc. v. Mademoiselle Knitwear, Inc., 8:4.1
L.L. Bean, 11:1.8
LLCs. *See* Limited liability companies (LLCs)
Loans
    collateral, 1:3.3, 1:4.5
    commercial, 1:4.5
    friends/family, 1:4.3
    revolving, 1:4.5

- secured, 1:4.5
- term, 1:4.5
- unsecured, 1:4.3, 1:4.5

Lock-up agreements
- equity investors, 1:3.2
- IPO process, 21:6.2

Lockheed Martin, 20:4.2[A]
Lockheed Martin Corp. v. Network Solutions, Inc., 7:3.4[B][2]
Logos, 2:6.2, 8:5. *See also* Trademarks
Lohan, Lindsay, 6:5.1, 18:4.2
Lolli and Pops, 11:1.7
Long-arm statutes, 7:3.1
Lord & Taylor
- fashion influencers, 15:7.2

L'Oréal, 15:4.3[A]
Loss, risk of
- retailer-vendor arrangements, 11:2.4

Louboutin
- *Christian Louboutin S.A. v. Yves Saint Laurent America Holding, Inc.*, 2:10.9[A]

Louis Vuitton
- Chen, Steven, 7:3.4[B][2]
- Chewy Vuiton dog toy, 2:10.8, 7:3.2
- Chinese e-commerce websites, 9:2
- design patents, 3:6.1
- fashion show, 13:4
- interlocking LV logo, 2:3
- La Haute Maroquinerie salons, 9:2
- *Louis Vuitton Malletier S.A. v. Haute Diggity Dog, LLC,* 2:10.8, 7:3.2
- *Louis Vuitton Malletier S.A. v. Hyundai Motor America,* 2:8
- *Louis Vuitton v. Akanoc Solutions, Inc.*, 7:3.4[B][2]
- MSG, 7:3.4[B][2]
- Section 337 Investigation, 2:9.5

Louis Vuitton North America Inc. v. Joon Ma, 6:5.1
Louis XIV shoes, 2:10.9[A]
LOVE ANGEL MUSIC BABY, 2:4.5
Loyalty programs for customers, 11:1.1
LPs. *See* Limited partnerships (LPs)
Lucky Brand Apparel, 22:1
Lululemon
- pima cotton, 15:5.2

Lululemon Athletica Canada Inc., 3:6.1
- Astro pant, 3:6.1

Luxury brands
exclusive distribution, retailer-vendor arrangements, 11:2.1
Michael Kors, 22:1
trademarks, duty to protect, 2:12
Luxury fashion
boutiques, 11:1.5
collaborative consumption (rent or borrow) e-commerce business model, 11:1.7
e-commerce, 11:1.5
Farfetch Limited, 11:1.5
Luxury goods. *See also* Louis Vuitton; Ralph Lauren
bling, 9:2
Brunello Cucinelli S.p.A., 21:5
China, e-commerce websites rolled out in, 9:2
consumption of, 9:2
core categories, 9:2
counterfeiting, 7:1
defined, 9:2
e-commerce, 9:2
globalization, 9:2
Hermes, 9:2, 14:2.1
luxury and fashion design, 9:2
Michael Kors Holdings Limited, 9:2
Salvatore Ferragamo S.p.A., 21:2.2
LVMH, 9:2

M

M. J. Soffe LLC., 3:6.1
Ma, Joon, 6:5.1
Macy's, 4:2, 11:1.1, 15:4.2[E]
enforcement of FTC labeling regulations, 15:4.2[E]
license agreement dispute, 10:2.2[A]
redesign of mobile app, 14:1
Made in America
entry of merchandise, 19:3
Made in USA labeling, 9:1, 9:3
false advertising, 15:4.2[F]
Made-to-order fashion, 11:1.10
Madrid Protocol, 2:6.3[G], 2:15.2, App. 2B
Magic Leap, 3:6.2[C]
Maidenform Brands, Inc., 3:6.1
Mail-order retailers, 11:1.8
Maker's Row, 9:1

Malaysia
Gucci America, Inc. v. Curveal Fashion, 7:3.3[C]
Malnourished person standard, 16:5
Managed Solutions Group, Inc. (MSG), 7:3.4[B][2]
Manufacturing, 9:1 *et seq. See also* Design
generally, 9:1
additive, 9:2
CMT, 9:3
cottage industry, 9:3
CPSC, 9:5.1
disasters, 9:5.2
domestic, 9:3
domestic manufacturing, statistics, 9:1
federal regulation, 9:5.1
flammability standards for fabrics and textiles, 9:5.1
full package, 9:3
General Certificate of Conformity, 9:5.1
global apparel manufacturing industry, 9:1
in-house, 9:3
industry initiatives, 9:5.2
labor costs, 9:1
license agreements, 10:2
Made in the U.S.A., 9:1, 9:3
on-demand apparel manufacturing, 9:1
options, 9:3
process, 9:1
product hazards, identification of, 9:5.1
product safety standards, 9:5.1
start-up companies, 9:3
state regulation, 9:5.1
statistics, 9:1
supply contracts, 9:4, App. 9A
technological advances, 9:1, 9:2
Transparency Pledge, 9:5.2
U.S. apparel manufacturing industry, 9:1
vertically integrated, 9:3, 10:3, 12:4
voluntary product safety standards, 9:5.1
Marilyn Monroe, LLC, 18:4.3
Marimar Textiles, Inc. v. Jude Clothing & Accessories Corp., 6:5.1
Markdown allowances, retailer-vendor arrangements, 11:2.2
Marketing, license agreements, 10:2.2[G]
Marketing challenges
internet retailers, 11:1.7
Marketing channels factor, 2:7.2[C]

Marketing Your Mobile App: Get It Right from the Start (FTC), 14:3.2
Markings requirements, country of origin, 19:6.4
Marks. *See* Trademarks
Marshall Field & Co., 4:2
Marshall's, 11:1.4[B]
Martha Steward Living Omnimedia (MSLO)
  license agreement dispute, 10:2.2[A]
Mass customization, 11:1.10
Massachusetts
  e-commerce and mobile e-commerce regulation, 14:3.2[A]
MasterCard, 7:3.4[B][1], 7:4.2, 14:4
  Payment Card Industry (PCI) Standards Council, 14:4
Material costs
  sourcing decisions, design process, 9:3
Mattel, Inc. v. MGA Entertainment, Inc., 6:2.3
Matz, A. Howard, 20:5.4
Mazer v. Stein, 4:3.2[A]
McCartney, Stella, 2:4.4
McMahon, Collen, 7:3.3[C]
MCW v. Badbusinessbureau.com., 15:7.3
MD&A, prospectus, 21:4.5
Medical leave, FMLA, 16:4.4
Menlo Ventures, 1:4.7
Men's Warehouse, 22:1
Merchandise augmentation
  going out of business sales (GOB sales), 23:5.2[B][1][b]
Mergers, 22:3.1
Metatagging, 2:11.1
Metatags, trademarks as, 2:11.1
#MeToo laws, 16:4
Mexico
  IPR Center (National Intellectual Property Rights Coordination Center), 7:2
  national team soccer jerseys, 19:8.1
Meyer v. Uber Technologies, Inc., 14:3.1
Michael Kors
  acquisition of Versace, 22:1, 22:2.1, 22:4
Michael Kors Holdings Limited, 9:2
Miche Bag, LLC v. Ayers, 4:9.2, 4:9.3[B], 4:9.4
Microsoft
  wearable technology, 3:6.2[C]
Midler v. Ford Motor Co., 18:4.1
Millennials, 11:1.10
Millinery Creators' Guild, 4:2

Minimum wage, 16:2.1
Ministry of Supply, 9:1
Minors. *See* Child labor laws
Misappropriation, 6:1 *et seq. See also* Unfair competition
    generally, 6:1
    California, 6:2.2
    Motschenbacher v. R.J. Reynolds Tobacco Co., 18:4.1
    New York, 6:3.1[B]
Mislabeling/misbranding cosmetic products, 15:4.3
Misleading advertising, 15:2.5. *See also* False advertising
Missguided, 11:1
Missoni collection, 11:1.3
Missoni S.p.A., 3:6.1
Mobile App for Kids: Disclosure Still Not Making the Grade (FTC), 14:3.2
Mobile apps, 14:2.2, 14:3.2, 14:3.2[A]
    discovery apps, 14:1
    IDS (permanent identification markers), 14:3.2
    Macy's, 14:1
    Marketing Your Mobile App: Get It Right from the Start (FTC), 14:3.2
    Mobile App for Kids: Disclosure Still Not Making the Grade (FTC), 14:3.2
    personal shopping apps, 14:1
    retail sales, 11:1
Mobile commerce, 14:1 *et seq. See also* E-commerce
    generally, 14:1
    browsewrap agreements, 14:3.1
    CAN-SPAM, 14:3.4
    clickwrap agreements, 14:3.1
    conditions of use, hyperlink, 14:3.1
    contract issues, 14:3.1
    data privacy, 14:3.2
    I Agree button, 14:3.1
    IDS (permanent identification markers), 14:3.2
    implementation section, business plan, 1:1.2[E]
    international presence, 14:1
    international regulation, 14:3.2[A]
    legal issues, 14:3
    mobile payments, 14:4
    payment methods, 14:4
    physical presence requirement, abolishment of, 14:3.3
    platform development, 14:2
    private privacy litigation, 14:3.2[B]
    sales statistics, 14:2.2

Mobile commerce (*cont'd*)
    security issues, 14:3.2
    smartphones, 14:1, 14:2.2, 14:3.2
    state regulation, 14:3.2[A]
    state taxation and *South Dakota v. Wayfair*, 14:3.3
    trademark infringement. *See* Search engine and Internet advertising, trademark infringement
    websites, 14:2
Mobile devices
    e-commerce, payment methods, 14:4
Mobile wallets, 14:4
Model Uniform Commercial Code
    Article 2, 11:2
Models. *See also* Publicity rights
    underweight, 16:5
Modern Appealing Clothing v. Ivanka Trump Marks, LLC, 6:2.1
Mon Cheri Bridals Inc. v. Wen Wu, 4:3.1
Monetary relief
    counterfeiting, 7:3.5
    patent infringement, 3:4.2[A]
    trademark infringement, 2:9.2
        attorneys' fees, 2:9.2[C]
        costs of action, 2:9.2[C]
        defendant's profits, 2:9.2[A]
        plaintiff's damages, 2:9.2[B]
Monogrammed jewelry, 6:2.1
Monroe, Marilyn, 18:4.3
Mood boards, 9:3
Morals clause
    publicity rights, 18:5
Motion pictures, copyright protection, 4:2
Motor oil, grape scent, 2:6.2
Motown Record Corp. v. Hormel & Co., 18:2
Motschenbacher v. R.J. Reynolds Tobacco Co., 18:4.1
Movie characters, copyright infringement, 4:7.2[D]
MovieBuff.com, 2:11.1
MSG. *See* Managed Solutions Group, Inc. (MSG)
Multi Time Machine, Inc. v. Amazon.com, 2:7.2[A]
Multifibre Arrangement (MFA), 19:1
Munsingwear, Inc. v. Jockey International, Inc., 2:7.2[B]
Musical works, copyright protection, 4:2
Myanmar (formerly known as Burma)
    economic sanctions, 19:9.1

N

NAD. *See* National Advertising Division (NAD)
NAFTA. *See* North American Free Trade Agreement (NAFTA)
Naked licensing, 2:10.7
Name.com LLC, 2:15.1
Names. *See also* Domain names; Personal names; Sale transactions (fashion companies/brands acquisitions); Trademarks
    corporations, 1:2.4
    doing business as, 1:2.2, 16:2.1
    general partnerships, 1:2.3
    LLCs, 1:2.7
    LPs, 1:2.8
Napoleon III, 18:1
NARB. *See* National Advertising Review Board (NARB)
Nasty Gal, 23:1
National Advertising Division (NAD), 15:2.6, 15:4.2[B], 15:6
National Advertising Review Board (NARB), 15:6
National Basketball Association v. New World Creation, 2:3
National Consumer Protection Week, 7:4.3
National Intellectual Property Rights Coordination Center, 7:2
National Labor Relations Act (NLRA)
    social media usage, 16:8
National Labor Relations Board (NLRB), 16:8
    bargaining units, 16:7
    social media usage, 16:8
National Retail Federation's annual Big Show conference (New York, 2016), 11:1.9
National Securities Markets Improvement Act, 1:4.7
Natural key word search
    search engine advertising, 2:11.2
Natural products
    100% natural or all natural, 15:2.3, 15:4.2[E]
NatureLuxe Mousse Mascara, Proctor & Gamble, 15:2.6
Nawab jackets by Canalli, 9:2
Negative covenants, 22:5.2
Neiman Marcus Last Call, 11:1.4[C]
Net sales, royalties, 10:2.2[E]
Network, of contacts, 1:1.1
Network Solutions, Inc.
    Lockheed Martin Corp. v. Network Solutions, Inc, 7:3.4[B][2]
New Balance
    Dashnaw v. New Balance Athletics, Inc., 15:4.2[F]
New business ventures. *See* Fashion companies (new business ventures)

New Jersey
  e-commerce and mobile e-commerce regulation, 14:3.2[A]
New Kids on the Block v. News America Publishing, Inc., 2:10.5
New World Creation, 2:3
New York. *See also* New York City
  Child labor laws, 16:3.2
  Chloé v. Queen Bee of Beverly Hills, LLC, 7:3.1[A]
  e-commerce and mobile e-commerce regulation, 14:3.2[A]
  Gucci America, Inc. v. Curveal Fashion, 7:3.3[C]
  Gucci America, Inc. v. Frontline Processing Corp., 7:3.1[B]
  long-arm statute, 7:3.1
  manufacturing, 9:1
  non-competition agreements, 17:4.1
  OSHA-approved state plans, 9:5.1
  publicity rights, 18:4.2
    Civil Rights Law, sections 50 & 51, 18:3, 18:4.2
    early development of, 18:3
  Triangle Shirtwaist Factory fire, 9:5.2
  unfair competition, 6:3.1
    common law, 6:3.1
    missappropration, 6:3.1[B]
    passing off, 6:3.1[A]
    statutory law, 6:3.2
  wages and hours, 16:2.1
New York City. *See also* Real estate
  Police Department, counterfeit seizures, 7:2
  Times Square, 13:3.7
  Zoning Resolution, 13:3.7
New Zealand
  design law protections, 5:5.4
Newport News Holdings Corp. v. Virtual City Vision, Inc., 2:10.6
Nguyen v Barnes & Noble Inc., 14:3.1
Nieman Marcus InCircle members, 11:1.1
Nike
  3D printing, 9:1
  Already LLC v. Nike, Inc, 2:10.1
  Apple Inc., 3:6.2[C]
  Bauer Bros. LLC v. Nike, Inc, 2:10.1
  Chattanoga Manufacturing, Inc. v. Nike Inc., 2:10.6
  Converse, 3:6.1
  design patents, number of, 3:6.1
  Iran, 19:9.1
  Jordan, 2:10.6
  Just Do It slogan, 2:3

Kasky v. Nike, Inc., 15:2.1
Michael Jordan, 17:2.4
Nike + iPod Sports Kit, 3:6.2[C]
swoosh logo, 2:6.2
Nike v. Enter Play Sports, Inc., 6:5.1
NLRB. *See* National Labor Relations Board (NLRB)
No-transfer periods, equity investors, 1:3.2
Nominative fair use doctrine, 2:10.5. *See also* Fair use doctrine
Non-commercial speech, false advertising, 15:2.1
Non-competition agreements, 17:4
generally, 17:4.1
enforcement, 17:4.1
forfeiture for competition provisions, 17:4.1
garden leave provisions, 17:4.1
non-disparagement agreement, 17:4.2
non-interference agreement, 17:4.2
non-solicitation agreement (anti-raid agreement), 17:4.2
reasonableness of restriction, 17:4.1
validity and enforcement under state law, 17:4.1
Non-disclosure agreement (NDAs)
violations, illustrative cases, 6:5.1
Non-distinctive marks, 2:3
Non-distinctive trade dress, 2:5
Non-issuers, FCPA enforcement, 20:5.1
Non-monetary breaches
assumption of real property lease (non-residential) and bankruptcy, 23:4.2[B][1][b]
Non-price vertical agreements
antitrust, 12:4.2
Non-priming debtor in possession financing
liquidity, bankruptcy cases, 23:2.3[C]
Non-prosecution agreements (NPAs), 20:4
Non-qualified deferred compensation plans, compliance (Section 409A coverage)
employment agreements, 17:2.3
Non-recourse factoring, 1:4.4
Nonassignability of leases
assignment of real property lease (non-residential) and bankruptcy, 23:4.2[C][2]
Nondisclosure agreements
sale transactions (fashion companies/brands acquisitions), 22:2.1
Nordstrom, 9:5.1, 18:5
Nordstrom Local, 11:1.7

Nordstrom Rack, 11:1.4[C]
North American Free Trade Agreement (NAFTA), 19:2.2, 19:6
  recordkeeping requirements, importers, 19:2.2
North Face Apparel Corp. v. Fujian Sharing Import & Export Ltd. Co., 7:3.3[A]
North Korea
  economic sanctions, 19:9.1
  HTSUS, classification of imported merchandise, 19:4
Notice of Allowance, PTO, 2:6.3[D], 3:3.4
NPAs. *See* Non-prosecution agreements (NPAs)
NSI. *See* Network Solutions, Inc.
Nu Skin case study
  FCPA enforcement, 20:4.3
Numbers, in trademarks, 2:4.1

O

Oakley, Inc., 3:6.1, 3:6.2[B], 3:6.2[C]
  smart glasses, 3:6.2[C]
Oakley, Inc. v. Predator Outdoor Products, LLC, 3:6.2[B]
Oakley, Inc. v. Talitor Far East Co. Ltd., 3:6.2[B]
Oath, patent applications, 3:3.1
Obama, Barack, 3:3.1, 14:3.4
Occulus VR (now a division of Facebook), 3:6.2[C]
Occupational Safety and Health Act (OSHA), 9:5.1
Ocean Medallion by Carnival Cruise Lines, 3:6.2[C]
OFF 5th, Saks Fifth Avenue's, 11:1.4[C]
Off-price stores, 11:1.4
Office of Foreign Assets Control (OFAC)
  economic sanctions, 19:9.1
  Specially Designated Nationals and Blocked Persons list, 19:9.1
Officer. *See* Director and officer
Old Navy, 2:7.2[C], 11:1.2, 18:4.1
OMbra biosensing sports bra, 3:6.2[C]
Omega Global Design logo, 8:5
Omega S.A. v. Costco Wholesale Corp., 8:3.4, 8:3.5, 8:5
Omin-channel retail strategy, 11:1
Omni-channel retailing, 11:1.9
OMsignal, Inc., 3:6.2[C]
On Davis v. The Gap, Inc., 4:8.1
On-demand apparel manufacturing, 9:1
Onassis v. Christian Dior-New York, Inc., 18:4.2

One for One mission, TOMS, 1:2.6
1-800 Contacts, Inc., 2:11.2
100% natural products, 15:2.3, 15:4.2[E]
100-stockholder limitation, 1:2.5
Online application system, PTO, 2:6.3[B]
Online auction sites, counterfeiting, 7:3.4[B]
Online auctions fashion offerings e-commerce business model, 11:1.7
Online flash sale sites, 11:1.7
Online sales, 11:1.9
Operating agreements, LLC, 1:2.7
Operation In Our Sites, 7:2
Operation In Our Sites VII, 7:2
Opinion versus fact, false advertising, 15:2.3
Opposition proceedings, trademark registration, 2:6.3[E]
Oral-B products, 15:6
Ordinary observer test, 4:7.2[A]
ORDRE
  online discounts and markdowns, 11:2.2
Organic brand diversification, 22:1
Organic Foods Production Act, 15:4.3[A]
Organisation for Economic Cooperation and Development (OECD), 20:2
Organizational structure. *See also* Corporations; Fashion companies (new business ventures); General partnerships; Limited liability companies (LLCs); Sole proprietorships
  co-ops, 1:2.9
  divisions, 1:2.11
  factors in choosing, 1:2.1
  initial considerations, 1:2.1
  LPs, 1:2.8
  subsidiaries, 1:2.11
Origin rules. *See* Country of origin rules
Originality test, copyright protection, 4:3.1
OSHA (Occupational Safety and Health Administration), 9:5.1
O'Shea case, 20:5.4
Outlet stores. *See* Factory outlets
Outside sales, overtime exemption, 16:2.2[F]
Overpromotion by retailers at discount prices, 11:2.2
Oversecured creditors, right to post-petition interest
  post-petition value creation, bankruptcy cases, 23:4.1[B][2]
Overstock.com
  Hines v. Overstock.com Inc., 14:3.1
Overtime exemptions. *See* Wages and hours

Ownership
- copyrights, 4:5, 4:6.2
- failure to transfer ownership of goods, 8:4.2
- intellectual property, employee agreements, 17:2.4
- interest, fee estate, 13:2.2

P

Panalpina, 20:5.2
Pantomimes, copyright protection, 4:2
Parfums Givenchy, Inc. v. Drug Emporium, Inc., 8:3.1
Paris
- eighteenth century, 9:2
- Louis Vuitton workshops, 9:2

Paris Convention for the Protection of Industrial Property, 3:5.2
Paris Fashion Week, 13:4
Parody defense, 2:10.8, 7:3.2
Partnerships. *See also* General partnerships
- agreements, 1:2.3, 1:2.7, 1:2.8
- limited, 1:2.8

Passing off
- New York, 6:3.1[A]

Patagonia, Inc., 4:6.1, 9:5.2
Patent agents, 3:3.4
Patent applications, 3:3
- AIA, 3:3.1
- costs and fees, 3:3.3
- declaration, 3:3.1
- drawings, 3:3.1, 3:3.5
- early filing, 3:3.1
- employers, 3:3.1
- examination, PTO, 3:3.4
- oath, 3:3.1
- rejection, 3:3.4
- requirements, 3:3.1
- written specification, 3:3.1

Patent Cooperation Treaty (PCT), 3:5.2
Patent exhaustion doctrine, 8:1, 8:2.4
Patent infringement
- described, 3:4.1
- eyewear, 3:6.2[B]
- footwear, 3:6.1
- injunctive relief, 3:4.2[B]
- monetary relief, 3:4.2[A]

prejudgment interest, 3:4.2[D]
remedies, 3:4.2
Section 337 investigations, 3:5.1
shoes, 3:6.2[B]
willful, enhanced damages, 3:4.2[E]
Patent pending, 3:3.6
Patent prosecution, 3:3.4
Patent protection
outside United States, 3:5.2
territoriality, 3:5
United States, 3:5.1
Patents, 3:1 *et seq. See also* Design patents; Patent applications; PTO (U.S. Patent and Trademark Office); Utility patents
generally, 3:1
aesthetic beauty of an article, courts shifting away from, 3:2.2
exhaustion doctrine, 8:1, 8:2.4
false marking, 3:3.6
first sale doctrine, 8:2.4
infringement. *See* Patent infringement
international designs. *See* International design law protections
patent applications, 3:3
trends in fashion related patents, 3:1
wearable technology and, 3:2.1, 3:6.2[C]
Pay-per-click, search engine advertising model, 2:11.2
Payment Card Industry (PCI) Standards Council, 14:4
Payment methods, mobile commerce/e-commerce, 14:4
Payment terms, retailer-vendor arrangements, 11:2.5
PayPal
accounts, counterfeiters, 7:2
e-commerce, 14:4
electronic shopping cart, 14:2.1
Operation in Our Sites, 7:2
Purchase Protection program, 7:4.2
PCT. *See* Patent Cooperation Treaty (PCT)
Penalties, customs laws, 19:8
detention orders, 19:8.1
forfeitures, 19:8.1
fraud, 19:8.2
gross negligence, 19:8.2
mitigation guidelines, 19:8.2
monetary penalties, 19:8.2
negligence, 19:8.2
seizures, 19:8.1
self-disclosure, 19:8.2
statistics, 19:8, 19:8.1

Per se illegal arrangements, 12:3, 12:4.2[C]
Percentage rent, brick-and-mortar lease, 13:3.5
  gross revenues, sample definition, 13:3.5
Perfect 10 v. Visa International Service Association, 7:3.4[B][1]
Perfume
  Amarige, 8:3.1
  Chanel No. 5, 2:4.1
  Parfums Givenchy, Inc. v. Drug Emporium, Inc., 8:3.1
  pets, 2:10.8
  scents, trademark registration, 2:6.2
  TIMMY HOLEDIGGER, 2:10.8
Permanent injunction, trademark infringement, 2:9.1[A]
Perry, Katy
  Joseph Tierney (a.k.a. Rime) v. Moschino SpA, 2:10.5
Perry Ellis, 22:1
Personal funds, 1:4.2
Personal information
  data breach settlements, 14:3.2[A]
Personal jurisdiction, over counterfeiters, 7:3.1
Personal liability
  limited, 1:2.4, 1:2.7, 1:2.8
  unlimited, 1:2.2, 1:2.3, 1:2.8
Personal names
  intellectual property rights, 1:1.1
  trademarks, 2:4.2
Personal shopping apps, 14:1
Personal subscription/subscription box e-commerce business model, 11:1.7
Personalization of services, retail stores, 11:1.10
Persuasion to deal
  antitrust, 12:4.1[C]
Pet perfume, 2:10.8
Peter Pan Fabrics, Inc. v. Martin Weiner Corp., 4:3.2[C]
Pfaudler v. Pfaudler Co., 18:4.2
Pharmaceuticals, *Inwood* decision, 7:3.4[A]
Philanthropy, fashion business model methodologies connected to, 11:1.10
Philips Oral Healthcare, Inc., 15:6
Phillips-Van Heusen Corporation, 9:5.2, 10:1
Physical presence requirement, state taxation
  abolishment of, 14:3.3
Physical space, brick-and-mortar lease provisions, 13:2.1
Pictorial works, copyright protection, 4:2
Piercing corporate veil, 1:2.3, 1:2.10
Piggyback registration rights, 1:3.2, 22:3.2[B]

Pima cotton, 15:5.2
Pinterest, 15:7, 18:3
  ancillary agreements, 22:4
Plaid color scheme, Burberry, 2:8.2, 7:3.2
Planning fashion companies, 1:1.1. *See also* Fashion companies (new business ventures)
Playboy Enterprises, Inc. v. Welles, 2:10.5
Playgirl Magazine, 18:4.2
Playmate of the Year, 2:10.5
PMSI. *See* Purchase money security interest in goods (PMSI)
Point of novelty test, 3:4.1, 3:6.1
Point-of-sale confusion, 2:7.2[B]
Polaris, 9:5.1
Polaroid Corporation v. Polarad Electronics Corporation, 2:7.2[A]
Political office
  unfair competition lawsuits, 6:2.1
Polo Fashions, Inc. v. Craftex, Inc., 2:7.2[B]
Polo insignia, Ralph Lauren's, 2:3
Poor man's copyright, 4:6
Pop-up shops, trial, 11:1.9
Pop-up stores, 1:1.1, 11:1.6, 13:1, 13:2.2
Pornography, CAN-SPAM, 14:3.4
Poshmark, 1:4.7
Post-closing indemnities, 22:5.3
Post-closing working capital adjustment provisions, 22:3.3
Post-petition value creation
  first day relief, bankruptcy cases, 23:4.1[B]
    cram-down situations, 23:4.1[B][2]
    oversecured creditors, right to post-petition interest, 23:4.1[B][2]
    prepetition liens, 23:4.1[B][1]
    proceeds, defined, 23:4.1[B][1]
    revenue source, 23:4.1[B][1]
Post-sale confusion doctrine, 2:7.2[B], 7:3.2
Potential buyers, 22:2.1
Potik, Fima, 6:5.1
The Power of Trademarks exhibit (National Investors Hall of Fame, Alexandria, Virginia), 7:4.3
Prada SpA, 9:2
Pre-owned or vintage fashion offerings e-commerce business model, 11:1.7
Pre-ticketing, 12:4.1[B]
Preemptive rights, equity investors, 1:3.2
Preferential rules of origin, 19:6.3

Preferred stock
convertible, 1:3.2, 1:3.3, 1:4.3, 1:4.6, 1:4.7
described, 1:3.2
Pregnancy Discrimination Act, 16:4.3
Prejudgment interest, 3:4.2[D]
Preliminary injunction, trademark infringement, 2:9.1[B]
Preparatory steps, fashion companies, 1:1.1. *See also* Fashion companies (new business ventures)
Prepetition liens
post-petition value creation, bankruptcy cases, 23:4.1[B][1]
Preproduction processes, 9:3, 10:2.2[D]
Price discrimination, antitrust, 12:5
Primary line, price discrimination, 12:5
Priming debtor in possession financing
liquidity, bankruptcy cases, 23:2.3[C]
Principal Register, trademark application, 2:6.1
Printing, 3D, 9:1
Prior art, 3:4.1
Canada's Industrial Design Act (CIDA), 5:5.5
defined, 3:2.1
searches, 3:3.2
Prior use, trademarks, 2:10.1
Prior works, copyright protection, 4:3.1
Privacy
data breach settlements, 14:3.2[A]
mobile commerce/e-commerce, 14:3.2
private privacy litigation, 14:3.2[B]
rights. *See* Publicity rights
Privacy on the Go: Recommendations for the Mobile Ecosystem (California DOJ), 14:3.2[A]
Privacy on the Go Report, 14:3.2[A]
Privacy protections
state attorney general, 14:3.2[A]
Private co-existence agreements, 2:13:1
Private equity financing, 1:4.8
Private equity portfolio companies
fiduciary duties, bankruptcy cases, 23:2.1[C]
Private label brands, 11:1.3
Private label products, 11:1.1
Private privacy litigation, 14:3.2[B]
Private self-regulation, false advertising, 15:6
Proceeds, defined
post-petition value creation, bankruptcy cases, 23:4.1[B][1]

Proctor & Gamble, 15:6
NatureLuxe Mousse Mascara, Proctor & Gamble, 15:2.6
Proctor & Gamble Co. v. Haughen, 15:7.1
Product lines
brand name, 1:1.1
business description section, 1:1.2[B]
defining, 1:1.1
divisions, 1:2.11
Product safety standards, manufacturing, 9:5.1
enforcement and civil penalties, 9:5.1
industry initiatives, 9:5.2
Transparency Pledge, 9:5.2
Production. *See also* Design; Manufacturing
construction specifications, 9:3
costs, 9:3
design process, 9:3
finishing stage, 9:3
license agreements, 10:2.2[D]
preproduction development, 10:2.2[D]
preproduction processes, 9:3, 10:2.2[D]
samples, 9:3
spec sheet, 9:3
technical drawings, 9:3
Profits
copyright infringement, 4:9.3
counterfeiting, 7:3.5[A]
trademark infringement, 2:9.3
Progressive encroachment doctrine, 2:10.6
Promotional programs
antitrust, 12:4.1[E]
Proof of concept, 1:4.2
Property of the estate
first day relief, bankruptcy cases, 23:4.1[A]
Prospectus, IPO, 21:4
business section, 21:4.6
capitalization, 21:4.4
compensation, 21:4.7
dilution, 21:4.4
drafting, 21:4
financial information, 21:4.4, 21:4.11
management section, 21:4.7
MD&A, 21:4.5
plain English, 21:4.2
principal requirements, 21:4

Prospectus, IPO (*cont'd*)
risk factors, 21:4.2, App. 21A
securities section, 21:4.9
stockholders section, 21:4.8
summary, 21:4.1
underwriting, 21:4.10
use of proceeds, 21:4.3
Prosser, Professor, 18:3
Proximity payments, 14:4
PTO (U.S. Patent and Trademark Office). *See also* Patents; Trademarks
fraud in trademark registration, 2:10.3
goods and services classification, App. 2A
international classification of goods and services, 2:6.3[B], App. 2A
Notice of Allowance, 2:6.3[D], 3:3.4
online application system, 2:6.3[B]
patent application examination, 3:3.4
patent's issued, statistics, 3:6.2
TEAS Plus application, 2:6.3[B]
trademark application examination, 2:6.3[D]
Trademark ID Manual, 2:6.3[D]
Trademark Official Gazette, 2:6.3[D], 2:6.3[E]
trademark search, 2:6.3[A]
TTAB, 2:6.3[D], 2:6.3[E]
utility patents, 3:6.2
Public benefit corporation, 1:2.6
Public companies, acquisition of, 22:3.1
Public company tender offer, 22:7.2
Public education, counterfeiting, 7:4.3
Public interest, trademark infringement, 2:9.1[B]
Public Interest Registry, 7:3.3[A]
Public international organizations, 20:5.4
Public notice, LLC formation, 1:2.7
Public offering. *See* IPO (initial public offering)
Publicity rights, 18:1
generally, 18:1, 18:2
celebrities, 18:1 *et seq.*
copyright, distinguished from publicity rights, 18:2
history of, 18:3
implications for fashion industry, 18:5
models, 18:1 *et seq.*
overview, 18:2

practical implications, 18:5
celebrity's image on apparel, 18:5
copyright and right of publicity, 18:5
images of celebrities appearing on apparel, 18:5
infringement challenges, 18:5
licensing, 18:5
morals clause, 18:5
social media campaigns, 18:5
privacy protections (Professor William Prosser), 18:3
right of publicity law, overview, 18:2
risks involved, 18:5
state right of publicity law, examples, 18:4
California, 18:4.1
Indiana, 18:4.3
New York, 18:3, 18:4.2
trademark, distinguished from publicity rights, 18:2
Puma SE v. Forever 21, Inc., 2:10.9[C]
Purchase money security interest in goods (PMSI)
consignments and bankruptcy, 23:4.5[A][2]
consignor does not obtain PMSI, 23:4.5[A][3]
Purchase orders, retailer-vendor arrangements, 11:2.3
Purchase price, 22:3.3
sale transactions (fashion companies/brands acquisitions), 22:3.2
Purchase price adjustment mechanisms, 22:3.3
Purchase Protection program, 7:4.2
PayPal, 7:4.2
Put options, 1:3.2
PVH Corp., 9:5.2, 10:1
Pyramid model, 9:2

Q

Qualitex Company v. Jacobson Products Co., 2:10.9
Quality control, 2:10.7, 2:14, 10:2.2[D]
Quality King Distributors, Inc. v. L'anza Research International, Inc., 8:3.2
Quality of defendant's product, confusion analysis, 2:7.2[C]
Quick Response codes, 7:4.1
Quill Corp. v. North Dakota, 14:3.3
Quiznos fast food franchise, 15:7.1
Qurate, 11:1.8
QVC, 11:1.8

R

Racketeer Influenced and Corrupt Organizations Act (RICO), 7:3.4[B]
Radio Frequency Identification (RFID) tags, 3:6.2[C], 7:4.1, 11:2.6
RAE Systems, Inc., 20:5.2
Ralph Lauren, 21:2.2
    fast fashion, 11:1
    FCPA enforcement, case study, 20:4.1
    overpromotion by retailers at discount prices, 11:2.2
    personal name trademark, 2:4.2
    polo insignia, 2:3
    pyramid model, 9:2
    sales, after runway shows, 11:1
    Societe Yves Saint Laurent Couture S.A. v. Societe Louis Dreyfus Retail Management S.A. (France), 5:4.1
Ready-to-wear (RTW), 9:3
Real estate. *See also* Brick-and-mortar lease provisions
    generally, 13:1
    brokers, 13:2.1
    e-commerce sites, 13:1
    emerging brands, 13:1
    fashion shows, 13:4
    lease provisions, drafting, 13:2.1, 13:3
        additional rent, 13:3.5
        additional rent, non-recurring payments of, 13:3.5
        after-hours charges or requirements, 13:3.8
        alterations, 13:3.8
        assignment/sublease provisions, 13:3.9
        exclusive use, 13:3.4
        expansion of space, 13:3.1
        fixed rent, 13:3.5
        gross revenues, sample definition of, 13:3.5
        leased premises, alterations to, 13:3.8
        loading docks, 13:3.8
        operational requirements detailed in lease, 13:3.8
        other provisions, 13:3.10
        other tenants, future interactions with, 13:3.8
        percentage rent, 13:3.5
        practical considerations; alterations, 13:3.8
        rent, 13:3.5
        rent abatements, 13:3.2, 13:3.6
        signage, 13:3.7
        soft costs, 13:3.8

space, 13:3.1
surrender space, 13:3.1
term, 13:3.2
termination right, 13:3.2
use provisions, 13:3.3
use restrictions, 13:3.4
visibility, 13:3.7
leases and licenses distinguished, 13:2.2
New York City, 13:1
real property interests, 13:2.2
soft costs, 13:3.8
suitable space, 13:2.1
zoning requirements, 13:3.7
Real property interests, 13:2.2. *See also* Brick-and-mortar lease provisions
Real property leases (non-residential) and bankruptcy, 23:4.2
assignment, 23:4.2[C]
adequate assurance, 23:4.2[C][1]
designation rights, 23:4.2[C][4]
nonassignability of leases, 23:4.2[C][2]
shopping center leases, 23:4.2[C][3]
assumption, 23:4.2[B]
adequate assurance, 23:4.2[B][2]
cure and compensation, 23:4.2[B][1]
deadline, 23:4.2[A]
defaults, 23:4.2[B][1]
extensions available, 23:4.2[A]
going dark clause, 23:4.2[B][1][b]
ipso facto clauses, 23:4.2[B][1][a]
non-monetary breaches, 23:4.2[B][1][b]
continuous use provisions, 23:5.2[B][1][d]
damages cap, 23:4.2[D]
executory contracts, 23:4.2
going dark provisions, 23:5.2[B][1][d]
going out of business sales (GOB sales), lease restrictions, 23:5.2[B][1][d]
landlord is debtor, 23:4.2[F]
rejection, 23:4.2[D]
damages cap, Bankruptcy Code section 502(b)(6), 23:4.2[D]
deadline, 23:4.2[A]
extensions available, 23:4.2[A]
rent obligations, 23:4.2[E]
stub rent, 23:4.2[E]
RealReal, 11:1.7, 11:1.9, 11:1.10
Reason analysis rule, 12:4.1[A], 12:4.2[C]

Reasonable care, importer responsibilities, 19:2.1
  generally, 19:2.1[A]
  forced labor, 19:2.1[B]
  intellectual property rights, 19:2.1[C]
Rebates, direct
  antitrust, 12:4.1[E]
Rebecca Minkoff, 9:1
Reclamation
  first day relief, bankruptcy cases, 23:3.2[D]
Reconciliation, imported merchandise, 19:5.6
Recordkeeping requirements, importers, 19:2.2
Recourse factoring, 1:4.4
Recreational Equipment Inc., 1:2.9
Red shoes, *Louboutin* case, 2:10.9[A]
Reebok, 3:6.2[B], 17:2.4
  DMX Series 2000 Cushioning Technology, 3:6.2[B]
ReFashioner, 11:1.7
Reference Guide on Survey Research (Diamond), 2:7.2[C]
Reformation, 11:1.9, 11:1.10
RefScale measurement, 11:1.10
Refusal to deal
  antitrust, 12:4.1[C]
Registered Design Act of 1949, 5:4.2
Registering trademarks. *See* Trademark registrations
Registration rights
  defined, 1:3.2
  demand, 1:3.2
  piggyback, 1:3.2, 22:3.2[B]
Registration statement, IPO, 21:3.1
Regulation
  manufacturing process, 9:5.1
  privacy, mobile commerce/e-commerce, 14:3.2[A]
Regulation A+, SEC, 1:4.7
Regulation Crowdfunding, SEC, 1:4.7
Regulation D, SEC, 1:4.7
Rejection
  of patent applications, 3:3.4
  of trademark applications, 2:6.3[D]
Related parties
  valuation, imported merchandise, 19:5.4
Remedies
  copyright infringement, 4:9
  false advertising, 15:4.1[D]
  patent infringement, 3:4.2
  trademark infringement, 2:9

accounting of profits, 2:9.3
attorneys' fees, 2:9.2[C]
balance of the hardships, 2:9.1[B]
costs of action, 2:9.2[C]
defendant's profits, 2:9.2[A]
domain names, 2:9.4
injunctive relief, 2:9.1
ITC's Section 337 investigations, 2:9.5
likelihood of irreparable harm, 2:9.1[B]
likelihood of success on the merits, 2:9.1[B]
monetary relief, 2:9.2
permanent injunction, 2:9.1[A]
plaintiff's damages, 2:9.2[B]
preliminary injunction, 2:9.1[B]
public interest, 2:9.1[B]

Renewal
of copyright registrations, 4:6.2
of trademark registrations, 2:6.3[F]

Rent, brick-and-mortar lease provisions, 13:3.5

Rent abatements, 13:3.2, 13:3.6

Rent obligations
real property leases (non-residential) and bankruptcy, 23:4.2[E]

Rent the Runway, 11:1.7

Reorganization
Chapter 11 reorganization, 23:5.1

Reporting provisions, license agreements, 10:2.2[F]

Representations and warranties
acquisition agreements, 22:5.1, App. 22B
license agreements, 10:2.2[K]

Resale price maintenance (RPM)
antitrust, 12:4.1[A]

Resource Guide to the U.S. Foreign Corrupt Practices Act
generally, 20:3.1[B]
crafting an effective compliance program, 20:5.6
enforcement, issue spotting, 20:5
entertainment, 20:5.5
foreign officials, 20:5.4
gifts, 20:5.5
responding to a potential violation, 20:5.7
successor liability, 20:5.3
third-party payments, 20:5.2

Responsive web design (RWD), 14:2.2

Restatement of Torts, 2:7.2[A]

Restore Online Shoppers' Confidence Act (ROSCA), 14:4

Restraint, of counterfeiters' assets, 7:3.3[B]

Restrictive non-competition agreements. *See* Non-competition agreements
Restructuring. *See also headings under Bankruptcy*
Retail Dive Survey, 11:1.9
Retail sales. *See also* Brick-and-mortar retail stores; Department stores; E-commerce
generally, 11:1, 11:4
Amazon effect, 11:1.7, 11:4
Amazon Effect, 11:1.7
Black Friday sales, 11:1
boutiques, 11:1.5
broad cultural phenomena, 11:1.10
catalog, 11:1.8
customer analytics, 11:1.7
direct-to-consumers, 11:2
discount department stores, 11:1.3
distribution agreements, 11:3
e-commerce, 11:1
e-commerce business models, 11:1.7
economical individualized clothing, 11:1.10
factory outlets, 11:1.4[A]
fast fashion companies, 11:1
fitting rooms, 11:1.10
flag-ship store, 11:1.1, 11:1.9
guideshops, 11:1.9
home shopping (television) retailers, 11:1.8
implementation section, business plan, 1:1.2[E]
in-store technology, 11:1.10
innovative brands, 11:1.10
Internet retailers, 11:1.7
made-to-order fashion, 11:1.10
mail-order, 11:1.8
marketing challenges, 11:1.7
mass customization, 11:1.10
mobile applications (mobile apps), 11:1
off-price stores, 11:1.4
omni-channel retail strategy, 11:1
omni-channel retailing, 11:1.9
online flash sale sites, 11:1.7
online sales, 11:1.9
personalization of services, 11:1.10
pop-up shops, trial, 11:1.9
pop-up stores, 1:1.1, 11:1.6, 13:1, 13:2.2
retail stores as destinations and experiences, 11:1.10
shipping and delivery terms, retailer-vendor arrangements, 11:2.4

shopping for the experience, 11:1.10
specialty stores, 11:1.2
statistics, 11:1
sustainable manufacturing, 11:1.10
technology advancements, impact of, 11:1
television retailers, 11:1.8
younger consumers, 11:1.10
Retail stores
as destinations and experiences, 11:1.10
in-store technology, 11:1.10
license agreements, 10:3
development of stores, 10:3.2
nature, 10:3.1
other terms, 10:3.3
royalties, 10:3.3
scope, 10:3.1
personalization of services, 11:1.10
Retailer-owned off-price stores, 11:1.4[C]
Retailer-vendor arrangements, 11:2
acceptance of goods, 11:2.5
chargebacks, 11:2.6
consignments, 11:2.7
delivery terms, 11:2.4
discounts, 11:2.2
electronic data interchange (EDI) technology systems, 11:2.1
exclusive distribution, 11:2.1
markdown allowances, 11:2.2
online discounts and markdowns, 11:2.2
overpromotion by retailers at discount prices, 11:2.2
payment terms, 11:2.5
purchase orders, 11:2.3
risk of loss, 11:2.4
shipping terms, 11:2.4
Stock keeping unit (SKU), 11:2.1
Universal Product Code (UPC) requirements, 11:2.1
vendor standards, 11:2.1
Retailers
manufacturer's General Certificate of Conformity, 9:5.1
Retirement plan participation
employment agreements, 17:2.3
Revenue source
post-petition value creation, bankruptcy cases, 23:4.1[B][1]
Reverse break-up fee, 22:6
Reverse confusion, 2:7.2[B]
Reverse triangular merger, 22:3.1

Revolve Group, LLC, 21:1, 21:4.2
Revolving loan, 1:4.5
RFID. *See* Radio Frequency Identification (RFID) tags
Right of publicity law, overview. *See* Publicity rights
Rights. *See also* Copyright, generally; Publicity rights; Registration rights
    appraisal, 1:3.2
    buy-out, 10:2.2[K]
    co-sale, 1:3.2
    consent, equity investors, 1:3.2
    consumer-rights movement, 15:3
    creative control, 1:3.2
    derivative suits, 1:3.2
    drag-along, 1:3.2, 22:3.4[B]
    first negotiation, 10:2.2[B]
    first offer, 1:3.2, 10:2.2[B], 22:3.4[B]
    first refusal, 1:3.2, 10:2.2[B], 22:3.4[B]
    inspection, 1:3.2
    intellectual property, 10:2.2[H]
    preemptive, equity investors, 1:3.2
    royalty, 22:3.4[B]
    tag-along, 1:3.2, 22:3.4[B]
    termination, 22:6
    types of
        first refusal, real estate expansion options, 13:3.1
        publicity rights. *See* Publicity rights
        termination, lease provision, 13:3.2
Rihanna's Fenty Shoe Collection
    LaChapelle v. Fenty, 4:3.3
    Puma SE v. Forever 21, Inc., 2:10.9[C]
Rime
    Joseph Tierney (a.k.a. "Rime") v. Moschino SpA, 2:10.5
Risk of loss, retailer-vendor arrangements, 11:2.4
Road show. *See also* IPO (initial public offering)
    IPO (initial public offering), 21:3.2, 21:5
Robinson-Patman Act, 12:5
Robotic systems, 9:2, 18:4.1
Rodriguez, Carlos, 20:3.1[B]
Roger Cleveland Golf Company v. Prince, 7:3.4[B][2], 7:3.5[B]
RogueBlock, 7:4.2
The Rolling Stones, 18:5
ROSCA. *See* Restore Online Shoppers' Confidence Act (ROSCA)
Rose-patterned fabric, Folio Impressions, 4:3.3
Rosen, Andrew, 1:3.2
Rosetta Stone Ltd. v. Google Inc., 2:11.2

Ross Dress for Less, 11:1.4[B]
Royalties
acquisitions/sale transactions, 22:3.4[B]
imported merchandise, 19:5.2
license agreements, 10:2.2[E]
license agreements, retail stores, 10:3.3
RoyaltySource Intellectual Property Database, 2:14
RPM. *See* Resale price maintenance (RPM)
RTW. *See* Ready-to-wear (RTW)
Rue La La, 11:1.7
Rue21, 23:2.3[A][3]
Rule 501, 1:4.7
Rule 504, 1:4.7
Rule 505, 1:4.7
Rule 506, 1:4.7
Rule on Care Labeling of Textile Wearing Apparel and Certain Piece Goods, 9:5.1
Runoff coverage
bankruptcy cases, preparation for, 23:2.2
Runway shows, sales after, 11:1
Russia
economic sanctions, 19:9.1
RWS. *See* Responsive web design (RWD)

S

S corporation
described, 1:2.5
preferred stock, 1:3.2
saferproducts.gov database, 9:5.1
Saint Laurent. *See* Yves Saint Laurent
Saks Fifth Avenue's OFF 5th, 11:1.4[C]
Sale of products. *See* License agreements; Retail sales
Sale transactions (fashion companies/brands acquisitions), 22:1 *et seq. See also* Acquisition agreements
generally, 22:1
ancillary agreements, 22:4
auction process, 22:2
breach, insurance policy to cover losses, 22:5.1
buyer promissory notes, 22:3.2[C]
cash purchase price, 22:3.2[A]
clean team, 22:2.2
closing conditions, 22:6
conglomeratization trend, 22:1

Sale transactions (fashion companies/brands acquisitions) (*cont'd*)
- contingent payment mechanisms, 22:3.4
- diversification by fast fashion powerhouses, 22:1
- drag-along rights, 22:3.4[B]
- due diligence, 22:2.2
- earn-outs, 22:3.4[A], App. 22A
- EBITDA, 22:3.4[B]
- equities securities of buyer, 22:3.2[B]
- escrow amounts, 22:5.4
- exclusive negotiations, 22:2.2
- exclusivity agreements, 22:2.1
- final bid package, 22:2.1
- financial buyers, 22:2
- first offer rights, 22:3.4[B]
- first refusal rights, 22:3.4[B]
- Form 10-K (SEC), 22:5.1
- illustrative acquisitions, 22:7
- indemnities, 22:5.3
- interval between signing and closing, 22:6
- IPO compared to, 22:1
- joint venture agreement, 22:3.4[B]
- leaked information in auction process, 22:2.1
- mergers, 22:3.1
- multiple bidders, 22:2.1
- nondisclosure agreements, 22:2.1
- organic brand diversification, 22:1
- potential buyers, 22:2.1
- public companies
  - acquisition of, 22:3.1
  - disclosure requirements, 22:5.1
- public company tender offer, 22:7.2
- purchase price, 22:3.2, 22:3.3
- purchase price adjustment mechanisms, 22:3.3
- royalty rights, 22:3.4[B]
- simultaneous signing and closing, 22:5.2, 22:6
- spinoff of division or subsidiary, 22:3.1
- statistics, 22:1
- stock purchase agreement, 22:7.1
- strategic acquisitions, 22:1
- strategic buyers, 22:1, 22:2, 22:2.2
- structure, 22:3
- tag-along rights, 22:3.4[B]
- tender offer, 22:6
- termination rights, 22:6
- third-party sales, 22:3.4[B]
- unsuccessful acquisitions, 22:1

Sales representatives, 16:6
    as independent contractors, 16:6
    classification of, 16:6
Sales volume, royalties, 10:2.2[E]
Salinger v. Colting, 2:9.1[B]
Salvatore Ferragamo S.p.A., 21:2.2
Samples, production, 9:3
Samsung
    smartphone design battle with Apple, 3:6.1
    White v. Samsung Electronics America, Inc., 18:4.1
Sanctions, economic, 19:9.1
SBA. *See* Small Business Administration (SBA)
SBICs. *See* Small business investment companies (SBICs)
Scent Lok brand, 15:2.4
Schedule C, 1:2.2
Schedule K-1, 1:2.3, 1:2.5
Schreiber v. Dunabin, 7:3.4[B][2]
Schumer, Charles, 4:4
Scott, Jeremy, 2:10.5
Sculptural works, copyright protection, 4:2
Seamans, Scott
    design patent, App. 3A–1
    utility patent, App. 3B–1
Search engine and Internet advertising, trademark infringement, 2:11 *et seq.*
    generally, 2:11
    aspirational customers, 2:11.2
    confusion, 2:11.2
    hashtags, use of trademarks in, 2:11.3
    infringement claims, 2:11.2
    likelihood-of-confusion multifactor test, 2:11.2
    metatags, trademarks as, 2:11.1
    natural key word search, 2:11.2
    pay-per-click advertising model, 2:11.2
    sponsored links, 2:11.2
    sponsorship of goods, 2:11.2
    Troika factors, 2:11.2
Sears, Roebuck & Co., 3:6.1, 11:1.1
    enforcement of FTC labeling regulations, 15:4.2[E]
Seasonal collections
    design teams, 9:3
Seasonal fluctuation of inventory, 23:2.3[A][1]
SEC Form 10-K
    sale transactions, disclosure requirements for public companies, 22:5.1

SEC (U.S. Securities and Exchange Commission). *See also* Foreign Corrupt Practices Act (FCPA); IPO (initial public offering)
- *Avon* case study, 20:4.2
- Electronic Data Gathering, Analysis and Retrieval (EDGAR) System, 21:2.2
- FCPA enforcement, generally, 20:4–20:5
- Form 8-A, registration statement, 21:6.3
- going public, 21:1
- IPO review, 21:3.1
- *Ralph Lauren* case study, 20:4.1
- registration rights, 1:3.2
- Regulation A+ rules, 1:4.7
- Regulation Crowdfunding rules, 1:4.7
- Regulation D rules, 1:4.7
- Resource Guide. *See* Resource Guide to the U.S. Foreign Corrupt Practices Act
- Rule 501, 1:4.7
- Rule 504, 1:4.7
- Rule 505, 1:4.7
- Rule 506, 1:4.7
- Watergate investigation, 20:2

Second Restatement of Torts
- unfair competition, federal, 6:4.1

Secondary liability, trademark infringement, 7:3.4[B]

Secondary line, price discrimination, 12:5

Secondary meaning, trademarks, 2:4.2

Secretary of State, Delaware, 1:2.3, 1:2.4, 1:2.7, 1:2.8

Section 107 of U.S. Code, Article 17, 4:8.1

Section 337 Investigations, ITC, 2:9.5, 3:5.1

Section 349, General Business Law, 6:3.2

Section 363 of Bankruptcy Code, sales authorized by, 23:5.2
- advantages for buyers and sellers, 23:5.2[B]
- conditions required, 23:5.2[B]
- credit bidding, 23:5.2[B]
- going out of business sales (GOB sales), 23:5.2[B][1]
  - generally, 23:5.2[B][1]
  - continuous use provisions, 23:5.2[B][1][d]
  - duration, 23:5.2[B][1][c]
  - federal law compliance, 23:5.2[B][1][a]
  - going dark provisions, 23:5.2[B][1][d]
  - lease restrictions, 23:5.2[B][1][d]
  - merchandise augmentation, 23:5.2[B][1][b]
  - state law compliance, 23:5.2[B][1][a]
- section 363 sales, basics, 23:5.2[A]

Section 409A, non-qualified deferred compensation plans, compliance
internal Revenue Code Section 409A and, 17:2.3
Section 1301, Copyright Act, 4:4
Section 17200, California Business and Professions Code, 6:2.1
Secured loans, 1:4.5
Securities Act of 1933, 1:4.7, 21:2.3
Securities and Exchange Commission. *See* SEC (U.S. Securities and Exchange Commission)
Securities Exchange Act of 1934, 20:3.1[A]
section 12, 20:5.1
Securities section, IPO prospectus, 21:4.9
Security. *See also* Customs and Border Protection (CBP)
Bureau of Industry and Security, 19:9.2
cyber security, 14:3.4, 21:2.3, 21:4.2
Department of Homeland Security, 19:2
mobile commerce/e-commerce, 14:3.2
Security deposits, real property interests, 13:2.3
Seizures, CBP, 19:8.1
Sell-Off Compliance Agreement, 8:3.3, 8:4.1
Sellers
section 363 of Bankruptcy Code, sales authorized by, 23:5.2[B]
Selling fashion companies. *See* Sale transactions (fashion companies/ brands acquisitions)
Selna, James V., 20:5.4
Senior security interest in consigned goods
consignments and bankruptcy, 23:4.5[A][2]
Sensor technologies/include all smart items
smart fabrics, 3:6.2[C]
Sensors and smart wearable technology, 3:6.2[C]
Separability doctrine, 4:3.2
Sephora, 11:1.7, 11:1.9
Sephora Collection at Coachella 2018, 11:1.10
Sephora Studios, 11:1.10
Service marks, 2:3. *See also* Trademarks
Services and goods. *See also* Trademarks
classification, PTO, 2:6.3[B], App. 2A
Sewbots, 9:1
Sex claims, BFOQ defense, 16:4.2
Sgouros v. TransUnion Corp, 14:3.1
Shaped fit sizing system, Levi Strauss & Co., 3:6.2[B]
Shareholders. *See* Stockholders
Shark Tank, 1:1.1
Shaw Family Archives, 18:4.3

Sherman Act, 4:2. *See also* Antitrust
antitrust claims, 12:2
Fashion Originator's Guild, 4:2
horizontal relationships, 12:3
vertical relationships, 12:4
Shippers
first day relief, bankruptcy cases, 23:3.2[C]
Shipping
internet retailers, free shipping option, 11:1.7
Shipping terms, retailer-vendor arrangements, 11:2.4
international commercial terms or inco terms, 11:2.4
ShoeDazzle, 11:1.7
Shoes. *See* Footwear
Shop within a shop, 13:2.2
Shopping center leases
assignment of real property lease (non-residential) and bankruptcy, 23:4.2[C][3]
Shopping for the experience, 11:1.10
Showrooming practice, 14:1
Signage, brick-and-mortar lease provisions, 13:3.7
Signing
interval between signing and closing, 22:6
simultaneous signing and closing, 22:5.2, 22:6
Similarity, copyright infringement, 4:7.2
Similarity of marks, confusion analysis, 2:7.2[C]
Simpson v. Union Oil Co., 12:4.1[C]
Simultaneous signing and closing, 22:5.2, 22:6
Singapore
design law protections, 5:5.6
Skechers, 3:6.1, 15:4.1[C]
adidas America Inc. v. Skechers USA, Inc., 2:9.1[B]
SKU. *See* Stock keeping unit (SKU)
Skunk Works trademark, 7:3.4[B][2]
S&M-themed photo series, 4:3.3
Small Business Administration (SBA), 1:1.2, 1:4.8
Small Business Credit Survey Report of 2017, 1:1.1
Small business investment companies (SBICs), 1:4.8
Small Business Investor Alliance, 1:4.8
Smart fabrics, 3:6.2[C]
Smart glasses, 3:6.2[C]
Smart ski and snowboard goggles, 3:6.2[C]
Smart watch, 3:6.2[C]
Smart wearables, 3:6.2[C]
Smartphones, 14:1, 14:2.2, 14:3.2
Apple's design battle with Samsung, 3:6.1

Smells, trademark registration, 2:6.2
Sneakers. *See* Footwear
Social impact/social benefit, fashion business model methodologies connected to, 11:1.10
Social media campaigns
  publicity rights, 18:5
Social media developments, 1:1.1
Social media platforms
  employment and labor issues, 16:8
  Facebook, 15:7, 16:8
  Facebook, ancillary agreements, 22:4
  false advertising, 15:7
  fashion influencers, 15:7.2
  FTC oversight, 15:7.2
  harassment, 16:8
  Pinterest, 15:7, 18:3
  Pinterest, ancillary agreements, 22:4
  Twitter, 15:7, 16:8, 18:3
    character limit on messages, 15:7.2
  Twitter, ancillary agreements, 22:4
  YouTube, 15:7, 18:3
Social media usage
  Civil Rights Act of 1964, Title VII, 16:8
  employee policies to conduct appropriate online activity, 16:8
  Facebook, 16:8
  labor and employment, 16:8
  National Labor Relations Act (NLRA), 16:8
  National Labor Relations Board (NLRB), 16:8
Societe Yves Saint Laurent Couture S.A. v. Societe Louis Dreyfus Retail Management S.A. (France), 5:4.1
Soft luxury, 9:2
Software
  counterfeit, unfair competition lawsuits, 6:2.1
SoftWear Automation, 9:1
Sole proprietorships
  described, 1:2.2
  disadvantages, 1:2.2
  general partnerships compared to, 1:2.3
  LLC compared to, 1:2.7
Solvency determination
  fiduciary duties, bankruptcy cases, 23:2.1[B]
Song-Beverly Credit Card Act, 14:3.2[B]
Sony
  wearable technology, 3:6.2[C]
Sony Interactive Entertainment, 3:6.2[C]

Sophia & Chloe, Inc. v. Brighton Collectibles, LLC, 4:7.2[B]
Sound recordings, copyright protection, 4:2
Sounds, trademark registration, 2:6.2
Source confusion, 2:7.2[B]
Sources and uses table, 1:1.1[G]
Sourcing decisions, design process, 9:3
South Dakota v. Wayfair, 14:3.2[A]
South Korea
  U.S. e-commerce retailers expansion into, 14:1
Space, brick-and-mortar lease provisions, 13:2.1
Spam, CAN-SPAM, 14:3.4
Spec sheet
  preproduction process, 9:3
Specht v. Netscape Communications Corp., 14:3.1
Specially Designated Nationals and Blocked Persons, 19:9.1
Specialty stores, 11:1.2
Spectravest, Inc. v. Mervyn's Inc., 4:7.2[B]
Speech, false advertising, 15:2.1
Spinoff of division or subsidiary, 22:3.1
Spirit Airlines, 15:7.2
Spoiled Brats images, 4:7.1
Sponsored links
  search engine advertising, 2:11.2
Sponsorship of goods
  search engine advertising, trademark infringement, 2:11.2
Sports Authority, 23:1, 23:4.5[A][3]
Spotted Friend, LLC v. Vigme, Inc., 6:5.1
Sprig, 1:4.3
Standing
  lack of standing, trademark infringement defense, 2:10.2
Standing of creditors
  fiduciary duties, bankruptcy cases, 23:2.1[A]
Standstill agreements, 1:4.7, 22:2.3
Standstill provisions, 1:3.2, 22:2.3
Staples, 9:1
Star Athletica LLC v. Varsity Brands, Inc., 4:1, 4:3.2[D]
Star Fabrics, Inc. v. DKJY, 4:3.1
Start-up companies
  manufacturing decisions, 9:3
Start-ups. *See also* Fashion companies (new business ventures)
  generally, 1:1.1
  drafting business plan. *See* Business plan
  financing, 1:4
  strategic acquisition of fashion companies, 22:1
Starting fashion companies. *See* Fashion companies (new business ventures)

State attorney general
    privacy protections, 14:3.2[A]
State child labor laws, 16:3.2
State law
    going out of business sales (GOB sales), 23:5.2[B][1][a]
State regulation
    manufacturing process, 9:5.1
    mobile commerce/e-commerce, 14:3.2[A]
State taxation
    Quill Corp. v. North Dakota, 14:3.3
    South Dakota v. Wayfair, 14:3.2[A]
Statue of Liberty, 3:2.2
Statutory damages
    copyright infringement, 4:9.3[B]
    counterfeiting, 7:3.5[B]
Statutory unfair competition law, New York, 6:3.2
Stella McCartney, 2:4.4
Steve Madden, 3:6.1
    Dolce Vita Holdings, Inc., acquisition of, 22:7.1
    Eliya, Inc. v. Steven Madden, Ltd., 2:10.9[B]
Stevens Linen Associates, Inc. v. Mastercraft Corp., 4:9.3[A]
Stitch Fix, 11:1.7, 21:1
Stock keeping unit (SKU), 11:2.1
Stock purchase agreement, 22:7.1
Stockholders. *See also* Corporations; IPO (initial public offering)
    agreements, 1:2.4, 1:3.2, 21:4.8
    appraisal rights, 1:3.2
    board observers, 1:3.2
    Board of directors fiduciary duties, 1:2.4, 1:2.5, 1:2.8
    C corporation, 1:2.4
    controlling, 1:3.2
    corporation employees, 1:2.4
    defined, 1:2.4
    derivative suits, 1:3.2
    diffusion, 1:3.2
    double taxation, 1:2.4, 1:2.5
    drag-along rights, 1:3.2, 22:3.4[B]
    inspection rights, 1:3.2
    limited personal liability, 1:2.7
    meetings, 1:2.4, 1:2.11
    no-transfer periods, 1:3.2
    100-stockholder limitation, 1:2.5
    rights agreements, 1:3.2
    S corporation, 1:2.5
    section, IPO prospectus, 21:4.8

Stored Communications Act
    Google violations under, 14:3.2[B]
Stratasys Ltd., 9:1
Strategic acquisitions, 22:1
Strategic buyers, 22:2
    sale transactions (fashion companies/brands acquisitions), 22:1, 22:2.2
Strength of mark, confusion analysis, 2:7.2[C]
Stuart Weitzman, 3:6.1, 22:1
Stub rent
    obligations, Bankruptcy Code section 365(d)(3), 23:2.4[B]
    real property leases (non-residential), 23:4.2[E]
Style piracy, 4:2
Sublease/assignment provisions, brick-and-mortar lease, 13:3.9
Sublicensing, 10:2.2[A]
Subscription box e-commerce model, 11:1.7
Subsidiaries, organizational structure, 1:2.11
Subsidiary or division, spinoffs, 22:3.1
Substantial nexus, state taxation, 14:3.3
Substantial similarity, copyright infringement, 4:7.2
Subway
    Quiznos v. Subway TV Add Challenge, 15:7.1
Success on the merits, 2:9.1[B], 2:10.8
Successive filtering approach, 4:7.2[C]
Successor liability, FCPA enforcement, 20:5.3
Suggested retail prices
    antitrust, 12:4.1[B]
Supplementary works, 4:5
Supply chain risks
    FCPA enforcement, 20:4.4
        distributors, 20:4.4[C]
        third-party manufacturers, 20:4.4[A]
        transportation service providers, 20:4.4[B]
Supply contracts, manufacturing, 9:4, App. 9A
The Supremes, 18:2
Sustainable Apparel Coalition, 9:5.2
Sustainable manufacturing, 11:1.10
Sweatshops, 16:3.3
Swift, Taylor, 15:2.6
Swoosh logo, Nike, 2:6.2
Syncor International, 20:5.3
Syria
    economic sanctions, 19:9.1

T

Tablets, 14:2.2. *See also* Smartphones
Tag-along rights, 1:3.2, 22:3.4[B]
Tapestry, Inc., 22:7.2
Target Corporation, 11:1.3
  Cat & Jack, 11:1.3
  chargebacks, 11:2.6
  data breach class action settlement, 14:3.2[A]
  international designers, collaboration with, 11:1.3
Target market
  business description section, business plan, 1:1.2[B]
  identifying, 1:1.1
  industry and market analysis section, business plan, 1:1.2[C]
Targeted venture capital search, 1:4.7
Tariff Act of 1930, 19:2.1, 19:2.2, 19:8.2
Tariffs
  GATT, 19:1
  Harmonized Tariff Schedule, 19:4, 19:6.3, App. 19B
Tarnishment, trademark dilution, 2:8.2
Tax forms
  Form 1040, 1:2.2, 1:2.5
  Form 1065, 1:2.3
  Form 1120, 1:2.4
  Form 2553, 1:2.5
  Form 8832, 1:2.7
  Schedule C, 1:2.2
  Schedule K-1, 1:2.3, 1:2.5
Taxes
  C corporations, 1:2.4
  divisions, 1:2.11
  double taxation, 1:2.4, 1:2.5
  employment agreements, 17:2.3
  general partnerships, 1:2.3
  gift, 1:4.3
  LLCs, 1:2.7
  loans from friends/family, 1:4.3
  LPs, 1:2.8
  S corporations, 1:2.5
  sole proprietorships, 1:2.2
  subsidiaries, 1:3.2
TDRA. *See* Trademark Dilution Revision Act of 2006 (TDRA)
TEAS Plus application, 2:6.3[B]
Tech packs, 9:3
Technical drawings, preproduction process, 9:3

Technology
electronic data interchange (EDI) technology systems, 11:2.1
fashion technology companies, 1:1.1, 1:2.1, 1:4.6
holograms, 7:4.1, 8:5
manufacturing process, 9:2
Quick Response codes, 7:4.1
retail sales, developments, 11:1
retail stores, in-store technology, 11:1.10
retailers, online discounts and markdowns, 11:2.2
RFID tags, 3:6.2[C], 7:4.1, 11:2.6
robotic systems, 9:2, 18:4.1
3D printing, 9:1
utility patents, fashion/technology integration, 3:6.2[C]
vendors, 11:2.1
wearable technology, 3:2.1, 3:6.2[C]
Technology advancements, impact on retail sales, 11:1
Technology and fashion, modern intersections (case study), 3:6.2[C]
Télécommunications d'Haiti S.A., 20:3.1
Television retailers, 11:1.8
Temporary restraining order (TRO), 7:3.3
Tenants. *See* Brick-and-mortar lease provisions
Tender offer
public company, 22:7.2
sale transactions (fashion companies/brands acquisitions), 22:6
Term
brick-and-mortar lease provisions, 13:3.2
design patents, 3:3.5
employment agreements, 17:2.2
license agreements, 10:2.2[C]
utility patents, 3:3.5
Term loan financing
liquidity, bankruptcy cases, 23:2.3[A][2]
Term loans, 1:4.5
Term sheets
angel investors, 1:4.6
manufacture/sale of products, 10:2.1
venture capitalists, 1:4.7
Termination of employment agreements
change in control provision/golden parachute, 17:2.3
termination for good reason, 17:2.2
termination with or without cause, 17:2.2
Termination of license agreements, 10:2.2[I]
Termination rights
break-up fees, 22:6
brick-and-mortar lease, 13:3.2

sale transactions, 22:6
termination fees, 22:6
Territorial restrictions, antitrust, 12:4.2[B]
Territoriality, patent protection, 3:5
Texas, Laredo
e-commerce counterfeiting, federal law enforcement, 7:2
Textile and apparel rules of origin, 19:6.2
Textile Fiber Products Identification Act, 9:5.1, 15:2.6, 19:6.4
Textiles
flammability standards for fabrics and textiles, 9:5.1
Textiles and apparel, rules of origin, 19:6.2
Thallmic Labs, Inc., 3:6.2[C]
The Children's Place, 3:6.1
Theory, 1:3.2
They're Real! mascara, Benefit Cosmetics, 15:2.6
Third-party e-commerce platform service providers, 14:2.1
Third-party manufacturers, FCPA enforcement actions, 20:4.4[A]
Third-party payments, FCPA enforcement, 20:5.2
Third-party releases
bankruptcy cases, preparation for, 23:2.4[A]
Third-party sale transactions (fashion companies/brands acquisitions), 22:3.4[B]
Thomson Compumark, 2:6.3[B]
3D printing, 9:1
threeASFOUR, 9:1
Tianyuan Garments Company, 9:1
Tiffany, 2:4.2
blue box, 2:5, 2:6.2
Tiffany (NJ) Inc. v. eBay, Inc, 7:3.4[B], 7:3.4[B][2]
trade dress, 2:5, 2:6.2
Tiffany & Co. v. Costco Wholesale Corp., 2:7.2[C]
Timeline, IPO, 21:3
Times Square (New York City), 13:3.7
Times Three Clothier, LLC, 3:6.1
TIMMY HOLEDIGGER pet perfume, 2:10.8
Titan Corporation, 20:5.3
Title, employment agreements, 17:2.1
T.J. Maxx, 11:1.4[B]
TJX, 8:4.1
TLDs. *See* Top-level domains (TLDs)
TLRA. *See* Trademark Law Revision Act of 1988 (TLRA)
Todd v. Montana Silversmiths, Inc., 4:3.1, 4:3.3
Tom Ford
fast fashion, 11:1
sales, after runway shows, 11:1

Tommy Hilfiger, 13:4
Tommy Hilfiger Licensing Inc. v. Nature Labs, LLC, 2:10.8
TOMMY HILFIGER mark, 2:10.8
TOMS, 1:2.6, 11:1.10
Too, Inc. v. Kohl's Department Stores, Inc., 8:4.2
Too, Inc. v. The TJX Cos., Inc., 8:4.1
Top-level domains (TLDs), 2:15.1, 14:2.1
Tory Burch company
    Burch v. Burch, 6:5.3
    personal name trademark, 2:4.2
Toxic Substance Control Act, 15:2.6
Traction, 1:4.7
Trade dress
    Chewy Vuiton dog toy, 2:10.8, 7:3.2
    defined, 2:5
    distinctiveness, 2:5
    Lanham Act, 6:4.1
    non-distinctive, 2:5
Trade secrets
    California, 6:2.3
    Defend Trade Secrets Act (DTSA)
        generally, 6:4.2
        claims, illustrative cases, 6:5.1
        ex parte civil seizure provision, 6:4.2
    illustrative cases, 6:5.1
    Nike v. Enter Play Sports, Inc., 6:5.1
Trademark
    distinguished from publicity rights, 18:2
Trademark Act of 1881, 2:2
Trademark Act of 1920, 15:3
Trademark Act of 1946. *See* Lanham Act (Trademark Act of 1946)
Trademark applications
    appeals, 2:6.3[D]
    examination, PTO, 2:6.3[D]
    intent-to-use, 2:6.3[C]
    rejection, 2:6.3[D]
    use-based, 2:6.3[C]
Trademark dilution
    by blurring, 2:8.1
    by tarnishment, 2:8.2
    defined, 2:8
    FTDA, 2:2, 2:8
    parody defense, 7:3.2
    TDRA, 2:2, 2:8, 2:10.5
Trademark Dilution Revision Act of 2006 (TDRA), 2:2, 2:8, 2:10.5

Trademark ID Manual, PTO, 2:6.3[D]
Trademark infringement, 2:7 *et seq.* *See also* Confusion, likelihood of; Counterfeiting
accounting of profits, 2:9.3
aesthetic functionality doctrine, 2:10.9
Burberry plaid color scheme, 2:8.2, 7:3.2
Champion T-shirts, 2:3
claims, 2:11.2
colors, 2:8.2, 2:10.9[A], 7:3.2
Confusion Factors, 2:7.2, 8:4.1
contributory, 7:3.4
defenses, 2:10
aesthetic functionality, 2:10.9
invalidity of trademark, 2:10.1
laches, 2:10.6
lack of standing, 2:10.2
naked licensing, 2:10.7
nominative fair use, 2:10.5
parody, 2:10.8
procurement fraud, 2:10.3
unclean hands, 2:10.4
first sale doctrine, 8:2.3
FTDA, 2:2, 2:8
injunctive relief, 2:9.1
Inwood decision and its progeny, 7:3.4[A]
ITC, 2:9.5
JA Apparel, 2:4.2
Lanham Act, 2:7
metatagging, 2:11.1
metatags, trademarks as, 2:11.1
monetary relief, 2:9.2
attorneys' fees, 2:9.2[C]
costs of action, 2:9.2[C]
defendant's profits, 2:9.2[A]
plaintiff's damages, 2:9.2[B]
naked licensing, 2:10.7
NBA v. New World Creation, 2:3
nominative fair use doctrine, 2:10.5
parody defense, 7:3.2
progressive encroachment doctrine, 2:10.6
remedies, 2:9
accounting of profits, 2:9.3
attorneys' fees, 2:9.2[C]
balance of the hardships, 2:9.1[B]
costs of action, 2:9.2[C]

Trademark infringement, remedies (*cont'd*)
defendant's profits, 2:9.2[A]
domain names, 2:9.4
injunctive relief, 2:9.1
ITC's Section 337 investigations, 2:9.5
likelihood of irreparable harm, 2:9.1[B]
likelihood of success on the merits, 2:9.1[B]
monetary relief, 2:9.2
permanent injunction, 2:9.1[A]
plaintiff's damages, 2:9.2[B]
preliminary injunction, 2:9.1[B]
public interest, 2:9.1[B]
search engine advertising, 2:11
search engine and Internet advertising, 2:11
secondary liability, Internet context, 7:3.4[B]
trademark validity, 2:10.1
Troika factors, 2:11.2
unclean hands, 2:10.4
vigilance in protection, 2:12
Trademark Law Revision Act of 1988 (TLRA), 2:2
Trademark licensees
licensor is debtor and bankruptcy, 23:4.4[C][2]
Trademark Official Gazette, 2:6.3[E]
Trademark registrations
canceling, 2:6.3[F]
constructive use concept, 2:2
DuPont factors, 2:6.1
fraud, 2:10.3
international aspects, 2:6.3[G], 2:15, App. 2B
logos, 2:6.2
Madrid Protocol, 2:6.3[G], 2:15.2, App. 2B
opposition proceedings, 2:6.3[E]
overview of process, 2:6.3
perfume scents, 2:6.2
post-registration, 2:6.3[F]
renewal, 2:6.3[F]
smells, 2:6.2
sounds, 2:6.2
third-party standing, 2:6.3[E]
what can be registered, 2:6.2
Trademark Trial and Appeal Board (TTAB), 2:6.3[D], 2:6.3[E]
Trademarks, 2:1 *et seq.*, 10:2.2[H]. *See also* Confusion, likelihood of; Lanham Act (Trademark Act of 1946); PTO (U.S. Patent and Trademark Office); Trademark infringement
generally, 2:1

abandoned, 2:6.3[F], 2:10.7
Anticounterfeiting Consumer Protection Act, 2:2
Bebe Stores, Inc., 22:3.4[B]
brand names, 1:1.1
cease-and-desist order, 2:13
certification marks, 2:3
COACH, 2:6.1, 2:6.2
collective marks, 2:3
colors, 2:8.2, 2:10.9[A], 7:3.2
common phrases, 2:4.4
deceptive words, 2:4.5
defined, 2:3
distinctiveness, 2:3, 2:7.1
duty to protect mark, 2:12
enforcement strategy, 2:13
establishing trademark entitled to protection, 2:7.1
federal trademark statutes, 2:3, 2:6.2, 6:4.2
first sale doctrine, 8:2.3
foreign words, 2:43
FTDA, 2:2, 2:8
functions, 2:1
generic terms, 2:4.4
geographic locations as, 2:3, 2:4.3, 2:43
Gucci, 2:4.2
history, 2:2
incongruous phrases, 2:4.4
incontestable status, 2:7.1, 2:10.1
infringement complaints, 2:13:1
intellectual property, 2:2
international designs. *See* International design law protections
international issues, 2:15
International Trademark Association, 7:4.3
Joseph Abboud, 2:4.2
legislative history, 2:2
letters in, 2:4.1
licensing requirements, 2:14
logos, 2:6.2
numbers in, 2:4.1
personal names, 2:4.2
primary meaning, 2:3
prior use, 2:10.1
quality control, 2:10.7, 2:14, 10:2.2[D]
recurring issues, 2:4
searches, 2:6.3[A]
secondary meaning, 2:3, 2:4.2, 6:3.1[A]

Trademarks (*cont'd*)
service marks, 2:3
shoe design, 2:10.9[B], 2:10.9[C]
Skunk Works, 7:3.4[B][2]
types, 2:3
union label, 2:3
validity, 2:10.1
woolmark, 2:3
Trading market, IPO preparation, 21:2.2
Traditional factoring, 1:4.4
Trafficking by federal contractors and subcontractors, 16:2.5
Trainees or interns, unpaid, 16:2.3
Transfer restrictions, equity investors, 1:3.2
Transition services agreements
ancillary agreements, 22:4
Transparency Pledge, 9:5.2
Transportation service providers, FCPA enforcement actions, 20:4.4[B]
Trendstop, 9:3
Trial pop-up shops, 11:1.9
Triangle Shirtwaist Factory fire, New York, 9:5.2
Triangular merger, 22:3.1
TRO. *See* Temporary restraining order (TRO)
Troika factors, 2:11.2
True People brand, 2:9.1[B]
True People mark, 2:9.1[B]
True Religion Apparel, 3:6.1, 7:3.5[B]
True sales
liquidity, bankruptcy cases, 23:2.3[A][3]
Trump, Donald, 6:2.1
Trump, Ivanka
Modern Appealing Clothing v. Ivanka Trump Marks, LLC, 6:2.1
Trump Administration
economic sanctions, 19:9.1
Truth in Lending Act, 14:4
TSG Consumer Partners, 1:4.8
TTAB. *See* Trademark Trial and Appeal Board (TTAB)
Turkmenistan cotton, customs seizure and forfeiture, 19:8.1
TWEEDS trademark, 2:4.4
Twitter, 15:7, 15:7.2, 16:8, 18:3
ancillary agreements, 22:4
character limit on messages, 15:7.2
Tying agreements, antitrust, 12:4.2[C]
TYR Sport Inc. v. Warnaco Swimwear, 15:2.3

U

Uber
    Meyer v. Uber Technologies, Inc., 14:3.1
UCC-1 financing statement
    Consignments and bankruptcy, 23:4.5[A][2]
UDRP. *See* Uniform Domain-Name Dispute-Resolution Policy (UDRP)
UDTP. *See* Uniform Deceptive Trade Practices Act (UDTP)
uFaker, Inc., 7:4.1
UGG boots, 19:4
Ukraine, Crimea Region
    economic sanctions, 19:9.1
Unclean hands defense, 2:10.4, 15:4.1[E]
Under Armour, Inc., 3:6.1, 3:6.2[A]
Undercapitalization, corporate veil, 1:2.10
Underwriters and underwriting, IPOs
    due diligence, 21:2.1
    prospectus, 21:4.10
Underwriting agreement, IPO, 21:6.2
Unfair competition, 6:1 *et seq. See also* Misappropriation
    generally, 6:1
    Burch v. Burch, 6:5.3
    California, 6:2
    Defend Trade Secrets Act (DTSA), 6:4.2
    federal law, 6:4
    illustrative cases, 6:5.2, 6:5.3
    J. Crew Group Inc. v. Fenton, 6:5.2
    New York law, 6:3
Unfair labor practices, 16:2.5. *See also* Employment and labor issues
Uniform Commercial Code (UCC), 11:2, 11:2.3
    Article 9, consignments in bankruptcy, 23:4.5[A]
Uniform Deceptive Trade Practices Act (UDTP), 15:5
    Little UDTP Act jurisdictions, 15:5.2
Uniform Domain-Name Dispute-Resolution Policy (UDRP), 2:15.1, 14:2.1
Uniform Trade Secrets Act (UTSA)
    California Trade Secrets Act (CUTSA), 6:2.3
Union Carbide Corp. v. Ever-Ready, Inc., 2:7.2[C]
Union label, 2:3
Unions
    bargaining units, labor and employment, 16:7
United Arab emirates
    design law protections, 5:5.8
United International Bureaux for the Protection of Intellectual Property, 2:15.1

United Kingdom
as European Union member state, 5:2
Brexit, 5:4.2
design law protections, 5:4.2
U.S. e-commerce retailers expansion into, 14:1
United Nations
International Labour Organization, 9:5.2
public international organizations, 20:3.1[B]
WIPO, 2:6.3[G], 2:15.1
World Intellectual Property Organization (WIPO), 2:6.3[G], 2:15.1, 5:3
United States Court of International Trade, 19:3, 19:4, 19:7
United States Department of Agriculture (USDA), 15:4.3[A]
United States Patent and Trademark Office. *See* PTO (U.S. Patent and Trademark Office)
United States Securities and Exchange Commission. *See* SEC (U.S. Securities and Exchange Commission)
United States (U.S.)
apparel manufacturing industry, 9:1
Made in the U.S.A., 9:1, 9:3
patent protection, 3:5.1
United States v. Esquenazi, 20:3.1[B]
United States v. Inn Foods, Inc., 19:8.2
United States v. Kay, 20:3.1[B]
United States v. King, 20:3.1[B]
United States v. Zhao, 7:2
Universal Product Code (UPC) requirements, 11:2.1
University of Pittsburgh v. Champion Products, Inc., 2:3
Unlimited personal liability, 1:2.2, 1:2.3, 1:2.8
Unpaid trainees or interns, 16:2.3
Unreal Campaign, 7:4.3
Unsecured loans, 1:4.3, 1:4.5
Untuckit, 11:1
UPC. *See* Universal Product Code (UPC) requirements
Urban Outfitters, Inc. v. BCBG Max Azria Group, Inc., 2:7.2[C], 2:9.1[B]
Urbanization
luxury sector, 9:2
U.S. *See* United States (U.S.)
U.S. Constitution
Article 1, section 8: copyright protection, 4:2
Article III, 14:3.2[A], 14:3.4[B], 19:7
lack of standing, trademark infringement defense, 2:10.2
First Amendment, 2:10.8, 4:8.1, 15:2.1, 18:3
patent and copyright clause, 2:2

U.S.-Mexico-Canada Agreement (USMCA), 19:6
U.S.A. Dawgs, Inc., 3:6.1
USA Patriot Act, 7:2
USDA. *See* United States Department of Agriculture (USDA)
Use-based trademark applications, 2:6.3[C]
Use of proceeds, IPO prospectus, 21:4.3
Use provisions, brick-and-mortar lease, 13:3.3
Use restrictions, brick-and-mortar lease, 13:3.4
Useful articles, separability doctrine, 4:3.2[B]
Uses and sources table, 1:1.1[G]
Utility patent applications
    AIA, 3:3.1
    costs and fees, 3:3.3
    declaration, 3:3.1
    drawings, 3:3.1, 3:3.5
    early filing, 3:3.1
    employers, 3:3.1
    examination, PTO, 3:3.4
    oath, 3:3.1
    pendency, 3:3.5
    prior art searches, 3:3.2
    requirements, 3:3.1
    written specification, 3:3.1
Utility patents. *See also* Patents
    generally, 3:7
    applications. *See* Utility patent applications
    described, 3:2.1
    examples, App. 3B–1, App. 3B–2
    fashion/technology integration, 3:6.2[C]
    number, 3:6.2[A]
    requirements, 3:2.1
    RFIDs, 3:6.2[C]
    samples, 3:2.1, 3:6.2[B]
    term, 3:3.5
    uses, 3:6.2[B]

V

Validity, trademark, 2:10.1. *See also* Trademark infringement
Valuation, imported merchandise, 19:5
    alternative means of, 19:5.5
    assists, 19:5.1
    buying agents, 19:5.3
    computed value, 19:5.5

Valuation, imported merchandise (*cont'd*)
deductive value, 19:5.5
fall back method, 19:5.5
related parties, 19:5.4
royalties, 19:5.2
transaction value of identical or similar merchandise, 19:5.5
Van Herpen, Iris, 9:1
Vandal Eyes, 2:10.5
Vendor-retailer arrangements. *See* Retailer-vendor arrangements
Vendor standards, retail, 11:2.1
Venture capital investors
angel investors compared to, 1:4.6, 1:4.7
benefits, 1:4.7
C corporations, 1:2.4, 1:2.8
convertible preferred stock, 1:4.7
described, 1:4.7
fashion technology companies, 1:1.1
LLCs, 1:2.7
Regulation A+ rules, 1:4.7
Regulation Crowdfunding, SEC, 1:4.7
Regulation D rules, 1:4.7
representation on Board of directors, 1:3.2, 1:4.7
Venue considerations
bankruptcy cases, preparation for, 23:2.4
Versace, 22:5.4
Michael Kors acquisition of, 22:1, 22:2.1, 22:4
Versace, Donatella, 22:4
Versace Beck, Allegra, 22:4
Vertical price restraints
antitrust, 12:4.1
Vertical relationships, antitrust, 12:4
non-price vertical agreements, 12:4.2
vertical price restraints, 12:4.1
Vertically integrated manufacturers, 9:3, 10:3, 12:4
Vessel Hull Act, 4:4
Victor Woolen Products of America, Inc., 19:5.4
Vietnam
global apparel manufacturing industry, 9:1
Vintage or pre-owned fashion offerings e-commerce model, 11:1.7
Visa, Inc., 7:3.4[B], 7:3.4[B][1], 7:4.2, 14:4
Payment Card Industry (PCI) Standards Council, 14:4
Perfect 10 v. Visa International Service Association, 7:3.4[B][1]
Visa International Service Association
Perfect 10 v. Visa International Service Association, 7:3.4[B][1]

VisaNet, 7:3.4[B]
Visibility, brick-and-mortar lease provisions, 13:3.7
Vogue
  underweight models, 16:5
von Metternich, Pauline, 18:1
VWP of America v. United States, 19:5.4

W

Wage and Hour Division, 16:2.3
Wages and hours, 16:2. *See also* Employment and labor issues
  California, 16:2.1
  Federal Labor Standards Act (FLSA), 16:2 *et seq.*
  home worker restrictions, 16:2.4
  hot goods, 16:2.5
  interns, 16:2.3
  minimum wage, 16:2.1
  minors, 16:3.1
  New York, 16:2.1
  overtime exemptions, 16:2.2
    administrative exemption, 16:2.2[B]
    combination exemption, 16:2.2[G]
    computer professional exemption, 16:2.2[E]
    creative professional exemption, 16:2.2[D]
    executive exemption, 16:2.2[A]
    highly compensated employee exemption, 16:2.2[H]
    learned professional exemption, 16:2.2[C]
    outside sales exemption, 16:2.2[F]
  overview, 16:2.1
  trafficking by federal contractors and subcontractors, 16:2.5
  trainees or interns, unpaid, 16:2.3
  unfair labor practices, combating, 16:2.5
  unpaid trainees or interns, 16:2.3
Wal-Mart Stores, 11:1.3
Walgreens, 3:6.1
Wall Street Journal, 10:2.2[E]
Wallace China Company, 2:10.9
Walmart
  chargebacks, 11:2.6
Wang, Alexander, 2:4.2
Warby Parker, 1:4.7, 11:1, 11:1.9, 11:1.10
Warehousemen
  first day relief, bankruptcy cases, 23:3.2[C]

Warnaco Group, 15:2.3
Warranties and representations
    acquisition agreements, 22:5.1, App. 22B
    license agreements, 10:2.2[K]
Warren, Samuel, 18:3
Watches
    holograms, 8:5
    Multi Time Machine, Inc. v. Amazon.com, 2:7.2[A]
    Omega S.A. v. Costco Wholesale Corp., 8:3.4, 8:3.5, 8:5
Watergate investigation, 20:2
Waterproof breathable materials, 3:6.2[A]
Wayfair
    South Dakota v. Wayfair, 14:3.2[A]
Wearable technology, 3:2.1, 3:6.2[C]
Wearing apparel
    flammability standards for fabrics and textiles, 9:5.1
Webrooming practice, 14:1
Websites. *See also* Domain names; E-commerce; eBay; Internet; Social media platforms
    auction sites, counterfeiting, 7:3.4[B]
    Chloé v. Queen Bee of Beverly Hills, LLC, 7:3.1[A]
    CopyCatClubs.com, 7:3.4[B][2]
    counterfeit goods, 7:3.1[A]
    mobile commerce, 14:2.2
    North Face Apparel Corp. v. Fujian Sharing Import & Export Ltd., 7:3.3[A]
    Operation In Our Sites, 7:2
    Operation In Our Sites VII, 7:2
    saferproducts.gov database, 9:5.1
Welles, Terri, 2:10.5
Wen Wu, 4:3.1
What Goes Around Comes Around (WGACA), 2:11.3
White v. Samsung Electronics America, Inc., 18:4.1
Whole Foods, 11:1.7
Willful patent infringement, 3:4.2[E]
WIPO. *See* World Intellectual Property Organization (WIPO)
Women
    FMLA, 16:4.4
    Pregnancy Discrimination Act, 16:4.3
    sex claims, BFOQ defense, 16:4.2
    underweight models, 16:5
Wool Products Labeling Act, 9:5.1, 15:2.6, 19:6.4
Woolmark, certification mark, 2:3
Work streams, IPO preparation, 21:2.3
Worker Safety Initiative, Bangladesh, 9:5.2

Workers' compensation programs
first day relief, bankruptcy cases, 23:3.2[B]
Workplace Code of Conduct, FLA, 9:5.2
Works for hire, copyrights, 4:5
World Anti-Counterfeiting Day (June 6, 2018), 7:4.3
World Cup, 2018
NIke and Iran, 19:9.1
World Customs Organization (WCO)
classification of imported merchandise, 19:4
Explanatory Notes, 19:4
World Health Organization (WHO)
malnourished person standard, 16:5
World Intellectual Property Organization (WIPO), 2:6.3[G], 2:15.1, 5:3
World Trade Organization, 19:1, 20:3.1[B]
Wormser, 8:4.2
Worth, Charles Frederick, 18:1
Written specification, patent applications, 3:3.1

Y

Yik Yak, 1:4.3
Yoga apparel, Lululemon Athletica Canada Inc., 3:6.1
Yoga pant, 3:2.2
Younger consumers, 11:1.10
YouTube, 15:7, 18:3
Yummie Tummie, 3:6.1
Yurman Designs v. PAJ, 2:5
Yves Saint Laurent
Louboutin case, 2:10.9[A]
Societe Yves Saint Laurent Couture S.A. v. Societe Louis Dreyfus Retail Management S.A. (France), 5:4.1

Z

Zacchini v. Scripps-Howard Broadcasting Co., 18:3
Zappos, 14:3.1, 14:3.2[B]
In re Zappos.com Inc., Customer Data Security Breach Litigation, 14:3.2[B]
Zara, 9:3, 11:1
"05," athletic jerseys, 2:4.1
Zoning requirements, 13:3.7